The Complete
BIBLICAL LIBRARY

The Complete BIBLICAL LIBRARY

THE NEW TESTAMENT GREEK-ENGLISH DICTIONARY

Lambda–Omicron
Word Numbers
2948–3664

The Complete BIBLICAL LIBRARY

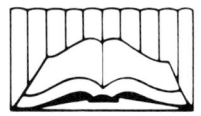

The Complete Biblical Library, part 1, a 16-volume study series on the New Testament. Volume 14: GREEK-ENGLISH DICTIONARY, LAMBDA—OMICRON, Word Numbers 2948–3664. World copyright ©1986 by Thoralf Gilbrant and Tor Inge Gilbrant. © Published 1990 by THE COMPLETE BIBLICAL LIBRARY, Springfield, Missouri 65802, U.S.A. All rights reserved. No part of this publication may be reproduced or transmitted in any form or by any means, electronic or mechanical, including photocopy, recording, or any information storage and retrieval system, without permission in writing from the publisher. Printed in the United States of America 1990 by R.R. Donnelley and Sons Company, Chicago, Illinois 60606. Library of Congress Catalog Card Number 90-85590 International Standard Book Number 0-88243-374-1.

INTERNATIONAL EDITOR
Thoralf Gilbrant

Executive Editor: Ralph W. Harris, M.A.
Computer Systems: Tor Inge Gilbrant

National Editor: Stanley M. Horton, Th.D
Managing Editor: Gayle Garrity Seaver, J.D.

Greek-English Dictionary
Editor: Denis W. Vinyard, M.Div.
Associate Editor: Donald F. Williams, M.Div.

NATIONAL EDITORS

NORWAY
Erling Utnem, Bishop
Arthur Berg, B.D.

DENMARK
Jorgen Glenthoj, Th.M.

HOLLAND
Herman ter Welle, Pastor
Henk Courtz, Drs.

FINLAND
Aapelii Saarisalo, Ph.D.
Valter Luoto, Pastor
Matti Liljequist, B.D.
Toivo Koilo, cand.mag.

SWEDEN
Hugo Odeberg, Ph.D., D.D.
Bertil E. Gartner, D.D.
Thorsten Kjall, M.A.
Stig Wikstrom, D.Th.M.

Project Coordinator: William G. Eastlake

THE COMPLETE BIBLICAL LIBRARY
International and Interdenominational Bible Study System

THE NEW TESTAMENT
Study Bible, Greek-English Dictionary, Harmony of the Gospels

THE OLD TESTAMENT
Study Bible, Hebrew-English Dictionary

THE BIBLE ENCYCLOPEDIA

THE NEW TESTAMENT GREEK-ENGLISH DICTIONARY

Lambda–Omicron
Word Numbers
2948–3664

THE COMPLETE BIBLICAL LIBRARY
Springfield, Missouri, U.S.A.

Table of Contents

	Page
Personnel	5
Greek and Hebrew Alphabets	9
Introduction	10
Greek-English Dictionary	19
Manuscripts	433
Egyptian Papyri	433
Major Codices	435
Majuscules and Minuscules	436
Early Versions	436
Early Church Fathers	437
Books of the Old and New Testament	439
Books of the Apocrypha and Pseudepigrapha	440
Orders and Tractates of the Mishnah and the Talmud	441
Bibliography	442
Resource Tools	442
Modern Greek Texts	442
General Bibliography	443
General References Sources by Title	455
Literature of Antiquity	457

Personnel

INTERNATIONAL EDITOR
Thoralf Gilbrant

Executive Editor: Ralph W. Harris, M.A.

National Editor: Stanley M. Horton, Th.D.

Managing Editor: Gayle A. Seaver, J.D.

Greek-English Dictionary Editor: Denis W. Vinyard, M.Div.

Greek-English Dictionary Associate Editor: Donald F. Williams, M.Div.

BOARD OF REVIEW

John D. Bechtle, D.Min.
Daniel L. Black, Th.D.
David Alan Black, D.Theol.
David R. Bundrick, Th.M.
Vernon D. Doerksen, Th.D.
Thomas E. Friskney, B.D.
Timothy P. Jenney, M.A.

Fred R. Johnson, Ph.D.
Erich H. Kiehl, Th.D.
Oliver McMahan, D.Min.
Siegfried S. Schatzmann, Ph.D.
Virgil Warren, Ph.D.
William C. Williams, Ph.D.
Barney D. Wimer, Ph.D.

STAFF

Senior Editors: Gary L. Leggett, M.A.; Dorothy B. Morris

Editorial Team: Paul S. Ash, B.A., GED Technical Editor; David A. Baca, B.A.; Patti J. Christensen; Faye Faucett; Charlotte L. Gribben; Susan Hall; Melvin M.S. Ho, M.Div.; Gilberto Huerta, M.A.; Carlos E. Johnson, Jr., M.A., GED Background Research; Debra K. King, B.A.; Robert F. Land, B.A., GED Background Research; Gregory A. Lint, M.Div., Septuagint Research; Charles F. Lynch, M.Div., GED Technical Editor; Paul J. Martin, M.A.; Michael Ritchie, M.Div.; Marietta L. Vinyard; Karen D. Wuertz, M.Div.

Production Coordinator, Study Bible, and GED Layout Artist: Cynthia D. Riemenschneider

Art Director: Terry Van Someren, B.F.A.

Word Processing and Secretarial: Sonja Jensen; Rochelle L. Holman; Therese Ritchie; Rachel Wisehart Harvey, B.A.

Personnel Continued

Volume 14 Contributors

The following writers contributed research and original manuscripts for the word studies in Volume 14.

Daniel E. Albrecht, M.A.	Dale Cornett, M.Div.
Donald L. Alexander, Ph.D.	Roger D. Cotton, Th.D.
Arden C. Autry, Ph.D.	Wilber T. Dayton, Th.D.
Gerard A. Bachke, D.E.A.	John D. Deisher, Jr., M.Div.
Carolyn D. Baker, M.Div.	David M. Dippold, M.A.
Donald E. Baldwin, Ph.D.	Vernon D. Doerksen, Th.D.
Richard P. Belcher, Ph.D.	Joseph R. Flower, B.A.
Daniel L. Black, Th.D.	Kenneth K. Foreman, Th.D.
Bill Brown, Ph.D.	Karen Franklin, M.Div.
Robert C. Buswell, D.Min.	Thomas E. Friskney, B.D.
Timothy B. Cargal, M.A.	John S. Gerlicher, Th.M.
John E. Carlson, B.A.	M. Fred Haltom, D.Min.
Gary G. Cohen, Th.D.	Ralph C. Hampton, Jr., M.Div.
Oral Edmond Collins, Ph.D.	Greg Hands, Th.M.

Samuel G. Hardman, M.A.

Walter D. Hatchner, B.A.

James Allen Hewett, Ph.D.

Fred R. Johnson, Ph.D.

Gerald Kath, M.Div.

Charles F. Lynch, M.Div.

David C. Macy, Th.M.

Grady W. Manley, M.A.

Gerald L. Mattingly, Ph.D.

Oliver McMahan, D.Min.

Terri L. C. Melton, B.A.

Johnny V. Miller, Th.D.

Stasie T. Nicholaides, M.Div.

R. Wade Paschal, Ph.D.

James D. Price, Ph.D.

Michael K. Ritchie, M.Div.

Bernard Rossier, Ph.D.

Siegfried S. Schatzmann, Ph.D.

James B. Shelton, Ph.D.

B. Maurice Stout, Th.M.

Roger J. Stronstad, M.C.S.

Edmund L. Tedeschi, M.A.

Michael B. VanDoren, D.Min.

Denis W. Vinyard, M.Div.

Jim Williams

William C. Williams, Ph.D.

Joseph P. Wilser, Th.D.

B. D. Wimer, Ph.D.

Paul O. Wright, Th.D.

Richard A. Young, Ph.D.

Greek and Hebrew Alphabets

Greek

A	α	alpha	a	(f<u>a</u>ther)
B	β	beta	b	
Γ	γ	gamma	g	(<u>g</u>ot)
Δ	δ	delta	d	
E	ε	epsilon	e	(g<u>e</u>t)
Z	ζ	zeta	z	dz (lea<u>d</u>s)
H	η	eta	ē	(<u>a</u>te)
Θ	θ	theta	th	(<u>th</u>in)
I	ι	iota	i	(s<u>i</u>n or mach<u>i</u>ne)
K	κ	kappa	k	
Λ	λ	lambda	l	
M	μ	mu	m	
N	ν	nu	n	
Ξ	ξ	xi	x	
O	ο	omicron	o	(l<u>o</u>t)
Π	π	pi	p	
P	ϱ	rho	r	
Σ	σ,ς[1]	sigma	s	
T	τ	tau	t	
Y	υ	upsilon	u	German ü
Φ	φ	phi	ph	(<u>ph</u>ilosophy)
X	χ	chi	ch	(<u>ch</u>aos)
Ψ	ψ	psi	ps	(li<u>ps</u>)
Ω	ω	omega	ō	(<u>o</u>cean)

Hebrew

א		aleph	ʾ [2]	
ב, בּ		beth	b, v	
ג, גּ		gimel	g, gh	
ד, דּ		daleth	d, dh	(<u>th</u>ey)[3]
ה		he	h	
ו		waw	w	
ז		zayin	z	
ח		heth	ch	(kh)
ט		teth	ṭ	
י		yodh	y	
כ, ךּ	כּ	kaph	k, kh	
ל		lamedh	l	
מ	ם	mem	m	
נ	ן	nun	n	
ס		samekh	ṣ	
ע		ayin	ʿ	
פ, ףּ	פּ	pe	p, ph	
צ	ץ	sadhe	ts	
ק		qoph	q	
ר		resh	r	
שׂ		sin	s	
שׁ		shin	sh	
ת, תּ		taw	t, th	(<u>th</u>ing)[3]

Hebrew Vowels

ָ	ā	father			u	rule	ֵי	ê	they
ַ	a	dam	ֹ	ō	role	ָה	âh	ah
ֶ	e	men	וּ	û	tune	ֲ	ă	hat
ֵ	ē	they	וֹ	ô	hole	ֱ	ě	met
	i	pin	ִי	î	machine	ְ	ᵉ	av<u>e</u>rage
ָ	o	roll	ֵי	ê	they	ֳ	ŏ	not

Greek Pronunciation Rules

Before another g, or before a k or a ch, g is pronounced and spelled with an n, in the transliteration of the Greek word.

In the Greek, **s** is written at the end of a word, elsewhere it appears as σ. The rough breathing mark (ʽ) indicates that an h-sound is to be pronounced before the initial vowel or diphthong. The smooth breathing mark (ʼ) indicates that no such h-sound is to be pronounced.

There are three accents, the acute (´), the circumflex (῀) and the grave (`). These stand over a vowel and indicate that stress in pronunciation is to be placed on the syllable having any one of the accents.

Pronouncing Diphthongs

ai is pronounced like ai in aisle
ei is pronounced like ei in eight
oi is pronounced like oi in oil
au is pronounced like ow in cow

eu is pronounced like eu in feud
ou is pronounced like oo in food
ui is pronounced like ui in suite (sweet)

1. Where two forms of a letter are given, the one at the right is used at the end of a **word**.
2. Not represented in transliteration when the initial letter.
3. Letters underscored represent pronunciation of the second form only.

Introduction

The 6 volumes of the *Greek-English Dictionary* form 1 division of the 16-volume *Complete Biblical Library*. The first division, called the *Study Bible*, is composed of nine volumes. Each one contains an *Interlinear*. It uses a *comparative* Greek text which includes both the *Textus Receptus* and variants from the modern critical texts. All the major variants are found here, plus a multitude of the less significant ones. For our purposes *variant* means a reading which differs from the *Textus Receptus*. A *Textual Apparatus* shows the manuscript background of the variants.

On the page which faces the *Interlinear* is the *Verse-by-Verse Commentary* and the *Various Versions* column. From nearly 100 versions, in addition to the King James Version, the column shows different ways phrases have been translated.

The six-volume *Greek-English Dictionary* is a fitting companion for the *Study Bible*. They are closely linked by a numerical system which identifies each Greek word. The number is placed above the word in the *Interlinear* and is repeated in the *Dictionary* which lists the words in alphabetical order. By this system a person may easily go from the *Study Bible* to an in-depth study in the *Dictionary*. Such an arrangement makes this Greek dictionary as usable for the layman as for the scholar.

Such a combination of Biblical and theological material has not been produced in any previous work. *The Complete Biblical Library* is special because it employs a system which is usable by those who have little or no knowledge of Greek, yet will appeal to theologians at the highest level of scholarship. For all who use this work, it will open wider the door to the richness of the original text of the New Testament.

The *Greek-English Dictionary* is by itself a unique tool. It provides information the user could not obtain without consulting many lexical and theological books. Here all the information is available, saving a great deal of research time for students, ministers, and scholars.

FEATURES OF THE GREEK-ENGLISH DICTIONARY
1. Greek Words of the New Testament
2. Cognate/Synonym Research
3. Septuagint Section
4. Grammatical Forms
5. Greek-English Concordance
6. Word Studies
7. Resource Tools

GREEK WORDS OF THE NEW TESTAMENT

Every Greek word which appears in our *Interlinear* of the New Testament is listed in its alphabetical and numerical order. It is referred to as the "entry word." Including proper nouns, there are more than 5,500 of these. The assigned number also appears above the word each time it occurs in the *Interlinear* of the *Study Bible*. Those who wish more information about a word found in the *Interlinear* can easily locate the word in the *Dictionary* by using this "lexical number," as it is called. The word first appears in its Greek form. As a help to pronunciation, the English transliteration is given. Next appears the grammatical form of the word, such as verb, noun, etc. Finally, the basic meaning or meanings of the word are given.

COGNATE/SYNONYM RESEARCH

Here a majority of the entire vocabulary of the New Testament is subdivided into two main groupings. The first consists of words which have numerous cognates and synonyms, listed by their Greek spelling, English pronunciation, and lexical number. Under them are shown the terms which are related to them, either by descent (cognates) or by meaning (synonyms).

The second group is referred to as cross-reference words. This category was introduced so the long list of cognates which appears with some words would not have to be repeated over and over. The notation *Cross-reference* simply indicates that the reader is being directed to an entry word where there is an extensive listing of related cognates.

Cognates

In analyzing a language the term *cognate* refers to words which share a common derivation or descent. In most languages a verb serves as the root word from which a variety of cognates or related terms (nouns, adjectives, adverbs, etc.) descend. For example, the English words *save*, *savior*, *savings*, *safe*, and *safety* all are cognates; that is, they share a common ancestry.

Considering the cognates of a word is very useful, since words of a common family often share similar characteristics. This is especially helpful in studying the Greek language, where a cognate of a particular word may be used more frequently than the word itself. Knowing the meanings of other members of a cognate "family" helps to define a word from that family which occurs infrequently.

For example, the noun *hagiotēs* occurs only once in the New Testament, at Hebrews 12:10, and is quite rare in both the classical Greek and Septuagint literature. However, the related cognates *hagiazō* ("to sanctify, be holy") and *hagios* ("holy") occur often. One may infer, therefore, that the rare term *hagiotēs* shares with its cognates some overlap in its range of meaning. (The KJV translates it "holiness.")

Synonyms

In this work synonyms are words which have meanings similar to that of the entry word. Thus they are helpful in ascertaining the full meaning of a particular term. In addition, the synonym list indicates the various terms a New Testament writer had available to him. If the Holy Spirit guided the writer to choose one term over another in a given context, it may be important to understand why He did so. It is possible that in some contexts word choice might be simply a matter of style, but on other occasions the choice of one word over another might be very significant.

For example, John 1:12 states that as many as received Jesus as Saviour, "to them gave he power (*exousia*) to become the sons of God." Although several other Greek words have meanings similar to *exousia*, such as *dunamis* ("power, ability") and *ischus* ("strength, power, might"), only *exousia* carries the idea of "authority" or "right" which the context of this verse requires. Use of the English word *power* by the King James' translators tends to cloud the truth conveyed by this text; namely, there is no innate strength or might resident in man which can make him a child of God. Only faith in Christ grants one the "right" or "authority" to become a member of the family of God.

Remember, however, that no two words have exactly the same meaning. The term *semantic range* may be the most accurate description of the actual concept. This expression refers to the range of meanings each word has, depending on how it is used in a specific context. This being true, in order to do an accurate and adequate word study it is important to compare words whose semantic ranges overlap to a significant degree. The synonym lists make such a study possible.

To avoid serious errors in using the cognate/synonym lists a word of warning may be proper at this point. For example, consider *kērux* ("envoy, herald, messenger") and a synonym, *angelos* ("angel, envoy, messenger"). Although some of their meanings are the same, it is absolutely incorrect to infer that *kērux* means "angel." The full significance of "semantic ranges" must be considered. One should not attach all the meanings of a cognate or a synonym to an entry word. The context helps to determine the specific meaning.

The editors of this massive work feel compelled to present a word of caution to those who use *The Complete Biblical Library's Greek-English Dictionary* and *Study Bible*. These volumes contain a vast amount of facts and information, but all this needs to be analyzed and synthesized before valid conclusions and applications can be derived. Note the following:

(1) While it is true that study of how a word was used over an extended period of time can help define its semantic range (i.e., the parameter of possible meanings a word may have), it will not necessarily disclose its specific meaning in a certain passage. In addition, a word which has a "literal" or "technical" meaning in one place may not have the same meaning every time it is used. For example, the Greek term *sarx*, which is one word used to refer to the human body (1 Peter 4:1), at different times refers to the "flesh" which covers the bones (Luke 24:39), to the human or physical nature (Romans 9:3), or to that aspect of man's fallen nature, i.e., the "flesh," which is subject to sin (Romans 8:3-8).

(2) A study of the historical etymology, including the root components and the cognates and synonyms of a word, does not necessarily determine its exact meaning.

(3) Tracing a word from one language to another (e.g., Hebrew to Greek, Latin to Greek, Greek to English, even Koine Greek to modern Greek) is no guarantee that the specific meaning of the term in its New Testament usage has been discovered.

(4) A Greek word may often have a wide range of meaning. This range is not only present within a particular type of literature (e.g., classical or New Testament) but also throughout the historical use and development of the word. Considering a word's use from one period to another is helpful, and studying all the uses of a word in a given body of literature such as the New Testament is illuminating. However, one must be careful not to impart

Introduction Continued

the entire breadth of meaning to a word everywhere it occurs.

All of these elements of research are of value and can shed light on how the word was used and what it meant in a variety of contexts. Therefore, in doing word studies consideration of the context must work together with the other elements mentioned above to yield a proper understanding of a specific term in a given passage.

This warning must not be allowed to discourage or confuse anyone who is seeking to understand the Bible better through a study of the languages in which it was originally written. Rather, it should be recognized that haphazard treatment of the Scriptures is a mistake that can have eternal consequences. Let this encourage all teachers and students of the Word of God to approach their studies with cautious humility in the effort to "rightly divide the word of truth."

THE SEPTUAGINT SECTION

The Septuagint version is the translation of the Hebrew Old Testament into the Greek Language. The title "Septuagint" (known also by the abbreviation LXX) is derived from the Latin term *septuaginta*, "seventy." This version came into being because of the spread of the Greek language throughout the then-known world. In the Fourth Century B.C. the armies of Alexander the Great swept across the earth, conquering all his enemies and bringing the Greek Empire to its zenith of power. Greek became the universal language.

The earliest written tradition that provides information concerning the origin and history of the Septuagint is the *Letter of Aristeas* (First or Second Century B.C.). This letter claims to be contemporary with the translation of the Torah by 72 Jewish elders who were gathered in Alexandria, Egypt, under the direction of Ptolemy II Philadelphus, ruler of Egypt (285-246 B.C.), hence the title LXX. Many historical inaccuracies and inconsistencies in the letter of Aristeas have caused some modern scholars to reject the reliability of much of the letter's contents. Another explanation is that this title was given to symbolize the 70 elders that accompanied Moses up Mount Sinai (Exodus 24:1,9).

Because of the Assyrian and Babylonian conquests several centuries before, thousands of Jews had been scattered to the far reaches of the empire, and by this time, in the Third Century B.C., Greek had become their everyday language.

Two factors helped to bring the Septuagint version into existence: (1) Some have given credit to Ptolemy II. It is thought that his interest in books led him to encourage the production of the Septuagint (he has also been credited with initiating the development of the great library at Alexandria, Egypt). (2) A more likely explanation, however, was the compelling need of the large number of Greek-speaking Jews at Alexandria and elsewhere who wished to have a text of the Old Testament they could read.

The Septuagint is important because it provides the Hebrew background for so many important Greek words of the New Testament. The Septuagint was of great significance to Greek culture, for through it the riches of the Old Testament were opened to the Greek mind for the first time.

The prominence of the Septuagint in the Early Church also greatly influenced the spread of Christianity and the development of Christian theology—for three reasons: (1) The extensive use of the Septuagint had spread ideas and themes to which the early Christian message could easily be attached. (2) The Septuagint provided a readily accessible pool of theological terminology which could be adapted by the Christian community in communicating the gospel to the Greek mind. (3) A majority of the citations and allusions to the Old Testament found in the New Testament are from the Septuagint.

It is well known that the language of the New Testament is not the classical Greek but the simpler, common, and international Koine Greek from the Hellenistic period of the time of Alexander the Great. But this is not the only characteristic of the New Testament Greek language. Words of deep theological significance in the New Testament text derive much of their content and meaning, not from the secular Greek use of the word, but from the Old Testament use in the history of revelation. In fact, many of these Greek words adopted a Hebrew meaning and spiritual dimension. Words which had little religious significance in secular Greek were used in the Septuagint to express the deep spiritual meaning of their Hebrew equivalents in the Hebrew Old Testament. (For an illustration of this see later information under the heading "Example of Use.")

Features of the Septuagint Section

In the opinion of the editors it is important to provide the information necessary to gain an adequate understanding of the way Old Testament themes, ideas, motifs, and vocabulary were transmitted through the Septuagint version into the Greek mind and the New Testament. Furthermore, this section will provide a bridge between the New Testament *Study Bible* and *Greek-English Dictionary* and the Old Testament *Study Bible* and *Hebrew-English Dictionary*, projected companion projects which will be forthcoming.

The research in this section is based upon the work *A Concordance to the Septuagint*, 3 volumes, edited by Edwin Hatch and Henry A. Redpath, Oxford: The Clarendon Press, 1897, 1906. Reprint, Grand Rapids: Baker Book House, 1983.

Hebrew Words

The first element of the Septuagint section is the Hebrew word(s) and the appropriate transliteration (pronunciation). Provided under each entry word, they represent the terms of the Hebrew Scriptures translated by that Greek word in the Septuagint version.

Note that the relatively small number of Hebrew phrases of two or more words translated by one Greek word are not included. Primarily this is due to the need to maintain a tightly controlled numerical reference system for the *Hebrew-English Dictionary*. In addition, not all words appearing in the Greek New Testament are present in the Septuagint version. Also omitted are any references to Greek particles, conjunctions, prepositions, numerals, or articles.

Hebrew Word Numbers

The second element of the Septuagint section is the number assigned to the Hebrew words. As mentioned earlier, the study system enables the student to move easily between the Old and New Testaments. This number will appear with the word in the *Hebrew-English Dictionary*. Numbers preceded by an *A* identify Aramaic words.

Short Hebrew Word Definitions

The third element of this section provides a brief definition of the Hebrew word and representative references where the Septuagint translates that Hebrew word by the Greek word shown above. This presentation seeks to provide definitions for the Hebrew words which are sensitive to the particular context of the passage cited.

For a more complete treatment of these words see the standard but somewhat dated work by Francis Brown, S.R. Driver, and Charles A. Briggs (*The New Brown-Driver-Briggs—Gesenius Hebrew and English Lexicon*. 1906. Reprint. Peabody, MA: Hendrickson Publishers. 1979). This edition is recommended over the Oxford edition because of its index which allows the student to find the Hebrew word under consideration and directs him to the page and column where the word is found in the lexicon. Furthermore, the Hendrickson edition is also indexed to *Strong's Exhaustive Concordance of the Bible*. The other recommended standard English work is the more recent, though less exhaustive, work by William Holladay (*A Concise Hebrew and Aramaic Lexicon of the Old Testament*. Leiden: E.J. Brill. 1988).

Verb Stems

Occasionally the primary meaning of a Hebrew verb differs from the meaning of that verb in the specific context of the Old Testament verse(s) cited in our research. In these cases the general definition is given first and is followed by the meaning of the specific form or stem being cited (e.g., qal, niphal, piel, etc.). For example: *shālam* (8396), Be complete, sound; piel: repay, return (Dt 7:10, 2 Sm 3:39).

Those who are not familiar with the Hebrew or Aramaic verb stems may want to refer to one of the following grammars: Lambdin, Thomas O. *Introduction to Biblical Hebrew* (New York: Charles Scribner and Sons. 1971); Seow, C.L. *A Grammar for Biblical Hebrew* (Nashville: Abingdon Press. 1987); Gesenius, Wilhelm. *Gesenius' Hebrew Grammar*. 2d English ed., ed. and rev. by E. Kautzsch and A. E. Cowley. (Oxford: Clarendon Press. 1910); Johns, Alger F. *A Short Grammar of Biblical Aramaic*. Rev. ed. (Berrien Springs, MI: Andrews University Printers. 1972).

Biblical and Apocryphal References

These references are simply a representative list of the places in the Septuagint where the given Hebrew word is translated by the Greek word cited. It is not an exhaustive list. For such a list see Hatch and Redpath's *A Concordance to the Septuagint* cited above.

The chapter and verse arrangements of the

Introduction Continued

Septuagint are sometimes different from the English Bible. When this occurs the Septuagint references are placed in brackets or parentheses immediately following the English Bible reference (e.g., Jeremiah 40:5 [47:5]). The Septuagint references are primarily shown according to *The Septuagint with Apocrypha: Greek and English* by Sir Lancelot Brenton, 1851. This work has been reprinted by both Zondervan Publishing House and Hendrickson Publishers and is the only complete English translation of the Septuagint available.

The names of Bible books are shown as they appear in the English Bible. The books affected by this include: 1 and 2 Samuel, which appear as 1 and 2 Kings in the Septuagint; 1 and 2 Kings, which appear as 3 and 4 Kings in the Septuagint; and Ezra, which appears as 2 Esdras in the Septuagint. References to the Theodotion text of Daniel have not been included.

At times a particular Greek rendering may have appeared in only one text. In these cases notations have been provided about the Greek text in which that particular rendering may be found.

As a result of the editing that the Septuagint received in both Jewish and Christian circles after the beginning of the Christian Era, the Septuagint text found in most modern editions does not reflect a single textual tradition. The recovery of a pure text is impossible. Rather, the text of modern printed editions represents the text of one or more of the following three uncials (ancient manuscripts of the Bible from the Third—Tenth Century A.D., written in all capital letters, on parchment or vellum, and bound in book form): Codex Alexandrinus (A) of the Fifth Century A.D.; Codex Sinaiticus (S or Aleph), of the Fourth Century A.D.; and Codex Vaticanus (B), of the Fourth Century A.D. Of the three the Vaticanus text enjoys the place of greatest stature.

In addition to the three texts mentioned above, there are references to the Sixtine Edition in the research part of the Septuagint section. Of the earlier editions the Sixtine is one of the most important. Published under the orders of Pope Sixtus V in 1568 (hence the title "Sixtine"), it was based primarily on the Codex Vaticanus, and any gaps were filled with readings from the Codex Alexandrinus. This edition became the basis for almost all other printed editions in the 300 years which followed its publishing.

For those Greek words which were used to translate five or less Hebrew words in the Septuagint, references are included to Sirach (also known as the Wisdom of Jesus the Son of Sirach, or also Ecclesiasticus), an apochryphal book of the Old Testament. These will provide additional examples of the way the Hebrew language and thought patterns were transmitted into Greek during the Intertestamental Period. Three primary copies of Sirach exist: the Greek of the Septuagint, the Syriac of the Peshitta, and the Hebrew fragments. The content of the book indicates that it was written prior to the Maccabean Revolt in 168 B.C., probably between 195 and 171 B.C.

Why Use the Septuagint?

How can study of the Septuagint increase one's understanding of the New Testament? (1) Most of the Old Testament quotes found in the New Testament come from the Septuagint. (2) More often than actual quotes, allusions to the Septuagint version appear in the New Testament. One such instance is John's use of the phrase *egō eimi* (John 8:58). This term comes directly from the Septuagint's translation of Exodus 3:14 where God reveals himself to Moses as the "I AM." (3) When interpreting specific New Testament passages, the Septuagint can provide the necessary link with the Old Testament which is essential for understanding certain New Testament terms, themes, and concepts.

Example of Use

The most common New Testament word for "law" is *nomos*. In secular Greek *nomos* primarily meant "common usage, custom, or universal principle." This gradually was modified to become what we refer to as "law." *Nomos* also came to mean a law as established by the governing body of a community or country. Through the Septuagint, however, an entirely new dimension for this word was added in the New Testament.

This new dimension came as the result of translating the Old Testament term *tôrāh* by the Greek word *nomos*. To the Jews *tôrāh* was the embodiment of their religion. It was used of the guidance and revelation of God himself, as communicated by the priests and prophets. The priestly instruction concerning the ceremonies and rituals was roughly equivalent to the Greek concept of *nomos*. In the Prophets, however, *tôrāh* was used as parallel in concept with "the word of the Lord" (Isaiah 1:10), and in this use embodied the principles of religion, God's purposes for His people, and the broad guidelines for ethics and morality.

When one comes to the word *nomos* in the Gospel of John, for instance, it is important to know that the word is used exclusively with the Old Testament concept of *tôrāh* in mind. On the other hand, Paul often uses *nomos* in both the common Greek manner, and less frequently in the manner of the Septuagint as equivalent to *tôrāh*. Without understanding the Jewish background of *nomos* as transmitted through the Septuagint, the student of the New Testament would be unaware of this important distinction.

GRAMMATICAL FORMS

In this section of the *Greek-English Dictionary* are listed the various and specific forms which an entry word takes in the text of the New Testament. For example, in the Greek language a noun will have different spellings, depending on how it functions in the sentence (as the subject, direct object, indirect object, etc.). A verb will be spelled differently, depending on whether it is present tense, future tense, singular, plural, etc. The list of grammatical forms simply represents the specific spelling and function in the context of particular verses. Notice the grammatical forms for the word *apostolē* (645):

1. *apostolēs* gen sing fem
2. *apostolēn* acc sing fem

The numbers on the left are a simple listing of the various forms the entry word will have throughout the New Testament. (Note that the word for "apostleship" never appears in the New Testament with its lexical spelling *apostolē*; it appears in the two forms shown above). Next the Greek spelling is shown, along with its English transliteration.

The third element, *gen sing fem*, shows the parsing for each form; that is, the specific information concerning the word's grammatical function in a given context. For example, the first grammatical form shows the word is used in the *gen*itive case, that it is *sing*ular in number, and that it is a *fem*inine noun.

Below is a complete listing of all the abbreviations used in this section (they also appear with the word in the *Interlinear* of the *Study Bible* volumes).

Parts of Speech
prs-pron = personal pronoun
rel-pron = relative pronoun
indef-pron = indefinite pronoun
intr-pron = interrogative pronoun
dem-pron = demonstrative pronoun
noun
verb
inf = infinitive
part = participle
adj = adjective
num = number
art = definite article
prep = preposition
conj = conjunction
partic = particle
intrj = interjection
card = cardinal (number)
ord = ordinal (number)
comp = comparative (adjective)
sup = superlative (adjective)
name
name-adj = name-adjective
name-adv = name-adverb

Mood
indic = indicative
subj = subjunctive
opt = optative
impr = imperative

Tense
pres = present
imperf = imperfect
fut = future
aor = aorist
perf = perfect
plperf = pluperfect

Voice
act = active
mid = middle
pass = passive

Case
nom = nominative
gen = genitive
dat = dative
acc = accusative
voc = vocative

Gender
masc = masculine
fem = feminine
neu = neuter

Person
1 = first person

Introduction Continued

2 = second person
3 = third person

Number
sing = singular
pl = plural

Following is a partial list of the more popular Greek grammars. They are identified as advanced, intermediate, and beginner works.

Blass, F. and A. Debrunner. *A Greek Grammar of the New Testament and Other Early Christian Literature.* Trans. by R.W. Funk. Chicago: Chicago University Press. 1961. (Advanced)

Dana, H.E. and J.R. Mantey. *A Manual Grammar of the Greek New Testament.* New York: Macmillan. 1927. (Intermediate-beginner)

Moulton, J.H., W.F. Howard and N. Turner. *A Grammar of New Testament Greek.* 4 vols. Edinburgh: T. and T. Clark. (Advanced)

Robertson, A.T. *A Grammar of the Greek New Testament in the Light of Historical Research.* Nashville: Broadman Press. 1934. (Advanced)

Story, J. Lyle and Cullen I.K. Story. *Greek to Me: Learning New Testament Through Memory Visualization.* San Francisco: Harper and Row. 1979. (Beginner)

Summers, R. *Essentials of New Testament Greek.* Nashville: Broadman Press. 1950. (Beginner)

Zerwick, M. *Biblical Greek Illustrated by Examples.* Rome: Scripta Pontificii Instituti Biblici. 1963. (Intermediate-advanced)

THE GREEK-ENGLISH CONCORDANCE

This lists all the places the entry word occurs in the KJV New Testament and how it is translated. Furthermore, variants to the KJV are included and identified by bold grammatical form numbers. There is a line for each entry, which includes part of the verse, the word being considered, and the Scripture reference.

Each entry is preceded by a number which identifies the grammatical form (see under "Grammatical Forms" above). Each occurrence of the word itself appears in boldface type so the student may see how it is translated in each context. (Some Greek words of the New Testament are translated by several English words because the context may change the meaning to some degree.) A parenthetical *NT* appears when the entry word can not be precisely translated in English.

Along with the other features, this part of the Dictionary is of great value. A person is able to study a Greek word in every context where it appears in the New Testament. This is the major source of information concerning the basic meaning of a word, and the varied significance it has in different contexts.

WORD STUDIES

The word studies are a focal point and the most prominent feature of the *Greek-English Dictionary.* Here the meaning and use of each Greek word of the New Testament are traced back to secular Greek sources and to the Septuagint. Most important of all, each Greek word is discussed with reference to its meaning within New Testament contexts.

Word Study Procedures

All Greek words found in the New Testament, including the variants to the *Textus Receptus*, have been listed in a dual order, both alphabetical and numerical. The more significant words are discussed in detail. Writers of the word studies have been asked to follow a uniform style so there will be a logical sequence.

First, the usage of the word in nonbiblical Greek literature is described under the heading "Classical Greek." For the purposes of the *Dictionary* this information reports how the entry word was used in secular Greek from as early as the Eighth Century B.C. (e.g., Homer) through the period of the New Testament's authorship. The discussion includes Greek poetry, historical accounts, inscriptions, ostraca, papyri, etc. This usage provides a good basis for understanding the word's significance in the New Testament.

The Septuagint version (*LXX*, see discussion regarding this version) is the next focus of research and study. This Greek translation of the Old Testament was the one used in the First Century A.D. and was a major resource for the New Testament writers. Just as a study of classical Greek literature yields information about the meaning of the Greek words used in the New Testament, study of a term's use within the context of the Septuagint provides additional insights. Moreover (as described earlier in the "Septuagint Section"), comparing a Greek term with the Hebrew word or words it translated may supply further understanding of what certain Greek terms meant to the New Testament writers.

Note: sometimes the Septuagint references are different from those in our English Bible. When this occurs, they follow in brackets or parentheses.

Finally, the study deals with how the word was used in the New Testament itself. This is the most significant factor, since the context is of major importance in determining the meaning of a word.

Sometimes in a word study the writer lists the number of times the word appears in the New Testament. This number may not coincide with the number of occurrences in the *Concordance*. The reason is that variants from the *Textus Receptus* are included in the *Concordance*.

Citations in Text and Bibliography

Our writers, researchers, and editors have cited a wide variety of sources in the word studies. In order to provide consistency in the usage of such a broad range of sources, both in text and in the Bibliography, some adaptations of basic principles have been made.

The fundamental rule concerning citations in text throughout this work is that when there is a reference to another source, the first element of information leads the reader directly to the correct place in the applicable subsection of the Bibliography, with one exception noted below for signed articles.

In-text references to individual books, commentaries, and periodicals are by last name of author, shortened title, volume, and/or page number. Therefore these will be found in the General Bibliography under the author.

Lexicons, dictionaries, and encyclopedias are cited in text by the title of the set, the entry word, and for long articles a volume and page number. In references to signed articles the author's name is listed first, followed by the entry word and title of the set. However, the reader will find this resource along with the others listed above in the Bibliography under "General Reference Sources by Title."

Where a word study refers to the word under discussion in another source, the Greek word is not repeated; only the cited source is given, plus the page number if applicable. For example, the reader may see simply (*Bauer*) in the word study on "agathos." This directs the reader to the article on "agathos" in *Bauer*.

Writings of antiquity are cited differently from modern works, first stating author and title, then usually book, section, and line. In the Bibliography, works of antiquity, early church fathers, the Apocrypha, pseudepigrapha, and Jewish literature are categorized in a section entitled "Literature of Antiquity." This covers secular and noncanonical literature from about the Fifth Century B.C. to the end of the Medieval Period, approximately A.D. 1500.

RESOURCE TOOLS

There are available many other fine works prepared by outstanding scholars. Of these we have selected six standard works which students may consult if they wish to do further research:

STRONG'S = Strong, James. *The Exhaustive Concordance of the Bible*. 1890. Reprint. Nashville: Abingdon Press. 1977.

BAUER = Bauer, Walter, William F. Arndt, and F. Wilbur Gingrich. *A Greek-English Lexicon of the New Testament and other Early Christian Literature*. Rev. ed. by F. Wilbur Gingrich and Frederick W. Danker. Chicago: The University of Chicago Press. 1979.

COLIN BROWN = Brown, Colin, ed. *The New International Dictionary of New Testament Theology*. 4 vols. Grand Rapids: Zondervan Publishing House. 1975.

KITTEL = Kittel, G., and G. Friedrich. *Theological Dictionary of the New Testament*. Trans. by G. W. Bromiley. 10 vols. Grand Rapids: William B. Eerdmans Publishing Co. 1972.

LIDDELL-SCOTT = Liddell, H. G., and R. Scott. *A Greek-English Lexicon*. 9th. ed. Ed. by H. Stuart Jones and R. McKenzie. Oxford: Clarendon. 1940.

MOULTON-MILLIGAN = Moulton, J. H., and G. Milligan. *The Vocabulary of the Greek Testament Illustrated from the Papyri and Other Non-Literary Sources*. London: Hodder and Stoughton. 1914–1930. Reprint. Grand Rapids: William B. Eerdmans Publishing Co. 1985.

They will be listed as follows, by number for Strong's and volume and page for all others: Strong; Bauer; Moulton-Milligan; Kittel; Liddell-Scott; and Colin Brown.

Each has its own special approach and will add to a student's understanding of the New Testament. When any of these six cross-references do not appear, it means that work does not discuss that particular word to any significant degree.

2948. λαγχάνω lanchanō verb
Obtain by lot, obtain, receive, appoint.

SYNONYM:
κληρόω klēroō (2793)

לָכַד lākhadh (4058), Take (1 Sm 14:47).

1. ἔλαχεν elachen 3sing indic aor act
2. λάχωμεν lachōmen 1pl subj aor act
3. λαχοῦσιν lachousin dat pl masc part aor act
4. ἔλαχε elache 3sing indic aor act

1	his lot was to burn incense when he went into the...	Luke 1:9
2	Let us not rend it, but cast lots for it,............	John 19:24
1	and had obtained part of this ministry.............	Acts 1:17
3	to them that have obtained like precious faith......	2 Pt 1:1

Classical Greek
In classical Greek *lanchanō* means "to attain." The attainment, however, is not by one's own effort. For example, an official would decide, by lots, the order of a hearing. Normally it does not mean "to cast lots" but "to receive or obtain by lot."

Septuagint Usage
In the Septuagint *lanchanō* translates *lākhad* which means "capture," "seize," or "take (by lot)." In Joshua 7:14 the NASB says, "And it shall be that the tribe which the LORD *takes by lot* shall come near by families."

New Testament Usage
In the New Testament the word occurs four times. The word means "to obtain by lot" in Luke 1:9. Zechariah, not by his own effort, obtained the once-in-a-lifetime privilege of ministering at the altar of incense in the temple. The word also was used to mean to "receive," "appoint," or "obtain" as in Acts 1:17 where Judas was made an apostle by the Lord Jesus. Similarly, Vine clearly explains 2 Peter 1:1 when he says that Christians *have obtained* a like precious faith by its being allotted to them. They did not acquire it for themselves, but it came by divine grace, an act independent of human control (*Expository Dictionary of New Testament Words*, "Obtain"). Last, the word infrequently means "to cast lots" as in John 19:24 where it is used of the soldiers casting lots to determine who would receive the seamless garment of Jesus.

STRONG 2975, BAUER 462, MOULTON-MILLIGAN 368, KITTEL 4:1-2, LIDDELL-SCOTT 1022-23, COLIN BROWN 1:478.

2949. Λάζαρος Lazaros name
Lazarus.

1. Λάζαρος Lazaros nom masc
2. Λάζαρον Lazaron acc masc
3. Λάζαρε Lazare voc masc

1	And there was a certain beggar named Lazarus,....	Luke 16:20
2	seeth Abraham afar off, and Lazarus in his bosom.....	16:23
2	Abraham, have mercy on me, and send Lazarus,........	16:24
1	thy good things, and likewise Lazarus evil things:......	16:25
1	Now a certain man was sick, named Lazarus,......	John 11:1
1	whose brother Lazarus was sick......................	11:2
2	Jesus loved Martha, and her sister, and Lazarus........	11:5
1	Our friend Lazarus sleepeth;........................	11:11
1	said Jesus unto them plainly, Lazarus is dead..........	11:14
3	he cried with a loud voice, Lazarus, come forth........	11:43
1	where Lazarus was which had been dead,..............	12:1
1	Lazarus was one of them that sat at the table.........	12:2
2	but that they might see Lazarus also,.................	12:9
2	that they might put Lazarus also to death;............	12:10
2	with him when he called Lazarus out of his grave,.....	12:17

Two men are so named in the New Testament. One is the poor beggar in the parable (Luke 16:19ff.), and the other is the brother of Mary and Martha whom Jesus raised from the dead (John 11:1ff.).

2950. λάθρα lathra adv
Secretly, covertly, without knowledge of.

1. λάθρα lathra

1	Joseph ... was minded to put her away privily.......	Matt 1:19
1	Herod, when he had privily called the wise men,........	2:7
1	went her way, and called Mary her sister secretly,..	John 11:28
1	and now do they thrust us out privily? nay verily;..	Acts 16:37

This adverb is derived from the root *lath* which means "unnoticed" or "unknown." The related verb *lanthanō* (2963) means "to escape notice" or "to lie hidden." When Joseph learned of Mary's pregnancy, he decided to divorce her secretly (Matthew 1:19). Herod met secretly with the Magi to determine the time when they saw the star (Matthew 2:7). Mary told Martha "secretly" that Jesus had come to see her (John 11:28). When Paul and Silas were told they could leave the prison at Philippi Paul refused to leave secretly because they were unlawfully beaten (Acts 16:37).

STRONG 2977, BAUER 462, MOULTON-MILLIGAN 368, LIDDELL-SCOTT 1023.

2951. λαῖλαψ lailaps noun

Whirlwind, tempestuous wind, fierce gust of wind.

SYNONYM:
θύελλα thuella (2343)

סוּפָה sûphāh (5679), Storm (Jb 21:18).

סַעַר saʻar (5787), Storm (Jer 25:32 [32:32]).

סְעָרָה seʻārāh (5788), Whirlwind (Jb 38:1).

1. λαῖλαψ lailaps nom sing fem
2. λαίλαπος lailapos gen sing fem

1 And there arose a great **storm** of wind, ... Mark 4:37
1 And there came down **a storm** of wind on the lake; .. Luke 8:23
2 clouds that are carried with a **tempest**; .... 2 Pt 2:17

The Septuagint and New Testament use *lailaps* both literally and symbolically. A literal whirlwind or tempestuous wind was the source of the Lord's answer to Job (Job 38:1). A literal storm was also the experience that the Lord used to test the faith of the disciples (Mark 4:35-44; Luke 8:22-25).

The symbolic use of *lailaps* is found in Job 21:18 where Job described the wicked as "stubble before the wind, and as chaff that the *storm* carrieth away." Peter described false teachers as "wells without water, clouds that are carried with a *tempest*; to whom the mist of darkness is reserved for ever" (2 Peter 2:17). These two metaphors describe the false teachers' lack of substance and their instability and evanescence. The end of such is nothing short of hell itself.

STRONG 2978, BAUER 462-63, MOULTON-MILLIGAN 368, LIDDELL-SCOTT 1024, COLIN BROWN 3:1003.

2952. λακτίζω laktizō verb

To kick, strike with the heel, struggle.

1. λακτίζειν laktizein inf pres act

1 it is hard for thee to **kick** against the pricks. .... Acts 9:5
1 it is hard for thee to **kick** against the pricks. 26:14

Classical Greek

This verb was used initially in classical Greek to describe "kicking" with the heel or foot. It was used with regard to both men and animals. Later the word developed the more abstract meaning of "struggle."

New Testament Usage

In the New Testament it is used as part of the proverb which Jesus spoke to Paul when He said that it was hard for him "to *kick* against the pricks" (Acts 26:14). The pricks or goads were sharp sticks used to prod oxen in their work. If the ox kicked back, he would only needlessly injure himself. This common Greek proverb was often used figuratively to speak of unreasonable resistance. Thus it was as useless for Paul (Saul) to continue in the wrong way as it would be for a stubborn ox to attempt to leave the furrow (Patch, "Goad," *International Standard Bible Encyclopedia*, 2:491). Jesus meant that Paul should yield to the conviction of the Holy Spirit and believe in Jesus. Paul's mention of his guilt concerning Stephen's death indicates that Stephen's life and death may have contributed to this conviction (Acts 22:20).

STRONG 2979, BAUER 463, MOULTON-MILLIGAN 368, KITTEL 4:3, LIDDELL-SCOTT 1025.

2953. λαλέω laleō verb

Speak, proclaim, say, utter sounds.

COGNATES:
ἀλάλητος alalētos (213)
ἄλαλος alalos (214)
ἀνεκλάλητος aneklalētos (410)
διαλαλέω dialaleō (1249)
ἐκλαλέω eklaleō (1570)
καταγγέλλω katangellō (2576)
καταλαλέω katalaleō (2605)
λαλιά lalia (2954)
μογγιλάλος mongilalos (3287B)
μογιλάλος mogilalos (3288)
προσλαλέω proslaleō (4212)
συλλαλέω sullaleō (4665)

SYNONYMS:
διαλέγομαι dialegomai (1250)
ἐρεύγομαι ereugomai (2027)
λέγω legō (2978)
ὁμιλέω homileō (3519)
φημί phēmi (5183)
φθέγγομαι phthengomai (5187)
φωνέω phōneō (5291)

אָמַר ʼāmar (569), Qal: say (Nm 26:1, 2 Kgs 20:14, Ez 33:10); hithpael: boast (Ps 94:4 [93:4]).

λαλέω 2953

אֵמֶר 'ēmer (571), Words (Jb 34:37).

דָּבַר dāvar (1744), Qal: speak, talk (Dt 5:1, Ps 15:2 [14:2], Zec 1:9); niphal: speak to one another (Mal 3:16); piel: speak, say (Nm 5:4ff., 2 Kgs 1:15ff., Ez 3:1); pual: be spoken (Ps 87:3 [86:3]); be spoken for (S/S 8:8); hithpael: speak (Nm 7:89).

דָּבָר dāvār (1745), Word, report (Ex 32:28, 1 Kgs 10:7, Jon 3:3).

חָשַׁב chāshav (2913), Plan (Jer 36:3 [43:3]—Codex Alexandrinus only).

מִלָּה millāh (4543), Talking, speech (Jb 29:9,22).

מָלַל mālal (4589), Piel: say, utter (Jb 8:2, Ps 106:2 [105:2]).

מְלַל mᵉlal (A4590), Pael: speak (Dn 7:8,11,20,25—Aramaic).

נָבָא nāvā' (5187), Hithpael: prophesy (1 Kgs 22:8).

נָגַד nāghadh (5222), Hiphil: told (Est 4:9).

סָפַר sāphar (5807), Count; piel: tell (Ps 145:6 [144:6]).

פָּגַע pāgha' (6534), Entreat (Gn 23:8).

צָוָה tsāwâh (6943), Piel: command (Nm 15:36—Codex Alexandrinus only).

קָרָא qārā' (7410), Cry, proclaim (1 Kgs 13:32, 2 Kgs 23:16, Zec 7:7).

רִיב rîv (7662), Contend (Jer 2:29).

1. λαλῶ lalō 1sing indic/subj pres act
2. λαλεῖ lalei 3sing indic pres act
3. λαλεῖς laleis 2sing indic pres act
4. λαλοῦμεν laloumen 1pl indic pres act
5. λαλοῦσιν lalousin 3pl indic pres act
6. λαλῇ lalē 3sing subj pres act
7. λαλῶσιν lalōsin 3pl subj pres act
8. λάλει lalei 2sing impr pres act
9. λαλείτω laleitō 3sing impr pres act
10. λαλεῖτε laleite 2pl impr pres act
11. λαλείτωσαν laleitōsan 3pl impr pres act
12. λαλῶν lalōn nom sing masc part pres act
13. λαλοῦντος lalountos gen sing masc part pres act
14. λαλοῦντι lalounti dat sing masc part pres act
15. λαλοῦντα lalounta acc sing masc part pres act
16. λαλοῦντες lalountes nom pl masc part pres act
17. λαλούντων lalountōn gen pl masc part pres act
18. λαλοῦντας lalountas acc pl masc part pres act
19. λαλοῦσα lalousa nom sing fem part pres act
20. λαλούσης lalousēs gen sing fem part pres act
21. λαλοῦσαν lalousan acc sing fem part pres act
22. λαλοῦσαι lalousai nom pl fem part pres act
23. λαλοῦν laloun nom/acc sing neu part pres act
24. λαλεῖν lalein inf pres act
25. λαλήσω lalēsō 1sing indic/subj fut/aor act
26. ἐλάλησα elalēsa 1sing indic aor act
27. ἐλάλησεν elalēsen 3sing indic aor act
28. ἐλαλήσαμεν elalēsamen 1pl indic aor act
29. ἐλαλήσατε elalēsate 2pl indic aor act
30. ἐλάλησαν elalēsan 3pl indic aor act
31. λαλήσῃ lalēsē 3sing subj aor act
32. λαλήσητε lalēsēte 2pl subj aor act
33. λαλήσωσιν lalēsōsin 3pl subj aor act
34. λαλήσας lalēsas nom sing masc part aor act
35. λαλήσαντος lalēsantos gen sing masc part aor act
36. λαλήσαντες lalēsantes nom pl masc part aor act
37. λαλῆσαι lalēsai inf aor act
38. λελάληκα lelalēka 1sing indic perf act
39. λελάληκεν lelalēken 3sing indic perf act
40. λαλήσει lalēsei 3sing indic fut act
41. λαλήσομεν lalēsomen 1pl indic fut act
42. λαλήσουσιν lalēsousin 3pl indic fut act
43. λαλήσετε lalēsete 2pl indic fut act
44. ἐλάλουν elaloun 1/3sing/pl indic imperf act
45. ἐλάλει elalei 3sing indic imperf act
46. ἐλαλοῦμεν elaloumen 1pl indic imperf act
47. λαλεῖται laleitai 3sing indic pres mid
48. λαλούμενον laloumenon nom/acc sing masc/neu part pres mid
49. λαλουμένη laloumenē nom sing fem part pres mid
50. λαλουμένοις laloumenois dat pl neu part pres mid
51. λαλεῖσθαι laleisthai inf pres mid
52. ἐλαλήθη elalēthē 3sing indic aor pass
53. λαληθείς lalētheis nom sing masc part aor pass
54. λαληθείσης lalētheisēs gen sing fem part aor pass
55. λαληθέντος lalēthentos gen sing neu part aor pass
56. λαληθέντων lalēthentōn gen pl neu part aor pass
57. λαληθῆναι lalēthēnai inf aor pass
58. λελάληται lelalētai 3sing indic perf mid
59. λελαλημένοις lelalēmenois dat pl neu part perf mid
60. λαληθήσεται lalēthēsetai 3sing indic fut pass
61. λαληθησομένων lalēthēsomenōn gen pl neu part fut pass

13	While he **spake** these things unto them,	Matt 9:18
27	And when the devil was cast out, the dumb **spake**:	9:33
43	take no thought how or what ye **shall speak**:	10:19
43	for it shall be given you ... what ye **shall speak**.	10:19
16	For it is not ye that **speak**, but the Spirit	10:20
23	the Spirit of your Father which **speaketh** in you.	10:20
24	that the blind and dumb both **spake** and saw.	12:22
24	how can ye, being evil, **speak** good things?	12:34
2	of the abundance of the heart the mouth **speaketh**.	12:34
33	That every idle word that men shall **speak**,	12:36
13	While he yet **talked** to the people,	12:46
37	brethren stood without, desiring to **speak** with him.	12:46
37	thy mother and ... desiring to **speak** with thee.	12:47
27	And he **spake** many things unto them in parables,	13:3
3	Why **speakest** thou unto them in parables?	13:10
1	Therefore **speak** I to them in parables:	13:13
27	Another parable **spake** he unto them;	13:33
27	**spake** Jesus unto the multitude in parables;	13:34
45	and without a parable **spake** he not unto them:	13:34
27	But straightway Jesus **spake** unto them, saying,	14:27
18	when they saw the dumb to **speak**,	15:31
13	While he yet **spake**, ... cloud overshadowed them:	17:5
27	**spake** Jesus to the multitude, and to his disciples;	23:1
60	also this, ... be told for a memorial of her.	26:13
13	And while he yet **spake**, lo, Judas, ... came,	26:47
27	And Jesus came and **spake** unto them, saying,	28:18

λαλέω 2953

24	and suffered not the devils **to speak**,	Mark 1:34
45	and he **preached** the word unto them.	2:2
2	Why **doth** this man thus **speak** blasphemies?	2:7
45	And with many such parables **spake** he the word	4:33
45	But without a parable **spake** he not unto them:	4:34
13	While he yet **spake**, there came from the ruler	5:35
48	As soon as Jesus heard the word that **was spoken**,	5:36
27	And immediately he **talked** with them,	6:50
45	his tongue was loosed, and he **spake** plain.	7:35
24	both the deaf to hear, and the dumb **to speak**.	7:37
45	And he **spake** that **saying** openly.	8:32
31	he wist not what **to say**; for they were sore afraid.	9:6
2	but believes that what **he says** is going (NASB)	11:23
24	began **to speak** to them in parables: (NASB)	12:1
32	take no thought beforehand what ye **shall speak**,	13:11
10	shall be given you in that hour, that **speak** ye:	13:11
16	for it is not ye **that speak**, but the Holy Ghost.	13:11
60	this also that she hath done **shall be spoken of**	14:9
45	But Peter kept **saying** insistently, (NASB)	14:31
13	immediately, while he yet **spake**, cometh Judas,	14:43
42	they **shall speak** with new tongues;	16:17
37	So then after the Lord **had spoken** unto them,	16:19
37	I am Gabriel, ... and am sent **to speak** unto thee,	Luke 1:19
37	behold, thou shalt be dumb, and not able **to speak**,	1:20
37	when he came out, he could not **speak** unto them:	1:22
59	of those things which were **told** her from the Lord.	1:45
27	As he **spake** to our fathers, to Abraham,	1:55
45	his tongue loosed, and he **spake**, and praised God.	1:64
27	As he **spake** by the mouth of his holy prophets,	1:70
44	the shepherds **said** to one another, (NIV)	2:15
55	saying which **was told** them concerning this child.	2:17
56	things which **were told** them by the shepherds.	2:18
52	they had heard and seen, as it **was told** unto them.	2:20
50	at those things which **were spoken** of him.	2:33
45	and **spake** of him to all them that looked for	2:38
27	the saying which he **spake** unto them.	2:50
24	And he rebuking them suffered them not **to speak**:	4:41
12	when he had left **speaking**, he said unto Simon,	5:4
2	saying, Who is this which **speaketh** blasphemies?	5:21
2	of the abundance of the heart his mouth **speaketh**.	6:45
24	And he that was dead sat up, and began **to speak**.	7:15
13	While he yet **spake**, there cometh one from the	8:49
45	and **spake** unto them of the kingdom of God,	9:11
27	when the devil was gone out, the dumb **spake**;	11:14
37	And as he **spake**, a certain Pharisee besought him	11:37
29	and that which ye **have spoken** in the ear in closets	12:3
13	And while he yet **spake**, behold a multitude,	22:47
13	immediately, while he yet **spake**, the cock crew.	22:60
27	remember how he **spake** unto you ... in Galilee.	24:6
30	to believe all that the prophets **have spoken**:	24:25
45	while he **talked with** us by the way,	24:32
17	as they thus **spake**, Jesus himself stood in the midst	24:36
26	These are the words which I **spake** unto you,	24:44
13	And the two disciples heard him **speak**,	John 1:37
4	We **speak** that we do know,	3:11
2	and **speaketh** of the earth:	3:31
2	whom God hath sent **speaketh** the words of God:	3:34
12	Jesus saith unto her, I that **speak** unto thee am he.	4:26
45	and marvelled that he **talked** with the woman:	4:27
3	What seekest thou? or, Why **talkest** thou with her?	4:27
1	the words that I **speak** unto you, they are spirit,	6:63
45	no man **spake** openly of him for fear of the Jews.	7:13
1	whether it be of God, or whether I **speak** of myself.	7:17
12	He that **speaketh** of himself seeketh his own glory:	7:18
2	he **speaketh** boldly, and they say nothing unto him.	7:26
27	officers answered, Never man **spake** like this man.	7:46
27	Then **spake** Jesus again unto them, saying,	8:12
27	These words **spake** Jesus in the treasury,	8:20
1	the same that I **said** unto you from the beginning.	8:25
24	I have many things **to say** and to judge of you:	8:26
1	these I **speak** to the world." (NASB)	8:26
1	as my Father hath taught me, I **speak** these things.	8:28
13	As he **spake** these words, many believed on him.	8:30
1	I **speak** that which I have seen with my Father:	8:38
38	seek to kill me, a man that **hath told** you the truth,	8:40
6	When he **speaketh** a lie, he **speaketh** of his own:	8:44
2	When he **speaketh** a lie, he **speaketh** of his own:	8:44
40	he is of age; ask him: he **shall speak** for himself.	John 9:21
39	We know that God **spake** unto Moses:	9:29
12	and it is he that **talketh** with thee.	9:37
45	what things they were which he **spake** unto them.	10:6
39	others said, An angel **spake** to him.	12:29
27	These things **spake** Jesus, and departed,	12:36
27	Esaias, when he saw his glory, and **spake** of him.	12:41
26	one that judgeth him: the word that I **have spoken**,	12:48
26	For I **have** not **spoken** of myself;	12:49
25	what I should say, and what I **should speak**.	12:49
1	whatsoever I **speak** therefore, ... the Father said	12:50
1	even as the Father said unto me, so I **speak**.	12:50
1	words that I **speak** unto you I speak not of myself:	14:10
1	words that I speak unto you I **speak** not of myself:	14:10
38	These things **have I spoken** unto you,	14:25
25	Hereafter I **will** not **talk** much with you:	14:30
38	ye are clean through the word which I **have spoken**	15:3
38	These things **have I spoken** unto you,	15:11
26	If I had not come and **spoken** unto them,	15:22
38	These things **have I spoken** unto you,	16:1
38	But these things **have I told** you,	16:4
38	But because I **have said** these things unto you,	16:6
40	for he **shall** not **speak** of himself;	16:13
40	but whatsoever he shall hear, that **shall he speak**:	16:13
2	A little while? we cannot tell what he **saith**.	16:18
38	These things **have I spoken** unto you in proverbs:	16:25
25	when I **shall** no more **speak** unto you in proverbs,	16:25
3	now **speakest** thou plainly, ... speakest no proverb.	16:29
38	These things **have I spoken** unto you,	16:33
27	These words **spake** Jesus,	17:1
1	and these things I **speak** in the world,	17:13
26	Jesus answered him, I **spake** openly to the world;	18:20
26	and in secret have I **said** nothing.	18:20
26	ask them ... what I **have said** unto them:	18:21
26	If I **have spoken** evil, bear witness of the evil:	18:23
3	**Speakest** thou not unto me?	19:10
24	and began **to speak** with other tongues,	Acts 2:4
17	every man heard them **speak** in his own language.	2:6
16	Behold, are not all these **which speak** Galilaeans?	2:7
17	**speak** in our tongues the wonderful works of God.	2:11
27	He seeing this before **spake** of the resurrection	2:31
27	which God **hath spoken** by the mouth ... prophets	3:21
31	hear in all things whatsoever he **shall say** unto you.	3:22
30	those that follow after, as many as **have spoken**,	3:24
17	And as they **spake** unto the people,	4:1
24	that they **speak** henceforth to no man in this name.	4:17
24	For we cannot but **speak** ... which we have seen	4:20
24	that with all boldness they **may speak** thy word,	4:29
44	and they **spake** the word of God with boldness.	4:31
10	Go, stand and **speak** in the temple to the people	5:20
24	that they **should** not **speak** in the name of Jesus,	5:40
45	resist the wisdom and the spirit by which he **spake**.	6:10
13	**speak** blasphemous words against Moses,	6:11
12	This man ceaseth not **to speak** blasphemous words	6:13
27	And God **spake** on this wise,	7:6
13	the angel which **spake** to him in the mount Sina,	7:38
12	as he had appointed, **speaking** unto Moses,	7:44
36	had testified and **preached** the word of the Lord,	8:25
27	And the angel of the Lord **spake** unto Philip,	8:26
60	and it **shall be told** thee what thou must do.	9:6
27	and that he **had spoken** to him,	9:27
45	and disputed against the Grecians:	9:29
40	he **shall tell** thee what thou oughtest to do.	10:6
12	angel which **spake** unto Cornelius was departed,	10:7
40	who, when he cometh, **shall speak** unto thee.	10:32
13	While Peter yet **spake** these words,	10:44
17	heard them **speak** with tongues, and magnify God.	10:46
40	Who **shall tell** thee words,	11:14
24	as I began **to speak**, the Holy Ghost fell on them,	11:15
16	**preaching** the word to none but unto the Jews	11:19
44	**spake** unto the Grecians, preaching the Lord Jesus.	11:20
57	**might be preached** to them the next sabbath.	13:42
50	talked ... against what Paul **was saying** (NIV)	13:45
57	word of God should first **have been spoken** to you:	13:46
37	into the synagogue of the Jews, and so **spake**,	14:1
13	The same heard Paul **speak**:	14:9
36	And when they **had preached** the word in Perga,	14:25

22

37	and were forbidden of the Holy Ghost **to preach**	Acts 16:6
46	and **spake** unto the women which resorted thither	16:13
50	she attended unto the things which **were spoken**	16:14
30	And they **spake** unto him the word of the Lord,	16:32
49	what this new doctrine, whereof thou **speakest**, is?	17:19
8	Be not afraid, but **speak,** and hold not thy peace:	18:9
45	**spake** and taught diligently the things of the Lord,	18:25
44	and they **spake** with tongues, and prophesied	19:6
16	**speaking** perverse things, to draw away disciples	20:30
37	I beseech thee, suffer me **to speak** unto the people	21:39
13	they heard not the voice of him that **spake** to me	22:9
60	go into Damascus; and there it **shall be told** thee	22:10
35	And when he **had** so **said,** there arose a dissension	23:7
27	but if a spirit or an angel **hath spoken** to him,	23:9
37	who hath something **to say** unto thee	23:18
21	I heard a voice **speaking** unto me,	26:14
30	the prophets and Moses **did say** should come:	26:22
1	before whom also I **speak** freely:	26:26
44	they **talked** between themselves, saying,	26:31
58	that it shall be even as it **was told** me	27:25
27	neither any ... showed or **spake** any harm of thee	28:21
27	Well **spake** the Holy Ghost by Esaias the prophet	28:25
2	it **saith** to them who are under the law:	Rom 3:19
1	brethren, for I **speak** to them that know the law,	7:1
24	For I will not dare **to speak** of any of those things	15:18
4	we **speak** wisdom among them that are perfect:	1 Co 2:6
4	But we **speak** the wisdom of God in a mystery,	2:7
4	Which things also we **speak,**	2:13
37	could not **speak** unto you as unto spiritual,	3:1
1	**Say** I these things as a man?	9:8
12	that no man **speaking** by the Spirit of God	12:3
5	**do** all **speak** with tongues? do all interpret?	12:30
1	Though I **speak** with the tongues of men	13:1
44	When I was a child, I **spake** as a child,	13:11
12	For he that **speaketh** in an unknown tongue	14:2
2	in an unknown tongue **speaketh** not unto men,	14:2
2	howbeit in the spirit he **speaketh** mysteries.	14:2
2	that prophesieth **speaketh** unto men to edification,	14:3
12	**speaketh** in an unknown tongue edifieth himself;	14:4
24	I would that ye all **spake** with tongues,	14:5
12	prophesieth than he that **speaketh** with tongues;	14:5
12	if I come unto you **speaking** with tongues,	14:6
25	except I **shall speak** to you either by revelation,	14:6
48	how shall it be known what **is spoken**?	14:9
16	for ye **shall speak** into the air	14:9
14	I shall be unto him that **speaketh** a barbarian,	14:11
12	and he that **speaketh** shall be a barbarian unto me	14:11
12	let him that **speaketh** in an unknown tongue pray	14:13
12	I **speak** with tongues more than ye all:	14:18
37	Yet in the church I had rather **speak** five words	14:19
25	and other lips **will** I **speak** unto this people;	14:21
7	together into one place, and all **speak** with tongues,	14:23
2	If any man **speak** in an unknown tongue,	14:27
9	and let him **speak** to himself, and to God.	14:28
11	Let the prophets **speak** two or three,	14:29
24	for it is not permitted unto them **to speak;**	14:34
24	for it is a shame for women **to speak** in the church.	14:35
24	and forbid not **to speak** with tongues.	14:39
1	I **speak** this to your shame. (NASB)	15:34
4	in the sight of God **speak** we in Christ.	2 Co 2:17
26	I believed, and therefore have I **spoken;**	4:13
4	we also believe, and therefore **speak;**	4:13
28	but as we **spake** all things to you in truth,	7:14
1	That which I **speak,** I **speak** it not after the Lord,	11:17
1	That which I **speak,** I **speak** it not after the Lord,	11:17
1	ministers of Christ? I **speak** as a fool I am more;	11:23
37	which it is not lawful for a man **to utter.**	12:4
4	we **speak** before God in Christ:	12:19
13	Since ye seek a proof of Christ **speaking** in me,	13:3
10	**speak** every man truth with his neighbour:	Eph 4:25
16	**Speaking** to yourselves in psalms and hymns	5:19
37	I may **speak** boldly, as I ought **to speak.**	6:20
24	much more bold **to speak** the word without fear.	Phlp 1:14
37	**to speak** the mystery of Christ,	Col 4:3
37	That I may make it manifest, as I ought **to speak.**	4:4
24	so that we need not **to speak** any thing.	1 Th 1:8
37	we were bold in our God **to speak** unto you	2:2
4	even so we **speak;** not as pleasing men, but God,	1 Th 2:4
37	**to speak** to the Gentiles that they might be saved,	2:16
22	**speaking** things which they ought not	1 Tm 5:13
8	But **speak** thou ... which become sound doctrine:	Tit 2:1
8	These things **speak,** and exhort, and rebuke	2:15
34	who at sundry times and in divers manners **spake**	Heb 1:1
27	Hath in **these** last days spoken unto us by his Son,	1:2
53	For if the word **spoken** by angels was stedfast,	2:2
51	which at the first began **to be spoken** by the Lord,	2:3
4	the world to come, whereof we **speak.**	2:5
61	of those things which were **to be spoken after;**	3:5
45	not afterward **have spoken** of another day.	4:8
34	but he that **said** unto him, Thou art my Son,	5:5
4	that accompany salvation, though we thus **speak.**	6:9
27	tribe Moses **spake** nothing concerning priesthood.	7:14
54	Moses **had spoken** every precept to all the people	9:19
47	and by it he being dead yet **speaketh.**	11:4
52	**it was said,** That in Isaac shall thy seed be called:	11:18
14	that **speaketh** better things than that of Abel.	12:24
15	See that ye refuse not him that **speaketh.**	12:25
30	who **have spoken** unto you the word of God:	13:7
37	let every man be swift to hear, slow **to speak,**	Jas 1:19
10	So **speak** ye, and so do, as they that shall be judged	2:12
30	who **have spoken** in the name of the Lord,	5:10
37	and his lips that they **speak** no guile:	1 Pt 3:10
2	If any man **speak,**	4:11
30	but holy men of God **spake** as they were moved	2 Pt 1:21
12	**speaking** in them of these things;	3:16
5	therefore **speak** they of the world,	1 Jn 4:5
37	I trust to come unto you, and **speak** face to face,	2 Jn 1:12
41	shortly see thee, and we **shall speak** face to face.	3 Jn 1:14
30	ungodly deeds ... and of all their hard speeches	Jude 1:15
2	and their mouth **speaketh** great swelling words,	1:16
27	And I turned to see the voice that **spake** with me	Rev 1:12
20	was as it were of a trumpet **talking** with me;	4:1
30	seven thunders **uttered** their voices.	10:3
30	when the seven thunders had **uttered** their voices,	10:4
30	Seal up those ... which the seven thunders **uttered,**	10:4
19	And the voice which I heard from heaven **were**	10:8
23	a mouth **speaking** great things and blasphemies;	13:5
45	two horns like a lamb, and he **spake** as a dragon.	13:11
31	that the image of the beast **should** both **speak,**	13:15
27	and **talked** with me, saying unto me, Come hither;	17:1
27	and **talked** with me, saying, Come hither,	21:9
12	And he **that talked** with me had a golden reed	21:15

Classical Greek

Laleō, "to speak, to say, to communicate" (see also *legō* [2978]), is a most common word in antiquity. As a result it has a broad range of meaning and import (e.g., "to say, to chatter [especially of animals], to babble, to sound [a musical instrument]" or "to chirp" [of locusts]) (*Liddell-Scott*; cf. DeBrunner, "legō," *Kittel*, 4:76f.).

In classical Greek the meanings "to babble" (as an infant) and "to croon" (as a nurse) (cf. the English word *lullaby*) or "to whisper" were common (see also *Bauer*). The term became especially significant in philosophical discussions later (see *logos* [3030]). Most authorities agree, however, that *laleō* points to the external sound rather than to the content of what is said (*Moulton-Milligan*).

Septuagint Usage

The versatility of *laleō* is mirrored by the Septuagint. Eleven Hebrew terms are translated by *laleō*, but the most popular equivalent is undisputably the term *dāvar* in its various tenses. It frequently refers to the Lord's speaking to someone (e.g., Genesis 12:4; 16:13; 17:3,22) or to a human conversation (Genesis 19:14; 20:8). The prophetic proclamation is depicted as *lalein* (Jeremiah 26:16 [LXX 33:16]; cf. Jeremiah 1:9), particularly in Ezekiel (12:23; 20:27) which often uses the formula "I the LORD have spoken" (*egō kurios lelalēka*; 21:17,32; 23:34; 26:5; 30:12).

In this sense *laleō* joins the company of *logos*, *legō*, and others which are instrumental in telling the story of God's revelation to His people. The usage of these terms indicates that God's primary method of revelation was through the spoken word, either in a covenant agreement or prophetic revelation (cf. Hebrews 1:1f.). Thus what God declares through His prophets and leaders may mean judgment or salvation, prosperity or disaster. His word becomes event; He speaks the universe into existence and controls the events of history down to the smallest detail (e.g., Psalm 147:16,18 [LXX 146:16,18]). (See Klappert, "Word," *Colin Brown*, 3:1090.)

New Testament Usage

The use of *laleō* in the New Testament is thoroughly shaped by its heritage in the Old. The Gospels and Acts are responsible for about two-thirds of the occurrences in the New Testament. The emphasis of *laleō* upon the physical nature of speech is apparent in some texts (e.g., Matthew 15:31; Luke 1:20; 7:15; Acts 2:6,11; cf. above), but the message of what was spoken is more important (e.g., Luke 24:25; Acts 3:24; 9:6).

Jesus spoke (*laleō*) as no man had ever spoken (John 7:46). This statement is basic to any understanding of *laleō/legō/logos* in the New Testament. Those who do not believe in Him cannot understand His message; His sheep, though, know His voice (John 10:4-6; cf. 12:36-41). Jesus spoke not of himself; He said what the Father had instructed Him to say (John 12:49,50; 14:10). The Spirit, too, speaks what He hears from the Father (John 16:13ff.). Jesus' words from the Father bring joy (John 15:11), salvation (15:22), safety (cf. 16:1,4), and peace (16:33).

The gospel message, *ton logon* (*tou theou*, "of God"; *tou kuriou* "of the Lord"), is regularly the object of the verb *laleō* in Acts (4:29,31; 8:25; 11:19; 13:46). "To proclaim (*lalein*) the word (*ton logon*)" is thus gospel proclamation. Furthermore, in the new community of God charismatic utterances are clearly a miracle of speech (*laleō*) rather than hearing (*akouō* [189]) (e.g., Acts 2:4,6; 10:46; cf. Ephesians 5:19). Here we see the tendency of *laleō* to bring out the externality of sound rather than its specific meaning (cf. 1 Corinthians 12:30; 13:1; chapter 14 passim). The New Testament associates prophetic utterance with *laleō* (Acts 3:21f.; cf. 19:6; 2 Peter 1:21).

Paul, like Luke, under the guidance of the Spirit used *laleō* to describe his gospel proclamation (e.g., 1 Corinthians 2:6f.,13; 2 Corinthians 2:17; 4:13; Ephesians 6:20; 1 Thessalonians 2:2) or to refer to his instruction for the household of faith (1 Corinthians 3:1; cf. 2 Corinthians 11:17).

The writer of Hebrews invested *laleō* with certain theological nuances. God's communication with mankind is portrayed in *laleō* language (e.g., Hebrews 1:1,2; 11:4), and he links it to the covenant (2:2; 12:25; cf. 13:7) and the Law (9:19; cf. 2:2,3). Prophetic forecasts are expressed in terms of *laleō* (3:5; 4:8). Of course, the Old Testament background of God's words and covenant message plays a vital role in the entire letter.

Elsewhere the Spirit moves the writer of Revelation to use *laleō* in connection with angelic messages (17:1; 21:9,15), prophetic visions, and voices from heaven (i.e., "God"; Revelation 1:12; 4:1; 10:4,8). But it also describes the speaking of the beast (13:5,11,15).

Much of the New Testament's teaching and explanation of what God has accomplished in Christ is related in *laleō* language. God's people are a "people of the ear" (e.g., see Deuteronomy 6:4,5 the basic tenet of Israel's religion) rather than the eye. His word to man is summarized in Jesus Christ—*ho logos* ("The Word"). God acts through His Word within the history of Israel. He creates with His Word. He reveals His will through His prophetic spokesmen. This Word guides and warns; it saves and restores. The disciple is responsible not only to listen to what God says, but he or she must act upon it (cf. Luke 8:21).

STRONG 2980, BAUER 463-64, MOULTON-MILLIGAN

368, Kittel 4:3-5,69-136, Liddell-Scott 1025-26, Colin Brown 3:1081,1106,1109.

2954. λαλιά lalia noun
Pronunciation, dialect, accent, speech, talk, utterance.
Cognate:
λαλέω laleō (2953)
Synonym:
λόγος logos (3030)

אֹמֶר 'ômer (199), Speech (Ps 19:3 [18:3]).
בָּטָא bāṭā' (1017II) Talk (Sir 5:13).
דִּבָּה dibbāh (1730), Rumor (Sir 42:11).
דָּבָר dāvār (1745), Words (Dn 10:6,9).
מִדְבָּר midhbār (4199), Mouth (S/S 4:3).
שִׂיחַ sîach (7945), Talking (Sir 13:11).

1. λαλιά lalia nom sing fem
2. λαλιάν lalian acc sing fem

1 thou also art one ... for thy **speech** bewrayeth thee. Matt 26:73
1 art a Galilaean, and thy **speech** agreeth thereto.... Mark 14:70
2 Now we believe, not because of thy **saying**:......... John 4:42
2 Why do ye not understand my **speech**?................ 8:43

Classical Greek and Septuagint Usage
In classical Greek *lalia* denotes a "style of speech" (cf. Matthew 26:73; Mark 14:70). Later the word meant "talkativeness" or "chatter." It can denote "sound rather than meaning" and therefore can be used of a "crying" baby. In the Septuagint *lalia* is used to translate the common Hebrew word *dāvār* which is translated "word" over 770 times and "saying" over 30 times.

New Testament Usage
In the New Testament the word can mean "speech," "dialect," or "accent." During the trials of Christ, Peter's "speech" (i.e., his "accent" as the RSV says in Matthew 26:73; Mark 14:70) gave away his identity. Galileans spoke a dialect of Aramaic that had significant differences in pronunciation. Another nuance of the word is simply "speech," "talk," or "conversation." In John 4:42 the woman at the well returned to the city and testified about Jesus. Some of the townspeople said, "Now we believe, not because of thy *saying*." Trench comments on John 8:43 by saying, "To hear his 'word' *logos* can be nothing else than to give room to his truth in the heart. They who will not do this must fail to understand his 'speech,' (*lalia*), the outward form and utterance which his 'word' assumes" (*Synonyms of the New Testament*, p.289).

Strong 2981, Bauer 464, Moulton-Milligan 368-69, Liddell-Scott 1025-26.

2955. λαμά lama adv
Why?
1. λαμά lama
2. λιμά lima
3. λεμά lema
4. λαμμᾶ lamma

1 saying, Eli, Eli, **lama** sabachthani?................. Matt 27:46
4 saying, Eloi, Eloi, **lama** sabachthani?............. Mark 15:34

This is an Aramaic word which is the interrogative "why?" In Hebrew the term is spelled *lāmāh*, in Aramaic, *lēma*. It is only used in Matthew 27:46 and Mark 15:34 where Jesus cried from the cross, "Why hast thou forsaken me?" This is a quotation of Psalm 22:1.

Strong 2982, Bauer 464, Moulton-Milligan 369.

2956. λαμβάνω lambanō verb
Take, take hold of, grasp, seize; receive, get, obtain.
Cognates:
ἀναλαμβάνω analambanō (351)
ἀνάλημψις analēmpsis (352)
ἀνάληψις analēpsis (352B)
ἀνεπίληπτος anepilēptos (421)
ἀντιλαμβάνομαι antilambanomai (479)
ἀντίλημψις antilēmpsis (481)
ἀπολαμβάνω apolambanō (612)
ἀπροσωπολήμπτως aprosōpolēmptōs (671B)
ἀπροσωπολήπτως aprosōpolēptōs (672)
ἐπιλαμβάνομαι epilambanomai (1934)
εὐλαβέομαι eulabeomai (2106)
καταλαμβάνω katalambanō (2608)
μεταλαμβάνω metalambanō (3205)
μετάληψις metalēpsis (3206)
παραλαμβάνω paralambanō (3741)
προλαμβάνω prolambanō (4160)
προσλαμβάνω proslambanō (4213)
πρόσληψις proslēpsis (4214)
συλλαμβάνω sullambanō (4666)
συμπαραλαμβάνω sumparalambanō (4689)
συμπεριλαμβάνω sumperilambanō (4694)
συναντιλαμβάνομαι sunantilambanomai (4729)
ὑπολαμβάνω hupolambanō (5112)
Synonyms:
αἱρετίζω hairetizō (139)
αἱρέω haireō (141)
αἴρω airō (142)
ἀναδέχομαι anadechomai (322)
ἀναιρέω anaireō (335)
ἀπαίρω apairō (518)
ἀπέχω apechō (563)
ἀπολαμβάνω apolambanō (612)
ἀποφέρω apopherō (661)

λαμβάνω 2956

ἁρπάζω harpazō (720)
ἀφαιρέω aphaireō (844)
βαστάζω bastazō (934)
δέχομαι dechomai (1203)
δράσσομαι drassomai (1399)
εἰσδέχομαι eisdechomai (1509)
ἐκβάλλω ekballō (1531)
ἐκλέγομαι eklegomai (1573)
ἐξαιρέω exaireō (1791)
ἐξαίρω exairō (1792)
ἐπιδέχομαι epidechomai (1911)
ἐπιλαμβάνομαι epilambanomai (1934)
ἐπιλέγω epilegō (1935B)
ἔχω echō (2174)
καταλαμβάνω katalambanō (2608)
κομίζω komizō (2837)
κρατέω krateō (2875)
κρίνω krinō (2892)
μεταλαμβάνω metalambanō (3205)
παραδέχομαι paradechomai (3720)
παραλαμβάνω paralambanō (3741)
παραφέρω parapherō (3772)
περιαιρέω periaireō (3877)
πιάζω piazō (3945)
προσδέχομαι prosdechomai (4185)
προσλαμβάνω proslambanō (4213)
προχειρίζομαι procheirizomai (4258)
συλλαμβάνω sullambanō (4666)
συναρπάζω sunarpazō (4734B)
ὑποδέχομαι hupodechomai (5103)

אָחַז 'āchaz (270), Seize, take hold (Ex 15:14f., Jb 16:12 [16:13], Is 21:3).

אָרַשׂ 'āras (806), Piel: betroth (Dt 28:30).

בּוֹא bô' (971), Go, come; hiphil: bring (Ps 78:71 [77:71]).

הֵא hē' (1953), Here (Gn 47:23).

חָזַק châzaq (2480), Be strong; hiphil: hold (Jgs 7:20—Codex Alexandrinus only).

חָלַק châlaq (2606), Take a portion (2 Chr 28:21).

יָצָא yātsâ' (3428), Go out, come out; hiphil: bring out (2 Chr 16:2, Ezr 1:7).

יָרַשׁ yārash (3542), Take possession of (Jer 32:23 [39:23]).

יָשַׁב yāshav (3553), Sit, dwell; hiphil: marry (Ezr 10:2—only some Sinaiticus texts).

לָכַד lākhadh (4058), Qal: take, capture (Nm 32:41f., 2 Chr 28:18, Jer 34:22 [41:22]); niphal: be captured (Jer 48:1,41 [31:1,41]).

לָקַח lāqach (4089), Qal: take (Ex 29:19ff., 1 Kgs 11:34f., Ez 5:1ff.); niphal: be taken, be captured (1 Sm 4:11,17,19, Ez 33:6); pual: be taken (Gn 3:19,23, Is 52:5); hophal: be brought, be taken (Gn 18:4, Is 49:24f.).

מְכוּרָה mᵉkhûrāh (4489), Origin (Ez 29:14).

מָלֵא mālē' (4527), Fill (1 Kgs 18:33).

מַלְקוֹחַ malqôach (4596), Plunder (Is 49:25).

מָצָא mātsâ' (4834), Reach (Is 10:10).

מִקָּח miqqāch (4889), Taking (2 Chr 19:7).

מַשְׂאֵת mas'ēth (5020), Burden (Zep 3:18).

נָכָה nākhâh (5409), Hiphil: attack (Jos 15:16).

נָפַל nāphal (5489), Fall; hiphil: cast (1 Chr 24:31).

נָשָׂא nāsâ' (5558), Qal: bear, take (Nm 18:22f., 1 Chr 23:22, Jer 31:19 [38:19]); niphal: be carried (Is 39:6, Dn 11:12); piel: support (Ezr 1:4); take away (Am 4:2); hiphil: bring (2 Sm 17:13).

נְשָׂא nᵉsâ' (A5559), Take (Ezr 5:15—Aramaic).

נָשַׂג nāsagh (5560), Hiphil: overtake (Ps 69:24 [68:24]—only some Sinaiticus texts).

סוּר sûr (5681), Take off (Est 8:2).

עָדָה 'ādhâh (5917), Adorn oneself (Jer 31:4 [38:4]).

עָלָה 'ālâh (6148), Prompt (2 Kgs 12:4—Codex Vaticanus only).

פּוּק pûq (6572), Hiphil: obtain (Prv 18:22).

צוּר tsûr (6961), Bind (Dt 14:25).

קַבֵּל qabbēl (A7187), Pael: receive (Dn 2:6—Aramaic).

קוּם qûm (7251), Arise; hiphil: raise up (Am 2:11).

קָרֵב qārēv (7414), Come near; hiphil: bring near (Nm 3:6).

קָרַע qāra' (7458), Tear (1 Kgs 11:12f.).

שִׂים sîm (7947), Lay, put, set; give (Is 57:11).

שָׁבָה shāvâh (8091), Carry away (2 Chr 14:15).

תָּפַשׂ tāphas (8945), Qal: take (Is 36:1); niphal: be seized (Jer 51:32 [28:32]).

1. λαμβάνετε lambanete 2pl indic/impr pres act
2. λαμβάνω lambanō 1sing indic pres act
3. λαμβάνεις lambaneis 2sing indic pres act
4. λαμβάνει lambanei 3sing indic pres act
5. λαμβάνομεν lambanomen 1pl indic pres act
6. λαμβάνουσιν lambanousin 3pl indic pres act
7. λαμβάνῃ lambanē 3sing subj pres act
8. λαμβάνων lambanōn nom sing masc part pres act
9. λαμβάνοντες lambanontes nom pl masc part pres act
10. λαμβάνειν lambanein inf pres act
11. λαμβανέτω lambanetō 3sing impr pres act
12. ἔλαβον elabon 1/3sing/pl indic aor act
13. ἔλαβες elabes 2sing indic aor act
14. ἔλαβεν elaben 3sing indic aor act
15. ἐλάβομεν elabomen 1pl indic aor act
16. ἐλάβετε elabete 2pl indic aor act
17. λάβω labō 1sing subj aor act
18. λάβῃ labē 3sing subj aor act
19. λάβωμεν labōmen 1pl subj aor act
20. λάβητε labēte 2pl subj aor act
21. λάβωσιν labōsin 3pl subj aor act
22. λάβοι laboi 3sing opt aor act
23. λάβε labe 2sing impr aor act
24. λάβετε labete 2pl impr aor act
25. λαβών labōn nom sing masc part aor act
26. λαβόντα labonta acc sing masc part aor act

λαμβάνω 2956

27. λαβόντες labontes nom pl masc part aor act
28. λαβόντας labontas acc pl masc part aor act
29. λαβοῦσα labousa nom sing fem part aor act
30. λαβοῦσαι labousai nom pl fem part aor act
31. λαβεῖν labein inf aor act
32. εἴληφα eilēpha 1sing indic perf act
33. εἴληφας eilēphas 2sing indic perf act
34. εἴληφεν eilēphen 3sing indic perf act
35. εἰληφώς eilēphōs nom sing masc part perf act
36. ἐλάμβανον elambanon 3pl indic imperf act
37. λαμβανόμενος lambanomenos
        nom sing masc part pres mid
38. λαμβανόμενον lambanomenon
        nom/acc sing neu part pres mid
39. λήψεται lēpsetai 3sing indic fut mid
40. ληψόμεθα lēpsometha 1pl indic fut mid
41. λήψεσθε lēpsesthe 2pl indic fut mid
42. λήψονται lēpsontai 3pl indic fut mid
43. ἔλαβε elabe 3sing indic aor act
44. λαβέτω labetō 3sing impr aor act
45. λήμψεται lēmpsetai 3sing indic fut mid
46. λημψόμεθα lēmpsometha 1pl indic fut mid
47. λήμψεσθε lēmpsesthe 2pl indic fut mid
48. λήμψονται lēmpsontai 3pl indic fut mid

31	sue thee ... and **take** away thy coat,	Matt 5:40
4	For every one that asketh **receiveth**;	7:8
14	saying, Himself **took** our infirmities,	8:17
16	freely ye **have received**, freely give.	10:8
4	he that **taketh** not his cross, and followeth after me,	10:38
39	**shall receive** a prophet's reward;	10:41
39	**shall receive** a righteous man's reward.	10:41
12	and **held** a council against him,	12:14
8	heareth the word, and anon with joy **receiveth** it;	13:20
25	like to a grain of mustard seed, which a man **took**,	13:31
29	like unto leaven, which a woman **took**,	13:33
25	and **took** the five loaves, and the two fishes,	14:19
31	It is not meet **to take** the children's bread,	15:26
25	And he **took** the seven loaves and the fishes,	15:36
31	his disciples ... they had forgotten **to take** bread,	16:5
15	It is because we **have taken** no bread?	16:7
16	because ye **have brought** no bread?	16:8
16	and how many baskets ye **took up**?	16:9
16	and how many baskets ye **took up**?	16:10
9	they that **received** tribute money came to Peter,	17:24
6	of whom do the kings of the earth **take** custom	17:25
25	that **take**, and give unto them for me and thee.	17:27
39	for my name's sake, **shall receive** a hundredfold,	19:29
41	and whatsoever is right, that **shall ye receive**.	20:7
12	they **received** every man a penny.	20:9
42	supposed that they **should have received** more;	20:10
12	and they likewise **received** every man a penny.	20:10
27	And when they **had received** it,	20:11
41	ask in prayer, believing, ye **shall receive**.	21:22
31	that they **might receive** the fruits of it.	21:34
27	And the husbandmen **took** his servants,	21:35
27	they **caught** him, and cast him out of the vineyard,	21:39
12	Then went the Pharisees, and **took** counsel	22:15
41	therefore ye **shall receive** the greater damnation.	23:14
30	likened unto ten virgins, which **took** their lamps,	25:1
30	They that were foolish **took** their lamps,	25:3
12	took their lamps, and **took** no oil with them:	25:3
12	the wise **took** oil in their vessels with their lamps.	25:4
25	Then he that **had received** the five talents	25:16
25	**had received** one went and digged in the earth,	25:18
25	And so he that **had received** five talents came	25:20
25	also that **had received** two talents came and said,	25:22
35	which **had received** the one talent came and said,	25:24
25	Jesus **took** bread, and blessed it, and brake it,	Matt 26:26
24	and said, Take, eat; this is my body.	26:26
25	And he **took** the cup, and gave thanks,	26:27
27	**take** the sword shall perish with the sword.	26:52
12	**took** counsel against Jesus to put him to death:	27:1
27	And the chief priests **took** the silver pieces,	27:6
27	And they **took** counsel, and bought with them	27:7
12	And they **took** the thirty pieces of silver,	27:9
25	but that rather a tumult was made, he **took** water,	27:24
12	and **took** the reed, and smote him on the head.	27:30
25	straightway one of them ran, and **took** a sponge,	27:48
25	And when Joseph **had taken** the body,	27:59
27	assembled with the elders, and **had taken** counsel,	28:12
27	they **took** the money, and did as they were taught:	28:15
6	immediately **receive** it with gladness;	Mark 4:16
25	And when he **had taken** the five loaves,	6:41
31	for it is not meet **to take** the children's bread,	7:27
25	and he **took** the seven loaves, and gave thanks,	8:6
31	Now the disciples had forgotten **to take** bread,	8:14
25	he **took** a child, and set him in the midst of them:	9:36
18	he **shall receive** an hundredfold now in this time,	10:30
1	believe that ye **receive** them, ... ye shall have them.	11:24
18	that he **might receive** ... the fruit of the vineyard.	12:2
27	And they **caught** him, and beat him,	12:3
27	And they **took** him, and killed him,	12:8
18	that his brother **should take** his wife,	12:19
14	were seven brethren: and the first **took** a wife,	12:20
14	And the second **took** her, and died,	12:21
12	And the seven **had** her, and left no seed:	12:22
42	these **shall receive** greater damnation.	12:40
25	And as they did eat, Jesus **took** bread, and blessed,	14:22
24	gave to them, and said, Take, eat: this is my body.	14:22
25	he **took** the cup, and when he had given thanks,	14:23
12	And the officers **received** Him with slaps (NASB)	14:65
14	gave him to drink wine ... but he **received** it not.	15:23
15	have toiled all the night, and **have taken** nothing:	Luke 5:5
14	And they were all amazed, (NT)	5:26
14	house of God, and **did take** and eat the showbread,	6:4
31	those from whom you expect **to receive**, (NASB)	6:34
14	there **came** a fear **on all**: and they glorified God,	7:16
25	Then he **took** the five loaves and the two fishes,	9:16
4	lo, a spirit **taketh** him, and he suddenly crieth out;	9:39
4	For every one that asketh **receiveth**;	11:10
25	is like a grain of mustard seed, which a man **took**,	13:19
29	a woman **took** and hid in three measures of meal,	13:21
18	Who shall not **receive** many times (NASB)	18:30
31	into a far country **to receive** for himself a kingdom,	19:12
26	he was returned, **having received** the kingdom,	19:15
3	neither **acceptest** thou the person of any,	20:21
18	that his brother **should take** his wife,	20:28
25	the first **took** a wife, and died without children.	20:29
14	the second **took** her to wife, and he died childless.	20:30
14	third **took** her; and in like manner the seven also:	20:31
42	the same **shall receive** greater damnation.	20:47
24	**Take** this, and divide it among yourselves:	22:17
25	And he **took** bread, and gave thanks, and brake it,	22:19
25	he **took** bread, and blessed it, ... and gave to them,	24:30
25	And he **took** it, and did eat before them,	24:43
12	But as many as **received** him,	John 1:12
15	And of his fulness **have** all we **received**,	1:16
1	and ye **receive** not our witness.	3:11
10	A man can **receive** nothing, except it be given him	3:27
4	and no man **receiveth** his testimony.	3:32
25	He that **hath received** his testimony	3:33
4	And he that reapeth **receiveth** wages,	4:36
2	But I **receive** not testimony from man:	5:34
2	I **receive** not honour from men.	5:41
1	come in my Father's name, and ye **receive** me not:	5:43
41	shall come in his own name, him ye **will receive**.	5:43
9	which **receive** honour one of another,	5:44
18	that every one of them **may take** a little.	6:7
14	And Jesus **took** the loaves;	6:11
31	Then they willingly **received** him into the ship:	6:21
4	If a man on the sabbath day **receive** circumcision,	7:23
10	which they that believe on him should **receive**:	7:39
17	I lay down my life, that **I might take** it again.	10:17
31	and I have power **to take** it again.	10:18

λαμβάνω 2956

12	This commandment have I **received** of my Father.	John 10:18
29	Then **took** Mary a pound of ointment of spikenard,...	12:3
12	**Took** branches of palm trees,........................	12:13
8	He that rejecteth me, and **receiveth** not my words,....	12:48
25	and **took** a towel, and girded himself..................	13:4
14	and had **taken** his garments,.........................	13:12
8	He that **receiveth** whomsoever I send receiveth me;...	13:20
4	He that receiveth whomsoever I send **receiveth** me;...	13:20
8	he that **receiveth** me receiveth him that sent me......	13:20
4	he that receiveth me **receiveth** him that sent me......	13:20
4	He **took** and gave it to Judas, (NASB)................	13:26
25	**having received** the sop went immediately out:.......	13:30
31	the Spirit of truth; whom the world cannot **receive**,...	14:17
39	He shall glorify me: for he **shall receive** of mine,.....	16:14
39	therefore said I, that he **shall take** of mine,..........	16:15
41	ask, and ye **shall receive**, that your joy may be full....	16:24
12	given ... the words ... and they have **received** them,...	17:8
25	**having received** a band of men and officers...........	18:3
24	**Take** ye him, and judge him according to your law....	18:31
14	Pilate therefore **took** Jesus, and scourged him.........	19:1
24	Pilate saith unto them, **Take** ye him,.................	19:6
12	**took** his garments, and made four parts,.............	19:23
14	that disciple **took** her unto his own home.............	19:27
14	When Jesus therefore **had received** the vinegar,.......	19:30
12	Then **took** they the body of Jesus,....................	19:40
24	and saith unto them, **Receive** ye the Holy Ghost:.....	20:22
4	**taketh** bread, and giveth them, and fish likewise......	21:13
41	But ye **shall receive** power,...........................	Acts 1:8
22	and his bishopric let another **take**....................	1:20
31	he **may take** part of this ministry and apostleship,.....	1:25
27	ye **have taken**, and by wicked hands have crucified.....	2:23
25	and **having received** of the Father the promise.........	2:33
41	and ye **shall receive** the gift of the Holy Ghost.........	2:38
31	he began asking to **receive** alms (NASB).............	3:3
31	expecting **to receive** something of them...............	3:5
16	have **received** the law by the disposition of angels,....	7:53
21	that they **might receive** the Holy Ghost...............	8:15
36	hands on them, and they **received** the Holy Ghost.....	8:17
7	I lay hands, he **may receive** the Holy Ghost...........	8:19
25	when he **had received** meat, he was strengthened......	9:19
27	Then the disciples **took** him by night,.................	9:25
31	believeth in him **shall receive** remission of sins........	10:43
12	which have **received** the Holy Ghost as well as we?....	10:47
31	**to take** out of them a people for his name.............	15:14
25	and **took** and circumcised him because of the Jews....	16:3
35	Who, **having received** such a charge,.................	16:24
27	And when they **had taken** security of Jason,.........	17:9
27	and **receiving** a commandment unto Silas............	17:15
16	said unto them, Have ye **received** the Holy Ghost.....	19:2
12	ministry, which I **have received** of the Lord Jesus,....	20:24
10	It is more blessed to give than **to receive**.............	20:35
14	But after two years Porcius Festus **came**.............	24:27
22	and have licence to answer for himself.................	25:16
25	**having received** authority from the chief priests;......	26:10
31	that they **may receive** forgiveness of sins,.............	26:18
25	And when he had thus spoken, he **took** bread,.......	27:35
14	he thanked God, and **took** courage...................	28:15
15	By whom we **have received** grace and apostleship,..	Rom 1:5
14	And he **received** the sign of circumcision,.............	4:11
15	by whom we **have** now **received** the atonement........	5:11
9	much more they which **receive** abundance of grace.....	5:17
29	But sin, **taking** occasion by the commandment,........	7:8
29	For sin, **taking** occasion by the commandment,.......	7:11
16	not **received** the spirit of bondage again to fear;.......	8:15
16	but ye **have received** the Spirit of adoption,............	8:15
42	and they that resist **shall receive** to themselves.......	13:2
15	Now we have **received**, not the spirit of the world,	1 Co 2:12
39	and every man **shall receive** his own reward..........	3:8
39	any man's work abide ... he **shall receive** a reward.....	3:14
13	and what hast thou that thou didst not **receive**?.......	4:7
13	now if thou **didst receive** it, why dost thou glory,.....	4:7
25	dost thou glory, as if thou **hadst** not **received** it?......	4:7
4	run in a race run all, but one **receiveth** the prize?.....	9:24
21	Now they do it **to obtain** a corruptible crown;.........	9:25
34	There hath no temptation **taken** you but such as.....	10:13
14	same night in which he was betrayed **took** bread:.....	11:23
24	**Take**, eat: this is my body,............................	11:24
18	interpret, that the church **may receive** edifying.....	1 Co 14:5
1	or if ye **receive** another spirit,.......................	2 Co 11:4
16	which ye **have** not **received**,.........................	11:4
25	**taking** wages of them, to do you service.............	11:8
4	if a man devour you, if a man **take** of you,..........	11:20
12	five times **received** I forty stripes save one...........	11:24
12	nevertheless, being crafty, I **caught** you with guile.....	12:16
4	no matter to me: God **accepteth** no man's person:...	Gal 2:6
16	**Received** ye the Spirit by the works of the law,........	3:2
19	that we **might receive** the promise of the Spirit........	3:14
25	and **took** upon him the form of a servant,...........	Phlp 2:7
12	Not as though I had already **attained**,................	3:12
16	touching whom ye **received** commandments:.........	Col 4:10
38	if it **be received** with thanksgiving:..................	1 Tm 4:4
8	When I **call** to remembrance the unfeigned faith...	2 Tm 1:5
14	**received** a just recompence of reward;...............	Heb 2:2
29	first began to be spoken by the Lord, (NT)...........	2:3
19	unto the throne ... that we **may obtain** mercy,........	4:16
37	For every high priest **taken** from among men........	5:1
4	And no man **taketh** this honour unto himself,........	5:4
9	who **receive** the office of the priesthood,.............	7:5
6	And here men that die **receive** tithes;................	7:8
8	who **receiveth** tithes, payed tithes in Abraham........	7:9
21	**might receive** the promise of eternal inheritance......	9:15
25	he **took** the blood of calves and of goats,............	9:19
31	that we **have received** the knowledge of the truth,....	10:26
10	to go out into a place which he should after **receive** ..	11:8
14	Through faith also Sara herself **received** strength......	11:11
27	not **having received** the promises,...................	11:13
27	which the Egyptians assaying **to do** were drowned....	11:29
12	Women **received** their dead raised to life again:......	11:35
12	others **had** trial of cruel mockings and scourgings,....	11:36
39	For let not that man think that he **shall receive**......	Jas 1:7
39	when he is tried, he **shall receive** the crown of life,.....	1:12
40	**we shall receive** the greater condemnation............	3:1
1	Ye ask, and **receive** not, because ye ask amiss,........	4:3
18	until he **receive** the early and latter rain.............	5:7
24	**Take**, my brethren, the prophets, who have spoken....	5:10
14	As every man **hath received** the gift,................	1 Pt 4:10
25	forgotten that he was purged from his (NT)........	2 Pt 1:9
25	**received** from God the Father honour and glory,......	1:17
16	But the anointing which ye **have received** of him....	1 Jn 2:27
5	And whatsoever we ask, we **receive** of him,..........	3:22
5	If we **receive** the witness of men,....................	5:9
15	**have received** a commandment from the Father.....	2 Jn 1:4
1	not this doctrine, **receive** him not into your house,....	1:10
9	they went forth, **taking** nothing of the Gentiles.....	3 Jn 1:7
8	which no man knoweth saving he that **receiveth** it...	Rev 2:17
32	even as I **received** of my Father.....................	2:27
33	Remember therefore how thou **hast received**.........	3:3
18	fast which thou hast, that no man **take** thy crown....	3:11
31	worthy, ... **to receive** glory and honour and power:.....	4:11
34	he came and **took** the book out of the right hand......	5:7
14	And when he **had taken** the book,....................	5:8
31	Thou art worthy **to take** the book,...................	5:9
31	the Lamb that was slain **to receive** power,...........	5:12
31	him that sat thereon **to take** peace from the earth,.....	6:4
34	the angel **took** the censer, and filled it with fire......	8:5
23	Go and **take** the little book which is open...........	10:8
23	And he said unto me, **Take** it, and eat it up;.........	10:9
12	And I **took** the little book out of the angel's hand,...	10:10
33	because thou **hast taken** to thee thy great power,.....	11:17
4	**receive** his mark in his forehead, or in his hand,......	14:9
4	and whosoever **receiveth** the mark of his name.......	14:11
12	ten kings, which have **received** no kingdom as yet;....	17:12
6	but **receive** power as kings one hour with the beast...	17:12
20	and that ye **receive** not of her plagues................	18:4
28	them that **had received** the mark of the beast,.......	19:20
12	neither his image, neither **had received** his mark.....	20:4
11	let him **take** the water of life freely..................	22:17

Classical Greek

Lambanō—actively meaning "to take," passively "to receive"—is the principal component of numerous compounds in antiquity and is consequently a widely used term with a diverse range of meaning (e.g., *analambanō* [351], *epilambanomai* [1934], *metalambanō* [3205], etc.). *Liddell-Scott* gives over 20 nuances for *lambanō*. The classical usage may emphasize the active sense, "to take, grasp" (Delling, "lambanō," *Kittel*, 4:5 note 1), but the passive sense, "to receive, acquire," is also attested. Delling notes that in religious statements "God can receive (*lambanō*) nothing because He possesses all things" (ibid., 4:5). Other meanings attested in classical literature include "to seize, to overtake, to discover, to apprehend, to receive in marriage, to reach, attain" (see also *Moulton-Milligan* for a summary of papyri usage).

Septuagint Usage
Lambanō translates over 30 Hebrew expressions, most commonly the various tense forms of *lāqach*. "God *took* the man, and put him into the garden of Eden" (Genesis 2:15; cf. 2:21,22 of Adam's ribs). The "sons of God" "took" women from the "daughters of men" (NIV, "married"; Genesis 6:2; passim the Old Testament). There may be a sexual reference in Genesis 20:2,3 (of Abimelech's "taking" of Sarah), although "marriage" may be equally correct. God "takes" Israel as His people (Exodus 6:7). *Lambanō* occurs in God's instructions concerning offerings and consecrations (Exodus chapter 29; cf. Numbers 16:6,15,17,39,46,47). The "seizing" of battle spoils is typically related by *lambanō* (1 Maccabees 5:3,22,28,35,51).

New Testament Usage
Lambanō occurs over 250 times in the Greek New Testament. It occurs regularly within the Gospel narratives: of a literal taking (Matthew 5:40; 26:26); of taking a wife (Luke 20:28f.); of receiving eternal life (Mark 10:30). It is most common in Matthew and John; Luke often uses synonyms (e.g., cf. Mark 4:16/Luke 8:13, *dechomai* [1203]; Mark 9:36/Luke 9:47). Paul (over 30 times) did not assign *lambanō* to the same position of importance as other New Testament writers; however, it was still useful for characterizing Christian experience. (Cf. 1 Corinthians 4:7, "What do you [the Corinthians] have that you did not receive [from God]?" NIV.)

Theologically, John especially included the term in his thesis' overall framework that Jesus and His message must be "received." That reception cannot take place apart from God's granting insight (e.g., John 3:11,27,32,33). Other writers agree that men receive forgiveness, mercy, and grace from God (Acts 10:43; Romans 1:5; Hebrews 4:16).

The Holy Spirit's relationship to the believer is at times viewed on the premise that He has been *received* (John 20:22; Acts 8:15; 19:2; 1 Corinthians 2:12; 2 Corinthians 11:4; Galatians 3:2). The same holds true for other promises and gifts of God (e.g., Romans 5:11, "atonement"; Romans 8:15, "the Spirit of adoption"; Hebrews 9:15, "promise of eternal inheritance"; cf. Mark 10:30; James 1:12). In fact, everything is a gift from God (1 Corinthians 4:7; cf. Revelation 22:17).

Jesus himself had taken upon himself the form of a servant (Philippians 2:7). He received His commission from the Father (John 10:18; cf. Revelation 2:28), and He is worthy to receive all power and riches (Revelation 5:12), glory and honor (Revelation 4:11). To all who receive Him He grants the right to become God's children (John 1:12; cf. 5:43; 13:20).

STRONG 2983, BAUER 464-65, MOULTON-MILLIGAN 369, KITTEL 4:5-7, LIDDELL-SCOTT 1026-27, COLIN BROWN 3:747-51.

2957. Λάμεχ Lamech name
Lamech.

1. Λάμεχ Lamech masc

1 which was the son of Lamech, ... Luke 3:36

The son of Methuselah in the genealogy of Jesus (Luke 3:36).

2958. λαμπάς lampas noun
Torch, lamp, glowing manifestation.
COGNATE:
 λάμπω lampō (2962)
SYNONYM:
 λύχνος luchnos (3060)

לַפִּיד lappîdh (4083), Lightning (Ex 20:18); torch (Jgs 15:4, Is 62:1).

1. λαμπάς lampas nom sing fem
2. λαμπάδες lampades nom pl fem
3. λαμπάδων lampadōn gen pl fem
4. λαμπάδας lampadas acc pl fem

4 likened unto ten virgins, which took their lamps, ... Matt 25:1
4 They that were foolish took their lamps, ... 25:3
3 the wise took oil in their vessels with their lamps...... 25:4

4 all those virgins arose, and trimmed their **lamps**.... Matt 25:7
2 Give us of your oil; for our **lamps** are gone out........ 25:8
3 cometh thither with **lanterns** and torches ....John 18:3
2 And there were many **lights** in the upper chamber, Acts 20:8
2 seven **lamps** of fire burning before the throne,....... Rev 4:5
1 great star from heaven, burning as it were **a lamp**,...... 8:10

Classical Greek
In classical Greek *lampas* is a "torch" or "lamp." This was a resinous pinewood torch or a ceramic lamp used with olive oil and a wick. It was lit during a festal procession or when a leader made an official visit to a city.

Septuagint Usage
In the Septuagint *lampas* is used to translate the Hebrew *lappîdh*, a "torch" like Gideon (Judges 7:16,20) and Samson (Judges 15:5,6) used in their exploits. The word also describes something that was brilliant (Ezekiel 1:13), e.g., a "flaming torch" symbolizing judgment (Zechariah 12:6) and the presence of God (Genesis 15:17).

New Testament Usage
In the New Testament the word is used five times in the Parable of the Ten Virgins (Matthew 25:1-8). Alfred Edersheim says, "The lamps consisted of a round receptacle for pitch or oil for the wick. This was placed in a shallow cup or deep saucer . . . which was fastened by a pointed end into a long wooden pole, on which it was borne aloft" (*Life and Times of Jesus the Messiah*, 2:455). The torch was used for general illumination as seen in the arrest in the Garden of Gethsemane (John 18:3). The reference in Acts 20:8 is to the typical small ceramic lamp containing olive oil for fuel and a wick for the flame which provided light in the upper room at Troas. In Revelation the word is used to describe a heavenly manifestation before the throne of God (4:5) and the great star that fell from heaven during the third trumpet judgment (8:10).

Strong 2985, Bauer 465, Moulton-Milligan 369-70, Kittel 4:16-28, Liddell-Scott 1027, Colin Brown 2:484-86.

2959. λαμπρός lampros adj
Bright, shining, radiant, brilliant, opulent, clear.
Cognate:
λάμπω lampō (2962)
Synonyms:
λευκός leukos (2996)
φωτεινός phōteinos (5296)

1. λαμπρόν **lampron** nom/acc sing masc/neu
2. λαμπρός **lampros** nom sing masc
3. λαμπρᾷ **lampra** dat sing fem
4. λαμπράν **lampran** acc sing fem
5. λαμπρά **lampra** nom/acc pl neu

4 mocked him, and arrayed him in a **gorgeous** robe, Luke 23:11
3 behold, a man stood before me in **bright** clothing,.. Acts 10:30
3 a man with a gold ring, in **goodly** apparel,........... Jas 2:2
4 have respect to him that weareth the **gay** clothing,..... 2:3
1 seven angels ... clothed in pure and **white** linen,.... Rev 15:6
5 things which were dainty and **goodly** are departed..... 18:14
1 should be arrayed in fine linen, clean and **white**:....... 19:8
1 a pure river of water of life, **clear** as crystal,.......... 22:1
2 and the **bright** and morning star...................... 22:16

Classical Greek
In the classical period the sense of *lampros* was "bright" (e.g., clothes) or "radiant" (e.g., sun or stars). In metaphoric usages it communicated the sense of "clear" (e.g., a witness) or "fresh" (e.g., a breeze). With reference to people it meant "well known" or "illustrious." In the Koine period it meant "shining" (e.g., land) or "illustrious" (e.g., a brother). It also was used as an adjective to describe miracles (cf. *Liddell-Scott* for references to the above examples).

Septuagint Usage
There are seven occurrences of *lampros* in the Septuagint: however, none of them are canonical. In those texts in which it does appear it refers to the "radiant" quality of Wisdom (Wisdom of Solomon 6:12) or to "elegant" food (Sirach 29:22). It is an image of cheer in some cases (Sirach 30:25, "cheerful heart," RSV; cf. our English idiom "beam" with pride, joy, etc.).

New Testament Usage
In the New Testament the word *lampros* is translated six different ways by the KJV in the nine times it occurs. Frequently the word is used as an adjective to describe clothes. It was used to describe the "splendid" robe that was put on Jesus when He was sent to Pilate (Luke 23:11), the "brilliant" dress of an angelic messenger (Acts 10:30), and the "fine" apparel that someone might wear to a meeting of the church (James 2:2,3). Also, the wife of the Lamb will be dressed in "elegant" fine white linen for Him (Revelation 19:8; cf. 15:6). The word also is used to describe the "opulence" and luxuries of the Babylon which is to come (Revelation 18:14). The river of water of life in the New Jerusalem will be "clear" and transparent as crystal (Revelation 22:1). Last, Jesus himself is called the "bright" and morning star (Revelation 22:16).

Strong 2986, Bauer 465-66, Moulton-Milligan 370, Kittel 4:16-28, Liddell-Scott 1028, Colin Brown 2:484,486.

2960. λαμπρότης lamprotēs noun
Brightness, brilliance, splendor.
CROSS-REFERENCE:
    λάμπω lampō (2962)

הָדָר hādhār (1994), Majesty (Ps 110:3 [109:3]).

נֹעַם nō'am (5461), Favor (Ps 90:17 [89:17]).

1. λαμπρότητα lamprotēta acc sing fem

1 above the **brightness** of the sun,............... Acts 26:13

Classical Greek
In classical Greek *lamprotēs* is used to describe the "splendor" of weapons. Its figurative sense is "magnanimity" or "largeheartedness." It is also used as a title of honor.

Septuagint Usage
The Septuagint uses *lamprotēs* to translate *hādhār* which, in the marginal rendering of the NASB in Psalm 110:3 (LXX 109:3), is translated as the "splendor" of holiness. In Isaiah 60:3 the nations will be drawn to the "brilliance" of the dawn of God. The apocryphal Book of Baruch uses *lamprotēs* as an image of God's salvation (4:24; cf. 5:3).

New Testament Usage
The New Testament uses *lamprotēs* only once (Acts 26:13). In this verse the glory of the Lord Jesus Christ on the Damascus Road when Saul was converted is described as "above the *brightness* of the sun" (cf. Acts 9:3; 22:9,11).

STRONG 2987, BAUER 466, MOULTON-MILLIGAN 370, LIDDELL-SCOTT 1028, COLIN BROWN 2:484-86.

2961. λαμπρῶς lamprōs adv
Splendidly, magnificently, lavishly, brilliantly.
CROSS-REFERENCE:
    λάμπω lampō (2962)

1. λαμπρῶς lamprōs

1 rich man, ... and fared **sumptuously** every day:..... Luke 16:19

This adverb is only used once in the New Testament. In Luke's account of the rich man and Lazarus, Jesus said that "there was a certain rich man, which was clothed in purple and fine linen, and fared *sumptuously* every day" (Luke 16:19). This rich man's wealth was evident by what he wore and how he lived.

STRONG 2988, BAUER 466, MOULTON-MILLIGAN 370, COLIN BROWN 2:484,486.

2962. λάμπω lampō verb
To shine, shine forth, illumine.

COGNATES:
    ἐκλάμπω eklampō (1571)
    λαμπάς lampas (2958)
    λαμπρός lampros (2959)
    λαμπρότης lamprotēs (2960)
    λαμπρῶς lamprōs (2961)
    περιλάμπω perilampō (3897)

SYNONYMS:
    ἀστράπτω astraptō (791)
    αὐγάζω augazō (820)
    ἐπιφαύσκω epiphauskō (2001)
    φαίνω phainō (5154)
    φωτίζω phōtizō (5297)

נָגַהּ nāghahh (5226), Shine (Is 9:2).

נֹגַהּ nōghahh (5227), Light (Prv 4:18).

צָחַח tsāchach (6972), Be white (Lam 4:7).

1. λάμπει lampei 3sing indic pres act
2. ἔλαμψεν elampsen 3sing indic aor act
3. λαμψάτω lampsatō 3sing impr aor act
4. λάμψαι lampsai inf aor act
5. λάμψει lampsei 3sing indic fut act

1 and it giveth **light** unto all that are in the house..... Matt 5:15
3 Let your light so **shine** before men,.................. 5:16
2 and his face did **shine** as the sun,..................... 17:2
1 **shineth** unto the other part under heaven;......... Luke 17:24
2 and a light **shined** in the prison:..................... Acts 12:7
4 who commanded the light to **shine** out of darkness,..2 Co 4:6
2 **shine** out of darkness, hath **shined** in our hearts,........ 4:6

Classical Greek and Septuagint Usage
In the classical Greek *lampō* means "shine" or "give light." Figuratively it is used to describe someone who was "famous." The Septuagint uses *lampō* to translate the Hebrew word *nāghahh* in two of the four times *lampō* occurs. Proverbs 4:18 describes the "path of the just" as a "shining light" that shines brightly each day until perfection is reached. Another metaphoric use can be found in Isaiah 9:2. Isaiah prophesied of the birth of the coming Messiah for those who "dwell in the land of the shadow of death, upon them hath the light *shined*."

New Testament Usage
At the Transfiguration Jesus' countenance "shined forth" (Matthew 17:2). A shining light also accompanied an angel of the Lord in Acts 12:7. *Lampō* is used of the initiation of salvation; just as God caused light to shine into the original darkness (Genesis 1:3), even so has God caused the light of Christ's salvation to shine into a lost man's dark heart (2 Corinthians 4:6). Just as a lamp on a lampstand gives light to a house, even so is a Christian to cause his "light to shine" in order that God might be glorified (Matthew 5:15,16). Last, the second coming of Christ will illuminate the sky like lightning does, for the glory of the second advent will be beheld by all men (Luke 17:24).

λανθάνω 2963

Strong 2989, Bauer 466, Moulton-Milligan 370, Kittel 4:16-28, Liddell-Scott 1028, Colin Brown 2:484-86, 496.

2963. λανθάνω lanthanō verb
Lie hidden, be hidden, be unaware.

COGNATES:
ἀληθεύω alētheuō (224)
ἐκλανθάνομαι eklanthanomai (1572)
ἐπιλανθάνομαι epilanthanomai (1935)

SYNONYMS:
ἀποκρύπτω apokruptō (607)
καλύπτω kaluptō (2543)
κρύπτω kruptō (2900)
παρακαλύπτω parakaluptō (3732)
περικαλύπτω perikaluptō (3891)
συγκαλύπτω sunkaluptō (4631)

כָּחַד kāchadh (3701), Niphal: be hidden (2 Sm 18:13).

מָעַל māʻal (4760), Act unfaithfully, be unfaithful (Lv 5:15, Nm 5:27).

עָדַר ʻādhar (5952), Niphal: be lacking, be missing (2 Sm 17:22, Is 40:26).

עָלַם ʻālam (6180), Niphal: be hidden (Lv 5:3,4, Nm 5:13, Jb 28:21).

1. **λανθάνει** lanthanei 3sing indic pres act
2. **λανθανέτω** lanthanetō 3sing impr pres act
3. **λανθάνειν** lanthanein inf pres act
4. **ἔλαθεν** elathen 3sing indic aor act
5. **ἔλαθον** elathon 3pl indic aor act
6. **λαθεῖν** lathein inf aor act

```
6 have no man know it: but he could not be hid...... Mark 7:24
4 And when the woman saw that she was not hid,.... Luke 8:47
3 that none of these things are hidden from him;.... Acts 26:26
5 thereby some have entertained angels unawares..... Heb 13:2
1 For this they willingly are ignorant of,............ 2 Pt 3:5
2 But, beloved, be not ignorant of this one thing,......... 3:8
```

Septuagint Usage
Lanthanō appears in the Septuagint 17 times and expresses a variety of actions. For example, Leviticus 4:13; 5:3,4,15 use this verb to describe unintentional sins that are committed by a group or by an individual that are temporarily hidden from public attention. In contrast, Numbers 5:13 refers to an intentional sin that is deliberately hidden. In a sobering discussion of divine justice, Job 34:21 says that God observes all the sins of mankind (literally, "nothing of what they do *has escaped* Him").

New Testament Usage
In the New Testament lanthanō appears six times. It expresses the concept of physical concealment (i.e., someone or something is actually hidden) and the contrast between ignorance and knowledge (i.e., something is hidden or not hidden from the mind). The former meaning is seen in Mark 7:24 which records that Jesus could find no privacy from the crowds ("he could not be hid" or "escape notice"). The other five appearances of *lanthanō* illustrate the latter meaning. Luke 8:47 records that the touch of the woman with a hemorrhage did not escape Jesus' notice.

By stating that "none of these things *are hidden*," Paul pointed to the public nature of the Gospel events (Acts 26:26). Those who practiced self-deception and willful ignorance were chastised in 2 Peter 3:5,8. Finally, Hebrews 13:2 observes that some people have entertained angels without knowing it ("unawares"). Although this verse alludes to Genesis 18:3; 19:2, the Greek world also believed in the possibility of conversing with angels who came to earth incognito.

Strong 2990, Bauer 466, Moulton-Milligan 370, Liddell-Scott 1028-29.

2964. λαξευτός laxeutos adj
Hewn or cut in stone.

פִּסְגָּה pisgāh (6695), Pisgah (Dt 4:49).

1. **λαξευτῷ** laxeutō dat sing neu

```
1 and laid it in a sepulchre that was hewn in stone,...Luke 23:53
```

This adjective describes that which is "cut in stone." It is derived from *las*, "stone," and *xeō*, "to scrape." It appears only once in the Septuagint at Deuteronomy 4:49, a reference to the "springs of *Pisgah*." The Septuagint's rendering of this proper noun with *laxeutos* may be geographically significant in determining whether the Pisgah was an entire mountain range or a single peak (see LaSor, "Pisgah," *International Standard Bible Encyclopedia*, 3:873, for further discussion of this). The only use of *laxeutos* in the New Testament is in Luke 23:53 where the tomb of Joseph of Arimathea where Jesus was buried is described as "a sepulchre that was *hewn in stone*."

Strong 2991, Bauer 466, Moulton-Milligan 370, Liddell-Scott 1029.

2965. Λαοδίκεια Laodikeia name
Laodicea.

1. **Λαοδικείας** Laodikeias gen fem
2. **Λαοδικείᾳ** Laodikeia dat fem
3. **Λαοδίκειαν** Laodikeian acc fem

2 conflict I have for you, and for them at **Laodicea**,	Col 2:1
2 them that are in **Laodicea** and them in Hierapolis.	4:13
2 Salute the brethren which are in **Laodicea**,	4:15
1 that ye likewise read the epistle from **Laodicea**.	4:16
1 Grace be with thee. Amen. (NT)	1 Tm 6:21
3 and unto Philadelphia, and unto **Laodicea**.	Rev 1:11
2 And to ... the church in **Laodicea** (NASB)	3:14

City in Asia Minor near Colossae; recipients of a Pauline epistle (either lost or the present day Epistle to the Ephesians; Colossians 4:16), and a message from the Risen Lord (Revelation 3:14).

2966. Λαοδικεύς Laodikeus name-adj

Laodicean.

1. Λαοδικέων Laodikeōn gen pl masc

1 it be read also in the church of the **Laodiceans**;	Col 4:16
1 And unto ... the church of the **Laodiceans** write;	Rev 3:14

Resident of Laodicea (Colossians 4:16).

2967. λαός laos noun

People, nation, crowd, general populace.

SYNONYMS:
- γλῶσσα glōssa (1094)
- δῆμος dēmos (1211B)
- ἔθνος ethnos (1477)
- ὄχλος ochlos (3657)
- πλῆθος plēthos (3988)
- φυλή phulē (5279)

אָדָם 'ādhām (119), Man (1 Sm 24:9 [24:10]).
אֻמָּה 'ummāh (531), Nation (Ps 117:1 [116:1]).
אֻמָּה 'ummāh (A532), Nation (Dn 3:4—Aramaic).
אֱנוֹשׁ 'ěnôsh (596), Man (Jgs 18:22—Codex Alexandrinus only).
בַּיִת bayith (1041), House (Ex 8:9).
בֵּן bēn (1158), Son (Ex 4:23).
גּוֹי gôy (1504), Nation (Jos 4:1, Is 9:3, Zec 14:14).
הָמוֹן hāmôn (2066), Multitude (Jb 31:34—Codex Alexandrinus only).
טַף taph (3054), Children (Jgs 21:10—Codex Alexandrinus only).
לְאֹם lᵉ'ōm (3947), People (Gn 25:23, Ps 2:1, Prv 14:28).
מַחֲנֶה machăneh (4402), Army (Jos 10:5).
מָקוֹם māqôm (4887), Place (Ru 4:10).
מִשְׁפָּחָה mishpāchāh (5121), Nation (Na 3:4).
עֶבֶד 'evedh (5860), Servant (1 Kgs 8:36—Codex Alexandrinus only).
עַם 'am (6194I), People (Ex 12:33f., 1 Sm 14:26ff., Mi 6:2f.).
צֹאן tsō'n (6887), Flock (Jer 23:3).

קָהָל qāhāl (7235), Assembly (1 Kgs 12:3, 2 Chr 30:24).

1. λαός laos nom sing masc
2. λαοῦ laou gen sing masc
3. λαῷ laō dat sing masc
4. λαόν laon acc sing masc
5. λαοί laoi nom pl masc
6. λαῶν laōn gen pl masc
7. λαοῖς laois dat pl masc

4	for he shall save his **people** from their sins.	Matt 1:21
2	the chief priests and scribes of the **people** together,	2:4
4	a Governor, that shall rule my **people** Israel.	2:6
1	The **people** which sat in darkness saw great light;	4:16
3	and all manner of disease among the **people**.	4:23
3	every sickness and every disease among the **people**.	9:35
2	For this **people's** heart is waxed gross,	13:15
1	**people** draweth nigh unto me with their mouth,	15:8
2	the chief priests and the elders of the **people**	21:23
2	and the scribes, and the elders of the **people**,	26:3
3	lest there be an uproar among the **people**.	26:5
2	from the chief priests and elders of the **people**.	26:47
2	all the chief priests and elders of the **people**	27:1
1	Then answered all the **people**, and said,	27:25
3	steal him away, and say unto the **people**,	27:64
1	This **people** honoureth me with their lips,	Mark 7:6
4	they feared the **people**:	11:32
2	the feast day, lest there be an uproar of the **people**.	14:2
2	the whole multitude of the **people** were praying	Luke 1:10
4	to make ready a **people** prepared for the Lord.	1:17
1	And the **people** waited for Zacharias,	1:21
3	for he hath visited and redeemed his **people**,	1:68
3	To give knowledge of salvation unto his **people**	1:77
3	tidings of great joy, which shall be to all **people**.	2:10
6	thou hast prepared before the face of all **people**;	2:31
2	and the glory of thy **people** Israel.	2:32
2	And as the **people** were in expectation,	3:15
4	many other things ... preached he unto the **people**.	3:18
4	Now when all the **people** were baptized,	3:21
2	and a great multitude of **people** out of all Judaea	6:17
2	ended all his sayings in the audience of the **people**,	7:1
4	and, That God hath visited his **people**.	7:16
1	all the **people** that heard him, and the publicans,	7:29
2	she declared unto him before all the **people**	8:47
4	should go and buy meat for all this **people**.	9:13
1	and all the **people**, when they saw it, gave praise	18:43
2	and the chief of the **people** sought to destroy him,	19:47
1	for all the **people** were very attentive to hear him.	19:48
4	as he taught the **people** in the temple,	20:1
1	and if we say, Of men; all the **people** will stone us:	20:6
4	Then began he to speak to the **people** this parable;	20:9
4	to lay hands on him; and they feared the **people**:	20:19
2	could not take hold of his words before the **people**:	20:26
2	Then in the audience of all the **people** he said	20:45
3	distress in the land, and wrath upon this **people**.	21:23
1	all the **people** came early in the morning to him;	21:38
4	how they might kill him; ... they feared the **people**.	22:2
2	The elders of the **people** and the chief priests and	22:66
4	He stirreth up the **people**,	23:5
4	the chief priests and the rulers and the **people**,	23:13
4	as one that perverteth the **people**:	23:14
2	there followed him a great company of **people**,	23:27
1	And the **people** stood beholding.	23:35
2	a prophet mighty ... before God and all the **people**:	24:19
1	and all the **people** came unto him;	John 8:2
2	that one man should die for the **people**,	11:50
2	expedient that one man should die for the **people**,	18:14
4	and having favour with all the **people**.	Acts 2:47
1	all the **people** saw him walking and praising God:	3:9
1	all the **people** ran together unto them in the porch	3:11
4	he answered unto the **people**, Ye men of Israel,	3:12
2	shall be destroyed from among the **people**.	3:23
4	And as they spake unto the **people**,	4:1
4	Being grieved that they taught the **people**,	4:2

λαός 2967

2	Ye rulers of the **people**, and elders of Israel,	Acts 4:8
3	known unto you all, and to all the **people** of Israel,	4:10
4	But that it spread no further among the **people**,	4:17
4	because of the **people**: for all men glorified God	4:21
5	and the **people** imagine vain things?	4:25
7	Pilate, with the Gentiles, and the **people** of Israel,	4:27
3	signs and wonders wrought among the **people**;	5:12
1	but the **people** magnified them.	5:13
3	Go, stand and speak in the temple to the **people**	5:20
4	standing in the temple, and teaching the **people**.	5:25
4	without violence: for they feared the **people**,	5:26
3	had in reputation among all the **people**,	5:34
4	and drew away much **people** after him:	5:37
3	did great wonders and miracles among the **people**.	6:8
4	And they stirred up the **people**, and the elders,	6:12
1	the **people** grew and multiplied in Egypt,	7:17
2	the affliction of my **people** which is in Egypt,	7:34
3	which gave much alms to the **people**,	10:2
3	Not to all the **people**, but unto witnesses chosen	10:41
3	And he commanded us to preach unto the **people**,	10:42
3	after Easter to bring him forth to the **people**.	12:4
2	from all the expectation of the **people** of the Jews.	12:11
4	any word of exhortation for the **people**, say on.	13:15
2	The God of this **people** of Israel chose our fathers,	13:17
3	exalted the **people** when they dwelt as strangers	13:17
3	baptism of repentance to all the **people** of Israel.	13:24
4	who are his witnesses unto the **people**.	13:31
4	to take out of them a **people** for his name.	15:14
1	for I have much **people** in this city.	18:10
3	saying unto the **people**,	19:4
2	teacheth all men every where against the **people**,	21:28
2	and the **people** ran together: and they took Paul,	21:30
3	For the multitude of the **people** followed after,	21:36
4	I beseech thee, suffer me to speak unto the **people**.	21:39
3	and beckoned with the hand unto the **people**.	21:40
2	Thou shalt not speak evil of the ruler of thy **people**.	23:5
2	Delivering thee from the **people**,	26:17
3	and should show light unto the **people**,	26:23
3	I have committed nothing against the **people**,	28:17
4	Saying, Go unto this **people**, and say,	28:26
2	For the heart of this **people** is waxed gross,	28:27
4	call them my **people**, which were not my **people**;	Rom 9:25
4	I will call them my **people**, which were not	9:25
1	it was said unto them, Ye are not my **people**;	9:26
4	hands unto a disobedient and gainsaying **people**.	10:21
4	I say then, Hath God cast away his **people**?	11:1
4	God hath not cast away his **people**	11:2
2	he saith, Rejoice, ye Gentiles, with his **people**.	15:10
5	Praise the Lord, ... and laud him, all ye **people**.	15:11
1	The **people** sat down to eat and drink,	1 Co 10:7
3	and other lips will I speak unto this **people**;	14:21
1	I will be their God, and they shall be my **people**.	2 Co 6:16
4	and purify unto himself a peculiar **people**,	Tit 2:14
2	to make reconciliation for the sins of the **people**.	Heb 2:17
3	remaineth therefore a rest to the **people** of God.	4:9
2	for the **people**, so also for himself, to offer for sins.	5:3
4	have a commandment to take tithes of the **people**	7:5
1	for under it the **people** received the law,	7:11
2	first for his own sins, and then for the **people**'s:	7:27
4	and they shall be to me a **people**:	8:10
2	for himself, and for the errors of the **people**:	9:7
3	Moses had spoken every precept to all the **people**	9:19
3	and sprinkled both the book, and all the **people**,	9:19
4	And again, The Lord shall judge his **people**.	10:30
3	rather to suffer affliction with the **people** of God,	11:25
4	he might sanctify the **people** with his own blood,	13:12
1	priesthood, an holy nation, a peculiar **people**;	1 Pt 2:9
1	Which in time past were not a **people**,	2:10
1	were not a **people**, but are now the **people** of God:	2:10
3	there were false prophets also among the **people**,	2 Pt 2:1
4	having saved the **people** out of the land of Egypt,	Jude 1:5
2	and tongue, and **people**, and nation;	Rev 5:9
6	all nations, and kindreds, and **people**, and tongues,	7:9
7	Thou must prophesy again before many **peoples**,	10:11
6	the **people** and kindreds and tongues and nations	11:9
4	every tribe, **people**, language and nation (NIV)	13:7
4	nation, and kindred, and tongue, and **people**,	14:6
5	**peoples**, and multitudes, and nations, and tongues.	Rev 17:15
1	voice from heaven, ... Come out of her, my **people**,	18:4
5	will dwell with them, and they shall be his **people**,	21:3

Classical Greek

The origin of *laos* is uncertain. At its outset *laos* meant "a crowd of people, a group, an army." The definition of *laos* as a "military troop," however, slowly disappeared. Gradually the term came to indicate any group of people, a "population," the "public." In this respect *laos* acquired formal and reverent tones.

Septuagint Usage

Such formal or reverent association may have influenced the Septuagint translators to afford *laos* with a unique status. The Greek *ho laos* (singular) came to denote the chosen "people" of God—i.e., Israel. The expression occurs about 2,000 times in the Septuagint, most often with this unique sense. *Laos* is the equivalent of the Hebrew *'am*, "people," whereas *ethnē* (see 1477), "nations, peoples," ordinarily indicates a Hebrew counterpart of *gôy/gôyim*, "the peoples," especially the Gentiles. *Laos* appears to have been reserved for denoting the "people of God," but not other peoples, and *ethnē* is utilized for the "nations," but not Israel.

At times Israel is called *'am yehwāh*, "the people of Yahweh." But far more consistently (about 300 times) the Lord himself calls Israel *'ammî*, "my people." Whenever Israel violated the covenant, the most severe punishment exacted by God was to "disown" His people. They were no longer called *'ammî*, "my people," but *lō' 'ammî*, "not my people" (cf. Hosea 1:9). The prophet envisioned a time when God would once again call the people *'ammî* (Hosea 2:1,23).

New Testament Usage

The New Testament writers, prompted by the Spirit, pick up on and modify the Septuagint's uses of *laos*. However, this is not the only use of *laōs* in the New Testament. In about 140 occurrences it departs from the Septuagintal distinctive and uses *laos* to indicate human beings in general (cf. Strathmann, "laos," *Kittel*, 4:50,51 who sees this as a more regular occurrence in Luke-Acts; but cf. Paul Minear, *Images of the Church in the New Testament*, pp.67ff.). The plural *laoi* is even more rare (eight times; e.g., Luke 2:31; Acts 4:25; Revelation 7:9). The most ordinary construction is with the article; thus "the people" is a wooden, albeit better, translation (ibid.; the articular construction is often found in Luke [e.g., 2:10,31; 6:17]).

The "people" are peculiarly God's people, the nation of Israel (e.g., Matthew 1:21; 2:6; John 11:50; 18:14; Acts 13:17,24). God has not rejected His people (Romans 11:2), however disobedient they have been (Romans 10:21). The nations (*ta ethna*) are now, however, coheirs with the nation Israel (Acts 15:14; Romans 15:10,11)—the Church is the new people of God (2 Corinthians 6:16; Titus 2:14; cf. Strathmann, "laos," *Kittel*, 4:54).

The author of Hebrews mirrors such thinking. Just as everything in the old covenant was a temporary representative of the new covenant (e.g., priesthood, sacrifice, offering system, law), so too, national, biological Israel as God's people is replaced or superseded by the Christian community, the new people of God. This takes place not on the biological level but on the level of faith (cf. John 8:12-59). Hebrews 4:9; 5:3; 10:30; 13:12 assume such a relationship. Christ as High Priest has offered himself for the sins of the people (7:5ff.; 11ff.; 9:7); He has offered himself on behalf of the people, once for all (Hebrews 9:28; 10:10).

First Peter, likewise, recognizes that Christ has transformed *ta ethna* (cf. 2:12) (the nations/ Gentiles) into a chosen race (*genos* [1079]), a royal priesthood, a holy nation (*ethnē*), a people (*laos*) belonging to God (2:9). Those who were "not a people" are now *laos theou*, "God's people" (2:10; cf. Hosea 1:9).

Revelation indicates that God's people(s) (*laoi*, 21:3; cf. 18:4) are comprised of "every kindred, and tongue, and *people*, and nation" (5:9; cf. 7:9; 14:6). Again, any national or physical interpretation of *laos* is dubious. Christ has died for all peoples to make a people for God (cf. Luke 2:31,32).

STRONG 2992, BAUER 466-67, MOULTON-MILLIGAN 370-71, KITTEL 4:29-57, LIDDELL-SCOTT 1029-30, COLIN BROWN 2:795-801,805.

2968. λάρυγξ larunx noun
Throat, larynx, gullet.

גָּרוֹן gārôn (1671), Throat (Pss 5:9, 69:3 [68:3], 115:7 [113:15]).

חֵךְ chēkh (2541), Palate, mouth (Jb 12:11, Ps 119:103 [118:103]).

מַלְקוֹחַ malqôach (4596), Jaws (Ps 22:15 [21:15]).

1. λάρυγξ larunx nom sing masc
1 Their throat is an open sepulchre; .... Rom 3:13

This noun is used only one time in the New Testament and means "throat" or "larynx." Paul, who used it metaphorically of speech, said concerning the wicked that "their *throat* is an open sepulchre; with their tongues they have used deceit; the poison of asps is under their lips" (Romans 3:13). Paul may have been alluding to Psalm 5:9 where the Septuagint uses this same word. David likewise said of the wicked that "there is no faithfulness in their mouth; their inward part is very wickedness; their *throat* is an open sepulchre; they flatter with their tongue" (Psalm 5:9). The reference to the throat as an open "sepulchre" (grave, tomb) depicts the uncleanness and filth which characterizes the speech of the wicked and leads to death.

STRONG 2995, BAUER 467, KITTEL 4:57-58, LIDDELL-SCOTT 1031.

2969. Λασαία Lasaia name
Lasea.

1. Λασαία Lasaia nom fem
1 fair havens; nigh whereunto was the city of Lasea... Acts 27:8

A city on the southern coast of the island of Crete (Acts 27:8).

2970. λάσκω laskō verb
Crack, burst open, burst apart.

1. ἐλάκησεν elakēsen 3sing indic aor act
1 falling headlong, he burst asunder in the midst, ... Acts 1:18

This verb, which means "to crack" or "burst open," is related to the verb *elakēsa*. In Acts 1:18 Luke, speaking of Judas' death, said that "he *burst asunder* in the midst, and all his bowels gushed out." What began as a suicide by hanging probably turned into something much more gruesome; perhaps the limb broke and Judas' body fell into a pit or chasm, causing such mutilation (cf. Archer, *Encyclopedia of Bible Difficulties*, p.344). Another explanation of the incident involves the word *apanchomai* (515), translated "hanged" at Matthew 27:5 in the KJV. Evidence suggests that in the time of Christ "hanging" was a reference to both crucifixion, impalement, and literal hanging by the neck. If Judas impaled himself on a sharpened stake, it is quite easy to see how his bowels "gushed out." The church father Papias, however, stated that Judas actually swelled up after hanging himself (see Horton, *Complete Biblical Library, Matthew*, p.611)—perhaps to the extent that his bowels burst and gushed out. It should be noted that *Bauer* claims the source of *elakōsen* in Acts 1:18 is *lakaō* rather than *laskō*. The verb *lakaō* means "to blister" or "burst."

STRONG 2997, BAUER 467,
MOULTON-MILLIGAN 371,
LIDDELL-SCOTT 1031.

2971. λατομέω latomeō verb

To cut stones, shape stones, hew out of rock.

חָצָה chātsâh (2779), Qal: hew out, something dug (1 Chr 22:2, Neh 9:25, Is 22:16; pual: be hewn (Is 51:1).

כָּרָה kārâh (3868), Dig (Ex 21:33).

1. ἐλατόμησεν elatomēsen 3sing indic aor act
2. λελατομημένον lelatomēmenon
   nom/acc sing neu part perf mid

1 new tomb, which he **had hewn** out in the rock:.....Matt 27:60
2 in a sepulchre which **was hewn** out of a rock,......Mark 15:46

This verb is a compound of *las*, "stone," and *temnō*, "to cut," and means "to cut stones." The Septuagint uses the noun form *latomos*, "stonecutter," and the infinitive *latomēsai*, "to cut," in 1 Chronicles 22:2. This verse relates how David "set masons *to hew* wrought stones to build the house of God." This verb is only used twice in the New Testament where it refers to the tomb of Joseph of Arimathea. Joseph took the body of Jesus "and laid it in his own new tomb, which *he had hewn out* in the rock" (Matthew 27:60; cf. Mark 15:46 and Luke 23:53).

STRONG 2998, BAUER 467, MOULTON-MILLIGAN 371, LIDDELL-SCOTT 1031.

2972. λατρεία latreia noun

Service, ministry, worship of God.
CROSS-REFERENCE:
   λατρεύω latreuō (2973)

עֲבֹדָה 'ăvōdhāh (5865), Service, ceremony (Ex 12:25,26, 13:5).

1. λατρείας latreias gen/acc sing/pl fem
2. λατρεία latreia nom sing fem
3. λατρείαν latreian acc sing fem

3 killeth you will think that he doeth God service.... John 16:2
2 and the giving of the law, and the service of God,...Rom 9:4
3 which is your reasonable service..................... 12:1
1 had also ordinances of divine service,............... Heb 9:1
1 first tabernacle, accomplishing the service of God....... 9:6

Classical Greek
This noun appears in classical Greek from the Fifth Century B.C., usually referring to the "service" of a hired laborer, or metaphorically, to the "business" or "duties" of everyday life (*Liddell-Scott*). *Latreia* also developed a religious significance as "service" to the Greek gods in the forms of worship and offerings. It is this sense of the word that is carried into Biblical usage.

Septuagint Usage
Latreia is used both in the Septuagint and in the New Testament of service or ministry rendered to God. It is closely related to *thrēskeia* (2333) in meaning. The nation of Israel was commanded to keep the *service* of the Passover (Exodus 12:25,26).

New Testament Usage
In the New Testament the writer to the Hebrews said that the first covenant had "ordinances of divine *service*" (Hebrews 9:1) and that the priests accomplished the "*service* of God" in the first tabernacle (Hebrews 9:6). Paul likewise said that to Israel "pertaineth ... the *service* of God" (Romans 9:4).

Jesus must have shocked His disciples when He said that the time would come when "whosoever killeth you will think that he doeth God *service*" (John 16:2). Paul had originally thought he was serving God when he persecuted Christians (Acts 26:9-11). *Latreia* is also used in Romans 12:1. "The *service* which Christians are to offer consists in the fashioning of their inner lives and their outward physical conduct in a way which plainly distinguishes them from the world and which corresponds to the will of God" (Strathmann, "latreia," *Kittel*, 4:65).

STRONG 2999, BAUER 467, MOULTON-MILLIGAN 371, KITTEL 4:58-65, LIDDELL-SCOTT 1032, COLIN BROWN 3:549-51.

2973. λατρεύω latreuō verb

Serve, worship.
COGNATE:
   λατρεία latreia (2972)
SYNONYMS:
   διακονέω diakoneō (1241)
   δουλεύω douleuō (1392)
   θεραπεύω therapeuō (2300)

λειτουργέω leitourgeō (2982)
ὑπηρετέω hupēreteō (5094)

עָבַד 'āvadh (5856), Serve (Dt 10:12, Jos 24:14f., 2 Kgs 17:12).

פְּלַח pᵉlach (A6643), Serve (Dn 3:12, 6:16, 7:14—Aramaic).

שָׁרַת shārath (8664), Piel: minister, serve (Nm 16:9, Ez 20:32).

1. λατρεύω latreuō 1sing indic pres act
2. λατρεύουσιν latreuousin 3pl indic pres act
3. λατρεύωμεν latreuōmen 1pl subj pres act
4. λατρεύοντα latreuonta acc sing masc part pres act
5. λατρεύοντες latreuontes nom pl masc part pres act
6. λατρεύοντας latreuontas acc pl masc part pres act
7. λατρεύουσα latreuousa nom sing fem part pres act
8. λατρεῦον latreuon nom/acc sing neu part pres act
9. λατρεύειν latreuein inf pres act
10. ἐλάτρευσαν elatreusan 3pl indic aor act
11. λατρεύσεις latreuseis 2sing indic fut act
12. λατρεύσουσιν latreusousin 3pl indic fut act
13. λατρεύομεν latreuomen 1pl indic pres act

```
11  worship the Lord ... and him only shalt thou serve. Matt 4:10
 9  being delivered ... might serve him without fear,....Luke 1:74
 7  served God with fastings and prayers night ... day......  2:37
11  worship the Lord ... and him only shalt thou serve.....  4:8
12  shall they come forth, and serve me in this place....Acts 7:7
 9  and gave them up to worship the host of heaven;......  7:42
 1  so worship I the God of my fathers,.................   24:14
 8  instantly serving God day and night, hope to come....  26:7
 1  the angel of God, whose I am, and whom I serve,....   27:23
 1  I serve with my spirit in the gospel of his Son,..... Rom 1:9
10  and served the creature more than the Creator,........   1:25
 5  the circumcision, which worship God in the spirit,.. Phlp 3:3
 1  I thank God, whom I serve from my forefathers ... 2 Tm 1:3
 2  Who serve unto the example and shadow..........Heb 8:5
 4  could not make him that did the service perfect,......   9:9
 9  from dead works to serve the living God?.............   9:14
 6  because that the worshippers once purged...........   10:2
 3  we may serve God acceptably with reverence........   12:28
 5  have no right to eat which serve the tabernacle......   13:10
 2  and serve him day and night in his temple:......... Rev 7:15
12  and his servants shall serve him:....................   22:3
```

Classical Greek

The verb *latreuō* is related to the noun *latron*, "reward"; in secular Greek it initially meant "to work for payment." Over time, however, the idea of payment gave way to the idea of service. Subsequently, it is often translated "to serve," and it may refer to either physical labor or to other types of work and service, including the service or worship of a deity in a cultic setting. In secular Greek the equivalent noun *latreia* means "work for hire" as well as "service, cultic service."

Septuagint Usage

Latreuō in almost every case in the Septuagint translates the Hebrew verb *'āvadh*, "to work, serve, perform the tasks of a servant/slave." This verb is, however, also translated *douleuō* (1392), "to be a slave, to serve as a slave." Consequently, the fact that the Septuagint chiefly employs *latreuō* when the Hebrew reads *'āvadh* for the religious, cultic service is significant for understanding *latreuō* in the New Testament. When God gave Moses the task of leading the people out of Egypt, He also indicated that the objective of the Exodus was that "ye shall *serve* God upon this mountain" (Exodus 3:12). The same issue of divine service was also at stake in the conflict between Moses and Pharaoh. God repeatedly told the ruler of Egypt: "Let my son (Israel) go, so he may *worship* (*latreuō*) me" (Exodus 4:23, NIV; cf. 8:1,20; 9:1,13). But Pharaoh only refused. Again, behind the conflict lies the issue of whether Israel would be allowed to perform cultic/sacral worship and offerings. *Latreuō* thus parallels the idea of offering sacrifice to God.

New Testament Usage

The New Testament incorporates the religious use of *latreuō*. Except for several instances in which the issue is serving foreign gods (Acts 7:42; Romans 1:25), the verb is employed exclusively for serving the only God—the Father of Jesus Christ. While many texts are directly influenced by the cultic setting of the Old Testament (e.g., Luke 2:37; Acts 7:7,42; Hebrews 8:5; 9:9; 10:2; 13:10), this cultic aspect is transmitted in other places in which the term carries a more developed and extended meaning. In these cases *latreuō* can refer to "serving" God in prayer or in one's life (e.g., Acts 24:14; Romans 1:9; Philippians 3:3).

The Epistle to the Hebrews frequently recalls the cultic service of the Old Testament in the desert tabernacle. When it does, the verb *latreuō* depicts the priestly offering service; but more extensively *latreuō* describes the participation of all people in the "worship" service. *Ho latreuōn*, "the worshiper," is particularly concerned with the rituals prescribed by the Law (*Bauer*; Hebrews 9:9; 10:2; cf. 8:5; 13:10). But to this same author the cultic system of the old covenant is only temporary; it finds its end and fulfillment in the substitutional self-sacrifice of Christ, the final offering. His sacrifice enables us to "serve" the living God with awe and reverence (Hebrews 9:14; 12:22-28).

Paul referred to his missionary preaching of the gospel as his service to God (Romans 1:9). Paul rendered this service with his "whole heart" (*en to pneumati mou*; cf. Romans 12:1; Philippians 3:3, the use of the noun *latreia* [2972]).

In citations and allusions to the Old Testament, as well as independent sayings of the New Testament, *latreuō* functions in the more narrow sense of "to pray, to worship" (e.g., Matthew 4:10; Luke 2:37; 4:8; Revelation 22:3; cf. 7:15). While *latreuō* thus has its background in the Old Testament ritual worship service of the temple, its use broadens in the New Testament to include service to God in prayer and worship. Now *latreuō* finds truest expression in the life and witness of the believer. The explanation of this development lies in Christ's self-sacrifice. It is reiterated by Paul's statement: "Do you not know that your body is a temple of the Holy Spirit, who is in you, whom you have received from God?" (1 Corinthians 6:19, NIV).

STRONG 3000, BAUER 467, MOULTON-MILLIGAN 371, KITTEL 4:58-65, LIDDELL-SCOTT 1032, COLIN BROWN 3:549-50.

2974. λάχανον lachanon noun
Vegetable, herb.
SYNONYM:
βοτάνη botanē (1001)

יָרָק yārāq (3536), Vegetable (1 Kgs 21:2 [20:2]).

יֶרֶק yereq (3537), Green plant, green herb (Gn 9:3, Ps 37:2 [36:2]).

1. λάχανον lachanon nom/acc sing neu
2. λαχάνων lachanōn gen pl neu
3. λάχανα lachana nom/acc pl neu

2 the greatest among **herbs**, and becometh a tree,....Matt 13:32
2 and becometh greater than all **herbs**,...............Mark 4:32
1 for ye tithe mint and rue and all manner of **herbs**, Luke 11:42
3 eat all things: another, who is weak, eateth **herbs**...Rom 14:2

Classical Greek and Septuagint Usage
This noun is used of herbs and vegetables cultivated in a field or garden, sold in the market, and prepared in the kitchen (Bornkamm, "lachanon," *Kittel*, 4:65). Hence, *lachanon* are not wild but domesticated plants (*Liddell-Scott*). The Septuagint uses *lachanon* to refer to the vegetables which God said Noah could eat with the meat of animals (Genesis 9:3).

New Testament Usage
Paul spoke of the weaker brother who abstained from meat and ate only "herbs" (Romans 14:2). While vegetarian practices were common in many groups—including those of a philosophical, academic, and religious nature (Bornkamm, "lachanon," *Kittel*, 4:67)—Paul did not allow condemnation of those who ate meat. At the same time, those who ate meat were not allowed to offend those who did not. "Paul quickly disposes of the general question of the 'intrinsic' rights or wrongs of freedom or abstinence" (ibid.).

Jesus compared the kingdom of heaven to a mustard seed which when planted would grow to become the "greatest among *herbs*" (Matthew 13:32; Mark 4:32). Jesus also rebuked the Pharisees because they tithed of "mint and rue and all manner of *herbs*, and pass(ed) over judgment and the love of God" (Luke 11:42; compare the discussion under *kuminon* [2924]).

STRONG 3001, BAUER 467, MOULTON-MILLIGAN 371, KITTEL 4:65-67, LIDDELL-SCOTT 1032.

2975. Λεββαῖος Lebbaios name
Lebbeus.

1. Λεββαῖος Lebbaios nom masc

1 James the son of Alphaeus, and **Lebbaeus**,.........Matt 10:3

One of the 12 apostles, also known as Thaddeus or Judas (not Iscariot; Matthew 10:3; Mark 3:18).

2976. λεγεών legeōn noun
Legion, a vast number.

1. λεγεών legeōn nom sing fem
2. λεγεῶνα legeōna acc sing fem
3. λεγεῶνας legeōnas acc pl fem
4. λεγιών legiōn nom sing fem
5. λεγιῶνα legiōna acc sing fem
6. λεγιῶνας legiōnas acc pl fem
7. λεγιώνων legiōnōn gen pl fem

3 give me more than twelve **legions** of angels?......Matt 26:53
2 was possessed with the devil, and had the **legion**,...Mark 5:15

This is the word used for the Roman legion of soldiers and is spelled *legiōn* or *legeōn*. The number of soldiers in a legion varied at different times in the history of the Roman Empire. The republican army which conquered the world had legions of 4,500 men which included: 1,200 spearmen, 1,200 experienced soldiers, 1,200 light armored troops, 600 veteran reserves, and 300 cavalry (Gealy, "Legion," *The Interpreter's Dictionary of the Bible*, 3:110). The number of soldiers in a legion was later increased to about 7,000. Although the legions originally consisted of property-owning citizens, they were later made up of professional soldiers.

New Testament Usage

Jewish writers used the word *legeōn* to refer to angelic hosts without number. This is also the meaning of the word in the New Testament where it refers to a vast host of demons and angels. When Jesus confronted the demon-possessed man in the country of the Gadarenes, He asked the demon who spoke through the man: "What is thy name? And he answered, saying, My name is *Legion*: for we are many" (Mark 5:9; cf. Luke 8:30). While one cannot determine exactly how many demons were involved, they did go into 2,000 hogs.

When Jesus was arrested in the Garden of Gethsemane, He rebuked Peter for cutting off the ear of the servant of the high priest saying, "Put up again thy sword into his place: for all they that take the sword shall perish with the sword. Thinkest thou that I cannot now pray to my Father, and he shall presently give me more than twelve *legions* of angels?" (Matthew 26:52,53). This vast number could have exceeded 72,000 angels. In light of the knowledge that *1* angel destroyed 185,000 Assyrian troops (cf. 2 Kings 19:35), 12 legions of angels would have provided more than enough power to deliver Jesus from the hands of His captors.

STRONG 3003, BAUER 467-68, MOULTON-MILLIGAN 371, KITTEL 4:68-69, LIDDELL-SCOTT 1033.

2977. Λεγεών Legeōn name
Legion.

1. **Λεγεών** Legeōn nom masc
2. **Λεγιών** Legiōn nom masc

1 saying, My name is Legion: for we are many........ Mark 5:9
1 And he said, Legion: because many devils were..... Luke 8:30

The name of the demon in the man from Gadara, indicating the presence of many (Mark 5:9,15).

2978. λέγω legō verb
Say, speak, tell, ask, answer, order, call.

COGNATES:
αἰσχρολογία aischrologia (148)
ἀντιλέγω antilegō (480)
γενεαλογέω genealogeō (1068)
γενεαλογία genealogia (1069)
διαλέγομαι dialegomai (1250)
διάλεκτος dialektos (1252)
διαλογίζομαι dialogizomai (1254)
ἐλλογέω ellogeō (1664)
ἐπιλέγω epilegō (1935B)
κακολογέω kakologeō (2522)
καταλέγω katalegō (2609)
λόγος logos (3030)
ὁμολογέω homologeō (3533)
παραλέγομαι paralegomai (3742)
παραλογίζομαι paralogizomai (3745)
προλέγω prolegō (4161)
συλλέγω sullegō (4667)
συναρμολογέω sunarmologeō (4734)
χρηστολογία chrēstologia (5377)

SYNONYMS:
αἰτέω aiteō (153)
ἀναγγέλλω anangellō (310)
ἀνατίθημι anatithēmi (392)
ἀπαγγέλλω apangellō (514)
ἀποδείκνυμι apodeiknumi (579)
ἀποκρίνω apokrinō (605B)
δέομαι deomai (1183)
διαλέγομαι dialegomai (1250)
διαμαρτύρομαι diamarturomai (1257)
διαστέλλω diastellō (1285)
διατάσσω diatassō (1293)
διηγέομαι diēgeomai (1328)
ἐκδιηγέομαι ekdiēgeomai (1542)
ἐμφανίζω emphanizō (1702)
ἐντέλλομαι entellomai (1765)
ἐντυγχάνω entunchanō (1777)
ἐξαιτέω exaiteō (1793)
ἐξηγέομαι exēgeomai (1817)
ἐξορκίζω exorkizō (1828)
ἐπερωτάω eperōtaō (1890)
ἐπιλέγω epilegō (1935B)
ἐπιτάσσω epitassō (1988)
ἐπονομάζω eponomazō (2012)
ἐρεύγομαι ereugomai (2027)
ἐρωτάω erōtaō (2049)
καλέω kaleō (2535)
καταγγέλλω katangellō (2576)
κελεύω keleuō (2724)
κηρύσσω kērussō (2756)
λαλέω laleō (2953)
ὁμιλέω homileō (3519)
ὀνομάζω onomazō (3550)
ὁρκίζω horkizō (3589)
παραγγέλλω parangellō (3715)
παραιτέομαι paraiteomai (3729)
παρακαλέω parakaleō (3731)
προσαγορεύω prosagoreuō (4174)
προστάσσω prostassō (4225)
πυνθάνομαι punthanomai (4299)
συντάσσω suntassō (4781)
τάσσω tassō (4872)
φημί phēmi (5183)
φθέγγομαι phthengomai (5187)
φωνέω phōneō (5291)
χρηματίζω chrēmatizō (5372)

אֹמֶר 'ômer (199), Word, address (Hb 3:9).

אָמַר 'āmar (569), Qal: say (Gn 1:22, 1 Sm 5:10, Ez 36:4); niphal: be said (Nm 21:14).

λέγω 2978

אָמַר 'āmar (A570), Say (Ezr 5:11, Dn 2:7, 6:20—Aramaic).

אֵמֶר 'ēmer (571), Word (Jos 24:27).

בָּטָה bāṭāh (1017I), Speak (Prv 12:18).

דָּבַר dāvar (1744), Qal: say (Ex 6:29, Nm 32:27, Jer 38:20 [45:20]); piel: say, speak (Ex 12:31, Prv 23:9, Jer 25:3).

דָּבָר dāvār (1745), Word, command (Gn 44:10, Est 8:14, Jb 11:2).

מִצְוָה mitswāh (4851), Command (Est 3:3).

מָשַׁל māshal (5090), Qal: quote a proverb (Ez 18:3); piel: speak a parable (Ez 20:49).

נְאֻם nā'am (5176), Say, declare (Nm 14:28, 2 Kgs 22:19, Zec 12:1).

סָפַר sāphar (5807), Piel: state (Is 43:26).

1. λέγω legō 1sing indic/subj pres act
2. λέγετε legete 2pl indic/impr pres act
3. λέγουσιν legousin dat pl masc/neu indic/part pres act
4. λέγεις legeis 2sing indic pres act
5. λέγει legei 3sing indic pres act
6. λέγομεν legomen 1pl indic pres act
7. λέγῃ legē 3sing subj pres act
8. λέγωμεν legōmen 1pl subj pres act
9. λέγητε legēte 2pl subj pres act
10. λέγωσιν legōsin 3pl subj pres act
11. λέγε lege 2sing impr pres act
12. λεγέτω legetō 3sing impr pres act
13. λέγοντα legonta nom/acc sing/pl masc/neu part pres act
14. λέγοντος legontos gen sing masc/neu part pres act
15. λέγων legōn nom sing masc part pres act
16. λέγοντες legontes nom pl masc part pres act
17. λεγόντων legontōn gen pl masc part pres act
18. λέγοντας legontas acc pl masc part pres act
19. λέγουσα legousa nom sing fem part pres act
20. λεγούσης legousēs gen sing fem part pres act
21. λέγουσαν legousan acc sing fem part pres act
22. λέγουσαι legousai nom pl fem part pres act
23. λέγον legon nom/acc sing neu part pres act
24. λέγειν legein inf pres act
25. ἔλεγον elegon 1/3sing/pl indic imperf act
26. ἔλεγεν elegen 3sing indic imperf act
27. ἐλέγετε elegete 2pl indic imperf act
28. λέγεται legetai 3sing indic pres mid
29. λεγόμενον legomenon nom/acc sing masc/neu part pres mid
30. λεγόμενος legomenos nom sing masc part pres mid
31. λεγομένου legomenou gen sing masc part pres mid
32. λεγόμενοι legomenoi nom pl masc part pres mid
33. λεγομένη legomenē nom sing fem part pres mid
34. λεγομένης legomenēs gen sing fem part pres mid
35. λεγομένην legomenēn acc sing fem part pres mid
36. λεγομένοις legomenois dat pl neu part pres mid
37. λεγόμενα legomena nom/acc pl neu part pres mid
38. λέγεσθαι legesthai inf pres mid
39. λέγοντι legonti dat sing masc part pres act
40. ἔλεγαν elegan 1/3sing/pl indic act
41. λεγομένων legomenōn gen pl fem part pres mid

30	of whom was born Jesus, who is **called** Christ.	Matt 1:16
15	**saying**, Joseph, thou son of David,	1:20
14	spoken of the Lord by the prophet, **saying**,	1:22
16	**Saying**, Where is he that is born King of the Jews?	2:2
15	angel of the Lord ... **saying**, Arise,	2:13
14	**saying**, Out of Egypt have I called my son.	2:15
14	fulfilled ... spoken by Jeremy the prophet, **saying**,	2:17
15	**Saying**, Arise, and take the young child	2:20
35	And he came and dwelt in a city **called** Nazareth:	2:23
15	And **saying**, Repent ye: for the kingdom ... at hand.	3:2
14	spoken of by the prophet Esaias, **saying**,	3:3
24	And think not **to say** within yourselves,	3:9
1	have Abraham to our father: for **I say** unto you,	3:9
15	But John forbad him, **saying**,	3:14
19	And lo a voice from heaven, **saying**,	3:17
5	And **saith** unto him, If thou be the Son of God,	4:6
5	**saith** unto him, All these things will I give thee,	4:9
5	Then **saith** Jesus unto him, Get thee hence, Satan:	4:10
14	was spoken by Esaias the prophet, **saying**,	4:14
24	From that time Jesus began to preach, and **to say**,	4:17
29	saw two brethren, Simon **called** Peter, and Andrew	4:18
5	And he **saith** unto them, Follow me,	4:19
15	he opened his mouth, and taught them, **saying**,	5:2
1	For verily **I say** unto you, Till heaven and earth	5:18
1	For **I say** unto you, That except your righteousness	5:20
1	But **I say** unto you, That whosoever is angry	5:22
1	Verily **I say** unto thee, ... no means come out	5:26
1	But **I say** unto you, ... whosoever looketh on	5:28
1	But **I say** unto you, ... shall put away his wife,	5:32
1	But **I say** unto you, Swear not at all;	5:34
1	But **I say** unto you, That ye resist not evil:	5:39
1	But **I say** unto you, Love your enemies,	5:44
1	Verily **I say** unto you, They have their reward.	6:2
1	Verily **I say** unto you, They have their reward.	6:5
1	Verily **I say** unto you, They have their reward.	6:16
1	Therefore **I say** unto you,	6:25
1	And yet **I say** unto you, That even Solomon	6:29
16	Therefore take no thought, **saying**, What ... we eat?	6:31
15	Not every one that **saith** unto me, Lord, Lord,	7:21
15	there came a leper and worshipped him, **saying**,	8:2
15	**saying**, I will; be thou clean.	8:3
5	And Jesus **saith** unto him, See thou tell no man;	8:4
15	And **saying**, Lord, my servant lieth at home sick	8:6
5	Jesus **saith** unto him, I will come and heal him.	8:7
1	and **I say** to this man, Go, and he goeth;	8:9
1	Verily **I say** unto you, ... not found so great faith,	8:10
1	And **I say** unto you, That many shall come	8:11
14	**saying**, Himself took our infirmities,	8:17
5	And Jesus **saith** unto him, The foxes have holes,	8:20
5	But Jesus **said** to him, "Follow Me; (NASB)	8:22
16	**saying**, Lord, save us: we perish.	8:25
5	And **he saith** unto them, Why are ye fearful,	8:26
16	But the men marvelled, **saying**,	8:27
16	And, behold, they cried out, **saying**,	8:29
16	So the devils besought him, **saying**,	8:31
5	then **saith** he to the sick of the palsy,	9:6
29	he saw a man, **named** Matthew,	9:9
5	and he **saith** unto him, Follow me,	9:9
25	they said to His disciples, (NASB)	9:11
16	Then came to him the disciples of John, **saying**,	9:14
15	a certain ruler, and worshipped him, **saying**,	9:18
26	For **she said** within herself,	9:21
5	**He said** unto them, Give place,	9:24
16	and **saying**, Thou son of David, have mercy on us.	9:27
5	and Jesus **saith** unto them,	9:28
3	**They said** unto him, Yea, Lord.	9:28
15	**saying**, According to your faith be it unto you.	9:29
15	**saying**, See that no man know it.	9:30

λέγω 2978

16	saying, It was never so seen in Israel.	Matt 9:33
25	But the Pharisees said, He casteth out devils	9:34
5	Then saith he unto his disciples,	9:37
30	The first, Simon, who is called Peter,	10:2
15	Jesus ... and commanded them, saying,	10:5
16	preach, saying, The kingdom of heaven is at hand.	10:7
1	Verily I say unto you, It shall be more tolerable	10:15
1	for verily I say unto you, ... the cities of Israel,	10:23
1	What I tell you in darkness, that speak ye in light:	10:27
1	verily I say unto you, ... in no wise lose his reward.	10:42
24	Jesus began to say unto the multitudes	11:7
1	yea, I say unto you, and more than a prophet.	11:9
1	Verily I say unto you, Among them that are born	11:11
3	And saying, We have piped unto you,	11:17
3	John came ... and they say, He hath a devil.	11:18
3	The Son of man came eating ... and they say,	11:19
1	But I say unto you, ... more tolerable for Tyre	11:22
1	But I say unto you, ... more tolerable for ... Sodom	11:24
1	But I say unto you, That in this place is one greater	12:6
16	saying, Is it lawful to heal on the sabbath days?	12:10
5	Then saith he to the man, Stretch forth thine hand.	12:13
14	spoken by Esaias the prophet, saying,	12:17
25	And all the people were amazed, and said,	12:23
1	Wherefore I say unto you,	12:31
1	But I say unto you, That every idle word	12:36
16	saying, Master, we would see a sign from thee.	12:38
5	Then he saith, I will return into my house	12:44
39	answered the one who was telling (NASB)	12:48
15	saying, Behold, a sower went forth to sow;	13:3
19	is fulfilled the prophecy of Esaias, which saith,	13:14
1	For verily I say unto you,	13:17
15	Another parable put he forth unto them, saying,	13:24
3	And the slaves said to him, (NASB)	13:28
15	Another parable put he forth unto them, saying,	13:31
14	which was spoken by the prophet, saying,	13:35
16	and his disciples came unto him, saying,	13:36
5	Jesus saith unto them, Have ye understood	13:51
3	They say unto him, Yea, Lord.	13:51
24	insomuch that they were astonished, and said,	13:54
28	is not his mother called Mary?	13:55
26	For John said unto him, It is not lawful for thee	14:4
16	his disciples came to him, saying,	14:15
3	they say unto him, We have here but five loaves,	14:17
16	saying, It is a spirit; and they cried out for fear.	14:26
15	But straightway Jesus spake unto them, saying,	14:27
15	he cried, saying, Lord, save me.	14:30
5	Jesus ... caught him, and said unto him,	14:31
16	came and worshipped him, saying,	14:33
16	came to Jesus scribes and Pharisees, ... saying,	15:1
15	For God commanded, saying,	15:4
2	But ye say, Whosoever shall say to his father or	15:5
15	well did Esaias prophesy of you, saying,	15:7
3	Then the disciples came and said to Him, (NASB)	15:12
19	saying, Have mercy on me, O Lord,	15:22
16	saying, Send her away; for she crieth after us.	15:23
19	Then came she and worshipped him, saying,	15:25
3	And his disciples say unto him,	15:33
5	Jesus saith unto them, How many loaves have ye?	15:34
2	When it is evening, ye say,	16:2
16	And they reasoned among themselves, saying,	16:7
15	he asked his disciples, saying, Whom do men say	16:13
3	Whom do men say that I the Son of man am?	16:13
5	He saith unto them, But whom say ye that I am?	16:15
2	He saith unto them, But whom say ye that I am?	16:15
1	And I say also unto thee, That thou art Peter,	16:18
15	saying, Be it far from thee, Lord:	16:22
1	Verily I say unto you,	16:28
19	and behold a voice out of the cloud, which said,	17:5
15	Jesus ... saying, Tell the vision to no man,	17:9
16	And his disciples asked him, saying,	17:10
3	Why then say the scribes that Elias must first come?	17:10
1	But I say unto you, That Elias is come already,	17:12
15	a certain man, kneeling down to him, and saying,	17:14
5	And He said to them, (NASB)	17:20
1	for verily I say unto you,	17:20
5	He saith, Yes. ... Jesus prevented him,	17:25
15	Jesus ... saying, What thinkest thou, Simon?	17:25
5	Peter saith unto him, Of strangers.	Matt 17:26
16	same time came the disciples unto Jesus, saying,	18:1
1	And said, Verily I say unto you,	18:3
1	for I say unto you, That in heaven their angels	18:10
1	And if so be that he find it, verily I say unto you,	18:13
1	Verily I say unto you,	18:18
1	Again I say unto you,	18:19
5	Jesus saith unto him, I say not unto thee,	18:22
1	Jesus saith unto him, I say not unto thee,	18:22
15	and worshipped him, saying, Lord,	18:26
15	and took him by the throat, saying,	18:28
15	saying, Have patience with me, and I will pay thee	18:29
5	after that he had called him, said unto him,	18:32
16	Pharisees ... tempting him, and saying unto him,	19:3
3	They say unto him, Why did Moses then command	19:7
5	He saith unto them,	19:8
1	And I say unto you,	19:9
3	His disciples say unto him, If the case	19:10
4	And he said unto him, Why callest thou me good?	19:17
5	He saith unto them, Which? Jesus said,	19:18
5	The young man saith unto him, All these ... I kept	19:20
1	Jesus unto his disciples, Verily I say unto you,	19:23
1	And again I say unto you, It is easier for a camel	19:24
16	amazed, saying, Who then can be saved?	19:25
1	And Jesus said unto them, Verily I say unto you,	19:28
5	others standing idle, and saith unto them,	20:6
3	They say unto him, Because no man hath hired us,	20:7
5	He saith unto them, Go ye also into the vineyard;	20:7
5	the lord of the vineyard saith unto his steward,	20:8
16	Saying, These last have wrought but one hour,	20:12
5	She saith unto him, Grant that these my two sons	20:21
3	They say unto him, We are able.	20:22
5	saith unto them, Ye shall drink indeed of my cup,	20:23
16	cried out, saying, Have mercy on us, O Lord,	20:30
16	but they cried the more, saying, Have mercy on us,	20:31
3	They say unto him, Lord, that our eyes ... opened.	20:33
15	Saying unto them, Go into the village	21:2
14	fulfilled which was spoken by the prophet, saying,	21:4
16	cried, saying, Hosanna to the son of David:	21:9
19	all the city was moved, saying, Who is this?	21:10
25	And the multitude said, This is Jesus the prophet	21:11
5	And said unto them, It is written,	21:13
18	and saying, Hosanna to the son of David;	21:15
3	and said unto him, Hearest thou what these say?	21:16
5	Jesus saith unto them, Yea; have ye never read,	21:16
5	and said unto it, Let no fruit grow on thee	21:19
16	the disciples saw it, they marvelled, saying,	21:20
1	Verily I say unto you, If ye have faith,	21:21
16	came unto him as he was teaching, and said,	21:23
16	And they reasoned with themselves, saying,	21:25
1	Neither tell I you by what authority I do these	21:27
3	They say unto him, The first.	21:31
5	Jesus saith unto them, Verily I say unto you,	21:31
1	Jesus saith unto them, Verily I say unto you,	21:31
15	But last of all he sent unto them his son, saying,	21:37
3	They say unto him, He will miserably destroy	21:41
5	Jesus saith unto them, Did ye never read	21:42
1	Therefore say I unto you,	21:43
5	they perceived that he spake of them.	21:45
15	spake unto them again by parables, and said,	22:1
15	Again, he sent forth other servants, saying,	22:4
5	saith he to his servants, The wedding is ready,	22:8
5	And he saith unto him, Friend,	22:12
16	saying, Master, we know that thou art true,	22:16
5	And he saith unto them, Whose is this image	22:20
3	They say unto him, Caesar's.	22:21
5	Then saith he unto them,	22:21
16	Sadducees, which say that there is no resurrection,	22:23
16	Saying, Master, Moses said, If a man die,	22:24
14	which was spoken unto you by God, saying,	22:31
15	asked him a question, tempting him, and saying,	22:35
15	Saying, What think ye of Christ?	22:42
3	They say unto him, The son of David.	22:42
5	He saith unto them, How then doth David in spirit	22:43
15	David in spirit call him Lord, saying,	22:43
15	Saying, The scribes and the Pharisees	23:2
3	for they say, and do not.	23:3

41

λέγω 2978

16	Woe unto you, ye blind guides, which say,	Matt	23:16
2	And say, If we had been in the days		23:30
1	Verily I say unto you, All these things shall come		23:36
1	For I say unto you, Ye shall not see me henceforth,		23:39
1	See ye not all these things? verily I say unto you,		24:2
16	the disciples came to him privately, saying,		24:3
16	many shall come in my name, saying, I am Christ;		24:5
1	Verily I say unto you, This generation		24:34
1	Verily I say unto you,		24:47
22	But the wise answered, saying, Not so;		25:9
22	other virgins, saying, Lord, Lord, open to us.		25:11
1	Verily I say unto you, I know you not.		25:12
15	saying, Lord, thou deliveredst unto me five talents:		25:20
16	Then shall the righteous answer him, saying,		25:37
1	the King shall answer ... Verily I say unto you,		25:40
16	Then shall they also answer him, saying,		25:44
15	Then shall he answer them, saying,		25:45
1	answer them, saying, Verily I say unto you,		25:45
31	the high priest, who was called Caiaphas,		26:3
25	But they said, Not on the feast day,		26:5
16	saying, To what purpose is this waste?		26:8
1	Verily I say unto you,		26:13
30	Then one of the twelve, called Judas Iscariot,		26:14
16	the disciples came to Jesus, saying unto him,		26:17
5	The Master saith, My time is at hand;		26:18
1	And as they did eat, he said, Verily I say unto you,		26:21
24	and began every one of them to say unto him,		26:22
5	Master, is it I? He said unto him, Thou hast said.		26:25
15	and gave thanks, and gave it to them, saying,		26:27
1	But I say unto you, I will not drink henceforth		26:29
5	Then saith Jesus unto them,		26:31
1	Jesus said unto him, Verily I say unto thee,		26:34
5	Peter said unto him, Though I should die		26:35
29	Jesus with them unto a place called Gethsemane,		26:36
5	and saith unto the disciples, Sit ye here,		26:36
5	Then saith he unto them, My soul is ... sorrowful,		26:38
15	and fell on his face, and prayed, saying,		26:39
5	and saith unto Peter, What, could ye not watch		26:40
15	saying, O my Father, if this cup may not pass away		26:42
5	cometh he to his disciples, and saith unto them,		26:45
15	saying, Whomsoever I shall kiss, that same is he:		26:48
5	Then said Jesus unto him,		26:52
5	Jesus said unto him, Thou hast said:		26:64
1	nevertheless I say unto you, Hereafter shall ye see		26:64
15	Then the high priest rent his clothes, saying,		26:65
16	Saying, Prophesy unto us, thou Christ,		26:68
19	and a damsel came unto him, saying,		26:69
15	But he denied before them all, saying,		26:70
4	denied before them ... I know not what thou sayest.		26:70
5	and said unto them that were there,		26:71
15	Saying, I have sinned in that I have betrayed		27:4
14	which was spoken by Jeremy the prophet, saying,		27:9
15	and the governor asked him, saying,		27:11
4	And Jesus said unto him, Thou sayest.		27:11
5	Then said Pilate unto him, Hearest thou not		27:13
29	they had then a notable prisoner, called Barabbas.		27:16
29	Barabbas, or Jesus which is called Christ?		27:17
19	his wife sent unto him, saying,		27:19
5	Pilate saith ... What shall I do then with Jesus		27:22
29	do then with Jesus which is called Christ?		27:22
3	They all say unto him, Let him be crucified.		27:22
16	But they cried out the more, saying,		27:23
15	and washed his hands before the multitude, saying,		27:24
16	and mocked him, saying, Hail, King of the Jews!		27:29
29	when they were come unto a place called Golgotha,		27:33
30	Golgotha, that is to say, a place of a skull,		27:33
16	And saying, Thou that destroyest the temple,		27:40
25	mocking him, with the scribes and elders, said,		27:41
15	saying, Eli, Eli, lama sabachthani?		27:46
25	when they heard that, said,		27:47
25	The rest said, Let be, let us see whether Elias will		27:49
16	saw the earthquake, ... they feared greatly, saying,		27:54
16	Saying, Sir, we remember that that deceiver said,		27:63
15	behold, Jesus met them, saying, All hail.		28:9
5	Then said Jesus unto them, Be not afraid:		28:10
16	Saying, Say ye, His disciples came by night,		28:13
15	And Jesus came and spake unto them, saying,		28:18

15	And preached, saying, There cometh one mightier	Mark	1:7
15	And saying, The time is fulfilled,		1:15
15	Saying, Let us alone; what have we to do		1:24
15	And Jesus rebuked him, saying, Hold thy peace,		1:25
18	saying, What thing is this?		1:27
3	lay sick of a fever, and anon they tell him of her.		1:30
3	they said unto him, All men seek for thee.		1:37
5	he said unto them, Let us go into the next towns,		1:38
15	kneeling down to him, and saying unto him,		1:40
5	and saith unto him, I will; be thou clean.		1:41
5	saith unto him, See thou say nothing to any man:		1:44
5	saw their faith, he said unto the sick of the palsy,		2:5
5	said to them, "Why are you reasoning (NASB)		2:8
5	he saith to the sick of the palsy,		2:10
1	I say unto thee, Arise, and take up thy bed,		2:11
18	saying, We never saw it on this fashion.		2:12
5	and said unto him, Follow me. And he arose		2:14
25	and said unto his disciples, How is it		2:16
5	When Jesus heard it, he saith unto them,		2:17
3	and they come and say unto him,		2:18
25	And the Pharisees said unto him, Behold,		2:24
26	And he said unto them, Have ye never read		2:25
26	said unto them, The sabbath was made for man,		2:27
5	saith unto the man which had the withered hand,		3:3
5	And he saith unto them, Is it lawful to do good		3:4
5	he saith unto the man, Stretch forth thine hand.		3:5
13	fell down before him, and cried, saying,		3:11
25	they went out to lay hold on him: for they said,		3:21
25	the scribes which came down from Jerusalem said,		3:22
26	and said unto them in parables, How can Satan		3:23
1	Verily I say unto you, All sins shall be forgiven		3:28
25	Because they said, He hath an unclean spirit.		3:30
3	multitude ... said to Him, (NASB)		3:32
15	And he answered them, saying,		3:33
5	and said, Behold my mother and my brethren!		3:34
26	and said unto them in his doctrine,		4:2
26	And he said unto them, He that hath ears to hear,		4:9
26	And he said unto them,		4:11
5	And he said unto them, Know ye not this parable?		4:13
26	And he said unto them, Is a candle brought		4:21
26	And he said unto them, Take heed what ye hear:		4:24
26	And he said, So is the kingdom of God,		4:26
26	And he said, Whereunto shall we liken		4:30
5	when the even was come, he saith unto them,		4:35
3	and they awake him, and say unto him, Master,		4:38
25	they feared exceedingly, and said one to another,		4:41
5	and crying out with a loud voice, he said, (NASB)		5:7
26	For he said unto him, Come out of the man,		5:8
15	saying, My name is Legion: for we are many.		5:9
16	And all the devils besought him, saying,		5:12
5	Jesus suffered him not, but saith unto him,		5:19
15	And besought him greatly, saying,		5:23
26	For she said, If I may touch but his clothes,		5:28
26	turned him about in the press, and said,		5:30
25	And his disciples said unto him,		5:31
4	and sayest thou, Who touched me?		5:31
16	certain which said, Thy daughter is dead:		5:35
5	he saith unto the ruler of the synagogue,		5:36
5	And when he was come in, he saith unto them,		5:39
5	he took the damsel by the hand, and said unto her,		5:41
1	Talitha cumi; ... I say unto thee, arise.		5:41
16	and many hearing him were astonished, saying,		6:2
26	But Jesus said unto them, A prophet is not		6:4
26	And he said unto them, In what place ... ye enter		6:10
1	Verily I say unto you, It shall be more tolerable		6:11
26	for his name was spread abroad: and he said,		6:14
25	Others said, That it is Elias.		6:15
25	And others said, That it is a prophet,		6:15
26	he said, "John, the man I beheaded, (NIV)		6:16
26	For John had said unto Herod, It is not lawful		6:18
19	with haste unto the king, and asked, saying,		6:25
5	And he said to them, (NASB)		6:31
3	his disciples came unto him, and said,		6:35
3	And they say unto him, Shall we go and buy		6:37
5	He saith unto them, How many loaves have ye?		6:38
3	when they knew, they say, Five, and two fishes.		6:38
5	and saith unto them, Be of good cheer: it is I;		6:50

λέγω 2978

26	And he **said** unto them, Full well ye reject	Mark 7:9
2	But ye **say**, If a man shall say to his father or	7:11
26	he **said** unto them, Hearken unto me every one	7:14
5	And he **saith** unto them,	7:18
26	And he **said**, That which cometh out of the man,	7:20
26	And He **was saying** to her, (NASB)	7:27
5	And she answered and **said** unto him, Yes, Lord;	7:28
5	and **saith** unto him, Ephphatha, that is, Be opened.	7:34
10	gave them orders not to **tell** anyone; (NASB)	7:36
16	And were beyond measure astonished, **saying**,	7:37
5	Jesus called his disciples, ... and **saith** unto them,	8:1
5	he sighed deeply in his spirit, and **saith**,	8:12
1	verily **I say** unto you, There shall no sign	8:12
15	And he charged them, **saying**, Take heed,	8:15
16	And they reasoned among themselves, **saying**,	8:16
5	And when Jesus knew it, he **saith** unto them,	8:17
3	They **say** unto him, Twelve.	8:19
3	And they **said** to Him, (NASB)	8:20
26	And **he said** unto them, ... ye do not understand?	8:21
26	he looked up, and **said**, I see men as trees, walking.	8:24
15	And he sent him away to his house, **saying**,	8:26
15	**saying** unto them, Whom do men say that I am?	8:27
3	**saying** unto them, Whom do men say that I am?	8:27
16	told Him **saying** John the Baptist; (NASB)	8:28
5	he **saith** unto them, But whom say ye that I am?	8:29
2	he saith unto them, But whom **say** ye that I am?	8:29
5	And Peter answereth and **saith** unto him,	8:29
10	charged them that they **should tell** no man of him.	8:30
15	rebuked Peter, **saying**, Get thee behind me, Satan:	8:33
26	And he **said** unto them, Verily I say unto you,	9:1
1	And he said unto them, Verily **I say** unto you,	9:1
5	And Peter answered and **said** to Jesus, Master,	9:5
19	and a voice came out of the cloud, **saying**,	9:7
16	And they asked him, **saying**, Why say the scribes	9:11
3	Why **say** the scribes that Elias must first come?	9:11
1	But **I say** unto you, That Elias is indeed come,	9:13
5	He answereth him, and **saith**,	9:19
26	and **said** with tears, Lord, I believe;	9:24
15	he rebuked the foul spirit, **saying** unto him,	9:25
24	as one dead; insomuch that many **said**, He is dead.	9:26
26	For he taught his disciples, and **said** unto them,	9:31
5	and called the twelve, and **saith** unto them,	9:35
15	And John answered him, **saying**, Master,	9:38
1	verily **I say** unto you, he shall not lose his reward.	9:41
5	And he **saith** unto them,	10:11
1	Verily **I say** unto you,	10:15
4	Jesus said unto him, Why **callest thou** me good?	10:18
5	looked round about, and **saith** unto his disciples,	10:23
5	But Jesus answereth again, and **saith** unto them,	10:24
16	**saying** among themselves, Who then can be saved?	10:26
5	And Jesus looking upon them **saith**,	10:27
24	Then Peter began **to say** unto him,	10:28
1	Jesus answered and said, Verily **I say** unto you,	10:29
24	and began **to tell** them what things should happen	10:32
16	come unto him, **saying**, Master,	10:35
5	But Jesus called them to him, and **saith** unto them,	10:42
24	he began to cry out, and **say**, Jesus,	10:47
16	And they call the blind man, **saying** unto him,	10:49
5	And Jesus answered and **said** unto him,	10:51
5	And **saith** unto them, Go ... into the village	11:2
25	certain of them that stood there **said** unto them,	11:5
16	cried, **saying**, Hosanna; Blessed is he that cometh	11:9
15	And he taught, **saying** unto them, Is it not written,	11:17
5	And Peter calling to remembrance **saith** unto him,	11:21
5	And Jesus answering **saith** unto them,	11:22
1	For verily **I say** unto you,	11:23
5	but shall believe that those things which he **saith**	11:23
1	Therefore **I say** unto you,	11:24
3	And **say** unto him, By what authority doest thou	11:28
16	And they reasoned with themselves, **saying**,	11:31
3	And they answered and **said** unto Jesus,	11:33
5	And Jesus answering **saith** unto them,	11:33
1	Neither do I **tell** you by what authority I do these	11:33
24	And he began **to speak** unto them by parables.	12:1
15	one son, ... he sent him also last unto them, **saying**,	12:6
3	And when they were come, they **say** unto him,	12:14
5	And they brought it. And he **saith** unto them,	12:16
3	the Sadducees, which **say** there is no resurrection;	Mark 12:18
16	unto him the Sadducees, ... asked him, **saying**,	12:18
15	how in the bush God spake unto him, **saying**,	12:26
26	And Jesus answered and **said**,	12:35
3	How **say** the scribes that Christ is the son of David?..	12:35
5	David therefore himself **calleth** him Lord;	12:37
26	And he **said** unto them in his doctrine,	12:38
5	called unto him his disciples, and **saith** unto them,	12:43
1	and saith unto them, Verily **I say** unto you,	12:43
5	one of his disciples **saith** unto him, Master,	13:1
24	And Jesus answering them began **to say**,	13:5
16	**saying**, I am Christ; and shall deceive many.	13:6
1	**I say** unto you, that this generation shall not pass,	13:30
1	And what **I say** unto you I say unto all, Watch.	13:37
1	And what I say unto you **I say** unto all, Watch.	13:37
25	But they **said**, Not on the feast day,	14:2
16	indignation within themselves, and **said**,	14:4
1	Verily **I say** unto you, Wheresoever this gospel	14:9
3	his disciples **said** unto him, Where wilt thou	14:12
5	and **saith** unto them, Go ye into the city,	14:13
5	The Master **saith**, Where is the guestchamber,	14:14
1	And as they sat and did eat, Jesus said, Verily **I say** ..	14:18
24	they began to be sorrowful, and **to say** unto him	14:19
1	Verily **I say** unto you, I will drink no more of	14:25
5	And Jesus **saith** unto them, All ye shall be offended ..	14:27
5	Jesus **saith** unto him, Verily I say unto thee,	14:30
1	Jesus saith unto him, Verily **I say** unto thee,	14:30
26	But he **spake** the more vehemently, If I should die ...	14:31
25	I will not deny thee ... Likewise also **said** they all.	14:31
5	and he **saith** to his disciples, Sit ye here,	14:32
5	**saith** unto them, My soul is exceeding sorrowful	14:34
26	And he **said**, Abba, Father, all things are possible	14:36
5	and **saith** unto Peter, Simon, sleepest thou?	14:37
5	he cometh the third time, and **saith** unto them,	14:41
15	**saying**, Whomsoever I shall kiss, that same is he;	14:44
5	and **saith**, Master, master; and kissed him.	14:45
16	and bare false witness against him, **saying**,	14:57
14	We heard him **say**, I will destroy this temple	14:58
15	stood up in the midst, and asked Jesus, **saying**,	14:60
5	and **said** unto him, Art thou the Christ,	14:61
5	Then the high priest rent his clothes, and **saith**,	14:63
24	and to buffet him, and **to say** unto him, Prophesy:	14:65
5	she looked upon him, and **said**, And thou also	14:67
15	But he denied, **saying**, I know not,	14:68
4	I know not, neither understand I what thou **sayest**.	14:68
24	and began **to say** to them that stood by,	14:69
25	they that stood by **said** again to Peter,	14:70
2	**saying**, I know not this man of whom ye speak.	14:71
5	And answering He **said** to him, (NASB)	15:2
4	And he answering said unto him, Thou **sayest** it.	15:2
15	asked him again, **saying**, Answerest thou nothing?	15:4
30	And there was one **named** Barabbas,	15:7
15	But Pilate answered them, **saying**,	15:9
26	Pilate **was saying** to them, (NASB)	15:12
2	do unto him whom ye **call** the King of the Jews?	15:12
26	Then Pilate **said** ... Why, what evil hath he done?	15:14
19	And the scripture was fulfilled, which **saith**,	15:28
16	wagging their heads, and **saying**, Ah,	15:29
25	**said** among themselves with the scribes,	15:31
15	**saying**, Eloi, Eloi, lama sabachthani?	15:34
25	when they heard it, **said**, Behold, he calleth Elias.	15:35
15	**saying**, Let alone; let us see whether Elias will	15:36
25	And they **said** among themselves, Who shall roll	16:3
5	And he **saith** unto them, Be not affrighted:	16:6
19	and hid herself five months, **saying**,	Luke 1:24
15	**saying**, His name is John. And they marvelled all.	1:63
16	heard them laid them up in their hearts, **saying**,	1:66
15	filled with the Holy Ghost, and prophesied, **saying**,	1:67
17	of the heavenly host praising God, and **saying**,	2:13
14	book of the words of Esaias the prophet, **saying**,	3:4
26	Then **said** he to the multitude that came forth	3:7
24	and begin not **to say** within yourselves,	3:8
1	I have Abraham to our father: for **I say** unto you,	3:8
16	people asked him, **saying**, What shall we do then?	3:10
5	He answereth and **saith** unto them,	3:11
16	And the soldiers likewise demanded of him, **saying**,	3:14
15	John answered, **saying** unto them all,	3:16

43

λέγω 2978

21	and a voice came from heaven, which **said**,	Luke 3:22
15	And Jesus answered him, **saying**, It is written,	4:4
24	And he began **to say** unto them,	4:21
25	And they **said**, Is not this Joseph's son?	4:22
1	And he said, Verily, I **say** unto you,	4:24
1	I **tell** you of a truth, many widows were in Israel	4:25
15	**Saying**, Let us alone; what have we to do with	4:34
15	And Jesus rebuked him, **saying**, Hold thy peace,	4:35
16	**saying**, What a word is this! for with authority	4:36
13	and **saying**, Thou art Christ the Son of God.	4:41
15	**saying**, Depart from me; for I am a sinful man,	5:8
15	and besought him, **saying**, Lord, if thou wilt,	5:12
15	touched him, **saying**, "I am willing; (NASB)	5:13
16	**saying**, Who is this which speaketh blasphemies?	5:21
1	he said unto the sick of the palsy, I **say** unto thee,	5:24
16	glorified God, and were filled with fear, **saying**,	5:26
16	**saying**, Why do ye eat and drink with publicans	5:30
26	And he **spake** also a parable unto them;	5:36
5	desireth new: for he **saith**, The old is better.	5:39
26	And he **said** unto them, That the Son of man	6:5
26	and **said**, Blessed be ye poor:	6:20
1	But I **say** unto you which hear, Love your enemies,	6:27
24	Either how canst thou **say** to thy brother, Brother,	6:42
1	Lord, Lord, and do not the things which I **say**?	6:46
16	they besought him instantly, **saying**,	7:4
15	the centurion sent friends to him, **saying** unto him,	7:6
1	and I **say** unto one, Go, and he goeth;	7:8
1	I **say** unto you, I have not found so great faith,	7:9
1	And he said, Young man, I **say** unto thee, Arise.	7:14
16	**saying**, That a great prophet is risen up among us;	7:16
15	**saying**, Art thou he that should come?	7:19
15	John Baptist hath sent us unto thee, **saying**,	7:20
24	he began **to speak** unto the people concerning John,	7:24
1	I **say** unto you, and much more than a prophet.	7:26
1	For I **say** unto you, Among those that are born	7:28
3	and calling one to another, and **saying**,	7:32
2	For John ... came ... and ye **say**, He hath a devil.	7:33
2	and ye **say**, Behold a gluttonous man,	7:34
15	**saying**, This man, if he were a prophet,	7:39
1	Wherefore I **say** unto thee, Her sins,	7:47
24	And they that sat at meat with him began **to say**	7:49
15	And when he **had said** these things, he cried,	8:8
16	And his disciples asked him, **saying**,	8:9
17	And it was told him by certain which **said**,	8:20
16	and awoke him, **saying**, Master, master, we perish.	8:24
16	they being afraid wondered, **saying** one to another,	8:25
15	And Jesus asked him, **saying**, What is thy name?	8:30
15	be with him: but Jesus sent him away, **saying**,	8:38
4	and press thee, and **sayest** thou, Who touched me?	8:45
15	**saying** to him, Thy daughter is dead;	8:49
15	But when Jesus heard it, he answered him, **saying**,	8:50
15	by the hand, and called, **saying**, Maid, arise.	8:54
38	he was perplexed, because that it was **said** of some,	9:7
15	**saying**, Whom say the people that I am?	9:18
3	he asked them, ... Whom **say** the people that I am?	9:18
2	He said unto them, But whom **say** ye that I am?	9:20
24	instructed them not **to tell** this to anyone, (NASB)	9:21
26	he said to them all, If any man will come after me,	9:23
1	I **tell** you of a truth, there be some standing here,	9:27
25	Who appeared in glory, and **spake** of his decease	9:31
5	and one for Elias: not knowing what he **said**.	9:33
14	While he thus **spake**, there came a cloud,	9:34
19	And there came a voice out of the cloud, **saying**,	9:35
15	**saying**, Master, I beseech thee, look upon my son:	9:38
26	Therefore **said** he unto them, ... harvest ... is great,	10:2
2	And into whatsoever house ye enter, first **say**,	10:5
2	heal the sick that are therein, and **say** unto them,	10:9
1	But I **say** unto you, that it shall be more tolerable	10:12
16	And the seventy returned again with joy, **saying**,	10:17
1	For I **tell** you, that many prophets and kings	10:24
15	lawyer stood up, and tempted him, **saying**, Master,	10:25
2	And he said unto them, When ye pray, **say**,	11:2
1	I **say** unto you, Though he will not rise and give	11:8
1	And I **say** unto you, Ask, and it shall be given you;	11:9
2	ye **say** that I cast out devils through Beelzebub.	11:18
5	seeking rest; and finding none, he **saith**,	11:24
24	And it came to pass, as he **spake** these things,	11:27
24	he began **to say**, This is an evil generation:	Luke 11:29
5	one of the lawyers, and **said** unto him, Master,	11:45
15	Master, thus **saying** thou reproachest us also.	11:45
1	verily I **say** unto you, It shall be required of this	11:51
14	And as he **said** these things unto them,	11:53
24	he began **to say** unto his disciples first of all,	12:1
1	And I **say** unto you my friends,	12:4
1	to cast into hell; yea, I **say** unto you, Fear him.	12:5
1	Also I **say** unto you, Whosoever shall confess me	12:8
15	And he spake a parable unto them, **saying**,	12:16
15	he thought within himself, **saying**, What shall I do,	12:17
1	said unto his disciples, Therefore I **say** unto you,	12:22
1	they toil not, they spin not; and yet I **say** unto you,	12:27
1	verily I **say** unto you, that he shall gird himself,	12:37
4	**speakest** thou this parable unto us, or even to all?	12:41
1	Of a truth **say** unto you, that he will make him	12:44
1	I **tell** you, Nay; but rather division:	12:51
26	And he **said** also to the people,	12:54
2	straightway ye **say**, There cometh a shower;	12:54
2	And when ye see the south wind blow, ye **say**,	12:55
1	I **tell** thee, thou shalt not depart thence,	12:59
1	I **tell** you, Nay: but, except ye repent,	13:3
1	I **tell** you, Nay: but, except ye repent,	13:5
26	He **spake** also this parable;	13:6
5	And he answering **said** unto him, Lord,	13:8
26	and **said** unto the people, There are six days in	13:14
14	And when he **had said** these things,	13:17
26	Then **said** he, ... what is the kingdom of God like?	13:18
1	for many, I **say** unto you, will seek to enter in,	13:24
16	and to knock at the door, **saying**, Lord, Lord,	13:25
24	Then shall ye begin **to say**,	13:26
1	But he shall say, I **tell** you, I know you not	13:27
16	**saying** unto him, Get thee out, and depart hence:	13:31
1	and verily I **say** unto you, Ye shall not see me,	13:35
15	spake unto the lawyers and Pharisees, **saying**,	14:3
26	he **put forth** a parable to those which were bidden,	14:7
15	they chose out the chief rooms; **saying** unto them,	14:7
26	Then **said** he also to him that bade him,	14:12
1	For I **say** unto you, That none of those men	14:24
16	**Saying**, This man began to build,	14:30
16	And the Pharisees and scribes murmured, **saying**,	15:2
15	And he spake this parable unto them, **saying**,	15:3
15	**saying** unto them, Rejoice with me;	15:6
1	I **say** unto you, that likewise joy shall be in heaven	15:7
19	**saying**, Rejoice with me; for I have found the piece	15:9
1	Likewise, I **say** unto you, there is joy	15:10
26	And he **said** also unto his disciples,	16:1
26	lord's debtors unto him, and **said** unto the first,	16:5
5	**said** unto him, Take thy bill, and write fourscore.	16:7
1	And I **say** unto you, Make to yourselves friends	16:9
5	Abraham **saith** unto him, They have Moses and	16:29
15	and seven times in a day turn again to thee, **saying**,	17:4
27	ye **might say** unto this sycamine tree,	17:6
2	**say**, We are unprofitable servants:	17:10
16	and **said**, Jesus, Master, have mercy on us.	17:13
1	I **tell** you, in that night there shall be two	17:34
3	they answered and **said** unto him, Where, Lord?	17:37
26	And he **spake** a parable unto them to this end,	18:1
15	**Saying**, There was in a city a judge, ... not God,	18:2
19	**saying**, Avenge me of mine adversary.	18:3
5	the Lord said, Hear what the unjust judge **saith**.	18:6
1	I **tell** you that he will avenge them speedily.	18:8
15	but smote upon his breast, **saying**, God be merciful	18:13
1	I **tell** you, this man went down to his house	18:14
15	But Jesus called for them, **saying**, (NASB)	18:16
1	Verily I **say** unto you, Whosoever shall not receive	18:17
15	asked him, **saying**, Good Master, what shall I do	18:18
4	Jesus said unto him, Why **callest** thou me good?	18:19
1	And he said unto them, Verily I **say** unto you,	18:29
37	neither knew they the things which **were spoken**.	18:34
15	And he cried, **saying**, Jesus, thou son of David,	18:38
15	**Saying**, What wilt thou that I shall do unto thee?	18:41
16	And when they saw it, they all murmured, **saying**,	19:7
16	**saying**, We will not have this man to reign over us.	19:14
15	**saying**, Lord, thy pound hath gained ten pounds.	19:16
15	**saying**, Lord, thy pound hath gained five pounds.	19:18
15	And another came, **saying**, Lord, behold, here is	19:20

λέγω 2978

5	And he **saith** unto him, Out of thine own mouth .. Luke	19:22
1	I **say** unto you, That unto every one which hath	19:26
15	**saying**, Go into the village opposite you, (NASB)	19:30
16	**Saying**, Blessed be the King that cometh	19:38
1	he answered and said unto them, I **tell** you that,	19:40
15	**Saying**, If thou hadst known, even thou, at least in	19:42
15	**Saying** unto them, It is written, My house is	19:46
16	And spake unto him, **saying**, ... by what authority	20:2
16	And they reasoned with themselves, **saying**,	20:5
1	Neither **tell** I you by what authority I do these	20:8
24	Then began he **to speak** to the people this parable;	20:9
16	**saying**, This is the heir: come, let us kill him,	20:14
16	And they asked him, **saying**, Master, we know	20:21
4	we know that thou **sayest** and teachest rightly,	20:21
16	**Saying**, Master, Moses wrote unto us,	20:28
5	when he **calleth** the Lord the God of Abraham,	20:37
3	How say they that Christ is David's son?	20:41
5	And David himself **saith** in the book of Psalms,	20:42
1	And he said, Of a truth I say unto you,	21:3
17	And as some **spake** of the temple,	21:5
16	**saying**, Master, but when shall these things be?	21:7
16	many shall come in my name, **saying**, I am Christ;	21:8
26	**said** he unto them, Nation shall rise against nation,	21:10
1	Verily I **say** ... This generation shall not pass away,	21:32
33	feast of unleavened bread ... **called** the Passover.	22:1
5	Master **saith** unto thee, Where is ... guestchamber,	22:11
1	For I **say** unto you, I will not eat any more thereof,	22:16
1	For I **say** unto you, I will not drink of the fruit	22:18
15	and gave unto them, **saying**, This is my body	22:19
15	Likewise also the cup after supper, **saying**,	22:20
1	And he said, I **tell** thee, Peter,	22:34
1	For I **say** unto you, that this that is written must	22:37
15	**Saying**, Father, if thou be willing, remove this cup	22:42
30	behold a multitude, and he that **was called** Judas,	22:47
15	he denied him, **saying**, Woman, I know him not.	22:57
15	another confidently affirmed, **saying**,	22:59
4	And Peter said, Man, I know not what thou **sayest**...	22:60
16	**saying**, Prophesy, who is it that smote thee?	22:64
25	And many other things blasphemously **spake** they	22:65
16	and led him into their council, **saying**,	22:66
2	And he said unto them, Ye **say** that I am.	22:70
16	And they began to accuse him, **saying**,	23:2
13	**saying** that he himself is Christ a King.	23:2
15	And Pilate asked him, **saying**,	23:3
4	And he answered him and said, Thou **sayest** it.	23:3
16	And they were the more fierce, **saying**,	23:5
16	cried out all at once, **saying**, Away with this man,	23:18
16	But they cried, **saying**, Crucify him, crucify him.	23:21
24	Then shall they begin **to say** to the mountains,	23:30
26	Then **said** Jesus, Father, forgive them;	23:34
16	And the rulers also with them derided him, **saying**,	23:35
16	**saying**, If thou be the king of the Jews, save thyself.	23:37
15	**saying**, If thou be Christ, save thyself and us.	23:39
15	But the other answering rebuked him, **saying**,	23:40
26	And he **said** unto Jesus, Lord, remember me	23:42
1	And Jesus said unto him, Verily I **say** unto thee,	23:43
15	**saying**, Certainly this was a righteous man.	23:47
15	**Saying**, The Son of man must be delivered	24:7
25	which **told** these things unto the apostles.	24:10
22	**saying**, that they had also seen a vision of angels,	24:23
3	a vision of angels, which **said** that he was alive.	24:23
16	But they constrained him, **saying**, Abide with us:	24:29
18	**Saying**, The Lord is risen indeed,	24:34
5	stood in the midst of them, and **saith** unto them,	24:36
15	John bare witness of him, and cried, **saying**, John	1:15
5	Art thou Elias? And he **saith**, I am not.	1:21
4	What **sayest** thou of thyself?	1:22
15	John answered them, **saying**, I baptize with water:	1:26
5	John seeth Jesus coming unto him, and **saith**,	1:29
15	And John bare record, **saying**,	1:32
5	And looking upon Jesus as he walked, he **saith**,	1:36
5	and saw them following, and **saith** unto them,	1:38
28	Rabbi, which **is to say**, being interpreted, Master,	1:38
5	He **saith** unto them, Come and see.	1:39
5	and **saith** unto him, We have found the Messias,	1:41
5	and findeth Philip, and **saith** unto him, Follow me.	1:43
5	Philip findeth Nathanael, and **saith** unto him,	1:45
5	Philip **saith** unto him, Come and see. John	1:46
5	Jesus saw Nathanael ... and **saith** of him,	1:47
5	Nathanael **saith** ... Whence knowest thou me?	1:48
5	Nathanael answered and **saith** unto him, Rabbi,	1:49
5	And he **saith** unto him,	1:51
1	Verily, verily, I **say** unto you,	1:51
5	the mother of Jesus **saith** unto him,	2:3
5	Jesus **saith** unto her, Woman,	2:4
5	His mother **saith** unto the servants,	2:5
7	Whatsoever he **saith** unto you, do it.	2:5
5	Jesus **saith** unto them,	2:7
5	And he **saith** unto them, Draw out now,	2:8
5	And **saith** unto him,	2:10
26	But he **spake** of the temple of his body.	2:21
26	his disciples remembered that he **had said** this	2:22
1	Verily, verily, I **say** unto thee,	3:3
5	Nicodemus **saith** unto him,	3:4
1	Jesus answered, Verily, verily, I **say** unto thee,	3:5
1	Verily, verily, I **say** unto thee,	3:11
35	to a city of Samaria, which is **called** Sychar,	4:5
5	Jesus **saith** unto her, Give me to drink.	4:7
5	Then **saith** the woman of Samaria unto him,	4:9
15	and who it is that **saith** to thee, Give me to drink;	4:10
5	The woman **saith** unto him, Sir,	4:11
5	The woman **saith** unto him, Sir, give me this water,	4:15
5	Jesus **saith** unto her, Go, call thy husband,	4:16
5	Jesus said unto her, Thou hast well said,	4:17
5	The woman **saith** unto him, Sir,	4:19
2	and ye **say**, that in Jerusalem is the place	4:20
5	Jesus **saith** unto her, Woman, believe me,	4:21
5	The woman **saith** unto him, ... Messias cometh,	4:25
30	I know that Messias cometh, which is **called** Christ:	4:25
5	Jesus **saith** unto her, I that speak unto thee am he.	4:26
5	went her way into the city, and **saith** to the men,	4:28
16	his disciples prayed him, **saying**, Master, eat.	4:31
25	Therefore **said** the disciples one to another,	4:33
5	Jesus **saith** unto them,	4:34
2	**Say** not ye, There are yet four months,	4:35
1	behold, I **say** unto you, Lift up your eyes,	4:35
25	And **said** unto the woman, Now we believe,	4:42
5	The nobleman **saith** unto him,	4:49
5	Jesus **saith** unto him, Go thy way; thy son liveth.	4:50
16	his servants met him, and told him, **saying**,	4:51
5	he **saith** unto him, Wilt thou be made whole?	5:6
5	Jesus **saith** unto him, Rise, take up thy bed,	5:8
25	The Jews therefore **said** unto him that was cured,	5:10
26	but **said** also that God was his Father,	5:18
26	Jesus therefore answered and **was saying** (NASB)	5:19
1	Verily, verily, I **say** unto you,	5:19
1	Verily, verily, I **say** unto you,	5:24
1	Verily, verily, I **say** unto you,	5:25
1	but these things I **say**, that ye might be saved.	5:34
5	he **saith** unto Philip, Whence shall we buy bread,	6:5
26	And this he **said** to prove him:	6:6
5	Andrew, Simon Peter's brother, **saith** unto him,	6:8
5	When they were filled, he **said** unto his disciples,	6:12
25	Then those men, when they had seen ... **said**,	6:14
5	But he **saith** unto them, It is I; be not afraid.	6:20
1	and said, Verily, verily, I **say** unto you,	6:26
1	Verily, verily, I **say** unto you,	6:32
25	And they **said**, Is not this Jesus, the son of Joseph,	6:42
5	he **saith**, I came down from heaven?	6:42
1	Verily, verily, I **say** unto you,	6:47
16	Jews therefore strove among themselves, **saying**,	6:52
1	Verily, verily, I **say** unto you,	6:53
26	And he **said**, Therefore said I unto you,	6:65
26	He **spake** of Judas Iscariot the son of Simon:	6:71
5	Then Jesus **said** unto them,	7:6
25	sought him at the feast, and **said**, Where is he?	7:11
25	for some **said**, He is a good man:	7:12
25	others **said**, Nay; but he deceiveth the people.	7:12
16	And the Jews marvelled, **saying**,	7:15
25	Then **said** some of them of Jerusalem,	7:25
3	he speaketh boldly, and they **say** nothing unto him.	7:26
15	cried Jesus in the temple as he taught, **saying**,	7:28
25	And many of the people believed on him, and **said**,	7:31
15	Jesus stood and cried, **saying**, If any man thirst,	7:37

45

λέγω 2978

25	Many ... said, Of a truth this is the Prophet.	John 7:40
25	Others said, This is the Christ.	7:41
25	But some said, Shall Christ come out of Galilee?	7:41
5	Nicodemus saith unto them,	7:50
3	They say unto him, Master,	8:4
4	that such should be stoned: but what sayest thou?	8:5
25	This they said, tempting him,	8:6
15	Then spake Jesus again unto them, saying,	8:12
25	Then said they unto him, Where is thy Father?	8:19
25	Then said the Jews, Will he kill himself?	8:22
5	because he saith, Whither I go, ye cannot come.	8:22
26	was saying ... , "You are from below, (NASB)	8:23
25	Then said they unto him, Who art thou?	8:25
1	and I speak to the world those things	8:26
26	understood not that he spake ... of the Father.	8:27
26	Then said Jesus to those Jews which believed	8:31
4	how sayest thou, Ye shall be made free?	8:33
1	Verily, verily, I say unto you,	8:34
5	Abraham is our father. Jesus saith unto them,	8:39
1	because I tell you the truth, ye believe me not.	8:45
1	And if I say the truth, why do ye not believe me?	8:46
6	Say we not well that thou art a Samaritan,	8:48
1	Verily, verily, I say unto you,	8:51
4	thou sayest, If a man keep my saying,	8:52
2	of whom ye say, that he is your God:	8:54
1	Verily, verily, I say unto you,	8:58
16	And his disciples asked him, saying, Master,	9:2
25	said, Is not this he that sat and begged?	9:8
25	Some said, This is he: ... but he said, I am he.	9:9
25	still others were saying, "No, (NASB)	9:9
26	others said, He is like him: but he said, I am he.	9:9
25	Therefore said they unto him,	9:10
30	A man that is called Jesus made clay,	9:11
5	Where is he? He said, I know not.	9:12
25	Therefore said some of the Pharisees,	9:16
25	This man is not of God, ... Others said,	9:16
3	They say unto the blind man again,	9:17
4	sayest thou of him, that he hath opened thine eyes?	9:17
16	And they asked them, saying, Is this your son,	9:19
2	Is this your son, who ye say was born blind?	9:19
2	now ye say, We see; therefore your sin remaineth.	9:41
1	Verily, verily, I say unto you,	10:1
1	Verily, verily, I say unto you,	10:7
25	And many of them said, He hath a devil,	10:20
25	Others said, These are not the words of	10:21
25	Then came the Jews ... and said unto him,	10:24
16	The Jews answered him, saying,	10:33
2	Say ye of him, whom the Father hath sanctified,	10:36
25	And many resorted unto him, and said,	10:41
22	Therefore his sisters sent unto him, saying,	11:3
5	Then after that saith he to his disciples,	11:7
3	His disciples say unto him, Master,	11:8
5	and after that he saith unto them,	11:11
5	thought ... he had spoken of taking of rest in sleep.	11:13
30	Then said Thomas, which is called Didymus,	11:16
5	Jesus saith unto her,	11:23
5	Martha saith unto him,	11:24
5	She saith unto him, Yea, Lord: I believe	11:27
16	saying, She goeth unto the grave to weep there.	11:31
19	she fell down at his feet, saying unto him, Lord,	11:32
3	They said unto him, Lord, come and see.	11:34
25	Then said the Jews, Behold how he loved him!	11:36
5	Jesus said, Take ye away the stone.	11:39
5	Martha, ... saith unto him, Lord,	11:39
5	Jesus saith unto her,	11:40
5	Jesus saith unto them, Loose him, and let him go.	11:44
25	gathered ... a council, and said,	11:47
35	near to the wilderness, into a city called Ephraim,	11:54
25	and spake among themselves,	11:56
5	Then saith one of his disciples, Judas Iscariot,	12:4
16	and desired him, saying, Sir, we would see Jesus.	12:21
5	Philip cometh and telleth Andrew:	12:22
3	and again Andrew and Philip tell Jesus.	12:22
15	Jesus answered them, saying, The hour is come,	12:23
1	Verily, verily, I say unto you,	12:24
26	people ... that stood by, ... said that it thundered:	12:29
25	others said, An angel spake to him.	12:29
26	This he said, signifying what death he should die.	John 12:33
4	that Christ abideth for ever: and how sayest thou,	12:34
5	and Peter saith unto him,	13:6
5	Peter saith unto him,	13:8
5	Simon Peter saith unto him, Lord,	13:9
5	Jesus saith unto him,	13:10
2	Ye call me Master and Lord: and ye say well;	13:13
1	Verily, verily, I say unto you,	13:16
1	I speak not of you all:	13:18
1	Now I tell you before it come,	13:19
1	Verily, verily, I say unto you,	13:20
1	Verily, verily, I say unto you,	13:21
5	the disciples ... doubting of whom he spake.	13:22
5	therefore gestured to him, and said (NASB)	13:24
5	he should ask who it should be of whom he spake.	13:24
5	He then lying on Jesus' breast saith unto him,	13:25
5	said Jesus unto him, That thou doest, do quickly.	13:27
5	that Jesus had said unto him,	13:29
5	Therefore, when he was gone out, Jesus said,	13:31
1	as I said unto the Jews, ... so now I say to you.	13:33
5	Simon Peter said unto him, Lord,	13:36
5	Peter said unto him,	13:37
1	Verily, verily, I say unto thee,	13:38
5	Thomas saith unto him,	14:5
5	Jesus saith unto him, I am the way,	14:6
5	Philip saith unto him, Lord, show us the Father,	14:8
5	Jesus saith unto him,	14:9
4	and how sayest thou then, Show us the Father?	14:9
1	words that I say to you I do not speak (NASB)	14:10
1	Verily, verily, I say unto you,	14:12
5	Judas saith unto him, not Iscariot, Lord,	14:22
1	Henceforth I call you not servants;	15:15
1	Nevertheless I tell you the truth;	16:7
24	I have yet many things to say unto you,	16:12
5	What is this that he saith unto us, A little while,	16:17
25	They said therefore, What is this that he saith,	16:18
5	What is this that he saith, A little while?	16:18
1	Verily, verily, I say unto you,	16:20
1	Verily, verily, I say unto you,	16:23
1	and I say not unto you, that I will pray	16:26
3	His disciples said unto him,	16:29
4	now speakest ... plainly, and speakest no proverb.	16:29
5	said to them, "Whom do ye seek?" (NASB)	18:4
5	Jesus saith unto them, I am he.	18:5
5	saith the damsel that kept the door unto Peter,	18:17
5	one of this man's disciples? He saith, I am not.	18:17
5	saith, Did not I see thee in the garden with him?	18:26
4	Sayest thou this thing of thyself,	18:34
4	Jesus answered, Thou sayest that I am a king.	18:37
5	Pilate saith unto him, What is truth?	18:38
5	went out again unto the Jews, and saith unto them,	18:38
16	saying, Not this man, but Barabbas.	18:40
25	And said, Hail, King of the Jews!	19:3
5	saith unto them, Behold, I bring him forth to you,	19:4
5	And Pilate saith unto them, Behold the man!	19:5
16	they cried out, saying, Crucify him, crucify him.	19:6
5	Pilate saith unto them, Take ye him,	19:6
5	and saith unto Jesus, Whence art thou?	19:9
5	Then saith Pilate unto him, Speakest thou not	19:10
16	The Jews cried out, saying, If thou let this man go,	19:12
29	in a place that is called the Pavement,	19:13
5	and he saith unto the Jews, Behold your King!	19:14
5	Pilate saith unto them, Shall I crucify your King?	19:15
29	into a place called the place of a skull,	19:17
28	which is called in the Hebrew Golgotha:	19:17
25	Then said the chief priests of the Jews to Pilate,	19:21
19	that the scripture might be fulfilled, which saith,	19:24
5	he saith unto his mother, Woman, behold thy son!	19:26
5	Then saith he to the disciple, Behold thy mother!	19:27
5	that the scripture might be fulfilled, saith, I thirst.	19:28
5	knoweth that he saith true, that ye might believe.	19:35
5	And again another scripture saith,	19:37
5	disciple, whom Jesus loved, and saith unto them,	20:2
3	they say unto her, Woman, why weepest thou?	20:13
5	She saith unto them,	20:13
5	Jesus saith unto her, Woman, why weepest thou?	20:15
5	saith unto him, Sir, if thou have borne him hence,	20:15

λέγω 2978

5	Jesus **saith** unto her, Mary.	John 20:16
5	She turned herself, and **saith** unto him, Rabboni;	20:16
28	**saith** unto him, Rabboni; which **is to say**, Master.	20:16
5	Jesus **saith** unto her, Touch me not;	20:17
5	and **saith** unto them, Peace be unto you.	20:19
5	and **saith** unto them, Receive ye the Holy Ghost:	20:22
30	But Thomas, one of the twelve, **called** Didymus,	20:24
25	The other disciples therefore **said** unto him,	20:25
5	Then **saith** he to Thomas, Reach hither thy finger,	20:27
5	Jesus **saith** unto him,	20:29
30	Simon Peter, and Thomas **called** Didymus,	21:2
5	Simon Peter **saith** unto them, I go a fishing.	21:3
3	They **say** unto him, We also go with thee.	21:3
5	Jesus **saith** unto them, Children, have ye any meat?	21:5
5	that disciple whom Jesus loved **saith** unto Peter,	21:7
5	Jesus **saith** unto them,	21:10
5	Jesus **saith** unto them, Come and dine.	21:12
5	Jesus **saith** to Simon Peter,	21:15
5	He **saith** unto him, Yea, Lord; thou knowest	21:15
5	He **saith** unto him, Feed my lambs.	21:15
5	He **saith** to him again the second time,	21:16
5	He **saith** unto him, Yea, Lord; thou knowest	21:16
5	He **saith** unto him, Feed my sheep.	21:16
5	He **saith** unto him the third time,	21:17
5	And he **said** to Him, "Lord, (NASB)	21:17
5	Jesus **saith** unto him, Feed my sheep.	21:17
1	Verily, verily, I **say** unto thee,	21:18
5	he **saith** unto him, Follow me.	21:19
5	Peter seeing him **saith** to Jesus,	21:21
5	Jesus **saith** unto him,	21:22
15	**speaking** of the things pertaining to the kingdom	Acts 1:3
16	they asked of him, **saying**, Lord,	1:6
16	**saying** one to another, ... are not all ... Galilaeans?	2:7
16	**saying** one to another, What meaneth this?	2:12
25	Others mocking **said**, ... men are full of new wine.	2:13
5	it shall come to pass in the last days, **saith** God,	2:17
5	For David **speaketh** concerning him,	2:25
5	but he **saith** himself, The Lord said unto my Lord,	2:34
15	did he testify and exhort, **saying**, Save yourselves	2:40
35	the gate of the temple which is **called** Beautiful,	3:2
15	God made with our fathers, **saying** unto Abraham,	3:25
16	**Saying**, What shall we do to these men?	4:16
26	neither **said** any of them that ought of the things	4:32
16	**Saying**, The prison truly found we shut	5:23
15	Then came one and told them, **saying**, Behold,	5:25
15	**Saying**, Did not we straitly command you	5:28
15	Theudas, **boasting** himself to be somebody;	5:36
1	And now I **say** unto you, Refrain from these men,	5:38
34	which **is called** the synagogue of the Libertines,	6:9
18	Then they suborned men, which **said**,	6:11
18	And set up false witnesses, which **said**,	6:13
14	For we have heard him **say**, that this Jesus	6:14
5	temples made with hands; as **saith** the prophet,	7:48
5	what house will ye build me? **saith** the Lord:	7:49
13	and **saying**, Lord Jesus, receive my spirit.	7:59
36	gave heed unto those things which Philip **spake**,	8:6
15	**giving out** that himself was some great one:	8:9
16	**saying**, This man is the great power of God.	8:10
15	**Saying**, Give me also this power,	8:19
15	**saying**, Arise, and go toward the south	8:26
5	I pray thee, of whom **speaketh** the prophet this?	8:34
21	and heard a voice **saying** unto him, Saul, Saul,	9:4
25	But all that heard him were amazed, and **said**;	9:21
28	which by interpretation is **called** Dorcas:	9:36
15	But Peter took him up, **saying**, Stand up;	10:26
24	that I **should** not call any man common or unclean.	10:28
16	**Saying**, Thou wentest in to men uncircumcised,	11:3
15	and expounded it by order unto them, **saying**,	11:4
20	a voice **saying** unto me, Arise, Peter; slay and eat.	11:7
26	the word of the Lord, how that he **said**,	11:16
16	they held their peace, and glorified God, **saying**,	11:18
15	**saying**, Arise up quickly.	12:7
5	he **saith** unto him, Cast thy garment about thee,	12:8
25	Then **said** they, It is his angel.	12:15
16	the rulers of the synagogue sent unto them, **saying**,	13:15
2	any word of exhortation for the people, **say on**.	13:15
26	And as John fulfilled his course, he **said**,	13:25
5	Wherefore he **saith** also in another psalm,	Acts 13:35
36	and spake against those things which **were spoken**	13:45
16	**saying** in the speech of Lycaonia,	14:11
16	And **saying**, Sirs, why do ye these things?	14:15
16	these **sayings** scarce restrained they the people,	14:18
16	of the sect of the Pharisees which believed, **saying**,	15:5
15	**saying**, Men and brethren, hearken unto me:	15:13
5	**saith** the Lord, who doeth all these things.	15:17
16	**saying**, Ye must be circumcised, and keep the law:	15:24
15	**saying**, Come over into Macedonia, and help us.	16:9
19	when she was baptized, ... she besought us, **saying**,	16:15
19	The same followed Paul and us, and cried, **saying**,	16:17
15	But Paul cried with a loud voice, **saying**,	16:28
16	sent the serjeants, **saying**, Let those men go.	16:35
16	**saying** that there is another king, one Jesus.	17:7
25	of the Stoicks, encountered him. And some **said**,	17:18
24	What will this babbler **say**?	17:18
16	**saying**, May we know what this new doctrine,	17:19
24	but either to **tell**, or to hear some new thing.	17:21
16	**Saying**, This fellow persuadeth men	18:13
15	**saying** unto the people,	19:4
16	**saying**, We adjure you by Jesus	19:13
15	**saying** that they be no gods,	19:26
16	cried out, **saying**, Great is Diana of the Ephesians.	19:28
23	**saying** that bonds and afflictions abide me.	20:23
25	who **said** to Paul through the Spirit,	21:4
5	Thus **saith** the Holy Ghost,	21:11
15	**saying** that they ought not to circumcise	21:21
6	Do therefore this that we **say** to thee:	21:23
5	he **said** unto the chief captain, May I speak	21:37
15	he spake unto them in the Hebrew tongue, **saying**,	21:40
20	and heard a voice **saying** unto me, Saul, Saul,	22:7
13	And saw him **saying** unto me, Make haste,	22:18
16	and then lifted up their voices, and **said**,	22:22
15	**saying**, Take heed what thou doest:	22:26
11	**Tell** me, art thou a Roman? He said, Yea.	22:27
3	For the Sadducees **say** that there is no resurrection,	23:8
16	and strove, **saying**, We find no evil in this man:	23:9
16	**saying** that they would neither eat nor drink till	23:12
24	**to say** before thee what they had against him.	23:30
15	Tertullus began to accuse him, **saying**,	24:2
24	the governor had beckoned unto him **to speak**,	24:10
3	that after the way which **they call** heresy,	24:14
15	Festus declared Paul's cause ... **saying**,	25:14
25	I asked him whether he would go to Jerusalem,	25:20
24	Thou art permitted **to speak** for thyself.	26:1
21	I heard a voice **saying** to me (NASB)	26:14
21	and **saying** in the Hebrew tongue, Saul, Saul,	26:14
15	**saying** none other things than those which	26:22
16	they talked between themselves, **saying**,	26:31
15	And **said** unto them, Sirs, I perceive	27:10
36	than those things which **were spoken** by Paul.	27:11
15	**Saying**, Fear not, Paul;	27:24
15	Paul besought them all to take meat, **saying**,	27:33
25	they **said** among themselves,	28:4
25	changed their minds, and **said** that he was a god.	28:6
26	when they were come together, he **said** unto them,	28:17
36	And some believed the things which **were spoken**,	28:24
23	**Saying**, Go unto this people, and say,	28:26
15	that **sayest** a man should not commit adultery,	Rom 2:22
1	Is God unrighteous ... I **speak** as a man	3:5
24	and as some affirm that we **say**, Let us do evil,	3:8
5	we know that what things soever the law **saith**,	3:19
5	For what **saith** the scripture?	4:3
5	David also **describeth** the blessedness of the man,	4:6
6	for we **say** that faith was reckoned to Abraham	4:9
1	I **speak** after the manner of men	6:19
26	for I had not known lust, except the law **had said**,	7:7
1	I **say** the truth in Christ, I lie not,	9:1
5	For he **saith** to Moses, I will have mercy	9:15
5	For the scripture **saith** unto Pharaoh,	9:17
5	As he **saith** also in Osee,	9:25
5	righteousness ... of faith **speaketh** on this wise,	10:6
5	But what **saith** it? The word is nigh thee,	10:8
5	the scripture **saith**, Whosoever believeth on him	10:11
5	Esaias **saith**, Lord, who hath believed our report?	10:16
1	But I **say**, Have they not heard?	10:18

47

λέγω 2978

1	But I say, Did not Israel know?................	Rom 10:19
5	First Moses **saith**, I will provoke you to jealousy.....	10:19
5	But Esaias is very bold, and **saith**,...................	10:20
5	But to Israel he **saith**,...............................	10:21
1	I **say** then, Hath God cast away his people?.........	11:1
5	Wot ye not what the scripture **saith** of Elias?........	11:2
15	maketh intercession to God against Israel, **saying**,....	11:2
5	But what **saith** the answer of God unto him?.........	11:4
5	And David **saith**, Let their table be made a snare,....	11:9
1	I **say** then, Have they stumbled that they should......	11:11
1	For I **speak** to you Gentiles,.........................	11:13
1	For I **say**, through the grace given unto me,.........	12:3
5	Vengeance is mine; I will repay, **saith** the Lord......	12:19
5	**saith** the Lord, every knee shall bow to me,..........	14:11
1	Now I **say** that Jesus Christ was a minister...........	15:8
5	And again he **saith**, Rejoice, ye Gentiles,............	15:10
5	Esaias **saith**, There shall be a root of Jesse,.........	15:12
9	that ye all **speak** the same thing,...................	1 Co 1:10
1	Now this I **say**, that every one of you **saith**,.........	1:12
5	Now this I **say**, that every one of you **saith**,.........	1:12
7	For while one **saith**, I am of Paul;....................	3:4
1	I **speak** to your shame. Is it so,......................	6:5
1	But I **speak** this by permission,......................	7:6
1	I **say** therefore to the unmarried and widows,.........	7:8
1	But to the rest **speak** I, not the Lord:................	7:12
1	And this I **speak** for your own profit;.................	7:35
32	For though there be that are **called** gods,............	8:5
5	or **saith** not the law the same also?...................	9:8
5	Or **saith** he it altogether for our sakes?..............	9:10
1	I **speak** as to wise men; judge ye what I say.........	10:15
1	Conscience, I **say**, not thine own, but of the other:...	10:29
15	also he took the cup, when he had supped, **saying**,....	11:25
5	no ... by the Spirit of God **calleth** Jesus accursed:....	12:3
4	seeing he understandeth not what thou **sayest**?.......	14:16
5	for all that will they not hear me, **saith** the Lord.....	14:21
5	to be under obedience, as also **saith** the law.........	14:34
3	**say** some among you that there is no resurrection....	15:12
1	I **speak** this to your shame...........................	15:34
1	I **show** you a mystery; We shall not all sleep,.......	15:51
5	For he **saith**, I have heard thee in a time accepted,	2 Co 6:2
1	I **speak** as unto my children, be ye also enlarged.....	6:13
5	come out ... and be ye separate, **saith** the Lord,......	6:17
5	my sons and daughters, **saith** the Lord Almighty......	6:18
1	I **speak** not this to condemn you:.....................	7:3
1	I **speak** not by commandment,......................	8:8
25	that, as I **said**, ye may be ready:.....................	9:3
8	we that we **say** not, ye should be ashamed...........	9:4
1	I **say** again, Let no man think me a fool;.............	11:16
1	I **speak** as concerning reproach,......................	11:21
1	I **speak** foolishly, I am bold also......................	11:21
1	As we said before, so **say** I now again,...............	Gal 1:9
1	Brethren, I **speak** after the manner of men;..........	3:15
5	He **saith** not, And to seeds, as of many;..............	3:16
1	this I **say**, that the covenant, that was confirmed......	3:17
1	Now I **say**, That the heir, as long as he is a child,.....	4:1
2	**Tell** me, ye that desire to be under the law,...........	4:21
5	Nevertheless what **saith** the scripture?................	4:30
1	I Paul **say** unto you, that if ye be circumcised,........	5:2
1	This I **say** then, Walk in the Spirit,...................	5:16
32	Gentiles ... who are **called** Uncircumcision...........	Eph 2:11
34	which is **called** the Circumcision in the flesh.........	2:11
5	Wherefore he **saith**, When he ascended up on high,....	4:8
1	This I **say** therefore, and testify in the Lord,.........	4:17
24	For it is a shame even to **speak** of those things.......	5:12
5	Wherefore he **saith**, Awake thou that sleepest,.......	5:14
1	but I **speak** concerning Christ and the church.........	5:32
25	For many walk, of whom I **have told** you often,.....	Phlp 3:18
1	told you often, and now **tell** you even weeping,......	3:18
1	Not that I **speak** in respect of want:..................	4:11
1	And this I **say**, lest any man should beguile you.....	Col 2:4
30	And Jesus, which is **called** Justus,....................	4:11
6	For this we **say** unto you by the word of the Lord,	1 Th 4:15
10	For when they shall **say**, Peace and safety;...........	5:3
29	and exalteth himself above all that is **called** God,...	2 Th 2:4
25	when I was yet with you, I **told** you these things?.....	2:5
3	understanding neither what they **say**,...............	1 Tm 1:7
1	I **speak** the truth in Christ, and lie not;..............	2:7
5	Now the Spirit **speaketh** expressly,.................	1 Tm 4:1
5	the scripture **saith**, Thou shalt not muzzle the ox......	5:18
1	Consider what I **say**;..............................	2 Tm 2:7
16	**saying** that the resurrection is past already;...........	2:18
24	having no evil thing **to say** of you...................	Tit 2:8
1	albeit I do not **say** to thee how thou owest unto me	Phlm 1:19
1	knowing that thou wilt also do more than I **say**.......	1:21
5	he **saith**, And let all the angels ... worship him......	Heb 1:6
5	And of the angels he **saith**,.........................	1:7
15	But one in a certain place testified, **saying**,............	2:6
15	**Saying**, I will declare thy name.....................	2:12
5	Wherefore as the Holy Ghost **saith**,..................	3:7
38	While it is **said**, To day if ye will hear his voice,......	3:15
15	Again, he limiteth a certain day, **saying** in David,.....	4:7
5	As he **saith** also in another place,.....................	5:6
24	Of whom we have many things **to say**,...............	5:11
15	**Saying**, Surely blessing I will bless thee,...............	6:14
38	and not **be called** after the order of Aaron?.........	7:11
28	For he of whom these things **are spoken**............	7:13
14	but this with an oath by him that **said** unto him,......	7:21
36	of the things which we **have spoken** this is the sum:....	8:1
5	For finding fault with them, he **saith**,................	8:8
5	Behold, the days come, **saith** the Lord,.............	8:8
5	and I regarded them not, **saith** the Lord.............	8:9
5	the house of Israel after those days, **saith** the Lord;....	8:10
15	every man his brother, **saying**, Know the Lord:........	8:11
24	In that he **saith**, A new covenant, he hath made......	8:13
28	and the showbread; which is **called** the sanctuary.....	9:2
33	the tabernacle which is **called** the Holiest of all;.......	9:3
24	of which we cannot now **speak** particularly..........	9:5
15	**Saying**, This is the blood of the testament............	9:20
5	when he cometh into the world, he **saith**,...........	10:5
15	Above when he **said**,...............................	10:8
5	make with them after those days, **saith** the Lord,.....	10:16
5	I will recompense, **saith** the Lord...................	10:30
16	For they that **say** such things declare plainly.........	11:14
38	refused **to be called** the son of Pharaoh's daughter;...	11:24
1	And what **shall** I more **say**?........................	11:32
15	but now he hath promised, **saying**,.................	12:26
24	So that we may boldly **say**, The Lord is my helper,...	13:6
12	**Let** no man **say** when he is tempted,................	Jas 1:13
7	a man **say** he hath faith, and have not works?........	2:14
19	And the scripture was fulfilled which **saith**,..........	2:23
5	Do ye think that the scripture **saith** in vain,..........	4:5
5	But he giveth more grace. Wherefore he **saith**,......	4:6
16	Go to now, ye that **say**, To day or to morrow........	4:13
24	For that ye ought **to say**, If the Lord will, we shall....	4:15
16	And **saying**, Where is the promise of his coming?.....	2 Pt 3:4
15	He that **saith**, I know him,........................	1 Jn 2:4
15	He that **saith** he abideth in him.....................	2:6
15	that **saith** he is in the light, and hateth his brother,....	2:9
1	is a sin unto death: I **do not say** that he shall pray.....	5:16
2	receive him not ... neither bid him God speed:.....	2 Jn 1:10
15	For he that **biddeth** him God speed is partaker........	1:11
15	seventh from Adam, prophesied of these, **saying**,...	Jude 1:14
25	**told** you there should be mockers in the last time,.....	1:18
5	the beginning and the ending, **saith** the Lord,......	Rev 1:8
20	**Saying**, I am Alpha and Omega,.....................	1:11
15	he laid his right hand upon me, **saying** unto me,......	1:17
5	These things **saith** he that holdeth the seven stars.....	2:1
18	those who **call** themselves apostles (NASB)........	2:2
5	hear what the Spirit **saith** unto the churches;.........	2:7
5	These things **saith** the first and the last,.............	2:8
17	the blasphemy of them which **say** they are Jews,.....	2:9
5	hear what the Spirit **saith** unto the churches;.........	2:11
5	These things **saith** he which hath the sharp sword.....	2:12
5	hear what the Spirit **saith** unto the churches;.........	2:17
5	These things **saith** the Son of God;.................	2:18
21	woman Jezebel, which **calleth** herself a prophetess,....	2:20
1	But unto you I **say**, and unto the rest in Thyatira,.....	2:24
3	have not known the depths of Satan, as they **speak**;...	2:24
5	hear what the Spirit **saith** unto the churches.........	2:29
5	These things **saith** he that hath the seven Spirits......	3:1
5	hear what the Spirit **saith** unto the churches..........	3:6
5	These things **saith** he that is holy, he that is true,.....	3:7
17	which **say** they are Jews, and are not, but do lie;......	3:9
5	hear what the Spirit **saith** unto the churches..........	3:13

5	saith the Amen, the faithful and true witness,	Rev 3:14
4	Because thou sayest, I am rich,	3:17
5	hear what the Spirit **saith** unto the churches.	3:22
19	were of a trumpet talking with me; which **said**,	4:1
13	and they rest not day and night, **saying**, Holy,	4:8
16	cast their crowns before the throne, **saying**,	4:10
5	And one of the elders **saith** unto me, Weep not:	5:5
16	And they sung a new song, **saying**,	5:9
16	**Saying** with a loud voice, Worthy is the Lamb	5:12
18	heard I **saying**, Blessing, and honour, and glory,	5:13
25	And the four beasts **said**, Amen.	5:14
14	one of the four beasts **saying**, Come and see.	6:1
14	I heard the second beast **say**, Come and see.	6:3
14	I heard the third beast **say**, Come and see.	6:5
21	I heard a voice in the midst of the four beasts **say**,	6:6
21	I heard the voice of the fourth beast **say**,	6:7
16	And they cried with a loud voice, **saying**,	6:10
3	And **said** to the mountains and rocks, Fall on us,	6:16
15	**Saying**, Hurt not the earth, neither the sea,	7:3
16	with a loud voice, **saying**, Salvation to our God	7:10
16	**Saying**, Amen: Blessing, and glory, and wisdom,	7:12
15	And one of the elders answered, **saying** unto me,	7:13
28	And the name of the star is **called** Wormwood:	8:11
14	the midst of heaven, **saying** with a loud voice, Woe,	8:13
21	**Saying** to the sixth angel which had the trumpet,	9:14
21	and I heard a voice from heaven **saying** unto me,	10:4
19	spake unto me again, and **said**,	10:8
15	And I went unto the angel, and **said** unto him,	10:9
5	And he **said** unto me, Take it, and eat it up;	10:9
5	And he **said** unto me, Thou must prophesy again	10:11
3	And they **said** to me, "You must prophesy (NASB)	10:11
15	angel stood, **saying**, Rise, and measure the temple	11:1
21	heard a great voice from heaven **saying** unto them,	11:12
22	and there were great voices in heaven, **saying**,	11:15
16	**Saying**, We give thee thanks, O Lord God	11:17
21	And I heard a loud voice **saying** in heaven,	12:10
16	and they worshipped the beast, **saying**,	13:4
15	**saying** to them that dwell on the earth,	13:14
13	**Saying** with a loud voice, Fear God, and give glory	14:7
15	followed another angel, **saying**, Babylon is fallen,	14:8
15	followed them, **saying** with a loud voice,	14:9
20	And I heard a voice from heaven **saying** unto me,	14:13
5	Yea, **saith** the Spirit,	14:13
15	**saying**, Thrust in thy sharp sickle,	14:18
16	**saying**, Great and marvellous are thy works,	15:3
20	And I heard a great voice out of the temple **saying**	16:1
14	And I heard the angel of the waters **say**,	16:5
14	And I heard another out of the altar **say**,	16:7
19	a great voice ... from the throne, **saying**, It is done.	16:17
15	and talked with me, **saying** unto me, Come hither;	17:1
5	he **saith** unto me, The waters which thou sawest,	17:15
15	he cried mightily with a strong voice, **saying**,	18:2
21	And I heard another voice from heaven, **saying**,	18:4
5	for she **saith** in her heart, I sit a queen,	18:7
16	afar off for the fear of her torment, **saying**, Alas,	18:10
16	And **saying**, Alas, alas, that great city,	18:16
16	**saying**, What city is like unto this great city!	18:18
16	and cried, weeping and wailing, **saying**, Alas,	18:19
15	a great millstone, and cast it into the sea, **saying**,	18:21
14	voice of much people in heaven, **saying**, Alleluia;	19:1
16	and worshipped God that sat on the throne, **saying**,	19:4
19	And a voice came out of the throne, **saying**,	19:5
18	the voice of mighty thunderings, **saying**, Alleluia:	19:6
5	And he **saith** unto me, Write,	19:9
5	**saith** unto me, These are the true sayings of God.	19:9
5	And he **said** unto me, See thou do it not:	19:10
15	**saying** to all the fowls that fly in the midst	19:17
20	And I heard a great voice out of heaven **saying**,	21:3
5	And he **said** unto me, Write:	21:5
15	and talked with me, **saying**, Come hither,	21:9
5	Then **saith** he unto me, See thou do it not:	22:9
5	And he **saith** unto me, Seal not the sayings	22:10
3	And the Spirit and the bride **say**, Come.	Rev 22:17
5	He which testifieth these things **saith**,	22:20

Classical Greek

The common verb *legō* has the general meaning of "say" or "speak," but it assumes a variety of specific meanings depending on context. In pre-classical Greek *legō* means "to gather," "to count," or "to enumerate." Eventually the word took on the meaning "to narrate," and later *legō* expressed the ordinary action of "speaking." Along with several compound verbs, the important word *logos* (3030), "word," derives from *legō*.

Septuagint Usage

The Hebrew word *'āmar*, whose general meaning is "to say," appears nearly 5,000 times in the Old Testament. In the Septuagint *'āmar* is translated by *legō* more than 1,300 times. Both *'āmar* and the Septuagint's usage of *legō* required a wide range of translations, as is true with *legō* in classical and New Testament Greek.

New Testament Usage

Legō appears in the New Testament over 1,300 times as the general verb for "saying" or "telling" both orally and in writing. The latter is seen in the way the New Testament writers introduce Old Testament quotations (e.g., Romans 10:16, "Isaiah saith"). Special ways of uttering words, all of which are renderings of *legō*, include asking (Matthew 9:14), answering (Matthew 19:8), ordering (Luke 6:46), assuring (Matthew 11:22), maintaining (Matthew 22:23), reporting (Luke 9:31), and naming (Matthew 27:33).

A distinction must be made between *legō* and *laleō* (2953), another Greek verb that means "to give forth sounds" or "to speak." *Laleō* refers primarily to the actual sound or pronunciation of words, while *legō* has reference to the meaning and substance of the words. This distinction is clear when both words are used together, as in Matthew 13:3 (cf. John 8:43).

STRONG 3004, BAUER 468-70, MOULTON-MILLIGAN 372, KITTEL 4:69-136, LIDDELL-SCOTT 1033-34, COLIN BROWN 3:1081-82,1087,1106-7.

2979. λεῖμμα leimma noun

Remnant, that which is left.

COGNATE:
    λείπω leipō (2981)

SYNONYM:
    κατάλειμμα kataleimma (2610)

שְׁאֵרִית sheʾērîth (8086), Remnant (2 Kgs 19:4—Codex Alexandrinus only).

1. λεῖμμα leimma nom/acc sing neu

1 is a remnant according to the election of grace..... Rom 11:5

Classical Greek
This noun is related to the verb *leipō* (2981), "to leave," and speaks of "that which is left," "the remnant." "The compounds *hupoleimma, kataleimma,* and *perileimma* have the same sense" (Schrenk, "leimma," *Kittel*, 4:195).

Septuagint Usage
The Septuagint uses *leimma* to refer to the forces of Israel in Jerusalem. When Sennacherib invaded the land and threatened to destroy Jerusalem, King Hezekiah asked Isaiah to pray for "the remnant" who were left (2 Kings 19:4 [LXX 4 Kings 19:4]). Those left in Israel under Gedaliah (Jeremiah 40) were the "remnant." When they went to Egypt, no remnant remained (in Israel). Then, those who returned from Babylon became the "remnant" (Herntrich, "leimma," *Kittel*, 4:197). *Leimma* is a two-edged sword in Isaiah's writings. He prophesied that a remnant would return, a promise of hope. Involved in this, however, Isaiah was prophesying that only a remnant would return. Hence, *leimma* speaks of salvation and judgment at the same time.

New Testament Usage
The only New Testament use of *leimma* is in Romans 11:5 where Paul said of Israel: "Even so then at this present time also there is a *remnant* according to the election of grace." God has always preserved a remnant who would serve Him. The remnant is grounded in God's action (ibid., 4:204). Paul saw the partial fulfillment of the remnant prophecies in his day and wrote of it in Romans 9—11. Those who are now part of the remnant are people who put their faith in Jesus Christ. God will again deal with His people Israel when He establishes the Messianic Kingdom (ibid., 4:209ff.). Some believe that the "remnant" (Isaiah 1:9) are those whom God has called, together with the Gentiles, into the churches of Christ (Günther and Krienke, "Remnant," *Colin Brown*, 3:252).

STRONG 3005, BAUER 470, MOULTON-MILLIGAN 372, KITTEL 4:194-214, LIDDELL-SCOTT 1035, COLIN BROWN 3:247-54.

2980. λεῖος leios adj
Smooth, level.

חָלָק chālāq (2607), Smooth (Gn 27:11).

חַלֻּק challuq (2612), Smooth (1 Sm 17:40—Sixtine Edition only).

1. λείας leias acc pl fem

1 and the rough ways shall be made smooth;.........Luke 3:5

Classical Greek and Septuagint Usage
This adjective was used in classical Greek from the Eighth Century B.C. to describe anything that was "smooth" to the touch (*Liddell-Scott*). It was used of clothing, stone, topographical features, water, animal and human skin (hairless), and even the sound of a voice; all of these literal uses had a positive connotation. It was also used in the Septuagint to refer to that which was literally "smooth" (to the touch). Jacob said that he feared pretending to be Esau because "Esau my brother is a hairy man, and I am a *smooth* man" (Genesis 27:11). When David went to fight Goliath, "he chose him five *smooth* stones out of the brook" (1 Samuel 17:40 [LXX 1 Kings 17:40]).

New Testament Usage
The only use of this adjective in the New Testament is in reference to the ministry of John the Baptist: "Prepare ye the way of the Lord, make his paths straight. Every valley shall be filled, and every mountain and hill shall be brought low; and the crooked shall be made straight, and the rough ways shall be made *smooth*" (Luke 3:4,5). The adjective *leios* is uniquely used here in a parabolic way to speak of repentance. The ideas found here are taken from Isaiah 40:3-5, although the Septuagint does not use *leios* in that passage. The imagery is that of making a highway for the coming king. New roads would be made which would be level, straight, and smooth. In a spiritual sense, John and his listeners were to prepare a highway for the Lord which would result in a repentant nation that would receive its Messiah.

STRONG 3006, BAUER 470, MOULTON-MILLIGAN 372, KITTEL 4:193, LIDDELL-SCOTT 1035.

2981. λείπω leipō verb
Leave, lack, be in need (or) want (of).

COGNATES:
  ἀδιάλειπτος adialeiptos (87)
  ἀδιαλείπτως adialeiptōs (88)
  ἀνέκλειπτος anekleiptos (411)
  ἀπολείπω apoleipō (614)
  διαλείπω dialeipō (1251)
  ἐγκαταλείπω enkataleipō (1452)
  ἐκλείπω ekleipō (1574)

ἐπιλείπω epileipō (1936)
ἐπίλοιπος epiloipos (1939)
κατάλειμμα kataleimma (2610)
καταλείπω kataleipō (2611)
κατάλοιπος kataloipos (2615)
λεῖμμα leimma (2979)
λοιπός loipos (3036)
περιλείπομαι perileipomai (3898)
ὑπόλειμμα hupoleimma (5112B)
ὑπολείπω hupoleipō (5113)

SYNONYM:
ὑστερέω hustereō (5139)

לוּז lûz (4005), Hiphil: be out of one's sight (Prv 4:21).

פָּרַד pāradh (6754), Niphal: be separated (Prv 19:4 [19:1]).

1. **λείπει** leipei 3sing indic pres act
2. **λείπῃ** leipē 3sing subj pres act
3. **λείποντα** leiponta nom/acc pl neu part pres act
4. **λείπεται** leipetai 3sing indic pres mid
5. **λειπόμενοι** leipomenoi nom pl masc part pres mid

1 Yet **lackest** thou one thing: sell all that thou hast,	Luke 18:22
3 shouldest set in order the things that **are wanting**,	Tit 1:5
2 that nothing **be wanting** unto them.	3:13
5 ye may be perfect and entire, **wanting** nothing.	Jas 1:4
4 If any of you **lack** wisdom, let him ask of God,	1:5
5 or sister be naked, and **destitute** of daily food,	2:15

Classical Greek and Septuagint Usage

Since the time of Homer the verb *leipō* has meant "to leave" or "to leave behind." Related terms include the important verb *kataleipō* (2611); the nouns *leimma* (2979) and *kataleimma* (2610), both meaning "remnant" or "residue"; and the adjective *loipos* (3036), "remaining" or "other." The Septuagint uses *leipō* in the active sense of "leaving someone or something behind" (Job 4:11). *Leipō* and its derivatives also appear in the Septuagint with the passive sense of "being abandoned or left behind" (Proverbs 4:21). Although none of these words take on a technical religious meaning in Greek usage, the teaching about the remnant of Israel is conveyed in the Septuagint largely through *leipō* and its word family. (See, for example, Isaiah 7:3 [Shear-Jashub means "a remnant will return"]; compare Romans 11:5.)

New Testament Usage

Leipō also carries the idea of being inferior, falling short, or being in need of something. In the New Testament *leipō* appears six times, always meaning "to lack" or "to be in want of." In Titus 3:13 Paul admonished his younger colleague to be hospitable and offer assistance to Zenas and Apollos, making sure "that nothing *be wanting* unto them." Reference to a deficiency in material needs is also found in James 2:15 where the King James Version renders a form of *leipō* as "destitute."

Titus was ordered to "set in order the things *that are wanting*" (Titus 1:5), presumably a reference to the lack of organization or leadership in the young church on Crete. Of more importance is James' desire that faith eventually eliminate spiritual shortcomings in the lives of his readers (James 1:4). Indeed, James 1:5 observes that those who lack wisdom will find that God is able to eliminate this deficiency. The final, and perhaps the most familiar, verse in which *leipō* appears is Luke 18:22 where Jesus shocked the "rich young ruler" by noting that this man lacked one thing, a willingness to part with his wealth.

STRONG 3007, BAUER 470, MOULTON-MILLIGAN 372, LIDDELL-SCOTT 1035-36, COLIN BROWN 3:247-48,251,253.

2982. λειτουργέω leitourgeō verb

To serve or minister to God or man.

COGNATES:
ἐργάζομαι ergazomai (2021)
λειτουργία leitourgia (2983)
λειτουργικός leitourgikos (2984)
λειτουργός leitourgos (2985)

SYNONYMS:
διακονέω diakoneō (1241)
δουλεύω douleuō (1392)
θεραπεύω therapeuō (2300)
λατρεύω latreuō (2973)
ὑπηρετέω hupēreteō (5094)

כָּהַן kāhan (3667), Piel: serve as a priest (2 Chr 11:14).

עָבַד ʿāvadh (5856), Serve, minister (Nm 4:37, Dt 18:5, 2 Chr 35:3).

עֲבֹדָה ʿăvōdhāh (5865), Service (1 Chr 23:28,32).

צָבָא tsāvāʾ (6892), Perform a service (Nm 8:24—Codex Alexandrinus only).

צָבָא tsāvāʾ (6893), Service (Nm 4:3,39,43).

שָׁרַת shārath (8664), Piel: minister, serve (Ex 29:30, 2 Chr 29:11, Ez 44:15ff.).

1. **λειτουργῶν** leitourgōn nom sing masc part pres act
2. **λειτουργούντων** leitourgountōn gen pl masc part pres act
3. **λειτουργῆσαι** leitourgēsai inf aor act

2 As they **ministered** to the Lord, and fasted,	Acts 13:2
3 duty is also **to minister** unto them in carnal things.	Rom 15:27
1 And every priest standeth daily **ministering**	Heb 10:11

Classical Greek

In classical literature *leitourgeō* was used in three ways. In a political sense it was first used to refer to those who served society in a political office at their own expense. Later it referred to anyone who served in public office. In reference to religion *leitourgeō* is used to refer to those involved in the pagan religions, including temple employees as well as priests. This verb is also used in a general sense to refer to the rendering of any service to another, such as slaves to masters, employees to employers, and even friends to one another.

Septuagint Usage

The Septuagint uses *leitourgeō* to refer to the service of the priests who were to "*minister in the holy place*" (Exodus 29:30) and of the ministry of the Levites (Numbers 18:2). Most frequently it translates the Hebrew term *'āvadh* meaning "work, serve, worship." When Korah and other Levites despised their priestly service and were jealous of the leadership positions of Moses and Aaron, God rebuked them saying: "Seemeth it but a small thing unto you, that the God of Israel hath separated you from the congregation of Israel, to bring you near to himself *to do the service* of the tabernacle of the LORD, and to stand before the congregation to minister unto them?" (Numbers 16:9).

New Testament Usage

Luke recorded that the prophets and teachers at Antioch "*ministered* to the Lord, and fasted" (Acts 13:2). R.C.H. Lenski interpreted this to be a reference to the ministry of these men in a local church service (*The Interpretation of the Acts of the Apostles*, p.494). However, this ministering to the Lord may be a reference to prayer, as in the case of Anna who served by prayer and fasting (Luke 2:37). Paul used *leitourgeō* to refer to ministering to the material needs of the saints (Romans 15:27).

The writer to the Hebrews used *leitourgeō* to refer to the "ministering" of the priests. Clearly, the entire Epistle to the Hebrews is deeply rooted in Old Testament ideology, culture, and tradition. From this frame of reference, then, the writer portrayed the person and the work of Jesus Christ. The priestly service which included bringing forth offerings to the Lord in the Old Testament serves as a picture of the priestly ministry of Jesus who offers himself for the sins of mankind. For the writer of this epistle, the system of divine service enacted under the old covenant finds its fulfillment in the work of Christ (8:2,6; 9:21,24; 10:11f.) who is the mediator of a new covenant (8:6; 9:15). However, unlike the priestly service of the Old Testament, Jesus did not enter "into the holy places made with hands, which are the figures of the true; but into heaven itself, now to appear in the presence of God for us" (9:24).

Likewise, while priests were required to present daily offerings and sacrifices, Jesus "offered one sacrifice for sins for ever" and "sat down on the right hand of God" (10:11f.). Therefore, the ministry of Christ is the only service which is now in effect and the only one which brings reconciliation and life.

In addition, the Book of Hebrews uses other members of the *leitourgeō* word group. For example, in Hebrews 1:7 the angels are referred to as "ministers," *leitourgous* (see 2985), and in 1:14 they are called "ministering (*leitourgika* [see 2984]) spirits" commissioned by God to assist those about to inherit salvation. In a similar fashion Paul described himself as a minister of the gospel of salvation, a priest of the Lord Jesus Christ whose holy service was to proclaim the "gospel of God" to a people who might become an acceptable offering to God (cf. Romans 15:16). Obviously this "offering" was not a redemption offering but a thanksgiving offering, and thus the priestly service Paul rendered to the Lord was a constant sacrifice of thanksgiving for the work of His Son on the Cross (cf. Philippians 2:17).

STRONG 3008, BAUER 470-71, MOULTON-MILLIGAN 372-73, KITTEL 4:215-29, LIDDELL-SCOTT 1036, COLIN BROWN 3:551-53.

2983. λειτουργία leitourgia noun

Service, ministry.

COGNATE:
λειτουργέω leitourgeō (2982)

SYNONYM:
διακονία diakonia (1242)

מְלָאכָה *mᵉlā'khāh* (4536), Work (1 Chr 26:30).
עֲבֹדָה *'ăvōdhāh* (5865), Service (Nm 18:4, 1 Chr 28:13, 2 Chr 35:15).
פָּלְחָן *polchān* (A6646), Service (Ezr 7:19—Aramaic).
פְּעֻלָּה *pᵉ'ullah* (6715), Labor (Ez 29:20).
צָבָה *tsāvâh* (6898), Service (Nm 8:24—Codex Alexandrinus only).

1. λειτουργίας leitourgias gen sing fem
2. λειτουργίᾳ leitourgia dat sing fem

```
1 days of his ministration were accomplished,......... Luke 1:23
1 For the administration of this service................ 2 Co 9:12
2 offered upon the sacrifice and service of your faith,..Phlp 2:17
1 to supply your lack of service toward me............. 2:30
1 now hath he obtained a more excellent ministry,..... Heb 8:6
1 the tabernacle, and all the vessels of the ministry....... 9:21
```

Classical Greek

Leitourgia, related to the verb *leitourgeō* (2982), is a compound of *leitos* ("of" or "for the people") and the root *erg-* ("to do work"). Thus *leitourgia* is any "work or service done on behalf of the public, a public service, a public duty" (the "public" being a political unity) (Strathmann, "leitourgeō," *Kittel,* 4:216).

The expression enjoyed status as a technical political term used to describe a public service or duty discharged by the richer citizens (*Liddell-Scott;* cf. Strathmann, "leitougeō," *Kittel,* 4:216). Popularly *leitourgia* could refer to any type of service rendered; this did not necessarily have to be for the sake of the public. Papyri show the idea of religious "service, ministry" was known, and they indicate that drift toward a technical religious sense was occurring (ibid., 4:218f.; cf. *Moulton-Milligan*).

Septuagint Usage

Leitourgia appears 45 times (cf. the verb about 100 times) in the Septuagint. The predominant Hebrew original (36 out of 41 times) is *ʿăvōdhāh* (cf. *ʿāvadh*), "service, worship, work," especially cultic.

The term is employed for the various tabernacle duties of the Levites (e.g., Numbers 4:24,27; 7:5; 16:9; 1 Chronicles 6:32; 9:13; passim) and of royal service (2 Samuel 19:18 [LXX 2 Kings 19:18], no Hebrew). Following the building of the temple Solomon reorganized the priests for "duties" in the temple (2 Chronicles 8:14). The priests and Levites became associated with the various duties (2 Chronicles 31:2,4,16). *Leitourgia* departs from its cultic moorings to the more general sense of "ministry" in the apocryphal Wisdom of Solomon (18:21). Still it retains its cultic nuance for the most part (Sirach 50:19; 2 Maccabees 3:3; 4:14). In a rare usage in Ezekiel 29:20 God declared that Nebuchadnezzar was in His *leitourgias,* "service" (Hebrew *peʿullāh;* manuscript Alexandrinus reads *douleias* [see 1391], "servitude, slavery").

It is noteworthy that the Septuagint has thoroughly reshaped the meaning of *leitourgia.* There is a complete absence of the technical political use so common in secular Greek. The duty or service is invariably directed to God himself via the tabernacle/temple cultus. Nonetheless, there was probably some influence by this older, formal idea. The people indirectly are the recipients of the priestly duties, but only as God is affected by them (the spirit of sacrifice rather that the sacrifice itself is, of course, what God accepts). (Cf. Strathmann, "leitourgeō," *Kittel,* 4:219-222; see also the discussion of cultic ministry in Rabbinic Judaism by Meyer, "leitourgeō," *Kittel,* 4:222ff.)

New Testament Usage

Six occurrences of *leitourgia* are found in the New Testament (cf. the verb three times). Luke 1:23, itself cast in a broader Septuagintal setting, uses *leitourgia* in a purely cultic sense of the priestly "duty" of Zechariah to burn incense in the sanctuary. Paul tied *leitourgia* to the "ministry" of financially or materially supporting missionaries (2 Corinthians 9:12). He saw the gospel worker as engaged in *leitourgia* "of Christ" (Philippians 2:30). He recognized a relationship between *leitourgia* and the cultic system (Philippians 2:17), and he may have acknowledged the more classical political concept that *leitourgia* benefits a "public," in this case God's people. At the same time *leitourgia* is, as in the Old Testament, directed to God (in thanksgiving) (2 Corinthians 9:12).

In what sense, then, can the Christian engage in divine service, in *leitourgia*? The most important elements of the service of Christians in the Early Church were the preaching of the gospel and the participation in the ordinances of baptism and the Lord's Supper. These activities represented an exercising of the new life in Christ which had been imparted by grace through the working of the Holy Spirit. "Divine service," therefore, is a work of the Spirit whereby believers are gathered to appear before the face of God through preaching of the Word and other means of grace. In this holy communion of the saints, the community of God participates in the act of worship and further ministers to the Lord by offering sacrifices of thanksgiving. At the heart of this is the profound realization that new life, divine service, and fellowship with God is through Christ alone. With this as the foundation, the Christian then continues his *leitourgia* by ministering to the people around him in ways which imitate and emulate the life of Jesus.

STRONG 3009, BAUER 471, MOULTON-MILLIGAN 373, KITTEL 4:215-29, LIDDELL-SCOTT 1036-37, COLIN BROWN 3:551-53.

2984. λειτουργικός leitourgikos adj

Ministry pertaining to service, engaged in holy service.

λειτουργός 2985

CROSS-REFERENCE:
λειτουργέω leitourgeō (2982)

עֲבֹדָה 'ăvōdhāh (5865), Service, work (Nm 4:26, 7:5).

שָׁרֵת shārēth (8665), Ministry, service (Nm 4:12, 2 Chr 24:14).

1. λειτουργικά leitourgika nom/acc pl neu

1 Are they not all **ministering** spirits, ... Heb 1:14

This word relates to the performance of service or ministry. The Septuagint uses *leitourgikos* to refer to the ministering of Aaron (Exodus 31:10), the Levites (Numbers 7:5), and the Gershonites (Numbers 9:26). The only New Testament usage is in reference to angels who are called "*ministering*" spirits, sent forth to minister for them who shall be heirs of salvation (Hebrews 1:14). (Compare the noun *leitourgos* [2985].) *Leitourgikos* is used also of holy vessels in Numbers 4:12,26 and 2 Chronicles 24:14.

STRONG 3010, BAUER 471, MOULTON-MILLIGAN 373, KITTEL 4:231, LIDDELL-SCOTT 1036, COLIN BROWN 3:551-53.

2985. λειτουργός leitourgos noun
Minister, servant.

COGNATE:
λειτουργέω leitourgeō (2982)
SYNONYMS:
διάκονος diakonos (1243)
θεράπων therapōn (2301)
ὑπηρέτης hupēretēs (5095)

לִיץ līts (4054), Mock; hiphil: officer (Sir 10:2).

פְּלַח peˈlach (A6643), Servant (Ezr 7:24—Aramaic).

שָׁרַת shārath (8664), Piel: servant, minister (2 Kgs 4:43, Ps 103:21 [102:21], Is 61:6).

1. λειτουργός leitourgos nom sing masc
2. λειτουργόν leitourgon acc sing masc
3. λειτουργοί leitourgoi nom pl masc
4. λειτουργούς leitourgous acc pl masc

3 for they are God's **ministers**, ... Rom 13:6
2 That I should be the **minister** of Jesus Christ 15:16
2 and he that **ministered** to my wants. .... Phlp 2:25
4 and his **ministers** a flame of fire. .... Heb 1:7
1 A **minister** of the sanctuary, ... 8:2

Classical Greek
This noun is used in classical Greek literature to refer to governmental and public servants, to priests and prophets in pagan religions, and to angels as spiritual ministers of God. It is also used of demons, calling them "servants" of the signs of zodiac (Strathmann, "leitourgos," *Kittel*, 4:229). In a general sense it denotes one who served with manual labor (whether a carpenter, workman, or private servant, etc.; cf. *Liddell-Scott*).

Septuagint Usage
In the Septuagint *leitourgos* refers both to the servants who were ministering to King Solomon when the Queen of Sheba visited (1 Kings 10:5 [LXX 3 Kings 10:5]) and to the priests as ministers of God (Nehemiah 10:39). Isaiah spoke of a future time of glory for Israel when the Gentiles would refer to Jews as "ministers of our God" (Isaiah 61:6). (See also Psalm 103:21 [LXX 102:21].)

New Testament Usage
The New Testament exhibits a continuation of the classical and Septuagintal uses of *leitourgos*. The writer to the Hebrews referred to angels as the ministers of God (Hebrews 1:7) and to our high priest Jesus as "the *minister* of the sanctuary, and of the true tabernacle, which the Lord pitched, and not man" (Hebrews 8:2). The apostle Paul referred to himself as "the *minister* of Jesus Christ to the Gentiles" (Romans 15:16). *Leitourgos* has a more sacral overtone than does *diakonos* (1243) (Strathmann, "leitourgos," *Kittel*, 4:229,230). Paul spoke of Epaphroditus as a *servant* of the church at Philippi who ministered to his needs (Philippians 2:25). Paul also considered human rulers as "God's ministers" (Romans 13:6) in that they serve God by punishing those who do evil.

STRONG 3011, BAUER 471, MOULTON-MILLIGAN 373, KITTEL 4:229-31, LIDDELL-SCOTT 1036-37, COLIN BROWN 3:551-53.

2986. λέντιον lention noun
Linen cloth, towel, apron.

1. λεντίῳ lentiō dat sing neu
2. λέντιον lention nom/acc sing neu

2 and took a **towel**, and girded himself. .... John 13:4
1 and to wipe them with the **towel** 13:5

The noun *lention* is translated "linen cloth (or towel)" in the New Testament and in classical Greek. It is used in classical Greek to refer to an attendant at a public bath, to a servant (male or female) preparing himself to serve by putting on a linen towel or apron around the waist, and at least once to a woman preparing to wash someone's feet (cf. *Bauer*). In the New Testament the word occurs only in John 13:4 on the occasion of the Last Supper when Jesus " . . . riseth from supper, and laid aside his garments; and took a *towel* (*lention*), and girded himself." This was done in preparation to washing the disciples' feet, certainly the act of a servant.

Strong 3012, Bauer 471, Moulton-Milligan 374, Liddell-Scott 1038.

2987. λεπίς lepis noun
Fish scales.

פַּח pach (6584), Plate (Nm 16:38).

קַשְׂקֶשֶׂת qasqeseth (7474), Scale (Lv 11:10,12, Dt 14:10).

1. λεπίδες lepides nom pl fem
1 there fell from his eyes as it had been scales:........Acts 9:18

Classical Greek
This word refers to many things that can be described as a thin layer, such as the skin of an onion, a scale of a fish or a snake, or a shell (as an eggshell). It is even used of flakes that fly from hammered copper, or snowflakes.

Septuagint Usage
In the Septuagint the noun *lepis* is translated as "fish scales." In both Leviticus 11:9 and Deuteronomy 14:9 the text indicates God's instructions as to which sea creatures are "clean" and which are "unclean." Those which had "scales" were to be considered "clean."

New Testament Usage
In the New Testament there is only one occurrence of the word *lepis*. In Acts 9:18, upon the conversion of Saul and his meeting with Ananias in Damascus, Ananias laid his hands on the blind Saul, "and immediately there fell from his eyes as it had been *scales (lepis)*: and he received sight forthwith." The expression draws on medical terminology. The term "descaling" derives from the removal of a growth of skin covering the eye and causing blindness (Bornkamm, "lepis," *Kittel*, 4:232). Whether God used this condition or another cannot be determined. However, Paul's blindness was supernaturally imposed and removed.

Strong 3013, Bauer 471, Moulton-Milligan 374, Kittel 4:232-33, Liddell-Scott 1039.

2988. λέπρα lepra noun
Leprosy, scaliness.
Cross-Reference:
λεπρός lepros (2989)

צָרַעַת tsāra'ath (7168), Leprosy, infectious skin disease (Lv 13:2f.,11-13, 2 Kgs 5:3).

1. λέπρα lepra nom sing fem
2. λέπρας lepras gen sing fem
1 And immediately his **leprosy** was cleansed..........Matt 8:3
1 immediately the **leprosy** departed from him,........ Mark 1:42
2 was in a certain city, behold a man full of **leprosy**:.. Luke 5:12
1 And immediately the **leprosy** departed from him........ 5:13

Classical Greek
In classical Greek *lepra* refers to psoriasis (cf. *Bauer*). Herodotus and medical authors used *lepra* to describe a cutaneous disease which gave a scaly or bumpy texture to the skin. It was associated with *leuke*, a whitish affliction of the skin. The skin had an absence of pigment resulting in an irregularly pale color or white patches.

Septuagint Usage
The Septuagint uses *lepra* for *tsāra'ath*, which is found especially in Leviticus 13f., or *negha'-tsāra'ath* (Leviticus 13:20). When Moses put his hand in his cloak and drew it out (the sign to Pharaoh), it is described as "leprous as snow" (Exodus 4:6). Miriam's judgment for rebelling against Moses' authority in Numbers 12:10 is described the same way.

New Testament Usage
In the New Testament the term *lepra* is reserved for the disease of leprosy. While the word is used primarily for leprosy in the sense normally understood, it also may have been used in a few instances to describe a lesser inflammatory skin condition such as psoriasis, ringworm, or favus (Matthew 8:3; Mark 1:42; Luke 5:12; cf. *Bauer*). "But the precise medical identification of the disease does not affect our estimation of the accounts of healings" (Michaelis, "lepra," *Kittel*, 4:233). Luke notes the advanced state of the leper who said to Jesus, "If thou wilt, thou canst make me clean." Luke records that he was "full of leprosy" (Luke 5:12).

Even though the disease may have been a much more severe form of psoriasis, it was actually thought of in New Testament times as a "scourge," as the word *lepra* indicates in its Hebrew background. Apparently caused by a microorganism, the disease caused the formation of ulcers or lesions in the skin followed by loss of sensation of feeling. In some cases this condition could lead to the loss of the extremities due to the absence of the sense of feeling.

Because of the fear associated with contracting this disease, lepers were required to keep a distance of at least 6 feet away from people—or if the wind came from their direction, at least 100 feet.

In the New Testament, whenever one was healed of the disease the person is always (with one exception, Luke 17:15) referred to as having been "cleansed" rather than "healed." This probably was due to the idea prevalent among the Hebrew people that sin was a major cause of leprosy, and therefore one was not healed as in the case of other diseases but rather was cleansed as by the removal of sin from the life.

STRONG 3014, BAUER 471, KITTEL 4:233-34, LIDDELL-SCOTT 1039, COLIN BROWN 2:464,466.

2989. λεπρός lepros adj
Scaly, leprous; leper.

COGNATE:
λέπρα lepra (2988)

צָרַע tsāraʿ (7164), Qal: be leprous, be diseased (Lv 13:44f., Nm 5:2); pual: leper, diseased person (Lv 14:2, 2 Sm 3:29); be leprous (2 Chr 26:20f.).

1. λεπρός lepros nom sing masc
2. λεπροῦ leprou gen sing masc
3. λεπροί leproi nom pl masc
4. λεπρούς leprous acc pl masc

1 there came a leper and worshipped him, saying,	Matt 8:2
4 Heal the sick, cleanse the lepers, raise the dead,	10:8
3 the lepers are cleansed, and the deaf hear,	11:5
2 in Bethany, in the house of Simon the leper,	26:6
1 And there came a leper to him, beseeching him,	Mark 1:40
2 being in Bethany in the house of Simon the leper,	14:3
3 many lepers were in Israel in the time of Eliseus	Luke 4:27
3 the lepers are cleansed, the deaf hear,	7:22
3 there met him ten men that were lepers,	17:12

Classical Greek
Lepros is related to the verb *lepō*, "to scale, to peel, to strip off" (as husks from corn). The adjective (cf. the noun *lepra* [2988], "leprosy, skin disease") means "scaly, scabby." It may refer to an uneven surface of any kind (e.g., a road), but it usually denotes a leprous, infectious condition of the skin (Michaelis, "lepra," *Kittel*, 4:233).

Septuagint Usage
Lepros occurs as an equivalent to *tsāraʿ* (not necessarily "leprous") in the Septuagint, a term used for various skin diseases (used 14 times; cf. *lepra*, 37 times, especially Leviticus chapter 13). We find it descriptive of the leprous individual with an "infectious (skin) disease" (Leviticus 13:45, NIV). Certain regulations were enacted to prevent the spread of these diseases (Leviticus 14:2,3; 22:4). Such a condition rendered the individual "unclean," and it jeopardized the health and well-being of the entire community (Numbers 5:2). Symbolically "leprosy" was a sign of judgment (cf. 2 Kings 5:27 [LXX 4 Kings 5:27; *lepra*]; 2 Chronicles 26:20ff.). Naaman was delivered of leprosy as a sign of God's presence (2 Kings 5:14 [LXX 4 Kings 5:14]).

New Testament Usage
Lepros occurs only in the Synoptic Gospels in the New Testament (nine times) where it is always used substantively, hence, "leper." Here too the term may indicate a wider range of skin diseases than just "leprosy." It may be picking up on the same Old Testament understanding (cf. Mark 1:40 *katharizō* [2483]; Luke 4:27). The most important observation to be gleaned in the New Testament is that Jesus' coming to heal or cleanse lepers was a recognized sign of the arrival of messianic salvation (Luke 7:22).

STRONG 3015, BAUER 472, KITTEL 4:233-34, LIDDELL-SCOTT 1039, COLIN BROWN 2:463-64.

2990. λεπτόν lepton adj
Mite.

דַּק daq (1911), Thin (Gn 41:6f., Lv 13:30); gentle (1 Kgs 19:12).

דָּקַק dāqaq (1914), Qal: grind small (Dt 9:21); hiphil: beat small, beat to powder (Ex 30:36, 2 Chr 34:7).

כָּתַת kāthath (3936), Somthing shattered (Is 30:14).

נָפַץ nāphats (5492), Crush; pual: be crushed (Is 27:9).

רִיק rîq (7672), Empty (Jer 51:34 [28:34]).

רֵיק rêq (7673), Empty (Gn 41:27).

רַק raq (7828), Lean (Gn 41:19f.,27).

1. λεπτόν lepton nom/acc sing neu
2. λεπτά lepta nom/acc pl neu

2 and she threw in two mites, which make a farthing.	Mark 12:42
1 till thou hast paid the very last mite.	Luke 12:59
2 a certain poor widow casting in thither two mites.	21:2

The word *lepton* (neuter of *leptos*) is the noun form of the verb *leipō* (2981) which means "to strip or peel bark off a tree." The usual result of peeling bark off trees was small, thin pieces of bark, and hence the noun form meant "thin," "small," and many other synonyms of the same. In the New Testament *lepton* is translated "mite." In each of its locations (Mark 12:42; Luke 12:59; 21:2) *lepton* is the widow's *mite*, referring to the smallest coin available for use in New Testament times.

STRONG 3016, BAUER 472 (see "leptos"), MOULTON-MILLIGAN 374, LIDDELL-SCOTT 1039-40 (see "leptos"), COLIN BROWN 2:850.

2991. Λευί Leui name
Levi.

1. Λευί Leui masc

1 which was the son of Levi,	Luke 3:24
1 which was the son of Levi,	3:29
1 And verily they that are of the sons of Levi,	Heb 7:5
1 Levi also, ... payed tithes in Abraham.	7:9
1 Of the tribe of Levi were sealed twelve thousand.	Rev 7:7

Four men are known by this name. The first is the son of Jacob, who headed one of the 12 tribes of Israel (Revelation 7:7). Two others are found in the genealogy of Jesus; the son of Melchi (Luke 3:24), and the son of Simeon (Luke 3:29). The fourth is one of the 12 apostles, also called Matthew (Mark 2:14; cf. Matthew 9:9).

2992. Λευίς Leuis name
Levi.

1. Λευίς Leuis nom masc
2. Λευίν Leuin acc masc

2 he saw Levi the son of Alphaeus sitting	Mark 2:14
2 he went forth, and saw a publican, named Levi,	Luke 5:27
1 And Levi made him a great feast in his own house:	5:29

Alternate spelling of *Leui* (2991).

2993. Λευίτης Leuitēs name
Levites.

1. Λευίτης Leuitēs nom sing masc
2. Λευίτας Leuitas acc pl masc

1 And likewise a Levite, when he was at the place,	Luke 10:32
2 when the Jews sent priests and Levites	John 1:19
1 Joses, ... a Levite, and of the country of Cyprus,	Acts 4:36

The descendants of Levi who performed priestly services in Israel; used of Barnabas (Acts 4:36).

2994. Λευιτικός Leuitikos name-adj
Levitical.

1. Λευιτικῆς Leuitikēs gen fem

1 If ... perfection were by the Levitical priesthood,	Heb 7:11

Descriptive title of the priesthood in Israel (Hebrews 7:11).

2995. λευκαίνω leukainō verb
Make white.
COGNATE:
λευκός leukos (2996)

לָבֵן lāvēn (3967), Hiphil: be white, make white (Ps 51:7 [50:7], Is 1:18, Jl 1:7).

לָבָן lāvān (3968), White (Lv 13:19).

1. ἐλεύκαναν eleukanan 3pl indic aor act
2. λευκᾶναι leukanai inf aor act

2 as snow; so as no fuller on earth can white them.	Mark 9:3
1 and made them white in the blood of the Lamb.	Rev 7:14

In the New Testament the verb *leukainō*, along with its noun form *leukos* (2996), conveys the meaning of lightening the color of someone or something until the object in question becomes white. The verb *leukainō* is used only twice, in Mark 9:3 and Revelation 7:14.

A literal use of the term is found in the Markan passage which describes the transfiguration of Jesus before Peter and John. In this verse Jesus' clothing is described as being "exceeding white as snow; so as no fuller on earth can *white* (*leukainō*) them." In the Revelation passage a figurative meaning is employed. The identity of the multitude arrayed in white robes is questioned. The response in Revelation 7:14 is, "These are they which came out of great tribulation, and have washed their robes, and made them *white* (*leukainō*) in the blood of the Lamb."

STRONG 3021, BAUER 472, MOULTON-MILLIGAN 374, KITTEL 4:241-50, LIDDELL-SCOTT 1041.

2996. λευκός leukos adj
White, brilliant, shining.
COGNATE:
λευκαίνω leukainō (2995)
SYNONYMS:
λαμπρός lampros (2959)
φωτεινός phōteinos (5296)

חוּם chûm (2439), White (Gn 30:35—Sixtine Edition only).

לָבָן lāvān (3968), White (Gn 30:37, Lv 13:19ff., Zec 6:3).

נְקֵא neqē' (A5528), Pure (Dn 7:9—Aramaic).

נָקֹד nāqōdh (5532), Speckled (Gn 30:32—Codex Alexandrinus only).

עָקֹד 'āqōdh (6362), Striped (Gn 31:8).

צַח tsach (6970), Radiant (S/S 5:10).

1. λευκόν leukon nom/acc sing masc/neu
2. λευκοῖς leukois dat pl masc/neu
3. λευκός leukos nom sing masc
4. λευκή leukē nom sing fem
5. λευκῇ leukē dat sing fem
6. λευκήν leukēn acc sing fem
7. λευκαί leukai nom pl fem

8. λευκάς leukas acc pl fem
9. λευκά leuka nom/acc pl neu
10. λευκαῖς leukais dat pl fem

6	thou canst not make one hair **white** or black.......	Matt 5:36
9	and his raiment was **white** as the light.................	17:2
1	was like lightning, and his raiment **white** as snow:.....	28:3
9	raiment became shining, exceeding **white** as snow;..	Mark 9:3
6	on the right side, clothed in a long **white** garment;.....	16:5
3	and his raiment was **white** and glistering............	Luke 9:29
7	for they are **white** already to harvest.................	John 4:35
2	And seeth two angels in **white** sitting......................	20:12
5	behold, two men stood by them in **white** apparel;....	Acts 1:10
7	His head and his hairs were **white** like wool,.........	Rev 1:14
1	his hairs were white like wool, as **white** as snow;......	1:14
6	and will give him a **white** stone,.......................	2:17
2	shall walk with me in **white**: for they are worthy......	3:4
2	the same shall be clothed in **white** raiment;.............	3:5
9	and **white** raiment, that thou mayest be clothed,......	3:18
2	elders sitting, clothed in **white** raiment;.................	4:4
3	And I saw, and behold a **white** horse:.................	6:2
7	**white** robes were given unto every one of them;.......	6:11
8	before the Lamb, clothed with **white** robes,.............	7:9
8	What are these which are arrayed in **white** robes?......	7:13
4	And I looked, and behold a **white** cloud,..............	14:14
3	I saw heaven opened, and behold a **white** horse;......	19:11
2	upon **white** horses, clothed in fine linen,..............	19:14
1	clothed in fine linen, **white** and clean..................	19:14
1	I saw a great **white** throne, and him that sat on it,.....	20:11

The adjective *leukos* comes from a root that means "bright" or "radiant" and is the general term for the color white. As an expression of color *leukos* is somewhat vague since it covers various shades of white and gray.

Classical Greek
In classical Greek *leukos* describes, among other things, the color of snow, hair, stones, clothing, and dust. Like the opposite color *melas* ("black"), *leukos* assumes a figurative meaning, with the former symbolizing that which is morally evil and the latter symbolizing purity, holiness, and divinity. In classical texts *leukos* is the color of sacrificial animals and priestly clothing. Indeed, Plato suggests that the color white is pleasing to the gods (cf. *Liddell-Scott*).

Septuagint Usage
The religious practices of the Hebrews indicate that they held white in similar esteem. In addition to its ordinary literal usages, *leukos* appears in the Septuagint as the color of priestly garments. Figuratively *leukos* symbolizes purification from sin (Psalm 51:7 [LXX 50:7]; Isaiah 1:18), and a vision of God is dominated by the color *leukos* (Daniel 7:9).

New Testament Usage
Given this rich background, it is not surprising to learn that nearly all of the 23 appearances of *leukos* in the New Testament use the term symbolically. Matthew 5:36 refers to ordinary white hair, and John 4:35 reports Jesus' statement about the white (golden-white) fields that are ready for harvest. Both Revelation 2:17 ("a white stone") and Revelation 6:2 ("a white horse") use *leukos* in a symbolic way, the former representing innocence or purity and the latter representing conquest.

Apart from the four instances mentioned in the previous paragraph, the New Testament uses *leukos* as the color associated with heaven. Most references are to white clothing, as in the descriptions of the transfiguration of Jesus, the post-Resurrection appearances of angels, or the heavenly citizens in the Book of Revelation. (See, for example, Matthew 17:2; Matthew 28:3; Acts 1:10; Revelation 3:4,5.) Even the throne of God is white (Revelation 20:11). Revelation 1:14 portrays the victorious Christ in terms reminiscent of the Ancient of Days in Daniel 7:9; both of these scenes are dominated by white.

STRONG 3022, BAUER 472, MOULTON-MILLIGAN 374, KITTEL 4:241-50, LIDDELL-SCOTT 1042, COLIN BROWN 1:204.

2997. λέων leōn noun
Lion.

אֲרִי 'ărî (761), Lion (Nm 24:9, 2 Chr 9:18f., Am 5:19).
אַרְיֵה 'aryēh (765), Lion (Gn 49:9, 1 Kgs 13:28, Is 35:9).
אַרְיֵה 'aryēh (A767), Lion (Dn 6:17,19f.,24—Aramaic).
כְּפִיר kᵉphîr (3841), Lion (Ps 35:17 [34:17], Ez 19:3, Na 2:13).
לָבִיא lāvî' (3965), Lion (Dt 33:20, Jb 4:11).
לַיִשׁ layish (4055), Lion (Prv 30:30 [24:65]).
שַׁחַל shachal (8256), Lion (Jb 10:16, 28:8, Prv 26:13).

1. λέων leōn nom sing masc
2. λέοντος leontos gen sing masc
3. λέοντι leonti dat sing masc
4. λεόντων leontōn gen pl masc

2	and I was delivered out of the mouth **of the lion**....	2 Tm 4:17
4	obtained promises, stopped the mouths **of lions**,....	Heb 11:33
1	the devil, as a roaring **lion**, walketh about,..........	1 Pt 5:8
3	And the first beast was like **a lion**,..................	Rev 4:7
1	behold, the **Lion** of the tribe of Juda,.................	5:5
4	and their teeth were as the teeth **of lions**..............	9:8
4	the heads of the horses were as the heads **of lions**;.....	9:17
1	cried with a loud voice, as when **a lion** roareth:.......	10:3
2	and his mouth as the mouth **of a lion**:.................	13:2

Classical Greek
Leōn is used of a savage, of a brave man, of Leo (the zodiac sign), and of a literal lion. Since the days of Homer *leōn* has been used in literature in symbolic form. In pre-Christian literature the word is normally used as a symbol of power and courage. Some pre-Christian religions used

the lion (or at least its body) as an icon for the faith. "The Babylonian Nergal as the god of the glowing sun is given the bodily shape of a lion; this god is mentioned in 2 Kings 17:30 because its worship spread to Samaria" (Michaelis, "leōn," *Kittel*, 4:251).

Septuagint Usage
The Septuagint mentions the lion over 100 times. There are many occurrences where *leōn* is used figuratively. In Genesis 49:9 it is used as a symbol of the tribe of Judah. In other places it is used to symbolize the predatory characteristics of people (cf. Numbers 23:24) and as a symbol of strength (cf. Numbers 24:9; Deuteronomy 33:20). Occasionally *leōn* is also used literally: of the lion killed by Samson (Judges 14:5); of the ornamental lions which decorated the temple furnishings (1 Kings 7:29 [LXX 3 Kings 7:29]) and Solomon's throne (1 Kings 10:19 [LXX 3 Kings 10:19]); and the lions Daniel faced for his refusal to cease praying (Daniel 6:7; passim).

New Testament Usage
Leōn is used nine times in the New Testament. In every case but one (Hebrews 11:33) the term is used symbolically. In the Hebrews passage the reference is made to the Old Testament heroes who "stopped the mouths of lions," a reference to Daniel 6:17ff. In each of the other references *leōn* is used as a symbol or in a figurative sense. (See 1 Peter 5:8; Revelation 4:7; 9:8,17; 10:3; and 13:2.) In 2 Timothy 4:17 Paul stated he was "delivered out of the mouth of the lion" meaning "from danger."

The New Testament's symbolic usage of this term seems to emphasize three characteristics of the lion: strength, courage, and cruelty. In using the first two of these characteristics the New Testament writers referred to the strength and courage of persons or groups, especially in Revelation as it refers to future conditions. In Revelation 5:5 Jesus is the lion from the tribe of Judah (cf. Genesis 49:9). However, in the 1 Peter passage the reference is to the devil who walks about like a "roaring lion." Here the reference is to the third characteristic, cruelty.

STRONG 3023, BAUER 472, MOULTON-MILLIGAN 374, KITTEL 4:251-53, LIDDELL-SCOTT 1043, COLIN BROWN 1:118.

2998. λήθη lēthē noun
Forgetfulness.

מַעַל ma'al (4761), Trespass, unfaithfulness (Lv 5:15, Nm 5:27).

שָׁכַח shākhach (8319), Forget (Dt 8:19).

1. λήθην **lēthēn** acc sing fem

1 and hath forgotten that he was purged .... 2 Pt 1:9

The noun *lēthē* is related to the verbs: *lēthō*, which is usually translated "escape notice," and *lēthomai*, usually translated "forget." *Lēthē* appears only once in the New Testament (2 Peter 1:9) where Peter instructed his readers they were acting as if they had "forgotten" their redemption if they did not display Christian characteristics (cf. 2 Peter 1:5-8).

STRONG 3024, BAUER 472, MOULTON-MILLIGAN 374, LIDDELL-SCOTT 1044, COLIN BROWN 3:231.

2999. ληνός lēnos noun
Winepress.

גַּת gath (1708), Winepress (Neh 13:15, Is 63:2, Lam 1:15).

גִּתִּית gittîth (1713), Gittith (Pss 8:title, 84:title).

דֶּמַע dema' (1892), Vintage (Ex 22:29).

יֶקֶב yeqev (3449), Winepress, vat (Nm 18:27, Prv 3:10, Jl 2:24).

מַמְּגֻרָה mamm^eghurāh (4601), Granary (Jl 1:17).

רַהַט rāhaṭ (7584), Watering trough (Gn 30:38—Sixtine Edition only).

1. ληνός **lēnos** nom sing fem
2. ληνοῦ **lēnou** gen sing fem
3. ληνόν **lēnon** acc sing fem

3 and digged a **winepress** in it, and built a tower, ... Matt 21:33
3 cast it into the great **winepress** of the wrath of God. Rev 14:19
1 And the **winepress** was trodden without the city, ... 14:20
2 and blood came out of the **winepress**, ... 14:20
3 treadeth the **winepress** of the fierceness and wrath 19:15

This noun is translated "winepress" in all four occurrences in the New Testament (Matthew 21:33; Revelation 14:19,20; 19:15). However, some believe that in the Matthew passage *lēnos* refers to only a part of the winepress. There (Matthew 21:33) Jesus told a parable in which a landowner dug a "winepress." This usage suggests that *lēnos* refers to the lower trough or vat which was in the ground and into which the grapejuice flowed following the actual pressing of the grapes. (On this see Thayer, *A Greek-English Lexicon*.) In Revelation treading the winepress is figurative of the wrath of God being poured out as the juice pours out of the grapes when trodden down.

STRONG 3025, BAUER 473, MOULTON-MILLIGAN 374, KITTEL 4:254-57, LIDDELL-SCOTT 1045.

3000. λῆρος lēros noun
Idle talk, nonsense.

1. λῆρος **lēros** nom sing masc

1 And their words seemed to them as idle tales,..... Luke 24:11

The only place *lēros* is found in the New Testament is in Luke 24:11. In this passage the word is translated as "idle talk or tales" denoting such other ideas as "nonsense," "foolishness," or "words which make no sense." The word is used in connection with the story of the Resurrection which Mary Magdalene, Joanna, Mary (the mother of James), and other women told to the apostles and which the apostles disbelieved at first.

STRONG 3026, BAUER 473, MOULTON-MILLIGAN 375, LIDDELL-SCOTT 1046.

3001. λῃστής lēstēs noun
Plunderer, robber; false teacher.

SYNONYM:
κλέπτης kleptēs (2785)

גְּדוּד gᵉdhûdh (1447), Raider, bandit (Jer 18:22, Hos 7:1).

פָּרִיץ pārîts (6782), Robber (Jer 7:11).

שָׁדַד shādhadh (8161), Robber (Ob 5).

1. λῃστής **lēstēs** nom sing masc
2. λῃστήν **lēstēn** acc sing masc
3. λῃσταί **lēstai** nom pl masc
4. λῃστῶν **lēstōn** gen pl masc
5. λῃσταῖς **lēstais** dat pl masc
6. λῃστάς **lēstas** acc pl masc

4 but ye have made it a den of **thieves**............... Matt 21:13
2 Are ye come out as against a **thief** with swords........ 26:55
3 Then were there two **thieves** crucified with him,....... 27:38
3 The **thieves** also, which were crucified with him,...... 27:44
4 but ye have made it a den of **thieves**............. Mark 11:17
2 Are ye come out, as against a **thief**, with swords....... 14:48
6 And with them they crucify two **thieves**;................ 15:27
5 from Jerusalem to Jericho, and fell among **thieves**, Luke 10:30
6 neighbour unto him that fell among the **thieves**?....... 10:36
4 but ye have made it a den of **thieves**................. 19:46
2 Be ye come out, as against a **thief**, with swords....... 22:52
1 the same is a thief and a **robber**.................... John 10:1
3 that ever came before me are thieves and **robbers**:..... 10:8
1 but Barabbas. Now Barabbas was a **robber**............. 18:40
4 in perils of waters, in perils **of robbers**,............ 2 Co 11:26

Classical Greek
This term is related to the verb *leizomai*, "to gain as plunder," and does not "unconditionally imply lack of honesty" (Rengstorf, "lēstēs," *Kittel*, 4:257). It is used of soldiers who, according to the custom of antiquity, were permitted to plunder their victims. It does, however, favor the bad sense, and it enjoys a special place in reference to pirates and buccaneers (cf. *Liddell-Scott*). Significantly, Josephus applied the term consistently to the Zealot party of Judaism who hoped to violently overthrow their Roman oppressors (Josephus *Wars of the Jews* 2.13.3; *Antiquities* 14.9.2). Rengstorf also notes that Rabbinic Judaism may have also borrowed the term in a similar fashion referring to Zealots (ibid., 4:258). The term can also mean "robber."

Septuagint Usage
Out of four instances of *lēstēs* in the Septuagint with Hebrew originals, three Hebrew terms are used. "Bandits" (Hosea 7:1), "robbers" (Jeremiah 7:11; Obadiah 1:5), and "invaders" (Jeremiah 18:22) are the New International Version's translations of *lēstēs*. Inherent in each of these is the idea of violent, forceful action, whether stealing or plundering. The apocryphal Letter of Jeremiah further confirms such nuances of violence. It conjoins it with war (15,18, cf. 57f.).

New Testament Usage
Except for one instance in 2 Corinthians (11:26, "bandits," NIV), *lēstēs* occurs exclusively in the Gospels. Each of the Synoptic Evangelists makes a considerable point of the fact that Jesus was not a *lēstēs*. This is not to say that He was ever regarded as a "thief" or "robber"; rather, what is at stake for them is an understanding of *lēstēs* similar to Josephus' and Rabbinic Judaism. Jesus was in no way a political zealot; those who crucified Him charged Him with that crime and executed Him as such.

The denouncement of such a misconception of Jesus' mission is lucid (e.g., Matthew 26:55; Mark 14:48; Luke 22:52; cf. Acts 5:36,37). The soldiers did not need swords to take Jesus as they would a violent insurrectionist. Elsewhere we are given clues that Jesus' kingdom is neither earthly nor political. The hierarchy, however, accused Him of "subverting our nation" (Luke 23:2, NIV), "inciting ... rebellion" (Luke 23:14, NIV).

The description of Barabbas in John as a *lēstēs* is telling. Here we see evidence that Barabbas—described as "in prison with the insurrectionists" by Mark (15:7, NIV; Greek *stasiastōn* [see 4564B])—was actually a political prisoner, a Zealot-type bandit rather than a common thief (cf. Mark 15:7; John 18:40). Jesus himself rejected all such violent false messiahs (John 10:1). The people, however, chose such a one in the person of Barabbas instead of the true Messiah, Jesus.

The irony continues in that Jesus was crucified between two *lēstai* who were "under the same sentence" as He (Luke 23:40, NIV; cf. the charges 23:2,14). The religious leadership is characterized as having completely misinterpreted Jesus' mission and purpose to establish God's kingdom—the rule of God in the lives of men and women. They themselves are the real *lēstai* (Matthew 21:13; Mark 11:17; Luke 19:46) who have forced the holy temple of God to become a "den" for their own merchandising, i.e., plundering of God's people (cf. John 10:1). The true believer will recognize the "thieves and robbers" who would try to lead the children of God away (John 10:8). These invaders bring death and destruction; only Jesus brings life (John 10:10).

STRONG 3027, BAUER 473, MOULTON-MILLIGAN 375, KITTEL 4:257-62, LIDDELL-SCOTT 1046, COLIN BROWN 3:377-79.

3002. λῆψις lēpsis noun

Receiving, credit, receipt.

1. λήψεως lēpseōs gen sing fem
2. λήμψεως lēmpseōs gen sing fem

1 as concerning giving and receiving,................. Phlp 4:15

Lēpsis appears only in Philippians 4:15 where it refers to the apostle Paul's appreciation for the generosity of the Philippians. It was they alone who entered in a partnership financially with him in his ministry: "When I departed from Macedonia, no church communicated with me as concerning giving and *receiving* (*lēpsis*), but ye only."

STRONG 3028, BAUER 473 (see "lēmpsis"), MOULTON-MILLIGAN 374, LIDDELL-SCOTT 1046.

3003. λίαν lian adv

Exceedingly, greatly, very.

SYNONYMS:
σφοδρός sphodros (4822)
σφοδρῶς sphodrōs (4823)

מְאֹד meʾōdh (4108), Very, exceedingly (Gn 1:31, 2 Sm 2:17, Jer 48:29 [31:29]).

מָה māh (4242), How (Ps 139:17 [138:17]).

1. λίαν lian

1 was mocked of the wise men, was **exceeding** wroth,..Matt 2:16
1 devil taketh ... into an **exceeding** high mountain,........ 4:8
1 **exceeding** fierce, so that no man might pass by......... 8:28
1 insomuch that the governor marvelled **greatly**.......... 27:14
1 **Very** early in the morning, (NIV)................ Mark 1:35
1 and they were **sore** amazed in themselves........... Mark 6:51
1 raiment became shining, **exceeding** white as snow;...... 9:3
1 **very** early in the morning the first day of the week,.... 16:2
1 when Herod saw Jesus, he was **exceeding** glad:.....Luke 23:8
1 I was not a whit behind the very **chiefest** apostles. 2 Co 11:5
1 in nothing am I behind the very **chiefest** apostles,...... 12:11
1 for he hath **greatly** withstood our words............ 2 Tm 4:15
1 I rejoiced **greatly** that I found of thy children........ 2 Jn 1:4
1 For I rejoiced **greatly**, when the brethren came......3 Jn 1:3

Lian, an adverb appearing from Homer (spelled *liēn*) on and often in the Septuagint and Josephus, is used to intensify the verb, adjective, or adverb that it modifies. It is used with a verb in such places as 2 Timothy 4:15, "greatly withstood," Matthew 2:16, "was exceeding wroth," and Matthew 27:14, "marveled greatly." *Lian* is also used to modify adjectives ("exceeding white," Mark 9:3; "exceeding high," Matthew 4:8; "exceeding fierce," Matthew 8:28) and adverbs ("great while," Mark 1:35; "very early," Mark 16:2).

Sometimes *lian* is further intensified by being compounded with the preposition *huper* (5065) (cf. *huperlian* [5082B]). It appears in this compound form in 2 Corinthians 11:5 and 12:11, "very chiefest" ("superlative," RSV).

STRONG 3029, BAUER 473, MOULTON-MILLIGAN 375, LIDDELL-SCOTT 1046-47.

3004. λίβανος libanos noun

Frankincense, frankincense tree.

CROSS-REFERENCE:
λιβανωτός libanōtos (3005)

לְבֹנָה leᵛōnāh (3972), Frankincense, incense (Lv 2:1f., S/S 3:6, Is 60:6).

1. λίβανον libanon acc sing masc

1 gold, and **frankincense**, and myrrh.................. Matt 2:11
1 and **frankincense**, and wine, and oil, and fine flour, Rev 18:13

In classical Greek the noun *libanos* is used both of the frankincense tree which grows in Arabia and India as well as of the white resinous gum which comes from varieties of this tree. In the ancient world frankincense was used for both medicinal and cultic purposes. As with myrrh, it was often used as a precious gift to the gods. The Greek term is a transliteration of the Hebrew word *leᵛōnāh*, used often in the Old Testament (e.g., Leviticus 2:1; Isaiah 60:6). This incense was used often in the sacrificial ritual of Israel.

The term appears twice in the New Testament. Together with gold and myrrh, it was brought as a precious gift by the Magi to the infant Christ child (Matthew 2:11). In Revelation 18:13 it is listed with other valuable merchandise destroyed with the fall of Babylon.

STRONG 3030, BAUER 473, MOULTON-MILLIGAN 375, KITTEL 4:263-64, LIDDELL-SCOTT 1047, COLIN BROWN 2:293-95.

3005. λιβανωτός libanōtos noun
Frankincense, censer.
COGNATE:
λίβανος libanos (3004)
SYNONYM:
θυμιατήριον thumiatērion (2346)
לְבֹנָה lᵉvōnāh (3972), Frankincense (1 Chr 9:29).

1. λιβανωτόν libanōton acc sing masc

1 another angel came ... having a golden censer; .... Rev 8:3
1 the angel took the censer, and filled it with fire 8:5

In classical Greek *libanōtos* refers to frankincense, the gum of the *libanos* (3004), "frankincense," tree used to burn sacrifices. The term is also used of the frankincense market (*Liddell-Scott*). *Libanōtos* appears two times in the Septuagint: at 1 Chronicles 9:29 where frankincense is included as part of the temple ritual, and at 3 Maccabees 5:2 where it is mentioned as a drug. The term appears twice in one setting in the New Testament. In Revelation 8:3,5, the "censer" in which incense was burned (in this case a golden censer) represents the prayers of saints being offered up to God.

STRONG 3031, BAUER 473, MOULTON-MILLIGAN 375, KITTEL 4:263-64, LIDDELL-SCOTT 1047, COLIN BROWN 2:293-95.

3006. Λιβερτῖνος Libertinos name
Libertines.

1. Λιβερτίνων Libertinōn gen pl masc

1 which is called the synagogue of the Libertines, ... Acts 6:9

Name of a synagogue in Jerusalem, perhaps attended by former slaves (Acts 6:9).

3007. Λιβύη Libuē name
Libya.

1. Λιβύης Libuēs gen fem

1 and in the parts of Libya about Cyrene, ... Acts 2:10

North African country west of Egypt; Jews from this area were in Jerusalem on the Day of Pentecost (Acts 2:10).

3008. λιθάζω lithazō verb
To stone, throw stones.
COGNATE:
λίθος lithos (3010B)
SYNONYMS:
καταλιθάζω katalithazō (2612)
λιθοβολέω lithoboleō (3010)

סָקַל sāqal (5820), Piel: throw stones (2 Sm 16:13).

1. λιθάζομεν lithazomen 1pl indic pres act
2. λιθάζετε lithazete 2pl indic pres act
3. λιθάσωσιν lithasōsin 3pl subj aor act
4. λιθάσαντες lithasantes nom pl masc part aor act
5. λιθάσαι lithasai inf aor act
6. ἐλιθάσθην elithasthēn 1sing indic aor pass
7. ἐλιθάσθησαν elithasthēsan 3pl indic aor pass
8. λιθασθῶσιν lithasthōsin 3pl subj aor pass
9. λιθάζειν lithazein inf pres act

9 commanded us to stone such women; (NASB) ...... John 8:5
3 Then the Jews took up stones again to stone him. 10:31
2 for which of those works do ye stone me? 10:32
1 For a good work we stone thee not; 10:33
5 the Jews of late sought to stone thee; 11:8
8 lest they should have been stoned. .... Acts 5:26
4 and, having stoned Paul, drew him out of the city, ... 14:19
6 Thrice was I beaten with rods, once was I stoned, .. 2 Co 11:25
7 They were stoned, they were sawn asunder, ... Heb 11:37

Appearing from Anaxandrides and Aristotle (Fourth Century B.C.) on *lithazō*, a verb related to the noun *lithos* (3010B), "stone," means "to fling stones." The word appears eight times in the New Testament, always referring to the means of execution by stoning. Jesus was threatened with being stoned (John 10:31-33; 11:8), as were the apostles (Acts 5:26; 14:19; 2 Corinthians 11:25). *Lithazō* does not occur in the Septuagint. The term used there for stoning is its synonym, *lithoboleō* (3010), "to cast stones" (Leviticus 20:2,27), a compound verb which is also found in the New Testament (Acts 7:58).

STRONG 3034, BAUER 473-74, MOULTON-MILLIGAN 375, KITTEL 4:267-68, LIDDELL-SCOTT 1048.

3009. λίθινος lithinos adj
(Made of) stone.
CROSS-REFERENCE:
λίθος lithos (3010B)

אֶבֶן 'even (63), Stone (Ex 34:4, Dt 9:10, Ez 11:19).
אֶבֶן 'even (A64), Stone (Ezr 6:4—Aramaic [Codex Vaticanus only]).
שֵׁשׁ shēsh (8667), Marble (Est 1:6).

1. λίθιναι lithinai nom pl fem

2. λιθίναις lithinais dat pl fem
3. λίθινα lithina nom/acc pl neu

1 And there were set there six waterpots **of stone**,..... John 2:6
2 not in tables **of stone**, but in fleshly tables.......... 2 Co 3:3
3 idols of gold, and silver, and brass, and **stone**,....... Rev 9:20

Classical Greek
The adjective *lithinos*, "of stone," is related to the noun *lithos* (3010B), "stone." *Lithos* is a general term that refers to a stone of any kind or size; *lithinos* is used in the same general way in classical and Biblical Greek to describe the material out of which a variety of items were made—troughs, presses, bowls, etc.

Septuagint Usage
The Septuagint uses *lithinos* in Genesis 35:14 to describe Jacob's "pillar of stone." *Lithinos* appears in a number of passages that refer to the "tables of stone" upon which the Law was inscribed. (See Exodus 24:12; 31:18, etc.) The Septuagint also uses *lithinos* in a figurative way in Ezekiel 11:19 and 36:26, passages in which God promises to replace the "stony heart" (i.e., a heart with no feeling) of the exiled Israelites with a "heart of flesh."

New Testament Usage
Lithinos appears in the New Testament three times and is used both literally and figuratively. John 2:6 notes, in passing, that the six large waterpots in Cana of Galilee were made "of stone." In addition to gold, silver, brass, and wood, some of the idols mentioned in Revelation 9:20 were made "of stone."

Most important is the figurative use of *lithinos* in 2 Corinthians 3:3. In this passage Paul described the Christian as an "epistle of Christ" (i.e., a living account of the gospel) that has been written in the flesh of the human heart, not on "tables (tablets) of stone" like the Old Testament law. (Compare the imagery of 2 Corinthians 3:3 with the Ezekiel passages mentioned above.)

STRONG 3035, BAUER 474, MOULTON-MILLIGAN 375, KITTEL 4:268-80, LIDDELL-SCOTT 1048, COLIN BROWN 3:390.

3010. λιθοβολέω lithoboleō verb
To pelt with stones, kill by stoning, stone.
COGNATE:
  λίθος lithos (3010B)
SYNONYMS:
  καταλιθάζω katalithazō (2612)
  λιθάζω lithazō (3008)

סָקַל sāqal (5820), Qal: stone (Ex 8:26, Dt 22:21, 1 Sm 30:6); niphal: be stoned (Ex 19:13, 21:28f.,32); pual: be stoned (1 Kgs 21:14 [20:14]).

רָגַם rāgham (7563), Stone (Lv 20:2, Dt 21:21, 2 Chr 24:21).

1. λιθοβολοῦσα litholobousa
    nom sing fem part pres act
2. ἐλιθοβόλησαν elithobolēsan 3pl indic aor act
3. λιθοβολήσαντες lithobolēsantes
    nom pl masc part aor act
4. λιθοβολῆσαι lithobolēsai inf aor act
5. ἐλιθοβόλουν elithoboloun 3pl indic imperf act
6. λιθοβολεῖσθαι litholoboleisthai inf pres mid
7. λιθοβοληθήσεται litholobolēthēsetai
    3sing indic fut pass

2 beat one, and killed another, and **stoned** another... Matt 21:35
1 and **stonest** them which are sent unto thee,............ 23:37
3 and at him they **cast stones**,...................... Mark 12:4
1 and **stonest** them that are sent unto thee;.......... Luke 13:34
6 that such **should be stoned**: but what sayest thou? ... John 8:5
5 And cast him out of the city, and **stoned** him:....... Acts 7:58
5 And they **stoned** Stephen, calling upon God,.......... 7:59
4 to use them despitefully, and **to stone** them,.......... 14:5
7 it **shall be stoned**, or thrust through with a dart:.... Heb 12:20

Lithoboleō, a compound verb formed by the noun *lithos* (3010B), "stone," and *boleō* ("to throw, toss"), means "to throw stones." A second meaning of the word is "to kill by stoning." In the Septuagint it is the usual term for execution by stoning (Deuteronomy 13:10). In the New Testament it is used in reference to the stoning (killing) the prophets (Matthew 23:37; Luke 13:34) and Stephen (Acts 7:58,59). In Iconium both the Jews and the Gentiles sought to kill Paul and Barnabas by stoning (Acts 14:5).

STRONG 3036, BAUER 474, MOULTON-MILLIGAN 375, KITTEL 4:267-68, LIDDELL-SCOTT 1048.

3010B. λίθος lithos noun
Stone.
COGNATES:
  καταλιθάζω katalithazō (2612)
  λιθάζω lithazō (3008)
  λίθινος lithinos (3009)
  λιθοβολέω lithoboleō (3010)
  χρυσόλιθος chrusolithos (5390)
SYNONYMS:
  πέτρα petra (3934)
  ψῆφος psēphos (5421)

אֶבֶן 'even (63), Stone (Ex 28:10, 1 Kgs 10:10f.); hailstone (Ez 13:11).

אֶבֶן 'even (A64), Stone (Ezr 5:8, Dn 2:34f., 6:17—Aramaic).

כֶּתֶם kethem (3929), Gold (Is 13:12).

λίθος 3010B

מַצֵּבָה matstsēvāh (4838), Pillar (Ex 24:4).

סָקַל sāqal (5820), Stoning (Ex 19:13, 21:28).

פְּנִינִים peninîm (6689), Ruby or coral (Lam 4:7).

צְרוֹר tserôr (7155), Small stone (2 Sm 17:13).

רָגַם rāgham (7563), Stone (Lv 24:16).

1. λίθος lithos nom sing masc
2. λίθου lithou gen sing masc
3. λίθῳ lithō dat sing masc
4. λίθον lithon acc sing masc
5. λίθοι lithoi nom pl masc
6. λίθων lithōn gen pl masc
7. λίθοις lithois dat pl masc
8. λίθους lithous acc pl masc

6	God is able of these **stones** to raise up children	Matt 3:9
5	command that these **stones** be made bread.	4:3
4	lest at any time thou dash thy foot against **a stone**	4:6
4	if his son ask bread, will he give him **a stone**?	7:9
4	The **stone** which the builders rejected,	21:42
4	whosoever shall fall on this **stone** shall be broken:	21:44
1	shall not be left here one **stone** upon another,	24:2
4	shall not be left here one **stone** upon another,	24:2
4	rolled a great **stone** to the door of the sepulchre,	27:60
4	sealing the **stone**, and setting a watch.	27:66
4	and came and rolled back the **stone** from the door,	28:2
7	crying, and cutting himself **with stones**.	Mark 5:5
1	that a **millstone** were hanged about his neck,	9:42
4	The **stone** which the builders rejected	12:10
5	see what manner of **stones** and what buildings	13:1
1	there shall not be left one **stone** upon another,	13:2
3	there shall not be left one **stone** upon another,	13:2
4	and rolled **a stone** unto the door of the sepulchre.	15:46
4	Who shall roll us away the **stone** from the door	16:3
1	the **stone** was rolled away: for it was very great.	16:4
6	That God is able of these **stones** to raise up	Luke 3:8
3	command this **stone** that it be made bread.	4:3
4	lest at any time thou dash thy foot against **a stone**.	4:11
4	a son shall ask bread ... will he give him **a stone**?	11:11
1	for him if a **millstone** were hung (NASB)	17:2
5	their peace, the **stones** would immediately cry out.	19:40
3	shall not leave in thee one **stone** upon another;	19:44
3	shall not leave in thee one **stone** upon another;	19:44
4	The **stone** which the builders rejected,	20:17
4	shall fall upon that **stone** shall be broken:	20:18
7	how it was adorned with goodly **stones** and gifts,	21:5
1	there shall not be left one **stone** upon another,	21:6
3	there shall not be left one **stone** upon another,	21:6
2	he was withdrawn from them about **a stone's** cast,	22:41
4	found the **stone** rolled away from the sepulchre.	24:2
4	without sin ... let him first cast **a stone** at her.	John 8:7
8	Then took they up **stones** to cast at him:	8:59
8	Then the Jews took up **stones** again to stone him.	10:31
1	It was a cave, and **a stone** lay upon it.	11:38
4	Jesus said, Take ye away the **stone**.	11:39
4	the **stone** from the place where the dead was laid.	11:41
4	and seeth the **stone** taken away from the sepulchre.	20:1
1	the **stone** which was set at nought of you builders,	Acts 4:11
3	or silver, or **stone**, graven by art and man's device.	17:29
3	For they stumbled at that **stumblingstone**.	Rom 9:32
4	I lay in Sion a **stumblingstone** and rock of offence:	9:33
8	gold, silver, precious **stones**, wood, hay, stubble;	1 Co 3:12
7	written and engraven in **stones**, was glorious,	2 Co 3:7
4	To whom coming, as unto a living **stone**,	1 Pt 2:4
5	also, as lively **stones**, are built up a spiritual house,	2:5
4	Behold, I lay in Sion a chief corner **stone**,	2:6
4	the **stone** which the builders disallowed,	2:7
1	And a **stone** of stumbling, and a rock of offence,	2:8
3	was to look upon like a jasper and a sardine **stone**:	Rev 4:3
3	decked with gold and precious **stones** and pearls,	17:4
2	and precious **stones**, and of pearls, and fine linen,	18:12
3	decked with gold, and precious **stones**, and pearls!	18:16
4	mighty angel took up **a stone** like a great millstone,	Rev 18:21
3	and her light was like unto **a stone** most precious,	21:11
3	even like a jasper **stone**, clear as crystal;	21:11
3	were garnished with all manner of precious **stones**.	21:19

Classical Greek

In classical Greek *lithos* denotes not only the common "stone" but also "precious stones, marble." In addition *lithos* held a special function in Athens where it was used for the "rostra" or "tribunes" in a judgment seat (*bēma* [961]), altars, or in the marketplace (*Liddell-Scott*). The normal understanding, though, was simply "a stone."

Septuagint Usage

Though a wide variety of Hebrew words are translated by *lithos*, *'even* is the most common. The literal usage dominates (e.g., Genesis 35:14, of an altar; Exodus 15:5, of a sinking stone; Leviticus 14:40, of the stones of a house). The combination *timon lithon*, "precious stone(s)" is also frequent (e.g., 2 Chronicles 9:1; 3:6). A figurative understanding of certain texts naturally developed since "Rock" was a familiar epithet for God (e.g., Psalm 95:1 [LXX 94:1], the Hebrew here is *tsur* and the Septuagint is not *lithos*, but the idea is the same; cf. Isaiah 28:16; Daniel 2:34f.; see Josephus *Antiquities* 2.12.1). Evidence from later Judaism suggests that many of the Old Testament passages that are applied to Christ in the New Testament were already associated with the Messiah (on all of the above see Jeremias, "lithos," *Kittel*, 4:272,268-280).

New Testament Usage

Besides the literal use of *lithos* (e.g., Luke 17:2; 19:44; John 8:59; 10:31; of "precious stones," Revelation 17:4; 18:12), the New Testament picks up on the connection between *lithos* and God's messianic salvation and applies the stone image directly to Jesus (e.g., Matthew 21:42; Mark 12:10; Luke 20:17f.; Acts 4:11/Psalm 118:22; cf. Romans 9:32,33/Isaiah 8:14; 28:16; see on this Bruce, *New Testament Development of Old Testament Themes*, pp.63-65). (Cf. *akrogōniaios* [202], "cornerstone," Ephesians 2:20; 1 Peter 2:6/Isaiah 28:16.)

The stone imagery is further applied to believers. The "stones" which God can raise up as Abraham's children (Matthew 3:9; Luke 3:8) may be a veiled reference to the tradition that Abraham, the "rock" would have descendants hewn out of the rock (cf. Isaiah 51:1,2 the probable basis of this tradition; Jeremias, "lithos," *Kittel*, 4:271).

Believers are "living stone(s)" according to 1 Peter, just as Christ is the Living Stone (2:4,5). Christ is also the "rock of offense" predicted by Isaiah 8:14. To believers, however, He is the "cornerstone" (NIV, "capstone"), literally, "head of the corner," who will vindicate them (1 Peter 2:6-8).

STRONG 3037, BAUER 474, MOULTON-MILLIGAN 375-76, KITTEL 4:268-80, LIDDELL-SCOTT 1049, COLIN BROWN 3:390-91,393-94.

3011. λιθόστρωτον lithostrōton adj
Pavement, mosaic.

רָצַף rātsaph (7821), Inlaid (S/S 3:10).

רִצְפָה ritsᵉphāh (7826), Pavement (2 Chr 7:3, Est 1:6).

1. λιθόστρωτον lithostrōton acc masc
1 in a place that is called the Pavement,............John 19:13

Lithostrōtos is a compound adjective formed from the noun *lithos* (3010B), "stone," and the adjective *strōtos*, "spread, paved." The term is used substantively of a floor or pavement often made of small varied-colored stones inlaid into a mosaic pattern. In the Septuagint *lithostrōtos* is used of the floor of the outer court of Solomon's Temple (2 Chronicles 7:3), the garden court of Ahasuerus' palace (Esther 1:6), and metaphorically of Solomon's sedan chair as a "pavement (mosaic)" of love (Song of Solomon 3:10). Its only appearance in the New Testament refers to a mosaic floor or porch in Pilate's judgment hall, i.e., the Praetorium of Herod's former palace along the west wall of Jerusalem (John 19:13).

STRONG 3038, BAUER 474, MOULTON-MILLIGAN 376, LIDDELL-SCOTT 1049.

3012. λίθος lithos
See word study at number 3010B.

3013. λικμάω likmaō verb
Crush, grind to powder.

זָרָה zārâh (2306), Qal: winnow (Ru 3:2); niphal: be scattered (Ez 36:19); piel: scatter, disperse (Jer 31:10 [38:10], 49:32 [30:32], Ez 29:12).

מִזְרֶה mizreh (4348), Fork (Is 30:24).

נוּעַ nûaʿ (5309), Waver, shake; niphal: be shaken (Am 9:9); hiphil: shake (Am 9:9).

סָחָה sāchâh (5688), Piel: scrape (Ez 26:4).

שָׂעַר sāʿar (7994), Piel: sweep away (Jb 27:21).

1. λικμήσει likmēsei 3sing indic fut act
1 it will grind him to powder.........................Matt 21:44
1 it shall fall, it will grind him to powder............Luke 20:18

Classical Greek
In its earliest occurrences in classical Greek the verb *likmaō* means "to winnow," i.e., "to separate wheat from chaff." The noun *likmos*, "winnowing basket," is related to this verb. Beginning with Homer and continuing through the classical period, *likmaō* retains this definition in Greek literature but takes on additional meanings in Septuagint and New Testament usage.

Septuagint Usage
In the Septuagint *likmaō* normally translates the Hebrew word *zārâh*, "to winnow." The winnowing can be literal (Ruth 3:2) or figurative (Amos 9:9). Used figuratively, winnowing almost always refers to judgment. Judgment is also expressed in another rendering of *likmaō*, "to blow apart" or "to scatter," as in Job 27:21 and Ezekiel 36:19. From the idea of scattering that which is worthless (i.e., chaff) comes a final definition for this verb, "to grind to powder" or "to destroy," as in Daniel 2:44. This translation of *likmaō* also connotes judgment.

New Testament Usage
Likmaō appears in the New Testament only twice (Matthew 21:44; Luke 20:18), but its translation in these parallel verses is debatable. A reference to winnowing does not seem to fit their overall meaning since the falling stone would be more likely to destroy than to winnow. Both the meaning of the passages and a similar use of *likmaō* in a post-New Testament text indicate that this verb can be translated "to crush" or "to grind to powder" (cf. *Bauer*). No matter which rendering is accepted, the New Testament uses of *likmaō* create a vivid picture of judgment.

STRONG 3039, BAUER 474-75, MOULTON-MILLIGAN 376, KITTEL 4:280-81, LIDDELL-SCOTT 1050.

3014. λιμήν limēn noun
Harbor, retreat, haven.

מָחוֹז māchôz (4366), Haven (Ps 107:30 [106:30]).

1. λιμένος limenos gen sing masc
2. λιμένα limena acc sing masc
3. λιμένας limenas acc pl masc

λίμην 3015

3 came unto a place which is called The fair havens;	Acts 27:8
1 the haven was not commodious to winter in,	27:12
2 attain to Phenice, ... which is an haven of Crete,	27:12

In classical Greek the noun *limēn* means "a harbor, a place of refuge from the sea." Metaphorically it is used of "a place of refuge, a retreat." Interestingly enough, *limēn* is also used of the womb as a place of safety. Its only usage in the New Testament is Acts 27:8,12. In verse 8 it is used with *kalos* (2541), "good, fair," to form a proper name, "Fair Havens" ("good harbors"), the name of a bay near Lasea on the southern coast of the island of Crete. In verse 12 "Fair Havens" is called a "harbor" as is the safer "harbor" of Phoenix, also on the southern shore of Crete but farther west.

STRONG 3040, BAUER 475, MOULTON-MILLIGAN 376, LIDDELL-SCOTT 1050.

3015. λίμνη limnē noun

Lake, pool.

SYNONYM:
θάλασσα thalassa (2258)

אֲגַם ʾăgham (95), Pool (Ps 114:78 [113:8]).

בְּרֵכָה bᵉrēkhāh (1320), Pool (S/S 7:4).

1. λίμνης limnēs gen sing fem
2. λίμνῃ limnē dat sing fem
3. λίμνην limnēn acc sing fem
4. λίμνη limnē nom sing fem

3 he stood by the lake of Gennesaret,	Luke 5:1
3 And saw two ships standing by the lake:	5:2
1 Let us go over unto the other side of the lake.	8:22
3 and there came down a storm of wind on the lake;	8:23
3 down a steep place into the lake, and were choked.	8:33
3 These both were cast alive into a lake of fire	Rev 19:20
3 the devil that deceived them was cast into the lake	20:10
3 And death and hell were cast into the lake of fire.	20:14
4 the second death, the lake of fire (NASB)	20:14
3 was ... in the book of life was cast into the lake	20:15
2 shall have their part in the lake which burneth	21:8

Used from Homer on, *limnē*, meaning "pool" or "lake," appears also in the Septuagint (Psalms 107:35 [LXX 106:35]; 114:8 [113:8]; Song of Solomon 7:4). In the New Testament it is used literally by Luke to refer to the "*lake* of Gennesaret," that is, the Sea of Galilee (Luke 5:1ff.; 8:22ff.). The other Gospel writers use *thalassa* (2258), "*sea* of Galilee" (Matthew 4:18; Mark 1:16; John 6:1). The Sea of Galilee has had many names over the centuries. In the Old Testament it was called "the sea of Chinnereth" (Numbers 34:11), and in the intertestamental period it was called the Sea or Lake of Gennesar (1 Maccabees 11:67; Josephus *Wars of the Jews* 3.10.15). The names "Lake of Gennesar or Gennesaret" are taken from the plain of Gennesaret which adjoins the northwestern shore. In Revelation, John used *limnē* of the place of eternal judgment, the "*lake* of fire" (19:20; 21:8,10ff.).

STRONG 3041, BAUER 475, MOULTON-MILLIGAN 376, LIDDELL-SCOTT 1050, COLIN BROWN 3:992.

3016. λιμός limos noun

Hunger, famine.

כָּפָן kāphān (3846), Famine (Jb 30:3).

רָעָב rāʿāv (7743), Famine (Gn 41:30, 2 Kgs 8:1, Jer 21:9).

רָעֵב rāʿēv (7744), Hungry (Is 8:21).

רְעָבוֹן rᵉʿāvôn (7745), Famine (Ps 37:19 [36:19]).

1. λιμός limos nom sing masc
2. λιμῷ limō dat sing masc
3. λιμόν limon acc sing masc
4. λιμοί limoi nom pl masc

4 and there shall be famines, and pestilences,	Matt 24:7
4 and there shall be famines and troubles:	Mark 13:8
1 when great famine was throughout all the land;	Luke 4:25
1 there arose a mighty famine in that land;	15:14
2 have bread enough ... and I perish with hunger!	15:17
4 earthquakes shall be in divers places, and famines,	21:11
1 Now there came a dearth over all the land of Egypt	Acts 7:11
3 should be great dearth throughout all the world:	11:28
1 or famine, or nakedness, or peril, or sword?	Rom 8:35
2 in hunger and thirst, in fastings often,	2 Co 11:27
2 to kill with sword, and with hunger,	Rev 6:8
1 in one day, death, and mourning, and famine;	18:8

Classical Greek
In classical Greek *limos* can refer to a literal "hunger" or "famine," and in a metaphoric sense one's mind might be said to be "hungry, starved." Famine was greatly feared in the ancient world and was often a consequence of drought (e.g., Genesis 12:10; 26:1) or war (e.g., 2 Kings 6:25; 7:4; 25:3).

Septuagint Usage
The Septuagint employs the formula *ho limos epi tēs gēs*, "famine upon the earth" (Genesis 45:6; 2 Kings 8:1 [LXX 4 Kings 8:1]; 2 Chronicles 6:28), or it might be a famine "in" (*en*) the land. Ordinarily *rāʿāv* is the Hebrew for "famine." Amos 8:11 provides an example of a metaphoric use. The famine to be experienced by Israel will be a famine/starvation to hear the word of the Lord. War, famine, and plague are a familiar trio in the Old Testament (Jeremiah 32:36 [LXX 39:36]; 42:16 [49:16]); many times these were seen as judgments from God (e.g., Jeremiah 14:12; Ezekiel 14:13).

New Testament Usage

Famine is an apocalyptic sign of distress according to the New Testament (Matthew 24:7; parallel Mark 13:8; Luke 21:11; Revelation 6:8; 18:8). The New Testament recalls several incidents of famine from the Old Testament (Luke 4:25; Acts 7:11/Genesis 41:54). On occasion, prophets foresaw famine (cf. Elijah, 1 Kings 17:1ff.; Joseph's interpretation of Pharaoh's dream, Genesis 41; cf. Ezekiel's word from the Lord, 5:12; Agabus, Acts 11:28). Famine is also symbolic of extreme hardship (Romans 8:35; 2 Corinthians 11:27).

STRONG 3042, BAUER 475, MOULTON-MILLIGAN 376, KITTEL 6:12-22, LIDDELL-SCOTT 1051, COLIN BROWN 2:264-66.

3017. λίνον linon noun

Flax, linen, wick.

SYNONYM:
σινδών sindōn (4471)

בַּד badh (940), Linen (1 Sm 22:18—Codex Alexandrinus only).

פֵּשֶׁת pēsheth (6844), Linen, flax (Dt 22:11, Prv 31:13, Is 19:9).

פִּשְׁתָּה pishtāh (6845), Flax (Ex 9:31); wick (Is 42:3).

1. λίνον linon nom/acc sing neu

1 and smoking **flax** shall he not quench, ... Matt 12:20
1 seven angels ... clothed in pure and white **linen**, ... Rev 15:6

The noun *linon* means "flax," but it can also refer to anything made from flax, such as linen cloth, fish line, fishnet, thread, cord, or lamp wicks. In the Septuagint *linon* is used of both flax (Exodus 9:31) and linen cloth (Deuteronomy 22:11). The term appears twice in the New Testament: once of linen clothing (Revelation 15:6) and once of a flax lamp wick (Matthew 12:20, a quote from Isaiah 42:3). Another term, *bussos* (1033), usually translated "fine linen," was cloth made of a species of fine, costly, Egyptian flax (Luke 16:19; cf. also *bussinos* [1032], "made of fine linen," Revelation 18:12). The same is true of *sindōn* (4471).

STRONG 3043, BAUER 475, MOULTON-MILLIGAN 376, LIDDELL-SCOTT 1051.

3018. Λῖνος Linos name

Linus.

1. Λῖνος Linos nom masc

1 Eubulus greeteth thee, and Pudens, and **Linus**, ... 2 Tm 4:21

Companion of Paul who sent a greeting to Timothy (2 Timothy 4:21).

3019. λιπαρός liparos adj

Fat, oily; rich, bright, luxury.

שָׁמֵן shāmēn (8469), Fertile (Neh 9:35).

1. λιπαρά lipara nom/acc pl neu

1 things which were **dainty** and goodly are departed ... Rev 18:14

Classical Greek

In classical Greek *liparos* appears frequently. It is used literally of foods cooked in "oil" or "grease" and of objects and human skin which have been rubbed with "oil" to make them shine. Figuratively it can signify the "shininess" or "brilliance" of something; the "fertility and productivity of land, prosperity, health"; or "luxurious living."

Septuagint Usage

In the Septuagint the three occurrences of *liparos* translate the Hebrew word *shāmēn* which means "fat" or "rich." In Judges 3:29 it refers to the "robust vigor" of defeated warriors. Nehemiah 9:35 and Isaiah 30:23 use it of the "fertility" of Palestine and the resultant "prosperity" which the Lord had bestowed on Israel.

New Testament Usage

The only New Testament usage of *liparos* is Revelation 18:14. In this passage it is used figuratively of the luxurious living of "Babylon the Great." The hour of her judgment is foretold. The ripe, harvest fruit which she longed for in the deepest reaches of her soul will depart, and her "luxury" and "brilliance" will pass away of themselves. They will never be found in her again. Most likely *liparos* here refers in a general way to the richness of Babylon's life-style, although some commentators have felt that it refers more specifically to her diet of rich food.

STRONG 3045, BAUER 475, LIDDELL-SCOTT 1052.

3020. λίτρα litra noun

Pound, a silver coin.

1. λίτραν litran acc sing fem
2. λίτρας litras acc pl fem

1 Then took Mary **a pound** of ointment of spikenard, John 12:3
2 myrrh and aloes, about an hundred **pound** weight. 19:39

Litra referred originally to a silver coin of Sicily and later to a measure of weight which was 12 ounces or "one pound" (Latin, *libra*, from which the abbreviation "lb." is derived). *Litra* is also used as a measure of size, a drinking cup holding "one *litra*." The basic metric measure, litre (liter), originates from this term.

Litra occurs only twice in the New Testament, both times in John's Gospel (12:3; 19:39). In either case it may refer to a weight of precious ointment or a liquid measure of capacity, i.e., the Roman pound of almost 12 ounces weight.

STRONG 3046, BAUER 475, MOULTON-MILLIGAN 377, LIDDELL-SCOTT 1054.

3021. λίψ lips noun
Southwest wind, area from which the southwest wind blows, hence, the west or the south.

דָּרוֹם dārôm (1924), South (Dt 33:23).

מַעֲרָב ma'arāv (4790), West side (2 Chr 32:30).

נֶגֶב neghev (5221), Negev, south (Gn 20:1, Jos 18:14, Ez 47:19).

תֵּימָן têmān (8816), South (Nm 2:10, Is 43:6); south wind (Ps 78:26 [77:26]).

1. λίβα **liba** acc sing masc

1 and lieth toward the **south west** and north west..... Acts 27:12

Though *lips* appears in classical Greek from Herodotus (Fifth Century B.C.) on, it is a hapax legomenon in the New Testament. The term signifies a southwest wind or the area from which a southwest wind comes. It came to mean south, southwest, or even west. Stars appearing in the western horizon were spoken of as being in that position of the heavens. In the Septuagint the term almost always means "south" (Genesis 13:14). The one New Testament usage is Acts 27:12; the harbor of Phoenix faced "*southwest* and northwest."

STRONG 3047, BAUER 475, MOULTON-MILLIGAN 377, LIDDELL-SCOTT 1055.

3021B. λογεία logeia noun
Collection (of money).
CROSS-REFERENCE:
λόγος logos (3030)

1. λογείας **logeias** gen sing fem
2. λογεῖαι **logeiai** nom pl fem

This is a variant spelling of *logia*. See the word study at number 3022.

3022. λογία logia noun
Collection (of money).
CROSS-REFERENCE:
λόγος logos (3030)

1. λογίας **logias** gen sing fem
2. λογίαι **logiai** nom pl fem

1 Now concerning the **collection** for the saints,....... 1 Co 16:1
2 that there be no **gatherings** when I come.............. 16:2

Appearing by the Third Century B.C., the noun *logeia* (*logia* in later manuscripts) is related to the verb *legō* (2978), "to collect, gather," and the noun *logos* (3030), "word," or *logenō*. *Logeia* was once a puzzling word to scholars, but in the 20th Century the discovery of the papyri has revealed usage where it means "collection" (cf. *Moulton-Milligan*; Kittel, "logeia," *Kittel*, 4:282). In secular usage the word may refer to all kinds of contributions and sometimes to special tax levies, but it is used frequently of collections and levies made for religious purposes (cf. *Bauer*; *Liddell-Scott*). It appears twice in the same context in the New Testament (1 Corinthians 16:1,2) for the "collection" of money which Paul was promoting for the poor saints in Judea.

STRONG 3048, BAUER 475 (see "logeia"), MOULTON-MILLIGAN 377, KITTEL 4:282-83 (see "logeia"), LIDDELL-SCOTT 1055, COLIN BROWN 3:751-52 (see "logeia").

3023. λογίζομαι logizomai verb
Reckon, calculate, take inventory, count, consider.
COGNATES:
    ἀναλογίζω analogizō (355)
    λογισμός logismos (3027)
    συλλογίζομαι sullogizomai (4668)
SYNONYMS:
    ἀναλογίζω analogizō (355)
    βλέπω blepō (984)
    βουλεύομαι bouleuomai (1003)
    διαλογίζομαι dialogizomai (1254)
    δοκέω dokeō (1374)
    εἶδον eidon (1481)
    ἐνθυμέομαι enthumeomai (1744)
    ἐπιβλέπω epiblepō (1899)
    ἔχω echō (2174)
    ἡγέομαι hēgeomai (2216)
    κατανοέω katanoeō (2627)
    κρίνω krinō (2892)
    νοέω noeō (3401)

νομίζω nomizō (3406)
οἴομαι oiomai (3496)
συμβάλλω sumballō (4671)
συμβουλεύω sumbouleuō (4674)
συμψηφίζω sumpsēphizō (4711)
ὑπολαμβάνω hupolambanō (5112)
φρονέω phroneō (5262)
ψηφίζω psēphizō (5420)

הָיָה hāyâh (2030), Be; were (2 Sm 19:43).

חָשַׁב chāshav (2913), Qal: reckon (Gn 15:6); plan, devise (2 Sm 14:13, Jer 11:19); niphal: be reckoned, be considered (Nm 18:27, Ps 106:31 [105:31], Is 32:15); piel: calculate, plan (Lv 27:23, Prv 16:9 [16:1], Na 1:9).

מָנָה mānâh (4630), Count; niphal: be counted, be numbered (2 Chr 5:6, Is 53:12).

קָרָא qārā' (7410), Call; niphal: be called (Dt 3:13).

שׁוּב shûv (8178), Return; remember (Is 44:19).

1. λογίζεσθε logizesthe 2pl indic/impr pres mid
2. λογίζομαι logizomai 1sing indic pres mid
3. λογίζῃ logizē 2sing indic pres mid
4. λογίζεται logizetai 3sing indic pres mid
5. λογιζόμεθα logizometha 1pl indic pres mid
6. λογιζέσθω logizesthō 3sing impr pres mid
7. λογιζόμενος logizomenos nom sing masc part pres mid
8. λογιζομένῳ logizomenō dat sing masc part pres mid
9. λογιζομένους logizomenous acc pl masc part pres mid
10. λογίζεσθαι logizesthai inf pres mid
11. ἐλογίσθη elogisthē 3sing indic aor pass
12. ἐλογίσθημεν elogisthēmen 1pl indic aor pass
13. λογίσηται logisētai 3sing subj aor mid
14. λογισθείη logistheiē 3sing opt aor pass
15. λογισάμενος logisamenos nom sing masc part aor mid
16. λογισθῆναι logisthēnai inf aor pass
17. λογίσασθαι logisasthai inf aor mid
18. λογισθήσεται logisthēsetai 3sing indic fut pass
19. ἐλογιζόμην elogizomēn 1sing indic imperf mid
20. ἐλογίζοντο elogizonto 3pl indic imperf pass

20	And they **reasoned** with themselves, saying,	Mark 11:31
11	And he **was numbered** with the transgressors.	15:28
11	And he **was reckoned** among the transgressors:	Luke 22:37
1	nor do you **take into account** that it is (NASB)	John 11:50
16	the great goddess Diana should be despised,	Acts 19:27
3	And **thinkest** thou this, O man,	Rom 2:3
18	his uncircumcision **be counted** for circumcision?	2:26
5	Therefore we **conclude** that a man is justified	3:28
11	and it **was counted** unto him for righteousness.	4:3
4	is the reward not **reckoned** of grace, but of debt.	4:4
4	his faith **is counted** for righteousness.	4:5
4	whom God **imputeth** righteousness without works,	4:6
13	the man to whom the Lord will not **impute** sin.	4:8
11	faith **was reckoned** to Abraham for righteousness.	4:9
11	How **was** it then **reckoned**?	4:10
16	righteousness might **be imputed** unto them also:	4:11
11	therefore it **was imputed** to him for righteousness.	4:22
11	not ... his sake alone, that it **was imputed** to him;	4:23
10	But for us also, to whom it shall **be imputed**,	Rom 4:24
1	Likewise **reckon** ye also yourselves to be dead.	6:11
2	For I **reckon** that the sufferings of this present time	8:18
12	we **are accounted** as sheep for the slaughter.	8:36
4	children of the promise **are counted** for the seed.	9:8
8	but to him that **esteemeth** any thing to be unclean,	14:14
6	Let a man so **account** of us,	1 Co 4:1
4	is not easily provoked, **thinketh** no evil;	13:5
19	I understood as a child, I **thought** as a child:	13:11
17	of ourselves **to think** any thing as of ourselves;	2 Co 3:5
7	not **imputing** their trespasses unto them;	5:19
2	wherewith I **think** to be bold against some,	10:2
9	**think** of us as if we walked according to the flesh.	10:2
6	let him of himself **think** this again,	10:7
6	Let such an one **think** this, that, such as we are	10:11
2	For I **suppose** I was not a whit behind	11:5
13	lest any man **should think** of me above that	12:6
11	and it **was counted** unto him for righteousness.	Gal 3:6
2	Brethren, I **count** not myself to have apprehended:	Phlp 3:13
1	and if there be any praise, **think** on these things.	4:8
14	I pray God that it may not **be laid** to their charge.	2 Tm 4:16
15	**Accounting** that God was able to raise him up,	Heb 11:19
11	and it **was imputed** unto him for righteousness:	Jas 2:23
2	Silvanus, a faithful brother unto you, as I **suppose**,	1 Pt 5:12

Classical Greek

This deponent verb (middle/passive in form, active in function) occurs throughout the literature of antiquity, and it is attested as early as Thucydides, Plato, Xenophon, and Herodotus. In one sense *logizomai* is a commercial technical term meaning "to charge to the account of, to credit." Along with this are other business and numerical senses: "to calculate, compute, figure." This is regularly the usage attested in papyri (cf. *Moulton-Milligan*; cf. Heidland, "logizomai," *Kittel*, 4:284).

A second distinct definition of *logizomai* in classical and Hellenistic Greek does not concern business dealings. In this sense it still means "to calculate, evaluate, consider" and adds the ideas of "to expect, to conclude (by reasoning), to infer" (*Liddell-Scott*; cf. the corresponding noun *logismos*, "calculating, reasoning").

Septuagint Usage

Logizomai is fairly common in the Septuagint—both canonical and apocryphal material—occurring over 100 times, usually for the Hebrew *chāshav* ("to think, account," e.g., Genesis 15:6; Leviticus 7:18; Numbers 18:27). In texts without a Hebrew original it is most common in the Wisdom of Solomon (e.g., 3:2,10) and the Maccabean writings (1 Maccabees 2:52; 3:52; 2 Maccabees 6:12; 3 Maccabees 4:4; 4 Maccabees 3:15).

J. Eichler observes that *logizomai*, which in secular Greek denoted nonreligious or commercial activity, receives a "new and personal slant" in the Septuagint ("Think," *Colin Brown*, 3:823). "To think, consider" involves also personal feeling as well as objective reckoning. It can describe man's relationship to God and God's intentions for man (e.g., 2 Samuel 14:4 [LXX 2 Kings 14:4]; Jeremiah 29:11 [LXX 36:11]; cf. Jeremiah 49:20 [LXX 29:20]; 50:45 [27:45]; cf. ibid., 3:824).

New Testament Usage

Logizomai is easily detected as a Pauline favorite (34 times out of 41 total). Elsewhere it occurs in Mark 15:28 and Luke 22:37 (in an application of Isaiah 53:12 to Jesus), in John 11:50 (in a nontheological sense), and in Acts 19:27 and 1 Peter 5:12. James 2:23 is an Old Testament text (Genesis 15:6) applied to a discussion of righteousness (see below). The use in Hebrews 11:19 resembles the Septuagintal nuance that *logizomai* involves both objective logic and heartfelt emotion. Abraham *logizetai* ("reckoned") that God could raise the dead (Isaac). Here *logizomai* closely resembles faith (cf. 11:17; the Hebrew idea of *chāshav* is probably coming through).

Whereas Jesus was "reckoned" among the transgressors, i.e., He was "charged with" humanity's sins (Mark 15:28 = Isaiah 53:12; Luke 22:37; cf. 2 Corinthians 5:21), righteousness has been "credited" (NIV) to believers through faith (cf. Romans 3:27f.; 4:23f.). Here again *logizesthai*, "to reckon," is not merely an intellectual act; it involves emotion and feeling (*chashab*). The classic example offered of this truth is Abraham who "believed God, and it was *credited* to him as righteousness" (Romans 4:3,9,22, NIV). Throughout the chapter the emphasis is clear that God "figures" righteousness apart from works or keeping the Law (4:6).

Moreover, this whole concept was foreseen by the Holy Scriptures (Galatians 3:8). The argument that God "credits" believers with righteousness revolves around Genesis 15:6 (e.g., Romans 4:3,6,10,22f.; Galatians 3:6), the account of the Abrahamic covenant. Abraham, instead of being a perfect example of someone who was justified by keeping the Law, was justified by remaining "faithful" (Galatians 3:9). God has never in the past and will never in the future "credit" righteousness on the basis of keeping the Law. Thus the Gentiles who do not have the Law are included in God's promise to Abraham (i.e., they may become "Abraham's children" by faith in Christ; Galatians 3:8,10-15).

STRONG 3049, BAUER 475-76, MOULTON-MILLIGAN 377-78, KITTEL 4:284-92, LIDDELL-SCOTT 1055, COLIN BROWN 3:822-26.

3024. λογικός logikos adj

Spiritual, reasonable, rational.

CROSS-REFERENCE:
λόγος logos (3030)

1. **λογικήν** logikēn acc sing fem
2. **λογικόν** logikon nom/acc sing neu

1 which is your **reasonable** service.................... Rom 12:1
2 babes, desire the sincere milk of the word,.......... 1 Pt 2:2

Classical Greek

The adjective *logikos* is derived from the same root as *logos* (3030), "word." The most common meaning of *logikos* in secular Greek is "reasonable, rational." *Logikos* was popular among philosophers such as Philo, who used it often, but usually reflecting the meaning "spiritual" (*Bauer*). Spiritual can be understood both as "supernatural" and as "metaphoric" (as opposed to literal). *Logikos* does not occur in the Septuagint.

New Testament Usage

Logikos is found in two locations in the New Testament. Romans 12:1 has the term in Paul's admonition to believers to present their bodies as sacrifices, alive, holy, and acceptable to God. This he called their "*logikēn* service." Most interpreters read *logikos* as "spiritual." Others prefer the translation "reasonable," the normal understanding in secular Greek. From the latter's viewpoint the meaning is that the presentation of the believer's body to God for service (cf. Romans 6:13) is to be a rational, reasonable sacrifice. Those preferring the figurative sense—"spiritual"—see worship as no longer external ritual but internal, spiritual service to God.

In 1 Peter 2:2 *logikos* occurs in an admonition to believers to crave as infants the pure "milk" of the Word of God and to grow toward salvation through it. Here translators are once again divided over whether *logikos* should be translated as an adjective—the "pure 'spiritual' milk"—or as a substantive—the "pure milk of 'the word' of God."

The context may favor the last translation since immediately before 2:2, in 1:25, Peter had just spoken of the "word of the Lord" that stands forever (Isaiah 40:6-8). But this, however, is not proof that *logikos* in 2:2 must be understood in a way not otherwise attested, either in secular Greek or in the New Testament.

Therefore, every indication is that *logikos* is best translated as "spiritual" or "reasonable." In that case, "spiritual" is probably preferable. Still, an element of rationality is inherent in the term, and it implies believers are rational beings.

STRONG 3050, BAUER 476, MOULTON-MILLIGAN 378, KITTEL 4:142-43, LIDDELL-SCOTT 1056, COLIN BROWN 3:1081,1105,1118-19.

3025. λόγιον logion noun
A little word, brief utterance, divine oracle.
CROSS-REFERENCE:
λόγος logos (3030)

אֵמֶר 'ēmer (571), Word (Nm 24:16, Pss 19:14 [18:14], 107:11 [106:11]).

אִמְרָה 'imrāh (577), Word (Dt 33:9, Pss 12:6 [11:6], 119:116 [118:116]).

דָּבָר dāvār (1745), Word (Ps 119:169 [118:169], Is 28:13).

מַשָּׂאָה massā'āh (5018), Cloud of smoke (Is 30:27).

1. **λογίων logiōn** gen pl neu
2. **λόγια logia** nom/acc pl neu

2 who received the lively **oracles** to give unto us:......Acts 7:38
2 that unto them were committed the **oracles** of God. Rom 3:2
1 the first principles of the **oracles** of God;............Heb 5:12
2 let him speak as the **oracles** of God;................1 Pt 4:11

Classical Greek
Logion is a diminutive of *logos* (3030), "word," which in turn is a verbal noun from *legō* (2978), "to say, speak." This neuter noun generally denotes "a saying." In classical Greek (from Euripides and Herodotus on) it is used primarily of brief oracles given by a god, usually of sayings or oracles of antiquity.

Septuagint Usage
In the Septuagint *logion* is used for any word or utterance of God, whether prophecy (Isaiah 28:13), promise (Psalm 119:58 [LXX 118:58]), or precept (Deuteronomy 33:9). It is one of several related terms David employed in his great psalm concerning the Word of God (119:11,38,67 [LXX 118:11,38,67], etc.). Only once is *logion* used of the words of man (Psalm 19:14 [LXX 18:14]). Philo spoke of the Decalogue as the "ten *logia*." A closely related term with *logion* in the Septuagint is *logeion*, used of the breastplate of the high priest which he wore when he appeared before or consulted with God (Exodus 28:15; Leviticus 8:8).

New Testament Usage
Logion occurs four times in the New Testament: twice of the contents and precepts of the Mosaic system (Acts 7:38; Romans 3:2), once of the basics of the Judeo-Christian faith (Hebrews 5:12), and once of the utterances of God through Christians gifted to proclaim His truth (1 Peter 4:11).

In early Christian literature (ca. Second Century A.D.) *logion* was used of the sayings of Jesus (Polycarp, *Epistle to the Philippians*, 7:1), the writings of the New Testament (Ignatius, *Epistle to the Smyrnaeans*, 3, longer version), as well as the oracles of God throughout all of Scripture (Clement of Rome, *First Epistle to the Corinthians*, 53:1).

STRONG 3051, BAUER 476, MOULTON-MILLIGAN 378, KITTEL 4:137-41, LIDDELL-SCOTT 1056, COLIN BROWN 3:1081,1106,1118.

3026. λόγιος logios adj
Learned, eloquent.
CROSS-REFERENCE:
λόγος logos (3030)

1. **λόγιος logios** nom sing masc

1 an **eloquent** man, and mighty in the scriptures,.....Acts 18:24

Classical Greek
From the time of Pindar (ca. 518 B.C.) *logios* appears in classical Greek writings. Sometimes it describes someone who is knowledgeable in a specific subject: "a storyteller," "a narrator," or "a professional" such as a physician. On other occasions it refers to an individual's skill with words (*logois*) and is used to mean "eloquent."

New Testament Usage
Septuagint writers never employed the term, and it is used only once in the New Testament, in Acts 18:24. Here Luke used it to describe Apollos as an *anēr logios*, a man who is either "eloquent" or "learned."

Some debate has arisen among Biblical scholars over the translation of the word in this verse. Because the first-century Jewish writers, Josephus and Philo, use it preponderately in the sense of "knowledgeable, educated, cultured" or "learned," most Biblical philologists prefer the translation "learned" (cf. Kittel, "logios," *Kittel*, 4:136).

Most of the older commentators seem to prefer "eloquence" because Acts 18:25 refers to Apollos as one who "was habitually speaking while he was seething in his spirit" (free translation). In the context, however, this is most likely a reference to his enthusiasm and not to his effectiveness.

References to Apollos in 1 Corinthians 1:12 and 3:5 are also sometimes used to support the idea that Apollos was eloquent, but they are also easily harmonized with the belief that Luke referred to Apollos as a man learned in Greek culture. Most recent commentators cite "learned" as the best translation. It is probable that Apollos was both learned and eloquent.

STRONG 3052, BAUER 476, MOULTON-MILLIGAN 378, KITTEL 4:136-37, LIDDELL-SCOTT 1056, COLIN BROWN 3:1081,1106,1117.

3027. λογισμός logismos noun

Thoughts, imaginations, reasoning, calculation.

COGNATE:
λογίζομαι logizomai (3023)

SYNONYMS:
διαλογισμός dialogismos (1255)
διανόημα dianoēma (1264)
διάνοια dianoia (1265)
ἐνθύμησις enthumēsis (1745)
ἔννοια ennoia (1755)
ἐπίνοια epinoia (1948)
νόημα noēma (3402)
νοῦς nous (3426)
σύνεσις sunesis (4757)

חָשַׁב chāshav (2913), Plot (Na 1:11).
חֶשְׁבּוֹן cheshbôn (2918), Explanation (Eccl 7:27 [7:28]); planning (Eccl 9:10).
חִשָּׁבוֹן chishshāvôn (2920), Device (Eccl 7:29 [7:30]).
מַחֲשָׁבָה machăshāvāh (4422I), Plan, scheme (Prv 6:18, Jer 18:11).

1. λογισμῶν logismōn gen pl masc
2. λογισμούς logismous acc pl masc

1 and their thoughts the mean while accusing .... Rom 2:15
2 Casting down **imaginations**, ... 2 Co 10:5

Classical Greek

Logismos appears in classical Greek from the Fifth Century B.C. onward. As a technical term in arithmetic it refers to either an "act of computation" or "the results of the computation." In more general usage it came to denote: (1) "the reasoning process"; (2) "a particular argument"; and (3) "man's ability to reason." The Stoic philosophers used it technically to designate man's highest activity, "reasoning" in a specific situation in a man's consciousness and behavior.

Septuagint Usage

The term appears over 100 times in the Septuagint but only 30 times in the canonical books. It is found over 70 times in 4 Maccabees and 12 times in the apocryphal Wisdom literature. These uses reflect the Stoic meaning. In its canonical use *logismos* translates the Hebrew *cheshbôn* which emphasizes "the creative and planning functions of reason," human (Psalm 33:10 [LXX 32:10]) or divine (Psalm 33:11 [LXX 32:11]). Fifteen of the canonical references depict evil thoughts and plans against God or His people.

Sometimes *logismos* signifies the "determination arrived at" in a judicial decision, either divine (Jeremiah 49:20 [LXX 29:20]; 50:45 [27:45]; 51:29 [28:29]) or human (Jeremiah 49:30 [30:30]). In Proverbs 15:22 it refers to the rationalizations of men who reject authority; in Jeremiah 18:18 the original bookkeeping use of the term is applied figuratively to the Jews' vengeful desire to settle accounts with Jeremiah.

New Testament Usage

Paul accounts for the only two uses of *logismos* in the New Testament. In Romans 2:15 it indicates the "moral judgments" of conscience which are in agreement with God's righteous requirements even though they are formulated by pagans who never heard the Mosaic law. In 2 Corinthians 10:5 Paul used *logismos* of the negative judgments his opponents had made against him. The context indicates they were presumptuous in their estimate of their own rational powers. They had built a fortress of self-glorifying thoughts and had cut themselves off from God. Their stronghold can be penetrated only by the divine revelation manifest in the Cross and in the teaching and discipline of Christ's apostolic preacher.

STRONG 3053, BAUER 476-77, MOULTON-MILLIGAN 378, KITTEL 4:284-92, LIDDELL-SCOTT 1056, COLIN BROWN 3:822-24.

3028. λογομαχέω logomacheō verb

To dispute about words, to wrangle about trivial matters.

CROSS-REFERENCES:
λόγος logos (3030)
μάχομαι machomai (3136)

1. λογομαχεῖν logomachein inf pres act

1 that they strive not **about words** to no profit, ... 2 Tm 2:14

The verb *logomacheō*, "to dispute about words, to war verbally about trivial matters," is a compound of *logos* (3030), "word, saying," and *machomai* (3136), "to war, dispute." The noun forms are *logomachos*, "a disputer about words," and *logomachia* (3029), "a verbal dispute about words." *Logomacheō* is a hapax legomenon in the New Testament. Paul warned Timothy about the futility and destructiveness of wrangling over trivial matters (2 Timothy 2:14).

STRONG 3054, BAUER 477, KITTEL 4:143,
LIDDELL-SCOTT 1056, COLIN BROWN 3:1119.

3029. λογομαχία logomachia noun

Word battle, war of words, dispute about words.

CROSS-REFERENCES:
λόγος logos (3030)
μάχομαι machomai (3136)

1. λογομαχίας logomachias acc pl fem

1 but doting about questions and strifes of words, ... 1 Tm 6:4

Appearing from the First Century B.C., the noun *logomachia* is a compound of *logos* (3030), "word, saying," and *machē* (3135), a "fight, combat" (either a physical battle with arms or a battle fought without arms, i.e., a dispute or quarrel between individuals at variance). The compound means "a battle of words, hair splitting, a disputing about trivial matters." *Logomachia* appears only once in the New Testament, in the plural (1 Timothy 6:4). Paul warned of the destructive nature of this kind of argumentation.

STRONG 3055, BAUER 477, KITTEL 4:143,
LIDDELL-SCOTT 1056, COLIN BROWN 3:1119.

3030. λόγος logos noun

Word, subject, matter, thing, statement, declaration, speech, message, proclamation, et al.

COGNATES:
ἀγενεαλόγητος agenealogētos (35)
ἄλογος alogos (247)
ἀναλογία analogia (354)
ἀναπολόγητος anapologētos (377)
ἀντιλογία antilogia (482)
ἀπολογέομαι apologeomai (620)
ἀπολογία apologia (621)
βαττολογέω battologeō (938)
γενεαλογέω genealogeō (1068)
γενεαλογία genealogia (1069)
δίλογος dilogos (1345)
λέγω legō (2978)
λογεία logeia (3021B)
λογία logia (3022)
λογικός logikos (3024)
λόγιον logion (3025)
λόγιος logios (3026)
λογομαχέω logomacheō (3028)
λογομαχία logomachia (3029)
ματαιολογία mataiologia (3122)
ματαιολόγος mataiologos (3123)
μωρολογία mōrologia (3335)
πιθανολογία pithanologia (3947)
πολυλογία polulogia (4040)
σπερμολόγος spermologos (4544)
στρατολογέω stratologeō (4609)
ψευδολόγος pseudologos (5408)

SYNONYMS:
κήρυγμα kērugma (2754)
λαλιά lalia (2954)
ῥῆμα rhēma (4343)

אָמַר 'āmar (569), Saying (2 Kgs 17:13—Codex Vaticanus only).
אֵמֶר 'ēmer (571), Word (Prv 1:2, 16:24, 22:21).
אִמְרָה 'imrāh (577), Speech, word (Gn 4:23, Ps 119:154 [118:154], Is 28:23).
דָּבַר dāvar (1744), Qal: speak, ask (Prv 16:13, Mi 7:3); piel: speak, utter (2 Sm 20:18, Neh 6:12, Jer 20:8).
דָּבָר dāvār (1745), Word (Dt 31:1, Jer 22:1f.); act (2 Kgs 15:11).
דִּבְרָה divrāh (1750), Because, on account of (Eccl 8:2).
דַּבֶּרֶת dabbereth (1755), Direction (Dt 33:3).
מַאֲמָר ma'ămār (4124), Decree (Est 9:32).
מִלָּה millāh (4543), Word (2 Sm 23:2, Jb 19:2, Prv 23:9).
מִלָּה millāh (A4544), Word (Dn 2:9, 4:31 [4:28], 7:11—Aramaic).
מִצְוָה mitswāh (4851), Commandment (Jgs 2:17).
נְבוּאָה nevû'āh (5191), Prophecy (2 Chr 9:29).
פֶּה peh (6552), Mouth; command, word (1 Sm 15:24, 1 Chr 12:23).
פִּתְגָם pithgām (6851), Edict (Est 1:20).
קוֹל qôl (7249), Voice (Jer 38:20 [45:20]).
שָׂפָה sāphāh (8004), Speech (Prv 16:21).
שֵׁבֶט shēvet (8101), Rod (Is 11:4).
תְּבוּנָה tevûnāh (8722), Understanding (Prv 5:1).
תּוֹרָה tôrāh (8784), Commandment (Prv 7:2).

1. λόγος logos nom sing masc
2. λόγου logou gen sing masc
3. λόγῳ logō dat sing masc
4. λόγον logon acc sing masc
5. λόγοι logoi nom pl masc
6. λόγων logōn gen pl masc
7. λόγοις logois dat pl masc
8. λόγους logous acc pl masc

2 saving **for the cause of fornication**, ... Matt 5:32
1 let your **communication** be, Yea, yea; Nay, nay: 5:37
8 Therefore whosoever heareth these **sayings** of mine, . . . 7:24
8 And every one that heareth these **sayings** of mine, ... 7:26
8 when Jesus had ended these **sayings**, ... 7:28
4 but speak the **word** only, ... 8:8
3 he cast out the spirits with his **word**, ... 8:16
8 shall not receive you, nor hear your **words**, ... 10:14
4 whosoever speaketh **a word** against the Son of man, . . . 12:32

λόγος 3030

4	shall give **account** thereof in the day of judgment...	Matt 12:36
6	For by thy **words** thou shalt be justified,	12:37
6	and by thy **words** thou shalt be condemned.	12:37
4	When any one heareth the **word** of the kingdom,	13:19
4	the same is he that heareth the **word**,	13:20
4	persecution ariseth because of the **word**,	13:21
4	is he that heareth the **word**;	13:22
4	choke the **word**, and he becometh unfruitful.	13:22
4	is he that heareth the **word**, and understandeth it;	13:23
4	you invalidated the **word** of God for (NASB)	15:6
4	were offended, after they heard this **saying**?	15:12
4	But he answered her not a **word**.	15:23
4	king, which would take **account** of his servants.	18:23
8	that when Jesus had finished these **sayings**,	19:1
4	All men cannot receive this **saying**,	19:11
4	But when the young man heard that **saying**,	19:22
4	I also will ask you one **thing**, which if ye tell me,	21:24
3	how they might entangle him in his **talk**.	22:15
4	And no man was able to answer him a **word**,	22:46
5	but my **words** shall not pass away.	24:35
4	the lord ... cometh, and **reckoneth** with them.	25:19
8	when Jesus had finished all these **sayings**,	26:1
4	and prayed the third time, saying the same **words**.	26:44
1	this **saying** is commonly reported among the Jews	28:15
4	publish it much, and to blaze abroad the **matter**,	Mark 1:45
4	and he preached the **word** unto them.	2:2
4	The sower soweth the **word**.	4:14
1	they by the way side, where the **word** is sown;	4:15
4	Satan ... and taketh away the **word** that was sown	4:15
4	who, when they have heard the **word**,	4:16
4	or persecution ariseth for the **word's** sake,	4:17
4	are sown among thorns; such as hear the **word**,	4:18
4	choke the **word**, and it becometh unfruitful.	4:19
4	such as hear the **word**, and receive it,	4:20
4	And with many such parables spake he the **word**	4:33
4	As soon as Jesus heard the **word** that was spoken,	5:36
4	Making the **word** of God of none effect	7:13
4	And he said unto her, For this **saying** go thy way;	7:29
4	And he spake that **saying** openly.	8:32
8	shall be ashamed of me and of my **words**	8:38
4	And they kept that **saying** with themselves,	9:10
3	he was sad at that **saying**, and went away grieved:	10:22
7	And the disciples were astonished at his **words**.	10:24
4	I will also ask of you one **question**, and answer me,	11:29
3	they send unto him ... to catch him in his **words**.	12:13
5	but my **words** shall not pass away.	13:31
4	went away, and prayed, and spake the same **words**.	14:39
4	confirming the **word** with signs following. Amen.	16:20
2	were eyewitnesses, and ministers of the **word**;	Luke 1:2
6	thou mightest know the certainty of **those things**,	1:4
7	be dumb, ... because thou believest not my **words**,	1:20
3	when she saw him, she was troubled at his **saying**,	1:29
6	As it is written in the book of the **words** of Esaias	3:4
7	and wondered at the gracious **words**	4:22
1	at his doctrine: for his **word** was with power.	4:32
1	saying, What a **word** is this! for with authority	4:36
4	people pressed upon him to hear the **word** of God,	5:1
1	But so much the more went there a **fame** abroad	5:15
6	and heareth my **sayings**, and doeth them,	6:47
3	but say in a **word**, and my servant shall be healed.	7:7
1	**rumour** of him went forth throughout all Judaea,	7:17
1	the parable is this: The seed is the **word** of God.	8:11
4	and taketh away the **word** out of their hearts,	8:12
4	which, when they hear, receive the **word** with joy;	8:13
4	having heard the **word**, keep it,	8:15
4	these which hear the **word** of God, and do it.	8:21
8	shall be ashamed of me and of my **words**,	9:26
8	to pass about an eight days after these **sayings**,	9:28
8	Let these **sayings** sink down into your ears:	9:44
4	which also sat at Jesus' feet, and heard his **word**.	10:39
4	blessed ... that hear the **word** of God, and keep it.	11:28
4	And whosoever shall speak a **word** against the Son	12:10
4	give an **account** of thy stewardship;	16:2
4	I will also ask you one **thing**; and answer me:	20:3
2	that they might take hold of his **words**,	20:20
5	but my **words** shall not pass away.	21:33
2	And Peter remembered the **word** of the Lord,	22:61
7	Then he questioned with him in many **words**;	Luke 23:9
5	What manner of **communications** are these	24:17
3	which was a prophet mighty in deed and **word**	24:19
5	These are the **words** which I spake unto you,	24:44
1	In the beginning was the **Word**,	John 1:1
1	the **Word** was with God, and the Word was God.	1:1
1	the Word was with God, and the **Word** was God.	1:1
1	the **Word** was made flesh, and dwelt among us,	1:14
3	and the **word** which Jesus had said.	2:22
1	And herein is that **saying** true,	4:37
4	believed on him for the **saying** of the woman,	4:39
4	And many more believed because of his own **word**;	4:41
3	the man believed the **word** that Jesus had spoken	4:50
4	He that heareth my **word**,	5:24
4	And ye have not his **word** abiding in you:	5:38
1	This is an hard **saying**; who can hear it?	6:60
1	What manner of **saying** is this that he said,	7:36
4	when they heard this **saying**,	7:40
3	If ye continue in my **word**,	8:31
1	kill me, because my **word** hath no place in you.	8:37
4	even because ye cannot hear my **word**.	8:43
4	If a man keep my **word**, he shall never see death.	8:51
4	thou sayest, If a man keep my **saying**,	8:52
4	but I know him, and keep his **saying**.	8:55
8	was a division ... among the Jews for these **sayings**.	10:19
1	unto whom the **word** of God came,	10:35
1	That the **saying** of Esaias the prophet	12:38
1	one that judgeth him: the **word** that I have spoken,	12:48
4	If a man love me, he will keep my **words**:	14:23
8	He that loveth me not keepeth not my **sayings**:	14:24
1	**word** which ye hear is not mine, but the Father's	14:24
4	ye are clean through the **word** which I have spoken	15:3
2	Remember the **word** that I said unto you,	15:20
1	if they have kept my **saying**,	15:20
1	that the **word** might be fulfilled that is written	15:25
4	gavest them me; and they have kept thy **word**.	17:6
4	I have given them thy **word**;	17:14
1	Sanctify them through thy truth: thy **word** is truth.	17:17
2	which shall believe on me through their **word**;	17:20
1	That the **saying** might be fulfilled, which he spake,	18:9
1	That the **saying** of Jesus might be fulfilled,	18:32
4	When Pilate therefore heard that **saying**,	19:8
4	When Pilate therefore heard that **saying**,	19:13
1	Then went this **saying** abroad among the brethren,	21:23
4	The former **treatise** have I made, O Theophilus,	Acts 1:1
8	Ye men of Israel, hear these **words**;	2:22
7	with many other **words** did he testify and exhort,	2:40
4	they that gladly received his **word** were baptized:	2:41
4	many of them which heard the **word** believed;	4:4
4	that with all boldness they may speak thy **word**,	4:29
4	and they spake the **word** of God with boldness.	4:31
8	And Ananias hearing these **words** fell down,	5:5
8	and the chief priests heard these **things**,	5:24
4	not reason that we should leave the **word** of God,	6:2
2	to prayer, and to the ministry of the **word**.	6:4
1	And the **saying** pleased the whole multitude:	6:5
1	And the **word** of God increased;	6:7
7	and was mighty in **words** and in deeds.	7:22
3	Then fled Moses at this **saying**,	7:29
4	went every where preaching the **word**.	8:4
4	heard that Samaria had received the **word** of God,	8:14
3	Thou hast neither part nor lot in this **matter**:	8:21
4	had testified and preached the **word** of the Lord,	8:25
3	I ask therefore for what **intent** ye have sent for me?	10:29
4	**word** which God sent unto the children of Israel,	10:36
4	Holy Ghost fell on all them which heard the **word**.	10:44
4	the Gentiles had also received the **word** of God.	11:1
4	preaching the **word** to none but unto the Jews	11:19
1	Then **tidings** of these things came unto the ears	11:22
1	But the **word** of God grew and multiplied.	12:24
4	they preached the **word** of God in the synagogues	13:5
4	and desired to hear the **word** of God.	13:7
1	any **word** of exhortation for the people, say on.	13:15
1	to you is the **word** of this salvation sent.	13:26
4	the whole city together to hear the **word** of God.	13:44
4	**word** of God should first have been spoken to you:	13:46
4	they were glad, and glorified the **word** of the Lord:	13:48

74

λόγος 3030

1	And the **word** of the Lord was published	Acts 13:49
3	which gave testimony unto the **word** of his grace,	14:3
2	Mercurius, because he was the chief **speaker**.	14:12
4	And when they had preached the **word** in Perga,	14:25
2	elders came together for to consider of this **matter**.	15:6
4	by my mouth should hear the **word** of the gospel,	15:7
5	And to this agree the **words** of the prophets;	15:15
7	that certain ... have troubled you with **words**,	15:24
2	who shall also tell you the same things by **mouth**.	15:27
2	exhorted the brethren with many **words**,	15:32
4	teaching and preaching the **word** of the Lord,	15:35
4	in every city where we have preached the **word**	15:36
4	forbidden ... to preach the **word** in Asia,	16:6
4	And they spake unto him the **word** of the Lord,	16:32
8	the keeper of the prison told this **saying** to Paul,	16:36
4	they received the **word** with all readiness of mind,	17:11
1	the **word** of God was preached of Paul at Berea,	17:13
3	Paul began devoting ... to the **word** (NASB)	18:5
4	teaching the **word** of God among them.	18:11
4	**reason** would that I should bear with you:	18:14
2	But if it be a question of **words** and names,	18:15
4	so that all they which dwelt in Asia heard the **word**	19:10
1	So mightily grew the **word** of God and prevailed.	19:20
4	have **a matter** against any man, the law is open,	19:38
4	whereby we may give an **account** of this concourse.	19:40
3	speaking many **words** of encouragement (NIV)	20:2
4	and continued his **speech** until midnight.	20:7
4	consider my life of any **account** (NASB)	20:24
3	and to the **word** of his grace,	20:32
6	and to remember the **words** of the Lord Jesus,	20:35
3	Sorrowing most of all for the **words** ... he spake,	20:38
2	And they gave him audience unto this **word**,	22:22
7	That thou mightest be justified in thy **sayings**,	Rom 3:4
1	as though the **word** of God hath taken none effect.	9:6
1	For this is the **word** of promise,	9:9
4	For he will finish the **work**,	9:28
4	because a short **work** will the Lord make	9:28
3	it is briefly comprehended in this **saying**,	13:9
4	every ... of us shall give **account** of himself to God.	14:12
3	to make the Gentiles obedient, by **word** and deed,	15:18
3	by him, in all **utterance**, and in all knowledge;	1 Co 1:5
2	to preach the gospel: not with wisdom of **words**,	1:17
1	the **preaching** of the cross is to them that perish	1:18
2	came not with excellency of **speech** or of wisdom,	2:1
2	And my **speech** and my preaching was not	2:4
7	my preaching was not with enticing **words**	2:4
7	not in the **words** which man's wisdom teacheth,	2:13
4	not the **speech** of them which are puffed up,	4:19
3	the kingdom of God is not in **word**, but in power.	4:20
1	to one is given by the Spirit the **word** of wisdom;	12:8
1	another the **word** of knowledge by the same Spirit;	12:8
4	utter by the tongue **words** easy to be understood,	14:9
8	Yet in the church I had rather speak five **words**	14:19
8	than ten thousand **words** in an unknown tongue.	14:19
1	What? came the **word** of God out from you?	14:36
3	if ye keep in memory what I preached unto you,	15:2
1	then shall be brought to pass the **saying**	15:54
1	our **word** toward you was not yea and nay.	2 Co 1:18
4	which corrupt the **word** of God:	2:17
4	nor handling the **word** of God deceitfully;	4:2
4	hath committed unto us the **word** of reconciliation.	5:19
3	By the **word** of truth, by the power of God,	6:7
3	in faith, and **utterance**, and knowledge,	8:7
1	and his **speech** contemptible.	10:10
3	as we are in **word** by letters when we are absent,	10:11
3	But though I be rude in **speech**,	11:6
3	For all the law is fulfilled in one **word**,	Gal 5:14
4	Let him that is taught in the **word**	6:6
4	also trusted, after that ye heard the **word** of truth,	Eph 1:13
1	Let no corrupt **communication** proceed	4:29
7	Let no man deceive you with vain **words**:	5:6
1	And for me, that **utterance** may be given unto me,	6:19
4	much more bold to speak the **word** without fear.	Phlp 1:14
4	Holding forth the **word** of life;	2:16
4	as **concerning** giving and receiving,	4:15
4	but I desire fruit that may abound to your **account**.	4:17
3	whereof ye heard before in the **word**	Col 1:5
4	is given to me for you, to fulfil the **word** of God;	Col 1:25
4	have indeed **a show** of wisdom in will worship,	2:23
1	Let the **word** of Christ dwell in you richly	3:16
3	And whatsoever ye do in **word** or deed,	3:17
2	that God would open unto us a door of **utterance**,	4:3
1	Let your **speech** be alway with grace,	4:6
3	For our gospel came not unto you in **word** only,	1 Th 1:5
1	having received the **word** in much affliction,	1:6
1	For from you sounded out the **word** of the Lord	1:8
3	For neither at any time used we flattering **words**,	2:5
4	ye received the **word** of God which ye heard of us,	2:13
4	ye received it not as the **word** of men,	2:13
4	but as it is in truth, the **word** of God,	2:13
3	For this we say unto you by the **word** of the Lord,	4:15
7	Wherefore comfort one another with these **words**.	4:18
2	or be troubled, neither by spirit, nor by **word**,	2 Th 2:2
2	whether by **word**, or our epistle.	2:15
3	and stablish you in every good **word** and work.	2:17
1	that the **word** of the Lord may have free course,	3:1
3	And if any man obey not our **word** by this epistle,	3:14
1	a faithful **saying**, and worthy of all acceptation,	1 Tm 1:15
1	This is a true **saying**, ... he desireth a good work.	3:1
2	For it is sanctified by the **word** of God and prayer.	4:5
7	nourished up in the **words** of faith	4:6
1	a faithful **saying** and worthy of all acceptation.	4:9
3	in **word**, in conversation, in charity, in spirit,	4:12
3	especially they who labour in the **word**	5:17
7	and consent not to wholesome **words**,	6:3
6	Hold fast the form of sound **words**,	2 Tm 1:13
1	but the **word** of God is not bound.	2:9
1	It is a faithful **saying**: For if we be dead with him,	2:11
4	rightly dividing the **word** of truth.	2:15
1	And their **word** will eat as doth a canker:	2:17
4	Preach the **word**; be instant in season,	4:2
7	for he hath greatly withstood our **words**.	4:15
4	But hath in due times manifested his **word**	Tit 1:3
2	Holding fast the faithful **word**	1:9
1	that the **word** of God be not blasphemed.	2:5
4	Sound **speech**, that cannot be condemned;	2:8
1	This is a faithful **saying**,	3:8
1	For if the **word** spoken by angels was stedfast,	Heb 2:2
1	but the **word** preached did not profit them,	4:2
1	For the **word** of God is quick, and powerful,	4:12
1	to whom we must give **account**. (NIV)	4:13
1	Of whom we have many things to say,	5:11
2	is unskilful in the **word** of righteousness:	5:13
4	leaving the principles of the **doctrine** of Christ,	6:1
1	but the **word** of the oath, which was since the law,	7:28
4	the **word** should not be spoken to them any more:	12:19
4	who have spoken unto you the **word** of God:	13:7
4	as they that must give **account**,	13:17
2	brethren, suffer the **word** of exhortation:	13:22
3	Of his own will begat he us with the **word** of truth,	Jas 1:18
1	and receive with meekness the engrafted **word**,	1:21
2	But be ye doers **of the word**, and not hearers only,	1:22
2	For if any be a hearer **of the word**, and not a doer,	1:23
3	offend not in **word**, the same is a perfect man,	3:2
2	Being born again, ... by the **word** of God,	1 Pt 1:23
3	even to them which stumble at the **word**,	2:8
3	that, if any obey not the **word**,	3:1
2	they also may without the **word** be won	3:1
4	to every man that asketh you a **reason** of the hope	3:15
4	shall give **account** to him that is ready to judge	4:5
4	We have also a more sure **word** of prophecy;	2 Pt 1:19
7	with feigned **words** make merchandise of you:	2:3
3	that by the **word** of God the heavens were of old,	3:5
3	the earth, ... by the same **word** are kept in store,	3:7
2	and our hands have handled, of the **Word** of life;	1 Jn 1:1
1	we make him a liar, and his **word** is not in us.	1:10
4	But whoso keepeth his **word**,	2:5
1	the **word** which ye have heard from the beginning.	2:7
1	ye are strong, and the **word** of God abideth in you,	2:14
3	My little children, let us not love in **word**,	3:18
1	the Father, the **Word**, and the Holy Ghost:	5:7
7	prating against us with malicious **words**:	3 Jn 1:10
4	Who bare record of the **word** of God,	Rev 1:2
8	and they that hear the **words** of this prophecy,	1:3

75

4 for the **word** of God, and for the testimony of Jesus..Rev	1:9
4 hast kept my **word**, and hast not denied my name.......	3:8
4 Because thou hast kept the **word** of my patience,.......	3:10
4 souls of them that were slain for the **word** of God,.....	6:9
4 and by the **word** of their testimony;...................	12:11
5 until the **words** of God shall be fulfilled (NASB)......	17:17
5 saith unto me, These are the true **sayings** of God.....	19:9
1 and his name is called The **Word** of God..............	19:13
4 for the witness of Jesus, and for the **word** of God,.....	20:4
5 Write: for these **words** are true and faithful...........	21:5
5 These **sayings** are faithful and true:...................	22:6
8 keepeth the **sayings** of the prophecy of this book......	22:7
8 and of them which keep the **sayings** of this book.....	22:9
8 Seal not the **sayings** of the prophecy of this book:.....	22:10
8 I testify unto every man that heareth the **words**........	22:18
6 from the **words** of the book of this prophecy,..........	22:19

Classical Greek

Logos is derived from the root *leg* which means "to gather up, to count, to speak." In secular Greek *logos* has a broad semantic range. It can stand for "word, conversation, utterance, language, opinion," and more. Initially there was no distinguishing characteristic between *logos* and other similar terms. For example, *muthos* (3316) became distinct and gradually came to denote fictitious stories; *epos* (2015) signified the epic literature. *Logos* became most important in the void between such words. *Logos* is often synonymous with *rhēma* (4343), "word, speech" (see Fries, "Word," *Colin Brown*, 3:1081).

Quite early in classical Greek *logos* became a favorite term in philosophical discussions. The Greek philosophical "logos" terminology originated with Heracleitus, a philosopher from Ephesus (ca. 535 to ca. 475 B.C.). His basic idea was that everything in this world is undergoing transformation, "everything flows." Still, existence is not in a totally chaotic state because of a controlling principle, a pattern from which everything is formed. At this point Heracleitus incorporated *logos* into his philosophical vocabulary as the regulating and controlling principle of existence—the rational and unchangeable law which governs every change. *Logos* connects humanity with the cosmos, with itself, and with deity, "the One in all." He infrequently called this law or force "justice" or "harmony"; but ordinarily he termed it *logos*. On a few occasions he termed it God (cf., ibid.).

Heracleitus' *logos* concept is one of the basic, central thoughts of Greek philosophy. The concept was never completely discarded. Greek philosophies, especially Stoicism, continued to be influenced by it throughout the centuries. Plato (ca. 427–347 B.C.) on one occasion presented *logos* as an expression for the divine power which he credited with setting the world in motion. The Greeks also saw *logos* as the creating and controlling power of God, the power which created the universe and which sustained it.

The precise understanding of *logos* varies among the different thinkers. Because of dualism's controlling impact upon Greek philosophy, and due to the accompanying theory that the immaterial divine cannot come in direct contact with the material world, *logos* was understood as a connecting link between God and the universe, a manifestation of the divine principle in the world. According to Stoic thinking *logos* is a divine "thought" as well as the light of reason which is dispersed in the world, "world reason" (cf. Kleinknecht, "legō," *Kittel*, 4:84f.).

Notwithstanding the error and superstition of these ancient concepts, the *logos* concept still remains as one of Greek philosophy's loftiest thoughts. Such a standing made *logos* a suitable choice of the Holy Spirit when John wrote his Gospel. Just as Paul sought to relate his gospel message to the idea of an unknown God in Athens (Acts 17:23), John introduced his Gospel by referring to the *logos* concept which was so well-known among Greeks. Everyone associated this concept with something great or significant. It would have been difficult to find any other philosophical concept which would attract similar attention and invoke interest from those seeking a meaning to life. Such seekers could receive the light and life of Jesus Christ, the Word of God.

Old Testament Background

On the other hand, it is evident that more of the background of the *logos* doctrine of the New Testament is to be found within the Jewish context. To the Hebrew mentality the "word" could involve more than a mere remark or comment. The expressed word could be considered irrevocable at times, an almost independent entity. It could go beyond the limits of what is normally understood with speech and could be perceived almost as a "being" of its own. On several occasions in the Old Testament the "word" is hypostatized, i.e., it is perceived as real, or personified.

While the dominant earlier trend in scholarship was to see *logos* in John as a loanword from Hellenistic thought, it is now becoming clear that the definition receives its heritage mainly from the Old Testament and from Judaism. One need not go outside of Scripture itself to find the origin and background of the definition. The term *logos* itself is Greek, and it must, of course, often be understood in its common, everyday meaning in the New Testament. But what the *logos* doctrine in the New Testament involves has been shaped far more by the revelation of God in the Old Testament than by a Greek philosophical speculation.

Septuagint Usage

The most usual term for "word" in the Septuagint is *dāvār* which, however, has a substantially different range of meaning than *logos*. The "word" lies at the heart of salvation history and revelation. All the depth of meaning of *dāvār* must not be overlooked. *Dāvār* implies not only word but action. Therefore, no real difference exists between what God says, i.e., His word, and what He does. God speaks through the prophets and through acts of history. All of salvation history recorded by the Holy Scriptures, in words as well as deeds, in proclamation as well as history, is the Word which God speaks to the world.

The Word of God is preexistent and eternal in heaven (Psalm 119:89 [LXX 118:89]). From heaven it is sent out (Psalms 107:20 [LXX 106:20]; 147:15 [146:15]), and to there it returns when it has fulfilled its mission (Isaiah 55:11).

In the same way as "wisdom" is personified (Proverbs 28:25f.), the word in the Old Testament is often something pointing beyond a mere thought or idea. It becomes personalized but *never* in the full sense in which John used *Logos* in John 1:1-18. Eventually the Word is realized to be the One who was to come with the message of God and for whom Israel was waiting.

While *logos* was commonly used as a translation for *dāvār* in the historical books, the prophetic writings use *rhēma* most often. (Both of these are later utilized in the New Testament: *logos* over 300 times; *rhēma* over 70 times.)

New Testament Usage

As seen above, the meaning of *logos* in the New Testament has been shaped far more by the Old Testament concept of *dāvār* than any philosophical usage of the ancient world. Although *logos* accommodates itself to philosophic language, it is in no respect to be understood philosophically from the Christian perspective. That the Word became flesh is the enormous distinction between speculation about existence and confrontation with the very Author of life.

Naturally not every occurrence of *logos* in the New Testament is theologically important. The normal, secular sense of "word, speech, message," and so on, is readily discernible (e.g., Matthew 5:37; 12:36; Mark 5:36). In some cases it may refer to the Old Testament Scriptures (e.g., Matthew 15:6). Nevertheless, the dominant idea underlying New Testament usage is that the "word" equals two things: (1) the gospel message and (2) Christ himself (John 1:1-18).

The "word" (*ton logon*, often as a direct object, sometimes plural) is Jesus' message of the Kingdom's arrival and demands (Mark 1:45; 4:14ff. with parallels). His words are eternal (Matthew 24:35); they challenge and disturb (Matthew 15:12; 19:22; Mark 8:32; 10:22).

Luke, more than any other Synoptic writer, viewed the *logos* as the gospel message. The "word" includes the message about Jesus' death, resurrection, ascension, His power and desire to forgive sins, and the summons to godly living. Luke regularly qualified the "word" as "of God" (*tou theou*; 5:1, of Jesus' preaching; 8:11, the seed, i.e., the Word of God; 8:21; 11:28), or "of the Lord" (e.g., Luke 22:61; Acts 8:25; 19:10). The Book of Acts reflects a similar attitude. However, instead of being a reference to Jesus' preaching, the "word of God" is a Christian proclamation about Jesus by the early disciples (Acts 4:29,31; 6:2; 8:14; 13:5; 17:13). Its impact in some ways represents the growth of the Church (Acts 6:7; 13:49). *Logos* is the word of salvation (Acts 13:26) and grace (Acts 14:3; cf. 20:32). "Good news" went out to the Gentiles as the "word of God" (Acts 15:7).

Paul joined with Luke and others in describing the "word of God" as Christian proclamation (1 Corinthians 14:36; 2 Corinthians 2:17; 4:2; Titus 1:3); a proclamation of reconciliation (2 Corinthians 5:19; Philippians 1:14; Colossians 1:25). It is furthermore the "word of Christ" (Colossians 3:16) that continues to guide and interest believers (cf. 2 Timothy 2:9,15). Paul knew this "word" is truth (Ephesians 1:13; Colossians 1:5; 2 Timothy 2:15) and life (Philippians 2:16).

The close relationship between Jesus and the Word outside of Johannine literature is noted by J.N. Sanders. He directs our attention to the verb *kērussō* (2756), "to preach," which can take as its object "the word" (Romans 10:8; 2 Timothy 4:2), "the gospel" (Galatians 2:2; Colossians 1:23; 1 Thessalonians 2:9), "Jesus" (2 Corinthians 11:4), "Christ" (1 Corinthians 1:23; 15:12), and "Jesus Christ" (2 Corinthians 1:9) ("The Word," *Interpreter's Dictionary of the Bible*, 4:871). Jesus was "powerful in deed and word" was the estimate of the Emmaus disciples. Paul echoed that Christ is the "power" of God (1 Corinthians 1:24).

Readers of the New Testament particularly associate the identification of Jesus as the Word with John's Gospel (1:1-18). Note how carefully John described the eternal existence of the Word in John 1:1-3. Two other Johannine texts that merit attention in this regard are 1 John 1:1 and Revelation 19:13.

John 1:1-14 portrays Jesus as the Word—God made flesh. The basis for John's understanding was the word of the Old Testament, although he could resonate with Hellenistic philosophical ideas. But John knew first and foremost the creative Word of the Old Testament who gives and sustains life. He has come in the flesh as God's ultimate Word/Act (cf. Hebrews 1:1,2). The Word is not merely personified; He is a human being, fully God and fully man. Jesus is also the Word of life which has been heard, seen with eyes, and touched with hands (1 John 1:1). He is the bearer of eternal life who invites believers to fellowship with the Father.

"The Word of God" mounts upon the white horse of Revelation 19:11 (see verse 13). He is none other than Jesus Christ (in Revelation 1:13-16 the description of the "one like unto the Son of man" is very similar; this figure is clearly Christ). He is "Faithful and True" (19:11); He is "KING OF KINGS AND LORD OF LORDS" (19:16).

Thus in the New Testament two ideas converge. One, Jesus, the Eternal Word, has become God incarnate. As the Word He does and says what His Father says. He is the Old Testament realization of the prophetic words of God through the prophets. He is the creative Word who creates new life in the believer. His power sustains, and His word saves.

Second, the Word with which believers are entrusted is none other than the same message of salvation as was entrusted to the early disciples. The Word is the announcement of God's final speaking to us through His Son (Hebrews 1:1ff.). True believers are responsible to proclaim His Word—the message of Jesus—to all people.

STRONG 3056, BAUER 477-79, MOULTON-MILLIGAN 379, KITTEL 4:69-136, LIDDELL-SCOTT 1057-59, COLIN BROWN 3:1081-87,1106,1108-10,1112, 1119-23.

3031. λόγχη lonchē noun
A spear, spearhead.

חֶרֶב cherev (2820), Sword (Jb 41:26 [41:17]).
מְחִי mᵉchî (4374), Blow (Ez 26:9 [26:8]).
רַב rav (7522), Archer (Jb 16:13 [16:14]).
רֹמַח rōmach (7709), Spear (Neh 4:13,16,21, Ez 39:9).

1. λόγχῃ lonchē dat sing fem
2. λόγχην lonchēn acc sing fem

1 one of the soldiers **with a spear** pierced his side,.... John 19:34

Appearing from Pindar (ca. Fifth Century B.C.) on, *lonchē* refers to a spear or lance; originally to the iron head or point of the spear (1 Samuel 17:7). In the New Testament this term appears only in John 19:34 (the Lord was pierced in the side with a lance, a long slender spear) and in the disputed text of Matthew 27:49.

STRONG 3057, BAUER 479, MOULTON-MILLIGAN 380, LIDDELL-SCOTT 1059.

3032. λοιδορέω loidoreō verb
To abuse, revile, reproach, rail at.
COGNATES:
  ἀντιλοιδορέω antiloidoreō (483)
  λοιδορία loidoria (3033)
  λοίδορος loidoros (3034)
SYNONYMS:
  βλασφημέω blasphēmeō (980)
  κακολογέω kakologeō (2522)
  καταλαλέω katalaleō (2605)
  ὀνειδίζω oneidizō (3542)
  ὑβρίζω hubrizō (5036)

גָּעַר gāʻar (1647), Rebuke (Jer 29:27 [36:27]—Codex Sinaiticus only).
רִיב rîv (7662), Quarrel, contend (Ex 17:2, Nm 20:3, Dt 33:8).

1. λοιδορεῖς loidoreis 2sing indic pres act
2. ἐλοιδόρησαν eloidorēsan 3pl indic aor act
3. λοιδορούμενος loidoroumenos
    nom sing masc part pres mid
4. λοιδορούμενοι loidoroumenoi
    nom pl masc part pres mid

2 Then they **reviled** him, and said,................ John 9:28
1 **Revilest** thou God's high priest?................ Acts 23:4

4 **being reviled**, we bless; .... 1 Co 4:12
3 Who, when he **was reviled**, reviled not again; .... 1 Pt 2:23

Loidoreō is a strong verb meaning "to rebuke harshly, to revile sharply." Appearing from Pindar (ca. Fifth Century B.C.) on, it occurs several times in the Septuagint (e.g., Genesis 49:23). This verb is used four times in the New Testament. The blind man was reviled by his inquisitors (John 9:28), and Paul was accused of being abusive to the high priest (Acts 23:4). In 1 Corinthians 4:12 Paul used this term as a contrast to "bless." Peter wrote that Christ did not respond to reviling (*loidoreō*) by reviling in return (*antiloidoreō* [483], 1 Peter 2:23).

STRONG 3058, BAUER 479, MOULTON-MILLIGAN 380, KITTEL 4:293-94, LIDDELL-SCOTT 1060, COLIN BROWN 3:346-47.

3033. λοιδορία loidoria noun
Railing, reviling, slander.
COGNATE:
λοιδορέω loidoreō (3032)
SYNONYM:
βλασφημία blasphēmia (981)
דִּבָּה dibbāh (1730), Slander (Prv 10:18).
מְרִיבָה merîvāh (4971), Meribah (Nm 20:24).
רִיב rîv (7663), Quarrel, strife (Ex 17:7, Prv 20:3).

1. **λοιδορίας** loidorias gen sing fem
2. **λοιδορίαν** loidorian acc sing fem

1 occasion to the adversary to **speak reproachfully**..... 1 Tm 5:14
2 Not rendering evil for evil, or **railing for railing**: .... 1 Pt 3:9
1 Not rendering evil for evil, or **railing for railing**: 3:9

Loidoria is a noun form of the verb *loidoreō*, "to revile, reproach, heap abuse on" (cf. also *loidoros* [3034], "a railer, reviler"). This noun, which first appears in Aristophanes (ca. Fifth Century B.C.), is found several times in the Septuagint (e.g., Exodus 17:7). It appears only twice in the New Testament: of the opportunities for an enemy "to speak reproachfully" against younger Christian women because of their misbehavior (1 Timothy 5:14) and of the Christian who should not reciprocate "railing for railing" (1 Peter 3:9, note also the similar usage of the verb *loidoreō* in 2:23).

STRONG 3059, BAUER 479, MOULTON-MILLIGAN 380, KITTEL 4:293-94, LIDDELL-SCOTT 1060, COLIN BROWN 3:346.

3034. λοίδορος loidoros noun
An abusive person, reviler, slanderer.

CROSS-REFERENCE:
λοιδορέω loidoreō (3032)
מָדוֹן mādhôn (4209II) Contention, quarrel (Prv 25:24, 26:21, 27:15).

1. **λοίδορος** loidoros nom sing masc
2. **λοίδοροι** loidoroi nom pl masc

1 a fornicator, or covetous, or an idolater, or a **railer**, 1 Co 5:11
2 nor drunkards, nor **revilers**, nor extortioners, ... 6:10

The noun *loidoros*, first appearing in Euripides (ca. Fifth Century B.C.), is the noun form of the verb *loidoreō* (3032) and means "a reviler, an abusive person, one who gives verbal reproach." The term appears twice in the New Testament, both times in 1 Corinthians (5:11; 6:10). Paul included it in a list with such types of persons as covetous, drunkards, and extortioners.

STRONG 3060, BAUER 479, MOULTON-MILLIGAN 380, KITTEL 4:293-94, LIDDELL-SCOTT 1060, COLIN BROWN 3:346-47.

3035. λοιμός loimos noun
Plague, pestilence, pest.

1. **λοιμόν** loimon acc sing masc
2. **λοιμοί** loimoi nom pl masc

2 and there shall be famines, and **pestilences**, ... Matt 24:7
2 great earthquakes ... and famines, and **pestilences**; .. Luke 21:11
1 For we have found this man a **pestilent** fellow, ... Acts 24:5

Classical Greek
Throughout the classical period *loimos* was used in two ways. Literally it designated "plagues" and was used in association with war, hunger, and famine. This literal use was dominant. Occasionally, however, it was used figuratively of people who are "pests."

New Testament Usage
Of the three occurrences in the New Testament, two employ the term literally, when Jesus listed plagues among the signs of the last days (Matthew 24:7; Luke 21:11). In Acts 24:5 the orator Tertullus, when speaking to Felix, applied the term to Paul identifying him as a restless, evil troublemaker, a plague on society.

STRONG 3061, BAUER 479, MOULTON-MILLIGAN 380, LIDDELL-SCOTT 1060.

3036. λοιπός loipos adj
Remaining, over, from now, rest, other.
COGNATE:
λείπω leipō (2981)
SYNONYMS:
κατάλοιπος kataloipos (2615)
τέλος telos (4904)

יָתַר yāthar (3613), Qal: the rest (1 Sm 15:15); niphal: remainder, rest (Lv 2:3, Jos 17:2, Ez 34:18).

יֶתֶר yether (3615), The rest (1 Kgs 15:7, 2 Kgs 15:26, 2 Chr 28:26).

כֹּל kōl (3725), All (1 Sm 8:5).

פֵּאָה pē'āh (6523), Corner (Lv 23:22).

שָׁאַר shā'ar (8080), Niphal: be left (Zec 11:9).

שְׁאָר sheʾār (8081), Rest, other (Ezr 4:7, Est 9:16).

שְׁאֵרִית sheʾērîth (8086), Rest (Ez 36:5).

1. λοιπῶν loipōn gen pl masc/fem/neu
2. λοιποῖς loipois dat pl masc/neu
3. λοιποί loipoi nom pl masc
4. λοιπούς loipous acc pl masc
5. λοιπαί loipai nom pl fem
6. λοιπάς loipas acc pl fem
7. λοιποῦ loipou gen sing neu
8. λοιπόν loipon nom/acc sing neu
9. λοιπά loipa nom/acc pl neu

3	And the **remnant** took his servants,	Matt 22:6
5	Afterward came also the **other** virgins,	25:11
8	Sleep on **now**, and take your rest:	26:45
3	The **rest** said, Let be, let us see whether Elias will	27:49
9	and the lusts of **other** things entering in,	Mark 4:19
8	Sleep on **now**, and take your rest: it is enough,	14:41
2	And they went and told it unto the **residue**:	16:13
2	but to **others** in parables;	Luke 8:10
1	why take ye thought for the **rest**?	12:26
4	that they were righteous, and despised **others**:	18:9
3	God, I thank thee, that I am not as **other** men are,	18:11
2	these things unto the eleven, and to all the **rest**.	24:9
5	and **other** women that were with them,	24:10
4	and said unto Peter and to the **rest** of the apostles,	Acts 2:37
1	And of the **rest** durst no man join himself to them:	5:13
1	of Jason, and of the **other**, they let them go.	17:9
8	hope that we should be saved was **then** taken	27:20
4	And the **rest**, some on boards,	27:44
3	**others** also, which had diseases in the island,	28:9
2	fruit among you ... even as among **other** Gentiles.	Rom 1:13
3	election hath obtained it, and the **rest** were blinded:	11:7
8	besides, I know not whether I baptized any **other**.	1 Co 1:16
8	Moreover it is required in stewards,	4:2
2	But to the **rest** speak I, not the Lord:	7:12
8	it **remaineth**, that both they that have wives	7:29
3	lead about a sister, a wife, as well as **other** apostles,	9:5
9	And the **rest** will I set in order when I come.	11:34
1	it may chance of wheat, or of **some other** grain:	15:37
6	is it wherein ye were inferior to **other** churches,	2 Co 12:13
2	to all **other**, that, if I come again, I will not spare:	13:2
8	**Finally**, brethren, farewell. Be perfect,	13:11
3	And the **other** Jews dissembled likewise with him;	Gal 2:13
7	From **henceforth** let no man trouble me:	6:17
3	by nature the children of wrath, even as **others**.	Eph 2:3
9	that ye henceforth walk not as **other** Gentiles walk,	4:17
8	**Finally**, my brethren, be strong in the Lord,	6:10
2	manifest in all the palace, and in all **other** places;	Phlp 1:13
8	**Finally**, my brethren, rejoice in the Lord.	3:1
1	Clement also, and with **other** my fellowlabourers,	4:3
8	**Finally**, brethren, whatsoever things are true,	4:8
8	**Furthermore** then we beseech you, brethren,	1 Th 4:1
3	ye sorrow not, even as **others** which have no hope.	4:13
3	Therefore let us not sleep, as do **others**;	5:6
8	**Finally**, brethren, pray for us,	2 Th 3:1
1	rebuke before all, that **others** also may fear.	1 Tm 5:20
8	**Henceforth** there is laid up for me a crown	2 Tm 4:8
8	From **henceforth** expecting till his enemies	Heb 10:13
6	as they do also the **other** scriptures,	2 Pt 3:16
2	But unto you I say, and unto the **rest** in Thyatira,	Rev 2:24
9	watchful, and strengthen the things which **remain**,	Rev 3:2
1	**other** voices of the trumpet of the three angels,	8:13
3	And the **rest** of the men which were not killed	9:20
3	and the **remnant** were affrighted,	11:13
1	went to make war with the **remnant** of her seed,	12:17
3	And the **remnant** were slain with the sword	19:21
3	But the **rest** of the dead lived not again until	20:5

Classical Greek
Loipos first appears in classical Greek in Pindar (ca. 518 B.C.). It is employed as an adjective meaning either "remaining" or "other." When used as a pronoun it means "others." Sometimes it functions as a noun and is translated "the rest." On occasion the noun refers to an individual's "descendants" (cf. *Liddell-Scott*).

Septuagint Usage
In the Septuagint *loipos* is used primarily to translate forms of *yāthar*. For example, "the rest of the acts of" (1 Kings 11:41 [LXX 3 Kings 11:41]; 2 Kings 15:6 [LXX 4 Kings 15:6]); "what remains of the flesh" (Exodus 29:34). In most of its other appearances it translates *shā'ar* and refers to a "remnant" of something: of Jews (Jeremiah 43:5), of nations (Ezekiel 36:5), of a piece of wood for carving an idol (Isaiah 44:17).

New Testament Usage
The term is used in the Gospels, Acts, the Epistles, and Revelation in the same manner as in the Septuagint and the classical writers. In several passages it functions as a pronoun meaning "others" (Luke 8:10). Most frequently it is employed as a noun and is translated by the KJV as "the remnant" (Matthew 22:6), "the residue" (Mark 16:13), "the rest" (1 Corinthians 7:12), or "the other" (2 Peter 3:16). Once it is translated "things which remain" (Revelation 3:2).

STRONG 3062, BAUER 479-80, MOULTON-MILLIGAN 380, LIDDELL-SCOTT 1060, COLIN BROWN 3:247-48, 251-53.

3037. Λουκᾶς Loukas name
Luke.

1. Λουκᾶς Loukas nom masc
2. Λουκᾶν Loukan acc masc
3. Λουκᾶ Louka gen masc

1	**Luke**, the beloved physician, and Demas,	Col 4:14
1	Only **Luke** is with me.	2 Tm 4:11
1	Aristarchus, Demas, **Lucas**, my fellowlabourers.	Phlm 1:24

The beloved physician and companion of Paul (Colossians 4:14); he wrote the third Gospel and the Book of Acts.

3038. Λούκιος Loukios name
Lucius.

1. Λούκιος Loukios nom masc

1 and **Lucius** of Cyrene, and Manaen,	Acts 13:1
1 Timotheus my workfellow, and **Lucius**, and Jason,	Rom 16:21

Christian teacher or prophet at Antioch (Acts 13:1); he sent a greeting to the Christians in Rome (Romans 16:21).

3039. λουτρόν loutron noun
Bath, washing, cleansing.

COGNATE:
  λούω louō (3040)

SYNONYM:
  βαπτισμός baptismos (903)

רַחְצָה rachtsāh (7650), Washing (S/S 4:2, 6:6 [6:5]).

1. λουτροῦ loutrou gen sing neu
2. λουτρῷ loutrō dat sing neu

2 cleanse it with the **washing** of water by the word,	Eph 5:26
1 by the **washing** of regeneration,	Tit 3:5

Classical Greek
In Homer the word appears as *loetron* and in Doric Greek as *lōtron*. Later it became *lutron* and basically refers to "a full bath" in contrast to other terms used for washing clothes or parts of the body. In the course of time it came to be used of the "bathhouse, the place of bathing," or "the water used for the bath." The term appears widely in the literature of the ancient world. Ritual bathing for cleansing from defilement picked up through death, sexual intercourse, menstruation, birth, miscarriages, sickness, insanity, etc. is found in Greece, Asia Minor, Syria, Egypt, and Palestine. In pagan religions it was seen as a magic ritual and often became a cheap means of moral cleansing. In paganism, however, it was never associated with any kind of a conversion experience.

Septuagint Usage
Loutron is found only twice in the Septuagint: once in the Song of Solomon (4:2) in a comparison of teeth with that of a sheep fresh from washing; once in Sirach (34:25) where ritual cleansing after defilement from contact with a dead person is allegorized as a reference to purification by fasting.

In Judaism the pagan tendency toward permissive moral cleansing was offset by the insistent message of the prophets which demanded that true repentance and conversion must accompany ritual and ceremonial washings (Jeremiah 2:22). This emphasis on the necessity of inner cleansing also plays a large part in Philo's works (cf. *Bauer*).

New Testament Usage
Loutron appears only twice in the New Testament. In Ephesians 5:26 it is used symbolically of Christ's provision of salvation for the Church. Paul spoke of "the *washing* of water by the word."

In Titus 3:5 Paul contrasted the righteous works of men with the saving mercy of God which is effected by the Holy Spirit's "*washing* of regeneration" (*palingenesia* [3686]) and "renewal" (*anakainōsis* [340]).

STRONG 3067, BAUER 480, MOULTON-MILLIGAN 381, KITTEL 4:295-307, LIDDELL-SCOTT 1061, COLIN BROWN 1:150-53.

3040. λούω louō verb
Wash, bathe.

COGNATES:
  ἀπολούω apolouō (622)
  λουτρόν loutron (3039)

SYNONYMS:
  ἀπολούω apolouō (622)
  ἀπονίπτω aponiptō (627)
  ἀποπλύνω apoplunō (631)
  βαπτίζω baptizō (901)
  νίπτω niptō (3400)
  πλύνω plunō (4010)

רָחַץ rāchats (7647), Qal: wash, bathe (Ex 40:12, Lv 15:11, 2 Kgs 5:10); pual: be washed (Ez 16:4).

שָׁחָה shāchâh (8246), Hiphil: drench (Ps 6:6).

1. ἔλουσεν elousen 3sing indic aor act
2. λούσαντι lousanti dat sing masc part aor act
3. λούσαντες lousantes nom pl masc part aor act
4. λουσαμένη lousamenē nom sing fem part aor mid
5. λελουμένος leloumenos nom sing masc part perf mid
6. λελουμένοι leloumenoi nom pl masc part perf mid
7. λελουσμένοι lelousmenoi nom pl masc part perf mid

5 He that is **washed** needeth not save to wash his feet,	John 13:10
3 whom when they had **washed**,	Acts 9:37
1 and **washed** their stripes;	16:33
6 and our bodies **washed** with pure water.	Heb 10:22
4 sow that was **washed** to her wallowing in the mire.	2 Pt 2:22
2 and **washed** us from our sins in his own blood,	Rev 1:5

Classical Greek and Septuagint Usage
Louō means "to bathe an entire body" as distinguished from washing a part of the body (*niptō* [3400]) or from washing inanimate objects such as clothes (*plunō* [4010]). In classical Greek the word is used both for routine bathing and for ritual purification. Both of these

uses are also found in the Septuagint where *louō* frequently translates *rāchats*. It is especially common in the requirements for ceremonial bathing under the Mosaic law (e.g., Leviticus 14–16).

New Testament Usage
In the New Testament the word is used both literally and figuratively. Three times it refers to normal physical cleansing: Acts 9:37; 16:33; 2 Peter 2:22. Twice it refers to a ceremonial bath. In John 13:10 the Lord Jesus referred to the customary ritual bath which preceded the Passover meal. Since all had bathed (*louō*), they needed only to have their feet washed (*niptō*). Hebrews 10:22 refers to the baptism ritual as a washing of the body which represents by an outward act the cleansing that has taken place internally as a result of Christ's blood. Finally, in Revelation 1:5 *louō* is used completely figuratively referring to the complete cleansing of the sinner by the blood of Christ.

STRONG 3068, BAUER 480-81, MOULTON-MILLIGAN 381, KITTEL 4:295-307, LIDDELL-SCOTT 1061-62, COLIN BROWN 1:150-54.

3041. Λύδδα Ludda name
Lydda.

1. Λύδδης Luddēs gen fem
2. Λύδδαν Luddan acc fem
3. Λύδδας Luddas gen fem
4. Λύδδα Ludda acc fem

2 came down also to the saints which dwelt at **Lydda**...Acts 9:32
2 And all that dwelt at **Lydda** and Saron saw him,........ 9:35
1 And forasmuch as **Lydda** was nigh to Joppa,............ 9:38

City southeast of Joppa where Peter healed Aeneas of paralysis (Acts 9:32ff.).

3042. Λυδία Ludia name
Lydia.

1. Λυδία Ludia nom fem
2. Λυδίαν Ludian acc fem

1 a certain woman named **Lydia**, a seller of purple,...Acts 16:14
2 and entered into the house of **Lydia**:................. 16:40

A woman from Thyatira who sold purple fabrics, she was Paul's first convert in Macedonia (Acts 16:14).

3043. Λυκαονία Lukaonia name
Lycaonia.

1. Λυκαονίας Lukaonias gen fem

1 and fled unto Lystra and Derbe, cities of **Lycaonia**, Acts 14:6

Province in Asia Minor visited by Paul on his first missionary journey (Acts 14:6).

3044. Λυκαονιστί
Lukaonisti name-adv
Lycaonian.

1. Λυκαονιστί Lukaonisti

1 saying in the speech of **Lycaonia**,................Acts 14:11

Belonging to Lycaonia; used of their language (Acts 14:11).

3045. Λυκία Lukia name
Lycia.

1. Λυκίας Lukias gen fem

1 had sailed ... we came to Myra, a city of **Lycia**......Acts 27:5

District on the southern coast of Asia Minor visited by Paul on his journey to Rome (Acts 27:5).

3046. λύκος lukos noun
Wolf.

דֹּב dōv (1726), Bear (Prv 28:15).

זְאֵב zeʾēv (2146), Wolf (Gn 49:27, Is 11:6, Hb 1:8).

1. λύκος lukos nom sing masc
2. λύκον lukon acc sing masc
3. λύκοι lukoi nom pl masc
4. λύκων lukōn gen pl masc

3 but inwardly they are ravening **wolves**...............Matt 7:15
4 I send you forth as sheep in the midst of **wolves**:...... 10:16
4 behold, I send you forth as lambs among **wolves**....Luke 10:3
2 seeth the **wolf** coming, and leaveth the sheep,.....John 10:12
1 the **wolf** catcheth them, and scattereth the sheep:...... 10:12
3 shall grievous **wolves** enter in among you,..........Acts 20:29

Classical Greek
Lukos denotes a "wolf," the large, violent member of the canine family. For the most part, ancient Greeks used the term literally. But a popular idiom, "to see a wolf," meant to be (so terrified as to be) unable to speak (cf. *Liddell-Scott*). The compound *lukotharsēs* means "bold as a wolf." The verb *lukoō* means "to tear, rip" like a wolf. The strength, voracity, and predatory nature of this animal were well-known (ibid.).

Septuagint Usage
In the Septuagint the corresponding Hebrew for *lukos* is normally (six times out of seven)

zeʾēv, "wolf" (*canis lupus, canis pallipes*). Of these the figurative use dominates (e.g., Genesis 49:27; Habakkuk 1:8; Zephaniah 3:3). The relationship or contrast between the villainous, predatory wolf and the passive, harmless lamb provides a sharp image of the evil men who prey on the poor and oppressed (Ezekiel 22:27). Later, the peace of the messianic kingdom is exemplified in a new relationship between these natural enemies (Isaiah 11:6; 65:25; cf. Sirach 13:17).

New Testament Usage
Of its six instances in the New Testament the image of wolves as wicked opponents of God's flock (i.e., sheep, Matthew 7:15; 10:16 with parallels; Acts 20:29) is seen.

A literal use occurs in John 10:12, but again the overall metaphoric tone of the passage as a whole echoes the image of the wolf as an evil force that can scatter "the sheep." The emphasis in the text, however, is that Jesus is the Good Shepherd who, unlike a hired shepherd, lays down His life to prevent such a catastrophe (John 10:11). Jesus used the wolf to symbolize the enmity His disciples would encounter in the world. Jesus told His disciples He was sending them as sheep or lambs "in the midst of *wolves*" (Matthew 10:16; cf. Luke 10:3). Therefore, in the midst of such men all disciples of Jesus must be "wise as serpents, and harmless as doves" (Matthew 10:16; cf. Luke 10:3).

Jesus called the false prophets who were to come "wolves." They may be disguised in "sheep's clothing" in order to infiltrate Christ's flock, but "inwardly they are ravening *wolves*" (Matthew 7:15). The flock of sheep (body of Christ) is especially in danger if one such "wolf" among them acts as a teacher or spiritual guide. Paul used this same picture in his address to the Ephesian elders: "For I know this, that after my departing shall grievous *wolves* enter in among you, not sparing the flock. Also of your own selves shall men arise, speaking perverse things, to draw away disciples after them" (Acts 20:29,30).

STRONG 3074, BAUER 481, MOULTON-MILLIGAN 381, KITTEL 4:308-11, LIDDELL-SCOTT 1064-65, COLIN BROWN 1:118.

3047. λυμαίνομαι lumainomai verb
Destroy, ravage.

בָּקַק bāqaq (1265), Polel: devastate (Jer 51:2 [28:2]).
כִּרְסֵם kirsēm (3894), Piel: ravage (Ps 80:13 [79:13]).
סָלַף sālaph (5751), Piel: subvert, ruin (Ex 23:8, Prv 19:3 [18:22]).
רָצַץ rātsats (7827), Cut off; piel: oppress (2 Chr 16:10).
שָׁחַת shāchath (8271), Piel: waste, ruin (Prv 23:8, Jer 48:18 [31:18]); hiphil: destroy (Prv 18:9, Is 65:25); hophal: be polluted (Prv 25:26).
תָּעַב tāʿav (8911), Piel: abhor (Ez 16:25).

1. ἐλυμαίνετο elumaineto 3sing indic imperf mid
1 As for Saul, he **made havock** of the church,......... Acts 8:3

Classical Greek
The word *lumainomai* suggests a pattern of wanton, wasteful destruction. It is related to the classical word *lumē* which means "an outrage." The verb is used in classical Greek for "injury," whether to a physical body through gluttony or to a nation through the devastation of warfare. It describes both physical and moral damage.

Septuagint Usage
The word occurs often in the Septuagint. It depicts merciless slaughter (Amos 1:11), the ravages of warfare (Jeremiah 28:2; 31:18 [LXX 48:18]), the wasting of a hedge by wild boars (Psalm 80:13 [LXX 79:13]), the pollution of a spring (Proverbs 25:26), the corruption of morals through bribery (Exodus 23:8), and the marring of beauty through immorality (Ezekiel 16:25). The result is always harmful destruction.

New Testament Usage
The tense of the verb in Acts 8:3, the only New Testament occurrence of *lumainomai* (*elumaineto*, imperfect), pictures Saul's repeated attempts to ravage and make "havoc" of the churches through fierce, savage persecution.

STRONG 3075, BAUER 481 (see "lumainō"), MOULTON-MILLIGAN 381-82, KITTEL 4:312, LIDDELL-SCOTT 1065.

3048. λυπέω lupeō verb
Grieve, distress, sorrow, pain (someone), mourn, be sorrowful, sad.

COGNATES:
ἄλυπος alupos (251)
λύπη lupē (3049)
περίλυπος perilupos (3899)
συλλυπέω sullupeō (4669)

SYNONYMS:
ὀδυνάομαι odunaomai (3463)
πενθέω pentheō (3858)

אָבֵל ʾāvēl (58), Mourning (Est 6:12).

λύπη 3049

בְּאֵשׁ beʾēsh (A921), Be distressed (Dn 6:14—Aramaic).

דַּוָּי dawwāy (1794), Faint (Lam 1:22).

חָרָה chārâh (2835), Be angry (Jon 4:4,9).

כְּאֵב keʾēv (3629), Pain (Jer 15:18).

לָאָה lāʾâh (3942), Be tired; hiphil: make weary (Mi 6:3).

עָצַב ʿātsav (6321), Niphal: be grieved (Gn 45:5, 2 Sm 19:2).

קָצַף qātsaph (7395), Qal: be angry (1 Sm 29:4, Est 2:21, Is 57:17); hithpael: be enraged (Is 8:21).

רָגַז rāghaz (7553), Be troubled, be enraged (Is 32:11, Ez 16:43).

רוּד rûdh (7586), Hiphil: be restless (Ps 55:2 [54:2]).

רַע raʿ (7737I), Heavy (Prv 25:20).

רָעַע rāʿaʿ (7778), Be evil; hiphil: be displeased (Jon 4:1).

1. λυπῶ lupō 1sing indic pres act
2. λυπεῖτε lupeite 2pl impr pres act
3. ἐλύπησα elupēsa 1sing indic aor act
4. ἐλύπησεν elupēsen 3sing indic aor act
5. λελύπηκεν lelupēken 3sing indic perf act
6. λυπεῖται lupeitai 3sing indic pres mid
7. λυπῆσθε lupēsthe 2pl subj pres mid
8. λυπούμενος lupoumenos
   nom sing masc part pres mid
9. λυπούμενοι lupoumenoi
   nom pl masc part pres mid
10. λυπεῖσθαι lupeisthai inf pres mid
11. ἐλυπήθη elupēthē 3sing indic aor pass
12. ἐλυπήθητε elupēthēte 2pl indic aor pass
13. ἐλυπήθησαν elupēthēsan 3pl indic aor pass
14. λυπηθῆτε lupēthēte 2pl subj aor pass
15. λυπηθέντες lupēthentes nom pl masc part aor pass
16. λυπηθῆναι lupēthēnai inf aor pass
17. λυπηθήσεσθε lupēthēsesthe 2pl indic fut pass
18. λυπηθείς lupētheis nom sing masc part aor pass

11	And the king was sorry:	Matt 14:9
13	And they were exceeding sorry.	17:23
13	they were very sorry, and came and told ... lord all	18:31
8	went away sorrowful: for he had great possessions.	19:22
9	And they were exceeding sorrowful,	26:22
10	and began to be sorrowful and very heavy.	26:37
8	went away grieved: for he had great possessions.	Mark 10:22
10	they began to be sorrowful, and to say unto him	14:19
17	the world shall rejoice: and ye shall be sorrowful,	John 16:20
11	Peter was grieved because he said unto him	21:17
6	But if thy brother be grieved with thy meat,	Rom 14:15
1	For if I make you sorry,	2 Co 2:2
8	but the same which is made sorry by me?	2:2
14	not that ye should be grieved,	2:4
5	if any have caused sorrow,	2:5
5	if any have caused grief, he hath not grieved me,	2:5
9	As sorrowful, yet alway rejoicing;	6:10
3	For though I made you sorry with a letter,	7:8
4	that the same epistle hath made you sorry,	7:8
12	Now I rejoice, not that ye were made sorry,	7:9
12	but that ye sorrowed to repentance:	7:9
12	for ye were made sorry after a godly manner,	7:11
16	that ye sorrowed after a godly sort,	7:11
2	And grieve not the holy Spirit of God,	Eph 4:30
7	ye sorrow not, even as others which have no hope.	1 Th 4:13
15	ye are in heaviness through manifold temptations:	1 Pt 1:6

Classical Greek and Septuagint Usage

Lupeō is a general term for "sorrow," encompassing various expressions of grief (cf. *thrēneō* [2331], "to lament"; *koptō* [2847], "to smite the breast in grief"; *pentheō* [3858], "to mourn passionately"). It may refer to outward mourning or simply to sad feelings. It is commonly used to designate heaviness of heart.

In the papyri its use ranges from grief over the loss of a loved one to sadness over the loss of a cloak (*Moulton-Milligan*). It is also used of the general troubles of a steward (ibid.). The Septuagint reflects the same general usage, ranging from mourning over death (2 Samuel 19:2 [LXX 2 Kings 19:2]) to a feeling of reluctance to give to the poor (Deuteronomy 15:10).

New Testament Usage

In the New Testament *lupeō* is used in all its variations. It denotes deep sorrow, for example, in the Lord's praying in Gethsemane (Matthew 26:37), the disciples' reaction to His death (Matthew 17:23; John 16:20), and Herod's response to the demand for John the Baptist's head (Matthew 14:9). It denotes sorrow over sin, both by the Holy Spirit (Ephesians 4:30) and by the true penitent (2 Corinthians 7:11). But the rich young ruler sorrowed instead of repenting (Matthew 19:22). While it is the opposite of joy or rejoicing (*chairō* [5299], 2 Corinthians 6:10), it is possible to experience joy along with sorrow because of the hope ahead (1 Peter 1:6). Less intensely, *lupeō* refers to the hurt feelings brothers may experience over disagreements or disappointments (Romans 14:15; 2 Corinthians 2:2,4,5).

STRONG 3076, BAUER 481, MOULTON-MILLIGAN 382, KITTEL 4:313-22, LIDDELL-SCOTT 1065-66, COLIN BROWN 2:419-20.

3049. λύπη lupē noun

Sadness, grief, pain (of mind or body), sorrow, affliction.

COGNATE:
λυπέω lupeō (3048)

SYNONYMS:
ὀδύνη odunē (3464)
πένθος penthos (3859)

דַּוָּי dawwāy (1794), Sick (Is 1:5).

יָגוֹן yāghôn (3123), Sorrow (Gn 42:38, Is 35:10, 51:11).

מַעֲצֵבָה maʿătsēvâh (4782), Torment (Is 50:11).

עֶצֶב 'etsev (6325), Pain, sorrow (Gn 3:16, Prv 10:22).

עִצָּבוֹן 'itstsāvôn (6328), Pain, toil (Gn 3:16f., 5:29).

עַצֶּבֶת 'atstseveth (6329), Trouble, sorrow (Prv 10:10, 15:13).

רָעָה rā'āh (7750), Sorrow (Gn 44:29).

תּוּגָה tûghāh (8755), Grief (Prv 10:1).

1. λύπη **lupē** nom sing fem
2. λύπης **lupēs** gen sing fem
3. λύπῃ **lupē** dat sing fem
4. λύπην **lupēn** acc sing fem
5. λύπας **lupas** acc pl fem

```
2 he found them sleeping for sorrow,............Luke 22:45
1 sorrow hath filled your heart....................John 16:6
1 but your sorrow shall be turned into joy..............16:20
4 A woman when she is in travail hath sorrow,..........16:21
4 And ye now therefore have sorrow:....................16:22
1 great heaviness and continual sorrow in my heart....Rom 9:2
3 that I would not come again to you in heaviness.....2 Co 2:1
4 sorrow from them of whom I ought to rejoice;..........2:3
3 should be swallowed up with overmuch sorrow...........2:7
1 For godly sorrow worketh repentance to salvation......7:10
1 but the sorrow of the world worketh death.............7:10
2 so let him give; not grudgingly, or of necessity:.....9:7
4 lest I should have sorrow upon sorrow..............Php 2:27
3 lest I should have sorrow upon sorrow................2:27
2 for the present seemeth to be joyous, but grievous: Heb 12:11
5 if a man for conscience toward God endure grief,... 1 Pt 2:19
```

Classical Greek

Lupē, a noun appearing from Aeschylus (ca. Fifth Century B.C.) on, is used both of the pain of body and pain of mind, though more often it means the subjective feelings of sorrow, vexation, and grief. Objectively, it may denote an annoyance or affliction. The verb form of *lupē* is *lupeō* (3048), "to give pain, to make sorrowful."

Septuagint Usage

In the Septuagint *lupē* translates several different Hebrew words that refer to the pain of childbirth (Genesis 3:16) and the painful toil of physical labor (Genesis 5:29). At other times it describes the sorrow of bereavement (Genesis 42:38), the grief of a mother caused by the foolishness of her son (Proverbs 10:1), the pain of poverty (Proverbs 31:6,7 [Hebrew: "bitter of soul"]), and spiritual anguish due to sin (Isaiah 1:5).

New Testament Usage

Lupē appears 16 times in the New Testament. Its usage falls into several categories. It is used of pain in childbirth (John 16:21) and the sorrow of bereavement (John 16:6). It also refers to the personal mental distress Paul felt in view of the continual unbelief of his people Israel (Romans 9:2, here used with the synonym *odunē* [3464], "sorrow, pain"). Elsewhere it refers to the pain of heart one may have over the actions and attitudes of personal friends (2 Corinthians 2:1,3) and the grief caused by persecution (1 Peter 2:19).

Paul contrasted the godly sorrow or grief which leads to repentance with the sorrow of the world (2 Corinthians 7:10). Luke 22:45 states that in Gethsemane the disciples were "sleeping for *lupē*." One does not ordinarily think of grief causing sleepiness, but perhaps the idea is that the disciples were psychologically exhausted, "worn out by grief" (*NEB*). It had been a long night, and they had heard strange things in the upper room about betrayal and denial. They had a sense of foreboding. *Lupē* may carry the idea of grudging action. Paul exhorted the Corinthian believers to give cheerfully, not "grudgingly" ("out of *lupē*," 2 Corinthians 9:7).

STRONG 3077, BAUER 482, MOULTON-MILLIGAN 382, KITTEL 4:313-22, LIDDELL-SCOTT 1065-66, COLIN BROWN 2:419-21.

3050. Λυσανίας **Lusanias** name

Lysanias.

1. Λυσανίου **Lusaniou** gen masc

```
1 and Lysanias the tetrarch of Abilene,..............Luke 3:1
```

The tetrarch of Abilene at the beginning of the ministry of John the Baptist (Luke 3:1).

3051. Λυσίας **Lusias** name

Lysias.

1. Λυσίας **Lusias** nom masc

```
1 Claudius Lysias unto the most excellent governor...Acts 23:26
1 But the chief captain Lysias came upon us,............24:7
1 When Lysias the chief captain shall come down,.......24:22
```

Surname of Claudius (see 2777) the Roman official in Jerusalem at the time of Paul's arrest (Acts 23:26; 24:7,22).

3052. λύσις **lusis** noun

Release, deliverance, separation, divorce (in marriage).
CROSS-REFERENCE:
λύω luō (3061)

פֵּשֶׁר pēsher (6842), Interpretation (Eccl 8:1 [7:30]).

1. λύσιν **lusin** acc sing fem

```
1 Art thou bound unto a wife? seek not to be loosed. 1 Co 7:27
```

The term *lusis*, used from Homer on, is a noun form of the verb *luō* (3061), "to release, loosen, untie, ransom." The noun means "loosing" and is used, among other things, of deliverance from guilt (expiation), of release from financial obligation, of death (the soul's release from the body), of the unraveling of a plot (of a drama) or saying (interpretation, Ecclesiastes 8:1 [LXX 7:30]), and of divorce (a loosening of the marriage bond). Its one appearance in the New Testament has to do with the dissolution of marriage, i.e., divorce (1 Corinthians 7:27).

STRONG 3080, BAUER 482, MOULTON-MILLIGAN 382, LIDDELL-SCOTT 1066-67, COLIN BROWN 3:177,188.

3053. λυσιτελέω lusiteleō verb
To be advantageous, profitable, useful.
CROSS-REFERENCES:
λύω luō (3061)
τελέω teleō (4903)

1. λυσιτελεῖ lusitelei 3sing indic pres act

1 It were better for him that a millstone were hanged Luke 17:2

Lusiteleō appears from Herodotus (ca. Fifth Century B.C.) on. It can also be found in the apocryphal portion of the Septuagint. This verb is a compound of *luō* (3061), "to loosen" or "release," hence "to pay," and *telos* (4904), "dues, toll, taxes." It means "to pay what is due" or "to pay expenses incurred," hence "to be profitable, useful." In its single appearance in the New Testament it is used in the impersonal form, "it is better, it profits" (Luke 17:2). Jesus knew "stumbling blocks" were inevitable (Luke 17:1), but He sternly warned the disciples against being the cause of another person's sin. It would be "better" for a tempter to suffer drowning than to suffer the judgment that awaits anyone who offends "one of these little ones" (Luke 17:2).

STRONG 3081, BAUER 482, MOULTON-MILLIGAN 382, LIDDELL-SCOTT 1067.

3054. Λύστρα Lustra name
Lystra.

1. Λύστραν Lustran acc sing fem
2. Λύστροις Lustrois dat pl neu

1 and fled unto **Lystra** and Derbe, cities of Lycaonia, Acts 14:6
2 And there sat a certain man at **Lystra**, ... 14:8
1 they returned again to **Lystra**, and to Iconium, ... 14:21
1 Then came he to Derbe and **Lystra**: 16:1
2 by the brethren that were at **Lystra** and Iconium. 16:2
2 came unto me at Antioch, at Iconium, at **Lystra**; .... 2 Tm 3:11

City in the province of Lycaonia (see 3043) where Paul healed a lame man (Acts 14:8ff.) and met Timothy (Acts 16:1ff.).

3055. λύτρον lutron noun
A loosener, ransom, redemption price.
COGNATE:
λυτρόω lutroō (3056)
SYNONYM:
ἀντίλυτρον antilutron (484)

גָּאַל gā'al (1381), Redeem (Lv 27:31).
גְּאֻלָּה geʾullāh (1383), Redemption (Lv 25:24,51f.).
כֹּפֶר kōpher (3853), Ransom (Ex 21:30, Nm 35:31, Prv 13:8).
מְחִיר māhîr (4248), Price (Is 45:13).
פָּדָה pādhāh (6540), Qal: redeem (Nm 18:15); hophal: be redeemed (Lv 19:20).
פְּדוּיִם peḏhûyim (6543), Ransom (Nm 3:51).
פִּדְיוֹן pidhyōn (6548I), Redemption (Ex 21:30).

1. λύτρον lutron nom/acc sing neu

1 and to give his life **a ransom** for many............. Matt 20:28
1 to minister, and to give his life **a ransom** for many. Mark 10:45

Classical Greek
Lutron in secular Greek denotes the ransom price paid in order to free a slave or a prisoner of war. The word sometimes occurs in religious contexts. At times *lutron* has the sense of "recompense, compensation," the price paid in exchange for something bought or won.

Septuagint Usage
The Septuagint reads the singular "ransom" (*lutron*) only three times; in every other case it has the plural. Each form translates one of several Hebrew words for "redemption" or "ransom": *kōpher*, *pidhyōn*, *geʾullāh*, and others. The redemption price might be an offering (Exodus 13:13-15; 34:20) or a sum of money (Exodus 30:13-16; Numbers 3:46-51; 18:15f.). In the Septuagint *lutron* often implies a sense of value. It may speak of a ransom for someone's life (Exodus 21:30), the redemption price of a slave (Leviticus 19:20), the purchase price of a field (Leviticus 25:24), or the payment demanded for the release of prisoners of war (Isaiah 45:13).

New Testament Usage
Lutron occurs only twice in the New Testament (Matthew 20:28; parallel Mark 10:45). In both cases the interpretation is somewhat guided by the preposition *anti* (470), with the resultant meaning of "ransom *for, instead of.*" Here we see the vicarious nature of Christ's sacrifice

most clearly: He came "to give his life a *ransom for* many" (Mark 10:45).

See also the word study on *antilutron* (484), the compound of *anti* and *lutron* (1 Timothy 2:6).

STRONG 3083, BAUER 482, MOULTON-MILLIGAN 382-83, KITTEL 4:328-35,340-49, LIDDELL-SCOTT 1067, COLIN BROWN 3:189-92,194-97.

3056. λυτρόω lutroō verb
Redeem by paying a ransom, set free, rescue.
COGNATES:
  ἀντίλυτρον antilutron (484)
  ἀπολύτρωσις apolutrōsis (623)
  λύτρον lutron (3055)
  λύτρωσις lutrōsis (3057)
  λυτρωτής lutrōtēs (3058)
SYNONYMS:
  ἀπαλλάσσω apallassō (521)
  ἀπολύω apoluō (624)
  διασῴζω diasōzō (1289)
  ἐλευθερόω eleutheroō (1646)
  ἐξαιρέω exaireō (1791)
  ἐπιλύω epiluō (1941)
  λύω luō (3061)
  ῥύομαι rhuomai (4363)
  σῴζω sōzō (4834)

גָּאַל gā'al (1381), Qal: redeem, rescue (Lv 25:48, Ps 72:14 [71:14], Is 43:1); niphal: be redeemed (Lv 25:30, 27:27f.).

עָרַף 'āraph (6438), Break the neck (Ex 13:13).

פָּדָה pādhâh (6540), Qal: redeem (Ex 34:20, 2 Sm 7:23, Jer 31:11 [38:11]); niphal: be freed (Lv 19:20).

פָּלַט pālaṭ (6647), Deliverance (Ps 32:7 [31:7]).

פָּעָה pā'âh (6709), Open; deliver (Ps 144:10 [143:10]).

פָּרַק pāraq (6811), Deliver, free (Pss 7:2, 136:24 [135:24], Lam 5:8).

פְּרַק pᵉraq (A6812), Break away from (Dn 4:27 [4:24]—Aramaic).

קָנָה qānâh (7353), Purchase (Ex 15:16).

שָׂגַב sāghav (7891), Be high; piel: protect (Ps 59:1 [58:1]).

שֵׁיזִב shêziv (A8288), Deliver (Dn 6:27—Aramaic).

1. λυτροῦσθαι lutrousthai inf pres mid
2. ἐλυτρώθητε elutrōthēte 2pl indic aor pass
3. λυτρώσηται lutrōsētai 3sing subj aor mid

1 it had been he which should have **redeemed** Israel: Luke 24:21
3 that he might **redeem** us from all iniquity,............ Tit 2:14
2 that ye were not **redeemed** with corruptible things,... 1 Pt 1:18

Classical Greek
Lutroō (only in the middle/passive voice in our literature; cf. *Bauer*) has two principle meanings in antiquity, one active and the other passive. Thus, it means actively "to free after payment of ransom" or passively "to be freed by ransom, purchased by ransom." The expression can occur in reference to freed prisoners of war or released slaves.

Septuagint Usage
Used throughout the Septuagint, *lutroomai* corresponds to nine different Hebrew terms. Two, however, usually stand behind it: *gā'al* and *pādhâh*. *Lutroomai* speaks of God's act of freeing the Israelites enslaved to the Egyptians (Exodus 6:6; cf. 15:13,16; Deuteronomy 7:8; 9:26; cf. also Leviticus 19:20 of the ransom price of a slave). It is also employed in reference to the practice of "redeeming" the land which belongs to God, not men (Leviticus 25:23; cf. 25:24-34). In this sense it is associated with the idea of Jubilee.

"Redeeming" also involved the payment of a sum or the offering of a sacrifice for the life of an animal or firstborn child. The payment acknowledged God's ownership (Exodus 13:13,15,16). God's acts of deliverance occurred on the personal as well as the corporate level. He redeemed David from his "troubles" (2 Samuel 4:9 [LXX 2 Kings 4:9]; 1 Kings 1:29 [LXX 3 Kings 1:29]; Psalm 103:4 [LXX 102:4]) just as He "rescued" Israel (1 Chronicles 17:21; Psalm 25:22 [LXX 24:22]).

Büchsel suggests that "Redemption in later Jewish usage (Rabbinic) is always the redemption of Israel from the dominion of Gentile peoples . . . The decisive New Testament concept of redemption from sins is not found" ("lutroō," *Kittel*, 4:350). Such a statement overlooks the probable influence of such Old Testament texts as Psalms 26:11; 103:4; 119:134; 130:8; Sirach 51:2; and Daniel (Theodotion) 4:24 if the author is suggesting that "redemption from sin" was an invention of the New Testament. The general thought, however, is valid, as the prophetic writings testify (Jeremiah 15:21; Lamentations 5:8; Zephaniah 3:15) and as extra-Biblical sources indicate (e.g., Psalms of Solomon 9:1; 12:6). A major title for God is "Redeemer" (Proverbs 23:11; Isaiah 41:14; 43:14; 44:24; Jeremiah 50:34; 1 Maccabees 4:11). This may also indicate an emphasis upon God as deliverer from the oppressor (Brown, "Redemption," *Colin Brown*, 3:194).

New Testament Usage
The redemptive activity in the New Testament (verb three times) is solely that of God or Christ (Büchsel, "lutroō," *Kittel*, 4:350).

λύτρωσις 3057

Jesus came in order (*hina* [2419]) to give His life as a ransom (*lutron*) for (*anti* [470]) the many (Mark 10:45). He is the "Redemption" (*lutrōsis* [3057]) of Jerusalem. His disciples expected that He would redeem Israel (Luke 24:21; cf. Luke 1:68; 2:38). Clearly this involves deliverance from enemies and oppressors (e.g., Luke 1:71-74), but it also means forgiveness of sins (Luke 1:77, "forgiveness" *aphesis* [852]; cf. 4:18, "deliverance to the captives," *aphesis*). Jesus brings redemption, salvation, forgiveness, and freedom to those who trust in His name.

Titus 2:14 is another affirmation that Christ's giving (*didōmi* [1319]) of himself (in sacrifice; cf. Galatians 1:4, on behalf of the believers' sins; Mark 10:45) redeems believers from all wickedness (cf. Psalm 130:8). Christ's death on the cross is the price paid to free believers from the power of sin and to empower them through His Spirit to live a pure life.

The sacrificial imagery of redemption (cf. Exodus 13:13; Numbers 18:15) is mirrored by 1 Peter 1:18,19. Those who believe are not bought with silver or gold but with something more valuable, the very life—the priceless blood, as a lamb without blemish or defect—of Christ. This freed those who had followed ancient traditions from their former empty way of life, and it releases believers today from following the traditions of men (cf. Hebrews 9:11ff., the same sacrificial imagery).

STRONG 3084, BAUER 482-83, MOULTON-MILLIGAN 383, KITTEL 4:328-35,349-51, LIDDELL-SCOTT 1067, COLIN BROWN 3:189-90,192.

3057. λύτρωσις lutrōsis noun
Release, deliverance, redemption.
CROSS-REFERENCE:
λυτρόω lutroō (3056)

גְּאוּלִים gᵉʾûlîm (1376), Redemption (Is 63:4).

גְּאֻלָּה gᵉʾullāh (1383), Redemption (Lv 25:29).

פָּדָה pādhāh (6540), Redeem (Nm 18:16).

פְּדוּת pᵉdhûth (6545), Redemption (Pss 111:9 [110:9], 130:7 [129:7]).

פִּדְיוֹן pidhyōn (6548I), Redemption (Ps 49:8 [48:8]).

1. λύτρωσιν lutrōsin acc sing fem

1 for he hath visited and redeemed his people, ... Luke 1:68
1 all them that looked for redemption in Jerusalem. 2:38
1 having obtained eternal redemption for us. .... Heb 9:12

In the New Testament *lutrōsis* is used in reference to the anticipated deliverance or redemption by God of the nation of Israel from its oppressors (Luke 1:68; 2:38). This idea is linked to God's grace and the resulting redemption of Israel, thus *lutrōsis* can overlap with *sōtēria* (4843), "salvation" or "deliverance" (see Büchsel, "lutrōsis," *Kittel*, 4:351).

Hebrews 9:12 speaks of deliverance ("redemption") from sin as a result of the redemptive work of Christ. While here the sense of ransoming is uncertain, the word *lutrōsis* itself is similar to *lutroō* (3056), "freed as a result of a paid ransom."

STRONG 3085, BAUER 483, MOULTON-MILLIGAN 383, KITTEL 4:328-35,351, LIDDELL-SCOTT 1067, COLIN BROWN 3:189-90,193,198-99.

3058. λυτρωτής lutrōtēs noun
Liberator, redeemer, deliverer.
CROSS-REFERENCE:
λυτρόω lutroō (3056)

גָּאַל gāʾal (1381), Redeemer (Pss 19:14 [18:14], 78:35 [77:35]).

1. λυτρωτήν lutrōtēn acc sing masc

1 and a deliverer by the hand of the angel .... Acts 7:35

Apparently *lutrōtēs* is found only in Biblical Greek (*Bauer*) and in the New Testament only in Acts 7:35. In Stephen's speech he described Moses as both ruler and "deliverer" (*lutrōtēs*) sent by God to deliver Israel from Egypt. The parallel between Moses and Jesus is evident here. Schneider ("Redemption," *Colin Brown*, 3:199) says that the point of Stephen's argument was "to show that the Jews' treatment of Jesus is consistent with the Jews' attitude to divinely appointed leaders and deliverers down the ages."

STRONG 3086, BAUER 483, MOULTON-MILLIGAN 383, KITTEL 4:328-35,351, LIDDELL-SCOTT 1067, COLIN BROWN 3:189-90,193,199.

3059. λυχνία luchnia noun
Lampstand.
CROSS-REFERENCE:
λύχνος luchnos (3060)

מְנוֹרָה mᵉnôrāh (4645), Lampstand (Ex 31:8, Nm 8:2ff., 2 Chr 4:7).

1. λυχνίας luchnias gen/acc sing/pl fem
2. λυχνία luchnia nom sing fem
3. λυχνίαν luchnian acc sing fem
4. λυχνίαι luchniai nom pl fem
5. λυχνιῶν luchniōn gen pl fem

3 but on **a candlestick**; and it giveth light unto all	Matt	5:15
3 a candle ... and not to be set on **a candlestick**?	Mark	4:21
1 but setteth it on **a candlestick**,	Luke	8:16
3 neither under a bushel, but on **a candlestick**,		11:33
2 the first, wherein was the **candlestick**,	Heb	9:2
1 And being turned, I saw seven golden **candlesticks**;	Rev	1:12
5 And in the midst of the seven **candlesticks**		1:13
1 seven stars ... and the seven golden **candlesticks**.		1:20
4 and the seven **candlesticks** which thou sawest		1:20
5 in the midst of the seven golden **candlesticks**;		2:1
3 and will remove thy **candlestick** out of his place,		2:5
4 the two olive trees, and the two **candlesticks**		11:4

This is the ordinary word for the stand upon which a "lamp" (*luchnos* [3060]) was placed. Such a lampstand was elevated and thus helped to extend the light. The translation of *luchnia* as "candlestick" is highly unlikely since there is no evidence of a lamp that did not use oil in either the Old or New Testaments (cf. Hasel, "Lamp," *International Standard Bible Encyclopedia*, 3:68f.).

The vital function of lamps and lampstands in the ancient world was taken for granted. It was in such a context that Jesus illustrated the role of His disciples in the world (Matthew 5:15; Mark 4:21; Luke 8:16; 11:33). "The disciples are to have an illuminating effect upon their environment," even as the lamp set on its stand lights up the darkness (Hahn, "Light," *Colin Brown*, 2:487). In Revelation (1:12,13,20; 2:1,5) the seven churches are spoken of as seven golden *luchnia*.

STRONG 3087, BAUER 483, MOULTON-MILLIGAN 383, KITTEL 4:324-27, LIDDELL-SCOTT 1068, COLIN BROWN 2:486-87.

3060. λύχνος luchnos noun
Lamp.
COGNATE:
λυχνία luchnia (3059)
SYNONYM:
λαμπάς lampas (2958)

נִיר nîr (5402), Lamp (2 Kgs 8:19, 2 Chr 21:7).
נֵר nēr (5552), Lamp (Ex 27:20, 2 Chr 13:11, Zec 4:2).

1. **λύχνος** luchnos nom sing masc
2. **λύχνου** luchnou gen sing masc
3. **λύχνῳ** luchnō dat sing masc
4. **λύχνον** luchnon acc sing masc
5. **λύχνοι** luchnoi nom pl masc

4 Neither do men light **a candle**, ... under a bushel,	Matt	5:15
1 The **light** of the body is the eye:		6:22
1 Is a **candle** brought to be put under a bushel,	Mark	4:21
4 No man, when he hath lighted **a candle**,	Luke	8:16
4 No man, when he hath lighted **a candle**,		11:33
1 The **light** of the body is the eye:		11:34
1 the bright shining of a **candle** doth give thee light.		11:36
5 loins be girded about, and your **lights** burning;		12:35
4 if she lose one piece, doth not light **a candle**,		15:8
1 He was a burning and a shining **light**:	John	5:35
3 as unto **a light** that shineth in a dark place,	2 Pt	1:19
2 **light of a candle** shall shine no more at all in thee;	Rev	18:23
1 and the Lamb is the **light** thereof.		21:23
2 shall be no night there; and they need no **candle**,		22:5

Classical Greek
Luchnos denotes a lamp (probably oil-burning) or the light of a lamp. Usually this consisted of a small ceramic open bowl which could be carried in the hand or placed upon a "lampstand" (*luchnia* [3059], not "candlestick," KJV; Hebrew *mᵉnôrāh*). The important role of lamps in everyday life led to its usage in figurative as well as literal language.

Septuagint Usage
The Septuagint indicates that *luchnos* translated *nēr* or one of its cognates. The gold lampstand with seven "lamps" played a significant part in the tabernacle (Exodus 25:37; cf. verses 31-40). These lamps were to be lit continually during the period of darkness (see Exodus 27:20ff; 30:7ff.; cf. 1 Samuel 3:3 [LXX 1 Kings 3:3]). Thus they were integral to religious life. A figurative use probably refers to David as the "lamp" of Israel; however, this may also be referring back to the lamp of the tabernacle which might be extinguished if David the warrior were to die (2 Samuel [LXX 2 Kings] 21:17; cf. 22:29, of God the light/lamp of David; cf. Psalm 18:28 [LXX 17:28]; Zechariah 4:2).

New Testament Usage
The New Testament has both literal and figurative instances of *luchnos* (14 times). No one would place a lighted lamp under a container (Luke 8:16; 11:33; cf. Matthew 5:15; Luke 15:8), and in the New Jerusalem inhabitants will not need lamps or even the sun (Revelation 22:5; cf. 18:23; 21:23). Figuratively *luchnos* denotes some kind of inner quality or attitude (Luke 11:34), or it suggests preparedness to keep lamps lit (Luke 12:35). The prophetic word is like a "light that shineth in a dark place" (2 Peter 1:19).

STRONG 3088, BAUER 483, MOULTON-MILLIGAN 383, KITTEL 4:324-27, LIDDELL-SCOTT 1068, COLIN BROWN 2:486-87,495-96.

3061. λύω luō verb
Loose, untie, set free, destroy, break up, abolish.
COGNATES:
ἀνάλυσις analusis (357)
ἀναλύω analuō (358)
ἀπόλλυμι apollumi (616)

λύω 3061

ἀπολύω apoluō (624)
διαλύω dialuō (1256)
ἐκλύω ekluō (1577)
ἐπιλύω epiluō (1941)
καταλύω kataluō (2617)
λύσις lusis (3052)
λυσιτελέω lusiteleō (3053)

SYNONYMS:

ἀναλύω analuō (358)
ἀνατρέπω anatrepō (394)
ἀνίημι aniēmi (445)
ἀπαλλάσσω apallassō (521)
ἀπόλλυμι apollumi (616)
ἀπολύω apoluō (624)
ἀφανίζω aphanizō (846)
διαφθείρω diaphtheirō (1305)
ἐδαφίζω edaphizō (1467)
ἐλευθερόω eleutheroō (1646)
ἐξαιρέω exaireō (1791)
ἐπιλύω epiluō (1941)
καθαιρέω kathaireō (2479)
κατάγνυμι katagnumi (2579)
κατακλάω kataklaō (2592)
καταλύω kataluō (2617)
καταργέω katargeō (2643)
κατασκάπτω kataskaptō (2649)
καταστρέφω katastrephō (2660)
καταφθείρω kataphtheirō (2673)
κενόω kenoō (2729)
κλάω klaō (2779)
λυτρόω lutroō (3056)
ὀλοθρεύω olothreuō (3508)
πορθέω portheō (4058)
ῥήγνυμι rhēgnumi (4342)
συνθλάω sunthlaō (4767)
συνθρύπτω sunthruptō (4769)
συντρίβω suntribō (4789)
φθείρω phtheirō (5188)

נָשָׂא nāsâ' (5558), Lift, carry; accept (Jb 42:9).

נָשַׁל nāshal (5577), Take off (Ex 3:5).

נָתַר nāthar (5609), Hiphil: release, set free (Pss 105:20 [104:20], 146:7 [145:7]).

סְתַר sᵉthar (A5849), Destroy (Ezr 5:12—Aramaic [Codex Vaticanus only]).

פָּתַח pāthach (6858), Qal: open (Gn 42:27, Is 14:17); niphal: be loosened (Is 5:27); piel: loose, free (Jb 39:5, Is 58:6, Jer 40:4 [47:4]).

רָצָה rātsâh (7813), Pardon; niphal: be pardoned (Is 40:2).

שְׁרָה shᵉrâh (A8639), Be loosened (Dn 3:25—Aramaic).

1. λύει luei 3sing indic pres act
2. λύετε luete 2pl indic pres act
3. λύουσιν luousin 3pl indic pres act
4. λύοντες luontes nom pl masc part pres act
5. λυόντων luontōn gen pl masc part pres act
6. ἔλυσεν elusen 3sing indic aor act
7. λύσω lusō 1sing subj aor act
8. λύσῃς lusēs 2sing subj aor act
9. λύσῃ lusē 3sing subj aor act
10. λύσητε lusēte 2pl subj aor act
11. λῦσον luson 2sing impr aor act
12. λύσατε lusate 2pl impr aor act
13. λύσας lusas nom sing masc part aor act
14. λύσαντες lusantes nom pl masc part aor act
15. λῦσαι lusai inf aor act
16. ἔλυεν eluen 3sing indic imperf act
17. λυομένων luomenōn gen pl neu part pres mid
18. ἐλύθη eluthē 3sing indic aor pass
19. ἐλύθησαν eluthēsan 3pl indic aor pass
20. λυθῇ luthē 3sing subj aor pass
21. λυθείσης lutheisēs gen sing fem part aor pass
22. λυθῆναι luthēnai inf aor pass
23. λέλυσαι lelusai 2sing indic perf mid
24. λελυμένον lelumenon nom/acc sing neu part perf mid
25. λελυμένα lelumena nom/acc pl neu part perf mid
26. λυθήσεται luthēsetai 3sing indic fut pass
27. λυθήσονται luthēsontai 3pl indic fut pass
28. ἐλύετο elueto 3sing indic imperf pass
29. λύσαντι lusanti dat sing masc part aor act

9 Whosoever therefore **shall break** one of these least Matt 5:19
8 thou shalt **loose** on earth shall be **loosed** in heaven.... 16:19
24 thou shalt **loose** on earth shall be **loosed** in heaven.... 16:19
10 whatsoever ye shall **loose** on earth................ 18:18
25 ye shall **loose** on earth shall be **loosed** in heaven...... 18:18
14 **loose** them, and bring them unto me................. 21:2
15 shoes I am not worthy to stoop down and **unloose**. Mark 1:7
18 and the string of his tongue **was loosed**,.............. 7:35
14 find a colt tied, ... **loose** him, and bring him.......... 11:2
3 found the colt tied ... and they **loose** him............ 11:4
4 What do ye, **loosing** the colt?....................... 11:5
15 latchet of whose shoes I am not worthy **to unloose**: Luke 3:16
1 on the sabbath **loose** his ox or his ass from the stall,... 13:15
22 **be loosed** from this bond on the sabbath day?........ 13:16
14 find a colt tied, ... **loose** him, and bring him hither.... 19:30
2 And if any man ask you, Why **do** ye **loose** him?...... 19:31
5 And as they were **loosing** the colt,................... 19:33
2 owners ... said unto them, Why **loose** ye the colt?.... 19:33
7 whose shoe's latchet I am not worthy **to unloose**....John 1:27
12 **Destroy** this temple, and in three days I will raise..... 2:19
16 because he not only **had broken** the sabbath,......... 5:18
20 that the law of Moses should not **be broken**;.......... 7:23
22 and the scripture cannot **be broken**;.................. 10:35
12 Jesus saith unto them, **Loose** him, and let him go..... 11:44
13 having **loosed** the pains of death:................... Acts 2:24
11 Put off thy shoes from thy feet:...................... 7:33
15 whose shoes of his feet I am not worthy **to loose**...... 13:25
21 Now when the congregation **was broken up**,.......... 13:43
6 he **loosed** him from his bands,..................... 22:30
9 that he might **loose** him:......................... 24:26
28 **was broken** with the violence of the waves.......... 27:41
23 Art thou **loosed** from a wife? seek not a wife....... 1 Co 7:27
13 and hath **broken down** the middle wall of partition.. Eph 2:14
27 and the elements **shall melt** with fervent heat,...... 2 Pt 3:10
17 Seeing then that all these things **shall be dissolved**,..... 3:11
27 the heavens being on fire **shall be dissolved**,.......... 3:12
9 that he might **destroy** the works of the devil....... 1 Jn 3:8
29 and **released** us from our sins (NASB)............ Rev 1:5
15 to open the book, and **to loose** the seals thereof?..... 5:2
15 open the book, and **to loose** the seven seals thereof.... 5:5
11 **Loose** the four angels which are bound............... 9:14
19 the four angels **were loosed**, which were prepared...... 9:15
22 and after that he must **be loosed** a little season....... 20:3
26 Satan **shall be loosed** out of his prison,............... 20:7

Classical Greek

In classical Greek *luō* generally means "loose, release, set free" and "open." It is used of the release from pain, hardship, and fear which the gods would grant to man. Its broad range of meanings includes: "*to loose* the limbs, knees, i.e., *unnerve, enfeeble,* and often in Homer, *to slay, kill*" (*Liddell-Scott*).

Septuagint Usage

Within the canonical writings of the Septuagint *luō* appears 16 times translating 7 different Hebrew words. Each time a nuance of the definition "loose, release" can be seen. The most frequent Hebrew word it translates is *pāthach*. In Genesis 42:27 a sack is "opened." Job 39:5 speaks of releasing an animal, and Isaiah 5:27 uses it of undoing a belt (cf. Judith 6:14; 9:2; 3 Maccabees 6:27,29).

Other Hebrew words which *luō* translates are *nāshal* (Exodus 3:5; Joshua 5:15), *nāthar* (Psalms 105:20 [LXX 104:20]; 146:7 [145:7]); *sethar* (Ezra 5:12) and *rātsâh* (Isaiah 40:2). One Aramaic word, *sherâ*, is translated by *luō* (Daniel 3:25). It means "loosed" in the sense of "unhindered."

In Job 42:9 *luō* is used to translate *nāsâ'*. This Hebrew word is found over 650 times in the Old Testament, but only here is it translated by *luō*. The Lord "loosed" Job, the Hebrew translation being that He "lifted up the face of Job" in the sense of accepting him.

New Testament Usage

The New Testament's use of *luō* largely accords with the common definitions found in classical and Septuagintal sources. However, the term occurs in many passages which are charged with theological implication.

Luō is used of John the Baptist's recognized unworthiness to "loose, untie" the thongs of Jesus' sandals, an event recounted by three evangelists and again in Acts (Mark 1:7; Luke 3:16; John 1:27; Acts 13:25). The image here serves to show that John regarded himself as totally inferior to the Lord. He did not even consider himself worthy to perform the menial task of the slave, even though he was 6 months older than Jesus; normally this would give him priority. To put it in other terms, he saw himself as less than a slave when compared to Jesus.

Besides the literal idea of "untying" something or "freeing" someone (e.g., Mark 11:2ff.; Luke 13:15; 19:30ff.; Acts 22:30), the idea of "unloosing" or "freeing" is also applied to Jesus' ministry. "Bonds" which restrain proper speech were "loosed" (Mark 7:35). Luke saw this as evidence that Jesus was breaking the power of Satan (Luke 13:16, note the word play in verse 15; Acts 2:24, of Jesus' breaking the throes of death; see also 1 John 3:8). "Loosing" also concerns the power of the Church to administer discipline, including the power to interpret the Law. Forgiveness too—on the individual as well as the corporate level—is within the power of the believer. Thus the decisions of the Church are endorsed by heaven (i.e., God) and are determinative for the community of God on earth (Matthew 16:19f.; 18:18). (Note that in rabbinic and Old Testament usage [cf. Isaiah 22:22] the terms "bind" and "loose" refer to rules of conduct [Hebrew *hālākhâh*]; therefore, many commentators believe the "keys" represent the internal authority of the Church to discipline its own. If so, these passages do not refer to spiritual "binding and loosing" which is so frequently the mistaken assumption of many. Jesus' promise to Peter does not mean God will be "bound" by anything man says, but that things done according to God's will have a "binding" validity. [Cf. Guthrie and Motyer, *New Bible Commentary*, p.837.])

Paul declared that Jesus has "broken down" the barrier, the middle wall of partition, that formerly separated Jews and Gentiles (Ephesians 2:14). Second Peter speaks of the coming end when the heavens and earth will be "burned up" (3:10,11,12).

In an unparalleled New Testament use, Paul employed *luō* in reference to being "loosed" ("divorced," NIV) from a woman (1 Corinthians 7:27).

STRONG 3089, BAUER 483-84, MOULTON-MILLIGAN 384, KITTEL 2:60-61; 4:328-37,
LIDDELL-SCOTT 1068-69, COLIN BROWN 2:732; 3:177,179-81,183-89.

3062. Λωΐς Lōis name

Lois.

1. Λωΐδι Lōidi dat fem

1 which dwelt first in thy grandmother Lois,..........2 Tm 1:5

The grandmother of Timothy noted for her sincere faith (2 Timothy 1:5).

3063. Λώτ Lōt name

Lot.

1. Λώτ Lōt masc

Λώτ 3063

1 Likewise also as it was in the days **of Lot;** .... Luke 17:28
1 But the same day that **Lot** went out of Sodom 17:29
1 Remember **Lot's** wife. 17:32
1 And delivered just **Lot,** .... 2 Pt 2:7

The nephew of Abraham who lived a righteous life in the midst of a wicked generation (Luke 17:28ff.; 2 Peter 2:7).

3064. Μάαθ Maath name
Maath.

1. Μάαθ Maath masc
1 Which was the son of Maath, ... Luke 3:26

The son of Mattathias in the genealogy of Jesus (Luke 3:26).

3064B. Μαγαδάν Magadan name
Magadan.

1. Μαγαδάν Magadan fem
1 and came to the region of Magadan. (NASB) ...... Matt 15:39

Variant of *Magdala* (3065).

3065. Μαγδαλά Magdala name
Magdala.

1. Μαγδαλά Magdala fem
1 and came into the coasts of Magdala. .... Matt 15:39

Home of Mary Magdalene on the western shore of the Sea of Galilee (Matthew 15:39).

3066. Μαγδαληνός Magdalēnos name
Magdalene.

1. Μαγδαληνή Magdalēnē nom fem
2. Μαγδαληνῇ Magdalēnē dat fem

1 Among which was Mary Magdalene, and Mary ..... Matt 27:56
1 there was Mary Magdalene, and the other Mary, ... 27:61
1 came Mary Magdalene and the other Mary to see 28:1
1 afar off: among whom was Mary Magdalene, ... Mark 15:40
1 Mary Magdalene and Mary the mother of Joses 15:47
1 And when the sabbath was past, Mary Magdalene, ... 16:1
2 he appeared first to Mary Magdalene, ... 16:9
1 Mary called Magdalene, out of whom ... devils, ... Luke 8:2
1 It was Mary Magdalene, and Joanna, and Mary the ... 24:10
1 Mary the wife of Cleophas, and Mary Magdalene .. John 19:25
1 The first day ... cometh Mary Magdalene early, ... John 20:1
1 Mary Magdalene came and told the disciples 20:18

Surname of a certain Mary from Magdala who was present at both the cross and empty tomb of Christ (Matthew 27:56; 28:1).

3066B. Μαγεδών Magedōn name
Mageddon.

1. Μαγεδών Magedōn

The site of the gathering of the ungodly for the war of the great day of God (Revelation 16:16); possibly Mount Megiddo. (See *Armageddōn* [711].)

3067. μαγεία mageia noun
Magic, sorcery.

COGNATE:
μαγεύω mageuō (3068)

SYNONYM:
φαρμακεία pharmakeia (5169)

1. μαγείαις mageiais dat pl fem
1 of long time he had bewitched them with sorceries... Acts 8:11

Classical Greek
Mageia is the work of a sorcerer or magician whether genuine or fraudulent. It is related to the word *magos* (3069), which originally identified members of the Persian priestly caste (Magians), but it came to be used commonly in classical Greek of those who possessed (supposedly) supernatural knowledge and power and who put it to work for a religious cause (cf. *Liddell-Scott*). The word is not found in the Septuagint.

New Testament Usage
This term is found only once in the New Testament, Acts 8:11, where it describes the astonishing work ("sorceries") of Simon. What

specifically those works entailed is unknown, but they had impressed the Samaritans for some time and had gained Simon a considerable following. However, the work of God through Philip amazed even Simon (Acts 8:13), perhaps exposing the true source (demonic) or true character (fraudulent) of his works.

STRONG 3095, BAUER 484, MOULTON-MILLIGAN 385 (see "magia"), KITTEL 4:359, LIDDELL-SCOTT 1071, COLIN BROWN 2:552,557-58.

3068. μαγεύω mageuō verb
Practice magic, use sorcery.
COGNATES:
μαγεία mageia (3067)
μάγος magos (3069)

1. μαγεύων mageuōn nom sing masc part pres act

1 which beforetime in the same city used sorcery,...... Acts 8:9

This verb, related to the noun *magos* (3069), "magus, magician," can refer to doing the work of the *magos* or belonging to the order of *magoi* (Delling, "mageuō," *Kittel*, 4:359). In the New Testament it occurs only in Acts 8:9 in reference to Simon Magus. Delling asserts that this use of *mageuō*, together with *mageia* (3067) (activity of the *magos*; i.e., "magic") in 8:11, stresses the distinction between Simon's influence through the practice of his magical arts and the possession of the genuine Spirit of God.

STRONG 3096, BAUER 484, MOULTON-MILLIGAN 385, KITTEL 4:359, LIDDELL-SCOTT 1071, COLIN BROWN 2:552,557-58.

3069. μάγος magos noun
Magus, sorcerer.
COGNATE:
μαγεύω mageuō (3068)
SYNONYMS:
φαρμακεύς pharmakeus (5170)
φάρμακος pharmakos (5171)

אַשָּׁף 'ashshāph (853), Conjurer (Dn 2:2).

אָשַׁף 'āshaph (A854), Conjurer (Dn 2:10—Aramaic).

1. μάγος magos nom sing masc
2. μάγον magon acc sing masc
3. μάγοι magoi nom pl masc
4. μάγων magōn gen pl masc
5. μάγους magous acc pl masc

3 there came **wise men** from the east to Jerusalem,.... Matt 2:1
5 Herod, when he had privily called the **wise men**,........ 2:7
4 when he saw that he was mocked of the **wise men**,...... 2:16
4 which he had diligently inquired of the **wise men**.... Matt 2:16
2 they found a certain **sorcerer**, a false prophet,...... Acts 13:6
1 But Elymas the **sorcerer** for so is his name............ 13:8

Classical Greek
The word *magos* (plural, *magi*) is derived from the title given to the wise men or religious leaders of the Babylonians (Chaldeans), Medes, and Persians. The term subsequently came to be applied to those who claimed to possess or use supernatural knowledge and power, to all magicians, and then figuratively to those who deceived others with such claims.

The Magi were originally a tribe of the Medes, a hereditary priesthood, who served as teachers, priests, physicians, astrologers, soothsayers, interpreters of dreams, prophets, etc. (cf. *Liddell-Scott*). They were absorbed by Zoroastrianism in the Sixth Century B.C. and retained their religious supremacy despite conquest first by the Persians and later by the Parthians. They evolved into the ruling political body which controlled the choice of the Parthian king (Delling, "magos," *Kittel*, 4:356).

Septuagint Usage
The Septuagint use of *magos* or *magoi* is limited almost exclusively to the Book of Daniel which records several instances where Babylonian kings called for both Daniel and the Magi to interpret dreams and visions (Daniel 1:20; 2:2,10,27; 5:7,11,15). Daniel's wisdom was superior to that of the Magi with the result that he was elevated to the position of *Rab-Mag*, head of the Magi (Daniel 2:48).

New Testament Usage
It is possible this relationship between Daniel and the Magi explains the geographical origin of the Magi who searched for Christ at His birth (Matthew 2:1, passim). It is possible that Daniel could have been a source of prophetic interest and knowledge for the Parthian (Persian) Magi and that the Magi who visited Jesus were in fact from Parthia. Another possibility is that the Magi were from Arabia, because the gifts they brought (especially gold and frankincense) are often associated in the Old Testament with caravan trains from Midian and from Sheba, both of which were in Arabia.

Perhaps a better explanation is that the Magi were from Babylon. A large colony of Jews had settled in Babylon after the Exile in 586 B.C. From these Jews it is possible Babylonian astrologers could have learned of the Jewish messianic expectations. It is also true the Babylonians were known for their astrological knowledge. They could have easily seen the star in the East and later followed it to Bethlehem (along with an indeterminate number of others who saw this phenomenon and journeyed to worship the newborn King; cf. Matthew 2:1f.).

While the Magi are not specifically identified (except as those coming from the East [Matthew 2:1], and by implication, as those who watched the heavenly bodies), the use of the term suggests a respected class of Middle Easterners who came as far as a few weeks' camel journey to find the Messiah and new King.

The term is used quite differently in Acts 13:6,8 to identify an apostate Jew named Elymas who made use of occult powers or else outright deceit to establish himself as an effective practitioner of the black arts. In a dramatic manner Paul exposed his deceit.

STRONG 3097, BAUER 484-45, MOULTON-MILLIGAN 385, KITTEL 4:356-59, LIDDELL-SCOTT 1071, COLIN BROWN 2:552,557,561.

3070. Μαγώγ Magōg name

Magog.

1. Μαγώγ Magōg masc

1 Gog and **Magog**, to gather them together to battle: Rev 20:8

One of the ungodly nations rallied for the final confrontation after the millennium (Revelation 20:8). (See *Gōg* [1130].)

3071. Μαδιάμ Madiam name

Midian.

1. Μαδιάμ Madiam masc

1 and was a stranger in the land of **Madian**, ... Acts 7:29

The land east of the Sinai Peninsula in Arabia where Moses fled after killing an Egyptian (Acts 7:29; cf. Exodus 2:15).

3072. μαθητεύω mathēteuō verb

Become a disciple, make a disciple of.
COGNATE:
 μανθάνω manthanō (3101)
SYNONYMS:
 διδάσκω didaskō (1315)
 κατηχέω katēcheō (2697)
 παιδεύω paideuō (3674)
 παραδίδωμι paradidōmi (3722)
 συμβιβάζω sumbibazō (4673)

1. ἐμαθήτευσεν emathēteusen 3sing indic aor act
2. μαθητεύσατε mathēteusate 2pl impr aor act
3. μαθητεύσαντες mathēteusantes nom pl masc part aor act
4. μαθητευθείς mathēteutheis nom sing masc part aor pass
5. ἐμαθητεύθη emathēteuthē 3sing indic aor pass

4 which is **instructed** unto the kingdom of heaven .... Matt 13:52
1 Joseph, who also himself was Jesus' **disciple**: 27:57
2 Go ye therefore, and **teach** all nations, ... 28:19
3 had preached the gospel ... and **had taught** many, ... Acts 14:21

Classical Greek
In classical Greek *mathēteuō*, related to *mathētēs* (3073), means "to be or become a pupil." The verb is not used in the Septuagint and only sparsely in the papyri.

New Testament Usage
In the New Testament it is used only once in a more general sense (one who "*was* Jesus' *disciple*," Matthew 27:57). Three times it is used with the more specialized meaning of making disciples (Matthew 13:52; 28:19; Acts 14:21).

In the Lord's Great Commission (Matthew 28:19,20) the command is not to *go*, *baptize*, or *teach*, but to *make disciples* (*mathēteusate*). "Discipling," therefore, is a more comprehensive term than "teaching" (*didaskō* [1315]), involving a commitment of the will as well as an exercise of the intellect. Baptizing (evangelism) and teaching (education) are primary elements of the discipling process.

STRONG 3100, BAUER 485, MOULTON-MILLIGAN 385, KITTEL 4:461, LIDDELL-SCOTT 1072.

3073. μαθητής mathētēs noun

Learner, pupil, disciple.
CROSS-REFERENCE:
 μανθάνω manthanō (3101)

אַלּוּף 'allûph (443), Ally (Jer 13:21—Codex Alexandrinus only).

1. μαθητής mathētēs nom sing masc
2. μαθητοῦ mathētou gen sing masc
3. μαθητῇ mathētē dat sing masc
4. μαθητήν mathētēn acc sing masc
5. μαθηταί mathētai nom pl masc
6. μαθητῶν mathētōn gen pl masc
7. μαθηταῖς mathētais dat pl masc
8. μαθητάς mathētas acc pl masc

5 and when he was set, his **disciples** came unto him: .. Matt 5:1
6 And another of his **disciples** said unto him, ... 8:21
5 entered into a ship, his **disciples** followed him. 8:23
5 And his **disciples** came to him, and awoke him, ... 8:25
7 came and sat down with him and his **disciples**. 9:10
7 they said unto his **disciples**, ... 9:11
5 Then came to him the **disciples** of John, saying, ... 9:14
5 Why do we ... fast oft, but thy **disciples** fast not? 9:14
5 and followed him, and so did his **disciples**. 9:19

μαθητής 3073

7	Then saith he unto his **disciples**,	Matt 9:37
8	when he had called unto him his twelve **disciples**,	10:1
1	The **disciple** is not above his master,	10:24
3	It is enough for the **disciple** ... be as his master,	10:25
2	a cup of cold water only in the name **of a disciple**,	10:42
7	made an end of commanding his twelve **disciples**,	11:1
6	John had heard ... he sent two of his **disciples**,	11:2
5	and his **disciples** were an hungred,	12:1
5	Behold, thy **disciples** do that which is not lawful	12:2
8	he stretched forth his hand toward his **disciples**,	12:49
5	And the **disciples** came, and said unto him,	13:10
5	and his **disciples** came unto him, saying,	13:36
5	And his **disciples** came, and took up the body,	14:12
5	when it was evening, his **disciples** came to him,	14:15
7	and gave the loaves to his **disciples**,	14:19
5	and the **disciples** to the multitude.	14:19
8	Jesus constrained his **disciples** to get into a ship,	14:22
5	And when the **disciples** saw him walking on the sea,	14:26
5	Why do thy **disciples** transgress the tradition	15:2
5	Then came his **disciples**, and said unto him,	15:12
5	And his **disciples** came and besought him,	15:23
8	Then Jesus called his **disciples** unto him, and said,	15:32
5	And his **disciples** say unto him,	15:33
7	and brake them, and gave to his **disciples**,	15:36
5	and the **disciples** to the multitude.	15:36
5	And when his **disciples** were come to the other side,	16:5
8	he asked his **disciples**, saying, Whom do men say	16:13
7	charged he his **disciples** that they should tell no	16:20
7	began Jesus to show unto his **disciples**,	16:21
7	Then said Jesus unto his **disciples**,	16:24
5	when the **disciples** heard it, they fell on their face,	17:6
5	And his **disciples** asked him, saying,	17:10
5	Then the **disciples** understood	17:13
7	And I brought him to thy **disciples**,	17:16
5	Then came the **disciples** to Jesus apart, and said,	17:19
5	At the same time came the **disciples** unto Jesus,	18:1
5	His **disciples** say unto him, If the case	19:10
5	little children, ... and the **disciples** rebuked them.	19:13
7	Then said Jesus unto his **disciples**,	19:23
5	When his **disciples** heard it, they were ... amazed,	19:25
8	took the twelve **disciples** apart in the way,	20:17
8	then sent Jesus two **disciples**,	21:1
5	the **disciples** went, and did as Jesus commanded	21:6
5	And when the **disciples** saw it, they marvelled,	21:20
8	unto him their **disciples** with the Herodians,	22:16
7	spake Jesus to the multitude, and to his **disciples**,	23:1
5	and his **disciples** came to him for to show him	24:1
5	the **disciples** came unto him privately, saying,	24:3
7	Jesus had finished ... he said unto his **disciples**,	26:1
5	But when his **disciples** saw it, they had indignation,	26:8
5	the **disciples** came to Jesus, saying unto him,	26:17
6	keep the passover at thy house with my **disciples**.	26:18
5	And the **disciples** did as Jesus had appointed them;	26:19
6	reclining ... with the twelve **disciples**. (NASB)	26:20
7	blessed it, and brake it, and gave it to the **disciples**,	26:26
7	Likewise also said all the **disciples**.	26:35
7	and saith unto the **disciples**, Sit ye here,	26:36
8	cometh unto the **disciples**, and findeth them asleep,	26:40
8	cometh he to his **disciples**, and saith unto them,	26:45
5	Then all the **disciples** forsook him, and fled.	26:56
5	lest his **disciples** come by night, and steal him	27:64
7	and tell his **disciples** that he is risen from the dead;	28:7
7	and did run to bring his **disciples** word.	28:8
8	And as they went to tell his **disciples**,	28:9
5	His **disciples** came by night, and stole him	28:13
5	Then the eleven **disciples** went away into Galilee,	28:16
7	also together with Jesus and his **disciples**:	Mark 2:15
7	they said unto his **disciples**, How is it	2:16
5	**disciples** of John and of the Pharisees used to fast:	2:18
5	Why do the **disciples** of John and ... Pharisees fast,	2:18
5	John's **disciples** and the **disciples** of (NASB)	2:18
5	the Pharisees fast, but thy **disciples** fast not?	2:18
5	his **disciples** began, ... to pluck the ears of corn.	2:23
6	But Jesus withdrew himself with his **disciples**	3:7
7	And he spake to his **disciples**,	3:9
7	he expounded all things to his **disciples**.	4:34
5	And his **disciples** said unto him,	5:31
5	and his **disciples** follow him.	Mark 6:1
5	And when his **disciples** heard of it,	6:29
5	his **disciples** came unto him, and said,	6:35
7	and gave them to his **disciples** to set before them;	6:41
8	he constrained his **disciples** to get into the ship,	6:45
6	And when they saw some of his **disciples** eat bread	7:2
5	Why walk not thy **disciples** according to	7:5
5	his **disciples** asked him concerning the parable.	7:17
8	Jesus called his **disciples** unto him,	8:1
5	And his **disciples** answered him,	8:4
7	and gave to his **disciples** to set before them;	8:6
6	he entered into a ship with his **disciples**,	8:10
5	And Jesus went out, and his **disciples**,	8:27
8	and by the way he asked his **disciples**,	8:27
8	he had turned about and looked on his **disciples**,	8:33
7	called the people unto him with his **disciples** also,	8:34
8	And when he came to his **disciples**,	9:14
7	thy **disciples** that they should cast him out;	9:18
5	**disciples** asked him privately, Why could not we	9:28
8	For he taught his **disciples**, and said unto them,	9:31
5	And in the house his **disciples** asked him again	10:10
5	and his **disciples** rebuked those that brought them.	10:13
7	looked round about, and saith unto his **disciples**,	10:23
5	And the **disciples** were astonished at his words.	10:24
6	and as he went out of Jericho with his **disciples**	10:46
6	he sendeth forth two of his **disciples**,	11:1
5	And his **disciples** heard it.	11:14
8	And he called unto him his **disciples**,	12:43
6	one of his **disciples** saith unto him, Master,	13:1
5	his **disciples** said unto him, Where wilt thou	14:12
6	And he sendeth forth two of his **disciples**,	14:13
6	where I shall eat the passover with my **disciples**?	14:14
5	his **disciples** went forth, and came into the city,	14:16
7	and he saith to his **disciples**, Sit ye here,	14:32
7	tell his **disciples** and Peter that he goeth before you	16:7
8	and Pharisees murmured against his **disciples**,	Luke 5:30
5	Why do the **disciples** of John fast often,	5:33
5	his **disciples** plucked the ears of corn, and did eat,	6:1
8	he called unto him his **disciples**:	6:13
6	and the company of his **disciples**,	6:17
8	And he lifted up his eyes on his **disciples**,	6:20
1	The **disciple** is not above his master:	6:40
5	and many of his **disciples** went with him,	7:11
5	And the **disciples** of John showed him of all these:	7:18
6	And John calling unto him two of his **disciples**	7:19
5	**disciples** asked him, ... What might this parable be?	8:9
5	that he went into a ship with his **disciples**:	8:22
8	Then he called his twelve **disciples** together,	9:1
8	And he said to his **disciples**,	9:14
7	gave to the **disciples** to set before the multitude.	9:16
5	his **disciples** were with him: and he asked them,	9:18
8	And I besought thy **disciples** to cast him out;	9:40
8	he said unto his **disciples**,	9:43
5	And when his **disciples** James and John saw this,	9:54
8	turned him unto his **disciples**, and said privately,	10:23
6	when he ceased, one of his **disciples** said unto him,	11:1
8	teach us to pray, as John also taught his **disciples**.	11:1
8	he began to say unto his **disciples** first of all,	12:1
8	said unto his **disciples**, Therefore I say unto you,	12:22
1	and his own life also, he cannot be my **disciple**.	14:26
1	doth not bear his cross, ... cannot be my **disciple**.	14:27
1	that forsaketh not all ... he cannot be my **disciple**.	14:33
8	And he said also unto his **disciples**,	16:1
8	Then said he unto the **disciples**,	17:1
8	And he said unto the **disciples**, The days will come,	17:22
5	but when his **disciples** saw it, they rebuked them.	18:15
6	the mount of Olives, he sent two of his **disciples**,	19:29
6	whole multitude of the **disciples** began to rejoice	19:37
7	said unto him, Master, rebuke thy **disciples**.	19:39
7	in the audience of all ... he said unto his **disciples**,	20:45
6	where I shall eat the passover with my **disciples**?	22:11
5	mount of Olives; ... his **disciples** also followed him.	22:39
8	rose up from prayer, and was come to his **disciples**,	22:45
6	next day after John stood, and two of his **disciples**;	John 1:35
5	And the two **disciples** heard him speak,	1:37
5	Jesus was called, and his **disciples**, to the marriage.	2:2
5	and his **disciples** believed on him.	2:11

96

5 his mother, and his brethren, and his **disciples**:	John	2:12
5 And his **disciples** remembered that it was written,		2:17
5 his **disciples** remembered that he had said this		2:22
5 Jesus and his **disciples** into the land of Judaea;		3:22
6 between some of John's **disciples** and the Jews		3:25
8 Jesus made and baptized more **disciples** than John,		4:1
5 Jesus himself baptized not, but his **disciples**,		4:2
5 For his **disciples** were gone away unto the city		4:8
5 And upon this came his **disciples**,		4:27
5 In the mean while his **disciples** prayed him,		4:31
5 Therefore said the **disciples** one to another,		4:33
6 and there he sat with his **disciples**.		6:3
6 One of his **disciples**, Andrew,		6:8
7 he distributed to the **disciples**,		6:11
5 and the **disciples** to them that were set down;		6:11
7 When they were filled, he said unto his **disciples**,		6:12
5 his **disciples** went down unto the sea,		6:16
5 save that one whereinto his **disciples** were entered,		6:22
7 that Jesus went not with his **disciples** into the boat,		6:22
5 but that his **disciples** were gone away alone;		6:22
5 saw that Jesus was not there, neither his **disciples**,		6:24
6 Many therefore of his **disciples**,		6:60
5 knew in himself that his **disciples** murmured at it,		6:61
6 From that time many of his **disciples** went back,		6:66
5 **disciples** also may see the works that thou doest		7:3
5 in my word, then are ye my **disciples** indeed;		8:31
5 And his **disciples** asked him, saying, Master,		9:2
5 will ye also be his **disciples**?		9:27
1 Thou art his **disciple**; but we are Moses' **disciples**.		9:28
5 Thou art his **disciple**; but we are Moses' **disciples**.		9:28
7 Then after that saith he to his **disciples**,		11:7
5 His **disciples** say unto him, Master,		11:8
5 Then said his **disciples**,		11:12
6 and there continued with his **disciples**.		11:54
6 Then saith one of his **disciples**, Judas Iscariot,		12:4
5 These things understood not his **disciples**		12:16
6 and began to wash the **disciples**' feet,		13:5
5 Then the **disciples** looked one on another,		13:22
6 was leaning on Jesus' bosom one of his **disciples**,		13:23
5 By this shall all men know that ye are my **disciples**,		13:35
5 bear much fruit; so shall ye be my **disciples**.		15:8
6 Then said some of his **disciples** among themselves,		16:17
5 His **disciples** said unto him,		16:29
7 he went forth with his **disciples**		18:1
5 a garden, ... which he entered, and his **disciples**.		18:1
6 Jesus ofttimes resorted thither with his **disciples**.		18:2
1 Peter followed Jesus, and so did another **disciple**:		18:15
1 that **disciple** was known unto the high priest,		18:15
1 Then went out that other **disciple**,		18:16
6 Art not thou also one of this man's **disciples**?		18:17
6 The high priest then asked Jesus of his **disciples**,		18:19
6 Art not thou also one of his **disciples**? He denied it,		18:25
4 and the **disciple** standing by, whom he loved,		19:26
3 Then saith he to the **disciple**, Behold thy mother!		19:27
1 that **disciple** took her unto his own home.		19:27
1 Joseph of Arimathaea, being a **disciple** of Jesus,		19:38
4 cometh to Simon Peter, and to the other **disciple**,		20:2
1 and that other **disciple**, and came to the sepulchre.		20:3
1 and the other **disciple** did outrun Peter,		20:4
1 Then went in also that other **disciple**,		20:8
5 **disciples** went away again unto their own home.		20:10
7 Mary Magdalene came and told the **disciples**		20:18
5 when the doors were shut where the **disciples** were		20:19
5 Then were the **disciples** glad, ... they saw the Lord.		20:20
5 The other **disciples** therefore said unto him,		20:25
5 after eight days again his **disciples** were within,		20:26
6 signs ... did Jesus in the presence of his **disciples**,		20:30
7 again to the **disciples** at the sea of Tiberias;		21:1
6 the sons of Zebedee, and two other of his **disciples**.		21:2
5 but the **disciples** knew not that it was Jesus.		21:4
1 that **disciple** whom Jesus loved saith unto Peter,		21:7
5 And the other **disciples** came in a little ship;		21:8
6 none of the **disciples** durst ask him, Who art thou?		21:12
7 third time ... Jesus shewed himself to his **disciples**,		21:14
4 seeth the **disciple** whom Jesus loved following,		21:20
1 that that **disciple** should not die:		21:23
1 This is the **disciple** which testifieth of these things,		21:24
6 Peter stood up in the midst of the **disciples**,	Acts	1:15
6 when the number of the **disciples** was multiplied,		6:1
6 called the multitude of the **disciples** unto them,		6:2
6 and the number of the **disciples** multiplied		6:7
8 and slaughter against the **disciples** of the Lord,		9:1
1 And there was a certain **disciple** at Damascus,		9:10
6 Then was Saul certain days with the **disciples**		9:19
5 Then the **disciples** took him by night,		9:25
7 he assayed to join himself to the **disciples**:		9:26
1 and believed not that he was a **disciple**.		9:26
5 and the **disciples** had heard that Peter was at,		9:38
8 the **disciples** were called Christians first in Antioch.		11:26
6 the **disciples**, every man according to his ability,		11:29
5 And the **disciples** were filled with joy,		13:52
6 Howbeit, as the **disciples** stood round about him,		14:20
6 Confirming the souls of the **disciples**,		14:22
7 And there they abode long time with the **disciples**.		14:28
6 to put a yoke upon the neck of the **disciples**,		15:10
1 and, behold, a certain **disciple** was there,		16:1
8 strengthening all the **disciples**.		18:23
7 exhorting the **disciples** to receive him:		18:27
8 came to Ephesus: and finding certain **disciples**,		19:1
8 departed from them, and separated the **disciples**,		19:9
5 the **disciples** suffered him not.		19:30
8 Paul called unto him the **disciples**,		20:1
6 when the **disciples** came together to break bread,		20:7
8 speaking ... to draw away **disciples** after them.		20:30
8 And finding **disciples**, we tarried there seven days:		21:4
6 with us also certain of the **disciples** of Caesarea,		21:16
3 with them one Mnason of Cyprus, an old **disciple**,		21:16

Classical Greek

Mathētēs, constructed from the stem *math* (cf. the verb *manthanō*), means "learner, pupil." By implication, the existence of a *mathētēs* signals the presence of a *didaskalos* (1314), "teacher." Thus the learner-teacher unit is a relationship in which knowledge, tradition, behavior, and/or values are transmitted from the teacher to the pupil.

Implicit in the expression is a "direct dependence of the one under instruction upon an authority superior in knowledge" (Rengstorf, "mathētēs," *Kittel*, 4:416). Papyri evidence shows that *mathētēs* functioned in a semitechnical sense for "apprentice" (ibid.; cf. *Moulton-Milligan*). Here there is a drift of *mathētēs* toward "disciple." It is easy to see how such language was suitable in regard to philosophical speculation and different schools of thought. "To learn" is to experience knowledge accessible only through "teaching." These ideas, concepts, truths, or facts are otherwise unobtainable (Muller, "Disciple," *Colin Brown*, 1:483f.).

Although the verb *manthanō*, "I learn" (Hebrew *lāmadh*), occurs around 40 times in the Septuagint, the noun *mathētēs* occurs only in possibly variant readings (Jeremiah 13:21 [Hebrew *'allûph*]).

Old Testament Background

It is not accidental that the Hebrew word *talmîdh*, which became the fixed word for "disciple" in Judaism, appears quite infrequently in the Old Testament and never with any special significance. The reason for this is due to the nature of the Old Testament itself. The Old Testament contains the inspired words of God to man and is God's distinct revelation. Men were not to look to other men for knowledge, not even to the prophets who were only mouthpieces for God. "In the sphere of revelation there is no place for the establishment of a master-disciple relation, nor is there the possibility of setting up a human word alongside the Word of God" (Rengstorf, "mathētēs," *Kittel*, 4:431). In no way does the Old Testament permit the idea of "masters" (even Moses) who instructed the people in God's Word, for God (the only Master) gave His Word through His chosen instruments.

With the close of the Old Testament canon, however, it became necessary for the Jews to devote themselves wholeheartedly to the study of God's Word. Those who excelled in studying the Law, the Torah, and the oral tradition surrounding the Torah were rabbis; those who studied under them were known as *talmîdhîm* (disciples). Because of the comprehensive knowledge of the rabbis, the *talmîdh* devoted himself entirely to his rabbi not only as one who learned but also as one who served.

There are close links between the development of rabbinic practice and the influence of Hellenism, especially in terms of teaching methods and the development of schools of tradition (ibid., 4:437-440). The most significant rabbinic "schools" were those of Hillel (ca. 60 B.C. to A.D. 20); Shammai (ca. 30 B.C. to A.D. 10); Gamaliel I, the grandson of Hillel, who taught Paul as a boy (Acts 22:3); and Akiba (ca. A.D. 50 to ca. 135).

Although the Pharisees were primarily concerned with the practical implications of the Torah and not theoretical reasoning about the Torah, it is apparent from Mark 2:18 (and parallels) that even the Pharisees may have had some disciples (cf. also Matthew 12:27 where "your children" may refer to disciples of the Pharisees).

New Testament Usage

The overall word group occurs in a broad range of New Testament literature; the noun, however, does not. It is restricted to the four Gospels and Acts. The concept of discipleship is, moreover, conveyed by other terms such as *akoulutheō* (188), "I follow," and *opisō* (3557), "behind, after."

One of the most common names for Jesus was "Teacher" (*didaskalos* [1314]), in other words, "Rabbi" (Mark 9:5; 11:21; John 1:38; 20:16). He was "The Teacher of Israel" (note the presence of the article in the Greek) who was sent from God (Luke 7:40; John 3:2,10; 13:13f.). To follow (*akoulutheō*) Jesus of Nazareth, to be His disciple, was no easy matter (Matthew 8:19-23; cf. 10:37; Luke 14:26,27,33). The disciple of the Great Teacher must be willing to imitate his teacher, not simply in knowledge but in behavior, life-style, and suffering (Matthew 10:24f.; cf. Mark 10:32).

Unlike other rabbis, Jesus' disciples did not choose Him—He chose them; He called them (*kaleō* [2535]; cf. John 2:2; 6:65). The "disciples" were not a group restricted to the 12 disciples/apostles appointed by Jesus. Already in the Gospels it included a much larger group of followers. The Twelve were selected by Jesus from this larger group for the purpose (*hina* [2419]) of "being with him (Jesus)" (Mark 3:13,14). They were also to be "sent out" (*apostellō* [643]) to preach, to have authority, and to cast out demons.

The task of the disciple, then, was to do the things Jesus did and to be like Him. He sent them out to preach repentance and to heal the sick (Luke 9:1,2,6). The Seventy, likewise, were sent out to heal the sick and to repeat the actions of Jesus (Luke 10:1-20). Unlike the pupil-teacher relationship of Hellenism which strove to make the disciple a teacher, in the Christian understanding there is only one teacher who is also Lord. Consequently, the work of the disciple is not to propagate knowledge but to serve (cf. Mark 10:45). Jesus exemplified this, especially at the Last Supper. It was the Teacher and Lord who washed the feet of His disciples as an example of humility for them to follow (John 13:12-17).

The basis for discipleship is faith (John 2:11; 6:61-69; cf. 7:3; 8:30). Belief will result in action like the Master. True discipleship holds to Jesus' teaching (John 8:31). The mark of discipleship is obedience to Jesus' command to "love one another" (John 13:34).

The term *disciple* is not restricted to those who follow Jesus. John the Baptist had disciples who evidently were bound by a sense of obligation and devotion to the Baptist's teachings (which Jesus endorsed because they pointed to Him; Matthew 11:2; Mark 6:29; Luke 11:1; cf. Mark 2:18; John 3:25-28). The Pharisees too were regarded as having disciples (Matthew 22:16; Mark 2:18). They regarded themselves as disciples of Moses (John 9:28). These were attachments, not of loyalty to a person but to a line of reasoning and dogma (cf. Mark 7:5).

Mathētēs was not applied to the new community of God until Acts 6:1 in Luke's second volume. Even in the election of Judas' replacement and the coming of the Spirit, the followers were not called *mathētai* (plural; but cf. *apostoloi* [see 646], "apostles"). "Disciple" was the name for the new believers of the good news that Jesus is the Messiah (Acts 6:1,7; cf. 5:42). They were the "Lord's disciples" (Acts 9:1) and were later called "Christians" (Acts 11:26). *Disciples* in Acts, therefore, has a broader connotation of general allegiance to God.

Possibly the reference to "disciples" in Acts 19:1 refers to disciples of John the Baptist at Ephesus who had been baptized by John (Acts 19:3) but were not converted. However, since *mathētēs* elsewhere in Acts always refers to Christians, it is more likely that the disciples Paul met in Ephesus were indeed Christians but had not experienced the baptism in the Holy Spirit (cf. Horton, *Complete Biblical Library, Acts*, p.445).

STRONG 3101, BAUER 485-86, MOULTON-MILLIGAN 385, KITTEL 4:415-60, LIDDELL-SCOTT 1072, COLIN BROWN 1:483-87,489-90.

3074. μαθήτρια mathētria noun
Disciple, learner, pupil (female).
CROSS-REFERENCE:
μανθάνω manthanō (3101)

1. μαθήτρια mathētria nom sing fem

1 was at Joppa a certain **disciple** named Tabitha,...... Acts 9:36

This word is the feminine counterpart to *mathētēs* (3073), "disciple" related to the verb *manthanō*, "to learn." This rare feminine form is only found in Greek literature from the First Century B.C. This is likely the result of the general exclusion of women from many organized forms of education in the ancient world.

In the New Testament *mathētria* is found only in Acts 9:36. It refers to Tabitha and identifies her as a "disciple" (of Jesus) or the near equivalent, a Christian (woman) (see Rengstorf, "mathētria," *Kittel*, 4:460f.).

STRONG 3102, BAUER 486, MOULTON-MILLIGAN 385, KITTEL 4:460-61, LIDDELL-SCOTT 1072.

3075. Μαθουσαλά Mathousala name
Methuselah.

1. Μαθουσαλά Mathousala masc

1 Which was the son **of Mathusala**,................... Luke 3:37

The son of Enoch in the genealogy of Jesus (Luke 3:37).

3076. Μαϊνάν Mainan name
Menan.

1. Μαϊνάν Mainan masc
2. Μεννά Menna masc

1 which was the son **of Menan**,...................... Luke 3:31

The son of Mattatha in the genealogy of Jesus (Luke 3:31).

3077. μαίνομαι mainomai verb
Mad, be out of one's mind, rave, be out of control.
COGNATES:
ἐμμαίνομαι emmainomai (1679)
μανία mania (3102)
SYNONYM:
ἐξίστημι existēmi (1822)

הָלַל hālal (2054), Praise; hithpoel: go mad (Jer 25:16 [32:16]).

שָׁגַע shāgha' (8154), Pual: madman (Jer 29:26 [36:26]).

1. μαίνομαι mainomai 1sing indic pres mid
2. μαίνῃ mainē 2sing indic pres mid
3. μαίνεται mainetai 3sing indic pres mid
4. μαίνεσθε mainesthe 2pl indic pres mid

3 He hath a devil, and **is mad**; why hear ye him?.... John 10:20
2 And they said unto her, Thou **art mad**............. Acts 12:15
2 Paul, **thou art beside thyself**;...................... 26:24
1 But he said, **I am not mad**, most noble Festus;........ 26:25
4 or unbelievers, will they not say that ye **are mad**?.. 1 Co 14:23

Classical Greek
Mainomai generally means "to be mad, beside oneself" or "to be in a frenzy." In classical Greek the word is used with a variety of meanings. Homer used *mainomai* to describe the rage in a marital dispute. Eusebius used it of one "mad" with wine (*Liddell-Scott*). *Mainomai*

is also used to describe the "madness" of an uncontrolled fire, the effect of uncontrolled ulcers, and even a vine that "madly" continues producing fruit (ibid.).

Septuagint Usage
There are seven instances of *mainomai* in the Septuagint, only two of which are canonical (Jeremiah 25:16 [LXX 32:16]; 29:26 [36:26]). God makes men "mad" (not angry) when He pours out His wrath. Antiochus considered Eleazar's willingness to undergo torture rather than denounce his religion as madness (4 Maccabees 8:5; cf. 10:13).

New Testament Usage
Mainomai occurs only five times in the New Testament. In John 10:20 the Jews accused Jesus of having a devil and used *mainomai* to describe Him as being "mad." Upon hearing the incredible news of Peter's presence, Mary's household accused Rhoda of being "mad" (Acts 12:15). *Mainomai* can also be used of one who allows his better judgment to be overcome by his enthusiasm as in Acts 26:24 where Festus accused Paul of being "mad" or beside himself with much learning. This usage is parallel to that of the Roman emperor who rebuked Appianus for using violent language by saying "we are accustomed to bring to their senses those who are mad or besides themselves" (*Moulton-Milligan*).

STRONG 3105, BAUER 486, MOULTON-MILLIGAN 385, KITTEL 4:360-61, LIDDELL-SCOTT 1073, COLIN BROWN 1:527-30; 3:230.

3078. μακαρίζω makarizō verb
Pronounce happy or blessed, fortunate.

COGNATES:
μακάριος makarios (3079)
μακαρισμός makarismos (3080)

אָשַׁר 'āshar (861), Piel: call one blessed (Jb 29:11, Mal 3:12); leader (Is 9:16); pual: be called blessed (Ps 41:2 [40:2]).

אַשְׁרֵי 'ashrê (869), Blessed (Ps 144:15 [143:15]).

1. μακαρίζομεν makarizomen 1pl indic pres act
2. μακαριοῦσιν makariousin 3pl indic fut act

2 henceforth all generations **shall call** me **blessed**...... Luke 1:48
1 Behold, we **count** them **happy** which endure.......... Jas 5:11

Classical Greek and Septuagint Usage
The verb *makarizō* means "to count or pronounce someone to be happy," "to bless," or "to congratulate someone." The classical Greek uses the word in the same sense as the Septuagint and New Testament. The Septuagint reflects this meaning when Leah said "the daughters will call me blessed" (Genesis 30:13). *Makarizō* occurs numerous times with the same sense (Job 29:11; Psalms 41:2; 72:17 [LXX 40:2; 71:17]). Often it is the Lord that "blesses" one, in that He bestows blessings or favors upon men. When the word is used with men as subject, the sense is more often that of counting or pronouncing one to be blessed. The papyri refer to one born under favorable planetary signs as "born under much *blessing*" (*Moulton-Milligan*).

New Testament Usage
Makarizō occurs only two times in the Greek New Testament. Luke used *makarizō* in the same sense as the Septuagint in Mary's Magnificat: "All generations shall call me blessed" (Luke 1:48). The sense here is that all men will recognize God's blessing and favor upon her and will congratulate her, holding her in high esteem. James says that "we count them happy (*makarizō*)" who endure affliction (James 5:11). *Makarizō* does not refer to joy or delight in experiencing the persecution but to the blessing gained by enduring the pressures of affliction.

STRONG 3106, BAUER 486, MOULTON-MILLIGAN 386, KITTEL 4:362-70, LIDDELL-SCOTT 1073-74, COLIN BROWN 1:215-16.

3079. μακάριος makarios adj
Blessed, fortunate, happy.

COGNATE:
μακαρίζω makarizō (3078)

SYNONYM:
εὐλογητός eulogētos (2109)

אֹשֶׁר 'ōsher (865), Happy (Gn 30:13).

אַשְׁרֵי 'ashrê (869), Happy, blessed (2 Chr 9:7, Ps 65:4 [64:4], Is 32:20).

1. μακάριον makarion nom/acc sing masc/neu
2. μακάριος makarios nom sing masc
3. μακαρίου makariou gen sing masc
4. μακάριοι makarioi nom pl masc
5. μακαρία makaria nom sing fem
6. μακαρίαν makarian acc sing fem
7. μακάριαι makariai nom pl fem
8. μακαριωτέρα makariōtera comp nom sing fem

4 **Blessed** are the poor in spirit:..................... Matt 5:3
4 **Blessed** are they that mourn:........................ 5:4
4 **Blessed** are the meek: ... shall inherit the earth........ 5:5
4 **Blessed** are they which do hunger and thirst........... 5:6
4 **Blessed** are the merciful: ... shall obtain mercy......... 5:7

4	Blessed are the pure in heart: ... shall see God.	Matt 5:8
4	Blessed are the peacemakers: ... children of God.	5:9
4	Blessed are they which are persecuted	5:10
4	Blessed are ye, when men shall revile you,	5:11
2	And blessed is he, whosoever shall not be offended.	11:6
4	But blessed are your eyes, for they see:	13:16
2	Blessed art thou, Simon Barjona:	16:17
2	Blessed is that servant, whom his lord ... find so	24:46
5	And blessed is she that believed:	Luke 1:45
4	Blessed be ye poor: for yours is the kingdom	6:20
4	Blessed are ye that hunger now: ... shall be filled.	6:21
4	Blessed are ye that weep now: for ye shall laugh.	6:21
4	Blessed are ye, when men shall hate you,	6:22
2	And blessed is he, whosoever shall not be offended	7:23
4	Blessed are the eyes which see ... things that ye see:	10:23
5	Blessed is the womb that bare thee,	11:27
4	blessed ... that hear the word of God, and keep it.	11:28
4	Blessed are those servants,	12:37
4	and find them so, blessed are those servants.	12:38
2	Blessed is that servant, whom his lord when he	12:43
2	thou shalt be blessed; for they cannot recompense	14:14
2	Blessed is he that shall eat bread in the kingdom	14:15
7	Blessed are the barren,	23:29
4	happy are ye if ye do them.	John 13:17
4	blessed are they that have not seen,	20:29
1	It is more blessed to give than to receive.	Acts 20:35
1	I think myself happy, king Agrippa,	26:2
4	Blessed are they whose iniquities are forgiven,	Rom 4:7
2	Blessed is ... to whom the Lord will not impute sin.	4:8
2	Happy is he that condemneth not himself	14:22
8	she is happier if she so abide, after my judgment:	1 Co 7:40
3	the glorious gospel of the blessed God,	1 Tm 1:11
2	who is the blessed and only Potentate,	6:15
6	Looking for that blessed hope,	Tit 2:13
2	Blessed is the man that endureth temptation:	Jas 1:12
2	this man shall be blessed in his deed.	1:25
4	if ye suffer for righteousness' sake, happy are ye:	1 Pt 3:14
4	happy are ye; for the spirit of glory and of God	4:14
2	Blessed is he that readeth, and they that hear	Rev 1:3
4	Blessed are the dead which die in the Lord	14:13
2	I come as a thief. Blessed is he that watcheth,	16:15
4	Write, Blessed are they which are called	19:9
2	Blessed ... that hath part in the first resurrection:	20:6
2	blessed is he that keepeth the sayings	22:7
4	Blessed are they that do his commandments,	22:14

Classical Greek

Makarios is a longer form of *makar* in classical Greek. The one who is *makarios* is "happy, fortunate, blessed." The idea is that he is secure from life's hardships (*Liddell-Scott*). Very often *makarios* occurs in a formal construction: "Happy is the one who . . . ." *Makarios* may denote an exhortation or a pronouncement; thus "congratulations" might even be a suitable translation (Becker, "Blessing," *Colin Brown*, 1:215).

Septuagint Usage

Such formulaic constructs—often called beatitudes—are popular in the Septuagint, e.g., where *makarios* translates *'esher* (e.g., Psalms 1:1; 34:8; 40:4 [LXX 33:8; 39:4]; Proverbs 8:32; Sirach 14:1). Israel as a nation is "fortunate" (Deuteronomy 33:29; Psalms 144:15; 146:5 [LXX 143:15; 145:5]). "Blessedness" (either in the sense of pronouncement or as an exhortation) is the lot of those who hope in the Lord and who are the objects of His grace, His unmerited favor (Job 5:17; Psalms 34:8; 40:4 [LXX 33:8; 39:4]; cf. 128:1 [127:1]; Sirach 26:1).

New Testament Usage

The most well-known example of *makarios* in the New Testament is the beatitudes of Jesus' Sermon on the Mount (Matthew 5:3-11; Luke 6:20,21, etc.). Matthew and Luke are in fact responsible for 28 out of 50 instances of *makarios* (not found in Mark). Every Gospel text of the Sermon follows a beatitude-type formula, "Blessed are . . . " or "O, the fullness of the blessing of . . . . " The condition of the gracious favor of God (implied) is for the present (Luke 6:20,21, "now" is read here). However, the immediacy of the pronouncement does not exclude the possibility that its realization may be future (Titus 2:13; Revelation 20:6). This seems especially apparent for those who are "fortunate" or who are "to be happy" in the circumstance of persecution (Luke 6:22; cf. other indications of future "blessedness" in James 1:12; Revelation 14:13; 19:9; 20:6).

"Blessed" is pronounced upon those who act. Here the idea of pronouncement clearly converges with exhortation (John 13:17; cf. Matthew 5:7; Luke 11:28; James 1:25; Revelation 1:3). "Congratulations" are extended to those who receive prophetic insight from God (Matthew 13:16; 16:17; Luke 10:23; 11:28) or who trust in God's—himself called "blessed" (1 Timothy 1:11)—words (Luke 1:45; John 20:29; Revelation 22:7; cf. Revelation 1:3). Those who have experienced forgiveness through Christ are indeed "blessed" (Romans 4:7,8).

STRONG 3107, BAUER 486-87, MOULTON-MILLIGAN 386, KITTEL 4:362-70, LIDDELL-SCOTT 1073-74, COLIN BROWN 1:215-16.

3080. μακαρισμός makarismos noun

To declare blessedness, ascribe blessing, a felicitation.

CROSS-REFERENCE:
μακαρίζω makarizō (3078)

1. μακαρισμός makarismos nom sing masc
2. μακαρισμόν makarismon acc sing masc

2	David also describeth the blessedness of the man,	Rom 4:6
1	this blessedness then upon the circumcision only,	4:9
1	Where is then the blessedness ye spake of?	Gal 4:15

In the New Testament *makarismos* and the group of words of which it is a part (*makarios* [3079], *makarizō* [3078]) generally denote the particular joy that accrues to the person as a result of salvation (see Hauck, "makarismos," *Kittel*, 4:367). The sense of ascribing or pronouncing blessing on a person is the way Romans 4:6 uses *makarismos*. Here Paul refers to David's pronouncement of blessing on those whom God has reckoned righteous. Similarly, the Galatians (4:15) were reminded of their previous sense of having been blessed by Paul's message of the gospel. That is, they had declared or considered themselves blessed, happy.

STRONG 3108, BAUER 487, MOULTON-MILLIGAN 386, KITTEL 4:362-70, LIDDELL-SCOTT 1074, COLIN BROWN 1:215-16.

3081. Μακεδονία Makedonia name
Macedonia.

1. **Μακεδονία** Makedonia nom fem
2. **Μακεδονίας** Makedonias gen fem
3. **Μακεδονίᾳ** Makedonia dat fem
4. **Μακεδονίαν** Makedonian acc fem

4	saying, Come over into **Macedonia**, and help us.....	Acts 16:9
4	we endeavoured to go into **Macedonia**,................	16:10
2	which is the chief city of that part of **Macedonia**,......	16:12
2	Silas and Timotheus were come from **Macedonia**,......	18:5
4	when he had passed through **Macedonia**...............	19:21
4	So he sent into **Macedonia** two of them...............	19:22
4	and departed for to go into **Macedonia**...............	20:1
2	he purposed to return through **Macedonia**............	20:3
1	For it hath pleased them of **Macedonia** and Achaia	Rom 15:26
4	when I shall pass through **Macedonia**:..............	1 Co 16:5
4	for I do pass through **Macedonia**....................	16:5
4	And to pass by you into **Macedonia**,...............	2 Co 1:16
2	and to come again out of **Macedonia** unto you,........	1:16
4	I went from thence into **Macedonia**.....................	2:13
4	For, when we were come into **Macedonia**,.............	7:5
2	grace ... bestowed on the churches **of Macedonia**;.......	8:1
2	brethren which came from **Macedonia** supplied:........	11:9
2	when I departed from **Macedonia**,.................	Phlp 4:15
3	to all that believe in **Macedonia** and Achaia.........	1 Th 1:7
3	out the word ... not only in **Macedonia** and Achaia,.....	1:8
3	all the brethren which are in all **Macedonia**:...........	4:10
4	abide ... at Ephesus, when I went into **Macedonia**,..	1 Tm 1:3

Roman province north of Greece, bordering the Adriatic and Aegean Seas; visited by Paul on his second missionary journey (Acts 16:9ff.).

3082. Μακεδών Makedōn name
Macedonian.

1. **Μακεδών** Makedōn nom sing masc
2. **Μακεδόνος** Makedonos gen sing masc
3. **Μακεδόνες** Makedones nom pl masc
4. **Μακεδόσιν** Makedosin dat pl masc
5. **Μακεδόνας** Makedonas acc pl masc

1	There stood a man **of Macedonia**, and prayed him,	Acts 16:9
5	men of **Macedonia**, Paul's companions in travel,.......	19:29
2	one Aristarchus, **a Macedonian** of Thessalonica,........	27:2
4	for which I boast of you to them **of Macedonia**,.....	2 Co 9:2
3	Lest haply if they **of Macedonia** come with me,.........	9:4

Native of Macedonia; of Gaius and Aristarchus (Acts 19:29).

3083. μάκελλον makellon noun
Meat market, food market, provision market.

1. **μακέλλῳ** makellō dat sing neu

1	Whatsoever is sold in the **shambles**, that eat,.......	1 Co 10:25

Classical Greek

Appearing from about 400 B.C., the noun *makellon* properly denotes "an enclosure, grating, fenced place, settlement." The term may perhaps be traced back to the Hebrew word *miklah*, "enclosure, fold" (Schneider, "makellon," *Kittel*, 4:370). It was used from the Third Century B.C. on for a meat or food market (*Bauer*). In a Greek city the meat market was part of or a section of the larger food market, the *makellon*. In the larger cities throughout ancient Greece, there was a rectangular centralized court bordered by pillars in which there were booths for the selling of food. This was known as the *makellon*. Chapels for cultic worship, adorned with statuary, were often in close proximity.

New Testament Usage

The term *makellon* does not appear in the Septuagint, and it is found only once in the New Testament (1 Corinthians 10:25). But the usage here is very significant. A Latin inscription which contains the word *macellum* (for the Greek *makellon*), dating back to the time of Paul, has been found in the excavations of Corinth. It was to this *makellon* that Paul referred when he wrote of meat purchased at the marketplace ("shambles," KJV). Since the meat being sold normally came from a pagan temple sacrifice, Paul urged caution in the exercise of Christian liberty for conscience' sake.

STRONG 3111, BAUER 487, MOULTON-MILLIGAN 386, KITTEL 4:370-72, LIDDELL-SCOTT 1074 (see "makellos").

3084. μακράν makran adv
Far, far off, distant.

COGNATES:
  μακρόθεν makrothen (3085)
  μακροθυμέω makrothumeō (3086)

μακροθυμία makrothumia (3087)
μακροθύμως makrothumōs (3088)
μακρός makros (3089)
μακροχρόνιος makrochronios (3090)

אָרֵךְ 'ārēkh (773), Be long (Ez 12:22—Codex Alexandrinus only).

מֶרְחָק merchāq (4963), Distance (2 Sm 15:17).

סוּר ṣûr (5681), Depart (Prv 13:19).

רָחוֹק rāchôq (7632), Far (1 Kgs 8:46, Ps 119:155 [118:155], Ez 6:12).

רַחִיק rachîq (A7635), Away (Ezr 6:6—Aramaic).

רָחַק rāchaq (7651), Qal: be far (Dt 14:24); hiphil: go far away, drive far away (Ex 8:28, Jos 3:16); be at a great distance (Prv 22:15).

1. μακράν makran

1 And there was a **good way off** from them............	Matt 8:30
1 Thou art not **far** from the kingdom of God........	Mark 12:34
1 And when he was now not **far** from the house,......	Luke 7:6
1 But when he was yet a **great way off**,.................	15:20
1 for they were not **far** from land,...................	John 21:8
1 though he be not **far** from every one of us:........	Acts 17:27
1 for I will send thee **far hence** unto the Gentiles........	22:21

Classical Greek

As the adverbial form of the adjective *makros* (3089), *makran* denotes a sense of distance both spatially and temporally. From the Fifth Century B.C. onward the classical writers used *makran* both figuratively and literally to mean "far (away)." These authors also employed *makran* in the sense of time to connote something not temporally imminent. For the Greeks *makran* could also be used as a preposition to mean "far away from someone or something."

Septuagint Usage

Makran occurs more than 30 times in the Septuagint. It is normally a translation of various forms of the Hebrew stem *rāchaq*, "to withdraw." The spatial sense is frequently used literally (e.g., Genesis 44:4; Numbers 14:24). Several figurative connotations are also used. *Makran* may refer to the distance of the individual from God (Jeremiah 2:5), the fact that salvation or righteousness is far off (Isaiah 46:12), or something that is far off or unattainable (Deuteronomy 30:11). Referring to the temporal, *makran* may speak of the length of time, such as, "the days are prolonged" (Ezekiel 12:22).

New Testament Usage

In the New Testament *makran* is used both literally (to denote place) and metaphorically. Matthew 8:30 refers to the place of the swine as a "good way off" (*makran*). The disciples on the lake, in John 21:8, "were not *far* (*makran*) from land." In an account of Paul's commissioning, *makran* indicates a distant destination, "I will send you far away to the Gentiles" (Acts 22:21, RSV).

The figurative usage of *makran* in the New Testament in some ways expresses a reversal of the Septuagintal usage. In the Septuagint it frequently connoted the remoteness of God from humankind. *Makran* in the New Testament, however, often reveals the removal of the separation between God and the individual. A scribe is said to be not far from the kingdom of God (Mark 12:34). According to Acts 17:27 God is "not far from every one of us." Ephesians 2:13,17 recalls that Gentiles who were once "far off" (*makran*) from God have been brought near and united to those (Jewish Christians) from whom they had been separated. (See Preisker, "makran," *Kittel*, 4:372-74; and *Bauer*.)

STRONG 3112, BAUER 487, MOULTON-MILLIGAN 386, KITTEL 4:372-74, LIDDELL-SCOTT 1074, COLIN BROWN 2:52-54.

3085. μακρόθεν makrothen adv

From afar, from a distance.

COGNATE:
μακράν makran (3084)

SYNONYM:
πόρρωθεν porrhōthen (4066)

מֶרְחָק merchāq (4963), Afar, distant (Ps 138:6 [137:6], Jer 4:16, 6:20).

רָחוֹק rāchôq (7632), Distant, far (Dt 29:22, Jos 9:6, 2 Chr 6:32).

רָחַק rāchaq (7651), Be far, be distant; hiphil: some distance away (Gn 21:16—Sixtine Edition only).

1. μακρόθεν makrothen

1 But Peter followed him **afar** off...................	Matt 26:58
1 And many women were there beholding **afar** off,......	27:55
1 he saw Jesus **afar** off, he ran and worshipped him,..	Mark 5:6
1 for divers of them came **from far**.................	8:3
1 And seeing a fig tree **afar** off having leaves,...........	11:13
1 And Peter followed him **afar off**,.....................	14:54
1 There were also women looking on **afar off**:...........	15:40
1 seeth Abraham **afar** off, and Lazarus in his bosom.	Luke 16:23
1 And the publican, standing **afar off**,...................	18:13
1 high priest's house. And Peter followed **afar off**........	22:54
1 the women that followed him ... stood **afar off**,........	23:49
1 Standing **afar** off for the fear of her torment,.......	Rev 18:10
1 shall stand **afar** off for the fear of her torment,........	18:15
1 sailors, and as many as trade by sea, stood **afar off**,...	18:17

From the root *makros* (3089), "long, distant," *makrothen* is used both figuratively and literally in the New Testament. It indicates a place that is removed in distance from another location. For instance, in Mark 11:13 Jesus saw a fig tree

μακροθυμέω 3086

from a distance; some of the crowd of Mark 8:3 had come from afar; Peter followed from a distance into the high priest's court (Mark 14:54; Luke 22:54).

To illustrate a figurative usage of *makrothen*, Preisker ("makrothen," *Kittel*, 4:373) points to the Synoptic texts (Matthew 27:55; Mark 15:40; Luke 23:49) that describe the women that stood far off from the Cross. The word here "does not so much fix their location as express the pious awe and sense of distance which grips the women when they are confronted by what God does at the cross" (ibid.). Revelation 18:10,15,17 portray onlookers to God's judgment; only from afar (the sense of being removed, of distance) dare they watch.

STRONG 3113, BAUER 487-88, MOULTON-MILLIGAN 386, KITTEL 4:372-74, LIDDELL-SCOTT 1074.

3086. μακροθυμέω
makrothumeō verb
Long-suffering, forbearing, persevere, endure, show patience.

COGNATES:
θυμόω thumoō (2350)
μακράν makran (3084)
μακροθυμία makrothumia (3087)
μακροθύμως makrothumōs (3088)

אָפַק 'āphaq (681), Hithpael: be patient (Sir 32:18).

אָרֵךְ 'ārēkh (773), Be long; hiphil: prolong (Eccl 8:12—only some Sinaiticus texts).

1. **μακροθυμεῖ** makrothumei 3sing indic pres act
2. **μακροθυμεῖτε** makrothumeite 2pl impr pres act
3. **μακροθυμῶν** makrothumōn
   nom sing masc part pres act
4. **μακροθύμησον** makrothumēson 2sing impr aor act
5. **μακροθυμήσατε** makrothumēsate 2pl impr aor act
6. **μακροθυμήσας** makrothumēsas
   nom sing masc part aor act

4	have patience with me, and I will pay thee all.	Matt 18:26
4	Have patience with me, and I will pay thee all.	18:29
3	his own elect, ... though he bear long with them?	Luke 18:7
1	Charity **suffereth long**, and is kind;	1 Co 13:4
2	support the weak, **be patient** toward all men.	1 Th 5:14
6	And so, after he **had patiently endured**,	Heb 6:15
5	Be patient therefore, brethren,	Jas 5:7
3	and hath **long patience** for it,	5:7
5	Be ye also **patient**; stablish your hearts:	5:8
1	but is **longsuffering** to us-ward,	2 Pt 3:9

Septuagint Usage
Makrothumeō is used in the Septuagint to translate two Hebrew words meaning "be patient," "suffer long," or "endure." Job says he will not live forever to "persevere in" or "endure" his affliction (Job 7:16). Proverbs describes a merciful man as one who "displays patience" with others (19:11). God is said to delay His wrath or "suffer long" with the sinner in hope that he may repent (Sirach 35:19).

New Testament Usage
The New Testament uses *makrothumeō* concerning men to mean: (1) "be patient with, wait for someone" or (2) "endure, persevere, or suffer long." The steward begged his master to "be patient" or "forbear" foreclosure (Matthew 18:26,29). Paul exhorted the Christian to "show patience" to those who cause him frustration and impatience (1 Thessalonians 5:14). Love demonstrates this quality (1 Corinthians 13:4). James expressed the second sense by exhorting Christians to "endure" suffering patiently, to "persevere" until the coming of the Lord (James 5:7,8). God also must "suffer" or "endure" the transgressions of men. Peter said the delay in God's judgment is not because God is hesitant or dilatory (*bradunei* [see 1012]) but is a demonstration that God "suffers long" (*makrothumeō*) the sins and infidelities of man (2 Peter 3:9).

STRONG 3114, BAUER 488, MOULTON-MILLIGAN 386, KITTEL 4:374-87, LIDDELL-SCOTT 1074-75, COLIN BROWN 2:768-72.

3087. μακροθυμία **makrothumia** noun
Long-suffering, forbearance, patience, endurance.

CROSS-REFERENCES:
θυμόω thumoō (2350)
μακράν makran (3084)
μακροθυμέω makrothumeō (3086)

1. **μακροθυμία** makrothumia nom sing fem
2. **μακροθυμίας** makrothumias gen sing fem
3. **μακροθυμίᾳ** makrothumia dat sing fem
4. **μακροθυμίαν** makrothumian acc sing fem

2	his goodness and forbearance and **longsuffering**;	Rom 2:4
3	endured with much **longsuffering** the vessels	9:22
3	By pureness, by knowledge, by **longsuffering**,	2 Co 6:6
1	peace, **longsuffering**, gentleness, goodness, faith,	Gal 5:22
2	with **longsuffering**, forbearing one another in love;	Eph 4:2
4	unto all **patience** and **longsuffering** with joyfulness;	Col 1:11
4	humbleness of mind, meekness, **longsuffering**;	3:12
4	Jesus Christ might show forth all **longsuffering**,	1 Tm 1:16
3	purpose, faith, longsuffering, charity, **patience**,	2 Tm 3:10
3	rebuke, exhort with all **longsuffering** and doctrine.	4:2
2	through faith and **patience** inherit the promises.	Heb 6:12
2	an example of suffering affliction, and of **patience**,	Jas 5:10
1	when once the **longsuffering** of God waited	1 Pt 3:20
4	that the **longsuffering** of our Lord is salvation;	2 Pt 3:15

Makrothumia (related to *makrothumos*) is a noun formed from the two words *makros* (3089), "long," and *thumos* (2349), "heart, mind" (in the sense of "spirit, feelings, disposition"). It means "patience, endurance" when used as an object and "long-suffering, forbearance" when used as a subject.

Septuagint Usage
Makrothumia occurs five times in the Septuagint. The adjective form *makrothumos* is more common. Only two texts have Hebrew equivalents behind them (Proverbs 25:15; Jeremiah 15:15 of God's patience; cf. Nehemiah 9:17; Nahum 1:3). The principal idea is that it is a virtue to have patience toward others (Sirach 5:11; Jeremiah 15:15) or "endurance, patient persistence" (1 Maccabees 8:4).

New Testament Usage
The New Testament echoes much of the Old Testament usage. God's patience is designed to lead men and women to repentance and salvation (Romans 2:4; 9:22; 1 Timothy 1:16; 2 Peter 3:15). From the New Testament perspective this has always been the case, even in the example of Noah (1 Peter 3:20).

Believers are urged to exhibit *makrothumia* toward others as a "fruit of the Spirit" (Galatians 5:22). It is a quality of love (*agapē* [26], cf. 1 Corinthians 13:4; Ephesians 4:2; Colossians 3:12; cf. 2 Timothy 4:2). This is in contrast to the unbridled passion that takes the law into one's own hands in order to seek revenge. It means being patient and lenient toward others even when self-vindication may appear justified. Moreover, it is conjoined with faith in the certainty of God's promise (2 Timothy 3:10; Hebrews 6:12). *Makrothumia* also speaks of "endurance, patient waiting for God in the face of adversity" (2 Corinthians 6:6; James 5:10).

STRONG 3115, BAUER 488, MOULTON-MILLIGAN 386, KITTEL 4:374-87, LIDDELL-SCOTT 1074-75, COLIN BROWN 2:764-71,776.

3088. μακροθύμως makrothumōs adv
Patiently.
CROSS-REFERENCES:
  θυμόω thumoō (2350)
  μακράν makran (3084)
  μακροθυμέω makrothumeō (3086)

1. μακροθύμως makrothumōs

1 wherefore I beseech thee to hear me **patiently**...... Acts 26:3

An adverbial form, *makrothumōs* occurs only one time in the Greek New Testament (Acts 26:3). It does not appear in the adverbial form in the Septuagint although the adjective form *makrothumos* occurs often. *Liddell-Scott* does not cite a single occurrence of the word in classical Greek, nor does *Moulton-Milligan* cite any occurrence in the papyri literature.

For insight into the meaning of the adverb *makrothumōs* one may look at the kindred verb *makrothumeō* (3086) or the adjective form *makrothumos*. Both the verb and adjective support the basic concept that *makrothumōs* describes actions that are "patient, forbearing, slow to anger." In Acts 26:3 Paul asked Agrippa that he be patient (*makrothumōs*) in hearing him and that he reserve judgment. Above all Paul was concerned that Agrippa allow him ample time to present what Agrippa needed to know.

STRONG 3116, BAUER 488, KITTEL 4:374-87, LIDDELL-SCOTT 1074-75, COLIN BROWN 2:768-69.

3089. μακρός makros adj
Long, distant, far.
CROSS-REFERENCE:
  μακράν makran (3084)

אָרֵךְ 'ārēkh (773), Be long (Ez 12:22).
אָרֵךְ 'ārēkh (774), Long (Ez 17:3).
אֹרֶךְ 'ōrekh (775), Long life (Jb 12:12—Codex Alexandrinus only).
אָרֹךְ 'ārōkh (776), Longer (Jb 11:9).
רָחוֹק rāchôq (7632), Far (Ez 12:27).

1. μακράν makran acc sing fem
2. μακρά makra nom/acc pl neu

2 and for a pretence make **long** prayer:............. Matt 23:14
2 and for a pretence make **long** prayers:............ Mark 12:40
1 and took his journey into a **far** country,.......... Luke 15:13
1 into a **far** country to receive for himself a kingdom,.... 19:12
2 and for a show make **long** prayers:................ 20:47
1 and to your children, and to all that are **afar off**,.... Acts 2:39
1 now in Christ Jesus ye who sometimes were **far off**... Eph 2:13
1 and preached peace to you which were **afar off**,......... 2:17

Classical Greek
This adjective, like its adverbial form *makran* (3084), is used to express the extension of both time and space. When applied to time it may mean "long-lasting" or "enduring." Referring to space the meaning again denotes "distant, far," or it may mean "far-stretching" or even "tall, lofty" or "deep" (*Liddell-Scott*).

New Testament Usage
In the New Testament *makros* was used by Jesus when He denounced the scribes for the hypocritical pretense of their long prayers (Mark 12:40; Luke 20:47). It was also used

by Luke to refer to space when speaking of a far or distant country, as in the Parable of the Prodigal Son (Luke 15:13) and the Parable of the Ten Talents (Luke 19:12).

STRONG 3117, BAUER 488, MOULTON-MILLIGAN 386, LIDDELL-SCOTT 1075.

3090. μακροχρόνιος
makrochronios adj

Long-lived.

CROSS-REFERENCES:
μακράν makran (3084)
χρόνος chronos (5385)

1. μακροχρόνιος makrochronios nom sing masc

1 and thou mayest **live long** on the earth............. Eph 6:3

This is a compound adjective consisting of the two words, *makros* (3089), "long," and *chronos* (5385), "time." In its use in classical Greek, the Septuagint, and its single occurrence in the New Testament it means "long-lived." Ephesians 6:3 alludes to the promise of the Decalogue (cf. Exodus 20:12; Deuteronomy 5:16) of long life.

STRONG 3118, BAUER 488, MOULTON-MILLIGAN 386, LIDDELL-SCOTT 1075.

3091. μαλακία malakia noun

Weakness, softness; ailment, sickness, infirmity.

COGNATE:
μαλακός malakos (3092)

SYNONYMS:
ἄρρωστος arrhōstos (726)
ἀσθένεια astheneia (763)
νόσος nosos (3417)

אָסוֹן 'āsôn (625), Harm (Gn 42:4, 44:29).

חֳלִי chŏlî (2582), Sickness, illness (Dt 7:15, 2 Chr 21:15, Is 38:9).

מַחֲלָה machălāh (4382), Sickness (Ex 23:25).

מַחֲלֻיִים machăluyîm (4387), Wounded (2 Chr 24:25).

מַכְאוֹב makh'ôv (4480), Pain (2 Chr 6:29).

תַּחֲלֻאִים tachălu'îm (8794), Pain (2 Chr 21:19).

1. μαλακίαν malakian acc sing fem

1 and all manner of **disease** among the people........ Matt 4:23
1 and healing every sickness and every **disease**........... 9:35
1 to heal ... sickness and all manner of **disease**........... 10:1

Classical Greek

Classical writers used *malakia* to speak of "softness, delicacy, effiminacy." It describes both moral and physical weakness. They also used it to refer to the "calmness" of the sea. References in later papyri to physical sickness are reflected in the New Testament and Septuagint as well (*Bauer*).

Septuagint Usage

In the Septuagint *malakia* (15 times) occurs only in the canonical writings. Although it translates four Hebrew expressions (usually *chŏlî/machălāh*), *malakia* denotes "disease" or "illness" almost every time (e.g., Exodus 23:25; Deuteronomy 7:15; 2 Chronicles 21:15,18). The two exceptions to this are Genesis 42:4 and 44:29, both references to Jacob's concern that Benjamin would be "harmed" (Hebrew '*āsôn*) if he went to Egypt with his brothers.

New Testament Usage

Malakia appears only three times in the New Testament, each time in Matthew. Jesus passed through Galilee and other towns healing every illness (*nosos* [3417]) and every "sickness or disease" (*malakia*) among the people (Matthew 4:24; cf. 9:35; 10:1). It is part and parcel of preaching the Kingdom's arrival, and it is a sign of God's authority over such evils. Jesus passed on this authority to His disciples (Matthew 10:1; cf. Mark 16:17,18).

STRONG 3119, BAUER 488, MOULTON-MILLIGAN 387, KITTEL 4:1091-98, LIDDELL-SCOTT 1076, COLIN BROWN 3:996-97,999.

3092. μαλακός malakos adj

Soft.

CROSS-REFERENCE:
μαλακία malakia (3091)

רַךְ rakh (7679), Soft (Prv 25:15).

1. μαλακοί malakoi nom pl masc
2. μαλακοῖς malakois dat pl neu
3. μαλακά malaka nom/acc pl neu

2 A man clothed in **soft** raiment?.................... Matt 11:8
3 they that wear soft clothing are in kings' houses....... 11:8
2 to see? A man clothed in **soft** raiment?............. Luke 7:25
1 nor idolaters, nor adulterers, nor **effeminate**,........ 1 Co 6:9

Classical Greek

This is the word for "soft" or "soft to the touch." Throughout classical Greek *malakos* is used (1) of things, such as clothes, and (2) of persons, especially to denote catamites, those who allow themselves passively to be used homosexually.

New Testament Usage

Both classical senses are employed in the New Testament. Matthew 11:8 (twice) and Luke 7:25 use *malakos* when speaking of clothing. The Baptist's clothes were not of a soft texture like the raiment of the rich.

In 1 Corinthians 6:9 *malakos* is used in the metaphoric sense. Here it refers to persons who are "soft." The rendering "effeminate" (*malakos*) designates the passive partner of a homosexual relationship, and "abusers of themselves with mankind" (*malakos* and *arsenokoitēs* [727]) denotes both the passive and active homosexual partners. (See Barrett, *Harper's New Testament Commentaries, 1 Corinthians*, p.140.)

STRONG 3120, BAUER 488, MOULTON-MILLIGAN 387, LIDDELL-SCOTT 1076-77.

3093. Μαλελεήλ Maleleēl name

Mahalaleel.

1. Μαλελεήλ Maleleēl masc

1 which was the son of **Maleleel**,..................... Luke 3:37

The son of Cainan in the genealogy of Jesus (Luke 3:37).

3094. μάλιστα malista adv

Especially, most of all, particularly.

1. μάλιστα malista sup

1 Sorrowing **most of all** for the words ... he spake,.... Acts 20:38
1 and **specially** before thee, O king Agrippa,............. 25:26
1 **Especially** because I know thee to be expert........... 26:3
1 **especially** unto them who are of the household....... Gal 6:10
1 **chiefly** they that are of Caesar's household.......... Phlp 4:22
1 Saviour of all men, **specially** of those that believe... 1 Tm 4:10
1 and **specially** for those of his own house,................ 5:8
1 **especially** they who labour in the word................. 5:17
1 and the books, but **especially** the parchments........ 2 Tm 4:13
1 and deceivers, **specially** they of the circumcision:...... Tit 1:10
1 a brother beloved, **specially** to me,.................. Phlm 1:16
1 But **chiefly** them that walk after the flesh........... 2 Pt 2:10

This word is used as the superlative of the adverb *mala*, "very, very much," in Greek literature. It can mean "especially, most, most of all, above all, particularly, (very) greatly, chiefly." The New Testament uses *malista* 12 times. It is most frequently translated "(e)specially" in the King James Version (Acts 25:26; 26:3; Galatians 6:10; 1 Timothy 4:10; 5:8,17).

STRONG 3122, BAUER 488-89, MOULTON-MILLIGAN 387, LIDDELL-SCOTT 1078.

3095. μᾶλλον mallon adv

More than, much, rather, on the contrary, instead of.

SYNONYM:
περισσοτέρως perissoterōs (3917)

1. μᾶλλον mallon comp

1 Are ye not **much** better than they?................. Matt 6:26
1 shall he not **much more** clothe you,.................... 6:30
1 how much **more** shall your Father ... in heaven...... 7:11
1 go **rather** to the lost sheep of the house of Israel...... 10:6
1 **much more** shall they call them of his household?..... 10:25
1 but **rather** fear him which is able to destroy........... 10:28
1 I say unto you, he rejoiceth **more** of that sheep,...... 18:13
1 but go ye **rather** to them that sell,..................... 25:9
1 but that **rather** a tumult was made, he took water,..... 27:24
1 but **rather** grew worse,........................... Mark 5:26
1 so much the **more** a great deal they published it;....... 7:36
1 better for him that a millstone (NT)................... 9:42
1 but he cried the **more** a great deal,................... 10:48
1 But he spake the **more** vehemently, If I should die..... 14:31
1 that he should **rather** release Barabbas unto him...... 15:11
1 But so much the **more** went there a fame abroad.... Luke 5:15
1 but **rather** rejoice, because your names are written.... 10:20
1 how much **more** shall your heavenly Father give....... 11:13
1 how much **more** are ye better than the fowls?......... 12:24
1 how much **more** will he clothe you,................... 12:28
1 but he cried so much the **more**, Thou son of David,... 18:39
1 and men loved darkness **rather** than light,........... John 3:19
1 Therefore the Jews sought the **more** to kill him,........ 5:18
1 For they loved the praise of men **more** 12:43
1 Pilate ... heard that saying, he was the **more** afraid;.... 19:8
1 to hearken unto you **more** than unto God,.......... Acts 4:19
1 And believers were the **more** added to the Lord,....... 5:14
1 We ought to obey God **rather** than men................ 5:29
1 But Saul increased the **more** in strength,............... 9:22
1 It is **more** blessed to give than to receive............. 20:35
1 spake in the Hebrew ... they kept the **more** silence:.... 22:2
1 the centurion believed the master ... **more**........... 27:11
1 Much **more** then, being now justified by his blood,.. Rom 5:9
1 much **more**, being reconciled,......................... 5:10
1 much **more** the grace of God, and the gift by grace,.... 5:15
1 much **more** they which receive abundance of grace..... 5:17
1 yea **rather**, that is risen again,........................ 8:34
1 how much **more** their fulness?........................ 11:12
1 how much **more** shall these, which be the natural...... 11:24
1 judge one another any **more**: but judge this **rather**,.... 14:13
1 ye are puffed up, and have not **rather** mourned,..... 1 Co 5:2
1 Why do ye not **rather** take wrong?...................... 6:7
1 do ye not **rather** suffer yourselves to be defrauded?..... 6:7
1 but if thou mayest be made free, use it **rather**.......... 7:21
1 If others be partakers ... are not we **rather**?............ 9:12
1 I would **rather** die than have (NIV).................... 9:15
1 Nay, much **more** those members of the body,.......... 12:22
1 but **rather** that ye may prophesy....................... 14:1
1 spake with tongues, but **rather** that ye prophesied:..... 14:5
1 I speak with tongues **more** than ye all:................ 14:18
1 that contrariwise ye ought **rather** to forgive him,.... 2 Co 2:7
1 the ministration of the spirit be **rather** glorious?......... 3:8
1 much **more** doth the ministration of righteousness...... 3:9
1 much **more** that which remaineth is glorious........... 3:11
1 and willing **rather** to be absent from the body,........... 5:8
1 so that I rejoiced the **more**............................. 7:7
1 exceedingly the **more** joyed we for the joy of Titus,..... 7:13
1 therefore will I **rather** glory in my infirmities,......... 12:9
1 ye have known God, or **rather** are known of God,... Gal 4:9
1 **more** children than she which hath an husband.......... 4:27
1 that stole steal no **more**: but **rather** let him labour,... Eph 4:28
1 but **rather** giving of thanks............................. 5:4
1 have no fellowship ... but **rather** reprove them.......... 5:11
1 this I pray, that your love may abound yet **more**.... Phlp 1:9
1 **more** and **more** in knowledge and in all judgment;....... 1:9
1 **rather** unto the furtherance of the gospel;.............. 1:12
1 depart, and to be with Christ; which is **far** better:...... 1:23
1 but now much **more** in my absence,.................... 2:12
1 If any ... might trust in the flesh, I **more**:............... 3:4
1 so ye would abound **more** and **more**.............. 1 Th 4:1
1 beseech you, ... that ye increase **more** and **more**;.... 4:10
1 **rather** than godly edifying which is in faith: so do... 1 Tm 1:4
1 not despise them, ... but **rather** do them service,....... 6:2
1 lovers of pleasures **more** than lovers of God;......... 2 Tm 3:4
1 Yet for love's sake I **rather** beseech thee,............ Phlm 1:9
1 **specially** to me, but how much **more** unto thee,......... 1:16
1 How much **more** shall the blood of Christ,.......... Heb 9:14

1 so much the **more**, as ye see the day approaching...	Heb 10:25
1 **rather** to suffer affliction with the people of God,	11:25
1 **rather** be in subjection unto the Father of spirits,	12:9
1 but let it **rather** be healed.	12:13
1 much **more** shall not we escape,	12:25
1 Wherefore the **rather**, brethren, give diligence	2 Pt 1:10

Mallon is the comparative of the adverb *mala*. This word occurs numerous times in classical Greek, in the Septuagint, and in the Greek New Testament. *Mallon* occurs in several different types of grammatical constructions that vary the sense of the word slightly. As one of its uses, *mallon* sometimes strengthens the word with which it occurs, as in Mark 10:48, "But he shouted *all the more*" (NIV) (*pollō mallon*). *Mallon* is also used in a comparative sense as in "are ye not *much* better than they" (Matthew 6:26). In Matthew 10:5-7 *mallon* has an adversative sense: Do not go to the Gentiles or Samaritans, but "on the contrary" (rather) go to the lost sheep of Israel (also Matthew 10:28; 25:9). The idea "instead of" is often present, as in the last reference cited, and especially in 1 Corinthians 6:7 where Paul said, "Why do you not accept wrong at the hand of your fellowman *instead of* taking them to civil law courts" (literal translation). Paul clearly gave the idea, by using *mallon*, that one option is preferable to the others.

STRONG 3123, BAUER 489, MOULTON-MILLIGAN 387, LIDDELL-SCOTT 1078.

3096. Μάλχος Malchos name
Malchus.

1. Μάλχος Malchos nom masc

1 The servant's name was **Malchus**.	John 18:10

The high priest's slave whom Peter struck with a sword during the arrest of Jesus (John 18:10).

3097. μάμμη mammē noun
A grandmother.

1. μάμμῃ mammē dat sing fem

1 which dwelt first in thy **grandmother** Lois,	2 Tm 1:5

In the earlier Greek writings *mammē* functioned primarily as the name an infant or young child used for its mother. The name came to denote a grandmother in later Greek and in the Septuagint (cf. 4 Maccabees 16:9). In the New Testament *mammē* is found only in 2 Timothy 1:5 and is rightly translated "grandmother." Here it is mentioned together with *mētēr* (3251), the standard word for "mother," when praising the faith of both Timothy's grandmother and mother.

STRONG 3125, BAUER 490, MOULTON-MILLIGAN 387, LIDDELL-SCOTT 1078.

3098. μαμωνᾶς mamōnas noun
Wealth, property.

SYNONYMS:
κτῆμα ktēma (2905)
πλοῦτος ploutos (4009)
χρῆμα chrēma (5371)

1. μαμωνᾶ mamōna gen sing masc
2. μαμωνᾷ mamōna dat sing masc
3. μαμμωνᾷ mammōna dat sing masc

3 Ye cannot serve God and **mammon**.	Matt 6:24
1 Make to yourselves friends of the **mammon**	Luke 16:9
2 not been faithful in the unrighteous **mammon**,	16:11
2 Ye cannot serve God and **mammon**.	16:13

Mamōnas, "wealth, property, material goods," is actually a transliteration of the Aramaic noun *mamon*. The Greek word is unique to the New Testament and later writings affected by it (e.g., 2 Clement 6:1; cf. *Bauer*). Hauck points out that the Aramaic underlying the entire saying of Luke 16:9ff. would have contained a pun, because the words for faith, to believe, trust, and genuine belong to the same stem as *mamōnas* (often translated "Mammon," KJV; cf. "mamōnas," *Kittel*, 4:388-390).

Intertestamental Period
Mamōnas does not occur in the Septuagint, although it is found in other Jewish writings such as the Mishnah (Aboth 2.12 [*Bauer* has 2.17]; Sanhedrin 1.1), Talmud, and perhaps in the writings of Qumran Damascus Document 14:20, "property." Hauck further shows usages in the Targums (Aramaic paraphrases of the Old Testament as well as other sources) and rabbinic literature which indicate that mammon could signify "property, goods." A negative nuance of "dishonest profit" recurs frequently ("mamōnas," *Kittel*, 4:389).

New Testament Usage
Mamōnas appears four times in the New Testament, each on the lips of Jesus. In the parallel passages of Matthew 6:24 and Luke 16:13 "mammon" is personified as something to "serve, be enslaved to" instead of serving God. The other texts appear in Luke's Gospel in the same context (16:9,11). The qualifying term "unrighteous" reflects the negative connotation.

The overall understanding of *mamōnas* is that it represents the materialistic wealth of the world. Such "security" is not to be trusted, for in the judgment it will offer no comfort. The idea is essentially the same as in the saying, "Don't store up treasures on earth, but store your treasures in heaven" (Matthew 6:19,20; free translation). The near relationship of this comment to a mammon saying in Matthew 6:24 is not coincidental (cf. Matthew 19:21; Luke 6:45; 12:33,34).

The injunction in Luke 16:9-11 regarding the proper handling of mammon ("worldly wealth," NIV) is followed by the example of mishandling of wealth by the rich man. He was more concerned with selfish earthly gain than he was in responsible administration of what God had given him (cf. 16:12).

STRONG 3126, BAUER 490, MOULTON-MILLIGAN 387, KITTEL 4:388-90, LIDDELL-SCOTT 1078, COLIN BROWN 2:836-37,852.

3099. Μαναήν Manaēn name
Manaen.

1. Μαναήν Manaēn masc

1 and Lucius of Cyrene, and **Manaen,**............ Acts 13:1

The foster-brother of Herod Antipas; he was either a prophet or a teacher in the church at Antioch (Acts 13:1).

3100. Μανασσῆς Manassēs name
Manasseh.

1. Μανασσῆς Manassēs nom masc
2. Μανασσῆ Manassē gen/acc masc

2 And Ezekias begat **Manasses;**............... Matt 1:10
1 and **Manasses** begat Amon;................. 1:10
2 tribe **of Manasses** were sealed twelve thousand....... Rev 7:6

The son of Hezekiah in the genealogy of Jesus (Matthew 1:10); one of the 12 tribes of Israel (Revelation 7:6).

3101. μανθάνω manthanō verb
Learn, understand, find out, discover, know.

COGNATES:
καταμανθάνω katamanthanō (2618)
μαθητεύω mathēteuō (3072)
μαθητής mathētēs (3073)
μαθήτρια mathētria (3074)
συμμαθητής summathētēs (4678)

אָלַף 'ālaph (509), Learn (Prv 22:25).
יָגַע yāghēʿ (3129), Labor (Is 47:12).
יָדַע yādhaʿ (3156), Find out (Ex 2:4).
לָמַד lāmadh (4064), Qal: learn (Dt 5:1, Ps 119:7 [118:7], Ez 19:3); piel: teach (Jer 9:5).
לִמֻּד limmudh (4065), Accustomed (Jer 13:23).
לָקַח lāqach (4089), Take, learn (Sir 16:24).
שָׁמַע shāmaʿ (8471), Hear, learn (Sir 8:9).
תַּלְמִיד talmîdh (8856), Pupil (1 Chr 25:8).

1. μανθάνουσιν manthanousin 3pl indic pres act
2. μανθάνωσιν manthanōsin 3pl subj pres act
3. μανθανέτω manthanetō 3sing impr pres act
4. μανθανέτωσαν manthanetōsan 3pl impr pres act
5. μανθάνοντα manthanonta
   nom/acc pl neu part pres act
6. ἔμαθον emathon 1sing indic aor act
7. ἔμαθες emathes 2sing indic aor act
8. ἔμαθεν emathen 3sing indic aor act
9. ἐμάθετε emathete 2pl indic aor act
10. μάθητε mathēte 2pl subj aor act
11. μάθετε mathete 2pl impr aor act
12. μαθών mathōn nom sing masc part aor act
13. μαθεῖν mathein inf aor act
14. μεμαθηκώς memathēkōs
    nom sing masc part perf act

11 But go ye and **learn** what that meaneth,.......... Matt 9:13
11 and **learn** of me; for I am meek and lowly in heart:.. 11:29
11 Now **learn** a parable of the fig tree;.............. 24:32
11 Now **learn** a parable of the fig tree;......... Mark 13:28
12 and **hath learned** of the Father, cometh unto me....John 6:45
14 knoweth this man letters, **having never learned?**....... 7:15
12 **having understood** that he was a Roman..........Acts 23:27
9 contrary to the doctrine which ye have **learned;**.... Rom 16:17
10 that ye **might learn** in us not to think of men above 1 Co 4:6
2 all **may learn,** and all may be comforted............. 14:31
13 And if they will **learn** any thing,................... 14:35
13 This only would I **learn** of you,.................... Gal 3:2
9 But ye have not so **learned** Christ;................ Eph 4:20
9 which ye **have** both **learned,** and received,........ Phlp 4:9
6 for I **have learned,** in whatsoever state I am,......... 4:11
9 also **learned** of Epaphras our dear fellowservant,.... Col 1:7
3 Let the woman **learn** in silence with all subjection. 1 Tm 2:11
4 let them **learn** first to show piety at home,.......... 5:4
1 And withal they **learn** to be idle,................... 5:13
5 **learning,** and never able to come to the knowledge 2 Tm 3:7
7 which thou **hast learned** and hast been assured of,.... 3:14
7 knowing of whom thou **hast learned** them;............ 3:14
4 **learn** to maintain good works for necessary uses,.... Tit 3:14
8 Though he were a Son, yet **learned** he obedience... Heb 5:8
13 and no man could **learn** that song but......... Rev 14:3

Classical Greek and Septuagint Usage
Manthanō occurs in classical Greek with various meanings such as "to learn by instruction, practice, or experience." It can also mean "to acquire the habit" or "to understand." The Septuagint uses *manthanō* to translate three different Hebrew words. In Exodus 2:4 Miriam watched in order to "learn by observation" (*manthanō*) what would happen to Moses. The Israelites were to hear God's word so they

might "learn by practice" or "acquire the habit" (*manthanō*) of obeying God (Deuteronomy 4:10; 5:1; 14:23). In Deuteronomy 17:19 the people are to read God's Word and "learn."

New Testament Usage
In the Greek New Testament *manthanō* means "to learn by investigation" (Matthew 9:13) and "to learn from instruction" (Matthew 11:29; Colossians 1:7). Jesus is said to be a man of letters although He had never "studied" or "attended (a rabbinical) school" (John 7:15). *Manthanō* means "to understand" in Acts 23:27. In Galatians 3:2 Paul wished to "find out" (*manthanō*) whether Galatians had been justified by works or by faith. The widow's children were to "learn" or "practice" (*manthanō*) at home in providing for needy parents or kinfolk (1 Timothy 5:4).

STRONG 3129, BAUER 490, MOULTON-MILLIGAN 387-88, KITTEL 4:390-413, LIDDELL-SCOTT 1078-79, COLIN BROWN 1:483-87.

3102. μανία mania noun
Madness, insanity.

CROSS-REFERENCE:
μαίνομαι mainomai (3077)

מַשְׂטֵמָה maṭēmāh (5028), Hostility (Hos 9:8).

1. μανίαν manian acc sing fem

1 Paul, ... much learning doth make thee mad....... Acts 26:24

Classical Greek
The classical meaning of *mania* is "madness" or "frenzy." It is also used in a general sense of "mad passion," "rage," or "fury." There are occasions when it is used specifically for "enthusiasm" or "bacchic frenzy."

Intertestamental Period
In the Second Century B.C. it also denoted "delirium" and at times a weakened sense of "eccentricity," "queerness," or "excitement." Thus is it found in this unedited Tebtunis papyrus: "You seem to have gone mad, for you pay no regard to yourself and have gone off your head" (*Moulton-Milligan*).

New Testament Usage
It is in this somewhat weakened sense that the only use of *mania* appears in the New Testament in Acts 26:24. The reader is helped in understanding the meaning of the term as Luke in the next verse expressed the opposite as being "truth" and "soberness." "Truth" denotes absolutes and reality, and "soberness" conveys rationality and mental soundness as a Christian manifests this nature in good judgment and self-control. The heathen governor Festus found Paul's witness to the gospel, including the Resurrection, difficult to comprehend. He was forced to the conclusion that the prisoner's mind had become affected. Actually, Festus was the one with a confused mind, not Paul. However, to Festus it all made no sense. There was only one word for it, *mania*.

STRONG 3130, BAUER 490, MOULTON-MILLIGAN 388, LIDDELL-SCOTT 1079, COLIN BROWN 1:528-29.

3103. μάννα manna noun
Manna.

מָן mān (4620), Manna (Nm 11:6f., Jos 5:11, Ps 78:24 [77:24]).

מִנְחָה minchāh (4647), Grain offering (Jer 17:26, 41:5 [48:5]).

1. μάννα manna neu

1 Our fathers did eat **manna** in the desert;............ John 6:31
1 Your fathers did eat **manna** in the wilderness,.......... 6:49
1 not as your fathers did eat **manna**, and are dead:....... 6:58
1 wherein was the golden pot that had **manna**,........ Heb 9:4
1 will I give to eat of the hidden **manna**,.............. Rev 2:17

Classical Greek
Perhaps *manna* (neuter, indeclinable) is related to the same Greek feminine form *manna*, meaning "little grain, granule." But the form more likely is dependent upon the Hebrew word *mān*, the miraculous food God supplied to the Israelites during their wilderness wanderings. Papyri and current study also indicate that *manna* comes in a natural way from a tamarisk tree. This substance has no food value and was used in medical preparations to stop nosebleeding (*Moulton-Milligan*).

Septuagint Usage
The Septuagint consistently translates *mān* as *manna* except for Exodus (16:31-33,35) where the direct transliteration occurs. Its name may have originally developed out of the question asked by the Israelites when they first encountered manna, "What (*mān*) is it?" The Hebrew word *minchāh*, "gift, tribute" (used of the offerings of Leviticus 2), also stands behind *manna* in some versions of the Septuagint (Jeremiah 17:26; 41:5 [LXX 48:5]; Ezekiel 46 passim). The correct form here is *manna* (e.g., Ezekiel 45:25; 46:5,7,11).

New Testament Usage
To fully appreciate the New Testament understanding of *manna* (five times) it is crucial

to examine the Jewish traditions about *manna*'s significance. God, through His Holy Spirit, accommodated himself to speak in a language and in concepts fully intelligible to first-century peoples; at the same time He challenged their thinking. Thus the idea of Jesus as the "Bread of Heaven" (i.e., the *manna*) is an allusion to popular Jewish thinking (cf. Merkel, "Bread," *Colin Brown*, 1:252f.) as well as a development of Old Testament concepts. *Manna* as "bread from heaven" is based upon Psalm 78:24: "He rained down manna for the people to eat, he gave them the grain of heaven" (NIV). Psalm 105:40 also contributed to this understanding: "They asked, and he brought them quail and satisfied them with the bread of heaven" (NIV).

Later Judaism speculated that in the Messianic Age manna would again "descend" (e.g., 2 Baruch 29:8; cf. Revelation 2:17, of hidden manna for those who overcome). C.H. Dodd notes that the "renewal of the gift of manna becomes a fixed feature of Jewish eschatological expectation" (*Interpretation of the Fourth Gospel*, p.335, see note 2). Manna was divine food. Now, however, Jesus, the True Bread (= *manna*), had come down (*katabainō*) from heaven (John 6:33,41,50,51,58) as God's divine food (John 6:32). But He is "food" of a different spiritual kind (John 6:48-59; cf. 6:31; 1 Corinthians 10:3). Jesus picked up on this in a way that radically challenged customary Jewish speculation. Although manna was indeed miraculous food, it possessed no power to bring eternal life; it merely sustained present existence (cf. John 6:26: Jesus downplayed their response to the physical satisfaction of His previous miracle of feeding 5,000). Jesus brings eternal life as the "living Bread from heaven" (John 6:35,48; cf. Deuteronomy 8:3). The world cannot understand this (6:52) apart from the enabling of the Spirit (6:65).

Hebrews 9:4 refers to the container of manna that was placed in the ark of the covenant along with Aaron's budding rod and the tablets of the Law (Exodus 16:32f.; Deuteronomy 10:3-5; 1 Kings 8:9).

Believers partake of the Bread of Life only by faith in Christ (John 6:28f.). Those who have eaten and drank of the Son of Man are not to go around looking for signs to sustain them (i.e., so they might believe, cf. John 6:30). Even seeing signs is not enough to promote belief (John 6:36); instead there must be faith that Christ has come in the flesh (John 6:41,42). Those who believe soon discover that to partake of this flesh/bread is to share in the life which Jesus gives on behalf of the world (John 6:51). The difficulty of receiving this is evident in that many disciples found the saying "hard" (6:60) and no longer followed Jesus (John 6:66); i.e., they quit being disciples. They did not believe in Him. We must continually partake of this bread to live forever (John 6:58).

STRONG 3131, BAUER 490-91, MOULTON-MILLIGAN 388, KITTEL 4:462-66, LIDDELL-SCOTT 1079, COLIN BROWN 1:252-53.

3104. μαντεύομαι manteuomai verb
Soothsaying, fortune-telling, practice divination.
SYNONYM:
προφητεύω prophēteuō (4253)
מִקְסָם miqsām (4901), Divination (Ez 12:24).
קָסַם qāsam (7364), Use divination, divine (Dt 18:10, Ez 21:21, Mi 3:11).
קֶסֶם qesem (7365), Divination (Ez 13:6).

1. μαντευομένη manteuomenē
nom sing fem part pres mid
1 brought her masters much gain by **soothsaying:** ..... Acts 16:16

Classical Greek and Septuagint Usage
The classical background of *manteuomai* may be seen with these three shades of meaning: (1) "to divine, prophesy, deliver an oracle"; (2) "to presage, forebode, surmise"; of animals, "to scent"; (3) "to seek divinations, to consult an oracle." It is used in an impersonal way in the passive sense meaning an oracle that is given or delivered. The word, which in the Septuagint is always used of lying prophets or divination contrary to the Law (Deuteronomy 18:10), has again a sinister connotation in its only occurrence in the New Testament (Acts 16:16).

New Testament Usage
In Acts 16:16 the meaning of the participial use of *manteuomai* is brought out as other words are analyzed which identify the nature of the damsel who makes the response reported here. She had a "spirit of divination"; literally, "a spirit, a Python." Python, in Greek mythology, was the serpent which guarded Delphi. According to the legend, Apollo descended from Olympus in order to select a site for his shrine and oracle. Having fixed upon a spot on the southern side of Mount Parnassus, he found it guarded by a vast and terrifying serpent which he slew with an arrow and permitted its body "to rot"

(*puthein*) in the sun. Therefore, the serpent was named *Python* (see 4294) ("rotting"). Later the name *Python* was used to designate a prophetic demon, and subsequently, soothsayers. (The soothsaying maiden in the temple of Delphi was called a pythoness.) Therefore, the heathen inhabitants of Philippi regarded the woman as inspired by Apollo; and Luke, in recording this case, employed the term which would naturally suggest itself to a Greek physician: "a Python-spirit" as if possessing the temporary madness of the priestess under the influence of the god.

STRONG 3132, BAUER 491, MOULTON-MILLIGAN 388, LIDDELL-SCOTT 1079-80, COLIN BROWN 3:74,81.

3105. μαραίνω marainō verb
Fade away, wither.

יָבֵשׁ yāvēsh (3111), Piel: wither (Jb 15:30).

1. μαρανθήσεται maranthēsetai 3sing indic fut pass

1 so also shall the rich man **fade away** in his ways...... Jas 1:11

Classical Greek
Both the literal and figurative meanings of *marainō* can be found in classical Greek. The literal meaning is "to put out, quench, extinguish"; as a passive form, "to die away, burn low." The metaphoric use is "to quench, to weaken, to cause to waste or pine away"; as a passive form it means "to die away, waste away, languish."

Septuagint Usage
In the Septuagint *marainō* can signify specifically to quench fire (in keeping with its original meaning; cf. Job 15:30) or, in the passive, the dying out of a fire. It is used variously in the active voice as meaning "to quench, waste, wear out" and in the passive, "to waste away." *Marainō* can include many kinds of enfeeblement and decay. Hence it is often found in epitaphs on tombs. It is also used of the abating of wind.

New Testament Usage
James follows the Septuagint use in 1:11 where he compared the transitory glory of a rich man to the fading beauty of the flowers on the Palestinian plains (cf. Job 24:24). As quickly as the beauty of the flowers fades under the intense heat of the south wind, the sirocco, so does the glory, popularity, and wealth of a rich man vanish with the brevity of his existence.

Peter employed the negative use of the word in 1 Peter 1:4 translated as "that fadeth not away." Vincent comments, "The loveliness of the heavenly inheritance is described as exempt from the blight that attaches to earthly bloom" (*Word Studies in the New Testament*, 1:630). This "unwithering" attribute of Peter's text refers to grace and beauty.

In light of either James 1:11 or 1 Peter 1:4 the Christian, rich or poor, comprehends the true nature of riches. They are temporary, as temporary as cut flowers under the burning heat of the sun.

STRONG 3133, BAUER 491, MOULTON-MILLIGAN 388, LIDDELL-SCOTT 1080.

3106. μαράν maran noun
Our Lord (has come), Our Lord (come).

1. μαράν maran masc
2. μαράνα marana masc

1 let him be Anathema **Maranatha**................. 1 Co 16:22

The word *maran* is best understood as an integral element of the phrase *maranatha*. This expression is a Greek transliteration of two Aramaic words which may be separated as *maran* ("our Lord") *atha* ("has come") or *marana* ("our Lord") *tha* ("come"). Thus one is a declaration, the other an invocation. Not found in the Septuagint *maranatha* occurs only once in the New Testament, 1 Corinthians 16:22.

This term also appears in *Didache* 10:6, an early Christian document, at the close of what some consider to be a eucharistic prayer: "Let grace come and let this world pass away. Hosannah to the God of David. If any man be holy, let him come! if any may be not, let him repent: *Maran atha*, Amen." (Cf. Revelation 22:20, "come, Lord Jesus" which is followed by the same wish for blessing as 1 Corinthians 16:23.)

Support seems to favor the reading *Marana tha*, "Our Lord Come!" as the correct separation. The Greek text and context both suggest an invocation rather than a declaration. Philippians 4:5, "the Lord is at hand," ("near," NIV) may echo the same thought.

Most exegetes consider the expression to have originated in the early congregation in Jerusalem and to have been accepted later by the Gentile Christian assemblies along with other Hebrew and Aramaic liturgical forms. The title "Lord" should then be understood from a Jewish perspective. Along with other references it indicates that from the very outset Jesus Christ was worshiped as Lord. (See also *atha* [109].)

STRONG 3134, BAUER 491 (see "maran atha"), MOULTON-MILLIGAN 388 (see "maranatha"), KITTEL 4:466-72 (see "maranatha"), LIDDELL-SCOTT 1080 (see "maran atha), COLIN BROWN 2:895-98 (see "maran atha").

3107. μαργαρίτης margaritēs noun
A pearl.

1. μαργαρίτου margaritou gen sing masc
2. μαργαρίτην margaritēn acc sing masc
3. μαργαρῖται margaritai nom pl masc
4. μαργαρίταις margaritais dat pl masc
5. μαργαρίτας margaritas acc pl masc
6. μαργαρίτῃ margaritē dat sing masc
7. μαργαριτῶν margaritōn gen pl masc

```
5  neither cast ye your pearls before swine,............Matt 7:6
5  is like unto a merchant man, seeking goodly pearls:....  13:45
2  Who, when he had found one pearl of great price,.....    13:46
4  not with broided hair, or gold, or pearls,............ 1 Tm 2:9
4  decked with gold and precious stones and pearls,... Rev 17:4
1  and precious stones, of pearls, and fine linen,.....     18:12
4  decked with gold, and precious stones, and pearls!.....  18:16
3  And the twelve gates were twelve pearls:.............    21:21
1  twelve pearls: every several gate was of one pearl:.....  21:21
```

Classical Greek
The pearl (*margaritēs*) in the ancient Greco-Roman world was normally placed on the level of precious stones. Pearls were quite expensive, and because of this the word *margaritēs* later was used figuratively to denote anything of great worth. While the Septuagint does not use *margaritēs*, the ancient Jews used the metaphor of pearls to indicate valuable sayings (cf. *Bauer*).

New Testament Usage
In the New Testament *margaritēs* is used both literally (1 Timothy 2:9) and figuratively (Matthew 7:6). Usually it indicates something of great worth, as in Revelation 17:4; 18:12,16 when used with precious stones, and in Matthew 13:45,46 in reference to something of exceeding worth. A figurative usage is seen in the proverb (Matthew 7:6) that exhorts believers not to cast "pearls" before swine.

STRONG 3135, BAUER 491, KITTEL 4:472-73, LIDDELL-SCOTT 1080, COLIN BROWN 3:394.

3108. Μάρθα Martha name
Martha.

1. Μάρθα Martha nom fem
2. Μάρθας Marthas gen fem
3. Μάρθαν Marthan acc fem

```
1  and a certain woman named Martha received him..Luke 10:38
1  But Martha was cumbered about much serving,........    10:40
1  And Jesus answered and said unto her, Martha,......    10:41
1  Martha, Martha, thou art careful and troubled.....    10:41
2  Bethany, the town of Mary and her sister Martha.   John 11:1
3  Jesus loved Martha, and her sister, and Lazarus......    11:5
3  And many of the Jews came to Martha and Mary,....    11:19
1  Then Martha, ... went and met him:.................    11:20
1  Then said Martha unto Jesus, Lord,................    11:21
1  Martha saith unto him,............................    11:24
1  but was in that place where Martha met him.........    11:30
1  Martha, the sister of him that was dead, saith........    11:39
1  they made him a supper; and Martha served:..........    12:2
```

The sister of Mary and Lazarus from Bethany, whom Jesus loved (Luke 10:38ff.; John 11:5,21).

3109. Μαρία Maria name
Mary.

1. Μαρία Maria nom fem
2. Μαρίας Marias gen fem
3. Μαρίᾳ Maria dat fem
4. Μαρίαν Marian acc fem

```
2  And Jacob begat Joseph the husband of Mary,......Matt 1:16
2  When as his mother Mary was espoused to Joseph,.....  1:18
4  do not be afraid to take Mary as your (NASB).........  1:20
2  they saw the young child with Mary his mother,.....  2:11
1  Among which was Mary Magdalene, and Mary........    27:56
1  and Mary the mother of James and Joses,.............    27:56
1  there was Mary Magdalene, and the other Mary,.....    27:61
1  there was Mary Magdalene, and the other Mary,.....    27:61
1  came Mary Magdalene and the other Mary to see.....    28:1
1  came Mary Magdalene and the other Mary to see.....    28:1
2  Is not this the carpenter, the son of Mary,........Mark 6:3
1  afar off: among whom was Mary Magdalene,..........    15:40
1  and Mary the mother of James the less and of Joses,..    15:40
1  Mary Magdalene and Mary the mother of Joses.......    15:47
1  Mary Magdalene and Mary the mother of Joses.......    15:47
1  And when the sabbath was past, Mary Magdalene,....    16:1
1  and Mary the mother of James, and Salome,.........    16:1
3  he appeared first to Mary Magdalene,................    16:9
2  that, when Elisabeth heard the salutation of Mary,...Luke 1:41
1  Mary called Magdalene, out of whom ... devils,........  8:2
1  And she had a sister called Mary,....................    10:39
1  and Mary hath chosen that good part,................    10:42
1  It was Mary Magdalene, and Joanna, and Mary the....    24:10
1  and Joanna, and Mary the mother of James, and.....    24:10
2  Bethany, the town of Mary and her sister Martha.   John 11:1
1  It was that Mary which anointed the Lord............    11:2
4  And many of the Jews came to Martha and Mary,....    11:19
1  but Mary sat still in the house....................    11:20
4  went her way, and called Mary her sister secretly,....    11:28
4  when they saw Mary, that she rose up hastily........    11:31
1  Then when Mary was come where Jesus was,.........    11:32
4  Then many of the Jews which came to Mary,........    11:45
1  Then took Mary a pound of ointment of spikenard,....    12:3
1  Mary the wife of Cleophas, and Mary Magdalene.....    19:25
1  Mary the wife of Cleophas, and Mary Magdalene.....    19:25
1  The first day ... cometh Mary Magdalene early,.....    20:1
1  But Mary stood without at the sepulchre weeping:.....    20:11
1  Jesus saith unto her, Mary.........................    20:16
1  Mary Magdalene came and told the disciples..........    20:18
3  Mary the mother of Jesus, and with his brethren.....Acts 1:14
2  he came to the house of Mary the mother of John,....    12:12
```

Μαριάμ 3110

Seven women bear this name in the New Testament. The mother of Jesus (Matthew 1:16) and the Magdalene (Luke 8:2; see 3066) are perhaps the better known. The mother of James and Joses was so named (Matthew 27:56), as was the wife of Cleophas (John 19:25). They may be the same woman, since both are identified near the cross of Christ. The sister of Martha and Lazarus was also named Mary (Luke 10:39). Little is known of John Mark's mother (Acts 12:12), or of a certain Christian greeted by Paul (Romans 16:6).

3110. Μαριάμ Mariam name
Mary.

1. Μαριάμ Mariam fem

1 fear not to take unto thee **Mary** thy wife:	Matt 1:20
1 is not his mother called **Mary**?	13:55
1 and the virgin's name was **Mary**.	Luke 1:27
1 And the angel said unto her, Fear not, **Mary**:	1:30
1 Then said **Mary** unto the angel, How shall this be,	1:34
1 And **Mary** said, Behold the handmaid of the Lord;	1:38
1 And **Mary** arose in those days,	1:39
1 And **Mary** said, My soul doth magnify the Lord,	1:46
1 And **Mary** abode with her about three months,	1:56
1 To be taxed with **Mary** his espoused wife,	2:5
1 And they came with haste, and found **Mary**,	2:16
1 But **Mary** kept all these things, and pondered them	2:19
1 Simeon blessed ... and said unto **Mary** his mother,	2:34
1 Greet **Mary**, who bestowed much labour on us.	Rom 16:6

Variant form of *Maria* (3109).

3111. Μάρκος Markos name
Mark.

1. Μάρκος Markos nom masc
2. Μάρκου Markou gen masc
3. Μάρκον Markon acc masc

2 of John, whose surname was **Mark**;	Acts 12:12
3 took with them John, whose surname was **Mark**.	12:25
3 take with them John, whose surname was **Mark**.	15:37
3 so Barnabas took **Mark**, and sailed unto Cyprus;	15:39
1 my fellowprisoner saluteth you, and **Marcus**,	Col 4:10
3 Take **Mark**, and bring him with thee:	2 Tm 4:11
1 **Marcus**, Aristarchus, ... Lucas, my fellowlabourers.	Phlm 1:24
1 saluteth you; and so doth **Marcus** my son.	1 Pt 5:13

The surname of John, the cousin of Barnabas (Acts 12:12; Colossians 4:10); he wrote the Gospel of Mark.

3112. μάρμαρος marmaros noun
Marble.

1. μαρμάρου marmarou gen sing masc

1 precious wood, and of brass, and iron, and **marble**,	Rev 18:12

In early Greek literature *marmaros* denotes a "boulder" or "block of rock." In later literature, due to the influence of *marmairō*, "to glisten or sparkle," the word refers to crystalline rock or glistening stone as marble. In the New Testament *marmaros* occurs only once, in Revelation 18:12. Here marble is one item among many of the merchants' listed cargoes.

STRONG 3139, BAUER 492, MOULTON-MILLIGAN 389, LIDDELL-SCOTT 1081.

3113. μαρτυρέω martureō verb
Bear witness, be a witness, testify.

COGNATES:
- ἀμάρτυρος amarturos (265)
- διαμαρτύρομαι diamarturomai (1257)
- ἐπιμαρτυρέω epimartureō (1942)
- καταμαρτυρέω katamartureō (2619)
- μαρτυρία marturia (3114)
- μαρτύριον marturion (3115)
- μάρτυς martus (3116)
- προμαρτύρω promarturō (4162)
- συμμαρτυρέω summartureō (4679)
- συνεπιμαρτυρέω sunepimartureō (4751)
- ψευδομαρτυρέω pseudomartureō (5410)
- ψευδομαρτυρία pseudomarturia (5411)
- ψευδόμαρτυς pseudomartus (5412)

SYNONYMS:
- διαμαρτύρομαι diamarturomai (1257)
- ἐπιμαρτυρέω epimartureō (1942)

עֵד 'ēdh (5915), Witness (Gn 31:48, Dt 19:18, 31:21).

עוּד 'ûdh (5967), Hiphil: admonish (Lam 2:13).

עָנָה 'ānâh (6257), Answer; testimony (Nm 35:30—Codex Vaticanus only).

1. μαρτυρῶ marturō 1sing indic/subj pres act
2. μαρτυρεῖς martureis 2sing indic pres act
3. μαρτυρεῖ marturei 3sing indic pres act
4. μαρτυροῦμεν marturoumen 1pl indic pres act
5. μαρτυρεῖτε martureite 2pl indic pres act
6. μαρτυροῦσιν marturousin 3pl indic pres act
7. μαρτυρῶν marturōn nom sing masc part pres act
8. μαρτυροῦντος marturountos
  gen sing masc part pres act
9. μαρτυροῦντι marturounti
  dat sing masc part pres act
10. μαρτυροῦντες marturountes
  nom pl masc part pres act
11. μαρτυρούντων marturountōn
  gen pl masc part pres act
12. μαρτυρούσης marturousēs
  gen sing fem part pres act
13. μαρτυροῦσαι marturousai
  nom pl fem part pres act
14. μαρτυροῦν marturoun
  nom/acc sing neu part pres act
15. μαρτυρεῖν marturein inf pres act

μαρτυρέω 3113

16. ἐμαρτύρησεν emarturēsen 3sing indic aor act
17. ἐμαρτυρήσαμεν emarturēsamen 1pl indic aor act
18. ἐμαρτύρησαν emarturēsan 3pl indic aor act
19. μαρτυρήσω marturēsō 1sing subj aor act
20. μαρτυρήσῃ marturēsē 3sing subj aor act
21. μαρτύρησον marturēson 2sing impr aor act
22. μαρτυρήσας marturēsas
    nom sing masc part aor act
23. μαρτυρήσαντος marturēsantos
    gen sing masc part aor act
24. μαρτυρῆσαι marturēsai inf aor act
25. μεμαρτύρηκα memarturēka 1sing indic perf act
26. μεμαρτύρηκας memarturēkas
    2sing indic perf act
27. μεμαρτύρηκεν memarturēken
    3sing indic perf act
28. μαρτυρήσει marturēsei 3sing indic fut act
29. ἐμαρτύρει emarturei 3sing indic imperf act
30. ἐμαρτύρουν emarturoun 3pl indic imperf act
31. μαρτύρομαι marturomai 1sing indic pres mid
32. μαρτυρούμενος marturoumenos
    nom sing masc part pres mid
33. μαρτυρούμενοι marturoumenoi
    nom pl masc part pres mid
34. μαρτυρουμένους marturoumenous
    acc pl masc part pres mid
35. μαρτυρουμένη marturoumenē
    nom sing fem part pres mid
36. ἐμαρτυρήθη emarturēthē 3sing indic aor pass
37. ἐμαρτυρήθησαν emarturēthēsan
    3pl indic aor pass
38. μαρτυρηθέντες marturēthentes
    nom pl masc part aor pass
39. μεμαρτύρηται memarturētai 3sing indic perf mid
40. ἐμαρτυρεῖτο emartureito 3sing indic imperf pass
41. μαρτυρεῖται martureitai 3sing indic pres mid
42. μαρτυρόμενος marturomenos
    nom sing masc part pres mid
43. μαρτυρόμενοι marturomenoi
    nom pl masc part pres mid

5	Wherefore ye be witnesses unto yourselves,	Matt 23:31
30	And all have him witness,	Luke 4:22
5	Truly ye bear witness that ye allow the deeds of	11:48
20	to bear witness of the Light,	John 1:7
20	but was sent to bear witness of that Light.	1:8
3	John bare witness of him, and cried, saying,	1:15
16	And John bare record, saying,	1:32
25	I saw, and bare record that this is the Son of God.	1:34
20	And needed not that any should testify of man:	2:25
4	and testify that we have seen;	3:11
26	to whom thou barest witness, behold,	3:26
5	Ye yourselves bear me witness, that I said,	3:28
3	what he hath seen and heard, that he testifieth;	3:32
12	which testified, He told me all that ever I did.	4:39
16	For Jesus himself testified,	4:44
1	If I bear witness of myself, my witness is not true.	5:31
7	There is another that beareth witness of me;	5:32
3	that the witness which he witnesseth of me is true.	5:32
27	sent unto John, and he bare witness unto the truth.	5:33
3	the same works that I do, bear witness of me,	5:36
27	the Father himself, ... hath borne witness of me.	5:37
13	and they are they which testify of me.	5:39
1	but me it hateth, because I testify of it,	7:7
2	Thou bearest record of thyself;	John 8:13
1	Though I bear record of myself,	8:14
7	I am one that bear witness of myself,	8:18
3	and the Father that sent me beareth witness of me.	8:18
3	in my Father's name, they bear witness of me.	10:25
29	The people therefore ... bare record.	12:17
16	he was troubled in spirit, and testified, and said,	13:21
28	the Spirit of truth, ... he shall testify of me:	15:26
5	And ye also shall bear witness,	15:27
21	If I have spoken evil, bear witness of the evil:	18:23
19	that I should bear witness unto the truth.	18:37
27	he that saw it bare record, and his record is true:	19:35
7	This is the disciple which testifieth of these things,	21:24
34	look ye out among you seven men of honest report,	Acts 6:3
32	of good report among all the nation of the Jews,	10:22
6	To him give all the prophets witness,	10:43
22	to whom also he gave testimony, and said,	13:22
9	which gave testimony unto the word of his grace,	14:3
16	bare them witness, giving them the Holy Ghost,	15:8
40	Which was well reported of by the brethren	16:2
31	Wherefore I take you to record this day,	20:26
3	As also the high priest doth bear me witness,	22:5
32	having a good report of all the Jews	22:12
24	so must thou bear witness also at Rome.	23:11
15	if they would testify, that after the most straitest	26:5
32	witnessing both to small and great,	26:22
35	being witnessed by the law and the prophets;	Rom 3:21
1	I bear them record that they have a zeal of God,	10:2
17	we have testified of God that he raised up Christ:	1 Co 15:15
1	For to their power, I bear record,	2 Co 8:3
1	the blessedness ye spake of? for I bear you record,	Gal 4:15
31	For I testify again to every man that is circumcised,	5:3
31	This I say therefore, and testify in the Lord,	Eph 4:17
1	bear him record, that he hath a great zeal for you,	Col 4:13
33	encouraging, conforting and urging you (NIV)	1 Th 2:12
35	Well reported of for good works;	1 Tm 5:10
23	before Pontius Pilate witnessed a good confession;	6:13
32	of whom it is witnessed that he liveth.	Heb 7:8
3	For he testifieth, Thou art a priest for ever	7:17
3	Whereof the Holy Ghost also is a witness to us:	10:15
37	For by it the elders obtained a good report,	11:2
36	he obtained witness that he was righteous,	11:4
8	God testifying of his gifts:	11:4
39	for before his translation he had this testimony,	11:5
38	having obtained a good report through faith,	11:39
4	and we have seen it, and bear witness,	1 Jn 1:2
4	and do testify that the Father sent the Son	4:14
14	And it is the Spirit that beareth witness,	5:6
10	For there are three that bear record in heaven,	5:7
10	And there are three that bear witness in earth,	5:8
27	this is the witness of God which he hath testified	5:9
27	believeth not the record that God gave of his Son.	5:10
11	when the brethren came and testified of the truth	3 Jn 1:3
18	borne witness of thy charity before the church;	1:6
39	Demetrius hath good report of all men,	1:12
4	of the truth itself: yea, and we also bear record;	1:12
16	Who bare record of the word of God,	Rev 1:2
24	I Jesus have sent mine angel to testify unto you	22:16
1	I testify to everyone who hears (NASB)	22:18
7	He which testifieth these things saith,	22:20

Classical Greek

Known from the time of Herodotus (Fifth Century B.C.), *martureō* (cf. *marturion* [3115], *martus* [3116], *marturia* [3114]) is primarily a legal term meaning "to bear witness, give testimony, testify." Generally this was understood in a positive sense of "to witness on behalf of." Such testimony is predicated upon personal experience. The "witness" (*martus*) either saw, heard, or by another sense experienced some event. The sphere of the language includes virtually every kind of official witness: verbal, written, or otherwise (see *Moulton-Milligan* for examples of ordinary usage).

In addition to its use in a legal sense *martureō* also appears in other spheres. *Martureō* is used of declaring a particular viewpoint, attitude, or conviction. The philosophers adopted *martureō* in this manner to speak of their "giving evidence" for their "truths, doctrines, and principles" (Coenen, "Witness," *Colin Brown*, 3:1039f.).

Septuagint Usage

Martureō appears infrequently in the Septuagint (17 times), often without rendering a Hebrew term (e.g., Genesis 31:44,48; Deuteronomy 19:15; and in the Apocrypha 3 times). When there is a Hebrew word being rendered by *martureō* it is in every instance except one (Numbers 35:30) a form of *'ûdh*, "to witness, give testimony."

In the above passage the legal overtones are clearly present. Jacob erected an altar "to witness" the agreement between himself and Laban (Genesis 31:47; cf. Joshua 22:27ff.; 1 Maccabees 2:37). "To witness" is not some subjective enterprise; rather, it rests upon truth, experience. It is a serious crime to violate the integrity of a testimony (Deuteronomy 19:15). The witness, like Jacob's pile of stones, may be a tangible reminder of a former agreement (of a song, Deuteronomy 31:19,21).

New Testament Usage

Coenen observes that the word group first acquired specific theological import in the New Testament (ibid., 3:1042; cf. the compounds *diamartureō*, *summartureō*, et al.). The verb is unevenly distributed in the New Testament.

Synoptic Gospels

Of the Synoptic Gospels only Matthew and Luke use it, and then only once each in independent material (Matthew 23:31; Luke 4:22). The precise sense of *matureō* in Luke 4:22 is of some dispute—the dative *autō* (see 840) may either be interpreted "for him" or "against him." In the remainder of the New Testament, Luke (in Acts) and John (in his Gospel and his letters) show a more theologically influenced understanding of *martureō*.

Johannine Literature

John, in contrast to the Synoptics, made *martureō* a central term in his gospel. This term always has a legal meaning which carries over into his epistles as well. John considered his own role as that of "witness" to the wonderful story of Jesus (John 21:24; cf. 1 John 1:2; 4:14; 2 John 3; Revelation 1:2; 22:18). John the Baptist is portrayed as a "witness" to Jesus (John 1:7,8,15,32; 5:33), and Jesus himself "testified" to His identity by what He did (John 5:36; 10:25). It is His purpose as the Father's emissary to testify to the truth which confronts the world (John 18:37). The Father, in turn, testifies to Jesus as the truth (John 5:37; 8:18), as do the Scriptures (John 5:39; cf. Hebrews 10:15). The Spirit will testify about Jesus when He is sent from the Father (John 5:26; cf. 1 John 5:6,7). Surprisingly, John does not make use of the cognate terms *martus* or *marturion*, a "witness" or "testimony." *Marturia*, however, is integral to the themes developed by *martureō* (cf. John 1:7,19ff.; 5:31ff.).

Acts Account

In Acts, Luke developed the idea of "to witness" (cf. Luke 24:48). The gospel message is "testified to" by the powerful signs and wonders (Acts 14:3). But more significantly, Paul "must bear witness" (*dei martureō*) in Rome (Acts 23:11). This characterizes the mission of the Church and echoes the mandate given by Jesus to "make disciples of all nations, baptizing them in the name of the Father and of the Son and of the Holy Spirit" (Matthew 28:19, NIV). The disciples became "witnesses" (*marturēs*) whose chief task was to proclaim Christ to all peoples. Their witnessing is eternal truth (e.g., Luke 24:48; Acts 1:8,22).

Pauline Epistles

In Pauline literature *martureō* assumes an almost technical quality. He wrote that "we have testified of God that He raised up Christ" (1 Corinthians 15:15; cf. of Jesus' own role as one who testified before [*epi* (1894)] Pilate [1 Timothy 6:13]). Paul did, however, use *martureō* frequently in a nontheological sense (e.g., Romans 10:2; 2 Corinthians 8:3; Colossians 4:13).

Hebrews

For the author of Hebrews it is chiefly God who "testifies" and confirms the faith of men (Coenen notes the use of the passive in Hebrews suggests divine action, especially in chapter 11, e.g., verses 2,4,5). God confirms the faith of those who hold on to their faith in spite of circumstances or appearances.

Like the classical usage suggests, the New Testament understanding of "to witness, to testify" is based upon the assumption that experience—sight, sound, touch—is the basis of witness. Thus, there is no room for subjective speculation in the historical Christian faith. The incarnation, ministry, death, resurrection, and ascension of Jesus were witnessed by the early disciples and apostles. (Just as an aside, it is fascinating to note that Luke used five optical terms to emphasize the visible nature of the Ascension in only two verses.) If these events were not witnessed—in the tangible sense of that word—the entire Christian faith is grounded upon myth rather than truth. It is against such heresy that the apostle John wrote: "That which was from the beginning, which we have heard, which we have seen with our eyes, which we have looked at and our hands have touched—this we proclaim concerning the Word of life" (1 John 1:1, NIV).

STRONG 3140, BAUER 492-93, MOULTON-MILLIGAN 389, KITTEL 4:474-508, LIDDELL-SCOTT 1082, COLIN BROWN 3:1038,1041-47,1203.

3114. μαρτυρία marturia noun

Testimony, evidence.

COGNATE:
μαρτυρέω martureō (3113)

SYNONYM:
μαρτύριον marturion (3115)

מוֹעֵד môʻēdh (4287), Appointed time (1 Sm 9:24—Codex Alexandrinus only).

עֵד ʻēdh (5915), Witness (Ex 20:16, Dt 5:20).

עֵדוּת ʻēdhûth (5925), Testimony (Ps 19:7 [18:7]).

שָׂהֲדוּ sāhădhû (A7904), Sahadutha, witness (Gn 31:47).

1. μαρτυρία marturia nom sing fem
2. μαρτυρίας marturias gen sing fem
3. μαρτυρίαν marturian acc sing fem
4. μαρτυρίαι marturiai nom pl fem

3	chief priests and all the council sought for witness	Mark 14:55
4	but their witness agreed not together.	14:56
1	But neither so did their witness agree together.	14:59
2	And they said, What need we any further witness?	Luke 22:71
3	The same came for a witness,	John 1:7
1	And this is the record of John,	1:19
3	and ye receive not our witness.	3:11
3	and no man receiveth his testimony.	3:32
3	He that hath received his testimony	3:33
1	If I bear witness of myself, my witness is not true.	5:31
1	that the witness which he witnesseth of me is true.	5:32
3	But I receive not testimony from man:	5:34
3	But I have greater witness than that of John:	5:36
1	bearest record of thyself; thy record is not true.	8:13
1	I bear record of myself, yet my record is true:	8:14
1	that the testimony of two men is true.	8:17
1	he that saw it bare record, and his record is true:	19:35
1	and we know that his testimony is true.	21:24
3	they will not receive thy testimony concerning me.	Acts 22:18
3	Moreover he must have a good report	1 Tm 3:7
1	This witness is true. Wherefore rebuke them	Tit 1:13
3	If we receive the witness of men,	1 Jn 5:9
1	the witness of God is greater:	5:9
1	this is the witness of God which he hath testified	5:9
3	He that believeth ... hath the witness in himself:	5:10
3	believeth not the record that God gave of his Son.	5:10
1	And this is the record,	5:11
1	and ye know that our record is true.	3 Jn 1:12
3	and of the testimony of Jesus Christ,	Rev 1:2
3	for the word of God, and for the testimony of Jesus	1:9
3	and for the testimony which they held:	6:9
3	And when they shall have finished their testimony,	11:7
2	and by the word of their testimony;	12:11
3	and have the testimony of Jesus Christ.	12:17
3	of thy brethren that have the testimony of Jesus:	19:10
1	for the testimony of Jesus is the spirit of prophecy.	19:10
3	them that were beheaded for the witness of Jesus,	20:4

Classical Greek

The noun *marturia* occurs in secular Greek as a legal term taken from the language of the courtroom. This term, as well as its related terms, revolves around the concept of "testimony" for or against someone. Gradually the word group acquired a broader sense, and it moved into other spheres besides the legal. Thus *marturia* can be used in reference to a moral view or philosophical conviction. For example, Stoic philosophers regarded themselves as "witnesses" of divine truths that they had discovered. In this respect they also referred to their adversities and difficulties as confirmation (i.e., "testimony") of the teachings they espoused.

Septuagint Usage

The larger word group is well represented in the Septuagint. The noun *marturion* (3115), "testimony," appears over 275 times and *martus* (3116), "witness," over 50 times. The noun *marturia*, however, occurs only seven times in the canonical material and five times in the Apocrypha. The verb *martureō* (3113), "to witness, testify," is found a limited number of times as well (17 times). Moreover, various compounds are utilized. Many Hebrew words are rendered by *marturia*, usually ʻēdh (cf. the verb ʻûdh, in the hiphil).

Israel was concerned that judgments should be founded upon solid, valid evidence. Testimonies in criminal cases were admissible as evidence upon the basis of two or three witnesses whose testimonies had been heard and corroborated (Deuteronomy 17:6; 19:15). False witnesses were severely punished (Deuteronomy 19:16f.). The commandment of the Decalogue: "Thou shalt not bear false witness against thy neighbor" (Exodus 20:16), which often carries the more general interpretation, "Thou shalt not lie," was undoubtedly originally understood in a legal sense.

People were called to witness legal transactions, such as the purchase of something or a marriage (Ruth 4:9f.). God was often invoked as a witness of the covenant (Genesis 31:50; passim).

Any concept of "testimony, witness" as involving a missionary effort is relatively foreign to the Old Testament. This aspect of witness is not found until the New Testament. A trace of the idea, though, may underlie Isaiah 55:4 which refers to the coming Messiah as a witness to all nations. Of particular interest too is Isaiah 43:9-13 and 44:7-11. In these texts the setting is a courtroom scene in which the Lord is Judge. All the nations will summon their witnesses on behalf of their gods, while the chosen people of God will testify to the one, true, and living God who chose them, led them, and delivered them from the clutches of peril.

New Testament Usage

The noun *marturia* occurs over 35 times in the New Testament where for the first time there is a link between "witness" and "proclamation." But in an ordinary sense false witnesses were paid by the religious authorities to bring false charges against Jesus (Matthew 26:59f.; Mark 14:57f.), just as there was false testimony solicited against Stephen (Acts 6:13f.; 7:58). Regarding congregational discipline, witnesses were necessary for bringing charges against someone. This corresponds to the Old Testament practice of having two or three witnesses (Matthew 18:16; 1 Timothy 5:19). Three visits, suggestive of three witnesses, were needed before Paul was ready to exercise his authority in disciplining the assembly in Corinth (2 Corinthians 13:1).

The legal dimension of witness joins with the historical aspects of testimony in the New Testament. Testimony is grounded upon experience. Luke emphasized the historical basis of the early faith and stressed that the disciples could testify about the reality of things which had taken place. Furthermore, they could interpret the significance of these events. The word *witness* often carries a double sense: "eyewitness and proclaimer." Under such conditions "witness" is virtually identical with "apostle." The apostle-witness has a divine call to testify; he has been a follower of Jesus from the beginning (Luke 24:47f.; Acts 1:8,21,22). It is assumed that these witnesses receive a special empowerment from the Spirit for witnessing (Luke 24:49; Acts 1:8). This missionary task has a universal scope; it is not only directed to the Jewish people, all peoples are invited to hear the good news (Acts 1:8). The apostles "testify" of the life, ministry, death, resurrection, and ascension of Jesus (Acts 10:39ff.; cf. 1:22; 2:32; 3:15; 5:31). Furthermore, they testify that Jesus will be the judge in the last days (Acts 10:42).

Others besides the 12 apostles were called witnesses by Luke; among these Paul was the most obvious and significant. He was an eyewitness to the risen Lord as a result of the Damascus experience. He was also a "witness" (*martus*) like Stephen, one who was called upon to suffer or even die for the Cross. Probably it is from such texts as Acts 22:20 that the Church came to give the term *martus,* "witness," the technical sense of "one who died for his/her testimony."

The writings of John emphasize that the testimony of Jesus was grounded upon His actions (John 15:27; 21:24). But this points to a greater truth: who Jesus is. He is the Son of God (John 1:34) from eternity (John 1:15); He is the Saviour of the world, light in a dark dying world (1:1-9; 5:36f.). Jesus brings eternal life (1 John 4:14; 5:11; cf. John 10:25; 15:26). It is important to remember that John stressed "witness" in the sense of Jewish law as he stressed that Jesus is truly the divine Son and agent of the Father.

The apostles were eyewitnesses of historical fact; but at the same time a purely historical concept of witness was expanded. The New Testament concept of witness includes its missionary thrust. All believers can become witnesses to the truth of Jesus Christ even though they have not personally seen the events of Jesus' life, death, or resurrection in a literal sense. The historical truth becomes imbedded in proclamation, i.e., the preaching of Jesus Christ.

The Revelation of John indicates that believers become witnesses when they serve in a missionary capacity; they are uniquely "witnesses" (*marturēs*) when such service costs them their lives (Revelation 11:3; 17:6). The Church later called these martyrs; however, in Revelation such persons are martyrs *because* of their testimony, not martyrs simply because they are believers who die. The latter line of thinking occurred only in the successive years of church history.

The apostles were fully aware of the tremendous responsibility of being "witnesses of God." They could not refrain from speaking what they had seen and heard (Acts 4:20). But neither could they add anything to the message to which they testified. Any "lies," however well-meaning, would be injurious to the truth; thus Paul says that if Christ had not risen from the dead then the apostles would be actually false witnesses of God since they testified of the Resurrection (1 Corinthians 15:15). "But now is Christ risen" (verse 20). It is not possible to make a more solemn statement about the sincerity of apostolic testimony.

The testimony of the apostles is a witness of Jesus Christ. Their testimony combines with God's own witness of His Son as well as with Jesus' own testimony. In John's Gospel there are seven "testimonies" about Jesus: (1) of the Father (5:27; 8:18); (2) of the Son (8:13,14; 14:35); (3) of the Spirit (15:26); (4) of the Scriptures (5:39); (5) of Jesus' works (5:36; 10:25); (6) of John the Baptist (1:7; 3:26; 5:33-36); (7) of the disciples (21:24; cf. 15:27).

Jesus is the great witness/testimony of God to humanity. He is the "faithful and true witness" (Revelation 3:14; cf. 1:5). He testifies to the truth (John 18:37; cf. 14:6) and to that which He has seen and heard from the Father (John 3:32). More importantly, Jesus testifies through His death of God's love for all mankind (1 Timothy 2:6; cf. John 3:16). In the Book of Revelation a frequent phrase is "the testimony of Jesus" (1:2,9; 12:17; 19:10; 20:4). This expression, in almost every case, joins with "the word of God"; consequently, it denotes the Christian revelation of truth. "The testimony of Jesus" is also the testimony of the Spirit concerning Jesus.

STRONG 3141, BAUER 493, MOULTON-MILLIGAN 389-90, KITTEL 4:474-508, LIDDELL-SCOTT 1082, COLIN BROWN 3:1038-46.

3115. μαρτύριον marturion noun

Testimony, witness, proof, evidence.

COGNATE:
μαρτυρέω martureō (3113)

SYNONYM:
μαρτυρία marturia (3114)

מוֹעֵד môʻēdh (4287), Meeting (Ex 29:4,10, Nm 4:3f., 1 Chr 9:21).

עֵד ʻēdh (5915), Witness (Gn 31:44, Jos 22:27f., Is 55:4).

עֵדָה ʻēdhāh (5921), Testimony, warning (Dt 4:45, 2 Kgs 17:15, Ps 119:2, 14,22 [118:2,14,22]).

עֵדוּת ʻēdhûth (5925), Testimony (Ex 25:21f., Nm 17:7f., 2 Chr 23:11).

תְּעוּדָה teʻûdhāh (8914), Attestation (Ru 4:7).

1. μαρτύριον marturion nom/acc sing neu
2. μαρτυρίου marturiou gen sing neu

1	and offer the gift ... for a testimony unto them.	Matt 8:4
1	for a testimony against them and the Gentiles.	10:18
1	in all the world for a witness unto all nations;	24:14
1	Moses commanded, for a testimony unto them.	Mark 1:44
1	shake off the dust under your feet for a testimony	6:11
1	before rulers ... for a testimony against them.	13:9
1	as Moses commanded, for a testimony unto them.	Luke 5:14
1	dust from your feet for a testimony against them.	9:5
1	And it shall turn to you for a testimony.	21:13
1	witness of the resurrection of the Lord Jesus:	Acts 4:33
2	had the tabernacle of witness in the wilderness,	7:44
1	as the testimony of Christ was confirmed in you:	1 Co 1:6
1	declaring unto you the testimony of God.	2:1
1	rejoicing is this, the testimony of our conscience,	2 Co 1:12
1	our testimony among you was believed in that day...	2 Th 1:10
1	a ransom for all, to be testified in due time.	1 Tm 2:6
1	Be not ... ashamed of the testimony of our Lord,	2 Tm 1:8
1	was faithful ... for a testimony of those things	Heb 3:5
1	and the rust of them shall be a witness against you,	Jas 5:3
2	tabernacle of the testimony in heaven was opened:	Rev 15:5

Classical Greek

This noun generally denotes that which serves as testimony, evidence, or proof. Among the classical authors *marturion*, unlike the rest of its word group, seldom if ever refers to the legal realm of witness. It denotes the objective testimony, its content, or a piece of evidence—proof which can confirm a fact or statement (see Strathmann, "marturion," *Kittel*, 4:474-508).

Septuagint Usage

In the Septuagint *marturion* occurs more than 290 times (250, *Kittel*) but mostly in Exodus, Leviticus, and Numbers. It refers to the two tablets of the testimony, the Sinaitic commandments (Exodus 31:18; 32:15); the tent of the testimony (Exodus 29:4,10ff.; 40:42ff.; Leviticus 4:4ff.; Numbers 4:25ff.); and the ark of the testimony (Exodus 40:3; 5:21; Leviticus 16:2; Numbers 4:5). As God's self-testimony contained in the Mosaic covenant, *marturion* is a way of knowing God. Josephus and Philo used *marturion* more in the manner of the classical authors than the expanded connotation of the Septuagint (see Coenen, "Witness," *Colin Brown*, 3:1038-47).

New Testament Usage

There are 20 occurrences of *marturion* in the New Testament. Most are in the Pauline letters and the Synoptics. Strathmann identifies three categories of meaning for *marturion* in the New Testament: (1) "witness for the prosecution," (2) "witness to something," (3) "witness in the active sense" ("marturion," *Kittel*, 4:502ff.). The first meaning has less to do with content than it does with testimony as a means of proof to indict someone. In James 5:3 the rust on the gold and silver will be an evidence, a witness for the prosecution against the rich who do not show mercy to the poor. The shaking of dust from the disciples' feet in Mark 6:11 and Luke 9:15 functions similarly in that the act is a witness (*marturion*) against those who do not welcome the disciples. Mark 1:44, Matthew 8:4, and Luke 5:14 also refer to a proof: the healed man's offering or sacrifice. The offering was to serve as a witness to the priest that the man was healed.

The second category, "witness to something," is particularly shaped, even imbued with new meaning and content, by the Pauline literature. First Corinthians 1:6 and 2:1 do not indicate a literal witness of proof, namely, documentation or a piece of evidence. Here *marturion* is "the *witness* of Christ" (1 Corinthians 1:6) and "the *witness* of God" (2:1). In these cases it specifically refers to the message of salvation proclaimed, the gospel. (See also 2 Thessalonians 1:10; 1 Timothy 2:6; 2 Timothy 1:8 [cf. Coenen, "Witness," *Colin Brown*, 3:1043].)

Thirdly, *marturion* may mean "witness in the active sense." Moses' faithfulness was for a *witness* of those things which were to be spoken. Hebrews 3:5 tells of Moses' faithfulness in his attesting to the people that which he had received from God. Bruce suggests that in this use of *marturion*, "There may be an echo of the repeated references to the ... 'tent of testimony' in Numbers 12:4,5,10" (Bruce, *New International Commentary on the New Testament, Hebrews*, p.58).

STRONG 3142, BAUER 493-4, MOULTON-MILLIGAN 390, KITTEL 4:474-508, LIDDELL-SCOTT 1082, COLIN BROWN 3:1038-40,1042-4.

3115B. μαρτύρομαι marturomai
Call to witness, testify, affirm.

CROSS-REFERENCE:
μαρτυρέω martureō (3113)

Classical Greek and Septuagint Usage
This verb can be found in classical Greek from the Fifth Century B.C. and generally means "call to witness" (*Liddell-Scott*). It was used of "invoking" the gods as well as to "call one to witness" something (ibid.). It does not appears in the canonical portions of the Septuagint. However, in 1 Maccabees 2:56 it is used of one who had to *bear witness* for the entire congregation of Israel.

New Testament Usage
In the New Testament *marturomai* is used once by Luke and twice by Paul. In Acts 20:26 Paul addressed the Ephesian elders telling them, "I *take* you *to record* this day, that I am pure from the blood of all men." Paul called on the Ephesian elders to "bear witness" to the manner in which he declared the gospel, i.e., excluding no one. Again in Galatians 5:3 Paul declared how he himself "testified" to everyone concerning the law of Moses, and in Ephesians 4:17 he "*testified* in the Lord" that those who are regenerated in Christ should not live as though they were not. In these two verses he is giving affirmation to important truths.

STRONG 3143, BAUER 494, MOULTON-MILLIGAN 390, KITTEL 4:510-12, LIDDELL-SCOTT 1082, COLIN BROWN 3:1038.

3116. μάρτυς martus noun
Witness, observer.

CROSS-REFERENCE:
μαρτυρέω martureō (3113)

עֵד 'ēdh (5915), Witness (Nm 35:30, Prv 12:17, Is 8:2).

1. μάρτυς martus nom sing masc
2. μάρτυρος marturos gen sing masc
3. μάρτυρα martura acc sing masc
4. μάρτυρες martures nom pl masc
5. μαρτύρων marturōn gen pl masc
6. μάρτυσιν martusin dat pl masc
7. μάρτυρας marturas acc pl masc

5	that in the mouth of two or three **witnesses**	Matt 18:16
5	what further need have we **of witnesses**?	26:65
5	and saith, What need we any further **witnesses**?	Mark 14:63
4	So you testify that you approve (NIV)	Luke 11:48
4	And ye are **witnesses** of these things	24:48
4	ye shall be **witnesses** unto me both in Jerusalem,	Acts 1:8
3	to be **a witness** with us of his resurrection	1:22
4	hath God raised up, whereof we all are **witnesses**	2:32
4	raised from the dead; whereof we are **witnesses**	3:15
4	And we are his **witnesses** of these things;	5:32
7	And set up false **witnesses**, which said,	6:13
4	and the **witnesses** laid down their clothes	7:58
4	And we are **witnesses** of all things	10:39
6	but unto **witnesses** chosen before of God,	10:41
4	who are his **witnesses** unto the people.	13:31

1	For thou shalt be his **witness** unto all men	Acts 22:15
2	when the blood of thy **martyr** Stephen was shed,	22:20
3	to make thee a minister and a **witness**	26:16
1	God is my **witness**, whom I serve with my spirit	Rom 1:9
3	Moreover I call God for a **record** upon my soul,	2 Co 1:23
5	In the mouth of two or three **witnesses**	13:1
1	For God is my **record**, how greatly I long after you	Phlp 1:8
1	nor a cloak of covetousness; God is **witness**:	1 Th 2:5
4	Ye are **witnesses**, and God also,	2:10
5	an accusation, but before two or three **witnesses**.	1 Tm 5:19
5	professed a good profession before many **witnesses**.	6:12
5	that thou hast heard of me among many **witnesses**,	2 Tm 2:2
6	died without mercy under two or three **witnesses**:	Heb 10:28
5	compassed about with so great a cloud **of witnesses**,	12:1
1	and a **witness** of the sufferings of Christ,	1 Pt 5:1
1	And from Jesus Christ, who is the faithful **witness**,	Rev 1:5
1	even in those days wherein Antipas was ... **martyr**,	2:13
1	saith the Amen, the faithful and true **witness**,	3:14
6	And I will give power unto my two **witnesses**,	11:3
5	and with the blood of the **martyrs** of Jesus:	17:6

Classical Greek

For the classical authors *martus* (also the Aeolic form *martur* [not found in the New Testament]) denoted a "witness," especially a legal witness. The "witness" was one who preferably had "seen" something. Greeks believed that hearing was a less reliable testimony than seeing, even in the religious context.

Septuagint Usage

For the translators of the Septuagint *martus* essentially replaced the Hebrew term *'ēdh*, "witness." The role of the "witness" was primarily legal here too. Thus two or three witnesses were necessary before the death penalty could be carried out (Deuteronomy 17:6; cf. 19:15); moreover, the "witnesses" were to be the first to mete out the penalty (verse 7). God was often invoked as a "witness" (Genesis 31:44; 1 Samuel [LXX 1 Kings] 12:5,6; 20:23; Psalm 89:37 [88:37]; Jeremiah 42:5 [49:5]). And God himself called witnesses (Isaiah 8:2; 43:10,12). In contrast to the Greeks, Israel regarded "hearing" as a major medium of God's revelation (see e.g., Deuteronomy 6:4; articles on *akouō* [189], *horaō* [3571]).

Lying was especially despised in the religion of Israel. The false witness is one of the six things hated by the Lord (Proverbs 6:19). Such criminal actions will not go unpunished (Proverbs 19:5,9; 21:28). The plot of one apocryphal book, Susanna, concerns false witnesses who testify against the righteous Susanna. Oddly, very little *martus* language is present (cf. verse 40). The concept of a "martyr" as one who "witnessed unto death" was not known in either the apocryphal or canonical material.

New Testament Usage

Thayer gives us a typical arrangement of the New Testament uses in three senses: legal, historical, and ethical (cf. *Greek-English Lexicon*). In the legal sense (Matthew 18:16; 26:65; Mark 14:63; Acts 6:13; 7:58; 2 Corinthians 13:1; 1 Timothy 5:19; Hebrews 10:28) it carries the literal value of witness, including the reference to false witnesses in Acts 6:13. The plural is very common in writings to introduce the names of "witnesses" to any contract or legal document.

In the historical sense (Acts 10:41; 1 Timothy 6:12; 2 Timothy 2:2; Hebrews 12:1) the witness is an observer of a historical event. It may be with a genitive of the object (Luke 24:48; Acts 1:22; 2:32; 3:15; 5:32; 10:39; 26:16; 1 Peter 5:1); or with a genitive of the possessor, one who testifies for one (Acts 1:8; 13:31); or with a genitive of the possessor and of the object (Acts 5:32); or to be a witness for one, serve him by testimony (Luke 11:48; Acts 1:8; 22:15). He is said to be a witness to whom appeal is made (Romans 1:9; 2 Corinthians 1:23; Philippians 1:8; 1 Thessalonians 2:5,10); the faithful interpreters of God's counsels are called God's witnesses (Revelation 1:5; 3:14; 11:3).

In the ethical sense those who undergo a violent death as martyrs are called witnesses of Jesus (Acts 22:20; Revelation 2:13; 17:6). These were willing to seal their testimony with their blood. (Although similar acts of "martyrdom" are attested elsewhere [e.g., 4 Maccabees], the term *martus* did not acquire the technical sense of "martyr" until the New Testament.)

STRONG 3144, BAUER 494, MOULTON-MILLIGAN 390, KITTEL 4:474-508, LIDDELL-SCOTT 1082, COLIN BROWN 3:1038,1041-44,1046-47.

3117. μασσάομαι massaomai verb

To chew, bite, gnaw.

לֶחֶם lechem (4035), Food (Jb 30:4).

1. ἐμασσῶντο emassōnto 3pl indic imperf mid
2. ἐμασῶντο emasōnto 3pl indic imperf mid

1	and they **gnawed** their tongues for pain,	Rev 16:10

The verb *massaomai* (also spelled *masaomai*) is related to *massō*, "to squeeze or knead," and both are from the root *maō*, "to touch." In Greek literature *massaomai* can mean "to bite, chew, consume, eat, or devour." The New Testament only employs *massaomai* once, in Revelation 16:10 where men "gnawed (*massaomai*) their tongues for pain." This agonizing and expressive behavior is the result of the pouring out of the fifth vial on the throne of the beast and the subsequent darkness that will cover the kingdom of the beast (see Schneider, "massaomai," *Kittel*, 4:514,515).

STRONG 3145, BAUER 495, MOULTON-MILLIGAN 390, KITTEL 4:514-15, LIDDELL-SCOTT 1082.

3118. μαστιγόω mastigoō verb

Scourge, whip, flog, chastise.
COGNATES:
    μαστίζω mastizō (3119)
    μάστιξ mastix (3120)
SYNONYMS:
    μαστίζω mastizō (3119)
    παίω paiō (3680)
    πατάσσω patassō (3822)
    πλήσσω plēssō (4001)
    τύπτω tuptō (5021)
    φραγελλόω phragelloō (5253)

כָּתַשׁ kāthash (3935), Pound (Prv 27:22).

נָגַע nāgha‛ (5236), Qal: be plagued (Ps 73:14 [72:14]); pual: be plagued (Ps 73:5 [72:5]).

נָכָה nākhâh (5409), Hiphil: strike (2 Chr 25:16, Jer 5:3); blow (Prv 17:10; hophal: be beaten (Ex 5:14,16).

שָׂטַם sāṭam (7929), Persecute (Jb 30:21).

1. **μαστιγοῖ mastigoi** 3sing indic pres act
2. **ἐμαστίγωσεν emastigōsen** 3sing indic aor act
3. **μαστιγώσαντες mastigōsantes** nom pl masc part aor act
4. **μαστιγῶσαι mastigōsai** inf aor act
5. **μαστιγώσετε mastigōsete** 2pl indic fut act
6. **μαστιγώσουσιν mastigōsousin** 3pl indic fut act

```
6 and they will scourge you in their synagogues;..... Matt 10:17
4 to mock, and to scourge, and to crucify him:.......... 20:19
5 some of them shall ye scourge in your synagogues,..... 23:34
6 And they shall mock him, and shall scourge him,.. Mark 10:34
3 And they shall scourge him, and put him to death: Luke 18:33
2 Pilate therefore took Jesus, and scourged him...... John 19:1
1 and scourgeth every son whom he receiveth........Heb 12:6
```

Classical Greek and Septuagint Usage

Mastigoō, "to whip, flog, or beat," is generally associated with punishment or discipline in classical Greek but is also used to describe unjustifiable "torment" or "mistreatment." The variation appears in references to Roman or Jewish authorities administering the punishment. It appears over 25 times in the Septuagint usually to translate the Hebrew *nākhâh* meaning "to strike or smite." Typically it is used in the sense of unwarranted beating (cf. Exodus 5:14), but for certain transgressions of the Law it was justified (Deuteronomy 25:2). Occasionally it is also used as a general term for fighting (cf. 1 Kings 12:24 [LXX 3 Kings 12:24]).

New Testament Usage

"Scourge" is a common New Testament translation of *mastigoō*. It was the normal and legal preliminary to crucifixion. In the case of Jesus (Luke 23:22) it was inflicted before the sentence of crucifixion was pronounced. Pilate hoped to avert the extreme punishment and satisfy the Jews at the same time.

The Jewish method of scourging, as described in the Mishnah, was by the use of 3 thongs of leather, the offender receiving 13 stripes on the bare breast and 13 on each shoulder (cf. the "forty stripes save one," as administered to Paul 5 times [2 Corinthians 11:24]).

In the New Testament *mastigoō* describes flogging as a punishment decreed by the synagogue (Matthew 10:17; 23:34; cf. Deuteronomy 25:2ff.). It denotes the beating given those condemned to death (Matthew 20:19; Mark 10:34; Luke 18:33; John 19:1). In other writings it is noted as punishment for those caught cheating in athletic contests. An interesting example of this verb occurs in Papyri Fiorentine I 61:59 (A.D. 85) where the prefect, having pronounced the accused deserving of being scourged, released him as a mark of favor to the multitude (*Moulton-Milligan*). (See Matthew 27:26; Mark 15:15; John 19:1. Matthew and Mark use the verb *phragelloō* [5253] which occurs only in these two instances. John used the more common Greek word *mastigoō*.)

Figuratively the verb denotes specifically God's action of "chastising" and training by afflictions (Hebrews 12:6; cf. Proverbs 3:12; Jeremiah 5:3).

STRONG 3146, BAUER 495, MOULTON-MILLIGAN 390, KITTEL 4:515-18, LIDDELL-SCOTT 1083, COLIN BROWN 1:161-64.

3119. μαστίζω mastizō verb

To scourge, whip, flog.
COGNATE:
    μαστιγόω mastigoō (3118)
SYNONYMS:
    μαστιγόω mastigoō (3118)
    παίω paiō (3680)
    πατάσσω patassō (3822)
    πλήσσω plēssō (4001)
    τύπτω tuptō (5021)
    φραγελλόω phragelloō (5253)

נָכָה nākhâh (5409), Hiphil: strike (Nm 22:25).

1. **μαστίζειν mastizein** inf pres act

1 lawful for you to **scourge** a man that is a Roman,.. Acts 22:25

Classical Greek
Very close in meaning to *mastigoō* (3118), "to whip, scourge, chastise," *mastizō* is a verb denoting "to whip, beat, or strike" with some type of whip. *Mastizō* is linked with the noun *mastix* (3120), "a whip, scourge." It occurs frequently among classical authors, particularly in the writings of Homer (ca. Eighth-Sixth Century B.C.), and was used both literally and figuratively. When used figuratively it can mean "to torment, to plague," or even "to lash with words" (Schneider, "mastizō," *Kittel*, 4:515).

Septuagint Usage
Mastizō does not occur with the same frequency in the Septuagint as does *mastigoō*. It does, however, occur once in Numbers 22:25 (for the Hebrew word *nākhâh*, "smote") describing the second time Balaam struck the ass. The term also occurs in the Wisdom of Solomon 5:11 and 3 Maccabees 2:21.

New Testament Usage
As in the Septuagint, *mastigoō* is more common in the New Testament than is *mastizō*. The only instance of *mastizō* is in Acts 22:25 where Paul was scourged. His offense was ambiguous to the Roman officials. Thus, they intended to use torture to force him to clarify or confess his crime. Since he had not been convicted of any crime, this was not technically punishment (ibid.). However, the inquiry was abruptly halted when Paul revealed his Roman citizenship. A Roman citizen might in some cases be punished by scourging following a conviction, but it was illegal to scourge a citizen as a part of interrogation (Bruce, *New International Commentary on the New Testament, Acts*, p.421).

Bruce distinguishes between this attempted scourging and Paul's other beatings. "Paul had been beaten with rods on three occasions ... and five times he had been sentenced to the disciplinary lash inflicted by Jewish authority, but neither of these penalties has the murderous quality of the 'flagellum' " (ibid., see also p.420). The "flagellum," the Latin equivalent for *mastix*, was a terrible instrument of torture. When used in the hands of the Romans, it could result in death or permanent maiming (see Embry, "Beat, Chastise, Scourge," *Colin Brown*, 1:161-164; also, Greenberg, "Scourging," *The Interpreter's Dictionary of the Bible*, 4:245f.).

STRONG 3147, BAUER 495, MOULTON-MILLIGAN 390, KITTEL 4:515-18, LIDDELL-SCOTT 1083, COLIN BROWN 1:161-62.

3120. μάστιξ mastix noun
Whip, lash, (examine someone by) scourging, torment, suffering.
CROSS-REFERENCE:
μαστιγόω mastigoō (3118)

מַכְאוֹב makh'ôv (4480), Sorrow (Ps 32:10 [31:10]).
מַכָּה makkāh (4485), One who smites (Is 50:6); wound (Jer 6:7).
נֶגַע negha' (5237), Blow (Ps 39:10 [38:10]); plague (Ps 91:10 [90:10]).
נֵכֶה nēkheh (5411), Attacker (Ps 35:15 [34:15]).
צֶלַע tsela' (7028), Falling (Ps 38:17 [37:17]).
שֵׁבֶט shēvet (8101), Rod (Jb 21:9).
שׁוֹט shôt (8199), Whip (1 Kgs 12:11,14, Prv 26:3, Na 3:2).
שֶׁפֶט shephet (8572), Judgment (Prv 19:29).

1. μάστιγος **mastigos** gen sing fem
2. μαστίγων **mastigōn** gen pl fem
3. μάστιξιν **mastixin** dat pl fem
4. μάστιγας **mastigas** acc pl fem

4 for to touch him, as many as had **plagues**........... Mark 3:10
1 felt in her body that she was healed of that **plague**...... 5:29
1 go in peace, and be whole of thy **plague**............... 5:34
2 he cured many of their infirmities and **plagues**,...... Luke 7:21
3 bade that he should be examined by **scourging**;..... Acts 22:24
2 others had trial of cruel mockings and **scourgings**,.. Heb 11:36

Classical Greek and Septuagint Usage
In classical Greek *mastix* denotes a "whip, scourge, horsewhip." It is also used metaphorically to mean "scourge, plague; the lash of eloquence" (*Liddell-Scott*). Occasionally in the late Second Century B.C. it was used in the sense of "policeman." Many of the Egyptian gods were pictured as carrying whips. It appears over 25 times in the Septuagint where it is usually used literally of a "whip" (cf. 1 Kings 12:11 [LXX 3 Kings 12:11]; 2 Chronicles 10:11). Occasionally it is also used metaphorically of "sorrows" (Psalms 32:10 [LXX 31:10]; 38:17 [37:17]).

New Testament Usage
Just as with the verb *mastigoō* (3118), the noun *mastix* retains its classical and Septuagintal meanings in the New Testament. There was some distinction between the Roman method and that of the Jews. The New Testament usage in Acts 22:24 refers to the Roman method in which the person was stripped and tied in a bending posture to a pillar or stretched on a

frame. The scourge was made of leather thongs, weighted with sharp pieces of bond or lead, which tore the flesh of both the back and the breast. Eusebius records his having witnessed the suffering of martyrs who died under this treatment. The context of Acts 22:24 reminds the reader that scourging of Roman citizens was prohibited by the Porcian law of 197 B.C. In Hebrews 11:36 *mastix* is employed of the sufferings of saints in the Old Testament times (cf. also 1 Kings 12:11,14). Among the Hebrews the usual mode, legal or domestic, was that of beating with a rod (cf. 2 Corinthians 11:25) or leather thongs.

The figurative usage is "sharp pain, torment, or suffering" sent by God to men as bodily illness or disease (Mark 3:10; 5:29,34; Luke 7:21; cf. Job 5:21; Psalms 39:10; 89:32).

The use of a scourge was a legal procedure with slaves, but a free man could not legally be so treated. *Mastix* is used mostly in the plural in situations concerned with examining someone by scourging (Acts 22:24; Hebrews 11:36; cf. Isaiah 50:6).

STRONG 3148, BAUER 495, MOULTON-MILLIGAN 390, KITTEL 4:518-19,1091-98, LIDDELL-SCOTT 1083, COLIN BROWN 1:161-63.

3121. μαστός mastos noun
Breast.

דּוֹד dôdh (1782), Love (S/S 1:2,4, 4:10, 7:12).

שַׁד shadh (8157), Breast (S/S 7:3, Is 32:12, Hos 9:14).

שֹׁד shōdh (8159), Breast (Jb 24:9, Is 66:11).

1. μαστοί mastoi nom pl masc
2. μαστοῖς mastois dat pl masc

1 and the **paps** which thou hast sucked. . . . . Luke 11:27
1 Blessed are ... the **paps** which never gave suck. 23:29
2 and girt about the **paps** with a golden girdle. . . . . Rev 1:13

Mastos is a noun denoting breast. In the classical literature *mastos* can refer to either the breast of a man or woman, or it may indicate the upper body. It can also be used figuratively of a hill or cup-shaped object. In the New Testament *mastos* occurs three times in the plural form, rendered each time by the KJV as "paps." Both Luke 11:27, "the *paps* which thou hast sucked," and Luke 23:29, "the *paps* which never gave suck," refer to a mother's breasts. Revelation 1:13, "girt about the paps with a golden girdle," denotes the upper body of a man (Motyer, "Body," *Colin Brown*, 1:232-242, especially p.240).

STRONG 3149, BAUER 495, MOULTON-MILLIGAN 391, LIDDELL-SCOTT 1083.

3122. ματαιολογία mataiologia noun
Empty, vain or idle talk.
CROSS-REFERENCES:
λόγος logos (3030)
ματαιόω mataioō (3126)

1. ματαιολογίαν mataiologian acc sing fem

1 have turned aside unto **vain jangling**; . . . . 1 Tm 1:6

This adjective is related to the noun *mataiologos* (3123) and means "empty prattle, vain speaking, fruitless discussion," etc. Its single occurrence in the New Testament (1 Timothy 1:6) refers to the kind of fruitless speech and teachings of those who have turned from the goal of the commandment, love, and from the "faith unfeigned" (verse 5). The result is that they do not understand what they say nor what they affirm (verse 7); they only generate "meaningless talk" (NIV) or "vain jangling" (*mataiologia*).

STRONG 3150, BAUER 495, MOULTON-MILLIGAN 391, KITTEL 4:524, LIDDELL-SCOTT 1084, COLIN BROWN 1:550,552.

3123. ματαιολόγος mataiologos adj
An idle, senseless talker, (idly talking).
CROSS-REFERENCES:
λόγος logos (3030)
ματαιόω mataioō (3126)

1. ματαιολόγοι mataiologoi nom pl masc

1 are many unruly and **vain talkers** and deceivers, ... Tit 1:10

Mataiologos comes from *mataios* (3124), "folly, fault," and *legō* (2978), "to speak," and is used both as an adjective ("idly talking") and as a noun ("idle, empty talker"). In its only occurrence in the New Testament, Titus 1:10, it is used in the latter sense. Here it refers to those who utter empty, senseless things. Such were the many "empty talkers" (*mataiologoi*) of whom Titus was warned. "The idea of worthlessness associated in the Jewish mind with heathen idols" may be implied (see Guthrie, *Tyndale New Testament Commentaries*, 14:187).

STRONG 3151, BAUER 495, MOULTON-MILLIGAN 391, KITTEL 4:524, LIDDELL-SCOTT 1084, COLIN BROWN 1:550,552.

3124. μάταιος mataios adj
Vain, useless, idle, empty, worthless, foolish.

COGNATE:
ματαιόω mataioō (3126)

SYNONYM:
κενός kenos (2727)

אָוֶן 'āwen (201), Evildoer (Hos 6:8 [6:9]).

אַכְזִיב 'akhzîv (398), Achzib (Mi 1:14).

אֱלִיל 'ĕlîl (462), Worthless (Zec 11:17).

הֶבֶל hevel (1961), Idol (2 Kgs 16:13); vanity (Prv 31:30, Jer 10:3).

חַטָּאת chaṭṭā'th (2496I), Sin (1 Kgs 16:2).

חִנָּם chinnām (2703), Without cause (Prv 26:2).

כָּזָב kāzāv (3695), Lie (Ez 13:6ff., Hos 12:1, Zep 3:13).

רִיק rêq (7673), Something vain (Prv 12:11).

שָׂעִיר sā'îr (7988), Goat-demon, satyr (Lv 17:7, 2 Chr 11:15).

שָׁוְא shaw' (8175), Vain (Ex 20:7, Ps 60:11 [59:11], Mal 3:14).

תֹּהוּ tōhû (8744), Nothingness; empty argument (Is 59:4).

1. μάταιοι mataioi nom pl masc/fem
2. μάταιος mataios nom sing masc
3. ματαία mataia nom sing fem
4. ματαίας mataias gen sing fem
5. ματαίων mataiōn gen pl neu

5 turn from these **vanities** unto the living God, ... Acts 14:15
1 the thoughts of the wise, that they are **vain**. .... 1 Co 3:20
3 And if Christ be not raised, your faith is **vain**; 15:17
1 for they are unprofitable and **vain**. .... Tit 3:9
2 this man's religion is **vain**. .... Jas 1:26
4 from your **vain** conversation received by tradition .... 1 Pt 1:18

Classical Greek
Outside of Biblical Greek the adjective *mataios* has two basic meanings: (1) It denotes the appearance of something as distinct from its essence, and it suggests the "deceptive" quality of something; (2) *Mataios* refers to the "ineffectiveness" or "uselessness" of something. In this latter sense it is often translated as "vain, without purpose." *Mataios* at times joins the company of *kenos* (2727), "empty" (Trench, *Synonyms of the New Testament*, p.180, observes such pairing in Aristotle and Plutarch).

Septuagint Usage
The same construction is not infrequent in the Septuagint (e.g., Job 20:18; Hosea 12:1; Micah 1:14), where *mataios* translates as many as 11 different Hebrew expressions. Ordinarily *hevel* and *shaw'* stand behind it (both meaning "worthless, in vain, without result, empty").

Mataios assumes a decidedly negative and religious quality in the Septuagint; in fact, the plural substantive form (*hoi mataioi*) is simply another way of saying "idols" (e.g., Leviticus 17:7; 1 Kings [LXX 3 Kings] 16:2,7; 2 Kings [4 Kings] 17:15, of Jereboam's sin of idolatry; passim).

The implicit deceit of idols is also suggested by *mataios* (cf. Psalms 5:9; 12:2; 24:4 [LXX 11:2; 23:4]). Moreover, the Hebrew is *kāzāv*, which means "lie." The deception of *mataios* is ultimately destructive (e.g., Proverbs 21:6; Amos 2:4). The deceitfulness of riches is equal to idolatry (Isaiah 2:28), and man's self-reliance is "useless" (Psalm 60:11 [LXX 59:11]; cf. 94:11 [LXX 93:11]). False prophets are pictured as leading Israel astray by their "worthless, deceptive" visions and prophecies (Ezekiel 13:6,9,19; 22:28). (See also the word *mataiotēs* [3125] in the Septuagint, especially in Ecclesiastes 2:1,11; Psalms and Proverbs.)

New Testament Usage
The extreme negative quality of *mataios* found in the Septuagint is also seen in the New Testament. The use in Acts 14:15 is undoubtedly a reference to the implied idolatry of the Lycaonian people who mistook Paul and Barnabas for "gods" (cf. 1 Peter 1:18). It is fundamental to Paul's thought that the Lord knows the "futility" and "uselessness" of human wisdom (1 Corinthians 3:20; cf. Psalm 94:11). Paul stressed how "futile" faith would be if the Resurrection were not a historical reality (1 Corinthians 15:17). The imagery of idolatry may lie behind James' explanation that religion without controlling one's tongue is "worthless" (James 1:26).

STRONG 3152, BAUER 495, MOULTON-MILLIGAN 391, KITTEL 4:519-22, LIDDELL-SCOTT 1084, COLIN BROWN 1:549-52.

3125. ματαιότης mataiotēs noun
Vanity, futility, worthlessness; depravity.

CROSS-REFERENCE:
ματαιόω mataioō (3126)

הֶבֶל hevel (1961), Futility, vanity (Ps 78:33 [77:33], Eccl 2:1, 8:14).

הַוָּה hawwāh (2010), Destruction (Ps 52:7).

רִיק rîq (7672), Something vain (Ps 4:2).

שָׁוְא shaw' (8175), Vanity, lies (Pss 119:37 [118:37], 139:20 [138:20], 144:8 [143:8]).

1. ματαιότητος mataiotētos gen sing fem
2. ματαιότητι mataiotēti dat sing fem

2 For the creature was made subject to **vanity**, ... Rom 8:20

ματαιόω 3126

2 as other Gentiles walk, in the **vanity** of their mind, ... Eph 4:17
1 when they speak great swelling words **of vanity**, ... 2 Pt 2:18

Classical Greek
The general sense of *mataiotēs* indicates a lack of or attainment of true purpose (see *Moulton-Milligan*). Classical Greek writings rarely use *mataiotēs* and its cognates. Its word group includes both *mataios* (3124), "folly, fault," and *matia*, "vain effort," and can mean "deceptive, fictitious, groundless." It can also mean "in vain, ineffectual, purposeless, pointless." *Mataiotēs* implies a particular set of values, a religious or moral standard, a norm by which truth is measured. When something is *mataiotēs* then, it is by implication something contrary to the norm, unexpected, something that ought not to be. In addition, it refers to something that is worthless due to its deceptive or ineffectual quality (Tiedtke, "Empty," *Colin Brown*, 1:549-553; Bauernfeind, "*mataiotēs*," *Kittel*, 4:519-524).

Septuagint Usage
While *mataiotēs* is rare in secular literature, it is used frequently in the Septuagint, especially in the Psalms and Ecclesiastes. It occurs more than 30 times in the latter (see 1:2; 2:1). Most commonly, *mataiotēs* is a translation of the Hebrew word *hevel*, "vanity, nothingness," but there are a variety of Hebrew words that describe different facets of "nothingness." These words generally speak of ways in which human beings can resist the reality of God. In Ecclesiastes, however, the Preacher is keenly aware of the futility and vanity of the human life and thought that ignores God and His commandments. A tone of lamenting tragedy for the vanity of everything runs through the book (see Tiedtke, "Empty," *Colin Brown*, 1:551).

New Testament Usage
In the New Testament *mataiotēs* occurs three times. Romans 8:20 "is a valid commentary on (Ecclesiastes)," says Bauernfeind. "It tells us plainly that the state of *mataiotēs* (vanity) exists, and also that this has a beginning and an end" (Bauernfeind, "*mataiotēs*," *Kittel*, 4:423). Here the whole creation is seen as subjected to frustration and vanity, awaiting with groans and painful travail its redemption from vanity (Romans 8:19,22). Thayer says that here *mataiotēs* connotes "frailty" and "want of vigor" (*Greek-English Lexicon*).

In Ephesians 4:17 the sense is more of perverseness or depravity of mind which affects the way of life. Here *mataiotēs* ("vanity, futility") of the mind is a characteristic of those who are alienated from the life of God. Paul exhorts believers to live no longer as those marked by such vanity. The speech of false teachers is described in 2 Peter 2:18. It is "great swelling words of *vanity* (*mataiotēs*)." The connotation of *mataiotēs* here is of something devoid of truth and appropriateness, "loud boasts of folly" (RSV).

STRONG 3153, BAUER 495, MOULTON-MILLIGAN 391, KITTEL 4:523, LIDDELL-SCOTT 1084, COLIN BROWN 1:549-52.

3126. ματαιόω mataioō verb
Render futile or foolish, vain.

COGNATES:
    ματαιολογία mataiologia (3122)
    ματαιολόγος mataiologos (3123)
    μάταιος mataios (3124)
    ματαιότης mataiotēs (3125)
    μάτην matēn (3127)

בָּעַר bāʿar (1220), Burn; niphal: be stupid (Jer 51:17 [28:17]).

הָבַל hāval (1960), Qal: become worthless (Jer 2:5); hiphil: lead into futility (Jer 23:16).

סָכַל sākhal (5721), Niphal: do something foolish (1 Chr 21:8); hiphil: act like a fool (1 Sm 26:21).

1. ἐματαιώθησαν emataiōthēsan 3pl indic aor pass

1 but **became vain** in their imaginations, ... Rom 1:21

This word may occur in the active sense, "to present what is vain" or "to deceive." However, its more common usage is passive, "to be given up to vanity." Used once in the New Testament, in Romans 1:21, it occurs in the passive sense. Here *mataioō* describes those who have become vain in their reasoning. Their thoughts are empty or foolish. This futility is in contrast to glorifying and thankfulness that should have been the response to the revelation of God (1:19). The sense of cause and effect is implied.

STRONG 3154, BAUER 495, KITTEL 4:523, LIDDELL-SCOTT 1084, COLIN BROWN 1:549,551-52.

3127. μάτην matēn adv
In vain, fruitless.

COGNATE:
    ματαιόω mataioō (3126)
SYNONYM:
    κενῶς kenōs (2732)

אָוֶן ʾāwen (201), Nothing (Is 41:29).

הֶבֶל hevel (1961), Vanity (Ps 39:6 [38:6]).
חִנָּם chinnām (2703), Without cause (Ps 35:7 [34:7], Prv 3:30).
שָׁוְא shawe' (8175), Falsely (Ps 41:6 [40:6]).
שֶׁקֶר sheqer (8632), Lie (Jer 8:8).

1. μάτην matēn

1 But in vain they do worship me,	Matt 15:9
1 Howbeit in vain do they worship me,	Mark 7:7

The adverb *matēn*, according to Bauernfeind, may have one of three meanings: "in vain"; "groundlessly, pointlessly"; or "deceitfully" ("matēn," *Kittel*, 4:523f.). Drawing from Isaiah 29:13, Matthew 15:9 and Mark 7:7 indicate that "hypocrites" worship *in vain* (*matēn*); it is a futile attempt. Despite their words, worship is pointless for those whose hearts are far from God.

STRONG 3155, BAUER 495-96, MOULTON-MILLIGAN 391, KITTEL 4:523-24, LIDDELL-SCOTT 1084, COLIN BROWN 1:549-50,552.

3128. Ματθαῖος Matthaios name

Matthew.

1. Ματθαῖος Matthaios nom masc
2. Ματθαῖον Matthaion acc masc
3. Μαθθαῖος Maththaios nom masc
4. Μαθθαῖον Maththaion acc masc

2 he saw a man, named **Matthew**,	Matt 9:9
1 Philip, and Bartholomew; Thomas, and **Matthew**	10:3
2 and Bartholomew, and **Matthew**, and Thomas,	Mark 3:18
2 **Matthew** and Thomas, James the son of Alphaeus,	Luke 6:15
1 and **Matthew**, James the son of Alphaeus,	Acts 1:13

A tax collector called to be one of the 12 apostles (Matthew 9:9); he wrote the gospel bearing his name.

3129. Ματθάν Matthan name

Matthan.

1. Ματθάν Matthan masc

1 and Eleazar begat **Matthan**;	Matt 1:15
1 and **Matthan** begat Jacob;	1:15

The son of Eleazar in the genealogy of Jesus (Matthew 1:15).

3130. Ματθάτ Matthat name

Matthat.

1. Ματθάτ Matthat masc
2. Μαθθάτ Maththat masc

1 Which was the son of **Matthat**,	Luke 3:24
1 which was the son of **Matthat**,	3:29

Two men in the genealogy of Jesus bear this name, and both had a father named Levi (Luke 3:24,29).

3131. Ματθίας Matthias name

Matthias.

1. Ματθίαν Matthian acc masc
2. Μαθθίαν Maththian acc masc

1 Joseph ... who was surnamed Justus, and **Matthias**...	Acts 1:23
1 and the lot fell upon **Matthias**;	1:26

Name of the disciple chosen to fill the apostolic office vacated by Judas Iscariot (Acts 1:23,26).

3132. Ματταθά Mattatha name

Mattatha.

1. Ματταθά Mattatha masc

1 which was the son of **Mattatha**,	Luke 3:31

The son of Nathan in the genealogy of Jesus (Luke 3:31).

3133. Ματταθίας Mattathias name

Mattathias.

1. Ματταθίου Mattathiou gen masc

1 Which was the son of **Mattathias**,	Luke 3:25
1 which was the son of **Mattathias**,	3:26

The son of Amos, and the son of Semei in the genealogy of Jesus (Luke 3:25,26).

3134. μάχαιρα machaira noun

A (small) sword, large knife.
COGNATE:
μάχομαι machomai (3136)
SYNONYM:
ῥομφαία rhomphaia (4358)

בַּרְזֶל barzel (1298), Iron (Is 10:34).
חֲנִית chănîth (2698), Spear (Jb 39:23).
חֶרֶב cherev (2820), Sword (Gn 34:25f., 2 Sm 15:14, Is 34:5f.).
מַאֲכֶלֶת ma'ăkheleth (4121), Knife (Gn 22:6,10).

1. μάχαιρα machaira nom sing fem
2. μαχαίρας machairas gen sing fem
3. μαχαίρᾳ machaira dat sing fem
4. μάχαιραν machairan acc sing fem
5. μάχαιραι machairai nom pl fem

6. μαχαιρῶν machairōn gen pl fem
7. μαχαίρης machairēs gen sing fem
8. μαχαίρῃ machairē dat sing fem

4	I came not to send peace, but **a sword**.	Matt 10:34
6	with him a great multitude with **swords** and staves,	26:47
4	stretched out his hand, and drew his **sword**,	26:51
4	Put up again thy **sword** into his place:	26:52
4	take the **sword** shall perish with the **sword**.	26:52
3	take the sword shall perish with the **sword**.	26:52
6	with **swords** and staves for to take me?	26:55
6	with him a great multitude with **swords** and staves,	Mark 14:43
4	And one of them that stood by drew a **sword**,	14:47
6	with **swords** and with staves to take me?	14:48
2	And they shall fall by the edge of the **sword**,	Luke 21:24
4	no **sword**, let him sell his garment, and buy one.	22:36
5	And they said, Lord, behold, here are two **swords**.	22:38
3	they said ... Lord, shall we smite with the **sword**?	22:49
6	come ... as against a thief, with **swords** and staves?	22:52
4	Then Simon Peter having **a sword** drew it,	John 18:10
4	Put up thy **sword** into the sheath:	18:11
3	killed James the brother of John with the **sword**.	Acts 12:2
4	drew out his **sword**, and would have killed himself,	16:27
1	or famine, or nakedness, or peril, or **sword**?	Rom 8:35
4	for he beareth not the **sword** in vain:	13:4
4	the **sword** of the Spirit, which is the word of God:	Eph 6:17
4	and sharper than any twoedged **sword**,	Heb 4:12
2	escaped the edge of the **sword**,	11:34
2	were tempted, were slain with the **sword**:	11:37
1	and there was given unto him a great **sword**.	Rev 6:4
3	he that killeth with the **sword** must be killed	13:10
3	with the sword must be killed with the **sword**.	13:10
2	to the beast, which had the wound by a **sword**,	13:14

Classical Greek
Related to *machē* (3135), "a fight," and *machomai* (3136), "to fight," *machaira* is a noun denoting "sword" or "large knife." The word was commonly used in classical Greek from Homer forward. Its earliest usage includes that of a large knife used for slaughtering and sacrificing animals, for cutting up meat, and for the occupational purposes of tanning or even gardening. Later *machaira* also came to denote a weapon, particularly a small sword or dagger. *Rhomphaia* (4358), "sword, spear," normally meant a larger weapon (see Wevers, "Sword," *Interpreter's Dictionary of the Bible*, 4:469f.; and Michaelis, "machaira," *Kittel*, 4:524-527).

Septuagint Usage
The Septuagint employs *machaira* frequently, over 180 times. It is typically a rendering of the Hebrew word *cherev* (the Septuagint also routinely uses *rhomphaia* for *cherev*). In the Septuagint *machaira* generally denotes a literal weapon, a small sword (Exodus 17:13). Seldom, however, does it refer to a knife as it does in Joshua 5:2. Nor is it often used figuratively as it is in Psalm 57:4 (LXX 56:4) and Isaiah 49:2.

New Testament Usage
With possibly one exception, each of the 29 times that *machaira* occurs in the New Testament it denotes a sword either literally or figuratively. The one exception (Hebrews 4:12) is a figurative reference to the priest's or butcher's knife. Thayer suggests at least three ways in which this word is used (*Greek-English Lexicon*). It is, of course, used in a literal sense to denote a weapon for making or repelling an attack, as in the Gospel reports of the arrest of Jesus. In these accounts Jesus' opponents have swords (Matthew 26:47,55; see parallels); a disciple uses a sword in Jesus' defense (Mark 26:51); and Jesus both rebukes and warns concerning swords in Matthew 26:52 (cf. Revelation 13:10).

Machaira is also used in a metonymical sense to denote the power and authority of a governing official or judge. To "bear the sword" (Romans 13:4) then, symbolizes an authority's power to punish, the power over life and death. Closely connected to this is the connotation of violent death at the hands of rulers (Acts 12:2) or even as a result of war or persecution (Luke 21:24; Romans 8:35; Hebrews 11:34).

In a metaphoric sense *machaira* can be used to mean "violence, dissension," or the "disruption of peace" as used in the saying of Jesus, "Do not suppose that I have come to bring peace to the earth. I did not come to bring peace, but a sword" (Matthew 10:34, NIV).

The term "Word of God" is also metaphorically linked to *machaira* in at least two senses. Ephesians 6:17 pictures the "*sword* of the Spirit" as complementary to the spiritual "armor of God." While Hebrews 4:12 makes a similar comparison between *machaira* and "Word of God," the function is different. Here a "sword" is not used as a part of spiritual weaponry, nor is it used as a sword (*rhomphaia*) as in Revelation 1:16; 2:12,16; 19:15,21. Rather its function is to discern the heart, to lay open the secret human intentions and thoughts. "Hence *machaira* is not a sword," asserts Michaelis; "to cut the joints and marrow one does not use a sword. The picture is that of the knife used by the priest or butcher, or even perhaps the surgeon" ("macharia," *Kittel*, 4:527; see also Brown, "War," *Colin Brown*, 3:958-967, especially p.967).

STRONG 3162, BAUER 496, MOULTON-MILLIGAN 391, KITTEL 4:524-27, LIDDELL-SCOTT 1085, COLIN BROWN 3:958,967.

3135. μάχη *machē* noun
A fight, quarrel, battle, conflict.

COGNATE:
μάχομαι machomai (3136)
SYNONYMS:
ἀντιλογία antilogia (482)
ἐριθεία eritheia (2036)
ἔρις eris (2038)
πόλεμος polemos (4031)
στάσις stasis (4565)
φιλονεικία philoneikia (5216)

מָדוֹן mādhôn (4209II) Quarrel (Prv 26:20).
מִלְחָמָה milchāmāh (4560), Battle (Jb 38:23).
מַצָּה matstsāh (4844), Strife (Is 58:4).
מְרִיבָה merîvāh (4970), Strife (Gn 13:8).
צָבָא tsāvā' (6893), War (Jos 4:13).
רִיב rîv (7662), Plead a case (Prv 25:8).
רִיב rîv (7663), Strife (Gn 13:7, 2 Sm 22:44, Prv 26:21).

1. **μάχαι** machai nom pl fem
2. **μάχας** machas acc pl fem

1	without were **fightings**, within were fears............	2 Co 7:5
2	knowing that they do gender **strifes**................	2 Tm 2:23
2	and **contentions**, and **strivings** about the law;.........	Tit 3:9
1	From whence come **wars** and **fightings** among you?...	Jas 4:1

This noun is related to *machomai* (3136), "to fight," and is used in the Greek literature to denote both a physical combat or contest as well as verbal dispute. In the four New Testament occurrences *machē* is only used in the plural form.

It is doubtful that *machē* signifies any physical fights in its New Testament usage. However, Bauernfeind suggests that Paul may have implied exposure to physical threats in 2 Corinthians 7:5 (Bauernfeind, "*machē*," *Kittel*, 4:527f.). Also, James 4:1 most likely refers to spiritual "wars and fightings." Both 2 Timothy 2:23 and Titus 3:9 connect verbal quarrels, "strivings" (*machē*), in a negative way to senseless questions. Similarly, James 4:1 points to human passions as a cause of *machē*.

STRONG 3163, BAUER 496, MOULTON-MILLIGAN 391, KITTEL 4:527-28, LIDDELL-SCOTT 1085, COLIN BROWN 3:958-59,963.

3136. μάχομαι machomai verb

Fight, contend, dispute.
COGNATES:
ἄμαχος amachos (267)
διαμάχομαι diamachomai (1258)
θεομαχέω theomacheō (2290)
θεομάχος theomachos (2291)
θηριομαχέω thēriomacheō (2318)
θυμομαχέω thumomacheō (2348)
λογομαχέω logomacheō (3028)
λογομαχία logomachia (3029)
μάχαιρα machaira (3134)
μάχη machē (3135)

SYNONYMS:
ἀγωνίζομαι agōnizomai (74)
πολεμέω polemeō (4030)
πυκτεύω pukteuō (4296)

חָרֵב chārēv (2817), Dry up, destroy; niphal: fight together (2 Kgs 3:23).
חָרָה chārâh (2835), Niphal: be angry (S/S 1:6).
לָחַם lācham (4032), Niphal: fight (2 Chr 27:5).
נָכָה nākhâh (5409), Hiphil: kill (Jos 9:18).
נָצָה nātsâh (5510), Niphal: strive, fight (Ex 21:22, Lv 24:10, 2 Sm 14:6).
רִיב rîv (7662), Quarrel, contend (Gn 26:20,22, Neh 5:7, Is 27:8).

1. **μάχεσθε** machesthe 2pl indic pres mid
2. **μαχομένοις** machomenois dat pl masc part pres mid
3. **μάχεσθαι** machesthai inf pres mid
4. **ἐμάχοντο** emachonto 3pl indic imperf mid

4	The Jews therefore **strove** among themselves,......	John 6:52
2	he showed himself unto them as they **strove**,......	Acts 7:26
3	And the servant of the Lord must not **strive**;......	2 Tm 2:24
1	ye **fight** and war, yet ye have not,..................	Jas 4:2

Classical Greek

In classical Greek *machomai*, a deponent verb, means "to fight, contend," especially in battle (cf. *machē* [3135], a "fight, contest, battle" hence, "strife, contention, quarrel"). The verb is usually used of armies engaged in battle, occasionally of one-on-one combat. The word is related to *machaira* (3134), a large knife, dagger, or small sword. It came to mean "to contend, struggle," as in a sporting contest, hence "to make an effort" or "to wrangle, dispute, quarrel," e.g., "to engage in a war of words" or "opinions," as in a legal dispute.

Septuagint Usage

The Septuagint uses this term often as a translation of *rîv* ("to strive, contend"); primarily it means "to contend with words" (e.g., Genesis 31:36). The verb *rîv* also developed legalistic connotations, hence it could also mean "conduct a lawsuit." There has been significant research concerning this use of *rîv* that has designated it as an important genre in prophetic literature. In communicating the seriousness of His charges against Israel, God used the form of "lawsuit" known to the people of that time (cf. Gemsler, "The *RIB*—or Controversy—Pattern in Hebrew Mentality," pp.120-137). According to Gemsler *rîv* took on a specialized meaning in prohetic literature: "a controversy in which Israel's God summons and accuses, threatens and decides against his chosen people" (ibid., pp.128f.). Examples of the use of *rîv* (both noun and verb) as part of this "lawsuit" genre can be found in Exodus 21:18f.; Nehemiah 5:7; Isaiah 27:8; Hosea 4 passim.

New Testament Usage
In the New Testament *machomai* is used of one-on-one physical combat (Acts 7:26) and of a battle of words, such as "to argue" (John 6:52), "to quarrel" (2 Timothy 2:24). The compound *diamachomai* (1258) indicates "to dispute heatedly, argue fiercely" (Acts 23:9; the *Textus Receptus* uses *theomacheō* [2290], "to fight against God").

The term is at times synonymous with *polemeō* (4030), "to war, fight," hence "to quarrel, wrangle." The two are used together in James 4:2, *polemeō* referring more to protracted hostile action or quarreling and *machomai* to sudden verbal outburst.

STRONG 3164, BAUER 496, MOULTON-MILLIGAN 391-92, KITTEL 4:527-28, LIDDELL-SCOTT 1085-86, COLIN BROWN 3:959,963.

3137. μεγαλαυχέω megalaucheō verb
Boast, become proud, arrogant.
CROSS-REFERENCE:
μέγας megas (3144)

גָּבַהּ gāvahh (1391), Be haughty (Ez 16:50, Zep 3:11).
עָרַץ 'ārats (6442), Terrify (Ps 10:18 [9:39]).

1. μεγαλαυχεῖ megalauchei 3sing indic pres act
1 a little member, and **boasteth great things**............ Jas 3:5

From two words *megala*, "great things," and *aucheō* (842B), "to lift up the neck, to boast," *megalaucheō* is found both in the compound form and as two separate words. In the Septuagint *megalaucheō* means "to boast great things, to bear one's self loftily in speech or action" (see Psalm 10:18 [LXX 9:39]; Ezekiel 16:50; Zephaniah 3:11). In the New Testament (only in James 3:5) the word denotes any kind of boastful language that hurts, provokes, or stirs up strife in others.

STRONG 3166, BAUER 496, MOULTON-MILLIGAN 392, LIDDELL-SCOTT 1086.

3138. μεγαλεῖος megaleios adj
Grand, magnificent; great things, wonderful works.
CROSS-REFERENCE:
μέγας megas (3144)

גָּדוֹל gādhôl (1448), Great (Ps 71:19 [70:19]).
גֹּדֶל gōdhel (1465), Greatness (Dt 11:2).
עֲלִילָה 'ălîlāh (6173), Deed (Ps 105:1 [104:1]—only some Sinaiticus texts).

1. μεγαλεῖα megaleia nom/acc pl neu
1 For he that is mighty hath done to me **great things**; Luke 1:49
1 speak in our tongues the **wonderful works** of God.... Acts 2:11

Classical Greek
The adjective *megaleios*, related to the word *megas* (3144), "great," is used in classical Greek for "majestic, magnificent, august, excellent, pompous, splendid, wonderful." It is descriptive of rulers and the epiphany of the gods (*Liddell-Scott*).

Septuagint Usage
The Septuagint often uses this term as a translation of *gōdhel* (meaning "great," i.e., "great things or greatness"). It is used this way to refer to God's perfections and His marvelous acts (Deuteronomy 11:2; Psalm 79:11 [LXX 78:11]; see also Sirach 42:21).

New Testament Usage
In the New Testament the term occurs only twice, both times in Luke's writings. In the Magnificat, Mary reflects on the "great things" of God; i.e., His excellencies and marvelous doings (Luke 1:49). This is reminiscent of the Hebrew *gōdhel* ("excellent greatness, mighty acts") in the Psalms (e.g., 79:11; 150:2). On the Day of Pentecost Jews from all parts of the empire who were living in Jerusalem heard in their own language the apostles speak of the "wonderful works" of God (Acts 2:11). What these wonderful works (*megaleios*) were, however, is not specifically stated.

STRONG 3167, BAUER 496, MOULTON-MILLIGAN 392, KITTEL 4:541, LIDDELL-SCOTT 1086, COLIN BROWN 2:425.

3139. μεγαλειότης megaleiotēs noun
Greatness, grandeur, magnificence, majesty.
COGNATE:
μέγας megas (3144)
SYNONYM:
μεγαλωσύνη megalōsunē (3142)

רְבוּ rᵉvû (A7533), Greatness (Dn 7:27—Aramaic).
תִּפְאֶרֶת tiph'ereth (8930), Honor (Jer 33:9 [40:9]).

1. μεγαλειότητος megaleiotētos gen sing fem
2. μεγαλειότητι megaleiotēti dat sing fem
3. μεγαλειότητα megaleiotēta acc sing fem

2 they were all amazed at the **mighty power** of God... Luke 9:43

3 and her **magnificence** should be destroyed,......... Acts 19:27
1 but were eyewitnesses of his **majesty**................ 2 Pt 1:16

In classical Greek this noun is used to offer divine ascriptions to their pagan gods, hence "greatness, majesty, magnificence." There is a different usage in the canonical portions of the Septuagint. Jeremiah 33:9 (LXX 40:9) describes how the captors of Israel will come to view their captives when God restores them. In Daniel's dream of the four beasts the kingdom of the Most High will be given "greatness." In the New Testament *megaleiotēs* is used similarly to classical Greek where it describes attributes of pagan gods or God. Luke 9:43 refers to the majesty or "mighty power" (*magaleiotēs*) of God. Second Peter 1:16 speaks of the magnificent splendor of Christ made visible to the eyewitnesses of the Transfiguration. The only other occurrence of this term in the New Testament is found in Acts 19:27 when Demetrius speaks of his fear that Paul's preaching would destroy the "magnificence" of Artemis (Diana).

STRONG 3168, BAUER 496, MOULTON-MILLIGAN 392, KITTEL 4:541-42, LIDDELL-SCOTT 1086, COLIN BROWN 2:424-26.

3140. μεγαλοπρεπής

megaloprepēs adj
Magnificent, splendid, excellent, majestic.

CROSS-REFERENCES:
μέγας megas (3144)
πρέπω prepō (4100)

גַּאֲוָה ga'ăwāh (1375), Majesty (Dt 33:26).

1. μεγαλοπρεποῦς megaloprepous gen sing fem

1 came such a voice to him from the **excellent glory**,.. 2 Pt 1:17

Megaloprepēs comes from two words: *megas* (3144), "great," and *prepō* (4100), "to be conspicuous, seemly, or fitting." It is used to speak of that which is great, noble, magnificent, magnanimous, or exalted. In classical Greek it is used of both men and animals; however, in the Septuagint it is used only of God's reign as King of Israel (cf. Deuteronomy 33:26; 2 Maccabees 8:15; 3 Maccabees 2:9). The New Testament uses *megaloprepēs* only once (2 Peter 1:17). Here it refers to God whose voice came to Christ from the magnificent or "excellent" (*megaloprepēs*) glory on the Mount of Transfiguration.

STRONG 3169, BAUER 497, MOULTON-MILLIGAN 392, KITTEL 4:542-43, LIDDELL-SCOTT 1087.

3141. μεγαλύνω megalunō verb

Magnify, enlarge, lengthen, extol, magnify, make great, praise.

COGNATE:
μέγας megas (3144)

SYNONYMS:
δοξάζω doxazō (1386)
πλατύνω platunō (3975)

גָּבַר gāvar (1428), Hiphil: prevail (Ps 12:4 [11:4]).

גָּדוֹל gādhôl (1448), Great (2 Sm 5:10, Ps 57:10 [56:10], Ez 9:9).

גָּדַל gādhal (1461), Qal: be valued, be magnified (1 Sm 26:24, Ps 40:16 [39:16], Zec 12:7); piel: make great, magnify (Gn 12:2, 2 Chr 1:1, Ps 69:30 [68:30]); hiphil: magnify, magnify oneself (Gn 19:19, Jb 19:5, Jer 48:26 [31:26]); hithpael: magnify oneself (Ez 38:23).

גָּדֵל gādhēl (1462), Growing (1 Sm 2:26).

מִגְדֹּל mighdōyl (4165), Tower, great (2 Sm 22:51).

פָּלָא pālā' (6623), Be too hard; piel: fulfill or perform a special vow (Nm 15:3,8).

רָבַב rāvav (7525), Be many (Ps 104:24 [103:24]).

רָבָה rāvâh (7528), Be several times more (Gn 43:34).

רְבָה rᵉvâh (A7529), Become great; pael: give great honors (Dn 2:48—Aramaic).

שָׂרַר sārar (8049), Rule (Prv 8:16).

1. **μεγαλύνει** megalunei 3sing indic pres act
2. **μεγαλύνουσιν** megalunousin 3pl indic pres act
3. **μεγαλυνόντων** megalunontōn gen pl masc part pres act
4. **ἐμεγάλυνεν** emegalunen 3sing indic imperf/aor act
5. **μεγαλυνθῆναι** megalunthēnai inf aor pass
6. **μεγαλυνθήσεται** megalunthēsetai 3sing indic fut pass
7. **ἐμεγαλύνετο** emegaluneto 3sing indic imperf pass

2 and **enlarge** the borders of their garments,......... Matt 23:5
1 And Mary said, My soul doth **magnify** the Lord,.... Luke 1:46
4 how the Lord **had showed great** mercy upon her;....... 1:58
4 but the people **magnified** them...................... Acts 5:13
3 heard them speak with tongues, and **magnify** God...... 10:46
7 and the name of the Lord Jesus **was magnified**......... 19:17
5 that we **shall be enlarged** by you................... 2 Co 10:15
6 so now also Christ **shall be magnified** in my body,... Phlp 1:20

Classical Greek

In classical Greek the verb *megalunō* (related to *megas* [3144], "great") means "to make great, powerful; to make great by word, extol, magnify." It also has the meaning of "to exaggerate" and "to aggravate" (as to aggravate a crime).

Septuagint Usage

In the Septuagint *megalunō* is normally used for the Hebrew *gādhal*, "to make great" (cf. Genesis 12:2; Psalm 40:16 [LXX 39:16]), having several possible translations; i.e., "to grow" (1 Samuel 2:21 [LXX 1 Kings 2:21]), "to make precious, valuable" (1 Samuel 26:24 [LXX 1 Kings 26:24]), "to exalt" (1 Chronicles 29:25), "to make great" (1 Chronicles 29:12). Often *megalunō* is used in reference to magnifying or extolling God (Genesis 19:19; Psalms 35:27 [LXX 34:27]; 70:4 [69:4]; Sirach 43:31). *Megalunō* also translates the Hebrew *gāvar* ("to make mighty, prevail," Psalm 12:4 [LXX 11:4]), *pālā'* ("to separate, distinguish, make wonderful, consecrate" as in performing a vow, Numbers 15:3,8), and *rāvav* ("to be many, manifold," Psalm 104:24 [LXX 103:24]).

New Testament Usage
In the New Testament *megalunō* is used in a variety of ways. It is used in the physical sense of "to lengthen," as in lengthening a tassel (Matthew 23:5). It is most often used in the sense of "to extol, magnify," e.g., "to make great by word, to acclaim." Mary echoed the Psalms when she spoke in her Magnificat of magnifying, or making great, the Lord (Luke 1:46). In the days of the Early Church the apostles were "magnified" ("highly regarded," NIV) by the common people (Acts 5:13). Paul desired that his (along with his associates') ministry be built up, enlarged, or magnified with the rightful respect of the Corinthians (2 Corinthians 10:15). A purpose for the exercise of tongues is to extol God (Acts 10:46). Paul desired that Jesus be made great, i.e., exalted or magnified, in his body, whether by life or death (Philippians 1:20; cf. Acts 19:17).

STRONG 3170, BAUER 497, MOULTON-MILLIGAN 392, KITTEL 4:543, LIDDELL-SCOTT 1088, COLIN BROWN 2:424-25.

3141B. μεγάλως megalōs adv
Greatly.

CROSS-REFERENCE:
μέγας megas (3144)

גָּדוֹל gādhôl (1448), Great (1 Chr 29:9, Neh 12:43).

פָּלָא pālā' (6623), Be too hard; hiphil: make a special vow (Nm 6:2).

רֹב rōv (7524), Abundance; all (Jb 4:14).

1. μεγάλως megalōs
1 But I rejoiced in the Lord greatly, ... Phlp 4:10

Megalōs is an adverb used as early as Homer. Related to the adjective *megas* (3144), "great," *megalōs* is used to strengthen a verb. It is so employed in its only appearance in the New Testament (Philippians 4:10). Here Paul "expresses his joy with regard to the Church's real and tangible interest in him" (Muller, *New International Commentary on the New Testament, Philippians and Philemon*, p.145). He emphasized that he was "greatly" (*megalōs*) rejoicing in the Lord as a result of the gifts sent him by the Philippian church. "The gifts symbolized for Paul Christian love and sympathy in the Church" (ibid.).

STRONG 3171, BAUER 497, MOULTON-MILLIGAN 392, LIDDELL-SCOTT 1088.

3142. μεγαλωσύνη megalōsunē noun
Majesty, greatness.

COGNATE:
μέγας megas (3144)

SYNONYM:
μεγαλειότης megaleiotēs (3139)

אַדֶּרֶת 'addereth (152), Glory (Zec 11:3).

גְּבוּרָה gᵉvûrāh (A1401), Power (Dn 2:20—Aramaic).

גְּדוּלָה gᵉdhûlāh (1449I), Something great, greatness (2 Sm 7:21, 1 Chr 17:19, Ps 145:3 [144:3]).

גָּדַל gādhal (1461), Hiphil: be magnificent (1 Chr 22:5).

גֹּדֶל gōdhel (1465), Greatness (Dt 32:3, Ps 150:2).

מִגְדָּל mighdāl (4166), Tower (Prv 18:10).

תִּפְאֶרֶת tiph'ereth (8930), Honor (Jer 33:9 [40:9]—Codex Sinaiticus only).

1. μεγαλωσύνη megalōsunē nom sing fem
2. μεγαλωσύνης megalōsunēs gen sing fem

2 sat down on the right hand of the **Majesty** on high; ... Heb 1:3
2 the throne of the **Majesty** in the heavens; 8:1
1 be glory and **majesty**, dominion and power, ... Jude 1:25

Megalōsunē, a noun built on the word *megas* (3144), "great," is used only in Biblical and early church writings. It carries the meaning of "loftiness, greatness, majesty."

Septuagint Usage
In the Septuagint the term is used of the majesty of God. It is the translation of the Hebrew *gōdhel* ("greatness," cf. Deuteronomy 32:3; Psalm 79:11 [LXX 78:11]) and *gᵉdhûlāh* ("greatness," cf. 2 Samuel 7:23 [LXX 2 Kings 7:23]; Psalm 145:3,6 [Psalm 144:3,6]) (see also Wisdom of Solomon 18:24; Sirach 39:15).

New Testament Usage
The term occurs three times in the New Testament. The writer to the Hebrews used it twice as a periphrasis, a divine name for God himself, expressing the idea of God in His greatness. "*Majesty* on high" (Hebrews 1:3)

and "*Majesty* in the heavens" (Hebrews 8:1) emphasize the super-and extramundane position and glory of God. Jude used *megalōsunē* in his great benediction (verse 25, "... glory and *majesty*, [*megalōsunē*] dominion and power ...").

In the postapostolic period it continued to be used as a divine attribute (1 Clement 16:2; 27:4) and in benedictions (1 Clement 20:12; 61:3; Martyrdom of Polycarp 20:2; 21:1; cf. *Bauer*).

STRONG 3172, BAUER 497, MOULTON-MILLIGAN 392, KITTEL 4:544, LIDDELL-SCOTT 1088, COLIN BROWN 2:424-26.

3143. μεγάλως megalōs adv
See word study at number 3141B.

3144. μέγας megas adj
Large, great.

COGNATES:
μεγαλαυχέω megalaucheō (3137)
μεγαλεῖος megaleios (3138)
μεγαλειότης megaleiotēs (3139)
μεγαλοπρεπής megaloprepēs (3140)
μεγαλύνω megalunō (3141)
μεγάλως megalōs (3141B)
μεγαλωσύνη megalōsunē (3142)
μέγεθος megethos (3145)
μεγιστάν megistan (3146)
μέγιστος megistos (3147)
μειζότερος meizoteros (3156)
μείζων meizōn (3157)

SYNONYMS:
ἱκανός hikanos (2401)
πολύς polus (4044)

אַדִּיר 'addîr (116), Mighty, stately (Is 33:21 [33:22], Ez 17:23).

אַדֶּרֶת 'addereth (152), Splendid (Ez 17:8).

גָּדוֹל gādhôl (1448), Great, large (Dt 4:6ff., 1 Sm 6:14f., Jer 11:16).

גְּדוּלָּה gᵉdhûllāh (1449II) Something great (1 Chr 17:21).

גָּדַל gādhal (1461), Qal: be great (Jb 2:13); hiphil: do something more (1 Sm 20:41).

גָּדֵל gādhēl (1462), Great; rich (Gn 26:13).

גֹּדֶל gōdhel (1465), Greatness (Nm 14:19).

הָמוֹן hāmôn (2066), Crowd, masses (Is 5:14).

יָרֵא yārē' (3486), Fear; niphal: be awesome, be feared (Jb 37:22, Is 18:7).

כָּבֵד kāvēdh (3632), Be heavy; be grievous (Gn 18:20).

כָּבֵד kāvēdh (3633), Great (Gn 50:9); grievous (Gn 50:11).

מְאֹד mᵉ'ōdh (4108), Power, strength; loudness (Ex 19:16).

מַרְבֶּה marbeh (4928), Increase (Is 9:7).

עָצוּם 'ātsûm (6335), Mighty (Is 60:22).

עֲצִיב 'ătsîv (A6336), Anguish (Dn 6:20—Aramaic).

פָּלָא pālā' (6623), Niphal: be too wonderful (Jb 42:3).

פֶּלֶא pele' (6624), Wonderful (Is 9:6).

צוּר tsûr (6962), Rock (Is 26:4).

רֹאשׁ rō'sh (7513), Head; officer (2 Chr 24:11).

רַב rav (7521), Severe, great (Nm 11:33, Neh 9:27, Ps 22:25 [21:25]).

רַב rav (A7523), Great (Ezr 4:10, 5:8, Dn 7:2—Aramaic).

רָבָה rāvâh (7528), Increase (Jb 10:17).

רְבָה rᵉvâh (A7529), Be strong, grow strong (Dn 4:11,20 [4:8,17—Aramaic]).

רוּם rûm (7597), Be high; be loud (Dt 27:14).

שַׂגִּיא saggî' (A7895), Great (Dn 2:31—Aramaic).

1. μεγάλῳ megalō dat sing masc/neu
2. μέγας megas nom sing masc
3. μεγάλου megalou gen sing masc
4. μέγαν megan acc sing masc
5. μεγάλοι megaloi nom pl masc
6. μεγάλων megalōn gen pl masc
7. μεγάλοις megalois dat pl masc
8. μεγάλους megalous acc pl masc
9. μεγάλη megalē nom sing fem
10. μεγάλης megalēs gen sing fem
11. μεγάλῃ megalē dat sing fem
12. μεγάλην megalēn acc sing fem
13. μεγάλαι megalai nom pl fem
14. μεγάλαις megalais dat pl fem
15. μεγάλας megalas acc pl fem
16. μέγα mega nom/acc sing neu
17. μεγάλα megala nom/acc pl neu

12	saw the star, ... rejoiced with exceeding **great** joy...	Matt 2:10
16	The people which sat in darkness saw **great** light;	4:16
2	shall be called **great** in the kingdom of heaven	5:19
3	by Jerusalem; for it is the city of the **great** King	5:35
9	and it fell: and **great** was the fall of it	7:27
2	And, behold, there arose a **great** tempest in the sea,	8:24
9	rebuked the winds ... and there was a **great** calm	8:26
9	**great** is thy faith: be it unto thee even as thou wilt	15:28
5	they that are **great** exercise authority upon them	20:25
2	but whosoever will be **great** among you,	20:26
9	which is the **great** commandment in the law?	22:36
9	This is the first and **great** commandment	22:38
9	For then shall be **great** tribulation,	24:21
17	and shall show **great** signs and wonders;	24:24
10	send his angels with a **great** sound of a trumpet,	24:31
11	about the ninth hour Jesus cried with a **loud** voice,	27:46
11	Jesus, when he had cried again with a **loud** voice,	27:50
4	rolled a **great** stone to the door of the sepulchre,	27:60
2	And, behold, there was a **great** earthquake:	28:2
10	quickly from the sepulchre with fear and **great** joy;	28:8
11	and cried with a **loud** voice, he came out of him...	Mark 1:26
8	and shooteth out **great** branches;	4:32
9	And there arose a **great** storm of wind,	4:37
9	And the wind ceased, and there was a **great** calm.	4:39
4	they feared **exceedingly**, and said one to another,	4:41
11	And cried with a **loud** voice, and said,	5:7
9	unto the mountains a **great** herd of swine feeding.	5:11

μέγας 3144

11	they were astonished with a **great** astonishment....	Mark 5:42
5	and their **great ones** exercise authority upon them.....	10:42
2	but whosoever will be **great** among you,.............	10:43
15	Seest thou these **great** buildings?.....................	13:2
16	And he will show you a **large** upper room...........	14:15
11	at the ninth hour Jesus cried with a **loud** voice,.......	15:34
12	Jesus cried with a **loud** voice, ... gave up the ghost....	15:37
2	the stone was rolled away: for it was very **great**......	16:4
2	For he shall be **great** in the sight of the Lord,.....	Luke 1:15
2	He shall be **great**, and shall be called the Son of......	1:32
11	And she spake out with a **loud** voice, and said,.........	1:42
17	For the Mighty One has done **great things** (NASB)....	1:49
4	angel of the Lord ... and they were **sore** afraid.........	2:9
12	behold, I bring you good tidings of **great** joy,.........	2:10
2	when **great** famine was throughout all the land;........	4:25
11	and cried out with a **loud** voice,......................	4:33
1	wife's mother was taken with a **great** fever;...........	4:38
12	And Levi made him **a great** feast in his own house:....	5:29
16	it fell; and the ruin of that house was **great**............	6:49
2	saying, That a **great** prophet is risen up among us;.....	7:16
11	fell down before him, and with a **loud** voice said,.....	8:28
1	for they were taken with **great** fear:...................	8:37
2	is least among you all, the same shall be **great**.........	9:48
16	and it grew, and waxed **a great** tree;..................	13:19
16	certain man made a **great** supper, and bade many:.....	14:16
16	between us and you there is a **great** gulf fixed:.......	16:26
10	turned back, and with a **loud** voice glorified God,....	17:15
11	began to rejoice and praise God with a **loud** voice	19:37
5	And **great** earthquakes shall be in divers places,......	21:11
17	and fearful sights and **great** signs shall there be......	21:11
9	for there shall be **great** distress in the land,..........	21:23
16	he shall show you **a large** upper room furnished:.....	22:12
14	And they were instant with **loud** voices,...............	23:23
11	And when Jesus had cried with a **loud** voice,..........	23:46
10	and returned to Jerusalem with **great** joy:.............	24:52
3	the sea arose by reason of a **great** wind that blew.	John 6:18
11	In the last day, that **great** day of the feast,............	7:37
11	he cried with a **loud** voice, Lazarus, come forth.......	11:43
9	for that sabbath day was an **high** day,................	19:31
6	and drew the net to land full of **great** fishes,.........	21:11
12	**great** and notable day of the Lord come:............	Acts 2:20
11	And **with great** power gave the apostles witness.......	4:33
9	and **great** grace was upon them all....................	4:33
2	and **great** fear came on all them that heard...........	5:5
2	And **great** fear came upon all the church,...........	5:11
17	did **great** wonders and miracles among the people.....	6:8
9	land of Egypt and Chanaan, and **great** affliction:.......	7:11
11	cried out with a **loud** voice, and stopped their ears,....	7:57
11	And he kneeled down, and cried with a **loud** voice,.....	7:60
2	And at that time there was a **great** persecution.......	8:1
4	and made **great** lamentation over him.................	8:2
11	For unclean spirits, crying with **loud** voice,...........	8:7
9	And there was **great** joy in that city..................	8:8
4	giving out that himself was some **great one**:...........	8:9
3	they all gave heed, from the least to the **greatest**,.....	8:10
9	saying, This man is the **great** power of God...........	8:10
15	as he observed signs and **great** miracles (NASB).......	8:13
12	a **great** sheet knit at the four corners,.................	10:11
12	as it had been a **great** sheet,........................	11:5
4	should be **great** dearth throughout all the world:.....	11:28
11	Said **with a loud** voice, Stand upright on thy feet.....	14:10
12	and they caused **great** joy unto all the brethren.......	15:3
2	And suddenly there was a **great** earthquake,.........	16:26
11	But Paul cried with a **loud** voice, saying,............	16:28
10	but also that the temple of the **great** goddess Diana..	19:27
9	cried out, saying, **Great** is Diana of the Ephesians.....	19:28
9	cried out, **Great** is Diana of the Ephesians............	19:34
10	is a worshipper of the **great** goddess Diana,..........	19:35
9	And there arose a **great** cry:........................	23:9
1	witnessing both to small and **great**,..................	26:22
11	Festus said **with a loud** voice, Paul,...................	26:24
1	whether in a short or **long** time (NASB).............	26:29
9	**great** heaviness and continual sorrow in my heart...	Rom 9:2
16	**a great thing** if we shall reap your carnal things? ...	1 Co 9:11
9	For a **great** door and effectual is opened unto me,....	16:9
16	no **great thing** if his ministers also be transformed	2 Co 11:15
16	This is a **great** mystery:...........................	Eph 5:32
16	**great** is the mystery of godliness:..................	1 Tm 3:16
2	But godliness with contentment is **great** gain...........	6:6
11	But in a **great** house ... not only vessels of gold ...	2 Tm 2:20
3	and the glorious appearing of the **great** God........	Tit 2:13
4	Seeing then that we have a **great** high priest,.......	Heb 4:14
3	all shall know me, from the least to the **greatest**.......	8:11
4	And having an **high** priest over the house of God;....	10:21
12	which hath **great** recompense of reward..............	10:35
2	By faith Moses, when he was come **to years**,.........	11:24
4	our Lord Jesus, that **great** shepherd of the sheep,.....	13:20
17	and yet it boasts of **great things**. (NASB)..........	Jas 3:5
10	unto the judgment of the **great** day................	Jude 1:6
12	heard behind me a **great** voice, as of a trumpet,.....	Rev 1:10
12	commit adultery with her into **great** tribulation,........	2:22
11	I saw a strong angel proclaiming with a **loud** voice,....	5:2
11	Saying with a **loud** voice, Worthy is the Lamb........	5:12
9	and there was given unto him a **great** sword..........	6:4
11	And they cried with a **loud** voice, saying,.............	6:10
2	and, lo, there was **a great** earthquake;................	6:12
3	when she is shaken of a **mighty** wind.................	6:13
9	For the **great** day of his wrath is come;..............	6:17
11	and he cried with a **loud** voice to the four angels,.....	7:2
11	with a **loud** voice, saying, Salvation to our God........	7:10
10	These are they which came out of **great** tribulation,...	7:14
16	and as it were a **great** mountain burning with fire.....	8:8
2	and there fell a **great** star from heaven,..............	8:10
11	the midst of heaven, saying with a **loud** voice, Woe,...	8:13
10	out of the pit, as the smoke of a **great** furnace;........	9:2
1	which are bound in the **great** river Euphrates........	9:14
11	cried with a **loud** voice, as when a lion roareth:......	10:3
10	dead bodies shall lie in the street of the **great** city,...	11:8
2	and **great** fear fell upon them which saw them.........	11:11
12	heard a **great** voice from heaven saying unto them,...	11:12
2	And the same hour was there **a great** earthquake,....	11:13
13	and there were **great** voices in heaven, saying,........	11:15
12	because thou hast taken to thee thy **great** power,......	11:17
7	and them that fear thy name, small and **great**;........	11:18
9	thunderings, and an earthquake, and **great** hail.......	11:19
16	And there appeared a **great** wonder in heaven;.......	12:1
2	wonder in heaven; and behold a **great** red dragon,...	12:3
2	the **great** dragon was cast out, that old serpent,......	12:9
12	And I heard a **loud** voice saying in heaven,..........	12:10
4	devil is come down unto you, having **great** wrath,....	12:12
3	the woman were given two wings of a **great** eagle,...	12:14
12	his power, and his seat, and **great** authority...........	13:2
17	a mouth speaking **great things** and blasphemies;......	13:5
17	**great** wonders, so that he maketh fire come down	13:13
8	And he causeth all, both small and **great**,.............	13:16
10	and as the voice of a **great** thunder:.................	14:2
11	with a **loud** voice, Fear God, and give glory to him;..	14:7
9	saying, Babylon is fallen, is fallen, that **great** city,....	14:8
11	followed them, saying with a **loud** voice,.............	14:9
11	with a **loud** voice to him that sat on the cloud,........	14:15
11	with a **loud** cry to him that had the sharp sickle,.....	14:18
12	cast it into the **great** winepress of the wrath of God...	14:19
16	saw another sign in heaven, **great** and marvellous,....	15:1
17	saying, **Great** and marvellous are thy works,.........	15:3
10	And I heard a **great** voice out of the temple saying ...	16:1
16	And men were scorched with **great** heat,.............	16:9
4	his vial upon the **great** river Euphrates;.............	16:12
10	to the battle of that **great** day of God Almighty......	16:14
9	came a **great** voice out of the temple of heaven,.....	16:17
2	and lightnings; and there was **a great** earthquake,....	16:18
2	so mighty an earthquake, and so **great**...............	16:18
8	And the **great** city was divided into three parts,.......	16:19
9	**great** Babylon came in remembrance before God,.......	16:19
9	there fell upon men a **great** hail out of heaven,......	16:21
9	hail; for the plague thereof was exceeding **great**.......	16:21
10	show unto thee the judgment of the **great** whore	17:1
9	MYSTERY, BABYLON THE **GREAT**,................	17:5
16	when I saw her, I wondered with **great** admiration....	17:6
9	the woman which thou sawest is that **great** city,......	17:18
12	I saw another angel ... having **great** power,...........	18:1
11	he cried mightily with a **strong** voice, saying,.........	18:2
9	a strong voice, saying, Babylon the **great** is fallen,....	18:2
9	saying, Alas, alas that **great** city Babylon,............	18:10
9	And saying, Alas, alas, that **great** city,................	18:16

11	saying, What city is like unto this **great** city!........	Rev 18:18
9	and wailing, saying, Alas, alas, that **great** city,........	18:19
4	mighty angel took up a stone like a **great** millstone,...	18:21
9	shall that **great** city Babylon be thrown down,........	18:21
12	And after these things I heard a **great** voice..........	19:1
12	for he hath judged the **great** whore,..................	19:2
5	and ye that fear him, both small and **great**...........	19:5
11	standing in the sun; and he cried with a **loud** voice,..	19:17
3	together unto the supper of the **great** God;..........	19:17
6	all men, both free and bond, both small and **great**....	19:18
12	having the key ... and a **great** chain in his hand.......	20:1
4	I saw a **great** white throne, and him that sat on it,...	20:11
8	And I saw the dead, small and **great**,................	20:12
10	And I heard a **great** voice out of heaven saying,......	21:3
16	away in the spirit to a **great** and high mountain,......	21:10
12	and showed me that **great** city, the holy Jerusalem,...	21:10
16	had a wall **great** and high, and had twelve gates,.....	21:12

Classical Greek

This extremely important and versatile adjective generally means "great," though the precise sense of this varies depending on the context. Something "large" in size may be *megas*; *megas* may also refer to any degree of something, such as "great kindness" or "great strength." Spatially, a distance may be "great"; a gulf may be "broad" or a road "long." *Megas* denotes figuratively the power, influence, or fame of individuals. A "great" individual is respected, important, and powerful. Rulers might receive the epithet "the Great" (e.g., Herod the Great) as did deities. Emotions too are described as *megas* ("intense, extreme"; e.g., fear, love, hate, desire). (Cf. *Liddell-Scott*; Grundmann, "megas," *Kittel*, 4:529f.) *Liddell-Scott* notes the important role of *megalōs* (3141B) (the adverbial form, "greatly") and *meizōn* (3157) (the comparative form, "greater"). Moreover, *megas* is integral to numerous compound forms.

Septuagint Usage

Twenty-four Hebrew expressions or constructions are rendered by *megas* in the Septuagint. The dominant counterpart is *gādhôl*. We see a wide range of meaning, from "becoming great, rich" (e.g., Genesis 26:13) to "great" (of mercy, Numbers 14:19). God himself is "great" (Deuteronomy 3:24; Isaiah 26:4; 33:21), as is His strength (Deuteronomy 4:37). A "loud" sound is *megas*; a "bright" light, too (cf. Exodus 19:16; Isaiah 9:2). *Megas* is the opposite of *mikros* (3262).

New Testament Usage

The New Testament usage largely accords with the classical pattern; however, there are some distinguishing theological overtones which merit attention. We observe regularly the classical sense of "great" in terms of a "loud" voice or sound (e.g., Mark 5:7; 15:34; Acts 7:57; Revelation 1:10, passim). Emotions, likewise, are described as "great" (of awe/fear, Luke 2:9; of joy, Luke 2:10; 24:52; Acts 15:3; of rage, Revelation 12:12). Individuals or deities are, like the classical understanding, great (Luke 1:15,32; Acts 19:27ff., of Artemis [Diana] the Ephesian goddess). Qualities may be great (of faith, Matthew 15:28); God's mysteries are as well (Ephesians 5:32; 1 Timothy 3:16).

God alone is the Great God (Titus 2:13); His great power accomplishes mighty miracles (Acts 8:10; cf. Matthew 24:24; Acts 8:13). Jesus is referred to as the "*great* high priest" (Hebrews 4:14; 10:21) and the "*great* shepherd of the sheep" (Hebrews 13:20). *Megas* may signal the importance or significance of some event or principle (Matthew 22:36; John 7:37; 19:31). This becomes particularly interesting in reference to the great Day of the Lord (see below).

Great and small—the mighty and the weak—are often found in the same context. Kingdom standards reverse the world's (Luke 9:48; cf. Mark 10:43; cf. the comparative form in Matthew 18:1; Luke 9:46). True greatness is discovered in humility and trust—childlike trust—in God (Matthew 18:3f.). Thus we become His children (ibid., 4:531f.). "Great and small," in addition, is a stock phrase denoting the totality of humanity (Acts 26:22; Revelation 11:18; 13:16).

To describe the last day, the day of God's eschatological judgment as the "great day" is to capture the import of that event. Perhaps a phrase borrowed from the Old Testament (cf. Zephaniah 1:14; Joel 2:31), it is consistently held to be the climax of history, the final judgment (*krisis* [2893], Jude 6) in which God will execute His wrath (*orgē* [3572], Revelation 6:17) upon the ungodly. Jesus referred to the "*great* tribulation" which would come upon the earth during those days (Matthew 24:21) as well as the "*great* signs" which would accompany its arrival (Matthew 24:24). Before this takes place, however, God invites everyone willing to "call upon the name of the Lord" to escape the coming wrath and instead to experience salvation and to share in the great banquet, the "marriage supper of the Lamb" (Revelation 19:9).

STRONG 3173, BAUER 497-98, MOULTON-MILLIGAN 392-93, KITTEL 4:529-41, LIDDELL-SCOTT 1088-89, COLIN BROWN 2:424-26,429.

μέγεθος 3145

3145. μέγεθος megethos noun
Greatness.
CROSS-REFERENCE:
μέγας megas (3144)

גֹּבַהּ gōvahh (1394), Height (Ez 19:11).

גָּדוֹל gādhôl (1448), Greatness (Ex 15:16).

קוֹמָה qômāh (7253), Height, stature (1 Sm 16:7, S/S 7:7, Ez 31:5).

1. μέγεθος megethos nom/acc sing neu

1 And what is the exceeding **greatness** of his power.... **Eph 1:19**

Classical Greek and Septuagint Usage
From *megas* (3144), *megethos* is a noun denoting greatness. It can refer, when used literally, to size. Figuratively it is employed to describe the nature of God or even that which is in some way connected to God, such as the martyrs or Christianity itself (*Bauer*). *Megethos* was also commonly used as a ceremonial title to mean "your highness" or "the Perfect" (cf. *Moulton-Milligan*). It appears 11 times in the canonical portions of the Septuagint, sometimes describing God (Exodus 15:16) or men (1 Samuel 16:7 [LXX 1 Kings 16:7]) or even the height of tall objects (1 Kings 6:23 [LXX 3 Kings 6:23]; 2 Kings 19:23 [LXX 4 Kings 19:23]; Ezekiel 19:11).

New Testament Usage
In Ephesians 1:19, the only occurrence of the term in the New Testament, *megethos* refers to the power of God. The writer wanted his readers to know the "exceeding *greatness*" of God's power toward those who believe. Here the text utilizes the combined strength of two words—*huperballō* (5072), "surpass, go beyond," and *megethos*—to emphasize the immeasurably, outstanding, surpassing greatness of the divine power (see Grundmann, "megethos," *Kittel*, 4:544).

STRONG 3174, BAUER 498, MOULTON-MILLIGAN 393, KITTEL 4:544, LIDDELL-SCOTT 1089.

3146. μεγιστάν megistan noun
A noble, magnate, great one.
CROSS-REFERENCE:
μέγας megas (3144)

אַדִּיר 'addîr (116), Officer (Na 2:5).

גָּדוֹל gādhôl (1448), Noble, great man (Jon 3:7, Na 3:10).

רַבְרְבָנִין ravrᵉvānîn (A7550), Nobles (Dn 5:23, 6:17—Aramaic).

שַׂר sar (8015), Prince (2 Chr 36:18, Prv 8:16).

1. μεγιστᾶνες megistanes nom pl masc
2. μεγιστᾶσιν megistasin dat pl masc

2 Herod on his birthday made a supper to his **lords**, .. **Mark 6:21**
1 And the kings of the earth, and the **great men**, ... **Rev 6:15**
1 for thy merchants were the **great men** of the earth; **18:23**

Classical Greek and Septuagint Usage
Megistan is a noun belonging to the *megas* word group (3144) and is used in the same superlative sense as *megistos* (3147), "greatest." *Megistan* refers literally to a person, "the great(est) one." It is however most commonly used in the plural, *megistanes*, to denote the "grandees, magnates, nobles, chief persons" of a city, or of a people, or even the associates or the courtiers of a king. The only occurrence of the singular *megistan* in the Septuagint is Sirach 4:7; the other 33 occurrences use the plural form usually referring to the "people" of Israel (cf. Joshua 14:8; Judges 7:5; 9:29; Isaiah 54:10).

New Testament Usage
Each of the three occurrences of *megistan* in the New Testament (Mark 6:21; Revelation 6:15; 18:23) is in the plural form. K.H. Bartels suggests that *megistan* is used as a title in Mark 6:21 describing the rank and office of some of those mentioned in Herod's entourage, "his lords" ("First," *Colin Brown*, 1:664-67). The "great men" (*megistan*) referred to in Revelation 6:15 are among those listed in connection with judgment. No one is above (or below) the judgment of God, whether a Roman governor, noble, or other magnate. Even the greatest person is subject to God's judgment.

STRONG 3175, BAUER 498, MOULTON-MILLIGAN 393, LIDDELL-SCOTT 1089.

3147. μέγιστος megistos adj
Very great, greatest.
CROSS-REFERENCE:
μέγας megas (3144)

1. μέγιστα megista sup nom/acc pl neu

1 **exceeding great** and precious promises: .... **2 Pt 1:4**

Megistos functions as a superlative of *megas* (3144), "great." While it is found frequently in other contemporary Greek sources it is employed only once in the New Testament (2 Peter 1:4). Here it is used to describe the divine promises as "exceeding great." The meaning of "more than great" is to be understood. This greatness refers specifically to the efficacy of these promises to bring about the believer's participation in the divine nature, i.e., Christ's work of restoring and renewing the image of God in the life of the Christian.

STRONG 3176, BAUER 498, MOULTON-MILLIGAN 393, LIDDELL-SCOTT 1089.

3148. μεθερμηνεύω
methermēneuō verb
Being interpreted, translate.

COGNATE:
ἑρμηνεύω hermēneuō (2043)

SYNONYMS:
διερμηνεύω diermēneuō (1323)
ἑρμηνεύω hermēneuō (2043)

1. **μεθερμηνεύεται methermēneuetai**
   3sing indic pres mid
2. **μεθερμηνευόμενον methermēneuomenon**
   nom/acc sing neu part pres mid
3. **μεθερμηνευόμενος methermēneuomenos**
   nom sing masc part pres mid

2 which being interpreted is, God with us............ Matt 1:23
2 Talitha cumi; which is, being interpreted, Damsel,...Mark 5:41
2 which is, being interpreted, The place of a skull....... 15:22
2 which is, being interpreted, My God, my God,......... 15:34
2 Rabbi, (which translated means Teacher), (NASB).. John 1:38
2 the Messias, which is, being interpreted, the Christ...... 1:41
2 which is, being interpreted, The son of consolation,.. Acts 4:36
1 for so is his name by interpretation................. 13:8

The verb *methermēneuō* means "to translate," specifically "to change" or "translate" from one language to another. According to Vine it comes from two words: *meta* (3196), implying change, and *hermēneuō* (2043), which means "to speak plainly" (Expository Dictionary, "Interpret"). The latter comes from Hermes, the Greek name of the pagan god Mercury, who was regarded as the messenger of the gods. (Paul was called "Hermes" in Acts 14:12 because of the eloquence of his speech.)

Methermēneuō, "being interpreted" or "is ... by interpretation," is used in the passive voice in the New Testament in conjunction with names and titles (i.e., *Immanuel*, Matthew 1:23; *Golgotha*, Mark 15:22; *Barnabas*, Acts 4:36; and *Elymas*, Acts 13:8). In Mark 5:41; 15:34; and John 1:42, the verb *methermēneuō* is rendered "is ... by interpretation," or literally "is interpreted."

STRONG 3177, BAUER 498, MOULTON-MILLIGAN 393, LIDDELL-SCOTT 1090, COLIN BROWN 1:579-80.

3149. μέθη methē noun
Strong drink, drunkenness.

COGNATE:
μεθύω methuō (3155)

SYNONYMS:
κραιπάλη kraipalē (2870)
οἰνοφλυγία oinophlugia (3495)

עָסִיס 'āsîs (6302), New wine (Jl 1:5).

שָׁכַר shākhar (8335), Become drunk (Hg 1:6).

שֵׁכָר shēkhār (8336), Strong drink (Prv 20:1, 31:6 [24:74]).

שִׁכָּרוֹן shikkārôn (8337), Drunkenness (Ez 23:33, 39:19).

1. **μέθῃ methē** dat sing fem
2. **μέθαι methai** nom pl fem
3. **μέθαις methais** dat pl fem

1 surfeiting, and drunkenness, and cares of this life,.. Luke 21:34
3 not in rioting and drunkenness,................... Rom 13:13
2 Envyings, murders, drunkenness, revellings,......... Gal 5:21

Classical Greek and Septuagint Usage
The noun *methē* denotes a "strong or potent drink" (corresponding to *methu*, "wine," especially old wine). *Methē* also indicates the state of "drunkenness" or "chronic intoxication." Wine is frequently paired with "strong drink" in the Old Testament and at least once in the New Testament at Luke 1:15 (Greek *sikera* [4463]) where drunkenness is recognized as a potential problem and is warned against (cf. Proverbs 20:1; 31:6 [LXX 24:74]). *Methē* is also used in the Septuagint at Joel 1:5 to translate "new wine," which is also capable of intoxication.

New Testament Usage
The New Testament is consistent with the Old Testament in its warnings against "drunkenness." All three New Testament occurrences of *methē* indicate the state of "drunkenness" without necessarily referring to the specific cause of intoxication. Jesus warned that those who are given to "drunkenness" will not be prepared to stand before the Son of Man (Luke 21:34). In Romans 13:13 Paul echoed that same warning; no one can fulfill the "lusts" of "the flesh" if they want to "walk in the Spirit" (cf. verses 11-14; Galatians 5:21).

STRONG 3178, BAUER 498, MOULTON-MILLIGAN 393-94, KITTEL 4:545-48, LIDDELL-SCOTT 1090.

3150. μεθίστημι methistēmi verb
Remove, transfer, change the place of, depose, pervert.

COGNATE:
ἵστημι histēmi (2449)

SYNONYMS:
κινέω kineō (2767)
μετατίθημι metatithēmi (3216)

מוֹט môṭ (4267), Waver; be removed (Is 54:10).

מוּשׁ mûsh (4318), Depart (Is 54:10).

מָסָה māṣāh (4678), Hiphil: make melt (Jos 14:8).

סוּר sûr (5681), Qal: turn aside (1 Sm 6:12, Is 59:15); be removed (2 Kgs 12:3); hiphil: remove, take away (Jgs 9:29, 2 Chr 15:16, Am 5:23).

עֲדָה 'ădāh (A5918), Remove (Dn 2:21—Aramaic).

פָּנָה pānāh (6680), Turn away (Dt 30:17).

1. μεθιστάνειν methistanein inf pres act
2. μετέστησεν metestēsen 3sing indic aor act
3. μεταστήσας metastēsas nom sing masc part aor act
4. μετασταθῶ metastathō 1sing subj aor pass
5. μεθιστάναι methistanai inf pres act

```
4 that, when I am put out of the stewardship,........ Luke 16:4
3 And when he had removed him,................... Acts 13:22
2 hath persuaded and turned away much people,......... 19:26
1 have all faith, so that I could remove mountains,... 1 Co 13:2
2 and hath translated us into the kingdom............. Col 1:13
```

Classical Greek
Methistēmi (later form is *methistanō*, 1 Corinthians 13:2) is composed of *meta* (3196), which in compound words means either "to associate with" or "to exchange," and *histēmi* (2449), "to stand" or "to place." In classical Greek it means "to transpose, transfer, or remove from one place or situation to another." It can also mean "to remove from life," hence, "to put to death."

Septuagint Usage
Its usage in the Septuagint is varied, being the translation of several different Hebrew words. It is used of removing or deposing rulers (Daniel 2:21; 1 Maccabees 11:63), removing things (2 Kings 12:3 [LXX 4 Kings 12:3]), and removing people (2 Kings 17:23 [LXX 4 Kings 17:23]).

New Testament Usage
In the New Testament the term is used of removing mountains (1 Corinthians 13:2; cf. Isaiah 54:10), removing from office (Luke 16:4), changing another's position, misleading, perverting (Acts 19:26; cf. Joshua 14:8), and transplanting as from one kingdom into another (Colossians 1:13; cf. 2 Kings 17:23). Acts 13:22 may mean either "to remove from office" or "to put to death" (cf. Daniel 2:21); both were true of Saul.

In postapostolic times *methistēmi* was used of changing things (Hermas *Vision* 1.3.4) and of removing from ecclesiastical office (1 Clement 44:5; cf. *Bauer*).

STRONG 3179, BAUER 498-99, MOULTON-MILLIGAN 394 (see "methistanō"), LIDDELL-SCOTT 1090-91.

3151. μεθοδεία methodeia noun
Method, strategy, scheming, craftiness, planned deceitful procedure.
CROSS-REFERENCE:
ὁδός hodos (3461)

1. μεθοδείαν methodeian acc sing fem
2. μεθοδείας methodeias acc pl fem

```
2 be able to stand against the wiles of the devil........ Eph 6:11
```

Classical Greek and Septuagint Usage
Methodeia, also spelled *methodia*, denotes in the favorable sense a "strategy," a "clear-sighted procedure," or a "method." In the unfavorable sense *methodeia* denotes a "trick," "stratagem," or "wiles" with intent to lure, deceive, and ensnare.

The word cannot be found in writings prior to the New Testament but is found in papyri dating A.D. 421 and later. The verb form of the word is used, however, by Polybius, Diodorus, and the Septuagint (cf. 2 Samuel 19:27 [LXX 2 Kings 19:27]) and means "to deal craftily" (see Abbott, *The International Critical Commentary*, *Ephesians*).

New Testament Usage
In the New Testament *methodeia* is used in two places: Ephesians 4:14 and 6:11, both in an unfavorable sense. In Ephesians 4:14 *methodeia* is used in reference to those individuals who deliberately, skillfully, and maliciously plan and develop a "strategy" of error to circumvent, distort, confuse, and deceive the followers of Christ so they might be lured away from the true Faith. In Ephesians 6:11 *methodeia* refers to those "schemes," "strategies," "wiles," or "tactics" that the devil himself uses to make war and destroy believers.

STRONG 3180, BAUER 499, MOULTON-MILLIGAN 394 (see "methodia"), KITTEL 5:102-3, LIDDELL-SCOTT 1091, COLIN BROWN 3:935,943.

3152. μεθόριον methorion noun
Borders, boundary, a region included within boundaries.
SYNONYM:
ὅριον horion (3588)

1. μεθόρια methoria nom/acc pl neu

```
1 and went into the borders of Tyre and Sidon,...... Mark 7:24
```

The term *methorion* is the neuter form of *methorios*, meaning "border," and comes from two words: *meta* (3196), meaning "with," and *horion* (3588) which means "the border of a country or district." It is also used metaphorically in classical Greek meaning "limit" (*Liddell-Scott*). It is only found once in the Septuagint, at Joshua 19:25, where it is used literally of tribal borders. Its single occurrence in the New Testament is Mark 7:24 where *methoria* is used to describe Jesus' going into the "borders," "region," or "vicinity" of Tyre and Sidon.

STRONG 3181, BAUER 499, MOULTON-MILLIGAN 394, LIDDELL-SCOTT 1091 (see "methorios").

3153. μεθύσκομαι methuskomai verb
To become drunk, intoxicated.
CROSS-REFERENCE:
μεθύω methuō (3155)

רְוָיָה rᵉwāyāh (7596), Overflow (Ps 23:5 [22:5]).

שָׁכַר shākhar (8335), Be drunk; piel: make drunk (Jer 51:7 [28:7], Hb 2:15).

שָׁתָה shāthâh (8686), Drink (Prv 4:17).

1. μεθύσκεσθε methuskesthe 2pl impr pres mid
2. μεθυσκόμενοι methuskomenoi
          nom pl masc part pres mid
3. μεθύσκεσθαι methuskesthai inf pres mid

3 and to eat and drink, and **to be drunken;**.........Luke 12:45
1 And **be not drunk** with wine, wherein is excess;......Eph 5:18
2 they that be drunken **are drunken** in the night.......1 Th 5:7

Classical Greek and Septuagint Usage
Methuskomai is the passive form of *methuskō* and is related to *methuō* (3155), "to drink to intoxication". While both the active and passive forms of *methuskō* appear throughout classical and Septuagintal Greek, only the passive appears in the New Testament. Most commonly, this word group refers to intoxication from drinking wine, but occasionally *methuskomai* is used of being "filled" with food (Hosea 14:8, Septuagint only) or power (cf. *Liddell-Scott*).

New Testament Usage
All three New Testament occurrences refer to the process of becoming intoxicated. Both Jesus and Paul warned against becoming drunk in view of the imminent return of Christ (Luke 12:45; 1 Thessalonians 5:7; cf. Luke 21:34). The time of the Lord's second coming is not known, but what is known is that only the "sober" can have any "hope of salvation" (1 Thessalonians 5:8). Paul equated sobriety with being wise and with being full of the Spirit so that praise overflowed from the heart. This is contrasted with being "drunk with wine, wherein is excess" (Ephesians 5:18,19).

STRONG 3182, BAUER 499 (see "methuskō"), MOULTON-MILLIGAN 394 (see "methuskō"), KITTEL 4:545-48, LIDDELL-SCOTT 1091 (see "methuskō"), COLIN BROWN 1:513 (see "methuskō").

3154. μέθυσος methusos noun
Drunken, drunkard.
CROSS-REFERENCE:
μεθύω methuō (3155)

סָבָא sāvā' (5617), Drunkard (Prv 23:21).

שִׁכּוֹר shikkôr (8318), Drunkard (Prv 26:9).

1. μέθυσος methusos nom sing masc
2. μέθυσοι methusoi nom pl masc

1 or a railer, or **a drunkard**, or an extortioner;........1 Co 5:11
2 Nor thieves, nor covetous, nor **drunkards**,..............6:10

In classical Greek and the Septuagint *methusos* is always used to describe one who is "drunk with wine." Although it is an adjective, *methusos* is employed in the New Testament as a noun: (1) in the singular in 1 Corinthians 5:11, referring to a "drunkard," and (2) in the plural in 1 Corinthians 6:10, meaning "drunkards."

STRONG 3183, BAUER 499, MOULTON-MILLIGAN 394, KITTEL 4:545-48, LIDDELL-SCOTT 1091, COLIN BROWN 1:513.

3155. μεθύω methuō verb
Be drunk, drink to intoxication.
COGNATES:
μέθη methē (3149)
μεθύσκομαι methuskomai (3153)
μέθυσος methusos (3154)

הָלַם hālam (2056), Strike; be overcome (Is 28:1).

רָוָה rāwâh (7588), Qal: give drink to someone (Ps 36:8 [35:8]); drink one's fill (Jer 46:10 [26:10]); piel: drench, be soaked (Ps 65:10 [64:10], Is 34:5); hiphil: water (Is 55:10); satisfy (Jer 31:25 [38:25]).

רָוֶה rāweh (7589), Watered (Is 58:11).

שׁוּק shûq (8224), Polel: water (Ps 65:9 [64:9]).

שִׁכּוֹר shikkôr (8318), Drunk, drunken (1 Sm 1:13, Is 19:14).

שָׁכַר shākhar (8335), Qal: become drunk, be drunk (Gn 9:21, Is 51:21); hiphil: make drunk (Dt 32:42, Jer 48:26 [31:26]); hithpael: be drunk (1 Sm 1:14).

1. μεθύει methuei 3sing indic pres act
2. μεθύουσιν methuousin 3pl indic pres act
3. μεθυόντων methuontōn gen pl masc part pres act
4. μεθύουσαν methuousan acc sing fem part pres act
5. ἐμεθύσθησαν emethusthēsan 3pl indic aor pass
6. μεθυσθῶσιν methusthōsin 3pl subj aor pass

3	and to eat and drink with the **drunken**;	Matt 24:49
6	and when men **have well drunk**,	John 2:10
2	For these **are** not **drunken**, as ye suppose,	Acts 2:15
1	and one is hungry, and another **is drunken**.	1 Co 11:21
2	they that **be drunken** are drunken in the night.	1 Th 5:7
5	the inhabitants of the earth **have been made drunk**	Rev 17:2
4	the woman **drunken** with the blood of the saints,	17:6

Classical Greek
In classical Greek the *methuō* word group (*methuskomai* [3153], *methē* [3149], *methusos* [3154]) is used literally of "drunkenness" or "intoxication." Equally significant is the figurative sense. To be drunk is to be so full of something as to lose focus and rationality. It signals the excess of something and its debilitating effect.

Septuagint Usage
The Septuagint also uses *methuō* and its cognates for literal drunkenness (e.g., Genesis 9:21; Proverbs 20:1; Isaiah 19:14; Ezekiel 23:33; Joel 1:5). Figuratively the verb *methuskō* describes the sword of the Lord which is "drunk" from the blood of those slain by His wrath (Isaiah 34:5-7). In Psalm 65:9,10 (LXX 64:9,10) *methuō* depicts the heavy, soaking, refreshing rain of God which sustains the earth. Here we see the idea of saturation emerge with a positive connotation.

New Testament Usage
The New Testament witnesses to six instances of *methuō*. Figuratively it refers to the intoxication of the cohorts of the great prostitute. These have been seduced by lust for power, influence, and money. Their desires, like strong drink, have affected their ability to see clearly or to reason rationally (Revelation 17:2). The prostitute herself is drunk from the blood of the saints. This speaks of the excessive slaughter of God's people (Revelation 17:6). Ordinarily, however, a literal use of the verb appears. A negative connotation underlies most instances (e.g., Matthew 24:49; 1 Thessalonians 5:7; cf. John 2:10; see also the vice lists of Romans 13, Galatians 5).

Strong 3184, Bauer 499, Moulton-Milligan 394, Kittel 4:545-48, Liddell-Scott 1092, Colin Brown 1:513-14.

3156. μειζότερος meizoteros adj
Greater.
Cross-Reference:
μέγας megas (3144)

1. μειζοτέραν meizoteran comp acc sing fem

1	I have no **greater** joy than to hear that my children	3 Jn 1:4

A double comparative of *megas* (3144), which means "great," *meizoteros* is found only in 3 John 4. Here it is used by John who wrote he had no "greater" joy than to hear that his children were walking in the truth.

Strong 3186, Bauer 497-98 (see "megas").

3157. μείζων meizōn adj
Greater, even more, of greater degree.
Cross-Reference:
μέγας megas (3144)

1. μείζονα meizona comp nom/acc sing/pl masc/fem/neu
2. μείζων meizōn comp nom sing masc/fem
3. μείζονος meizonos comp gen sing masc/fem
4. μείζονες meizones comp nom pl masc
5. μείζω meizō comp nom/acc sing/pl fem/neu
6. μείζονας meizonas comp acc pl fem
7. μεῖζον meizon comp nom/acc sing neu

2	there hath not risen **a greater** than John the Baptist:	Matt 11:11
2	least in the kingdom of heaven is **greater** than he	11:11
2	That in this place is one **greater** than the temple	12:6
7	the **greatest** among herbs, and becometh a tree,	13:32
2	Who is the **greatest** in the kingdom of heaven?	18:1
2	the same is **greatest** in the kingdom of heaven.	18:4
7	but they cried the **more**, saying, Have mercy on us,	20:31
2	he that is **greatest** among you shall be your servant	23:11
2	Ye fools and blind: for whether is **greater**,	23:17
7	Ye fools and blind: for whether is **greater**, the gift,	23:19
7	and becometh **greater** than all herbs,	Mark 4:32
2	they had disputed ... who should be the **greatest**.	9:34
2	none other commandment **greater** than these	12:31
2	is not **a greater** prophet than John the Baptist:	Luke 7:28
2	is least in the kingdom of God is **greater** than he	7:28
2	which of them should be **greatest**.	9:46
6	I will pull down my barns, and build **greater**;	12:18
2	which of them should be accounted the **greatest**.	22:24
2	shall not be so: but he that is **greatest** among you,	22:26
2	For whether is **greater**, he that sitteth at meat,	22:27
5	thou shalt see **greater** things than these.	John 1:50
2	Art thou **greater** than our father Jacob,	4:12
1	and he will show him **greater** works than these,	5:20
5	But I have **greater** witness than that of John:	5:36
2	Art thou **greater** than our father Abraham,	8:53
7	My Father, ... is **greater** than all;	10:29
2	The servant is not **greater** than his lord;	13:16
2	neither he that is sent **greater** than he that sent	13:16
1	and **greater** works than these shall he do;	14:12
2	for my Father is **greater** than I	14:28
1	**Greater** love hath no man than this,	15:13
2	The servant is not **greater** than his lord.	15:20
1	he that delivered me ... hath the **greater** sin.	19:11
2	The elder shall serve the younger.	Rom 9:12
1	But earnestly desire the **greater** gifts. (NASB)	1 Co 12:31
2	these three; but the **greatest** of these is charity.	13:13
2	for **greater** is he that prophesieth	14:5
3	because he could swear by no **greater**,	Heb 6:13
3	For men verily swear by the **greater**:	6:16
3	by a **greater** and more perfect tabernacle,	9:11
1	Esteeming the reproach of Christ **greater** riches	11:26
7	we shall receive the **greater** condemnation.	Jas 3:1
1	But he giveth **more** grace. Wherefore he saith,	4:6
4	angels, which are **greater** in power and might,	2 Pt 2:11
2	heart condemn us, God is **greater** than our heart,	1 Jn 3:20
2	because **greater** is he that is in you,	4:4
2	the witness of God is **greater**:	5:9

Meizōn, "greater," is the comparative degree of *megas* (3144), "great," in reference to a wide range of connotations (e.g., great size, rank, external form, degree or intensity of feeling, wind, loudness etc.). *Meizōn* is used in the neuter plural in John 1:50 referring to "greater things" and in John 14:12, "greater works" (literally, "greater things"). In 1 Corinthians 12:31 it translated "the best." The idea of "greater degree" is reflected in Romans 9:12 in the words, "The *elder* shall serve the younger."

A form of *meizōn* functions as an adverb with the meaning "all the more" in Matthew 20:31. It is also used in the superlative degree to mean "greatest" (cf. Matthew 18:1,4; Mark 9:34; 1 Corinthians 13:13).

STRONG 3187, BAUER 497-98 (see "megas"), MOULTON-MILLIGAN 394, LIDDELL-SCOTT 1088-89 (see "megas"), COLIN BROWN 2:425-27.

3158. μέλαν melan adj
Ink.

1. μέλανος melanos gen sing neu
2. μέλανι melani dat sing neu

2 written not with **ink**, but with the Spirit	2 Co 3:3
1 I would not write with paper and **ink**:	2 Jn 1:12
1 but I will not with **ink** and pen write unto thee:	3 Jn 1:13

Melan is the neuter of the adjective *melas* (3159) which means "black." *Melan* is used to indicate "ink" in 2 Corinthians 3:3; 2 John 12; and 3 John 13. *Melas* is used of anything dark in color as opposed to *leukos* (2996), "white" (Matthew 5:36). Later Christian literature called the devil "the black one" (Angel, "Black," Colin Brown, 1:204).

STRONG 3188, BAUER 499-500 (see "melas"), MOULTON-MILLIGAN 395 (see "melas"), KITTEL 4:549-51 (see "melas"), LIDDELL-SCOTT 1095, COLIN BROWN 1:203-4.

3159. μέλας melas adj
Black, dark.

חַכְלִלוּת chakhlilûth (2548), Redness (Prv 23:29).
שָׁחֹר shāchōr (8265), Black (Lv 13:37, S/S 1:5, Zec 6:2,6).

1. μέλας melas nom sing masc
2. μέλαιναν melainan acc sing fem

2 thou canst not make one hair white or **black**.	Matt 5:36
1 And I beheld, and lo a **black** horse;	Rev 6:5
1 and the sun became **black** as sackcloth of hair,	6:12

Classical Greek
In classical usage *melas* is an adjective meaning "black" or "dark," the opposite of *leukos* (2996), "white" or "light, bright, dazzling." It is used of such things as dark wine and dark skin. The term includes the cultic meaning of "sinister, terrible, unlucky" (e.g., black magic). The neuter substantive *melan* (3158) is used for ink made of soot or sepia (e.g., India ink) (cf. 2 Corinthians 3:3; 2 John 12; 3 John 13).

Septuagint Usage
The Septuagint uses this adjective as a translation of the Hebrew term *shāchōr* meaning "black" or "swarthy" (Leviticus 13:31, "black hair"; Song of Solomon 1:5, "black," meaning "dark skin color"; 5:11, "black as a raven"; Zechariah 6:2, "black horses").

New Testament Usage
In Matthew 5:36 *leukos* is contrasted with *melas* ("white or black" in the sense of "aged or youthful"). It is also used of the apocalyptic black horse (Revelation 6:5; cf. Zechariah 6:2) and of the darkening of the sun, comparing it to the color of sackcloth (Revelation 6:12). Sackcloth (*sakkos* [4383], from the Hebrew *saq*) was a dark, coarse covering used for mourning.

In postapostolic times the word was often used in the cultic sense of evil. Metaphorically *melas* relates to *skoteinos* (4507), "full of darkness" or "covered with darkness," as *leukos* does to *phōteinos* (5296), "full of light" or "composed of light."

STRONG 3189, BAUER 499-500, MOULTON-MILLIGAN 395, KITTEL 4:549-51, LIDDELL-SCOTT 1095-96, COLIN BROWN 1:203.

3159B. Μελεά Melea name
Melea.

1. Μελεά Melea masc

The son of Menan in the genealogy of Jesus (Luke 3:31).

3160. Μελεᾶς Meleas name
Melea.

1. Μελεᾶ Melea gen masc

1 Which was the son **of Melea**,	Luke 3:31

Form of *Melea* (3159B).

3161. μελετάω meletaō verb
Practice, take care of, devise, meditate upon.
CROSS-REFERENCE:
μέλω melō (3169)

בִּין bîn (1032), Discern (Jb 6:30).

דָּבַר dāvar (1744), Piel: speak (Ps 37:30 [36:30]—only some Sinaiticus texts).

הָגָה hāghâh (1965), Qal: meditate, plot (Jos 1:8, Ps 38:12 [37:12], Is 33:18); poel: conceive (Is 59:13).

הֶגֶה hegheh (1966), Sigh (Ps 90:9 [89:9]).

שִׂיחַ sîach (7943), Qal: meditate (Ps 119:148 [118:148]); pilpel: muse (Ps 143:5 [142:5]).

שָׁעָה shāʻâh (8541), Have regard for (Ps 119:117 [118:117]).

שָׁעַע shāʻaʻ (8551), Pilpel: delight in something (Ps 119:70 [118:70]); hithpalpel: delight in something (Ps 119:16,47 [118:16,47]).

1. μελέτα meleta 2sing impr pres act
2. μελετᾶτε meletate 2pl impr pres act
3. ἐμελέτησαν emeletēsan 3pl indic aor act

2	what ye shall speak, neither do ye **premeditate**:	Mark 13:11
3	and the people **imagine** vain things?	Acts 4:25
1	**Meditate upon** these things;	1 Tm 4:15

Classical Greek
In classical Greek the primary meaning of the verb *meletaō* is "to take thought for, attend to, care for." It can also mean "to exercise" or "to practice," for example, an orator who practices speaking or reviews a speech in his mind before addressing an audience.

Septuagint Usage
The Septuagint uses *meletaō* mainly to translate *hāghâh* which means "to meditate" or "ponder" on something by talking to oneself. The Lord spoke to Joshua and advised him to meditate on the Book (the Torah) day and night (Joshua 1:8). The same is said of the righteous man (Psalm 1:2). The Psalmist meditated on the precepts, decrees, and promises of the Lord (Psalm 119:15,48,148 [LXX 118:15,48,148]).

New Testament Usage
Meletaō occurs only three times in the New Testament. In Mark 13:11 the King James Version translates *meletaō* with "premeditate." The idea is that the disciples should not "rack their brains" when they are brought to trial because the Holy Spirit will give them wisdom and words to say. Acts 4:25 is a literal quotation of Psalm 2:1 from the Septuagint. In this place it is best rendered by "plan" or "plot." Timothy was exhorted to meditate on a number of things including the public reading of Scripture, preaching, and teaching (1 Timothy 4:15).

Following the use of *meletaō* in some papyri, it would be preferable to translate the passage, "Exercise yourself in (practice, cultivate) these things" (*Moulton-Milligan*).

STRONG 3191, BAUER 500, MOULTON-MILLIGAN 395, LIDDELL-SCOTT 1096-97.

3162. μέλι meli noun
Honey.

דְּבַשׁ devash (1756), Honey, honeycomb (Ex 13:5, 1 Sm 14:27, Ez 16:13).

נֹפֶת nōpheth (5499), Honey (Prv 5:3).

1. μέλι meli nom/acc sing neu

1	and his meat was locusts and wild **honey**	Matt 3:4
1	and he did eat locusts and wild **honey**;	Mark 1:6
1	but it shall be in thy mouth sweet as **honey**	Rev 10:9
1	and it was in my mouth sweet as **honey**:	10:10

Classical Greek
As early as the time of Homer it is apparent that honey was an important commodity. Honey was as essential as sugar is today. It was used in medicine, in cosmetics, and also in preserving food.

Septuagint Usage
Meli appears over 50 times in the Septuagint, frequently in connection with God's promise to Israel that she would come to "a land flowing with milk and honey" (e.g., Exodus 3:8); i.e., a land full of sweetness. The use of honey as a metaphor for sweetness continued on into the time of the Old Testament apocryphal writings where it is used especially in Ecclesiasticus. Honey was not only sweet but could be used for nourishment as well.

New Testament Usage
Two of the four occurrences of *meli* in the New Testament refer to the austere life-style of John the Baptist who ate "locusts and wild *honey*" (Matthew 3:4; Mark 1:6). In the Book of Revelation, John the apostle was instructed to eat a book which would taste as "sweet as honey" in his mouth but would make his "belly bitter" (Revelation 10:9,10). This figurative use of *meli* is reminiscent of Ezekiel who also "ate" a book, causing both sweetness and bitterness (Ezekiel 2:9—3:3). The sweetness and bitterness represent the mixture of blessings and woes that both Ezekiel and John were called to prophetically proclaim to God's people. Some manuscripts of Luke 24:42 record that Jesus' final meal before His ascension was fish and honey.

STRONG 3192, BAUER 500, MOULTON-MILLIGAN 395, KITTEL 4:552-54, LIDDELL-SCOTT 1097.

3163. μελίσσιος melissios adj
Made by bees, honeycomb.

1. μελισσίου melissiou gen sing neu
1 a piece of a broiled fish, and of an honeycomb..... Luke 24:42

From *melissa*, "bee," the noun *melissios* signifies that which is "made by bees." *Melissios* is found in Luke 24:42 in many ancient Greek manuscripts and is translated into the King James Version referring to Jesus' final meal with His disciples. It is not found in some early Greek manuscripts and is omitted by many English translations (e.g., NIV, RSV, NASB).

STRONG 3193, BAUER 500, MOULTON-MILLIGAN 395, KITTEL 4:552-54 (see "meli"), LIDDELL-SCOTT 1098 (see "melissaios").

3164. Μελίτη Melitē name
Melita.

1. Μελίτη Melitē nom fem
1 then they knew that the island was called Melita.... Acts 28:1

Mediterranean island south of Italy; Paul performed healing miracles here on his way to Rome (Acts 28:1ff.).

3165. μέλλω mellō verb
Be about to, be on the point of, intend, purpose, must, intend, delay.

אַחֲרוֹן 'achārôn (315), Last (Jb 19:25).
עָתִיד 'āthîdh (6503), Ready (Jb 3:8).

1. **μέλλω** mellō 1sing indic pres act
2. **μέλλεις** melleis 2sing indic pres act
3. **μέλλει** mellei 3sing indic pres act
4. **μέλλομεν** mellomen 1pl indic pres act
5. **μέλλετε** mellete 2pl indic pres act
6. **μέλλουσιν** mellousin 3pl indic pres act
7. **μέλλῃ** mellē 3sing subj pres act
8. **μέλλοντα** mellonta
    nom/acc sing/pl masc/neu part pres act
9. **μέλλοντος** mellontos
    gen sing masc/neu part pres act
10. **μέλλοντι** mellonti dat sing masc/neu part pres act
11. **μελλόντων** mellontōn
    gen pl masc/neu part pres act
12. **μέλλων** mellōn nom sing masc part pres act
13. **μέλλοντες** mellontes nom pl masc part pres act
14. **μέλλοντας** mellontas acc pl masc part pres act
15. **μελλούσης** mellousēs gen sing fem part pres act
16. **μέλλουσαν** mellousan acc sing fem part pres act
17. **μέλλον** mellon nom/acc sing neu part pres act
18. **μέλλειν** mellein inf pres act
19. **μελλήσετε** mellēsete 2pl indic fut act
20. **ἔμελλον** emellon 1/3sing/pl indic imperf act
21. **ἤμελλεν** ēmellen 3sing indic imperf act
22. **ἔμελλεν** emellen 3sing indic imperf act
23. **μελλήσω** mellēsō 1sing indic fut act
24. **ἤμελλον** ēmellon 1/3sing/pl indic imperf act
25. **ἔμελλες** emelles 2sing indic imperf act

3	for Herod is going to search for the Child (NASB)	Matt 2:13
15	who ... warned you to flee from the wrath **to come**?	3:7
12	this is Elias, which was for **to come**.	11:14
10	neither in this world, neither in the world **to come**.	12:32
3	For the Son of man **shall come** in the glory	16:27
3	Likewise **shall** also the Son of man suffer of them.	17:12
3	The Son of man **shall be betrayed**	17:22
12	Jesus **was about to go up** (NASB)	20:17
1	Are ye able to drink of the cup that I **shall drink** of,	20:22
19	And ye **shall hear** of wars and rumours of wars:	24:6
8	and began to tell them what things **should happen**	Mark 10:32
7	be the sign when all these things **shall be fulfilled**?	13:4
15	warned you to flee from the wrath **to come**?	Luke 3:7
21	who was dear unto him, was sick, and **ready** to die.	7:2
22	decease which he **should accomplish** at Jerusalem.	9:31
3	**shall be delivered** into the hands of men.	9:44
22	city and place, whither he himself **would come**.	10:1
17	and if it bears fruit **next year**, fine; (NASB)	13:9
21	tree to see him: for he **was to pass** that way.	19:4
3	the kingdom of God **should** immediately appear.	19:11
7	what sign ... when these things **shall come to pass**?	21:7
8	to escape all these things that **shall come to pass**,	21:36
12	which of them it was that **should do** this thing.	22:23
12	it had been he which **should have redeemed** Israel:	24:21
21	for he **was at the point of** death.	John 4:47
22	for he himself knew what he **would do**.	6:6
6	that they **would come** and take him by force,	6:15
21	Judas ... for it was that he **should betray** him,	6:71
3	Whither **will he go**, that we shall not find him?	7:35
3	**will he go** unto the dispersed among the Gentiles,	7:35
20	which they that believe on him **should receive**:	7:39
22	prophesied that Jesus **should die** for that nation;	11:51
12	Iscariot, Simon's son, which **should betray** him,	12:4
21	This he said, signifying what death he **should die**.	12:33
2	how is it that thou **wilt manifest** thyself unto us,	14:22
21	signifying what death he **should die**.	18:32
14	**about** to go into the temple asked an alms.	Acts 3:3
5	what ye **intend to do** as touching these men.	5:35
18	**should be** great dearth throughout all the world:	11:28
22	And when Herod **would have brought** him forth,	12:6
8	now no more to return to corruption, (NT)	13:34
22	drew out his sword, and **would have killed** himself,	16:27
3	he **will judge** the world in righteousness	17:31
9	And when Paul **was now about** to open his mouth,	18:14
18	and her magnificence **should be destroyed**,	19:27
10	as he **was about** to sail into Syria,	20:3
12	**ready** to depart on the morrow;	20:7
13	sailed unto Assos, there **intending** to take in Paul:	20:13
12	**minding** himself to go afoot.	20:13
6	that they **should see** his face no more.	20:38
20	And when the seven days **were almost ended**,	21:27
12	And as Paul **was to be led** into the castle,	21:37
2	now why **tarriest thou**? arise, and be baptized,	22:16
2	"What are you **about to do**? (NASB)	22:26
13	departed ... which **should have examined** him:	22:29
3	God **shall smite** thee, thou whited wall:	23:3
14	as though ye **would inquire** something more	23:15
13	**would inquire** somewhat of him more perfectly.	23:20

8	and **should** have been killed of them:	Acts 23:27
18	the Jews laid wait for the man, (NT)	23:30
18	that there **shall** be a resurrection of the dead,	24:15
9	righteousness, temperance, and judgment **to come**,	24:25
18	and that he himself **would** depart shortly thither.	25:4
12	because I **shall** answer for myself this day	26:2
11	the prophets and Moses did say **should** come:	26:22
3	and **should** show light unto the people,	26:23
13	**meaning** to sail by the coasts of Asia;	27:2
18	I perceive that this voyage **will** be with hurt	27:10
11	they **would** have cast anchors out of the foreship,	27:30
22	And while the day **was** coming on,	27:33
18	they looked when he **should** have swollen,	28:6
3	But for us also, to whom it **shall** be imputed,	Rom 4:24
9	who is the figure of him that was **to come**.	5:14
5	For if ye live after the flesh, ye **shall** die:	8:13
16	the glory which **shall** be revealed in us.	8:18
8	nor **things** present, nor **things to come**,	8:38
8	or things present, or **things to come**; all are yours;	1 Co 3:22
16	shut up unto the faith which **should** ... be revealed.	Gal 3:23
10	this world, but also in that which **is to come**:	Eph 1:21
11	Which are a shadow of things **to come**;	Col 2:17
4	told you before that we **should** suffer tribulation;	1 Th 3:4
11	**should hereafter** believe on him to life everlasting.	1 Tm 1:16
15	of the life that now is, and of that which is **to come**.	4:8
17	a good foundation against the **time to come**,	6:19
9	Christ, who **shall** judge the quick and the dead	2 Tm 4:1
14	minister for them who **shall** be heirs of salvation?	Heb 1:14
16	the world **to come**, whereof we speak.	2:5
9	word of God, and the powers of the world **to come**,	6:5
12	when he **was about** to make the tabernacle:	8:5
11	an high priest of good things **to come**,	9:11
11	the law having a shadow of good things **to come**,	10:1
9	which **shall** devour the adversaries.	10:27
21	to go out into a place which he **should** after receive..	11:8
11	blessed Jacob and Esau concerning **things to come**.	11:20
16	no continuing city, but we seek one **to come**.	13:14
13	as they that **shall** be judged by the law of liberty.	Jas 2:12
15	also a partaker of the glory that **shall** be revealed:	1 Pt 5:1
23	Therefore, I shall always be **ready** (NASB)	2 Pt 1:12
11	those that **after** should live ungodly;	2:6
3	and the things which **shall** be hereafter;	Rev 1:19
2	Fear none of those things which thou **shalt** suffer:	2:10
3	the devil **shall** cast some of you into prison,	2:10
3	the things which remain, that **are ready** to die:	3:2
15	temptation, which **shall** come upon all the world,	3:10
1	art lukewarm, ... I **will** spue thee out of my mouth.	3:16
13	their brethren, that **should** be killed as they were,	6:11
11	of the three angels, which **are yet** to sound!	8:13
20	I **was about** to write: and I heard a voice	10:4
7	the seventh angel, when he **shall begin** to sound,	10:7
15	the woman which **was ready** to be delivered,	12:4
3	who **was** to rule all nations with a rod of iron:	12:5
3	and **shall** ascend out of the bottomless pit,	17:8

Classical Greek
In classical Greek the verb *mellō* means "to be about, to be destined" or "likely to." It indicates that something is about to be done with a strong probability in the present or the future.

Septuagint Usage
In the Septuagint the meaning is the same. Joseph's brothers prepared a gift for "they heard that they *should* eat bread there" (Genesis 43:25). The Lord saw Moses' inhibition to be His mouthpiece and told him, "I will be with thy mouth, and teach thee what thou *shalt* say" (Exodus 4:12). Job mentioned those "who *are ready* to raise up their mourning" when he cursed the day of his birth (Job 3:8).

Intertestamental Period
The intertestamental period, during which time Israel was constantly subject to foreign domination and pagan authority, saw the Jews develop a new understanding of history which made use of *mellō* in two ways. First, *mellō* became strongly deterministic in character: in spite of the present persecution and suppression that Israel was undergoing, it was inevitable that God would one day triumph over all His enemies and crush them. Second, and in connection with this, *mellō* could therefore refer to the last time or end time (cf. Job 19:25 when Job's redeemer would stand at the last time) or the age to come. The Jews therefore had a dualistic view of history expressed in the Old Testament pseudepigraphal book of 4 Ezra 7:50: "The Most High has not made one age but two." They contrasted present history, this age (*ho aiōn houtos*), with the future reign of the Messiah, the age to come (*ho aiōn mellōn*), when God would vindicate His people.

New Testament Usage
Although the New Testament is not deterministic in a way that would violate an individual's free will, the New Testament uses *mellō* in a way that the degree of probability of something happening is so great that it can be spoken of as inevitable, such as "the glory which shall be revealed" (Romans 8:18; 1 Peter 5:1). When the disciples asked Jesus concerning the things which were to be fulfilled (Mark 13:4; Luke 21:7), there was no doubt that they would be fulfilled.

Mellō may also denote an intended action: "Herod *will* seek the young child" (Matthew 2:13; see John 6:15). *Mellō* can also indicate an action that necessarily follows a divine decree: "Likewise *shall* also the Son of man suffer of them" (Matthew 17:12; see Matthew 17:22; Luke 9:44; or Acts 26:22 where the words of the prophets *must* come to pass). In one place in the New Testament *mellō* has the meaning "to delay": "And now what are you waiting for?" (Acts 22:16, NIV).

STRONG 3195, BAUER 500-501, MOULTON-MILLIGAN 395-96, LIDDELL-SCOTT 1099, COLIN BROWN 1:325-27.

3166. μέλος *melos* noun
Member, body, part, limb.

הֶגֶה *hegheh* (1966), Mourning (Ez 2:10).

מִזְמוֹר mizmôr (4344), Musical tune (Sir 44:5).

נֵתַח nēthach (5592), Piece (Ex 29:17, Lv 8:20 [8:19], Ez 24:6).

שִׁיר shîr (8302), Melody (Sir 40:21).

1. μέλος melos nom/acc sing neu
2. μέλη melē nom/acc pl neu
3. μελῶν melōn gen pl neu
4. μέλεσιν melesin dat pl neu

3 that one of thy **members** should perish,	Matt	5:29
3 that one of thy **members** should perish,		5:30
2 Neither yield ye your **members** as instruments	Rom	6:13
2 and your **members** as instruments of righteousness		6:13
2 for as ye have yielded your **members**		6:19
2 even so now yield your **members**		6:19
4 did work in our **members** to bring forth fruit		7:5
4 But I see another law in my **members**,		7:23
4 captivity to the law of sin which is in my **members**.		7:23
2 For as we have many **members** in one body,		12:4
2 and all **members** have not the same office:		12:4
2 and every one **members** one of another.		12:5
2 that your bodies are the **members** of Christ?	1 Co	6:15
2 shall I then take the **members** of Christ,		6:15
2 and make them the **members** of an harlot?		6:15
2 For as the body is one, and hath many **members**,		12:12
2 and all the **members** of that one body,		12:12
1 For the body is not one **member**, but many.		12:14
2 the **members** every one of them in the body,		12:18
1 if they were all one **member**, where ... the body?		12:19
2 now are they many **members**, yet but one body.		12:20
2 Nay, much more those **members** of the body,		12:22
2 but that the **members** should have the same care		12:25
1 And whether one **member** suffer,		12:26
2 all the **members** suffer with it;		12:26
1 or one **member** be honoured,		12:26
2 all the **members** rejoice with it.		12:26
2 are the body of Christ, and **members** in particular.		12:27
2 for we are **members** of one another.	Eph	4:25
2 For we are **members** of his body, of his flesh,		5:30
2 your **members** which are upon the earth;	Col	3:5
1 Even so the tongue is a little **member**,	Jas	3:5
4 so is the tongue among our **members**,		3:6
4 even of your lusts that war in your **members**?		4:1

Classical Greek
In classical Greek the primary meaning of *melos* is "limb" or "part" of the body. The early Greek writers used *melos* only in the plural. It was also used for a musical member or phrase, the melody of an instrument, or the music to which a song is set (cf. *Liddell-Scott*).

Septuagint Usage
In the Septuagint *melos* is the translation of the Hebrew *nēthach* which has the identical meaning of "member" or "limb" of the body. Referring to sacrifices, the expression *kata melē* denotes the cutting of an animal "into pieces" (Exodus 29:17; Leviticus 1:6,12; 8:19). In its secondary musical meaning *melos* has the sense of a lament or mournful song (Ezekiel 2:10; Micah 2:4).

Melos assumes grave importance in the apocryphal books of the Maccabees, because those Jews who remained faithful to God had to endure martyrdom, or at the least the members of their bodies would be maimed or mutilated (e.g., 4 Maccabees 10:20).

New Testament Usage
The New Testament retains only the primary meaning of *melos*. Sometimes it is used in a literal sense. Paul, for example, exhorted the Roman Christians not to offer the parts of their bodies to sin, as instruments of wickedness (Romans 6:13; see 6:19). James reminds us that "the tongue is a little member, and boasteth great things" (James 3:5,6; cf. 3:6; see also Matthew 5:29,30).

Melos appears in a figurative sense in Paul's epistles, a rather common device in his time. The Church as the body of Christ is composed of individual members (Romans 12:4,5; 1 Corinthians 12:12-37; Ephesians 4:25). In 1 Corinthians 6:15 the bodies of Christians are called the "members of Christ." This emphasis by Paul was meant to underscore the repugnance of having sexual relations with a prostitute.

STRONG 3196, BAUER 501-2, MOULTON-MILLIGAN 396, KITTEL 4:555-68, LIDDELL-SCOTT 1099, COLIN BROWN 1:229,231.

3167. Μελχί Melchi name
Melchi.

CROSS-REFERENCE:
ἐπιμελέομαι epimeleomai (1944)

1. Μελχί Melchi masc

1 which was the son **of Melchi**,	Luke	3:24
1 Which was the son **of Melchi**,		3:28

The son of Janna, and the son of Addi in the genealogy of Jesus (Luke 3:24,28).

3168. Μελχισέδεκ Melchisedek name
Melchizedek.

1. Μελχισέδεκ Melchisedek masc

1 a priest for ever after the order **of Melchisedec**.	Heb	5:6
1 an high priest after the order **of Melchisedec**.		5:10
1 high priest for ever after the order **of Melchisedec**.		6:20
1 For this **Melchisedec**, king of Salem,		7:1
1 loins of his father, when **Melchisedec** met him.		7:10
1 priest should rise after the order **of Melchisedec**,		7:11
1 after the similitude of **Melchisedec** there ariseth		7:15
1 a priest for ever after the order **of Melchisedec**,		7:17
1 a priest for ever after the order **of Melchisedec**:		7:21

Old Testament king-priest who foreshadowed the royal priesthood of Christ (Hebrews 5:6).

3169. μέλω melō verb
To be an object of care or thought, to care about.

μεμβράνα 3170

COGNATES:
  ἐπιμέλεια epimeleia (1943)
  ἐπιμελέομαι epimeleomai (1944)
  ἐπιμελῶς epimelōs (1945)
  μελετάω meletaō (3161)
  προμελετάω prometeaō (4163)

SYNONYM:
  μεριμνάω merimnaō (3179)

חֵפֶץ chēphets (2761), Pleasure (Jb 22:3).

1. **μέλει melei** 3sing indic pres act
2. **μελέτω meletō** 3sing impr pres act
3. **ἔμελεν emelen** 3sing indic imperf act

1 neither **carest** thou for any man:		Matt 22:16
1 Master, **carest** thou not that we perish?		Mark 4:38
1 we know that thou art true, and **carest** for no man:		12:14
1 dost thou not **care** that my sister hath left me		Luke 10:40
1 he is an hireling, and **careth** not for the sheep		John 10:13
3 This he said, not that he **cared** for the poor;		12:6
3 And Gallio **cared** for none of those things.		Acts 18:17
2 Art thou called being a servant? **care** not for it:		1 Co 7:21
1 **Doth** God take **care** for oxen?		9:9
1 all your **care** upon him; for he **careth** for you.		1 Pt 5:7

Classical Greek

This verb occurs from Homer onward in the classical, Septuagintal, and New Testamental Greek texts. In classical Greek literature it is used either (1) in the middle voice, with the meaning "to be an object of care" or "to be an object of thought," or (2) in the active voice, with the meaning "to care for" or "to take an interest in" (cf. *Liddell-Scott*). Except for its use as a present active infinitive, the active voice almost always occurs in the third person singular or plural (*melei*), denoting the object or objects of care or thought (ibid.).

Homer provided one such example where *melō* was used in the third person singular of the imperfect tense with a negative particle: *ouk emelen moi tauta metallēsai*, "It was not an object of care to me, to ask these things" (*Odyssey* 16.465; cf. *Liddell-Scott*). In the active voice, *melō* always requires a direct object. For example, in Homer's *Iliad* (5.708; cf. ibid.) *melō* occurs as a perfect participle with its direct object in the genitive: *mega ploutoio memēlōs*, "having had care for great riches." "Having had care" translates the participle with its direct object being "great riches."

Septuagint Usage

In the Septuagint *melō* occurs in five passages, with Job 22:3 as the only undisputed canonical verse. In this passage *melō* is used in the active voice: "For what does it matter (*Ti gar melei*) to the Lord if you are blameless in your works?" In Isaiah 59:5 (Codex Sinaiticus) *melō* also occurs in the active voice, and that in a participial form: "The one who cares (*melon*) for their eggs to eat." The remaining four passages are located in the apocryphal books (e.g., Tobit 10:5 [Codex Sinaiticus]; Wisdom of Solomon 12:13; 1 Maccabees 14:42,43 [Codices Alexandrinus and Sinaiticus]).

New Testament Usage

In the New Testament *melō* is found ten times, occurring only in the active voice (Matthew 22:16; Mark 4:38; 12:14; Luke 10:40; John 10:13; 12:6; Acts 18:17; 1 Corinthians 7:21; 9:9; 1 Peter 5:7). In all but two of these passages (1 Corinthians 9:9; 1 Peter 5:7), *melō* is used with a negative particle.

An example of this may be seen at Matthew 22:16: "And they sent out unto him their disciples with the Herodians, saying, Master, we know that thou art true, and teachest the way of God in truth, neither *carest* thou for any *man*" (*kai ou melei soi peri oudenos*; cf. its parallel, Mark 12:14).

One of *melō*'s only uses without a negative particle reads, "Casting all your care upon him; for he *careth* for you" (*hoti autō melei peri humōn*, literally, "for to Him it is an object of care concerning you" [1 Peter 5:7]). First Corinthians 7:21 provides the only occurrence of this verb in the imperative mood: "Art thou called *being* a servant? *care* not for it" (*mē soi meletō*).

STRONG 3199, BAUER 500 (see "melei"),
MOULTON-MILLIGAN 395 (see "melei"),
LIDDELL-SCOTT 1100, COLIN BROWN 1:276,278.

3170. μεμβράνα membrana noun
Parchment.

1. **μεμβράνας membranas** acc pl fem

1 and the books, but especially the **parchments**	2 Tm 4:13

Membrana is a Latin loanword ("membrāna," from which we get the English word *membrane*) which refers to a "skin covering" or "parchment." Parchment is said to have been developed by Eumenes II of Pergamum (197–158 B.C.). Parchment was made by soaking goat or sheep skins in lime and then scraping them to remove the hair. After they were washed, dried, and stretched on frames, the skins were rubbed smooth with fine chalk and pumice stone. Vellum, a superior grade of parchment, was made from the skin of calves or kids (Williams, "Parchment," *Interpreter's Dictionary of the Bible*, 3:658). By Paul's time parchment was preferred over papyrus for its durability. In 2 Timothy 4:13 the word *membrana* is used by Paul to ask Timothy to bring him "the parchments," a probable reference to the scrolls of Old Testament Scriptures or his own personal documents.

STRONG 3200, BAUER 502, MOULTON-MILLIGAN 396, LIDDELL-SCOTT 1100.

3171. μέμφομαι memphomai verb
To blame, to find fault, to chide.

COGNATES:
  ἄμεμπτος amemptos (271)
  μεμψίμοιρος mempsimoiros (3172)

1. **μέμφεται** memphetai 3sing indic pres mid
2. **μεμφόμενος** memphomenos
     nom sing masc part pres mid
3. **ἐμέμψαντο** emempsanto 3pl indic aor mid

3 with unwashen, hands, they **found fault**............	Mark 7:2
1 wilt say then unto me, Why doth he yet **find fault**?..	Rom 9:19
2 For **finding fault** with them, he saith,...............	Heb 8:8

Memphomai is a verb which means "to blame" or "to find fault with" and overlaps a great deal in meaning with the verb *mōmaomai* (3331). It is found in Mark 7:2; Romans 9:19; and Hebrews 8:8. Mark 7:2 tells how the Pharisees found fault with Jesus' disciples for eating with unwashed hands, a violation of Jewish tradition. In Romans 9:19 *memphomai* is translated, "Why doth he (God) yet *find fault*? For who hath resisted his will?" Hebrews 8:8 insists that it was not God's covenant with Israel that was faulty, but a new covenant was necessary because He "found fault" in the Jewish people.

STRONG 3201, BAUER 502, MOULTON-MILLIGAN 396, KITTEL 4:571, LIDDELL-SCOTT 1101, COLIN BROWN 2:143-45.

3172. μεμψίμοιρος mempsimoiros adj
Faultfinding, complaining, discontented, criticizing.

CROSS-REFERENCE:
  μέμφομαι memphomai (3171)

1. **μεμψίμοιροι** mempsimoiroi nom pl masc

1 These are murmurers, **complainers**,................ Jude 1:16

Mempsimoiros means "one who complains" or literally, "complaining of one's lot." *Mempsimoiros* comes from two words: *memphomai* (3171), "to blame," and *moira*, "a fate" or "one's lot." The word occurs only once in the New Testament, in Jude 16, where it has the meaning of "complainers," "grumblers," or "malcontents."

STRONG 3202, BAUER 502, MOULTON-MILLIGAN 396, KITTEL 4:571,574, LIDDELL-SCOTT 1101, COLIN BROWN 2:143,145.

3173. μέν men conj
No meaning without correlating particle.

1. **μέν** men

1 I **indeed** baptize you with water unto repentance:....	Matt 3:11
1 harvest **truly** is plenteous, ... the labourers are few;.....	9:37
1 And if the house be worthy, (NT)....................	10:13
1 when he sowed, **some** seeds fell by the way side,......	13:4
1 and brought forth fruit, **some** an hundredfold,.........	13:8
1 some an hundredfold, some sixty, some thirty. (NT)...	13:23
1 Which **indeed** is the least of all seeds:................	13:32
1 ye can discern the face of the sky; (NT).............	16:3
1 **Some** say that thou art John the Baptist:..............	16:14
1 Elias **truly** shall first come, and restore all things......	17:11
1 saith unto them, Ye shall drink **indeed** of my cup,.....	20:23
1 and beat **one**, and killed another,.....................	21:35
1 **one** to his farm, another to his merchandise:..........	22:5
1 he to his servants, The wedding is ready, (NT)........	22:8
1 which **indeed** appear beautiful outward,...............	23:27
1 ye also outwardly appear righteous (NT).............	23:28
1 And unto **one** he gave five talents, to another two,.....	25:15
1 And he shall set the sheep on his right hand, (NT)....	25:33
1 The Son of man goeth as it is written of him: (NT)....	26:24
1 the spirit **indeed** is willing, but the flesh is weak.......	26:41
1 I **indeed** have baptized you with water:................	Mark 1:8
1 as he sowed, **some** fell by the way side,................	4:4
1 Elias **verily** cometh first, and restoreth all things;.......	9:12
1 Ye shall **indeed** drink of the cup that I drink of;.......	10:39
1 and many others; beating **some**, and killing **some**.....	12:5
1 Son of man **indeed** goeth, as it is written of him:......	14:21
1 The spirit **truly** is ready, but the flesh is weak........	14:38
1 So then after the Lord had spoken unto them,........	16:19
1 I **indeed** baptize you with water;....................	Luke 3:16
1 many other things in his exhortation (NT).............	3:18
1 **some** fell by the way side; and it was trodden..........	8:5
1 harvest **truly** is great, but the labourers are few:.......	10:2
1 if the son of peace be there, (NT)....................	10:6
1 **indeed** killed them, and ye build their sepulchres......	11:48
1 And if it bear fruit, well: (NT).......................	13:9
1 **truly** the Son of man goeth, as it was determined:.....	22:22
1 **one** on the right hand, and the other on the left........	23:33
1 we **indeed** justly; ... but this ... done nothing amiss.....	23:41
1 and rested the sabbath day (NT).....................	23:56
1 for **some** said, He is a good man:....................	John 7:12
1 John did no miracle: but all things (NT).............	10:41
1 he abode two days still in the same place (NT)........	11:6
1 Of sin, because they believe not on me; (NT).........	16:9
1 And ye now therefore have sorrow: (NT).............	16:22
1 These things therefore the soldiers did. (NT).........	19:24
1 and brake the legs of the first, (NT).................	19:32
1 And many other signs **truly** did Jesus.................	20:30
1 The former treatise have I made, (NT)..............	Acts 1:1
1 For John **truly** baptized with water;..................	1:5
1 When they therefore were come together, (NT).......	1:6
1 purchased a field with the reward of iniquity; (NT)....	1:18
1 they that gladly received his word (NT)..............	2:41
1 to be killed, and you disowned them (NIV) (NT)......	3:13
1 the heaven must receive until the times (NT).........	3:21
1 For Moses **truly** said unto the fathers,................	3:22
1 for that **indeed** a notable miracle hath been done......	4:16
1 The prison **truly** found we shut with all safety,........	5:23
1 they departed from the presence (NT)................	5:41

μέν 3173

1 Therefore they that were scattered (NT)	Acts	8:4
1 And they, when they had testified (NT)		8:25
1 hearing a voice, but seeing no man. (NT)		9:7
1 Then had the churches rest (NT)		9:31
1 John **indeed** baptized with water;		11:16
1 Now they which were scattered abroad (NT)		11:19
1 Peter therefore was kept in prison: (NT)		12:5
1 So they, being sent forth by the Holy Ghost, (NT)		13:4
1 For David, after he had served (NT)		13:36
1 Long time therefore abode they (NT)		14:3
1 part held with the Jews, and part (NT)		14:4
1 And they called Barnabas, Jupiter; (NT)		14:12
1 And being brought on their way (NT)		15:3
1 So when they were dismissed, (NT)		15:30
1 so were the churches established (NT)		16:5
1 Therefore many of them believed; (NT)		17:12
1 disputed he in the synagogue with the Jews, (NT)		17:17
1 And the times of this ignorance (NT)		17:30
1 the resurrection of the dead, some mocked: (NT)		17:32
1 If it were a matter of wrong (NT)		18:14
1 John **verily** baptized ... baptism of repentance,		19:4
1 "Jesus I know, and Paul I know (NIV) (NT)		19:15
1 Some therefore cried one thing, (NT)		19:32
1 Demetrius, and the craftsmen which (NT)		19:38
1 I am a man which am a Jew of Tarsus, (NT)		21:39
1 I am **verily** a man which am a Jew, born in Tarsus,		22:3
1 And they that were with me saw **indeed** the light,		22:9
1 For the Sadducees say that (NT)		23:8
1 he took him, and brought him to (NT)		23:18
1 So the chief captain then let the young (NT)		23:22
1 Then the soldiers, as it was commanded (NT)		23:31
1 But Festus answered, that Paul should (NT)		25:4
1 For if I be an offender, (NT)		25:11
1 My manner of life from my youth, (NT)		26:4
1 I **verily** thought with myself,		26:9
1 Sirs, ye should have hearkened unto me, (NT)		27:21
1 ship aground; and the forepart stuck fast, (NT)		27:41
1 And the rest, some on boards, (NT)		27:44
1 And he shook off the beast into the fire, (NT)		28:5
1 for as concerning this sect, (NT)		28:22
1 And some believed the things (NT)		28:24
1 I thank my God through Jesus Christ (NT)	Rom	1:8
1 To them who by patient continuance (NT)		2:7
1 contentious, and do not obey the truth, (NT)		2:8
1 circumcision **verily** profiteth, if thou keep the law:		2:25
1 Much every way: chiefly, because that (NT)		3:2
1 for **on the one hand** the judgment arose (NASB)		5:16
1 reckon ye ... yourselves to be dead **indeed** unto sin,		6:11
1 Wherefore the law is holy, (NT)		7:12
1 So then, **on the one hand** I myself (NASB)		7:25
1 the body is dead because of sin,		8:10
1 heirs of God, and joint-heirs with Christ; (NT)		8:17
1 of the same lump to make **one** vessel unto honour,		9:21
1 my heart's desire and prayer to God (NT)		10:1
1 inasmuch as I am the apostle of the Gentiles, (NT)		11:13
1 on them which fell, severity; (NT)		11:22
1 As concerning the gospel, (NT)		11:28
1 For one believeth that he may eat all things: (NT)		14:2
1 One man esteemeth one day above another: (NT)		14:5
1 All things **indeed** are pure;		14:20
1 yet I would have you wise unto that (NT)		16:19
1 I am of Paul; and I of Apollos; (NT)	1 Co	1:12
1 the cross is to them that perish foolishness; (NT)		1:18
1 unto the Jews a stumblingblock, (NT)		1:23
1 But he that is spiritual judgeth all things, (NT)		2:15
1 For while one saith, I am of Paul; (NT)		3:4
1 I **verily**, as absent in body, but present in spirit,		5:3
1 If then ye have judgments of things (NT)		6:4
1 Now therefore there is utterly a fault (NT)		6:7
1 one after this manner, and another after that. (NT)		7:7
1 they which run in a race run all, (NT)		9:24
1 Now they do it to obtain a corruptible crown; (NT)		9:25
1 For a man **indeed** ought not to cover his head,		11:7
1 if a man have long hair, it is a shame (NT)		11:14
1 For first **of all**, when ye come together		11:18
1 and one is hungry, and another is drunken. (NT)		11:21
1 to one is given by the Spirit the word (NT)		12:8
1 now are they many members, (NT)	1 Co	12:20
1 God hath set some in the church, (NT)		12:28
1 For thou **verily** givest thanks well,		14:17
1 but there is one kind of flesh of men, (NT)		15:39
1 but the glory of the celestial is one, (NT)		15:40
1 We shall not all sleep, but we shall (NT)		15:51
1 To the **one** we are the savour of death unto death;	2 Co	2:16
1 So then death worketh in us, but life in you. (NT)		4:12
1 For **indeed** he accepted the exhortation;		8:17
1 For as touching the ministering to the saints, (NT)		9:1
1 who in presence am base among you, (NT)		10:1
1 For his letters, say they, are weighty (NT)		10:10
1 For if he that cometh preacheth another (NT)		11:4
1 necessary, though it is not profitable; (NASB) (NT)		12:1
1 **Truly** the signs of an apostle were wrought		12:12
1 Howbeit then, when ye knew not God, (NT)	Gal	4:8
1 But he who was of the bondwoman (NT)		4:23
1 the one from the mount Sinai, (NT)		4:24
1 And he gave **some**, apostles; and some, prophets;	Eph	4:11
1 Some **indeed** preach Christ even of envy	Phlp	1:15
1 The one preach Christ of contention, (NT)		1:16
1 which is to them an evident token (NT)		1:28
1 Him therefore I hope to send presently, (NT)		2:23
1 to me **indeed** is not grievous, but for you it is safe		3:1
1 forgetting those things which are behind, (NT)		3:13
1 have **indeed** a show of wisdom in will worship,	Col	2:23
1 come unto you, even I Paul, once and again;	1 Th	2:18
1 Jesus Christ, who hath abolished death, (NT)	2 Tm	1:10
1 and **some** to honour, and some to dishonour.		2:20
1 And they shall turn away their ears (NT)		4:4
1 Unto the pure all things are pure: (NT)	Tit	1:15
1 And of the angels he saith, (NT)	Heb	1:7
1 And Moses **verily** was faithful in all his house,		3:5
1 For men **verily** swear by the greater:		6:16
1 first being by interpretation King (NT)		7:2
1 And **verily** they that are of the sons of Levi,		7:5
1 **In the one case**, the tenth is collected (NIV)		7:8
1 If therefore perfection were by the Levitical (NT)		7:11
1 there is **verily** a disannulling of the commandment		7:18
1 For those priests were made without an oath; (NT)		7:21
1 And they **truly** were many priests,		7:23
1 For if he were on earth, he should not (NT)		8:4
1 Then **verily** the first covenant had also ordinances		9:1
1 the priests went always into the first (NT)		9:6
1 that the patterns of things in the heavens (NT)		9:23
1 And every priest standeth daily ministering (NT)		10:11
1 Partly, whilst ye were made a gazingstock, (NT)		10:33
1 **truly**, if they had been mindful of that country		11:15
1 have had fathers of our flesh (NT)		12:9
1 For they **verily** for a few days chastened us		12:10
1 All discipline for the moment seems (NASB) (NT)		12:11
1 no chastening for the present seemeth (NT)		12:11
1 wisdom that is from above is first pure, (NT)	Jas	3:17
1 Who **verily** was foreordained before ... the world,	1 Pt	1:20
1 as unto a living stone, disallowed **indeed** of men,		2:4
1 by him for the punishment of evildoers, (NT)		2:14
1 being put to death in the flesh, (NT)		3:18
1 might be judged according to men (NT)		4:6
1 on their part he is evil spoken of, (NT)		4:14
1 Likewise also these filthy dreamers (NT)	Jude	1:8
1 evil of those things which they know not: (NT)		1:10
1 of **some** have compassion, making a difference:		1:22

Classical Greek and Septuagint Usage

Men is a very common affirmative particle in classical Greek which is usually left untranslated in English. It does not appear as frequently in New Testament Greek, and it occurs very rarely in the Septuagint. Sometimes it is used to express certainty by the speaker or writer, but more often it is used to correlate one phrase with another that is introduced by *de* (1156) (cf. *Liddell-Scott*).

New Testament Usage

In the New Testament *men* is also usually linked with another particle, *de*, to show strong contrast and can be translated (rather clumsily) "on the one hand . . . on the other hand": "I (*men*, on the one hand) am of Paul; I (*de*, on the other hand) of Apollos . . . " (1 Corinthians 1:12). Most translators omit the first particle *men* and translate the second *de* simply "but" (see Matthew 3:11; 9:37; etc.). In some cases *men* and *de* can be rendered by "some . . . others." "Some sided with the Jews, others with the apostles" (Acts 14:4, NIV; see Matthew 16:14; John 7:12; etc.).

Men appears sometimes without any other particle when the contrast is supplied from the context (2 Corinthians 12:12; Colossians 2:23; etc.). *Men* is also frequently combined with the particle *oun* (3631) to denote continuation, "When (*men oun*) they had testified . . . " (Acts 8:25; see Acts 9:31; 15:30; etc.), or to summarize or sum up what precedes.

STRONG 3303, BAUER 502-3, MOULTON-MILLIGAN 396, LIDDELL-SCOTT 1101-2.

3173B. μενοῦν menoun partic

On the contrary; certainly; indeed; that's right, but.

1. μενοῦν menoun

1	"On the contrary, blessed are those (NASB)	Luke 11:28
1	On the contrary, who are you, O man, (NASB)	Rom 9:20
1	More than that, I count all (NASB) (NT)	Phlp 3:8

The correlative particle *men* (3173) and the inferential particle *oun* (3631) combine to make this word. It functions to relate what has been said before with something that is to follow. Its translation is determined by the sense of the context in which it appears.

In Romans 9:20 it means "on the contrary." In Luke 11:28 it means "yes, but": "*Yea, rather*, blessed are they that hear the word of God, and keep it."

BAUER 503, MOULTON-MILLIGAN 396.

3174. μενοῦνγε menounge partic

Rather, on the contrary, indeed.

1. μενοῦνγε menounge

1	But he said, Yea rather, blessed are they that hear	Luke 11:28
1	Nay but, O man, who art thou that repliest	Rom 9:20
1	Yes verily, their sound went into all the earth,	10:18
1	Yea doubtless, and I count all things but loss	Phlp 3:8

Menounge is a compound particle formed by three particles: *men* (3173), *oun* (3631), and *ge* (1058). Used to introduce a correction or an emphasis, *menounge* is often found in answers to questions or in responses to statements or views which one wishes to correct or refine. This is the sense of the word in Luke 11:28, Romans 9:20, and 10:18. In each place *menounge* could be translated "rather" or "on the contrary." In Philippians 3:8 *menounge* is combined with *alla* (233) to give a sense of "indeed" ("Yea doubtless," KJV). Here Paul did not correct his previous statement in 3:7 but used *alla menounge* to introduce 3:8 which emphasizes the truth of 3:7.

STRONG 3304, BAUER 503, MOULTON-MILLIGAN 396-97, LIDDELL-SCOTT 1102.

3175. μέντοι mentoi partic

Nevertheless, yet, but, actually.

1. μέντοι mentoi

1	yet no man said, What seekest thou?	John 4:27
1	Howbeit no man spake openly of him for fear	7:13
1	among the chief rulers also many believed (NT)	12:42
1	saw the linen clothes lying; yet went he not in	20:5
1	but the disciples knew not that it was Jesus	21:4
1	Nevertheless the foundation of God standeth sure,	2 Tm 2:19
1	If, however, you are fulfilling the royal law,	Jas 2:8
1	Likewise also these filthy dreamers defile the flesh,	Jude 1:8

Mentoi is a combination of two particles, *men* (3173) and *toi* (*toi* is an enclitic particle that is used to affirm what has been previously said by way of contrast, e.g., "certainly, truly"). As a strengthened form of *men* it is often used to give strong emphasis to a fact, or notice to an added point. The word is found in the New Testament with the sense of a conjunction: "nevertheless," "yet," or in a weakened sense of the word "but" (John 4:27; 7:13; 12:42; 20:5; 21:4; 2 Timothy 2:19). *Mentoi* also functions as an adverb and is translated "likewise" (Jude 8, taken together with the adverb *homoiōs* [3530B] which means "likewise"). As an adverb *mentoi* can also be rendered "really" or "actually" (the sense in James 2:8, but left untranslated in KJV).

STRONG 3305, BAUER 503, MOULTON-MILLIGAN 397, LIDDELL-SCOTT 1102.

3176. μένω menō verb

Remain, stay, stand fast, dwell, abide, continue, wait, last, endure, be permanent.

μένω 3176

COGNATES:
ἀναμένω anamenō (360)
διαμένω diamenō (1259)
ἐμμένω emmenō (1682)
ἐπιμένω epimenō (1946)
καταμένω katamenō (2620)
μονή monē (3301)
παραμένω paramenō (3748)
περιμένω perimenō (3900)
προσμένω prosmenō (4215)
συμπαραμένω sumparamenō (4690)
ὑπομένω hupomenō (5116)

SYNONYMS:
ἀπολείπω apoleipō (614)
αὐλίζομαι aulizomai (829)
διαμένω diamenō (1259)
διατελέω diateleō (1294)
διατρίβω diatribō (1298)
εἰμί eimi (1498)
ἐκδέχομαι ekdechomai (1538)
ἐμμένω emmenō (1682)
ἐπιμένω epimenō (1946)
καθίζω kathizō (2495)
καταμένω katamenō (2620)
κατασκηνόω kataskēnoō (2651)
κατοικέω katoikeō (2700)
οἰκέω oikeō (3474)
παραμένω paramenō (3748)
περιλείπομαι perileipomai (3898)
σκηνόω skēnoō (4492)
ὑπομένω hupomenō (5116)

אָחַר 'āchar (310), Piel: stay up (Is 5:11).

אָרַךְ 'ārēkh (773), Hiphil: prolong (Eccl 7:15 [7:16]).

הָיָה hāyâh (2030), Be; endure (Ps 89:36 [88:36]).

חָכָה châkhâh (2542), Piel: wait (2 Kgs 7:9, Is 8:17, 30:18).

יָחַל yāchal (3282), Hiphil: waste time (2 Sm 18:14—Codex Vaticanus only).

יָצָא yātsâ' (3428), Go out (1 Sm 20:11).

יָשַׁב yāshav (3553), Remain, endure (Gn 24:55, Ps 102:12 [101:12], Zec 14:10).

כּוּן kûn (3679), Stand firm, be established; niphal: be at hand (Jb 15:23).

כָּתַר kāthar (3932), Piel: bear with someone (Jb 36:2).

לִין lîn (4053), Spend the night (Jgs 19:9—Codex Alexandrinus only).

עָמַד 'āmadh (6198), Endure, stand (Ps 111:3 [110:3], Is 46:7); be unchanged (Lv 13:5).

קָוָה qāwâh (7245), Piel: look for, expect (Is 5:2,4,7).

קוּם qûm (7251), Stand (Nm 30:5, Prv 19:21, Is 32:8).

קַיָּם qayyām (A7290B) Enduring (Dn 6:26—Aramaic).

קָרָא qārā' (7410), Call; niphal: be mentioned (Is 14:20).

1. **μένει** menei 3sing indic pres act
2. **μένετε** menete 2pl indic/impr pres act
3. **μένω** menō 1sing indic pres act
4. **μένεις** meneis 2sing indic pres act
5. **μένομεν** menomen 1pl indic pres act
6. **μένουσιν** menousin 3pl indic pres act
7. **μένῃ** menē 3sing subj pres act
8. **μένε** mene 2sing impr pres act
9. **μενέτω** menetō 3sing impr pres act
10. **μένων** menōn nom sing masc part pres act
11. **μένοντος** menontos gen sing masc part pres act
12. **μένοντα** menonta acc sing masc part pres act
13. **μένουσαν** menousan acc sing fem part pres act
14. **μένον** menon nom/acc sing neu part pres act
15. **μένειν** menein inf pres act
16. **ἔμεινεν** emeinen 3sing indic aor act
17. **ἐμείναμεν** emeinamen 1pl indic aor act
18. **ἔμειναν** emeinan 3pl indic aor act
19. **μείνῃ** meinē 3sing subj aor act
20. **μείνητε** meinēte 2pl subj aor act
21. **μείνωσιν** meinōsin 3pl subj aor act
22. **μεῖνον** meinon 2sing impr aor act
23. **μείνατε** meinate 2pl impr aor act
24. **μείναντες** meinantes nom pl masc part aor act
25. **μεῖναι** meinai inf aor act
26. **μεμενήκεισαν** memenēkeisan 3pl indic plperf act
27. **μενῶ** menō 1sing indic fut act
28. **μενεῖτε** meneite 2pl indic fut act
29. **ἔμενεν** emenen 3sing indic imperf act
30. **ἔμενον** emenon 3pl indic imperf act
31. **μένητε** menēte 2pl subj pres act
32. **μενεῖ** menei 3sing indic fut act

23	who ... worthy; and there **abide** till ye go thence.	Matt 10:11
18	in Sodom, it would have **remained** until this day.	11:23
23	**tarry** ye here, and watch with me.	26:38
2	there **abide** till ye depart from that place.	Mark 6:10
23	sorrowful unto death: **tarry** ye here, and watch.	14:34
16	And Mary **abode** with her about three months,	Luke 1:56
29	neither **abode** in any house, but in the tombs.	8:27
2	And whatsoever house ye enter into, there **abide**,	9:4
2	in the same house **remain**, eating and drinking.	10:7
25	come down; for to day I must **abide** at thy house.	19:5
22	But they constrained him, saying, **Abide** with us:	24:29
25	And he went in to **tarry** with them.	24:29
16	from heaven like a dove, and it **abode** upon him.	John 1:32
14	see the Spirit descending, and **remaining** on him,	1:33
4	Master, where **dwellest** thou?	1:38
1	They came and saw where he **dwelt**,	1:39
18	and **abode** with him that day:	1:39
18	and they **continued** there not many days.	2:12
1	but the wrath of God **abideth** on him.	3:36
25	they besought him that he would **tarry** with them:	4:40
16	and he **abode** there two days.	4:40
12	And ye have not his word **abiding** in you:	5:38
13	for that meat which **endureth** unto everlasting life,	6:27
1	drinketh my blood, **dwelleth** in me, and I in him.	6:56
16	he **abode** still in Galilee.	7:9
20	If ye **continue** in my word,	8:31
1	And the servant **abideth** not in the house for ever:	8:35
1	servant **abideth** not ... but the Son **abideth** ever.	8:35
1	now ye say, We see; therefore your sin **remaineth**.	9:41
16	and there he **abode**.	10:40
16	he **abode** two days still in the same place	11:6
16	and there He **stayed** with the disciples (NASB)	11:54
1	Except a corn ... die, it **abideth** alone.	12:24
1	heard out of the law that Christ **abideth** for ever:	12:34
19	believeth on me should not **abide** in darkness.	12:46
10	Father that **dwelleth** in me, he doeth the works.	14:10
7	Comforter, that he may **abide** with you for ever;	14:16
1	for he **dwelleth** with you, and shall be in you.	14:17

#	Reference	Verse
10	being yet **present** with you.	John 14:25
23	**Abide** in me, and I in you.	15:4
19	bear fruit of itself, except it **abide** in the vine;	15:4
20	no more can ye, except ye **abide** in me.	15:4
10	He that **abideth** in me, and I in him,	15:5
19	If a man **abide** not in me, he is cast forth	15:6
20	If ye **abide** in me, and my words abide in you,	15:7
19	If ye abide in me, and my words **abide** in you,	15:7
23	so have I loved you: **continue** ye in my love.	15:9
28	keep ... commandments, ye **shall abide** in my love;	15:10
3	ye shall abide in my love; ... and **abide** in his love.	15:10
19	that my joy **might remain** in you,	15:11
7	and that your fruit **should remain**:	15:16
19	that the bodies **should** not **remain** upon the cross	19:31
15	If I will that he **tarry** till I come,	21:22
15	but, If I will that he **tarry till I come**,	21:23
14	Whiles it **remained**, was it not thine own?	Acts 5:4
29	Whiles it remained, was it not **thine own**?	5:4
25	it came to pass, that he **tarried** many days in Joppa	9:43
23	come into my house, and **abide** there.	16:15
29	he **abode** with them, and wrought:	18:3
25	they desired him **to tarry** longer time with them,	18:20
30	These going before **tarried for** us at Troas.	20:5
24	and **tarried** at Trogyllium;	20:15
6	saying that bonds and afflictions **abide** me.	20:23
17	to Ptolemais, ... and **abode** with them one day.	21:7
17	into the house of Philip ... and **abode** with him.	21:8
21	Except these **abide** in the ship, ye cannot be saved.	27:31
16	the forepart stuck fast, and **remained** unmoveable,	27:41
15	**to dwell** by himself with a soldier that kept him.	28:16
16	Paul **dwelt** two whole years in his own ... house,	28:30
7	purpose of God according to election **might stand**,	Rom 9:11
32	If any man's work **abide** which he hath built	1 Co 3:14
21	It is good for them if they **abide** even as I.	7:8
9	But and if she depart, **let her remain** unmarried,	7:11
9	**abide** in the same calling wherein he was called.	7:20
9	wherein he is called, therein **abide** with God.	7:24
19	she is happier if she so **abide**, after my judgment:	7:40
1	And now **abideth** faith, hope, charity, these three;	13:13
6	of whom the greater part **remain** unto this present,	15:6
14	much more that which **remaineth** is glorious.	2 Co 3:11
1	for until this day **remaineth** the same veil untaken	3:14
1	his righteousness **remaineth** for ever.	9:9
27	having this confidence, I know that I **shall abide**	Phlp 1:25
21	if they **continue** in faith and charity and holiness	1 Tm 2:15
1	yet he **abideth** faithful: he cannot deny himself.	2 Tm 2:13
8	But **continue** thou in ... which thou hast learned	3:14
16	Erastus **abode** at Corinth:	4:20
1	**abideth** a priest continually.	Heb 7:3
15	But this man, because he **continueth** ever,	7:24
13	in heaven a better and an **enduring** substance.	10:34
19	those things which cannot be shaken **may remain**.	12:27
9	Let brotherly love **continue**.	13:1
13	For here have we no **continuing** city,	13:14
11	word of God, which liveth and **abideth** for ever.	1 Pt 1:23
1	But the word of the Lord **endureth** for ever.	1:25
15	He that saith he **abideth** in him	1 Jn 2:6
1	He that loveth his brother **abideth** in the light,	2:10
1	ye are strong, and the word of God **abideth** in you,	2:14
1	but he that doeth the will of God **abideth** for ever.	2:17
26	they would no doubt **have continued** with us:	2:19
9	**Let** that therefore **abide** in you,	2:24
19	heard from the beginning **shall remain** in you,	2:24
28	also **shall continue** in the Son, and in the Father.	2:24
1	which ye have received of him **abideth** in you,	2:27
28	even as it hath taught you, ye **shall abide** in him.	2:27
2	And now, little children, **abide** in him;	2:28
10	Whosoever **abideth** in him sinneth not:	3:6
1	for his seed **remaineth** in him: and he cannot sin,	3:9
1	He that loveth not his brother **abideth** in death.	3:14
13	that no murderer hath eternal life **abiding** in him.	3:15
1	how **dwelleth** the love of God in him?	3:17
1	that keepeth his commandments **dwelleth** in him,	3:24
1	And hereby we know that he **abideth** in us,	3:24
1	If we love one another, God **dwelleth** in us,	4:12
5	Hereby know we that we **dwell** in him,	4:13
1	God **dwelleth** in him, and he in God.	4:15
10	and he that **dwelleth** in love dwelleth in God,	1 Jn 4:16
1	and he that dwelleth in love **dwelleth** in God,	4:16
1	**abides** in God, and God abides in him. (NASB)	4:16
13	For the truth's sake, which **dwelleth** in us,	2 Jn 1:2
10	and **abideth** not in the doctrine of Christ,	1:9
10	He that **abideth** in the doctrine of Christ,	1:9
25	when he cometh, he must **continue** a short space	Rev 17:10

Classical Greek and Septuagint Usage

In classical Greek the verb *menō* means "to remain" in a place, "to stay," or "to tarry." It also frequently carries the metaphoric meaning of being in a "sphere" or quality of life. In the Septuagint *menō* has basically the same meaning as in classical Greek. It is often used to translate two Hebrew verbs, *qum* and *'āmadh*, both having as their primary meaning "to stand." As with classical Greek there is the metaphoric meaning of "sphere" or "quality," e.g., to "remain" in a vow is to validate the vow, to make it meaningful (Numbers 30:5).

In the Septuagint *menō* is also significant in reference to God and to people and things relating to God. God is the abiding one. He is distinct from our changing world because of His characteristic of immutability. To say that God is immutable does not mean, as in Greek philosophy, that God cannot be moved (e.g., by prayer) or is static; instead, immutability denotes God's steadfastness to His people. The eternalness of God's Word and His love expresses the never-ending quality of our relationship with Him. He is the God who endures forever (Daniel 6:26); His counsel remains (Isaiah 14:24); His Word stands forever (Isaiah 40:8); and the new heavens and new earth He is going to create will endure before Him (Isaiah 66:22).

New Testament Usage

In the New Testament, besides the common meaning of staying or abiding in a place (see Matthew 10:11; Luke 1:56; etc.), *menō* refers to the same concept of the immutability of God, the things of God, and the sphere of God. The Word of God stands forever (1 Peter 1:23,25); Jesus abides forever (John 12:34); and so does the new covenant (2 Corinthians 3:11). Unbelievers abide in darkness and death (John 12:46; 1 John 3:14), but Christians abide in Christ (John 6:56; 15:4-7). As a result the anointing, eternal life, love, and truth remain in the believer (1 John 2:27; 3:15,17; 2 John 2). The use of *menō* to describe the believer's relationship with Christ is particularly Johannine and parallels Paul's phrase *en christō*, "in Christ."

μερίζω 3177

STRONG 3306, BAUER 503-4, MOULTON-MILLIGAN 397, KITTEL 4:574-76, LIDDELL-SCOTT 1103, COLIN BROWN 3:223-25.

3177. μερίζω merizō verb
Divide, separate, share, distribute, apportion.

COGNATES:
διαμερίζω diamerizō (1260)
διαμερισμός diamerismos (1261)
μερίς meris (3179B)
μερισμός merismos (3180)
μεριστής meristēs (3181)
μέρος meros (3183)
πολυμερῶς polumerōs (4041)
συμμερίζω summerizō (4680)

SYNONYMS:
ἀποδιορίζω apodiorizō (587)
ἀπώλεια apōleia (677)
ἀφορίζω aphorizō (866)
διαδίδωμι diadidōmi (1233)
διαιρέω diaireō (1238)
διακρίνω diakrinō (1246)
διαμερίζω diamerizō (1260)
διαχωρίζω diachōrizō (1310)
δίδωμι didōmi (1319)
κοινωνέω koinōneō (2814)
κρίνω krinō (2892)
μεταδίδωμι metadidōmi (3200)
σχίζω schizō (4829)
χωρίζω chōrizō (5398)

גְּבוּל gᵉvûl (1397), Border (Jos 13:27—Codex Alexandrinus only).

חָלַק chālaq (2606), Qal: share, distribute (1 Sm 30:24, Neh 13:13); niphal: be divided (Nm 26:53,55f., 1 Kgs 16:21); piel: divide (Ex 15:9, Jos 13:7, Is 53:12).

חֵלֶק chēleq (2610), Portion (Dt 18:8).

חֶלְקָה chelqāh (2614), Portion (Dt 33:21).

חָצָה chātsâh (2779), Qal: divide (Jb 41:6 [40:25]); niphal: be parceled out (Dn 11:4).

כָּתַב kāthav (3918), Write; describe (Jos 18:6).

מַחְלְקוֹת machlᵉqôth (4392), Hammahlekoth (1 Sm 23:28).

נָחַל nāchal (5336), Qal: inherit (Prv 14:18); hiphil: endow, give for an inheritance (Prv 8:21, Jer 12:14).

נַחֲלָה nachălāh (5338), Inheritance (Prv 19:14).

1. ἐμέρισεν emerisen 3sing indic aor act
2. ἐμερίσθη emeristhē 3sing indic aor pass
3. μερισθῇ meristhē 3sing subj aor pass
4. μερισθεῖσα meristheisa nom sing fem part aor pass
5. μερίσασθαι merisasthai inf aor mid
6. μεμέρισται memeristai 3sing indic perf mid
7. μεμέρικεν memeriken 3sing indic perf act

4	Every kingdom **divided** against itself ... desolation;	Matt 12:25
4	and every city or house **divided** against itself,	12:25
2	Satan cast out Satan, he is **divided** against himself;	12:26
3	And if a kingdom be **divided** against itself,	Mark 3:24
3	And if a house be **divided** against itself,	3:25
6	if Satan rise up against himself, and be **divided**,	3:26
1	and the two fishes **divided** he among them all.	Mark 6:41
5	that he **divide** the inheritance with me.	Luke 12:13
1	God hath **dealt** to every man the measure of faith.	Rom 12:3
6	Is Christ **divided**? was Paul crucified for you?	1 Co 1:13
1	But as God hath **distributed** to every man,	7:17
6	is **difference** also between a wife and a virgin.	7:34
1	of the rule which God hath **distributed** to us,	2 Co 10:13
1	To whom also Abraham **gave** a tenth part of all;	Heb 7:2

Classical Greek
The primary meaning of *merizō* is "to divide." The suffix, *-izō*, involves the idea of causation, i.e., "to cause or make a division." A secondary meaning of *merizō* is "to share something with someone," such as the distribution of the tithe of produce to the priests or the distribution of parental property to the children.

Septuagint Usage
In the Septuagint *merizō* describes God's command to divide Canaan among the 12 tribes (Joshua 13:7-27; 14:5). It is also used to describe the distribution of the spoils of battle (1 Samuel 30:24 [LXX 1 Kings 30:24]) and how God provided "portions" for the priests (Levites) to live on since they had no part of the inherited land (Deuteronomy 18:8). In spite of all that God gave, Israel persisted in her unfaithfulness to Him and was punished for her divided heart (Hosea 10:2).

New Testament Usage
In addition to the Septuagint, the New Testament uses *merizō* to show that division may destroy (see Matthew 12:25,26). Thus, there is a moral element in the term. As in the Septuagint, the New Testament uses *merizō* to describe the spiritual problem of carnal hearts divided by devotion to God and to the world. However, *merizō* does *not* contain the judicial or legal aspect of separation as *krisis* (2893) does.

Merizō is the most inclusive of its four related terms in the New Testament. It includes a simple separation as well as a violent tearing apart. *Merizō* and *diaireō* (1238) can be interchanged in the division and distribution of an estate (Luke 15:12). Two other related words appear to show different ways that division may occur. *Aphorizō* (866), "to divide by setting boundaries, to exclude someone or something," and *chōrizō* (5398), "to divide by separation, divorce, or departure," clearly are limited in their scope compared with *merizō*. *Schizō* (4829), from which the English word *schism* is derived, consistently involves a harsh or violent means of division.

STRONG 3307, BAUER 504, MOULTON-MILLIGAN 397, LIDDELL-SCOTT 1103-4.

3178. μέριμνα merimna noun

Care, concern, anxiety.

CROSS-REFERENCE:
μεριμνάω merimnaō (3179)

דְּאָגָה dᵉʾāghāh (1722), Care, anxiety (Sir 42:9).
יְהָב yᵉhāv (3163), Burden (Ps 55:22 [54:22]).

1. μέριμνα merimna nom sing fem
2. μέριμναν merimnan acc sing fem
3. μέριμναι merimnai nom pl fem
4. μεριμνῶν merimnōn gen pl fem
5. μερίμναις merimnais dat pl fem

1 and the **care** of this world,		Matt 13:22
3 And the **cares** of this world,		Mark 4:19
4 and are choked with **cares** and riches and pleasures		Luke 8:14
5 surfeiting, and drunkenness, and **cares** of this life,		21:34
1 the **care** of all the churches.		2 Co 11:28
2 Casting all your **care** upon him; for he careth		1 Pt 5:7

Classical Greek and Septuagint Usage

Merimna is a common word used in classical Greek literature from the time of Hesiod. It is used 12 times in the Septuagint to express the burden of anxious care, apprehension (e.g., Psalm 55:22 [LXX 54:22]; Job 11:18) and distress (Sirach 31:1,2).

New Testament Usage

Merimna is used six times in the New Testament and often means the foolish or selfish "anxiety" caused by lack of trust in God or by ambition for merely temporal satisfactions. It can also refer to a proper "concern" for those persons or matters placed in one's "care." Paul's "care" for the churches he had established was a responsible concern for their spiritual health (2 Corinthians 11:28). All other New Testament occurrences of *merimna* have a negative connotation, referring to the sort of worries and anxieties that hinder spiritual health and that need to be submitted to God (Matthew 13:22; Mark 4:19; Luke 8:14; 21:34; 1 Peter 5:7).

STRONG 3308, BAUER 504, MOULTON-MILLIGAN 397, KITTEL 4:589-93, LIDDELL-SCOTT 1104, COLIN BROWN 1:276-78.

3179. μεριμνάω merimnaō verb

Be anxious, care for, be concerned about.

COGNATES:
ἀμέριμνος amerimnos (273)
μέριμνα merimna (3178)
προμεριμνάω promerimnaō (4164)

SYNONYMS:
ἀδημονέω adēmoneō (84)
μέλω melō (3169)
μετεωρίζομαι meteōrizomai (3219)

דָּאַג dāʾagh (1720), Be sorry (Ps 38:18 [37:18]).
כָּעַס kāʿas (3832), Be angry (Ez 16:42).
עֶצֶב ʿetsev (6325), Labor (Prv 14:23).
עָשָׂה ʿāsāh (6449), Work (Ex 5:9).
רָגַז rāghaz (7553), Be disturbed (2 Sm 7:10, 1 Chr 7:9).
שָׁעָה shāʿāh (8541), Pay attention (Ex 5:9).

1. μεριμνᾶτε merimnate 2pl indic/impr pres act
2. μεριμνᾷς merimnas 2sing indic pres act
3. μεριμνᾷ merimna 3sing indic pres act
4. μεριμνῶσιν merimnōsin 3pl subj pres act
5. μεριμνῶν merimnōn nom sing masc part pres act
6. μεριμνήσητε merimnēsēte 2pl subj aor act
7. μεριμνήσει merimnēsei 3sing indic fut act

1 **Take** no **thought** for your life, what ye shall eat,		Matt 6:25
5 Which of you **by taking thought** can add one cubit		6:27
1 And why **take** ye **thought** for raiment?		6:28
6 Therefore **take** no **thought**, saying, What ... we eat?		6:31
6 **Take** therefore no **thought** for the morrow:		6:34
7 morrow **shall take thought** for the things of itself.		6:34
6 **take** no **thought** how or what ye shall speak:		10:19
2 thou art **careful** and troubled about many things:		Luke 10:41
1 **take** ye no **thought** how or what ... ye shall answer,		12:11
1 I say unto you, **Take** no **thought** for your life,		12:22
5 And which of you **with taking thought** can add		12:25
2 why **take** ye **thought** for the rest?		12:26
3 **careth** for the things that belong to the Lord,		1 Co 7:32
3 **careth** for the things that are of the world,		7:33
3 **careth** for the things of the Lord,		7:34
3 that is married **careth** for the things of the world,		7:34
4 but that the members should **have** the same **care**		12:25
7 who will naturally **care** for your state.		Phlp 2:20
1 **Be careful** for nothing;		4:6

Classical Greek

In secular Greek *merimnaō* means "have consideration or concern for something or someone," either oneself or others. It can additionally indicate anxious concern, worry, care; this can be both for the present and the future. Such concern might also prove cumbersome.

Septuagint Usage

In the Septuagint the Hebrew has no directly corresponding word for *merimnaō*: six terms lie behind only seven texts. Pharaoh attempted to redirect the concerns of the Israelites by increasing their work (Exodus 5:9). Anxiety over life issues, such as threats from enemies, is frequently expressed by *merimnaō* (2 Samuel 7:10 [LXX 2 Kings 7:10]; 1 Chronicles 17:9). Sin causes distress and anxiety (Psalm 38:18 [LXX 37:18]; cf. Ezekiel 16:42, of God's distress over Israel's sin).

New Testament Usage

The distribution of *merimnaō* in the New Testament is concentrated in the Synoptics and Pauline literature. It occurs only in Matthew (six times) and Luke (five times) in the Gospels. Each of these is parallel with one another except for Luke 10:41. Outside of the Gospels only Paul uses *merimnaō* (seven times). His usage is concentrated too: five times in 1 Corinthians and twice in Philippians.

The Gospel texts concern the unnecessary anxiety experienced over daily needs such as food and clothing. God will take care of His children (Matthew 6:25ff.; Luke 12:11ff.; cf. Luke 10:41 of Martha's anxiety). Moreover, one's anxiety will not change anything (e.g., Luke 12:25).

Paul used *merimnaō* four times (together with another member of the word group, *amerimnos* [273], "not anxious; free from care, worry, concern") in 1 Corinthians 7 in his discussion about marriage and sexual mores. The opening verse to the paragraph containing every instance sets the stage for interpreting *merimnaō*: "I would like you to be *free from concern*" (*amerimnos*, verse 32, NIV).

Keeping in mind that this is the foundation for Paul's subsequent argument, one should be careful not to see being anxious "for the things of the Lord" (1 Corinthians 7:32) as somehow to be preferred to being anxious about "the things of the world." The key to understanding this lies in the problem of those who had gone overboard with their newfound faith at the expense of their sexual responsibility to their mates (e.g., 7:1-24). These are those anxious about "the things of the Lord." Paul did not want the Corinthians to view Christian commitment as requiring neglect of marital relationships (e.g., 7:12-15,17,20,23; cf. 39). Thus to be anxious about "the things of the Lord" is not a virtue; rather, as Paul plainly states, he wants both unmarried and married alike "to be free from concern" (7:32, NIV).

Moreover, being concerned about "the things of the world" should not be seen as a totally negative position; Paul was simply stating the facts. Practically speaking, Paul did not want the Corinthians to get hung up over whether they were married or unmarried—which is precisely what modern interpreters succeed in doing too! Marriage will indeed bring "troubles" (*thlipsis* [2324]); that is a fact of life. However, theologically speaking Paul did not see marriage as inferior in any way.

As fellow members of the body of Christ we should have concern for one another (1 Corinthians 12:25; cf. Philippians 2:20). Paul's advice to the believers at Philippi echoed Christ: "Do not be anxious about anything" (Philippians 4:6, NIV). God is the God of peace (4:9); He will guard the believers' hearts and minds and grant them peace (verse 7).

STRONG 3309, BAUER 505, MOULTON-MILLIGAN 398, KITTEL 4:589-93, LIDDELL-SCOTT 1104, COLIN BROWN 1:276-78.

3179B. μερίς *meris* noun
Part, portion, division.
CROSS-REFERENCE:
μερίζω *merizō* (3177)

חָלַק *chālaq* (2606), Distribute, divide; piel: scatter (Lam 4:16).

חֵלֶק *chēleq* (2610), Portion, property (Dt 18:1, 2 Kgs 9:36f., Ez 45:7).

חֶלְקָה *chelqāh* (2614), Piece, plot (Gn 33:19, 2 Kgs 9:25f., Am 4:7).

חֲלֻקָּה *chăluqqāh* (2615), Division (2 Chr 35:5).

מַחֲלֹקֶת *machălōqeth* (4393), Division (Neh 11:36).

מָנָה *mānâh* (4630), Portion (Lv 7:33 [7:23], 1 Sm 1:4f., Est 9:22).

מְנָת *menāth* (4669), Portion (2 Chr 31:3f., Neh 13:10); prey (Ps 63:10 [62:10]).

מַשְׂאֵת *mas'ēth* (5020), Portion (Gn 43:34).

נֹא *nō'* (5169), Thebes (Na 3:8).

נַחֲלָה *nachălāh* (5338), Inheritance (Jos 18:7, Prv 20:21).

נֵתַח *nēthach* (5592), Piece (Jgs 19:29—Codex Alexandrinus only).

פְּלַגָּה *pelaggāh* (6634), Division (Jgs 5:15).

קָצֶה *qātseh* (7381), End (Ru 3:7).

1. μερίς *meris* nom sing fem
2. μερίδος *meridos* gen sing fem
3. μερίδα *merida* acc sing fem

3 and Mary hath chosen that good **part**,............. Luke 10:42
1 Thou hast neither **part** nor lot in this matter:........ Acts 8:21
2 which is the chief city of that **part** of Macedonia,...... 16:12
1 or what **part** hath he that believeth with an infidel? 2 Co 6:15
3 to be **partakers** of the inheritance of the saints........ Col 1:12

Classical Greek
The primary meaning of *meris* is "part." It describes the results of a division without reference to size. In its secular use the word describes someone's allotment or portion of a mine, a tax assessment, and a contribution. Geographically it refers to a portion of a field or cemetery. Politically it may be any subdivision of a country or one of its party factions. In speech the term refers to the separate points to be made, while in grammar it is the analysis of a sentence into its component parts. In

measurement *meris* is one unit of the scale. In religion it shows the part that different persons perform during the sacred ceremony.

Septuagint Usage

In the Septuagint *meris* is used most often for the Hebrew *chēleq* to describe the apportionment of Canaan among the 12 tribes (Joshua 14:4). Its meaning overlaps with *klēros* (2792) and *klēronomia* (2790) when it refers to that portion of an estate distributed among the heirs. The word is used in a moral sense when it warns against taking part in adulterous behaviors in order to show that punishment is the portion of the evildoers (Psalm 50:18 [LXX 49:18]). Spiritually, God is the *meris* of the saints (Psalm 16:5 [LXX 15:5]), and "the Lord's *portion* is his people" (Deuteronomy 32:9).

New Testament Usage

In the New Testament the word is used almost exclusively in a spiritual sense. For example, Mary chose the "good *part*" (Luke 10:42). It defines what "part" a believer has with an infidel (2 Corinthians 6:15). In addition, belonging to the kingdom of Christ is a "part" of the saints' inheritance (Colossians 1:12). Peter's rebuke of Simon (Acts 8:21) is a kind of excommunication, "You have no *part* or share in this ministry, because your heart is not right before God" (NIV). Its only other occurrence is geographical in meaning (Acts 16:12).

Strong 3310, Bauer 505, Moulton-Milligan 398, Liddell-Scott 1104, Colin Brown 2:303-4.

3180. μερισμός merismos noun

Distribution, division, separation.

Cross-Reference:
μερίζω merizō (3177)

מַחְלְקָה machleqāh (A4391), Order (Ezr 6:18—Aramaic).

מַחֲלֹקֶת machălōqeth (4393), Division (Jos 11:23).

1. μερισμοῦ merismou gen sing masc
2. μερισμοῖς merismois dat pl masc

2 gifts of the Holy Ghost, according to his own will?.. Heb 2:4
1 even to the **dividing asunder** of soul and spirit,......... 4:12

The term *merismos* is related to the noun *meris* (3179B) which means "part" or "portion." *Merismos* refers to the act of dividing the whole into parts. This can emphasize a "distribution" or "division." Both occurrences of the word in the New Testament are in Hebrews. In 2:4 the "gifts" of the Holy Spirit are actually "distributions" or "apportionments" of the Spirit, apparently meaning distinct manifestations of the Spirit's power by which God confirmed the preaching of the gospel.

In Hebrews 4:12 *merismos* is translated "dividing asunder." There are some who believe this emphasizes the power of the Word of God to separate the spiritual part of man from his innermost nature; however others suggest that the writer was making no such distinction. F.F. Bruce says that what is meant in that verse is "the word of God probes the inmost recesses of our spiritual being and brings the subconscious motives to light" (*New International Commentary on the New Testament, Hebrews*, p.82). The passage is not necessarily trying to make a distinction between body components, but is perhaps saying that God's Word can discriminate between man's thoughts and intents.

Strong 3311, Bauer 505, Moulton-Milligan 398, Liddell-Scott 1104.

3181. μεριστής meristēs noun

A divider, arbitrator, distributor.

Cross-Reference:
μερίζω merizō (3177)

1. μεριστήν meristēn acc sing masc

1 Man, who made me a judge or **a divider** over you? Luke 12:14

Meristēs, which means "a divider," is related to the more common word *merismos* (3180), which denotes "a division" or "partition" (from *meros* [3183], "a part").

Meristēs is found in the New Testament only at Luke 12:14 where Jesus responded to someone in the crowd who had asked Him to arbitrate a dispute between him and his brother over an inheritance. Jesus replied, "Man, who made me a judge or *a divider* over you?" The New International Version renders *meristēs* "arbiter."

Strong 3312, Bauer 505, Moulton-Milligan 398, Liddell-Scott 1104.

3182. μερίς meris noun

See the word study at number 3179B.

3183. μέρος meros noun

Part, share, portion, piece, allotment.
Cross-Reference:
μερίζω merizō (3177)

μέρος 3183

בָּזָא bāzā' (994), Divide (Is 18:7).

הֲלָךְ hălākh (A2052), Toll (Ezr 4:20—Aramaic).

חֵלֶק chēleq (2610), Reward (Eccl 5:18).

יָד yādh (3135), Hand; one part of many, fraction (Gn 47:24, Neh 11:1); projecting piece of a frame, tenon (Ex 26:19).

יַרְכָה yarkāh (3526), Rear (Ex 26:22).

מוּל mûl (4272II) Front (Nm 8:2f.).

מִן min (4623), From (2 Chr 36:7).

מִן min (A4624), Of (Dn 2:23,41f.—Aramaic).

מִקְצוֹעַ miqtsôa‘ (4903II) Corner (Ez 46:21).

נַחֲלָה nachălāh (5338), Inheritance (Prv 17:2).

עֵבֶר ‘ēver (5884), Side (Ex 32:15).

פֵּאָה pē'āh (6523), Corner (Ex 25:26 [25:25]); side, border (Jos 18:20, Ez 47:20).

פֶּלֶךְ pelekh (6662), District (Neh 3:15—Sixtine Edition only).

פַּעַם pa‘am (6718), Foot (1 Kgs 7:30).

צַד tsadh (6917), Beside, side (Jos 3:16, 1 Sm 6:8, 2 Sm 13:34).

צֵלָע tsēlā‘ (7029), Side (Ex 26:26,35).

קֵץ qēts (7377), Remote part (Is 37:24).

קָצֶה qātseh (7381), Edge, border (Nm 22:36, Jos 15:2, 2 Kgs 7:8).

קָצָה qātsāh (7382), Edge, tip (Ex 28:7, 1 Kgs 6:24).

קְצָת qᵉtsāth (7406), End (Ex 38:5 [38:24]); some, part (Neh 7:70, Dn 1:2).

קְצָת qᵉtsāth (A7407), Part (Dn 2:42—Aramaic).

רֶבַע reva‘ (7542), Side, direction (Ez 1:8, 10:11, 43:16).

רוּחַ rûach (7593), Wind, breath; side (Jer 52:23).

שָׂפָה sāphāh (8004), Lip; edge (Jos 12:2).

1. **μέρος** meros nom/acc sing neu
2. **μέρους** merous gen sing neu
3. **μέρει** merei dat sing neu
4. **μέρη** merē nom/acc pl neu

4	he turned aside into the **parts** of Galilee:	Matt 2:22
4	and departed into the **coasts** of Tyre and Sidon.	15:21
4	Jesus came into the **coasts** of Caesarea Philippi,	16:13
1	and appoint him his **portion** with the hypocrites:	24:51
4	and came into the **parts** of Dalmanutha.	Mark 8:10
1	be full of light, having no **part** dark,	Luke 11:36
1	will appoint him his **portion** with the unbelievers.	12:46
1	give me the **portion** of goods that falleth to me.	15:12
1	And they gave him a **piece** of a broiled fish,	24:42
1	If I wash thee not, thou hast no **part** with me.	John 13:8
4	took his garments, and made four **parts**,	19:23
1	and made four parts, to every soldier **a part**;	19:23
4	Cast the net on the right **side** of the ship,	21:6
4	and in the **parts** of Libya about Cyrene,	Acts 2:10
1	and brought a certain **part**,	5:2
4	Paul having passed through the upper **coasts**	19:1
1	So that not only this our **craft** is in danger	19:27
4	And when he had gone over those **parts**,	20:2
1	one **part** were Sadducees, and the other Pharisees,	23:6
2	the scribes that were of the Pharisees' **part** arose,	23:9
2	that blindness in **part** is happened to Israel,	Rom 11:25
2	written the more boldly unto you in **some sort**,	15:15
2	if first I be **somewhat** filled with your company.	15:24
1	be divisions among you; and I **partly** believe it.	1 Co 11:18
2	are the body of Christ, and members in **particular**.	12:27
2	For we know in **part**, and we prophesy in part.	13:9
2	For we know in part, and we prophesy in **part**.	13:9
2	then that which is in **part** shall be done away.	13:10
2	now I know in **part**; but then shall I know	13:12
1	and that by **course**; and let one interpret.	14:27
2	As also ye have acknowledged us in **part**,	2 Co 1:14
2	but in **part**: that I may not overcharge you all.	2:5
3	made glorious had no glory in this **respect**,	3:10
3	boasting of you should be in vain in this **behalf**;	9:3
4	descended first into the lower **parts** of the earth?	Eph 4:9
2	the effectual working in the measure of every **part**,	4:16
3	or in **respect** of an holyday, or of the new moon,	Col 2:16
1	of which we cannot now speak **particularly**.	Heb 9:5
3	but let him glorify God on this **behalf**.	1 Pt 4:16
4	And the great city was divided into three **parts**,	Rev 16:19
1	holy is he that hath **part** in the first resurrection:	20:6
1	shall have their **part** in the lake which burneth	21:8
1	God shall take away his **part** out of the book of life,	22:19

Classical Greek

Primarily *meros* means "part" or "piece" as contrasted to the whole. The word is rooted in Grecian mythology whose goddess of fate, Moira, was believed to be one of several deities who apportioned good and evil to men.

In its secular use *meros* has many shades of meaning, e.g., part of a body, building, land, district, and division of an army. Legally it describes a section of a document and identifies parties in a contract and court trial. In mathematics it describes fractions and is applied to the denominator as one part of a fraction. When objects or locations are being described it means "side" (cf. Exodus 26:26; John 21:6).

Unlike *meris* (3179B), *meros* has a special adverbial sense; e.g., *meros ti*, "in part," and *to pleistos meros*, "for the most part." Used with different prepositions it can mean "partly, alternately, specially," etc. Exact meanings must be determined from the context.

Septuagint Usage

Its primary meaning carries over into the Septuagint. While *meros* is used for several Hebrew nouns, its most common use is to express locality; i.e., border, edge of road, or piece of land. In addition, it occurs frequently in describing parts of the tabernacle and its furnishings (Exodus 26:5,19,21,22,25,26,35).

The religious use of the term is limited in the Septuagint, where it describes a part of God's ways with men (Job 26:14) and the discretion of the wise man who reveals only part of his thoughts (Proverbs 29:11).

New Testament Usage

In the New Testament *meros* is used most often to express physical locality, particularly with regards to the travels of Jesus and His disciples (cf. Matthew 2:22; 15:21; 16:13; Mark 8:10;

Acts 2:10). The locality described was not limited to the part of a country or region, but could also refer to the "side" of a boat. In Ephesians 4 Paul used *meros* to refer to the "lower *parts* of the earth" (verse 9) as well as to the "parts" of the "body" of which Christ is the head (verse 16).

Meros is also used figuratively to mean "share of something" or "allotment." This could have a negative connotation (e.g., the unfaithful servant was assigned a place among the unbelievers, Luke 12:46; cf. Revelation 21:6) or a positive promise (e.g., Luke 11:36; 1 Corinthians 13:9,10,12). Perhaps the most exciting example of this kind of promise was recorded by the apostle John: "Blessed and holy is he that hath *part* in the first resurrection: on such the second death hath no power, but they shall be priests of God and of Christ, and shall reign with him a thousand years" (Revelation 20:6).

STRONG 3313, BAUER 505-6, MOULTON-MILLIGAN 398-99, KITTEL 4:594-98, LIDDELL-SCOTT 1104-5, COLIN BROWN 2:303-4.

3184. μεσημβρία mesēmbria noun
Noon, midday, the south, toward the south.
COGNATE:
μέσος mesos (3189)
SYNONYM:
νότος notos (3421)

אוֹר 'ôr (214), Sunshine (Is 18:4).
נֶגֶב neghev (5221), Southward, south (Dn 8:4,9).
צָהַר tsāhar (6935), Hiphil: be noon (Sir 43:3).
צָהֳרַיִם tsohŏrayim (6937), Noon (Gn 43:16, 1 Kgs 18:26f., Jer 6:4).

1. μεσημβρίαν mesēmbrian acc sing fem
1 saying, Arise, and go toward the south .... Acts 8:26
1 and was come nigh unto Damascus about noon, ... 22:6

Mesēmbria is derived from two words: *mesos* (3189), "middle," and *hēmera* (2232), "a day." Literally *mesēmbria* means "middle day" and signifies "noon" as in Acts 22:6. *Mesēmbria* is also translated "the south" as in Acts 8:26, probably a reference to the position of the sun at midday. (Palestine is north of the equator.)

STRONG 3314, BAUER 506, MOULTON-MILLIGAN 399, LIDDELL-SCOTT 1105-6.

3185. μεσιτεύω mesiteuō verb
To act as a mediator, to give surety, guarantee a pledge, negotiate.

CROSS-REFERENCE:
μεσίτης mesitēs (3186)

1. ἐμεσίτευσεν emesiteusen 3sing indic aor act
1 confirmed it by an oath: .... Heb 6:17

Classical Greek
Mesiteuō and its cognate *mesitēs* (3186), "mediator, umpire," are used in three primary ways in classical Greek. The first is a technical sense meaning "to act as an umpire or peacemaker." Another usage which can be included in this technical sense involves a "deposit" or a "pledge" which is given to a sequester, a "pledge." A second sense given to the term is spatial and means "to occupy the middle place." The third sense means "to establish a relationship" between two unrelated parties, to "mediate" their coming together.

The earliest occurrence of the word is found in the writings of Polybius (Second Century B.C.) who employed it transitively with the meaning of to "mediate" or "negotiate." Intransitively the term meant "something that lies on deposit," as with a stockholder. It is also used in reference to "something lying between something else." Josephus (First Century A.D.) used it in reference to "acting as an arbiter" or "mediator" (*Antiquities* 7.8.5). Other extracanonical usages which come to us from the First Century include to "pledge" or "mortgage" property (cf. *Liddell-Scott*). *Mesiteuō* does not occur in the Septuagint.

New Testament Usage
In the New Testament the term is used one time, in Hebrews 6:17. Here it functions in the technical sense and could be translated "guarantee" or "pledge," although some versions (KJV, NIV) translate it "confirmed" while others (RSV, NASB) translate it "interpose." In this passage it is God who bears witness to himself as the Christian's guarantee that all His promises will be fulfilled. The Biblical record of how God has never failed to keep His covenants is a sure foundation for Christian faith (cf. verses 13-20).

STRONG 3315, BAUER 506, MOULTON-MILLIGAN 399, KITTEL 4:598-624, LIDDELL-SCOTT 1106, COLIN BROWN 1:373-75.

3186. μεσίτης mesitēs noun
Mediator, arbitrator.
CROSS-REFERENCE:
μεσιτεύω mesiteuō (3185)

μεσονύκτιον 3187

בֵּין bayin (1033), Between; umpire (Jb 9:33).

1. **μεσίτης** mesitēs nom sing masc
2. **μεσίτου** mesitou gen sing masc
3. **μεσίτῃ** mesitē dat sing masc

2 was ordained by angels in the hand of a **mediator**....	Gal 3:19
1 **mediator** is not a mediator of one, but God is one......	3:20
1 one God, and one **mediator** between God and men,	1 Tm 2:5
1 much also he is the **mediator** of a better covenant,...	Heb 8:6
1 he is the **mediator** of the new testament,...............	9:15
3 And to Jesus the **mediator** of the new covenant,.......	12:24

Classical Greek and Septuagint Usage

In classical Greek *mesitēs* denotes an arbitrator who settles disputes between two parties. It was his duty to bring the disputing parties to a decision of reconciliation. The term further depicted a "guarantor, surety," someone who placed himself under bond until a debt was paid. The word occurs only once in the Septuagint in Job 9:33 in the sense of "arbitrator."

New Testament Usage

A single *mesitēs* represents two parties. The New Testament declares that there is one God and one mediator between God and men—Jesus Christ (1 Timothy 2:5). Through Christ's death we are reconciled to God if we receive the reconciliation (2 Corinthians 5:18-20).

Jesus is God's representative to us, His delegate. At the same time He represents us before the Father. Jesus can assume such a mediative role because of His unique status as fully God and fully human. Moses mediated the imperfect Law (Galatians 3). *Mesitēs* also describes someone who is instrumental in transferring something from one person to another. Christ has mediated to us a new and better covenant (Hebrews 8:6; 9:15; 12:24) through which we are granted eternal life in communion with God.

STRONG 3316, BAUER 506-7, MOULTON-MILLIGAN 399, KITTEL 4:598-624, LIDDELL-SCOTT 1106, COLIN BROWN 1:372-76.

3187. μεσονύκτιον

mesonuktion noun

Midnight.

CROSS-REFERENCES:
μέσος mesos (3189)
νύξ nux (3433)

נֶשֶׁף nesheph (5582), Twilight (Is 59:10).

1. **μεσονυκτίου** mesonuktiou gen sing neu
2. **μεσονύκτιον** mesonuktion nom/acc sing neu

1 at even, or **at midnight**, or at the cockcrowing,....	Mark 13:35
1 and shall go unto him at **midnight**,................	Luke 11:5
2 And at **midnight** Paul and Silas prayed,............	Acts 16:25
1 and continued his speech until **midnight**...............	20:7

Mesonuktion is an adjective that comes from the words *mesos* (3189), "middle," and *nux* (3433), "night," and denotes "at (or of) midnight." The Romans divided the night into four watches: evening (*opsios* [3662]) 6—9 p.m., midnight (*mesonuktion*) 9 p.m.—midnight, cockcrow (*alektorophōnia* [217]) midnight—3 a.m., and morning (*prōinos* [4265]) 3—6 a.m. (Cf. Mark 13:35.)

Mesonuktion is used as a noun in Mark 13:35; Luke 11:5; Acts 16:25; and Acts 20:7, and means "midnight" in each text.

STRONG 3317, BAUER 507, MOULTON-MILLIGAN 399, LIDDELL-SCOTT 1107.

3188. Μεσοποταμία

Mesopotamia name

Mesopotamia.

1. **Μεσοποταμίᾳ** Mesopotamia dat fem
2. **Μεσοποταμίαν** Mesopotamian acc fem

2 and the dwellers in **Mesopotamia**, and in Judaea,....	Acts 2:9
1 in **Mesopotamia**, before he dwelt in Charran,...........	7:2

Region between the Tigris and Euphrates Rivers; Jews from this area were in Jerusalem on the Day of Pentecost (Acts 2:9).

3189. μέσος mesos adj

Middle, midst, in the middle, the middle object or person.

COGNATES:
μεσημβρία mesēmbria (3184)
μεσονύκτιον mesonuktion (3187)
μεσότοιχον mesotoichon (3190)
μεσουράνημα mesouranēma (3191)
μεσόω mesoō (3192)

בֵּין bayin (1033), Between (Ez 10:2).

גַּו gaw (A1489), Midst (Dn 3:24—Aramaic).

גֵּו gēw (1490), Back (Is 51:23).

חֲצִי chătsî (2783), Middle (Jos 10:13).

קֵץ qēts (7377), Farthest (2 Kgs 19:23).

קָצֶה qātseh (7381), Edge (2 Kgs 7:5).

קֶרֶב qerev (7419), Midst, among (Jos 1:11, Pss 78:28 [77:28], 82:1 [81:1]).

תָּוֶךְ tāwekh (8761), Midst, middle (Ex 14:16, 1 Kgs 8:64, Ez 22:19).

תִּיכוֹן tîkhôn (8814II) Middle (Ex 26:28, 1 Kgs 6:6, Ez 42:6).

1. μέσῳ **mesō** dat sing masc/neu
2. μέσος **mesos** nom sing masc
3. μέσης **mesēs** gen sing fem
4. μέσου **mesou** gen sing neu
5. μέσον **meson** nom/acc sing neu

1	I send you forth as sheep in the **midst** of wolves:..	Matt 10:16
5	his enemy came and sowed tares **among** the wheat,	13:25
4	and sever the wicked from **among** the just,	13:49
1	the daughter of Herodias danced **before** them,	14:6
5	But the ship was now in the **midst** of the sea,	14:24
1	a little child ... and set him in the **midst** of them,	18:2
1	two or three are ... there am I in the **midst** of them.	18:20
3	And at **midnight** there was a cry made,	25:6
5	saith unto the man ... Stand **forth**.	Mark 3:3
1	the ship was in the **midst** of the sea,	6:47
5	through the **midst** of the coasts of Decapolis.	7:31
1	he took a child, and set him in the **midst** of them:	9:36
5	And the high priest stood up in the **midst**,	14:60
1	in the temple, sitting in the **midst** of the doctors,	Luke 2:46
4	he passing through the **midst** of them went his way,	4:30
5	And when the devil had thrown him in the **midst**,	4:35
5	tiling with his couch into the **midst** before Jesus.	5:19
5	Rise up, and stand forth in the **midst**.	6:8
1	some fell **among** thorns; and the thorns sprang up	8:7
1	behold, I send you forth as lambs **among** wolves.	10:3
4	passed through the **midst** of Samaria and Galilee.	17:11
1	let them which are in the **midst** of it depart out;	21:21
1	but I am **among** you as he that serveth.	22:27
1	they had kindled a fire in the **midst** of the hall,	22:55
1	set down together, Peter sat down **among** them.	22:55
5	and the veil of the temple was rent in the **midst**.	23:45
1	Jesus himself stood in the **midst** of them,	24:36
2	standeth one **among** you, whom ye know not;	John 1:26
1	and when they had set her in the **midst**,	8:3
1	and the woman standing in the **midst**.	8:9
4	going through the **midst** of them, and so passed by.	8:59
5	on either side one, and Jesus in the **midst**.	19:18
5	came Jesus and stood in the **midst**,	20:19
5	stood in the **midst**, and said, Peace be unto you.	20:26
1	Peter stood up in the **midst** of the disciples,	Acts 1:15
2	falling headlong, he burst asunder in the **midst**,	1:18
1	which God did by him in the **midst** of you,	2:22
1	when they had set them in the **midst**, they asked,	4:7
1	Then Paul stood in the **midst** of Mars' hill,	17:22
4	So Paul departed from **among** them.	17:33
4	and to take him by force from **among** them,	23:10
3	At **midday**, O king, I saw in the way a light	26:13
1	Paul stood forth in the **midst** of them, and said,	27:21
5	about **midnight** the shipmen deemed that they	27:27
4	might be taken **away** from among you.	1 Co 5:2
5	that shall be able to judge **between** his brethren?	6:5
4	come out from **among** them, and be ye separate,	2 Co 6:17
1	in the **midst** of a crooked and perverse nation,	Phlp 2:15
4	and took it out of the **way**, nailing it to his cross;	Col 2:14
1	But we were gentle **among** you,	1 Th 2:7
4	until he be taken out of the **way**.	2 Th 2:7
1	in the **midst** of the church will I sing praise	Heb 2:12
1	And in the **midst** of the seven candlesticks	Rev 1:13
1	in the **midst** of the seven golden candlesticks;	2:1
1	which is in the **midst** of the paradise of God.	2:7
1	**midst** of the throne, and round about the throne,	4:6
1	in the **midst** of the throne and of the four beasts,	5:6
1	and in the **midst** of the elders, stood a Lamb	5:6
1	I heard a voice in the **midst** of the four beasts say,	6:6
5	the Lamb in the **center** of the throne (NASB)	7:17
1	In the **midst** of the street of it,	22:2

A common word, *mesos* can be an adjective, an adverb, or a noun. As an adjective denoting "middle," "in the middle," or "midst," *mesos* is normally in a prepositional phrase. In Luke 22:55, for example, "Peter sat down *among* them." In addition, *mesos* is used in reference to the rending of the veil "in the midst" in Luke 23:45. Used with the article, *mesos* can mean "the middle" of something or "among" something. Other technical uses do not change the basic meaning.

Mesos is also used adverbially in prepositional phrases and is rendered, for example, in 1 Corinthians 6:5, "between"; Matthew 13:25, "among"; Revelation 7:17, "in the midst"; Luke 4:30 and 17:11, "through the midst"; and in Luke 10:3, "in the midst," (RSV), "among" (KJV).

Strong 3319, Bauer 507-8, Moulton-Milligan 399-400, Liddell-Scott 1107, Colin Brown 1:372-73.

3190. μεσότοιχον mesotoichon noun
Middle wall, dividing wall.

Cognates:
μέσος mesos (3189)
περιέχω periechō (3886)
τεῖχος teichos (4886)

1. μεσότοιχον **mesotoichon** nom/acc sing neu

1 and hath broken down the **middle wall** of partition ... Eph 2:14

Mesotoichon comes from two words: *mesos* (3189), "middle," and *toichos* (4956), "a wall," hence the meaning "partition wall." Ephesians 2:14 is the only New Testament reference containing *mesotoichon*. Despite the view of some that the wall is between God and man, *mesotoichon* speaks figuratively of the "barrier" (literally the "middle wall") which represented the Law. This barrier kept the Gentiles from citizenship in Israel and made them foreigners to the covenants of promise; it created hostility and separation between the Gentile and the Jew. It was a "dividing wall" that was abolished by the Cross. The language here may be derived from the wall in the temple area which divided the courtyard of the Gentiles from the area which only Jews could enter.

Strong 3320, Bauer 508, Moulton-Milligan 400, Kittel 4:625, Liddell-Scott 1108, Colin Brown 3:795,948-49.

3191. μεσουράνημα
mesouranēma noun
Mid-heaven, zenith.

μεσόω 3192

CROSS-REFERENCES:
μέσος mesos (3189)
οὐρανός ouranos (3636)

1. μεσουρανήματι mesouranēmati dat sing neu

1 heard an angel flying through the **midst of heaven,**... Rev 8:13
1 And I saw another angel fly in the **midst of heaven,**.... 14:6
1 to all the fowls that fly in the **midst of heaven,**........ 19:17

From *mesos* (3189), "middle," and *ouranos* (3636), "heaven," *mesouranēma* denotes "midheaven," "the midst of the heavens," or "midair" (cf. Revelation 8:13; 14:6; and 19:17). In astronomy *mesouranēma* denotes the meridian or culmination, of the sun, for example.

STRONG 3321, BAUER 508, MOULTON-MILLIGAN 400, LIDDELL-SCOTT 1108.

3192. μεσόω mesoō verb

To be in the middle, be at the midpoint.

CROSS-REFERENCE:
μέσος mesos (3189)

חֲצִי chătsî (2783), Mid, the middle of something (Ex 12:29).

תִּיכוֹן tîkhôn (8814II) Middle (Jgs 7:19—Codex Alexandrinus only).

תְּקוּפָה tᵉqûphāh (8958), Turn (Ex 34:22).

1. μεσούσης mesousēs gen sing fem part pres act

1 Now about the **midst** of the feast Jesus went up.....John 7:14

Mesoō is the verbal form of the word *mesos* (3189) which denotes "middle," "in the middle," or "in the midst." *Mesoō* is used in John 7:14 which states that "about the midst" of the feast (the halfway point of the feast), Jesus went into the temple to teach. The feast referred to in this passage was probably the Feast of Tabernacles. Normally this feast was held 5 days after the Day of Atonement and lasted for a week as a time of general rejoicing.

STRONG 3322, BAUER 508, LIDDELL-SCOTT 1108.

3193. Μεσσίας Messias name

The Messiah, the Anointed One.

1. Μεσσίας Messias nom masc
2. Μεσσίαν Messian acc masc

2 and saith unto him, We have found the **Messias,**.... John 1:41
1 I know that **Messias** cometh, which is called Christ:..... 4:25

Messias is a Greek transliteration of the Hebrew word *māshîach* and is the root of the English word *Messiah*. *Messias* occurs twice in the New Testament, in John 1:41 and 4:25. Both the Septuagint and John use *Christos* (5382), "Anointed One," to translate *māshîach*.

Classical Greek

In its secular use, *christos* describes such common everyday activities as rubbing the body with oil after a bath, smearing poison on the points of arrows, painting, whitewashing, and using cosmetics. In the secular literature the word was anything but a title of honor. (For more information, especially about Jesus as Messiah, see the article on *Christos* [5382].)

Septuagint Usage

Like *christos*, the primary meaning of *māshîach* is "anointed one." In the Septuagint and Apocrypha it is often used to describe induction into an office. Its most common usage was the royal anointing of a king which ceremonially conferred on him the authority, power, and majesty of the office. This act of anointing was one of the most distinctive parts of the inaugural ceremony.

Religiously the word describes the act of consecrating the high priest and his assistants. It also describes the dedication of the tabernacle with the altar of burnt offering, the ark of the covenant, and the laver. These persons and objects were thus set apart by anointing for sacred purposes.

God called Cyrus, the Persian king, his "anointed" since he fulfilled the role of savior to Jewish exiles by permitting them to return to their homeland (Isaiah 45:1). God also anointed Isaiah with His Spirit (Isaiah 61:1) to endow him with power for the prophetic ministry. Jesus applied this Scripture passage to himself at the opening of His public ministry (Luke 4:16-21).

New Testament Usage

In John 1:35-51 there is the account of the calling of the first disciples. Although there is no clear evidence to indicate that the disciples had a fully developed understanding of what Jesus' messiahship actually meant, there is nonetheless the pronouncement, "We have found the Messiah" (verse 41). There is some speculation why this appears only in the Gospel of John. Perhaps John was giving an explanation of a distinctively Jewish term for his non-Jewish readers (cf. verse 38).

The only other occurrence of *Messias* is at John 4:25 where Jesus meets the Samaritan woman by Jacob's well (cf. verses 4-42). Like John and Andrew, the Samaritan woman was one who expressed her messianic expectancy. In verse 26 Jesus confirmed her hope by declaring, "I who speak to you am he" (NIV).

Strong 3323, Bauer 508, Moulton-Milligan 400, Colin Brown 2:334.

3194. μεστός mestos adj

Having full measure, fill with something, full of something.

Synonym:
πλήρης plērēs (3994)

מָלֵא māle' (4527), Be full, be complete (Ez 37:1, Na 1:10).

1. **μεστόν** meston nom/acc sing masc/neu
2. **μεστοί** mestoi nom pl masc
3. **μεστούς** mestous acc pl masc
4. **μεστή** mestē nom sing fem

2	but within ye are **full** of hypocrisy and iniquity.....	Matt 23:28
1	Now there was set a vessel **full** of vinegar:........	John 19:29
1	they put a sponge **full** of the sour wine (NASB).......	19:29
1	and drew the net to land **full** of great fishes,..........	21:11
3	**full** of envy, murder, debate, deceit, malignity;......	Rom 1:29
2	that ye also are **full** of goodness,.....................	15:14
4	it is an unruly evil, **full** of deadly poison.............	Jas 3:8
4	easy to be entreated, **full** of mercy and good fruits,.....	3:17
3	Having eyes **full** of adultery,.......................	2 Pt 2:14

Classical Greek and Septuagint Usage

Mestos, an adjective, is commonly translated "full" (with the sense of "having full measure"). *Mestos* is used literally in reference to the material world and metaphorically as applied to thoughts, feelings, evil things, or virtues. A typical example of its literal use in the Septuagint can be found at Ezekiel 37:1 where the prophet was put in a valley "*full* of bones" to prophecy to them.

New Testament Usage

In the New Testament *mestos* is used literally, for example, in John 19:29 which states, "There was set a vessel full of vinegar." John 21:11 speaks of a net "full" of fish.

Mestos is used metaphorically in Matthew 23:28 where Jesus described the scribes, Pharisees, and hypocrites who were "full" of hypocrisy and iniquity. Also, Paul spoke of those corrupt individuals who were "full" of unrighteousness, fornication, wickedness, covetousness, maliciousness, envy, murder, debate, deceit, etc. (Romans 1:29). Paul commended his brethren (Romans 15:14) by acknowledging that they were "full" of goodness, filled with all knowledge, and able to admonish one another. In contrast, James said that the tongue is "full" of deadly poison (James 3:8), while the wisdom from above is "full" of mercy and good fruits, without partiality, and without hypocrisy (James 3:17). Lastly, Peter described the ungodly as having eyes "full" of adultery, who cannot cease from sin (2 Peter 2:14).

Strong 3324, Bauer 508, Moulton-Milligan 400, Liddell-Scott 1108, Colin Brown 2:597.

3195. μεστόω mestoō verb

To fill full, to cause to bulge.

Synonyms:
ἀνταναπληρόω antanaplēroō (463)
γεμίζω gemizō (1065)
ἐμπίμπλημι empimplēmi (1689)
κορέννυμι korennumi (2853)
πληρόω plēroō (3997)
συμπληρόω sumplēroō (4696)
πληρόω plēroō (3997)
συμπληρόω sumplēroō (4696)

1. **μεμεστωμένοι** memestōmenoi
    nom pl masc part perf mid

1	These men are **full** of new wine...................	Acts 2:13

Mestoō is a verb that is related to the adjective *mestos* (3194) which means "full." *Mestoō* occurs in the New Testament only in Acts 2:13 and is translated as "full" (KJV) and "are filled with" (RSV). This word, describing the charge against the disciples who were speaking in tongues after being filled with the Spirit, carries the implication that their behavior was caused by drinking a great deal of wine.

Strong 3325, Bauer 508, Moulton-Milligan 400, Liddell-Scott 1108.

3196. μετά meta prep

With, after, behind, among.

1. **μεθ'** meth'
2. **μετ'** met'
3. **μετά** meta

3	And **after** they were brought to Babylon,...........	Matt 1:12
1	which being interpreted is, God **with** us................	1:23
2	he was troubled, and all Jerusalem **with** him...........	2:3
3	they saw the young child **with** Mary his mother,........	2:11
3	brethren, ... in a ship **with** Zebedee their father,........	4:21
2	whiles thou art in the way **with** him;..................	5:25
2	compel thee to go a mile, go **with** him twain..........	5:41
3	and shall sit down **with** Abraham, and Isaac,...........	8:11
3	Why eateth your Master **with** publicans and	9:11
2	as long as the bridegroom is **with** them?..............	9:15
2	what David did, ... when he was **with** him;......	12:3
2	neither for them which were **with** him,.............	12:4
2	He that is not **with** me is against me;.................	12:30
2	he that gathereth not **with** me scattereth abroad.......	12:30
3	shall rise in judgment **with** this generation,.........	12:41
3	shall rise up in the judgment **with** this generation,.....	12:42
1	and taketh **with** himself seven other spirits............	12:45
3	heareth the word, and anon **with** joy receiveth it;......	13:20
1	Whereupon he promised **with** an oath to give her whatsoever	14:7

μετά 3196

1	having **with** them those that were lame,	Matt 15:30
3	come in the glory of his Father **with** his angels;	16:27
1	And **after** six days Jesus taketh Peter, James, and	17:1
2	appeared ... Moses and Elias talking **with** him.	17:3
1	how long shall I be **with** you?	17:17
3	then take **with** thee one or two more,	18:16
3	king, which would take account of his servants.	18:23
3	If the case of the man be so **with** his wife,	19:10
3	agreed **with** the labourers for a penny a day,	20:2
3	the mother of Zebedee's children **with** her sons,	20:20
2	ye shall find an ass tied, and a colt **with** her:	21:2
3	unto him their disciples **with** the Herodians,	22:16
3	Immediately **after** the tribulation of those days	24:29
3	Son of man coming ... **with** power and great glory.	24:30
3	send his angels **with** a great sound of a trumpet,	24:31
3	and to eat and drink **with** the drunken;	24:49
3	and appoint him his portion **with** the hypocrites:	24:51
1	took their lamps, and took no oil **with** them:	25:3
3	the wise took oil in their vessels **with** their lamps.	25:4
2	that were ready went in **with** him to the marriage:	25:10
3	**After** a long time the lord of those servants cometh,	25:19
2	the lord ... cometh, and reckoneth **with** them.	25:19
2	and all the holy angels **with** him,	25:31
3	**after** two days is the feast of the passover,	26:2
1	For ye have the poor always **with** you;	26:11
3	keep the passover at thy house **with** my disciples.	26:18
3	the even was come, he sat down **with** the twelve.	26:20
2	He that dippeth his hand **with** me in the dish,	26:23
1	until that day when I drink it new **with** you	26:29
3	But **after** I am risen again, I will go before you	26:32
2	Jesus **with** them unto a place called Gethsemane,	26:36
2	tarry ye here, and watch **with** me.	26:38
2	What, could ye not watch **with** me one hour?	26:40
2	**with** him a great multitude with swords and staves,	26:47
2	with him a great multitude **with** swords and staves,	26:47
3	which were **with** Jesus stretched out his hand,	26:51
3	**with** swords and staves for to take me?	26:55
3	went in, and sat **with** the servants, to see the end.	26:58
3	Thou also wast **with** Jesus of Galilee.	26:69
3	This fellow was also **with** Jesus of Nazareth.	26:71
1	he denied **with** an oath, I do not know the man.	26:72
3	**after** a while came unto him they that stood by,	26:73
3	They gave him vinegar to drink mingled **with** gall:	27:34
3	priests mocking him, **with** the scribes and elders,	27:41
3	And came out of the graves **after** his resurrection,	27:53
2	when the centurion, and they that were **with** him,	27:54
3	next day, that **followed** the day of the preparation,	27:62
3	**After** three days I will rise again.	27:63
3	and along **with** the guard they set (NASB)	27:66
3	quickly from the sepulchre **with** fear and great joy;	28:8
3	And when they were assembled **with** the elders,	28:12
1	I am **with** you alway,	28:20
3	tempted of Satan; and was **with** the wild beasts;	Mark 1:13
3	Now **after** that John was put in prison,	1:14
3	father Zebedee in the ship **with** the hired servants,	1:20
3	house of Simon and Andrew, **with** James and John.	1:29
2	And Simon and they that were **with** him followed	1:36
3	Pharisees saw him eat **with** publicans and sinners,	2:16
3	he eateth and drinketh **with** publicans and sinners?	2:16
2	fast, while the bridegroom is **with** them?	2:19
1	as long as they have the bridegroom **with** them,	2:19
1	was an hungred, he, and they that were **with** him?	2:25
2	he had looked round about on them **with** anger,	3:5
3	and straightway took counsel **with** the Herodians	3:6
3	But Jesus withdrew himself **with** his disciples	3:7
3	he ordained twelve, that they should be **with** him,	3:14
3	immediately receive it **with** gladness;	4:16
2	And there were also **with** him other little ships.	4:36
2	prayed him that he might be **with** him.	5:18
2	Jesus went **with** him; and much people followed	5:24
2	He allowed no one to follow **with** Him, (NASB)	5:37
2	and them that were **with** him,	5:40
3	she came in straightway **with** haste unto the king,	6:25
2	And immediately he talked **with** them,	6:50
3	he entered into a ship **with** his disciples,	8:10
1	they in the ship **with** them more than one loaf.	8:14
3	and be killed, and **after** three days rise again.	8:31

3	in the glory of his Father **with** the holy angels.	Mark 8:38
1	And **after** six days Jesus taketh with him Peter,	9:2
1	no man any more, save Jesus only **with** themselves.	9:8
3	and said **with** tears, Lord, I believe;	9:24
3	and **after** three days he will rise." (NIV)	9:31
3	and children, and lands, **with** persecutions;	10:30
3	three days later He will rise (NASB) (NT)	10:34
3	he went out unto Bethany **with** the twelve.	11:11
2	**after** that tribulation, the sun shall be darkened,	13:24
3	coming in the clouds **with** great power and glory.	13:26
3	**After** two days was the feast of the passover,	14:1
1	For ye have the poor **with** you always,	14:7
3	where I shall eat the passover **with** my disciples?	14:14
3	And in the evening he cometh **with** the twelve.	14:17
2	One of you which eateth **with** me shall betray me.	14:18
3	But **after** that I am risen, I will go before you	14:28
3	And he taketh **with** him Peter and James and John,	14:33
2	**with** him a great multitude with swords and staves,	14:43
3	with him a great multitude **with** swords and staves,	14:43
3	**with** swords and with staves to take me?	14:48
3	and he sat **with** the servants, and warmed himself	14:54
3	of power, and coming in the clouds of heaven.	14:62
3	And thou also wast **with** Jesus of Nazareth.	14:67
3	And he denied it again. And a little **after**,	14:70
3	the chief priests held a consultation **with** the elders	15:1
3	one named Barabbas, which lay bound **with**	15:7
3	And he was numbered **with** the transgressors.	15:28
3	said among themselves **with** the scribes,	15:31
2	she went and told them that had been **with** him,	16:10
3	**After** that he appeared in another form unto two	16:12
3	So then **after** the Lord had spoken unto them,	16:19
3	And **after** those days his wife Elisabeth conceived,	Luke 1:24
3	Lord is **with** thee: blessed art thou among women.	1:28
3	and went into the hill country **with** haste,	1:39
2	how the Lord had showed great mercy **upon** her;	1:58
2	And the hand of the Lord was **with** him.	1:66
3	To perform the mercy promised **to** our fathers,	1:72
3	and had lived **with** an husband seven years	2:36
1	that **after** three days they found him in the temple,	2:46
3	he went down **with** them, and came to Nazareth,	2:51
3	And **after** these things he went forth,	5:27
2	publicans and of others that sat down **with** them.	5:29
3	do ye eat and drink **with** publicans and sinners?	5:30
2	fast, while the bridegroom is **with** them?	5:34
2	was an hungered, and they which were **with** him;	6:3
2	and gave also to them that were **with** him;	6:4
2	he came down **with** them, and stood in the plain,	6:17
2	Pharisees desired him that he would eat **with** him.	7:36
3	which, when they hear, receive the word **with** joy;	8:13
2	all denied, Peter and they that were **with** him said,	8:45
3	And it came to pass about an eight days **after** these	9:28
3	into a convulsion with foaming (NASB)	9:39
1	we forbad him, because he followeth not **with** us.	9:49
3	**After** these things the Lord appointed other	10:1
3	And the seventy returned again **with** joy, saying,	10:17
3	And he said, He that showed mercy **on** him.	10:37
2	and my children are **with** me in bed; I cannot rise	11:7
2	He that is not **with** me is against me:	11:23
2	and he that gathereth not **with** me scattereth.	11:23
3	in the judgment **with** the men of this generation,	11:31
3	**with** this generation, and shall condemn it:	11:32
3	and **after** that have no more that they can do.	12:4
3	**after** he hath killed hath power to cast into hell;	12:5
2	that he divide the inheritance **with** me.	12:13
3	will appoint him his portion **with** the unbelievers.	12:46
3	thou goest **with** thine adversary to the magistrate,	12:58
3	blood Pilate had mingled **with** their sacrifices.	13:1
2	and thou begin **with** shame to take the lowest room.	14:9
3	that cometh against him **with** twenty thousand?	14:31
2	not many days **after** the younger son gathered all	15:13
3	that I might make merry **with** my friends:	15:29
3	which hath devoured thy living **with** harlots,	15:30
3	thou art ever **with** me, and all that I have is thine.	15:31
3	and **afterward** thou shalt eat and drink?	17:8
3	turned back, and **with** a loud voice glorified God,	17:15
3	The kingdom of God cometh not **with** observation:	17:20
3	but **afterward** he said within himself,	18:4

μετά 3196

3	see the Son of man coming in a cloud **with** power	Luke 21:27
3	where I shall eat the passover **with** my disciples?	22:11
1	to eat this passover **with** you before I suffer:	22:15
3	Likewise also the cup **after** supper, saying,	22:20
2	the hand of him that betrayeth me is **with** me	22:21
2	which have continued **with** me in my temptations.	22:28
3	Lord, I am ready to go **with** thee, both into prison,	22:33
3	And he was reckoned **among** the transgressors:	22:37
3	come ... as against a thief, **with** swords and staves?	22:52
1	When I was daily **with** you in the temple,	22:53
3	And **after** a little while another saw him, and said,	22:58
2	Of a truth this fellow also was **with** him:	22:59
2	Herod and Pilate became friends **with** (NASB)	23:12
2	To day shalt thou be **with** me in paradise.	23:43
3	Why seek ye the living **among** the dead?	24:5
1	But they constrained him, saying, Abide **with** us:	24:29
2	And it came to pass, as he sat at meat **with** them,	24:30
3	and returned to Jerusalem **with** great joy:	24:52
3	After this he went down to Capernaum,	John 2:12
2	miracles that thou doest, except God be **with** him.	3:2
3	**After** these things came Jesus and his disciples	3:22
2	and there he tarried **with** them, and baptized.	3:22
3	**between** some of John's disciples and the Jews	3:25
3	he that was **with** thee beyond Jordan,	3:26
3	and marvelled that he talked **with** the woman:	4:27
2	What seekest thou? or, Why talkest thou **with** her?	4:27
3	Now **after** two days he departed thence,	4:43
3	**After** this there was a feast of the Jews;	5:1
3	whosoever then first **after** the troubling	5:4
3	**Afterward** Jesus findeth him in the temple,	5:14
3	**After** these things Jesus went over the sea	6:1
3	and there he sat **with** his disciples.	6:3
2	Murmur not **among** yourselves.	6:43
2	disciples went back, and walked no more **with** him.	6:66
3	**After** these things Jesus walked in Galilee:	7:1
1	Yet a little while am I **with** you,	7:33
2	And he that sent me is **with** me:	8:29
3	and it is he that talketh **with** thee.	9:37
2	Pharisees which were **with** him heard these words,	9:40
3	Then **after** that saith he to his disciples,	11:7
3	and **after** that he saith unto them,	11:11
2	Let us also go, that we may die **with** him.	11:16
2	The Jews then which were **with** her in the house,	11:31
3	and there continued **with** his disciples.	11:54
2	and spake **among** themselves,	11:56
1	For the poor always ye have **with** you;	12:8
2	**with** him when he called Lazarus out of his grave,	12:17
1	Yet a little while is the light **with** you.	12:35
3	but thou shalt know **hereafter**.	13:7
2	If I wash thee not, thou hast no part **with** me.	13:8
2	He that eateth bread **with** me	13:18
3	And **after** the sop Satan entered into him.	13:27
1	Little children, yet a little while I am **with** you.	13:33
1	Have I been so long time **with** you,	14:9
1	Comforter, that he may abide **with** you for ever;	14:16
1	Hereafter I will not talk much **with** you:	14:30
2	because ye have been **with** me from the beginning.	15:27
1	at the beginning, because I was **with** you.	16:4
2	Do ye inquire **among** yourselves of that I said,	16:19
2	yet I am not alone, because the Father is **with** me.	16:32
1	While I was **with** them in the world,	17:12
2	whom thou hast given me, be **with** me where I am;	17:24
3	Jesus ofttimes resorted thither **with** his disciples.	18:2
3	cometh thither **with** lanterns and torches	18:3
2	Judas also, which betrayed him, stood **with** them.	18:5
2	and Peter stood **with** them, and warmed himself.	18:18
2	saith, Did not I see thee in the garden **with** him?	18:26
2	and two others **with** him, on either side one,	19:18
3	After this, Jesus knowing that all ... accomplished,	19:28
3	And **after** this Joseph of Arimathaea,	19:38
3	and wound it in linen clothes **with** the spices,	19:40
3	the napkin, ... not lying **with** the linen clothes,	20:7
2	Thomas, ... was not **with** them when Jesus came.	20:24
1	**after** eight days again his disciples were within,	20:26
2	his disciples were within, and Thomas **with** them:	20:26
3	**After** these things Jesus showed himself again	21:1
3	**after** his passion by many infallible proofs,	Acts 1:3
3	baptized with the ... Ghost not many days **hence**.	Acts 1:5
3	and he was numbered **with** the eleven apostles.	1:26
3	shalt make me full of joy **with** thy countenance.	2:28
3	let me freely speak unto you of the patriarch (NT)	2:29
3	that **with** all boldness they may speak thy word,	4:29
3	and they spake the word of God **with** boldness.	4:31
3	and brought them **without** violence:	5:26
3	**After** this man rose up Judas of Galilee	5:37
3	and from thence, **when** his father was dead,	7:4
2	for a possession, and to his seed **after** him,	7:5
3	and **after** that shall they come forth, and serve me	7:7
2	sold Joseph into Egypt: but God was **with** him,	7:9
3	**with** the angel which spake to him	7:38
3	**with** Jesus into the possession of the Gentiles,	7:45
3	Then was Saul certain days **with** the disciples	9:19
2	**with** them coming in and going out at Jerusalem.	9:28
2	while she was **with** them.	9:39
3	**after** the baptism which John preached;	10:37
2	and healing all ... for God was **with** him.	10:38
3	and drink with him **after** he rose from the dead.	10:41
2	And the hand of the Lord was **with** them:	11:21
3	**after** Easter to bring him forth to the people.	12:4
3	And **after** the reading of the law and the prophets	13:15
3	and **with** an high arm brought he them out of it.	13:17
3	And **after** that he gave unto them judges	13:20
3	and **after** these things he gave (NASB)	13:20
2	But, behold, there cometh one **after** me,	13:25
3	and had prayed **with** fasting,	14:23
2	they rehearsed all that God had done **with** them,	14:27
2	declared all things that God had done **with** them.	15:4
3	**after** they had held their peace, James answered,	15:13
3	**After** this I will return,	15:16
2	go in peace from the brethren unto the apostles.	15:33
3	teaching and preaching ... **with** many others also.	15:35
3	And some days **after** Paul said unto Barnabas,	15:36
3	they received the word **with** all readiness of mind,	17:11
3	**After** these things Paul departed from Athens,	18:1
3	For I am **with** thee, and no man shall set on thee	18:10
2	believe on him which should come **after** him,	19:4
3	**After** I have been there, I must also see Rome.	19:21
3	And **after** the uproar was ceased,	20:1
3	from Philippi **after** the days of unleavened bread,	20:6
1	after what manner I have been **with** you	20:18
3	Serving the Lord **with** all humility of mind,	20:19
3	so that I might finish my course **with** joy,	20:24
3	that **after** my departing shall grievous wolves enter	20:29
3	to warn every one night and day **with** tears.	20:31
3	my necessities, and to them that were **with** me.	20:34
3	And **after** those days we took up our carriages,	21:15
3	And **after** five days Ananias the high priest	24:1
3	Ananias the high priest descended **with** the elders,	24:1
3	most noble Felix, **with** all thankfulness.	24:3
3	and **with** great violence took him away	24:7
3	neither **with** multitude, nor with tumult.	24:18
3	neither with multitude, nor **with** tumult.	24:18
3	And **after** certain days,	24:24
3	**after** three days he ascended from Caesarea	25:1
3	Festus, when he had conferred **with** the council,	25:12
3	Agrippa was come, and Bernice, **with** great pomp,	25:23
2	Whereupon as I went to Damascus **with** authority	26:12
3	I perceive that this voyage will be **with** hurt	27:10
2	But not long **after** there arose against it	27:14
3	God hath given thee all them that sail **with** thee.	27:24
3	And **after** three months we departed in a ship	28:11
3	and **after** one day the south wind blew,	28:13
3	And it came to pass, that **after** three days	28:17
3	**with** all confidence, no man forbidding him.	28:31
3	Rejoice with them that do rejoice,	Rom 12:15
3	and weep **with** them that weep.	12:15
3	If it be possible, ... live peaceably **with** all men.	12:18
3	he saith, Rejoice, ye Gentiles, **with** his people.	15:10
3	Now the God of peace be **with** you all. Amen.	15:33
1	The grace of our Lord Jesus Christ be **with** you.	16:20
3	The grace of our Lord Jesus Christ be **with** you all.	16:24
3	But brother goeth to law **with** brother,	I Co 6:6
1	because ye go to law one **with** another.	6:7
2	and she be pleased to dwell **with** him,	7:12

2	and if he be pleased to dwell **with** her,	1 Co 7:13
3	**After** the same manner also he took the cup,	11:25
3	for I look for him **with** the brethren.	16:11
3	desired him to come unto you **with** the brethren:	16:12
1	The grace of our Lord Jesus Christ be **with** you.	16:23
3	My love be **with** you all in Christ Jesus. Amen.	16:24
3	or what part hath he that believeth **with** an infidel?	2 Co 6:15
3	what agreement hath the temple of God **with** idols?	6:16
3	how **with** fear and trembling ye received him.	7:15
3	**with** much entreaty that we would receive the gift,	8:4
2	And we have sent **with** him the brother,	8:18
1	and the God of love and peace shall be **with** you.	13:11
3	the communion of the Holy Ghost, be **with** you all.	13:14
3	Then **after** three years I went up to Jerusalem	Gal 1:18
3	I went up again to Jerusalem **with** Barnabas,	2:1
3	he did eat **with** the Gentiles:	2:12
3	which was four hundred and thirty years **after**,	3:17
3	this Agar ... and is in bondage **with** her children.	4:25
3	shall not be heir **with** the son of the freewoman.	4:30
3	grace of our Lord Jesus Christ be **with** your spirit.	6:18
3	**With** all lowliness and meekness,	Eph 4:2
3	**with** longsuffering, forbearing one another in love;	4:2
3	speak every man truth **with** his neighbour:	4:25
3	that are your masters ... **with** fear and trembling,	6:5
2	**With** good will doing service, as to the Lord,	6:7
3	Peace be to the brethren, and love **with** faith,	6:23
3	Grace be **with** all them that love our Lord Jesus	6:24
3	Always in every prayer ... making request **with** joy,	Phlp 1:4
3	work out your own salvation **with** fear	2:12
3	Receive him therefore ... **with** all gladness;	2:29
3	laboured **with** me in the gospel, **with** Clement also,	4:3
3	by prayer and supplication **with** thanksgiving	4:6
1	do: and the God of peace shall be **with** you.	4:9
3	The grace of our Lord Jesus Christ be **with** you all.	4:23
3	unto all patience and longsuffering **with** joyfulness;	Col 1:11
1	Remember my bonds. Grace be **with** you. Amen.	4:18
3	received the word ... **with** joy of the Holy Ghost:	1 Th 1:6
3	coming of our Lord Jesus Christ **with** all his saints.	3:13
1	The grace of our Lord Jesus Christ be **with** you.	5:28
1	And to you who are troubled rest **with** us,	2 Th 1:7
2	be revealed from heaven **with** his mighty angels,	1:7
3	**with** quietness they work, and eat their own bread.	3:12
3	The Lord be **with** you all.	3:16
3	The grace of our Lord Jesus Christ be **with** you all.	3:18
3	**with** faith and love which is in Christ Jesus.	1 Tm 1:14
3	modest apparel, **with** shamefacedness and sobriety;	2:9
3	in faith and charity and holiness **with** sobriety.	2:15
3	having his children in subjection **with** all gravity;	3:4
3	**with** thanksgiving of them which believe	4:3
3	if it be received **with** thanksgiving:	4:4
3	**with** the laying on of the hands of the presbytery.	4:14
3	But godliness **with** contentment is great gain.	6:6
3	Grace be **with** thee. Amen.	6:21
3	salvation which is in Christ ... **with** eternal glory.	2 Tm 2:10
3	**with** them that call on the Lord out of a pure heart.	2:22
2	Only Luke is **with** me.	4:11
3	Take Mark, and bring him **with** thee:	4:11
3	The Lord Jesus Christ be **with** thy spirit.	4:22
1	Jesus Christ be **with** thy spirit. Grace be **with** you.	4:22
3	speak, and exhort, and rebuke **with** all authority.	Tit 2:15
3	**after** the first and second admonition reject;	3:10
2	All that are **with** me salute thee.	3:15
3	Grace be **with** you all. Amen.	3:15
3	grace of our Lord Jesus Christ be **with** your spirit.	Phlm 1:25
3	To day, **after** so long a time; as it is said,	Heb 4:7
3	not **afterward** have spoken of another day.	4:8
3	therefore draw near **with** confidence (NASB)	4:16
3	prayers and supplications **with** strong crying	5:7
3	but this **with** an oath by him that said unto him,	7:21
3	but the word of the oath, which was **since** the law,	7:28
3	will make **with** the house of Israel **after** those days,	8:10
3	And **after** the second veil, ... the Holiest of all;	9:3
3	blood of calves and of goats, **with** water,	9:19
3	once to die, but **after** this the judgment:	9:27
3	for **after** that he had said before,	10:15
3	is the covenant that I will make ... **after** those days,	10:16
3	**with** a true heart in full assurance of faith,	10:22
3	For if we sin wilfully **after** that	Heb 10:26
3	and took joyfully the spoiling of your goods, (NT)	10:34
3	dwelling in tabernacles **with** Isaac and Jacob,	11:9
2	when she had received the spies **with** peace.	11:31
3	Follow peace **with** all men, and holiness,	12:14
3	though he sought it carefully **with** tears.	12:17
3	we may serve God acceptably **with** reverence	12:28
3	that they may do it **with** joy, and not with grief:	13:17
1	**with** whom, if he come shortly, I will see you.	13:23
3	Grace be **with** you all. Amen.	13:25
3	the sufferings ... and the glory that should **follow**.	1 Pt 1:11
3	the hope that is in you **with** meekness and fear.	3:15
3	I will ... that ye may be able **after** my decease	2 Pt 1:15
1	that ye also may have fellowship **with** us:	1 Jn 1:3
3	and truly our fellowship is **with** the Father,	1:3
3	is with the Father, and **with** his Son Jesus Christ.	1:3
2	If we say that we have fellowship **with** him,	1:6
2	we have fellowship one **with** another,	1:7
3	they would no doubt have continued **with** us:	2:19
1	love is perfected **with** us, (NASB)	4:17
1	which dwelleth in us, and shall be **with** us for ever.	2 Jn 1:2
1	Grace be **with** you, mercy, and peace, from God	1:3
3	cometh with clouds; and every eye shall see him,	Rev 1:7
2	And I turned to see the voice that spake **with** me.	1:12
3	and the things which shall be **hereafter**;	1:19
2	and will fight **against** them with the sword	2:16
2	commit adultery **with** her into great tribulation,	2:22
3	shall walk **with** me in white: for they are worthy.	3:4
2	I will come in to him, and will sup **with** him,	3:20
2	and will sup with him, and he **with** me.	3:20
2	will I grant to sit **with** me in my throne,	3:21
3	and am set down with my Father in his throne.	3:21
3	**After** this I looked, and, behold,	4:1
2	was as it were of a trumpet talking **with** me;	4:1
3	I will show thee things which must be **hereafter**.	4:1
2	sat on him was Death, and Hell followed **with** him.	6:8
3	And **after** these things I saw four angels	7:1
3	**After** this I beheld, and, lo, a great multitude,	7:9
3	and, behold, there come two woes more **hereafter**.	9:12
2	And the voice ... from heaven spake **unto** me again,	10:8
2	shall make war **against** them, ... and kill them.	11:7
3	And **after** three days and an half the Spirit of life	11:11
3	Michael ... waging war **with** the dragon (NASB)	12:7
3	Satan, ... and his angels were cast out **with** him.	12:9
3	went to make war **with** the remnant of her seed,	12:17
2	the beast? who is able to make war **with** him?	13:4
3	it was given unto him to make war **with** the saints,	13:7
2	and **with** him an hundred forty and four thousand,	14:1
3	These are they which were not defiled **with** women;	14:4
2	their deeds follow **with** them." (NASB)	14:13
3	And **after** that I looked, and, behold, the temple	15:5
2	and talked **with** me, saying unto me, Come hither;	17:1
1	**With** whom the kings of the earth have	17:2
3	but receive power as kings one hour **with** the beast.	17:12
3	These shall make war **with** the Lamb,	17:14
2	are **with** him are called, and chosen, and faithful.	17:14
3	And **after** these things I saw another angel	18:1
2	the kings ... have committed fornication **with** her,	18:3
2	the kings ... and lived deliciously **with** her,	18:9
3	And **after** these things I heard a great voice	19:1
3	to make war **against** him that sat on the horse,	19:19
3	him that sat on the horse, and **against** his army.	19:19
3	beast was taken, and **with** him the false prophet	19:20
3	and **after** that he must be loosed a little season.	20:3
3	lived and reigned **with** Christ a thousand years.	20:4
2	and shall reign **with** him a thousand years.	20:6
3	Behold, the tabernacle of God is **with** men,	21:3
2	will dwell **with** them, and they shall be his people,	21:3
2	God himself shall be **with** them, and be their God,	21:3
2	and talked **with** me, saying, Come hither,	21:9
2	And he that talked **with** me had a golden reed	21:15
2	behold, I come quickly; and my reward is **with** me,	22:12
3	The grace of our Lord Jesus Christ be **with** you all.	22:21

The root meaning of *meta* is "mid" or "midst." According to Vine, "in the middle or midst" is usually translated by *mesos* (3189), and "withal (at the same time)" is usually translated by *hama* (258) (*Expository Dictionary*, "Midst," "Withal"). The word *meta* is related to these but primarily denotes association and accompaniment.

In the papyri, Septuagint, and the New Testament, the word usually appears in prepositional phrases with either the genitive or accusative case. *Meta* with the dative case does not occur in the New Testament, but Grecian poets used the word to describe any impersonal association of people as well as something held with (between) the hands.

In the New Testament *meta* with the genitive case is translated "with" over 380 times. The relationship of Jesus with His disciples, a bishop with his church, and God with His believers express intimate associations. Used with verbs of going or staying, the idea of accompaniment prevails. With verbs that express hostility, as an army fighting *with* its enemy, it means "against." The term also expresses personal emotions that are experienced in different situations, e.g., "with joy," "with shame," "with fear and trembling," and "with boldness." In a few instances it shows the means by which something is done, as "write with ink."

Meta with the accusative case, usually translated "after," has three principal meanings. First, it refers to a definite or indefinite time period, as after 6 days, or after a few days. Second, it means "pursuit," that is, to go *after* someone whether in a friendly or hostile manner. And third, it means "sequence or succession" whether of place (as in Hebrews 9:3, "after [behind] the second veil"); of time (as thereafter); or of worth or rank (as next to the gods).

STRONG 3326, BAUER 508-10, MOULTON-MILLIGAN 400-401, KITTEL 7:766-97, LIDDELL-SCOTT 1108-9, COLIN BROWN 3:1172-74,1182,1190,1201,1204-7.

3197. μεταβαίνω metabainō verb

Go across, pass over.

COGNATE:
  ὑπερβαίνω huperbainō (5070)
SYNONYMS:
  κινέω kineō (2767)
  φέρω pherō (5179)

1. **μεταβαίνετε** metabainete 2pl impr pres act
2. **μετέβη** metebē 3sing indic aor act
3. **μεταβῇ** metabē 3sing subj aor act
4. **μετάβηθι** metabēthi 2sing impr aor act
5. **μεταβάς** metabas nom sing masc part aor act
6. **μεταβέβηκεν** metabebēken 3sing indic perf act
7. **μεταβεβήκαμεν** metabebēkamen 1pl indic perf act
8. **μεταβήσεται** metabēsetai 3sing indic fut mid
9. **μετάβα** metaba 2sing impr aor act

3	that **he would depart** out of their coasts.	Matt 8:34
2	**he departed** thence to teach and to preach	11:1
5	And when he **was departed** thence,	12:9
5	And Jesus **departed** from thence,	15:29
4	**Remove** hence to yonder place;	17:20
8	say unto this mountain, ... and it shall remove;	17:20
1	**Go** not from house to house.	Luke 10:7
6	but **is passed** from death unto life.	John 5:24
4	**Depart** hence, and go into Judaea,	7:3
3	that he **should depart** out of this world	13:1
5	And he **departed** thence,	Acts 18:7
7	We know that we **have passed** from death unto life,.	1 Jn 3:14

Metabainō is a compound verb made up of the preposition *meta* (3196), "with" or "after," and *bainō*, "to go." Thus, it literally means "to go or pass over from one place to another."

Classical Greek

In classical Greek the word primarily means "to go away," "to remove," or "to depart." It describes the change when someone moves from one dwelling to another or makes a change in course or direction. In speaking and in writing, the word means "to pass on to another subject." In logic it is the process of making a transition or an inference based on an analogy or resemblance. In drama it is the changing fortunes of the actors as the plot unfolds.

The word does not appear in any of the canonical books of the Septuagint. None of the five apocryphal occurrences translate a Hebrew equivalent.

New Testament Usage

The New Testament uses *metabainō* predominantly in a geographical sense to show Jesus' movements from place to place during His traveling ministry (e.g., Matthew 12:9). It is also used to describe Jesus' departure from this world and His consequent return to His Father (e.g., John 13:1). While a change of physical location is basic to the word, a change from one condition or state of existence to another is denoted by the term.

In His teachings, Jesus used the word to illustrate the power of faith to remove mountains (Matthew 17:20) and to explain the theological concept of change from spiritual death to life through faith in Christ, as stated in John 5:24.

STRONG 3327, BAUER 510, MOULTON-MILLIGAN 401, KITTEL 1:523, LIDDELL-SCOTT 1109, COLIN BROWN 2:184,186.

3198. μεταβάλλω metaballō verb
To throw over, turn, change quickly, alter, vary.

CROSS-REFERENCE:
βάλλω ballō (900)

הָפַךְ hāphakh (2089), Qal: turn (Ex 10:19, Lv 13:3f., Jos 7:8); niphal: be turned (Ex 7:17,20, Lv 13:16f.).

חָוַר chāwar (2447), Grow pale (Is 29:22).

חָלַף chālaph (2599), Sweep by (Hb 1:11).

פָּשָׂה pāsâh (6831), Spread (Lv 13:7).

שׁוּב shûv (8178), Turn back (Jos 8:21—Codex Vaticanus only).

1. μεταβαλλόμενοι metaballomenoi
nom pl masc part pres mid
2. μεταβαλόμενοι metabalomenoi
nom pl masc part aor mid

1 changed their minds, and said that he was a god.... Acts 28:6

Metaballō, a compound, prepositional verb, comes from *meta* (3196), "with, change," and *ballō* (900) which means "to throw." *Metaballō* denotes the sense of turning or changing one's course, purpose, way, life, or mind. In Acts 28:6 *metaballomai*, the middle voice of *metaballō*, is used to indicate the Melita natives' quick "change of mind" concerning Paul when they saw that he had not been harmed by the venomous viper. Instead of thinking him a murderer, they said he was a god.

STRONG 3328, BAUER 510, MOULTON-MILLIGAN 401-2 (see "metaballomai"), LIDDELL-SCOTT 1109-10.

3199. μετάγω metagō verb
To turn about, direct, guide.

CROSS-REFERENCE:
ἄγω agō (70)

סָבַב sāvav (5621), Change hands (Sir 10:8).

סוּר sûr (5681), Turn aside; hiphil: depose (2 Chr 36:3).

שָׁבָה shāvâh (8091), Qal: take captive (1 Kgs 8:48); niphal: be carried away captive (1 Kgs 8:47, 2 Chr 6:37).

1. μετάγομεν metagomen 1pl indic pres act
2. μετάγεται metagetai 3sing indic pres mid

1 and we turn about their whole body................. Jas 3:3
2 yet are they turned about with a very small helm,....... 3:4

Metagō is found in the New Testament only at James 3:3,4 and is translated "to turn about" or "to guide." James used this term to describe the use of both the horse's bit and the rudder of a ship which, though small, are able to effectively "turn about" or direct large things. In the same way, James says, the tongue is a small thing but has enormous power or impact in life. Hence there is the need to control one's tongue so what is said may glorify God and edify other people.

STRONG 3329, BAUER 510, MOULTON-MILLIGAN 402, LIDDELL-SCOTT 1111.

3200. μεταδίδωμι metadidōmi verb
Give over, impart, share, bestow.

COGNATE:
δίδωμι didōmi (1319)

SYNONYMS:
διαδίδωμι diadidōmi (1233)
διαιρέω diaireō (1238)
διαμερίζω diamerizō (1260)
δίδωμι didōmi (1319)
δωρέομαι dōreomai (1426)
κοινωνέω koinōneō (2814)
μερίζω merizō (3177)
μετέχω metechō (3218)

שָׁבַר shāvar (8132), Break, buy; hiphil: sell (Prv 11:26).

1. μεταδιδούς metadidous nom sing masc part pres act
2. μεταδιδόναι metadidonai inf pres act
3. μεταδῶ metadō 1sing subj aor act
4. μεταδότω metadotō 3sing impr aor act
5. μεταδοῦναι metadounai inf aor act

4 two coats, let him impart to him that hath none;.... Luke 3:11
3 that I may impart unto you some spiritual gift,...... Rom 1:11
1 he that giveth, let him do it with simplicity;............ 12:8
2 that he may have to give to him that needeth........ Eph 4:28
5 we were willing to have imparted unto you,.......... 1 Th 2:8

Classical Greek and Septuagint Usage
In classical Greek *metadidōmi* can mean "to inform," "give a report," or "instruct." It can also mean "to transmit" a disease. *Metadidōmi* comes from two words: *meta* (3196), "with," and *didōmi* (1319), "to give." This compound indicates the giving or granting of something from the store or abundance of one's resources. Of the seven occurrences in the Septuagint, only one translates a Hebrew equivalent. In Proverbs 11:26 *metadidōmi* translates a form of *shāvar* which is used in this verse to mean "willing to sell." The motivation for such action is not greed or profit but a willingness to share rather than "hoard" one's prosperity.

New Testament Usage
In Luke 3:11 John the Baptist instructed those who had two tunics to "share" with him who had none. In Romans 1:11 Paul expressed his desire to see the Christians at Rome and to "impart" some spiritual gift so they might be strengthened in the Faith. Romans 12:8 states that if our gift in serving the members of the

body of Christ is "giving" (out of our own resources or the distribution of what has been contributed by others), we are to give generously and cheerfully.

Ephesians 4:28 tells us that the one who has been stealing must work with his hands in order to have something to "give" or "impart" to those who are in need. In 1 Thessalonians 2:8 Paul stated that he and his fellow apostles were glad to have "shared" or "imparted" the gospel of God as well as their lives with the Thessalonians because of their love for them.

STRONG 3330, BAUER 510-11, MOULTON-MILLIGAN 402, LIDDELL-SCOTT 1111, COLIN BROWN 2:40-41.

3201. μετάθεσις metathesis noun

Change of position, transformation, transfer, removal.
CROSS-REFERENCE:
μετατίθημι metatithēmi (3216)

1. **μετάθεσις** metathesis nom sing fem
2. **μεταθέσεως** metatheseōs gen sing fem
3. **μετάθεσιν** metathesin acc sing fem

1 there is made of necessity **a change** also of the law... Heb 7:12
2 for before his **translation** he had this testimony,....... 11:5
3 signifieth the **removing** of those things............... 12:27

Classical Greek and Septuagint Usage

The basic meaning of this noun is a change of position, e.g., between the states of sleeping and waking. *Metathesis* can also denote a figurative change of mind or opinion, or any change that implies a transference of one thing or from one place or side to another (cf. *Liddell-Scott*). It comes from two words: *meta* (3196), implying "change," and *tithēmi* (4935), which means "to put" or "to place." It does not appear in any of the canonical books of the Septuagint; however, it is used once at 2 Maccabees 11:24 where it describes the reluctance of the Jews to "change" their "manner of living" in accordance with the "customs of the Gentiles."

New Testament Usage

In the New Testament *metathesis* is found only in the Book of Hebrews. Hebrews 7:12 states that when there is a "change" of the priesthood there must also be a "change" of the Law. The verbal form of this word is found twice in Hebrews 11:5. We are told that "Enoch was taken up (*metetethē*) so that he should not see death; and he was not found, because God had taken (*metethēken*) him" (RSV). The KJV translates *metetethe* as "translation" in that verse. What both versions are describing is the transfer of Enoch directly from earth to the presence of God without dying first.

In Hebrews 12:27 *metathesis* is rendered "removing," speaking of the "removing" of that which can be "shaken" (created things) so "that those things that cannot be shaken may remain" (i.e., the Kingdom).

STRONG 3331, BAUER 511, MOULTON-MILLIGAN 402, KITTEL 8:161-62, LIDDELL-SCOTT 1111-12, COLIN BROWN 2:265-66.

3202. μεταίρω metairō verb

Go away, depart, transfer, remove.
COGNATE:
αἴρω airō (142)
SYNONYMS:
ἀναλύω analuō (358)
ἀναχωρέω anachōreō (400)
ἀπαλλάσσω apallassō (521)
ἀπέρχομαι aperchomai (562)
ἀποβαίνω apobainō (571)
ἀπολύω apoluō (624)
ἀποχωρέω apochōreō (666)
ἀφίημι aphiēmi (856)
ἀφίστημι aphistēmi (861)
διαχωρίζω diachōrizō (1310)
ἐγκαταλείπω enkataleipō (1452)
ἐξέρχομαι exerchomai (1814)
ἐξιέναι exienai (1821)
παράγω paragō (3717)
ὑπάγω hupagō (5055)
χωρέω chōreō (5397)

גָּלָה gālâh (1580), Go away, uncover; hiphil: carry into exile (2 Kgs 25:11).
נָסַע nāsa' (5450), Hiphil: bring out (Ps 80:8 [79:8]).
סוּג sûgh (5657), Go back; hiphil: move (Prv 22:28).
סוּר sûr (5681), Turn aside; hiphil: remove (2 Kgs 16:17).

1. **μετῆρεν** metēren 3sing indic aor act

1 finished these parables, he **departed** thence......... Matt 13:53
1 finished these sayings, he **departed** from Galilee,...... 19:1

In the transitive sense the verb *metairō* means "to lift up and remove from one place to another, to transfer." In the intransitive sense it means "to go away" or "to depart." In the Septuagint this word occurs four times (2 Kings [LXX 4 Kings] 16:17; 25:11; Psalm 79:9; Proverbs 22:28) and is used transitively. It occurs twice in the New Testament (Matthew 13:53; 19:1), and both times it is employed intransitively with regards to Jesus' practice of traveling to different regions to teach the multitudes that followed Him.

STRONG 3332, BAUER 511, MOULTON-MILLIGAN 402, LIDDELL-SCOTT 1112.

3203. μετακαλέομαι
metakaleomai verb

To summon, to send for, to call from one place to another.

COGNATE:
καλέω kaleō (2535)

SYNONYMS:
ἐπικαλέω epikaleō (1926)
καλέω kaleō (2535)
μεταπέμπομαι metapempomai (3213)
παρακαλέω parakaleō (3731)
προσκαλέομαι proskaleomai (4200)
συγκαλέω sunkaleō (4630)
φωνέω phōneō (5291)

קָרָא qārā' (7410), Call (Hos 11:1,2).

1. **μετεκαλέσατο** metekalesato 3sing indic aor mid
2. **μετακάλεσαι** metakalesai 2sing impr aor mid
3. **μετακαλέσομαι** metakalesomai 1sing indic fut mid

1	and called his father Jacob to him,	Acts 7:14
2	Send therefore to Joppa, and call hither Simon,	10:32
1	and called the elders of the church.	20:17
3	have a convenient season, I will call for thee.	24:25

This is a compound prepositional verb combining *meta* (3196), "change," with *kaleō* (2535), "to call." The verb *metakaleomai* is the middle voice form of *metakaleō* and denotes "to call to one's self" or "to send for." In the Septuagint the word occurs in Hosea 11:1,2 in connection with God's "call" to Israel. In the New Testament it is found exclusively in Acts (7:14; 10:32; 20:17; 24:25). The verb is always in the middle voice: Joseph sending for Jacob, Cornelius for Peter, Paul for the church leaders of Ephesus, and Felix for Paul, respectively.

STRONG 3333, BAUER 511 (see "metakaleō"), MOULTON-MILLIGAN 402-3 (see "metakaleō"), KITTEL 3:496, LIDDELL-SCOTT 1112 (see "metakaleō"), COLIN BROWN 1:273.

3204. μετακινέω metakineō verb

To move away, to be moved from a place, remove.

CROSS-REFERENCE:
κινέω kineō (2767)

מוֹט môṭ (4267), Be removed (Is 54:10).

נִדָּה niddāh (5257), Something unclean (Ezr 9:11).

נוּס nûṣ (5308), Flee; hiphil: put to flight (Dt 32:30).

נוּעַ nûa' (5309), Totter, wander; hiphil: cause to wander (2 Sm 15:20—Codex Vaticanus only).

סוּג sûgh (5657), Go back; hiphil: move (Dt 19:14).

1. **μετακινούμενοι** metakinoumenoi
    nom pl masc part pres mid

1	be not moved away from the hope of the gospel,	Col 1:23

Metakineō is a compound verb from *meta* (3196) and *kineō* (2767), "to set in motion" or "move." It is an uncommon word with the connotation of displacement. It occurs four times in the Septuagint in connection with the moving away of landmarks (Deuteronomy 19:14), enemies (Deuteronomy 32:30; Ezra 9:11 [LXX 2 Esdras 9:11]), and mountains (Isaiah 54:10). *Metakineō* is translated in Colossians 1:23 in the passive voice: "Be not *moved away* from the hope of the gospel." Other English versions translate the word in the middle voice ("Do not move yourself away"), thus emphasizing the believer's responsibility to remain steadfast in his faith.

STRONG 3334, BAUER 511, MOULTON-MILLIGAN 403, KITTEL 3:720, LIDDELL-SCOTT 1112.

3205. μεταλαμβάνω
metalambanō verb

Receive, take a share of, partake, obtain.

COGNATE:
λαμβάνω lambanō (2956)

SYNONYMS:
ἀναδέχομαι anadechomai (322)
ἀπέχω apechō (563)
ἀπολαμβάνω apolambanō (612)
δέχομαι dechomai (1203)
εἰσδέχομαι eisdechomai (1509)
ἐπιδέχομαι epidechomai (1911)
κομίζω komizō (2837)
λαμβάνω lambanō (2956)
παραδέχομαι paradechomai (3720)
παραλαμβάνω paralambanō (3741)
προσδέχομαι prosdechomai (4185)
προσλαμβάνω proslambanō (4213)
ὑποδέχομαι hupodechomai (5103)
ὑπολαμβάνω hupolambanō (5112)

1. **μεταλαμβάνει** metalambanei 3sing indic pres act
2. **μεταλαμβάνειν** metalambanein inf pres act
3. **μεταλαβών** metalabōn nom sing masc part aor act
4. **μεταλαβεῖν** metalabein inf aor act
5. **μετελάμβανον** metelambanon 3pl indic imperf act

5	did eat their meat with gladness	Acts 2:46
3	when I have a convenient season, I will call	24:25
4	Paul besought them all to take meat, saying,	27:33
4	I encourage you to take some food (NASB)	27:34
2	that laboureth must be first partaker of the fruits.	2 Tm 2:6
1	receiveth blessing from God:	Heb 6:7
4	that we might be partakers of his holiness.	12:10

Classical Greek and Septuagint Usage
Metalambanō is a compound verb formed from *meta* (3196) and *lambanō* (2956), "to take" or "to receive." It is usually used in classical Greek to refer to literally having or getting a physical portion or share of something. It can also be

found in a figurative sense meaning "have part in, participate in" activities or ideas that one is in agreement with (*Liddell-Scott*). *Metalambanō* does not appear in the canonical portions of the Septuagint, but it is used 14 times in apocryphal writings. Twelve of these occurrences are in Maccabees where *metalambanō* frequently means "receiving" information in the sense of hearing and understanding (cf. 2 Maccabees 4:21; 11:6; 12:5,8; 15:1) or perceiving (2 Maccabees 13:10).

New Testament Usage
In the New Testament, Acts 2:46 renders *metalambanō* "did eat" (KJV) or "partook" (RSV), i.e., shared in the meals. In Acts 24:25 *metalambanō* is translated "*when I have a convenient season*" or, more particularly, "when I have obtained time for receiving you and what you have to say" (free translation).

In 2 Timothy 2:6 and Hebrews 12:10 *metalambanō* is rendered "to be partaker (or partakers) of." Second Timothy uses it in connection with the farmer receiving a share of the crops, and in Hebrews 12:10 it describes the purpose of discipline in the life of a believer.

In Hebrews 6:7 *metalambanō* is used metaphorically of the earth "*receiving* a blessing from God" because it fulfilled divine purpose through producing vegetation after having been watered by the rain that He sent.

STRONG 3335, BAUER 511, MOULTON-MILLIGAN 403, KITTEL 4:10-11, LIDDELL-SCOTT 1113, COLIN BROWN 3:747,750.

3206. μετάληψις metalēpsis noun
Participation, taking, sharing.
CROSS-REFERENCE:
λαμβάνω lambanō (2956)

1. μετάληψιν metalēpsin acc sing fem
2. μετάλημψιν metalēmpsin acc sing fem

1 which God hath created to be received .... 1 Tm 4:3

Metalēpsis, also spelled *metalēmpsis*, is a noun that is related to the verb *metalambanō* (3205) and generally means "participation." Only in the New Testament does it refer to the "partaking" of food (1 Timothy 4:3). Paul used it in reference to certain foods that were prohibited by a false teaching regarding asceticism. Paul stated that all food could "be received" with thanksgiving and eaten without fear by the believer.

STRONG 3336, BAUER 511 (see "metalēmpsis"), MOULTON-MILLIGAN 403, KITTEL 4:11, LIDDELL-SCOTT 1113, COLIN BROWN 3:747,750.

3207. μεταλλάσσω metallassō verb
To exchange, alter, substitute.
COGNATE:
ἀλλάσσω allassō (234)
SYNONYM:
ἀλλάσσω allassō (234)

מוּת mûth (4322), Die (Est 2:7).

1. μετήλλαξαν metēllaxan 3pl indic aor act

1 Who changed the truth of God into a lie, ... Rom 1:25
1 for even their women did change the natural use 1:26

This is a compound verb made up of *meta* (3196) and *allassō* (234), "alter, change." The prefix *meta* often implies change. In addition, the root verb *allassō* is used several times to denote a fundamental or elemental change as in 1 Corinthians 15:51 where the thorough change in the body of the believer at Christ's coming is discussed. In Hebrews 1:12 *allassō* is used to describe the fundamental change to be made in the heavens at the destruction of the world.

Matallassō, in contrast to *allassō*, is an intensive compound meaning "to exchange" one thing for another. Romans 1:25 notes the "exchange" of the truth of God for a lie. In Romans 1:26 women "exchange" natural sexual relationships for that which is not according to nature. In the papyri an additional meaning is given to *metallassō* where it means "to die" or "to exchange by leaving" (cf. *Moulton-Milligan*).

STRONG 3337, BAUER 511, MOULTON-MILLIGAN 403, KITTEL 1:259, LIDDELL-SCOTT 1113, COLIN BROWN 3:166-67.

3208. μεταμέλομαι metamelomai verb
Regret, repent, feel sorry for.
COGNATE:
ἀμεταμέλητος ametamelētos (276)
SYNONYM:
μετανοέω metanoeō (3210)

אָשֵׁם 'āshēm (843), Be punished (Zec 11:5).

נָהַם nāham (5277), Groan (Prv 5:11).

נָחַם nācham (5341), Niphal: change one's mind, relent (Ex 13:17, Ps 106:45 [105:45], Jer 20:16).

קָצַף qātsaph (7395), Hithpael: be angry, repent (Sir 35:19).

1. μεταμέλομαι metamelomai 1sing indic pres mid
2. μετεμελήθητε metemelēthēte 2pl indic aor pass

μεταμοϱφόω 3209

3. μεταμεληθείς metamelētheis
   nom sing masc part aor pass
4. μεταμεληθήσεται metamelēthēsetai
   3sing indic fut pass
5. μετεμελόμην metemelomēn 1sing indic imperf mid

```
3 but afterward he repented, and went............. Matt 21:29
2 repented not afterward, that ye might believe him...... 21:32
3 he saw that he was condemned, repented himself,...... 27:3
1 I do not repent, though I did repent:.............. 2 Co 7:8
5 I do not repent, though I did repent:................ 7:8
4 The Lord sware and will not repent,............... Heb 7:21
```

Classical Greek
Metamelomai is composed of the two Greek terms *meta* (3196), "after," and *melō* (3169), "I care, I am concerned for." The basic meaning is "to feel regret, to repent, to feel sorrow." In classical Greek it can mean "to change one's mind," and it cannot always be clearly distinguished from *metanoeō* (3210), "I repent" (cf. Trench, *Synonyms of the New Testament*, p.256).

Septuagint Usage
The translators of the Septuagint used *metamelomai* to translate three Hebrew words, but one is most common (seven times out of nine)—the niphal of *nācham* ("to repent, be sorry"). *Metamelomai* suggests a "change of mind" (Exodus 13:17). It does not necessarily imply a sense of error, but it emphasizes the feeling of sorrow (e.g., 1 Samuel 15:35 [LXX 1 Kings 15:35], the Lord "repented" [regretted] He had made Saul king; cf. 1 Chronicles 21:15). In fact, God's great love and mercy may effect a change in His mind (Psalm 106:45 [LXX 105:45]), but His oath is unchangeable (Psalm 110:4 [LXX 109:4]).

New Testament Usage
Metamelomai does not join with *metanoeō* in the New Testament to describe conversion or repentance in the Biblical sense. In fact, some distinction may be preserved, as the example of Judas, who regretted (*metamelomai*) betraying Christ, suggests. He in no way is regarded as "repentant" in a spiritual sense (Matthew 27:3). Trench, quoting the English theologian Chillingworth, goes so far as to say that *metamelomai* in no way suggests any forgiveness of sins. Only *metanoia* (3211), he contends, signifies a "thorough change of the heart and soul, of the life and actions" (Trench, ibid.). However, Matthew hints at a relationship between *metamelomai* and repentance or at least the movement toward repentance (Matthew 21:32 of "repenting" [*metamelomai*] at the preaching of John the Baptist).

Paul's usage in 2 Corinthians 7:8 maintains a distinction between regret and repentance. Paul regretted his indicting letter to the Corinthians, but he does not attempt to alter its effect. In fact, if it led them to repentance he was delighted.

The Hebrews (7:21) citation of Psalm 110:4 emphasizes God's firm commitment, His absence of regret, in making Christ high priest. This reaffirms God's covenant and ensures His steadfast faithfulness and purpose.

STRONG 3338, BAUER 511, MOULTON-MILLIGAN 403, KITTEL 4:626-29, LIDDELL-SCOTT 1114, COLIN BROWN 1:356.

3209. μεταμοϱφόω
metamorphoō verb

Be changed in form, be transformed, be transfigured.

CROSS-REFERENCE:
μοϱφόω morphoō (3308)

1. μεταμοϱφούμεθα metamorphoumetha
   1pl indic pres mid
2. μεταμοϱφοῦσθε metamorphousthe
   2pl impr pres mid
3. μετεμοϱφώθη metemorphōthē 3sing indic aor pass

```
3 And was transfigured before them:................ Matt 17:2
3 mountain ... and he was transfigured before them....Mark 9:2
2 be ye transformed by the renewing of your mind,...Rom 12:2
1 are changed into the same image from glory........ 2 Co 3:18
```

Classical Greek
This is a compound from *meta* (3196), "change" (in compound words), and the verb *morphoō* (3308), "to give shape or form" (from *morphē* [3307], "form"). Thus, its definition is "to change forms, to transform." If used passively it means "to be transformed, altered in appearance." This includes external transformation (cf. the classical works of Apuleius and Ovid, *Metamorphoses* [a transliteration of the Greek into Latin]). The idea of being changed from one form to another is popular in ancient Greek literature. In Apuleius' *Golden Ass* the unfortunate main character is changed into an ass. Of course such a concept of physical change as a religious experience is preposterous from the New Testament understanding of internal transformation or of Christ's transfiguration (Liefield, "Transform," *Colin Brown*, 3:861f.; cf. *Moulton-Milligan*).

Septuagint Usage
The Septuagint offers only one versional reading of *metamorphoō*. Symmachus substitutes it

in Psalm 34:1 for *alloioō*, "to make different, change" (of David's "face," i.e., his disposition; David pretended he was insane). No versions use it in Exodus 34:29-35 of Moses' face which changed while he spoke with God on Sinai; but Paul spoke of a relationship to that event in 2 Corinthians 3:12-18.

New Testament Usage

Metamorphoō appears four times in the New Testament, always in the passive form. Mark (9:2) describes the "transformation" of Jesus and His clothes (cf. Matthew 17:2 which mentions only the transformation of His features). Luke does not include this term; perhaps, as Liefield suggests, it was because it invited pagan comparison ("Transform," *Colin Brown*, 3:862; cf. Behm, "metamorphoō," *Kittel*, 4:756f., on the use of the term in religions outside of the Bible). The reality of the Transfiguration is assumed by the writers of the New Testament and was unquestioned (2 Peter 1:16-18; Mark 9:9, it was *seen*). The significance of the event is, in part, its anticipation of the upcoming triumph of the Cross and Christ's glorification (for more on this see Liefield, "Transform," *Colin Brown*, 3:861f.).

Paul used *metamorphoō* in the internal sense in Romans 12:2. The believer is to "be transformed" through the "renewing" of his or her mind. Our goal is to become formed in Christ's image. Such renewal prepares us for godly Christian living (cf. 2 Corinthians 3:18).

STRONG 3339, BAUER 511, MOULTON-MILLIGAN 403, KITTEL 4:755-59, LIDDELL-SCOTT 1114, COLIN BROWN 3:861,864.

3210. μετανοέω metanoeō verb

To repent, change one's mind, be converted.

COGNATES:
ἀμετανόητος ametanoētos (277)
μετάνοια metanoia (3211)
νοέω noeō (3401)

SYNONYM:
μεταμέλομαι metamelomai (3208)

נָחַם nācham (5341), Niphal: change one's mind, relent (1 Sm 15:29, Jer 18:8, Jon 3:9).

שׁוּב shûv (8178), Return; qal: repent (Sir 48:15); hiphil: recall (Is 46:8).

1. μετανοῶ metanoō 1sing indic pres act
2. μετανοῆτε metanoēte 2pl subj pres act
3. μετανοεῖτε metanoeite 2pl impr pres act
4. μετανοοῦντι metanoounti dat sing masc part pres act
5. μετανοεῖν metanoein inf pres act
6. μετενόησεν metenoēsen 3sing indic aor act
7. μετενόησαν metenoēsan 3pl indic aor act
8. μετανοήσῃς metanoēsēs 2sing subj aor act
9. μετανοήσῃ metanoēsē 3sing subj aor act
10. μετανοήσωσιν metanoēsōsin 3pl subj aor act
11. μετανόησον metanoēson 2sing impr aor act
12. μετανοήσατε metanoēsate 2pl impr aor act
13. μετανοησάντων metanoēsantōn gen pl masc part aor act
14. μετανοήσουσιν metanoēsousin 3pl indic fut act
15. μετανοῶσιν metanoōsin 3pl subj pres act
16. μετανοήσητε metanoēsēte 2pl subj aor act
17. μετανοῆσαι metanoēsai inf aor act

3	**Repent** ye: for the kingdom of heaven is at hand...	Matt 3:2
3	**Repent:** for the kingdom of heaven is at hand...	4:17
7	upbraid the cities ... because **they repented** not:	11:20
7	they **would have repented** long ago in sackcloth	11:21
7	because **they repented** at the preaching of Jonas;	12:41
3	**repent** ye, and believe the gospel.	Mark 1:15
10	went out, and preached that men **should repent**.	6:12
7	they **had** a great while ago **repented,**	Luke 10:13
7	for they **repented** at the preaching of Jonas;	11:32
2	but, except ye **repent,** ye shall all likewise perish.	13:3
2	but, except ye **repent,** ye shall all likewise perish.	13:5
4	joy ... be in heaven over one sinner that **repenteth,**	15:7
4	there is joy ... over one sinner that **repenteth.**	15:10
14	went unto them from the dead, they **will repent.**	16:30
9	rebuke him; and if he **repent,** forgive him.	17:3
1	saying, I **repent;** thou shalt forgive him.	17:4
12	Then Peter said unto them, **Repent,**	Acts 2:38
12	**Repent** ye therefore, and be converted,	3:19
11	**Repent** therefore of this thy wickedness,	8:22
5	now commandeth all men every where to **repent:**	17:30
5	that they **should repent** and turn to God,	26:20
13	and **have** not **repented** of the uncleanness	2 Co 12:21
11	and **repent,** and do the first works;	Rev 2:5
8	will remove thy candlestick ... except **thou repent.**	2:5
11	**Repent;** or else I will come unto thee quickly,	2:16
9	And I gave her space **to repent** of her fornication;	2:21
6	gave her space to repent ... and **she repented** not.	2:21
17	I have given her time to **repent** (NIV)	2:21
10	great tribulation, except they **repent** of their deeds.	2:22
11	hast received and heard, and hold fast, and **repent.**	3:3
11	be zealous therefore, and **repent.**	3:19
7	not killed by these plagues yet **repented** not	9:20
7	Neither **repented** they of their murders,	9:21
7	and they **repented** not to give him glory.	16:9
7	blasphemed ... and **repented** not of their deeds.	16:11

Classical Greek and Septuagint Usage

The verb *metanoeō* is from *meta* (3196), "change" (in compound words), and *noeō* (3401), "to exercise the mind." In classical Greek it first meant "to perceive afterwards," as in the opposite of *pronoeō* (4165), "to consider in advance" (*Liddell-Scott*). Eventually it came to mean "change one's mind or purpose," and this usage was carried into the Septuagint. When Saul disputed Samuel's claim that the Lord had rejected Saul as king of Israel, Samuel reminded Saul that God "does not lie or *change his mind*; for he is not a man, that he should *change his mind*" (1 Samuel 15:29 [LXX 1 Kings 15:29], NIV; "repent," KJV). In a similar manner, Proverbs 20:25 notes the danger of "reconsidering" a vow after it has already been made. The use of *metanoeō* to mean "repent" in the sense of religious conversion is not found in the Septuagint.

New Testament Usage

The most extensive repentance is a thoroughgoing change in one's thinking, attitudes, and purpose. This is the deep-seated repentance spoken of in passages like Matthew 3:2 and Acts 3:19 where a thorough change of mind is urged. When compared to *metamelomai* (3208) (used 5 times), *metanoeō* (used over 30 times) is much more prevalent, especially when referring to repentance linked to salvation. This repentance is stronger than remorse or emotional regret. *Metanoeō* portrays a change of mind so effective that Luke 15:7,10 assumes salvation for a sinner who has "repented."

This "repentance" is required for entrance into the kingdom of heaven and is a subject of the apostolic preaching in Acts. Unfortunately, Jerome, the translator of the Vulgate, translated *metanoeō* in the imperative as "do penance."

STRONG 3340, BAUER 511-12, MOULTON-MILLIGAN 403-4, KITTEL 4:975-1008, LIDDELL-SCOTT 1115, COLIN BROWN 1:357-59.

3211. μετάνοια metanoia noun

Remorse, repentance, turning about, change of mind.

CROSS-REFERENCE:
μετανοέω metanoeō (3210)

1. **μετανοίας** metanoias gen sing fem
2. **μετάνοιαν** metanoian acc sing fem

1 Bring forth therefore fruits meet for **repentance**:	Matt 3:8
2 I indeed baptize you with water unto **repentance**:	3:11
2 not ... righteous, but sinners to **repentance**.	9:13
1 and preach the baptism **of repentance**	Mark 1:4
2 not to call the righteous, but sinners to **repentance**.	2:17
1 the baptism **of repentance** for the remission of sins;	Luke 3:3
1 Bring forth therefore fruits worthy **of repentance**,	3:8
2 not to call the righteous, but sinners to **repentance**.	5:32
1 ninety and nine just ... which need no **repentance**.	15:7
2 And that **repentance** and remission of sins	24:47
2 and a Saviour, for to give **repentance** to Israel,	Acts 5:31
2 the Gentiles granted **repentance** unto life.	11:18
1 baptism **of repentance** to all the people of Israel.	13:24
1 John ... baptized with the baptism **of repentance**,	19:4
2 **repentance** toward God, and faith toward our Lord..	20:21
1 turn to God, and do works meet for **repentance**.	26:20
2 the goodness of God leadeth thee to **repentance**?	Rom 2:4
2 but that ye sorrowed to **repentance**:	2 Co 7:9
2 For godly sorrow worketh **repentance** to salvation	7:10
2 if God peradventure will give them **repentance**	2 Tm 2:25
1 the foundation **of repentance** from dead works,	Heb 6:1
2 to renew them again unto **repentance**;	6:6
1 for he found no place **of repentance**,	12:17
2 but that all should come to **repentance**.	2 Pt 3:9

Classical Greek

Both the noun *metanoia* and the verb *metanoeō* (3210) in secular Greek primarily mean "to reconsider something, to regret." The term may indicate a change of mind (*nous* [3426]); nevertheless, in classical Greek literature these words never acquire the restricted sense of "repentance" that is so essential to the New Testament. The word group appears seldomly in classical writings, being more common in the vernacular of the people.

Septuagint Usage

The noun *metanoia* is not used at all in the Septuagint. The verb form *metanoeō*, however, does translate the Hebrew *nācham*, "have a change of heart, turn from a former attitude" (of God: 1 Samuel 15:29 [LXX 1 Kings 15:29]; Jeremiah 18:8; Joel 2:13f.; Amos 7:3,6; of men: Jeremiah 8:6).

The most remarkable feature of *metanoia*/*metanoeō* in the Septuagint, however, is that the chief Old Testament word for "repentance," the Hebrew *shûv*, "to turn," is not translated with *metanoeō* at all, but with *epistrephō* (1978) instead (e.g., Hosea 5:4; 6:1; Amos 4:6).

This is even more striking since *metanoia* becomes the principal New Testament word used to mean "repentance" (24 times), while the noun *epistrophē* (1979) occurs only once (Acts 15:3). The verb form *metanoeō* appears 34 times, while the verb *epistrephō* can be found about 40 times; but of these only about one-half are related to "turning" in the sense of religious conversion.

Some have tried to explain this peculiarity by the need for a precise distinction between a "a change of mind" (*meta-noia*) and the stronger idea of "turn around" conveyed by the Hebrew term *shûv*, especially as it was used in the prophetic writings. Although one concedes that the New Testament teaching concerning repentance involves a change of mind, this should not be viewed as in contrast or contradistinction to the Old Testament idea of repentance. The preaching of the prophets did not merely invite external repentance (through the rituals of religion); rather, their chief purpose was to effect a change of mind and heart in the people.

The most obvious explanation for the New Testament choice is that when the New Testament employs *metanoia* as a technical term for conversion, and when it understands *metanoeō* and *epistrephō* synonymously, this is because both of these terms were considered equal to the Hebrew *shûv/shûvah*. They both identify repentance as the same kind of spiritual, moral, and ethical change heralded by the prophets of the Old Testament. It is from this cast that John the Baptist is molded as he comes in the "spirit and power of Elijah" and urges his hearers, "Repent!" (cf. Matthew 3:2).

Any understanding of repentance (*metanoia/metanoeō*) in the New Testament must, therefore, first and foremost rest upon its Old Testament foundation. The concept of repentance plays a major role in the covenant relationship of the Old Testament. It is stressed through two avenues: the cultic ritual expression of repentance and the prophetic idea of internal change.

Old Testament Background

The Old Testament abounds with examples of ceremonial, ritual repentance. Confronted with adversity and threatened with the impending wrath of God, people repeatedly strove to avert such judgment through acts of repentance. When the adversity threatened the entire nation a solemn public fast was frequently proclaimed. This became a central feature of ceremonial repentance (1 Samuel 7:6; 2 Chronicles 20:3; Ezra 8:21; Nehemiah 1:4). A typical example of corporate repentance occurs in Joel 2:11-17. Israel with all its heart "turns" to the Lord with fasting, weeping, and mourning (Joel 2:12). Both the high and low, great and small, joined together, and the priests wept and cried out to the Lord: "Spare thy people, O Lord, and give not thine heritage to reproach, that the heathen should rule over them: wherefore should they say among the people, Where is their God?" (Joel 2:17).

Another sign of repentance was to tear one's garments, to don sackcloth, and to scatter ashes over one's head (Ezra 9:5; 1 Kings 21:27; Nehemiah 9:1; Daniel 9:3). Sometimes people would even make their beds in sackcloth and ashes (Isaiah 58:5; Esther 4:3). Loud cries and weeping often accompanied repentance (Nehemiah 1:4; Ezra 10:1; Hosea 7:14). Above all, repentance was accompanied by a confession of sins (Nehemiah 1:5-11; Daniel 9:3-19). This was especially true for corporate repentance (1 Samuel 7:6).

In the powerful preaching of the prophets, ritualistic repentance without genuine remorse and change came under intense attack. God demands repentance based upon a relationship with Him. At the same time, the prophetic indictment of ceremony should not always be taken as antiritualistic (Joel 2:12; Isaiah 22:12f.). The prophets were only insisting that the ceremonial aspects of repentance be subsumed to a personal, internal commitment to change.

The term *shûv* had been previously linked to turning to the Lord (Deuteronomy 4:30; 30:10; 1 Kings 8:47ff.; 2 Kings 23:25). But the concept of internal change became more crucially shaped by the preaching of the prophets. The thought of "returning to" God and His covenant purpose as well as the idea of "turning away from" sin and rebellion is inherent in *shûv*. Another distinctive mark of the prophet's urging of repentance was its demand for an entirely new attitude toward the Lord and His will. Repentance does not stop at a partial regret (Hosea 6:1-3). Just as sin is a turning away from God, the invitation to repent is an invitation to turn again to Him.

Ezekiel especially emphasized the necessity of individual, personal repentance instead of the more customary plea for corporate change (18:21,27; 33:9,11,14,15). He stressed personal guilt and responsibility. Other prophets used related concepts to reflect this same position. For example, Hosea saw sin as unfaithfulness in the "spiritual marriage" between the Lord and Israel (chapters 1—3). Isaiah spoke of sin in terms of sons who revolted against their fathers (chapters 1,2). Jeremiah simply called it sin to leave the Lord (1:16; 2:13,17,19; 5:7; etc.). In each of the prophets there is given ample evidence of the negative impact of sin upon the nation of Israel. Because the connection with the Lord was not intact, all other relationships became disjointed—with fellow men, with the family of God, with the governmental authorities, with surrounding nations, and so on.

The incentive to repent in order to escape God's judgment was increasingly limited because Israel's sin and rebellion grew larger and larger. Amos cried, "Hate the evil, and love the good" (5:15), but it was drowned out by his other warning of impending doom. The Lord could no longer forgive; His judgment could not be avoided even if one repented (Amos 5:16-27). Hosea saw the inevitability of judgment. Any suggestion of corporate repentance is remote:

"Their deeds do not permit them to return to their God" (Hosea 5:4, NIV). Nevertheless, God would preserve a faithful remnant through His judgments (Hosea 2:17-23; 3:5). The message of Isaiah was virtually identical to Hosea, but he emphasized that the judgment would come because of the people's refusal to repent (see chapters 1—39). Still a remnant would survive the judgment as a result of God's mercy (Isaiah 10:20f.).

Jeremiah in particular admonished the people of Israel with great fervor, calling them to repentance in the hope that they might be saved from the impending wrath and judgment of God (4:1; 26:3; 36:3,7). However, in his preaching there is a somewhat skeptical note: "Can the Ethiopian change his skin, or the leopard his spots? then may ye also do good, that are accustomed to do evil" (Jeremiah 13:23). Nevertheless, in the midst of such despair Jeremiah had an abiding, deep-seated confidence that God would make for himself a new people; He would restore the broken covenant and create a new faithfulness toward God by writing the Law in the hearts of the people (31:33).

At an increasing pace the prophets came to regard repentance as a work of the Lord, who through judgment and discipline was creating a holy and redeemed people for His name. The desire to return to God was viewed as an eschatological gift, the hope of the prophets (Jeremiah 24:7; 31:18). With Isaiah chapters 40—66 and Psalm 51 the thought of repentance finds its fullest expression. Repentance originated from the redeeming grace of God (Isaiah 44:22; Psalm 51:12). It is from this Old Testament understanding of repentance that the New Testament concept is drawn.

Intertestamental Period

In the period between the testaments, "conversion" became extremely "rules oriented" reflecting the legalism which pervaded all of Judaism during that time. The prophetic voice of men like Jeremiah, who called for personal repentance and return to the covenant will of God, gradually diminished. Sin was diminished to being understood only in terms of transgressing the Law, and the Law became less and less associated with the personal will of the Lord. Conversion that demanded a new heart and a new mind, a conversion that comes only through the grace of God, was almost entirely lost during this period in the history of Israel. In its place there came a religion of works which demanded legalistic obedience not only to the Law but to man-made traditions as well (cf. Mark 7:1-23). Yet with revivalistic hope, Malachi foretold of the coming of "Elijah the prophet" who would come before the "great and dreadful day of the LORD" (4:5,6).

New Testament Usage

The first cry to "repent" in the New Testament is on the lips of John the Baptist: "Repent ye: for the kingdom of heaven is at hand" (Matthew 3:2). It is important to notice that the imperative "Repent!" throughout the New Testament, is predicated upon the indicative "The kingdom of God is at hand!" This suggests that repentance is more a gift from God than a duty. The return to God is possible because God himself turns to us and redeems us and rescues us from the power of sin (Luke 1:76-79).

John the Baptist called for complete repentance. It was not limited to a turning away from certain sinful acts (Luke 3:12f.); rather, the totality of one's former life-style was to be dropped and replaced with one lived unto God. John's preaching, moreover, was directed to all peoples, both the "righteous" and the "unrighteous." The true nature of repentance is expressed in its fruits. (See also Filson, "John the Baptist," *International Standard Bible Encyclopedia*, 2:1108-1110.)

John's radical call to repentance was continued by Jesus (Matthew 12:41; cf. 11:20f.). Furthermore, Jesus based His summons on the same belief that it is a gift (see above). God makes repentance possible in Jesus: "I came not to call the righteous, but sinners to repentance" (Luke 5:32). In the life and ministry of Jesus, God demonstrates His goodness and invites sinners to share in His life (cf. Romans 2:4).

Faith in Jesus is the basis for repentance (Mark 1:15). Faith is the positive expression of repentance: we turn to God through Jesus, God's representative. Repentance not only means a radical break with one's former life, but first and foremost it is a positive, confident commitment to God's offer of salvation. To repent is to become a child of God (Matthew 18:1-3).

What is impossible with men is possible with God. He alone grants repentance (Mark 10:27). Repentance is simultaneously a summons to change and a gift for peace. Behind the invitation to repent stands the promise of a new start, forgiveness of sins, the gift of the Holy Spirit, and a new relationship with God (cf. Matthew 9:6; 3:11).

Apostolic preaching clearly summons men and women to repentance (Acts 2:38; 3:19; 5:31; 8:22; passim). According to Hebrews 6:1 repentance is an elementary principle of the faith. To repent is to turn away from evil (Acts 8:22; 3:26; Revelation 2:22; 9:20f.) and to return to God (Acts 20:21; 26:20; 1 Peter 2:25; Revelation 16:9). It is the response of man to the command (Acts 2:38; 17:30) and the gift of God (Acts 5:31; 11:18). Conversion is based on the revelation of salvation in Jesus Christ. It is an eschatological option that God offers prior to judgment (Acts 17:30f.). He grants a period of grace to allow men to repent, and He administers power to experience deliverance from the bondage of sin and evil through faith in Jesus. Repentance is, in its truest sense, "recreation" (2 Corinthians 5:17; Galatians 6:15).

STRONG 3341, BAUER 512, MOULTON-MILLIGAN 404, KITTEL 4:975-1008, LIDDELL-SCOTT 1115, COLIN BROWN 1:357-58.

3212. μεταξύ metaxu adv

In the midst, between, next, meanwhile.

1. μεταξύ metaxu

1 tell him his fault **between** thee and him alone:		Matt 18:15
1 whom ye slew **between** the temple and the altar		23:35
1 which perished **between** the altar and the temple:		Luke 11:51
1 **between** us and you there is a great gulf fixed:		16:26
1 In the **mean while** his disciples prayed him,		John 4:31
1 Peter was sleeping **between** two soldiers,		Acts 12:6
1 might be preached to them the **next** sabbath		13:42
1 And put no difference **between** us and them,		15:9
1 and their thoughts the mean while accusing (NT)		Rom 2:15

Classical Greek

In the classical Greek *metaxu* is primarily used in the sense of "after" or "next" rather than "between" (the *meta* [3196] meaning prevailing in this compound of *meta* and *xun* or *sun* [4713], "with").

Septuagint Usage

The Septuagint uses *metaxu* as "between" (Genesis 31:50, "God is witness betwixt me and thee"; cf. Wisdom of Solomon 18:23), "among" (Wisdom of Solomon 4:10), and "in the midst of" (Wisdom of Solomon 16:19).

New Testament Usage

In the New Testament *metaxu* has several different senses: (1) as a preposition of mutual relation, "one with another" (Matthew 18:15; Acts 15:9; Romans 2:15), (2) as a preposition of place or location, "between" (Matthew 23:35; Luke 11:51; 16:26; Acts 12:6), and (3) as a preposition of time, "meanwhile" (John 4:31), literally "in the week between."

The only New Testament usage of *metaxu* as "next" is in Acts 13:42, "The Gentiles besought that these words might be preached to them the *next* sabbath," but this sense is sometimes found for the word in later Greek writings.

STRONG 3342, BAUER 512-13, MOULTON-MILLIGAN 404, LIDDELL-SCOTT 1115.

3213. μεταπέμπομαι

metapempomai verb

To summon, send for, call for.

COGNATE:
πέμπω pempō (3854)

SYNONYMS:
ἐπικαλέω epikaleō (1926)
καλέω kaleō (2535)
μετακαλέομαι metakaleomai (3203)
παρακαλέω parakaleō (3731)
προσκαλέομαι proskaleomai (4200)
συγκαλέω sunkaleō (4630)
φωνέω phōneō (5291)

לָקַח lāqach (4089), Take; fetch (Gn 27:45).

נָחָה nāchâh (5328), Hiphil: bring (Nm 23:7).

1. μεταπεμπόμενος metapempomenos
  nom sing masc part pres mid
2. μετεπέμψατο metepempsato 3sing indic aor mid
3. μετεπέμψασθε metepempsasthe 2pl indic aor mid
4. μεταπέμψηται metapempsētai 3sing subj aor mid
5. μετάπεμψαι metapempsai 2sing impr aor mid
6. μεταπεμφθείς metapemphtheis
  nom sing masc part aor pass
7. μεταπέμψασθαι metapempsasthai inf aor mid
8. μεταπεμψάμενος metapempsamenos
  nom sing masc part aor mid

5 and **call for** one Simon, whose surname is Peter:		Acts 10:5
7 by an holy angel **to send for** thee into his house,		10:22
6 without gainsaying, as soon as I **was sent for**:		10:29
3 I ask therefore for what intent ye **have sent for** me?		10:29
5 Send men to Joppa, and **call for** Simon,		11:13
8 and when he had **exhorted** them (NASB)		20:1
2 **sent for** Paul, and heard him concerning the faith		24:24
1 wherefore he **sent for** him the oftener,		24:26
4 that he would **send for** him to Jerusalem,		25:3

The verb *metapempomai* occurs only in the Greek middle or passive voice in the New Testament. Of eight occurrences in the New Testament *metapempomai* is always translated "to call for" or "send for." The related verb *pempō* (3854) occurs over 80 times as the most general word for "send," compared to *apostellō* (643) which usually implies sending with a mission. The prefix *meta* (3196), "after," with the general word for "send," *pempō*, gives *metapempomai* a reflexive sense of "calling" back to oneself or "sending" for the purpose of bringing someone back to oneself. The Revised Standard Version translates *metapempomai* "fetch" in Acts 10:5 and 11:13, emphasizing the idea of bringing someone back to the one "calling" or "sending."

STRONG 3343, BAUER 513 (see "metapempō"), MOULTON-MILLIGAN 404, LIDDELL-SCOTT 1115 (see "metapempō").

3214. μεταστρέφω metastrephō verb
To turn about, transform, change.

COGNATE:
  στρέφω strephō (4613)
SYNONYMS:
  ἀλλάσσω allassō (234)
  διαστρέφω diastrephō (1288)
  μετασχηματίζω metaschēmatizō (3215)
  μετατίθημι metatithēmi (3216)
  στρέφω strephō (4613)

הָפַךְ hāphakh (2089), Qal: turn, change (Dt 23:5, Ps 105:25 [104:25], Zep 3:9); niphal: be changed, be turned (Ex 14:5, Lam 5:2, Jl 2:31).

סָבַב sāvav (5621), Turn; niphal: be turned over (Jer 6:12); hiphil: change (2 Chr 36:4).

1. **μεταστρέψαι** metastrepsai inf aor act
2. **μεταστραφήτω** metastraphētō 3sing impr aor pass
3. **μεταστραφήσεται** metastraphēsetai 3sing indic fut pass

3 The sun **shall be turned** into darkness,......... Acts 2:20
1 and would **pervert** the gospel of Christ.......... Gal 1:7
2 let your laughter **be turned** to mourning,......... Jas 4:9

This verb is a compound of *meta* (3196) plus *strephō* (4613). Other related compound verbs like *apostrephō* (648), *diastrephō* (1288), *epistrephō* (1978), and *hupostrephō* (5128) portray the same basic idea, but each prefix gives a different shade of meaning when used with the various Greek case combinations. *Metastrephō* is used three times in the New Testament. In Acts 2:20 it means to "turn" or "change" one thing into another; i.e., the sunlight into darkness. *Metastrephō* speaks of making a drastic change such as changing one thing into its opposite (see James 4:9, laughter turned into grief). In Galatians 1:7 Paul spoke of some preachers who wanted to "pervert" the gospel of Christ—denoting a negative change by misrepresentation or twisting of truth. All of these occurrences in the New Testament carry the same meaning, i.e., "to turn, to transform, to change" or "to change from one state to another" (cf. *Moulton-Milligan*).

STRONG 3344, BAUER 513, MOULTON-MILLIGAN 404, KITTEL 7:729, LIDDELL-SCOTT 1117.

3215. μετασχηματίζω metaschēmatizō verb
Change, fashion, figure, transform.

COGNATE:
  σχῆμα schēma (4828)
SYNONYMS:
  ἀλλάσσω allassō (234)
  μεταστρέφω metastrephō (3214)
  μετατίθημι metatithēmi (3216)
  στρέφω strephō (4613)

1. **μετεσχημάτισα** meteschēmatisa 1sing indic aor act
2. **μετασχηματίσει** metaschēmatisei 3sing indic fut act
3. **μετασχηματίζεται** metaschēmatizetai 3sing indic pres mid
4. **μετασχηματίζονται** metaschēmatizontai 3pl indic pres mid
5. **μετασχηματιζόμενοι** metaschēmatizomenoi nom pl masc part pres mid

1 in a figure **transferred** to myself and to Apollos..... 1 Co 4:6
5 **transforming themselves** into the apostles of Christ. 2 Co 11:13
3 Satan himself **is transformed** into an angel of light...... 11:14
4 no great thing if his ministers also **be transformed**...... 11:15
2 Who shall **change** our vile body,................Php 3:21

Classical Greek
This verb—a compound of *meta* (3196), "with," and *schēma* (4828), "outward form, figure, fashion"—in classical Greek has the meaning of "transforming, altering" or "changing" the outward appearance of a person or thing. It was also used in the field of astronomy to refer to the changing of the constellations (cf. *Liddell-Scott*).

Septuagint Usage
Metaschēmatizō is found in the Septuagint in 4 Maccabees 9:22 describing the transformation of the martyrs into incorruptibility. In the Symmachus version, 1 Samuel 28:8 (LXX 1 Kings 28:8) uses the verb in reference to the disguising of Saul.

New Testament Usage
The New Testament writers make a clear distinction between the verbs *metaschēmatizō* and *metamorphoō* (3209). While they share the first part of the compound, *meta*, there is a great difference between the meanings of the

root words *schēma* and *morphē* (3307). *Schēma* refers to that which is changeable, the outward "fashion" of a person or thing, e.g., a person's gestures, speech, clothing. *Morphē*, however, denotes the distinctive character, nature, the very essence of the person or thing. The verb used to express the kind of change which occurs in the Transfiguration is not *metaschēmatizō* but *metamorphoō*, a change deeper than Christ's clothing or merely the addition of a glow (Matthew 17:2). On the other hand, when Paul spoke of Satan becoming an angel of light, or of the false prophets transforming themselves into apostles, etc. (2 Corinthians 11:13-15), he used the verb *metaschēmatizō*, denoting by the choice that the change is an outward one only, not touching their essence.

Paul was the only New Testament writer to use this word. Besides the above mentioned references in 2 Corinthians, he used it two more times. In Philippians 3:21 it indicates the "change" that will occur in the bodies of believers upon their resurrection, and in 1 Corinthians 4:6 *metaschēmatizō* is used to denote the fashion in which Paul expressed himself.

STRONG 3345, BAUER 513, MOULTON-MILLIGAN 404, KITTEL 7:957-58, LIDDELL-SCOTT 1117, COLIN BROWN 1:708-10; 3:864.

3216. μετατίθημι metatithēmi verb

Carry over, transpose, exchange, change, translate, turn away.

COGNATES:
ἀμετάθετος ametathetos (274)
μετάθεσις metathesis (3201)
τίθημι tithēmi (4935)

SYNONYMS:
ἀλλάσσω allassō (234)
μεθίστημι methistēmi (3150)
μεταστρέφω metastrephō (3214)
μετασχηματίζω metaschēmatizō (3215)
στρέφω strephō (4613)

לָקַח lāqach (4089), Take (Gn 5:24).

מוֹט môṭ (4267), Fall (Ps 46:2 [45:2]).

סוּג sûgh (5657), Go back; hiphil: move (Dt 27:17, Prv 23:10, Hos 5:10).

סוּת sûth (5684), Hiphil: incite (1 Kgs 21:25 [20:25]).

פָּלָא pālā' (6623), Be too hard; hiphil: do something marvelous (Is 29:14).

שׁוּב shûv (8178), Return; be turned (Is 29:17).

1. μετατιθέντες metatithentes
   nom pl masc part pres act

2. μετέθηκεν metethēken 3sing indic aor act
3. μετατίθεσθε metatithesthe 2pl indic pres mid
4. μετατιθεμένης metatithemenēs
   gen sing fem part pres mid
5. μετετέθη metetethē 3sing indic aor pass
6. μετετέθησαν metetethēsan 3pl indic aor pass

6 And were carried over into Sychem,................Acts 7:16
3 I marvel that ye are so soon **removed** from him......Gal 1:6
4 For the priesthood **being changed**,.................Heb 7:12
5 Enoch **was translated** that he should not see death;....11:5
2 was not found, because God had **translated** him:.......11:5
1 **turning** the grace of our God into lasciviousness,....Jude 1:4

Classical Greek

In classical, secular Greek this verb (derived from *meta* [3196], "with, after," and *tithēmi* [4935], "to put, place") means "to bring to, set in another place," either literally or metaphorically. It is used to refer to the changing or altering of an agreement, a name, an opinion, as well as the changing of the office of high priest. Some additional meanings of the word are to change or transfer from one school of philosophy to another, to give oneself over to the Roman party, or to desert the army (see *Liddell-Scott*).

Septuagint Usage

In the Septuagint *metatithēmi* is used 17 times to translate 6 different Hebrew words. It translates the Hebrew *sûgh* meaning to "move" a boundary marker or boundary stone over a few feet and thus steal a strip of the neighbor's property (Deuteronomy 27:17). God "translated" (Hebrew *laqach*, "took") Enoch from earth to heaven (Genesis 5:24). Other uses include "warding off" an attack (3 Maccabees 1:16), "transplanting" people (Isaiah 29:14, where the Septuagint has a reading that differs from the Hebrew), and "turning away" (in the sense of apostasy) from the fathers (2 Maccabees 7:24).

New Testament Usage

The New Testament uses the verb six times. Stephen used it of transferring the bodies of some of the patriarchs from Egypt to Shechem (Acts 7:16). Paul used it to show surprise that the Galatians so soon deserted Him (God) who called them into the grace of Christ and turned away to "another gospel" (Galatians 1:6, where the Greek implies that their apostasy was not complete but was in progress; thus there was still opportunity for them to change their ways). Hebrews uses it once in 7:12 of a change in the priesthood (in the sense of passing it on from one person to another) and thus calling for a change in the Law. Then Hebrews uses it twice in 11:5 of the translation of Enoch to heaven without dying. This follows the Septuagint's usage of *metatithēmi* as "changing the position of, conveying to another place" (Genesis 5:24). Finally, Jude uses it nonliterally of "turning" ("perverting") the grace of God into lasciviousness or dissoluteness (Jude 4).

STRONG 3346, BAUER 513, MOULTON-MILLIGAN 404-5, KITTEL 8:161-62, LIDDELL-SCOTT 1117, COLIN BROWN 3:601-2.

3216B. μετατρέπω metatrepō verb
Turn around, be turned, be moved, overthrow.

CROSS-REFERENCE:
ἐπιτρέπω epitrepō (1994)

1. μετατραπήτω metatrapētō 3sing impr aor pass

1 let your laughter be turned into mourning, (NASB)...Jas 4:9

In this term the preposition *meta* (3196), "with, after, change," combines and intensifies the verb *trepō*, "to turn, direct, change." The term has several usages in classical Greek: "overthrow"; "turn back" or "away"; "change" (as in changing one's way of thinking); "turn oneself around"; and "look back," thus "care for" or "show regard for" (*Liddell-Scott*). In James 4:9 this verb is employed when the apostle commanded his readers to be radically changed. In their repentance, their mirth was to be "turned" or changed into mourning and their delight into dejection.

BAUER 513, MOULTON-MILLIGAN 405, LIDDELL-SCOTT 1117.

3217. μετέπειτα metepeita adv
Afterward, then, later.

1. μετέπειτα metepeita

1 For ye know how that afterward,............Heb 12:17

Metepeita occurs only in Hebrews 12:17 in the New Testament. This usage clearly refers to the time of Esau's attempt to receive his birthright, which was subsequent to the time when he sold it for food. The word is used sparingly in ancient literature and in the Septuagint. *Moulton-Milligan* documents occurrences in the papyri, translating *matepeita* "thereafter." According to Vine *metepeita* does not explicitly indicate an event immediately following the preceding as *hexēs* (1819) does in Luke 7:11 (*Expository Dictionary*, "After, Afterward").

STRONG 3347, BAUER 514, MOULTON-MILLIGAN 405, LIDDELL-SCOTT 1119.

3218. μετέχω metechō verb
Share, have a share, partake, participate.

COGNATES:
  ἔχω echō (2174)
  μετοχή metochē (3222)
  μέτοχος metochos (3223)
  συμμέτοχος summetochos (4681)
SYNONYMS:
  κοινωνέω koinōneō (2814)
  μερίζω merizō (3177)
  μεταδίδωμι metadidōmi (3200)

אֵת 'ēth (882), With (Prv 5:17).

1. μετέχω metechō 1sing indic pres act
2. μετέχομεν metechomen 1pl indic pres act
3. μετέχουσιν metechousin 3pl indic pres act
4. μετέχων metechōn nom sing masc part pres act
5. μετέχειν metechein inf pres act
6. μετέσχεν meteschen 3sing indic aor act
7. μετέσχηκεν meteschēken 3sing indic perf act

5 thresheth in hope should **be partaker** of his hope.... 1 Co 9:10
3 If others **be partakers** of this power over you,.......... 9:12
2 for we are all **partakers** of that one bread............. 10:17
5 ye cannot **be partakers** of the Lord's table,............ 10:21
1 For if I by grace **be a partaker**,..................... 10:30
6 he also himself likewise **took part** of the same;....... Heb 2:14
4 For every one **that useth** milk is unskilful............. 5:13
7 For he ... **pertaineth** to another tribe,................ 7:13

Classical Greek
In classical Greek *metechō* is frequently used to describe the partaking of something common in the relationship between two people or things. Philosophers used it to express a participation of an individual spirit in the universal spirit. The connection between the lower and the higher or between men and god(s) was also seen as participation.

Septuagint Usage
Although *metechō* rarely occurs in the Septuagint to translate a Hebrew equivalent, its basic meaning is "to share." In the papyri the same meaning is evident (cf. *Moulton-Milligan*).

New Testament Usage
Generally, in the New Testament *metechō* and *koinōneō* (2814) overlap in meaning. *Metechō* also means "to share" or "to participate in." Sharing in the life of the righteous with its various experiences is illustrated in the Lord's table (1 Corinthians 10:17,21). Paul spoke of sharing in the benefits and labors of the Christian life (1 Corinthians 9:10,12).

When referring to Christ's sharing (participating) in human life, Hebrews declares that He shared by His own flesh and blood (Hebrews 2:14). Belonging to a tribe also indicates His participation (Hebrews 7:13). Lastly, *metechō* ("participation") can mean "to eat," "to drink," or "to enjoy," especially regarding foods (cf. Hebrews 5:13).

STRONG 3348, BAUER 514, MOULTON-MILLIGAN 405, KITTEL 2:830-32, LIDDELL-SCOTT 1120, COLIN BROWN 1:635-36,639.

3219. μετεωρίζομαι
meteōrizomai verb
Anxious, troubled, unsettled, worried, be in suspense.

SYNONYMS:
ἀδημονέω adēmoneō (84)
μεριμνάω merimnaō (3179)

גָּבַהּ gāvahh (1391), Be high; hiphil: soar (Ob 4).

נָשָׂא nāsāʾ (5558), Lift up, carry; niphal: be raised (Mi 4:1).

רוּם rûm (7597), Qal: be haughty (Ps 131:1 [130:1]); rise (Ez 10:16); niphal: rise (Ez 10:19).

1. μετεωρίζεσθε meteōrizesthe 2pl impr pres mid
1 neither be ye of doubtful mind....................Luke 12:29

Classical Greek
In classical Greek and in the papyri *meteōrizomai* means "to raise on high," "to exalt," or "to suspend." It implies the suspending of an object or even a person in midair. Figuratively, *meteōrizomai* is used in two ways: (1) "to raise up someone by hope," "to lift up oneself," "to be proud or arrogant"; (2) "to be unsettled, anxious, tense" or "to be suspended between fear and hope" (*Liddell-Scott*).

Septuagint Usage
The Septuagint uses *meteōrizomai* concerning "the lifting up" of cherubim or the "mounting up" of an eagle (Ezekiel 10:16; Obadiah 4). Also it is used in the sense of "being exalted" as in the exaltation of the Lord's house (Micah 4:1). Being arrogant or exalted in one's own mind is the negative sense of the word (Psalm 131:1 [LXX 130:1]).

New Testament Usage
In the New Testament *meteōrizomai* is used only once (Luke 12:29). The context indicates the second and less familiar meaning of "being anxious, doubtful" or suspended between fear and hope. Jesus said that all who seek the kingdom of God first (Luke 12:31) will have no need to worry about all the things the "nations of the world seek after" (verse 30).

STRONG 3349, BAUER 514, MOULTON-MILLIGAN 405, KITTEL 4:630-31, LIDDELL-SCOTT 1120 (see "meteōrizō").

3220. μετοικεσία metoikesia noun
Deportation, migration, transportation.

CROSS-REFERENCE:
οἰκέω oikeō (3474)

גּוֹלָה gôlāh (1506), Exile, captivity (2 Kgs 24:16, 1 Chr 5:22, Na 3:10).

גָּלוּת gālûth (1588), Exiles (Ob 20).

מִשְׁבָּת mishbāth (5054), Ruin (Lam 1:7—only some Alexandrinus texts).

1. μετοικεσίας metoikesias gen sing fem
2. μετοικεσίαν metoikesian acc sing fem

1 about the time they were carried away to Babylon:...Matt 1:11
2 And after the deportation to Babylon,................. 1:12
1 from David until the carrying away into Babylon........ 1:17
1 and from the carrying away into Babylon............... 1:17

The noun *metoikesia* occurs only four times in the New Testament and only in Matthew's Gospel. It is a compound word from the prefix *meta* (3196), which means change, and *oikia* (3477) which denotes "house" or "dwelling." According to Louw and Nida these combine to produce the compound form *metoikesia* which means "to cause someone to move to another place, to change the place of his residence" or "to resettle" (*Greek-English Lexicon*, 1:732). In Matthew 1:11,13,17 (twice) *metoikesia* is used specifically in connection with the Jewish people who were "carried away" to another place of habitation ("deported" to Babylon as exiles) on account of their idolatry and lack of repentance towards God. In that era "resettling" conquered people was a common practice of nations which wanted to break the spirit of their subjects and to destroy their nationalistic ambitions. In Acts 7:4 the verb *metoikizō* (3221) refers to God's moving Abraham to another place. However, *metoikesia* is used exclusively in the New Testament for "deportation" of Jews by an enemy nation. This is in contrast to those Jews who were scattered to other parts of the world for other reasons (see *diaspora* [1284], 1 Peter 1:1).

STRONG 3350, BAUER 514, MOULTON-MILLIGAN 405, LIDDELL-SCOTT 1121, COLIN BROWN 1:685.

3221. μετοικίζω metoikizō verb
Transfer, move to another place, emigrate, resettle.
CROSS-REFERENCE:
οἰκέω oikeō (3474)

גָּלָה gālâh (1580), Qal: go into exile, depart (Lam 1:3, Hos 10:5); hiphil: carry away into exile, send into exile (1 Chr 5:6, Jer 20:4, Am 5:27).

גָּרַשׁ gārash (1691), Piel: drive out (Jgs 2:3—Codex Alexandrinus only).

1. μετῴκισεν metōkisen 3sing indic aor act
2. μετοικιῶ metoikiō 1sing indic fut act

1 removed him into this land, wherein ye now dwell....Acts 7:4
2 and I will carry you away beyond Babylon.............. 7:43

The verb *metoikizō* is related to the noun *metoikesia* (3220). *Metoikizō* means "moving and resettling in another place." In Acts 7:4 it is used to emphasize divine purpose and initiative when God led Abraham to move from Haran to Canaan upon the death of his father. God "removed" or "resettled" Abraham. It is also used to mean deportation by an antagonist as in Acts 7:43 where God spoke to Israel and alluded to His using an enemy king to "carry away" the Jews to Babylon. The documented occurrences in the papyri contain the same meaning (cf. *Moulton-Milligan*). According to Vine there are several Greek words that have variations of meaning: "to carry," "to bring," etc., but none seem to duplicate the verb *metoikizō* (*Expository Dictionary*, "Carry," "Remove").

STRONG 3351, BAUER 514, MOULTON-MILLIGAN 405, LIDDELL-SCOTT 1121.

3222. μετοχή metochē noun
Partnership, fellowship, sharing, common interest, participation.
COGNATE:
μετέχω metechō (3218)
SYNONYM:
κοινωνία koinōnia (2815)

חָבַר chāvar (2357), Be united; pual: compacted (Ps 122:3 [121:3]).

1. μετοχή metochē nom sing fem

1 fellowship ... righteousness with unrighteousness? .... 2 Co 6:14

The noun *metochē* occurs only one time in the New Testament. In 2 Corinthians 6:14 the absolute lack of "common interest" or ground for "fellowship" between righteousness (*dikaiosunē* [1336]) and lawlessness (*anomia* [455]) is emphasized. *Metochē* refers to the partnership, not the partners, emphasizing the active relationship based on shared purposes and activity more than the people involved. For this reason *Bauer* suggests "sharing" or "participation" as definitions. The bond between believers, however, is described by a different word, *koinōnia* (2815), the more common word for Christian "fellowship." Those who share a common heritage are described by the objective *metochos* (3223), "partakers of ... " (Hebrews 3:1,14).

STRONG 3352, BAUER 514, MOULTON-MILLIGAN 406, KITTEL 2:830-32, LIDDELL-SCOTT 1121, COLIN BROWN 1:635-39.

3223. μέτοχος metochos adj
Partaking, sharing, participating, a partner, a companion.
COGNATE:
μετέχω metechō (3218)
SYNONYMS:
ἑταῖρος hetairos (2062)
κοινωνός koinōnos (2817)
συγκοινωνός sunkoinōnos (4642)

חָבַר chāvar (2357), Qal: be joined (Hos 4:17); pual: compacted (Pss 122:3 [121:3]—Codex Alexandrinus only).

חָבֵר chāvēr (2358), Fellow, companion (Pss 45:7 [44:7], 119:63 [118:63], Eccl 4:10).

1. μέτοχοι metochoi nom pl masc
2. μετόχοις metochois dat pl masc
3. μετόχους metochous acc pl masc

2 And they beckoned unto their **partners**,............. Luke 5:7
3 with the oil of gladness above thy **fellows**............Heb 1:9
1 holy brethren, **partakers** of the heavenly calling,........ 3:1
1 For we are made **partakers** of Christ,................... 3:14
3 and were made **partakers** of the Holy Ghost,........... 6:4
1 chastisement, whereof all are **partakers**,................ 12:8

Classical Greek and Septuagint Usage
In classical Greek the meaning of *metochos* is related to the root *echō* (2174), "to have," as in a mystical having of a god. Later the idea developed of man the lower being participating (*metochos*) in the higher world of the divine. The Septuagint uses *metochos* infrequently. When used it primarily translates "friend," "companion," or "partner." However, *metochos* is more common in the papyri where it means "an associate," "colleague," or even "a joint owner" (*Moulton-Milligan*).

New Testament Usage
The New Testament, not unlike the Septuagint and the papyri, uses *metochos* as a noun to

mean "partner" or "colleague" (Luke 5:7). With the exception of Luke 5:7 *metochos* is found only in Hebrews and is normally an adjective meaning "sharing," "partaking," or "participating."

For example, Christians are called to be sharers or "partakers" in the "heavenly calling" (Hebrews 3:1). Hebrews also has the idea of participation in Christ with a particular focus on sharing in His sufferings and in His endurance (3:14; 6:4). A perseverance that holds fast to the Faith recognizes participation in the chastisement of true sonship (12:8).

STRONG 3353, BAUER 514, MOULTON-MILLIGAN 406, KITTEL 2:830-32, LIDDELL-SCOTT 1122, COLIN BROWN 1:635-36,639.

3224. μετρέω metreō verb

Measure.

COGNATES:
ἄμετρος ametros (278)
ἀντιμετρέω antimetreō (485)
μετρητής metrētēs (3225)
μετριοπαθέω metriopatheō (3226)
μετρίως metriōs (3227)
μέτρον metron (3228)
σιτομέτριον sitometrion (4475)

מָדַד mādhadh (4200), Measure (Nm 35:5, Ru 3:15, Is 40:12).

1. **μετρεῖτε** metreite 2pl indic pres act
2. **μετροῦντες** metrountes nom pl masc part pres act
3. **ἐμέτρησεν** emetrēsen 3sing indic aor act
4. **μετρήσῃς** metrēsēs 2sing subj aor act
5. **μετρήσῃ** metrēsē 3sing subj aor act
6. **μέτρησον** metrēson 2sing impr aor act
7. **μετρηθήσεται** metrēthēsetai 3sing indic fut pass

```
1 and with what measure ye mete, ... be measured.....Matt 7:2
7 it will be measured to you. (NASB)................... 7:2
1 with what measure ye mete, it shall be measured....Mark 4:24
7 measure ye mete, it shall be measured to you:.......... 4:24
1 For with the same measure that ye mete withal it...Luke 6:38
2 but they measuring themselves by themselves,......2 Co 10:12
6 and measure the temple of God, and the altar,..... Rev 11:1
4 But the court ... leave out, and measure it not;........ 11:2
5 had a golden reed to measure the city,................ 21:15
3 and he measured the city with the reed,................ 21:16
3 And he measured the wall thereof,...................... 21:17
```

Classical Greek and Septuagint Usage

This is a very common verb in classical Greek with a wide variety of meanings. *Liddell-Scott* cites many examples of *metreō* as a general word for "measure" of space, number (e.g., "count") and time. It is used only six times in the Septuagint, usually to translate the Hebrew term *mādhadh*, "measure." In Numbers 35:5 *metreō* is used as a "measure" of space in the instructions for the apportionment of the inheritance for the Levites. In Ruth 3:15 it is used as a "measure" of number when Boaz gave Ruth a very generous amount of the freshly harvested barley to show his goodwill toward her. *Metreō* is also used in a figurative sense of God's incomparable greatness. In Isaiah 40:12 the prophet rhetorically asked if there was anyone who could "measure" even the extent of God's creation, much less instruct the Creator (verses 13,14).

New Testament Usage

The nine occurrences of *metreō* in the New Testament also reflect a variety of usages. In the Synoptics, *metreō* is used figuratively as a "measure" of judgment. Jesus warned His disciples not to judge others, for the attitude they had toward others would affect the divine judgment they would receive (Matthew 7:2; Mark 4:24; Luke 6:38). Paul's use of *metreō* reflects a similar figurative sense as found in the Synoptics. In 2 Corinthians 10:12, he ironically disassociated himself with those who "measure" their character relatively, in relation to others; that is, they do not use a standard that is eternal and unchanging, namely, Christ Jesus. The five remaining occurrences of *metreō* are all in Revelation and each describes a "measure" of space (e.g., the "temple of God," 11:1; the "new Jerusalem," 21:15-17).

STRONG 3354, BAUER 514, MOULTON-MILLIGAN 406, KITTEL 4:632-34, LIDDELL-SCOTT 1122, COLIN BROWN 3:402.

3225. μετρητής metrētēs noun

Measurer, measure, a liquid measure.

CROSS-REFERENCE:
μετρέω metreō (3224)

בַּת bath (1352), Bath (2 Chr 4:5).
סְאָה sᵉʾāh (5613), Measure (1 Kgs 18:32).
פּוּרָה pûrāh (6576), Measure (Hg 2:16 [2:17]).

1. **μετρητάς** metrētas acc pl masc

```
1 containing two or three firkins apiece............... John 2:6
```

The noun *metrētēs* is related to the verb form *metreō* (3224). *Metrētēs* occurs three times in the canonical portions of the Septuagint (1 Kings 18:32 [LXX 3 Kings 18:32]; 2 Chronicles 4:5; Haggai 2:16) but only one time in the New Testament, in John 2:6 where it is translated "firkins" by the KJV. The word *metrētēs* refers to a utensil used for measuring liquids and contains about the same volume as the Hebrew *bath*: 72 sextarii, approximately 39 liters or 9 gallons (according to the writings of Josephus; cf. *Bauer*). Other archaeological research suggests a *bath* contained 22 liters, roughly half the size of the *bath* described by Josephus. Perhaps this supports the idea that originally the *bath* represented the capacity of water an Israelite "daughter" (Hebrew, *bath* also) could carry from the well to the house (Cook, "Weights and Measures," *International Standard Bible Encyclopedia*, 4:1050f.). In the papyri *metrētēs* came to mean a general word for measure, thus including more than the specific 72 sextarii technically assigned to it. The papyri indicate that two *metrētēs* of oil constitute an "ass' load." Using this system of measurement, tax officials could calculate duty tax by simply counting animals (cf. *Moulton-Milligan*).

STRONG 3355, BAUER 514, MOULTON-MILLIGAN 406, LIDDELL-SCOTT 1122, COLIN BROWN 3:403.

3226. μετριοπαθέω
metriopatheō verb
To have compassion, deal gently, to be gently disposed toward.

COGNATES:
μετρέω metreō (3224)
πάθος pathos (3669)

1. μετριοπαθεῖν metriopathein inf pres act

1 Who can have compassion on the ignorant,.......... Heb 5:2

The verb *metriopatheō* occurs only once in the New Testament (Hebrews 5:20). This word is derived from two words: *metriōs* (3227), implying moderation, and *paschō* (3819), "to suffer." The noun *pathēma* (3667) from a similar root refers to the things one has suffered or to the suffering itself. In reference to Christ, Hebrews 5:2 uses *metriopatheō* to indicate His "compassion" or "moderate bearing with" one's faults and infirmities. This word indicates the ability to consider another's failures and yet not vent a full degree of passion in the form of anger, displeasure, or grief. *Metriopatheō* does not occur in the Septuagint. The noun and adjective forms occur in ancient and papyri literature (*Moulton-Milligan*). Vine cites other words used in the New Testament that approach the same meaning as *metriopatheō* such as *makrothumeō* (3086), "to be long-suffering,"

oikteirō (3489), "to have pity," and *sumpatheō* (4685), "to suffer with" (*Expository Dictionary*, "Compassion," "Bear").

STRONG 3356, BAUER 514-15, MOULTON-MILLIGAN 406, LIDDELL-SCOTT 1122, COLIN BROWN 5:938.

3227. μετρίως metriōs adv
Moderately.

CROSS-REFERENCE:
μετρέω metreō (3224)

1. μετρίως metriōs

1 and were not a little comforted.................... Acts 20:12

Classical Greek and Septuagint Usage
While *metriōs* occurs only once in the New Testament, it does appear several times in classical Greek literature and once in the Septuagint (2 Maccabees 15:38). The word usually has the sense of "moderately, sufficiently" or "temperately." The adjective forms *metrios* or *metrion* also occur many times in classical Greek literature.

In the extra-Biblical literature *metriōs* has different shades of meaning which are not always obvious. There are quotations that suggest meanings that include "considerably" and "moderately" and an instance that has been interpreted to mean "virtuous" (*Moulton-Milligan*).

New Testament Usage
In Acts 20:12 the people were comforted "not" *metriōs*, "considerably, exceedingly, greatly," i.e., "not a little" (KJV). The meaning is quite obvious in this context.

STRONG 3357, BAUER 515, MOULTON-MILLIGAN 406-7, LIDDELL-SCOTT 1122.

3228. μέτρον metron noun
A measure.

COGNATE:
μετρέω metreō (3224)

SYNONYMS:
κόρος koros (2857)
σάτον saton (4424)
χοῖνιξ choinix (5354)

אֵיפָה 'êphāh (380), Measure, ephah (Dt 25:14, Ez 46:14, Zec 5:8ff.).

אַמָּה 'ammāh (527), Cubit (Ez 47:3).

בַּת bath (1352), Bath (2 Chr 2:10).

יָד yādh (3135), Hand; way (Ez 48:1—Codex Alexandrinus only).

מָדַד mādhadh (4200), Measure (Ez 42:20—Codex Alexandrinus only).

מִדָּה middāh (4201), Measure, section (Ex 26:2, Neh 3:19f., Ez 40:32f.).

מֵמַד memādh (4602), Measurement (Jb 38:5).

מְשׂוּרָה mesûrāh (5025), Measure (Ez 4:11,16).

סְאָה seʾāh (5613), Measure (Gn 18:6).

קָו qāw (7241), Measuring line, line (2 Kgs 21:13, Lam 2:8).

קָוֶה qāweh (7246), Measuring line (Zec 1:16).

שָׁלִישׁ shālîsh (8386), Measure (Ps 80:5 [79:5]).

1. μέτρου metrou gen sing neu
2. μέτρῳ metrō dat sing neu
3. μέτρον metron nom/acc sing neu

2	and with what **measure** ye mete, ... be measured....	Matt 7:2
3	Fill ye up then the **measure** of your fathers............	23:32
2	with what **measure** ye mete, it shall be measured...	Mark 4:24
3	good **measure**, pressed down, and shaken together,..	Luke 6:38
2	For with the same **measure** that ye mete withal it.......	6:38
1	for God giveth not the Spirit by **measure** unto him.	John 3:34
3	God hath dealt to every man the **measure** of faith.	Rom 12:3
3	but according to the **measure** of the rule............	2 Co 10:13
1	a **measure** to reach even unto you...................	10:13
3	grace according to the **measure** of the gift of Christ...	Eph 4:7
3	the **measure** of the stature of the fulness of Christ:......	4:13
2	the effectual working in the **measure** of every part,......	4:16
3	a gold **measuring** rod to measure (NASB)..........	Rev 21:15
3	according to the **measure** of a man,...................	21:17

Classical Greek
Metron occurs very frequently in classical Greek. The broad meaning includes the standard by which something is measured whether of content, space, length, or weight. The word may refer either to the standard of measure, i.e., the vessel, weight, or rule which is used as the tool for measuring. It may refer to the object which has been gauged—as a "measure" (*metron*) of barley. *Metron* may also be used to refer to abstract quantities as a "measure" of wisdom or of time. Men who were responsible for inspecting and maintaining the standards of measure were called *metronomoi*—a compound composed of *metron* and *nomos* (3414), "law."

Septuagint Usage
Metron is used over 50 times in the Septuagint. In Genesis 18:6 Abraham referred to "three *measures* of fine meal." The Levites were charged with many responsibilities in the tabernacle, including measuring quantities of items involved in the worship ceremony (1 Chronicles 23:29). Moulton-Milligan documents several occurrences of *metron* in the papyri literature. *Metron* refers to a "measure" of wheat, to a royal standard of "measure," and even to a "measure" of the pulse rate or heartbeat.

New Testament Usage
Metron also occurs several times in the New Testament. The word refers to the instrument used for measuring, whether a vessel measuring volume or a rod measuring length (cf. Matthew 7:2; Luke 6:38). In John 3:34 we are told that when God gives the Holy Spirit, He is not limited by some sort of "measure" (*metron*). It is also implied (Ephesians 4:7) that when God's grace is given according to the "measure of . . . Christ," there is an abundant and generous "measure." Most of the occurrences of *metron* in the New Testament refer to some figurative type of "measure" as in Romans 12:3 ("measure of faith"), and Ephesians 4:13 ("measure of the stature of the fulness of Christ").

STRONG 3358, BAUER 515, MOULTON-MILLIGAN 407, KITTEL 4:632-34, LIDDELL-SCOTT 1123, COLIN BROWN 3:402-4.

3229. μέτωπον metōpon noun
Forehead.

CROSS-REFERENCE:
πρόσωπον prosōpon (4241)

מֵצַח mētsach (4860), Forehead (1 Sm 17:49, 2 Chr 26:19f., Ez 9:4).

1. μετώπου metōpou gen sing neu
2. μέτωπον metōpon nom/acc sing neu
3. μετώπων metōpōn gen pl neu

3	sealed the servants of our God in their **foreheads**.....	Rev 7:3
3	which have not the seal of God in their **foreheads**.......	9:4
2	a mark in their right hand, or in their **foreheads**:......	13:16
3	his Father's name written in their **foreheads**............	14:1
1	receive his mark in his **forehead**, or in his hand,......	14:9
2	And upon her **forehead** was a name written,...........	17:5
2	his mark upon their **foreheads**, or in their hands;......	20:4
3	and his name shall be in their **foreheads**..............	22:4

The noun *metōpon* occurs eight times in the New Testament and only in the Book of Revelation. It is used to refer to the area of the face above the eyes known as the forehead. The word derives from *meta* (3196) and *ops*, "eye" (or "face"). The citations in Revelation 7:3; 9:4; 13:16; etc., may parallel a custom of identifying slaves by branding the forehead (*Moulton-Milligan*). All the occurrences of *metōpon* in Revelation refer to this mark in the forehead indicating ownership, identity, or association.

STRONG 3359, BAUER 516, MOULTON-MILLIGAN 407, LIDDELL-SCOTT 1123.

3230. μέχρι mechri prep
As far as, until, unto.

1. μέχρι mechri
2. μέχρις mechris

1	in Sodom, it would have remained **until** this day....	Matt 11:23
1	Let both grow together **until** the harvest:	13:30
1	commonly reported among the Jews **until** this day	28:15
2	generation ... not pass, **till** all these things be done.	Mark 13:30
1	Prophets were proclaimed **until** John; (NASB)	Luke 16:16
1	Four days ago I was fasting **until** this hour;	Acts 10:30
1	and continued his speech **until** midnight.	20:7
1	Nevertheless death reigned from Adam to Moses,	Rom 5:14
1	from Jerusalem, and round about **unto** Illyricum,	15:19
2	in labor **until** Christ is formed in you (NASB)	Gal 4:19
1	**Till** we all come in the unity of the faith,	Eph 4:13
1	and became obedient **unto** death,	Phlp 2:8
1	for the work of Christ he was nigh **unto** death,	2:30
1	**until** the appearing of our Lord Jesus Christ:	1 Tm 6:14
1	suffer trouble, as an evil doer, even **unto** bonds;	2 Tm 2:9
1	and the rejoicing of the hope firm **unto** the end.	Heb 3:6
1	beginning of our confidence stedfast **unto** the end;	3:14
1	imposed on them **until** the time of reformation.	9:10
2	not yet resisted **unto** blood, striving against sin.	12:4

Classical Greek
The term *mechri* is commonly used in classical Greek as an adverb, a preposition, and a conjunction. As an adverb it can be found before a preposition or another adverb of place or time, usually meaning "as far as." As a preposition it can be found before a genitive of place, time, or degree, usually meaning "even to, as far as." As a conjunction it means "until" or "as long as." (For specific examples of all of the above uses see *Liddell-Scott*).

Septuagint Usage
Mechri is also a word commonly used in the Septuagint; however, it was not used to translate a Hebrew term. In most cases it is used in reference to time. Joshua 4:23 recounts how God held back the waters of the Red Sea "until" the Israelites crossed into safety. Psalm 50:1 (LXX 49:1) also uses *mechri* as a conjunction connecting the time from the "rising of the sun *unto* the going down thereof." In Job 8:2 the phrase *mechri tinos*, "How long?" begins Bildad's affirmation of God's justice in his response to Job's accusations.

New Testament Usage
The New Testament uses *mechri* 17 times, usually as a conjunction, "until." *Mechri* is often used in reference to time (e.g., "until this day," Matthew 11:23; cf. 28:15; "until this hour," Acts 10:30; cf. 20:7; and "until" the time when something is done, Mark 13:30; cf. Hebrews 9:10). Another frequent use of *mechri* is as a preposition (before a genitive), "unto." In Romans 15:19 Paul used it in reference to place, "unto" (or "as far as") Illyricum; it could also be used figuratively of a state or condition (e.g., "unto death," Philippians 2:8,30; cf. Hebrews 3:6,14; and "unto" some type of suffering, 2 Timothy 2:9; Hebrews 12:4).

STRONG 3360, BAUER 515, MOULTON-MILLIGAN 407, LIDDELL-SCOTT 1123.

3231. μή mē partic
Not.

1. μή mē

1	Nor scrip for your journey, neither two coats,	Matt 10:10

Classical Greek
In classical Greek this negative particle is used for the negative of thought, i.e., negation that depends on a condition that is understood. It is distinct from *ou* (3620) which denies, while *mē* rejects. When one thinks a thing is not, *mē* is used. It is subjective, involving will and thought, not fact and statement (*Liddell-Scott*).

Septuagint Usage
The Septuagint generally uses *ou* for negative thought, particularly in Daniel where it occurs 36 times, while *mē* occurs 4 times (2:24; 4:19; 5:10; 9:19) and only in petition (e.g., in the formula "let not"). The Hebrew terms for *ou* and *mē* are *lō* and *'al*, respectively.

New Testament Usage
Emphatic negation is indicated when the objective *ou* is combined with the subjective *mē*: "By no means ye will complete the cities of Israel" (Matthew 10:23, literal translation); "By no means may ye enter into the Kingdom" (Matthew 18:3, literal translation).

Wish is expressed by *mē*: "God forbid," literally, "May it *not* be"—*mē genoito* (Romans 3:4). *Mē* is also used in hesitant questions where a negative answer is expected: "(*Not*) a stone he will give him?" (Matthew 7:9, literal sense). When *mē* introduces the question and *ou* negates the verb, however, the double negative calls for an affirmative answer.

STRONG 3361, BAUER 515-17, MOULTON-MILLIGAN 407-9, LIDDELL-SCOTT 1123-24.

3232. μήγε mēge partic
Otherwise.

1. μήγε mēge

1	otherwise ye have **no** reward of your Father	Matt 6:1
1	**else** the bottles break, and the wine runneth out,	9:17

1 if otherwise, then both the new maketh a rent,	Luke 5:36
1 else the new wine will burst the bottles,	5:37
1 shall rest upon it: if not, it shall turn to you again.	10:6
1 and if not, then after that thou shalt cut it down.	13:9
1 Or else, while the other is yet a great way off,	14:32
1 if otherwise, yet as a fool receive me,	2 Co 11:16

Mēge is a compound particle made up of the particle *mē* (3231) and the particle *ge* (1058). *Mē* appears in several compounds such as *mēde* (3234), a negative conjunction, and *mēdepote* (3236), "never." *Ge* is a particle that calls attention to the word it follows. *Ge* may emphasize or set bounds on the word it is associated with. *Mēge* appears in the New Testament in the formula *ei de mēge*. *Mēge* means "otherwise" as in Matthew 6:1, "Otherwise (*mēge*) ye have no reward." See 2 Corinthians 11:16 for a similar example.

BAUER 517, MOULTON-MILLIGAN 409.

3233. μηδαμῶς mēdamōs adv

No one, none, certainly not, by no means.

אֲהָהּ 'ăhāhh (159), Ah! (Ez 4:14, 20:49).

אַל 'al (414), No (Jgs 19:23—Codex Alexandrinus only).

אָנָּה 'onnāh (588), Oh, please (Jon 1:14).

1. μηδαμῶς mēdamōs

1 But Peter said, Not so, Lord;	Acts 10:14
1 But I said, Not so, Lord:	11:8

Classical Greek

Mēdamōs is the adverbial form of the adjective *mēdamos*. *Mēdamōs* is a compound form from the negative *mēde* (3234), "not," and *hamos*, "anyone, anything," with the meaning "not even one" (i.e., "no one") or when in the plural, "none" (*Liddell-Scott*). There are several related words that carry parallel meanings. Some of these are *mēdamē*, "nowhere" or "in no way"; *mēdaminos*, "good for nothing"; *mēdmothen*, "from no place."

Septuagint Usage

Mēdamōs occurs about 12 times in the Septuagint. Most of these occurrences are in 1 Samuel (LXX 1 Kings). In 1 Samuel 20:2 (LXX 1 Kings 20:2) Jonathan promised David, "My father will do nothing (*mēdamōs*) either great or small...." First Samuel 22:15 (LXX 1 Kings 22:15) also uses *mēdamōs* with the meaning "nothing." In 1 Samuel 26:11 (LXX 1 Kings 26:11) "no one" (*mēdamōs*) saw David take the spear from the side of King Saul (KJV, verse 12). *Moulton-Milligan* also documents several occurrences of *mēdamos* in the papyri.

New Testament Usage

There are only two occurrences of *mēdamōs* in the New Testament. In Acts 10:14 Peter replied to God's exhortation to eat from the selection of food, "Certainly not" (*mēdamōs*). (The KJV translates it "not so.") The second occurrence is in Acts 11:8 when Peter reported this same event to the church.

STRONG 3365, BAUER 517, MOULTON-MILLIGAN 409, LIDDELL-SCOTT 1124-25.

3234. μηδέ mēde adv

But not, nor, not even, neither.

1. μηδέ mēde
2. μηδ' mēd'

1 nor yet for your body, what ye shall put on	Matt 6:25
1 neither cast ye your pearls before swine,	7:6
1 Provide neither gold, nor silver, ... in your purses,	10:9
1 Provide neither gold, ... nor brass in your purses,	10:9
1 Nor scrip for your journey, neither two coats,	10:10
1 neither two coats, neither shoes, nor yet staves;	10:10
1 neither two coats, neither shoes, nor yet staves:	10:10
1 shall not receive you, nor hear your words,	10:14
1 not knowing the scriptures, nor the power of God.	22:29
1 Neither be ye called masters:	23:10
1 your flight be not ... neither on the sabbath day:	24:20
1 no, not so much as about the door:	Mark 2:2
1 that they could not even eat a meal. (NASB)	3:20
1 whosoever shall not receive you, nor hear you,	6:11
1 Neither go into the town, nor tell it to any	8:26
1 nor tell it to any in the town.	8:26
1 know not the scriptures, neither the power of God?	12:24
1 what ye shall speak, neither do ye premeditate:	13:11
1 neither enter therein, to take any thing out	13:15
1 Do violence to no man, neither accuse any falsely;	Luke 3:14
1 Carry neither purse, nor scrip, nor shoes:	10:4
1 neither for the body, what ye shall put on	12:22
1 neither did according to his will,	12:47
1 call not thy friends, nor thy brethren,	14:12
1 neither thy kinsmen, nor thy rich neighbours;	14:12
1 neither thy kinsmen, nor thy rich neighbours;	14:12
1 neither can they pass to us, ... from thence.	16:26
1 or, see there: go not after them, nor follow them.	17:23
1 that I thirst not, neither come hither to draw.	John 4:15
1 not your heart be troubled, neither let it be afraid.	14:27
1 not to speak at all nor teach in the name of Jesus...	Acts 4:18
1 neither to walk after the customs.	21:21
1 is no resurrection, neither angel, nor spirit:	23:8
1 Neither yield ye your members as instruments	Rom 6:13
1 neither having done any good or evil,	9:11
1 It is good neither to eat flesh, nor to drink wine,	14:21
1 nor any thing whereby thy brother stumbleth,	14:21
1 neither with the leaven of malice and wickedness;	1 Co 5:8
1 or an extortioner; with such an one no not to eat.	5:11
1 Neither be ye idolaters, as were some of them;	10:7
1 Neither let us commit fornication,	10:8
1 Neither let us tempt Christ,	10:9
1 Neither murmur ye,	10:10
1 nor handling the word of God deceitfully;	2 Co 4:2
1 do not give the devil an opportunity. (NASB)	Eph 4:27
1 not be once named among you, as becometh saints;	5:3
1 out of selfish ambition or vain conceit, (NIV)	Phlp 2:3
1 Touch not; taste not; handle not;	Col 2:21
1 Touch not; taste not; handle not;	2:21
1 from your composure or be disturbed (NASB)	2 Th 2:2

1 that if any would not work, neither should he eat.	2 Th 3:10
1 Neither give heed to fables	1 Tm 1:4
1 neither be partaker of other men's sins:	5:22
1 nor trust in uncertain riches, but in the living God,	6:17
1 the testimony of our Lord, nor of me his prisoner:	2 Tm 1:8
1 nor enslaved to much wine, (NASB)	Tit 2:3
1 nor faint when thou art rebuked of him:	Heb 12:5
1 be not afraid of their terror, neither be troubled;	1 Pt 3:14
1 not by constraint, but willingly;	5:2
2 Neither as being lords over God's heritage,	5:3
1 Love ... neither the things that are in the world.	1 Jn 2:15
1 neither in tongue; but in deed and in truth.	3:18

Classical Greek and Septuagint Usage

Mēde is a negative particle used as both a conjunction and an adverb. It is a compound of the negative particle *mē* (3231), "not," and the conjunction *de*, "but." *Mēde* used as a conjunction means "and not, but not," or "nor" and is used to connect independent clauses (*Liddell-Scott*). There are various combinations of *mēde* with other negative particles when clauses are coupled in different ways. *Mēde* may be repeated (*mēde . . . mēde*, "but not . . . nor"). In this construction the first *mēde* may serve either as an adverb or as a conjunction. *Mēte* (3250) may be followed by *mēde* (*mēte . . . mēde*, "neither . . . nor"). *Mēde* never occurs antecedent to *mēte* when used with it (ibid.). *Mē* may be followed by *mēde* (*mē . . . mēde*, "not . . . nor"). And in consecutive clauses *oude* (3624) may be followed by *mēde* (*oude . . . mēde*, "and not . . . nor"). When used as an adverb *mēde* may be joined with a single word or phrase meaning "not even" or "not either" (cf. *Bauer*). *Mēde* does not occur in the Septuagint but does occur in the papyri literature (cf. *Moulton-Milligan*).

New Testament Usage

Mēde occurs many times in the New Testament using several of the above examples. In Matthew 6:25 *mēde* continues the preceding negative, "Take no thought for your life . . . *nor yet* (*mēde*) for your body." In Luke 10:4 Jesus told the disciples to "Carry neither purse, nor scrip, *nor* (*mēde*) shoes." The conjunctive negative also occurs in 2 Thessalonians 3:10, "If any would not work, *neither* (*mēde*) should he eat." Mark 8:26 illustrates an example of repeating *mēde*: "*Neither* go into the town, *nor* tell (it) to any in the town" (cf. Matthew 10:10). *Mēde* can also be found as an adverb simply meaning "neither" (e.g., Acts 23:8; 1 Corinthians 5:8, and as part of a negative imperative "do not . . . " e.g., Romans 6:13; 9:11; 1 Corinthians 10:7; 2 Timothy 1:8).

STRONG 3366, BAUER 517-18, MOULTON-MILLIGAN 409, LIDDELL-SCOTT 1125.

3235. μηδείς mēdeis num

No, nobody, no one, none, nothing.

1. μηδενός mēdenos card gen masc/neu
2. μηδενί mēdeni card dat masc/neu
3. μηδείς mēdeis card nom masc
4. μηδένα mēdena card acc masc
5. μηδεμίαν mēdemian card acc fem
6. μηδέν mēden card nom/acc neu

2 See thou tell no man; but go thy way,	Matt 8:4
3 saying, See that no man know it.	9:30
2 should tell no man that he was Jesus the Christ.	16:20
2 Jesus ... saying, Tell the vision to no man,	17:9
6 Have thou nothing to do with that just man:	27:19
2 saith unto him, See thou say nothing to any man:	Mark 1:44
2 saith unto him, See thou say nothing to any man:	1:44
6 spent all that she had, and was nothing bettered,	5:26
3 charged them straitly that no man should know it;	5:43
6 commanded them that they should take nothing	6:8
2 And he charged them that they should tell no man:	7:36
2 charged them that they should tell no man of him:	8:30
2 he charged them that they should tell no man	9:9
3 No man eat fruit of thee hereafter for ever.	11:14
6 Exact no more than that which is appointed you.	Luke 3:13
4 Do violence to no man, neither accuse any falsely;	3:14
6 he came out of him, and hurt him not.	4:35
2 And he charged him to tell no man:	5:14
6 and do good, and lend, hoping for nothing again;	6:35
2 but he charged them that they should tell no man	8:56
6 he said unto them, Take nothing for your journey,	9:3
2 and commanded them to tell no man that thing;	9:21
4 nor shoes: and salute no man by the way.	10:4
4 and saw none but the woman, he said unto her,	John 8:10
2 that they speak henceforth to no man in this name.	Acts 4:17
6 finding nothing how they might punish them,	4:21
6 that none of these things which ye have spoken	8:24
4 hearing a voice, but seeing no man.	9:7
6 doubting nothing: for I have sent them.	10:20
4 that I should not call any man common or unclean.	10:28
6 Spirit bade me go with them, nothing doubting.	11:12
2 preaching the word to none but unto the Jews	11:19
5 And though they found no cause of death in him,	13:28
6 no greater burden than these necessary things;	15:28
6 Do thyself no harm: for we are all here.	16:28
6 ye ought to be quiet, and to do nothing rashly.	19:36
1 there being no cause whereby we may give	19:40
6 and concluded that they observe no such thing,	21:25
1 that we will eat nothing until we have slain Paul.	23:14
2 See thou tell no man that thou hast showed these	23:22
6 to have nothing laid to his charge worthy of death	23:29
4 and that he should forbid none of his acquaintance	24:23
5 without any delay on the morrow I sat	25:17
6 that he had committed nothing worthy of death,	25:25
6 and continued fasting, having taken nothing.	27:33
6 and saw no harm come to him,	28:6
5 because there was no cause of death in me.	28:18
2 Recompense to no man evil for evil.	Rom 12:17
2 Owe no man any thing,	13:8
6 Owe no man any thing,	13:8
2 So that ye come behind in no gift;	1 Co 1:7
3 Let no man deceive himself.	3:18
3 let no man glory in men. For all things are yours;	3:21
3 Let no man seek his own, ... wealth.	10:24
6 that eat, asking no question for conscience sake:	10:25
6 eat, asking no question for conscience sake.	10:27
5 Giving no offence in any thing,	2 Co 6:3
2 Giving no offence in any thing,	6:3
6 as having nothing, and yet possessing all things.	6:10
2 that ye might receive damage by us in nothing.	7:9
6 I was not a whit behind the very chiefest apostles.	11:5
6 Now I pray to God that ye do no evil;	13:7
6 think himself to be something, when he is nothing,	Gal 6:3
3 From henceforth let no man trouble me:	6:17

3	Let **no man** deceive you with vain words:	Eph 5:6
2	And in **nothing** terrified by your adversaries:	Phlp 1:28
6	Let **nothing** be done through strife or vainglory;	2:3
6	Be careful for **nothing**;	4:6
3	in order than **no one** may delude (NASB)	Col 2:4
3	Let **no man** beguile you of your reward	2:18
4	That **no man** should be moved by these afflictions:	1 Th 3:3
1	and that ye may have lack of **nothing**.	4:12
4	Let no man deceive you by **any** means:	2 Th 2:3
6	working **not at all**, but are busybodies.	3:11
3	Let **no man** despise thy youth;	1 Tm 4:12
5	give **none** occasion to the adversary	5:14
6	observe these things ... doing **nothing** by partiality.	5:21
2	Lay hands suddenly **on no man**,	5:22
6	He is proud, knowing **nothing**,	6:4
6	having **no** evil thing to say of you.	Tit 2:8
3	rebuke with all authority. Let **no man** despise thee.	2:15
4	To speak evil of **no man**, to be no brawlers,	3:2
6	that **nothing** be wanting unto them.	3:13
5	should have had **no** more conscience of sins.	Heb 10:2
2	ye may be perfect and entire, wanting **nothing**.	Jas 1:4
6	But let him ask in faith, **nothing** wavering.	1:6
3	Let **no man** say when he is tempted,	1:13
5	do well, and are not afraid with **any** amazement.	1 Pt 3:6
3	Little children, let **no man** deceive you:	1 Jn 3:7
6	they went forth, taking **nothing** of the Gentiles.	3 Jn 1:7
6	Fear **none** of those things which thou shalt suffer:	Rev 2:10
3	fast which thou hast, that **no man** take thy crown.	3:11

Classical Greek
This frequently emphatic adjective is actually a compound from the negative particle *mē* (3231), the conjunction *de* (1156), which together become a negative disjunctive conjunction (*mēde* and the noun *heis* [1506A], "one"). Originally the components were separated (*mēde heis*); gradually the elided form dominated. Together these result in the word *mēdeis*, meaning "no" or "none" when used as a noun and "nothing, no one, not one" when used in an absolute sense. In the neuter form, *mēden*, it means "not at all, by no means" (*Liddell-Scott*).

Septuagint Usage
Mēdeis (as well as the form *mētheis*) occurs in 11 Hebrew constructions in the Septuagint. No single term dominates, although it replaces *'îsh*, "someone, one, each one, no one" more than any other term (e.g., Exodus 16:19: "no one" is to keep manna overnight; cf. Exodus 34:3). The emphatic nature of *mēdeis* is apparent in some texts (e.g., 1 Kings 18:40 [LXX 3 Kings 18:40]).

New Testament Usage
Occurring in almost every book of the New Testament, *mēdeis* follows its basic range of definition. In most cases it functions in an absolute sense, i.e., "no one" or "nothing" (*mēden*) (e.g., Matthew 8:4; Mark 1:44; 6:8; Luke 5:14). As an adjective it means "no"; thus in Acts 13:28 we read that "no cause" for death was found in Jesus (cf. Acts 19:40). The emphatic sense is related in some texts. In these "not at all" or "in no way" are appropriate translations (e.g., Mark 5:26; Luke 4:35; Philippians 4:6; cf. *Bauer*).

STRONG 3367, BAUER 518, MOULTON-MILLIGAN 409, LIDDELL-SCOTT 1125.

3236. μηδέποτε mēdepote adv
Never.

1. μηδέποτε mēdepote

1 **never** able to come to the knowledge of the truth... 2 Tm 3:7

Mēdepote is composed from the negative particle *mēde* (3234), "and not," and the enclitic particle of time *pote* (4077), "once." *Mēdepote* does not occur in the Septuagint but does occur in the papyri (*Moulton-Milligan*). *Mēdepote* is used as a simple negative adverb with either the present, past, or future tenses meaning "never." It was used only once in the New Testament, in 2 Timothy 3:7, where Paul spoke of those in the last days who will "never" (*mēdepote*) come to the knowledge of the truth.

STRONG 3368, BAUER 518, MOULTON-MILLIGAN 409, LIDDELL-SCOTT 1125.

3237. μηδέπω mēdepō adv
Not yet.

1. μηδέπω mēdepō

1 being warned of God of things **not** seen as yet, ... Heb 11:7

Although the adverb *mēdepō* is found in Greek literature dating from the Fifth Century B.C., it is a hapax legomenon in the New Testament being found only at Hebrews 11:7. Here it has a temporal significance that modifies the action of the verb or participle and is best understood by the expression "not yet." By faith, Noah saw Him "who is invisible" (verse 27) and trusted in God enough to prepare for dangers "*not* seen *as yet*" (verse 7).

STRONG 3369, BAUER 518, MOULTON-MILLIGAN 409, LIDDELL-SCOTT 1125.

3238. Μῆδος Mēdos name
Mede.

1. Μῆδοι Mēdoi nom pl masc

1 Parthians, and **Medes**, and Elamites, ... Acts 2:9

Resident of Media; Jews from this area were in Jerusalem on the Day of Pentecost (Acts 2:9).

3238B. μηθέν mēthen adv
Nothing.

1. μηθέν mēthen

1 gone without eating, having taken **nothing**. (NASB) Acts 27:33

Mēthen is the neuter form of *mētheis*, an alternate spelling of *mēden*, "no one, nothing." The alternate spelling was common in inscriptions and papyri from the Third Century B.C. until the Second Century A.D. (*Liddell-Scott*). It rarely occurs after the beginning of the Christian era. The only occurrence in the New Testament is in some manuscripts at Acts 27:33 where it has the meaning "nothing." The *Textus Receptus* has *mēden* at this point.

BAUER 518, LIDDELL-SCOTT 1125.

3239. μηκέτι mēketi adv
No longer, no more, no further.

אַל ʾal (414), Not (Jb 41:8 [40:27]).

לֹא lōʾ (3940), Not (Jos 22:33).

1. μηκέτι mēketi

1 Let no fruit grow on thee **henceforward** for ever....Matt 21:19
1 Jesus could **no more** openly enter into the city,.....Mark 1:45
1 insomuch that there was **no room** to receive them,......2:2
1 come out of him, and enter **no more** into him..........9:25
1 No man eat fruit of thee **hereafter** for ever............11:14
1 do **not** trouble the Teacher anymore." (NASB)......Luke 8:49
1 sin **no more**, lest a worse thing come unto thee......John 5:14
1 Neither do I condemn thee: go, and sin **no more**.......8:11
1 that they speak **henceforth** to no man in this name...Acts 4:17
1 now **no more** to return to corruption,..................13:34
1 crying that he ought not to live **any longer**............25:24
1 that henceforth we should not serve sin.............. Rom 6:6
1 Let us not therefore judge one another **any more**:......14:13
1 But now having **no more** place in these parts,.........15:23
1 should not **henceforth** live unto themselves,.......... 2 Co 5:15
1 That we henceforth be **no more** children,............. Eph 4:14
1 that ye **henceforth** walk not as other Gentiles walk,.....4:17
1 Let him that stole steal **no more**:......................4:28
1 Wherefore when we could **no longer** forbear,........1 Th 3:1
1 For this cause, when I could **no longer** forbear,..........3:5
1 Drink **no longer** water, but use a little wine........ 1 Tm 5:23
1 That he **no longer** should live the rest of his time....1 Pt 4:2

This term is a combination of the negative particle *mē* (3231) and the adverb *eti* (2068), meaning "yet" or "still." It is used with the moods of possibility—the subjunctive, optative, or imperative: Mark 9:25: "Come out of him and *never* enter him *again*" (NIV, RSV); Mark 11:14: "May no one *ever* eat fruit from you *again*" (NIV, RSV; cf. Matthew 21:19; Luke 8:49; Romans 14:13; 2 Corinthians 5:15; Ephesians 4:14,28; 1 Timothy 5:23). It also occurs with the infinitive (Mark 1:45: "... insomuch that Jesus could *no more [no longer]* openly enter into the city"; cf. Acts 4:17; 25:24; Ephesians 4:17) or with the participle (Acts 13:34: "*no more* [never] to return to corruption"; cf. Romans 15:23; 1 Thessalonians 3:1,5).

STRONG 3371, BAUER 518, MOULTON-MILLIGAN 409, LIDDELL-SCOTT 1126.

3240. μῆκος mēkos noun
Length.

אֲרוּכָה ʾărûkhāh (749), Repair (2 Chr 24:13).

אֹרֶךְ ʾōrekh (775), Length (Ex 27:9,11, 2 Chr 3:3f., Ez 40:20).

1. μῆκος mēkos nom/acc sing neu

1 the breadth, and **length**, and depth, and height;......Eph 3:18
1 the **length** is as large as the breadth:............Rev 21:16
1 **length** and the breadth and the height ... are equal.....21:16

Classical Greek
Found in Greek literature from Homer onward, *mēkos* has several usages. It is used of space when referring to the *length* of a club or the *height* of a wall or the *length* as opposed to the depth of something. It is also used of time when referring to speech (e.g., a *long* speech). When describing size or degree it is translated "greatness" or "magnitude." In addition, it was used of longitude. The first line of a body of troops in close array is described by this term (cf. *Liddell-Scott*).

New Testament Usage
In its only New Testament occurrences (Ephesians 3:18 and Revelation 21:6) *mēkos* takes on the meaning of space and is translated "length." Paul spoke of linear space, the "length," as he prayed for the Ephesians to know the full magnitude of Christ's love (Ephesians 3:18). John, as he described the heavenly city of Jerusalem (Revelation 21), spoke of it as "foursquare": "The *length* is as large as the breadth (*platos* [3974])" (verse 16). Then, when he measured it, he added a third dimension: "The *length* and the breadth and the height of it are equal" (verse 16).

STRONG 3372, BAUER 518, MOULTON-MILLIGAN 409, LIDDELL-SCOTT 1126.

3241. μηκύνω mēkunō verb
To grow (long), lengthen, make long.

SYNONYMS:
αὐξάνω auxanō (831)
πλεονάζω pleonazō (3981)
φύω phuō (5289)

גָּדַל gādhal (1461), Grow, be great; piel: make grow (Is 44:14).

מָשַׁךְ māshakh (5082), Extend, pull; niphal: be delayed (Ez 12:25,28).

1. μηκύνηται **mēkunētai** 3sing subj pres mid
1 and the seed should spring and grow up,.......... Mark 4:27

Classical Greek and Septuagint Usage

Literally meaning "to lengthen," this word is related to the noun *mēkos* (3240), "length." *Mēkunō* has several usages in Greek literature. It is used in reference to the *lengthening* of a road, or the *lengthening* of time or life. In its passive form it is used in reference to the *lengthening* of a sickness, the *lengthening* of war or a battle, or the *lengthening* of the front rank of an army. It is also used of time with the meaning of "delay." In regards to composition it carries the sense of "enlarging," and in certain contexts it can mean "repeating something over and over again." It is used with the Greek word *boē* (988), "loud cry," signifying the *raising* of a loud cry. In grammar it refers to the *lengthening* of a syllable or a vowel, and in mathematics it refers to multiplication (cf. *Liddell-Scott*). It appears twice in the Septuagint with two different uses. In Ezekiel 12:25,28 *mēkunō* is used of "prolonging" time, and in Isaiah 44:14 it is used of a tree that "grows."

New Testament Usage

In the New Testament the only use of *mēkunō* is in reference to the *growing* of grain (Mark 4:27). In the parable of seed growing without the sower's assistance, Jesus depicted the process verbally: "The seed should spring and *grow up* (*mēkunetai*), he (the sower) knoweth not how" (Mark 4:27).

STRONG 3373, BAUER 518, MOULTON-MILLIGAN 409, LIDDELL-SCOTT 1126.

3242. μηλωτή mēlōtē noun
Sheepskin.

אַדֶּרֶת 'addereth (152), Mantle (1 Kgs 19:13,19, 2 Kgs 2:8,13f.).

1. μηλωταῖς **mēlōtais** dat pl fem
1 they wandered about in sheepskins and goatskins; ...Heb 11:37

Literally meaning "sheepskin" or "any rough, woolly skin," this New Testament hapax legomenon (occurring only in Hebrews 11:37) is related to *mēlon*, "sheep" or "goat." Some see the sheepskin as a prophetic garb indicating the prophet's austere life-style, his separation from the world, his need, affliction, and lonely life in the wilderness.

The clothing of some of the persecuted persons in the honor roll of faith (Hebrews 11) was "sheepskin." (The same term is used when referring to Elijah's mantle in 1 Kings 19:13,19 [LXX 3 Kings 19:13,19] and 2 Kings 2:8,13,14 [4 Kings 2:8,13,14]).

STRONG 3374, BAUER 518, MOULTON-MILLIGAN 410, LIDDELL-SCOTT 1127, COLIN BROWN 4:637-38.

3243. μήν mēn noun
Month.

COGNATES:
νεομηνία neomēnia (3363B)
νουμηνία noumēnia (3424)

חֹדֶשׁ chōdhesh (2414), Month (Ex 12:2, 1 Chr 27:1ff., Ez 24:1).

יֶרַח yerach (3505), Month (Dt 21:13, 1 Kgs 8:2, Jb 7:3).

יְרַח yᵉrach (A3508), Month (Ezr 6:15, Dn 4:29 [4:26]—Aramaic).

1. μήν **mēn** nom sing masc
2. μηνί **mēni** dat sing masc
3. μῆνα **mēna** acc sing masc
4. μῆνας **mēnas** acc pl masc

4 Elisabeth conceived, and hid herself five **months**,.... Luke 1:24
2 And in the sixth **month** the angel Gabriel was sent..... 1:26
1 and this is the sixth **month** with her,................ 1:36
4 And Mary abode with her about three **months**,......... 1:56
4 heaven was shut up three years and six **months**,...... 4:25
4 nourished up in his father's house three **months**:.... Acts 7:20
4 And he continued there a year and six **months**,....... 18:11
4 and spake boldly for the space of three **months**,..... 19:8
4 And there abode three **months**....................... 20:3
4 And after three **months** we departed in a ship........ 28:11
4 Ye observe days, and **months**, and times,............ Gal 4:10
4 by the space of three years and six **months**.......... Jas 5:17
4 but that they should be tormented five **months**:..... Rev 9:5
4 and their power was to hurt men five **months**......... 9:10
3 For an hour, and a day, and a **month**, and a year,... 9:15
4 shall they tread under foot forty and two **months**.... 11:2
4 given unto him to continue forty and two **months**.... 13:5
3 and yielded her fruit every **month**:................. 22:2

Mēn is a measure of time commonly referred to as "month." James 5:17 clearly illustrates the New Testament usage. When Elijah prayed that it not rain, there was no rain for "three years and six *months*" (cf. Luke 1:24,26,36,56; 4:25; Acts 7:20; 18:11; 19:8; 20:3; 28:11; Revelation 9:5,10,15, etc.).

In Galatians 4:10 Paul rebuked the Galatian readers for keeping certain "days, and *months*, and times, and years." The fault underlying these activities was quite likely a keeping of the Jewish new moon festival.

STRONG 3376, BAUER 518, MOULTON-MILLIGAN 410, KITTEL 4:638-42, LIDDELL-SCOTT 1093-94 (see "meis").

3244. μήν mēn partic
Surely, certainly, verily, assuredly.

1. μήν mēn

1 Saying, **Surely** blessing I will bless thee, ... Heb 6:14

This particle occurs frequently in classical Greek. It is used to strengthen either asseverations or adversatives, is found with interrogatives, and is used in idiomatic expressions with other particles (see *Liddell-Scott*). *Mēn* always follows the word that begins the clause, is frequently used with the imperative, and its meaning overlaps with that of *men* (3173), although it is a stronger term. *Mēn*, like *men*, is used to express the certainty of the speaker or writer but with more assurance. One New Testament example is Hebrews 6:14, a quotation of Genesis 22:17, where *mēn* is used with *ei* (1479) as an idiomatic phrase meaning "surely." (For etymological notes see Robertson, *Grammar of the Greek New Testament*, p.1150.)

STRONG 3375, BAUER 518, MOULTON-MILLIGAN 410, LIDDELL-SCOTT 1127.

3245. μηνύω mēnuō verb
Make known, disclose, show, declare, report, reveal.

SYNONYMS:
ἀναδείκνυμι anadeiknumi (320)
ἀποκαλύπτω apokaluptō (596)
γνωρίζω gnōrizō (1101)
δείκνυμι deiknumi (1161)
δηλόω dēloō (1207)
ἐμφανίζω emphanizō (1702)
φανερόω phaneroō (5157)

1. ἐμήνυσεν emēnusen 3sing indic aor act
2. μηνύσῃ mēnusē 3sing subj aor act
3. μηνύσαντα mēnusanta acc sing masc part aor act
4. μηνυθείσης mēnutheisēs gen sing fem part aor pass

1 even Moses **showed** at the bush, ... Luke 20:37
2 if any man knew where he were, he **should show** it, John 11:57
4 when it **was told** me how that the Jews laid wait .... Acts 23:30
3 eat not for his sake **that showed** it, ... 1 Co 10:28

Classical Greek
Mēnuō is related to the noun *mēnuma* meaning "information, indication." In pre-Bible usage the verb *mēnuō* is used to "report" runaway slaves, "report" military requisitions or secrets, and "report" items important to a king. It can also mean the "revealing" of information that is secret or within a person (cf. *Liddell-Scott*). The word also appears in the Septuagint, Josephus, and Philo.

Septuagint Usage
Mēnuō occurs only in the Maccabean writings of the Septuagint. "To inform" is the basic sense (2 Maccabees 3:7), but it can have strong negative overtones (2 Maccabees 6:11, "betrayed"; 14:37, "denounced").

New Testament Usage
Mēnuō occurs four times in the New Testament. In Luke 20:37 it refers to the "showing, appearing, revealing" of God in the burning bush to Moses. In John 11:57 the Pharisees and chief priests commanded that anyone who knew where Jesus was should "show" Him to them. In Acts 23:30 a plot against Paul was "reported" or "revealed" to him. And in 1 Corinthians 10:28 the emphasis is upon a sacrifice that is "declared" or "made known."

In each of the above occurrences the knowledge has a value that is desired or striven for. The action is not merely knowing as in *ginōskō* (1091), but the acquisition or declaration of something valued, desired, or striven for.

STRONG 3377, BAUER 519, MOULTON-MILLIGAN 410, LIDDELL-SCOTT 1128.

3246. μήποτε mēpote partic
Not ever, never, lest at anytime, perhaps, whether indeed.

1. μήποτε mēpote

1 **lest at any time** thou dash thy foot against a stone... Matt 4:6
1 **lest at any time** the adversary deliver thee 5:25
1 **lest** they trample them under their feet, ... 7:6
1 **lest at any time** they should see with their eyes 13:15
1 But he said, Nay; **lest** while ye gather up the tares, ... 13:29
1 not ... away fasting, **lest** they faint in the way 15:32
1 But the wise answered, saying, **Not so**; 25:9
1 **lest** his disciples come by night, and steal him 27:64
1 **lest at any time** they should be converted, ... Mark 4:12
1 the feast day, **lest** there be an uproar of the people.... 14:2
1 **whether** he were the Christ, or not; .... Luke 3:15
1 **lest at any time** thou dash thy foot against a stone...... 4:11
1 delivered from him; **lest** he hale thee to the judge, ... 12:58
1 **lest** a more honourable man than thou be bidden 14:8
1 call not thy friends, ... **lest** they also bid thee again, ... 14:12
1 **Lest haply**, after he hath laid the foundation, ... 14:29
1 **lest at any time** your hearts be overcharged 21:34
1 Do the rulers know **indeed** ... Christ? (NT) .... John 7:26
1 **lest haply** ye be found even to fight against God..... Acts 5:39
1 **lest** they should see with their eyes, ... 28:27
1 **if** God **peradventure** will give them repentance ...... 2 Tm 2:25
1 **lest at any time** we should let them slip .... Heb 2:1
1 **lest** there be in any of you an evil heart of unbelief, ... 3:12
1 Let us therefore fear, **lest**, a promise being left us 4:1
1 **otherwise** it is of no strength at all 9:17

Classical Greek and Septuagint Usage

Mēpote is formed from two words, *mē* (3231), "not," and *pote* (4077), "at any time." The meaning of these two words combined is the expression of a negative wish, command, condition, or question that covers a general amount of time, area, or persons. It occurs in literature prior to the New Testament as an adverb meaning "never" or as a conjunction meaning "lest ever" (*Liddell-Scott*). It is used especially in oaths and can also be found in prohibitions or warnings (ibid.). The compound *mēpote* does not appear in the Septuagint, however, *mēpote* does occur frequently as a conjunction indicating purpose (*Bauer*; cf. Genesis 38:23; Ezra 4:22 [LXX 2 Esdras 4:22]). Sometimes it can also mean simply "perhaps" in the sense of something less than definite (Genesis 24:5; cf. *Liddell-Scott*).

New Testament Usage

Mēpote occurs 25 times in the New Testament. Seventeen of these are in Matthew and Luke. It occurs 13 times with a command and is used as a general negation, e.g., Hebrews 9:17. In Matthew 5:25 it comes between a command and a qualifying expression about that which preceded: "Agree with thine adversary quickly, ... *lest at any time* the adversary deliver thee to the judge." It is also used as a prohibition reflecting the purpose of an action, e.g., Luke 12:58. In addition it is used with questions that express doubt about the outcome, e.g., John 7:26.

STRONG 3379, BAUER 519, MOULTON-MILLIGAN 410, LIDDELL-SCOTT 1129.

3247. μήπω mēpō adv

Not yet.

1. μήπω mēpō

1 For the children being **not yet** born,	Rom 9:11
1 into the holiest of all was **not yet** made manifest,	Heb 9:8

In Greek literature *mēpō* is used both as an adverb meaning "not yet" and as a conjunction meaning "lest yet" (*Liddell-Scott*). In the New Testament its usage is restricted to that of a temporal adverb which places negative limits upon an action. For example, children were "*not yet* born" (Romans 9:11); and the way into the sanctuary "was *not yet* made manifest" (Hebrews 9:8).

STRONG 3380, BAUER 519, MOULTON-MILLIGAN 410, LIDDELL-SCOTT 1129.

3248. μήπως mēpōs conj

Lest perhaps, lest in any way.

1. μήπως mēpōs

1 fearing **lest** we should have fallen upon rocks,	Acts 27:29
1 take heed **lest** he also spare not thee.	Rom 11:21
1 take heed **lest** by any means this liberty of yours	1 Co 8:9
1 **lest** that by any means,	9:27
1 **lest perhaps** such a one should be swallowed up	2 Co 2:7
1 **Lest haply** if they of Macedonia come with me,	9:4
1 But I fear, **lest** by any means,	11:3
1 For I fear, **lest**, when I come,	12:20
1 **lest** there be debates, envyings, wraths, strifes,	12:20
1 **lest** by any means I should run, ... in vain.	Gal 2:2
1 **lest** I have bestowed upon you labour in vain.	4:11
1 **lest** by some means the tempter have tempted you,	1 Th 3:5

Mēpōs, a conjunction, occurs after verbs of fear or apprehension to voice a speaker's negative reservation. Aside from Acts 27:29 (*Textus Receptus*) it is a Pauline term. Consider 2 Corinthians 12:20, "For I fear *lest*, when I come, I shall not find ..." (cf. 1 Corinthians 8:9; 2 Corinthians 11:3; Galatians 4:11; 1 Thessalonians 3:5).

Mēpōs may introduce a result clause with a negated perspective, as 2 Corinthians 2:7, "... *lest perhaps* such a one should be swallowed up" (cf. 9:4; 1 Corinthians 9:27).

STRONG 3381, BAUER 519, MOULTON-MILLIGAN 411, LIDDELL-SCOTT 1129.

3249. μηρός mēros noun

Thigh.

בֶּרֶךְ berekh (1314), Knee (Gn 50:23, Ez 7:17, 47:4).

יָרֵךְ yārēkh (3525), Thigh, side (Gn 32:25, Jgs 3:16, S/S 3:8).

יַרְכָּה yarkāh (3526), Remote area (Jgs 19:1).

כֶּסֶל keṣel (3814), Loins (Jb 15:27).

1. μηρόν mēron acc sing masc

1 on his vesture and on his **thigh** a name written,	Rev 19:16

A common word in classical Greek, *mēros* denotes *the upper part of the leg* upon which a sword might have hung (Homer *Iliad* 1.190; cf. *Liddell-Scott*). It is also used in reference to the thighbone and more generally the leg bone. *Mēros* occurs over 30 times in the Septuagint, usually to translate the Hebrew *yārēkh* meaning "thigh" (cf. Genesis 32:25; Exodus 32:27). Perhaps because of the close proximity of the thigh to the reproductive organs, children were considered offspring of their father's thigh (Genesis 46:26; Exodus 1:5; cf. Harrison, "Thigh," *International Standard Bible Encyclopedia*, 4:839). In the New Testament the word occurs only in Revelation 19:16. There the rider of the white horse, whose name is "the Word of God," has inscribed upon His *thigh* "King of Kings and Lord of Lords."

Strong 3382, Bauer 519, Moulton-Milligan 411, Liddell-Scott 1129.

3250. μήτε mēte conj
And not.

1. μήτε mēte

1	neither by heaven; for it is God's throne:	Matt 5:34
1	Nor by the earth; for it is his footstool:	5:35
1	neither by Jerusalem; ... the city of the great King.	5:35
1	Neither shalt thou swear by thy head,	5:36
1	For John came neither eating nor drinking,	11:18
1	For John came neither eating nor drinking,	11:18
1	so that they could not so much as eat bread.	Mark 3:20
1	For John the Baptist came neither eating bread nor	Luke 7:33
1	For John the Baptist came neither eating bread nor	7:33
1	Take nothing for your journey, neither staves,	9:3
1	neither staves, nor scrip, neither bread,	9:3
1	neither staves, nor scrip, neither bread,	9:3
1	neither money; neither have two coats apiece.	9:3
1	neither money; neither have two coats apiece.	9:3
1	is no resurrection, nor an angel, (NASB)	Acts 23:8
1	is no resurrection, neither angel, nor spirit:	23:8
1	neither eat nor drink till they had killed Paul.	23:12
1	neither eat nor drink till they had killed Paul.	23:12
1	will neither eat nor drink till they have killed him:	23:21
1	will neither eat nor drink till they have killed him:	23:21
1	when neither sun nor stars in many days appeared,	27:20
1	when neither sun nor stars in many days appeared,	27:20
1	Neither give place to the devil.	Eph 4:27
1	ye be not soon shaken in mind, or be troubled,	2 Th 2:2
1	or be troubled, neither by spirit, nor by word,	2:2
1	or be troubled, neither by spirit, nor by word,	2:2
1	nor by word, nor by letter as from us,	2:2
1	understanding neither what they say,	1 Tm 1:7
1	neither what they say, nor whereof they affirm.	1:7
1	having neither beginning of days, nor end of life;	Heb 7:3
1	having neither beginning of days, nor end of life;	7:3
1	swear not, neither by heaven, neither by the earth,	Jas 5:12
1	swear not, neither by heaven, neither by the earth,	5:12
1	neither by any other oath: but let your yea be yea;	5:12
1	not blow on the earth, nor on the sea,	Rev 7:1
1	blow on the earth, nor on the sea, nor on any tree.	7:1
1	Hurt not the earth, neither the sea, nor the trees,	7:3
1	Hurt not the earth, neither the sea, nor the trees,	7:3

Mē (3231), "not," is joined with *te* (4885), "and," to form a negative conjunction that frequently occurs in sequences (*mēte . . . mēte*, "neither . . . nor"; cf. *Liddell-Scott*). Consider Matthew 11:18, "For John came *neither* eating *nor* drinking" (cf. Luke 7:33; Acts 23:8,12,21; 27:20; Hebrews 7:3; Revelation 7:1,3).

The word is also used in sequences that amplify a negated thought. There, "*either . . . or . . . or*" may better accommodate idiomatic English. Examples include Matthew 5:34-36 (RSV): "Do not swear at all; *either* by heaven . . . , *or* by earth . . . , *or* by Jerusalem . . . , *or* by your head . . . " (cf. Luke 9:3; 2 Thessalonians 2:2; 1 Timothy 1:7; James 5:12). In Mark 3:20 (*Textus Receptus*) the term means "*not even.*"

Strong 3383, Bauer 519-20, Liddell-Scott 1129.

3251. μήτηρ mētēr noun
Mother, matron, city.

Cognates:
ἀμήτωρ amētōr (280)
μήτρα mētra (3253)
μητραλῴας mētralōas (3254)
μητρολῴας mētrolōas (3255)
μητρόπολις mētropolis (3255B)

אֵם 'ēm (525), Mother (Gn 28:2, 2 Kgs 4:19, Ez 19:2).

אִשָּׁה 'ishshāh (828), Wife, woman (2 Kgs 22:14, Is 45:10).

יָלַד yāladh (3314), Give birth (Jer 50:12 [27:12]).

1. μήτηρ mētēr nom sing fem
2. μητρός mētros gen sing fem
3. μητρί mētri dat sing fem
4. μητέρα mētera acc sing fem
5. μητέρας mēteras acc pl fem

2	When as his mother Mary was espoused to Joseph,	Matt 1:18
2	they saw the young child with Mary his mother,	2:11
4	and take the young child and his mother,	2:13
4	he took the young child and his mother by night,	2:14
4	and take the young child and his mother,	2:20
4	and took the young child and his mother,	2:21
2	and the daughter against her mother,	10:35
4	He that loveth father or mother more than me	10:37
1	behold, his mother and his brethren stood without,	12:46
1	thy mother and thy brethren stand without,	12:47
1	Who is my mother? and who are my brethren?	12:48
1	Behold my mother and my brethren!	12:49
1	the same is my brother, and sister, and mother.	12:50
1	is not his mother called Mary?	13:55
2	And she, being before instructed of her mother,	14:8
3	and she brought it to her mother.	14:11
4	Honour thy father and mother:	15:4
4	He that curseth father or mother,	15:4
3	Whosoever shall say to his father or his mother,	15:5
4	And honour not his father or his mother,	15:6
4	For this cause shall a man leave father and mother,	19:5
2	which were so born from their mother's womb:	19:12
4	Honour thy father and thy mother:	19:19
4	or brethren, or sisters, or father, or mother,	19:29
1	the mother of Zebedee's children with her sons,	20:20
1	and Mary the mother of James and Joses,	27:56
1	and the mother of Zebedee's children.	27:56
1	There came then his brethren and his mother,	Mark 3:31
1	thy mother and thy brethren without seek for thee.	3:32
1	saying, Who is my mother, or my brethren?	3:33
1	and said, Behold my mother and my brethren!	3:34
1	the same is my brother, and my sister, and mother.	3:35
4	he taketh the father and the mother of the damsel,	5:40
3	and said unto her mother, What shall I ask?	6:24
3	and the damsel gave it to her mother.	6:28
4	Moses said, Honour thy father and thy mother;	7:10
4	Whoso curseth father or mother, let him die	7:10
3	If a man shall say to his father or mother,	7:11
3	no more to do ought for his father or his mother;	7:12
4	leave his father and mother, and cleave to his wife;	10:7
4	Defraud not, Honour thy father and mother.	10:19
4	or father, or mother, or wife, or children,	10:29
5	houses, and brethren, and sisters, and mothers,	10:30
1	and Mary the mother of James the less and of Joses,	15:40
2	with ... Holy Ghost, even from his mother's womb.	Luke 1:15
1	that the mother of my Lord should come to me?	1:43

1	And his **mother** answered and said, Not so;	Luke 1:60
1	And Joseph and his **mother** marvelled	2:33
4	Simeon blessed ... and said unto Mary his **mother**,	2:34
1	and Joseph and his **mother** knew not of it.	2:43
1	and his **mother** said unto him, Son,	2:48
1	but his **mother** kept all these sayings in her heart.	2:51
3	the only son of his **mother**, and she was a widow:	7:12
3	And he delivered him to his **mother**.	7:15
1	Then came to him his **mother** and his brethren,	8:19
1	Thy **mother** and thy brethren stand without,	8:20
1	My **mother** and my brethren are these which hear	8:21
4	and the father and the **mother** of the maiden.	8:51
1	the **mother** against the daughter,	12:53
3	and the daughter against the **mother**;	12:53
4	hate not his father, and **mother**, and wife, and	14:26
4	Honour thy father and thy **mother**.	18:20
1	and the **mother** of Jesus was there:	John 2:1
1	the **mother** of Jesus saith unto him,	2:3
3	His **mother** saith unto the servants,	2:5
1	he, and his **mother**, and his brethren,	2:12
2	enter the second time into his **mother's** womb,	3:4
4	son of Joseph, whose father and **mother** we know?	6:42
1	Now there stood by the cross of Jesus his **mother**,	19:25
2	his **mother**, and his **mother's** sister,	19:25
4	When Jesus therefore saw his **mother**,	19:26
3	he saith unto his **mother**, Woman, behold thy son!	19:26
1	Then saith he to the disciple, Behold thy **mother**!	19:27
3	Mary the **mother** of Jesus, and with his brethren,	Acts 1:14
2	And a certain man lame from his **mother's** womb,	3:2
2	he came to the house of Mary the **mother** of John,	12:12
2	being a cripple from his **mother's** womb,	14:8
4	Salute Rufus ... and his **mother** and mine.	Rom 16:13
2	God, who separated me from my **mother's** womb,	Gal 1:15
1	is free, which is the **mother** of us all.	4:26
4	this cause shall a man leave his father and **mother**,	Eph 5:31
4	Honour thy father and **mother**;	6:2
5	elder women as **mothers**; the younger as sisters,	1 Tm 5:2
3	in thy grandmother Lois, and thy **mother** Eunice;	2 Tm 1:5
1	THE **MOTHER** OF HARLOTS	Rev 17:5

Classical Greek

Mētēr is common in classical Greek. Motherhood was highly regarded in ancient Greece. Mothers of sons fallen in battle were honored before a city's leading citizens (cf. *Bauer*). As a concept, *mētēr* goes beyond the immediate family context. It is also used of animals, of land (frequently, one's native land), and of the origin or source of events (*Liddell-Scott*).

The "mother earth" idea exerted a strong influence in Greek thought. *Mētēr* is also used figuratively to personify wisdom (especially Philo). Philosophers sometimes called matter the "mother and nurse of all" (to delineate the "underlying principle").

Septuagint Usage

Mētēr occurs over 300 times in the Septuagint. It nearly always translates the Hebrew term *'ēm* (forms of which mean "mother," "ancestors," "people," or "city"). The Old Testament is replete with notable mothers: Sarah, Hannah, Ruth, to name a few. *Mētēr* is used to designate a parent (Exodus 20:12, "Honor thy father and thy mother"), and it is used figuratively. For example, Israel is compared to a mother put away for divorcement; Yahweh refuses to put away the Nation (Isaiah 50:1); and God's people are called *mētēr* (Hosea 4:5).

New Testament Usage

Mētēr is freed in the New Testament from excessive myth and religious symbol. Emphasis is on what a good mother represents and what her place is in God's creation. Exodus 20:12 is reiterated (Matthew 15:4; Mark 7:10). Mothers of prominent sons are noted (for example, Mark 15:40). Jesus, however, disallowed an unreasonable elevation of His own earthly mother, Mary (Luke 11:27,28). Paul used the term loosely in Romans 16:13 calling Rufus' mother, "his mother and mine." Elderly ladies are to be treated as one's own mother (1 Timothy 5:2; plural of *mētēr*, "many mothers").

Generally *mētēr* is used literally in the sense of the parent. Qualities of mother or motherhood are applied in other contexts. Symbolic use of the word is minimal with Revelation 17:5, "BABYLON ... THE MOTHER OF HARLOTS" a prime example. While not directly using *mētēr*, other passages augment the New Testament ideal for her (Ephesians 5:22-27, the bride of Christ).

STRONG 3384, BAUER 520, MOULTON-MILLIGAN 411, KITTEL 4:642-44, LIDDELL-SCOTT 1129-30, COLIN BROWN 3:1068-70.

3252. μήτι mēti partic

Perhaps? is it? (usually untranslated).

1. μήτι mēti
2. μήτις mētis

1	Grapes are **not** gathered from thorn (NASB)	Matt 7:16
1	Is **not** this the son of David?	12:23
1	to say unto Him, "Surely **not** I, Lord?" (NASB)	26:22
1	"Surely it is **not** I, Rabbi?" He said to him,	26:25
1	A lamp is **not** brought to be put under (NASB)	Mark 4:21
1	one by one, "Surely **not** I?" (NASB)	14:19
1	"A blind man **cannot** guide a blind (NASB)	Luke 6:39
1	except we should go and buy meat for all this	9:13
1	Come, see a man, ... is **not** this the Christ?	John 4:29
1	He will **not** perform more signs than those (NASB)	7:31
1	"Surely He will **not** kill Himself, (NASB)	8:22
1	Pilate answered, "I am **not** a Jew, (NASB)	18:35
1	"Surely no one can refuse (NASB)	Acts 10:47
2	lest any of them should swim out, and escape.	27:42
1	how much more things that pertain to this life?	1 Co 6:3
1	one another, except by agreement (NASB)	7:5
1	Therefore I was **not** vacillating when I (NASB)	2 Co 1:17
1	Titus did **not** take any (NASB)	12:18
1	Christ is in you--unless **indeed** you fail (NASB)	13:5
1	Doth a fountain send forth ... sweet (NT)	Jas 3:11

This interrogative particle occurs in questions (typically direct, though an indirect question does occur in Luke 9:13) when the speaker anticipates a negative answer (*Bauer*). *Bauer* also notes that it is usually left untranslated and offers no clear-cut translation.

The word is a combination of *mē* (3231), "not," and *ti* (see 4948), "what?" It is best represented by casting the question at hand in such a way as to invite the reader to render a negative response. For example, "A blind man is not able to lead a blind man, *is he*?" (free translation, Luke 6:39, literally, "[*Not*] can a blind man guide?"); "Pilate responded, 'I am not a Jew, *am I*?' " (free translation, John 18:35, literally, "[*Not*] am I a Jew?"; cf. Acts 10:47; 2 Corinthians 1:17; James 3:11).

The expected negative response may not be valid. Judas, who betrayed Jesus, asked, "I am not he, *am I*, Rabbi?" (free translation, Matthew 26:25, literally, "[*Not*] am I, rabbi?"). History knows the answer. (Cf. Matthew 12:23; John 4:29; 8:22.)

STRONG 3385, BAUER 520, MOULTON-MILLIGAN 411, LIDDELL-SCOTT 1130.

3252B. μήτιγε mētige adv
Not even then, let alone.

1. μήτιγε mētige

Mētige is a combination of the particle *mēti* (3252) and *ge* (1058). *Mēti* is an interrogative particle usually left untranslated but used when the question expects a negative answer or when the questioner is in doubt concerning the answer (*Bauer*). *Ge* is a particle that is often untranslatable but is generally appended to a word to emphasize that particular word (*Bauer*). *Mētige* is not documented in the classical literature by *Liddell-Scott* nor in the Septuagint. However, it is found in the papyri sparingly (cf. *Moulton-Milligan*). The only time *mētige* is found in the New Testament is in 1 Corinthians 6:3, "Know ye not that ye shall judge angels? *how much more* (*mētige*) things that pertain to this life?"

STRONG 3386, BAUER 520, MOULTON-MILLIGAN 411.

3253. μήτρα mētra noun
Womb.
COGNATE:
 μήτηρ mētēr (3251)
SYNONYMS:
 γαστήρ gastēr (1057)
 κοιλία koilia (2809)

קָבָה qēvāh (7182), Body (Nm 25:8).

רֶחֶם rechem (7641I), Womb (Ex 13:2, Hos 9:14).
שֶׁגֶר shegher (8156), Firstborn (Ex 13:12).

1. μήτρας mētras gen sing fem
2. μήτραν mētran acc sing fem

2 Every male that openeth the **womb** shall be called...Luke 2:23
1 neither yet the deadness of Sarah's **womb**:..........Rom 4:19

Classical Greek
The noun *mētra* is related to the noun *mētēr* (3251), "mother." *Mētra* denotes the "womb" or more specifically the "entrance to the womb" (cf. *Liddell-Scott*). In classical Greek *mētra* is also applied to a pig's "paunch," and the "pith or heart of trees" (see *Liddell-Scott*). Related terms include *mētregchutēs*, a syringe for injections into the womb, and the adjective *mētridios* which applies to someone or something that is "fruitful" or "filled with seed" (*Liddell-Scott*).

Septuagint Usage
The Septuagint uses *mētra* more than 20 times. Genesis 20:18 records that "the Lord had fast closed up all the *wombs* (*mētra*) of the house of Abimelech." In reference to Leah, God "opened her *womb*" (*mētra*, Genesis 29:31). The papyri uses *mētra* in a similar way (cf. *Moulton-Milligan*).

New Testament Usage
Mētra occurs only two times in the New Testament, and both occurrences reflect the Old Testament usage. Luke used the term when he wrote of Christ's dedication to the Lord: "Every male that openeth the *womb* (*mētra*) shall be called holy to the Lord" (Luke 2:23). In Romans 4:19 Paul spoke of the "deadness of Sarah's *womb*" (*mētra*).

STRONG 3388, BAUER 520, MOULTON-MILLIGAN 411, LIDDELL-SCOTT 1130.

3254. μητραλῴας mētralōas noun
One who strikes his mother, matricide.
CROSS-REFERENCE:
 μήτηρ mētēr (3251)

1. μητραλῴαις mētralōais dat pl masc

1 for murderers of fathers and **murderers of mothers**,..1 Tm 1:9

Classical Greek and Septuagint Usage
Classical Greek uses this word with a variation in spelling, *mētraloias*. The noun *mētralōas* is a compound of *mētēr* (3251), "mother," and *aloiaō*, "tread, smite, crush," hence, "striking one's mother" or "matricide." *Mētralōas* does not occur in the Septuagint.

New Testament Usage
There is only one occurrence of *mētraloas* in the New Testament (1 Timothy 1:9). Paul cataloged a list of very wicked types of people. Referring to them he said, "The law is not made for a righteous man, but . . . for murderers of fathers (*patroloas* [3831B]) and *murderers of mothers* (*mētraloas*)." Note the parallel use of the words for murderers of fathers and mothers.

STRONG 3389, BAUER 520, MOULTON-MILLIGAN 411, LIDDELL-SCOTT 1130 (see "metroloas").

3255. μητρολῷας metroloas noun
One who murders his mother.
CROSS-REFERENCE:
μήτηρ mētēr (3251)

1. μητρολῷαις metrolōais dat pl masc

This word is an alternate spelling of *mētraloas*. See the word study at number 3254.

3255B. μητρόπολις metropolis noun
Mother-state, mother-city, capital city.
CROSS-REFERENCES:
μήτηρ mētēr (3251)
πόλις polis (4032)

1. μητρόπολις metropolis nom sing fem

Classical Greek
The noun *metropolis* is a combination of *mētēr* (3251), "mother," and *polis* (4032), "city, city-state." In classical Greek it denotes a "mother-state" (e.g., the relationship between Athens and her colonies), "mother-city" (meaning one's native place of origin), and "capital city" (*Liddell-Scott*).

Septuagint Usage
Metropolis occurs eight times in the Septuagint translating several different Hebrew terms. Usually *metropolis* is used to describe a literal "city" (Joshua 10:2; 15:13; 21:11; 2 Samuel 20:19 [LXX 2 Kings 20:19]), but at least one occurrence is figurative. Isaiah 1:26 records how God promised to refine and restore the faithful remnant among Israel, and they would be called "the *city* of righteousness." *Moulton-Milligan* documents occurrences in the papyri literature where *metropolis* probably refers to a major city.

New Testament Usage
The word *metropolis* occurs only once in a noncanonical subscription following 1 Timothy 6:21. Although this subscription is included in the Majority Text, several important manuscripts do not include it (e.g., Sinaiticus, Alexandrinus).

STRONG 3390, BAUER 520, MOULTON-MILLIGAN 411, LIDDELL-SCOTT 1130-31.

3256. μιαίνω miainō verb
Stain, defile, pollute, soil.
COGNATES:
ἀμίαντος amiantos (281)
μίασμα miasma (3257)
μιασμός miasmos (3258)
SYNONYMS:
κοινόω koinoō (2813)
μολύνω molunō (3298)
σπιλόω spiloō (4549)

זָנַח zānach (2269), Reject; hiphil: discard (2 Chr 29:19).

חָטָא chātā' (2490), Sin; hiphil: cause to sin (Dt 24:4 [24:6]).

חָלַל chālal (2591), Niphal: be profaned (Ez 7:24); piel: profane (Ex 20:25, Is 43:28, Ez 7:22).

חָנֵף chāneph (2714), Qal: be polluted (Jer 3:1); hiphil: pollute, corrupt (Jer 3:2, Dn 11:32).

טָמֵא ṭāmē' (3041), Qal: be unclean, be defiled (Lv 22:5, Ez 22:3f., Hg 2:13 [2:14]); niphal: defile oneself (Nm 5:14, Ez 23:13, Hos 5:3); piel: pronounce unclean, defile (Lv 13:3, Ps 79:1 [78:1], Ez 18:6); pual: defile oneself (Ez 4:14); hithpael: defile oneself, be defiled (Lv 18:30, Ez 20:7, Hos 9:4); hothpaal: be defiled (Dt 24:4 [24:6]).

טָמֵא ṭāmē' (3042), Defiled, unclean (Nm 6:12, Hg 2:14 [2:15]).

טֻמְאָה ṭum'āh (3043), Uncleanness (Nm 5:19).

1. μιαίνουσιν miainousin 3pl indic pres act
2. μιανθῶσιν mianthōsin 3pl subj aor pass
3. μεμίανται memiantai 3sing indic perf mid
4. μεμιαμένοις memiamenois dat pl masc part perf mid
5. μεμιαμμένοις memiammenois dat pl masc part perf mid
6. μεμιασμένοις memiasmenois dat pl masc part perf mid

2 not into the ... hall, lest they should be defiled;	John 18:28
6 but unto them that are defiled and unbelieving	Tit 1:15
3 but even their mind and conscience is defiled	1:15
2 trouble you, and thereby many be defiled;	Heb 12:15
1 Likewise also these filthy dreamers defile the flesh,	Jude 1:8

Classical Greek
In several early Greek writings *miainō* is used to describe the act of coloring something by painting or staining it. This use is morally neutral; however, other uses acquired negative meanings such as "taint, defile." Frequently

miainō is used of moral pollution and sometimes of religious defilement (cf. *Liddell-Scott*).

Septuagint Usage
In the Septuagint *miainō* is generally translated for the Hebrew *tāmē'* ("ritual uncleanness" or "defilement"). The word is used of sexual impurity (Numbers 5:13,20), dead things (Leviticus 5:3; Haggai 2:13), and religious ceremony (2 Chronicles 36:14; Isaiah 30:22). As in classical Greek, individuals (Genesis 34:5,13,27), the land (Leviticus 18:28; Numbers 5:3), and the sanctuary (Leviticus 15:31) can be defiled.

New Testament Usage
The New Testament moves from ritual (external) defilement to that of an inner quality. *Miainō* occurs 5 times compared to over 100 in the Septuagint. John 18:28 speaks of the Jews' refusal to enter Pilate's Hall in order to avoid defilement in terms of their Passover regulations. Unbelief results in defiled consciences (Titus 1:15) which taint everything these individuals contact. The perfect tense used indicates a continuing state of defilement.

Hebrews 12:14,15 warns against allowing bitterness ("Follow peace with all men," verse 14) to prevent seeing the Lord because of defilement (ingressive aorist, to enter into at a specified point in time). Here *miainō* is deeper than moral sin and indicates also a sinking back into filth. Jude 8 is introduced with the adverb *homoiōs* (3530B), "of similar drift" (the inhabitants of Sodom and Gomorrah, verse 7). These false teachers continually "*defile the flesh*" (*miainousin*, present active tense of *miainō* denoting continuous activity), disobeying God's commands.

STRONG 3392, BAUER 520, MOULTON-MILLIGAN 411, KITTEL 4:644-46, LIDDELL-SCOTT 1132, COLIN BROWN 1:447-49.

3257. μίασμα miasma noun
Defilement, corruption, pollution.
CROSS-REFERENCE:
μιαίνω miainō (3256)

בֶּצַע betsa' (1240), Gain (Ez 33:31).

פִּגּוּל piggûl (6533), Abomination (Lv 7:18 [7:8]).

שִׁקּוּץ shiqqûts (8617), Abomination (Jer 32:34 [39:34]).

1. μιάσματα miasmata nom/acc pl neu

1 after they have escaped the **pollutions** of the world .. 2 Pt 2:20

Classical Greek
Miasma is predominantly used in classical Greek to describe the moral "corruption" or "defilement" associated with criminal or scandalous actions (e.g., "taint of guilt," *Liddell-Scott*). This noun is related to the verb *miainō* (3256) which means "defile." Generally a person was considered to be defiled when a crime was committed. By definition, such sin involved a violation of accepted ritualistic practice. A kind of purification was often needed. It could even require bloodguilt (death as an appropriate penalty). Judges hindering the purification process are designated *miasma* (Antiphon *Tetralogies*). Philo (20 B.C. to A.D. 50) used it to mean ceremonial and then later moral uncleanness. *Miasma* is also common in Greek poetry (*Liddell-Scott*).

Septuagint Usage
In the Septuagint there are three occurrences of *miasma* which have Hebrew equivalents. *Miasma* translates *piggûl*, "uncleanness" ("abomination," KJV), in Leviticus 7:18 (LXX Leviticus 7:8) where the flesh of the sacrifice was not eaten promptly: "The soul that eateth of it shall bear his iniquity." Jeremiah 32:34 (LXX 39:34) describes the desecration of the temple as *shiqqûts*, "detestable" or "an idol" ("abomination," KJV). Ezekiel 33:31 portrays Israel as paying Yahweh lip service while engaging in self-serving activities (*betsa'* or "unjust gain," ["covetousness," KJV], literally "their cut").

New Testament Usage
In the New Testament *miasma* occurs only in 2 Peter 2:20. There the apostate or false teachers are described as those who, at one time, had escaped the "defilements" ("pollutions," KJV) of the *kosmos* (2862), i.e., the world value system, by *epignōsis* (1907) or a full knowledge of the Lord. A kindred word, *miasmos* (see 3258), is translated "uncleanness" in 2 Peter 2:10. False doctrine coupled with the arrogance of these men results in a gradual slipping back into sin. Here the later moral emphasis is seen in the broader meaning and heritage of the word. The body is quite literally defiled and given to passion.

STRONG 3393, BAUER 521, MOULTON-MILLIGAN 412, KITTEL 4:646-47, LIDDELL-SCOTT 1132, COLIN BROWN 1:447-48.

3258. μιασμός miasmos noun
Pollution, corruption, defilement (the act of).

COGNATE:
μιαίνω miainō (3256)
SYNONYM:
ἀλίσγημα alisgēma (232)

1. μιασμοῦ miasmou gen sing masc

1 that walk after the flesh in the lust **of uncleanness,** ...2 Pt 2:10

Classical Greek and Septuagint Usage

In classical literature *miasmos* is used to describe the "act" of defilement or corruption; hence it means "crime, scandal" (*Liddell-Scott*). *Miasma* (3257) is the noun form that describes "defilement" as the result of an action while *miasmos* is the noun that pictures the action or state that defiles or pollutes something. The related word *miasma* occurs in the Septuagint eight times while *miasmos* occurs only twice. In Wisdom of Solomon 14:26 accusations were made against men who engaged in "defiling of souls" (cf. 1 Maccabees 4:43).

New Testament Usage

In 2 Peter 2:10 *miasmos* occurs in the phrase, "the lust of *uncleanness*." This genitive might be more clearly translated "the desires to perform sin," or more literally, "to produce defilement." *Miasma* appears in 2 Peter 2:20 which speaks of "the pollutions (as a result of the act of sin) of the world." The differences in meaning are seen in these instances where each word makes its single appearance.

STRONG 3394, BAUER 521, KITTEL 4:647, LIDDELL-SCOTT 1132, COLIN BROWN 1:447-48.

3259. μίγμα migma noun

Mixture, compound.
CROSS-REFERENCE:
μίγνυμι mignumi (3260)

1. μίγμα migma nom/acc sing neu

1 and brought **a mixture** of myrrh and aloes, ... John 19:39

The noun *migma* occurs in classical literature frequently in a context referring to a "mixture" of medicines. An interesting extension of the word is *migmato pōlēs* which refers to a pharmacist and means "a mixture- or compound-seller" (cf. *Liddell-Scott*). A related form, *migmos*, also occurs in classical writings as an equivalent to *migma* (ibid.). *Migma* occurs in the Septuagint (Sirach 38:8), as does its related verb form *mignumi* (3260), "to mingle or mix something." Both the noun *migma* and the verb form *mignumi* are also found in the papyri (cf. *Moulton-Milligan*). In the New Testament John 19:39 is the only occurrence of *migma*. Here Nicodemus brought a "*mixture* of myrrh and aloes" to prepare the body of Jesus for burial.

STRONG 3395, BAUER 521, MOULTON-MILLIGAN 412, LIDDELL-SCOTT 1132.

3260. μίγνυμι mignumi verb

To mix, mingle, blend.
COGNATES:
μίγμα migma (3259)
συναναμίγνυμι sunanamignumi (4725)
SYNONYM:
κεράννυμι kerannumi (2738)

מָלַח mālach (4553), Salt; pual: be salted (Ex 30:35).
עָרַב 'ārav (6386), Pledge; hithpael: make a bargain (2 Kgs 18:23, Is 36:8); mingle (Ps 106:35 [105:35]).
שִׁית shîth (8308), Put (Gn 30:40).

1. ἔμιξεν emixen 3sing indic aor act
2. μεμιγμένον memigmenon
    acc sing masc part perf mid
3. μεμιγμένην memigmenēn
    acc sing fem part perf mid
4. μεμιγμένα memigmena
    nom/acc pl neu part perf mid

2 They gave him vinegar to drink **mingled with** gall: Matt 27:34
1 blood Pilate had **mingled** with their sacrifices....... Luke 13:1
4 there followed hail and fire **mingled with** blood, ... Rev 8:7
3 I saw as it were a sea of glass **mingled with** fire: 15:2

Classical Greek

The verb *mignumi* is also found with the variant spelling *meignumi* (*Liddell-Scott*; *Bauer*). *Mignumi* means "to mix up" or "blend" and may refer to mixing liquids, solids with liquids, or solids with solids. The word even refers to bringing together armies or individuals as in a battle, or to bringing people together for making acquaintance (cf. *Liddell-Scott*). *Mignumi* may refer to bringing people together in relationships for verbal communication and even for sexual intercourse (ibid.).

Septuagint Usage

Mignumi occurs in the Septuagint only six times. In Genesis 30:40 *mignumi* refers to "mixing" Jacob's cattle with Laban's. Exodus 30:34,35 speaks of "mixing" certain items to create a perfume. The same sense of meaning is found in the papyri (cf. *Moulton-Milligan*).

New Testament Usage

The New Testament has only four occurrences of the verb *mignumi*. Matthew 27:34 speaks of "vinegar to drink *mingled* (*mignumi*) with gall." In Luke 13:1 *mignumi* is used to describe Pilate's slaughter of the Galileans "whose blood Pilate had *mingled* (*mignumi*) with their

μικρόν 3261

sacrifices." Revelation 8:7 speaks of "hail and fire *mingled* (*mignumi*) with blood" (cf. Revelation 15:2).

STRONG 3396, BAUER 521, MOULTON-MILLIGAN 412, LIDDELL-SCOTT 1092 (see "meignumi").

3261. μικρόν mikron adv
A little while.
CROSS-REFERENCE:
μικρός mikros (3262)

1. μικρόν mikron

1	And he went **a little** farther, and fell on his face,	Matt 26:39
1	Little children, yet **a little while** I am with you.	John 13:33
1	Yet **a little while**, and the world seeth me no more;	14:19
1	**A little while**, and ye shall not see me:	16:16
1	and again, **a little while**, and ye shall see me,	16:16
1	**A little while**, and ye shall not see me:	16:17
1	and again, **a little while**, and ye shall see me:	16:17
1	What is this that he saith, **A little while**?	16:18
1	**A little while**, and ye shall not see me:	16:19
1	and again, **a little while**, and ye shall see me?	16:19
1	that I may boast myself **a little**.	2 Co 11:16
1	yet **a little while**, and he that shall come will come,	Heb 10:37

Technically *mikron* is the neuter singular form of the adjective *mikros* (3262). Although *Bauer* indicates the term is simply a substantival usage of the adjective, other lexicons treat *mikron* as a separate adverbial cognate. In all but two instances *mikron* functions as an adverb of time and is translated "a little while" (e.g., John 16:16). The only exceptions to this use are seen at Matthew 26:39 (cf. Mark 14:35) where it appears to be functioning adverbially in relation to the verb *proelthōn*: "He went *a little* further." (For other occurrences and uses of the neuter singular spelling of the adjective *mikros*, see *Bauer* and the word study at number 3262.)

STRONG 3397, BAUER 521, COLIN BROWN 2:429.

3262. μικρός mikros adj
Small, little, short.
COGNATE:
μικρόν mikron (3261)
SYNONYMS:
βρέφος brephos (1018)
νήπιος nēpios (3378)
ὀλίγος oligos (3504)
παιδάριον paidarion (3671)
παιδίον paidion (3676)
παῖς pais (3679)
τέκνον teknon (4891)

זְעֵיר zeʿêr (2275), Something little (Jb 36:2, Is 28:10,13).
זְעֵיר zeʿêr (A2276), Little (Dn 7:8—Aramaic).
מִיכַל mîkhal (4462), Brook (2 Sm 17:20).
מְעַט meʿaṭ (4746), Little, some (Gn 44:25, 2 Chr 12:7, Ez 11:16).
מִצְעָר mitsʿār (4867), Small (Gn 19:20).
צָעִיר tsāʿîr (7087), Least (Jgs 6:15—Codex Alexandrinus only).
צָעַר tsāʿar (7096), Something little (Zec 13:7).
קָטֹן qāṭōn (7277), Small, little (Gn 19:11, 1 Sm 2:19, 1 Kgs 8:64).
קָטָן qāṭān (7278), Small, little (Nm 22:18, 1 Kgs 17:13).
קָלַל qālal (7327), Be slight, be swift; niphal: be too light (Ez 8:17).
שֶׁצֶף shetseph (8611), Outburst (Is 54:8).

1. μικρόν mikron nom/acc sing masc/neu
2. μικρῶν mikrōn gen pl masc/neu
3. μικρός mikros nom sing masc
4. μικροῦ mikrou gen sing masc
5. μικρῷ mikrō dat sing masc
6. μικροῖς mikrois dat pl masc
7. μικρούς mikrous acc pl masc
8. μικροί mikroi nom pl masc
9. μικρά mikra nom sing fem
10. μικράν mikran acc sing fem
11. μικρότερος mikroteros comp nom sing masc
12. μικρότερον mikroteron comp nom/acc sing neu

2	shall give to drink unto one of these **little ones**	Matt 10:42
11	**least** in the kingdom of heaven is greater than he.	11:11
12	Which indeed is the **least** of all seeds:	13:32
2	But whoso shall offend one of these **little ones**	18:6
2	that ye despise not one of these **little ones**;	18:10
2	that one of these **little ones** should perish.	18:14
1	after **a while** came unto him they that stood by,	26:73
11	is **less** than all the seeds that be in the earth:	Mark 4:31
2	And whosoever shall offend one of these **little ones**	9:42
1	he went forward **a little**, and fell on the ground,	14:35
1	And he denied it again. And **a little** after,	14:70
4	and Mary the mother of James the **less** and of Joses,	15:40
11	but he that is **least** in the kingdom of God	Luke 7:28
11	is **least** among you all, the same shall be great.	9:48
1	Fear not, **little flock**; for it is your Father's good	12:32
2	than that he should offend one of these **little ones**.	17:2
3	not for the press, because he was **little** of stature.	19:3
1	Yet **a little while** am I with you,	John 7:33
1	Yet **a little while** is the light with you.	12:35
4	they all gave heed, from the **least** to the greatest,	Acts 8:10
5	witnessing both to **small** and great,	26:22
9	that **a little** leaven leaveneth the whole lump?	1 Co 5:6
1	ye could bear with me **a little** in my folly:	2 Co 11:1
9	**A little** leaven leaveneth the whole lump.	Gal 5:9
4	all shall know me, from the **least** to the greatest.	Heb 8:11
1	Even so the tongue is **a little** member,	Jas 3:5
10	no man can shut it: for thou hast **a little** strength,	Rev 3:8
1	that they should rest yet for **a little** season,	6:11
6	and them that fear thy name, **small** and great;	11:18
7	And he causeth all, both **small** and great,	13:16
8	ye that fear him, both **small** and great.	19:5
2	all men, both free and bond, both **small** and great.	19:18
1	and after that he must be loosed **a little** season.	20:3
7	And I saw the dead, **small** and great,	20:12

Classical Greek and Septuagint Usage
This word demonstrates a wide semantic range in both classical and Septuagintal Greek. It can

be found in classical Greek with reference to numerical quantity or amount of importance of persons, places, things, and even time (e.g., "short"; *Liddell-Scott*). *Mikros* is used over 150 times in the Septuagint to translate 18 different Hebrew terms. The Hebrew term most frequently translated by *mikros* is *qāṭān*, meaning "small" in a variety of ways: of a person's stature (Genesis 19:11), of amount (Numbers 22:18), of size (Deuteronomy 25:13); of importance (1 Chronicles 25:8; 26:13), of age (Jeremiah 6:13). *Mikros* is also found in Philo and Josephus.

New Testament Usage
In the New Testament *mikros* is used in two major ways: (1) to describe the diminutive height (Luke 19:3), age (Matthew 18:6,10,14), and influence (Matthew 10:42; Mark 9:42; Luke 17:2) of people; (2) to describe the size (Matthew 13:32; James 3:5), number (Luke 12:32), significance (Revelation 3:8), and length of time (Hebrews 10:37) of things.

Of special interest to students of the New Testament is the use of the word in the Gospels where *mikros* denotes the status of Christians in the world. While the incident in Matthew 18:6-10 was sparked by an encounter with children, its primary application was to members of the Christian community. They were considered, like the apostles before them (Matthew 10:42), "little"; that is, people of no significance in the eyes of the world. J. Schniewind comments that "the little ones are the lowly in the broadest sense, the poor, uneducated, the socially inferior" (Michel, "mikros," *Kittel*, 4:653, note 22). It is these special members of the body of Christ that Jesus went to great lengths to protect with His strict admonitions in Luke 17:2 and Matthew 18:6,7. The emphasis is heavily placed on the protection of the testimony and position of the "little" ones.

STRONG 3398, BAUER 521, MOULTON-MILLIGAN 412, KITTEL 4:648-59, LIDDELL-SCOTT 1133, COLIN BROWN 2:427-29.

3263. Μίλητος Milētos name
Miletus.

1. Μιλήτου Milētou gen fem
2. Μιλήτῳ Milētō dat fem
3. Μίλητον Milēton acc fem

3 and the next day we came to **Miletus**.............. Acts 20:15
1 And from **Miletus** he sent to Ephesus,............. Acts 20:17
2 but Trophimus have I left at **Miletum** sick......... 2 Tm 4:20

Seaport city in western Asia Minor where Paul bid farewell to the Ephesian elders (Acts 20:17ff.)

3264. μίλιον milion noun
A Roman mile.

1. μίλιον milion nom/acc sing neu

1 And whosoever shall compel thee to go a **mile**,..... Matt 5:41

Milion is a unit of measure. In Roman measure it is equivalent to 8 stades, 1,000 paces, or about 1,618 yards in English measure. Two related words carry the same idea. The verb *miliazō* means "to measure by mile or mark by milestone" (*Liddell-Scott*). The related noun form *miliasmos* refers to the act of measuring or marking off by miles (ibid.). Neither *milion* nor its related verb or noun appear in the Septuagint. The word is found in the papyri (cf. *Moulton-Milligan*). *Milion* occurs only one time in the New Testament. If one should "compel thee to go a *mile* (*milion*), go with him twain" (Matthew 5:41).

STRONG 3400, BAUER 521, MOULTON-MILLIGAN 412, LIDDELL-SCOTT 1134.

3265. μιμέομαι mimeomai verb
Imitate, represent, mimic, portray.
COGNATES:
μιμητής mimētēs (3266)
συμμιμητής summimētēs (4682)
SYNONYMS:
ἀκολουθέω akoloutheō (188)
ἐξακολουθέω exakoloutheō (1795)
ἐπακολουθέω epakoloutheō (1857)
κατακολουθέω katakoloutheō (2598)
παρακολουθέω parakoloutheō (3738)
συνακολουθέω sunakoloutheō (4721)

1. μιμοῦ mimou 2sing impr pres mid
2. μιμεῖσθε mimeisthe 2pl impr pres mid
3. μιμεῖσθαι mimeisthai inf pres mid

3 For yourselves know how ye ought **to follow** us:..... 2 Th 3:7
3 make ourselves an ensample unto you **to follow** us...... 3:9
2 whose faith **follow**, considering the end............. Heb 13:7
1 Beloved, **follow** not that which is evil,............... 3 Jn 1:11

Classical Greek
Mimeomai is one of the many members of the *mem-* stem word group. Basically this deponent verb means "represent, imitate, portray" and is frequently used in reference to the arts (i.e.,

sculpture, painting, music) and poetry (*Liddell-Scott*).

Septuagint Usage
Only one instance of *mimeomai* occurs in the canonical portions of the Septuagint, although even here the Hebrew is uncertain (Psalm 31:6 [LXX 30:6]). Otherwise it occurs twice in the Wisdom of Solomon (4:2; 15:9) and twice in 4 Maccabees (9:23; 13:9). In the Apocrypha the role of "imitation" is positive (of virtue, Wisdom of Solomon 4:2) and negative (of one who imitates the idol-makers, Wisdom of Solomon 15:9). In 4 Maccabees there is the foreshadowing of martyrdom; those dying for the religion of Israel urge others to "imitate" their dedication (4 Maccabees 9:23; cf. 13:9, for the sake of the Law).

New Testament Usage
The verb *mimeomai* occurs only four times in the New Testament, although the concept of "imitation" is present in the noun *mimētēs* (3266), "imitator." Paul used *mimeomai* twice in his second letter to the Thessalonians (3:7,9). He urged that they "imitate" us ("follow us, KJV). The point of imitation in this case concerned Paul and his coworkers' life-style: they were not idle or disruptive (*ataktos* [807]) in the community. From other texts it is clear that Paul's pattern for imitation was none other than Christ (1 Corinthians 11:1). Thus, those who imitated Paul were in fact imitating Christ (cf. Ephesians 5:1; 1 Thessalonians 1:6).

Conduct too (*anastrophē* [389]) was the concern of the writer of Hebrews who urged his readers to imitate the life-style of their leaders (13:7). John's third epistle also views "imitation" in terms of conduct. Good—the attribute of God—rather than evil was to be the object of imitation (3 John 11).

STRONG 3401, BAUER 521-22, MOULTON-MILLIGAN 412, KITTEL 4:659-74, LIDDELL-SCOTT 1134, COLIN BROWN 1:490-91.

3266. μιμητής mimētēs noun
Imitator, follower.
CROSS-REFERENCE:
μιμέομαι mimeomai (3265)

1. μιμηταί mimētai nom pl masc

1 Wherefore I beseech you, be ye **followers** of me..... 1 Co 4:16
1 Be ye **followers** of me, even as I also am of Christ..... 11:1
1 Be ye therefore **followers** of God, as dear children;.. Eph 5:1
1 And ye became **followers** of us, and of the Lord,....1 Th 1:6
1 For ye, brethren, became **followers** of the churches.. 1 Th 2:14
1 but **followers** of them who ... inherit the promises.... Heb 6:12
1 if ye be **followers** of that which is good?............ 1 Pt 3:13

Classical Greek
Related to the verb *mimeomai*, "to imitate," the noun *mimētēs* denotes "one who imitates, an actor." In a negative sense it means "imposter" or "forger" (*Liddell-Scott*). Despite the negative association, this word group became significant in the sphere of ethics. "Imitation" of what was good was desired above imitation of what was evil. Michaelis notes that the ideal relation between a teacher and a student or a parent and a child was expressed in *mimeomai* language ("mimeomai," *Kittel*, 4:661). The related term *mimesis* acquired special import in philosophical discussions regarding the origin of the world (ibid., pp.661ff.).

Septuagint Usage
Mimētēs does not occur in the Septuagint either in the canonical or apocryphal sources. The verb *mimeomai* and the term *mimētas* ("counterfeit copy") do appear in limited number, mostly in the Apocrypha (e.g., Wisdom of Solomon 4:2; 9:8; 4 Maccabees 9:23). That the Hebrew knows virtually no concept of imitation is clear in that the single canonical use (Psalm 31:6 [LXX 30:6]) has no Hebrew counterpart.

New Testament Usage
Apart from Hebrews 6:12 and 1 Peter 3:13 *mimētēs* is a uniquely Pauline expression (five times) in the New Testament. From the context of Paul's usage it is likely that *mimētēs* has ethical overtones. He encouraged his Corinthian readers to imitate his own lifestyle (1 Corinthians 4:16; 11:1). He was so concerned that this should take place that he sent Timothy to remind them of it (1 Corinthians 4:17). Apparently Paul taught such a life-style in all the churches. *Mimētēs* ("followers") here closely approximates the idea of disciple (*mathētēs* [3073]), and there are apparently links between living out this life-style and suffering for the gospel (cf. 1 Corinthians 4:12-15; 1 Thessalonians 2:14). The standard for imitation, however, is not Paul, but ultimately Christ, whom Paul imitated (1 Thessalonians 1:6). He could even suggest believers "become followers of God" and live a life of love and high moral integrity (Ephesians 5:1ff.). To further stress this concept, a new term comes into being in Philippians 3:17, *summimētēs* (4682), "imitators with" ("followers together," KJV).

The writer of Hebrews made the same ethical connection in his use of *mimētēs*. Believers are to imitate ("follow," KJV) those great saints whose faith and patience are exemplary (6:12).

Strong 3402, Bauer 522, Moulton-Milligan 412, Kittel 4:659-74, Liddell-Scott 1134, Colin Brown 1:490-91.

3267. μιμνῄσκω mimnēskō verb
To remember, call to mind, recall.

Cognates:
    ἀναμιμνῄσκω anamimnēskō (362)
    ἀνάμνησις anamnēsis (363)
    ἐπαναμιμνῄσκω epanamimnēskō (1863)
    μνεία mneia (3281)
    μνῆμα mnēma (3282)
    μνημεῖον mnēmeion (3283)
    μνήμη mnēmē (3284)
    μνημονεύω mnēmoneuō (3285)
    μνημόσυνον mnēmosunon (3286)
    ὑπομιμνῄσκω hupomimnēskō (5117)
    ὑπόμνησις hupomnēsis (5118)

Synonyms:
    ἀναμιμνῄσκω anamimnēskō (362)
    μνημονεύω mnēmoneuō (3285)
    ὑπομιμνῄσκω hupomimnēskō (5117)

זָכַר zākhar (2226), Qal: remember (Dt 9:7, Neh 5:19, Ps 105:5 [104:5]); niphal: be mentioned, be remembered (Jb 28:18, Ps 83:4 [82:4], Ez 18:24); hiphil: mention, invoke (1 Sm 4:18, Ps 71:16 [70:16], Is 48:1).

נָשָׂא nāsā' (5558), Lift up, take up (Gn 40:13,20, Ps 16:4 [15:4]).

עוּר 'āwar (5996), Hithpolel: arouse oneself (Is 64:7).

פָּקַד pāqadh (6734), Seek (Is 26:16).

1. μιμνῄσκῃ mimnēskē 2sing indic pres mid
2. μιμνῄσκεσθε mimnēskesthe 2pl impr pres mid

1 What is man, that thou art mindful of him?......... Heb 2:6
2 Remember them that are in bonds,................... 13:3

Classical Greek
Mimnēskō occurs in classical literature meaning "to remember" or "to call to mind." The middle-passive form *mimnēskomai* can be found in classical literature with the sense "to remind oneself" and hence, "to remember" (*Liddell-Scott*). The word also means "to bear in mind" or "to be mindful" of a situation. One might also "remember a thing aloud" or "mention" it (ibid.).

Septuagint Usage
There are numerous occurrences of the term in the Septuagint, where *mimnēskō* translates five Hebrew terms. The Hebrew term most frequently translated by *mimnēskō* is *zākhar*, generally meaning "remember." Because of God's perfect faithfulness, it is He who "remembers" His people (Genesis 8:1; Psalm 9:12) and His covenant with them (Exodus 2:24; Leviticus 26:42). For the people to keep His covenant they must "remember" and obey His commandments (Numbers 15:39,40). And the day will come when the faithful from "the ends of the world shall *remember* and turn unto the Lord: and all the kindreds of the nations shall worship before thee" (Psalm 22:27 [LXX 21:27]).

New Testament Usage
Bauer does not list this word in a lexical entry but treats it under the middle-passive form *mimnēskomai*. However, Thayer gives *mimnēskō* as the lexical entry and treats other words of similar root as if they were all forms of this verb (*Greek-English Lexicon*). *Mimnēskō* appears only twice in the New Testament, both times in Hebrews. In 2:6 the writer of Hebrews quotes Psalm 8:4: "What is man, that thou *art mindful* (literally, 'remember') of him?" Among the concluding remarks of this epistle there is an exhortation to "remember" those believers who were incarcerated for their faith in Jesus Christ by vicariously sharing in their suffering (Hebrews 13:3).

Strong 3403, Bauer 522 (see "mimnēskomai"), Moulton-Milligan 412-13 (see "mimnēskomai"), Kittel 4:675-78, Liddell-Scott 1135, Colin Brown 3:230,233,240-42,245.

3268. μισέω miseō verb
Hate, detest, abhor, prefer against.

זָעַם zā'am (2278), Be angry (Prv 22:14).

מָאַס mā'as (4128), Qal: despise, reject (Prv 15:32 [16:3], Is 33:15); niphal: be rejected (Is 54:6).

צָרַר tsārar (7173), Foe (Ps 74:4 [73:4]).

קוּם qûm (7251), Rise (Ps 74:23 [73:23]).

שָׂנֵא sānē' (7983), Qal: hate (Dt 7:10, Ps 69:14 [68:14], Am 5:10); niphal: be hated (Prv 14:20); piel: one who hates, enemy (Nm 10:35, 2 Sm 22:41, Ps 55:12 [54:12]).

שְׂנָא s^enā' (A7984), Enemy (Dn 4:19 [4:16])—Aramaic.

שִׂנְאָה sin'āh (7985), Hate (Dt 1:27).

שָׂנִיא sānî' (7986), Disliked (Dt 21:15).

שָׁאַף shā'aph (8079), Crush (Ez 36:3).

1. μισῶ misō 1sing indic pres act
2. μισεῖς miseis 2sing indic pres act
3. μισεῖ misei 3sing indic pres act
4. μισῇ misē 3sing subj pres act

5. **μισῶν** misōn nom sing masc part pres act
6. **μισοῦντες** misountes nom pl masc part pres act
7. **μισούντων** misountōn gen pl masc part pres act
8. **μισοῦσιν** misousin dat pl masc part pres act
9. **μισοῦντας** misountas acc pl masc part pres act
10. **μισεῖν** misein inf pres act
11. **ἐμίσησα** emisēsa 1sing indic aor act
12. **ἐμίσησας** emisēsas 2sing indic aor act
13. **ἐμίσησεν** emisēsen 3sing indic aor act
14. **ἐμίσησαν** emisēsan 3pl indic aor act
15. **μισήσωσιν** misēsōsin 3pl subj aor act
16. **μεμίσηκεν** memisēken 3sing indic perf act
17. **μεμισήκασιν** memisēkasin 3pl indic perf act
18. **μισήσεις** misēseis 2sing indic fut act
19. **μισήσει** misēsei 3sing indic fut act
20. **μισήσουσιν** misēsousin 3pl indic fut act
21. **ἐμίσουν** emisoun 3pl indic imperf act
22. **μισούμενοι** misoumenoi
 nom pl masc part pres mid
23. **μεμισημένου** memisēmenou
 gen sing neu part perf mid

18	love thy neighbour, and **hate** thine enemy.	Matt 5:43
9	But I say ... do good to them that **hate** you,	5:44
19	for either he will **hate** the one, and love the other;	6:24
22	ye shall be **hated** of all men for my name's sake:	10:22
22	ye shall be **hated** of all nations for my name's sake...	24:9
20	betray one another, and shall **hate** one another.	24:10
22	ye shall be **hated** of all men for my name's sake:	Mark 13:13
7	and from the hand of all that **hate** us;	Luke 1:71
15	Blessed are ye, when men shall **hate** you,	6:22
8	Love ... enemies, do good to them which **hate** you,	6:27
3	If any man come to me, and **hate** not his father,	14:26
19	for either he will **hate** the one, and love the other;	16:13
21	But his citizens **hated** him, and sent a message	19:14
22	ye shall be **hated** of all men for my name's sake:	21:17
3	For every one that doeth evil **hateth** the light,	John 3:20
10	The world cannot **hate** you; but me it hateth,	7:7
3	The world cannot **hate** you; but me it **hateth**,	7:7
5	and he that **hateth** his life in this world	12:25
3	If the world **hate** you, ye know that it hated me	15:18
16	ye know that it hated me before it **hated** you.	15:18
3	therefore the world **hateth** you.	15:19
5	He that **hateth** me **hateth** my Father also.	15:23
3	He that **hateth** me **hateth** my Father also.	15:23
17	but now have they both seen and **hated**	15:24
14	They **hated** me without a cause.	15:25
13	and the world hath **hated** them,	17:14
1	that do I not; but what I **hate**, that do I.	Rom 7:15
11	Jacob have I loved, but Esau have I **hated**.	9:13
13	For no man ever yet **hated** his own flesh;	Eph 5:29
6	hateful, and **hating** one another.	Tit 3:3
12	Thou hast loved righteousness, and **hated** iniquity;	Heb 1:9
5	that saith he is in the light, and **hateth** his brother,	1 Jn 2:9
5	But he that **hateth** his brother is in darkness,	2:11
3	Marvel not, my brethren, if the world **hate** you.	3:13
5	Whosoever **hateth** his brother is a murderer:	3:15
4	If a man say, I love God, and **hateth** his brother,	4:20
6	**hating** even the garment spotted by the flesh.	Jude 1:23
2	that thou **hatest** the deeds of the Nicolaitanes,	Rev 2:6
1	the deeds of the Nicolaitanes, which I also **hate**.	2:6
1	the doctrine of the Nicolaitanes, which thing I **hate**.	2:15
20	the ten horns ... these shall **hate** the whore,	17:16
23	and a cage of every unclean and **hateful** bird.	18:2

Classical Greek and Septuagint Usage

In classical Greek *miseō* primarily means "hate." It is frequently used with reference to hating someone (or a god), or being hated by someone (or by a god). In the Septuagint the word refers to an emotional impulse of men among themselves, either in a strong sense such as enmity (Genesis 26:27; Judges 11:7; 2 Samuel [LXX 2 Kings] 5:8; 13:22), or in a milder sense such as preference against (Genesis 29:31-33; Deuteronomy 21:15; Proverbs 19:7) or distaste (Deuteronomy 22:13; 24:3). In addition, *miseō* may mean "to slight" (Isaiah 60:15) or "to be unfriendly" (Exodus 20:5; Deuteronomy 7:10). Another occurrence states there is a divine command to overcome *hatred* (Leviticus 19:17). Furthermore, the word relates to God's hatred of sin and phony worship (Isaiah 1:11ff.; Amos 5:21).

New Testament Usage

In the New Testament the word occurs 41 times. It represents: (1) malicious feelings toward other people or things (Matthew 10:22; Luke 6:22,27); (2) a correct feeling of aversion from what is evil (Romans 7:15; Hebrews 1:9); and (3) a relative preference of one thing over another, especially concerning discipleship (Matthew 6:24; Luke 14:26; 16:13; John 12:25).

When God said "Jacob I loved, but Esau I *hated*" (Malachi 1:3; Romans 9:13), or when Jesus stated we must "hate" our family in order to follow Him (Luke 14:26), the idea of the term conveyed is "to prefer one over the other," not "to hate" in a literal sense.

STRONG 3404, BAUER 522-23, MOULTON-MILLIGAN 413, KITTEL 4:683-94, LIDDELL-SCOTT 1136, COLIN BROWN 1:555-57.

3269. μισθαποδοσία

misthapodosia noun
Recompense of reward, reward, punishment.
CROSS-REFERENCE:
 μισθόω misthoō (3273)

1. **μισθαποδοσίαν** misthapodosian acc sing fem

1	received a just **recompense** of reward;	Heb 2:2
1	which hath great **recompense** of reward.	10:35
1	he had respect unto the **recompense** of the reward.	11:26

This word is not used at all in classical Greek nor is it found anywhere in the Septuagint (*Bauer*). A related noun, *misthos* (3272), is used classically in the sense of "reward for work," "reimbursement," or "compensation for service" (cf. *Liddell-Scott*). It can also be seen as the proper reward for negative behavior, hence, "punishment" (*Bauer*).

New Testament Usage
In the New Testament *misthapodosia* occurs only three times, all of which are in Hebrews. In each case it denotes "recompense of reward." However, there are two nuances of meaning for this word. In Hebrews 10:35 and 11:26 the term refers to the reward which comes with the fullness of future salvation as a result of faith and steadfastness. In Hebrews 2:2 the word signifies "punishment" as a recompense to warn readers against not heeding the New Testament message of salvation which is greater than that of the Old Testament.

STRONG 3405, BAUER 523, KITTEL 4:695-728, LIDDELL-SCOTT 1136, COLIN BROWN 3:138,141,143.

3270. μισθαποδότης
misthapodotēs noun
One who pays wages, rewarder.
CROSS-REFERENCE:
μισθόω misthoō (3273)

1. μισθαποδότης misthapodotēs nom sing masc
1 he is **a rewarder** of them that diligently seek him.... Heb 11:6

Classical Greek
Misthapodotēs is a compound from *misthos* (3272), "wages," and *apodidōmi* (586), "to give back or restore." These combine to form the meaning "to pay wages." The noun form *misthapodotēs* has the ending *tēs* which emphasizes the one who does the action. Therefore, *misthapodotēs* is literally "one who pays wages." The noun *misthapodotēs* does not occur in the Septuagint but does occur in the papyri (cf. *Moulton-Milligan*).

New Testament Usage
In the New Testament *misthapodotēs* occurs only one time (Hebrews 11:6) while the related form *misthapodosia* (3269) occurs three times. *Misthapodosia* refers to the reward or wages while *misthapodotēs* refers to the person doing the paying, as in Hebrews 11:6, "he is a *rewarder* of them that diligently seek him."

STRONG 3406, BAUER 523, MOULTON-MILLIGAN 413, KITTEL 4:695-728, LIDDELL-SCOTT 1136, COLIN BROWN 3:138,141,143.

3271. μίσθιος misthios adj
Hired person, laborer.
CROSS-REFERENCE:
μισθόω misthoō (3273)

שָׂכִיר sākhîr (7957), Hired man (Lv 25:50).
שָׂכָר sākhar (7963), Hireling (Sir 7:20).

1. μίσθιοι misthioi nom pl masc
2. μισθίων misthiōn gen pl masc
1 **hired servants** of my father's have bread enough.... Luke 15:17
2 make me as one of thy **hired servants**............ 15:19

Classical Greek and Septuagint Usage
Misthios comes from the noun *misthos* (3272), "wages." The *misthios* is one who is a salaried person, a common laborer, or one who works for a daily wage. The Septuagint uses *misthios* in Leviticus 19:13 to refer to a person whose financial situation is so critical that he must be paid wages at the end of each day (a day laborer). Leviticus 25:50 uses *misthios* in reference to a "hired servant."

New Testament Usage
Misthios occurs only twice in the New Testament. The Prodigal Son spoke of the many "hired servants" (*misthios*) of his father's house (Luke 15:17). He asked later to be treated as one of his father's *misthios*, "hired servants" (Luke 15:19).

STRONG 3407, BAUER 523, MOULTON-MILLIGAN 413, KITTEL 4:695-728, LIDDELL-SCOTT 1136, COLIN BROWN 3:138-39.

3272. μισθός misthos noun
Payment, wages, reward, punishment.
COGNATE:
μισθόω misthoō (3273)
SYNONYM:
ὀψώνιον opsōnion (3664)

אֶשְׁכָּר 'eshkār (841), Payment (Ez 27:15).
אֶתְנַן 'ethnan (900), Hire (Is 23:18).
מְחִיר meᶜchîr (4379), Price (Mi 3:11).
מַשְׂכֹּרֶת maskōreth (5032), Wages (Gn 29:15, 31:7,41).
עִזְבוֹנִים ʿizvônîm (6014), Wares (Ez 27:27,33).
פֹּעַל poʿal (6714), Wages (Jb 7:2, Jer 22:13).
פְּעֻלָּה peᶜullah (6715), Wages (Lv 19:13).
שָׂכִיר sākhîr (7957), Hired man (Jb 7:1—Codex Alexandrinus only).
שָׂכָר sākhar (7963), Wages, reward (Gn 31:8, 2 Chr 15:7, Is 40:10).
שֶׂכֶר sekher (7966), Reward (Prv 11:18).

1. μισθός misthos nom sing masc
2. μισθοῦ misthou gen sing masc
3. μισθόν misthon acc sing masc

1 Rejoice, ... for great is your **reward** in heaven:...... Matt 5:12
3 love them which love you, what **reward** have ye?...... 5:46
3 otherwise ye have no **reward** of your Father............ 6:1

μισθός 3272

3	Verily I say unto you, They have their **reward**.	Matt 6:2
3	Verily I say unto you, They have their **reward**.	6:5
3	Verily I say unto you, They have their **reward**.	6:16
3	shall receive a prophet's **reward**;	10:41
3	shall receive a righteous man's **reward**.	10:41
3	verily I say ... he shall in no wise lose his **reward**.	10:42
3	Call the labourers, and give them their **hire**,	20:8
3	verily I say unto you, he shall not lose his **reward**.	Mark 9:41
1	for, behold, your **reward** is great in heaven:	Luke 6:23
1	and your **reward** shall be great,	6:35
2	for the labourer is worthy of his **hire**.	10:7
3	And he that reapeth receiveth **wages**,	John 4:36
2	purchased a field with the **reward** of iniquity;	Acts 1:18
1	is the **reward** not reckoned of grace, but of debt.	Rom 4:4
3	and every man shall receive his own **reward**	1 Co 3:8
3	any man's work abide ... he shall receive a **reward**.	3:14
3	For if I do this thing willingly, I have a **reward**:	9:17
1	What is my **reward** then?	9:18
2	And, The labourer is worthy of his **reward**.	1 Tm 5:18
1	Behold, the **hire** of the labourers who have reaped	Jas 5:4
3	And shall receive the **reward** of unrighteousness,	2 Pt 2:13
3	Balaam ... who loved the **wages** of unrighteousness;	2:15
3	but that we receive a full **reward**.	2 Jn 1:8
2	ran greedily after the error of Balaam for **reward**,	Jude 1:11
3	that thou shouldest give **reward** unto thy servants	Rev 11:18
1	behold, I come quickly; and my **reward** is with me,	22:12

The noun *misthos* in its basic sense denotes "payment for work or services." From this evolved the general idea of "reward, recompense, repayment" in both a positive and a negative sense. The term is utilized in both ways in classical as well as in the Septuagint. The New Testament also picks up on this understanding and uses it over 30 times. The term functions in an ordinary monetary sense and in the figurative sense of "reward." Figuratively, it can be used to describe the "reward" in the life to come.

Old Testament Background

The concept that God rewards and repays each individual according to his or her deeds is central and fundamental to our biblically revealed religion from its inception. God's holiness and righteousness are the basis for this. He rewards that which is good with life and "rewards" that which is evil with destruction. God's reward is just.

Both the negative and the positive dimensions of reward are expressed in the history of the Old Testament. Israel's relationship with God and His purpose determined its fate. The nation as well as individuals "reaped what it sowed." On the other hand, there is not an unalterable relationship between sin and its reward/consequences. Repentance will avert the judgment of God, and it opens the channel to forgiveness and grace (Jeremiah 19:1f.; Ezekiel 18:20f.).

Intertestamental Period

Within later Judaism (in certain groups) the concept of God's reward increasingly deteriorated from its Old Testament roots to the point where it regarded reward (merits) as something which could be "earned" and "stored." Through good deeds—especially prayer, fasting, and almsgiving—it was believed one could gain great reward if the total of the good deeds surpassed the evil deeds (violations of the Law and traditions). This vein of Judaism totally misinterpreted the Law and the prophetic idea of reward. The consequence of such an aberration was either an endless anxiety or uncertainty over one's relationship to God, or even worse, some groups within Judaism degenerated into a Pharisaic-like legalism which held that righteousness could be attained through good works. Such a narrow view perverts God's law and prevents others from experiencing God's mercy.

Septuagint Usage

Misthos occurs over 50 times in the Septuagint translating 6 Hebrew terms. The Hebrew term translated most frequently is *sākhar* meaning "wages." Usually *sākhar* was used of "wages" for actual work rendered (Genesis 29:15; 30:28; Exodus 2:9; Leviticus 19:13; Numbers 18:31; Jeremiah 22:13), but it could also be found in the figurative sense of the "wages" of good versus evil deeds (Proverbs 11:18). In Genesis 15:1 Abram was promised that God would be his "reward," and in Psalm 127:3 (LXX 126:3) children are said to be God's "reward" even before they are the mother's.

New Testament Usage

Misthos is used most often in the New Testament in a figurative and eschatological sense. In the Sermon on the Mount Jesus exhorted His disciples to rejoice in their earthly persecution for they, like the prophets, would receive their "reward" *in heaven* (Matthew 5:12; Luke 6:23). Likewise the believer's stewardship and sacrificial life-style on earth will be rewarded *in heaven* (Matthew 5:46; 6:1,2,5,16; cf. Luke 6:35). Those who support the work of Christ by supporting His disciples will also have a share in the heavenly "reward" (Matthew 10:40-42; cf. Mark 9:41). Paul reminded the Corinthians that "every man shall receive his own *reward* according to his own labor" (1 Corinthians 3:8; cf. 3:14; Revelation 11:18). Every person will receive a "reward" after his life on earth is done; however, not every "reward" will be desirable. Because of the direct relationship between conduct now and the coming reward, some will receive the "*reward* of iniquity" (Acts 1:18) and the "*wages* of unrighteousness" (2 Peter 2:13,15). It was Jesus who made the final appeal for urgency and integrity in the believer's earthly work when He said, "And, behold, I come quickly; and my *reward* is with me, to give to every man according as his work shall be" (Revelation 22:12).

As elsewhere, Jesus aligned himself with the prophets of the Old Testament. He advocated the view that individuals are responsible before God, and He reaffirmed that there is indeed "reward" for both the good and the evil (e.g., Matthew 6:19,20; 19:21; Romans 2:5,6). However, He reprimanded those who believed that righteousness could be earned or stored to one's account (see Romans 3:9 to 4:5). A believer's relationship to God is not some businesslike contract that depends on efforts and work; rather, it depends totally upon God's forgiveness and upon the redemption found in Jesus Christ.

This essential view is reiterated from different perspectives by the various inspired writers of the New Testament. In Romans 4:4,5 Paul advised that the believer's reward is not the result of an obligation. God justifies men by faith, not works. They are credited with righteousness apart from works (Romans 4:6). This does not, however, negate the twofold reward/judgment they will receive on the basis of works (e.g., Romans 2:1-10; 6:23; 2 Corinthians 5:10; Galatians 6:7f.). Forgiveness for sin as well as reward for good deeds are always gifts in the New Testament.

Christians may not receive their reward during this existence. In addition, their reward is not to have "gold and silver, fine homes, and fine clothes." Such an attitude is typical of the world's values. The believer's reward is to become like Christ and to be with Him eternally.

STRONG 3408, BAUER 523, MOULTON-MILLIGAN 413, KITTEL 4:695-728, LIDDELL-SCOTT 1137, COLIN BROWN 3:138-39,141-45.

3273. μισθόω misthoō verb

To let out for hire; hire.
COGNATES:
ἀντιμισθία antimisthia (486)
μισθαποδοσία misthapodosia (3269)
μισθαποδότης misthapodotēs (3270)
μίσθιος misthios (3271)
μισθός misthos (3272)
μίσθωμα misthōma (3274)
μισθωτός misthōtos (3275)

כָּרָה kārâh (3868), Buy (Hos 3:2).

סָכַר sākhar (5727), Hire (Ezr 4:5).

שָׂכִיר sākhîr (7957), Hired (Is 7:20).

שָׂכַר sākhar (7963), Hire (Dt 23:4, 2 Kgs 7:6, Is 46:6).

1. ἐμισθώσατο emisthōsato 3sing indic aor mid
2. μισθώσασθαι misthōsasthai inf aor mid

2 went out early in the morning **to hire labourers**.... Matt 20:1
1 They say unto him, Because no man **hath hired us**..... 20:7

Classical Greek
Misthoō occurs many times in classical literature. The word can be found in reference to "hiring out" people or "letting out" buildings or property, as in our current expression "to farm out." The middle form occurs with the meaning of "to hire," just as it does in the New Testament.

Septuagint Usage
The Septuagint uses the verb several times. Genesis 30:16 cites Leah's claim to "have hired" Jacob by giving Rachel some of her son's mandrakes. Deuteronomy 23:4 speaks of the enemies of Israel who "hired against thee Balaam the son of Beor." Note that the most common occurrences in the Septuagint are the middle form which means "to hire" rather than "to hire out." *Moulton-Milligan* documents occurrences in the papyri with both meanings.

New Testament Usage
In the New Testament *misthoō* does not occur in the active form meaning "to let out for hire." However, it does occur in the middle form in Matthew 20:1,7 with the sense of "to hire." Matthew 20:1 speaks of a man "which went out early in the morning *to hire* laborers into his vineyard."

STRONG 3409, BAUER 523, MOULTON-MILLIGAN 413-14, KITTEL 4:695-728, LIDDELL-SCOTT 1137, COLIN BROWN 3:138-39.

3274. μίσθωμα misthōma noun

Contract price, expense, rent, anything rented.
CROSS-REFERENCE:
μισθόω misthoō (3273)

אֶתְנָה 'ethnāh (898), Wages (Hos 2:12).

אֶתְנַן 'ethnan (900), Hire, payment (Dt 23:18, Ez 16:34, Mi 1:7).

נֵדֶה nēdheh (5256), Gift (Ez 16:33).

נָדָן nādhān (5262), Gift (Ez 16:33).

1. μισθώματι misthōmati dat sing neu

1 dwelt two whole years in his own **hired house**,......Acts 28:30

Classical Greek
This noun is derived from the verb *misthoō* (3273) which means "to hire." According to Louw and Nida *misthōma* is "that which has been rented or hired" (*Greek-English Lexicon*) or the price—either paid or received—for goods and services. *Liddell-Scott* cites the following examples which are typical of its use: a soldier's wage, a contract price for building construction, an allowance for public service rendered, and a doctor's fee.

Septuagint Usage
In the Septuagint the word is used 11 times, usually in connection with payment for the hiring of prostitutes (e.g., Deuteronomy 23:18; Ezekiel 16:31,33,34).

New Testament Usage
The word occurs only once in the New Testament (Acts 28:30) where Paul paid "rent" on a house for 2 years, meaning he lived on his own earnings ("at his own expense," RSV).

STRONG 3410, BAUER 523, MOULTON-MILLIGAN 414, KITTEL 4:695-728, LIDDELL-SCOTT 1137, COLIN BROWN 3:138-39.

3275. μισθωτός misthōtos adj
A hired person, laborer.
CROSS-REFERENCE:
μισθόω misthoō (3273)

שָׂכִיר sākhîr (7957), Hired servant, hireling (Lv 25:6, Jb 7:2, Is 16:14).

1. μισθωτός misthōtos nom sing masc
2. μισθωτῶν misthōtōn gen pl masc

2 father Zebedee in the ship with the **hired servants**,..Mark 1:20
1 But he that is an **hireling**, and not the shepherd,...John 10:12
1 The **hireling** fleeth, because he is an hireling,.......... 10:13
1 The **hireling** fleeth, because he is **an hireling**,.......... 10:13

Classical Greek
This word is the noun form of the verb *misthoō* (3273) which means "to hire." The masculine suffix *-tos* indicates a person, hence *misthōtos* is a hired worker employed for a particular task. In the papyri the term refers to the lessee or tenant (*Moulton-Milligan*).

Septuagint Usage
Misthōtos appears 20 times in the Septuagint where it is always used to translate *sākhîr*, meaning "hired servant" (Exodus 12:45; Leviticus 19:13; Deuteronomy 15:18).

New Testament Usage
In the New Testament *misthōtos* contrasts the hired man with the owner or employer. James and John's father Zebedee is contrasted with his "hired servants" (Mark 1:20); the true Shepherd stands in contrast to the "hireling" or the "hired hand" who is employed to tend the sheep (John 10:12,13); and the Prodigal Son contrasted his circumstance to that of the "hired servants" of his father (Luke 15:17).

STRONG 3411, BAUER 523, MOULTON-MILLIGAN 414, KITTEL 4:695-728, LIDDELL-SCOTT 1137, COLIN BROWN 3:138-44.

3276. Μιτυλήνη Mitulēnē name
Mytilene.

1. Μιτυλήνην Mitulēnēn acc fem

1 at Assos, we took him in, and came to **Mitylene**....Acts 20:14

Seaport city in western Asia Minor visited by Paul on his way to Jerusalem (Acts 20:14).

3277. Μιχαήλ Michaēl name
Michael.

1. Μιχαήλ Michaēl masc

1 Yet **Michael the archangel**, when contending........ Jude 1:9
1 **Michael and his angels** fought against the dragon;...Rev 12:7

Michaēl is the Greek form of the Hebrew proper name *Mîkhā'ēl* (which means "Who is like God?"); although the Hebrew name is rather common in the Old Testament (cf. the references in Achtemeier, "Michael," *Interpreter's Dictionary of the Bible*, 3:372,73), it only appears in the New Testament with reference to the angel Michael. This angel is mentioned only in Daniel (10:13,21 and 12:1) in the Old Testament and just twice in the New Testament (Jude 9 and Revelation 12:7). Jude 9 designates him as "the archangel." Despite these few references, Michael plays an important role in the elaborate angelologies of ancient Judaism and early Christianity. They made Michael along with Gabriel and Raphael the "angels of the presence," or "archangels" (from *archō* [751], "to rule," and *angelos* [32], "angel," and thus "ruling angels"), who stand before the very throne of God. According to some traditions there were as many as seven archangels (cf. 1 Enoch 20; Revelation 8:2).

Michael was the patron angel of Israel (Daniel 12:1). He came to the assistance of an angelic messenger sent to provide Daniel with the interpretation of a vision (Daniel 10:13). The "prince of the kingdom of Persia" had detained this angelic messenger since the vision foretold, among other things, the fall of the Medo-Persian Empire to the Greeks. Presumably this patron angel of Persia hoped to prevent the fall of the nation by not allowing the interpretation of the vision to come to Daniel. The choice of Michael to lead the celestial host against the "dragon" in the great eschatological battle (Revelation 12:7) probably stems from his role as patron of Israel and the prophecy in Daniel 12:1 that Michael would "stand up" in the "time of trouble."

This prophecy in Daniel 12:1 that Michael will bring deliverance to "every one that shall be found written in the book" also provides the impetus for the idea that he is the "recording angel" who keeps account of the "deeds of the children of Israel" (Ascension of Isaiah 9:22,23). Michael was also believed to be the guardian of Scripture and the angelic intermediary between God and Moses in the giving of the Law (Ascension of Isaiah 11:21 and elsewhere).

Jude 9 refers to another tradition that relates to Michael and Moses, namely that Michael was involved in a dispute with the devil for the body of Moses. According to Origen and others from the Patristic Era, this story was taken from the Assumption of Moses, although it is not found in any of the fragmentary copies of this work which have survived. For other traditions about Michael and citations where they are found, see Gaster, "Michael," *Interpreter's Dictionary of the Bible*, 3:373.

STRONG 3413, BAUER 524, MOULTON-MILLIGAN 414, COLIN BROWN 1:104.

3278. μνᾶ mna noun
Mina.

דַּרְכְּמוֹנִים dark^emônîm (1933), Drachmas (Ezr 2:69).

מָנֶה māneh (4632), Maneh or mina (Ez 45:12).

1. μνᾶ mna nom sing fem
2. μνᾶν mnan acc sing fem
3. μνᾶς mnas acc pl fem

```
3 his ten servants, and delivered them ten pounds,... Luke 19:13
1 saying, Lord, thy pound hath gained ten pounds........ 19:16
3 saying, Lord, thy pound hath gained ten pounds........ 19:16
1 saying, Lord, thy pound hath gained five pounds....... 19:18
3 saying, Lord, thy pound hath gained five pounds....... 19:18
1 Lord, behold, here is thy pound, which I have kept.... 19:20
2 Take from him the pound, and give it to him that..... 19:24
3 and give it to him that hath ten pounds............Luke 19:24
3 And they said unto him, Lord, he hath ten pounds..... 19:25
```

Classical Greek and Septuagint Usage
The *mina* is a Greek monetary unit of fluctuating value often influenced by the rate of exchange a money changer would accept. As a sum of money it was generally accepted to equal 100 drachmas of Greek currency and approximately 50 shekels in Hebrew weight. At the time of Christ the Greek drachma was about the same value as the Roman denarius. This word is used four times in the Septuagint (1 Kings 10:17 [LXX 3 Kings 10:17]; Ezra 2:69 [LXX 2 Esdras 2:69]; Nehemiah 7:71; Ezekiel 45:12) and six times in the New Testament (all of which are found in Luke 19).

New Testament Usage
In the Parable of the Pounds (Luke 19:11-27) the nobleman who gave a *mina* to each of 10 servants entrusted to each one enough money to pay the salary of 1 laborer for a little over 4 months. The servant who increased his funds tenfold earned enough to pay one laborer's wages for about 3 1/2 years. This kind of success, using the larger value of *mina*, seems consistent with the significance of his reward, i.e., rule over 10 cities. Thus this parable shows the high value of the efforts of those who work for the coming of the kingdom of Christ. (See also the word studies at *drachmē* [1400] and *dēnarion* [1214].)

STRONG 3414, BAUER 524, MOULTON-MILLIGAN 414, LIDDELL-SCOTT 1138.

3279. μνάομαι mnaomai verb
Be mindful of, woo, court.

1. ἐμνήσθην emnēsthēn 1sing indic aor pass
2. ἐμνήσθη emnēsthē 3sing indic aor pass
3. ἐμνήσθημεν emnēsthēmen 1pl indic aor pass
4. ἐμνήσθησαν emnēsthēsan 3pl indic aor pass
5. μνησθῶ mnēsthō 1sing subj aor pass
6. μνησθῇς mnēsthēs 2sing subj aor pass
7. μνήσθητι mnēsthēti 2sing impr aor pass
8. μνήσθητε mnēsthēte 2pl impr aor pass
9. μνησθῆναι mnēsthēnai inf aor pass
10. μέμνησθε memnēsthe 2pl indic perf mid
11. μεμνημένος memnēmenos
        nom sing masc part perf mid
12. μνησθήσομαι mnēsthēsomai 1sing indic fut pass

```
6 there rememberest that thy brother hath ought..... Matt 5:23
2 And Peter remembered the word of Jesus,........... 26:75
3 Saying, Sir, we remember that that deceiver said,..... 27:63
9 his servant Israel, in remembrance of his mercy;....Luke 1:54
9 the mercy ... and to remember his holy covenant;...... 1:72
```

7	remember that thou in thy lifetime receivedst thy	Luke 16:25
7	remember me when thou comest into thy kingdom....	23:42
8	remember how he spake unto you ... in Galilee,......	24:6
4	And they remembered his words,.....................	24:8
4	And his disciples remembered that it was written,..	John 2:17
4	his disciples remembered that he had said this.........	2:22
4	when Jesus was glorified, then remembered they......	12:16
4	alms are had in remembrance in the sight of God.	Acts 10:31
1	Then remembered I the word of the Lord,...........	11:16
10	brethren, that ye remember me in all things,......	1 Co 11:2
11	desiring to see thee, being mindful of thy tears,....	2 Tm 1:4
5	and their iniquities will I remember no more........	Heb 8:12
5	their sins and iniquities will I remember no more.....	10:17
9	may be mindful of the words which were spoken....	2 Pt 3:2
8	remember ye the words which were spoken before..	Jude 1:17
2	great Babylon came in remembrance before God,...	Rev 16:19

Classical Greek

Although *mnaomai* appears to be of uncertain origin, there is general agreement about the meaning of the term. *Liddell-Scott* state that its primary meaning in classical literature is "to be mindful of, to turn one's mind to a thing." After Homer the term was used to describe one's pursuit for appointment to an office or solicitation of a favor (ibid.). So, when a young man turned his mind to seeking a bride, *mnaomai* described the courtship process.

Bauer and *Moulton-Milligan* assign the term to *mnēsteuō* (3287), "I woo and win, I betroth, promise in marriage." Moulton (*The Analytical Greek Lexicon Revised*, "mnaomai," p.271) traces its origin to *mimnēskō* (3267), "I remember." The *New Englishman's Greek Concordance and Lexicon* also relates *mnaomai*, "bear in mind, recollect," to *mimnēskō*.

New Testament Usage

Whereas *mimnēskō* appears only twice in the New Testament, *mnaomai* appears 21 times. If any disciple "remembered" that a brother had a dispute with him, he should immediately seek reconciliation, even if it meant a temporary delay in his worship (Matthew 5:23,24). Peter "remembered" the prophetic words of Jesus after he had denied Him three times (Matthew 26:34). He "wept bitterly" because of realizing what he had done (Matthew 26:75). One of the thieves crucified alongside Jesus realized the just condemnation of his crimes and acknowledged the innocence of Jesus when he said, "Lord, *remember* me when thou comest into thy kingdom" (Luke 23:42).

In Acts 10 an angel told Cornelius that his prayers and offerings were "remembered" by God and would be answered. The answer came by Peter's realization and proclamation that the gospel and the Holy Spirit could be received by the Gentiles as well as the Jews (Acts 10:31ff.). Because of the finished work of Christ on the cross, the writer of Hebrews told of God's new covenant in which He would "*remember no more*" the sins and iniquities of believers (Hebrews 8:12; 10:17; cf. Jeremiah 31:31-34). Likewise, Peter wrote "to them that have obtained like precious faith with us through the righteousness of God and our Saviour Jesus Christ" (2 Peter 1:1), that they should "*be mindful of the words which were spoken before by the holy prophets, and of the commandment of us the apostles of the Lord*" in light of His second coming (2 Peter 3:2).

STRONG 3415, BAUER 524, MOULTON-MILLIGAN 415 (see "mnēsteuō"), LIDDELL-SCOTT 1138.

3280. Μνάσων Mnasōn name

Mnason.

1. Μνάσωνι Mnasōni dat masc

1 and brought with them one **Mnason** of Cyprus,..... Acts 21:16

Christian from Cyprus who provided lodging for Paul and his companions in Jerusalem (Acts 21:16).

3281. μνεία mneia noun

Mention, remembrance, recollection.

COGNATE:
 μιμνήσκω mimnēskō (3267)
SYNONYMS:
 ἀνάμνησις anamnēsis (363)
 μνήμη mnēmē (3284)
 ὑπόμνησις hupomnēsis (5118)

זָכַר zākhar (2226), Remember (Dt 7:18).

זֵכֶר zēkher (2228), Something to be remembered, memory (Ps 111:4 [110:4], Is 26:8).

1. μνεία mneia dat sing fem
2. μνείαν mneian acc sing fem

2	that without ceasing I make **mention** of you always ..	Rom 1:9
2	making **mention** of you in my prayers;..............	Eph 1:16
1	I thank my God upon every **remembrance** of you,...	Phlp 1:3
2	making **mention** of you in our prayers;.............	1 Th 1:2
2	and that ye have good **remembrance** of us always,.....	3:6
2	that without ceasing I have **remembrance** of thee	2 Tm 1:3
2	making **mention** of thee always in my prayers,......	Phlm 1:4

Classical Greek and Septuagint Usage

In classical Greek the meaning of *mneia* is "remembrance" or "mention." In the Septuagint it means "to think of," "to have in remembrance," "to mention someone." It also denotes a specific proclamation or action such as the Passover, or a definite acknowledgment of the saving action of God (Deuteronomy 7:18,19;

Psalm 111:4 [LXX 110:4]; Jeremiah 31:20 [LXX 38:20]).

New Testament Usage
In the New Testament *mneia* means "mention" or "remembrance." It is used only seven times and conveys specific reference to certain people in each case (e.g., Romans 1:9; Ephesians 1:16). Only Paul used *mneia*, and in six instances he related his prayerful intercession for brethren or congregations. The word implies that he "mentioned" their names while praying for their welfare. In the other instance, the Thessalonian church had Paul "in good remembrance" which includes the idea that there was a good relationship between them (1 Thessalonians 3:6).

STRONG 3417, BAUER 524, MOULTON-MILLIGAN 414, KITTEL 4:678-79, LIDDELL-SCOTT 1139, COLIN BROWN 3:230,238,242,246.

3282. μνῆμα mnēma noun

Tomb, grave, monument, memorial.
COGNATE:
μιμνῄσκω mimnēskō (3267)
SYNONYMS:
μνημεῖον mnēmeion (3283)
τάφος taphos (4876)

קְבוּרָה qᵉvûrāh (7185), Grave (Ez 32:23f.).
קֶבֶר qever (7197), Grave, tomb (Nm 19:16, 2 Chr 16:14, Is 65:4).

1. **μνῆμα** mnēma nom/acc sing neu
2. **μνήματι** mnēmati dat sing neu
3. **μνήμασιν** mnēmasin dat pl neu
4. **μνήματα** mnēmata nom/acc pl neu

```
3 he had his dwelling among the tombs. (NASB) ..... Mark 5:3
3 he was in the mountains, and in the tombs, ........... 5:5
2 and laid him in a tomb (NASB) .................... 15:46
1 they came to the tomb (NASB) ..................... 16:2
3 neither abode in any house, but in the tombs. ...... Luke 8:27
2 and laid it in a sepulchre that was hewn in stone, .... 23:53
1 in the morning, they came unto the sepulchre, ....... 24:1
1 and his sepulchre is with us unto this day. .......... Acts 2:29
2 and laid in the sepulchre that Abraham bought ....... 7:16
4 not suffer their dead bodies to be put in graves. .... Rev 11:9
```

Mnēma literally means "a sign of remembrance" for the dead. The Jews commonly used at least two types of tombs. First, there was the common burying ground used for the poor or stranger. Not every town had its own such burial place, resulting in funeral processions to carry the dead some distance (Luke 7:12ff.). Second, there were private family tombs in a cave, usually located in a garden of the rich or moderately well-to-do. Inscriptions were made on stones placed over the vaults and were thus "a sign of remembrance." The grave or tomb was marked by a stone and kept whitened in order to warn the passerby against defilement (Matthew 23:27; see Edersheim, *Life and Times of Jesus the Messiah*, 2:316).

In Mark 5:3 (and parallel Luke 8:27) the demoniac of the Gerasenes was living among the tombs. This was considered a sign of madness. Also, uncleanness and unclean spirits were thought to rule over the dead (Michel, "mnēma," *Kittel*, 4:680).

STRONG 3418, BAUER 524, MOULTON-MILLIGAN 414-15, KITTEL 4:679-80, LIDDELL-SCOTT 1139, COLIN BROWN 1:263-65; 3:230,238,246.

3283. μνημεῖον mnēmeion noun

Monument, memorial, grave, tomb, record, remembrance.
COGNATE:
μιμνῄσκω mimnēskō (3267)
SYNONYMS:
μνῆμα mnēma (3282)
τάφος taphos (4876)

קְבוּרָה qᵉvûrāh (7185), Grave (Gn 35:20).
קֶבֶר qever (7197), Sepulchre, tomb (Gn 23:6, Neh 2:3, Is 22:16).

1. **μνημεῖον** mnēmeion nom/acc sing neu
2. **μνημείου** mnēmeiou gen sing neu
3. **μνημείῳ** mnēmeiō dat sing neu
4. **μνημεῖα** mnēmeia nom/acc pl neu
5. **μνημείων** mnēmeiōn gen pl neu
6. **μνημείοις** mnēmeiois dat pl neu

```
5 two possessed with devils, coming out of the tombs, Matt 8:28
4 and garnish the sepulchres of the righteous, ......... 23:29
4 And the graves were opened; ....................... 27:52
5 And came out of the graves after his resurrection, ... 27:53
3 And laid it in his own new tomb, ................... 27:60
2 rolled a great stone to the door of the sepulchre, ... 27:60
2 quickly from the sepulchre with fear and great joy; .. 28:8
5 immediately there met him out of the tombs a man Mark 5:2
6 Who had his dwelling among the tombs; ............. 5:3
3 took up his corpse, and laid it in a tomb. ............ 6:29
3 and laid him in a sepulchre which was hewn out ..... 15:46
2 and rolled a stone unto the door of the sepulchre .... 15:46
1 came unto the sepulchre at the rising of the sun ..... 16:2
2 away the stone from the door of the sepulchre? ..... 16:3
1 entering into the sepulchre, they saw a young man ... 16:5
2 went out quickly, and fled from the sepulchre; ...... 16:8
4 for ye are as graves which appear not, ........... Luke 11:44
4 for ye build the sepulchres of the prophets, .......... 11:47
4 indeed killed them, and ye build their sepulchres .... 11:48
1 beheld the sepulchre, and how his body was laid. .... 23:55
2 found the stone rolled away from the sepulchre ..... 24:2
2 And returned from the sepulchre, ................... 24:9
1 Then arose Peter, and ran unto the sepulchre; ....... 24:12
1 women ... which were early at the sepulchre; ....... 24:22
1 of them which were with us went to the sepulchre, .. 24:24
6 in the which all that are in the graves shall hear .. John 5:28
3 he had lain in the grave four days already. .......... 11:17
1 saying, She goeth unto the grave to weep there. ..... 11:31
```

1 again groaning in himself cometh to the **grave**......	John 11:38
2 with him when he called Lazarus out of his **grave**,.....	12:17
1 and in the garden a new **sepulchre**,...................	19:41
1 for the **sepulchre** was nigh at hand...................	19:42
1 early, when it was yet dark, unto the **sepulchre**,.......	20:1
2 and seeth the stone taken away from the **sepulchre**.....	20:1
2 have taken away the Lord out of the **sepulchre**,.......	20:2
1 and that other disciple, and came to the **sepulchre**.....	20:3
1 and came first to the **sepulchre**......................	20:4
1 and went into the **sepulchre**,.........................	20:6
1 other disciple, which came first to the **sepulchre**,.......	20:8
1 But Mary stood without at the **sepulchre** weeping:.....	20:11
1 she stooped down, and looked into the **sepulchre**,......	20:11
1 and laid him in a **sepulchre**.........................	Acts 13:29

Mnēmeion is closely related to mnēma (3282) and is frequently used for "tomb." But according to Thayer, *mnēmeion* is "any visible object for preserving or recalling the memory of any person or thing; a sepulchral monument" (*Greek-English Lexicon*). With the exception of Joseph's sarcophagus (Genesis 50:26), coffins were not typically used by the Jews until after the Third Century B.C. From the Third Century B.C. onward, bone chests or ossuraries were often used to inter the bones after the body's decomposition (see Payne, "Burial," *International Standard Bible Encyclopedia*, 1:556-561). These mortuary chests often had memorial inscriptions written on them. Inscriptions were also graven on the great stone "rolled at the entrance of the cave or of the 'court' leading into the tomb" (Edersheim, *Life and Times of Jesus the Messiah*, 2:317; Luke 11:47; Acts 13:29).

In Matthew 23:27 (cf. Luke 11:44) Jesus called the Pharisees whitewashed tombs, meaning that they, like unrecognizable graves, were hiding their true nature (i.e., death and uncleanliness) (Michel, "mnēmeion," *Kittel*, 4:681).

STRONG 3419, BAUER 524, MOULTON-MILLIGAN 415, KITTEL 4:680-81, LIDDELL-SCOTT 1139, COLIN BROWN 1:263-65; 3:238,246.

3284. μνήμη mnēmē noun
Remembrance, memory.

COGNATE:
μιμνήσκω mimnēskō (3267)
SYNONYMS:
ἀνάμνησις anamnēsis (363)
μνεία mneia (3281)
ὑπόμνησις hupomnēsis (5118)

זֵכֶר zēkher (2228), Name, memory (Pss 30:4 [29:4], 145:7 [144:7], Prv 10:7).

זִכָּרוֹן zikkārôn (2230), Remembrance (Eccl 1:11).

1. μνήμην mnēmēn acc sing fem

1 to have these things always **in remembrance**..........	2 Pt 1:15

Used once in the New Testament in 2 Peter 1:15, *mnēmē* has the same meaning as *hupomnēsis* (5118) in verse 13 above. It means the "memory" one has of something. Emphasis is often given in a passage through use of related words with synonymous meanings. Peter's ministry of stirring up his readers to remember the truth would itself prompt them to further remembrance of the same after his death. The verb form of the noun *meēmē* is common (see *mimnēskō* [3267]).

STRONG 3420, BAUER 524-25, MOULTON-MILLIGAN 415, KITTEL 4:679, LIDDELL-SCOTT 1139, COLIN BROWN 3:230-31,238,240.

3285. μνημονεύω mnēmoneuō verb
Remember, recollect, recall, be mindful.

COGNATE:
μιμνήσκω mimnēskō (3267)
SYNONYMS:
ἀναμιμνήσκω anamimnēskō (362)
μιμνήσκω mimnēskō (3267)
ὑπομιμνήσκω hupomimnēskō (5117)

זָכַר zākhar (2226), Remember (Ex 13:3, 2 Kgs 9:25, Ps 63:6 [62:6]).

זֵכֶר zēkher (2228), Remembrance (Ps 6:5).

1. μνημονεύετε mnēmoneuete
    2pl indic/impr pres act
2. μνημονεύει mnēmoneuei 3sing indic pres act
3. μνημονεύωμεν mnēmoneuōmen 1pl subj pres act
4. μνημονεύητε mnēmoneuēte 2pl subj pres act
5. μνημόνευε mnēmoneue 2sing impr pres act
6. μνημονεύοντες mnēmoneuontes
    nom pl masc part pres act
7. μνημονεύειν mnēmoneuein inf pres act
8. ἐμνημόνευσεν emnēmoneusen 3sing indic aor act
9. ἐμνημόνευον emnēmoneuon 3pl indic imperf act
10. μνημονεύουσιν mnēmoneuousin
    3pl indic pres act

1 **remember** the five loaves of the five thousand,.....	Matt 16:9
1 having ears, hear ye not? and do ye not **remember**?	Mark 8:18
1 **Remember** Lot's wife............................	Luke 17:32
1 **Remember** the word that I said unto you,..........	John 15:20
4 ye **may remember** that I told you of them.............	16:4
2 she **remembereth** no more the anguish,................	16:21
6 Therefore watch, and **remember**,....................	Acts 20:31
7 and to **remember** the words of the Lord Jesus,.........	20:35
3 they would that we should **remember** the poor;.......	Gal 2:10
1 **remember**, that ye being in time past Gentiles.......	Eph 2:11
1 **Remember** my bonds. Grace be with you. Amen......	Col 4:18
6 **Remembering** without ceasing your work of faith,....	1 Th 1:3
1 For ye **remember**, brethren, our labour................	2:9
1 **Remember** ye not, that, ... I told you these things?	2 Th 2:5
5 **Remember** that Jesus Christ of the seed of David.....	2 Tm 2:8
9 truly, if they **had been mindful** of that country.....	Heb 11:15
8 By faith Joseph, when he died, **made mention**........	11:22
1 **Remember** them which have the rule over you,........	13:7

5 Remember therefore from whence thou art fallen,	Rev 2:5
5 Remember therefore how thou hast received	3:3
8 and God hath remembered her iniquities.	18:5

Classical Greek and Septuagint Usage

In classical Greek *mnēmoneuō* is translated as "remember," and in the Septuagint it means "remember, mention, recollect" (cf. Exodus 13:3; Isaiah 43:18). David often used the word "remember" with respect to God's goodness being cause for thanks and future trust. (See Psalms 105:5 [LXX 104:5, does not use *mnēmoneuō*]; 63:6 [62:6].)

New Testament Usage

In the New Testament *mnēmoneuō* usually implies a warning similar to "Now don't you forget," as shown in Luke 17:32, "*Remember Lot's wife*," and Revelation 2:5, "*Remember therefore from whence thou art fallen, and repent*." Both of these warnings were issued by Jesus. *Mnēmoneuō* implies exercise of memory and usually focuses on an object or person. The New Testament uses *mnēmoneuō* principally as a warning call to duty—a form of recollection and exercise of mind—as shown in Hebrews 13:7, "*Remember them which have the rule over you* . . . ." Only once in the New Testament is this verb used in the sense of beneficent care (Galatians 2:10).

A secondary meaning is "to make mention of" as found in Hebrews 11:22, whereby Joseph on his deathbed "remembered" the promise of God to give the land of Canaan to the seed of Abraham (Genesis 12:7; 13:15; 15:7). He also prophesied that Abraham's descendants would pass 400 years in bondage in a strange land and afterwards be brought out (Genesis 15:13,14).

STRONG 3421, BAUER 525, MOULTON-MILLIGAN 415, KITTEL 4:682-83, LIDDELL-SCOTT 1139, COLIN BROWN 3:230,240-43.

3286. μνημόσυνον

mnēmosunon noun

Memory, memorial, honorable remembrance.

CROSS-REFERENCE:
μιμνῄσκω mimnēskō (3267)

אַזְכָּרָה 'azkārāh (233), Memorial (Lv 2:2, 5:12, Nm 5:26).

זָכַר zākhar (2226), Remember; niphal: be remembered (Est 9:28 [9:27]); hiphil: remembrance (Sir 50:16).

זֵכֶר zēkher (2228), Memory, name (Dt 32:26, Ps 109:15 [108:15], Hos 12:5).

זִכָּרוֹן zikkārôn (2230), Reminder, memorial (Ex 13:9, Lv 23:24, Nm 5:15).

שֵׁם shēm (8428), Name; remembrance (Sir 49:1).

1. μνημόσυνον mnēmosunon nom/acc sing neu

1 also this, ... be told for **a memorial** of her.	Matt 26:13
1 done shall be spoken of for **a memorial** of her.	Mark 14:9
1 are come up for **a memorial** before God.	Acts 10:4

The neuter noun *mnēmosunon* is related to both *mnēmoneuō* (3285) and *mnēmē* (3284) and generally means "memorial" or "remembrance" of a thing (cf. *Liddell-Scott*). It appears over 50 times in the Septuagint, usually translating the Hebrew term *zēkher*, "remembrance, memorial" (cf. Exodus 3:15; Psalm 102:12 [LXX 101:12]; Isaiah 57:8), but is used only 3 times in the New Testament.

Mary, the sister of Lazarus (John 11:2), poured an alabaster vial of costly perfume upon Jesus. She was promised that such loving sacrifice would "be spoken *in memory of* her" (Matthew 26:13; Mark 14:9). In Acts 10:4 *mnēmosunon* means "a memorial offering." Cornelius' prayers and alms were a constant reminder to God of his sincere worship, much like the rising smoke from a grain offering was a *mnēmosunon*, "memorial" (Leviticus 2:2). *Mnēmosunon* can also mean "memory" as a mental faculty, such as in 1 Clement 45:8 (*Bauer*).

STRONG 3422, BAUER 525, MOULTON-MILLIGAN 415, LIDDELL-SCOTT 1139, COLIN BROWN 3:230,233,236,238,242.

3287. μνηστεύω mnēsteuō verb

Betroth, become engaged.

SYNONYM:
ἁρμόζω harmozō (712)

אָרַשׂ 'āras (806), Piel: betroth (Dt 20:7, Hos 2:19f.); pual: be betrothed (Dt 22:25,27f.).

1. μνηστευθείσης mnēsteutheisēs
  gen sing fem part aor pass

2. μεμνηστευμένῃ memnēsteumenē
  dat sing fem part perf mid

3. μεμνηστευμένην memnēsteumenēn
  acc sing fem part perf mid

4. ἐμνηστευμένῃ emnēsteumenē
  dat sing fem part perf mid

5. ἐμνηστευμένην emnēsteumenēn
  acc sing fem part perf mid

1 When as his mother Mary **was espoused** to Joseph,	Matt 1:18
3 virgin **espoused** to a man whose name was Joseph,	Luke 1:27
2 To be taxed with Mary his **espoused** wife,	2:5

Classical Greek and Septuagint Usage

The verb *mnēsteuō* is used in classical Greek meaning "seek in marriage" with the idea of a successful courtship leading to engagement (cf. *Liddell-Scott*). It consistently translates forms of the Hebrew *'āras* ("betroth") in the Septuagint (cf. Deuteronomy 20:7; 22:23,25,27,28) and appears three times in the New Testament (all of which refer to Mary and Joseph).

New Testament Usage
In the Jewish culture betrothal was more formal and binding than engagement is today. "Mary had been *betrothed* to Joseph, (and) before they came together she was found to be with child" (Matthew 1:18, RSV; Luke 1:27; 2:5). Betrothal was considered preparation for marriage but was legally binding. If the marriage did not take place because of a breach of contract (the dowry not paid to her parents, sexual infidelity, etc.), the young woman could not be married to another man until she was freed by due process and a certificate of divorce. The permanence and faithfulness expected of the betrothal bond are figuratively described in God's relationship with Israel: "I will *betroth* thee unto me forever; yea, I will *betroth* thee unto me in righteousness . . . I will even *betroth* thee unto me in faithfulness" (Hosea 2:19,20; cf. Bower and Knapp, "Marriage," *International Standard Bible Encyclopedia*, 3:263). This formality of betrothal generally was not entered into until the marriage was considered reasonably certain by the parents (see also Deuteronomy 22:23-28).

STRONG 3423, BAUER 525, MOULTON-MILLIGAN 415, LIDDELL-SCOTT 1140.

3287B. μογγιλάλος mongilalos adj
Speak with a hoarse voice, speaking with difficulty, speech impediment.
CROSS-REFERENCES:
λαλέω laleō (2953)
μόγις mogis (3289)

1. μογγιλάλον mongilalon acc sing masc

Mongilalos is a compound derived from *mongos*, "with a hoarse or hollow voice," and *laleō* (2953), "to speak." It is a rare word in all of Greek literature. It occurs in a few New Testament manuscripts at Mark 7:32. Because of the weak manuscript support many scholars agree that the proper reading should be *mogilalos* (3288), as in the *Textus Receptus*. *Mogilalos* comes from *mogis* (3289), "difficulty," and *laleō*, "to speak," and means "to speak with difficulty" or "to have a speech impediment." Some suggest that *mogilalos* is an atticistic correction for *mongilalos* (Blass and DeBrunner, *Greek Grammar of the New Testament*, p.19).

BAUER 525.

3288. μογιλάλος mogilalos adj
Speaking with difficulty, speech impediment.
CROSS-REFERENCES:
λαλέω laleō (2953)
μόγις mogis (3289)
אִלֵּם 'illēm (489), Dumb (Is 35:6).

1. μογιλάλον mogilalon acc sing masc

1 and had an impediment in his speech; .... Mark 7:32

Mogilalos comes from two Greek words, *mogis* (3289), "with difficulty," and *laleō* (2953), "to speak," and thus "to speak with difficulty." This word occurs only once in the New Testament in Mark 7:32. The older versions took its meaning from its only use in the Septuagint, "Then shall the lame man leap as a hart, and the tongue of the *dumb* sing . . ." (Isaiah 35:6). But in Mark the meaning is more in keeping with its common classical usage, that is, "speaking with difficulty, having an impediment in one's speech" (*Liddell-Scott*). In Mark 7:32 the man could not hear and had an "*impediment* in his speech," but after Jesus' touch, his condition (verse 35) is described by the words "he spoke plainly" (cf. verse 37).

STRONG 3424, BAUER 525, MOULTON-MILLIGAN 415, LIDDELL-SCOTT 1140, COLIN BROWN 1:428.

3289. μόγις mogis adv
Hardly, with difficulty, with toil and pain.
COGNATES:
μογγιλάλος mongilalos (3287B)
μογιλάλος mogilalos (3288)
SYNONYMS:
δυσκόλως duskolōs (1416)
μόλις molis (3296)

1. μόγις mogis

1 and bruising him hardly departeth from him......... Luke 9:39

This adverb is an early form of the Greek word *molis* (3296). *Mogis* and *molis* are used interchangeably throughout all Greek literature. The only New Testament occurrence of *mogis* is in Luke 9:39 where the disciples could not cast the demon spirit out of the boy whose father reported to Jesus, "It *scarcely* (*hardly*, KJV) ever leaves him" (NIV). The use of *mogis* here indicates that the continual debilitating possession the boy endured *scarcely* ever subsided; that is, the effects of the spirit upon him were almost continuous.

STRONG 3425, BAUER 525, MOULTON-MILLIGAN 415, KITTEL 4:735-36, LIDDELL-SCOTT 1140.

3290. μόδιος modios noun
A dry measure.

1. μόδιον modion acc sing masc

1 light a candle, and put it under **a bushel**,	Matt 5:15
1 Is a candle brought to be put under **a bushel**,	Mark 4:21
1 putteth it in a secret place, neither under **a bushel**,	Luke 11:33

Modios is a Latin word for a unit of dry measure equal roughly to 8 dry quarts or 1 peck. Jesus used this in His illustration: "Neither do men light a candle, and put it under a *bushel*, but on a candlestick . . . " (Matthew 5:15; Mark 4:21; Luke 11:33). These containers, which held 2 to 7 gallons, were common household items in those times.

STRONG 3426, BAUER 525, MOULTON-MILLIGAN 415, LIDDELL-SCOTT 1140.

3291. μοιχαλίς moichalis adj
Adulteress, adulterous.
CROSS-REFERENCE:
μοιχεύω moicheuō (3294)

נָאַף nā'aph (5178), Qal: commit adultry (Ez 16:38, 23:45); piel: adulteress, adulterer (Prv 30:20 [24:55], Hos 3:1, Mal 3:5).

1. μοιχαλίς moichalis nom sing fem
2. μοιχαλίδος moichalidos gen sing fem
3. μοιχαλίδι moichalidi dat sing fem
4. μοιχαλίδα moichalida acc sing fem
5. μοιχαλίδες moichalides nom pl fem

1 evil and **adulterous** generation seeketh after a sign;	Matt 12:39
1 wicked and **adulterous** generation seeketh ... sign;	16:4
3 in this **adulterous** and sinful generation;	Mark 8:38
1 she shall be called an **adulteress**:	Rom 7:3
4 so that she is no **adulteress**,	7:3
5 Ye adulterers and **adulteresses**,	Jas 4:4
2 Having eyes full **of adultery**,	2 Pt 2:14

This noun occurs seven times in the New Testament. It is a descriptive word depicting the kind of age we live in both literally and figuratively. It is often used in connection with other adjectives such as "evil," "sinful," and "wicked." "An evil and *adulterous* generation seeketh after a sign" (Matthew 12:39; 16:4; Mark 8:38). The gospel presents adultery not only as a matter of civil law (Romans 7:3, "She shall be called an *adulteress*"), but also a matter of the inner condition of the heart and life (cf. 2 Peter 2:14). Hosea described apostate Israel as being adulterous (e.g., Hosea 3:1) because she was unfaithful to God.

STRONG 3428, BAUER 526, MOULTON-MILLIGAN 415-16, KITTEL 4:729-35, LIDDELL-SCOTT 1141, COLIN BROWN 2:582.

3292. μοιχάομαι moichaomai verb
Commit adultery.
CROSS-REFERENCE:
μοιχεύω moicheuō (3294)

נָאוּפִים ni'ûphîm (5174), Adulteries (Ez 23:43—Codex Alexandrinus only).

נָאַף nā'aph (5178), Qal: commit adultery (Jer 5:7, 7:9, 23:14); piel: commit adultery, adulterer (Jer 3:8, 9:2, Ez 23:37).

1. μοιχᾶται moichatai 3sing indic pres mid
2. μοιχᾶσθαι moichasthai inf pres mid

2 causeth her **to commit adultery**:	Matt 5:32
1 marry her that is divorced **committeth adultery**.	5:32
1 and shall marry another, **committeth adultery**:	19:9
1 and whoso marrieth her ... doth **commit adultery**:	19:9
1 marry another, **committeth adultery** against her.	Mark 10:11
1 be married to another, she **committeth adultery**.	10:12

This verb and *moicheuō* (3294) are used interchangeably (*Liddell-Scott*). *Moichaomai* occurs only six times in the New Testament (e.g., Matthew 5:32; 19:9; Mark 10:11,12). Sexual intercourse outside of marriage is sin for both the married and the unmarried. Not only is lust the moral equivalent of adultery (Matthew 5:27-30), but divorce can be the cause of adultery as well (Matthew 5:31,32). A man who divorces his wife (or a wife who divorces her husband, Mark 10:12) commits *moichaomai*, that is, "causes her to commit adultery." Thus sexual fidelity in marriage is required by God (Genesis 2:23f.; Exodus 20:14) and vindicated by Christ (Matthew 19:9).

STRONG 3429, BAUER 526 (see "moichaō"), MOULTON-MILLIGAN 416, KITTEL 4:729-35 (see "moichaō"), LIDDELL-SCOTT 1141 (see "moichaō"), COLIN BROWN 2:582 (see "moichaō").

3293. μοιχεία moicheia noun
Adultery.
CROSS-REFERENCE:
μοιχεύω moicheuō (3294)

μοιχεία 3293

נָאֻפִים ni'ûphîm (5174), Adulteries (Jer 13:27).

נָאַף nā'aph (5178), Adultery (Hos 4:2).

נַאֲפוּפִים na'āphûphîm (5179), Adulterous look (Hos 2:2).

1. **μοιχεία** moicheia nom sing fem
2. **μοιχείᾳ** moicheia dat sing fem
3. **μοιχεῖαι** moicheiai nom pl fem

```
3  For out of the heart proceed ... adulteries, ........ Matt 15:19
3  evil thoughts, adulteries, fornications, murders, ..... Mark 7:21
3  greed, malice, deceit, lewdness, envy (NASB) (NT) ..... 7:22
2  brought unto him a woman taken in adultery; ....... John 8:3
1  Adultery, fornication, uncleanness, lasciviousness, ..... Gal 5:19
```

Classical Greek

Moicheia is the word for "adultery"; i.e., "illicit intercourse in which one of the parties is married" (cf. the verb *moicheuō* [3294]). In the ancient world marital fidelity was expected of the wife only. Acts of adultery between an unmarried man and a married woman or between two married individuals, however, were not tolerated. Yet, a married man's visit to a prostitute was not regarded as adultery. Thus the ancient world endorsed a double standard for determining adultery. This is radically different from the Biblical attitude where adultery is seen as a violation of the original, divinely instituted marriage bond (Genesis 2:23f.; Exodus 20:14).

Septuagint Usage

Moicheia (four times) and its cognates translate forms of *nā'aph* in the Septuagint (e.g., Jeremiah 13:27; Hosea 2:2; 4:2). A fundamental proposition of Old Testament sexual ethics is, "You shall not commit adultery," one of the Ten Commandments (*moicheuō*, Exodus 20:14). Such an act implicitly violates the sanctity of marriage. The punishment for adultery—for both parties—is death (Deuteronomy 22:22; cf. Ezekiel 16:40).

Figuratively "adultery" denotes the religious infidelity/unfaithfulness of Israel to her God (Jeremiah 2:2; 5:7; 9:2; Hosea 2:2). This is one of the most serious offenses in Israel's history. It directly violates the most fundamental tenet of Biblical religion, "The Lord our God is one" (Deuteronomy 6:4).

New Testament Usage

Moicheia occurs four times (including John 8:3) in the New Testament, although its cognates as well as the general concept are scattered throughout. *Moicheia* occurs in the parallel expression that adultery is a crime of the heart (Matthew 15:19; Mark 7:21). Jesus radicalizes this and suggests that committing adultery with the heart is as serious to God as the physical act itself because it is an act of inward impurity (cf. Matthew 5:27ff.). The scribes and the Pharisees brought to Jesus a woman who was caught in the act of adultery (John 8:3). Jesus forgave her. While Jesus may have taught that a man may put away his wife for reasons of adultery (Matthew 5:31f.), this in no way minimizes the evil of adultery.

The figurative understanding of adultery was applied to the "evil and adulterous generation" that sought for signs and yet were determined to kill Jesus (Matthew 12:39; 16:4; cf. Mark 8:38, of the entire "age"). The context of Luke 16:18 may indicate that a figurative understanding is preferred here too.

Paul regarded adultery as a serious infraction of Christian standards (he did not use *moicheia*, but its cognates). Adulterers will not inherit the kingdom of God (1 Corinthians 6:9, *moichos* [3295]).

The Epistles clearly break away from the accepted cultural norms by delivering a strong rebuke against the sin of adultery. Ephesians 5:5, for example, warns that no whoremonger or unclean person has any place in the kingdom of God. In 1 Corinthians 6:9 adultery and idolatry are placed on the same level, while in Romans 1:24-27 the deep moral decay of the Gentiles is seen as a punishment sent from God.

The false preaching of a supposed "liberty" that believers enjoy with respect to carnality and lewdness has always been a threat to the people of God. The "deeds of the Nicolaitans" (Revelation 2:6) and the so-called "doctrine of Balaam" (Revelation 2:14) sought to promote the toleration of the sin of adultery so prevalent in that day while encouraging Christians to adapt their own life-styles to that of the surrounding world. This doctrine was particularly seductive in Thyatira where it appeared in a spiritual disguise (Revelation 2:20). In each of these contexts the message was "Repent!" However, it is clear from the later chapters of the Book of Revelation that even the horrific judgments poured out in the last days will not cause men to repent of such sins (9:21). As a result, immoral men will be excluded from God's eternal realm (21:8,27; 22:14,15).

(See also the articles on *moichalis* [3291], *moicheuō* [3294], and *moichos* [3295].)

STRONG 3430, BAUER 526, MOULTON-MILLIGAN 416, KITTEL 4:729-35, LIDDELL-SCOTT 1141, COLIN BROWN 2:582.

3294. μοιχεύω moicheuō verb
Commit adultery.
COGNATES:
μοιχαλίς moichalis (3291)
μοιχάομαι moichaomai (3292)
μοιχεία moicheia (3293)
μοιχός moichos (3295)
SYNONYM:
πορνεύω porneuō (4062)

נאוּפִים niʾûphîm (5174), Adulteries (Ez 23:43).

נָאַף nāʾaph (5178), Qal: commit adultery, adultery (Lv 20:10, Dt 5:18, Jer 3:9); piel: commit adultery, adulterer (Hos 4:13f., 7:4).

1. μοιχεύεις moicheueis 2sing indic pres act
2. μοιχεύει moicheuei 3sing indic pres act
3. μοιχεύοντας moicheuontas
   acc pl masc part pres act
4. μοιχεύειν moicheuein inf pres act
5. ἐμοίχευσεν emoicheusen 3sing indic aor act
6. μοιχεύσῃς moicheusēs 2sing subj aor act
7. μοιχεύσεις moicheuseis 2sing indic fut act
8. μοιχευομένη moicheuomenē
   nom sing fem part pres mid
9. μοιχευομένην moicheuomenēn
   acc sing fem part pres mid
10. μοιχευθῆναι moicheuthēnai inf aor pass

7	Thou shalt not commit adultery:	Matt 5:27
5	committed adultery with her already in his heart.	5:28
10	makes her commit adultery; (NASB)	5:32
7	Thou shalt not commit adultery,	19:18
6	Do not commit adultery, Do not kill,	Mark 10:19
2	and marrieth another, committeth adultery:	Luke 16:18
2	put away from her husband committeth adultery	16:18
6	Do not commit adultery, Do not kill,	18:20
8	this woman was taken in adultery, in the very act.	John 8:4
4	that sayest a man should not commit adultery,	Rom 2:22
1	dost thou commit adultery?	2:22
7	Thou shalt not commit adultery,	13:9
6	For he that said, Do not commit adultery,	Jas 2:11
7	Now if thou commit no adultery, yet if thou kill,	2:11
3	commit adultery with her into great tribulation,	Rev 2:22

This verb occurs 14 times in the New Testament. The Scripture is consistent in insisting that sexual relations outside the marriage covenant are sin. *Moicheuō* may mean fornication (*porneia* [4061]) as well (John 8:4). "Thou shalt not *commit adultery*" (Exodus 20:14) is still God's absolute moral standard (Matthew 19:18; Mark 10:19; Romans 13:9; James 2:11). The Pharisees, like the culture around them, tended to minimize the evil of divorce and remarriage. Jesus upheld the sanctity of marriage as it was intended by God from creation: "Everyone who divorces his wife and marries another commits (*moicheuō*) *adultery*; and he who marries a woman divorced from her husband commits adultery" (Luke 16:18, RSV). Finally, marriage, with its demand for faithfulness and blessings of intimacy, is an analogy of our relationship with God. Adultery and idolatry are connected in a spiritual sense (Romans 2:22; Revelation 2:22).

STRONG 3431, BAUER 526, MOULTON-MILLIGAN 416, KITTEL 4:729-35, LIDDELL-SCOTT 1141, COLIN BROWN 2:582.

3295. μοιχός moichos noun
Adulterer.
CROSS-REFERENCE:
μοιχεύω moicheuō (3294)

נָאַף nāʾaph (5178), Qal: adulterer, commit adultery (Jb 24:15, Prv 6:32); piel: adulterer (Ps 50:18 [49:18], Is 57:3).

1. μοιχοί moichoi nom pl masc
2. μοιχούς moichous acc pl masc

1	unjust, adulterers, or even as this publican.	Luke 18:11
1	neither fornicators, nor idolaters, nor adulterers,	1 Co 6:9
2	but whoremongers and adulterers God will judge.	Heb 13:4
1	Ye adulterers and adulteresses,	Jas 4:4

This word occurs four times in the New Testament and refers to "the one who commits adultery." It is thus related to *moichalis* (3291), *moichaomai* (3292), and *moicheuō* (3294). The self-righteous Pharisee thanked God that he was not a *moichos* (Luke 18:11), yet his pride caused God to reject him. The *moichos*, "the violator of the marriage bond," is also excluded from inheriting the kingdom of God: "Know ye not that the unrighteous shall not inherit the kingdom of God? Be not deceived: neither fornicators, nor idolaters, nor *adulterers*, nor effeminate . . . " (1 Corinthians 6:9). Marriage must be held in honor "and the bed undefiled: but whoremongers and *adulterers* God will judge" (Hebrews 13:4). The apostolic preaching did not lower Jesus' standard or His assessment of adultery (see Hauck, "moicheuō," *Kittel*, 4:734).

STRONG 3432, BAUER 526, MOULTON-MILLIGAN 416, KITTEL 4:729-35, LIDDELL-SCOTT 1141, COLIN BROWN 2:582.

3296. μόλις molis adv
With difficulty, hardly, with toil.
SYNONYMS:
δυσκόλως duskolōs (1416)
μόγις mogis (3289)

1. μόλις molis

1	it mauls him, it scarcely leaves him. (NASB)	Luke 9:39
1	these sayings scarce restrained they the people,	Acts 14:18

| 1 and scarce were come over against Cnidus,..........Acts 27:7
| 1 And, **hardly** passing it, came unto a place............27:8
| 1 were **scarcely** able to get the ship's (NASB)............27:16
| 1 For **scarcely** for a righteous man will one die:.......Rom 5:7
| 1 And if the righteous **scarcely** be saved,.............1 Pt 4:18

This adverb is a post-Homeric related term of *mogis* (3289) (Liddell-Scott). It appears a few times in the Septuagint but is never used to translate a Hebrew original. In classical Greek the meaning is "scarcely, barely able to be done." The thought here is of struggle to attain something worthwhile only after great effort.

Molis is related to another Greek word, *mogis*, meaning "toil." This meaning is seen in Acts 27:7,8,16 where *molis* demonstrates the "toil" of laboring against the storm which eventually caused Paul's shipwreck. In Acts 14:18 *molis* is rendered "scarce," showing the hard work Paul and Barnabas had in convincing the people they were not gods. First Peter 4:18 suggests the narrow margin for error and danger of complacency by rendering *molis* as "*scarcely* be saved."

Small wonder then that Paul, in his own defense to the church at Corinth, told them he was "in labors more abundant" (2 Corinthians 11:23). *Molis* seems almost to be the byword of much of Paul's experience in the gospel. Some people would give up at the first sign of a struggle, but this was not true of the apostle Paul.

STRONG 3433, BAUER 526, MOULTON-MILLIGAN 416, KITTEL 4:735-36, LIDDELL-SCOTT 1142.

3297. Μολόχ Moloch name

Moloch.

1. Μολόχ Moloch masc

| 1 Yea, ye took up the tabernacle of **Moloch**,..........Acts 7:43

Heathen planetary god whose worship included child sacrifice (Acts 7:43).

3298. μολύνω molunō verb

Defile, soil, pollute, stain.

COGNATE:
μολυσμός molusmos (3299)
SYNONYMS:
κοινόω koinoō (2813)
μιαίνω miainō (3256)
σπιλόω spiloō (4549)

בּוּס bûs (983), Polel: trample down (Jer 12:10).

גָּאַל gā'al (1381), Redeem; niphal: be defiled (Is 59:3).

הָלַךְ hālakh (2050), Go, walk; be weak (Ez 7:17, 21:7).

חָנֵף chānēph (2714), Be godless (Jer 23:11).

טָבַל ṭāval (2991), Dip (Gn 37:31).

טָנַף ṭānaph (3047), Piel: soil (S/S 5:3).

פִּגּוּל piggûl (6533), Unclean meat (Is 65:4).

שָׁגֵל shāghēl (8151), Ravish; niphal: be ravished (Zec 14:2).

1. ἐμόλυναν emolunan 3pl indic aor act
2. μολύνεται molunetai 3sing indic pres mid
3. ἐμολύνθησαν emolunthēsan 3pl indic aor pass

| 2 and their conscience being weak is **defiled**...........1 Co 8:7
| 1 in Sardis which have not **defiled** their garments;......Rev 3:4
| 3 These are they which were not **defiled** with women;....14:4

Classical Greek
A frequent use of *molunō* in classical Greek is to soil or make dirty by mud or filthiness. Figuratively, it means spiritual defilement. There is some conjecture that its root is *melas* (3159), "black," but this view is not supported by leading scholarly works.

Septuagint Usage
Molunō appears 18 times in the Septuagint translating 9 different Hebrew terms. Frequently the idea of defilement is connected with blood. *Molunō* is used at Genesis 37:31 in reference to Joseph's brothers dipping his coat in goat's blood in order to convince their father that Joseph had been killed. God accused Israel of having their hands "defiled with blood" because of their corporate sins (Isaiah 59:3). In 1 Maccabees 1:37 the enemies of Israel "shed innocent blood" inside the sanctuary and "defiled" it. Another use of *molunō* is at Jeremiah 23:11 where God denounced both the lying prophets and priests as "profane."

New Testament Usage
In New Testament Greek *molunō* is generally used in a figurative sense speaking of a conscience defiled by sin (e.g., 1 Corinthians 8:7). The word is never used in a good sense (such as *miainō* [3256] which is sometimes translated as "defile") but means to be "stained" or tinged with another color as in the dyeing of cloth or glass. *Molunō* appears only three times in the New Testament and is used in Revelation 14:4 to specify the degree of purity of the 144,000 who were "not defiled (*molunō*) with women."

The New Testament is confined to moral and ethical "defilement," as shown in 1 Corinthians 8:7 and Revelation 3:4 where "a few names" have kept their garments clean from the pollution of the world and the flesh.

Strong 3435, Bauer 526-27, Moulton-Milligan 416, Kittel 4:736-37, Liddell-Scott 1142, Colin Brown 1:448-49.

3299. μολυσμός molusmos noun
Defilement, pollution, filthiness.
Cross-Reference:
μολύνω molunō (3298)

חֲנֻפָּה chănuppāh (2717), Ungodliness (Jer 23:15).

1. μολυσμοῦ molusmou gen sing masc
1 let us cleanse ourselves from all **filthiness** .... 2 Co 7:1

This noun is related to the verb *molunō* (3298) and is used only once in the New Testament, at 2 Corinthians 7:1: "Having therefore these promises, dearly beloved, let us cleanse ourselves from all *filthiness* of the flesh and spirit, perfecting holiness in the fear of God." We must prune from our lives "all sorts of filthiness, physical, moral, mental, ceremonial, 'of flesh and spirit' " (Robertson, *Word Pictures in the New Testament*, 4:238), that is, all defilement both outward and inward. The opposite of *molusmos* is aggressive and progressive holiness.

Strong 3436, Bauer 527, Moulton-Milligan 416, Kittel 4:737, Liddell-Scott 1142, Colin Brown 1:448-49.

3300. μομφή momphē noun
Complaint, blame, cause for quarrel.

1. μομφήν momphēn acc sing fem
1 if any man have a **quarrel** against any: .... Col 3:13

This is a very rare word occurring only in a Greek writer (Pindar) of the Fifth Century B.C. Its only occurrence in the New Testament is at Colossians 3:13: "Forbearing one another, and forgiving one another, if any man have a *quarrel* against any: even as Christ forgave you, so also do ye." Whatever "blame" or "cause for complaint" we have against another, we are to forgive. The ground for forgiving is that we have been forgiven by Christ. Thus, *momphē* indicates a cause for broken interpersonal relationships.

Strong 3437, Bauer 527, Kittel 4:571-74, Liddell-Scott 1143.

3301. μονή monē noun
Stay, abiding place.
Cross-Reference:
μένω menō (3176)

1. μονήν monēn acc sing fem
2. μοναί monai nom pl fem

2 In my Father's house are many **mansions**: .... John 14:2
1 come unto him, and make our **abode** with him. 14:23

Classical Greek and Septuagint Usage
The noun *monē* is related to the verb *menō* (3176) and has been commonly used throughout Greek literature. In the classical period it meant "a staying" or "tarrying," along with its opposite—"movement" or "exit out of a place." The idea of "persistence" and "continuance" is inherent within its meaning, and it is thus used for staying in service as opposed to leaving it. A second meaning of "abiding place" or "abode" was derived from its first usage to represent the place where one would "stay" or "tarry."

The Septuagint does not use this word except once in the Apocrypha where it means "permanence" (1 Maccabees 7:38). Other early Greek literature uses *monē* the same as the classical period but more frequently utilizes the second meaning of "a place to stay in." The papyri are an exception and used *monē* to denote: (1) technically in sureties, the appearance of certain persons (e.g., "requesting that they may be compelled to provide written security that they will *stay* and appear"); (2) a special place of residence such as a "monastery, mansion, or station" (*Moulton-Milligan*).

New Testament Usage
In the New Testament *monē* occurs only twice, both of these in John 14: "In my Father's house are many *mansions* (*monai*): if it were not so, I would have told you. I go to prepare a place for you" (verse 2); "Jesus answered and said unto him, If a man love me, he will keep my words: and my Father will love him, and we will come unto him, and make our *abode* (*monēn*) with him" (verse 23).

As one can see, these two statements correspond intentionally. In verse 2 we go up to Jesus and the Father. In verse 23 Jesus and the Father come down to us. The purpose of our going up and of Jesus' and the Father's coming down is the same: to take up residence. We with Jesus and the Father, and they with us. This provides a major theme of the Last Supper discourse (John 14—17).

Monē "seems to be deliberately chosen to express the fact that our earthly state is transitory and provisional compared with eternal and blessed being with God" (Hauck, "monē," *Kittel*, 4:580). Heaven is thus viewed as our permanent "dwelling place." There are many dwelling places in the Father's house. This blessed promise is fulfilled in death for all believers who die before the Second Coming (John 14:3,4) and for all other believers after the Rapture.

Salvation is the union of God with the believer. This union is shown to be a reality even before we go up to our "mansion." In verse 23 God comes down to abide within the believer who is loving and keeping the words of Jesus. Thus, salvation is a present reality but conditioned on loving and keeping the words of Jesus. Assurance of salvation is given to those who fulfill these conditions (1 John 2:3; 3:22,24; 5:3) and is characterized by fellowship, the result of God's *monē* with us.

STRONG 3438, BAUER 527, MOULTON-MILLIGAN 416, KITTEL 4:579-81, LIDDELL-SCOTT 1143, COLIN BROWN 3:224,229.

3302. μονογενής monogenēs adj

Only, unique, only-begotten.

CROSS-REFERENCES:
γίνομαι ginomai (1090)
μόνος monos (3304)

יָחִיד yāchîdh (3279), Lonely (Ps 25:16 [24:16]).

1. μονογενής monogenēs nom sing masc/fem
2. μονογενοῦς monogenous gen sing masc
3. μονογενῆ monogenē acc sing masc

```
1  the only son of his mother, and she was a widow:...Luke 7:12
1  had one only daughter, about twelve years of age,......   8:42
1  look upon my son: for he is mine only child............   9:38
2  the glory as of the only begotten of the Father,......John 1:14
1  hath seen God at any time; the only begotten Son,......   1:18
3  that he gave his only begotten Son,.................   3:16
2  in the name of the only begotten Son of God..........   3:18
3  offered up his only begotten son...................Heb 11:17
3  because that God sent his only begotten Son........ 1 Jn 4:9
```

Classical Greek

This adjective is a compound of *mono-* ("only") and *genēs* (cf. *genos* [1079], "race," from *ginomai* [1090], "to be born"); thus, *monogenēs* means "only-begotten," the "only one of its kind." It is known from around the Seventh Century B.C. The *mono-* prefix stresses the "only" aspect, i.e., it means "without brothers and sisters" (Büchsel, "monogenēs," *Kittel*, 4:738). It would be used to describe a "unique" form, place, or even manner of behavior (*Liddell-Scott*).

Septuagint Usage

Monogenēs occurs in the Septuagint 10 times, although some of these texts are questionable (e.g., Psalm 35:17 [LXX 34;17]; Baruch 4:16). The Hebrew translated by *monogenēs* is *yāchîdh*, which is also rendered by *agapētos* (27), "beloved," quite regularly in the Septuagint (e.g., Genesis 22:2,12,16). *Agapētos* and *monogenēs* appear together in Judges 11:34. Jephthah's daughter is described in the Septuagint as "beloved and an only-child." Under most circumstances the term *monogenēs* suggests an emphasis upon the relationship between the "only-begotten" one and his/her parents (cf. Tobit 6:10ff.; 8:17; cf. in the New Testament John 1:14,18; 3:16,18 of Jesus; see Büchsel, "monogenēs," *Kittel*, 4:739). The uniqueness of the only-begotten makes it possible that *monogenēs* stresses the incomparable aspect without necessarily making reference to a child's genealogical status (e.g., Psalms 22:20 [LXX 21:20]; 35:17 [34:17]).

New Testament Usage

The New Testament records *monogenēs* nine times. Three of these are in the Gospel of Luke and refer to the "only-begotten" children of ordinary people (Luke 7:12; 8:42; 9:38). Four are in the Gospel of John and refer to God's only-begotten Son, Jesus (John 1:14,18; 3:16,18). John continued this theme in his epistles (1 John 4:9).

In *A Textual Commentary of the Greek New Testament*, Bruce Metzger explains why some modern Greek texts, such as *Nestle-Aland 26th*, read "only-begotten *God*" at John 1:18. In addition to stating significant internal support, he says: "With the acquisition of p66 and p75 (two of the oldest papyri), both of which read *theos*, the external support of this reading had been notably strengthened" (p.198).

John is the only New Testament writer to apply the term *monogenēs* to Jesus. Under the guidance of the Holy Spirit he was undoubtedly making the correspondence between Jesus as the Son of God and us as His sons and daughters—His children (e.g., John 1:12; 11:52; 1 John 3:1,2,10; 5:2; Büchsel, "monogenēs," *Kittel*, 4:759). Christ, however, is the "only-begotten" in the sense of "unique, one-of-a-kind"; we become God's children by being "born again." The uniqueness of Jesus and the sentiment attached to the designation "only-begotten" demonstrate God's ultimate act of love in giving His Son on our behalf (John 3:16). In addition, it is one of the strongest expressions of the intimate relationship and unity shared by the Father and the Son.

In the Fourth Century, a heresy known as Arianism mistakenly saw *monogenēs* as a derivation related to the word *gennaō* (1074), which means "to beget, to generate, or to give birth." This inappropriate connection was used to support the false doctrine that Jesus was created by God and was not eternal with Him. However, the context of John's Gospel makes it clear that *monogenēs* is emphasizing the unique relationship between God the Son and God the Father, and not the physical birth of Jesus. Nowhere does the Bible teach that Jesus is a created being. On the contrary, the Scriptures reveal Jesus Christ to be the Second Person of the Trinity, coeternal with the Father and with the Holy Spirit. "For in him dwelleth all the fulness of the Godhead bodily" (Colossians 2:9). Jesus was with God in eternity past.

In addition, as the "only-begotten" of the Father, Jesus is not simply unique, He is the One who was with God from the beginning, the pre-existent, eternal Son (John 1:2; 8:58; 17:5,24). He did not *become* the "Son" of God at the Incarnation; He is the Son from eternity and remains so forever. This truth is a divine mystery which John did not attempt to fully explain. In one creed of the Church (the Nicene Creed) this mystery is stated as follows: Christ is "eternally begotten of the Father."

Outside of John, the Book of Hebrews applies *monogenēs* to Isaac. Isaac assumed such a standing because of his vital role in the promise of God to Abraham. Technically Abraham had other children (Ishmael), but Isaac was the only son of promise and the child of Abraham and Sarah (Genesis 22:2, the Septuagint reads *agapētos*, "beloved" here; the NIV translates the Hebrew "only son").

STRONG 3439, BAUER 527, MOULTON-MILLIGAN 416-17, KITTEL 4:737-41, LIDDELL-SCOTT 1144, COLIN BROWN 2:723-25.

3303. μόνον monon adv
Only, alone.
CROSS-REFERENCE:
μόνος monos (3304)

אַךְ 'akh (395), Only, but (Gn 27:13, 34:22f., Jb 2:6).
רַק raq (7828), Only (Gn 19:8, 24:8, 47:22).

1. μόνον monon

1	And if ye salute your brethren **only**,	Matt 5:47
1	but speak the word **only**,	8:8
1	If I **only** touch His garment, I shall (NASB)	9:21
1	a cup of cold water **only** in the name of a disciple,	10:42
1	that they might **only** touch the hem of his garment:	14:36
1	and found nothing thereon, but leaves **only**,	21:19
1	ye shall not **only** do this which is done to the fig	21:21
1	Be not afraid, **only** believe.	Mark 5:36
1	nothing for their journey, save a staff **only**;	6:8
1	believe **only**, and she shall be made whole.	Luke 8:50
1	because he not **only** had broken the sabbath,	John 5:18
1	And not for that nation **only**,	11:52
1	and they came not for Jesus' sake **only**,	12:9
1	not my feet **only**, but also my hands and my head.	13:9
1	Neither pray I for these **alone**,	17:20
1	**only** they were baptized in the name of the Lord.	Acts 8:16
1	preaching the word to none but ... the Jews **only**.	11:19
1	knowing **only** the baptism of John.	18:25
1	that not **alone** at Ephesus,	19:26
1	So that not **only** this our craft is in danger	19:27
1	for I am ready not to be bound **only**,	21:13
1	And Paul said, I would to God, that not **only** thou,	26:29
1	and much damage, not **only** of the lading and ship,	27:10
1	not **only** do the same, but have pleasure in them	Rom 1:32
1	Is he the God of the Jews **only**?	3:29
1	to them who are not of the circumcision **only**,	4:12
1	not to that **only** which is of the law,	4:16
1	Now it was not written for his sake **alone**,	4:23
1	And not **only** so, but we glory in tribulations also:	5:3
1	And not **only** so, but we also joy in God	5:11
1	And not **only** they, but ourselves also,	8:23
1	And not **only** this; but when Rebecca also had	9:10
1	not of the Jews **only**, but also of the Gentiles?	9:24
1	not **only** for wrath,	13:5
1	to be married to whom she will; **only** in the Lord.	1 Co 7:39
1	If in this life **only** we have hope in Christ,	15:19
1	And not by his coming **only**,	2 Co 7:7
1	not **only** to do, but also to be forward a year ago.	8:10
1	And not that **only**, but who was also chosen	8:19
1	not **only** in the sight of the Lord,	8:21
1	not **only** supplieth the want of the saints,	9:12
1	they had heard **only**, That he which persecuted us	Gal 1:23
1	**Only** they would that we should remember	2:10
1	This **only** would I learn of you,	3:2
1	and not **only** when I am present with you.	4:18
1	**only** use not liberty for an occasion to the flesh,	5:13
1	**only** lest they should suffer persecution	6:12
1	every name that is named, not **only** in this world,	Eph 1:21
1	**Only** let your conversation be as it becometh	Phlp 1:27
1	not **only** to believe on him, but also to suffer	1:29
1	ye have always obeyed, not as in my presence **only**,	2:12
1	but God had mercy on him; and not on him **only**,	2:27
1	For our gospel came not unto you in word **only**,	1 Th 1:5
1	out the word ... not **only** in Macedonia and Achaia,	1:8
1	not the gospel of God **only**, but also our own souls,	2:8
1	**only** he who now letteth will let,	2 Th 2:7
1	and not **only** idle, but tattlers also and busybodies,	1 Tm 5:13
1	there are not **only** vessels of gold and of silver,	2 Tm 2:20
1	shall give me at that day: and not to me **only**,	4:8
1	Which stood not **only** in meats and drinks,	Heb 9:10
1	Yet once more I shake not the earth **only**,	12:26
1	But be ye doers of the word, and not hearers **only**,	Jas 1:22
1	by works ... is justified, and not by faith **only**.	2:24
1	to your masters ... not **only** to the good and gentle,	1 Pt 2:18
1	the propitiation for our sins: and not for ours **only**,	1 Jn 2:2
1	not by water **only**, but by water and blood.	5:6
1	denying the **only** Lord God, and our Lord Jesus	Jude 1:4

The use of *monon* (the neuter of *monos* [3304]) as an adverb occurs 66 times in the New Testament with the meaning "only, alone."

It is used to show that something is limited (1 Corinthians 15:19, "If in this life *only* we have hope in Christ . . ."), or isolated (James 2:24, "Ye see then how that by works a man is justified, and not by faith *only*" [faith viewed in isolation]). *Monon* is used with negatives frequently meaning "not only" and is used in the common expression "not only . . . but also" as in Matthew 21:21, "If ye have faith, and doubt not, ye shall *not only* do this . . . to the fig tree, *but also* if ye shall say unto this mountain . . . ."

STRONG 3440, BAUER 527, MOULTON-MILLIGAN 417, LIDDELL-SCOTT 1145, COLIN BROWN 2:723-24.

3304. μόνος monos adj

Only, alone, solitary, no other.

COGNATES:
καταμόνας katamonas (2621)
μονογενής monogenēs (3302)
μόνον monon (3303)
μονόφθαλμος monophthalmos (3305)
μονόω monoō (3306)

אַךְ 'akh (395), Only (Gn 7:23, Jer 32:30 [39:30]).

בָּדָד bādhādh (945), Alone, lonely (Dt 32:12, 33:28, Lam 1:1).

רַק raq (7828), Only (Nm 12:2).

1. μόνον **monon** nom/acc sing masc/neu
2. μόνος **monos** nom sing masc
3. μόνου **monou** gen sing masc
4. μόνῳ **monō** dat sing masc
5. μόνοι **monoi** nom pl masc
6. μόνοις **monois** dat pl masc
7. μόνους **monous** acc pl masc
8. μόνην **monēn** acc sing fem
9. μόνα **mona** nom/acc pl neu
10. μόνας **monas** acc pl fem

4	It is written, Man shall not live by bread **alone**,....	Matt 4:4
4	worship the Lord ... and him **only** shalt thou serve.....	4:10
6	not lawful for him ... but **only** for the priests?........	12:4
2	when the evening was come, he was there **alone**......	14:23
1	they saw no man, save Jesus **only**....................	17:8
3	tell him his fault between thee and him **alone**:.........	18:15
2	no, not the angels of heaven, but my Father **only**...	24:36
10	And as soon as He was **alone**, (NASB)..........	Mark 4:10
2	midst of the sea, and he **alone** on the land...........	6:47
7	up into an high mountain apart **by themselves**:.........	9:2
1	no man any more, save Jesus **only** with themselves.....	9:8
4	That man shall not live by bread **alone**,..........	Luke 4:4
4	worship the Lord ... and him **only** shalt thou serve.....	4:8
2	Who can forgive sins, but God **alone**?..........	5:21
7	is not lawful to eat but for the priests **alone**?............	6:4
10	while He was praying **alone**, (NASB).................	9:18
2	when the voice was past, Jesus was found **alone**.......	9:36
8	not care that my sister hath left me to serve **alone**?...	10:40
9	he beheld the linen clothes laid **by themselves**,...............	24:12
2	Art thou **only** a stranger in Jerusalem,................	24:18
3	seek not the honour that cometh from God **only**?..	John 5:44
2	he departed again into a mountain himself **alone**.......	6:15
5	but that his disciples were gone away **alone**;.......	John 6:22
2	and Jesus was left **alone**,............................	8:9
2	my judgment is true: for I am not **alone**,...............	8:16
1	the Father hath not left me **alone**;...................	8:29
2	Except a corn ... die, it abideth **alone**:...............	12:24
1	every man to his own, and shall leave me **alone**:.....	16:32
2	yet I am not **alone**, because the Father is with me....	16:32
1	that they might know thee the **only** true God,........	17:3
2	and I am left **alone**, and they seek my life........	Rom 11:3
2	unto whom not **only** I give thanks,...................	16:4
4	To God **only** wise, be glory through Jesus Christ ...	16:27
2	Or I **only** and Barnabas, have not we power.......	1 Co 9:6
7	or came it unto you **only**?..........................	14:36
1	and then shall he have rejoicing in himself **alone**,...	Gal 6:4
5	no church communicated with me ... but ye **only**....	Phlp 4:15
5	These **only** are my fellowworkers...................	Col 4:11
5	we thought it good to be left at Athens **alone**;.....	1 Th 3:1
4	the **only** wise God, be honour and glory for ever ..	1 Tm 1:17
3	who is the blessed and **only** Potentate,................	6:15
2	Who **only** hath immortality..........................	6:16
2	**Only** Luke is with me............................	2 Tm 4:11
2	But into the second went the high priest **alone**......	Heb 9:7
2	whom I love in the truth; and not I **only**,...........	2 Jn 1:1
4	To the **only** wise God our Saviour,.................	Jude 1:25
7	but only those men which have not the seal of God	Rev 9:4
2	Lord, and glorify thy name? for thou **only** art holy:...	15:4

Classical Greek and Septuagint Usage

The adjective *monos* is commonly found in classical Greek meaning "alone." By implication and usage the idea of "without others" carries a sense of isolation and uniqueness (see examples in *Liddell-Scott*). It can be found over 160 times in the Septuagint where it most frequently translates some form or compound of l^evadh, also meaning "alone," from the verb bādhādh, "be separated or isolated." In Genesis 2:18 God said: "It is not good that the man should be *alone*," and in Psalm 51:4 (LXX 50:4) David prayed for cleansing after sinning with Bathsheba: "Against thee (God), thee *only*, have I sinned, and done this evil in thy sight."

New Testament Usage

Monos is found 48 times in the New Testament as an adjective, most often meaning "alone" (without a companion). Hebrews 9:7 refers to the high priest who "alone" goes into the Holy of Holies. No one else was allowed to enter.

Monos is also used to mean "left alone, forsaken, deprived of something." Jesus foretold: "Ye . . . shall leave me *alone*: and yet I am not *alone*, because the Father is with me" (John 16:32). Associated with this meaning is the idea of "isolated, by itself" as used in John 12:24: "Except a corn of wheat fall into the ground and die, it abideth *alone*."

Monos may also carry the idea of "standing alone, single in its kind, unique." This is especially evident when used with "God" as in 1 Timothy 1:17, "The *only* wise God"; and 6:15,16, "The blessed and *only* Potentate, the King of kings, and Lord of lords; who *only* hath immortality." This meaning is also common in the Septuagint as seen in Hezekiah's prayer in 2 Kings 19:15,19: "Thou art the God, even thou *alone*" (see also Psalm 86:10 [LXX 85:10]; Isaiah 37:20; John 5:44; 17:3, "The *only* true God and Jesus Christ . . . ").

STRONG 3441, BAUER 527, MOULTON-MILLIGAN 417, LIDDELL-SCOTT 1145, COLIN BROWN 2:716,723-24.

3305. μονόφθαλμος
monophthalmos adj
One-eyed, single-eyed.
CROSS-REFERENCES:
μόνος monos (3304)
ὀφθαλμός ophthalmos (3652)

1. μονόφθαλμον monophthalmon acc sing masc

1 it is better for thee to enter into life with **one eye,** Matt 18:9
1 to enter into the kingdom of God **with one eye,** . . . . . Mark 9:47

Early Greek writings use *monophthalmos* to refer to one who has lost an eye or only has one eye (e.g., the mythical Cyclops; cf. *Liddell-Scott*).

This word occurs only two times in the New Testament: "And if thine eye offend thee, pluck it out: it is better for thee to enter into the kingdom of God with *one eye*, than having two eyes to be cast into hell fire" (Mark 9:47; see also Matthew 18:9). Jesus used hyperbole, exaggeration for effect, to make His point: it is so important to enter into eternal life that radical spiritual surgery is demanded to remove the sin that prohibits participation in the Kingdom of God. Mark, like Matthew, also emphasizes the individual's responsibility for his or her own spiritual health.

STRONG 3442, BAUER 528, MOULTON-MILLIGAN 417, LIDDELL-SCOTT 1146.

3306. μονόω monoō verb
Be left alone, deserted, desolate.
CROSS-REFERENCE:
μόνος monos (3304)

1. μεμονωμένη memonōmenē
nom sing fem part perf mid

1 Now she that is a widow indeed, and **desolate,** . . . . . . 1 Tm 5:5

Monoō is a verb that occurs frequently in classical Greek generally meaning "make single" or "solitary," or as a passive, "to be left alone, forsaken" (*Liddell-Scott*). It does not appear in the Septuagint, but its related adjective *monos* (3304) occurs over 160 times. *Monoō* is used only once in the New Testament, in 1 Timothy 5:5: "Now she that is a widow indeed, and *desolate*, trusteth in God, and continueth in supplications and prayers night and day." In contrast to widows with children or relatives (see verse 4), the "desolate" widow was without children to care for her. The church supported this group of widows in Acts 6, and they in turn were to serve the church by caring for and training the younger wives.

STRONG 3443, BAUER 528, MOULTON-MILLIGAN 417, LIDDELL-SCOTT 1146.

3307. μορφή morphē noun
Form, outward appearance, shape.
COGNATE:
μορφόω morphoō (3308)
SYNONYMS:
εἶδος eidos (1482)
εἰκών eikōn (1494)
ἰδέα idea (2374)
μόρφωσις morphōsis (3309)
ὁμοίωμα homoiōma (3530)
σχῆμα schēma (4828)
τύπος tupos (5020)

צְלֵם ts^elēm (A7022), Facial expression (Dn 3:19—Aramaic).

תֹּאַר tō'ar (8717), Resemblance (Jgs 8:18—Codex Alexandrinus only).

תַּבְנִית tavnîth (8732), Form (Is 44:13).

תְּמוּנָה t^emûnāh (8874), Form (Jb 4:16).

1. μορφῇ morphē dat sing fem
2. μορφήν morphēn acc sing fem

1 After that he appeared in another **form** unto two . . Mark 16:12
1 Who, being in the **form** of God, ... Phlp 2:6
2 and took upon him the **form** of a servant, ... 2:7

Classical Greek
The definition of *morphē* is "form, manner, appearance." This may be the unique quality or aspect characterizing an individual or object. The term is used in classical Greek to describe the external appearance and form, nature, or condition in which a person appears.

Some aspects of Greek religion speculated that gods appeared in various human forms; furthermore, they thought that men could be transformed (*metamorphoō* [3209]) by the power of the gods into another form (e.g., Apuleius' *The Golden Ass* recounts such an episode). Much philosophical speculation existed about matter and form, substance and *morphē*. All of this, however, is of secondary importance for considering the New Testament understanding of *morphē*.

Septuagint Usage

Morphē occurs nine times in the Septuagint as a translation for various Hebrew terms: *tavnîth* (Isaiah 44:13, of the idol-worshiper who created an image/form of a man); *t^emûnāh* (Job 4:16, of physical form); *tselem* (Daniel 3:19, of Nebuchadnezzar's changed form [i.e., the external expression of his attitude]). The Septuagint never employs *morphē* in reference to the "form" of God; not even in its recounting of God's theophanies or in anthropomorphic terms (speaking about God in human terms; e.g., "the arm of God").

New Testament Usage

In the New Testament the noun *morphē* appears three times, in Mark 16:12 and Philippians 2:6,7. After the Resurrection, Jesus revealed himself "in another form" to the two travelers (cf. Luke 24:13f.). Here *morphē* is simply a visual form of something (Louw and Nida, *Greek-English Lexicon*, 1:587). It is the manner in which Christ appeared or looked to the disciples as compared to His preresurrection form.

In the Philippians text Paul contrasts *morphē theou* ("form of God") with *morphēn doulou* ("form of a servant or slave") to afford a premier theological/Christological statement that has been surrounded by controversy since it appeared. Here occurs one of the boldest statements about the nature of the Incarnation (see the word study on *kenoō* [2729]).

Paul declared in these verses (repeating what some refer to as the *Carmen Christi*, a hymn of the Early Church) that Jesus Christ was in the "form of God" (*morphē*); that is, the true "form" of His preexistent, divine, majestic, and glorious nature (cf. John 17:5). But Jesus relinquished this form of glory and took instead the "form" of a servant. Here "form" is not merely the external appearance or mode of existence by which He was observed by those around Him. Rather, *morphē* in these verses is "the nature or character of something, with emphasis upon *both* the internal and external form" (ibid., 1:586). His external form was totally reversed for our sakes; the King became a slave.

The parallelism between "the form of God" and "the form of a servant" in this hymn is important in understanding the meaning of *morphē* in Philippians 2:6,7. As Braumann states, the *en* ("in") does not mean that this form was somehow only an outer shell that was different from the essential nature of Christ. If this were true He would have been like an actor playing the part of someone who He was not ("Form," *Colin Brown*, 1:706). That Christ was in the "form of God" means that Christ's essential nature was divine. In the Incarnation Jesus exchanged the "form of God" for the "form of a servant." However, this does not suggest any change in the nature and essence of Jesus as God It was in the process of becoming the God-man He humiliated himself and took the form of a slave. The essence which appeared in the form of a servant remained the same. Jesus did not relinquish His deity, only its "form" of glory, power, and majesty. When He was transformed (*metamorphoō*) on the Mount of Transfiguration, His outward appearance changed to correspond with the internal glory and essence He always had.

STRONG 3444, BAUER 528, MOULTON-MILLIGAN 417-18, KITTEL 4:742-52, LIDDELL-SCOTT 1147, COLIN BROWN 1:705-8.

3308. μορφόω morphoō verb

Take on form, be formed, shape, fashion.
COGNATES:
μεταμορφόω metamorphoō (3209)
μορφή morphē (3307)
μόρφωσις morphōsis (3309)
συμμορφίζω summorphizō (4682B)
σύμμορφος summorphos (4683)
συμμορφόω summorphoō (4684)

1. μορφωθῇ **morphōthē** 3sing subj aor pass

1 again until Christ be formed in you, ... Gal 4:19

Classical Greek

In classical Greek *morphoō* means "to fashion" as an artist who "gives shape" to his material. Other words related to *morphoō* (*morphotēr*—"one who shapes"; *morphōma*—"outline" or "form" of a figure, etc.) stress the outward appearance rather than the inward essence or nature of something or someone. This sense of "outward appearance" for *morphoō* does not occur in the Bible. But a meaning which parallels its Biblical usage is found in classical literature and describes the "forming" of the embryo, as a child in the womb (*Bauer*).

Septuagint Usage

The Septuagint does not use the verb *morphoō* but uses the related term *plassō* (3972). (It is interesting to note that *plassō* is mostly utilized in the active voice ["God *formed* man," Genesis 2:7], but *morphoō* is predominant passive ["until Christ *be formed* in you," Galatians 4:19].)

New Testament Usage

The only New Testament occurrence is at Galatians 4:19. Here Paul used the analogy of a woman's travailing birth pangs to describe his intense desire and prayer that the nature and character of Christ "be formed" in the lives of the Galatian believers. In order that the *morphē* (3307), or essential nature of the Christ-life, may come into being in them, Christ must not only be in each of them, but must also grow or "be formed" in them. This process of maturity into Christlikeness is not a mere outward conformity to Christ but a progressive inward transformation of one's character. Christian growth through the Spirit's work is a major theme in Paul's writings.

The third-century church father Hippolytus underscored this image of Christian growth in his use of *morphoō*: "The true Christian is *being formed* by the instruction of the Lord" (Behm, "morphoō," *Kittel*, 4:753).

Strong 3445, Bauer 528, Moulton-Milligan 418, Kittel 4:752-54, Liddell-Scott 1147, Colin Brown 1:705,708.

3309. μόρφωσις morphōsis noun

Form, appearance, semblance, embodiment.

Cognate:
μορφόω morphoō (3308)

Synonyms:
εἶδος eidos (1482)
εἰκών eikōn (1494)
ἰδέα idea (2374)
μορφή morphē (3307)
ὁμοίωμα homoiōma (3530)
σχῆμα schēma (4828)
τύπος tupos (5020)

1. μόρφωσιν morphōsin acc sing fem

1 the form of knowledge and of the truth in the law... Rom 2:20
1 Having a form of godliness, but denying the power.. 2 Tm 3:5

Morphōsis is a verbal noun that denotes the activity of forming or shaping, e.g., the "shaping" or training of trees (cf. *Liddell-Scott*). It is absent from the Septuagint. In the New Testament it is used in the passive sense with the emphasis on the result of the forming, "the form."

The related word *morphē* (3307) also means "form" and denotes either that which is perceived (Mark 16:12) or the essential nature or character of something (Louw and Nida, *Greek-English Lexicon*, 1:586). *Schēma* (4828) also means "form" or "appearance," but focuses on the external and may actually be deceptive concerning the inward reality. As used in the New Testament, *morphōsis* shares nuances of meaning with both words.

Some have held that *morphōsis* denotes the objective outline of reality. However, Romans 2:20 seems to require a meaning such as "embodiment," not merely "an outline." In 2 Timothy 3:5 the meaning is clearly "outward appearance." The meaning is settled here by the contexts.

Strong 3446, Bauer 528, Moulton-Milligan 418, Kittel 4:754-55, Liddell-Scott 1147, Colin Brown 1:705,708.

3310. μοσχοποιέω moschopoieō verb

Make a calf.

Cross-References:
μόσχος moschos (3311)
ποιέω poieō (4020)

1. ἐμοσχοποίησαν emoschopoiēsan 3pl indic aor act

1 And they made a calf in those days,............... Acts 7:41

This verb is a compound of *moschos* (3311), "calf," and *poieō* (4020), "to make"; hence *moschopoieō* means "make a calf." According to *Bauer* it is found only in Christian writings. It occurs in the New Testament only at Acts 7:41: "And they *made a calf* in those days, and offered sacrifice unto the idol, and rejoiced in the works of their own hands." This term is formed from two separate words in Exodus 32:4 ("make" and "calf") and according to Blass (cf. *Moulton-Milligan*) is an example of the flexibility of the Greek language in forming new words. By creating this new word, Stephen highlighted the great sin of idolatry that plagued Israel and ultimately led to her being cast off by God and sent into exile.

Strong 3447, Bauer 528, Moulton-Milligan 418, Liddell-Scott 1148.

3311. μόσχος moschos noun

Calf, young bull.

Cross-Reference:
μοσχοποιέω moschopoieō (3310)

μουσικός 3312

בָּקָר bāqār (1267), Oxen, bull (Gn 20:14, 2 Chr 29:33, Jer 52:20).

עֵגֶל ʿēghel (5903), Calf (Ex 32:19f., Neh 9:18, Mi 6:6).

עֶגְלָה ʿeghlāh (5904), Young bull, bull (Hos 10:5).

פַּר par (6749), Bull, young bull (Lv 4:4f., Nm 29:20f., Ez 43:22f.).

שׁוֹר shôr (8228), Ox, calf (Dt 17:1, 1 Sm 15:3, Ps 106:19 [105:19]).

תּוֹר tôr (A8783), Bull (Ezr 6:17, 7:17-Aramaic).

1. **μόσχῳ** moschō dat sing masc
2. **μόσχον** moschon acc sing masc
3. **μόσχων** moschōn gen pl masc

```
2 And bring hither the fatted calf, and kill it; ........ Luke 15:23
2 and thy father hath killed the fatted calf, ............ 15:27
2 thou hast killed for him the fatted calf. ............. 15:30
3 Neither by the blood of goats and calves, ........... Heb 9:12
3 he took the blood of calves and of goats, ............. 9:19
1 and the second beast like a calf, .................... Rev 4:7
```

Classical Greek and Septuagint Usage
In classical Greek the noun *moschos* can be used for a "calf, young bull, ox," or "musk." *Moschos* is used in the Septuagint to translate various Hebrew terms: *bāqār* ("oxen," Genesis 12:16); *ʿeghlāh* ("calf," Exodus 32:4); *par* ("young bullock," Leviticus 4:3); and *shôr* ("bullock," Leviticus 9:4).

New Testament Usage
In the New Testament *moschos* is the fatted "calf" killed at the Prodigal Son's return (Luke 15:23,27,30). In Hebrews 9:12 *moschos* is used to refer to the "blood of goats and *calves*" that was necessarily sacrificed by the high priest in order to make atonement; however, the writer of Hebrews stated that Christ, as High Priest of the new covenant, entered the Holy Place by "his own blood." Hebrews 9:19 refers to the blood "of *calves* and of goats" used by Moses to mark the solemn inauguration of the old covenant with Israel (cf. Exodus 24). The sixth and final occurrence of *moschos* is in Revelation 4:7 (cf. Ezekiel 1:10) as an apocalyptic animal.

STRONG 3448, BAUER 528, MOULTON-MILLIGAN 418, KITTEL 4:760-62, LIDDELL-SCOTT 1148.

3312. μουσικός mousikos adj
Skilled in music, the musician.

זְמָר zᵉmār (A2254), Music (Dn 3:5,7,10,15—Aramaic).

מִזְמוֹר mizmôr (4344), Psalm; musical tune (Sir 44:5).

שִׁיר shîr (8302), Song (Gn 31:27, Ez 26:13).

1. **μουσικῶν** mousikōn gen pl masc

```
1 And the voice of harpers, and musicians, ........... Rev 18:22
```

The adjective *mousikos* generally means "musical." It is used of both persons ("musicians") and things ("harmonious"). As a substantive it may refer to either instrumentalists or vocalists, generally "persons skilled in music." In classical literature the term also includes men of letters and great accomplishments (*Liddell-Scott*) and sometimes denotes a special class of performers (*Moulton-Milligan*). In the Septuagint this word is applied to different kinds of music (Genesis 31:27; Daniel 3:5,7,10,15) and musicians (Ezekiel 26:13). The only use of this word in the New Testament is in Revelation 18:22. In describing the aftermath of the complete destruction of Babylon, there will be an eerie silence where the sounds of "harpers, and *musicians*, and of pipers, and trumpeters" were once enjoyed.

STRONG 3451, BAUER 528, MOULTON-MILLIGAN 418, LIDDELL-SCOTT 1148-49.

3313. μόχθος mochthos noun
Labor, toil, hardship, exertion.

SYNONYMS:
ἔργον ergon (2024)
κόπος kopos (2845)
ποίησις poiēsis (4022)
πόνος ponos (4051)

אָוֶן ʾāwen (201), Trouble (Nm 23:21).

יָגוֹן yāghôn (3123), Sorrow (Jer 20:18—only some Sinaiticus texts).

יְגִיעַ yᵉghîaʿ (3127), Labor, something worked for (Jer 3:24, Ez 23:29).

עָמָל ʿāmāl (6219), Labor (Eccl 2:10, 4:8f., 8:15).

פְּעֻלָּה pᵉʿullāh (6715), Recompense (Is 61:8).

פֶּרֶךְ perekh (6783), Severity, harshness (Lv 25:46, Ez 34:4).

תְּלָאָה tᵉlāʾāh (8843), Hardship (Ex 18:8, Nm 20:14, Neh 9:32).

1. **μόχθῳ** mochthō dat sing masc
2. **μόχθον** mochthon acc sing masc

```
1 In weariness and painfulness, in watchings often, ... 2 Co 11:27
2 ye remember, brethren, our labour and travail: ...... 1 Th 2:9
1 but wrought with labour and travail night and day, .. 2 Th 3:8
```

The noun *mochthos* is related to *mogis* (3289), "hardly, with difficulty," and is often found with *kopos* (2845), "toil." In classical Greek *mochthos* can mean "toil, hardship, distress," with the implication of "work," *ponos* (4051) (cf. *Liddell-Scott*). *Mochthos* is used in the Septuagint to translate several Hebrew terms meaning "labor" (Ecclesiastes 2:10; Isaiah

55:2) and "rigor" (Leviticus 25:43,46,53). *Mochthos* is used only three times in the New Testament (2 Corinthians 11:27, "painfulness"; 1 Thessalonians 2:9, "travail"; 2 Thessalonians 3:8, "travail") and always in close sequence to *kopos*. Paul presented a list of the things he endured throughout his ministry, not the least of which were "severe work" and "difficult labor."

STRONG 3449, BAUER 528, MOULTON-MILLIGAN 418, LIDDELL-SCOTT 1149, COLIN BROWN 1:262.

3314. μυελός muelos noun
Marrow.

חֵלֶב chēlev (2561), Fat (Gn 45:18).
מֹחַ mōach (4355), Marrow (Jb 21:24).

1. μυελῶν muelōn gen pl masc
1 of soul and spirit, and of the joints and marrow, ... Heb 4:12

Classical Greek and Septuagint Usage
Muelos denotes the "inmost part" of something. It is found in classical and Koine Greek, and three times in the Septuagint (Genesis 45:18; Job 21:24; 33:24). In classical Greek the word can be found meaning "brain" or "spinal cord" (*Liddell-Scott*). Marrow, however, is also considered good food (ibid.). The word can also be used metaphorically to mean the best available or good living. This is seen in Pharaoh's invitation to Jacob to come and participate in the *fat* (*muelon*) of the land (Genesis 45:18).

New Testament Usage
Muelos occurs only once in the New Testament. Hebrews 4:12 describes the function of the living Word of God to discern between the innermost aspects of man, "soul and spirit, and of the joints and marrow (*muelos*)." *Muelos* suggests the smallest division as applied to man's being. Nothing, however small, incidental, or hidden in the recesses of our being, can escape the judicial effect of the living Word of God.

STRONG 3452, BAUER 528, LIDDELL-SCOTT 1150.

3315. μυέω mueō verb
Initiate into (the mysteries), learn a secret, instruct, teach.

CROSS-REFERENCE:
μυστήριον mustērion (3328)

1. μεμύημαι memuēmai 1sing indic perf mid
1 every where and in all things I am instructed .... Phlp 4:12

Classical Greek
In classical Greek the word *mueō* is a term used frequently of the mystery religions, "to initiate into the mysteries" (see word study on *mustērion* [3328]). It was usually in the passive, "to be initiated" (*Liddell-Scott*). A large number of inscriptions in the papyri indicate the continued use in this technical sense throughout the Koine period (*Moulton-Milligan*). The word also came to be used in a general sense, "to instruct" or "to teach."

Septuagint Usage
The lone occurrence of *mueō* in the Septuagint is in 3 Maccabees 2:30 where the form is *memuēmenois* and refers to those initiated in the rites of Dionysius. *Mueō* may have developed from *muō*, "to shut" (the mouth) and thus to keep secret. The initiated were thoroughly instructed in the mysteries of the cults, but those secrets were kept from outsiders.

New Testament Usage
In the New Testament *mueō* is found only in Philippians 4:12 in connection with Paul's deprivations and sufferings. Paul may have used the word in its general sense to mean he had become accustomed to hardships and had "learned" to endure them, but it could also mean that in the midst of suffering he "learned the secret" of doing all things in the strength of Christ (cf. verse 13).

STRONG 3453, BAUER 529, MOULTON-MILLIGAN 418, KITTEL 4:828, LIDDELL-SCOTT 1150, COLIN BROWN 3:501.

3316. μῦθος muthos noun
Word, speech; tale, legend, myth, fable, fiction.

1. μύθοις muthois dat pl masc
2. μύθους muthous acc pl masc

1 give heed to fables and endless genealogies, ... 1 Tm 1:4
2 But refuse profane and old wives' fables, ... 4:7
2 from the truth, and shall be turned unto fables. ..... 2 Tm 4:4
1 Not giving heed to Jewish fables, ... Tit 1:14
1 For we have not followed cunningly devised fables, .. 2 Pt 1:16

Classical Greek
This noun is commonly used in classical Greek with a wide variety of meanings. In literature as early as Homer, *muthos* can be found referring to "words," especially those spoken, e.g., a "speech," "conversation," or "anything said" (*Liddell-Scott*). It is also used where there is no clear distinction of what is true or false, hence a "story, tale, fiction" (a well-known example

of which is Aesop's *fables*). *Muthos* appears twice in the Septuagint; both occurrences are noncanonical, and neither translate a Hebrew term (Wisdom of Solomon 17:4; Sirach 20:19, "tale").

New Testament Usage
This word occurs five times in the New Testament and always denotes a "false story" or "tale" (1 Timothy 1:4; 4:7; 2 Timothy 4:4; Titus 1:14; 2 Peter 1:16). When Paul used the term he was referring to what might be called "old wives' fables" (*Bauer*; cf. Plato who wrote about "old women who tell *stories*"). The "fables" Paul warned against were Jewish myths and stories concerning "endless genealogies" (1 Timothy 1:4; Titus 1:14). One characteristic of backsliders in the last days is that they shall not endure sound doctrine but will instead turn to "fables" (2 Timothy 4:3,4). Elsewhere, Peter solemnly reminded the readers of his letter that when he spoke of Jesus Christ, he was not transmitting "cunningly devised *fables*." On the contrary, he assured them that he was an eyewitness of His majesty (2 Peter 1:16f.).

STRONG 3454, BAUER 529, MOULTON-MILLIGAN 418-19, KITTEL 4:762-95, LIDDELL-SCOTT 1151, COLIN BROWN 2:643-45,647.

3317. μυκάομαι mukaomai verb
Roar (of lions), mooing (of cattle), bellow (of oxen).
SYNONYMS:
ἠχέω ēcheō (2255)
ὠρύομαι ōruomai (5445)

1. μυκᾶται mukatai 3sing indic pres mid
1 cried with a loud voice, as when a lion roareth:..... Rev 10:3

This verb is used only once in the New Testament, at Revelation 10:3. In classical Greek it is used to describe the sounds typically made by oxen or cattle. *Mukaomai* is used in some versions of the Septuagint in 1 Samuel 6:12 (LXX 1 Kings 6:12) for the "lowing" of cows; in Job 6:5 for the ox's "lowing." This suggests that the voice of the angel in Revelation 10:3 had "deep resonance which would demand the attention of those who heard" (Mounce, *New International Commentary on the New Testament, Revelation*, p.208). In Koine Greek this verb is also used for the roar of the sea (cf. *Moulton-Milligan*).

STRONG 3455, BAUER 529, MOULTON-MILLIGAN 419, LIDDELL-SCOTT 1151.

3318. μυκτηρίζω muktērizō verb
Turn up the nose at, treat with contempt, mock, ridicule, deride.

אַף 'aph (653), Nose (Ez 8:17).
בּוּז bûz (972), Despise (Prv 11:12, 23:9).
בָּזָה bāzâh (995), Despise (Prv 15:20).
הָתַל hāthal (2130), Piel: mock (1 Kgs 18:27).
לָעַב lāʻav (4073), Hiphil: mock (2 Chr 36:16).
לָעַג lāʻagh (4074), Nock (2 Kgs 19:21, Is 37:22, Jer 20:7).
נָאַץ nāʼats (5180), Spurn, despise (Prv 1:30, 15:5).

1. μυκτηρίζεται muktērizetai 3sing indic pres mid
1 Be not deceived; God is not mocked:................ Gal 6:7

Septuagint Usage
Muktērizō, a word that is rarely found outside of the Septuagint, occurs 15 times there. It is related to *muktēr*, "the nose." The action of "turning up the nose" or "sneering" at someone with contempt portrays the meaning of *muktērizō* (*Liddell-Scott*). It is frequently used in the Septuagint of the attitude of the fool toward his parents (Proverbs 15:5,20), of an ungodly person's actions toward the people of God (Psalms 44:13 [LXX 43:13]; 80:6 [79:6]), and of the attitude of those who reject God (Proverbs 1:30; 23:9).

New Testament Usage
Muktērizō occurs only once in the New Testament, at Galatians 6:7: "God is not *mocked*" or to be treated with contempt. One manuscript uses *muktērizō* in Luke 23:36, instead of using *empaizō* (1686), a closely related word, to describe the attitude and actions of the soldiers toward Christ at His crucifixion. See also *ekmuktērizō* (1579), a compound of *muktērizō* and used in Luke 23:35 of the peoples' attitude toward Christ.

STRONG 3456, BAUER 529, MOULTON-MILLIGAN 419, KITTEL 4:796, LIDDELL-SCOTT 1152, COLIN BROWN 3:341.

3319. μυλικός mulikos adj
Pertaining to a mill.

1. μυλικός mulikos nom sing masc
1 that a millstone were hanged about his neck,....... Mark 9:42
1 if a millstone were hung (NASB)................. Luke 17:2

Mulikos is an adjective meaning "that which pertains to a mill." *Mulikos* is used in Mark 9:42, Luke 17:2, and Revelation 18:21 with reference to the "stones (*lithos* [3010B]) of the mill," hence the "millstones." Matthew 18:18

and Mark 9:42 confirm that these stones which belong to the mill are indeed millstones by using the word *mulos* (3320), "millstone." There were at least two kinds of millstones—the one turned by hand (a common tool used to grind grain), referred to in Luke 17:35, "two women shall be grinding together"; the other turned by an ass or some other animal. The punishment of putting a huge millstone around the neck of an offender and casting him into the sea was reportedly practiced by the Roman ruler Augustus. The leaders of an insurrection under Judas of Galilee were executed in this manner (Edersheim, *Life and Times of Jesus the Messiah*, 2:120). (See also *mulos* [3320], "mill, millstone.")

STRONG 3457, BAUER 529, MOULTON-MILLIGAN 419, LIDDELL-SCOTT 1152, COLIN BROWN 3:390,394.

3319B. μύλινος mulinos adj
Belonging to the mill, made of millstone.

1. μύλινον mulinon acc sing masc

This is a variant spelling of *mulikos*. See the word study at number 3319.

3320. μύλος mulos noun
Millstone, mill.

רֵחַיִם rēchayim (7634), Mill, millstones (Ex 11:5, Dt 24:6 [24:8], Is 47:2).

1. μύλος mulos nom sing masc
2. μύλου mulou gen sing masc
3. μύλον mulon acc sing masc
4. μύλῳ mulō dat sing masc

1 it were better for him that a **millstone** were hanged Matt 18:6
1 a heavy **millstone** hung around his neck, (NASB) ... Mark 9:42
1 It were better for him that a **millstone** were hanged Luke 17:2
3 mighty angel took up a stone like a great **millstone**, Rev 18:21
2 the sound of a **millstone** shall be heard no more 18:22

Classical Greek and Septuagint Usage
In early Greek literature *mulē* is used to describe a "mill," frequently a "hand-mill" used by women (*Liddell-Scott*). In later Greek *mulos* denotes the same thing, frequently with a greater emphasis on the size of the millstone. In this it parallels the Hebrew *rēcheh* which it translates in the Septuagint in Exodus 11:5, Numbers 11:8, Deuteronomy 24:6, and Isaiah 47:2. *Rēcheh* is found only in the dual (*rēchayim*) indicating that the two stones of the mill were always in view even when the focus was on the mill as a unit.

New Testament Usage
In New Testament times mills were often made of two flat, circular stones. The lower stone was stationary. The movement of the upper stone against the lower produced the grinding that made flour from the grain. Small rotary handmills were usually operated by women or servants with the larger ones requiring two women to operate them (cf. Numbers 11:8; Matthew 24:41).

During the Second or First Century B.C., community mills often had stones 2 to 3 feet in diameter which required animal power to turn them (see Rasmussen, *International Standard Bible Encyclopedia*, 3:355f.). Matthew 18:6 refers to such a millstone as a *mulos onikos*, "a millstone of an ass," i.e., a millstone turned by a donkey. (See also Luke 17:2; Revelation 18:21,22.)

STRONG 3458, BAUER 529, MOULTON-MILLIGAN 419, LIDDELL-SCOTT 1152, COLIN BROWN 3:390,394.

3321. μύλων mulōn noun
Mill-house.

פְּקֻדָּה peqḍuddāh (6735), Oversight, visitation; prison (Jer 52:11).

1. μύλωνι mulōni dat sing masc

1 Two women shall be grinding at the **mill**; .... Matt 24:41

This noun, which refers to the very building itself, is used only once in the New Testament. In Matthew 24:41, a reference to the Second Coming, Jesus said that "two women shall be grinding at the *mill*." There were at least two methods of grinding meal at the commonplace mill—the one turned by hand, referred to in Luke 17:35 with the words "two women ... grinding together"; and the other turned by an animal (see *mulikos* [3319]).

STRONG 3459, BAUER 529, LIDDELL-SCOTT 1152-53.

3322. Μύρα Mura name
Myra.

1. Μύρα Mura nom/acc pl neu

1 had sailed ... we came to **Myra**, a city of Lycia..... Acts 27:5

Seaport city in southern Asia Minor where Paul changed ships on his way to Rome (Acts 27:5).

3323. μυριάς murias noun

Myriad (ten thousand), a vast number, innumerable.

1. **μυριάδες** muriades nom pl fem
2. **μυριάδων** muriadōn gen pl fem
3. **μυριάσιν** muriasin dat pl fem
4. **μυριάδας** muriadas acc pl fem

2 gathered ... an **innumerable multitude** of people,	....	Luke 12:1
4 and found it fifty **thousand** pieces of silver	....	Acts 19:19
1 many **thousands** of Jews there are which believe;	......	21:20
3 and to an **innumerable company** of angels,	....	Heb 12:22
3 the Lord cometh with **ten thousands** of his saints,	....	Jude 1:14
1 and the number of them was **myriads** (NASB)	....	Rev 5:11
2 **myriads** of myriads, and thousands (NASB)	....	5:11
1 horsemen were two hundred thousand **thousand**:	....	9:16
2 horsemen were two hundred thousand **thousand**:	....	9:16

This noun is used six times in the New Testament. It represents the number *10,000* (Acts 19:19, five *murias* = 50,000). It most often denotes a numberless host or vast numbers of men (Luke 12:1; Acts 21:20) or angels (Hebrews 12:22; Jude 14). Compare also *dismurias* (1357B), literally "two 10,000's," and its use together with *murias* in Revelation 9:16 as an apocalyptic number.

STRONG 3461, BAUER 529, MOULTON-MILLIGAN 419, LIDDELL-SCOTT 1153-54.

3324. μυρίζω murizō verb

Anoint (for burial), rub (with ointment or unguent).

SYNONYMS:
ἀλείφω aleiphō (216)
ἐπιχρίω epichriō (2009)
χρίω chriō (5383)

1. **μυρίσαι** murisai inf aor act

1 come aforehand **to anoint** my body to the burying. Mark 14:8

Murizō is used only once in the New Testament, in Mark 14:8, with the meaning of preparing a corpse for burial by anointing it with spices. This word is related to the noun *muron* (3326), "ointment." In the Mark 14 passage Mary of Bethany had a costly alabaster of *muron*, described as genuine nard (unadulterated and unmixed perfume). Its exact ingredients may be uncertain, but its special value is clear from the context. It is also uncertain whether Mary fully realized the significance of her action (i.e., anointing for burial); however, there is no doubt as to her sincere expression of pure devotion to Jesus. It was Jesus who interpreted her actions, for all onlookers, as the only preparation for His burial that He would receive. The only other attempt to anoint Jesus' body was made *after* His death (Mark 16:1).

STRONG 3462, BAUER 529, MOULTON-MILLIGAN 419, KITTEL 4:800-801, LIDDELL-SCOTT 1154.

3325. μύριοι murioi adj

Ten thousand; very numerous, innumerable, numberless, countless.

1. **μυρίους** murious acc pl masc
2. **μυρίων** muriōn gen pl neu

2 which owed him **ten thousand** talents.	....	Matt 18:24
1 though ye have **ten thousand** instructors in Christ,	...	1 Co 4:15
1 than **ten thousand** words in an unknown tongue.	....	14:19

Murioi, the plural of *murios*, denotes the number *10,000* when used before a collective substantive. However, since it is the largest of the Greek numbers, it can also mean "very numerous" or "innumerable." It is used in both senses in secular Greek, as well as in the Septuagint. In its three New Testament uses *murioi* seems to be used in the literal sense in Matthew 18:24—the unmerciful slave was forgiven the debt of 10,000 talents—but in the secondary sense of "innumerable" or "countless" in 1 Corinthians 4:15 and 14:19.

STRONG 3463, BAUER 529, MOULTON-MILLIGAN 419, LIDDELL-SCOTT 1154.

3326. μύρον muron noun

Ointment, perfume, sweet oil, unguent.

CROSS-REFERENCE:
σμύρνα smurna (4521)

בֶּשֶׂם besem (1336I), Spices (S/S 4:14).
מִרְקַחַת mirqachath (5005), Spices (1 Chr 9:30).
רָקַח rāqach (7836), Blend; pual: be blended (2 Chr 16:14).
רֹקַח rōqach (7838), Blend (Ex 30:25).
שֶׁמֶן shemen (8467), Oil (Prv 27:9, S/S 1:3, Am 6:6).

1. **μύρον** muron nom/acc sing neu
2. **μύρου** murou gen sing neu
3. **μύρῳ** murō dat sing neu
4. **μύρα** mura nom/acc pl neu

2 an alabaster box of very precious **ointment**,	....	Matt 26:7
1 For this **ointment** might have been sold for much,	.....	26:9
1 in that she hath poured this **ointment** on my body,	.....	26:12
2 box of **ointment** of spikenard very precious;	....	Mark 14:3
2 Why was this waste of the **ointment** made?	....	14:4
1 "For this **perfume** might have been sold (NASB)	......	14:5
2 brought an alabaster box **of ointment**,	....	Luke 7:37
3 and anointed them with the **ointment**.	....	7:38
3 this woman hath anointed my feet **with ointment**.	....	7:46

4 they returned, and prepared spices and **ointments**;	Luke 23:56
3 Mary which anointed the Lord with **ointment**,	John 11:2
2 Then took Mary a pound **of ointment** of spikenard,	12:3
2 house was filled with the odour of the **ointment**.	12:3
1 Why was not this **ointment** sold	12:5
1 And cinnamon, and odours, and **ointments**,	Rev 18:13

Classical Greek
Muron is the juicelike aromatic extract from plants, or perfumed oil. As a cosmetic *muron* could be translated "perfume." "Ointment" is perhaps a useful English translation, since *muron* was often medicinal and at times cultic in significance, being used for anointing (e.g., for burial). Another common use was in the embalming process (cf. *Bauer*).

Septuagint Usage
Muron occurs 18 times in the Septuagint. The Hebrew counterpart to *muron* is most regularly a form of *shemen*, usually denoting "oil" or "perfumed oil." A cultic use of *muron* in Israel's religion is attested on several occasions (e.g., Exodus 30:25, *rōqach*, "sacred anointing oil," NIV; 1 Chronicles 9:30, "spices," NIV; cf. Psalm 133:2 [LXX 132:2]). The cosmetic understanding occurs throughout the Song of Solomon (LXX Canticles) (e.g., 1:3; 4:10,14; cf. Wisdom of Solomon 2:7; Amos 6:6). Oils were a priceless commodity in the ancient world (Isaiah 39:2; cf. Revelation 18:13 and the context of the Gospel accounts).

New Testament Usage
Apart from a single reference in Revelation (18:13), *muron* occurs only in the four Gospels (13 times). The Synoptic Gospels record anointings of Jesus' head by Mary of Bethany. Matthew and Mark clearly link this anointing to Jesus' upcoming burial (Matthew 26:12; Mark 14:8).

The setting in Luke's Gospel is in the house of a Pharisee (also named Simon, cf. Matthew and Mark). Here The anointing of Jesus' feet by the unnamed woman signaled her recognition of Jesus as Lord. She stands in stark contrast to Simon who did not recognize Jesus (cf. Luke 7:44-47,49). John's Gospel, too, associates the anointing by Mary (of Bethany) of Jesus' feet (John 11:2) to be in preparation for His burial (John 12:7).

Burial practices of the New Testament period are reflected in these accounts. It was customary to first wash the body (Acts 9:37) and then anoint it with perfume (Mark 16:1). Fragrant spices were also enclosed in the wrappings around the corpse (cf. Mark 15:46; 16:1). Jesus' burial was hastily carried out because of the time of death (the Sabbath began at sunset); however, it was all unnecessary since He triumphed over the grave!

STRONG 3464, BAUER 529-30, MOULTON-MILLIGAN 419, KITTEL 4:800-801, LIDDELL-SCOTT 1155, COLIN BROWN 2:294-95.

3327. Μυσία Musia name
Mysia.

1. Μυσίαν Musian acc fem

1 After they were come to **Mysia**,	Acts 16:7
1 And they passing by **Mysia** came down to Troas.	16:8

Northwestern province in Asia Minor visited by Paul on his second missionary journey (Acts 16:7,8).

3328. μυστήριον mustērion noun
Secret, secret teaching, mystery, anything hidden or unrevealed.

CROSS-REFERENCE:
μυέω mueō (3315)

רָז rāz (A7611), Mystery (Dn 2:19f.,28ff.,47—Aramaic).

1. μυστήριον mustērion nom/acc sing neu
2. μυστηρίου mustēriou gen sing neu
3. μυστηρίῳ mustēriō dat sing neu
4. μυστηρίων mustēriōn gen pl neu
5. μυστήρια mustēria nom/acc pl neu

5 Because it is given unto you to know the **mysteries**	Matt 13:11
1 Unto you it is given to know the **mystery**	Mark 4:11
5 Unto you it is given to know the **mysteries**	Luke 8:10
1 that ye should be ignorant of this **mystery**,	Rom 11:25
2 according to the revelation of the **mystery**,	16:25
3 But we speak the wisdom of God in a **mystery**,	1 Co 2:7
4 and stewards of the **mysteries** of God.	4:1
5 and understand all **mysteries**, and all knowledge;	13:2
5 howbeit in the spirit he speaketh **mysteries**.	14:2
1 I show you a **mystery**; We shall not all sleep,	15:51
1 made known unto us the **mystery** of his will,	Eph 1:9
1 that by revelation he made known ... the **mystery**;	3:3
3 understand my knowledge in the **mystery** of Christ	3:4
2 all men see what is the fellowship of the **mystery**,	3:9
1 This is a great **mystery**:	5:32
1 to make known the **mystery** of the gospel,	6:19
1 Even the **mystery** which hath been hid from ages	Col 1:26
2 the glory of this **mystery** among the Gentiles;	1:27
2 to the acknowledgment of the **mystery** of God,	2:2
1 to speak the **mystery** of Christ,	4:3
1 For the **mystery** of iniquity doth already work:	2 Th 2:7
1 the **mystery** of the faith in a pure conscience.	1 Tm 3:9
1 great is the **mystery** of godliness:	3:16
1 The **mystery** of the seven stars which thou sawest	Rev 1:20
1 the **mystery** of God should be finished,	10:7
1 **MYSTERY, BABYLON THE GREAT,**	17:5
1 I will tell thee the **mystery** of the woman,	17:7

Classical Greek
The precise origin of *mustērion* is disputed, but it suggests that a silence is to be kept (e.g., a "secret rite," *Liddell-Scott*). Fenkerath suggests

that *mustērion* is from the verb *muō*, "to close, be shut" ("Secret," *Colin Brown*, 3:501). Bornkamm, however, thinks its etymology is uncertain ("mustērion," *Kittel*, 4:803).

The term is especially significant in the religious sphere in antiquity. There were "mystery cults" (from around the Seventh Century B.C. to the Fourth Century A.D.) which were typified by their secrecy; hence the term *mystery*. Basic features of the mysteries included this guarding of secrets; an initiation process, a view that the participants share—through a ritual act—in the life of the god; and a promise of cosmic salvation (ibid., 4:803-808).

These mystery cults gradually infiltrated philosophical circles with terminology, concepts, and speculation (e.g., Plato). Magic, too, shows indications of mystery influence. Furthermore, "mysteries" were those "secrets" that are disclosed to the Gnostic practitioner. Such knowledge came to be linked to redemption and to the power to escape the world (ibid., 4:811-813).

Septuagint Usage

The Septuagint presents a curious use of *mustērion*. Here we encounter, on the one hand, evidence that *mustērion* is especially a Hellenistic concept and relatively foreign to the Hebrew Scriptures. The majority of the documents reading *mustērion* are the noncanonical intertestamental writings that do not have Hebrew behind them. On the other hand, the evidence is plain that *mustērion* is potentially a concept recognized as early as Daniel as is reflected in the Aramaic word *rāz* (e.g., Daniel 2:18,19,27,30,47). *Rāz*, "secret, mystery," describes the mystery revealed to Daniel as the interpreter of Nebuchadnezzar's dream. Both the Septuagint version and Theodotion's version read *rāz* as *mustērion*. The extent to which these translations are imposing Hellenistic ideas is obviously debatable.

The important factor is that in Daniel we have evidence of the transition *mustērion* makes from the notion of "secret" to "revealed secret." Bornkamm remarks concerning this connection: "In Daniel *mustērion* takes on for the first time a sense which is important for the further development of the word, namely, that of an eschatological mystery, a concealed intimation of divinely ordained future events whose disclosure and interpretation is reserved for God alone . . . and for those inspired by His Spirit" (ibid., 4:814f.).

Thus we can see how mystery takes a quality of "divine." This, in turn, becomes a characteristic feature of apocalyptic literature (from *apokaluptō* [596], "I reveal," cf. the Apocalypse, i.e., the Book of Revelation). In this type of literature divine secrets of the future are revealed. In his Revelation John is the apocalyptic seer who reveals the secrets of the future. Thus these "secrets" are now "revealed secrets." We see the distinctive, then, that in the Biblical sense a mystery is not some unexplainable puzzle; rather, the "mystery" has now been openly revealed and can be potentially known by all.

New Testament Usage

Of the 27 uses of *mustērion* in the New Testament, 20 are attributed to Paul. Of the remaining seven, three occur in the Synoptic Gospels in parallel texts (Matthew 13:11; Mark 4:11; Luke 8:10); the other four appear in Revelation (1:20; 10:7; 17:5,7).

Jesus disclosed the secrets of the kingdom of God to those who came to Him in faith. The reception of such insight is firmly tied to repentance (Mark 4:11ff.). Unwilling ears will not hear the Kingdom's secrets, and covered eyes will not see (Matthew 13:11-15), because the message of the Kingdom is a summons to repent and believe. It demands perseverance in the face of adversity (Mark 4:17; Luke 8:15).

The greatest divine secret of all time is the now-revealed mystery of Christ who has come to redeem the world through His death on the cross (1 Corinthians 2:1,2; cf. verses 9,10). Also essential to this larger mystery is the radical revelation that this salvation is offered to the Jews and Gentiles on the same basis, which "has been made known" in the preaching (e.g., Ephesians 2:1f.; 3:3,4ff., especially verse 6). Paul regarded this revelation of the universal scope of God's redemption as his purpose (Ephesians 6:19; cf. Colossians 1:26,27; 4:3). Thus he could call himself the "apostle of the Gentiles" (Romans 11:13).

The "mystery of the faith" and the "mystery of godliness" (1 Timothy 3:9,16) are also linked to the revelation of Jesus Christ as the Saviour of the world. Note that following the statement "great is the mystery of godliness" we have the famous Christ-hymn that summarizes the gospel story of Jesus.

The idea that "mysteries" are now "revelations" is also represented in the Book of Revelation. John explained the "mystery" of the seven lampstands (Revelation 1:20). The mystery of God which is "completed" refers to the eschatological program already heralded by the prophets which is destined to reach its fulfillment (Revelation 10:7).

STRONG 3466, BAUER 530-31, MOULTON-MILLIGAN 420, KITTEL 4:802-27, LIDDELL-SCOTT 1156, COLIN BROWN 3:501-5.

3329. μυωπάζω muōpazō verb
To blink; to be shortsighted or nearsighted, see dimly.

1. μυωπάζων muōpazōn nom sing masc part pres act

1 But he ... is blind, and **cannot see afar off**,.......... 2 Pt 1:9

Though not found in Greek literature before its use in the New Testament (*Bauer*), the meaning of *muōpazō* is clear. Its noun form, *muōps*, was used by Aristotle for a "shortsighted" man, and the verb was used after New Testament times to mean "blink," "be nearsighted," or "see dimly." The meaning "to blink the eyes" seems to be drawn from the habit that nearsighted people have of squinting their eyes in order to see (cf. *Liddell-Scott*). The formal English word for nearsightedness, *myopia*, comes from this family of Greek words.

In its single New Testament use at 2 Peter 1:9, Peter wrote that anyone who lacks the eight spiritual qualities listed in verses 5 through 7 "is blind, and *cannot see afar off*." The literal meaning, "he is so near-sighted that he is blind" (*Bauer*), probably means that such a person is blind to spiritual and eternal things because his sight is limited only to the worldly things which are temporal and close at hand.

STRONG 3467, BAUER 531, MOULTON-MILLIGAN 420, LIDDELL-SCOTT 1157.

3330. μώλωψ mōlōps noun
Welt, bruise, mark from a blow.
SYNONYMS:
πληγή plēgē (3987)
τραύμα trauma (4973)

חַבּוּרָה chabbûrāh (2337), Wound (Ex 21:25, Ps 38:5 [37:5], Is 1:6).

1. μώλωπι mōlōpi dat sing masc

1 by whose **stripes** ye were healed................ 1 Pt 2:24

Classical Greek and Septuagint Usage
The word *mōlōps* appears frequently outside the New Testament for a wound or injury that raised a swelling or welt. It is occasionally used of such hurts as bee stings, mosquito bites, and blood clots (cf. *Liddell-Scott*), but most often represents the welts or swollen "stripes" that were left after a beating or whipping (cf. Exodus 21:25; Psalm 38:5 [LXX 37:5]; Isaiah 53:5).

New Testament Usage
The only New Testament use of this word is in 1 Peter 2:24, where Peter quoted Isaiah 53:5 asserting that we are "healed" by Jesus' "stripes." Actually the word is singular in both places, and it is suggested by some that Peter recalled the brutally scourged back of Jesus as a single mass of bloody welts. In the context Peter was citing Jesus' response to insult and beating as the model to be imitated by Christian slaves who might well be suffering from similar beatings by their masters.

STRONG 3468, BAUER 531, MOULTON-MILLIGAN 420, KITTEL 4:829, LIDDELL-SCOTT 1158.

3331. μωμάομαι mōmaomai verb
To find fault with, blame, criticize, discredit.

מְאוּם meʾûm (4113I), Abuse (Prv 9:7).

1. μωμηθῇ mōmēthē 3sing subj aor pass
2. μωμήσηται mōmēsētai 3sing subj aor mid

1 that **the ministry be not blamed:**............... 2 Co 6:3
2 Avoiding this, that no man should blame us............ 8:20

This common Greek verb is found only twice in the New Testament, both times in 2 Corinthians. In 6:3 Paul wrote of the precaution he had taken to avoid causing anyone to stumble at the gospel so that his ministry might not be "blamed" ("criticized" or "discredited"). Verses 4 through 10 describe his extraordinary personal labor and self-sacrifice to achieve these aims.

In 2 Corinthians 8 Paul said that he had arranged with certain churches for a trustworthy "brother" (verse 19) to travel with him as he delivered the financial gifts from the Gentile churches to the needy saints at Jerusalem. This practical precaution had been taken, he wrote, so "no man should *blame*" (*mōmaomai*) him (verse 20), or find any room to criticize him in his handling of their money.

STRONG 3469, BAUER 531, LIDDELL-SCOTT 1158.

3332. μῶμος mōmos noun
Blame, blemish, blot, defect, disgrace.

מְאוּם mᵉʾûm (4113I), Defect, blemish (Lv 21:17f., Dt 17:1, S/S 4:7).

1. μῶμοι mōmoi nom pl masc

1 Spots they are and **blemishes**,..................... **2 Pt 2:13**

Classical Greek and Septuagint Usage
This noun appears in classical Greek since the time of Homer (ca. Eighth Century B.C.) to describe "blame, reproach, or disgrace" that is put on someone (*Liddell-Scott*). As a "mark" or "brand" (ibid.) set on someone, it could also be regarded as a "blot" or "blemish." In Old Testament times the Mosaic Law forbade that a priest with any physical defect should offer a sacrifice to God and that any animal with a defect should be offered. The word used in the Septuagint for such a "blemish" in a priest (Leviticus 21:17-23) or animal (Leviticus 22:20-25, etc.) is *mōmos*. Occasionally the word was used for moral blemishes or defects.

New Testament Usage
In 2 Peter 2:13, the only New Testament use of this word, Peter described the ungodly false teachers of his day as "spots" (*spiloi* [see 4548]) and "blemishes" (*mōmoi*). These men were morally "branded" by their animallike sensuality and deceptive doctrines (verses 10-19), and, while so "blemished," their lives were totally unacceptable for service to God. Interestingly, Peter used the opposites of these two terms in 1 Peter 1:19 to describe Jesus as the "lamb without blemish (*amōmos* [297]) and without spot (*aspilos* [778])." Peter also used nearly identical language in 2 Peter 3:14, where he urged Christians, in light of final judgment, to make every effort to be found by Christ "without spot (*aspilos*) and blameless (*amōmētos*)."

STRONG 3470, BAUER 531, MOULTON-MILLIGAN 420, KITTEL 4:829-30, LIDDELL-SCOTT 1158.

3333. μωραίνω mōrainō verb
Make foolish, become foolish; make tasteless, become tasteless, insipid.

CROSS-REFERENCE:
μωρία mōria (3334)

בָּעַר bāʿar (1220), Burn; niphal: be stupid (Is 19:11, Jer 10:14).

סָכַל sākhal (5721), Niphal: do something foolish (2 Sm 24:10); piel: make into a fool (Is 44:25—Sixtine Edition only).

1. ἐμώρανεν emōranen 3sing indic aor act
2. ἐμωράνθησαν emōranthēsan 3pl indic aor pass
3. μωρανθῇ mōranthē 3sing subj aor pass

3 but if the salt have **lost his savour**,................. **Matt 5:13**
3 Salt is good: but if the salt have **lost his savour**,.... **Luke 14:34**
2 Professing ... to be wise, they **became fools**,......... **Rom 1:22**
1 not God **made foolish** the wisdom of this world?.... **1 Co 1:20**

Classical Greek
Appearing as early as Euripides (Fifth Century B.C.), this verb means "to be foolish" or, causally, "to be made foolish." It is related to *mōros* (3336), "dull, stupid, and sluggish," has been used to describe intellectual "dullness" and physical "laziness." A second function is to describe "useless" medicines or spices (e.g., salt may lose its savor; cf. Matthew 5:13; Luke 14:34) (Bertram, "mōrainō," *Kittel*, 4:832f. cites primary evidence; cf. *Bauer*).

Septuagint Usage
The Septuagint records *mōrainō* five times in the canonical Scriptures (for either *bāʿar* or *sākhal*) and one time in the Apocrypha (Sirach 23:14). David was convicted for his "foolish act" (*mōrainō*) of numbering Israel in disobedience to God (2 Samuel 24:10 [LXX 2 Kings 24:10]; cf. 1 Chronicles 21:1,8). God makes the counsel of men foolish (Isaiah 44:25; cf. 19:11); a similar contrast is made between God and idolatrous man in Jeremiah (10:11-15, especially verse 14; cf. 51:17 [LXX 28:17]). Thus "to make foolish" is God's response to mankind's arrogant, idolatrous "knowledge" (cf. the word study on *mōros* [3336]).

New Testament Usage
The four usages of *mōrainō* in the New Testament reflect the two distinct meanings encountered in classical Greek. Matthew (5:13) and Luke (14:34) both use *mōrainō* of salt that "has lost" its savor. Mark, in a related saying attributed to Jesus (9:50), reads *analos* (356), "without salt."

Paul receives credit for the two remaining instances of *mōrainō*. The context of Romans 1—idolatry—suggests that Paul was relating this to the Septuagintal idea that *mōrainō* is especially a consequence of arrogant idolatry (cf. especially Jeremiah 10:11-15; 51:17).

But in 1 Corinthians 1:20 Paul explained that the word of the Cross has "made foolish" the wisdom (*sophia* [4531]) of the world (*kosmos* [2862]). This, too, is reminiscent of the fact that man in his foolishness considers himself wise. The Cross—God's wisdom—appears utterly foolish to the mind set on the world's values. Such a person fails to realize that God is not usually at work in the lofty, powerful, and noble (the world's champions), but in the oppressed and powerless—the despised of the world (cf. 1 Corinthians 1:26-29).

STRONG 3471, BAUER 531, KITTEL 4:832-47, LIDDELL-SCOTT 1158, COLIN BROWN 3:1023,1025.

3334. μωρία *mōria* noun
Foolishness, silliness, absurdity.
COGNATES:
μωραίνω *mōrainō* (3333)
μωρολογία *mōrologia* (3335)
μωρός *mōros* (3336)
SYNONYMS:
ἄνοια *anoia* (452)
ἀφροσύνη *aphrosunē* (869)

1. **μωρία** *mōria* nom sing fem
2. **μωρίας** *mōrias* gen sing fem
3. **μωρίαν** *mōrian* acc sing fem

1 the cross is to them that perish **foolishness**;	1 Co 1:18
2 **foolishness** of preaching to save them that believe.	1:21
3 and unto the Greeks **foolishness**;	1:23
1 for they are **foolishness** unto him:	2:14
1 the wisdom of this world is **foolishness** with God.	3:19

Classical Greek
Mōria, a noun related to *mōros* (3336), means "foolishness, silliness." It can denote the extreme folly or even "absurdity" of an act or suggestion (e.g., the "foolishness" of illicit love, cf. [*Liddell-Scott*]).

Septuagint Usage
Mōria occurs only in the apocryphal document of Sirach (2 times) in the Septuagint. Both texts (20:31; 41:15) are repetitions of the same phrase. "The man who hides his *folly* (*mōria*) is better than the man who hides his wisdom" (free translation).

New Testament Usage
Mōria is almost as rare in the New Testament, where it occurs only five times, all in 1 Corinthians (1:18,21,23; 2:14; 3:19). It is set in striking contrast to *sophia* (4531)—the world's "wisdom." To those who are perishing (the unsaved) the message of the Cross is "absurd" (*mōria*). However, God chose this means to confound the "wisdom" of the world, because God detests the arrogant know-it-all attitude of men that prevents them from knowing God. It is utterly foolish from man's perspective that the death of a state-executed criminal was really the death of a powerful Messiah (to the Jews), or in fact the plan of the supremely wise God (to the Greeks).

God is contrasted with humanity; His spiritual ways appear to be "foolishness" to the unspiritual person (1 Corinthians 2:14), just as the Cross is "foolishness" from the world's point of view (1 Corinthians 1:18,21; 3:19). But God's "foolish ways" (*mōron*) are wiser (*sophōteron*) than those of men (1 Corinthians 1:25). In fact, God chose the "foolish things of the world" (*ta mōra tou kosmou*) to shame the wise (*sophoi*, 1 Corinthians 1:27).

STRONG 3472, BAUER 531, KITTEL 4:832-47, LIDDELL-SCOTT 1158, COLIN BROWN 3:1023,1025-26.

3335. μωρολογία *mōrologia* noun
Foolish talk, silly talk.
COGNATES:
λόγος *logos* (3030)
μωρία *mōria* (3334)

1. **μωρολογία** *mōrologia* nom sing fem

1 Neither filthiness, nor **foolish talking**, nor jesting,	Eph 5:4

The only New Testament use of *mōrologia* is in Ephesians 5:4, where Paul listed "foolish talk" among those activities which are totally inappropriate for Christians. The term is used by nonbiblical writers for "silly talk" in general, such as might come from the mouth of one who is of weak intellect, or even intoxicated (cf. *Liddell-Scott*). In Biblical writings, however, the term *fool* (*mōros* [3336]) often implies a willful blindness to the truth of God (see, for example, Psalm 94:8; Matthew 23:17,19; etc.). Therefore, Trench is probably right that the force of Paul's *mōrologia* "is that 'talk of fools' which is foolishness and sin together" (*Synonyms of the New Testament*, p.121).

STRONG 3473, BAUER 531, MOULTON-MILLIGAN 420, KITTEL 4:832-47, LIDDELL-SCOTT 1158.

3336. μωρός *mōros* adj
Foolish, stupid, dull.
COGNATE:
μωρία *mōria* (3334)
SYNONYMS:
ἀνόητος *anoētos* (451)

ἄσοφος asophos (775)
ἀσύνετος asunetos (795)
ἄφρων aphrōn (871)

אֱוִיל 'ĕwîl (188), Fool (Is 19:11).
כְּסִיל kesîl (3809), Fool (Sir 20:13).
נָבָל nāvāl (5210), Foolish, fool (Dt 32:6, Is 32:5).
נְבָלָה nevālāh (5214), Folly (Is 32:6).
סָכָל sākhāl (5722), Foolish (Jer 5:21).
פָּתָה pāthâh (6853), Fool (Sir 8:17).
שָׂכַל sākhal (7959), Hiphil: be wise (Ps 94:8 [93:8]).

1. μωρός mōros nom sing masc
2. μωρῷ mōrō dat sing masc
3. μωρέ mōre voc sing masc
4. μωροί mōroi nom pl masc
5. μωραί mōrai nom pl fem
6. μωράς mōras acc pl fem
7. μωρόν mōron nom/acc sing neu
8. μωρά mōra nom/acc pl neu

```
3 but whosoever shall say, Thou fool, .............. Matt 5:22
2 shall be likened unto a foolish man, ................. 7:26
4 Ye fools and blind: for whether is greater, ........... 23:17
4 Ye fools and blind: for whether is greater, the gift, .... 23:19
5 And five of them were wise, and five were foolish. .... 25:2
5 They that were foolish took their lamps, .............. 25:3
5 And the foolish said unto the wise, ................... 25:8
7 Because the foolishness of God is wiser than men;.. 1 Co 1:25
8 But God hath chosen the foolish things ................. 1:27
1 let him become a fool, that he may be wise. ........... 3:18
4 We are fools for Christ's sake, but ye are wise ......... 4:10
6 But foolish and unlearned questions avoid, ......... 2 Tm 2:23
6 But avoid foolish questions, and genealogies, ........ Tit 3:9
```

Classical Greek
Depending on the context and circumstances, the adjective *mōros* (see also *mōria* [3334]) takes on a variety of meanings. Essentially *mōros* suggests a deficiency of some kind; thus, in a context regarding intellectual matters *mōros* means "stupid, foolish" (in contrast to *sophos* [4533], "wise"). Used of medicines or spices (of salt, see *mōrainō* [3333]) it means "useless, ineffective." There is an implied unfavorable judgment in being called *mōros*. "Foolish" suggests inadequacy of both a mental and a physical nature (e.g., "sluggish") as well as being used in a spiritual sense (cf. *Liddell-Scott*).

Septuagint Usage
Although the canonical writings of the Septuagint make only limited use of *mōros*, the term is not without interest. To ignore God's past faithfulness and to abandon Him is "foolish" (Deuteronomy 32:6). This thought is repeated elsewhere with different shades of meaning (e.g., Psalm 94:8 [LXX 93:8]; Isaiah 32:6; Jeremiah 5:21ff.).

Sirach, an apocryphal Wisdom document, uses *mōros* as a thematic word 28 times. Here too foolishness is associated with mistrust of God (e.g., 16:23). This is additionally reflected in the wise versus foolish man's wisdom sayings (e.g., 20:13,16,20; 21:13f.).

New Testament Usage
The New Testament's use of *mōros* proves interesting. First, Matthew (7 out of 13 total times in the New Testament) connects *mōros* with the abusive Aramaic expression *rhaka* (4326). The precise meaning here is elusive, but it probably means "emptyhead" or (for those who take it to have a stronger meaning) "numskull." The *mōros* explanatory remark seems to add the sense of "godless." One should never allow anger to rule one's judgment (Matthew 5:22). The wise/fool contrast occurs in Matthew 7:26 as a second example of *mōros*' understanding. Here we see the possible influence of the Old Testament; the "wise" put into practice Jesus' words while the "foolish" do not (Matthew 7:24; cf. 25:3-8). A third related use is Jesus' indictment of the Pharisees and legal experts as "blind and foolish." Both terms refer to the spiritual deficiency of the "religious."

Paul used *mōros* in a slightly different way (see especially his use of *mōria*), although he did use it in its customary sense (2 Timothy 2:23; Titus 3:9). God's "foolishness" is wiser than mankind's wisdom. It finds its fullest expression in the Cross whose seeming failure is ridiculous to the world (cf. 1 Corinthians 3:18f.). Nevertheless, this is how God operates (1 Corinthians 1:27). The Cross appears foolish to man because there is nothing "powerful" or "intelligent" about it according to the world's standards. Furthermore, the fact that mankind can do nothing to contribute to this salvation frustrates his logic. Salvation is wholly dependent upon God in Christ. In the same vein Paul sarcastically compared his own "spirituality" with that of the Corinthians (1 Corinthians 4:10; cf. verses 9-13).

STRONG 3474, BAUER 531, MOULTON-MILLIGAN 420, KITTEL 4:832-47, LIDDELL-SCOTT 1158-59, COLIN BROWN 3:1023-26.

3337. Μωσῆς Mōsēs name
Moses.

1. Μωσῆς Mōsēs nom masc
2. Μωσέως Mōseōs gen masc

3. **Μωσεῖ** Mōsei dat masc
4. **Μωσῇ** Mōsē dat masc
5. **Μωσέα** Mōsea acc masc
6. **Μωσῆν** Mōsēn acc masc

1	and offer the gift that **Moses** commanded,	Matt 8:4
1	appeared ... **Moses** and Elias talking with him.	17:3
4	one for thee, and one for **Moses**, and one for Elias.	17:4
1	Why did **Moses** then command to give a writing	19:7
1	**Moses** because of the hardness of your hearts	19:8
1	**Moses** said, If a man die, having no children,	22:24
2	The scribes and the Pharisees sit in **Moses**' seat:	23:2
1	and offer ... those things which **Moses** commanded,	Mark 1:44
1	**Moses** said, Honour thy father and thy mother;	7:10
3	And there appeared unto them Elias with **Moses**:	9:4
3	one for thee, and one for **Moses**, and one for Elias.	9:5
1	he answered ... What did **Moses** command you?	10:3
1	**Moses** suffered to write a bill of divorcement,	10:4
1	Master, **Moses** wrote unto us,	12:19
2	have ye not read in the book of **Moses**,	12:26
2	according to the law of **Moses** were accomplished,	Luke 2:22
1	and offer ... according as **Moses** commanded,	5:14
1	with him two men, which were **Moses** and Elias:	9:30
3	one for thee, and one for **Moses**, and one for Elias:	9:33
5	have **Moses** and the prophets; let them hear them.	16:29
2	If they hear not **Moses** and the prophets,	16:31
1	Saying, Master, **Moses** wrote unto us,	20:28
1	even **Moses** showed at the bush,	20:37
2	And beginning at **Moses** and all the prophets,	24:27
2	fulfilled, which were written in the law of **Moses**,	24:44
2	For the law was given by **Moses**,	John 1:17
1	**Moses** in the law, and the prophets, did write,	1:45
1	as **Moses** lifted up the serpent in the wilderness,	3:14
1	there is one that accuseth you, even **Moses**,	5:45
4	For had ye believed **Moses**, ye ... believed me:	5:46
1	**Moses** gave you not that bread from heaven;	6:32
1	Did not **Moses** give you the law,	7:19
1	**Moses** therefore gave unto you circumcision;	7:22
2	not because it is of **Moses**, but of the fathers;	7:22
2	that the law of **Moses** should not be broken;	7:23
1	Now **Moses** in the law commanded us,	8:5
2	Thou art his disciple; but we are **Moses**' disciples.	9:28
4	We know that God spake unto **Moses**:	9:29
1	For **Moses** truly said unto the fathers,	Acts 3:22
6	speak blasphemous words against **Moses**,	6:11
1	In which time **Moses** was born,	7:20
1	And **Moses** was learned in all the wisdom	7:22
1	Then fled **Moses** at this saying,	7:29
1	When **Moses** saw it, he wondered at the sight:	7:31
1	Then **Moses** trembled, and durst not behold.	7:32
1	for as for this **Moses**, which brought us out	7:40
4	as he had appointed, speaking unto **Moses**,	7:44
2	ye could not be justified by the law of **Moses**.	13:39
1	For **Moses** of old time hath in every city	Acts 15:21
2	which are among the Gentiles to forsake **Moses**,	21:21
1	the prophets and **Moses** did say should come:	26:22
2	out of the law of **Moses**, and out of the prophets,	28:23
2	Nevertheless death reigned from Adam to **Moses**,	Rom 5:14
4	For he saith to **Moses**, I will have mercy	9:15
1	**Moses** describeth the righteousness ... of the law,	10:5
1	First **Moses** saith, I will provoke you to jealousy	10:19
2	For it is written in the law of **Moses**,	I Co 9:9
6	baptized unto **Moses** in the cloud and in the sea;	10:2
2	could not stedfastly behold the face of **Moses**	2 Co 3:7
1	And not as **Moses**, which put a veil over his face,	3:13
1	when **Moses** is read, the veil is upon their heart.	3:15
1	as also **Moses** was faithful in all his house.	Heb 3:2
6	was counted worthy of more glory than **Moses**,	3:3
1	And **Moses** verily was faithful in all his house,	3:5
2	howbeit not all that came out of Egypt by **Moses**.	3:16
1	tribe **Moses** spake nothing concerning priesthood.	7:14
1	as **Moses** was admonished of God	8:5
2	He that despised **Moses**' law died without mercy	10:28
1	By faith **Moses**, when he was born, was hid	11:23
1	By faith **Moses**, when he was come to years,	11:24
1	that **Moses** said, I exceedingly fear and quake:	12:21
2	Michael ... he disputed about the body of **Moses**,	Jude 1:9
2	And they sing the song of **Moses** the servant of God,	Rev 15:3

Leader of the Exodus and writer of the Pentateuch; he appeared with Elijah at the transfiguration of Jesus (Matthew 17:3ff.).

3338. Μωϋσῆς Mōusēs name

Moses.

1. **Μωϋσῆς** Mōusēs nom masc
2. **Μωϋσέως** Mōuseōs gen masc
3. **Μωϋσεῖ** Mōusei dat masc
4. **Μωϋσῆν** Mōusēn acc masc
5. **Μωϋσῇ** Mōusē dat masc
6. **Μωϋσεα** Mōusea acc masc

1	change the customs which **Moses** delivered us.	Acts 6:14
4	This **Moses** whom they refused,	7:35
1	This is that **Moses**,	7:37
2	be circumcised after the manner of **Moses**,	15:1
2	and to command them to keep the law of **Moses**.	15:5
3	Now as Jannes and Jambres withstood **Moses**,	2 Tm 3:8
2	**Moses** had spoken every precept to all the people	Heb 9:19

Variant spelling of *Mōsēs* (3337).

ν

3339. Ναασσών Naassōn name
Nahshon.

1. Ναασσών Naassōn masc

1 and Aminadab begat **Naasson**;	Matt 1:4
1 and **Naasson** begat Salmon;	1:4
1 which was the son of **Naasson**,	Luke 3:32

The son of Amminadab in the genealogy of Jesus (Matthew 1:4; Luke 3:32).

3340. Ναγγαί Nangai name
Naggai.

1. Ναγγαί Nangai masc

1 which was the son of **Nagge**,	Luke 3:25

The son of Maath in the genealogy of Jesus (Luke 3:25).

3341. Ναζαρέτ Nazaret name
Nazareth.

1. Ναζαρέτ Nazaret fem
2. Ναζαρά Nazara fem
3. Ναζαρέθ Nazareth fem
4. Ναζαράθ Nazarath fem

1 And he came and dwelt in a city called **Nazareth**:	Matt 2:23
1 And leaving **Nazareth**, ... dwelt in Capernaum,	4:13
1 This is Jesus the prophet of **Nazareth** of Galilee.	21:11
1 that Jesus came from **Nazareth** of Galilee,	Mark 1:9
1 unto a city of Galilee, named **Nazareth**,	Luke 1:26
1 out of the city of **Nazareth**, into Judaea,	2:4
1 returned into Galilee, to their own city **Nazareth**.	2:39
1 he went down with them, and came to **Nazareth**,	2:51
1 came to **Nazareth**, where he had been brought up:	4:16
1 Jesus of **Nazareth**, the son of Joseph.	John 1:45
1 Can there any good thing come out of **Nazareth**?	1:46
1 How God anointed Jesus of **Nazareth**	Acts 10:38

City in Galilee where Jesus, Mary, and Joseph resided (Luke 1:26; 2:4); it had a poor reputation (John 1:46).

3342. Ναζαρηνός Nazarēnos name-adj
Nazarene.

1. Ναζαρηνός Nazarēnos nom sing masc
2. Ναζαρηνοῦ Nazarēnou gen sing masc
3. Ναζαρηνόν Nazarēnon acc sing masc
4. Ναζαρηνέ Nazarēne voc sing masc

4 what have we ... with thee, thou Jesus of **Nazareth**?	Mark 1:24
2 And thou also wast with Jesus of **Nazareth**.	14:67
3 Ye seek Jesus of **Nazareth**, which was crucified:	16:6
4 Jesus of **Nazareth**? art thou come to destroy us?	Luke 4:34

Adjective meaning "coming from Nazareth"; said only of Jesus (Mark 1:24; Luke 24:19).

3343. Ναζωραῖος Nazōraios name
Nazarene.

1. Ναζωραῖος Nazōraios nom sing masc
2. Ναζωραίου Nazōraiou gen sing masc
3. Ναζωραῖον Nazōraion acc sing masc
4. Ναζωραίων Nazōraiōn gen pl masc

1 fulfilled ... He shall be called a **Nazarene**.	Matt 2:23
2 This fellow was also with Jesus of **Nazareth**.	26:71
1 And when he heard that it was Jesus of **Nazareth**,	Mark 10:47
1 they told him, that Jesus of **Nazareth** passeth by.	Luke 18:37
2 they said unto him, Concerning Jesus of **Nazareth**,	24:19
3 They answered him, Jesus of **Nazareth**.	John 18:5
3 Whom seek ye? And they said, Jesus of **Nazareth**.	18:7
1 JESUS OF **NAZARETH** THE KING OF ... JEWS.	19:19
3 Jesus of **Nazareth**, a man approved of God	Acts 2:22
2 In the name of Jesus Christ of **Nazareth** rise up	3:6
2 that by the name of Jesus Christ of **Nazareth**,	4:10
1 that this Jesus of **Nazareth** shall destroy this place,	6:14
1 I am Jesus of **Nazareth**, whom thou persecutest.	22:8
4 and a ringleader of the sect of the **Nazarenes**:	24:5
2 things contrary to the name of Jesus of **Nazareth**.	26:9

Title used of Jesus and by Jesus (Acts 22:8); applied also to His followers (Acts 24:5).

3344. Ναθάν Nathan name
Nathan.

1. Ναθάν Nathan masc
2. Ναθάμ Natham masc

1 which was the son of **Nathan**,	Luke 3:31

The son of David in the genealogy of Jesus (Luke 3:31).

3345. Ναθαναήλ Nathanaēl name

Nathanael.

1. Ναθαναήλ Nathanaēl masc

1 Philip findeth **Nathanael**, and saith unto him,	John 1:45
1 And **Nathanael** said unto him,	1:46
1 Jesus saw **Nathanael** coming to him,	1:47
1 **Nathanael** saith ... Whence knowest thou me?	1:48
1 **Nathanael** answered and saith unto him, Rabbi,	1:49
1 and **Nathanael** of Cana in Galilee,	21:2

Apostle from Cana in Galilee introduced to Jesus by Philip (John 1:45ff.; 21:2); also known as Bartholomew.

3346. ναί nai intrj

Yes, indeed, verily, of course, certainly.

1. ναί nai

1 let your communication be, Yea, yea; Nay, nay:	Matt 5:37
1 let your communication be, Yea, yea; Nay, nay:	5:37
1 They said unto him, Yea, Lord.	9:28
1 yea, I say unto you, and more than a prophet.	11:9
1 Even so, Father: for so it seemed good in thy sight.	11:26
1 They say unto him, Yea, Lord.	13:51
1 And she said, Truth, Lord: yet the dogs eat	15:27
1 He saith, Yes. ... Jesus prevented him,	17:25
1 Jesus saith unto them, Yea; have ye never read,	21:16
1 And she answered and said unto him, Yes, Lord:	Mark 7:28
1 But what went ye out for to see? A prophet? Yea,	Luke 7:26
1 hast revealed them unto babes: even so, Father,	10:21
1 verily I say unto you, It shall be required of this	11:51
1 to cast into hell; yea, I say unto you, Fear him.	12:5
1 She saith unto him, Yea, Lord; I believe	John 11:27
1 Yea, Lord; thou knowest that I love thee.	21:15
1 Yea, Lord; thou knowest that I love thee.	21:16
1 And she said, Yea, for so much.	Acts 5:8
1 Tell me, art thou a Roman? He said, Yea.	22:27
1 not also of the Gentiles? Yes, of the Gentiles also:	Rom 3:29
1 with me there should be yea yea, and nay nay?	2 Co 1:17
1 with me there should be yea yea, and nay nay?	1:17
1 our word toward you was not yea and nay.	1:18
1 was not yea and nay, but in him was yea.	1:19
1 was not yea and nay, but in him was yea.	1:19
1 For all the promises of God in him are yea,	1:20
1 Yes, and I ask you, loyal yokefellow, (NASB)	Phlp 4:3
1 Yea, brother, let me have joy of thee in the Lord:	Phlm 1:20
1 but let your yea be yea; and your nay, nay;	Jas 5:12
1 but let your yea be yea; and your nay, nay;	5:12
1 shall wail because of him. Even so, Amen.	Rev 1:7
1 Yea, saith the Spirit,	14:13
1 out of the altar say, Even so, Lord God Almighty,	16:7
1 He which testifieth ... Surely I come quickly.	22:20
1 I come quickly. Amen. Even so, come, Lord Jesus.	22:20

Classical Greek and Septuagint Usage

From the classical period on, *nai* has always carried the meaning or sense of strong affirmation and has had a wide variety of usages (cf. *Liddell-Scott*). *Nai* occurs in only a few texts in the Septuagint (seven times). It follows its regular use as a particle denoting affirmation (e.g., Genesis 17:19) or emphatic repetition (Judith 9:12).

New Testament Usage

In the New Testament the usages can be noted as follows: (1) an affirmative answer to the question of another (Matthew 9:28; 13:51; 21:16; John 11:27; 21:15,16: Acts 5:8; 22:27); (2) an affirmative answer to the question one has himself raised (Matthew 11:9; Luke 7:26; Romans 3:29; 2 Corinthians 1:19 [second use, and the question is in verse 17]; 2 Corinthians 1:20 [the question is again in verse 17]); (3) an affirmative agreement with the statement of another (Matthew 15:27; Mark 7:28; Revelation 16:7; 22:20 [second use]); (4) an emphatic affirmative by use of repetition (Matthew 5:37; James 5:12); and (5) an emphatic agreement with one's own assertion (Matthew 11:26; Luke 10:21; 11:51; 12:5; Philemon 20; Revelation 1:7; 14:13; 22:20 [first use]). *Nai* is also used with *ou* (3620), "no," to express inconsistency or uncertainty (2 Corinthians 1:17-19).

STRONG 3483, BAUER 532-33, MOULTON-MILLIGAN 422, LIDDELL-SCOTT 1159.

3347. Ναΐν Nain name

Nain.

1. Ναΐν Nain fem

1 that he went into a city called **Nain**;	Luke 7:11

City on Mount Tabor in Galilee where Jesus raised the widow's son from the dead (Luke 7:11).

3348. ναός naos noun

Temple, shrine.

SYNONYM:
ἱερόν hieron (2387)

אֵילָם 'êlām (365), Porch (1 Chr 28:11, 2 Chr 8:12, 29:7).
בַּיִת bayith (1041), House (1 Kgs 6:17).
דְּבִיר d⁰vîr (1735), Sanctuary (Ps 28:2 [27:2]).
הֵיכָל hêkhāl (2033), Temple, nave (2 Chr 3:17, Ps 65:4 [64:4], Ez 41:1).
הֵיכַל hêkhal (A2034), Temple (Ezr 5:14—Aramaic).

1. ναός naos nom sing masc
2. ναοῦ naou gen sing masc
3. ναῷ naō dat sing masc

4. ναόν naon acc sing masc
5. ναοῖς naois dat pl masc
6. ναούς naous acc pl masc

```
3 Whosoever shall swear by the temple, it is nothing; Matt 23:16
2 whosoever shall swear by the gold of the temple,......  23:16
1 the gold, or the temple that sanctifieth the gold?......  23:17
3 And whoso shall swear by the temple,................  23:21
2 whom ye slew between the temple and the altar........  23:35
4 This fellow said, I am able to destroy the temple......  26:61
3 And he cast down the pieces of silver in the temple,...  27:5
4 destroyest the temple, and buildest it in three days,....  27:40
2 behold, the veil of the temple was rent in twain.......  27:51
4 I will destroy this temple that is made with hands, Mark 14:58
4 thou that destroyest the temple, and buildest it........  15:29
2 And the veil of the temple was rent in twain..........  15:38
4 when he went into the temple of the Lord...........Luke 1:9
3 marvelled that he tarried so long in the temple..........  1:21
3 perceived that he had seen a vision in the temple:......  1:22
2 and the veil of the temple was rent in the midst......  23:45
4 Destroy this temple, and in three days I will raise...John 2:19
1 Forty and six years was this temple in building,.........  2:20
2 But he spake of the temple of his body.................  2:21
5 Howbeit the most High dwelleth not in temples.....Acts 7:48
5 dwelleth not in temples made with hands;.............  17:24
6 a silversmith, which made silver shrines for Diana,.....  19:24
1 Know ye not that ye are the temple of God,........ 1 Co 3:16
4 If any man defile the temple of God,................  3:17
1 for the temple of God is holy, which temple ye are......  3:17
1 is the temple of the Holy Ghost which is in you,........  6:19
3 what agreement hath the temple of God with idols? 2 Co 6:16
1 for ye are the temple of the living God;................  6:16
4 groweth unto an holy temple in the Lord:...........Eph 2:21
4 so that he as God sitteth in the temple of God,..... 2 Th 2:4
3 will I make a pillar in the temple of my God,........Rev 3:12
3 and serve him day and night in his temple:..............  7:15
4 and measure the temple of God, and the altar,........  11:1
2 the court which is without the temple leave out,......  11:2
1 And the temple of God was opened in heaven,........  11:19
3 was seen in his temple the ark of his testament:......  11:19
2 And another angel came out of the temple,...........  14:15
2 And another angel came out of the temple ...........  14:17
1 the temple of the tabernacle of the testimony..........  15:5
2 And the seven angels came out of the temple,........  15:6
1 the temple was filled with smoke from the glory.......  15:8
4 and no man was able to enter into the temple,........  15:8
2 And I heard a great voice out of the temple saying....  16:1
2 came a great voice out of the temple of heaven,......  16:17
4 And I saw no temple therein:........................  21:22
1 God Almighty and the Lamb are the temple of it......  21:22
```

Classical Greek

Classical writers specifically used the noun *naos* (perhaps from *naiō*, "to inhabit, dwell") to denote the "dwelling place of a god" (*Liddell-Scott*). Consequently the *naos* was the inner "sanctuary" of a temple in which the image of the god was placed (ibid.). It is often translated simply "temple," but the association with "sanctuary" should not be overlooked. The noun was regularly taken in the cultic sense, although the same does not hold true for the verb (Michel, "naos," *Kittel*, 4:880).

Septuagint Usage

Naos is relatively common in the Septuagint; however, it does not occur in the Pentateuch. Usually *hêkhāl* stands behind it, although *'êlām* is also used on several occasions, especially in Chronicles (e.g., 1 Chronicles 28:11; 2 Chronicles 8:12). *Hêkhāl* is a "palace" or "temple" or the "sanctuary" of a temple. Where *naos* is equated with it we often find "temple of the Lord" (e.g., 1 Samuel 1:9 [LXX 1 Kings 1:9]; 2 Chronicles 15:8; Ezekiel 8:16). It is God's "holy dwelling place" (Psalms 5:7; 11:4 [LXX 10:4]; Jonah 2:4). Nevertheless, *naos* is not reserved exclusively for God's temple. The author of the apocryphal 1 Esdras writes of Nebuchadnezzar's "temple" (1 Esdras 6:18ff.). *Hieros* (2388B), "temple," however, was generally used for pagan temples or the larger temple complex (as opposed to the inner Holy of Holies—*naos*—see 3 Maccabees 1:10).

New Testament Usage

In the light of the unique role of *naos* as a cultic technical term for the inner sanctuary of a deity, we can see why the religious leaders were so upset when they thought Jesus had made reference to destroying the Jerusalem Holy of Holies (Mark 14:58; cf. Matthew 26:61; John 2:19). Actually Jesus, as God incarnate, was referring to His own person as the dwelling place of God (John 2:21). The same idea of *naos* as God's abode is repeated in Acts 17:24: God does not dwell in man-made sanctuaries. The pagan understanding of *naos* is reflected in Acts 19:24, a reference to "shrines" which were made and sold by followers of the pagan goddess Artemis (Diana) (cf. 2 Corinthians 6:16).

Paul called the church in Corinth the *naos* of God (1 Corinthians 3:16; Ephesians 2:21) and also said that individual persons are the "temple" of the Holy Spirit (1 Corinthians 6:19; cf. 2 Corinthians 6:16).

The use of *naos* in 2 Thessalonians 2:4 is puzzling. The Antichrist sets himself up in God's "temple." Here the precise meaning is uncertain, although a literal understanding may be preferred. A "foretaste" of what the Antichrist may do is perhaps reflected by the incident of Caligula's (A.D. 40) attempts to have his statue erected in the Jerusalem temple (Bruce, *Word Biblical Commentary, 1 and 2 Thessalonians*, 45:168).

Naos occurs 16 times in Revelation. The residence of God is clearly intended. Here, however, the sanctuary is in heaven (Revelation 11:19; 14:17; 15:5). The same building imagery used in Ephesians is repeated here (Revelation 3:12; cf. Ephesians 2:21). From the heavenly sanctuary God's messengers dispense judgment

(Revelation 14:15,17; 15:5ff.; 16:1,17). The Holy of Holies in the new city of God, the heavenly Jerusalem, will be the Lord God Almighty and the Lamb instead of a material building.

In the Book of Revelation the Old Testament imagery of Ezekiel comes through clearly (cf. Ezekiel 40; Revelation 11:1f.). God's people will worship Him in this new community of God. Inherent in the concept of God's dwelling with His people and making them "his people" is the covenant idea of "I will be your God and you will be my people" (cf. Revelation 21:3). Believers can worship God night and day because we will become one with Him. He himself will be the temple and we will also be a part of it: "In him the whole building is joined together and rises to become a holy temple in the Lord. And in him you too are being built together to become a dwelling in which God lives by his Spirit" (Ephesians 2:21,22, NIV). Believers can thus experience the *future* union with God in the *present* through the power of the Holy Spirit.

STRONG 3485, BAUER 533-34, MOULTON-MILLIGAN 422, KITTEL 4:880-90, LIDDELL-SCOTT 1160, COLIN BROWN 1:781-85.

3349. Ναούμ Naoum name

Nahum.

1. Ναούμ Naoum masc

1 which was the son of Naum,...................... Luke 3:25

The son of Esli in the genealogy of Jesus (Luke 3:25).

3350. νάρδος nardos noun

(Spike)nard, oil of spikenard.

נֵרְדְּ nērdᵉ (5556), Perfume, nard (S/S 1:12, 4:13f.).

1. νάρδου nardou gen sing fem

1 box of ointment of spikenard very precious;....... Mark 14:3
1 Then took Mary a pound of ointment of spikenard, John 12:3

Classical Greek

Nardos refers to a fragrant and very valuable oil used as a perfume and for the anointing of important guests and persons. It was extracted from the *Nardostaychys Jatamansi* plant which was found in the Himalayan mountains. In the classical Greek *nardos* is used in reference both to the plant and to the oil from the plant.

Septuagint Usage

The Septuagint uses the word in the sense of the oil or perfume only (Song of Solomon 1:12; 4:13,14). In the 4:14 passage it is mentioned in a list of some of the other most valued ancient aromatics.

New Testament Usage

The two references in the New Testament (Mark 14:3 and John 12:3) refer also to the oil or perfume from the plant. In these passages great emphasis is given to the extreme value of the oil that was used to anoint Jesus. Obviously, it was of great value. The oil was so expensive because of the distance it had to be transported (from the Himalayan mountains), the difficulty of its transportation, the further difficulty of its preservation, and also because Jesus was anointed with the oil in its unadulterated form. According to R.K. Harrison, "The best spikenard was imported from India in scaled alabaster boxes, which were opened only on very special occasions" ("Nard," *International Standard Bible Encyclopedia*, 3:490f.).

STRONG 3487, BAUER 534, MOULTON-MILLIGAN 422, LIDDELL-SCOTT 1160.

3351. Νάρκισσος Narkissos name

Narcissus.

1. Ναρκίσσου Narkissou gen masc

1 Greet them that be of the household of Narcissus,..Rom 16:11

Recipient of a greeting from Paul (Romans 16:11).

3352. ναυαγέω nauageō verb

To experience shipwreck; to fail, be destroyed.

CROSS-REFERENCES:
ἄγω agō (70)
ναῦς naus (3354)

1. ἐναυάγησα enauagēsa 1sing indic aor act
2. ἐναυάγησαν enauagēsan 3pl indic aor act

1 once was I stoned, thrice I suffered shipwreck,..... 2 Co 11:25
2 concerning faith have made shipwreck:............. 1 Tm 1:19

The verb *nauageō* is probably a compound of *naus* (3354), "ship," and *anonumi*, "to break," and is a common Greek word in nonbiblical writings describing shipwrecks. In the New Testament the word is used twice by Paul, once literally and once figuratively. The literal use is in 2 Corinthians 11:25 where he included in the description of his sufferings as an apostle the fact that he "suffered shipwreck" three times. Of these three occasions we know nothing, since the shipwreck of Acts 27 took place after the writing of 2 Corinthians.

Paul used the term figuratively in 1 Timothy 1:19 when he wrote that some men, including Hymeneus and Alexander (verse 20), had "put away" their good consciences and were, as a result, "made shipwreck" concerning the Faith. By doing what their consciences told them was wrong, they had been wrecked, or destroyed, as far as the Christian faith was concerned.

STRONG 3489, BAUER 534, MOULTON-MILLIGAN 422, KITTEL 4:891, LIDDELL-SCOTT 1161.

3353. ναύκληρος nauklēros noun
Ship's owner; ship's captain, or commander.
CROSS-REFERENCES:
κληρόω klēroō (2793)
ναῦς naus (3354)

1. ναυκλήρῳ nauklērō dat sing masc

1 believed the master and the owner of the ship, ... Acts 27:11

In nonbiblical Greek a *nauklēros* usually describes the owner of a ship (*naus* [3354]) who leased his vessel out to transport passengers or cargo. Sometimes, though, it refers to the captain who commanded the vessel.

Either of these two meanings is possible for the only New Testament use of *nauklēros*, in Acts 27:11. It appears that the Alexandrian ship (27:6) on which Paul was placed was in the service of the Roman government, since verse 11 shows the Roman centurion had the final decision about whether or not to sail in rough weather. It is possible that the *nauklēros* was only the ship's captain and that perhaps the ship was government owned. However, since the ship's owner was often its captain, and since even the owner would probably be subject to the Roman centurion if the ship was in Roman service, it is just as likely that "owner of the ship" is the correct translation.

STRONG 3490, BAUER 534, MOULTON-MILLIGAN 422-23, LIDDELL-SCOTT 1161.

3354. ναῦς naus noun
Ship.
COGNATES:
ναυαγέω nauageō (3352)
ναύκληρος nauklēros (3353)
ναύτης nautēs (3355)

SYNONYM:
πλοῖον ploion (4003)

אֳנִי 'ŏnî (604), Ships, fleet (1 Kgs 9:26f., 10:11,22).
אֳנִיָּה 'ŏnîyāh (605), Ship, boat (2 Chr 9:21, Jb 9:26, Prv 31:14).
עֹפֶל 'ōphel (6308), Tumor (1 Sm 5:6).

1. ναῦν naun acc sing fem

1 ran the **ship** aground; and the forepart stuck fast, ... Acts 27:41

In early Greek literature *naus* is commonly used for "ship," specifically a larger sailing vessel (the English word *navy* comes from it, through the cognate Latin word for ship, *nāvis*). In the New Testament *ploion* (4003), "boat," is commonly used for both the smaller fishing vessels described in the Gospels and for those larger vessels described elsewhere, which might be properly called "ships" (Acts 20–28; James 3:4; Revelation 8:9; 18:19). Thus, in the New Testament *ploion* is a generic term for boats in general.

The sole New Testament use of *naus* is in Acts 27:41 which says "they ran the *ship* aground." Previously in the chapter Luke had repeatedly used the word *ploion* for this vessel, and many feel that Luke here changed terms because he was recalling a phrase which had been used by Homer for the beaching of a ship (*Odyssey* 9.148; cf. Blass, *Philology of the Gospels*, p.186).

STRONG 3491, BAUER 534, MOULTON-MILLIGAN 423, LIDDELL-SCOTT 1162.

3355. ναύτης nautēs noun
Sailor, seaman, mariner.
CROSS-REFERENCE:
ναῦς naus (3354)

1. ναῦται nautai nom pl masc
2. ναυτῶν nautōn gen pl masc

1 about midnight the **shipmen** deemed that they ...... Acts 27:27
2 as the **shipmen** were about to flee out of the ship, ... 27:30
1 **sailors**, and as many as trade by sea, stood afar off, Rev 18:17

Though occasionally meaning "a passenger at sea," the common meaning of *nautēs* (perhaps from *naus* [3354], "ship") in Greek literature is "shipman," referring to a sailor or seaman, one who makes his living on a ship (cf. *Liddell-Scott*). It is used in this way in Acts 27:27,30. These verses refer to the "sailors" on the ship that was wrecked on Malta while carrying Paul toward Rome.

In Revelation 18:17, the third and final New Testament occurrence, the word is used in the same way. Among those who mourn the fall of "Babylon" are those who make their living by the sea, including "sailors." Here the sailors seem to be specifically distinguished from the passengers or the "company in ships" (literally, "those sailing to a place").

STRONG 3492, BAUER 534, MOULTON-MILLIGAN 423, LIDDELL-SCOTT 1162.

3356. Ναχώρ Nachōr name
Nahor.

1. Ναχώρ Nachōr masc
1 which was the son **of Nachor**,................ Luke 3:34

The son of Serug in the genealogy of Jesus (Luke 3:34).

3357. νεανίας neanias noun
Young man, youth.
COGNATES:
νεανίσκος neaniskos (3358)
νέος neos (3363C)
SYNONYM:
νεανίσκος neaniskos (3358)

בָּחוּר bāchûr (1005), Young man, chosen man (Ru 3:10, 2 Sm 6:1, Prv 20:29).

בָּחַר bāchar (1013), Choice man (2 Sm 10:9—Codex Alexandrinus only).

יֶלֶד yeledh (3315), Youth (Dn 1:10).

נַעַר naʿar (5470), Lad, young man (1 Sm 20:37, Prv 7:7).

1. νεανίας neanias nom sing masc
2. νεανίου neaniou gen sing masc
3. νεανίαν neanian acc sing masc

2 at a **young man's** feet, whose name was Saul........Acts 7:58
1 And there sat in a window a certain **young man** 20:9
3 Bring this **young man** unto the chief captain:.......... 23:17
3 and prayed me to bring this **young man** unto thee,..... 23:18
3 So the chief captain then let the **young man** depart,.... 23:22

The noun *neanias* occurs five times in the New Testament, all in the Book of Acts. Luke described as a "young man" each of these three persons: (1) the pre-Christian Paul (Saul), at whose feet Stephen's murderers laid their garments (7:58); (2) Eutychus, who fell out of a third-story window in Troas while Paul was preaching (20:9); and (3) Paul's own nephew who overheard the plot against Paul's life in Jerusalem (23:17, and in some texts, verses 18 and 22).

The word tells us little about the actual age of these men, however. "Youth" was (and is) a relative term, and *neanias* was used elsewhere to cover a wide range of ages—from the upper teen years to an age in the lower forties (cf. *Bauer*). That Eutychus is also called a *pais* (3679), or "boy" (20:12), and Paul's nephew is also called a *neaniskos* (3358), the diminutive form of *neanias*, may indicate—though not conclusively—that they were on the younger side of the above scale.

STRONG 3494, BAUER 534, MOULTON-MILLIGAN 423, LIDDELL-SCOTT 1163.

3358. νεανίσκος neaniskos noun
Young man, youth, servant, attendant.
COGNATE:
νεανίας neanias (3357)
SYNONYM:
νεανίας neanias (3357)

אֱנוֹשׁ ʾĕnôsh (596), Man (Jos 2:1,23).

בָּחוּר bāchûr (1005), Young man, chosen one (Dt 32:25, Jgs 14:10, Jer 50:44 [27:44]).

בָּחַר bāchar (1013), Choice man (2 Sm 10:9—Codex Vaticanus only).

יֶלֶד yeledh (3315), Man, youth (Gn 4:23, Dn 1:4,13,15,17).

נַעַר naʿar (5470), Boy, young man (Gn 25:27, Lam 5:13); servant (1 Sm 9:27).

עֶלֶם ʿelem (6182), Youth (1 Sm 20:22).

1. νεανίσκος neaniskos nom sing masc
2. νεανίσκον neaniskon acc sing masc
3. νεανίσκε neaniske voc sing masc
4. νεανίσκοι neaniskoi nom pl masc

1 The **young man** saith unto him, All these ... I kept Matt 19:20
1 But when the **young man** heard that saying,........... 19:22
1 And there followed him a certain **young man**,..... Mark 14:51
4 and the **young men** laid hold on him:................. 14:51
2 they saw a **young man** sitting on the right side,........ 16:5
3 And he said, **Young man**, I say unto thee, Arise.....Luke 7:14
4 and your **young men** shall see visions,...............Acts 2:17
4 and the **young men** came in, and found her dead,....... 5:10
2 and asked me to lead this **young man** (NASB)......... 23:18
2 the commander let the **young man** go (NASB)......... 23:22
4 I write unto you, **young men**,.....................1 Jn 2:13
4 I have written unto you, **young men**,................... 2:14

Classical Greek
In classical Greek the primary meaning of *neaniskos* is "young man," though the specific age referred to covers a rather broad spectrum. In a few instances the word means "servant."

Septuagint Usage
The Septuagint uses *neaniskos* also in reference to "young man," but again the exact age range is not specific. For example, the word is used to speak of very young men (even "boys") in

Genesis 25:27, but also of young men who are certainly beyond their teens (Genesis 19:4).

New Testament Usage

The New Testament usages not only continue the primary definition of "young man," but also the indefiniteness as to any specific age. Among those referred to by *neaniskos* are the rich young ruler who inquired how he might have eternal life (Matthew 19:20-22); the "young man" in Gethsemane who lost the linen cloth covering his body to other "young men" (Mark 14:51 [both are referred to by *neaniskos*]); the widow's son whom Christ raised from the dead (Luke 7:14); the "young men" who will see visions (Acts 2:17—as contrasted to the old men who will dream dreams); and the "young men" addressed by John (1 John 2:13,14—as contrasted to the little children, *paidia* [see 3676], and the fathers, *pateres* [see 3824]). The definition of "servant" may be used in Acts 5:10, although those who buried Sapphira may simply have been "young men" of the congregation. The use of the word in Mark 16:5 in reference to an angel may very well speak of his appearance as a "young man" or his duty as a servant rather than his nature.

STRONG 3495, BAUER 534, MOULTON-MILLIGAN 423, LIDDELL-SCOTT 1164.

3359. Νεάπολις Neapolis name
Neapolis.

1. Νεάπολιν Neapolin acc fem
2. Νέαν Πόλιν Nean Polin acc fem

1 and the next day to **Neapolis**;............... Acts 16:11

Macedonian seaport city on the Aegean Sea visited by Paul on his second missionary journey (Acts 16:11).

3360. Νεεμάν Neeman name
Naaman.

1. Νεεμάν Neeman masc
2. Ναιμάν Naiman masc

1 none ... cleansed, saving **Naaman** the Syrian......... Luke 4:27

Syrian captain healed of leprosy by Elisha the prophet (Luke 4:27; cf. 2 Kings 5:1ff.).

3361. νεκρός nekros adj
Dead, lifeless, useless.

CROSS-REFERENCE:
νεκρόω nekroō (3362)

גָּוַע gāwaʿ (1510), Death (Sir 8:7).
הָרַג hāragh (2103), Slain ones (Ez 37:9).
חָלָל chālāl (2591), Slain (1 Sm 31:8, Ez 11:6).
מוּת mûth (4322), Dead (Gn 23:6, Ps 88:5 [87:5], Is 26:14).
נְבֵלָה nᵉvēlāh (5215), Carcass (Dt 28:26, Jer 19:7).
פֶּגֶר pegher (6538), Corpse (Is 34:3).

1. νεκρόν nekron nom/acc sing masc/neu
2. νεκρῶν nekrōn gen pl masc/neu
3. νεκρός nekros nom sing masc
4. νεκροῦ nekrou gen sing masc
5. νεκροί nekroi nom pl masc
6. νεκροῖς nekrois dat pl masc
7. νεκρούς nekrous acc pl masc
8. νεκρά nekra nom sing fem
9. νεκράν nekran acc sing fem

7 Follow me; and let the **dead** bury their dead.........	Matt	8:22
7 Follow me; and let the dead bury their **dead**...........		8:22
7 Heal the sick, cleanse the lepers, raise the **dead**,......		10:8
5 the deaf hear, the **dead** are raised up,....................		11:5
2 John the Baptist; he is risen from the **dead**;.............		14:2
2 until the Son of man be risen again from the **dead**.....		17:9
2 But as touching the resurrection of the **dead**,..........		22:31
2 God is not the God of the **dead**, but of the living.....		22:32
2 but are within full **of dead** men's bones,................		23:27
2 say unto the people, He is risen from the **dead**:.......		27:64
5 the keepers did shake, and became as **dead** men......		28:4
2 and tell his disciples that he is risen from the **dead**,..		28:7
2 That John the Baptist was risen from the **dead**,.....	Mark	6:14
2 John, whom I beheaded: he is risen from the **dead**......		6:16
2 till the Son of man were risen from the **dead**...........		9:9
2 what the rising from the **dead** should mean............		9:10
3 as one **dead**; insomuch that many said, He is dead......		9:26
2 For when they shall rise from the **dead**,................		12:25
2 And as touching the **dead**, that they rise:..............		12:26
2 not the God of the **dead**, but the God of the living:....		12:27
3 And he that was **dead** sat up, and began to speak...	Luke	7:15
5 the deaf hear, the **dead** are raised,......................		7:22
2 it was said ... that John was risen from the **dead**;.......		9:7
7 Jesus said unto him, Let the **dead** bury their dead:......		9:60
7 Jesus said unto him, Let the dead bury their **dead**:......		9:60
3 For this my son was **dead**, and is alive again;..........		15:24
3 for this thy brother was **dead**, and is alive again;......		15:32
2 went unto them from the **dead**, they will repent........		16:30
2 be persuaded, though one rose from the **dead**..........		16:31
2 and the resurrection from the **dead**,.....................		20:35
5 Now that the **dead** are raised,...........................		20:37
2 For he is not a God of the **dead**, but of the living:....		20:38
2 Why seek ye the living among the **dead**?...............		24:5
2 and to rise from the **dead** the third day:...............		24:46
2 When therefore he was risen from the **dead**,.........	John	2:22
7 For as the Father raiseth up the **dead**,..................		5:21
5 the **dead** shall hear the voice of the Son of God:.....		5:25
2 Lazarus was ... whom he raised from the **dead**.........		12:1
2 see Lazarus ... whom he had raised from the **dead**.....		12:9
2 called Lazarus ... and raised him from the **dead**,.......		12:17
2 that he must rise again from the **dead**...................		20:9
2 after that he was risen from the **dead**...................		21:14
2 whom God hath raised from the **dead**;................	Acts	3:15
2 through Jesus the resurrection from the **dead**..........		4:2
2 ye crucified, whom God raised from the **dead**,.........		4:10
9 and the young men came in, and found her **dead**,......		5:10
2 and drink with him after he rose from the **dead**........		10:41
2 ordained of God to be ... Judge of quick and **dead**.....		10:42
2 But God raised him from the **dead**:.....................		13:30
2 as concerning that he raised him up from the **dead**,....		13:34

νεκρός 3361

2 and risen again from the **dead**;	Acts 17:3
2 in that he hath raised him from the **dead**.	17:31
2 when they heard of the resurrection of the **dead**,	17:32
3 down from the third loft, and was taken up **dead**.	20:9
2 of the hope and resurrection of the **dead**	23:6
2 that there shall be a resurrection of the **dead**,	24:15
2 Touching the resurrection of the **dead**.	24:21
7 incredible ... that God should raise the **dead**?	26:8
2 should be the first that should rise from the **dead**,	26:23
1 swollen, or fallen down **dead** suddenly:	28:6
2 by the resurrection from the **dead**:	Rom 1:4
7 even God, who quickeneth the **dead**,	4:17
2 him that raised up Jesus our Lord from the **dead**;	4:24
2 that like as Christ was raised up from the **dead**	6:4
2 Knowing that Christ being raised from the **dead**	6:9
7 Likewise reckon ye also yourselves to be **dead**	6:11
2 as those that are alive from the **dead**,	6:13
2 even to him who is raised from the **dead**,	7:4
8 For without the law sin was **dead**.	7:8
1 if Christ be in you, the body is **dead** because of sin;	8:10
2 that raised up Jesus from the **dead** dwell in you,	8:11
2 he that raised up Christ from the **dead** shall also	8:11
2 that is, to bring up Christ again from the **dead**.	10:7
2 that God hath raised him from the **dead**,	10:9
2 the receiving of them be, but life from the **dead**?	11:15
2 that he might be Lord both of the **dead** and living.	14:9
2 if Christ be preached that he rose from the **dead**,	1 Co 15:12
2 that there is no resurrection of the **dead**?	15:12
2 But if there be no resurrection of the **dead**,	15:13
5 if so be that the **dead** rise not.	15:15
5 For if the **dead** rise not, then is not Christ raised:	15:16
2 But now is Christ risen from the **dead**,	15:20
2 by man came also the resurrection of the **dead**.	15:21
2 shall they do which are baptized for the **dead**,	15:29
5 baptized for the **dead**, if the **dead** rise not at all?	15:29
2 why are they then baptized for the **dead**?	15:29
5 what advantageth it me, if the **dead** rise not?	15:32
5 some man will say, How are the **dead** raised up?	15:35
2 So also is the resurrection of the **dead**.	15:42
5 and the **dead** shall be raised incorruptible,	15:52
7 but in God which raiseth the **dead**:	2 Co 1:9
2 God the Father, who raised him from the **dead**;	Gal 1:1
2 in Christ, when he raised him from the **dead**,	Eph 1:20
7 who were **dead** in trespasses and sins:	2:1
7 Even when we were **dead** in sins,	2:5
2 Awake thou that sleepest, and arise from the **dead**,	5:14
2 I might attain unto the resurrection of the **dead**.	Phlp 3:11
2 who is the beginning, the firstborn from the **dead**;	Col 1:18
2 of God, who hath raised him from the **dead**.	2:12
7 And you, being **dead** in your sins	2:13
2 whom he raised from the **dead**, even Jesus,	1 Th 1:10
5 and the **dead** in Christ shall rise first:	4:16
2 was raised from the **dead** according to my gospel:	2 Tm 2:8
7 Christ, who shall judge the quick and the **dead**	4:1
2 the foundation of repentance from **dead** works,	Heb 6:1
2 laying on of hands, and of resurrection of the **dead**,	6:2
2 purge your conscience from **dead** works	9:14
6 For a testament is of force after men are **dead**:	9:17
2 God was able to raise him up, even from the **dead**;	11:19
7 Women received their **dead** raised to life again:	11:35
2 that brought again from the **dead** our Lord Jesus,	13:20
8 faith, if it hath not works, is **dead**, being alone.	Jas 2:17
8 know, ... that faith without works is **dead**?	2:20
1 For as the body without the spirit is **dead**, so faith	2:26
8 so faith without works is **dead**.	2:26
2 by the resurrection of Jesus Christ from the **dead**,	1 Pt 1:3
2 God, that raised him up from the **dead**,	1:21
7 him that is ready to judge the quick and the **dead**.	4:5
6 the gospel preached also to them that are **dead**,	4:6
2 faithful witness, and the first begotten of the **dead**,	Rev 1:5
3 And when I saw him, I fell at his feet as **dead**.	1:17
3 I am he that liveth, and was **dead**;	1:18
3 the first and the last, which was **dead**, and is alive;	2:8
3 thou hast a name that thou livest, and art **dead**.	3:1
2 the time of the **dead**, that they should be judged,	11:18
5 Blessed are the **dead** which die in the Lord	14:13
4 the sea; and it became as the blood **of a dead** man;	16:3
2 But the rest of the **dead** lived not again until	Rev 20:5
7 And I saw the **dead**, small and great,	20:12
5 the **dead** were judged ... according to their works.	20:12
7 And the sea gave up the **dead** which were in it;	20:13
7 hell delivered up the **dead** which were in them:	20:13

Classical Greek

From the time of Homer and following *nekros* was a common word used to describe persons and animals that had died. It was probably used first as a noun, "dead body," and then later as an adjective, "dead." Its early occurrences as an adjective appear from 500 B.C. (cf. *Liddell-Scott*). A body without life (*psuchē* [5425]) was just a "corpse, inanimate, mere matter." However, *nekros* could also refer to the spirit or "shade" of the dead individual as a "dweller in the netherworld" (Homer *Odyssey* 10.526; cf. *Liddell-Scott*). The word's meaning also extended to include lifeless and inanimate "things" (*nekra*), such as stone and wood.

Figurative uses of *nekros* also appear in the classical period. Evil men were occasionally described as "dead"; Stoic philosophers picked up the term to describe false teachers as well as their words. Evidently "dead" meant "dying," or "leading to death," or perhaps "not life-giving." Similarly, wealth was said to be dead. Even the body, while still alive, came to be called "dead" in this same sense of "destined to die," and the soul (*psuchē*) was referred to as "death-bearing," because it was considered to be still carrying the body.

Septuagint Usage

In the Septuagint *nekros* is found over 80 times, mostly as a noun but sometimes as an adjective. It usually translates the Hebrew word *mûth*, "dead person," but also translates several other words suggestive of deceased persons or corpses. Sometimes the dead are pictured as going to a dark "underworld" (Hades) where there is—at least in relation to the world of the living—no consciousness (Psalms 88:3-12 [LXX 87:3-12]; 115:17 [113:25]; 143:3 [142:3]; Ecclesiastes 9:3-6) and no hope (Ecclesiastes 9:4; Isaiah 26:14). At other times there is the hint that the souls of the dead still exist and may be joined in their "pit" (Ezekiel 32:18-32, cf. 2 Samuel 12:23 [LXX 2 Kings 12:23] and Homer *Odyssey* 10.526 above) and that there is the possibility (Ezekiel 37:9), and even the hope (Isaiah 26:19, cf. Job 19:26; Daniel 12:2), of a resurrection to life.

New Testament Usage

In the New Testament *nekros* is found some 130 times. It is rarely used literally as an adjective ("dead"), but it occurs over 100 times as a noun in the literal sense. Occasionally it speaks of lifeless bodies which are buried (Matthew 8:22; Acts 5:10; etc.) or which are fit to be buried (Acts 20:9; 28:6; James 2:26; etc.). Most often, however, it is plural—"the dead (ones)"—and is used in the sense of the company of humans who have passed from this life into the next, and from this physical, bodily existence into the unseen realm of spirits, sometimes called Hades (Acts 2:31; Revelation 20:13).

In keeping with the more positive view of death in the New Testament, *nekros* is used over 80 times—almost two-thirds of its total usage—in connection with a resurrection "from" or "of" the dead. About half of these speak of Jesus' resurrection from "the dead," and about half speak of the resurrection of others, either individually (Luke 7:15,22; John 12:1,9,17; etc.) or all together (in the general resurrection—Matthew 22:31; Acts 24:15,21; 1 Corinthians 15:12,13,15,16,20,21,29,32,35,42,52; etc.). Not only are "the dead" to be raised, but also they will be judged alongside those who are still living when Christ returns (Acts 10:42; 2 Timothy 4:1; 1 Peter 4:5; Revelation 11:18; 20:12,13).

Only about one-sixth of the New Testament uses of *nekros* are figurative. Most of these use "dead" in the moral sense: spiritually dead in sins prior to acceptance of the gospel (Matthew 8:22; Luke 9:60 [first use]; John 5:25; Romans 6:13; 11:15; Ephesians 2:1,5; 5:14; Colossians 2:13) or, in the case of the Prodigal Son, prior to repentance (Luke 15:24,32). Sometimes things are dead or lifeless in the sense of "powerless" or "unproductive": faith without works (James 2:17,20,26); works without faith (Hebrews 6:1; 9:14); our bodies in the face of death (Romans 8:10). Even sin is said to be dead or powerless when apart from law (Romans 7:8). Similarly, in a good sense, the Christian is to be "dead to sin" (Romans 6:11, i.e., "inanimate toward") when it comes to committing sin or to feeling its guilt.

In Matthew 22:32 (and parallels) Jesus asserted that God is "not the God of the *dead*, but of the living." He was speaking of the ultimate lifelessness of nonexistence which the Sadducees imagined for the dead. Paul made it clear that Jesus is in fact "the Lord both of the *dead* and of the living" (Romans 14:9).

STRONG 3498, BAUER 534-35, MOULTON-MILLIGAN 423, KITTEL 4:892-94, LIDDELL-SCOTT 1165-66, COLIN BROWN 1:443-46.

3362. νεκρόω nekroō verb

To put to death, mortify, be worn out, impotent.

COGNATES:
νεκρός nekros (3361)
νέκρωσις nekrōsis (3363)

SYNONYMS:
ἀναιρέω anaireō (335)
ἀποκτείνω apokteinō (609)
ἀπόλλυμι apollumi (616)
διαχειρίζομαι diacheirizomai (1309)
θανατόω thanatoō (2266)
θύω thuō (2357)
σφάζω sphazō (4821)
φονεύω phoneuō (5244)

1. **νεκρώσατε** nekrōsate 2pl impr aor act
2. **νενεκρωμένου** nenekrōmenou
   gen sing masc part perf mid
3. **νενεκρωμένον** nenekrōmenon
   nom/acc sing neu part perf mid

3 he considered not his own body now **dead**,..........Rom 4:19
1 **Mortify** therefore your members which are...........Col 3:5
2 sprang there even of one, and him as good as **dead**, Heb 11:12

Classical Greek and Septuagint Usage

The verb *nekroō* has not been found in surviving Greek literature until after the classical period, although it is related to the adjective *nekros* (3361), "dead," which is well attested from classical times. Where it is found in classical usage it is often passive, meaning "worn out" or "impotent" (cf. *Bauer*). Likewise, *nekros* is found many times in the Septuagint, but *nekroō* is not used. When *nekroō* does appear in the Koine Greek of the Hellenistic period (the time during which the New Testament was written), it is used in both literal and figurative senses.

In a literal sense *nekroō* means "to put something or someone to death." Koine writers used the passive form of the verb to describe dead bodies. In some medical references the verb is used to describe the effects of disease on parts of the body. Other references are to the deadening effects of aging: the aging body is falling victim to the process which eventually leads to death. Thus the aged, exhausted body can be spoken of as "dead" in the sense of "as good as dead" (ibid.).

In a figurative sense *nekroō* means "to mortify, to treat as dead," or "to disregard." Such a figurative use is found in the writings of the Stoic philosophers (see Coenen, "nekros,"

Colin Brown, 1:443; Bultmann, "nekroō," Kittel, 4:894).

New Testament Usage

Nekroō is used three times in the New Testament. Two of these are in reference to Abraham's physical condition at the time of God's promise to give him a son. Romans 4:19 says that Abraham "considered not his own body now *dead*" (or "already dead," New King James Bible). Obviously Abraham was not dead in the strict sense of the word, but his body had aged and was "as good as dead" (NIV) with respect to ordinary expectations for becoming a father. Hebrews 11:12 describes Abraham as being "as good as *dead*" in the same sense. Both these references to Abraham's condition parallel nonbiblical ways of using *nekroō* to refer to the deadening effects of age (e.g., "impotency").

A third New Testament reference is Colossians 3:5. This verse tells believers to "mortify" their earthly "members," to "treat them as dead" as far as sinful desires of the flesh are concerned. Christians are to do this because they have died to self and been raised with Christ, and their true life is now in Him (Colossians 3:1-4; cf. 2 Corinthians 5:17). Therefore, they should not respond to the temptations of the flesh; they should disregard them and dismiss them as being dead. Treating sinful desires as dead is thus an act of obedience in response to the truth of the gospel, carried out in the power of the new life we have received in Jesus. This "putting to death" or "mortifying" is not the killing of the physical body but the submission of the whole self to the lordship of Jesus Christ.

STRONG 3499, BAUER 535, MOULTON-MILLIGAN 424, KITTEL 4:894, LIDDELL-SCOTT 1166, COLIN BROWN 1:443,445.

3363. νέκρωσις nekrōsis noun

A putting to death; deadness.
CROSS-REFERENCE:
νεκρόω nekroō (3362)

1. νέκρωσιν nekrōsin acc sing fem

1 neither yet the **deadness** of Sarah's womb: .... Rom 4:19
1 Always bearing about in the body the **dying** .... 2 Co 4:10

Nekrōsis in Hellenistic Greek is used in medical treatises to describe the process of mortification, the dying (loss of power, even withering) of parts of the body. In Romans 4:19 the word is similarly used to describe the "deadness" of Sarah's womb, her incapacity to bear a child. Neither Sarah's inability nor Abraham's own "dead" ("having died," from *nekroō* [3362]) body inhibited his faith in God's promise that they would produce a son in their old age.

The only other New Testament use of the word comes in 2 Corinthians 4:10, where Paul said that he was "always bearing about . . . the *dying* (*nekrōsis*) of the Lord Jesus" in his body. The verses following seem to explain his meaning: he was willing to expose himself to death, following Jesus' example, in order to demonstrate the life-giving power there is in Jesus.

Thus, as evidenced by its uses, *nekrōsis* can indicate both the process or act of dying (loss of strength, vitality) and the resultant state of death.

STRONG 3500, BAUER 535, MOULTON-MILLIGAN 424, KITTEL 4:895, LIDDELL-SCOTT 1166, COLIN BROWN 1:443,445.

3363B. νεομηνία neomēnia noun

The new moon.
CROSS-REFERENCES:
μήν mēn (3243)
νέος neos (3363C)

1. νεομηνίας neomēnias gen sing fem

This is an alternate spelling of *noumēnia*. See the word study at number 3424.

3363C. νέος neos adj

New, fresh, young.
COGNATES:
ἀνανεόω ananeoō (364)
νεανίας neanias (3357)
νεομηνία neomēnia (3363B)
νεοσσός neossos (3364)
νεότης neotēs (3366)
νεόφυτος neophutos (3367)
νεωκόρος neōkoros (3373)
νεωτερικός neōterikos (3374)
νουμηνία noumēnia (3424)
νουνεχῶς nounechōs (3425)
SYNONYMS:
ἄγναφος agnaphos (45)
καινός kainos (2508)
πρόσφατος prosphatos (4230)

אָבִיב 'āvîv (23), Abib (Ex 13:4, 23:15, Dt 16:1).
בִּכּוּרִים bikkûrîm (1101), Firstfruit (Nm 28:26).
חָדָשׁ chādhāsh (2413), New (Nm 28:26).

נַעַר na'ar (5470), Young, youth (Dt 28:50, 1 Chr 12:28, Is 65:20).

1. **νέον** neon nom/acc sing masc/neu
2. **νέος** neos nom sing masc
3. **νέας** neas gen/acc sing/pl fem·
4. **νεώτερος** neōteros comp nom sing masc
5. **νεώτεροι** neōteroi comp nom pl masc
6. **νεωτέρους** neōterous comp acc pl masc
7. **νεωτέρας** neōteras comp acc pl fem

1	Neither do men put **new** wine into old bottles:	Matt 9:17
1	but they put **new** wine into new bottles,	9:17
1	And no man putteth **new** wine into old bottles:	Mark 2:22
2	else the **new** wine doth burst the bottles,	2:22
1	but **new** wine must be put into new bottles.	2:22
1	And no man putteth **new** wine into old bottles;	Luke 5:37
2	the **new** wine will burst the bottles, and be spilled,	5:37
1	But **new** wine must be put into new bottles;	5:38
1	having drunk old wine straightway desireth **new**:	5:39
4	And the **younger** of them said to his father,	15:12
4	the **younger** son gathered all together,	15:13
4	is greatest among you, let him be as the **younger**;	22:26
4	When thou wast **young**, thou girdedst thyself,	John 21:18
5	And the **young men** arose, wound him up,	Acts 5:6
1	that ye may be **a new** lump, as ye are unleavened.	1 Co 5:7
1	And have put on the **new** man, which is renewed	Col 3:10
6	and the **young men** as brethren;	1 Tm 5:1
7	elder women as mothers; the **younger** as sisters,	5:2
7	But the **younger** widows refuse:	5:11
7	I will therefore that the **younger** women marry,	5:14
3	That they may teach the **young** women to be sober,	Tit 2:4
6	**Young** men likewise exhort to be sober minded.	2:6
3	And to Jesus the mediator of the **new** covenant,	Heb 12:24
5	ye **younger**, submit yourselves unto the elder.	1 Pt 5:5

Classical Greek
This versatile term has basically three functions in antiquity: (1) it describes something as "young, youthful"; (2) it refers to objects (a predominant use) which may be "new, fresh"; and (3) it functions as an adverb of time meaning "newly, recently" (*Liddell-Scott*). In the second sense *neos* and *kainos* (2508) overlap in meaning and *neos* suggests a "new" quality or essence (cf. Behm, "neos," *Kittel*, 4:896).

Septuagint Usage
In the Septuagint *neos* appears predominantly in the comparative form *neōteros* for as many as five Hebrew words. This does not include the six other terms translated by *neos*. On several occasions *neos* is the counterpart to 'āvîv. The reference in these cases is almost invariably to the month of Abib, the month in which Israel was led out of Egypt (i.e., Passover; Exodus 13:4; 23:15; 34:18; Deuteronomy 16:1; but cf. Leviticus 2:14).

Especially in Genesis *neōteros* ("youngest") refers to the youngest in a family, such as Benjamin (e.g., Genesis 44:2,12,30; throughout chapters 42–44) or David (1 Samuel 17:14 [LXX 1 Kings 17:14]; the apocryphal Psalm 151:1). It is also used to describe objects (e.g., "fresh/new" grain, Leviticus 23:14,16; 26:10) or "youth" in general (Isaiah 40:30).

New Testament Usage
The New Testament, likewise, contrasts "new" with "old" (*palaios* [3683]) in terms of the age of the objects. "Fresh" wineskins are needed for fresh wine (Matthew 9:17; Mark 2:22; cf. John 21:18). It is the younger brother (*neōteros*) who goes off and squanders his inheritance in the Parable of the Prodigal Son (Luke 15:12,13).

The social position of the young in contrast to the old in ancient culture may be detected in some texts. Elders (*presbuteroi* [see 4104]) were generally esteemed for their wisdom and experience in contrast to youth who were largely considered inexperienced and in need of training (cf. 1 Timothy 4:12, *neotēs*; 1 Timothy 5:1ff.). Youth were expected to follow the example and lead of older people (cf. Titus 2:4,6). How unlike present society which places so high a premium upon "youth" instead of "experience" (cf. 1 Peter 5:5 with above texts).

Jesus is the mediator of a "new" covenant (*neos diathēkē*) according to Hebrews 12:24. Here we note that *neos* shares territory with *kainos*, the ordinary term for this concept (e.g., Luke 22:20; 1 Corinthians 11:25; 2 Corinthians 3:6; Hebrews 8:8; 9:15). As a rule, however, *neos* does not have the same eschatological dimension as *kainos* (but cf. Colossians 3:10). "New" in this respect means "new" of a different kind, order, or nature (see *kainos* [2508]). But *neos* does carry a sense of being superior to the "old" (Hebrews 12:24). (Trench validly points out that *kainos* emphasizes quality while *neos*, time. However, this distinction is not to be pressed since something "fresh" is implicitly superior to something "old" [e.g., Leviticus 23:14,26]; *Synonyms of the New Testament*, pp.219ff.)

STRONG 3501, BAUER 535-36, MOULTON-MILLIGAN 424, KITTEL 4:896-99, LIDDELL-SCOTT 1169, COLIN BROWN 2:669-71,674-76.

3364. νεοσσός neossos noun
Young bird, chick (usually dove or pigeon), nesting.

COGNATES:
νέος neos (3363C)
νοσσιά nossia (3418)
νοσσίον nossion (3419)
νοσσός nossos (3419B)

1. νεοσσούς neossous acc pl masc
1 A pair of turtledoves, or two **young** pigeons......... Luke 2:24

Also spelled *nossos*, this word denotes the young offspring of a bird. Its only occurrence in the New Testament is in Luke 2:24. After her time of purification, Mary and Joseph offered the sacrifice prescribed in Leviticus 12:8—"a pair of turtledoves or two *young* (*neossous*) pigeons." The word *neossos* is found here in a quotation from the Septuagint.

STRONG 3502, BAUER 543 (see "nossos"), MOULTON-MILLIGAN 430 (see "nossos"), LIDDELL-SCOTT 1169.

3365. νέος neos
See word study at number 3363C.

3366. νεότης neotēs noun
Youth.
CROSS-REFERENCE:
νέος neos (3363C)

בְּחוּרוֹת bᵉchûrôth (1006), Youth (Eccl 12:1).
יַלְדוּת yaldhûth (3317), Childhood (Eccl 11:10).
נְעוּרִים nᵉʿûrîm (5454), Youth (Nm 30:4 [30:3], Ps 129:1f. [128:1f.], Jer 3:25).
נֹעַר nōʿar (5471), Youth (Jb 36:14, Ps 88:15 [87:15]).
עוֹד ʿôdh (5968), Still; life (Gn 48:15).
עֲלוּמִים ʿălûmîm (6156), Youthful vigor (Jb 20:11).
עַלְמָה ʿalmāh (6183), Maiden (Prv 30:19 [24:54]).
צְעִירָה tsᵉʿîrāh (7089), Youth (Gn 43:33).

1. νεότητος neotētos gen sing fem
1 All these things have I kept from my **youth** up:.... Matt 19:20
1 Master, all these have I observed from my **youth**... Mark 10:20
1 he said, All these have I kept from my **youth** up... Luke 18:21
1 My manner of life from my **youth**,................. Acts 26:4
1 Let no man despise thy **youth**;..................... 1 Tm 4:12

In Mark 10:20, Luke 18:21, and Acts 26:4 this noun refers to the early years of a person's life. In the Gospel texts the wealthy ruler claimed to have kept the commandments from his "youth." Paul likewise testified to having grown up in the strict manner of life taught by the Pharisees (Acts 26:4). Both the ruler and Paul were making statements about their religious training in their "youth."

In 1 Timothy 4:12 *neotēs* might be better thought of as "youthfulness" in a relative sense. Timothy was a grown man but younger than some to whom he was ministering. They should not despise his comparative "youth."

STRONG 3503, BAUER 536, MOULTON-MILLIGAN 424-25, LIDDELL-SCOTT 1170, COLIN BROWN 2:674-75.

3367. νεόφυτος neophutos adj
Newly planted, young plants; new convert, novice.
CROSS-REFERENCES:
νέος neos (3363C)
φύω phuō (5289)

נֶטַע neṭaʿ (5379), Plant (Jb 14:9, Is 5:7).
נְטִעִים nᵉṭiʿîm (5380), Plant (Ps 144:12 [143:12]).
שָׁתִיל shāthîl (8691), Plant (Ps 128:3 [127:3]).

1. νεόφυτον neophuton acc sing masc
1 Not **a novice**, lest being lifted up with pride he fall .. 1 Tm 3:6

Neophutos means "newly planted." In classical Greek this word is used commonly in speaking of newly planted vineyards or trees. Its one use in the New Testament, however, is metaphoric and refers to a person. First Timothy 3:6 describes a recent convert to Christian faith as a "novice" or "neophyte" (an English transliteration of the Greek word). Such a person is only recently established in the Faith, and just as a newly planted tree or vine, he or she requires time to become well rooted and strong. This makes the new convert especially vulnerable. For his own good, the novice should not be given authority over others in the church.

STRONG 3504, BAUER 536, MOULTON-MILLIGAN 425, LIDDELL-SCOTT 1170.

3367B. Νέρωνι Nerōni name

1. Νέρωνι Nerōni dat masc

Nero Claudius Caesar was an emperor of Rome (A.D. 54-68) notorious for his persecution of Christians. He is accused of using the bodies of Christians as torches in his garden and of clothing believers in animal skins in order to be attacked by dogs. The name *Nerōni* appears only in a variant addition at 2 Timothy 4:22.

3368. νεύω neuō verb
Incline (in any direction); nod toward, signal by nodding, beckon.

νεφέλη 3369

COGNATES:
διανεύω dianeuō (1263)
ἐκνεύω ekneuō (1580)
ἐννεύω enneuō (1754)
ἐπινεύω epineuō (1947)
κατανεύω kataneuō (2626)

SYNONYMS:
διανεύω dianeuō (1263)
κατανεύω kataneuō (2626)

1. **νεύει** neuei 3sing indic pres act
2. **νεύσαντος** neusantos gen sing masc part aor act

1 Simon Peter therefore **beckoned** to him,.............	John 13:24
2 the governor **had beckoned** unto him to speak,.....	Acts 24:10

In classical Greek the verb *neuō* generally means "to incline in any direction" (*Liddell-Scott*). When used in reference to the head, it means "to nod" as a signal, such as in motioning someone to speak. In this sense of "motioning toward" or "beckoning to" someone, *neuō* occurs in John 13:24 where Peter signaled with a nod ("beckoned") to the disciple nearest Jesus, prompting him to ask Jesus who the betrayer would be. In a similar way, the Roman governor Felix nodded ("beckoned") toward Paul to give him permission to speak in his own defense after his Jewish accusers had finished making their charges (Acts 24:10).

STRONG 3506, BAUER 536, MOULTON-MILLIGAN 425, LIDDELL-SCOTT 1171.

3369. νεφέλη nephelē noun
Cloud.

SYNONYM:
νέφος nephos (3371)

אֵד 'ēdh (105), Mist (Jb 36:27).

מַאֲפֵל ma'aphēl (4130), Darkness (Jos 24:7).

נָשִׂיא nāsî' (5563), Vapor, cloud (Ps 135:7 [134:7], Jer 10:13, 51:16 [28:16]).

עָב 'āv (5854), Cloud, clouds (1 Kgs 18:44f., Jb 26:8, Is 19:1).

עֲבֹת 'ăvōth (5895), Cloud (Ez 31:3,10,14).

עָנָן 'ānān (6281), Cloud (Nm 9:15ff., Neh 9:12, Ez 10:3).

עֲנָן 'ānān (A6283), Clouds (Dn 7:13—Aramaic).

שַׁחַק shachaq (8263), Skies (Pss 36:5 [35:5], 77:17 [76:16], 108:4 [107:4]).

1. **νεφέλη** nephelē nom sing fem
2. **νεφέλης** nephelēs gen sing fem
3. **νεφέλῃ** nephelē dat sing fem
4. **νεφέλην** nephelēn acc sing fem
5. **νεφέλαι** nephelai nom pl fem
6. **νεφελῶν** nephelōn gen pl fem
7. **νεφέλαις** nephelais dat pl fem

1 behold, a bright **cloud** overshadowed them:........	Matt 17:5
2 and behold a voice out of the **cloud**, which said,......	17:5
6 see the Son of man coming in the **clouds** of heaven....	24:30
6 of power, and coming in the **clouds** of heaven.........	26:64
1 And there was a **cloud** that overshadowed them:....	Mark 9:7
2 and a voice came out of the **cloud**, saying,............	9:7
7 coming in the **clouds** with great power and glory.....	13:26
6 of power, and coming in the **clouds** of heaven.........	14:62
1 there came a **cloud**, and overshadowed them:.......	Luke 9:34
4 and they feared as they entered into the **cloud**..........	9:34
2 And there came a voice out of the **cloud**, saying,......	9:35
4 When ye see a **cloud** rise out of the west,.............	12:54
3 see the Son of man coming in a **cloud** with power.....	21:27
1 and a **cloud** received him out of their sight.........	Acts 1:9
4 how that all our fathers were under the **cloud**,.....	1 Co 10:1
3 baptized unto Moses in the **cloud** and in the sea;.....	10:2
7 caught up together with them in the **clouds**,.........	1 Th 4:17
5 **clouds** that are carried with a tempest;..............	2 Pt 2:17
5 **clouds** they are without water,......................	Jude 1:12
6 cometh with **clouds**; and every eye shall see him,.....	Rev 1:7
4 come down from heaven, clothed with a **cloud**:........	10:1
3 And they ascended up to heaven in a **cloud**;..........	11:12
1 And I looked, and behold a white **cloud**,..............	14:14
4 upon the **cloud** one sat like unto the Son of man,....	14:14
2 with a loud voice to him that sat on the **cloud**,.......	14:15
4 And he that sat on the **cloud** thrust in his sickle.......	14:16

Classical Greek
In classical Greek *nephelē* occurs mostly in poetic writings (*Liddell-Scott*). It has multiple uses, including literal and figurative. Thus it stands for literal clouds or figuratively for something clouded, such as a memory (ibid.). *Nephelē* is related to *nephos* (3371) which describes a larger cloud mass.

Septuagint Usage
In the Septuagint *nephelē* is used of the "cloud" that accompanied the covenant of God with His people (Genesis 9:13-16). God used the pillar of "cloud" by day to direct the Israelites on their march out of Egypt (Exodus 13:21; see 1 Corinthians 10:1,2). The cloud also was used to protect Israel from her enemies (Exodus 14:19,20). At each special revelation, on the Tent of Meeting and Mt. Sinai, the "cloud" concealed and displayed God's presence and message to His people (cf. Exodus 19:9; 33:9,10; 40:34).

Occasionally the word *nephelē* is used in the Scriptures in a figurative way. For example, God's mercy and faithfulness "reacheth unto the *clouds*" (Psalm 36:5 [LXX 35:5]). God blots out transgression like a cloud (Isaiah 44:22); Judah's goodness is like a "morning cloud" (Hosea 6:5), and the Lord "rides" upon a "cloud" when He comes to judge (Isaiah 19:1).

New Testament Usage
In the New Testament very significant events took place in clouds. One such event was the transfiguration of Jesus Christ (Mark 9:7). The Acts account of the ascension of Christ says a

nephelē "received him out of their sight" (Acts 1:9). When Christ referred to His coming again, He said, "You will see the Son of Man sitting at the right hand of the Mighty One, and coming on the *clouds* of heaven" (Mark 14:62, NIV). The apostle Paul said that all believers "shall be caught up . . . in the clouds (*nephelais*), to meet the Lord in the air" (1 Thessalonians 4:17).

As in the Old Testament, these New Testament occurrences indicate that when God chose to do something very significant to, for, and with His people, He often did it within *nephelais* ("clouds").

STRONG 3507, BAUER 536-37, MOULTON-MILLIGAN 425, KITTEL 4:902-10, LIDDELL-SCOTT 1171, COLIN BROWN 3:1000,1003.

3370. Νεφθαλείμ Nephthaleim name
Naphtali.

1. **Νεφθαλείμ Nephthaleim** masc
2. **Νεφθαλίμ Nephthalim** masc

1 in the borders of Zabulon and **Nephthalim**:......... Matt 4:13
1 The land of Zabulon, and the land of **Nephthalim**,...... 4:15
1 tribe of **Nephthalim** were sealed twelve thousand..... Rev 7:6

Israelite tribe that settled in the northeastern corner of Palestine (Matthew 4:13).

3371. νέφος nephos noun
Cloud, cloud mass; mass of people, multitude.
SYNONYM:
   νεφέλη nephelē (3369)

נָשִׂיא nāsî' (5563), Cloud (Prv 25:14).
עָב 'āv (5854), Cloud (Jb 20:6, 38:34, Eccl 12:2).
עָנָן 'ānān (6281), Cloud (Jb 7:9, 26:8, 38:9).
שַׁחַק shachaq (8263), Cloud (Jb 36:28, Prv 8:28).

1. **νέφος nephos** nom/acc sing neu
1 compassed about with so great **a cloud** of witnesses, Heb 12:1

Classical Greek and Septuagint Usage
The noun *nephos* is the common word for a large mass of clouds, whereas *nephelē* (3369) is the common word for *cloud*. Though common in nonbiblical Greek and in the Septuagint, *nephos* is found but once in the New Testament. The latter term generally suggests specific clouds with definite shape that cover a part of the sky, whereas *nephos* indicates a large, dense cloud mass which covers the whole sky but which has no definite shape. Thus, *nephos* as a large cloud could be a symbol of darkness and blindness.

The distinction of meaning in the Septuagint is slight however, since *nephelē* and *nephos* generally translate the same Hebrew words.

Metaphorically *nephos* is used to describe a great mass of people. The word is also found, at least from the time of Homer, to mean "a cloud of men," for example, "a cloud of footmen" and "a cloud of Trojans" (*Iliad*, 4.274; 16.66; 23.133; cf. *Liddell-Scott*). Herodotus (8.109) records that Themistocles referred to the Persian armies defeated by the Greeks as "so great a cloud of men" (ibid.).

New Testament Usage
When Hebrews 12:1 speaks of "so great a *cloud* of witnesses," then, it is speaking of the great "mass" of Old Testament heroes who are cataloged in chapter 11, the testimony of whose lives encourage Christians to remain faithful to God whatever the cost.

STRONG 3509, BAUER 537, MOULTON-MILLIGAN 425, KITTEL 4:902-10, LIDDELL-SCOTT 1171, COLIN BROWN 3:1003.

3372. νεφρός nephros noun
Kidney; seat of emotion, mind.

כִּלְיָה kilyāh (3749), Kidney (Lv 3:4,10); mind, heart, or innermost part of man (Ps 26:2 [25:2], Jer 17:10).

1. **νεφρούς nephrous** acc pl masc
1 that I am he which searcheth the reins and hearts:... Rev 2:23

Classical Greek and Septuagint Usage
In secular Greek *nephros* commonly denotes "a kidney." Exodus and Leviticus in the Septuagint also use the word often when referring to sacrificial animals, the "kidneys" of which were among those parts which were to be offered on the altar.

The idea that certain emotions and psychological activities arise from organs of the body is common in Near Eastern thought. "The kidneys" ("reins," KJV) represented "the inner self" in general (Job 16:14; Psalm 16:7 [LXX 15:7]; Lamentations 3:13), or, more specifically, signified the innermost feelings and purposes of the mind, which only God sees (Psalms 7:9; 26:2 [LXX 25:2]; Jeremiah 11:20; 17:10; 20:12).

Nephros occurs four times in apocalyptic literature. It can refer to the seat of distress (1 Enoch 60:3), the seat of trouble (1 Enoch 68:3), the center of prudence (Testament of

Naphtali 2:8), or meditation (2 Baruch 48:39). (See Russell, *The Method and Message of Jewish Apocalyptic*, pp.144f.)

New Testament Usage

Jesus' statement in Revelation 2:23, the only New Testament use of *nephros*, strongly reflects the more common figurative use from the Septuagint. So in warning the permissive church at Thyatira, Jesus claimed the divine power to "search the *reins* (*nephros*) and hearts" and to give to everyone according to his works. Psalms and Jeremiah frequently couple the words "reins" and "hearts" (*kardia* [2559]), probably in the general sense of "minds and hearts," but Jesus seems to draw His specific thought and wording in the Revelation passage from Jeremiah 17:10.

STRONG 3510, BAUER 537, MOULTON-MILLIGAN 425, KITTEL 4:911, LIDDELL-SCOTT 1172.

3373. νεωκόρος neōkoros noun

Temple sweeper, temple keeper, temple guardian.

CROSS-REFERENCE:
νέος neos (3363C)

1. νεωκόρον neōkoron acc sing masc

1 is a **worshipper** of the great goddess Diana, ... Acts 19:35

Classical Greek

The noun *neōkoros* can be found in classical Greek literature from the Fourth Century B.C. to describe lowly laborers or slaves whose responsibility it was to keep pagan temples swept and clean, hence a "temple sweeper." The word also assumed a more positive position of "temple keeper," one who was put in charge of the regular operation and maintenance of a temple.

In literature from the First Century A.D. the word had been appropriated by some cities, especially in Asia Minor, as a proud title affirming that they had established and were maintaining temples to their patron gods or goddesses, or to the emperor (cf. *Liddell-Scott*). Thus, they had become temple "guardians" or "wardens."

New Testament Usage

The word is so used in Acts 19:35, its only New Testament usage. That the city clerk declared Ephesus to be the *neōkoros* of "the great goddess Diana (Artemis)" means that the Ephesians were the caretakers and preservers of the temple in the goddess' honor. Inscriptions and coins dating back into the First Century A.D. have confirmed, in language almost identical to Luke's, Ephesus' proud claim to be the *neōkoros* of Diana (Artemis). (See word study on *Artemis* [730].)

STRONG 3511, BAUER 537, MOULTON-MILLIGAN 425, LIDDELL-SCOTT 1172, COLIN BROWN 3:796.

3374. νεωτερικός neōterikos adj

Youthful.

CROSS-REFERENCE:
νέος neos (3363C)

1. νεωτερικάς neōterikas acc pl fem

1 Flee also **youthful** lusts: but follow righteousness, ... 2 Tm 2:22

Related to *neos* (3363C), "new, fresh, young" (through its comparative *neōteros*, "newer, fresher, younger"), *neōterikos* means "youthful," or "common or natural to a youth." In the New Testament the word is found only in 2 Timothy 2:22 where Paul told Timothy to "flee also *youthful* lusts." Compared to Paul, Timothy still fit the ancient category of a "young man" (see the words *neaniskos* [3358] and *neanias* [3357], and see 1 Timothy 4:12).

By "youthful lusts" Paul probably meant more than just improper sexual desires. Desires for power, prominence, possessions, action, excitement, confrontation, and novelty all combine to make young men naturally more vulnerable to being led astray by such adverse influences.

STRONG 3512, BAUER 537, MOULTON-MILLIGAN 425, LIDDELL-SCOTT 1172.

3375. νή nē intrj

(I swear or I affirm) by.

1. νή nē

1 I protest **by** your rejoicing which I have in Christ .. 1 Co 15:31

Classical Greek and Septuagint Usage

Nē is a Greek particle that is frequently used in classical and Septuagintal Greek to introduce an oath, vow, or solemn affirmation. The phrase *nē Dia*, "*by* Zeus," also appears as a rather common Greek expression to call a god as witness to the truthfulness of a sworn oath (see Link, "Swear," *Colin Brown*, 3:738) or to add emphasis to a statement, a question, or an answer to a question (*Liddell-Scott*). Both Septuagint uses of *nē* occur in Genesis 42 where

Joseph's vow (verse 15) and his subsequent strong declaration (verse 16) were both affirmed "*by* the life of Pharaoh." Papyri occurrences further support its continued use to introduce oaths (*Moulton-Milligan*).

New Testament Usage
In the New Testament *nē* is used only in 1 Corinthians 15:31 where it is translated "I protest by." It seems that Paul meant to affirm the fact of a bodily resurrection as forcefully as possible, and that he did so by solemnly calling as witness the Corinthians' own boasting about his exposure to death every day for the sake of the gospel. Such self-endangerment would be tragically foolish if Paul were not confident of a future resurrection. A more literal translation might be, "I die daily—*I swear* (or affirm) it *by* your boasting . . . ." In this case "your boasting" refers to Paul's boasting about the Corinthians as is demonstrated by the following clause, "which I have in Christ Jesus."
Strong 3513, Bauer 537, Moulton-Milligan 426, Liddell-Scott 1173, Colin Brown 3:738.

3376. νήθω nēthō verb
To spin.

טָוָה ṭāwâh (3011), Spin (Ex 35:25f.).

מַטְוֶה maṭweh (4436), Spun work (Ex 35:25).

שָׁזַר shāzar (8242), Hophal: twisted (Ex 26:31, 39:24 [36:32]).

1. νήθει nēthei 3sing indic pres act
2. νήθουσιν nēthousin 3pl indic pres act

1 they toil not, neither do they spin: .... Matt 6:28
1 the lilies ... they toil not, they spin not; .... Luke 12:27

Classical Greek
The verb *nēthō* is related to *neō* and can be found in classical Greek from the Fifth Century B.C. meaning "spin." The term occurs in such contexts as spiders spinning webs and clothmakers spinning fabrics.

In the ancient world spinning, the act of twisting fibers into a continuous thread, was accomplished using a spindle (a rod made of wood, bone, or some other material) with a hook on the end of it. Prepared fibers were held on a distaff, another stick held under the left arm, drawn through the hook, and spun by twisting the spindle. Proverbs 31:19 is illustrative: "In her hand she holds the distaff and grasps the spindle with her fingers" (NIV). In Palestine spinning was generally considered women's work (see Forbes, *Studies in Ancient Technology*, 4:151-171).

Septuagint Usage
In the Septuagint *nētho* appears only in Exodus (specifically chapters 26 and 35−39) where it describes the linen, scarlet, and goat-hair fabrics which had been "spun" by skilled women to make the tabernacle curtains and high-priestly clothing.

New Testament Usage
The word *nēthō* is found only twice in the New Testament. Both Matthew 6:28 and Luke 12:27 record Jesus' statement that the "lilies" of the field neither "toil" nor "spin." In these two passages Jesus stated that, though these relatively worthless flowers cannot labor to "spin" their own clothing, God himself provides them with a most beautiful covering; therefore, He certainly will not neglect the clothing needs of His own children.
Strong 3514, Bauer 537, Moulton-Milligan 426, Liddell-Scott 1173.

3377. νηπιάζω nēpiazō verb
To be a baby, to act like a baby.
Cross-Reference:
νήπιος nēpios (3378)

1. νηπιάζετε nēpiazete 2pl impr pres act

1 howbeit in malice be ye children, ... 1 Co 14:20

Classical Greek
Just as *nēpios* (3378), "baby, infant," is often used figuratively of someone who was babylike in any of a wide range of ways, so also the verb *nēpiazō* is capable of the same wide range of meanings. In addition to the literal meaning, "to be a baby," it is used even of adults to mean "to be babylike" or "childish" in either a negative or a positive sense. Positively it can mean to be innocent, sincere, guileless, or trusting, but more often it is used with a negative meaning, such as to be immature, helpless, foolish, inexperienced, unknowledgeable, or unskilled. *Nēpiazō* does not appear in the Septuagint.

New Testament Usage
In its only New Testament use, 1 Corinthians 14:20, Paul's precise intention may be somewhat difficult to grasp from the King James Version's rendering of two different Greek words by "children." The verse reads as follows: "Brethren, be not *children* (*paidia* [see 3676], 'little children') in understanding: howbeit in malice be ye *children* (*nēpiazō*, 'be babes'), but in

understanding be *men* (*teleioi* [see 4894], literally 'mature')." In scolding the Corinthians Paul exhorted them to stop thinking like little children (using *paidia* in a negative sense), but with regard to plotting and performing evil they need to be as innocent as "infants" (using *nēpiazō* in a positive sense).

STRONG 3515, BAUER 537, MOULTON-MILLIGAN 426, KITTEL 4:912-23, LIDDELL-SCOTT 1174.

3378. νήπιος nēpios adj
Infant, minor, child, childlike, innocent.

COGNATE:
νηπιάζω nēpiazō (3377)

SYNONYMS:
βρέφος brephos (1018)
μικρός mikros (3262)
παιδάριον paidarion (3671)
παιδίον paidion (3676)
παῖς pais (3679)
τέκνον teknon (4891)

טַף ṭaph (3054), Child (Ez 9:6).

נַעַר naʿar (5470), Child (Hos 11:1).

נֹעַר nōʿar (5471), Child (Jb 33:25).

עוֹלָל ʿôlāl (5985I), Child (Jer 6:11, 9:21).

עוֹלֵל ʿôlēl (5985II) Child (1 Sm 15:3).

פְּתִי pethî (6864), Simple one (Pss 19:7 [18:7], 119:130 [118:130], Prv 1:32).

1. **νήπιος nēpios** nom sing masc
2. **νηπίου nēpiou** gen sing masc
3. **νήπιοι nēpioi** nom pl masc
4. **νηπίων nēpiōn** gen pl masc
5. **νηπίοις nēpiois** dat pl masc

5 and hast revealed them unto **babes**.	Matt 11:25
4 Out of the mouth of **babes** and sucklings	21:16
5 hast revealed them **unto babes**: even so, Father;	Luke 10:21
4 An instructor of the foolish, a teacher of **babes**,	Rom 2:20
5 but as unto carnal, even as **unto babes** in Christ.	1 Co 3:1
1 When I was **a child**, I spake as a child,	13:11
1 When I was **a child**, I spake as **a child**,	13:11
1 I understood as **a child**, I thought as a child:	13:11
1 I understood as a child, I thought as **a child**:	13:11
2 when I became a man, I put away **childish** things.	13:11
1 Now I say, That the heir, as long as he is **a child**,	Gal 4:1
3 Even so we, when we were **children**,	4:3
3 That we henceforth be no more **children**,	Eph 4:14
1 unskilful in the word ... for he is **a babe**.	Heb 5:13

Classical Greek
This adjective appears frequently in Homeric literature as a substantive meaning "child, infant" (*Liddell-Scott*). In other Greek literature it is used of children up to puberty, and less frequently of the "young" of animals and plants (ibid.). Metaphorically *nēpios* means "childish" with regard to behavior, understanding, or bodily strength.

Septuagint Usage
The translators of the Septuagint typically used *nēpios* as an equivalent to ʿôlēl (or ʿôlāl), "child," and *pethî*, "a young, naive person" (easily deceived). Other words are also equated with *nēpios* (e.g., "little ones," Esther 8:11). The Septuagint uses *nēpios* both literally and figuratively. In 1 Samuel 15:3 (LXX 1 Kings 15:3) Samuel told Saul that God wanted all those of Amalek destroyed, even *infants*, as retribution for what Amalek did to Israel (cf. 1 Samuel 22:19 [LXX 1 Kings 22:19]). Examples of the figurative use of *nēpios* can be found in Psalms 17:4 (LXX 16:4), "babes," and 19:7 (18:7), "the simple" (cf. 119:130 [118:130]; Proverbs 1:32).

New Testament Usage
Jesus praised God because the manifestations of the Kingdom's arrival were revealed to *nēpioi*, "babes, infants" (Matthew 11:25; Luke 10:21). This figurative use confirms that the point of contact of Jesus' mission was not in terms of a theological dialogue with religiosity or even in terms of a religious explanation. Rather, God's message of salvation comes to the naive and untrained, the lowly and despised, to those dispossessed by society and not by the "wise" of the world.

The naive condition of the *nēpios* often warrants instruction. Hence in Paul's writings it carries a negative nuance as a sign of spiritual immaturity (1 Corinthians 3:1; cf. 13:11; Romans 2:20; Ephesians 4:14). The writer of Hebrews made this same connection between being an "infant" and being spiritually immature (Hebrews 5:13). He particularly linked this to teaching on righteousness.

Nēpios is never used in reference to our status as "children" of God. The term used in that case is *teknon* (4891). The use in Galatians clarifies this point. Paul considered—in his larger image of sonship—that infancy (*nēpios*) is a condition of "slavery under the basic principles of the world" (Galatians 4:1,3).

STRONG 3516, BAUER 537, MOULTON-MILLIGAN 426, KITTEL 4:912-23, LIDDELL-SCOTT 1174, COLIN BROWN 1:280-82.

3379. Νηρεύς Nēreus name
Nereus.

1. **Νηρέα Nērea** acc masc

1 Salute Philologus, and Julia, **Nereus**, and his sister,	Rom 16:15

Recipient of a greeting from Paul (Romans 16:15).

3380. Νηρί Nēri name
Neri.

1. Νηρί Nēri masc

1 which was the son of Neri,........................ Luke 3:27

The son of Melchi in the genealogy of Jesus (Luke 3:27).

3381. νησίον nēsion noun
Small island, islet.
SYNONYM:
νῆσος nēsos (3382)

1. νησίον nēsion nom/acc sing neu

1 under a certain island which is called Clauda,...... Acts 27:16

Some have considered this noun to be the diminutive form of nēsos (3382), "island." Literally it denotes a "small island"; however, evidence suggests that it is no longer considered to be a diminutive (cf. *Bauer*), and therefore the two terms may be interchangeable. The latter term is found in the Scriptures only in Acts 27:16 where Clauda ("Cauda" in many early manuscripts) is named as the "certain island" (but more accurately, a "certain small island") below which Paul's ship sailed when it was caught in a storm on the way to Rome. Apparently, Luke's intention was to contrast the small size of this island with those referred to elsewhere in Acts, since he used nēsos in all six of his other references to islands. Clauda is the modern Gavdho, or Gaudos, just south of Crete, and is only about 5 miles across.

STRONG 3519, BAUER 538, LIDDELL-SCOTT 1174-75.

3382. νῆσος nēsos noun
Island, isle.
SYNONYM:
νησίον nēsion (3381)

אִי 'î (339), Isle, island (Ps 72:10 [71:10], Is 42:10); coastland (Ez 27:3,6f.).

1. νῆσος nēsos nom sing fem
2. νήσου nēsou gen sing fem
3. νήσῳ nēsō dat sing fem
4. νῆσον nēson acc sing fem

4 when they had gone through the isle unto Paphos,..Acts 13:6
4 Howbeit we must be cast upon a certain island........ 27:26
1 then they knew that the island was called Melita....Acts 28:1
2 possessions of the chief man of the island,............ 28:7
3 others also, which had diseases in the island,.......... 28:9
3 ship of Alexandria, which had wintered in the isle,.... 28:11
3 was in the isle that is called Patmos,................. Rev 1:9
1 and every mountain and island were moved............ 6:14
1 And every island fled away,........................ 16:20

Related to *neō* ("to swim"), *nēsos* ("floating land") is the common word for "island" or "isle" in nonbiblical and Septuagint Greek. Six of its nine New Testament uses occur in the Book of Acts, where it is used once for the island of Cyprus (13:6) and five times for Melita (Malta), the island on which Paul was shipwrecked (27:26; 28:1,7,9,11). The three other uses are in Revelation. John stated that he was on "the isle . . . called Patmos" at the time he received his vision and commission (1:9-11). In addition, he twice spoke of the "islands" being moved out of their places on the day of God's wrath (6:14) and at the judgment of "Babylon" (16:20).

STRONG 3520, BAUER 538, MOULTON-MILLIGAN 426, LIDDELL-SCOTT 1175.

3383. νηστεία nēsteia noun
Fasting, going without food, going hungry; starving.
COGNATE:
νηστεύω nēsteuō (3384)
SYNONYMS:
ἄσιτος asitos (771)
νῆστις nēstis (3385)

צוֹם tsôm (6948), A fast, fasting (2 Chr 20:3, Is 58:5, Jl 2:12).

1. νηστείᾳ nēsteia dat sing fem
2. νηστείαν nēsteian acc sing fem
3. νηστειῶν nēsteiōn gen pl fem
4. νηστείαις nēsteiais dat pl fem

1 this kind goeth not out but by prayer and fasting...Matt 17:21
1 come forth by nothing, but by prayer and fasting....Mark 9:29
4 served God with fastings and prayers night ... day...Luke 2:37
3 and had prayed with fasting,...................... Acts 14:23
2 dangerous, because the fast was now already past,..... 27:9
1 that ye may give yourselves to fasting and prayer;...1 Co 7:5
4 in tumults, in labours, in watchings, in fastings;..... 2 Co 6:5
4 in hunger and thirst, in fastings often,................ 11:27

Classical Greek
Related to the verb *nēsteuō* (3384), the noun *nēsteia* was used from ancient times for both voluntary and involuntary fasting, and for both religious and nonreligious fasting. In the Fifth and Fourth Centuries B.C. Hippocrates and Aristotle were using the term to refer to men who were hungry (or starving) for lack of food.

But even in pagan circles *nēsteia* was frequently used of religious fastings. In the religions of the Greeks and Romans, worshipers often fasted to prepare for mystical encounters with their gods or in expectation of some blessing or power from them. In fact, every October the Athenians had a fertility festival, Thesmophoria, during which one day was set aside for women to fast in order to be more receptive to the powers of fertility from the goddess Demeter. This day was named *Hē Nēsteia*, "The Fast" (see Rothenberg, "Fast," *Colin Brown*, 1:611f.; and Behm, "nēstis," *Kittel*, 4:926). Fasting was also a common practice when people would mourn the dead.

Septuagint Usage

Nēsteia is found over 20 times in the Septuagint, nearly always translating the regular Hebrew word for "fast" or "fasting," *tsôm*. The references are always to religious fasts of some sort. Interestingly, this noun form is never used in the Septuagint for the Day of Atonement, the only Jewish fast mandated by the Law, though it is regularly so used by later Jewish writers (*Bauer*). Rather, the word is primarily used of private fasts which sought the Lord's favor or deliverance (2 Samuel 12:16 [LXX 2 Kings 12:16]; 2 Chronicles 20:3; Psalms 35:13 [LXX 34:13]; 69:10 [68:10]; 109:24 [108:24]; Daniel 9:3) or of public fasts which sought God's favor (Ezra 8:21 [LXX 2 Esdras 8:21]; Nehemiah 9:1; Jeremiah 36:6 [LXX 43:6]) or His forgiveness (Joel 1:14; 2:12,15; Jonah 3:5) for a nation or group of people. These fasts were nearly always accompanied by prayer and were usually intended to demonstrate the sincerity of the people who prayed. But even fasts could be insincere, and God sometimes rejected Israel's fasts precisely because they were not from the heart (Isaiah 1:14; 58:3-6; Zechariah 7:5).

New Testament Usage

Five of the eight New Testament uses of *nēsteia* link fasting with prayer, continuing the Old Testament emphasis. However, many Greek manuscripts omit any reference to fasting in three of these passages (Matthew 17:21; Mark 9:29; 1 Corinthians 7:5). Even if they were later additions to the text, they do show that the early Christians saw fasting as a means of strengthening prayer. Luke, however, said that the elderly prophetess Anna served God in the temple "with *fastings* and prayers night and day" (Luke 2:37), and he described how Paul and Barnabas "prayed with *fasting*" when they ordained elders in the cities of Asia Minor (Acts 14:23). Reflecting the current Jewish usage (see Philo and Josephus; cf. *Bauer*), Luke also referred to the Day of Atonement as "the fast" (*hē nēsteia*) in Acts 27:9.

What may be the only nonreligious uses of *nēsteia* in the New Testament are the two found in 2 Corinthians. In both 6:5 and 11:27 Paul included "fasting" in the description of the harsh circumstances he endured as a minister of God. The phrase "in fastings" probably means that he had endured some periods with an empty stomach. It may be that this was not by choice but simply because he had no access to food. The phrase "in hunger and thirst" is also listed in the latter passage and may suggest that the "fastings" were more lengthy periods of food deprivations. Some think, however, that these "fastings" were periods when Paul would voluntarily forego his meals so as not to interrupt his work of ministry.

STRONG 3521, BAUER 538, KITTEL 4:924-35, LIDDELL-SCOTT 1175, COLIN BROWN 1:611-12.

3384. νηστεύω nēsteuō verb

To fast, abstain from food.

COGNATES:
νηστεία nēsteia (3383)
νῆστις nēstis (3385)

צוֹם tsûm (6947), Fast (2 Sm 12:22f., Neh 1:4, Zec 7:5).

קָרָא qāra' (7410), Call; proclaim (1 Kgs 21:9 [20:9]).

1. νηστεύω nēsteuō 1sing indic pres act
2. νηστεύομεν nēsteuomen 1pl indic pres act
3. νηστεύουσιν nēsteuousin 3pl indic pres act
4. νηστεύητε nēsteuēte 2pl subj pres act
5. νηστεύων nēsteuōn nom sing masc part pres act
6. νηστεύοντες nēsteuontes
    nom pl masc part pres act
7. νηστευόντων nēsteuontōn
    gen pl masc part pres act
8. νηστεύειν nēsteuein inf pres act
9. νηστεύσας nēsteusas nom sing masc part aor act
10. νηστεύσαντες nēsteusantes
    nom pl masc part aor act
11. νηστεύσουσιν nēsteusousin 3pl indic fut act
12. νηστεῦσαι nēsteusai inf aor act

9	when he **had fasted** forty days and forty nights,	Matt 4:2
4	Moreover when ye **fast**, be not, as the hypocrites,	6:16
6	that they may appear unto men to **fast**.	6:16
5	But thou, when **thou fastest**, anoint thine head,	6:17
5	That thou appear not unto men to **fast**,	6:18
2	Why do we and the Pharisees **fast** oft,	9:14
3	Why do we ... **fast** oft, but thy disciples **fast** not?	9:14
11	bridegroom ... from them, and then **shall they fast**.	9:15
6	disciples of John and of the Pharisees used to **fast**:	Mark 2:18
3	Why do the disciples of John and ... Pharisees **fast**,	2:18
3	the Pharisees **fast**, but thy disciples **fast** not?	2:18
8	Can the children of the bridechamber **fast**,	2:19

8 have the bridegroom with them, they cannot fast...	Mark 2:19
11 and then shall they fast in those days..................	2:20
3 Why do the disciples of John fast often,............	Luke 5:33
8 Can ye make the children of the bridechamber fast,....	5:34
11 and then shall they fast in those days..................	5:35
1 I fast twice in the week, I give tithes of all...........	18:12
5 Four days ago I was fasting until this hour;........	Acts 10:30
7 As they ministered to the Lord, and fasted,..........	13:2
10 And when they had fasted and prayed,................	13:3

Classical Greek and Septuagint Usage

The verb *nēsteuō* is a compound of the prefix *nē-* ("not") and *esthiō* (2052), "to eat," and means "to not eat, to fast." In the pagan religions of the Hellenistic world to fast demonstrated one's fear of evil spirits. Furthermore, fasting prepared one to encounter a deity. The link between fear and preparation for a meeting with a god, therefore, is direct. Fasting was also practiced widely in conjunction with death. It was believed that eating and drinking while the soul of the dead person was still near brought the risk of demonic infection (Rothenberg, "Fast," *Colin Brown*, 1:611).

Nēsteuō is used in the Septuagint 18 out of 21 times to translate the Hebrew term *tsûm*, "fasting." A fast might be total (both food and drink) or partial (perhaps only food). A total fast might last only a day (cf. 2 Samuel 1:12 [LXX 2 Kings 1:12]). If the period extended into several days it was usually only a partial fast (cf. Esther 4:16).

During Jesus' day fasting was a typical rite practiced by pious Judaism. Both public and private fasting were common. The Law prescribed only one national fast per year in connection with the Day of Atonement (cf. Leviticus 16:29). It is simply called "the fast" in Acts 27:9, a suggestion of its importance.

New Testament Usage

The New Testament records *nēsteuō* 21 times (cf. *nēsteia*), all of which occur in the Gospels and Acts. The normal translation is "to fast." John the Baptist taught his disciples to fast (Mark 2:18), but Jesus was questioned because His disciples did not. To this query Jesus responded that the guests of the bridegroom cannot mourn while the bridegroom is still with them. "But the days will come, when the bridegroom shall be taken from them, and then shall they *fast*" (Matthew 9:15). This same passage records the comment made by John's disciples concerning the Pharisees' "much" fasting (Matthew 9:14). According to tradition the Pharisees fasted twice a week, Mondays and Thursdays (Luke 18:12; cf. Behm, "nēstis," *Kittel*, 4:930). Jesus condemned their hypocritical attitude of fasting for the sake of being seen by others. The purpose of the fast was not to be seen by men but by God—in secret. Therefore, Jesus advised that those who fast anoint themselves and bathe and not give the appearance of fasting. A fast is not a public performance; rather, it is a private act of divine worship.

Jesus began His own public ministry with a 40-day "fast" in the desert (Matthew 4:2). The Early Church also associated "fasting" with prayer (Acts 13:3; 14:23). This was especially true prior to the selection and sending of missionaries and with the appointment of "elders in every church" (Acts 14:23).

A fast in keeping with Biblical guidelines always involves prayer. The aged widow Anna was in the temple fasting and praying "day and night" (Luke 2:37). Following his conversion Paul (Saul) fasted and prayed after being led to Damascus (Acts 9:9,11).

STRONG 3522, BAUER 538, MOULTON-MILLIGAN 426, KITTEL 4:924-35, LIDDELL-SCOTT 1175, COLIN BROWN 1:611-13.

3385. νῆστις nēstis adj

Fasting, going without food; having an empty stomach, hungry.

COGNATE:
νηστεύω nēsteuō (3384)

SYNONYMS:
ἄσιτος asitos (771)
νηστεία nēsteia (3383)

טְוָת tᵉwāth (A3018), Fasting (Dn 6:18—Aramaic).

1. νήστεις nēsteis acc pl masc

1 and I will not send them away **fasting**,.............	Matt 15:32
1 if I send them away **fasting** to their own houses,....	Mark 8:3

Like its kindred verb *nēsteuō* (3384) and noun *nēsteia* (3383), in classical Greek the noun *nēstis* suggests a period of going without food, whether for religious or nonreligious purposes, and whether voluntarily or involuntarily. Unlike the general usage of the verb and noun forms, however, *nēstis* is not used for voluntary religious fasting in the New Testament. Both its New Testament uses refer to the same occasion. Before Jesus fed the 4,000 He expressed His reluctance to send the multitude away "fasting" (Matthew 15:32; Mark 8:3). The crowd had chosen to stay with Jesus for 3 days rather than to go home and eat. Jesus, moved with compassion, did not want to send them away with empty stomachs for fear that they would faint from weakness before they could reach their homes.

STRONG 3523, BAUER 538, MOULTON-MILLIGAN 426, KITTEL 4:924-35, LIDDELL-SCOTT 1175, COLIN BROWN 1:611-13.

3386. νηφάλεος nēphaleos adj

Sober, drinking no wine; temperate, clearheaded.

COGNATE:
νήφω nēphō (3387)
SYNONYM:
σώφρων sōphrōn (4850)

1. **νηφαλίους** nēphalious acc pl masc/fem
2. **νηφάλιον** nēphalion acc sing masc
3. **νηφαλέους** nēphaleous acc pl masc
4. **νηφάλεον** nēphaleon acc sing masc

4 vigilant, **sober**, of good behaviour,	1 Tm 3:2
3 grave, not slanderers, **sober**, faithful in all things,	3:11
1 That the aged men be **sober**, grave, temperate,	Tit 2:2

Classical Greek

Like its related verb *nēphō* (3387), the adjective *nēphaleos* (*nēphalios* in some manuscripts) is used outside the New Testament in both the literal and figurative sense of "sober." Literally the term means "to be free of wine" and is first used of inanimate things, such as drinks in which there was no wine and even of piles of wood in which there were no grapevine twigs. When used of persons it sometimes describes those who totally abstained from wine, and thus was the opposite of "intoxicated." Figuratively it is used to describe one who was clearheaded—free from rash, confused, or fanatical thinking—so as to be capable of sound judgment. In general it refers to someone who avoided sins of excess and who was, therefore, "moderate" or "restrained." "Sober" is probably the nearest English equivalent of *nēphaleos*, since it retains both the literal and figurative connotations of the word. This term is not found in the Septuagint.

New Testament Usage

All three New Testament uses of *nēphaleos* occur in the Pastoral Epistles, and each occurrence is within a list of character qualities which Paul required from respected members of the church. In the list of qualifications for bishops (1 Timothy 3:2) the word is not so accurately translated "vigilant" ("sober" in this verse is a translation of *sōphrōn* [4850]). (Note: the NIV and RSV translation of *nēphalios* as "temperate" in 1 Timothy 3:2.) Later in the chapter (at verse 11) *nēphaleos* is translated "sober" in the list of qualifications for the deacons' "wives" (or, perhaps, "women" deacons). The final appearance of the word, in Titus 2:2, called for Titus to teach the older men of the Cretan congregations to be "sober." The figurative meaning of the word is no doubt dominant in these three uses, especially in the first—since "not given to wine" occurs as a later qualification for bishops—but the literal meaning is probably not to be excluded from any of them.

STRONG 3524, BAUER 538, MOULTON-MILLIGAN 426, KITTEL 4:939-41 (see "nēphalios"), LIDDELL-SCOTT 1175, COLIN BROWN 1:513-15 (see "nēphalios").

3387. νήφω nēphō verb

Be sober, temperate, be well balanced, self-controlled.

COGNATES:
ἀνανήφω ananēphō (365)
ἐκνήφω eknēphō (1581)
νηφάλεος nēphaleos (3386)
SYNONYM:
σωφρονέω sōphroneō (4845)

1. **νήφωμεν** nēphōmen 1pl subj pres act
2. **νῆφε** nēphe 2sing impr pres act
3. **νήφοντες** nēphontes nom pl masc part pres act
4. **νήψατε** nēpsate 2pl impr aor act

1 let us not sleep, ... but let us watch and be **sober**.	1 Th 5:6
1 But let us, who are of the day, be **sober**,	5:8
2 But **watch** thou in all things,	2 Tm 4:5
3 gird up the loins of your mind, be **sober**,	1 Pt 1:13
4 be ye therefore sober, and **watch** unto prayer.	4:7
4 Be sober, be vigilant; because your adversary	5:8

Classical Greek

The verb *nēphō* basically means "to be sober" (in both a figurative and literal sense) in classical Greek. In the strictest literal sense it means "drink no wine"; however, its figurative uses have a broader range of meaning. It can mean "to be free of confusion, wary" (*Liddell-Scott*), or "self-controlled" (such as the discipline involved in athletic practice, cf. *Bauer*). It is not found in any writings of the Septuagint.

New Testament Usage

Nēphō occurs in the New Testament in Paul's first letter to the Thessalonians, his second letter to Timothy, and in the First Epistle of Peter. Remarkably, both Paul and Peter use *nēphō* in a figurative sense and in eschatological contexts (ibid.). Paul admonished his readers to be spiritually "sober" and to watch in order that they not be taken by surprise by the coming of the Day of the Lord, which will come as a thief (1 Thessalonians 5:6,8). Likewise, in 2 Timothy 4:5 the admonition to spiritual "sound-mindedness" (NIV, "keep your head") occurs in a larger context of warning against those who in the last days will not accept sound teaching.

Peter used *nēphō* twice in an eschatological context and once in a warning against the devil who seeks to devour all he can (1 Peter 5:8). Peter urged his listeners to be "clearheaded" (NIV, "self-controlled") and to "set your hope fully on the grace to be given you when Jesus Christ is revealed" (1 Peter 1:13, NIV). Again in 1 Peter 4:7, in light of the imminent end of all things, Peter advised his readers to "be ye therefore sober, and *watch* unto prayer."

STRONG 3525, BAUER 538-39, MOULTON-MILLIGAN 426-27, KITTEL 4:936-39, LIDDELL-SCOTT 1175, COLIN BROWN 1:514-15.

3388. Νίγερ Niger name

Niger.

1. Νίγερ Niger masc

1 as Barnabas, and Simeon that was called **Niger**,.... Acts 13:1

Surname of Simeon the prophet and teacher in Antioch (Acts 13:1).

3389. Νικάνωρ Nikanōr name

Nicanor.

1. Νικάνορα Nikanora acc masc

1 Philip, and Prochorus, and **Nicanor**, and Timon,..... Acts 6:5

One of the seven men chosen to be deacons in the Jerusalem church (Acts 6:5).

3390. νικάω nikaō verb

Be victorious, prevail, conquer, overcome, win.
COGNATES:
νίκη nikē (3391)
νῖκος nikos (3396)
ὑπερνικάω hupernikaō (5083)
זָכָה zākhâh (2218), Be blameless (Ps 51:4 [50:4]).
חָמַד chāmadh (2629), Lust (Prv 6:25).
נָצַח nātsach (5514), Piel: director of music (Hb 3:19).

1. νικᾷ nika 3sing indic pres act
2. νίκα nika 2sing impr pres act
3. νικῶν nikōn nom sing masc part pres act
4. νικῶντι nikōnti dat sing masc part pres act
5. νικῶντας nikōntas acc pl masc part pres act
6. ἐνίκησα enikēsa 1sing indic aor act
7. ἐνίκησεν enikēsen 3sing indic aor act
8. ἐνίκησαν enikēsan 3pl indic aor act
9. νικήσῃς nikēsēs 2sing subj aor act
10. νικήσῃ nikēsē 3sing subj aor act
11. νικήσασα nikēsasa nom sing fem part aor act
12. νικῆσαι nikēsai inf aor act
13. νενίκηκα nenikēka 1sing indic perf act
14. νενικήκατε nenikēkate 2pl indic perf act
15. νικήσει nikēsei 3sing indic fut act
16. νικῶ nikō 2sing impr pres mid
17. νικήσεις nikēseis 2sing indic fut act

```
10  shall come upon him, and overcome him, ........ Luke 11:22
13  but be of good cheer; I have overcome the world. John 16:33
 9  and mightest overcome when thou art judged. ...... Rom 3:4
16  Be not overcome of evil, ............................ 12:21
 2  but overcome evil with good. ........................ 12:21
14  because ye have overcome the wicked one. ....... 1 Jn 2:13
14  and ye have overcome the wicked one. ............. 2:14
14  are of God, ... and have overcome them: ........... 4:4
 1  whatsoever is born of God overcometh the world: .... 5:4
11  and this is the victory that overcometh the world, .. 5:4
 3  Who is he that overcometh the world, ............. 5:5
 4  that overcometh will I give to eat of the tree of life, Rev 2:7
 3  He that overcometh shall not be hurt .............. 2:11
 4  To him that overcometh will I give to eat .......... 2:17
 3  overcometh, and keepeth my works unto the end, .... 2:26
 3  He that overcometh, the same shall be clothed ...... 3:5
 3  Him that overcometh will I make a pillar .......... 3:12
 3  To him that overcometh will I grant to sit with me ... 3:21
 6  sit with me in my throne, even as I also overcame, ... 3:21
 7  Root of David, hath prevailed to open the book, .... 5:5
 3  and he went forth conquering, and to conquer. ..... 6:2
10  and he went forth conquering, and to conquer. ..... 6:2
15  and shall overcome them, and kill them. ........... 11:7
 8  And they overcame him by the blood of the Lamb, ... 12:11
12  make war with the saints, and to overcome them: ... 13:7
 5  them that had gotten the victory over the beast, .... 15:2
15  make war ... and the Lamb shall overcome them: ... 17:14
 3  He that overcometh shall inherit all things; ....... 21:7
```

Classical Greek

The verb *nikaō*, "to conquer, to overcome," as well as its cognate nouns *nikē* (3391) and *nikos* (3396), "victory," occur in both classical Greek and Biblical Greek. It can be commonly found in reference to the "winning, prevailing" of military battles, athletic contests, and political or social causes (see examples in *Liddell-Scott*). Frequently there is an implicit sense of "vanquishing" the opposition in order to "succeed." This sense of "overpowering" can often be found in reference to human emotions, passions, and miseries (ibid.). In any case, the word does not refer to being "victorious" without first enduring a struggle.

Septuagint Usage

Within the Old Testament the two ideas converge—Israel must fight for its national identity as well as struggle to be (spiritually) God's people. The terms *nikaō/nikos* occur only 26 and 12 times respectively in the Septuagint, essentially in the apocryphal portions. Moreover, the Hebrew lacks any direct equivalent to "victory." In those texts discussing "victory" the Old Testament uses forms of the verb *yāshaʻ*, "to save, deliver" (the name Joshua [= Jesus/*Iēsous*] is from this word).

The battle/victory motif is found on several occasions in both the Old and New Testaments. Practically all of salvation history is presented in Scripture as a struggle or war between God and the enemy in an effort to redeem lost creation and to "conquer" (*nikaō*) the powers of evil.

Old Testament Background

The background of the Biblical battle/victory motif is free of any of the influence of Hellenistic dualism. Furthermore, Scripture contains no myths of an evil force or power of a slightly less than divine character; there is no cosmological dualism such as one finds in Gnosticism. The Biblical creation story excludes by its nature the possibility of holding to a dualistic position. Revelation history as disclosed by the prophets knows no "anti-god" who wages war against the Lord God.

The Biblical battle/victory motif is based upon the concept that a rebellion has taken place within God's creation. The instigators of this revolt were God's own creatures. The rebellion began in the angelic realm, where Satan, a "prince" of the angels, enticed the angels to sin and to reject the authority of God (Jude 6; cf. 2 Peter 2:4). Satan also seduced mankind to join this rebellion (Genesis 3:11ff.) with the false promise "ye shall be as gods" (Genesis 3:5). When man desired to become "like God" he rejected the relationship God had planned for him.

The theme of victory in both the Old and New Testaments is governed by the idea that God is the sovereign and unconquerable Lord of His creation (Psalm 2:2-4). Through the sending of His Son, God will reestablish and demonstrate His dominion. He will crush creation's rebellion against Him. This occurs in part through the overcoming grace of Christ that atones for our sins and redeems us. It moreover results from His "triumphant" judgment at the manifestation of His power when He returns.

Throughout the Old Testament the Biblical discussion of "victory" largely centers around the external victories God won for His people on the battlefield. Here the "Day of the Lord" in a unique sense captures the heart of the battle/victory motif.

New Testament Usage

Through Christ, creation is restored to its original order (Romans 5:12-21; Ephesians 1:10; Colossians 1:20). Within this "new creation"—as Paul often said—everyone and everything will be subordinate to Christ, the "head" of all things (1 Corinthians 11:3; Ephesians 1:22,23; 4:15). God reconciles to himself all things in Christ, "whether they be things in earth, or things in heaven" (Colossians 1:20). Through Christ the presently divided creation will be united (Ephesians 1:10).

Scripture makes the outcome of the "battle" plain from the outset. A promise of victory is made on the same day as the Fall (Genesis 3:15). The battle is not between equals. The Lord God reveals His superior almighty power as He negates the power of sin and crushes Satan's rebellion. Far from regarding the devil as a "coequal" opponent of God, the Scriptures testify that Satan is simply a cowardly creature who trembles at the thought of the inevitable judgment to come (cf. Matthew 8:29; James 2:19).

But while victory is assured, the struggle is marked by violence, and the eternal destiny of each individual hangs in the balance. The power and seduction of sin are so great that many will succumb to its ploys; these are doomed to eternal punishment. Only a relatively few, however, will find the way to life (Matthew 7:13,14). The price is high for the one choosing to enter the narrow door (Luke 13:24).

The battle Christ waged with the "Prince of Darkness" was a real struggle. Christ conquered the "strong one," and He rescued humanity which had fallen into Satan's power. By "overcoming" death Christ in effect destroyed the one who had the power of death (Hebrews 2:14). Christ's victory on the cross was not merely a display of power, He secured a moral victory over the entire principle of sin. He "disarmed the powers and authorities, (and) he made a public spectacle of them, triumphing over them by the cross" (Colossians 2:15, NIV). In addition, as a result of Christ's victory on the cross, sin will have no part in eternity.

The discussion in the New Testament, however, is primarily focused upon God's victory over Satan and his evil forces (John 12:31; 1 Corinthians 15; Ephesians 6:11ff.; Colossians 2:15). These spiritual forces, nonetheless, are "incarnate" in those forces in the world that are anti-Christian, especially in the figures of the Antichrist, the beast, and the lawless one (2 Thessalonians 2:8; Revelation 19:15ff.).

The believer will share in the spoils of the Lord's victory. They are more than conquerors over the difficulties of life (Romans 8:37)—even in death (1 Corinthians 15:57)! Everyone who is born of God will overcome (*nikaō*) the world (1 John 5:4). The greatest promises are given to those who "overcome" (Revelation 2:7,11,17,26; 3:5,12,21; 21:7). This victory is won by faith (1 John 5:4) and by virtue of the "blood of the Lamb and the word of their (believers') testimony" (Revelation 12:11).

The Christian's victory is both present now and coming in the future. He may have personal victory over sin and sinful desires in this life (Romans 6:12,14; Galatians 5:16), but the New Testament also speaks of a final victory in which believers will participate. This ultimate victory occurs at the end-time coming of God's kingdom. It is the realization of the messianic promises of the Old Testament. It is the fulfillment of end-time prophecies made by the New Testament (e.g., Revelation, chapters 19–21). The miracles wrought by Jesus, His healing of the sick and the casting out of evil spirits, were signs and portents of the final victory (Mark 1:24; 5:7). Christ has already won the victory on the cross; the effects of this triumph, however, will not be fully realized until His return in glory (Revelation 20).

STRONG 3528, BAUER 539, MOULTON-MILLIGAN 427, KITTEL 4:942-45, LIDDELL-SCOTT 1176, COLIN BROWN 1:650,652.

Classical Greek

The word *nikē* (related to the noun, *nikos* [3396], and verb, *nikaō* [3390]) occurs often in secular Greek literature with applications ranging from superiority in any form of human rivalry, to the conquering and vanquishing of a foe in battle (*Liddell-Scott*). Some of the earliest expressions of facial happiness and bodily motion in Greek sculpture use the figure of the goddess of victory named *Nikē*—a winged figure with arms uplifted in the joyous celebration of triumph.

Septuagint Usage

In Biblical usage the focus of the word group is narrowed to victory over enemies, and victory is recognized as coming from God. In the Septuagint the battles are not won by the superiority of Israel's army but by God giving the enemy into their hands (Judges 7; 1 Chronicles 29:11).

New Testament Usage

In the New Testament the related verb *nikaō* occurs in the Gospels in the Parable of the Strong Man (Luke 11:22), showing our Lord's superiority over demonic power. In Romans (8:37; 12:21) the believers are victorious through Him. In 1 Corinthians 15 victory ultimately over even death is "given" by God to the Christian (verses 54-57; using *nikos*). In Revelation the ones overcoming (*nikōn* or *nikōnti*) through Christ will stand with Him in the final victory.

The only occurrence of the noun *nikē* in the New Testament is in 1 John 5:4. The power for personal "victory" over the evil forces of this world comes through faith in Christ Jesus.

STRONG 3529, BAUER 539, MOULTON-MILLIGAN 427, KITTEL 4:942-45, LIDDELL-SCOTT 1176, COLIN BROWN 1:650-51.

3391. νίκη nikē noun

Victory.

COGNATE:
νικάω nikaō (3390)

SYNONYM:
νῖκος nikos (3396)

נֶצַח nētsach (5516I), Victory (1 Chr 29:11—Codex Vaticanus only).

1. νίκη nikē nom sing fem

1 and this is the **victory** that overcometh the world, ... 1 Jn 5:4

3392. Νικόδημος Nikodēmos name

Nicodemus.

1. Νικόδημος Nikodēmos nom masc

1 a man of the Pharisees, named **Nicodemus**,	John 3:1
1 **Nicodemus** saith unto him,	3:4
1 **Nicodemus** answered and said unto him,	3:9
1 **Nicodemus** saith unto them,	7:50
1 And there came also **Nicodemus**,	19:39

Pharisee who visited Jesus at night (John 3:1ff.); he defended Jesus before the Pharisees and brought spices for Jesus' burial (John 7:50; 19:39).

3393. Νικολαΐτης Nikolaitēs name
Nicolaitan, follower of the sect of Nicolaus.

1. Νικολαϊτῶν Nikolaitōn gen pl masc

1 that thou hatest the deeds of the **Nicolaitanes**, ... Rev 2:6
1 them that hold the doctrine of the **Nicolaitanes**, ... 2:15

The Nicolaitans were a sect in the Early Church mentioned in the New Testament only in Revelation 2:6 and 15. While the letter to the church at Ephesus commended the Ephesians because they "hate(d) the deeds of the Nicolaitans," the letter to the church at Pergamos indicates they had within their community adherents to "the doctrine of the Nicolaitans."

Little is known of a certainty about this group. According to some of the apologists of the Post-Apostolic Church (most notably Clement of Alexandria and Irenaeus), the Nicolaitans were a Gnostic sect that traced its origins to "Nicolas of Antioch," one of the seven Hellenists chosen to oversee the "distribution" to the widows and orphans of the Jerusalem church (Acts 6:5). Although this argument draws indirect support from the fact that the Early Church tended to enhance the image of people mentioned in the New Testament rather than vilify them (see Donaldson, "Nicolaitans," *International Standard Bible Encyclopedia*, 3:533f.), most scholars now reject the view that there was any connection between this person and the later sect (as Donaldson finally concludes; cf. also Beck, "Nicolaitans," *Interpreter's Dictionary of the Bible*, 3:548). It seems there is a growing consensus that there may be no connection between the Nicolaitan sect mentioned in Revelation and the later Gnostic group of the same name.

An alternative explanation for the origin of the name of this sect is that it is a symbolic wordplay linked etymologically to the name "Balaam" (mentioned in Revelation 2:14). According to Thayer "Balaam" is seen as a derivative of the Hebrew *bālaʿ ʿam*, "destroyer of the people," whereas the Greek "Nicolas" derives from *nikos laos*, "conqueror of the people" (*Greek-English Lexicon*). There is widespread agreement that the "doctrine of Balaam ... to eat things sacrificed unto idols, and to commit fornication" (Revelation 2:14) is being presented here as the content of the "doctrine of the Nicolaitans," which already provides a link between "Balaam" and "Nicolaitan." Additionally, the symbolic name "Jezebel" is applied to a prophetess who was apparently preaching the same doctrine in the church at Thyatira (Revelation 2:20). If this symbolic explanation of the name is rejected as being overly speculative (as it is by many modern scholars; cf. Beck, *Interpreter's Dictionary of the Bible*, 3:548), then all that can be said is that the sect draws its name from an otherwise unknown Nicolaus (cf. *Oxford Dictionary of the Christian Church*, "Nicolaitians").

It has already been mentioned that the Nicolaitans in the Book of Revelation are probably not to be identified directly with the later Gnostic sect of this name. Apparently the group mentioned in Revelation was an antinomian sect who felt that Christian freedom permitted participation in aspects of Hellenistic society that involved eating food which had been offered to idols and participating in sexual immorality, even though both activities had been prohibited to Gentile Christians by the "Jerusalem Council" (Acts 15:28f.). The antinomian groups identified as "followers of Balaam" in 2 Peter 2:15 and Jude 11 may or may not be related to the Nicolaitans in Revelation 2 (see Donaldson, "Nicolatians," *International Standard Bible Encyclopedia*, 3:534 and Hemer, *The Letters to the Seven Churches*, pp.87-94).

STRONG 3531, BAUER 539, MOULTON-MILLIGAN 427, COLIN BROWN 2:676.

3394. Νικόλαος Nikolaos name
Nicolas.

1. Νικόλαον Nikolaon acc masc

1 and Parmenas, and **Nicolas** a proselyte of Antioch: .. Acts 6:5

Antiochian proselyte chosen to be a deacon in the Jerusalem church (Acts 6:5).

3395. Νικόπολις Nikopolis name
Nicopolis.

1. Νικοπόλεως Nikopoleōs gen fem
2. Νικόπολιν Nikopolin acc fem

2 be diligent to come unto me to **Nicopolis**: .... Tit 3:12

City on the western shore of Greece where Paul lodged for the winter (Titus 3:12).

3396. νῖκος nikos noun
Victory, conquest.

COGNATE:
νικάω nikaō (3390)
SYNONYM:
νίκη nikē (3391)

נֵצַח netsach (5516II) Forever, continually (2 Sm 2:26, Am 1:11); strength (Lam 3:18).

1. νῖκος nikos nom/acc sing neu

1 till he send forth judgment unto **victory**............	Matt 12:20
1 that is written, Death is swallowed up in **victory**....	1 Co 15:54
1 "Where, O death, is your **victory**? (NIV)..............	15:55
1 O grave, where is thy **victory**?........................	15:55
1 which giveth us the **victory** through our Lord Jesus....	15:57

Septuagint Usage

Though *nikē* (3391) is the common Greek word for "victory" in classical Greek, there is a preference for its later form and related term *nikos* in the Septuagint and in the New Testament (cf. *Liddell-Scott*). In the Septuagint *nikos* usually translates the Hebrew term *netsach*, "endurance, everlastingness." Second Samuel 2:26 (LXX 2 Kings 2:26) uses the phrase *eis nikos* (Hebrew, *lānetsach*), meaning "forever" (cf. Job 36:7; Amos 1:11). In Lamentations 3:18 Jeremiah spoke of how his "success, strength" (or "endurance of life") had vanished. When this idea is used as an attribute of God it means His "glory" (cf. 1 Chronicles 29:11, uses *nikē* in some manuscripts).

New Testament Usage

Three of the New Testament uses of *nikos* occur in quotations from the Old Testament; however, the Septuagint does not use *nikos* in any of these passages quoted.

Matthew 12:20 cites Isaiah's (42:3) prophecy about God's "Servant," Jesus, who would gently save men and "bring forth judgment unto truth." In Matthew, "unto *victory*" (*nikos*) is substituted for "unto truth," presumably drawing this thought from Isaiah's next verse (4), that the Lord "shall not fail" till His justice has triumphed forever.

The other three uses of *nikos* are in 1 Corinthians 15, where Paul saw the ultimate conquest of death. The future resurrection and immortality of Christians prove with surety that "Death is swallowed up in *victory*" (verse 54), and that God "giveth us the *victory* through our Lord Jesus Christ" (verse 57). So Paul challenged: "O grave, where is thy *victory*?" (verse 55). Verse 54 reflects the Hebrew of Isaiah 25:8, where *lānetsach* means "forever" in the sense of eternal "victory." First Corinthians 15:55 is taken from the Septuagint of Hosea 13:14 which reads, "Death, where is thy penalty? Hades, where is thy sting?" Paul, by substituting "victory" (*nikos*) for "penalty" (*dikē* [1343]), was again giving the meaning of the passage with accuracy (i.e., eternal outcome), though he was not citing it verbatim.

STRONG 3534, BAUER 539, KITTEL 4:942-45, LIDDELL-SCOTT 1176, COLIN BROWN 1:650.

3397. Νινευί Nineui name

Nineveh.

1. Νινευί Nineui fem
2. Νινευή Nineuē fem

1 The men of **Nineve** shall rise up in the judgment... Luke 11:32

Capital city of Assyria; the repentance of its citizens will condemn the unbelievers of Jesus' day (Luke 11:32).

3398. Νινευίτης Nineuitēs name

Ninevite.

1. Νινευῖται Nineuitai nom pl masc
2. Νινευίταις Nineuitais dat pl masc

1 The men of **Nineveh** shall rise in judgment.........	Matt 12:41
2 For as Jonas was a sign unto the **Ninevites**,.........	Luke 11:30

Resident of Nineveh (Matthew 12:41).

3399. νιπτήρ niptēr noun

Washbasin, washing vessel, basin.
CROSS-REFERENCE:
νίπτω niptō (3400)

1. νιπτῆρα niptēra acc sing masc

1 After that he poureth water into a **basin**,.......... John 13:5

In the New Testament *niptēr* is found only in John 13:5 where Jesus, while in the Upper Room on the eve of His death, poured water "into a *basin*" and washed the disciples' feet. Though derived from a common Greek verb—*niptō* (3400), the word for "wash" in verse 5—the noun *niptēr* is rare in Greek and Biblical literature.

This "washbasin" was likely one of the two vessels that had been made available for footwashing purposes by the master of the house. One early manuscript reads *podoniptēr*, "washbasin for feet," rather than *niptēr*, "washbasin." Jesus probably poured water from a pitcher over the feet of the apostles, rubbing the dust from their feet as He caught the water

νίπτω 3400

in this "basin" placed below. By performing this task which was normally reserved for low-ranking slaves, Jesus taught His disciples the greatness which is shown in humble service of others. Some suggest that in addition to modeling the humility Jesus expected His disciples to follow, He was also demonstrating a symbolic prophecy of the cleansing from sin made possible by His atoning death (see Opperwall, "Foot Washing," *International Standard Bible Encyclopedia*, 2:333).

STRONG 3537, BAUER 540, LIDDELL-SCOTT 1177.

3400. νίπτω niptō verb
Wash.

COGNATES:
- ἄνιπτος aniptos (447)
- ἀπονίπτω aponiptō (627)
- νιπτήρ niptēr (3399)

SYNONYMS:
- ἀπολούω apolouō (622)
- ἀπονίπτω aponiptō (627)
- ἀποπλύνω apoplunō (631)
- βαπτίζω baptizō (901)
- λούω louō (3040)
- πλύνω plunō (4010)

מָטָר māṯar (4442), Hiphil: rain (Jb 20:23).

רָחַץ rāchats (7647), Wash (Ex 30:19ff., 2 Chr 4:6, Ps 58:10 [57:10]).

שָׁטַף shāṯaph (8278), Qal: rinse (Lv 15:11); niphal: be rinsed (Lv 15:12).

1. **νίπτεις** nipteis 2sing indic pres act
2. **νίπτειν** niptein inf pres act
3. **ἔνιψα** enipsa 1sing indic aor act
4. **ἔνιψεν** enipsen 3sing indic aor act
5. **νίψω** nipsō 1sing subj aor act
6. **νίψῃς** nipsēs 2sing subj aor act
7. **νίπτονται** niptontai 3pl indic pres mid
8. **ἐνιψάμην** enipsamēn 1sing indic aor mid
9. **ἐνίψατο** enipsato 3sing indic aor mid
10. **νίψωνται** nipsōntai 3pl subj aor mid
11. **νίψαι** nipsai 2sing impr aor mid
12. **νιψάμενος** nipsamenos nom sing masc part aor mid
13. **νίψασθαι** nipsasthai inf aor mid

11	anoint thine head, and **wash** thy face;	Matt 6:17
7	for **they wash** not their hands when they eat bread.	15:2
10	except **they wash** their hands oft, eat not,	Mark 7:3
11	**wash** in the pool of Siloam,	John 9:7
9	and **washed**, and came seeing.	9:7
11	Go to the pool of Siloam, and **wash:**	9:11
12	and I went and **washed**, and I received sight.	9:11
8	clay upon mine eyes, and I **washed**, and do see.	9:15
2	and began **to wash** the disciples' feet,	13:5
1	Peter saith ... Lord, dost thou **wash** my feet?	13:6
6	Peter saith ... Thou **shalt** never **wash** my feet.	13:8
5	If I **wash** thee not, thou hast no part with me.	13:8
13	He that is washed needeth not save **to wash** his feet,	John 13:10
4	So after he **had washed** their feet,	13:12
3	I ... your Lord and Master, have **washed** your feet;	13:14
2	ye also ought **to wash** one another's feet.	13:14
4	if she **have washed** the saints' feet,	1 Tm 5:10

Classical Greek
Niptō is a variation of the verb *nizō* ("wash"). In classical Greek *nizō* commonly is used of washing parts of the body, such as hands and feet. It occasionally describes purging or cleansing (cf. *Liddell-Scott*).

Septuagint Usage
In the Septuagint *niptō* is used frequently for washing hands, feet, or face, and occasionally for rinsing. It is particularly used of the need for the high priest Aaron "to wash" in the water of the laver in the tabernacle (Exodus 30:18-21; cf. 40:31). It describes "rinsing" something with water, but even this can have religious significance (Leviticus 15:11,12). Washing one's hands can also be a symbolic gesture of innocence (Deuteronomy 21:6; cf. Psalms 26:6 [LXX 25:6]; 58:10 [57:10]; 73:13 [72:13]; Matthew 27:24).

New Testament Usage
In the New Testament *niptō* is used of washing parts of the body such as face, hands, feet, and eyes. A blind man washed his eyes after Jesus put clay on them for healing (John 9:7,11,15). The face was washed as part of the daily hygienic practice (Matthew 6:17). The hands were washed before eating as part of the ritual cleansing of Jewish tradition (Matthew 15:2; Mark 7:3). The feet were washed as part of Jewish custom for refreshing and cleansing after travel (John 13:5,6,8,10,12,14); the washing was usually done by a household servant. Jesus used foot washing as a striking example of the humble service Christians should render to one another (John 13:14). (Much has been written about the significance of "foot washing"; cf. Opperwall, "Foot Washing," *International Standard Bible Encyclopedia*, 2:333.) Because people wore open sandals on dusty roads, foot washing was a common courtesy provided for travelers by their host (cf. Genesis 18:4; 19:2; Judges 19:21). It was considered a menial task, even for a servant (cf. Mark 1:7). Jesus commended the woman who washed His feet with her tears and anointed them with nard; the host failed to be as gracious (Luke 7:36-50). Besides Jesus, there is only one other specific reference to foot washing made in the New Testament. In 1 Timothy 5:10 Paul said that a widow must "*have washed* the saints' feet."

This implies that accommodating travelers (i.e., for the sake of spreading the gospel) was one of the tasks of widows who were to be supported by the church. This simple practice of hospitality and humility eventually became a rite of the Early Church (ibid.).

STRONG 3538, BAUER 540, MOULTON-MILLIGAN 427, KITTEL 4:946-47, LIDDELL-SCOTT 1177, COLIN BROWN 1:153-54.

3401. νοέω noeō verb

Perceive, understand, realize, see, consider, take note of, think over.

COGNATES:
 ἄνοια anoia (452)
 διανόημα dianoēma (1264)
 διάνοια dianoia (1265)
 δυσνόητος dusnoētos (1418)
 ἔννοια ennoia (1755)
 ἐπίνοια epinoia (1948)
 εὐνοέω eunoeō (2113)
 εὔνοια eunoia (2114)
 κατανοέω katanoeō (2627)
 μετανοέω metanoeō (3210)
 νόημα noēma (3402)
 νουθετέω noutheteō (3423)
 νοῦς nous (3426)
 προνοέω pronoeō (4165)
 ὑπονοέω huponoeō (5120)
 ὑπόνοια huponoia (5121)

SYNONYMS:
 αἰσθάνομαι aisthanomai (143)
 ἀναλογίζω analogizō (355)
 βλέπω blepō (984)
 βουλεύομαι bouleuomai (1003)
 γινώσκω ginōskō (1091)
 διαλογίζομαι dialogizomai (1254)
 δοκέω dokeō (1374)
 εἶδον eidon (1481)
 ἐνθυμέομαι enthumeomai (1744)
 ἐπιβλέπω epiblepō (1899)
 ἐπιγινώσκω epiginōskō (1906)
 ἐπίσταμαι epistamai (1971)
 ἔχω echō (2174)
 ἡγέομαι hēgeomai (2216)
 θεωρέω theōreō (2311)
 καταλαμβάνω katalambanō (2608)
 κατανοέω katanoeō (2627)
 κρίνω krinō (2892)
 λογίζομαι logizomai (3023)
 νομίζω nomizō (3406)
 οἶδα oida (3471)
 οἴομαι oiomai (3496)
 ὁράω horaō (3571)
 παρακολουθέω parakoloutheō (3738)
 συμβάλλω sumballō (4671)
 συμβουλεύω sumbouleuō (4674)
 συνίημι suniēmi (4770)
 ὑπολαμβάνω hupolambanō (5112)
 ὑπονοέω huponoeō (5120)
 φρονέω phroneō (5262)

בִּין bîn (1032), Qal: perceive, understand (2 Sm 12:19, Prv 19:25, 29:19); hiphil: understand, learn (Prv 1:2, 8:5); hithpolel: observe (Jer 2:10).

עָשָׂה 'āsâh (6449), Do; be busy (Is 32:6).

שִׂים sîm (7947), Set, put, lay; consider (Is 47:7).

שָׂכַל sākhal (7959), Hiphil: teach, understand (Prv 16:23, Is 44:18); prosper (Jer 20:11).

שָׁחַת shāchath (8271), Hiphil: batter (2 Sm 20:15).

שִׁית shîth (8308), Put, set; pay attention (1 Sm 4:20).

1. **νοοῦμεν** nooumen 1pl indic pres act
2. **νοεῖτε** noeite 2pl indic pres act
3. **νόει** noei 2sing impr pres act
4. **νοείτω** noeitō 3sing impr pres act
5. **νοοῦντες** noountes nom pl masc part pres act
6. **νοήσωσιν** noēsōsin 3pl subj aor act
7. **νοῆσαι** noēsai inf aor act
8. **νοούμενα** nooumena nom/acc pl neu part pres mid

2	Do not ye yet **understand**,	Matt 15:17
2	Do ye not yet **understand**, neither remember	16:9
2	How is it that ye do not **understand**	16:11
4	whoso readeth, let him **understand**:	24:15
2	without understanding also? Do ye not **perceive**,	Mark 7:18
2	**perceive** ye not yet, neither understand?	8:17
4	let him that readeth **understand**,	13:14
6	nor **understand** with their heart, and be converted,	John 12:40
8	being **understood** by the things that are made,	Rom 1:20
7	**understand** my knowledge in the mystery of Christ	Eph 3:4
1	abundantly above all that we ask or **think**,	3:20
5	**understanding** neither what they say,	1 Tm 1:7
3	**Consider** what I say;	2 Tm 2:7
1	Through faith we **understand**	Heb 11:3

Classical Greek

Noeō broadly means "to perceive, to observe (with the eyes)" (*Liddell-Scott*). Essentially it involves the intellectual perception resulting from sight; it does not simply refer to someone's physical sight. Gradually it lost this association with visual perception altogether and came to mean "to understand." Another primary definition is "to think, suppose" and from that "to plan, to conceive" (ibid.). The noun related to *noeō* is *nous* (3426), "mind," an important philosophical/religious term in antiquity.

Septuagint Usage

The translators of the Septuagint selected *noeō* to translate six Hebrew words. The term's relation to mental understanding is apparent because it translates *bîn*, "to understand, to perceive, to realize," in 14 out of 24 occurrences having a Hebrew original (e.g., 2 Samuel 12:19 [LXX 2 Kings 12:19]; Job 15:9). *Noeō* is a popular word in the Wisdom literature of Proverbs. The purpose of Proverbs is, in fact, "for understanding words of insight" (1:2; cf. 1:3,6). At times *noeō* carries a hint of spiritual perception or faithfulness (Proverbs 28:5; 29:7;

Jeremiah 10:21; cf. Wisdom of Solomon 4:15, RSV). Otherwise, nonreligious usages are also attested (e.g., Jeremiah 2:10; 4 Maccabees 4:7).

New Testament Usage

The New Testament uses *noeō* in its common sense of "to realize, to see" (Matthew 15:17; Ephesians 3:20; 1 Timothy 1:7); however, this ability "to perceive" especially involves understanding the nature of Jesus' ministry (Matthew 16:9,11; Mark 8:17). Both Matthew and Mark include the curious explanatory remark, "Let the reader *understand* (*noeō*)" (Matthew 24:15; Mark 13:14). Here some measure of end-time insight may be expected.

A figurative location of spiritual understanding is the "heart" (John 12:40; cf. the Old Testament concept of 1 Samuel 4:20; Job 33:23; Isaiah 32:6; 44:18; 47:7). Paul argued that even the spiritual reality of "God's invisible qualities . . . have been clearly seen, being *understood* (*noeō*) from what has been made . . . " (Romans 1:20, NIV; cf. Hebrew 11:3, NIV, "by faith we *understand*"). Paul desired that his readers "understand" his knowledge by revelation of the "mystery of Christ"; that is, the Gentiles can become coheirs in the kingdom of God by faith (Ephesians 3:4). Paul also instructed Timothy to give consideration to all Paul said and wrote to him so that the Lord might give him "*understanding* in all things" (2 Timothy 2:7).

Strong 3539, Bauer 540, Moulton-Milligan 427-28, Kittel 4:948-51, Liddell-Scott 1177-78, Colin Brown 3:122-29,132-33.

3402. νόημα noēma noun

Mind, thought, device, purpose.

Cognate:
νοέω noeō (3401)

Synonyms:
γνώμη gnōmē (1100)
διαλογισμός dialogismos (1255)
διανόημα dianoēma (1264)
διάνοια dianoia (1265)
ἐνθύμησις enthumēsis (1745)
ἔννοια ennoia (1755)
ἐπίνοια epinoia (1948)
λογισμός logismos (3027)
νοῦς nous (3426)

1. νόημα noēma nom/acc sing neu
2. νοήματα noēmata nom/acc pl neu

2 for we are not ignorant of his **devices**............ 2 Co 2:11
2 But their **minds** were blinded:........................ 3:14
2 hath blinded the **minds** of them which believe not,...... 4:4
1 and bringing into captivity every **thought**.......... 2 Co 10:5
2 so your **minds** should be corrupted................... 11:3
2 shall keep your hearts and **minds** through Christ.....Phlp 4:7

Classical Greek and Septuagint Usage

In classical Greek *noēma* is used commonly of the activity of the mind and means "perception, thought, concept, purpose, idea, design." At times it refers to the mind itself as that which thinks. In the literature of philosophy *noēma* emphasizes thought as opposed to sensation. In the literature of rhetoric it emphasizes thought as expressed in literary form (see *Liddell-Scott*). In the Septuagint *noēma* occurs only three times in the Apocrypha, always of an "evil plan" (Sirach 21:11; Baruch 2:8; 3 Maccabees 5:30).

New Testament Usage

In the New Testament *noēma* was used only by the apostle Paul. Four times it refers to the mind: the minds of Jews that are hardened by unbelief (2 Corinthians 3:14); the minds of the lost that are blinded by Satan (2 Corinthians 4:4); the minds of Christians that may be "corrupted from the simplicity that is in Christ" (2 Corinthians 11:3); and the minds of Christians that are kept by the peace of God (Philippians 4:7). On one occasion *noēma* refers to the thoughts of Christians that should be brought into the obedience of Christ (2 Corinthians 10:5), and in another occurrence it refers to the "devices" (schemes, plots) of Satan by which he takes advantage of people (2 Corinthians 2:11).

Strong 3540, Bauer 540, Moulton-Milligan 428, Kittel 4:960-61, Liddell-Scott 1178-79, Colin Brown 3:122-25,128.

3403. νόθος nothos adj

Illegitimate child, bastard; baseborn, poorly bred; not genuine, counterfeit.

1. νόθοι nothoi nom pl masc

1 then are ye **bastards**, and not sons................ Heb 12:8

Classical Greek

In classical Greek literature *nothos* refers to a child that was born either illegitimately, i.e., out of wedlock, or as the child of a slave or concubine. It is also used in nonbiblical Greek writings for poorly bred persons, animals, or plants. Athenian writers sometimes used the term to describe someone whose mother or father was not an Athenian citizen (cf. *Liddell-Scott*). It can also denote persons, writings, or things which were "not genuine," i.e., "counterfeit." Its opposites are *eugenēs* (2083) and *gnēsios* (1097), "well-born, legitimate." Its only use in the Septuagint is in the apocryphal Wisdom of Solomon (4:3) where it refers to an "illegitimate child."

New Testament Usage
The only canonical use of *nothos* in Biblical writings is in Hebrews 12:8 where those who are not disciplined by the Lord are said to be "illegitimate children and not true sons" (NIV). ("Bastard" [KJV] was a more acceptable term in the days of King James than it is now.) Here the word is not used in its primary sense but in the secondary sense of "not genuine." Following the thought of Proverbs 3:11 and 12—that God chastens those He loves, just as does any father who genuinely loves his son—Hebrews stresses that such discipline from the Lord proves a person to be genuinely a child of God.

STRONG 3541, BAUER 540-41, MOULTON-MILLIGAN 428, LIDDELL-SCOTT 1178, COLIN BROWN 1:187-88.

3405. νομή nomē noun
Pasture, spreading.
CROSS-REFERENCE:
νόμος nomos (3414)

מַרְבֵּץ marbēts (4931), Lair (Zep 2:15 [3:1]).

מִרְעֶה mirʿeh (4992), Pasture (Gn 47:4, 1 Chr 4:41, Ez 34:18).

מַרְעִית marʿîth (4993), Pasture (Ps 95:7 [94:7], Is 49:9, Hos 13:6).

נָוֶה nāweh (5295), Pasture, habitation (Jer 23:3, 50:7,19 [27:7,19]).

נָוָה nāwāh (5297), Pasture, fold (Jer 23:10, Am 1:2, Zep 2:6).

1. νομήν nomēn acc sing fem

1 and shall go in and out, and find **pasture**......... John 10:9
1 And their word will eat as doth a canker:......... 2 Tm 2:17

Classical Greek
In classical Greek *nomē* denotes "pasturage," the food obtained by cattle from grazing in a pasture. Also it denotes the "feeding" or "grazing" of the cattle in a pasture. Figuratively it means "spreading out," as of cattle dispersing in a field, and then of "spreading" in general, as of a disease. In addition, *nomē* speaks of "division" or "distribution," and in legal documents it means "possession."

Septuagint Usage
Nomē translates three Hebrew terms in the Septuagint, most often a form of either *mirʿeh* or *nāwāh*, both meaning "pasture" (e.g., cf. Genesis 47:4 and Jeremiah 23:3, NIV). Figuratively, the earth is the "pasture" of God who is the Shepherd of His people ("flock") (e.g., Psalms 74:1 [LXX 73:1]; 79:13 [78:13]; 95:7 [94:7]; 100:3 [99:3]).

New Testament Usage
In the New Testament *nomē* refers to the spiritual nourishment available for God's people as they follow the true Shepherd—they can "go in and out and find *pasture*" (John 10:9). It also is used figuratively to refer to the spreading of false doctrine—"their teaching will *spread* like gangrene" (2 Timothy 2:17, NIV).

STRONG 3542, BAUER 541, MOULTON-MILLIGAN 428, LIDDELL-SCOTT 1178-79.

3406. νομίζω nomizō verb
Have in common use, use customarily; consider, regard, suppose, think, believe.
COGNATE:
νόμος nomos (3414)
SYNONYMS:
ἀναλογίζω analogizō (355)
βλέπω blepō (984)
βουλεύομαι bouleuomai (1003)
διαλογίζομαι dialogizomai (1254)
δοκέω dokeō (1374)
εἶδον eidon (1481)
ἐνθυμέομαι enthumeomai (1744)
ἐπιβλέπω epiblepō (1899)
ἔχω echō (2174)
ἡγέομαι hēgeomai (2216)
κατανοέω katanoeō (2627)
κρίνω krinō (2892)
λογίζομαι logizomai (3023)
νοέω noeō (3401)
οἴομαι oiomai (3496)
συμβάλλω sumballō (4671)
συμβουλεύω sumbouleuō (4674)
ὑπολαμβάνω hupolambanō (5112)
φρονέω phroneō (5262)

1. νομίζω nomizō 1sing indic pres act
2. νομίζει nomizei 3sing indic pres act
3. νομίζων nomizōn nom sing masc part pres act
4. νομιζόντων nomizontōn gen pl masc part pres act
5. νομίζειν nomizein inf pres act
6. ἐνόμισας enomisas 2sing indic aor act
7. ἐνόμισαν enomisan 3pl indic aor act
8. νομίσητε nomisēte 2pl subj aor act
9. νομίσαντες nomisantes nom pl masc part aor act
10. ἐνόμιζεν enomizen 3sing indic imperf act
11. ἐνόμιζον enomizon 3pl indic imperf act
12. ἐνομίζετο enomizeto 3sing indic imperf pass
13. νομίζοντες nomizontes nom pl masc part pres act
14. ἐνομίζομεν enomizomen 1pl indic imperf act

8	Think not that I am come to destroy the law,	Matt 5:17
8	Think not that I am come to send peace on earth:	10:34
7	supposed that they should have received more;	20:10
9	supposing him to have been in the company,	Luke 2:44
12	being as was supposed the son of Joseph,	3:23
10	he supposed his brethren would have understood	Acts 7:25
6	because thou hast thought that the gift of God	8:20
9	out of the city, supposing he had been dead.	14:19
12	where prayer was wont to be made;	16:13
3	supposing that the prisoners had been fled.	16:27
5	not to think that the Godhead is like unto gold,	17:29
11	supposed that Paul had brought into the temple.	21:29
1	I suppose therefore that this is good	1 Co 7:26
2	But if any man think that he behaveth himself	7:36
4	supposing that gain is godliness:	1 Tm 6:5

Classical Greek

The range of meaning of the verb *nomizō* is rather broad in Greek literature. It is related to *nomos* (3414), "law," and refers to legislators who "enact" or "make common use of" law. However, it especially refers to the customary nature or practice of some event, action, ritual, speech, or mannerism (*Liddell-Scott*). In addition, it refers to how one "considers" or "acknowledges" something or someone. Here the idea of customary action moves into the area of the treatment of that person or object. Thus it can even be used of "belief" (ibid.). For example, important persons may be "esteemed" or "held" in high regard.

Septuagint Usage

In the Septuagint *nomizō* occurs exclusively in the Apocrypha. For example, the writer of the Wisdom of Solomon mocked the foolish act of those who "regarded" the elements of the heavens and earth as gods (13:2; cf. 17:3). Of more common matters the author of Sirach said that many persons "regard" a loan as a windfall (29:4; cf. 2 Maccabees 7:19, of "common thinking").

New Testament Usage

The New Testament does not depart from the Septuagintal and classical uses of *nomizō*. In Acts 16:13 the word is used with the idea of the regular custom or practice of meeting for prayer outside of Philippi. In the other 14 occurrences it is translated "think, suppose," or "have the opinion." In every case, except for 1 Corinthians 7:26 and 36, that which the individual thought or supposed was untrue or incorrect (cf. e.g., Acts 7:25 of Moses' mistaken conjecture). Even when *nomizō* is used with the negative, the implication is that the people thought the opposite to be true. This signifies that a thought or opinion does not have to be true to be held in esteem.

STRONG 3543, BAUER 541, MOULTON-MILLIGAN 428, LIDDELL-SCOTT 1178-79.

3407. νομικός nomikos adj

Lawyer, legal expert, jurist, pertaining to the law.

COGNATE:
νόμος nomos (3414)

SYNONYM:
γραμματεύς grammateus (1116)

1. **νομικός** nomikos nom sing masc
2. **νομικόν** nomikon acc sing masc
3. **νομικοί** nomikoi nom pl masc
4. **νομικῶν** nomikōn gen pl masc
5. **νομικοῖς** nomikois dat pl masc
6. **νομικούς** nomikous acc pl masc
7. **νομικάς** nomikas acc pl fem

1	Then one of them, which was a lawyer, asked him	Matt 22:35
3	But the Pharisees and lawyers rejected the counsel	Luke 7:30
1	a certain lawyer stood up, and tempted him,	10:25
4	Then answered one of the lawyers,	11:45
5	And he said, Woe unto you also, ye lawyers!	11:46
5	Woe unto you, lawyers!	11:52
6	And Jesus answering spake unto the lawyers	14:3
7	and contentions, and strivings about the law;	Tit 3:9
2	Zenas the lawyer and Apollos on their journey	3:13

Classical Greek

Actually *nomikos* is an adjective meaning "relating to the law, legal matters," or "conventional." When used as a substantive it can mean "one who is learned in the law," hence, "lawyer, legal expert, jurist, notary" (*Liddell-Scott*). Classical usage favors the adjectival use; later occurrences show it functioning as a technical term for "lawyer" or "assessor" (see *Moulton-Milligan*).

Septuagint Usage

Only one instance of *nomikos* occurs in the Septuagint, and it is in the apocryphal 4 Maccabees where it functions as an adjective describing Eleazar, who was "*knowledgeable in the matters of the law*" (5:4). Here *nomikos* particularly concerns Eleazar's expertise in Jewish law.

New Testament Usage

The New Testament has all three of the above uses of *nomikos*. In Titus 3:9 it is used as an adjective to explain that the strivings were *nomikos*, "about the Law," referring to the entire Old Testament. In Titus 3:13 *nomikos* is used as a title for Zenas the "lawyer." Matthew and Luke use *nomikos* as a technical term for "lawyer." At times it is interchangeable with *grammateus* (1116), "scribe," and *nomodidaskalos* (3410), "doctor (teacher) of the law." It seems that *nomikos* is used in the contexts of administrating or understanding the law of Moses.

In New Testament times the *nomikoi* did three things. First, they had to study and interpret the Law. Due to the general nature of the Law, they clarified the Law in practical ways. Second, they taught the Law to the young Jewish men. Third, they had to act in decisions or questions about the Law. They acted as both judges and advisors to the court (see Hillyer, "Scribe," *Colin Brown,* 3:480).

STRONG 3544, BAUER 541, MOULTON-MILLIGAN 428-29, KITTEL 4:1088, LIDDELL-SCOTT 1178-79, COLIN BROWN 2:438,443,447; 3:477-80.

3408. νομίμως nomimōs adv
Lawfully, legally, according to the law, according to the rules; legitimately, properly, rightly.
CROSS-REFERENCE:
νόμος nomos (3414)

1. νομίμως nomimōs
1 know that the law is good, if a man use it **lawfully**; 1 Tm 1:8
1 yet is he not crowned, except he strive **lawfully**..... 2 Tm 2:5

The adverb form of the adjective *nomimos,* "lawful," is *nomimōs,* "lawfully." This adverb is used only twice in canonical writings, both times in the Pastoral Epistles. Paul used it with its more literal meaning of "legally, according to the rules" in 2 Timothy 2:5, when he said that an athlete must contend "lawfully" if he is to be crowned with the victor's wreath.

In 1 Timothy 1:8 Paul used one of the extended meanings of *nomimōs* in a play on words: "... the law (*nomos*) is good, if a man use it lawfully (*nomimōs*)." Paul pointed out that the value of the Law was in its restraint of wickedness, not in its ability to save. The Law, then, was good only when it was used legitimately, or properly, i.e., according to the way it was intended to be used.

STRONG 3545, BAUER 541, MOULTON-MILLIGAN 429, KITTEL 4:1088-89, LIDDELL-SCOTT 1178-79, COLIN BROWN 2:438,447.

3409. νόμισμα nomisma noun
Money, coin, legal tender; something with legal value; something sanctioned by law or by customary usage.
COGNATE:
νόμος nomos (3414)
SYNONYMS:
ἀργύριον argurion (688)
κέρμα kerma (2743)
χαλκός chalkos (5311)
χρῆμα chrēma (5371)
דַּרְכְּמוֹנִים dark*mônîm (1933), Drachmas (Neh 7:71—Sixtine Edition only).
דָּת dāth (1944), Commission (Ezr 8:36).

1. νόμισμα nomisma nom/acc sing neu
1 Show me the tribute **money**...................... Matt 22:19

The noun *nomisma* is related to the verb *nomizō* (3406) and is commonly used in classical Greek to mean "anything sanctioned by current or established usage, custom" (*Liddell-Scott*). A common example of its use is in reference to the "coin" or "money" that was used as legal tender in Jesus' day. The term *nomisma* is found in the New Testament only in Matthew 22:19 where Jesus requested His Pharisaical and Herodian tempters to show Him "the tribute money" (literally, "the legal money [*nomisma*] of the tax [*kēnsos* (2750)]"). The Roman denarius, a coin accepted for legal exchange by these Jews, bore the image of and an inscription to Tiberius Caesar. This underscored the propriety of returning it to him, through the tax, to pay for the benefits which the Roman government provided.

STRONG 3546, BAUER 541, MOULTON-MILLIGAN 429, LIDDELL-SCOTT 1179.

3410. νομοδιδάσκαλος
nomodidaskalos noun
Teacher of the law.
COGNATES:
διδάσκω didaskō (1315)
νόμος nomos (3414)

1. νομοδιδάσκαλος nomodidaskalos nom sing masc
2. νομοδιδάσκαλοι nomodidaskaloi nom pl masc

2 were Pharisees and **doctors of the law** sitting by,.....Luke 5:17
1 a Pharisee, named Gamaliel, **a doctor of the law,**.....Acts 5:34
2 Desiring to be **teachers of the law;**................. 1 Tm 1:7

Classical Greek
This expression, a compound of *nomos* (3414), "law," and *didaskalos* (1314), "teacher," occurs only in Christian literature of the New Testament and later literature (*Bauer*). It does not occur in the Septuagint. According to *Bauer,* however, the similar word *nomodidaktēs* does occur in classical literature (e.g., Plutarch; cf. *Liddell-Scott*).

New Testament Usage
In the New Testament *nomodidaskalos* denotes a "teacher of the law." Of the three usages in the New Testament, two clearly associate this

status with teaching the law of Moses. The Pharisees and "teachers of the law" (NIV) were challenged by Jesus' authority to forgive sins (Luke 5:17; cf. verse 21). Here that title seems somewhat negative because these same teachers who placed impossible burdens on the people did nothing to help them (cf. Luke 11:45). The term also describes Gamaliel, a respected "teacher of the law" and member of the Sanhedrin Council. He is portrayed positively as he virtually intercedes on behalf of the apostles (Acts 5:34ff.; cf. verse 40).

The third occurrence, in 1 Timothy 1:7, is difficult to interpret precisely. It could be a negative label for the false teachers in Ephesus that recalls the legalism of Judaism. Or, positively, it might highlight the inadequacy of the false teachers: "They want to be teachers of the law, but they do not know what they are talking about or what they so confidently affirm" (1 Timothy 1:7, NIV).

STRONG 3547, BAUER 541, MOULTON-MILLIGAN 429, KITTEL 2:159, LIDDELL-SCOTT 1179-80, COLIN BROWN 2:438,447; 3:477,480,765,768.

3411. νομοθεσία nomothesia noun
The giving of the Law, the law, legislation.
COGNATES:
νόμος nomos (3414)
τίθημι tithēmi (4935)

1. νομοθεσία nomothesia nom sing fem

1 and the **giving of the law,** and the service of God,... Rom 9:4

Classical Greek and Septuagint Usage
This is a compound word formed from *nomos* (3414), "law," and a derivative of *tithēmi* (4935), "to put, place, give." It has close association with *nomothetēs* (3413), the lawgiver, God. Among such classical writers as Plato and Aristotle *nomothesia* simply refers to "legislation" or (plural) "ordinances" enacted by civil authorities (*Liddell-Scott*). It has been used to signify both the act of giving the Law and the end result, which is the legislation or law itself. In the Jewish writings and the Septuagint *nomothesia* refers to the Mosaic law (only in 2 Maccabees 6:23; 4 Maccabees 5:35; 17:16).

New Testament Usage
The only instance of the word in the New Testament is in Romans 9:4. There *nomothesia* denotes the act of giving and the result of giving. Paul listed the privileges of the Israelites and mentioned *nomothesia* as one of them. As a privileged people, Israel had the Law. However, even the Gentiles could boast of having the Law if they wanted it. But only Israel could boast of receiving the Law by direct revelation from *nomothetēs*, "the Lawgiver." Thus Israel alone could boast of both having the Law, and receiving the Law by direct revelation. This was a great privilege given to Israel.

STRONG 3548, BAUER 541, MOULTON-MILLIGAN 429, KITTEL 4:1089, LIDDELL-SCOTT 1179-80, COLIN BROWN 2:438,445.

3412. νομοθετέω nomotheteō verb
To legislate, to enact law; to establish or settle by law.
COGNATES:
νόμος nomos (3414)
τίθημι tithēmi (4935)
יָרָה yārâh (3498), Hiphil: direct, teach (Dt 17:10, Pss 25:8 [24:8], 119:33 [118:33]).

1. νενομοθέτηται nenomothetētai
3sing indic perf mid
2. νενομοθέτητο nenomothetēto
3sing indic plperf pass

2 for under it the people **received the law,**............ Heb 7:11
1 which **was established** upon better promises............ 8:6

Classical Greek
From *nomos* (3414), "law," and *tithēmi* (4935), "put," *nomotheteō* means to "frame laws" or "to put something into law." The word appears from about 400 B.C. in the work of such classical writers as Lysias, Xenophon, and Plato. It continued in frequent use on into New Testament times. A general meaning of the term is "to legislate," sometimes in the sense of "enacting" laws in general and sometimes "establishing" something specific by law, or to settle something legally (see Gutbrod, "nomotheteō," *Kittel*, 4:1090).

Septuagint Usage
In 8 of its 11 Septuagint uses *nomotheteō* translates the hiphil form of the Hebrew verb *yārâh*, which, among other things, means "to instruct." The English translations "teach" (Exodus 24:12; Psalms 25:8,12 [LXX 24:8,12]; 27:11 [26:11]; 119:33,102 [118:33,102]) and "inform" (Deuteronomy 17:10) reflect the Hebrew reading in each case. It seems that since it was the Lord who was doing the teaching in each of the verses above, the Septuagint translators felt justified in strengthening the idea of "instruct" to that of "legislate." God's instructions were, after all, legally binding,

especially those which had been actually written into the Law. The particular form of the Hebrew *yārâh* used in Psalm 84:6 (LXX 83:6) can mean "the early rain" as well as "one who teaches." So the English translation "the rain" reflects a different interpretation of the Hebrew than that of the Septuagint writers who took it in the same sense as the seven passages above, "to teach." Two apocryphal uses (2 Maccabees 3:15; 4 Maccabees 5:25) refer to God as the One who "legislates" or who gives men laws to live by, thus reflecting the more common meaning of *nomotheteō*.

New Testament Usage

In the New Testament *nomotheteō* occurs twice, both times in Hebrews. Hebrews 7:11 states that the Hebrew people "received the law (*nomotheteō*)" under the Levitical priesthood, reflecting the word's normal passive meaning when used of people. Hebrews 8:6 says that "a better covenant... *was established* (*nomotheteō*) upon better promises," reflecting the word's normal passive meaning when used of things. The new covenant, legally established as the norm for life, supercedes the old covenant which was faulty and inferior.

STRONG 3549, BAUER 541-42, MOULTON-MILLIGAN 429, KITTEL 4:1090, LIDDELL-SCOTT 1180, COLIN BROWN 2:438,448.

3413. νομοθέτης nomothetēs noun

Lawgiver.
COGNATES:
νόμος nomos (3414)
τίθημι tithēmi (4935)

1. νομοθέτης nomothetēs nom sing masc

1 is one **lawgiver**, who is able to save and to destroy:... Jas 4:12

Nomothetēs is the noun related to the verb *nomotheteō* (3412) which means "to enact or give laws." Thus, a *nomothetēs* is a "lawgiver." It is used once in the Septuagint (Psalm 9:20) where David prayed to the Lord to appoint a "lawgiver" over the heathen and sinful men. The one occurrence of the noun in the New Testament, James 4:12, reminds Christians that there is one "lawgiver" of the ultimate law by which they are to live, and that He is also the judge of all who break that law. Therefore, Christians are not to act as judges over one another but are to humble themselves before the Lord, stop boasting, stop their selfish strife, and do what is right (cf. James 4).

STRONG 3550, BAUER 542, KITTEL 4:1089, LIDDELL-SCOTT 1180, COLIN BROWN 2:438,450.

3414. νόμος nomos noun

Law, rule, principle.
COGNATES:
ἀνομία anomia (455)
ἄνομος anomos (456)
ἀνόμως anomōs (457)
διανέμω dianemō (1262)
ἔννομος ennomos (1756)
κατακληρονομέω kataklēronomeō (2594B)
κληρονομέω klēronomeō (2789)
κληρονομία klēronomia (2790)
κληρονόμος klēronomos (2791)
νομή nomē (3405)
νομίζω nomizō (3406)
νομικός nomikos (3407)
νομίμως nomimōs (3408)
νόμισμα nomisma (3409)
νομοδιδάσκαλος nomodidaskalos (3410)
νομοθεσία nomothesia (3411)
νομοθετέω nomotheteō (3412)
νομοθέτης nomothetēs (3413)
οἰκονομέω oikonomeō (3483)
παρανομέω paranomeō (3752)
παρανομία paranomia (3753)
συγκληρονόμος sunklēronomos (4640)
SYNONYM:
ἔθος ethos (1478)

דָּבָר dāvār (1745), Words (Ps 119:57 [118:57]).

דָּת dāth (1944), Law, command (Est 1:13,15).

דָּת dāth (A1945), Command, law (Ezr 7:12, Dn 7:25—Aramaic).

חֹק chōq (2805), Statute, order (Jos 24:25, Jer 31:36 [38:36]).

חֻקָּה chuqqāh (2807), Law, statute (Ex 13:10, Nm 9:12, Jer 44:23 [51:23]).

מִצְוָה mitswāh (4851), Commandment (Prv 6:20).

מִשְׁפָּט mishpāṭ (5122), Judgment (Jer 49:12 [29:12]).

פִּתְגָם pithgām (6851), Edict (Est 1:20).

תּוֹרָה tôrāh (8784), Law (Lv 14:2, 2 Chr 17:9, Ps 119:1 [118:1]).

1. νόμος nomos nom sing masc
2. νόμου nomou gen sing masc
3. νόμῳ nomō dat sing masc
4. νόμον nomon acc sing masc
5. νόμους nomous acc pl masc

4 Think not that I am come to destroy the **law**,....... Matt 5:17
2 jot or one tittle shall in no wise pass from the **law**,..... 5:18
1 for this is the **law** and the prophets................... 7:12
1 all the prophets and the **law** prophesied until John..... 11:13
3 Or have ye not read in the **law**,...................... 12:5
3 which is the great commandment in the **law**?.......... 22:36
1 On these two commandments hang all the **law**........ 22:40
2 and have omitted the weightier matters of the **law**,.... 23:23
4 according to the **law** of Moses were accomplished,... Luke 2:22
3 As it is written in the **law** of the Lord,................ 2:23
3 a sacrifice according to ... in the **law** of the Lord,...... 2:24

νόμος 3414

2	Jesus, to do for him after the custom of the law,	Luke 2:27
4	had performed all things according to the law	2:39
3	What is written in the law? how readest thou?	10:26
1	The law and the prophets were until John:	16:16
2	and earth to pass, than one tittle of the law to fail.	16:17
3	fulfilled, which were written in the law of Moses,	24:44
1	For the law was given by Moses,	John 1:17
3	Moses in the law, and the prophets, did write,	1:45
4	Did not Moses give you the law,	7:19
4	and yet none of you keepeth the law?	7:19
1	that the law of Moses should not be broken;	7:23
4	this people who knoweth not the law are cursed.	7:49
1	Doth our law judge any man, before it hear him,	7:51
3	Now Moses in the law commanded us,	8:5
3	It is also written in your law,	8:17
3	Is it not written in your law, I said, Ye are gods?	10:34
2	heard out of the law that Christ abideth for ever:	12:34
3	word might be fulfilled that is written in their law,	15:25
4	Take ye him, and judge him according to your law.	18:31
4	We have a law, and by our law he ought to die,	19:7
4	We have a law, and by our law he ought to die,	19:7
2	words against this holy place, and the law:	Acts 6:13
4	have received the law by the disposition of angels,	7:53
2	And after the reading of the law and the prophets	13:15
3	from which ye could not be justified by the law	13:39
4	and to command them to keep the law of Moses.	15:5
4	saying, Ye must be circumcised, and keep the law:	15:24
4	to worship God contrary to the law.	18:13
2	question of words and names, and of your law,	18:15
2	and they are all zealous of the law:	21:20
4	thyself also walkest orderly, and keepest the law.	21:24
2	against the people, and the law, and this place:	21:28
2	taught according to the perfect manner of the law	22:3
4	one Ananias, a devout man according to the law,	22:12
4	for sittest thou to judge me after the law,	23:3
2	to be accused of questions of their law,	23:29
4	and would have judged according to our law.	24:6
4	believing all things which are written in the law	24:14
4	Neither against the law of the Jews,	25:8
2	out of the law of Moses, and out of the prophets,	28:23
3	have sinned in the law shall be judged by the law;	Rom 2:12
2	have sinned in the law shall be judged by the law;	2:12
2	For not the hearers of the law are just before God,	2:13
2	but the doers of the law shall be justified.	2:13
4	For when the Gentiles, which have not the law,	2:14
2	do by nature the things contained in the law,	2:14
4	having not the law, are a law unto themselves:	2:14
1	having not the law, are a law unto themselves:	2:14
2	show the work of the law written in their hearts,	2:15
3	restest in the law, and makest thy boast of God,	2:17
2	being instructed out of the law;	2:18
3	the form of knowledge and of the truth in the law.	2:20
3	Thou that makest thy boast of the law,	2:23
2	through breaking the law dishonourest thou God?	2:23
4	circumcision verily profiteth, if thou keep the law:	2:25
2	but if thou be a breaker of the law,	2:25
2	uncircumcision keep the righteousness of the law,	2:26
4	if it fulfil the law, judge thee, who by the letter	2:27
2	who by ... circumcision dost transgress the law?	2:27
1	we know that what things soever the law saith,	3:19
3	it saith to them who are under the law:	3:19
2	Therefore by the deeds of the law there shall no	3:20
2	for by the law is the knowledge of sin.	3:20
2	righteousness of God without the law is manifested,	3:21
2	being witnessed by the law and the prophets;	3:21
2	By what law? of works? Nay: ... by the law of faith.	3:27
2	By what law? of works? Nay: ... by the law of faith.	3:27
2	is justified by faith without the deeds of the law.	3:28
4	Do we then make void the law through faith?	3:31
4	God forbid: yea, we establish the law.	3:31
2	not to Abraham, or to his seed, through the law,	4:13
2	For if they which are of the law be heirs,	4:14
1	Because the law worketh wrath:	4:15
1	for where no law is, there is no transgression.	4:15
2	not to that only which is of the law,	4:16
2	For until the law sin was in the world:	5:13
2	but sin is not imputed when there is no law.	5:13
1	Moreover the law entered,	Rom 5:20
4	for ye are not under the law, but under grace.	6:14
4	shall we sin, because we are not under the law,	6:15
4	brethren, for I speak to them that know the law,	7:1
1	law hath dominion over a man as long as he liveth?	7:1
3	bound by the law to her husband so long as	7:2
2	she is loosed from the law of her husband.	7:2
2	she is free from that law;	7:3
3	are become dead to the law by the body of Christ;	7:4
2	the motions of sins, which were by the law,	7:5
2	But now we are delivered from the law,	7:6
1	What shall we say then? is the law sin?	7:7
2	I had not known sin, but by the law:	7:7
1	for I had not known lust, except the law had said,	7:7
2	For without the law sin was dead.	7:8
2	For I was alive without the law once:	7:9
1	Wherefore the law is holy,	7:12
1	For we know that the law is spiritual:	7:14
3	I consent unto the law that it is good.	7:16
4	I find then a law, that, when I would do good,	7:21
3	I delight in the law of God after the inward man:	7:22
4	But I see another law in my members,	7:23
3	warring against the law of my mind,	7:23
2	and bringing me into captivity to the law of sin	7:23
3	with the mind I myself serve the law of God;	7:25
3	but with the flesh the law of sin.	7:25
1	For the law of the Spirit of life in Christ Jesus	8:2
2	hath made me free from the law of sin and death.	8:2
2	For what the law could not do,	8:3
2	That the righteousness of the law might be fulfilled	8:4
3	for it is not subject to the law of God,	8:7
4	which followed after the law of righteousness,	9:31
4	hath not attained to the law of righteousness.	9:31
2	but as it were by the works of the law.	9:32
2	is the end of the law for righteousness to every one	10:4
2	describeth the righteousness which is of the law,	10:5
2	for he that loveth another hath fulfilled the law.	13:8
2	therefore love is the fulfilling of the law.	13:10
3	is bound by the law as long as her husband liveth;	1 Co 7:39
1	or saith not the law the same also?	9:8
3	For it is written in the law of Moses,	9:9
4	to them that are under the law, as under the law,	9:20
4	to them that are under the law, as under the law,	9:20
4	not being myself under the Law, (NASB)	9:20
4	that I might gain them that are under the law;	9:20
3	In the law it is written, With men of other tongues	14:21
1	to be under obedience, as also saith the law.	14:34
1	and the strength of sin is the law.	15:56
2	that a man is not justified by the works of the law,	Gal 2:16
2	and not by the works of the law:	2:16
2	by the works of the law shall no flesh be justified.	2:16
2	For I through the law am dead to the law,	2:19
2	For I through the law am dead to the law,	2:19
2	for if righteousness come by the law,	2:21
2	Received ye the Spirit by the works of the law,	3:2
2	doeth he it by the works of the law,	3:5
2	are of the works of the law are under the curse:	3:10
2	things which are written in the book of the law	3:10
3	no man is justified by the law in the sight of God,	3:11
1	And the law is not of faith:	3:12
2	Christ hath redeemed us from the curse of the law,	3:13
1	confirmed before of God in Christ, the law,	3:17
2	For if the inheritance be of the law,	3:18
1	Wherefore then serveth the law?	3:19
1	Is the law then against the promises of God?	3:21
1	had been a law given which could have given life,	3:21
2	verily righteousness should have been by the law.	3:21
4	But before faith came, we were kept under the law,	3:23
1	law was our schoolmaster to bring us unto Christ,	3:24
4	his Son, made of a woman, made under the law,	4:4
4	To redeem them that were under the law,	4:5
4	Tell me, ye that desire to be under the law,	4:21
4	desire to be under the law, do ye not hear the law?	4:21
4	that he is a debtor to do the whole law.	5:3
3	whosoever of you are justified by the law;	5:4
1	For all the law is fulfilled in one word,	5:14
4	if ye be led of the Spirit, ye are not under the law.	5:18

1	against such there is no law.	Gal 5:23
4	and so fulfil the law of Christ.	6:2
4	they themselves who are circumcised keep the law;	6:13
4	law of commandments contained in ordinances;	Eph 2:15
4	as touching the law, a Pharisee;	Phlp 3:5
3	touching the righteousness which is in the law,	3:6
2	mine own righteousness, which is of the law,	3:9
1	But we know that the law is good,	1 Tm 1:8
1	that the law is not made for a righteous man,	1:9
4	to take tithes of the people according to the law,	Heb 7:5
2	there is made of necessity a change also of the law.	7:12
4	not after the law of a carnal commandment,	7:16
1	For the law made nothing perfect,	7:19
1	law maketh men high priests which have infirmity;	7:28
4	but the word of the oath, which was since the law,	7:28
4	are priests that offer gifts according to the law:	8:4
5	I will put my laws into their mind,	8:10
4	when Moses had spoken ... according to the law,	9:19
4	almost all things are by the law purged with blood;	9:22
1	the law having a shadow of good things to come,	10:1
4	which are offered by the law;	10:8
5	I will put my laws into their hearts,	10:16
4	He that despised Moses' law died without mercy	10:28
4	But whoso looketh into the perfect law of liberty.	Jas 1:25
4	If ye fulfil the royal law according to the scripture,	2:8
2	and are convinced of the law as transgressors.	2:9
4	For whosoever shall keep the whole law,	2:10
2	thou art become a transgressor of the law.	2:11
2	as they that shall be judged by the law of liberty.	2:12
2	speaketh evil of the law, and judgeth the law:	4:11
4	speaketh evil of the law, and judgeth the law:	4:11
4	but if thou judge the law, thou art not a doer	4:11
2	thou art not a doer of the law, but a judge.	4:11

Classical Greek

The noun *nomos* is related to the verb *nēmō*, "to distribute, to divide." Some lexicons distinguish between *nomos* (accented on the first syllable, i.e., the "penult") and *nomos* (accented on the last syllable, i.e., the "ultima"), defining *nomos* as "pasture, apportionment, district, and sphere of command" (*Liddell-Scott*). From these meanings *nomos* was then used to denote "custom, that which is habitual practice, statute, ordinance made by authority and law" (ibid.). Inherent within all of these meanings is the idea of an authoritative apportionment that becomes an accepted statute. Eventually *nomos* came to be used to denote anything that was legally prescribed, regulated, or customarily practiced in any given society's social, cultural, and political structure. Its wide variety of uses attests its versatility of meaning: from local "customs" to civil "ordinances," from "martial law" to "general laws," and from rules of musical "composition" to "courses" of building masonry—just to give a few examples (cf. *Liddell-Scott*).

Nomos was an essential ingredient for the unity and success of the Greek city-state (*polis* [4032]). In the Fifth Century B.C. Greeks began to document and codify their laws. Soon *nomos* came to represent the law(s) enacted by the city-state governing body. It was administered by the judicial system. The idea of *nomos* as "custom" disappeared; *ethos* (1478), "custom," came to depict the commonly held, unwritten laws of society (see Esser, "Law," *Colin Brown*, 2:439).

Because laws were instituted through the actions of city government as a result of the political process, *nomos* was regarded principally from a human perspective. This human-centeredness contrasted the initial idea of *nomos* as a religious enactment. *Nomos* was linked to the divine, as is indicated by Greek philosophy which maintained this relationship.

Philosophy asserted that human laws could be imperfect. It offered as a solution obedience to the law of the universe that controlled the world (*kosmos*). Only when the mind (*nous*) of man attained harmony with the cosmic divine law could inner peace be achieved. In contrast to Biblical usage, therefore, secular Greek usage often regarded *nomos* as covering political, social, and religious territory (ibid.).

Septuagint Usage

Nomos occurs in the Septuagint over 400 times; about 200 of these lack a Hebrew original. On some occasions *nomos* translates *dāth* (16 times) and *chōq/chuqqāh* (12 times), but the predominant Hebrew word translated by *nomos* is *tôrāh*, "law, instruction."

Law in the Old Testament

Tôrāh occurs more than 200 times in the Old Testament. Its original stem is uncertain and it has many different meanings. It is the Word of God spoken by the prophets (Isaiah 1:10; 8:16,20; 30:9f.) and equals the duties and instructions of the priests (Haggai 2:11f.; Malachi 2:6f.). *Tôrāh* extensively denotes the truth of God's revelation (Isaiah 2:3; 42:24; 51:4,7; Micah 4:2). It also refers to the Law or the Ten Commandments, the Decalogue (Deuteronomy 27:3,8; 31:26), the Pentateuch (2 Chronicles 23:18), and includes other Old Testament teaching and instruction as well (2 Chronicles 17:9; Nehemiah 8). In general terms *tôrāh* also involves understanding divine teaching and law.

The Law expressed God's rule over Israel and His demands upon the lives of those He graciously called His own. Because Israel—God's people—was to have fellowship with the Holy God, they too must be holy (Leviticus 19:2; cf. 20:7). The Law provided the standard and expectations of God for His covenant people. It outlined the blessings that resulted from obedience and the curses that would come from rebellion.

The Law was fulfilled when the community, in response to God's redemptive grace, rejoiced and abandoned itself to being obedient to the will of God. Obedience is not a requirement before experiencing God's mercy; rather, it is a response of faith to the mercy received. Fulfilling the Law's requirements did not bring life in God; on the contrary, life was given to those who did not deserve it. Life came through the election and sanctification provided in the "blood of the covenant" (Exodus 24:8). This fundamental viewpoint shaped the understanding of the purpose and meaning of the Law (see Gutgrod, "nomos," *Kittel*, 4:1037).

1. The Law did not declare what Israel must do in order to become God's chosen people. Instead, the Law explained what behavior would destroy the existing relationship. This was verified in the form of the commandments: "Thou shalt not . . . . " As well, it explained the attitudes and actions that would strengthen the relationship. These were expressed in the form of the commandments: "Thou shalt . . . . "

2. The Law cautioned against certain behavior and offered practical advice. By encouraging obedience because of the benefit of doing so, *tôrāh* sought to eliminate transgressions. Deuteronomy especially reflects such a positive attitude toward the rewards of heartfelt obedience to God and devotion to His will. God's goodness and redemption are the bases for obedience, not threats (Deuteronomy 4:31-40; 5:6f.; cf. Exodus 20:2f.). God's great love for Israel was intended to cause Israel to respond in love and carry out the Law.

3. Keeping the Law was not simply to be an external commitment. The Law was to be followed "with all thine heart, and with all thy soul, and with all thy might" (Deuteronomy 6:5; cf. 10:12; 26:16).

4. Israel's religion, therefore, was not founded upon the necessity of keeping the Law in order to enter into fellowship with God. The promises of "reward" for keeping the Law (Deuteronomy 28:1-14), the sayings that to keep the commandments is "to live (by) in them" (Leviticus 18:5), were not enticements to faithfulness. These were to be regarded as promises to be experienced as Israel, through faithful obedience, continued in communion with God. The basis for this expectation was God's grace alone.

The ritual laws were primarily designed to carry out—especially in the atonement sacrifice—the covenant obligations that enabled the sinful nation to reestablish its relationship with the absolute and holy God through the offering of glory and thanksgiving (Exodus 25-30; Leviticus 1-4).

The moral laws were intended to guide the nation in its individual and social life (Exodus 24:12). They present a high ethical standard: "And what nation is there so great, that hath statutes and judgments so righteous as all this *law*, which I set before you this day?" (Deuteronomy 4:8).

Later in the history of Israel the prophets were sent from God to proclaim impending judgment on a backslidden people, who in unfaithfulness and disobedience had rejected the covenant. Idolatry, a denial of the first commandment, was a chief sin of this time. The prophets based their messages on the premise that Israel was the chosen people of God. Israel had seen the blessings of the Lord but it chose to fall away from God. The prophets lamented over Israel's apostasy (Isaiah 1:2; 5:1-7; Jeremiah 2:12-14; Hosea 7:13; Amos 2:9-12; 3:2). The nation's disregard for God's ordinances indicated its disdain of God. Such a "stiff-necked" attitude was thoroughly condemned by the prophets (Hosea 5:10; Amos 5:7; 5:10-12). Any superficial ritual carried out by the unrepentant and sinful was also condemned (Isaiah 1:12f.; Jeremiah 7:9f.; 8:7; Hosea 6:6; Amos 2:6-8; 8:4-14; Micah 6:7f.).

The prophets announced that Israel had broken its covenant relationship with God (Isaiah 24:5; Jeremiah 31:32; Hosea 6:7). Israel's future salvation could, as a result, only occur through a new divine intervention—the coming of Messiah. The redemption brought by the Messiah would establish a new and better covenant between God and His people (Isaiah 42:6; 49:8; 55:3; Jeremiah 31:31f.; 32:40; Ezekiel 16:60; Daniel 9:27; Malachi 3:1). The new covenant would not only be for Israel; the Gentiles would also share in the messianic salvation (Isaiah 42:6; 49:6).

The creative power of the Holy Spirit would "circumcise the hearts" of the members of this new covenant. God's law would be written on tablets of the heart rather than tablets of stone. The Lord himself would effect a new obedience and fulfillment that was in keeping with the original intent and purpose of the Law (Jeremiah 31:33; Ezekiel 36:26,27). The prophet's message was that the Servant of the Lord, through the offering of himself, would provide absolute forgiveness of sins, the basis of the new covenant (Isaiah 53:5-11; Jeremiah 31:34; 33:8; Ezekiel 36:25; Zechariah 13:1).

Law in the Intertestamental Period

In the time between the testaments the Law became increasingly looked to as the source of salvation. More and more emphasis was placed upon keeping the letter of the Law. The Law acquired such a place of prominence in Judaism that it was believed to provide the means to win God's grace as well as the means to remain in His favor.

From internal pressures within Judaism itself the religion of Israel drifted into a legalistic system that adopted the idea of earning salvation by works (law-keeping). This view permeates the pseudepigraphal and apocryphal literature.

Such a legalistic attitude toward a relationship with God and an obsession with fulfilling the letter of the law occurs especially in rabbinic Judaism. God's revelation was evaluated solely in terms of mankind's behavior and conduct. *Tôrāh* was regarded as the only site of God's revelation; consequently, any relationship with God was judged in terms of keeping the Law as reflected in the Pentateuch. The prophetical writings were evaluated in terms of the Law. Indeed the entire canon of the Old Testament was viewed in connection with the Law (cf. Matthew 7:12; 22:40).

Later Judaism might not have succeeded in totally keeping the requirements of the Law, but it did regard such compliance as theoretically possible (see Gerstner, "Law in the New Testament," *International Standard Bible Encyclopedia*, 3:90). Legalism developed because it was believed that life could be attained *only* by keeping the Law. It was hoped that one could offset one's transgressions by performing acts of "obedience," such as prayer, fasting, and almsgiving. If the balances favored good deeds then God would be obligated to save that person by his grace. God's grace was often praised, but in the context of legalistically causing this grace to occur. The Pharisees represented the most extreme form of such legalism. Two consequences might result from such extremism: anxious uncertainty about one's status before God or the opposite, i.e., arrogant self-righteousness and self-glorification.

It is crucial to understand the legalism of Judaism was quite distinct from the Old Testament appreciation of the Law. Only from this basis can we realize the nature of the struggle that Jesus and Paul waged. The Biblically revealed religion of the Old Testament in no way represents a legalistic religion, or a religion in which one could earn salvation. The Abrahamic covenant was of the same essence of obedience based upon faith as the covenant brought by Jesus (Galatians 3:8). God's covenant with Abraham was not declared void by the Law (Galatians 3:17). This implies that the Mosaic covenant was subordinate to Abraham's; both covenants were in effect in the religious life of Israel.

Only in this light can it be recognized that the entire Old Testament is a prelude to that which was to come. Israel's history and its religion anticipated the Church (Romans 15:4; 1 Corinthians 10:11; 2 Timothy 3:16; Hebrews 9:9).

New Testament Usage

In the New Testament *nomos* can only be understood in view of the Torah. *Nomos* occurs over 175 times in the New Testament; of these, no less than 113 are in Paul's writings, 75 of which occur in Romans and 32 in Galatians.

Law in the Gospels

Like *tôrāh* in the Old Testament, *nomos* includes many different nuances in the New Testament. In the Synoptic Gospels *nomos* stands for: (1) the Books of Moses (i.e., the Pentateuch; cf. Luke 24:44) and (2) the law of Moses as the guide for behavior before God. Although it is found in different applications in the New Testament, the Mosaic law is still understood in a threefold manner: (1) moral law, as summarized in the Decalogue; (2) ceremonial law, prescribing the rituals of the sacrificial system; and (3) civil or political law, guiding Israel's national and political life (ibid.). Jesus did not refer to oral tradition as *tôrāh/nomos*, as was customary in Judaism at this time; however, He occasionally used *nomos* to signify the entire Old Testament (John 10:34; 12:34; 15:25). The phrase "the Law and the Prophets" refers to the Old Testament canon. The Law and the Prophets recalls the demands of the Scriptures (Matthew 5:17; 7:12; 22:40). The "prophets and the law" emphasizes the promissory nature of Scripture (Matthew 11:13).

Jesus' relationship with the Law was both positive and negative. Such a dual attitude was not unique to Him but was typical of the prophets (see above). Jesus adamantly rejected the legalism of Judaism that had made the Law the mediator between God and man. This perversion of the Law had changed the relationship based originally upon grace into one dependent upon man's actions. Jesus stepped on the scene as the replacement of the Law. He is the only mediator (Matthew 5:17,18).

Jesus considered the covenant relationship between God and Israel as broken, just as the prophets had done before Him. Therefore Jesus summoned the entire nation to repent by offering to establish a new community of God based upon a new covenant. This is precisely what the prophets had prophesied would happen in the last days (Matthew 26:28). As the Old Testament initially intended, any relationship between God and humanity depends upon God's sovereign and free grace. Now God's redemptive act on behalf of a sinful people is accomplished in Christ Jesus (Luke 1:68f.).

The new covenant of Christ brought new implications to the Law of the "old" covenant. The burden of its ceremonial and civil aspects would be lifted because the sacrifices they required would be fulfilled by Jesus on Calvary (cf. Matthew 5:17). However, God's moral laws would never pass away (Matthew 5:18). Jesus not only fulfilled the moral law by obeying it, He charged any one who would follow Him to do the same (Matthew 5:48). Therefore the Sermon on the Mount was an intense reaffirmation of the moral law. Jesus condemned the scribes and Pharisees for neglecting these "weightier matters" (Matthew 23:23). Their zeal to legalistically follow ceremonial and civil law without "justice, mercy, and faith" was unable to give life or to grant a share in the kingdom Christ came to establish. Any notion of ceremonial righteousness by the Law was denounced (Matthew 23; Luke 11:39). The Law was unable to give life or to grant a share in the eschatological reign of God; only the fellowship based upon faith in Jesus permits this (Matthew 11:28-30). Therefore, tax-collectors and sinners who repented will enter God's kingdom before those who profess to "keep the law" (the Pharisees) (Luke 15:1f.; 18:9-14).

Jesus acknowledged fully the claim that the Law was the expression of God's will (Matthew 5:17-19). He recognized the Law when He forgave (Luke 7:40f.), and when He cared for the lost in an effort to restore their lives in accordance with the will of God (Luke 19:8; John 8:11). Jesus' forgiveness always rests upon the fact that as the sacrificial Lamb of God He carried the curse of the Law (death) which affects all mankind.

Nomos occurs 14 times in the Gospel of John in reference to the full Law, Torah (that is, to the Pentateuch). But first and foremost, in John's Gospel the Law is the revelation of God in the Old Testament. Law is not some ethical demand which seeks to dominate mankind. "For the *law* was given by Moses, but grace and truth came by Jesus Christ" (John 1:17). Jesus Christ is God's final and ultimate revelation of the truth of God.

Jesus enlisted several phrases to describe himself and His gift of salvation. These phrases were commonly used by Judaism in praise of the Law: the light (John 8:12; 9:5; 12:35); living water (chapter 4); the bread of life (chapter 6); the way, the truth, and the life (14:6).

At the same time that the Gospel of John highlights the contrast between Jesus and the Law, it also exhibits a positive interrelationship between Jesus and the Law. The Law testifies to Jesus (John 5:39f.; 7:19f.). He is the fulfillment of the Law (John 8:17; 10:34; 12:34; 15:25). True obedience to the law of Moses and the revealed will of God will lead to acknowledgment of Jesus as Lord (John 5:39f.; 8:39f.).

The early Jewish-Christian congregation in Jerusalem, for the most part, continued to live according to the framework of the Law as long as the temple cultus remained (until about A.D. 70; cf. Acts 21:20).

Law in the Early Church

The problem of law and grace came to the forefront with the advent of the Gentile mission. The Apostolic Council as recorded in Acts 15 (cf. Galatians 2) reveals the basic attitude of the Early Church. The Jerusalem Council debated whether or not righteousness could be provided by the Law. They concluded that righteousness could only be obtained by grace—this held true for Jew and Greek alike. Both had to trust in the grace of God (Acts 15:10,11; Galatians 2:16). The Gentiles were not required to submit to the "yoke" of the Law in order to participate in the new community of God. They were only under the Lordship of Christ and must follow His teaching and commandments (Matthew 28:20).

An extremist group within early Jewish Christianity, the "Judaizers," insisted that a Gentile convert must undergo circumcision and keep the law of Moses (i.e., live as a Jew) in order to be counted as one of God's people (Galatians 1:7; 2:4). In spite of the fact that the Apostolic Council in Jerusalem clearly rejected such a stance, the "Judaizers" continued to spread their teaching and attempted to undermine the work of Paul which presented a "gospel which was free from the Law." They even appealed to Jesus' obedience to the Law and that of the earliest church as "proof" of their position. They also probably contended that a gospel that was free from the Law would lead to lawlessness.

Law in Pauline Literature

The place of the Law is a principal theme in Paul's writings. Paul's instruction regarding the Law can only be interpreted against the background of his past life as a law-abiding Pharisee and against the prevalent Jewish understanding of the Law as the means to salvation and righteousness.

Paul showed an understanding of *nomos* that was variegated and complex rather than one-dimensional. For Paul *nomos* equaled the law of the Old Testament, including the Ten Commandments (Romans 13:8f.; 2:20f.; 7:7), the law of Moses in the extended sense (Romans 7:4; Galatians 4:4), and the single commands (Romans 7:2). More than anything else the Law was a power which demanded something from man, a power of the will that confronted man with its claims. Some claimed to "keep" and practice the Law (Romans 2:25; Galatians 5:3); consequently, "works of the law" is a frequent topic of discussion in Paul's writings. Works of the Law are those demands of the Law which the natural man performs in hope of fulfilling the Law and thus receiving "righteousness." The works-religion of Judaism was consequently devoid of any power to save according to the message "the just shall live by faith" found in the New Testament (cf. Habakkuk 2:4). Any concept of an earned righteousness is truly remote to the Bible (e.g., Romans 3:20,27,28; Galatians 2:16; Ephesians 2:9; Philippians 3:9).

Like Christ, Paul equated *nomos* with the Five Books of Moses, the Pentateuch (Romans 3:21; Galatians 4:21). Paul often distinguished between the "law" and the "prophets" of the Old Testament. His scriptural support for his arguments was often drawn from both groups (Romans 9:12,13; 10:5-21; 12:19,20; and elsewhere). The entire Old Testament was also regarded as *nomos* as well (1 Corinthians 14:21). *Nomos* also carries a general sense of a rule (Romans 7:21), a principle of power (the law of sin, Romans 7:25; the law of the Spirit, Romans 8:2; the law of the members and the mind, Romans 7:23).

Paul's writings are reminiscent of Jesus because he both endorsed and rejected the Law. To understand Paul's attitude toward the Law one must first examine his teaching about the Cross (Esser, "Law," *Colin Brown*, 2:445). For Paul the Cross is the axis around which everything else revolves (Romans 7:1f.; Galatians 2:19-21; Philippians 3:3-11).

With regard to Paul's negative attitude toward the Law, it can be noted that being freed from the power of the Law through the power of the Cross was a principal concern for Paul. This is reflected on many occasions in his writings; the letter to the Galatians especially has this as a theme. The struggle to be free from the Law should be considered under two headings.

First, Paul waged his greatest battle against an interpretation of the Law that would see it as a means of salvation (e.g., Pharisaism). Paul knew the inability to become righteous through "works" (Romans 3:20f.; Galatians 2:16). "If righteousness come by the *law*, then Christ is dead in vain" (Galatians 2:21). Paul rejected any hope of righteousness through the keeping of the Law when he encountered the risen Lord. He had to confess that all his "righteousness" (obtained by keeping the Law) was really worthless (Philippians 3:7f.). Paul, therefore, radically challenged his contemporaries within Judaism who believed the Law to be a way to salvation (Galatians 3:10-14).

Second, any attempt to obtain righteousness through the Law was, from Paul's point of view, a terrible sin that had set Israel over against the true righteous relationship proclaimed by the prophets. Even since the Abrahamic covenant righteousness depended upon God's election and grace, i.e., righteousness is by faith (Romans 4; Galatians 3). Paul denied that the Law had any power to bring life to the people (Galatians 3:21). A relationship with God cannot be earned. Judaism's hope of righteousness through the Law and Christianity's hope of a right relationship through faith are, thus, diametrically opposed to one another (Galatians 3:10; 4:22f.).

Those passages in Paul's letters that seem to imply that Moses' covenant—and the Old Testament—teaches two ways of salvation (faith/works) must be considered in light of Paul's accommodating himself to the argumentation of his opponents. Instead, Paul considered the statement "the just shall live by faith" as fundamental to all of his theology. Scripture as a whole is entirely in keeping with this teaching (Habakkuk 2:4; Romans 1:17).

Paul also rejected the power of the Law to make righteous because of its "weakness" and inability to overcome the power of sin and the sinful nature of man (Romans 8:3). The Law is able only to expose sin and condemn it (Romans 3:19,20; 7:7). The Law makes us aware of our sins and consequently shows us how we deserve the judgment and wrath of God (Romans 4:15; 5:13,14). Through the commandment, sin becomes "exceedingly sinful" (Romans 7:13).

Paul's rejection of a "works-righteousness" theology was also influenced by his understanding of God's saving activity in history. Paul took seriously Jesus' words: "For all the prophets and the law prophesied until John" (Matthew 11:13). Paul not only refused to compromise on his position that Gentiles do not need to "bear the yoke of the law," he also believed the same holds true for Jewish Christians (cf. Galatians 5:1; Philippians 3:3f; Colossians 2:16f.; cf. Acts 15:1; Galatians 2:1f.; cf. 1 Corinthians 9:20).

Paul would agree that Moses' law, with its commands and ordinances, was only "a shadow of good things to come" (Hebrews 10:1). That is to say, the reality of what the Law symbolized is realized in Christ (Colossians 2:17). Christ has "abolished . . . the law of commandments contained in ordinances" (Ephesians 2:15), He has "broken down the middle wall of partition between us," the dividing wall between Israel and the nations (Ephesians 2:14). Therefore, the abolishing of the Law and the instituting of the new covenant makes Jews and Gentiles "co-participants"—by faith—in the promises of God.

The freedom from the Law experienced by the believer was for Paul related to: (1) freedom from the condemning power of the Law for those who violate its commands (Galatians 3:13; Colossians 2:14); (2) freedom from the Law as the required expression of the Old Testament covenant (Romans 7:1f.; Galatians 3:23-25; 4:1-5; Ephesians 2:15); (3) freedom from the bondage of trying to obtain righteousness by works of the Law (Galatians 2:16; Philippians 3:7f.).

Paul fully confirmed and endorsed as valid the words of the Law as divine words of revelation. The Law expresses God's will: "Wherefore the *law* is holy, and the commandment holy, and just, and good" (Romans 7:12). In this regard the Law informs, instructs, and explains (Romans 2:18f.). God reveals His wrath through the Law (Romans 4:15); it shows our guilt before God (Romans 3:19f.). The Law's restraining force acted as a "schoolmaster" or "tutor" to prepare Israel for the redemption that comes in Christ (Galatians 3:23,25; 4:1-5). Originally the commandment was intended to bring life, not death (Romans 7:10; cf. Leviticus 18:5).

Furthermore, Paul wrote that Christ lived in full compliance with the demands of the Law (Galatians 4:4). Through His atoning death and substitutional sacrifice Christ satisfied all the legal demands for the punishment of offenders of the Law (Romans 3:25f.; Galatians 3:13; Colossians 2:14). Therefore, the Law itself was legally declared void, having been fulfilled in every way. Paul posed the question: "Do we then make void the law through faith? God forbid: yea, we establish the law" (Romans 3:31). The Law is further affirmed because its ethical demands are more fully met in the new obedience of the Church through the power of the Spirit. The Law is fulfilled by a life lived in love, the chief fruit of the Spirit (Galatians 5:22). "Love fulfills the law" (cf. Romans 13:8,10; Galatians 5:14). The fulfillment of the Law can only take place in the Church under the power of God himself, "which worketh in you both to will and to do of his good pleasure" (Philippians 2:13).

Law in the Epistle to the Hebrews

The relationship of the Law in light of the new covenant is a theme throughout the Letter to the Hebrews. There *nomos* primarily denotes the covenant agreement expressed in the Old Testament. The Law is evaluated in light of God's saving activity in history, and it belongs solely to the former agreement which was only a shadow of things to come (Hebrews 8:5f.; 9:23f.). During the period of the new covenant the salvation promised by the old is realized. The Law in the Book of Hebrews is not of crucial ethical importance as it was in Paul's epistles; rather, it is examined from its ritual and ceremonial side (Hebrews 8:1f.). The "law" includes the guidelines for priestly service and worship in the old covenant. Christ is presented as the reality of what these rituals were intended to represent (Hebrews 7:11). He is the ultimate expression of perfection, sanctification, and holiness. He is totally able to forgive sins and to provide ethical renewal (Hebrews 9:12,26; 10:14f.; 12:1f.). As the true High Priest, Christ offers the perfect sacrifice for sin. He restores fellowship with God and brings salvation to man. Much of this theme is woven around the fulfillment of prophecy and the fulfillment of the Law. As the Law is fulfilled it becomes replaced by the reality it represents (Hebrews 9:9-12).

Law in the Book of James

The Epistle of James has a distinct understanding of "law" (*nomos*). James speaks of the "perfect law of liberty" (1:25), the "royal law" (2:8). Both of these expressions are capsulized expressions of Old Testament law. Christianity, however, reduces the laws of that economy to the "perfect law of liberty." Therefore, the "law of liberty" equals the saving "word of truth" (James 1:18f.), the "engrafted word, which is able to save your souls" (1:21f.). This word is a creative and life-giving force which implants love as the fulfillment of the Law. Love creates doers of love and promotes loving acts of faith. The royal commandment is the commandment of love (2:8).

As this survey has shown, *nomos* in the New Testament is extremely diverse in its meaning. Simple secular definitions are inadequate. The background of *nomos* in the New Testament is the Old Testament concept of *tôrāh* and its revelation history. Furthermore, not only Paul and Jesus but all of the New Testament join with the Old Testament to present a unified understanding of the nature of God's holy law.

STRONG 3551, BAUER 542-43, MOULTON-MILLIGAN 429-30, KITTEL 4:1022-85, LIDDELL-SCOTT 1180, COLIN BROWN 2:437-50,455.

3415. νοσέω noseō verb

Beside, to have a morbid interest in, or an unhealthy desire for (something).

CROSS-REFERENCE:
νόσος nosos (3417)

1. νοσῶν nosōn nom sing masc part pres act

1 but **doting** about questions and strifes of words,.... 1 Tm 6:4

In its earliest occurrences *noseō* is a verb that means to be sick in body or mind. Later writings use it in the sense of "to take a morbid interest in" or "to have an unhealthy desire or craving for something." It is used twice in the Septuagint and only once in the New Testament. First Timothy 6:4 refers to someone who advocates a doctrine other than the healthy, godly teachings of Christ. Such a person is conceited, misunderstands the truth, and has an unhealthy craving or inordinate passion (*noseō*) for controversy that produces envy and strife.

STRONG 3552, BAUER 543, MOULTON-MILLIGAN 430, KITTEL 4:1091-98, LIDDELL-SCOTT 1181, COLIN BROWN 3:996-98.

3416. νόσημα nosēma noun

Disease, sickness.
COGNATE:
νόσος nosos (3417)
SYNONYMS:
ἀσθένεια astheneia (763)
νόσος nosos (3417)

1. νοσήματι nosēmati dat sing neu

1 was made whole of whatsoever **disease** he had....... John 5:4

Nosēma conveys essentially the same idea as *nosos* (3417), the common word for "disease, illness, sickness." *Nosēma* is found only in John 5:4 in the New Testament, which is a problem passage. Because the oldest copies of the Gospel of John do not have this verse and others mark it as questionable, many scholars have concluded that it is probably a true account that was added later to the Gospel of John to explain the people's belief. In John 5:4 the reference is simply to diseases of which people were supposedly healed, according to a tradition, if they were the first to enter the pool of Bethesda while it was stirring.

STRONG 3553, BAUER 543, KITTEL 4:1091-98, LIDDELL-SCOTT 1181, COLIN BROWN 3:996-98.

3417. νόσος nosos noun

Illness, sickness, disease.

νόσος 3417

COGNATES:
νοσέω noseō (3415)
νόσημα nosēma (3416)

SYNONYMS:
ἄῤῥωστος arrhōstos (726)
ἀσθένεια astheneia (763)
μαλακία malakia (3091)
νόσημα nosēma (3416)

חֳלִי chŏlî (2582), Sickness (2 Chr 21:19, Hos 5:13).

מַדְוֶה madhweh (4207), Disease (Dt 7:15).

מַחֲלֶה machăleh (4380), Disease (2 Chr 21:15).

מַחֲלָה machălāh (4382), Disease (Ex 15:26).

מַכָּה makkāh (4485), Sickness (Dt 28:59).

תַּחֲלֻאִים tachălu'îm (8794), Diseases (Dt 29:22, Dt 103:3 [102:3]).

1. **νόσον** noson acc sing fem
2. **νόσων** nosōn gen pl fem
3. **νόσοις** nosois dat pl fem
4. **νόσους** nosous acc pl fem

```
1  and healing all manner of sickness and ... disease ... Matt 4:23
3  that were taken with divers diseases and torments, .......  4:24
4  took our infirmities, and bare our sicknesses. ............  8:17
1  and healing every sickness and every disease ...........  9:35
1  gave them power ... to heal all manner of sickness ...  10:1
3  he healed many that were sick of divers diseases, ... Mark 1:34
4  power to heal sicknesses, and to cast out devils: ........  3:15
3  all they that had any sick with divers diseases ....... Luke 4:40
2  to hear him, and to be healed of their diseases; .........  6:17
2  he cured many of their infirmities and plagues, ..........  7:21
4  and authority over all devils, and to cure diseases. .....  9:1
4  and the diseases departed from them, .............. Acts 19:12
```

Classical Greek

In classical Greek the noun *nosos* and the cognate verb *noseō* (3415) are used primarily in connection with illness. It can also be used generally of "distress, anguish" and figuratively of character defects and mental illness.

Septuagint Usage

In the Septuagint *nosos* is used only 13 times. Its few occurrences are due in part to a preference for two other terms, *arrostia*, "not well, ill" (cf. *arrōstos* [726]), and *malakia* (3091), "weak, soft," and to the Old Testament's use of specific terms for specific illnesses instead of the general term "illness."

Old Testament Background

In the Old Testament illness is almost always considered from a religious point of view. Primary interest is not on the physical causes of illness nor its diagnosis, but rather on the relationship existing between God—who is Master of illness and health, life and death—and the one who is ill.

In Israelite thought illness was an evil and contrary to nature, something out of place in God's creation. But if sickness and weakness did affect human life, some believed it was because of sin. Mankind incurred God's wrath because of sin, and consequently, is under the power of evil forces. Thus, suffering and illness were seen as ordinary conditions for a fallen and sinful mankind. (See Harrison, "Disease," *Intenational Standard Bible Encyclopedia*, 1:955-960.)

The origin of illness can be traced back to the Fall. Death entered the world as a direct result of sin, and to the Hebrews illness merely signaled the beginning of death, something which sapped one's life force. In many of the Psalms it is clear that the sick person believed he was under the power of death. In the Hebrew idiom a person "becomes alive" when he regains his health. When the Psalmist described man as "afflicted and ready to die" from his youth on (88:15), he was not employing poetic exaggeration but acknowledging grim reality.

The Law stated that if the Israelites kept God's commands, He would not bring the diseases of Egypt on them (Exodus 15:26; 23:25; Deuteronomy 7:12,15). However, serious illness would afflict them if they broke the covenant (Leviticus 26:15,16; Deuteronomy 28:22,27,58-61). Found in this conditional promise is a clear cause and effect relationship between sin and sickness. But innocent people can also be afflicted. When David sinned by starting a census, it was not he alone but his nation that was heavily afflicted with pestilence (2 Samuel 24:15-17). Also, when he sinned with the wife of Uriah, their child died (2 Samuel 12:14).

The Book of Job also proves that the righteous also suffer illness. The dramatic lessons of this book strongly warn against adopting the view which Job's friends so eloquently asserted—and which was common among the Jews—that illness is always a result of one's personal sins.

To a limited degree the priests of Israel were skilled in medicine. Detailed instructions for the recognition and diagnosis of leprosy were provided to protect the nation from this disease (Leviticus 13). Hence the role of man in providing human assistance and nursing is not incompatible with the Law, even though the Lord himself was the healer of Israel (Exodus 15:26).

This healing power was also manifested through the prophets (e.g., Elijah and Elisha). Isaiah prophesied that the suffering Messiah would himself take our sicknesses; and healing is provided through His stripes (Isaiah 53:4,5). In the coming kingdom of the Messiah perfect health will reign: "No one living in Zion will say, 'I am ill' " (Isaiah 33:24, NIV).

New Testament Usage

In the New Testament *nosos* appears 12 times—11 times in the Synoptic Gospels and once in Acts (19:12). It is always used literally of physical illness. The verb *noseō* occurs only once, in a figurative sense of those who have a "morbid craving (*noseō*) for controversy and for disputes about words" (1 Timothy 6:4, RSV). In addition a cognate noun, *nosēma* (3416), occurs once (John 5:4).

Nosos is used parallel with the other general terms for sickness, *malakia* (3091), *mastix* (3120), *astheneia* (763), and the verb *astheneō* (764), in passages that describe Jesus' healing ministry. It should be noted that New Testament writers distinguished between natural diseases and demonically originated afflictions. Jews following the theology of the Old Testament understood sickness to be in the world because of sin which began at the Fall.

Healing testimonies comprise a large portion of the Gospels, showing Jesus spent much of His time ministering to the sick. Sick people gathered around Him, and people brought to him all who were ill with various diseases; those suffering severe pain, the demon possessed, those having seizures, and the paralyzed, and He healed them (Matthew 4:24). He also sent His disciples out with power and authority to heal (Matthew 10:8).

Jesus strongly opposed the teaching that sickness and disaster always occur as punishment for particular sins (cf. Luke 13:1ff.). Of the man who had been born blind He said, "Neither hath this man sinned nor his parents" (John 9:3). This does not mean Jesus did not believe these people were sinners; rather, it emphasizes that this man's blindness was not a direct result of any particular sin which he or his parents may have committed. Lazarus, the friend of Jesus, became ill not because he had sinned, but in order that through his resurrection the Son of Man might be glorified (John 11:1ff.).

Perhaps the most significant use of *nosos* is in Matthew 8:17 where Isaiah 53:4 is quoted in a quite literal Greek translation of the Hebrew. Matthew was inspired to choose *nosos* and *astheneia* instead of the Septuagint's "sin and hardships." The message here is that Jesus is the Messiah who provides deliverance from sickness and all effects of the Fall by taking the root cause—the sin of the world—on himself. This and the other uses of *nosos* serve as a reminder that though Christians may suffer the common experience of disease in this fallen world, God has provided for healing in Christ's atonement as one of the benefits of His many-faceted grace.

However, it would be very difficult to find the New Testament teaching that illness is in any way a blessing. It is considered quite natural that the one who is ill wishes to regain his health (Matthew 20:32f.; John 5:6). Illness is a by-product of living in a world placed under the curse of sin—as are suffering, sorrow, accidents, and death. The believer can expect the assistance and strength of God through all these, but nevertheless, they are a part of life. Thus even early Christians were afflicted by sickness. One of the best workers of the church "became sick and died" (Acts 9:37, NIV); one of Paul's coworkers "was ill, and almost died" (Philippians 2:27, NIV); and Trophimus had to be left in Miletus because he was sick (2 Timothy 4:20).

But the New Testament also teaches that illness is sometimes a judgment of God on sin, for example, Herod the king (Acts 12:23) and Elymas the sorcerer (Acts 13:11). Illness can also be a chastisement from the Lord on His children when they sin, to bring about repentance. For example, in Corinth many became sick and died because they did not recognize the body of the Lord. They were disciplined so they would not "be condemned with the world" (1 Corinthians 11:32). Even the action taken against the person involved in sexual immorality and delivered "unto Satan for the destruction of the flesh" was intended for his reflection, conversion, and ultimate salvation (1 Corinthians 5:5). Also, those who blasphemed could be disciplined in the same way (1 Timothy 1:20). This particular church discipline was to be conducted in the power of the Lord and stands in strong contrast to the gifts of healing (1 Corinthians 5:4).

In the New Testament illness is traced back to the Fall as in the Old Testament. Through sin death entered the world (Romans 5:12), and naturally, sickness also—the forerunner of death, and its physical cause. Because of the Fall the body of man is now a body of humiliation (Philippians 3:21); it is dead because of sin (Romans 8:10), and subject to death (Romans

8:11) and corruption (1 Corinthians 15:42). In its earthly nature, as flesh and blood, the body cannot inherit the eternal life of the kingdom of God without a radical transformation (1 Corinthians 15:50).

In the present state of the body it is impossible to sharply delineate between the condition of being sick and the condition of being healthy. The difference between "healthy" and "ill" is largely a difference in degree rather than a difference in nature. Perfect health belongs to the realm of eternity and cannot be achieved in the present life. This is why the Scriptures state that at the return of Christ the bodies of the believers will be changed "so that they will be like his glorious body" (Philippians 3:21, NIV). At the resurrection the mortal will clothe itself with the immortal (1 Corinthians 15:53). In the eternal state there is no death, sorrow, or suffering (Revelation 21:4), and the leaves of the tree of life will be for the healing of the nations (Revelation 22:2).

STRONG 3554, BAUER 543, MOULTON-MILLIGAN 430, KITTEL 4:1091-98, LIDDELL-SCOTT 1181, COLIN BROWN 3:996-99.

3418. νοσσιά nossia noun

Nest, brood of young birds, nestlings.
CROSS-REFERENCE:
νεοσσός neossos (3364)

חֹר chōr (2815), Lair (Na 2:12).

קֵן qēn (7348), Nest (Dt 22:6, Ps 84:3 [83:3], Ob 4).

1. νοσσιάν nossian acc sing fem

1 as a hen doth gather her **brood** under her wings,... Luke 13:34

Nossia refers to a "brood" of young birds or the "nest" they live in. Psalm 84:3 (LXX 83:3) in the Septuagint compares the altars of the Lord to the secure place which the swallow finds for her "nest"—a place to lay her young. The analogy further emphasizes the blessing of those who dwell in God's house.

In beautiful fulfillment of this imagery, Christ, who was God dwelling among men, whose body was the ultimate temple of God, cried out to Jerusalem that He desired to gather her children "as a hen doth gather her brood under her wings," but they rejected Him (Luke 13:34). The use of nossia reminds Christians that God loves them with a maternal love as well as a paternal love.

STRONG 3555, BAUER 543, MOULTON-MILLIGAN 430, LIDDELL-SCOTT 1181, COLIN BROWN 1:174.

3419. νοσσίον nossion noun

Young bird, chick.
CROSS-REFERENCE:
νεοσσός neossos (3364)

אֶפְרֹחַ 'ephrōach (686), Young ones (Ps 84:3 [83:3]).

1. νοσσία nossia nom/acc pl neu

1 as a hen gathereth her **chickens** under her wings,... Matt 23:37

Nossion's one occurrence at Matthew 23:37 corresponds to that of nossia at Luke 13:34. Jesus was lamenting over the people of Jerusalem because they would not let Him gather them as "chicks" under His (the "hen's") wings. He knew that because of their rejection they would receive the desolation of judgment. Matthew's inspired challenge is to praise Jesus as the Saviour who comes in the name of the Lord and thereby to be gathered as His chicks rather than be destroyed in the judgment.

STRONG 3556, BAUER 543, LIDDELL-SCOTT 1181.

3419B. νοσσός nossos noun

Young (of a bird).
CROSS-REFERENCE:
νεοσσός neossos (3364)

אֶפְרֹחַ 'ephrōach (686), Young, young ones (Dt 22:6, Jb 39:30).

בֵּן bēn (1158), Son; young one (Ps 147:9 [146:9]).

גּוֹזָל gôzāl (1501), Eagle (Dt 32:11).

יֶלֶד yeledh (3315), Young (Jb 38:41).

קֵן qēn (7348), Nest (Is 16:2).

1. νοσσούς nossous acc pl masc

1 "A pair of doves or two **young** pigeons." (NIV) ..... Luke 2:24

The word nossos is a variant spelling of neossos (3364). Neossos occurs from the time of Homer (ca. Eighth Century B.C.) and denotes (1) a young bird, a nestling, or even the yoke of an egg; (2) the young of any animal; or (3) a young child (Liddell-Scott). The shortened form does not appear until the Hellenistic period (cf. Bauer, ca. 300 B.C.–A.D. 300). The loss of the vowel reduced the number of syllables in the word and made it easier to pronounce. In the Epistle of Barnabas (11.3) nossos refers to fledgling birds which were taken from the nest (Liddell-Scott).

Nossos occurs in some of the older New Testament manuscripts at Luke 2:24. Joseph and Mary came to the temple to offer a sacrifice of a pair of turtledoves or two young pigeons according to the Law's provision for the poor (cf. Leviticus 12:8). The *Textus Receptus* has *neossos* at Luke 2:24.

BAUER 543, MOULTON-MILLIGAN 430, LIDDELL-SCOTT 1181.

3420. νοσφίζομαι nosphizomai verb

To put aside for oneself secretly, misappropriate, pilfer, embezzle.

לָקַח lāqach (4089), Take (Jos 7:1).

1. νοσφιζομένους nosphizomenous
acc pl masc part pres mid
2. ἐνοσφίσατο enosphisato 3sing indic aor mid
3. νοσφίσασθαι nosphisasthai inf aor mid

```
2  And kept back part of the price,................Acts 5:2
3  and to keep back part of the price of the land?........ 5:3
1  Not purloining, but showing all good fidelity;........Tit 2:10
```

Classical Greek

In early Homeric literature *nophizomai* means "turn away, forsake, abandon" (*Liddell-Scott*). In later classical Greek it means "set apart, separate." Its definition includes the sense of "putting aside for oneself," hence "depriving" or "robbing" another.

Septuagint Usage

Nosphizomai is used in the Septuagint only in Joshua 7:1 in a situation that corresponds well to its use in Acts 5:2,3. In Joshua 7:1 Achan secretly "set aside" for himself some of the spoils that the Lord had prohibited as dedicated objects for destruction. When Achan's sin was discovered he was put to death. Likewise, in Acts 5:2,3, Ananias and his wife "kept back" some of the price of a property he sold while claiming to give all the price to the apostles, thereby lying to the Holy Spirit. When they were exposed, both died under the judgment of God.

New Testament Usage

Titus 2:10, the only other New Testament use of the word, calls for slaves not to "purloin," pilfer, or steal from their masters. On the contrary, they should show all good faith so they will give a good testimony for the Saviour. The use of this word reminds Christians to be honest with their stewardship.

STRONG 3557, BAUER 543 (see "nosphizō"), MOULTON-MILLIGAN 430 (see "nosphizō"), LIDDELL-SCOTT 1182.

3421. νότος notos noun

South, south or south westerly wind, land of the South.

SYNONYM:
μεσημβρία mesēmbria (3184)

דָּרוֹם dārôm (1924), South (Eccl 1:6, Ez 40:27, 42:12f.).

כָּתֵף kātheph (3931I), Slope (Jos 15:8—Codex Vaticanus only).

נֶגֶב neghev (5221), South, the Negev (Ex 40:24, Jgs 1:9, Zec 14:4).

קָדִים qādhîm (7205), East (Ex 14:21, Jb 38:24, Ez 27:26).

תֵּימָן têmān (8816), South, south wind (Jb 39:26, S/S 4:16, Zec 6:6).

1. νότου notou gen sing masc
2. νότον noton acc sing masc

```
1  queen of the south shall rise up in the judgment...Matt 12:42
1  queen of the south shall rise up in the judgment...Luke 11:31
2  And when ye see the south wind blow, ye say,........ 12:55
1  shall come from the east, ... and from the south,...... 13:29
1  And when the south wind blew softly,.............Acts 27:13
1  and after one day the south wind blew,................ 28:13
1  on the north three gates; on the south three gates;..Rev 21:13
```

Classical Greek and Septuagint Usage

From antiquity this word has signified the direction known as "south" in classical use (e.g., Homer, Herodotus) and the Septuagint. For example, Psalm 126:4 (LXX 125:4) speaks longingly of the "streams of the south" (*notos*), here referring to the Negev or southern part of Israel. It could also mean the land of the South (*Bauer*). In the New Testament period *notos* continued in common usage, which is reflected both in the Oxyrhynchus and Tebtunis Papyri (First and Second Century A.D.) describing property as in the "south lane" and "south ... road" (*Moulton-Milligan*).

New Testament Usage

The New Testament uses the word *notos* seven times. In Revelation 21:13 where it describes the gates of the celestial city, it is used amid a citation of all four cardinal directions (*anatolē* [393], "east"; *borras* [998], "north"; *notos*, "south"; and *dusmē* [1417], "west"). Luke 13:29 likewise uses it in a listing of all four directions from which the redeemed would come to sit down in the kingdom of God.

Notos is also used to identify the wind blowing from the south in Luke 12:55, Acts 27:13, and 28:13. This wind, according to both ancient and modern custom, was named for the direction *from* which it blew, not for the direction in which it blows—as a careful examination of Acts 27:1-20 will confirm. Mariners claim that the wind spoken of in Acts 27:13 actually came from the southwest rather than from straight south. Nevertheless, the general name for this wind designated it a "south wind."

Matthew 12:42 and Luke 11:31 are parallel passages that use *notos* to refer to the land of the South from which the Queen of Sheba came. This is most probably Yemen in southwest Arabia. (The legendary connection with Ethiopia is probably wrong; cf. Hubbard, "Queen of Sheba," *International Standard Bible Encyclopedia*, 4:8-11.)

STRONG 3558, BAUER 544, MOULTON-MILLIGAN 430, LIDDELL-SCOTT 1182, COLIN BROWN 3:1000,1003.

3422. νουθεσία nouthesia noun

Admonition, warning, counsel, instruction.
CROSS-REFERENCE:
νουθετέω noutheteō (3423)

1. **νουθεσία** nouthesia dat sing fem
2. **νουθεσίαν** nouthesian acc sing fem

2 and they are written for our **admonition**, ... 1 Co 10:11
1 in the nurture and **admonition** of the Lord. .... Eph 6:4
2 after the first and second **admonition** reject; .... Tit 3:10

Classical Greek and Septuagint Usage

Nouthesia is the noun related to the more common verb *noutheteō* (3423), "to admonish, warn, instruct." It is a compound of the Greek words *nous* (3426), "mind," and *tithēmi* (4935), "to put," and is used of instruction with a view to correcting a person's actions and attitudes. This noun is not very common in early classical Greek but can be found in literature from the Fifth–Fourth Century B.C. Its single occurrence in the Septuagint is in the apocryphal Wisdom of Solomon where it refers to those who were "admonished" to obey God's laws.

New Testament Usage

The word *nouthesia* can refer to advising someone of the danger their actions entail, as in Titus 3:10. Thus, there is often the sense of warning. First Corinthians 10:11 says the judgments of Israel's unbelief and rebellion in the wilderness happened for our examples and "they are written for our *admonition*." Believers are admonished, instructed, and warned to correct their lives and to turn to the Lord continually in repentance and faith. In doing so they will not come under judgment and miss God's blessings.

The final New Testament use is Ephesians 6:4 where parents are challenged to bring up their children "in the nurture and *admonition* of the Lord." This is in contrast to provoking them to anger. This concept of *nouthesia* is important in these days when so much of society is impersonal. Families and the church family need this kind of personal discipleship and care for one another, for the erring brother, for the young convert, and for children, so all may grow in the fullness of Christ.

STRONG 3559, BAUER 544, MOULTON-MILLIGAN 430, KITTEL 4:1019-22, LIDDELL-SCOTT 1182, COLIN BROWN 1:568-69.

3423. νουθετέω noutheteō verb

Put in mind, admonish, warn, instruct.
COGNATES:
νοέω noeō (3401)
νουθεσία nouthesia (3422)
SYNONYMS:
ἐλέγχω elenchō (1638)
ἐπιπλήσσω epiplēssō (1954)
ἐπιτιμάω epitimaō (1992)

בִּין bîn (1032), Hithpolel: comprehend (Jb 38:18).
בִּינָה bînāh (1035), Understanding (Jb 34:16).
יָסַר yāṣar (3364), Piel: instruct (Jb 4:3).
כָּהָה kāhâh (3663), Piel: restrain (1 Sm 3:13).

1. **νουθετῶ** noutheto 1sing indic pres act
2. **νουθετεῖτε** noutheteite 2pl impr pres act
3. **νουθετῶν** nouthetōn nom sing masc part pres act
4. **νουθετοῦντες** nouthetountes
   nom pl masc part pres act
5. **νουθετοῦντας** nouthetountas
   acc pl masc part pres act
6. **νουθετεῖν** nouthetein inf pres act

3 to **warn** every one night and day with tears. .... Acts 20:31
6 able also to **admonish** one another. .... Rom 15:14
1 but as my beloved sons I **warn** you. .... 1 Co 4:14
4 **warning** every man, and teaching every man .... Col 1:28
4 teaching and **admonishing** one another in psalms 3:16
5 and are over you in the Lord, and **admonish** you; ... 1 Th 5:12
2 Now we exhort you, ... **warn** them that are unruly, ... 5:14
2 not as an enemy, but **admonish** him as a brother. .... 2 Th 3:15

Classical Greek

A compound of *nous* (3426), "mind," and a derivative of *tithēmi* (4935), "to put, place," *noutheteō* means "to put in mind." The action describes an influence exerted upon the mind and implies a prior resistance. *Noutheteō*, then, means "to admonish, warn, instruct," so as to redirect someone from wrong ways and correct his behavior (Selter, "Exhort," *Colin Brown*, 1:568). In classical Greek literature this verb is found especially in the tragic writers, such as Homer's *Iliad*, Eighth—Seventh Century B.C., and Aeschylus' *Prometheus Vinctus*, Sixth—Fifth Century B.C.

Septuagint Usage
With the exception of 1 Samuel 3:13 (LXX 1 Kings 3:13), where it means "to admonish" or "reprimand," *noutheteō* is used only in Job in the canonical portions of the Septuagint. In the active sense it means "to instruct" (Job 4:3), whereas the unusual passive sense, namely, to let oneself be taught, be reproved, gain insight, understand, is found in Job 23:15; 36:12; 37:14; 38:18.

New Testament Usage
In the New Testament *noutheteō* occurs seven times in the Pauline letters and once in Acts 20:31 where it carries the sense of "to warn." In Paul's usage the verb clearly has pedagogical implications. In Colossians 1:28 and 3:16 *noutheteō* is linked with *didaskō* (1315), "to teach," implying that the proclamation of Christ encompasses both teaching (shaping the intellect) and warning (shaping the will). The task of admonishing the church belongs to the leaders of the church (1 Thessalonians 5:12). Individual members who are disobedient need to be warned of the error of their ways, in order that they might be restored (1 Thessalonians 5:14; 2 Thessalonians 3:15). Believers are also called upon to admonish or instruct one another (Romans 15:14). Even though *noutheteō* carried the intention of shaping character and conduct, Paul never viewed it as synonymous with *paideuō* (3674), "to correct by discipline."

STRONG 3560, BAUER 544, MOULTON-MILLIGAN 430, KITTEL 4:1019-22, LIDDELL-SCOTT 1182-83, COLIN BROWN 1:567-68.

3424. νουμηνία noumēnia noun
New moon, beginning of the month, a festival associated with it.
CROSS-REFERENCES:
μήν mēn (3243)
νέος neos (3363C)

חֹדֶשׁ chōdhesh (2414), New moon (Nm 29:6, 2 Chr 31:3, Ez 46:1).

1. νουμηνίας noumēnias gen sing fem

1 or in respect of an holyday, or of the **new moon**, ... Col 2:16

Classical Greek and Septuagint Usage
Noumēnia is the contracted form of *neomēnia* (3363B) meaning "new moon"; i.e., the first appearance of the moon in a new cycle of phases. The new moon designated the beginning of a new month of the Jewish calendar. Both Jews and Gentiles had festivals at the first of the lunar month. Israel was told in Numbers 28:11 to offer sacrifices on the first of the month out of worship, faith, and gratefulness to the Lord.

New Testament Usage
In the one New Testament use of this word Christians are told not to let anyone judge them in regard to diet or a festival, a new moon, or a Sabbath Day (Colossians 2:16). These were only shadows of the Christ who has now come and is the reality that they had anticipated. Paul's letter opposes legalistic observance of rituals which hold people in bondage to self-made religion. Such legalism is held in contrast to the new life of God's fullness in Christ. The reference to new moon here reminds believers that observing sacred days is to be a matter of personal conscience and that it must be motivated by gratitude and faith in the Lord and not by fear or selfishness.

STRONG 3561, BAUER 544, MOULTON-MILLIGAN 430, LIDDELL-SCOTT 1183.

3425. νουνεχῶς nounechōs adv
Wisely, thoughtfully, discreetly, prudently.
CROSS-REFERENCE:
νέος neos (3363C)

1. νουνεχῶς nounechōs

1 And when Jesus saw that he answered **discreetly**, . . Mark 12:34

Classical Greek
Derived from a combination of *nous* (3426), "mind, understanding," and *echō* (2174), "to have," the adjective *nounechōs* means "sensibly, wisely, discreetly." In the classical Greek the cognate words *nounecheia* and *nounechēs* are found with meanings of "with understanding, sensible, discreet" as well as the related word *nounechontōs* meaning "sensibly" (*Liddell-Scott*).

New Testament Usage
In the New Testament *nounechōs* is found only once, at Mark 12:34. Here the scribe responded to Christ's instruction concerning the first and second commandments. Jesus perceived that he

had answered *nounechōs*, "with understanding" or "intelligently and thoughtfully." Consequently, Jesus responded that the scribe was "not far from the kingdom."

STRONG 3562, BAUER 544, MOULTON-MILLIGAN 430-31, KITTEL 2:816-27, LIDDELL-SCOTT 1183.

3426. νοῦς nous noun

Attitude, intellect, mind, thought, understanding.

COGNATE:
νοέω noeō (3401)

SYNONYMS:
διαλογισμός dialogismos (1255)
διανόημα dianoēma (1264)
διάνοια dianoia (1265)
ἐνθύμησις enthumēsis (1745)
ἔννοια ennoia (1755)
ἐπίνοια epinoia (1948)
λογισμός logismos (3027)
νόημα noēma (3402)
σύνεσις sunesis (4757)

אֹזֶן 'ōzen (238), Ear (Jb 33:16).

לֵב lēv (3949), Heart (Ex 7:23, Jos 14:7, Is 10:7).

רוּחַ rûach (7593), Spirit (Is 40:13).

1. νοῦς nous nom sing masc
2. νοός noos gen sing masc
3. νοΐ noi dat sing masc
4. νοῦν noun acc sing masc

4	Then opened he their **understanding**,	Luke 24:45
4	God gave them over to a reprobate **mind**,	Rom 1:28
2	warring against the law of my **mind**,	7:23
3	with the **mind** I myself serve the law of God;	7:25
4	For who hath known the **mind** of the Lord?	11:34
2	be ye transformed by the renewing of your **mind**,	12:2
3	Let every man be fully persuaded in his own **mind**.	14:5
3	in the same **mind** and in the same judgment.	1 Co 1:10
4	For who hath known the **mind** of the Lord,	2:16
4	But we have the **mind** of Christ.	2:16
1	spirit prayeth, but my **understanding** is unfruitful.	14:14
3	and I will pray with the **understanding** also:	14:15
3	and I will sing with the **understanding** also.	14:15
2	rather speak five words with my **understanding**,	14:19
2	as other Gentiles walk, in the vanity of their **mind**,	Eph 4:17
2	And be renewed in the spirit of your **mind**;	4:23
4	the peace of God, which passeth all **understanding**,	Phlp 4:7
2	vainly puffed up by his fleshly **mind**,	Col 2:18
2	That ye be not soon shaken in **mind**,	2 Th 2:2
4	Perverse disputings of men of corrupt **minds**,	1 Tm 6:5
4	these also resist the truth: men of corrupt **minds**,	2 Tm 3:8
1	but even their **mind** and conscience is defiled.	Tit 1:15
4	hath **understanding** count the number of the beast:	Rev 13:18
1	And here is the **mind** which hath wisdom.	17:9

Classical Greek

Nous appears as early as 1400–1200 B.C. and is found in Homer as a contracted form of *noos*. The original meaning was an "inner sense directed on an object, embracing 'sensation,' 'power of spiritual perception,' 'capacity for intellectual apprehension' " (Behm, "nous," *Kittel*, 4:952). The chief senses thus were "mind (the disposition), insight, understanding, thought," and related aspects usually in practical relationship to a particular object. Thus *nous* was "capable of embracing all the instruments of sensual and conceptual perception" (Harder, "Mind," *Colin Brown*, 3:122). These senses all continue in secular Greek usage through the New Testament period.

In philosophy *nous* specifically becomes the organ of knowledge, i.e., "the mind," a separate part of the total human being. To Plato the *nous* was the highest and most excellent part of tripartite man (Behm, "nous," *Kittel*, 4:954). The concept of mind becomes more theoretical than practical. Aristotle believed the sphere of *nous* was limited to perception, and he further linked it to reason (ibid.). It was the embodiment of the divine. Stoicism modified this concept and equated *nous* with reason and with God. Thus the later Stoic Epictetus defined *nous* as "God's being" (*Discourses* 2.8.1). The emperor Marcus Aurelius said the *nous* of a man is the *daimōn* (1136) (the divine power of element) within him, and this element is part of deity. Philo also equated *nous* with reason (Behm, "nous," *Kittel*, 4:955).

Septuagint Usage

In the Septuagint *nous* is relatively rare due to the lack of an equivalent concept in Hebrew thought. In its 32 appearances only 10 have Hebrew words behind them. In Hebrew thought the heart (*lēv* or *lēvāv*) was the organ of feeling (as felt in a change of beat), intellectual activities, and volition (Eichrodt, *Theology of the Old Testament*, 2:143). The translators of the Septuagint generally translated *lēv* with *kardia* (2559), "heart," whose figurative sense was also common in Greek. *Nous* translates *lēv* only six times, and such senses as "thoughts, disposition," and the general, nontechnical senses found in secular Greek are most evident (Exodus 7:23; Job 7:17; Isaiah 41:22).

The philosophical definition of *nous* as "mind" only appears in the later, noncanonical books (e.g., Wisdom of Solomon 4:12; 9:15; 3 Maccabees 1:25), and once in Isaiah 40:13 where Hebrew *rûach* stands behind it. In this verse, "Who has known the *mind* of the Lord," it is clear that God's "organ of knowledge" and His cognitive processes are in view. In the Stoic Fourth Maccabees *nous* is equated again with reason as the power controlling the emotions and body (1:35; 3:17).

Finally, on three occasions *nous* translates *'ōzen*, "ear," and it is likely that either a copyist's or translator's error has substituted *nous* for *ous* (3638B), "ear." Manuscript variations of this type are regular.

New Testament Usage

The New Testament follows the secular Greek and Septuagintal usage of *nous*. The philosophical senses are absent. *Nous* is primarily used by Paul (21 of 24 occurrences, 13 of them in Romans and 1 Corinthians alone). Paul probably used *nous* with his predominantly Greek readers because they were familiar with it. In the New Testament as a whole *kardia* and the Hebrew concept of the psychic man generally predominate. *Nous* then can indicate the mind, faculties of judgment, and insight.

The Holy Spirit inspired Paul to quote Isaiah 40:13 when the apostle defined the genuinely spiritual person (1 Corinthians 2:16). It is the individual who has the mind of Christ. Paul referred to the same verse in Isaiah's prophecy when he addressed the Roman assembly with respect to God's dealings with Israel (Romans 11:34). Paul utilized the statement from Isaiah to show how ludicrous it is for people to question the mind of the Lord and to attempt to be His counselor. The verse in Romans and the one in 1 Corinthians both use *nous* in the sense of having a particular mode of thinking and judgment. It certainly is foolish to question God's judgment. The only way a person can be truly spiritual is to think as God thinks.

Paul encouraged the Corinthian church members to all have the same mind (1 Corinthians 1:10). This verse is an integral part of the theme of the entire epistle which points to the key to unity in God's work, i.e., exalting the Lord Jesus Christ (1 Corinthians 1:10-31). If the Corinthians had done that they would not have experienced the many problems that plagued them, the problems Paul confronted in his correspondences to them.

This Greek word can also be used in the sense of opening one's mind to understand what God is doing. Jesus did precisely that for His disciples after His resurrection. He opened their minds so they could understand the Old Testament Scriptures (Luke 24:45-47) that said, "It behooved Christ to suffer, and to rise from the dead the third day: and that repentance and remission of sins should be preached in his name among all nations, beginning at Jerusalem." The last book of the Bible uses this Greek word in the same sense concerning the number of the Antichrist (Revelation 13:18). The mind with godly wisdom will understand the meaning from the context in this chapter. The same idea is found with respect to the seven heads of the beast on which the woman sits (Revelation 17:9). Again, the Holy Spirit will give clear understanding from the context.

The capacity for understanding spiritual truths can be seen with reference to the mind being able to recognize what is in accordance with God's plan and what is evil. Hence, the Scriptures speak of reprobate or unapproved minds that turn from worshiping the true God to worshiping the creature (Romans 1:28); of empty minds that live without the light of God (Ephesians 4:17); of proud minds that add to the Scriptures (Colossians 2:18); of corrupt minds which think wealth is a sign of godliness (1 Timothy 6:5); of depraved minds that oppose the truth (2 Timothy 3:8); and of defiled minds that consider everything impure (Titus 1:15).

Paul used this same Greek term to encourage the Roman Christians to be fully persuaded in their own minds as to what days they should set aside to worship God (Romans 14:5). He cautioned the Thessalonians not to be shaken in mind over false claims that the Lord already had returned and they were in the Tribulation period (2 Thessalonians 2:2).

In connection with corporate worship Paul spoke of the mind being "unfruitful" when he was praying in tongues (1 Corinthians 14:14). He encouraged the Corinthians to balance this praying with the "understanding" or with the mind, and he mentioned the same things about singing (1 Corinthians 14:15). He stressed the necessity of the mind understanding what was being spoken in tongues (1 Corinthians 14:19).

Paul encouraged the Philippian saints with the promise that the peace of God which surpasses all human understanding would guard them emotionally and intellectually (Philippians 4:7).

To the Romans Paul spoke of his own human mind that wanted to do what was right but could not without the grace of God (Romans 7:23), and of the progressive metamorphosis of the Christian mind that is dedicated to God's will (Romans 12:2).

Νύμφα 3426B

STRONG 3563, BAUER 544-55, MOULTON-MILLIGAN 431, KITTEL 4:951-60, LIDDELL-SCOTT 1180, COLIN BROWN 3:122-130.

3426B. Νύμφα Numpha name
Nymphas.

1. Νύμφαν Numphan acc fem

Laodicean Christian who received a greeting from Paul (Colossians 4:15).

3427. Νυμφᾶς Numphas name
Numphas.

1. Νυμφᾶν Numphan acc masc

1 the brethren which are in Laodicea, and **Nymphas**,... Col 4:15

Masculine form of *Numpha* (see 3426B). Colossians 4:15 has the accusative form (*Numphan*), which may be traced to either the masculine or feminine form.

3428. νύμφη numphē noun
Bride, daughter-in-law.

COGNATES:
νυμφίος numphios (3429)
νυμφών numphōn (3430)
בְּתוּלָה bᵉthûlāh (1359), Virgin, maiden (Jer 2:32, Jl 1:8).
כַּלָּה kallāh (3738), Daughter-in-law, daughter (Gn 38:16, Ru 2:20, Hos 4:13f.).

1. νύμφη numphē nom sing fem
2. νύμφης numphēs gen sing fem
3. νύμφην numphēn acc sing fem

3 and the **daughter in law** against her mother in law. Matt 10:35
3 the mother in law against her **daughter in law**,..... Luke 12:53
1 and the **daughter in law** against her mother in law...... 12:53
3 He that hath the **bride** is the bridegroom:.......... John 3:29
2 and the voice of the bridegroom and of the **bride**... Rev 18:23
3 prepared as a **bride** adorned for her husband......... 21:2
3 I will show thee the **bride**, the Lamb's wife........... 21:9
1 And the Spirit and the **bride** say, Come.............. 22:17

Classical Greek

The term *numphē* occurs very early in classical Greek. In the beginning it appears to have been connected with the Latin *nurus*. The Greeks did use the word with the sense "bride," but it had a far broader use as well and can be translated "young women, virgin, engaged," and "young wife." It is also used in connection with lower, female deities. Later *numphē* was used by the Gnostics in their sensual, erotic religious systems, and also concerning the community with their *sōtēr* (4842), "deities."

Septuagint Usage

In the Septuagint *numphē* translates the Hebrew *kallāh*. *Numphē* is the word used both in the Septuagint and the New Testament for "bride" and "daughter-in-law" in various references to weddings and family relationships. However, what is interesting is the figurative use of these common, ancient Near Eastern cultural settings to describe spiritual realities. In Micah 7:6 *numphē* is used of daughter-in-law against mother-in-law strife to describe unrestrained human nature of evil times. Jesus made a similar use of the term in reference to the divisions caused by the gospel as some receive while others reject (Matthew 10:35; Luke 12:53).

The Old Testament employs the bride-bridegroom relationship metaphorically, perhaps even allegorically, of the relationship between the Lord and Israel. Israel is described as the bride of the Lord or His lawful wife (Isaiah 49:18; 62:5; Jeremiah 2:2; Hosea 2:19f.). The rabbis also interpreted the Song of Solomon in this way. Jeremiah 7:34 and several other passages describe the judgment on the sinful nation of Israel in terms of the sound of joy from the participants at a wedding ceasing, as does Revelation 18:23 of the destruction of Babylon. However, Isaiah 62:5 says God rejoices over His people like a groom over a bride. John the Baptist picked up this common Old Testament theme when he said he rejoiced as a friend of the bridegroom to see the groom receive the bride. He said his joy was completed by seeing many people coming to believe in Jesus as the Christ (John 3:26-36).

New Testament Usage

In the New Testament *numphē* is almost always used metaphorically. The Old Testament imagery describing God and His chosen people has been transferred to Christ and the universal Christian church. As Isaiah 49:18 and 61:10 use *numphē* to describe God's people as His bride being prepared for Him, so the apostle John was inspired to describe the eternal fellowship of God with His people as a husband receiving his bride (Revelation 21:2,9). This marital imagery, which is not limited to contexts where *numphē* is used (e.g., Ephesians 5:22-32), is thus an important way the Lord has chosen to communicate His desire for intimate personal fellowship with all those who will accept His offer.

In both Mark 2:19 (cf. Matthew 9:15) and Luke 5:34f. Jesus referred to himself as the bridegroom, but He did not refer to believers as the "bride." Perhaps the earliest figurative reference in the New Testament to the Church as the "bride of Christ" is 2 Corinthians 11:2, where Paul pictured himself as the "best man": "For I am jealous over you with godly jealousy: for I have espoused you to one husband, that I may present you as a chaste *virgin* (*parthenos* [3795]) to Christ." The context shows how Paul based his remarks on the same marital imagery emphasized by the Old Testament prophets (i.e., Jeremiah, Ezekiel, Hosea) and on the relationship between Adam and Eve. Paul further developed the Adam-Eve typology in Ephesians 5:22-31, and he interpreted Genesis 2:24 ("the two shall become one") as a symbolic foreshadowing of the relationship between Christ and His Church (Ephesians 5:32; cf. Aune, "Bride of Christ," *International Standard Bible Encyclopedia*, 1:547).

In Revelation John applied the image of the "bride of Christ" to the "heavenly Jerusalem" which is a symbol for the Church (ibid.). The comparison of the "heavenly Jerusalem" as a bride adorned for her husband (cf. Isaiah 61:10) depicts the anticipated readiness of the Church for Jesus (Revelation 21:2; 22:17). (For other examples of similar imagery cf. Matthew 22:2-14 and 25:1-13.)

STRONG 3565, BAUER 545, MOULTON-MILLIGAN 431, KITTEL 4:1099-1106, LIDDELL-SCOTT 1184, COLIN BROWN 2:584-85.

3429. νυμφίος numphios noun
Bridegroom.

CROSS-REFERENCE:
νύμφη numphē (3428)

חָתָן chāthān (2968), Son-in-law, bridegroom (Neh 13:28, Ps 19:5 [18:5], Is 61:10).

1. **νυμφίος** numphios nom sing masc
2. **νυμφίου** numphiou gen sing masc
3. **νυμφίον** numphion acc sing masc

1	as long as the **bridegroom** is with them?	Matt 9:15
1	when the **bridegroom** shall be taken from them,	9:15
2	and went forth to meet the **bridegroom**.	25:1
2	While the **bridegroom** tarried, they all slumbered	25:5
1	the **bridegroom** cometh; go ye out to meet him.	25:6
1	And while they went to buy, the **bridegroom** came;	25:10
1	fast, while the **bridegroom** is with them?	Mark 2:19
3	as long as they have the **bridegroom** with them,	2:19
1	the **bridegroom** shall be taken away from them,	2:20
1	fast, while the **bridegroom** is with them?	Luke 5:34
1	the **bridegroom** shall be taken away from them,	5:35
3	the governor of the feast called the **bridegroom**,	John 2:9
1	He that hath the bride is the **bridegroom**:	3:29
2	but the friend of the **bridegroom**,	John 3:29
2	because of the **bridegroom's** voice:	3:29
2	and the voice of the **bridegroom** and of the bride	Rev 18:23

Classical Greek

The use of *numphios*, "bridegroom," is attested to from the time of Homer (Eighth Century B.C.). It carries the meaning of "bridegroom," "betrothed," and "young husband." In Homer's *Iliad* it refers to "one lately married" (cf. *Liddell-Scott*). In addition to the singular form the plural *numphiois* is used to signify the "bridal pair" (e.g., Euripides [Fifth Century B.C.]). Also, *numphios* is used adjectivally with the meaning "bridal." *Numphios* within Hellenism was used to convey the concept of the bride and bridegroom as analogous to the relationship of the Saviour and men, particularly within the realm of the Gnostic oriented structures (Günther, "Marriage," *Colin Brown*, 2:584).

Septuagint Usage

In the Septuagint *numphios*, used for the Hebrew *chāthān*, is found in the canonical literature as well as in the apocryphal writings of Baruch and 1 Maccabees. Besides the customary translation of "bridegroom," *numphios* also acquired another meaning, that of "son-in-law." In Judges 15:6 Samson is referred to as a *numphios*, "son-in-law" (cf. Judges 19:5; Nehemiah 13:28).

Elsewhere in the Septuagint *numphios* is translated as "bridegroom" and is used both literally and figuratively. Literally, Jeremiah spoke of the coming conditions of Israel and how, along with other occurrences, the voice of the "bridegroom" would be heard no more (Jeremiah 7:34; 16:9; 25:10). Later, when speaking of the return and restoration of Israel from her captivity, the picture is used of the voice of the "bridegroom" again being heard in the land. Symbolically, the implication is that of the loss and eventual regaining of joy by a people who had disobeyed God, who had repented, and who then were restored.

Figuratively, *numphios* is used with regard to the relationship between God and the nation of Israel. Isaiah 61:10 and 62:5 picture God as a *numphios*, "bridegroom." In this relationship Israel is God's bride. A prominent theme throughout these passages is that of the joy which is present in the relationship.

New Testament Usage

In the New Testament the various referents found in the classical writings (e.g., "young husband") and the Septuagint (e.g., "son-in-law") are absent. Only "bridegroom" is carried into the New Testament. However, this usage is primarily a reflection of the Jewish customs and concepts. The use of *numphios* in the New Testament is relatively rare, being found primarily in the Gospels and once in Revelation.

In the New Testament *numphios* is used both literally and figuratively. In John 2:9 and Revelation 18:23 *numphios* literally denotes "bridegroom." In John 3:29 the "bridegroom" is called aside by the master of the banquet in order to comment on the quality of the wine. In Revelation 18:23—at the fall of Babylon—the voice of the "bridegroom" will be heard no more in the city.

Figuratively, the two *numphios* usages (Matthew 9:15 with parallel passages and Matthew 25:1-13) offer a fulfillment of an Old Testament concept in the New Testament. However, the Old Testament references of the bride and bridegroom are to Israel and God (Isaiah 62:5), whereas the New Testament uses this imagery in referring to the community of believers and Christ. This use of "bridegroom" as it relates to the Messiah is unique to the New Testament.

Surrounding the imagery of the "bridegroom" are other important aspects that further study brings into focus. In John 3:39 reference is made to *ho philos tou numphiou*, "the friend of the bridegroom," who played a key role in the marriage picture. Further imagery of this concept of Christ as the "bridegroom" and the Church as the "bride" is found in the writings of Paul in 2 Corinthians 11:2 and Ephesians 5:22-32. Although *numphios* is not specifically found in these passages the picture is clearly one of the marriage relationship.

STRONG 3566, BAUER 545, MOULTON-MILLIGAN 431, KITTEL 4:1099-1106, LIDDELL-SCOTT 1184, COLIN BROWN 2:584-85.

3430. νυμφών numphōn noun

Wedding hall, bridechamber.

CROSS-REFERENCE:
νύμφη numphē (3428)

1. **νυμφῶνος** numphōnos gen sing masc
2. **νυμφών** numphōn nom sing masc

1 Can the children of the **bridechamber** mourn,....... Matt 9:15
2 the **wedding hall** was filled (NASB).................. 22:10
1 Can the children of the **bridechamber** fast,.......... Mark 2:19
1 Can ye make the children of the **bridechamber** fast, Luke 5:34

Classical Greek and Septuagint Usage

In classical Greek *numphōn* primarily denotes "bridechamber," that is, the room where a marriage is consummated. In the context of pagan worship *numphōn* is used of a temple where sexual fertility rites were conducted (Pausanias *Periegeta* 2.II.3; cf. *Liddell-Scott*). In another context *numphōn* is the name of a kind of water lily (ibid.). *Numphōn* does not appear in the canonical portions of the Septuagint but does occur twice in the Apocrypha where it means "bridechamber" (Tobit 6:13,16).

New Testament Usage

In Matthew 22:10 *numphōn* is the room where the wedding guests assemble to celebrate the marriage: "The *wedding hall* was filled with guests" (NIV). Otherwise, it appears only in the expression, "children of the *bridechamber*" (Matthew 9:15; Mark 2:19; Luke 5:34). This refers to those guests of the bridegroom closest to him who played a special role in the ceremonies (i.e., "bridegroom attendants"). The term appears here in a parable of Jesus in which He pointed out that the "children of the bridechamber" do not fast at the wedding ceremonies. (Feasting was practiced on such occasions.) Neither should the disciples of Jesus fast when Jesus was with them. The time would come when He would be taken away; then they would fast (Matthew 9:15).

STRONG 3567, BAUER 545, MOULTON-MILLIGAN 431, LIDDELL-SCOTT 1185, COLIN BROWN 2:584-85.

3431. νῦν nun adv

Now.

אַךְ 'akh (395), If (Jos 22:19).
אֵפוֹא 'ēphô' (660I), Then (Is 19:12).
הֵנָּה hēnnāh (2077), Until now (1 Sm 1:16).
הִנֵּה hinnēh (2079), Now (Nm 24:11).
כְּעַן ke'an (A3830), Now (Ezr 5:17, 6:6, Dn 2:23—Aramaic).
נָא nā' (5168), Now (Is 47:12).
נָא nā' (5167), Beseech (Is 64:9).
עַתָּה 'attāh (6498), Now (Gn 3:22 [3:23], 2 Chr 6:16f., Jer 18:11).

1. **νῦν** nun

1 not since the beginning of the world to **this** time,... Matt 24:21
1 behold, **now** ye have heard his blasphemy............. 26:65
1 let him **now** come down from the cross,............... 27:42

1	He trusted in God; let him deliver him **now**,	Matt 27:43
1	he shall receive an hundredfold **now** in this time,	Mark 10:30
1	of the creation which God created unto **this time**,	13:19
1	Let Christ the King ... descend **now** from the cross,	15:32
1	**henceforth** all generations shall call me blessed.	Luke 1:48
1	Lord, **now** lettest thou thy servant depart in peace,	2:29
1	Fear not; from **henceforth** thou shalt catch men.	5:10
1	Blessed are ye that hunger **now**: ... shall be filled.	6:21
1	Blessed are ye that weep **now**: for ye shall laugh.	6:21
1	Woe to you who are well-fed **now** (NASB)	6:25
1	Woe unto you that laugh **now**! for ye shall mourn	6:25
1	**Now** do ye Pharisees make clean the outside	11:39
1	**henceforth** there shall be five in one house	12:52
1	Lazarus evil things: but **now** he is comforted,	16:25
1	thy peace! but **now** they are hid from thine eyes.	19:42
1	from **now** on until the kingdom (NASB)	22:18
1	But **now**, he that hath a purse, let him take it,	22:36
1	"But from **now** on THE SON OF MAN (NASB)	22:69
1	And he saith unto them, Draw out **now**,	John 2:8
1	and he whom thou **now** hast is not thy husband:	4:18
1	But the hour cometh, and **now** is,	4:23
1	The hour is coming, and **now** is,	5:25
1	does He **now** say, "I have come (NASB)	6:42
1	But **now** ye seek to kill me,	8:40
1	**Now** we know that thou hast a devil.	8:52
1	But by what means he **now** seeth, we know not;	9:21
1	**now** ye say, We see; therefore your sin remaineth.	9:41
1	the Jews of **late** sought to stone thee;	11:8
1	But I know, that even **now**,	11:22
1	**Now** is my soul troubled; and what shall I say?	12:27
1	**Now** is the judgment of this world:	12:31
1	**now** shall the prince of this world be cast out.	12:31
1	**Now** is the Son of man glorified,	13:31
1	Whither I go, thou canst not follow me **now**;	13:36
1	And **now** I have told you before it come to pass,	14:29
1	but **now** they have no cloak for their sin.	15:22
1	but **now** have they both seen and hated	15:24
1	But **now** I go my way to him that sent me;	16:5
1	And ye **now** therefore have sorrow:	16:22
1	**now** speakest thou plainly, ... speakest no proverb.	16:29
1	**Now** are we sure that thou knowest all things,	16:30
1	Behold, the hour cometh, yea, is **now** come,	16:32
1	**now**, O Father, glorify thou me with thine own	17:5
1	**Now** they have known that all things ... are of thee.	17:7
1	And **now** come I to thee; and these things I speak	17:13
1	but **now** is my kingdom not from hence.	18:36
1	Bring of the fish which ye have **now** caught.	21:10
1	hath shed forth this, which ye **now** see and hear.	Acts 2:33
1	And **now**, brethren, ... through ignorance ye did it,	3:17
1	And **now**, Lord, behold their threatenings:	4:29
1	And **now** I say unto you, Refrain from these men,	5:38
1	removed him into this land, wherein ye **now** dwell.	7:4
1	And **now** come, I will send thee into Egypt.	7:34
1	ye have been **now** the betrayers and murderers:	7:52
1	**now** send men to Joppa, and call for one Simon,	10:5
1	**Now** therefore are we all here present before God,	10:33
1	**Now** I know of a surety,	12:11
1	**now**, behold, the hand of the Lord is upon thee,	13:11
1	who are **now** His witnesses (NASB)	13:31
1	**Now** therefore why tempt ye God,	15:10
1	**now** therefore depart, and go in peace.	16:36
1	and **now** do they thrust us out privily? nay verily;	16:37
1	**now** commandeth all men every where to repent:	17:30
1	from **henceforth** I will go unto the Gentiles.	18:6
1	And **now**, behold, I go bound in the spirit	20:22
1	And **now**, behold, I know that ye all,	20:25
1	And **now** I commend you to God (NASB)	20:32
1	hear ye my defence which I make **now** unto you.	22:1
1	And **now** why tarriest thou? arise, and be baptized,	22:16
1	**Now** therefore ye with the council signify	23:15
1	and **now** are they ready, looking for a promise	23:21
1	prove the things whereof they **now** accuse me.	24:13
1	Felix trembled, ... Go thy way for **this time**;	24:25
1	And **now** I stand and am judged for the hope	26:6
1	from the Gentiles, unto whom **now** I send thee,	26:17
1	And yet **now** I urge you (NASB)	27:22
1	To declare, I say, at **this time** his righteousness:	Rom 3:26
1	Much more then, being **now** justified by his blood,	Rom 5:9
1	by whom we have **now** received the atonement.	5:11
1	even so **now** yield your members	6:19
1	in those things whereof ye are **now** ashamed?	6:21
1	There is therefore **now** no condemnation	8:1
1	For I reckon that the sufferings of this **present time**	8:18
1	groaneth and travaileth in pain together until **now**.	8:22
1	Even so then at this **present time** also	11:5
1	have **now** obtained mercy through their unbelief:	11:30
1	Even so have these also **now** not believed,	11:31
1	they also may **now** be shown mercy. (NASB)	11:31
1	for **now** is our salvation nearer than when we	13:11
1	But **now** is made manifest,	16:26
1	not able to bear it, neither yet **now** are ye able.	1 Co 3:2
1	your children unclean; but **now** are they holy.	7:14
1	**now** are they many members, yet but one body,	12:20
1	but his will was not at all to come **at this time**;	16:12
1	from **now** on we recognize no man (NASB)	2 Co 5:16
1	yet **now** henceforth know we him no more.	5:16
1	behold, **now** is the accepted time;	6:2
1	behold, **now** is the day of salvation.	6:2
1	**Now** I rejoice, not that ye were made sorry,	7:9
1	But by an equality, that **now** at this time	8:14
1	**now** I write to them which heretofore have sinned,	13:2
1	**now** preacheth the faith which once he destroyed.	Gal 1:23
1	and the life which I **now** live in the flesh	2:20
1	are ye **now** made perfect by the flesh?	3:3
1	But **now**, after that ye have known God,	4:9
1	and answereth to Jerusalem which **now** is,	4:25
1	flesh persecuted ... Spirit, even so it is **now**.	4:29
1	that **now** worketh in the children of disobedience:	Eph 2:2
1	as it is **now** revealed unto his holy apostles	3:5
1	To the intent that **now** unto the principalities	3:10
1	but **now** are ye light in the Lord:	5:8
1	your fellowship ... from the first day until **now**;	Phlp 1:5
1	so **now** also Christ shall be magnified in my body,	1:20
1	the same conflict ... and **now** hear to be in me.	1:30
1	but **now** much more in my absence,	2:12
1	told you often, and **now** tell you even weeping,	3:18
1	Who **now** rejoice in my sufferings for you,	Col 1:24
1	but has **now** been manifested (NASB)	1:26
1	For **now** we live, if ye stand fast in the Lord.	1 Th 3:8
1	And **now** ye know what withholdeth	2 Th 2:6
1	having promise of the life that **now** is,	1 Tm 4:8
1	Charge them that are rich in **this** world,	6:17
1	But is **now** made manifest by the appearing	2 Tm 1:10
1	hath forsaken me, having loved this **present** world,	4:10
1	righteously, and godly, in this **present** world;	Tit 2:12
1	But **now** we see not yet all things put under him.	Heb 2:8
1	**now** he has obtained a ... ministry, (NASB)	8:6
1	of which we cannot **now** speak particularly.	9:5
1	**now** to appear in the presence of God for us:	9:24
1	**now** once in the end of the world hath he appeared	9:26
1	But as it is, they desire (NASB) (NT)	11:16
1	but **now** he hath promised, saying,	12:26
1	Go to **now**, ye that say, To day or to morrow	Jas 4:13
1	But **now** ye rejoice in your boastings:	4:16
1	Go to **now**, ye rich men, weep and howl	5:1
1	which are **now** reported unto you by them that	1 Pt 1:12
1	were not a people, but are **now** the people of God:	2:10
1	but **now** have obtained mercy.	2:10
1	but are **now** returned unto the Shepherd	2:25
1	whereunto even baptism doth also **now** save us	3:21
1	But the heavens and the earth, which are **now**,	2 Pt 3:7
1	To him be glory both **now** and for ever. Amen.	3:18
1	even **now** are there many antichrists;	1 Jn 2:18
1	And **now**, little children, abide in him;	2:28
1	Beloved, **now** are we the sons of God,	3:2
1	and even **now** already is it in the world.	4:3
1	And **now** I beseech thee, lady,	2 Jn 1:5
1	dominion and power, both **now** and for ever.	Jude 1:25

Classical Greek and Septuagint Usage

The adverb *nun*, "now," is a commonly used word with reference to time. It is found throughout classical writers such as Homer,

Sophocles, Herodotus, and Euripides, as well as in inscriptions, papyri, the Septuagint, Philo, and Josephus (see *Bauer* for specific examples).

In the classical writings a number of nuances are expressed with the use of *nun*. Not only does it express time in the sense of "this present moment" but also with the sense of "the present time generally" (*Liddell-Scott*). Additionally, *nun* is used: (a) to express time in the past; (b) to indicate the immediate sequence of one thing upon another, "then, therefore, thereafter"; (c) to show the sequence of one thing from another, "then, therefore"; (d) to strengthen or precipitate a command or call; (e) to strengthen a question, "what then?" The use of *nun* in the Septuagint is extensive, and it is used to translate a number of Hebrew words which relate to time.

New Testament Usage
In the New Testament a variety of nuances are present, carrying forward the Hebrew concepts of time. Approximately 140 instances of *nun* can be found, the majority located in the writings of Luke, John, and Paul. Although strictly an adverb, *nun* is also used as a noun and adjective. Perhaps the greatest use of *nun* is its literal representation of time in a variety of modes.

Translated "now," *nun* is used of the immediate present and to denote both a particular point in time as well as the extent of the time (*Bauer*). In this sense it occurs with a variety of verb tenses in order to give the constructions different nuances of meaning. In this way the writer could express himself according to his desire, e.g., using *nun* with the aorist tense to make a contrast with the past, denoting the action or condition as beginning in the present (ibid.; e.g., Romans 5:11, "we have now received the atonement," "reconciliation," NIV).

Nun is also used in conjunction with other particles such as *de* (1156), "but now"; *alla* (233), "but now"; *gar* (1056), "for now"; *oude eti*, "not even now," and *kai* (2504), "even now," as well as others. In addition to the emphasis being placed upon the immediate present, *nun* is used to direct attention to the situation at a given time, e.g., "For now we really live, if you stand firm in the Lord" (1 Thessalonians 3:8, NASB: also Acts 15:10).

Finally, when *nun* is found with the article it functions as an adjective or a substantive. Paul used *nun* adjectivally when he wrote to Timothy and Titus concerning "this present (*nun*) world" (1 Timothy 6:17, NIV; 2 Timothy 4:10; Titus 2:12). Peter also used *nun* in this way when he wrote about the "present (*nun*) heavens and earth" (2 Peter 3:7, NIV). It is seen as a substantive in 2 Corinthians 5:16: "So from *now* on we regard no one from a wordly point of view" (NIV). The substantival use is also seen in Romans 8:22 where the whole creation is said to be groaning until *nun*, "now; this present time" (see also Philippians 1:5 where Paul spoke of the believers' participation in the gospel "from the first day until *now* [*nun*]").

STRONG 3568, BAUER 545-46, MOULTON-MILLIGAN 431, KITTEL 4:1106-23, LIDDELL-SCOTT 1185, COLIN BROWN 3:833-34, 837, 841.

3432. νυνί nuni adv
Now.

1. νυνί nuni

1 But **now** the righteousness of God without the law	..	Rom 3:21
1 But **now** being made free from sin,		6:22
1 But **now** we are delivered from the law,		7:6
1 **Now** then it is no more I that do it,		7:17
1 But **now** having no more place in these parts,		15:23
1 But **now** I go unto Jerusalem to minister		15:25
1 **now** I have written unto you not to keep company,	..	1 Co 5:11
1 But **now** hath God set the members every one		12:18
1 And **now** abideth faith, hope, charity, these three;		13:13
1 **Now**, brethren, if I come unto you speaking with		14:6
1 But **now** is Christ risen from the dead,		15:20
1 **Now** therefore perform the doing of it;		2 Co 8:11
1 but **now** much more diligent,		8:22
1 **now** in Christ Jesus ye who sometimes were far off	...	Eph 2:13
1 yet **now** hath he reconciled		Col 1:21
1 but **now** is made manifest to his saints:		1:26
1 But **now** ye also put off all these; anger, wrath,		3:8
1 and **now** also a prisoner of Jesus Christ.		Phlm 1:9
1 but **now** profitable to thee and to me:		1:11
1 **now** hath he obtained a more excellent ministry,		Heb 8:6
1 **now** once at the consummation of the ages (NASB)		9:26
1 But **now** they desire a better country, that is,		11:16

The adverb *nuni*, "now," is the Attic form of the adverb *nun* (3431). Like *nun*, it is an adverb of time. Evidence from the papyri indicates that there is no essential difference between *nuni* and *nun* (*Bauer*). In the Koine papyri *nuni* appears as frequently as *nun*, but in the Biblical Koine it is less frequent, being found primarily in the Pauline epistles and Hebrews with some additional usage in Acts.

Nuni is found most extensively with the present tense, literally of time (Acts 24:13; Romans 15:23; 25:2; 2 Corinthians 8:22), but is also found with the perfect tense to indicate continuance (Romans 3:21; 6:22; cf. *Bauer*). Used with the aorist it indicates an accomplished act, "but now" (Ephesians 2:13; Colossians 1:22). In a rare use *nuni* occurs with the future tense meaning "listen *now*" to my defense (Acts 22:1). It can also introduce a real situation following an unreal statement (Hebrews 9:26; cf. *Bauer*).

STRONG 3570, BAUER 546, MOULTON-MILLIGAN 431, LIDDELL-SCOTT 1185, COLIN BROWN 3:833-34,837.

3433. νύξ nux noun

Night, at night, nighttime.

COGNATES:
μεσονύκτιον mesonuktion (3187)
νυχθήμερον nuchthēmeron (3436)

לַיְלָה laylāh (4050I), Night (Gn 30:16, 1 Sm 19:10, Ps 92:2 [91:2]).

לֵילִי lêlê (A4051), Night (Dn 2:19, 7:13—Aramaic).

נֶשֶׁף nesheph (5582), Twilight (Jb 3:9).

1. **νύξ nux** nom sing fem
2. **νυκτός nuktos** gen sing fem
3. **νυκτί nukti** dat sing fem
4. **νύκτα nukta** acc sing fem
5. **νύκτας nuktas** acc pl fem

2	he took the young child and his mother by **night**,	Matt 2:14
5	when he had fasted forty days and forty **nights**,	4:2
5	three days and three **nights** in the whale's belly;	12:40
5	the Son of man be three days and three **nights**	12:40
2	fourth watch of the **night** Jesus went unto them,	14:25
2	And at **midnight** there was a cry made,	25:6
3	All ye shall be offended because of me this **night**:	26:31
3	That this **night**, before the cock crow,	26:34
2	lest his disciples come by **night**, and steal him	27:64
2	His disciples came by **night**, and stole him	28:13
4	And should sleep, and rise **night** and day,	Mark 4:27
2	**night** and day, he was in the mountains,	5:5
2	fourth watch of the **night** he cometh unto them,	6:48
3	All ye shall be offended because of me this **night**:	14:27
3	That this day, even in this **night**, before the cock	14:30
2	keeping watch over their flock by **night**.	Luke 2:8
4	served God with fastings and prayers **night** ... day;	2:37
2	have toiled all the **night**, and have taken nothing:	5:5
3	fool, this **night** thy soul shall be required of thee:	12:20
3	in that **night** there shall be two men in one bed;	17:34
2	his own elect, which cry day and **night** unto him,	18:7
5	and at **night** he went out, and abode in the mount	21:37
2	The same came to Jesus by **night**,	John 3:2
2	he that came to Jesus by **night**, being one of them,	7:50
1	the **night** cometh, when no man can work.	9:4
3	But if a man walk in the **night**, he stumbleth,	11:10
1	went immediately out: and it was **night**.	13:30
2	which at the first came to Jesus by **night**,	19:39
3	and that **night** they caught nothing.	21:3
2	But the angel ... by **night** opened the prison doors,	Acts 5:19
2	they watched the gates day and **night** to kill him.	9:24
2	Then the disciples took him by **night**,	9:25
3	the same **night** Peter was sleeping	12:6
2	And a vision appeared to Paul in the **night**;	16:9
2	And he took them the same hour of the **night**,	16:33
2	sent away Paul and Silas by **night** unto Berea:	17:10
3	spake the Lord to Paul in the **night** by a vision,	18:9
4	to warn every one **night** and day with tears.	20:31
3	And the **night** following the Lord stood by him,	23:11
2	at the third hour of the **night**;	23:23
2	took Paul, and brought him by **night** to Antipatris.	Acts 23:31
4	instantly serving God day and **night**, hope to come.	26:7
3	For there stood by me this **night** the angel of God,	27:23
1	But when the fourteenth **night** was come,	27:27
2	about **midnight** the shipmen deemed that they	27:27
1	The **night** is far spent,	Rom 13:12
3	Jesus the same **night** in which he was betrayed	1 Co 11:23
2	labour and travail: for labouring **night** and day,	1 Th 2:9
2	**Night** and day praying exceedingly	3:10
3	day of the Lord so cometh as a thief in the **night**.	5:2
2	we are not of the **night**, nor of darkness.	5:5
2	For they that sleep sleep in the **night**;	5:7
2	they that be drunken are drunken in the **night**.	5:7
4	but wrought with labour and travail **night** and day,	2 Th 3:8
2	in supplications and prayers **night** and day.	1 Tm 5:5
2	remembrance of thee in my prayers **night** and day;	2 Tm 1:3
3	day of the Lord will come as a thief in the **night**;	2 Pt 3:10
2	and they rest not day and **night**, saying, Holy,	Rev 4:8
2	and serve him day and **night** in his temple:	7:15
1	not for a third part of it, and the **night** likewise.	8:12
2	which accused them before our God day and **night**.	12:10
2	and they have no rest day nor **night**,	14:11
2	and shall be tormented day and **night** for ever	20:10
1	not be shut ... for there shall be no **night** there.	21:25
1	shall be no **night** there; and they need no candle,	22:5

Classical Greek

In classical Greek *nux* means "night," the opposite of day. The word sometimes denotes time and sometimes darkness. In Old Testament times the night was divided into three watches, but by New Testament times it was commonly divided into four watches and 12 hours (Hill, "Night," *International Standard Bible Encyclopedia*, 3:535). The length of watches and hours varied according to the season of the year. As a proper noun *nux* is the name of the Greek goddess of night. *Nux* is sometimes used figuratively to mean "death" or some other calamitous circumstance (*Liddell-Scott*).

Septuagint Usage

In Old Testament thought night like day was created by God (Genesis 1:4,5). It is therefore not evil but good (Psalm 139:11,12 [LXX 138:11,12]). Nevertheless, darkness provides a cover for the actions of evil men (Job 36:20; Jeremiah 6:5). The use of *nux* in the expression "three days and three nights" should not be taken literally, for on the "third day" a man said he had not eaten for "three days and three nights" (1 Samuel 30:12,13 [LXX 1 Kings 30:12,13]). The statement may be understood as a pleonastic idiom meaning "three days." The idiom is common in the Bible (see especially Matthew 12:40; cf. 17:23). *Nux* is sometimes used figuratively for a time of gloom and despair (Micah 3:6).

New Testament Usage

Jesus used *nux* as a figure for a time coming when man cannot work (John 9:4). Used figuratively it refers to this present evil age (Romans 13:12). Elsewhere, the people of God are "sons of day" whereas those of this world are "sons of night" (1 Thessalonians 5:5). Similarly, God's people are not to be "of night" but awake, sober, and on the alert (verse 6).

STRONG 3571, BAUER 546, MOULTON-MILLIGAN 431-32, KITTEL 4:1123-26, LIDDELL-SCOTT 1185, COLIN BROWN 1:420-21.

3434. νύσσω nussō verb

Stab, pierce through, prick.
SYNONYMS:
διϊκνέομαι diikneomai (1332)
ἐκκεντέω ekkenteō (1561)

1. ἔνυξεν enuxen 3sing indic aor act

1 one of the soldiers with a spear **pierced** his side,... John 19:34

Classical Greek
In the classical period *nussō* meant: (a) "to touch with a sharp point, prick, pierce," (b) "to nudge with one's elbow," (c) "to prick an object to see its contents," (d) metaphorically, "to sting," and (e) "to impinge upon," especially with regard to sense impressions (*Liddell-Scott*).

It is found frequently in the writings of Homer, many times in reference to the receiving of a severe or deadly wound. *Nussō* can also be found in Philo, Josephus, and apocryphal writings. Plutarch (ca. First–Second Century A.D.) used *nusseiv* in referring to the use of a dagger in determining a person's condition, whether they were dead or alive (cf. *Bauer*).

Septuagint Usage
The word *nussō* occurs twice in the Septuagint, in the apocryphal writings of Sirach and 3 Maccabees. In 3 Maccabees a servant "shook" the king in order to wake him (5:14). In Sirach the reference is to a "wound" in the eye (22:19, note that the Syriac version reads *nosoi* where the Latin version reads *nussōn*).

New Testament Usage
In the New Testament there is only one occurrence of *nussō*. In John 19:34 the form *enuxen* is used to describe the soldier's use of a spear to "pierce" the side of Jesus resulting in the flow of blood and water.

STRONG 3572, BAUER 547, MOULTON-MILLIGAN 432, LIDDELL-SCOTT 1185.

3435. νυστάζω nustazō verb

To be half asleep, doze; to hang the head; to be idle.

דָּלַף dālaph (1872), Melt (Ps 119:28 [118:28]).
נוּם nûm (5305), Slumber (Ps 121:3f. [120:3f.], Is 5:27, Na 3:18).
רָדַם rādham (7578), Niphal: be in a deep sleep (Ps 76:6 [75:6]).
שֵׁנָה shēnāh (8524), Sleep (Prv 6:10, 24:33 [24:48]).

1. νυστάζει nustazei 3sing indic pres act
2. ἐνύσταξαν enustaxan 3pl indic aor act
3. νυστάξει nustaxei 3sing indic fut act

2 bridegroom tarried, they all **slumbered** and slept.... Matt 25:5
1 and their damnation **slumbereth** not................. 2 Pt 2:3

Classical Greek
In classical Greek *nustazō* primarily means "to become drowsy" or "to doze." As well, it sometimes denotes "to hang the head," as in "grow drowsy" (*Liddell-Scott*).

Septuagint Usage
In the Septuagint *nustazō* is used for taking a nap at midday (2 Samuel 4:5 [LXX 2 Kings 4:5]), the dozing or sleeping of the indolent (Isaiah 56:10), or dozing on the watch (Psalm 121:3,4 [LXX 120:3,4]; Nahum 3:18). *Nustazō* is found repeatedly in the expression "*become drowsy* and fall asleep" (Psalm 121:4 [LXX 120:4]; Isaiah 5:27). In Psalm 119:28 (LXX 118:28) *nustazō* means weariness of soul. In one text *nustazō* appears to be used figuratively for death (Psalm 76:6 [LXX 75:6]).

New Testament Usage
In the New Testament *nustazō* appears in Jesus' Parable of the Ten Virgins who "*became drowsy* and fell asleep" (Matthew 25:5, NIV). It appears in only one other passage, "Their destruction has not been *sleeping*" (2 Peter 2:3, NIV). Peter personified Destruction as the agent of God, wide awake and ready to act against the ungodly in due time.

STRONG 3573, BAUER 547, LIDDELL-SCOTT 1185-86.

3436. νυχθήμερον

nuchthēmeron noun

A day and a night.
CROSS-REFERENCES:
ἡμέρα hēmera (2232)
νύξ nux (3433)

1. νυχθήμερον nuchthēmeron nom/acc sing neu

1 **a night and a day** I have been in the deep;......... 2 Co 11:25

Found only in 2 Corinthians 11:25, *nuchthēmeron*, "a night and a day," is used adjectivally with reference to describing the length of time the apostle Paul spent in the sea. This word

3437. Νῶε Nōe name
Noah.

1. Νῶε Nōe masc

1 But as the days of **Noe** were, so shall also	Matt 24:37
1 until the day that **Noe** entered into the ark,	24:38
1 which was the son **of Noe,**	Luke 3:36
1 And as it was in the days **of Noe,** so shall it be also	17:26
1 until the day that **Noe** entered into the ark,	17:27
1 By faith **Noah,** ... moved with fear,	Heb 11:7
1 in the days **of Noah,** while the ark was a preparing,	1 Pt 3:20
1 but saved **Noah** the eighth person, a preacher	2 Pt 2:5

The son of Lamech in the genealogy of Jesus (Luke 3:36). This preacher of righteousness "by faith" constructed the ark by which his family was saved (2 Peter 2:5; Hebrews 11:7).

3438. νωθρός nōthros adj
Lazy, sluggish, indolent, dull.

SYNONYM:
ὀκνηρός oknēros (3499)

1. νωθροί nōthroi nom pl masc

1 hard to be uttered, seeing ye are **dull** of hearing	Heb 5:11
1 That ye be not **slothful,** but followers of them	6:12

Classical Greek and Septuagint Usage
During the classical period *nōthros* meant "leisurely or gradually falling into a deep sleep," often with reference to the mind and one's mental responsiveness (cf. *Liddell-Scott*). The word is rare in the writings of the Septuagint. In one example Sirach warns against "indolence" in work (Sirach 4:29).

New Testament Usage
In the New Testament *nōthros* is found only in the Book of Hebrews. The word conveys the idea of a lack or deficiency and refers to both a lack of receptivity to Christian truth and a general dullness or staleness concerning one's faith or spiritual fervor.

In Hebrews 5:11 the author wanted to share more concerning the depths of the truth of Jesus but felt unable to because his readers had become *nōthroi*, "dull" of hearing, and therefore in need of further elementary teaching. Hebrews 6:12 indicates the author was strongly concerned about the readers' "sluggishness" with regard to their faith and the perils of falling away. The author desired that they maintain the vitality of spiritual fervor so that through the dynamic of their faith, they would experience grace to inherit the promises of the Kingdom.

STRONG 3576, BAUER 547, MOULTON-MILLIGAN 432, KITTEL 4:1126, LIDDELL-SCOTT 1186.

3439. νῶτος nōtos noun
Back.

גַּב gav (1384), Rim (1 Kgs 7:33, Ez 1:18); back (Ez 10:12).

גֵּו gēw (1490), Back (Is 50:6).

כָּתֵף kātheph (3931I), Side (Jos 18:12, Ez 40:41).

מַפְרֶקֶת maphreqeth (4826), Neck (1 Sm 4:18).

מָתְנַיִם mothnayim (5158), Loins (Ps 69:23 [68:23]).

עֹרֶף ʻōreph (6439), Neck (Gn 49:8); back (2 Sm 22:41, Jer 48:29 [31:39]).

שְׁכֶם sheKhem (8327), Shoulder (Gn 9:23, Ps 81:6 [80:6]); back (Ps 21:12 [20:12]).

1. νῶτον nōton acc sing masc

1 and bow down their **back** alway	Rom 11:10

Nōtos primarily identifies that part of the anatomy of both humans and animals commonly referred to as the back. It occurs only once in the New Testament in Romans 11:10. According to Moulton this quote from the Septuagint version of Psalm 68:24 speaks figuratively of persons who bow the back under affliction (*Analytical Greek Lexicon,* "nōtos").

STRONG 3577, BAUER 547, MOULTON-MILLIGAN 432, LIDDELL-SCOTT 1187 (see "nōton").

3440. ξενία xenia noun
Hospitality, guest room.
CROSS-REFERENCE:
ξένος xenos (3443)

1. ξενίαν xenian acc sing fem

| 1 there came many to him into his **lodging**; | Acts 28:23 |
| 1 But withal prepare me also **a lodging**: | Phlm 1:22 |

Classical Greek and Septuagint Usage
In classical Greek the noun *xenia* is commonly used to describe the "hospitality" or "friendly relation" shown to a *xenos*, "stranger, guest-friend" (*Liddell-Scott*). Less frequently it is also used of the place where a guest might be received or entertained, hence, "guestchamber, guesthouse." The Septuagint uses *xenia* only once, in Sirach 29:27, where it is a place for housing a guest and is interchangeable with *oikia* (3477), "house."

New Testament Usage
In the New Testament *xenia* is used only twice: in Philemon 22 for the "lodging" (room) Philemon was to prepare for Paul, and in Acts 28:23 for the "lodging" (house) Paul stayed in at Rome. *Xenia* was not used by the New Testament writers for the virtue of "hospitality" that is a mark of Christianity (cf. *philoxenia* [5218]; Romans 12:13; Hebrews 13:2).

STRONG 3578, BAUER 547, MOULTON-MILLIGAN 433, KITTEL 5:1-36, LIDDELL-SCOTT 1188.

3441. ξενίζω xenizō verb
Receive or entertain a guest, be or make strange, shock or surprise (as with something strange).
CROSS-REFERENCE:
ξένος xenos (3443)

1. ξενίζοντα xenizonta nom/acc pl neu part pres act
2. ἐξένισεν exenisen 3sing indic aor act
3. ξενίσαντες xenisantes nom pl masc part aor act
4. ξενίζεται xenizetai 3sing indic pres mid
5. ξενίζονται xenizontai 3pl indic pres mid
6. ξενίζεσθε xenizesthe 2pl impr pres mid
7. ξενισθῶμεν xenisthōmen 1pl subj aor pass

4 He **lodgeth** with one Simon a tanner,	Acts 10:6
4 which was surnamed Peter, were **lodged** there.	10:18
2 Then called he them in, and **lodged** them.	10:23
4 he **is lodged** in the house of one Simon a tanner	10:32
1 thou bringest certain **strange** things to our ears:	17:20
7 an old disciple, with whom we **should lodge**.	21:16
2 received us, and **lodged** us three days courteously.	28:7
3 thereby some **have entertained** angels unawares.	Heb 13:2
5 they **think it strange** that ye run not with them	1 Pt 4:4
6 think it not **strange** concerning the fiery trial	4:12

Classical Greek
In classical Greek the verb *xenizō* is used of "receiving or entertaining someone as a guest" (*Liddell-Scott*). It is related to *xenos* (3443), "strange, stranger," and can also be found meaning "surprise, astonish by some strange sight" (ibid.).

Septuagint Usage
Jews in the Biblical period had an acute sense of the evils of being strangers and aliens, thus all the uses of *xenizō* in the Septuagint are negative. *Xenizō* refers to the wandering stranger (Sirach 29:25), or in Maccabees, to the strangeness of unusually cruel tortures (2 Maccabees 9:6; 3 Maccabees 7:3).

New Testament Usage
In the New Testament *xenizō* carries with it either neutral or positive connotations, unlike the strictly negative connotations in the Septuagint. It is used seven times to describe the temporary housing of a guest, especially one who is traveling in the Lord's service (see Acts 10:6; 21:16; 28:7; Hebrews 13:2). Three times it means "to consider something strange": in a missionary context in Acts 17:20, and in an apocalyptic setting in 1 Peter 4:4,12.

Strong 3579, Bauer 547-48, Moulton-Milligan 433, Kittel 5:1-36, Liddell-Scott 1188.

3442. ξενοδοχέω xenodocheō verb
Show hospitality.
CROSS-REFERENCE:
    ξένος xenos (3443)

1. ἐξενοδόχησεν exenodochēsen 3sing indic aor act

1 if she have lodged strangers,....................... 1 Tm 5:10

This word describes a host who entertains guests or strangers. *Xenodocheō* occurs only once in the New Testament in 1 Timothy 5:10. The apostle Paul listed several character traits of widows who could be supported by the church. Lodging strangers, i.e., "showing hospitality," was one of these important virtues and qualifications.

Strong 3580, Bauer 548, Moulton-Milligan 433, Liddell-Scott 1189, Colin Brown 1:686.

3443. ξένος xenos adj
Strange, foreign, alien.
COGNATES:
    ξενία xenia (3440)
    ξενίζω xenizō (3441)
    ξενοδοχέω xenodocheō (3442)
    φιλοξενία philoxenia (5218)
    φιλόξενος philoxenos (5219)
SYNONYMS:
    ἀλλότριος allotrios (243)
    παρεπίδημος parepidēmos (3789)
    πάροικος paroikos (3803)

אָרַח 'ārach (755), Wayfarer (2 Sm 12:4).

גֵּר gēr (1658), Stranger (Jb 31:32).

נָכְרִי nokhrî (5425), Foreigner, alien (Ru 2:10, Ps 69:8 [68:8], Lam 5:2).

קָרָא qārā' (7410), Invite (1 Sm 9:13).

1. ξένος xenos nom sing masc
2. ξένον xenon acc sing masc
3. ξένοι xenoi nom pl masc
4. ξένοις xenois dat pl masc
5. ξένους xenous acc pl masc
6. ξέναις xenais dat pl fem
7. ξένου xenou gen sing neu
8. ξένων xenōn gen pl neu

1 I was a stranger, and ye took me in:............... Matt 25:35
2 When saw we thee a stranger, and took thee in?...... 25:38
1 I was a stranger, and ye took me not in:............ 25:43
2 or a stranger, or naked, or sick, or in prison,...... 25:44
4 bought ... the potter's field, to bury strangers in:... 27:7
8 He seemeth to be a setter forth of strange gods:... Acts 17:18
3 For all the Athenians and strangers which were....... 17:21
1 Gaius mine host, and of the whole church,........Rom 16:23
3 and strangers from the covenants of promise,........ Eph 2:12
3 therefore ye are no more strangers and foreigners,...... 2:19
3 that they were strangers and pilgrims on the earth. Heb 11:13
6 carried about with divers and strange doctrines........ 13:9
7 as though some strange thing happened unto you:... 1 Pt 4:12
5 thou doest to the brethren, and to strangers;........ 3 Jn 1:5

Classical Greek
This is a common word used to express the idea of what is "strange, foreign," or even "surprising." There are two distinct usages of this term. First, when used as an adjective it describes something or someone as "foreign, unacquainted, or unusual." Second, when used substantively (as a noun) it refers generally to a "stranger." As an adjective *xenos* could be a "man from without, strange, hard to fathom, surprising, unsettling, sinister." As a noun, it could be a "stranger" who gives or receives hospitality (cf. Stahlin, "xenos," *Kittel*, 5:1).

Classical Greek writers applied the term to persons who gave and received hospitality, i.e., host and guest. The major emphasis was often placed on a guest who could be any visitor, traveler, foreigner, alien, refugee, wanderer, or beggar. Foreigners generally were not treated well in primitive times. All of these are in contrast to the idea of belonging as a family member or citizen. In religion, devotees were given hospitality, protection, and asylum, but foreign beliefs were refused as a corruption of morals. Because the gods were feared, strangers were shown hospitality as long as the moral beliefs and religious practices were not tampered with (Bietenhard, Foreign, *Colin Brown*, 1:686f.). In philosophy, the soul is a stranger in the world because its true home lies beyond this material realm (ibid., 1:687).

Septuagint Usage
Xenos is used 21 times in the Septuagint. Occasionally, it is used figuratively; for example, in Psalm 69:8 (LXX 68:8) David cried out in distress: "I am become a *stranger* unto my brethren, and an alien unto my mother's children." Usually *xenos* is used literally of "strangers." In a prayer for mercy Jeremiah said: "Our inheritance is turned to *strangers*, our houses to aliens" (Lamentations 5:2), where "strangers" refers to the captors of Israel. In 2 Samuel 15:19 (LXX 2 Kings 15:19) it is the exiles who are referred to as "strangers." In both Ruth 2:10 and 2 Samuel 12:4 (LXX 2 Kings 12:4) the "stranger" is one who is innocent, needy, and a traveler from a foreign land. And in Job 31:32 there is an exhortation to show hospitality to the "stranger" (cf.

according to the Mosaic law, Deuteronomy 24:14).

There are many other uses of "stranger" in the Old Testament that are relevant (but do not use *xenos*). For example, Abraham befriended the heavenly visitors (Genesis 18). Nationally, Israel was a stranger in Egypt (Exodus 22:21) and *xenos* from the other nations, i.e., the Gentiles. In religion, all that was strange or foreign was to be rejected as idolatry (Deuteronomy 4:15-28; Joshua 24:23; 1 Kings 11:1-13; Jeremiah 5:19, et al.). However, during the time of the Dispersion a great part of the people lived abroad as strangers, and consequently there was a mutual need of understanding between Jews and other groups of people, despite marked religious differences.

The word in the papyri is used very much like the descriptions above but also added is the idea of immigrants who were waiting to receive full citizenship (*Moulton-Milligan*).

New Testament Usage

In the New Testament *xenos* occurs 14 times. There are five distinct uses. First, it describes the stranger who is the outsider needing help (Matthew 25:35,38,43,44). Jews were commanded to help those who were foreigners since they had no way of providing for their own livelihood. One specific command was to leave whatever grain fell accidentally on the ground at harvest time and the grain in the corners of the fields (Leviticus 19:9,10). Ruth went to gather grain as a foreigner, knowing she would find some. Boaz was especially kind to her by letting her glean alongside his reapers (Ruth 2:7,8). Also, the Israelites were not to charge high interest to a foreigner. Second, it refers to strange (i.e., foreign) gods (Acts 17:18) and doctrines (Hebrews 13:9), that is to say, any other message besides the gospel of Jesus Christ which has brought salvation (Galatians 1:8,9). Third, it expresses something unusual or surprising (1 Peter 4:12). Peter told his audience not to be surprised at trials, because this is normal for the Christian. Fourth, Gentiles are described as estranged from the covenants of promise (Ephesians 2:12). That is, they were separated from Christ because the gospel came to the Jew first. Because of Israel's idolatry, the Word of the Lord was not spread among the nations as it should have been until the time of Christ and the apostles. And fifth, it describes the host who entertains others (Romans 16:23). This usage describes the one who opens his or her home to someone else (e.g., such as Gaius did for Paul). Even the widow was to show hospitality to the stranger (1 Timothy 5:10).

Hospitality among early Christians enabled the messengers of the gospel to travel and spread their message (Romans 12:13; Hebrews 13:2; 1 Peter 4:9; 3 John 5). Paul employed *xenos* with a theological sense in Ephesians 2:19 in his description of the presalvation status of his readers. Before their conversion they were *xenoi*, "strangers," and *paroikoi* (see 3803), "enemies," excluded from Israel, the people of God, "and strangers from the covenants of promise" (verse 12).

Xenos exhibits a further usage when applied to the status of believers on earth: they are *xenoi*, "strangers," and *parepidēmoi* (see 3789), "aliens," on earth (Hebrews 11:13; 1 Peter 1:17), but their citizenship is now in heaven (Philippians 3:20; cf. Galatians 4:26; Ephesians 2:6; Hebrews 11:15f.; 12:22f.; 13:14).

STRONG 3581, BAUER 548, MOULTON-MILLIGAN 433-34, KITTEL 5:1-36, LIDDELL-SCOTT 1189, COLIN BROWN 1:686-90.

3444. ξέστης xestēs noun
Pot, pitcher.

1. ξεστῶν xestōn gen pl masc

1 as the washing of cups, and **pots**, brazen vessels,	Mark 7:4
1 as the washing **of pots** and cups:	7:8

This word originally described a small unit of measure that was used for either dry or liquid contents (equalling about a pint [1/2 liter] or a little less; cf. *Moulton-Milligan*). It is also used to denote a "pitcher" or "jug" without any indication of the amount that it held (*Bauer*). It is in this latter sense that it is used in both of its occurrences in the New Testament (Mark 7:4,8). Mark includes *xestōn* with the similar word *potērion* (see 4080), "cups," as parts of a miscellaneous collection of kitchen utensils which, according to Jewish traditions, should be washed before they were used.

STRONG 3582, BAUER 548, MOULTON-MILLIGAN 434, LIDDELL-SCOTT 1189-90.

3445. ξηραίνω xērainō verb
Wither, dry up, dry out.
CROSS-REFERENCE:
    ξηρός xēros (3446)

חָרֵב chārēv (2817), Dry up (Is 19:6).

יָבֵשׁ yāvēsh (3111), Qal: dry up, wither (Gn 8:14, Ps 90:6 [89:6], Is 40:8); piel: dry up (Prv 17:22, Na 1:4); hiphil: dry up (Is 44:27, Ez 17:24, Jl 1:17).

נָשַׁת nāshath (5587), Be parched (Is 41:17).

שָׁאַף shā'aph (8079), Pant (Is 42:14).

שָׁמַד shāmadh (8436), Hiphil: destroy (Am 2:9).

1. ἐξήρανεν exēranen 3sing indic aor act
2. ξηραίνεται xērainetai 3sing indic pres mid
3. ἐξηράνθη exēranthē 3sing indic aor pass
4. ἐξήρανται exērantai 3sing indic perf mid
5. ἐξηραμμένην exērammenēn
   acc sing fem part perf mid

```
3  and because they had no root, they withered away. Matt 13:6
3  And presently the fig tree withered away.............. 21:19
3  How soon is the fig tree withered away!............... 21:20
5  there was a man there which had a withered...Mark 3:1
5  saith unto the man which had the withered hand,....... 3:3
3  and because it had no root, it withered away.......... 4:6
3  the fountain of her blood was dried up;............... 5:29
2  and gnasheth with his teeth, and pineth away;......... 9:18
5  they saw the fig tree dried up from the roots........ 11:20
4  the fig tree which thou cursedst is withered away.... 11:21
3  and as soon as it was sprung up, it withered away,.. Luke 8:6
3  he is cast forth as a branch, and is withered;....John 15:6
1  withereth the grass, and the flower thereof falleth,....Jas 1:11
3  The grass withereth,................................ 1 Pt 1:24
3  for the harvest of the earth is ripe................Rev 14:15
3  Euphrates; and the water thereof was dried up,........ 16:12
```

Classical Greek
In classical Greek *xērainō* denotes the "drying up" of land and plants, "dehydration" or "constipation" of animals and human beings. It also refers to "drying up" of a supply of liquid. In addition, *xērainō* is used metaphorically to describe suffering or paralysis.

Septuagint Usage
Xērainō is used over 60 times in the Septuagint to translate various Hebrew words that mean "to dry up or wither," "to make desolate," to dry up in the sense of "exhausting" a supply of liquid (or metaphorically, a source of life or strength), and "to destroy." Most uses are literal: of water that evaporates, or of grass that withers. The messianic Psalm 22 (LXX 21) describes Christ's strength drying up as His body became dehydrated and exhausted on the cross. The loss of strength and usefulness (i.e., "paralysis") underlies the major metaphorical use in the Septuagint and the New Testament. *Xērainō* is also used extensively in the Septuagint in a simile comparing the brief life of mortal man to grass that withers (cf. Psalm 129:6 [LXX 128:6]).

New Testament Usage
The New Testament uses *xērainō* much like the Septuagint. Twelve times it speaks of water or plants drying up, and once of the drying up of the issue of blood in the woman Jesus healed (Mark 5:29). The remaining uses are metaphorical for paralysis (Mark 3:1,3) or the "drying up" of the usefulness of the body (cf. Mark 9:18).

STRONG 3583, BAUER 548, MOULTON-MILLIGAN 434, LIDDELL-SCOTT 1190, COLIN BROWN 1:515.

3446. ξηρός xēros adj
Dry, withered.

CROSS-REFERENCE:
ξηραίνω xērainō (3445)

חָרָבָה chārāvāh (2824), Dry land, dry ground (Ex 14:21, Jos 3:17, Hg 2:6 [2:7]).

יָבֵשׁ yāvēsh (3112), Dry (Is 56:3, Ez 20:47, 37:4).

יַבָּשָׁה yabbāshāh (3114), Dry land (Ex 14:22, Ps 66:6 [65:6], Jon 2:10 [2:11]).

יַבֶּשֶׁת yabbesheth (3116), Dry ground, dry land (Ex 4:9, Ps 95:5 [94:5]).

צִיָּה tsîyāh (6993), Drought (Jb 24:19).

צָמַק tsāmaq (7054), Be dry (Hos 9:14).

תֵּבֵל tēvēl (8725), The earth (Sir 37:3).

1. ξηρῶν xērōn gen pl masc
2. ξηρά xēra nom sing fem
3. ξηρᾶς xēras gen sing fem
4. ξηράν xēran acc sing fem
5. ξηρῷ xērō dat sing neu

```
4  there was a man which had his hand withered...... Matt 12:10
4  for ye compass sea and land to make one proselyte,... 23:15
4  the man with the withered hand, (NASB).......... Mark 3:3
2  there was a man whose right hand was withered..... Luke 6:6
4  and said to the man which had the withered hand,...... 6:8
5  in a green tree, what shall be done in the dry?........ 23:31
1  impotent folk, of blind, halt, withered,............... John 5:3
3  they passed through the Red sea as by dry land:....Heb 11:29
```

Classical Greek
This word is a common term for showing the effects of the loss of natural fluids from living objects, especially those in the plant kingdom. It describes the drying up of cut grass as well as the withering of trees, branches, plants, and seeds (*Bauer*).

Septuagint Usage
In the Septuagint *xēros* translates several Hebrew terms meaning "dry." In the creation account of Genesis God gathered the waters together and the "*dry* land" was formed (Genesis 1:9). Then in Genesis 7:22 all those who lived on "*dry* land" died in the Flood. In Ezekiel 37:11 the prophet was commanded to

prophecy to the "*dry* bones," a metaphor that described the nation of Israel.

New Testament Usage

Xēros occurs seven times in the New Testament. Twice it refers to dry land (Matthew 23:15; Hebrews 11:29) and once to dry wood (Luke 23:31). It is used symbolically in the other references to describe a wasting disease or diseased state, e.g., a withered hand (Matthew 12:10; Mark 3:3; Luke 6:6,8) and paralysis (John 5:3).

STRONG 3584, BAUER 548, MOULTON-MILLIGAN 434, LIDDELL-SCOTT 1190, COLIN BROWN 1:515-16.

3447. ξύλινος xulinos adj

Wooden.

CROSS-REFERENCE:
ξύλον xulon (3448)

אָע 'āʿ (A651), Timber (Ezr 6:4—Aramaic).

עֵץ ʿēts (6320), Wooden, wood (Lv 15:12, Neh 8:4, Jer 28:13 [35:13]).

1. ξύλινα xulina nom/acc pl neu

1 vessels of gold ... but also of **wood** and of earth; .... 2 Tm 2:20
1 idols of gold, ... and brass, and stone, and of **wood**: .. Rev 9:20

This adjective is built on the stem of the Greek word *xulon* (3448) which means "wood," "tree," or "timber." The suffix *-inos* refers to the material or substance from which something is made. Hence, the primary meaning is "made of wood," i.e., "wooden" (cf. Greenlee, *A Concise Exegetical Grammar of New Testament Greek*, p.20). It is used in this sense in both places where it occurs in the New Testament (2 Timothy 2:20; Revelation 9:20).

STRONG 3585, BAUER 549, MOULTON-MILLIGAN 434, LIDDELL-SCOTT 1191.

3448. ξύλον xulon noun

Wood, timber, cross, tree.

COGNATE:
ξύλινος xulinos (3447)

SYNONYM:
σταυρός stauros (4567)

אָע 'āʿ (A651), Timber (Ezr 5:8, 6:11—Aramaic).

נַהֲלֹל nahălōl (5275), Water hole (Is 7:19).

סַד sadh (5649), Stocks (Jb 33:11).

עֵץ ʿēts (6320), Tree, timber (Gn 2:9, 2 Chr 2:8, Ez 31:4f.).

צֶלָע tsēlāʿ (7029), Plank (1 Kgs 6:15).

1. ξύλον xulon nom/acc sing neu
2. ξύλου xulou gen sing neu
3. ξύλῳ xulō dat sing neu
4. ξύλων xulōn gen pl neu
5. ξύλα xula nom/acc pl neu

4 with him a great multitude with swords and **staves**, Matt 26:47
4 with swords and **staves** for to take me? 26:55
4 with him a great multitude with swords and **staves**, Mark 14:43
4 with swords and with **staves** to take me? 14:48
4 come ... as against a thief, with swords and **staves**? Luke 22:52
3 For if they do these things in a green **tree**, ... 23:31
2 Jesus, whom ye slew and hanged on a **tree**............Acts 5:30
2 whom they slew and hanged on a **tree**: 10:39
2 they took him down from the **tree**, ... 13:29
1 and made their feet fast in the **stocks**. 16:24
5 gold, silver, precious stones, **wood**, hay, stubble; .....1 Co 3:12
2 Cursed is every one that hangeth on a **tree**: .... Gal 3:13
1 bare our sins in his own body on the **tree**, ... 1 Pt 2:24
2 that overcometh will I give to eat of the **tree** of life, Rev 2:7
1 purple, and silk, and scarlet, and all thyine **wood**, ... 18:12
2 and all manner vessels of most precious **wood**, ... 18:12
1 the **tree** of life, which bare twelve manner of fruits, ... 22:2
2 the leaves of the **tree** were for the healing 22:2
1 that they may have right to the **tree** of life, ... 22:14
2 take away his part from the **tree** of life (NASB) 22:19

Classical Greek

Classical Greek uses *xulon* to denote a "tree," a "piece of wood," "timber," etc. As a single piece of wood *xulon* may represent a variety of forms: "beam, post, or log" (*Liddell-Scott*). Moreover, *xulon* can refer to anything made of wood, including objects of punishment, such as "stocks, clubs, gallows, stakes," etc. A living "tree" is *xulon*, and metaphorically *xulon* recalls the inanimate restrictions of wood or its properties of strength (although in a negative sense, "stubbornness") (ibid.).

Septuagint Usage

In the Septuagint *xulon* most often translates *ʿēts*, "tree, wood." This can be a living "tree" that bears fruit (e.g., Genesis 1:29; Exodus 10:12,15), or "wood" that has been fashioned for construction purposes (e.g., Exodus 26:26; 27:1,6; Deuteronomy 20:20).

A particularly interesting use of *xulon* (often plural) is as a symbol of idolatry. Thus we read of gods of wood and stone which are worshiped and served (Deuteronomy 28:36,64; 29:17).

Also important religious symbols in the religion of Israel are the "tree of life" (Genesis 2:9; 3:22,24) and the "tree of the knowledge of good and evil" (Genesis 2:9,17). It is difficult to delineate precisely between the two. Apparently the "tree of life" continued to play a role in Israel's religion. We find allusions to it in Proverbs 3:18; 11:30; 13:12; 15:4 in canonical material and in 4 Maccabees 18:16 in the Apocrypha. In other Jewish writings outside of the canon it is also mentioned in 1 Enoch 24:4ff.; 2 Enoch 8:3ff.; 4 Esdras 8:52 (cf. Smick, "Tree of Knowledge, Tree of Life," *Interpreter's Dictionary of the Bible*, 4:901-903). We observe the recurrence of the interest in the "tree of life" in the New Testament (Revelation 2:7; 22:2,14,19; see below).

New Testament Usage

The New Testament's use of *xulon*, often translated merely "wood," needs to be qualified as to what this "wood" is. It may mean a stick or piece of wood, either living or dead. Or it can be used of a piece of wood cut for a specific purpose, such as the stocks in which Paul and Silas found themselves (Acts 16:24). The term acquires a sense not found before the New Testament when various writers use *xulon* as a metonym, i.e., "the Cross."

In Luke 23:31 Jesus used the imagery of a piece of wood to differentiate between His and the people of Israel's following of Jewish tradition. He referred to both groups as wood, but He called himself "living" wood, while the Jewish people were called "dead" wood. This is a use very close to the literal meaning and one the people would understand.

A distinctive New Testament use of *xulon* is its reference to "cross." In each instance where this occurs it is used exclusively of the cross upon which Jesus was crucified. This must be understood against the background of the Septuagint reading of Deuteronomy 21:22,23. A person who committed a crime and was executed often had his body hung on a tree for display. However, the body was not permitted to hang on the tree overnight. Luke used this imagery to show the shame of the Crucifixion (Acts 5:30). Paul referred to the curse invoked if this custom were neglected (Galatians 3:13) and applied it to Christ, who became accursed so those under the Law might be free from its curse and instead experience the promise made to Abraham, the gift of the Holy Spirit (Galatians 3:13,14).

John used *xulon* as a figure of speech in Revelation. The imagery pictured emerged from the history of the Jews and the Old Testament Scriptures. Later Judaism connected the restoration of paradise, including the tree of life, to be a task of Messiah. In paradise the "tree of life" would give the people the food of everlasting life (Revelation 22:2).

STRONG 3586, BAUER 549, MOULTON-MILLIGAN 434-35, KITTEL 5:37-41, LIDDELL-SCOTT 1191-92, COLIN BROWN 1:389-90; 3:865-66,868.

3449. ξυράω xuraō verb

Shave, shear, be shaved.

גָּלָה gālâh (1580), Piel: shave (Lv 14:9, Nm 6:9, Ez 44:20); pual: be shaved (Jer 41:5 [48:5]); hithpael: shave oneself (Lv 13:33).

גָּרַע gāraʿ (1686), Cut (Jer 48:37 [31:37]).

קָרַח qārach (7428), Qal: make oneself bald (Mi 1:16); niphal: shave one's head (Jer 16:6).

קָרְחָה qorchā (7433), Bald (Jer 48:37 [31:37]).

1. ξυρᾶσθαι xurasthai inf pres/aor mid
2. ξυρήσωνται xurēsōntai 3pl subj aor mid
3. ἐξυρημένῃ exurēmenē dat sing fem part perf mid
4. ξυρήσονται xurēsontai 3pl indic fut mid

2 that they may shave their heads: .... Acts 21:24
3 for that is even all one as if she were shaven. ...... 1 Co 11:5
1 be a shame for a woman to be shorn or shaven, ... 11:6

This word describes the practice of cutting hair or shaving one's beard or body throughout classical Greek and the Septuagint. In its noun form, *xurētēs*, it denotes a "barber," while *xuron* refers to "a razor." *Xuraō* and its alternate forms—*xureō*, *xurō*, and *xuraomai*—are more restricted in use than *keirō*. *Keirō* is the common word used for shearing sheep, and figuratively, for "a close shave" to express danger, and to "fleece" or "plunder" a country by cutting down its crops and fruit trees (*Liddell-Scott*).

Xuraō occurs three times in the New Testament. In Acts 21:24 it refers to cutting the hair after completion of a vow, and in 1 Corinthians 11:5,6 it refers to a woman disgracing her head by shaving her hair.

STRONG 3587, BAUER 549, MOULTON-MILLIGAN 435, LIDDELL-SCOTT 1192 (see "xureō").

O

3450. ὁ ho art
The.

1. τῶν tōn gen pl masc/fem/neu
2. τοῦ tou gen sing masc/neu
3. τῷ tō dat sing masc/neu
4. τοῖς tois dat pl masc/neu
5. ὁ ho nom sing masc
6. τόν ton acc sing masc
7. οἱ hoi nom pl masc
8. τούς tous acc pl masc
9. ἡ hē nom sing fem
10. τῆς tēs gen sing fem
11. τῇ tē dat sing fem
12. τήν tēn acc sing fem
13. αἱ hai nom pl fem
14. ταῖς tais dat pl fem
15. τάς tas acc pl fem
16. τό to nom/acc sing neu
17. τά ta nom/acc pl neu

```
10  when ye depart out of that house or city,......... Matt 10:14
3   came and told unto their lord all that was done....... 18:31
3   and give it unto him which hath ten talents.......... 25:28
3   but woe unto that man by whom the Son............ 26:24
10  the Son of man sitting on the right hand of power,... 26:64
3   was wont to release unto the people a prisoner,...... 27:15
2   else the new piece ... taketh away from the old,... Mark 2:21
4   Herod on his birthday made a supper to his lords,..... 6:21
11  word of God of none effect through your tradition,.... 7:13
3   take his wife, and raise up seed unto his brother...... 12:19
11  And the first day of unleavened bread,.............. 14:12
3   that by the word of God the heavens were of old,.. 2 Pt 3:5
```

The origin of the article *ho, hē, to* (the masculine, feminine, and neuter forms), meaning "the," is from the Greek word *hode* (3455), *hēde, tode* meaning "this, these," or "that, those." Over time it became weakened to mean simply "the" (Vaughan and Gideon, *Greek Grammar*, p.80). But the article is sometimes restored to its original force and origin and may be translated by various pronouns such as "this, that, some, others, ours, his," or "which."

In English there are two words known as "articles": the indefinite article "a" (or "an"), and the definite article "the." In Greek however, there is only the definite article *ho, hē, to*. Omitting the article before a word often gives that word an indefiniteness. Unfortunately, an English translation does not show the significance of the use or omission of the Greek article. It has many usages and possible meanings not translated.

The general rule for understanding the article is as follows: (1) the article placed before a word makes that word either *definite* (stressing its identity) or *generic* (the word is a general representative of a class or group); and (2) the omission of the article before a word makes that word *indefinite* ("a," "an") or *qualitative* (stressing its essence, character, and quality). For example, the omission of the article before "God" in "... and the Word was God" (John 1:1), gives the word "God" a qualitative meaning. That is, the Word is the essence of the divine nature of God. Thus, the Word, *logos* (3030), is "very God," not the indefinite "a god."

Frequently the article is used before a word to point it out in a distinctive way, distinguishing and contrasting one thing from another. In Acts 19:13, "We adjure you by (*the*) Jesus whom Paul preacheth," uses the article before "Jesus" to point out His distinctiveness and identity.

STRONG 3588, BAUER 549-52, MOULTON-MILLIGAN 436-37, LIDDELL-SCOTT 1193-95.

3451. ὀγδοήκοντα ogdoēkonta num
Eighty.

1. ὀγδοήκοντα ogdoēkonta card

```
1  said unto him, Take thy bill, and write fourscore... Luke 16:7
```

A cardinal numeral, this word is related to *oktō* (3501), "eight." It occurs numerous times in the Septuagint (e.g., Numbers 4:48; 1 Kings

3:1 [LXX 3 Kings 3:1]; 2 Kings 10:24 [LXX 4 Kings 10:24]; 2 Chronicles 14:8) and two times in the New Testament (Luke 2:37; 16:7). Luke 2:37 gives the age (or years of widowhood) of Anna the widowed prophetess who received the baby Jesus and His parents in the temple. In the Parable of the Dishonest Steward (Luke 16:1-13) the debtor who owed 100 measures of wheat was instructed by the dishonest steward to make a partial payment of 80 measures (Luke 16:7). The word specifies quantity, whether in number of years or amount of produce.

STRONG 3589, BAUER 552, MOULTON-MILLIGAN 437, LIDDELL-SCOTT 1196.

3452. ὀγδοηκοντατέσσαρες
ogdoēkontatessares num
Eighty-four.

1. ὀγδοηκοντατεσσάρων ogdoēkontatessarōn
card gen masc/fem/neu

1 she was a widow of about **fourscore and four** years,..Luke 2:37

This word is a combination of *ogdoēkonta* (3451), "eighty" (80), and *tessares* (4911B), "four" (4). Used only once in the New Testament, Luke 2:37 reports the age (or years of widowhood) of Anna the prophetess. Some Greek texts, including the *Nestle's Revised Edition* (1936) and the *Nestle-Aland 26th* separate the term into its two component parts.

LIDDELL-SCOTT 1196.

3453. ὄγδοος ogdoos num
Eighth.

1. ὄγδοος ogdoos ord nom sing masc
2. ὄγδοον ogdoon ord acc sing masc
3. ὀγδόῃ ogdoē ord dat sing fem

3 the **eighth** day they came to circumcise the child;....Luke 1:59
3 begat Isaac, and circumcised him the **eighth** day;.... Acts 7:8
2 but saved Noah the **eighth** person, a preacher...... 2 Pt 2:5
1 even he is the **eighth**, and is of the seven,.......... Rev 17:11
1 the seventh, chrysolyte; the **eighth**, beryl;............. 21:20

Ogdoos is an adjective that is used to express rank, e.g., the eighth. This meaning is consistent in the classical Greek, the inscriptions, papyri, the Septuagint, and the New Testament (*Bauer*).

Of five occurrences in the New Testament, two refer to the "eighth" day for circumcision (Luke 1:59; Acts 7:8); one refers to the "eighth" person, i.e., Noah (2 Peter 2:5); one to the prophesied ruler (Revelation 17:11); and one to the "eighth" foundation of the New Jerusalem, the Holy City, that John saw in his vision (Revelation 21:20).

STRONG 3590, BAUER 552-53, MOULTON-MILLIGAN 437, LIDDELL-SCOTT 1196, COLIN BROWN 2:692.

3454. ὄγκος onkos noun
Weight, mass, burden, impediment, body.
SYNONYM:
βάρος baros (916)

1. ὄγκον onkon acc sing masc

1 let us lay aside every **weight**,...................... Heb 12:1

Classical Greek
In the classical Greek literature the use of *onkos*, which refers to the "mass of a body" (whether the emphasis is on size, bulk, or weight), is the meaning that has bearing on the New Testament. *Onkos* describes the weight of a dead man's ashes as well as the weight of a child in the womb (*Liddell-Scott*). Similar to the term *baros* (916), "weight, burden," *onkos* can also refer to the particles of a body mass, i.e., the molecules.

New Testament Usage
Metaphorically, *onkos* refers in a negative sense to "inner spiritual weight which accrues to something" (Seeseman, "onkos," *Kittel*, 5:41) such as attitudes of pride, self-importance, and loftiness which, when observed in others, are sometimes hard to bear. The word occurs only once in the New Testament where the writer of Hebrews exhorted his readers to "lay aside every weight (*onkos*)..." (Hebrews 12:1) in order to run the Christian race without hindrance.

STRONG 3591, BAUER 553, MOULTON-MILLIGAN 437, KITTEL 5:41, LIDDELL-SCOTT 1197, COLIN BROWN 1:671,674.

3455. ὅδε hode dem-pron
This, that.

1. ὅδε hode nom sing masc
2. τῇδε tēde dat sing fem
3. τήνδε tēnde acc sing fem
4. τάδε tade acc pl neu

2 And **she** had a sister called Mary,.................Luke 10:39
1 Lazarus evil things: but now **he** is comforted,.......... 16:25
4 And they wrote letters by them after **this** manner;...Acts 15:23
4 **Thus** saith the Holy Ghost,........................ 21:11
3 To day or to morrow we will go into **such** a city,.....Jas 4:13
4 **These things** saith he that holdeth the seven stars.... Rev 2:1

4	These things saith the first and the last,	Rev 2:8
4	These things saith he which hath the sharp sword	2:12
4	These things saith the Son of God,	2:18
4	These things saith he that hath the seven Spirits	3:1
4	These things saith he that is holy, he that is true,	3:7
4	These things saith the Amen,	3:14

A demonstrative pronoun, *hode* is formed by adding the enclitic *de*, "but, and," to the definite article (*ho* [3450], *hē*, *to*, "the"; cf. *Liddell-Scott*). A term that overlaps in meaning with *houtos* (3642), "this," *hode* designates what is close or present and contrasts what is near with something more remote (ibid.).

The term is often used as a formula (*Bauer*) to introduce something of importance that was about to follow; e.g., the provisions of a testator's will (*Moulton-Milligan*), official proclamations of a king, or the holy utterances of a prophet (*Bauer*). It is used in this way in 8 of its 12 occurrences in the New Testament (Acts 15:23; Revelation 2:1,8,12,18; 3:1,7,14). In addition, *hode* is sometimes used as an adverb to mean "thus" or "such." It is used two times in the New Testament in this manner (Acts 21:11; James 4:13).

STRONG 3592, BAUER 553, MOULTON-MILLIGAN 437-38, LIDDELL-SCOTT 1197-98.

3456. ὁδεύω hodeuō verb

To make one's way, journey, travel.

SYNONYMS:
ἀποδημέω apodēmeō (584)
πορεύομαι poreuomai (4057)

הָלַךְ hālakh (2050), Walk (1 Kgs 6:12—Codex Alexandrinus only).

1. ὁδεύων hodeuōn nom sing masc part pres act

1 But a certain Samaritan, as he **journeyed**, ... Luke 10:33

The verb *hodeuō*, meaning "to go, travel, take a journey," appears in classical Greek from Homer on. It occurs three times in the Septuagint and always as a translation of the Hebrew verb *hālak*, "to go, come, walk" (1 Kings 6:12 [LXX 3 Kings 6:12]; Tobit 6:5; Wisdom of Solomon 5:7). Though the verb is a hapax legomenon (found only once, in Luke 10:33), the noun *hodos* (3461), "a way, road, highway," appears numerous times in the New Testament, both literally ("a road") and metaphorically ("a way of life"). In the Parable of the Good Samaritan (Luke 10:30-37), the Samaritan is said to have been "traveling, making his way" (present participle form of the verb). The priest was "coming down" (*katabainō* [2568]) from Jerusalem, the central place of worship and service in Israel, as was probably the Levite; however, this is evidently not the case with the Samaritan. He is mentioned as simply traveling. It may be significant that he is not mentioned as coming down from Jerusalem (since there was such animosity between Jews and Samaritans).

STRONG 3593, BAUER 553, MOULTON-MILLIGAN 438, LIDDELL-SCOTT 1198.

3457. ὁδηγέω hodēgeō verb

Lead one upon his way, guide, instruct.

COGNATES:
ὁδηγός hodēgos (3458)
ὁδός hodos (3461)

SYNONYMS:
ἄγω agō (70)
ἀνάγω anagō (319)
ἀπάγω apagō (516)
ἀποφέρω apopherō (661)
ἡγέομαι hēgeomai (2216)
κατευθύνω kateuthunō (2690)

דָּרַךְ dārakh (1931), Tread; hiphal: guide, lead (Pss 25:9 [24:9], 107:7 [106:7]); cause to go (Ps 119:35 [118:35]).

הָלַךְ hālakh (2050), Qal: go (2 Sm 7:23, 1 Chr 17:21); hiphil: lead (Jos 24:3, Ps 106:9 [105:9]).

יָצָא yātsā' (3428), Go out, come out; hiphil: bring out (Nm 24:8).

יָרָה yārâh (3498), Throw, shoot; Hiphil: teach (Pss 45:4 [44:4], 86:11 [85:11]).

נָהַג nāhagh (5268), Lead (Ps 80:1 [79:1]).

נָחָה nāchâh (5328), Qal: lead (Ex 15:13, Pss 60:9 [59:9], 139:24 [138:24]); hiphil: guide (Neh 9:19, Pss 23:3 [22:3], 78:72 [77:72]).

1. ὁδηγῇ hodēgē 3sing subj pres act
2. ὁδηγεῖν hodēgein inf pres act
3. ὁδηγήσῃ hodēgēsē 3sing subj aor act
4. ὁδηγήσει hodēgēsei 3sing indic fut act
5. ὁδηγεῖ hodēgei 3sing indic pres act

1	And if the blind **lead** the blind, both shall fall	Matt 15:14
2	Can the blind **lead** the blind?	Luke 6:39
4	Spirit of truth, ... he will **guide** you into all truth:	John 16:13
3	How can I, except some man should **guide** me?	Acts 8:31
4	shall **lead** them unto living fountains of waters:	Rev 7:17

Classical Greek

The verb *hodēgeō* is related to the noun *hodēgos* (3458), "leader, guide," and in classical Greek means "lead the way, guide." This meaning is consistent in both secular and sacred Greek writings (*Bauer*). *Hodēgeō* does not describe the person who must find his own way, but it describes the action of leading someone to a desired result.

Septuagint Usage

Hodēgeō occurs several times in the Septuagint, mostly in Psalms. In Psalm 108:10 (LXX 107:10) the Psalmist asks, "Who will *bring* me *into* the strong city?" In Psalm 23:3 (LXX 22:3) the Lord *guides* in paths of righteousness. In Psalm 25:5 (LXX 24:5) David prayed for the Lord to *lead* him into God's truth and to teach him. Israel experienced God's leading at the Exodus (Exodus 13:17; 15:13; Psalms 77:20 [LXX 76:20]; 105:9 [104:9]) (see also Michaelis, "hodēgeō," *Kittel*, 5:98). All of the references in the Wisdom of Solomon call those who are guides to interpret that which is needed to "guide" people (9:11; 10:10,17).

New Testament Usage

The word *hodēgeō* is used five times in the New Testament. All of these occurrences express a figurative use of the term; e.g., false teachers misleading others like a blind man *leading* another blind man (Matthew 15:14; Luke 6:39); the Holy Spirit of Truth, as a good teacher, *guiding* the disciples (and other believers) into the Truth (John 16:13); the Ethiopian eunuch who needed a human instructor to *guide* him to the meaning of the Scriptures he was reading (Acts 8:31); and the white-robed multitudes of saints whom the Lamb will *lead* to living fountains of waters (Revelation 7:17).

STRONG 3594, BAUER 553, MOULTON-MILLIGAN 438, KITTEL 5:97-102, LIDDELL-SCOTT 1198, COLIN BROWN 3:935-37,942.

3458. ὁδηγός hodēgos noun

Guide, leader.

COGNATES:
ὁδηγέω hodēgeō (3457)
ὁδός hodos (3461)

1. **ὁδηγοῦ hodēgou** gen sing masc
2. **ὁδηγόν hodēgon** acc sing masc
3. **ὁδηγοί hodēgoi** nom pl masc

3 Let them alone: they be blind **leaders** of the blind. Matt 15:14
3 Woe unto you, ye blind **guides**, which say,............ 23:16
3 Ye blind **guides**, which strain at a gnat,............... 23:24
1 which was **guide** to them that took Jesus............ Acts 1:16
2 confident that thou thyself art **a guide** of the blind,.. Rom 2:19

Classical Greek

In secular literature *hodēgos* is used of someone or something that guides, for example, a goddess or even a pilot boat (*Liddell-Scott*).

A *hodēgos* is the person who helps someone go from one place to another (*Bauer*). It says nothing about the manner of the movement, how one gets from one place to another.

New Testament Usage

Occurring five times in the New Testament the word *hodēgos* describes Judas, for example, who led the armed mob to capture Jesus. In four other occurrences in the New Testament *hodēgos* has a literal meaning (although "guide" and "blind" are used figuratively) that condemns the false guide who misleads those who trust in him, implicating the Pharisees in the charge (Matthew 15:14; 23:16,24). "In Romans 2:19, Paul characterizes the Jew instructed in the Law as one who presumes to be 'a guide to the blind' " (Ebel, "Walk," *Colin Brown*, 3:942).

STRONG 3595, BAUER 553, KITTEL 5:97-102, LIDDELL-SCOTT 1198, COLIN BROWN 3:935-37,939,942.

3459. ὁδοιπορέω hodoiporeō verb

Travel, be on a journey.

CROSS-REFERENCE:
ὁδός hodos (3461)

1. **ὁδοιπορούντων hodoiporountōn**
gen pl masc part pres act

1 On the morrow, as they **went on their journey,**..... Acts 10:9

Hodoiporeō is composed of *hodos* (3461), "a road, way, highway," and *poreō*, "I go." Thus its primary meaning is "I travel, I go on a journey" (*Bauer*). It can mean "walk" since this was the usual means of travel. It is used in this way in both the secular and sacred Greek literature.

In the New Testament the word appears only once, in Acts 10:9 where Luke narrated that Peter and his friends "traveled" from Joppa to the home of Cornelius in Caesarea. Perhaps it is a missionary term (Ebel, "Walk," *Colin Brown*, 3:941), although it would seem that Acts would contain such a term more frequently if this were true.

STRONG 3596, BAUER 553, MOULTON-MILLIGAN 438, LIDDELL-SCOTT 1198, COLIN BROWN 3:941.

3460. ὁδοιπορία hodoiporia noun

Journey, walking.

COGNATE:
ὁδός hodos (3461)

SYNONYM:
ὁδός hodos (3461)

1. ὁδοιπορίας hodoiporias gen sing fem
2. ὁδοιπορίαις hodoiporiais dat pl fem

1 Jesus therefore, being wearied with his **journey**, ... John 4:6
2 In **journeyings** often, in perils of waters, ... 2 Co 11:26

A cognate form of *hodoiporeō* (3459), "I travel," *hodoiporia* denotes the "trip" or "journey." Like its verb form, *hodoiporia* is used consistently in this way in both the secular and sacred Greek writings (*Bauer*). It can also mean "walking" since this was the common means of travel.

The word occurs two times in the New Testament. In John 4:6 Jesus took a trip through Samaria, and in 2 Corinthians 11:26 Paul mentioned his "many journeys" as part of a long list of the things he endured for Christ's sake.

STRONG 3597, BAUER 553, MOULTON-MILLIGAN 438, LIDDELL-SCOTT 1198.

3460B. ὁδοποιέω hodopoieō verb
Make a path, make a way.
CROSS-REFERENCES:
ὁδός hodos (3461)
ποιέω poieō (4020)

סָלַל sālal (5744), Heap up, pile up; extol (Ps 68:4 [67:4]).
פָּלַס pālas (6668), Piel: make a path (Ps 78:50 [77:50]).
פָּנָה pānâh (6680), Turn; piel: clear (Ps 80:9 [79:9]).

1. ὁδοποιεῖν hodopoiein inf pres act

The compound word *hodopoieō* (composed of the noun *hodos* [3461], "road, path," and the verb *poieō* [4020], "make, do") is found only one time in the New Testament, in Mark 2:23. Most Greek manuscripts show *hodon poien* rather than the single term *hodopoien* which occurs only in the Codex Vaticanus (B), the five miniscules of the f1 group, and a few others. Nevertheless, there is a great deal of both classical and Septuagintal support for the existence of the compound form. In classical literature it means "to make a road" or "to make fit for use." It describes troops "making a way" for themselves in a forest (*Liddell-Scott*). *Moulton-Milligan* says that in the Mark passage the verb should simply be translated "journey." (Cf. *hodoiporeō* [3459], "journey," in John 4:6 and 2 Corinthians 11:26.)

BAUER 553, MOULTON-MILLIGAN 438, LIDDELL-SCOTT 1198.

3461. ὁδός hodos noun
Road, way, highway.
COGNATES:
ἄμφοδον amphodon (294)
διέξοδος diexodos (1321)
εἴσοδος eisodos (1513)
ἔξοδος exodos (1825)
μεθοδεία methodeia (3151)
ὁδηγέω hodēgeō (3457)
ὁδηγός hodēgos (3458)
ὁδοιπορέω hodoiporeō (3459)
ὁδοιπορία hodoiporia (3460)
ὁδοποιέω hodopoieō (3460B)
πάροδος parodos (3800)
συνοδεύω sunodeuō (4772)
συνοδία sunodia (4773)
SYNONYMS:
ἀγωγή agōgē (71)
ἄμφοδον amphodon (294)
ἀναστροφή anastrophē (389)
ὁδοιπορία hodoiporia (3460)
πορεία poreia (4056)
ῥύμη rhumē (4362)
τρίβος tribos (4988)

אָרַח 'ārach (755), Walk (Jb 34:8—Codex Alexandrinus only).
אֹרַח 'ōrach (758), Path, way (Jb 33:11, Ps 119:101 [118:101], Is 26:8).
אֶרֶץ 'erets (800), Land (1 Kgs 18:6).
דָּרַךְ dārakh (1931), Tread (Jb 24:11).
דֶּרֶךְ derekh (1932), Way (Dt 2:8, 1 Kgs 13:10, Is 55:7ff.).
הָלִיךְ hālîkh (2048), Step (Jb 29:6).
חוּץ chûts (2445), Street (Prv 22:13, Jer 5:1); outside (Hos 7:1).
יוֹם yôm (3219), Day (Ps 37:18 [36:18]).
מָבוֹא māvô' (4136), Entrance (Ez 27:3—Codex Alexandrinus only).
מַהֲלָךְ mahălākh (4250), Journey (Jon 3:3).
מוֹעֵצָה mô'ētsāh (4292), Counsel (Mi 6:16).
מוֹרָד môrādh (4309), Descent (Jer 48:5 [31:5]).
מְסִלָּה mᵉsillāh (4697), Highway (Jgs 20:31, 2 Kgs 18:17, Is 33:8).
מַעְגָּל ma'gāl (4724), Path (Is 59:8).
מִצְוָה mitswāh (4851), Commandment (Ps 119:151 [118:151]).
מָקוֹם māqôm (4887), Space (1 Sm 26:13).
נְתִיבָה nᵉthîvāh (5594), Path (Prv 8:20—only some Sinaiticus texts).
רְחֹב rᵉchōv (7624), Street (Is 59:14).
שָׂדֶה sādheh (7898), Country (1 Sm 27:7).

1. ὁδός hodos nom sing fem
2. ὁδοῦ hodou gen sing fem
3. ὁδῷ hodō dat sing fem
4. ὁδόν hodon acc sing fem
5. ὁδοί hodoi nom pl fem

ὁδός 3461

6. ὁδῶν hodōn gen pl fem
7. ὁδοῖς hodois dat pl fem
8. ὁδούς hodous acc pl fem

2	they departed into their own country another way... Matt	2:12
4	Prepare ye the way of the Lord,	3:3
4	by the way of the sea, beyond Jordan,	4:15
3	whiles thou art in the way with him;	5:25
1	for wide is the gate, and broad is the way,	7:13
1	Because strait is the gate, and narrow is the way,	7:14
2	so that no man might pass by that way.	8:28
4	Go not into the way of the Gentiles,	10:5
4	Nor scrip for your journey, neither two coats,	10:10
4	which shall prepare thy way before thee.	11:10
4	when he sowed, some seeds fell by the way side,	13:4
4	This is he which received seed by the way side.	13:19
3	not ... away fasting, lest they faint in the way.	15:32
3	took the twelve disciples apart in the way,	20:17
4	behold, two blind men sitting by the way side,	20:30
3	great multitude spread their garments in the way;	21:8
3	cut ... branches ... and strowed them in the way.	21:8
2	when he saw a fig tree in the way, he came to it,	21:19
3	John came unto you in the way of righteousness,	21:32
6	Go ye therefore into the highways,	22:9
8	So those servants went out into the highways,	22:10
4	and teachest the way of God in truth,	22:16
4	which shall prepare thy way before thee. Mark	1:2
4	Prepare ye the way of the Lord,	1:3
4	disciples began to make their way (NASB)	2:23
4	as he sowed, some fell by the way side,	4:4
4	And these are they by the way side,	4:15
4	that they should take nothing for their journey,	6:8
3	them away fasting ... they will faint by the way:	8:3
3	and by the way he asked his disciples,	8:27
3	What was it that ye disputed ... by the way?	9:33
3	held their peace: for by the way they had disputed	9:34
4	And when he was gone forth into the way,	10:17
3	And they were in the way going up to Jerusalem;	10:32
4	Bartimaeus, ... sat by the highway side begging.	10:46
3	received his sight, and followed Jesus in the way.	10:52
4	And many spread their garments in the way:	11:8
4	branches off ... trees, and strowed them in the way.	11:8
4	but teachest the way of God in truth:	12:14
8	go before the face of the Lord to prepare his ways; Luke	1:76
4	to guide our feet into the way of peace.	1:79
4	went a day's journey; and they sought him among	2:44
4	Prepare ye the way of the Lord,	3:4
8	and the rough ways shall be made smooth;	3:5
4	which shall prepare thy way before thee.	7:27
4	fell by the way side; and it was trodden down,	8:5
4	Those by the way side are they that hear;	8:12
4	he said unto them, Take nothing for your journey,	9:3
4	And it came to pass, that, as they went in the way,	9:57
4	nor shoes: and salute no man by the way.	10:4
3	there came down a certain priest that way:	10:31
2	For a friend of mine in his journey is come to me,	11:6
3	adversary to the magistrate, as thou art in the way,	12:58
8	Go out into the highways and hedges,	14:23
4	a certain blind man sat by the way side begging:	18:35
3	as he went, they spread their clothes in the way.	19:36
4	but teachest the way of God truly:	20:21
3	while he talked with us by the way,	24:32
3	And they told what things were done in the way,	24:35
4	Make straight the way of the Lord, John	1:23
4	And whither I go ye know, and the way ye know.	14:4
4	and how can we know the way?	14:5
1	I am the way, the truth, and the life:	14:6
4	which is from Jerusalem a sabbath day's journey. Acts	1:12
8	Thou hast made known to me the ways of life;	2:28
4	way that goeth down from Jerusalem unto Gaza,	8:26
4	And as they went on their way,	8:36
4	and he went on his way rejoicing.	8:39
2	that if he found any of this way,	9:2
3	that appeared unto thee in the way as thou camest,	9:17
3	how he had seen the Lord in the way,	9:27
8	wilt thou not cease to pervert the right ways	13:10
7	suffered all nations to walk in their own ways. Acts	14:16
4	which show unto us the way of salvation.	16:17
4	This man was instructed in the way of the Lord;	18:25
4	expounded ... the way of God more perfectly.	18:26
4	but spake evil of that way before the multitude,	19:9
2	same time there arose no small stir about that way.	19:23
4	And I persecuted this way unto the death,	22:4
4	that after the way which they call heresy,	24:14
2	having more perfect knowledge of that way,	24:22
4	laying wait in the way to kill him.	25:3
4	I saw in the way a light from heaven,	26:13
7	Destruction and misery are in their ways: Rom	3:16
4	And the way of peace have they not known:	3:17
5	are his judgments, and his ways past finding out!	11:33
8	who shall bring you into remembrance of my ways.. I Co	4:17
4	and yet show I unto you a more excellent way.	12:31
4	our Lord Jesus Christ, direct our way unto you. 1 Th	3:11
8	and they have not known my ways. Heb	3:10
4	that the way into the holiest of all	9:8
4	a new and living way, which he hath consecrated	10:20
7	A double minded man is unstable in all his ways. Jas	1:8
3	messengers, and had sent them out another way?	2:25
2	the error of his way shall save a soul from death,	5:20
1	the way of truth shall be evil spoken of. 2 Pt	2:2
4	have forsaken the right way, and are gone astray,	2:15
3	following the way of Balaam the son of Bosor,	2:15
4	not to have known the way of righteousness,	2:21
3	for they have gone in the way of Cain, Jude	1:11
5	just and true are thy ways, thou King of saints. Rev	15:3
1	the way of the kings of the east might be prepared.	16:12

Classical Greek

In all the ancient Greek literature (classical papyri, Septuagint, New Testament, and Post-Apostolic Fathers) *hodos* refers to any "road" or "way" that carried ordinary traffic (*Bauer*; cf. Michaelis, "hodos," *Kittel*, 5:91). The word makes no distinction in the kind of road. It can denote a broad public highway for armies or chariots, a network of roads and trade routes that crisscross the land, a city street, a footpath in the country that lay through, beside, or between fields (ibid., 5:66), or a river channel.

Septuagint Usage

A very common word in the Septuagint, *hodos* occurs about 800 times. In most of these occurrences *hodos* translates the Hebrew term *derekh* from the root "to tread." As in classical usage, *hodos* is used in the Septuagint to describe the usual ungraded road or path where the surface has been packed down by the passing animals, pedestrians, and vehicles. *Hodos* also translates the Hebrew term m^eṣillāh, which is the common term for a constructed roadway, "that which is built up" (cf. Isaiah 62:10; Jeremiah 31:21).

During their Exodus, Israel traveled on the *hodos* of the king (Numbers 20:17); later the cities of Israel were connected with roadways to expedite the flight of accused killers (Deuteronomy 19:3). During the period of the judges, highways also connected places of corporate worship (Judges 20:31; 21:19). The longest known highway of ancient times was the famous "Silk Road" that ran from Rome to China (cf. Thiele, "Roads," *International Standard Bible Encyclopedia*, 4:201; cf. pp.199-203). Even though Jesus confined most of His earthly ministry to the region of Galilee, His teaching was easily spread throughout the Roman Empire because of the vast systems of roads they constructed.

New Testament Usage

In the New Testament *hodos* occurs about 100 times, 83 of which are translated "way." *Hodos* identifies only two specific roads in Palestine, the Jericho Road (Luke 10:30,31) and the desert road from Jerusalem to Gaza (Acts 8:26). The term has different meanings when used in prepositional phrases, e.g., "into (*eis*) the way," which means for the journey, traveling (Matthew 10:10), whether by water, land, or air; "in (*en*) the way," en route (Matthew 20:17; Mark 8:27); "before (*pro*) the way," further on or toward; and "out (*ek*) of the way," aside or beside (*Liddell-Scott*). Literally, *hodos* can refer to a road (Matthew 13:4) or a traveling route (Matthew 2:12), but it is predominantly used with a figurative sense in such expressions as "way of righteousness" (Matthew 21:32), "way of truth" (2 Peter 2:2), "way of peace" (Luke 1:79), and "way of salvation" (Acts 16:17).

Other examples include the "way of a day," which means a day's journey, or the distance a person would travel during one day (Luke 2:44); "way of a Sabbath" or the distance Jews were allowed to travel on a holy day (by tradition the rabbis limited this distance to 2000 cubits [3000 feet by Hellenistic measure, 3600 feet by Roman measure] from one's house; this distance seems to be based on Joshua 3:4 which defines the distance the people had to be behind the ark during their wilderness travel). It can also mean "way of the sea," meaning toward or along the shore (Matthew 4:15); "way of the Gentiles," referring to the region where they lived (Matthew 10:5); and "going the way of all the earth" which meant to die (Joshua 23:14).

Biblical writers were especially concerned with the way people lived. Therefore, they wrote of "going their own way," a general reference to the habits and behaviors of mankind (Proverbs 21:2) or animals such as the eagle and snake (Proverbs 30:19), locusts (Joel 2:25), and ants (Proverbs 6:6). The phrase "way of Cain" describes a misguided life (Jude 11); and the phrase "the two ways" depicts both the narrow passage to life and the broad way of darkness, destruction, and death (Matthew 7:13,14).

Related to Christianity, John the Baptist prepared the way for Jesus (Mark 1:2). Jesus is the Way into the (heavenly) sanctuary (Hebrews 9:8; 10:20), as well as the Way (John 14:6) to heaven. Christianity was called "the Way" (Acts 9:2; 22:4). The way of love is the "more excellent way" (1 Corinthians 12:31 to 13:13). The "way of Truth" as an expression of God's will is synonymous with *entolē* (1769), "commandment" (Michaelis, "hodos," *Kittel*, 5:51).

Particularly in the Book of Acts *hodos* is employed in the phrase "the way of God"—a general term for all that Christian preaching and activity represents. Thus, the "way of God" has a membership (9:2); it may be explained (18:26); some speak evil of it (19:9); it causes a stir in the community (19:23); it was the object of Saul's (Paul's) persecution (22:4); it is called heresy (24:14); and one can grow in the knowledge of it (24:22). From these varied uses it is clear this phrase denotes the entire Christian community and its beliefs.

STRONG 3598, BAUER 553-55, MOULTON-MILLIGAN 438, KITTEL 5:42,96, LIDDELL-SCOTT 1199, COLIN BROWN 3:935-37.

3462. ὀδούς odous noun

Tooth.

שֵׁן shēn (8514), Tooth (Ex 21:27, Ps 37:12 [36:12], Jl 1:6).

שֵׁן shēn (A8515), Tooth (Dn 7:5,7,19—Aramaic).

1. ὀδόντος odontos gen sing masc
2. ὀδόντα odonta acc sing masc
3. ὀδόντες odontes nom pl masc
4. ὀδόντων odontōn gen pl masc
5. ὀδόντας odontas acc pl masc

```
2  An eye for an eye, and a tooth for a tooth:.........Matt 5:38
1  An eye for an eye, and a tooth for a tooth:.............5:38
4  there shall be weeping and gnashing of teeth...........8:12
4  there shall be wailing and gnashing of teeth..........13:42
4  there shall be wailing and gnashing of teeth..........13:50
4  there shall be weeping and gnashing of teeth..........22:13
4  there shall be weeping and gnashing of teeth..........24:51
4  there shall be weeping and gnashing of teeth..........25:30
5  and he foameth, and gnasheth with his teeth,.....Mark 9:18
4  There shall be weeping and gnashing of teeth,....Luke 13:28
5  and they gnashed on him with their teeth...........Acts 7:54
3  and their teeth were as the teeth of lions..........Rev 9:8
```

Classical Greek

The primary use of *odous* is "tooth," i.e., an incisor or molar. This use is consistent in the classical and Septuagintal Greek. Metaphorically, the word refers to anything sharp or pointed—a prong or spike, the tooth of a saw, comb, or cogwheel, or the point of a plowshare. It is also used of the second vertebrae (or perhaps the first) in the neck, so called because of its shape (*Liddell-Scott*).

Septuagint Usage
In the Septuagint *odous* is frequently used to translate the Hebrew term *shēn*, "tooth, ivory." It is occasionally used literally (Numbers 11:33), but more often it is used figuratively. In Exodus 21:24 the Mosaic law required "tooth for tooth" as retribution for physical injury (cf. Leviticus 24:20; Deuteronomy 19:21). The phrase "gnashing of *teeth*" generally symbolizes uncontrollable anger and rage (Job 16:9; Psalms 35:16 [LXX 34:16]; 112:10 [110:10]) however, in the New Testament this same phrase usually describes anguish.

New Testament Usage
Odous occurs 11 times in the New Testament. Several times it refers literally to "teeth." These occurrences are in Matthew 5:38; Mark 9:18; Acts 7:54 and express intense pain or suffering. The phrase "gnashing of teeth" is used to describe the intense misery of those who are eternally exiled from heaven (cf. Matthew 8:12; 13:42,50; 22:13; 24:51; 25:30; Luke 13:28). In Revelation 9:8, in the plague of locusts from the pit, they are described as having the *teeth* of lions.

Strong 3599, Bauer 555, Moulton-Milligan 438, Liddell-Scott 1199, Colin Brown 2:421.

3463. ὀδυνάομαι odunaomai verb
Cause pain; feel pain, be tormented.
Cognate:
  ὀδύνη odunē (3464)
Synonyms:
  λυπέω lupeō (3048)
  πενθέω pentheō (3858)

דָּוֶה dāweh (1791), Faint (Lv 1:13).

חִיל chîl (2527), Agony (Zec 9:5).

מָרַר mārar (5006), Hiphil: be bitter (Zec 12:10).

1. **ὀδυνῶμαι odunōmai** 1sing indic pres mid
2. **ὀδυνᾶσαι odunasai** 2sing indic pres mid
3. **ὀδυνώμενοι odunōmenoi**
   nom pl masc part pres mid

```
3 thy father and I have sought thee sorrowing........Luke 2:48
1 cool my tongue; for I am tormented in this flame......16:24
2 but now he is comforted, and thou art tormented.......16:25
3 Sorrowing most of all for the words ... he spake,...Acts 20:38
```

The word *odunaō* means "to cause intense pain" in its active sense, or "to be anguished or tormented" in its passive sense. It is a word used in the New Testament only by Luke. Mary and Joseph were "consumed with grief" as any parent with a lost child would be (Luke 2:48). When Paul was to take leave of the Ephesian elders, they expressed their "anguish" on having to part with him (Acts 20:38). And in the Parable of the Rich Man and Lazarus the rich man was physically, mentally, and spiritually "tormented" in the flames of hell (Luke 16:24,25).

Strong 3600, Bauer 555 (see "odunaō"), Moulton-Milligan 438-39, Kittel 5:115, Liddell-Scott 1199 (see "odunaō").

3464. ὀδύνη odunē noun
Pain, grief, sorrow.
Cognate:
  ὀδυνάομαι odunaomai (3463)
Synonyms:
  λύπη lupē (3049)
  πένθος penthos (3859)

אֵבֶל 'ēvel (60), Mourning (Est 9:22—Codex Alexandrinus only).

אָוֶן 'āwen (201), Mourning (Dt 26:14).

בַּלָּהָה ballāhāh (1130), Terror (Jb 30:15).

דָּוֶה dāweh (1791), Faint (Lam 5:17).

דְּוַי dᵉway (1793), Languishing (Ps 41:3 [40:3]).

הַיָּה hayyāh (2031), Calamity (Jb 6:2).

יָגוֹן yāghôn (3123), Sorrow (Ps 31:10 [30:10], Is 35:10, Jer 8:18).

כָּאַב kā'av (3628), Be in pain; hiphil: hurt (Ez 28:24).

לַעֲנָה la'ănāh (4081), Wormwood (Jer 23:15).

מַדְוֶה madhweh (4207), Disease (Dt 28:60).

מָזוֹר māzôr (4334), Sore (Hos 5:13).

מַחַץ machats (4411), Wound (Is 30:26).

מַכְאוֹב makh'ôv (4480), Suffering (Ex 3:7 [3:8]).

מֶמֶר memer (4612), Bitterness (Prv 17:25).

מַר mar (4914), Bitter, bitterness (Jb 3:20, Is 38:15 [38:14], Am 8:10).

מְרִי mᵉrî (4967), Stubbornness (1 Sm 15:23).

מְרִירוּת mᵉrîrûth (4977), Bitterness (Ez 21:6).

מָרַר mārar (5006), Be bitter; hiphil: bitter weeping (Zec 12:10).

נֶגַע negha' (5237), Wound (Prv 6:33).

נְדֻדִים nᵉdhudhîm (5254), Tossing (Jb 7:4).

סוּפָה sûphāh (5679), Whirlwind (Jb 37:9).

עָמָל 'āmāl (6219), Trouble, misery (Jb 4:8, 7:3, 15:35).

עֳנִי 'ŏnî (6271), Affliction (Jb 30:16).
עֶצֶב 'etsev (6325), Toil (Ps 127:2 [126:2]).
עֹצֶב 'ōtsev (6327), Pain (Is 14:3).
פַּלָּצוּת pallātsûth (6671), Trembling (Jb 21:6).
רַעַשׁ ra'ash (7783), Trembling (Ez 12:18).
שַׂרְעַפִּים sar'appîm (8040), Anxiety (Ps 94:19 [93:19]).
תּוּגָה tûghāh (8755), Sorrow (Prv 17:21).

1. ὀδύνη odunē nom sing fem
2. ὀδύναις odunais dat pl fem

1 great heaviness and continual **sorrow** in my heart.... Rom 9:2
2 pierced themselves through with many **sorrows**...... 1 Tm 6:10

The literal translation of the word *odunē* is "pain." This may occur as either physical pain to the body, or as an emotional and mental pain of grief or distress. The only two occurrences of *odunē* in the New Testament are Romans 9:2 and 1 Timothy 6:10. In Romans Paul used this word to express his mental and emotional grief while knowing that his fellow Jews were shut off from salvation. This is expressed as sorrow, deep sorrow, a distress that knows no reconciliation. In 1 Timothy *odunē* is used for the severe and piercing "self-accusations and pangs of conscience which will smite those who defected out of love for money" (Hauck, "odunē," *Kittel*, 5:115). Again, this refers more to the emotional aspects of this word rather than physical aspects of such suffering.

STRONG 3601, BAUER 555, MOULTON-MILLIGAN 439, KITTEL 5:115, LIDDELL-SCOTT 1199.

3465. ὀδυρμός odurmos noun
Lamentation, mourning, wailing.
SYNONYM:
πένθος penthos (3859)

תַּמְרוּרִים tamrûrîm (8893), Bitterness (Jer 31:15 [38:15]).

1. ὀδυρμός odurmos nom sing masc
2. ὀδυρμόν odurmon acc sing masc

1 lamentation, and weeping, and great **mourning**,...... Matt 2:18
2 your **mourning**, your fervent mind toward me;...... 2 Co 7:7

Odurmos is a combination of the stem of *oduromai*, "I bewail, lament," and the suffix *-mos* which is often used to form verbal abstracts (Moulton and Howard, *Grammar of New Testament Greek*, 2:350). Thus, it means a "lamentation" or "mourning." It is used in this sense in both the secular and sacred Greek literature (*Liddell-Scott*). *Odurmos* conveys a more intense emotion of mourning than the terms *dakruon* (1139), "a tear," and *krazō* (2869), "I cry aloud, shout, or cry."

In its two occurrences in the New Testament the term expresses a very intense and deep sense of sorrow; e.g., Bethlehem mothers mourning the slaughter of their babies with loud and grievous lamentation (Matthew 2:18 quoting Jeremiah 31:15), and the Corinthian believers sorrowing unto repentance (2 Corinthians 7:7).

STRONG 3602, BAUER 555, MOULTON-MILLIGAN 439, KITTEL 5:116, LIDDELL-SCOTT 1199, COLIN BROWN 2:417.

3466. Ὀζίας Ozias name
Uzziah.

1. Ὀζίας Ozias nom masc
2. Ὀζίαν Ozian acc masc

2 and Josaphat begat Joram; and Joram begat **Ozias**;.. Matt 1:8
1 And **Ozias** begat Joatham;............................ 1:9

The son of Jehoram in the genealogy of Jesus (Matthew 1:8,9).

3467. ὄζω ozō verb
To smell, give off an odor, aroma.
COGNATES:
εὐωδία euōdia (2156)
ὀσμή osmē (3606)

בָּאַשׁ bā'ash (919), Stink (Ex 8:14).

1. ὄζει ozei 3sing indic pres act

1 he **stinketh**: for he hath been dead four days....... John 11:39

As a verb *ozō* means "to give off an odor" (*Bauer*). In a positive sense it is the fragrance of flowers or the sweet aroma of a perfumed body. Negatively it refers to something giving off a foul smell. Both secular and sacred writers use the term in these ways (*Liddell-Scott*). In its only occurrence in the New Testament *ozō* is used negatively when Martha commented about her dead brother, "Lord, by this time there will *be an odor*" (John 11:39, RSV). A similar instance in secular Greek reads, "The body emitting a pungent odor ... " (*Moulton-Milligan*).

STRONG 3605, BAUER 555, MOULTON-MILLIGAN 439, LIDDELL-SCOTT 1200.

3468. ὅθεν hothen adv
Whence, from where, from which, for which reason.

1. ὅθεν hothen

1 will return into my house from **whence** I came out; Matt	12:44
1 **Whereupon** he promised with an oath to give her whatsoever	14:7
1 and gathering **where** thou hast not strowed:	25:24
1 and gather **where** I have not strowed:	25:26
1 I will return unto my house **whence** I came out…..Luke	11:24
1 from **whence** they had been recommended……… Acts	14:26
1 **Whereupon**, O king Agrippa,	26:19
1 And **from thence** we fetched a compass,	28:13
1 **Wherefore** in all things it behoved him to be made…Heb	2:17
1 **Wherefore**, holy brethren, partakers	3:1
1 **Wherefore** he is able also to save them	7:25
1 **wherefore** it is of necessity that this man have	8:3
1 **Whereupon** neither the first testament was	9:18
1 from **whence** also he received him in a figure.	11:19
1 **whereby** we know that it is the last time. 1 Jn	2:18

Bauer cites three uses of *hothen*. First, it is an adverb "of place," "from which fact," and "for which reason." As an adverb of place, *hothen* indicates "from whatever source, from what manner" (*Liddell-Scott*). For example, in the Parable of the Talents the master was accused of harvesting crops "from" fields "where" he had not planted (Matthew 25:24,26); Paul left Syracuse "from whence" he then traveled to Rhegium on his way to Rome (Acts 28:13); and the demon went back to his house "from which" he had gone (Matthew 12:44; Luke 11:24).

Secondly, *hothen* is used as a literary device to express progression in one's arguments as in 1 John 2:18 where John reasoned, "*From which fact* we know it is the last days*" (free translation). Thirdly, *hothen* is used to express a reason. Placed at the beginning of a clause it is variously translated as "therefore, wherefore, so then, hence," etc. (Matthew 14:7; Acts 26:19; Hebrews 2:17; 3:1; 7:25; 8:3; 9:18; and 11:19).

STRONG 3606, BAUER 555, MOULTON-MILLIGAN 439, LIDDELL-SCOTT 1200.

3469. ὀθόνη othonē noun

Sheet, linen cloth, fine linen, sail of a ship.

1. ὀθόνην othonēn acc sing fem

1 a great **sheet** knit at the four corners, Acts	10:11
1 as it had been a great **sheet**,	11:5

Classical Greek
Othonē describes a relatively large linen cloth. In classical Greek, writings of Homer, and in the papyri *othonē* refers to "sails" on a ship and "fine linen" clothes, especially of women's dresses (*Liddell-Scott*). Liddell-Scott also reports one special use of the term to describe the membranes that enclose the pupil of the eye (cf. *Moulton-Milligan*).

Septuagint Usage
Othonē appears only three times in the Septuagint. In Judges 14:13 the cost for failing to solve Samson's riddle was "thirty *sheets* and thirty change of garments." Hosea's adulterous wife boasted of the "linen" and other gifts illicitly given by her lovers (Hosea 2:5; cf. verse 9).

Othonē overlaps in meaning with *lention* (2986), "cloth, napkin, towel," and *linon* (3017), "flax, linen," and things made from them; i.e., lamp wicks, garments, and fishnets (see *Bauer*, "lention," "linon").

New Testament Usage
In the New Testament the word occurs only in Acts 10:11 and 11:5 where in Peter's vision he saw a large "sheet" come down from heaven. The impact of this vision upon Peter and his ministry had far-reaching ramifications not only for Peter but for the ministry of the entire Early Church. This vision and the events that took place later in the home of Cornelius opened the way for greater understanding on the part of the early Jewish Christians regarding the status of Gentiles in the kingdom of God and in the local church.

STRONG 3607, BAUER 555, MOULTON-MILLIGAN 439, LIDDELL-SCOTT 1200.

3470. ὀθόνιον othonion noun

Linen cloth, fine linen, bandage, towel.

סָדִין sādhîn (5650), Garment (Jgs 14:13).
פֵּשֶׁת pēsheth (6844), Flax (Hos 2:5,9).

1. ὀθονίων othoniōn gen pl neu
2. ὀθονίοις othoniois dat pl neu
3. ὀθόνια othonia nom/acc pl neu

3 he beheld the **linen clothes** laid by themselves,…..Luke	24:12
2 and wound it in **linen clothes** with the spices,…… John	19:40
3 saw the **linen clothes** lying; yet went he not in………	20:5
3 and seeth the **linen clothes** lie,	20:6
1 the napkin, … not lying with the **linen clothes**,	20:7

Othonion is the diminutive form of *othonē* (3469); hence it describes a smaller cloth. It is used in the secular Greek literature for "towel," "linen cloths," and "linen bandages" for wounds (*Liddell-Scott*). Strips of "linen cloth" were also used in the preparation of corpses for burial (*Bauer*). All five of its uses in the New Testament designate the grave clothes; i.e., the strips of linen used to bind the corpse and secure the spices about it, which was the Jewish custom for burial (Luke 24:12; John 19:40, 20:5-7).

STRONG 3608, BAUER 555, MOULTON-MILLIGAN 439, LIDDELL-SCOTT 1200.

οἶδα 3471

3471. οἶδα oida verb
Know fully; understand, recognize.

Cognates:
εἶδον eidon (1481)
σύνοιδα sunoida (4774)

Synonyms:
αἰσθάνομαι aisthanomai (143)
γινώσκω ginōskō (1091)
γνωρίζω gnōrizō (1101)
εἶδον eidon (1481)
ἐπιγινώσκω epiginōskō (1906)
ἐπίσταμαι epistamai (1971)
καταλαμβάνω katalambanō (2608)
νοέω noeō (3401)
ὁράω horaō (3571)
παρακολουθέω parakoloutheō (3738)
συνίημι suniēmi (4770)

בִּין bîn (1032), Qal: perceive, understand (Jb 23:8, 42:3); hithpolel: understand (Jb 26:14).

דֵּעַ dēaʿ (1903), Opinion (Jb 32:10).

דַּעַת daʿath (1907), Intention, knowledge (Dt 4:42, Jb 21:14, Is 5:13).

זָכַר zākhar (2226), Remember; hiphil: acknowledge (Is 26:13).

חָזָה chāzâh (2463), See (Is 26:11).

חָכָם chākhām (2550), Skilled (2 Chr 2:7).

יָדַע yādhaʿ (3156), Qal: know (Ex 32:22f., 1 Sm 20:3, Jer 24:7); niphal: be known (Dt 21:1).

יְדַע yᵉdhaʿ (A3157), Know (Ezr 7:25, Dn 2:8—Aramaic).

נָכַר nākhar (5421), Recognize; piel: regard (Jb 34:19).

רָאָה rāʾâh (7495), See (Gn 39:3, Nm 35:23, Is 33:19).

שָׂעַר sāʿar (7994), Know about (Dt 32:17).

שָׁמַע shāmaʿ (8471), Hear (1 Kgs 20:31 [21:31]).

שָׁמַר shāmar (8490), Be careful (Jos 1:8).

1. ἴστε iste 2pl indic/impr perf act
2. οἶδα oida 1sing indic perf act
3. οἶδας oidas 2sing indic perf act
4. οἶδεν oiden 3sing indic perf act
5. οἴδαμεν oidamen 1pl indic perf act
6. οἴδατε oidate 2pl indic perf act
7. ἴσασι isasi 3pl indic perf act
8. οἴδασιν oidasin 3pl indic perf act
9. ᾔδειν ēdein 1sing indic plperf act
10. ᾔδεις ēdeis 2sing indic plperf act
11. ᾔδει ēdei 3sing indic plperf act
12. ᾔδειτε ēdeite 2pl indic plperf act
13. ᾔδεισαν ēdeisan 3pl indic plperf act
14. εἰδῶ eidō 1sing subj perf act
15. εἰδῇς eidēs 2sing subj perf act
16. εἰδῶμεν eidōmen 1pl subj perf act
17. εἰδῆτε eidēte 2pl subj perf act
18. εἰδώς eidōs nom sing masc part perf act
19. εἰδότι eidoti dat sing masc part perf act
20. εἰδότες eidotes nom pl masc part perf act
21. εἰδόσιν eidosin dat pl masc part perf act
22. εἰδότας eidotas acc pl masc part perf act
23. εἰδυῖα eiduia nom sing fem part perf act
24. εἰδότα eidota nom/acc pl neu part perf act
25. εἰδέναι eidenai inf perf act
26. εἰδήσουσιν eidēsousin 3pl indic fut act
27. εἴδῃ eidē 3sing subj perf act
28. ἴσασιν isasin 3pl indic perf act

4	your Father **knoweth** what things ye have need of,	Matt 6:8
4	your heavenly Father **knoweth** that ye have need	6:32
6	**know** how to give good gifts unto your children,	7:11
18	And Jesus **knowing** their thoughts said, (NASB)	9:4
17	that ye may **know** that the Son of man hath power	9:6
18	Jesus **knew** their thoughts, and said unto them,	12:25
3	**Knowest** thou that the Pharisees were offended,	15:12
6	Jesus answered and said, Ye **know** not what ye ask.	20:22
6	Ye **know** that the princes of the Gentiles	20:25
5	And they answered Jesus, and said, We cannot **tell**.	21:27
5	saying, Master, we **know** that thou art true,	22:16
20	not **knowing** the scriptures, nor the power of God.	22:29
4	But of that day and hour **knoweth** no man,	24:36
6	for ye **know** not what hour your Lord doth come.	24:42
11	that if the goodman of the house **had known**	24:43
2	Verily I say unto you, I **know** you not.	25:12
6	for ye **know** neither the day nor the hour	25:13
10	thou **knewest** that I reap where I sowed not,	25:26
6	Ye **know** that after two days is the feast	26:2
2	denied before them ... I **know** not what thou sayest	26:70
2	he denied with an oath, I do not **know** the man.	26:72
2	curse and to swear, saying, I **know** not the man.	26:74
11	For he **knew** that for envy they had delivered him.	27:18
6	go your way, make it as sure as ye **can**.	27:65
2	for I **know** that ye seek Jesus, which was crucified.	28:5
2	I **know** thee who thou art, the Holy One of God.	Mark 1:24
13	not the devils to speak, because **they knew** him.	1:34
17	that ye may **know** that the Son of man hath power	2:10
6	And he said unto them, **Know** ye not this parable?	4:13
4	spring and grow up, he **knoweth** not how.	4:27
23	and trembling, **knowing** what was done in her,	5:33
18	**knowing** that he was a just man and an holy,	6:20
11	he **wist** not what to say; for they were sore afraid.	9:6
3	Thou **knowest** the commandments,	10:19
6	Jesus said unto them, Ye **know** not what ye ask:	10:38
6	Ye **know** that they which are accounted to rule	10:42
5	answered and said unto Jesus, We cannot **tell**.	11:33
5	we **know** that thou art true, and carest for no man:	12:14
18	But he, **knowing** their hypocrisy, said unto them,	12:15
20	**know** not the scriptures, neither the power of God?	12:24
18	and **perceiving** that he had answered them well,	12:28
4	But of that day and that hour **knoweth** no man,	13:32
6	watch and pray: for ye **know** not when the time is,	13:33
6	ye **know** not when the master of the house cometh,	13:35
13	neither **wist** they what to answer him.	14:40
2	I **know** not, neither understand I what thou sayest.	14:68
2	saying, I **know** not this man of whom ye speak.	14:71
12	**wist** ye not that I must be about my Father's	Luke 2:49
2	I **know** thee who thou art; the Holy One of God.	4:34
13	not to speak: for they **knew** that he was Christ.	4:41
17	that ye may **know** that the Son of man hath power	5:24
11	But he **knew** their thoughts, and said to the man	6:8
20	laughed him to scorn, **knowing** that she was dead.	8:53
18	and one for Elias: not **knowing** what he said.	9:33
18	**knowing** what they were thinking (NASB)	9:47
6	Ye **know** not what manner of spirit ye are of.	9:55
6	**know** how to give good gifts unto your children:	11:13
18	But he, **knowing** their thoughts, said unto them,	11:17
8	men that walk over them are not **aware** of them.	11:44
4	your Father **knoweth** that ye have need of these	12:30
11	if the goodman of the house **had known** what hour	12:39
6	ye **can discern** the face of the sky and of the earth;	12:56
6	You **know** how to analyze the appearance (NASB)	12:56
2	say unto you, I **know** you not whence ye are:	13:25
2	I **know** you not whence ye are; depart from me,	13:27

310

οἶδα 3471

3	Thou **knowest** the commandments,	Luke 18:20
10	Thou **knewest** that I was an austere man,	19:22
25	answered, that they could not **tell** whence it was.	20:7
5	we **know** that thou sayest and teachest rightly,	20:21
25	thou shalt thrice deny that thou **knowest** me.	22:34
2	he denied him, saying, Woman, I **know** him not.	22:57
2	And Peter said, Man, I **know** not what thou sayest.	22:60
8	forgive them; for they **know** not what they do.	23:34
6	standeth one among you, whom ye **know** not;	John 1:26
9	And I **knew** him not:	1:31
9	And I **knew** him not:	1:33
11	and **knew** not whence it was:	2:9
13	but the servants which drew the water **knew**;	2:9
5	we **know** that thou art a teacher come from God:	3:2
3	but canst not **tell** whence it cometh,	3:8
5	We speak that we **do know**,	3:11
10	If thou **knewest** the gift of God,	4:10
6	Ye worship ye **know** not what:	4:22
5	we **know** what we worship:	4:22
2	I **know** that Messias cometh, which is called Christ:	4:25
6	I have meat to eat that ye **know** not of.	4:32
5	and **know** that this is indeed the Christ,	4:42
11	And he that was healed **wist** not who it was:	5:13
2	and I **know** that the witness ... is true.	5:32
11	for he himself **knew** what he would do.	6:6
5	son of Joseph, whose father and mother we **know**?	6:42
18	**knew** in himself that his disciples murmured at it,	6:61
11	For Jesus **knew** from the beginning who they were	6:64
4	How **knoweth** this man letters,	7:15
5	Howbeit we **know** this man whence he is:	7:27
6	Ye both **know** me, and ye know whence I am:	7:28
6	Ye both know me, and ye **know** whence I am:	7:28
6	but he that sent me is true, whom ye **know** not.	7:28
2	But I **know** him: for I am from him,	7:29
2	for I **know** whence I came, and whither I go;	8:14
2	ye cannot **tell** whence I come, and whither I go.	8:14
6	Ye neither **know** me, nor my Father:	8:19
12	if ye **had known** me, ... known my Father also.	8:19
12	ye should **have known** my Father also.	8:19
2	I **know** that ye are Abraham's seed;	8:37
2	Yet ye have not **known** him; but I **know** him:	8:55
2	if I should say, I **know** him not, I shall be a liar	8:55
2	but I **know** him, and keep his saying.	8:55
2	Where is he? He said, I **know** not.	9:12
5	We **know** that this is our son, ... he was born blind:	9:20
5	But by what means he now seeth, we **know** not;	9:21
5	or who hath opened his eyes, we **know** not:	9:21
5	we **know** that this man is a sinner.	9:24
2	Whether he be a sinner or no, I **know** not:	9:25
2	one thing I **know**, that, whereas I was blind,	9:25
5	We **know** that God spake unto Moses:	9:29
5	as for this fellow, we **know** not from whence he is.	9:29
6	that ye **know** not from whence he is,	9:30
5	Now we **know** that God heareth not sinners:	9:31
8	and the sheep follow him: for **they know** his voice.	10:4
8	for they **know** not the voice of strangers.	10:5
2	But I **know**, that even now,	11:22
2	I **know** that he shall rise again in the resurrection	11:24
9	And I **knew** that thou hearest me always:	11:42
6	said unto them, Ye **know** nothing at all,	11:49
4	for he that walketh in darkness **knoweth** not	12:35
2	I **know** that his commandment is life everlasting:	12:50
18	when Jesus **knew** that his hour was come	13:1
18	Jesus **knowing** that the Father had given all	13:3
3	What I do thou **knowest** not now;	13:7
11	For he **knew** who should betray him;	13:11
6	If ye **know** these things,	13:17
2	I **know** whom I have chosen;	13:18
6	And whither I go ye **know**, and the way ye know.	14:4
6	And whither I go ye know, and the way ye **know**.	14:4
5	Lord, we **know** not whither thou goest;	14:5
25	and how can we **know** the way?	14:5
12	you **would have known** My Father also; (NASB)	14:7
4	for the servant **knoweth** not what his lord doeth:	15:15
8	because they **know** not him that sent me.	15:21
5	A little while? we cannot **tell** what he saith.	16:18
5	Now are we **sure** that thou knowest all things,	16:30
3	Now are we sure that thou **knowest** all things,	John 16:30
11	Judas also, which betrayed him, **knew** the place:	18:2
18	**knowing** all things that should come upon him,	18:4
8	behold, they **know** what I said.	18:21
3	**knowest** thou not that I have power to crucify thee,	19:10
18	**knowing** that all things were now accomplished,	19:28
4	**knoweth** that he saith true, that ye might believe.	19:35
5	and we **know** not where they have laid him.	20:2
13	For as yet they **knew** not the scripture,	20:9
2	and I **know** not where they have laid him.	20:13
11	saw Jesus standing, and **knew** not that it was Jesus.	20:14
13	but the disciples **knew** not that it was Jesus.	21:4
20	**knowing** that it was the Lord.	21:12
3	Yea, Lord; thou **knowest** that I love thee.	21:15
3	Yea, Lord; thou **knowest** that I love thee.	21:16
3	he said unto him, Lord, thou **knowest** all things;	21:17
5	and we **know** that his testimony is true.	21:24
6	as ye yourselves also **know**:	Acts 2:22
18	**knowing** that God had sworn with an oath to him,	2:30
6	made this man strong, whom ye see and **know**:	3:16
2	I **wot** that through ignorance ye did it,	3:17
23	his wife, not **knowing** what was done, came in.	5:7
11	Till another king arose, which **knew** not Joseph.	7:18
5	we **wot** not what is become of him.	7:40
6	That word, I say, ye **know**,	10:37
11	and **wist** not that it was true which was done	12:9
2	Now I **know** of a surety,	12:11
13	for they **knew** all that his father was a Greek.	16:3
13	part **knew** not wherefore they were come together.	19:32
18	not **knowing** the things that shall befall me there:	20:22
2	And now, behold, I **know** that ye all,	20:25
2	For I **know** this, that after my departing	20:29
9	I **wist** not, brethren, that he was the high priest:	23:5
18	having more perfect **knowledge** of that way,	24:22
28	My manner of life ... **know** all the Jews;	26:4
2	I **know** that thou believest.	26:27
5	But we **are sure** that the judgment of God	Rom 2:2
5	we **know** that what things soever the law saith,	3:19
20	**knowing** that tribulation worketh patience;	5:3
20	**Knowing** that Christ being raised from the dead,	6:9
6	**Know** ye not, that to whom ye yield yourselves	6:16
9	for I **had** not **known** lust, except the law had said,	7:7
2	For we **know** that the law is spiritual:	7:14
2	For I **know** that in me that is, in my flesh,	7:18
5	For we **know** that the whole creation groaneth	8:22
5	we **know** not what we should pray for as we ought:	8:26
4	And he that searcheth the hearts **knoweth**	8:27
5	we **know** that all things work together for good	8:28
6	**Wot** ye not what the scripture saith of Elias?	11:2
20	**knowing** the time,	13:11
2	I **know**, and am persuaded by the Lord Jesus,	14:14
2	And I **am** sure, that, when I come unto you,	15:29
2	besides, I **know** not whether I baptized any other.	1 Co 1:16
25	I determined not **to know** any thing among you,	2:2
4	For what man **knoweth** the things of a man,	2:11
4	even so the things of God **knoweth** no man,	2:11
16	that we **might know** the things that are freely given	2:12
6	**Know** ye not that ye are the temple of God,	3:16
6	**Know** ye not that a little leaven leaveneth	5:6
6	not **know** that the saints shall judge the world?	6:2
6	**Know** ye not that we shall judge angels?	6:3
6	**Know** ye not that the unrighteous shall not inherit	6:9
6	**Know** ye not that your bodies are the members	6:15
6	**know** ye not that he which is joined to an harlot	6:16
6	What? **know** ye not that your body is the temple	6:19
3	For what **knowest** thou, O wife,	7:16
3	or how **knowest** thou, O man,	7:16
5	we **know** that we all have knowledge.	8:1
25	And if any man think that he **knoweth** any thing,	8:2
5	we **know** that an idol is nothing in the world,	8:4
6	Do ye not **know** that they which minister	9:13
6	**Know** ye not that they which run in a race run all,	9:24
25	But I would have you **know**,	11:3
6	Ye **know** that ye were Gentiles,	12:2
14	and **understand** all mysteries, and all knowledge;	13:2
14	Therefore if I **know** not the meaning of the voice,	14:11
4	seeing he **understandeth** not what thou sayest?	14:16

311

οἶδα 3471

20	know that your labour is not in vain in the Lord.	1 Co 15:58
6	brethren, ye know the house of Stephanas,	16:15
20	knowing, that as ye are partakers of the sufferings,	2 Co 1:7
20	Knowing that he which raised up the Lord Jesus	4:14
5	For we know that if our earthly house	5:1
20	knowing that, whilst we are at home in the body,	5:6
20	Knowing therefore the terror of the Lord,	5:11
5	henceforth know we no man after the flesh:	5:16
2	For I know the forwardness of your mind,	9:2
4	Wherefore? because I love you not? God knoweth.	11:11
4	our Lord Jesus Christ, ... knoweth that I lie not.	11:31
2	I knew a man in Christ above fourteen years ago,	12:2
2	whether in the body, I cannot tell;	12:2
2	or whether out of the body, I cannot tell:	12:2
4	out of the body, I cannot tell: God knoweth;	12:2
2	And I knew such a man,	12:3
2	I cannot tell: God knoweth;	12:3
4	I cannot tell: God knoweth;	12:3
20	Knowing that a man is not justified by the works	Gal 2:16
20	Howbeit then, when ye knew not God,	4:8
6	Ye know how ... I preached the gospel unto you	4:13
25	that ye may know what is the hope of his calling,	Eph 1:18
1	For this you know with certainty, (NASB)	5:5
20	Knowing ... whatsoever good thing any man doeth,	6:8
20	knowing that your Master also is in heaven;	6:9
17	But that ye also may know my affairs,	6:21
20	knowing that I am set for the defence of the gospel.	Phlp 1:17
2	For I know that this shall turn to my salvation	1:19
2	having this confidence, I know that I shall abide	1:25
2	I know both how to be abased, and ... to abound:	4:12
2	how to be abased, and I know how to abound:	4:12
6	Now ye Philippians know also,	4:15
25	that ye knew what great conflict I have for you,	Col 2:1
20	Knowing that of the Lord ye shall receive	3:24
20	knowing that ye also have a Master in heaven.	4:1
25	ye may know how ye ought to answer every man.	4:6
20	Knowing, brethren beloved, your election of God.	1 Th 1:4
6	as ye know what manner of men we were among	1:5
6	brethren, know our entrance in unto you,	2:1
6	were shamefully entreated, as ye know, at Philippi,	2:2
6	as ye know, nor a cloak of covetousness;	2:5
6	As ye know how we exhorted and comforted	2:11
6	yourselves know that we are appointed thereunto.	3:3
6	tribulation; even as it came to pass, and ye know.	3:4
6	For ye know what commandments we gave you	4:2
25	should know how to possess his vessel	4:4
24	even as the Gentiles which know not God:	4:5
6	For yourselves know perfectly that the day	5:2
25	to know them which labour among you,	5:12
21	taking vengeance on them that know not God,	2 Th 1:8
6	And now ye know what withholdeth	2:6
6	For yourselves know how ye ought to follow us:	3:7
5	But we know that the law is good,	1 Tm 1:8
18	Knowing this, ... law is not made for a righteous	1:9
4	For if a man know not how to rule his own house,	3:5
15	thou mayest know how thou oughtest to behave	3:15
2	not ashamed: for I know whom I have believed,	2 Tm 1:12
3	This thou knowest, that all they which are in Asia	1:15
18	knowing that they do gender strifes.	2:23
18	knowing of whom thou hast learned them;	3:14
3	from a child thou hast known the holy scriptures,	3:15
25	They profess that they know God;	Tit 1:16
18	Knowing that he that is such is subverted,	3:11
18	knowing that thou wilt also do more than I say.	Phlm 1:21
26	saying, Know the Lord: for all shall know me,	Heb 8:11
5	For we know him that hath said,	10:30
1	For ye know how that afterward,	12:17
1	This you know, my beloved (NASB)	Jas 1:19
20	knowing ... shall receive the greater condemnation.	3:1
6	know ye not that the friendship of the world is	4:4
19	Therefore to him that knoweth to do good,	4:17
20	Whom having not seen, ye love;	1 Pt 1:8
20	ye know that ye were not redeemed with ... gold,	1:18
20	blessing; knowing that ye are thereunto called,	3:9
20	knowing that the same afflictions are accomplished	5:9
22	always in remembrance ... though ye know them,	2 Pt 1:12
18	Knowing that ... I must put off this my tabernacle,	1:14
4	The Lord knoweth how to deliver the godly	2 Pt 2:9
4	in darkness, and knoweth not whither he goeth,	1 Jn 2:11
6	But ye have an unction ... and ye know all things.	2:20
6	I have not written unto you because ye know not,	2:21
6	because ye know it, and that no lie is of the truth.	2:21
17	If ye know that he is righteous,	2:29
5	but we know that, when he shall appear,	3:2
6	know that he was manifested to take away our sins;	3:5
5	We know that we have passed from death unto life,	3:14
6	and ye know that no murderer hath eternal life	3:15
17	that ye may know that ye have eternal life,	5:13
5	if we know that he hear us, whatsoever we ask,	5:15
5	we know that we have the petitions that we desired	5:15
5	We know that whosoever is born of God	5:18
5	And we know that we are of God,	5:19
5	And we know that the Son of God is come,	5:20
6	and ye know that our record is true.	3 Jn 1:12
22	in remembrance, though ye once knew this,	Jude 1:5
8	speak evil of those things which they know not:	1:10
2	know thy works, and thy labour, and thy patience,	Rev 2:2
2	I know thy works, and tribulation, and poverty,	2:9
2	I know thy works and where thou dwellest,	2:13
4	no one knows but he who receives it (NASB)	2:17
2	I know thy works, and charity, and service,	2:19
2	I know thy works, ... hast a name that thou livest,	3:1
2	I know thy works: ... set before thee an open door,	3:8
2	know thy works, that thou art neither cold nor hot:	3:15
3	and knowest not that thou art wretched,	3:17
3	And I said unto him, Sir, thou knowest.	7:14
18	because he knoweth that he hath but a short time.	12:12
4	a name written, that no man knew, but he himself.	19:12

Oida is the perfect form of *eidō*, which occurs so infrequently as to be archaic. *Eidō* does not occur in the active present form at all. Although *oida* is in the perfect tense it is translated as if it were a present, "I know." Yet the perfect idea of "possessed knowledge" rather than the present aspect of "acquiring knowledge" dominates the word's definition.

Classical Greek

Scholars maintain that a distinction existed between the perfective kind of knowledge denoted by *oida* and the progressive or "acquired" knowledge represented by *ginōskō* (1091), particularly in classical usage. To a large degree it is believed that this distinction carried over into the New Testament, although most scholars feel this distinction was breaking down or had broken down by the New Testament period. *Moulton-Milligan* states flatly that "the distinction between *oida* know and *ginōskō* come to know (cf. Lightfoot on Galatians 4:9 [sic]) cannot be pressed in Hellenistic Greek" (*Moulton-Milligan*).

From classical evidence we know that *oida* retains its proper sense of "to see" in the aorist tense (*eidon* [1481], *eidēnai*; cf. *idein*, etymologically related). Thus in the aorist form the idea of literal or mental sight is understood. Passively it could mean "to be visible, to appear" (*Liddell-Scott*). As already mentioned, the perfect form *oida* basically means "I know";

but under other conditions it can mean "to know how, to know for certain," or "to acknowledge" (as in a debt) (ibid.). Ordinarily the sense of the perfect (i.e., action completed) is lost; instead, the sense is of a continued completed state: "I know," not "I have come to know" (through experience or event).

Septuagint Usage

The Septuagint reveals that *oida* translates 12 Hebrew words, most frequently the word *yādhaʿ*, "I know," in its various conjugations. *Ginōskō* is also used to translate this Hebrew term. *Oida* can also translate *rāʾāh*, "I see" (e.g., Numbers 11:16; Ecclesiastes 5:7). The textual variation that occurs regularly when *oida* translates *rāʾāh* reveals the close relationship between *oida* and *idein*, "to see." The use of both *oida* and *ginōskō* to render a Hebrew infinitive absolute (usually translated emphatically) at 1 Samuel 20:3 (LXX 1 Kings 20:3) suggests that the Septuagint translators did not rigidly enforce the classical distinction between the two terms (Hebrew: *yādô ʿa yādaʿ*; Greek: *ginōskōn oiden*). Nonetheless, the "rule of thumb" was to separate the two concepts of knowing. Through its use of *oida* as an equivalent (however imprecise) of 12 Hebrew words or forms the Septuagint confirms that *oida* was a versatile term. This fact remains equally true in the New Testament.

New Testament Usage

In the New Testament the distinctive perfective sense of *oida* may have deteriorated slightly, and *ginōskō* and *oida* may be moving in the direction of considerable semantic overlap. For the most part, however, there are few surprises in over 300 occurrences of *oida*. Again, from a simplified point of view, *oida* means "to know."

People "know" one another, both in an intimate fashion (e.g., Matthew 26:72; Acts 7:18; 2 Corinthians 5:16) and in a general sense (John 1:26,31). Facts may "be known" (Matthew 25:13), or other intangible items like commandments (Luke 18:20) or mysteries (1 Corinthians 13:2) are "known."

Frequently *oida* is followed by an explanatory *hoti* (3617), "that": "We know *that* . . ." (Matthew 22:16; Luke 20:21; John 3:2; etc.). Paul used a similar device in his famous rhetorical question, "Do you not know that . . . ?" (Romans 6:16; 1 Corinthians 3:16; 5:6; 6:2,3; etc.). This construction often introduces material accepted as fact and may reflect the classical distinction inherent in *oida*.

"To know" is often expressed by "know-how." The aspiring church leader should "*know how* to manage his own household" (1 Timothy 3:5; cf. Matthew 7:11; Luke 11:13). In addition, at 1 Thessalonians 5:12, *oida* seems to indicate the idea of respect or appreciation.

Pauline Epistles

From a theological standpoint *oida* does have a limited role, most often from a negative stance. To "not know" God is tantamount to rejecting Him (Galatians 4:8; 1 Thessalonians 4:5). Those who "do not know God" (*tois mē eidosin theon*) will be punished (2 Thessalonians 1:8). These texts possibly draw from the Old Testament perspective that ignorance of God is characteristic of the pagan nations (e.g., Wisdom of Solomon 13:1ff.; Jeremiah 9:3,6). The punishment of the "ignorant," i.e., those who willfully reject God and His people, is also certain (cf. Psalm 79:6; Jeremiah 10:25). Israel, too, in her sinful condition does not "know" the Lord (cf. Isaiah 1:3). Simply professing to know God is not enough (Titus 1:16); true knowledge expresses itself in obedience to God and love for His people (1 John 2:3,4).

Usually believers are only implicitly spoken of as "knowing God." More often it is God who "knows" humanity (Galatians 4:9). He is the all-knowing One (2 Corinthians 11:11,31; 12:2,3). *Oida*-type knowing of Jesus (not *ginōskō*) plays only an insignificant part in Pauline theology. Only 1 Corinthians 2:2 and 2 Corinthians 5:16 provide allusions to knowing (*oida*) Christ. One is a reference to knowing the Christ of the Cross: "I . . . know nothing . . . except Jesus Christ and him crucified" (1 Corinthians 2:2, NIV). The other recalls the exalted Christ who was known (*oida*) according to the flesh, but is now known (*ginōskō*) only according to the perspective of the new man. "From now on we know (*oida*) no one *kata sarka*; although we knew (*egnōkamen*, aorist) Christ according to the flesh, but now we no longer know (*ginōskomen*) him in this way" (2 Corinthians 5:16, free translation). Here the interchange between *oida* and *ginōskō* can be cited as further evidence that these terms, in some cases, were used interchangeably by the time of the New Testament (see Burdick, *Oida and Ginōskō in* the Pauline Epistles, *New Dimensions in New Testament Study*, pp.344-356).

Johannine Literature

Perhaps the most theological benefit is derived from John's use of *oida*. The reality of a threat of Gnosticism upon the Johannine community is far from certain (despite Seesemann, "oida," *Kittel*, 5:116-118), and the role of *oida* in the alleged heresy is less than concrete. But, "knowing" is an integral motif in John's Gospel and letters. *Oida* is used for different types of knowledge: of human affairs and various facts (John 4:25; 6:42,61; 7:15; 9:20,25). Turner notes that *oida* occurs in primitive "creeds and dogmas (e.g., John 11:22,24; 1 John 2:29; 3:2,5)" (*Grammatical Insights*, pp.152ff.).

But *oida* is expressly used for the unique relationship that Jesus experiences with His Father. "Then Jesus, still teaching in the temple courts, cried out, 'Yes, you *know* (*oida*) me, and you *know* (*oida*) where I am from. I am not here on my own, but he who sent me is true. You do not *know* (*oida*) him, but I *know* (*oida*) him because I am from him and he sent me'" (John 7:28,29; NIV). The people may have indeed "known" Jesus and where he was from (John 6:42; 7:27), but they did not "know" God.

Jesus also described His relationship to His disciples in terms of "knowing": "I *know* whom I have chosen" (John 13:18). It is implied that the disciple's relationship to Jesus is one of "knowing"; nevertheless, it is deficient knowledge until the arrival of the Spirit: "If you really knew (*ginōskō*) me, you would know (*ginōskō*) my Father as well. From now on, you do know (*ginōskō*) him and have seen him" (John 14:7, NIV). Jesus makes the Father known. The disciples would also know (*ginōskō*) the Holy Spirit (John 14:15,16; cf. 20:14; 21:4). Here again we see the interplay between *ginōskō* and *oida*. One crucial point is that such "knowledge," either *ginōskō* or *oida*, is not experienced by the world (John 7:28; 8:14,19,54,55; 9:29; 14:17). This coincides with the broader concept that only those who know God—or rather are known by God (Galatians 4:9)—live a life which reflects this knowledge.

Oida, then, functions in a wide capacity and can have theological overtones under certain conditions. The classical distinction inherent in the perfect tense of *oida* is usually, but not always, present. Ultimately context must determine the answer to that question. As to the relationship between *ginōskō* and *oida*, there is no developed motif which pits one against the other. They undoubtedly move closer together as the classical distinction deteriorates. By the time of the New Testament they could be, but were not always, used interchangeably.

BAUER 555-56, MOULTON-MILLIGAN 439-40, KITTEL 5:116-19, LIDDELL-SCOTT 1201, COLIN BROWN 2:391.

3472. οἰκεῖος oikeios adj

Household; what is in or of or belongs to a house.

CROSS-REFERENCE:
οἰκέω oikeō (3474)

אַלּוּף 'allûph (443), Friend (Prv 17:9).
אֱנוֹשׁ 'ěnôsh (596), Men (Nm 25:5).
בַּיִת bayith (1041), House (Is 3:6).
דּוֹד dôdh (1782), Uncle (1 Sm 10:14ff., 14:50, Am 6:10).
שְׁאֵר she'ēr (8083), Relative (Lv 18:6, 25:49, Nm 27:11).
שַׁאֲרָה sha'ărāh (8084), Female relative (Lv 18:17).

1. οἰκεῖοι oikeioi nom pl masc
2. οἰκείων oikeiōn gen pl masc
3. οἰκείους oikeious acc pl masc

3 unto them who are of the **household** of faith......... Gal 6:10
1 with the saints, and of the **household** of God;........ Eph 2:19
2 and specially for those of his own **house**,........... 1 Tm 5:8

The adjective (used substantively in the New Testament) *oikeios* is derived from *oikos* (3486) and means "what is in or of a house, what belongs or is related to a house or household." Thus in 1 Timothy 5:8 the word denotes one's immediate family ("those of his own house" in specific contrast to someone else's), specifying that one should be certain they are provided for.

In the Early Church the believing community was spoken of as "a house" (*oikos*; e.g., Hebrews 3:1-6). Due to this understanding, *oikeios* is used in Ephesians 2:19 where the "household of God" signifies the same thing as the "household of faith" found in Galatians 6:10; i.e., the company of those reconciled to God through faith in Christ. The former assures the Gentiles that they are no longer foreigners but full-fledged members of the household of God. The latter reminds the believers of their Christian duty to fellow believers.

STRONG 3609, BAUER 556, MOULTON-MILLIGAN 440, KITTEL 5:134-35, LIDDELL-SCOTT 1202, COLIN BROWN 2:247,251.

3472B. οἰκετεία oiketeia noun

Household (of slaves).

CROSS-REFERENCE:
    οἰκέω oikeō (3474)

1. οἰκετείας oiketeias acc sing fem

1 put in charge of his **household**, (NASB) .... Matt 24:45

Classical Greek and Septuagint Usage

The noun *oiketeia* usually refers to the slaves or servants who work in a household, i.e., household slaves. It is used in one version of Job 1:3 (Symmachus) where it mentions that Job had a very large "household." The Septuagint uses *hupēresia* which, in this context, signifies a "body of servants" or a "retinue." Both Josephus (*Antiquities* 8.2.11) and Epictetus (*Enchiridion* 33.7) used it of domestic slavery (cf. *Bauer*).

New Testament Usage

Its only occurrence in the New Testament is in some manuscripts at Matthew 24:45, "Who then is a faithful and wise servant, whom his lord hath made ruler over his household?" The word here must refer to the household staff, not the family that owned the estate. The faithful servant was placed in charge over the other servants. The *Textus Receptus* has *therapeia* (2299) at Matthew 24:45.

BAUER 556-57, MOULTON-MILLIGAN 440, LIDDELL-SCOTT 1202.

3473. οἰκέτης oiketēs noun

House(hold) servant; servant.

COGNATE:
    οἰκέω oikeō (3474)

SYNONYMS:
    δοῦλος doulos (1395)
    παιδάριον paidarion (3671)
    παῖς pais (3679)

עֶבֶד 'evedh (5860), Servant, slave (Ex 21:26f., Dt 15:15, Prv 22:7).

1. οἰκέτης oiketēs nom sing masc
2. οἰκέτου oiketou gen sing masc
3. οἰκέτην oiketēn acc sing masc
4. οἰκετῶν oiketōn gen pl masc
5. οἰκέται oiketai nom pl masc

1 No **servant** can serve two masters: .... Luke 16:13
4 he called two of his household **servants**, ... Acts 10:7
3 Who art thou that judgest another man's **servant**? .. Rom 14:4
5 **Servants**, be subject to your masters with all fear; ... 1 Pt 2:18

Classical Greek and Septuagint Usage

The word *oiketēs* is related to *oikos* (3486), with the basic meaning, "one who lives in the same house with another and thus under the authority of the same householder." From this is derived the meaning "household servant, domestic." In the Septuagint this word substitutes for the Hebrew term *'evedh* ("slave, servant") and is frequently used in the Pentateuch, Joshua, and Proverbs. It is used once in Isaiah 36:9 and after that the word is not found in the Old Testament. This probably reflects the social change in the lives of the Jewish people during and after the Babylonian captivity.

New Testament Usage

The *oiketēs* contrasts with the *doulos* (1395), denoting one who had closer relations with the family. Aside from Acts 10:7, where the KJV translates the word as Cornelius' "household servants," it is rendered as "servant" in the balance of its locations in the New Testament: Luke 16:13, "No *servant* can serve two masters . . ."; Romans 14:4, "Who art thou that judgest another man's *servant*?"; and 1 Peter 2:18, "*Servants*, be subject to your masters . . . ."

STRONG 3610, BAUER 557, MOULTON-MILLIGAN 440, LIDDELL-SCOTT 1202, COLIN BROWN 2:509.

3474. οἰκέω oikeō verb

To inhabit, dwell (in), reside.

COGNATES:
    ἐγκατοικέω enkatoikeō (1453)
    ἐνοικέω enoikeō (1758)
    κατοικέω katoikeō (2700)
    μετοικεσία metoikesia (3220)
    μετοικίζω metoikizō (3221)
    οἰκεῖος oikeios (3472)
    οἰκετεία oiketeia (3472B)
    οἰκέτης oiketēs (3473)
    οἴκημα oikēma (3475)
    οἰκητήριον oikētērion (3476)
    οἰκία oikia (3477)
    οἰκιακός oikiakos (3478)
    οἰκοδεσποτέω oikodespoteō (3479)
    οἰκοδεσπότης oikodespotēs (3480)
    οἰκοδομέω oikodomeō (3481)
    οἰκονομέω oikonomeō (3483)
    οἶκος oikos (3486)
    οἰκουμένη oikoumenē (3487)
    οἰκουργός oikourgos (3487B)
    οἰκουρός oikouros (3488)
    πάροικος paroikos (3803)
    περιοικέω perioikeō (3902)
    περίοικος perioikos (3903)
    συνοικέω sunoikeō (4775)

SYNONYMS:
    αὐλίζομαι aulizomai (829)
    καθίζω kathizō (2495)
    καταμένω katamenō (2620)
    κατασκηνόω kataskēnoō (2651)
    κατοικέω katoikeō (2700)

μένω menō (3176)
σκηνόω skēnoō (4492)

אֱנוֹשׁ 'ĕnôsh (596), Men (Gn 24:13).

גּוּר gûr (1513), Reside (Jer 43:2 [50:2]).

דּוּר dûr (1806), Dwell (Ps 84:10 [83:10]).

דּוּר dûr (A1808), Live (Dn 4:1 [3:31], 6:25—Aramaic).

יָשַׁב yāshav (3553), Qal: stay, live (Gn 27:44, Jgs 9:41, Prv 21:9); niphal: be inhabited (Ex 16:35); hophal: be made to live (Is 5:8).

יְתִב yᵉthiv (A3603), Live (Ezr 4:17—Aramaic).

נָתַן nāthan (5598), Give; appoint (Neh 13:4).

שִׁיבָה shîvāh (8285), Stay (2 Sm 19:32).

שָׁכַן shākhan (8331), Dwell (Prv 10:30).

1. οἰκεῖ oikei 3sing indic pres act
2. οἰκῶν oikōn nom sing masc part pres act
3. οἰκοῦσα oikousa nom sing fem part pres act
4. οἰκεῖν oikein inf pres act
5. ὁμοιάζετε homoiazete 2pl indic pres act

3 is no more I that do it, but sin that **dwelleth** in me. Rom 7:17
1 in my flesh, **dwelleth** no good thing: 7:18
3 no more I that do it, but sin that **dwelleth** in me. 7:20
1 if so be that the Spirit of God **dwell** in you. 8:9
1 that raised up Jesus from the dead **dwell** in you, ... 8:11
1 and that the Spirit of God **dwelleth** in you? .... 1 Co 3:16
4 and she be pleased **to dwell** with him, ... 7:12
4 and if he be pleased **to dwell** with her, ... 7:13
2 **dwelling** in the light which no man can approach ... 1 Tm 6:16

The verb *oikeō* is related to *oikos* (3486), and from Homer on meant "to inhabit." When used transitively it means "to dwell (in), inhabit" as one would occupy a house. The Septuagint uses it to express cohabitation with a woman under a single roof (Deuteronomy 28:30), and it is in this sense that it is used in 1 Corinthians 7:12,13: " . . . and she be pleased *to dwell* with him . . . if he be pleased *to dwell* with her . . . ."

Elsewhere in the New Testament the verb is more frequently used metaphorically to denote relationships that are otherwise hard to conceive. It describes God "dwelling" in inaccessible light (1 Timothy 6:16), and the Spirit of God "dwelling" in the believer (Romans 8:9,11) or the church corporately (1 Corinthians 3:16). Paul said that "no good thing" could "dwell" in his carnal nature (Romans 7:18), and that sin "dwelt" in him (Romans 7:20).

STRONG 3611, BAUER 557, MOULTON-MILLIGAN 440, KITTEL 5:135-36, LIDDELL-SCOTT 1202-03, COLIN BROWN 2:247,250.

3475. οἴκημα oikēma noun
Dwelling place.

CROSS-REFERENCE:
οἰκέω oikeō (3474)

גַּב gav (1384), Shrine (Ez 16:24).

1. οἰκήματι oikēmati dat sing neu

1 and a light shined in the **prison**: .... Acts 12:7

The noun *oikēma* is related to *oikos* (3486) and denotes "dwelling place" or "habitation." It also refers to a "room, apartment," or "chambers" in Greek literature from the time of Herodotus on (cf. *Bauer*). It is used euphemistically for a brothel or a place for heathen worship, as in Ezekiel 16:24 (Septuagint), and euphemistically for a "prison" or a "prison cell" as in its only occurrence in the New Testament, Acts 12:7.

STRONG 3612, BAUER 557, MOULTON-MILLIGAN 440-41, LIDDELL-SCOTT 1203.

3476. οἰκητήριον oikētērion noun
Habitation, abode, dwelling-place.

COGNATE:
οἰκέω oikeō (3474)
SYNONYMS:
κατοικητήριον katoikētērion (2702)
κατοικία katoikia (2703)
σκηνή skēnē (4488)

1. οἰκητήριον oikētērion nom/acc sing neu

1 to be clothed upon with our **house** ... from heaven: .. 2 Co 5:2
1 but left their own **habitation**, ... Jude 1:6

The word *oikētērion* is related to *oikētēr*, "inhabitant," and *oikos* (3486), and denotes a "dwelling place, habitation." It is used twice in the Septuagint (2 Maccabees 11:2 and 3 Maccabees 2:15) and twice in the New Testament. In 2 Corinthians 5:2 it is used metaphorically of the glorified body of the transfigured Christian (" . . . our *house* which is from heaven"). Here Paul contrasted the eternal nature of the glorified body to the present human body which to him was a temporary tent (*skēnos* [4491]), mortal and limited. Jude 6 speaks of the angels who left their own "habitations"; i.e., the place where they dwelt. While the specific incident to which this verse refers is not without question (see *The Complete Biblical Library, Jude*, pp.459,461), what is apparent is that the place where the angels dwelt was somehow tied to their place of authority in the order God had established. Thus, when they left the place assigned to them it was tantamount to rebellion.

STRONG 3613, BAUER 557, MOULTON-MILLIGAN 441,

KITTEL 5:155, LIDDELL-SCOTT 1203, COLIN BROWN 3:814.

3477. οἰκία oikia noun

House, dwelling, household.

COGNATE:
  οἰκέω oikeō (3474)
SYNONYM:
  οἶκος oikos (3486)

אֹהֶל 'ōhel (164), Tent (Gn 25:27, Nm 19:14).

בַּיִת bayith (1041), House (Lv 14:41-49, Jgs 19:18, Jer 18:22).

חָצֵר chātsēr (2793), Court (Jer 37:21 [44:21]).

טַף taph (3054), Little one (Gn 50:21).

מָבוֹא māvô' (4136), Entrance (Jer 38:14 [45:14]).

מוֹשָׁב môshāv (4319), Dwelling place (Nm 31:10—Codex Vaticanus only).

1. **οἰκίας** oikias gen/acc sing/pl fem
2. **οἰκία** oikia nom sing fem
3. **οἰκίᾳ** oikia dat sing fem
4. **οἰκίαν** oikian acc sing fem
5. **οἰκιῶν** oikiōn gen pl fem

4	And when they were come into the **house**,	Matt 2:11
3	and it giveth light unto all that are in the **house**.	5:15
4	a wise man, which built his **house** upon a rock:	7:24
3	and the winds blew, and beat upon that **house**;	7:25
4	which built his **house** upon the sand:	7:26
3	and the winds blew, and beat upon that **house**;	7:27
3	Lord, my servant lieth at **home** sick of the palsy,	8:6
4	And when Jesus was come into Peter's **house**,	8:14
3	as Jesus sat at meat in the **house**,	9:10
4	And when Jesus came into the ruler's **house**,	9:23
4	And when he was come into the **house**,	9:28
4	And when ye come into an **house**, salute it.	10:12
2	**house** be worthy, let your peace come upon it:	10:13
1	when ye depart out of that **house** or city,	10:14
2	and every city or **house** divided against itself	12:25
4	else how can one enter into a strong man's **house**,	12:29
4	and then he will spoil his **house**.	12:29
1	The same day went Jesus out of the **house**,	13:1
4	sent the multitude away, and went into the **house**:	13:36
3	save in his own country, and in his own **house**.	13:57
4	And when he was come into the **house**,	17:25
1	And every one that hath forsaken **houses**,	19:29
1	hypocrites! for ye devour widows' **houses**,	23:14
1	not come down to take any thing out of his **house**:	24:17
4	not have suffered his **house** to be broken up.	24:43
3	in Bethany, in the **house** of Simon the leper,	26:6
4	they entered into the **house** of Simon and Andrew,	Mark 1:29
3	as Jesus sat at meat in his **house**,	2:15
2	And if a **house** be divided against itself,	3:25
2	be divided against itself, that **house** cannot stand.	3:25
4	No man can enter into a strong man's **house**,	3:27
4	and then he will spoil his **house**.	3:27
3	and among his own kin, and in his own **house**.	6:4
4	In what place soever ye enter into an **house**,	6:10
4	and entered into an **house**,	7:24
3	and being in the **house** he asked them,	9:33
3	And in the **house** his disciples asked him again	10:10
4	There is no man that hath left **house**,	10:29
1	**houses**, and brethren, and sisters, and mothers,	10:30
1	Which devour widows' **houses**,	12:40
4	is on the housetop not go down into the **house**,	13:15
1	neither enter ... to take any thing out of his **house**:	13:15
4	a man taking a far journey, who left his **house**,	Mark 13:34
1	ye know not when the master of the **house** cometh,	13:35
3	being in Bethany in the **house** of Simon the leper,	14:3
4	and entered into Simon's **house**.	Luke 4:38
3	And Levi made him a great feast in his own **house**:	5:29
4	He is like a man which built an **house**,	6:48
3	the stream beat vehemently upon that **house**,	6:48
4	is like a man ... built an **house** upon the earth;	6:49
1	it fell; and the ruin of that **house** was great.	6:49
1	And when he was now not far from the **house**,	7:6
4	And he went into the Pharisee's **house**,	7:36
3	that Jesus sat at meat in the Pharisee's **house**,	7:37
4	Seest thou this woman? I entered into thine **house**,	7:44
3	neither abode in any **house**, but in the tombs.	8:27
4	And when he came into the **house**, he suffered no	8:51
4	And whatsoever **house** ye enter into, there abide,	9:4
4	And into whatsoever **house** ye enter, first say,	10:5
3	in the same **house** remain, eating and drinking	10:7
1	Go not from **house** to house.	10:7
1	Go not from house to **house**.	10:7
4	Martha welcomed Him into her **home**. (NASB)	10:38
4	doth not light a candle, and sweep the **house**,	15:8
3	and as he came and drew nigh to the **house**,	15:25
4	be upon the housetop, and his stuff in the **house**,	17:31
4	There is no man that hath left **house**, or parents,	18:29
1	Which devour widows' **houses**,	20:47
4	follow him into the **house** where he entereth in.	22:10
1	And ye shall say unto the goodman of the **house**,	22:11
4	to the **house** of the high priest; (NASB)	22:54
2	and himself believed, and his whole **house**.	John 4:53
3	And the servant abideth not in the **house** for ever:	8:35
3	The Jews then which were with her in the **house**,	11:31
2	**house** was filled with the odour of the ointment.	12:3
3	In my Father's **house** are many mansions:	14:2
5	were possessors of lands or **houses** sold them,	Acts 4:34
3	inquire in the **house** of Judas for one called Saul,	9:11
4	and entered into the **house**;	9:17
2	whose **house** is by the sea side:	10:6
4	had made inquiry for Simon's **house**,	10:17
3	in the **house** of one Simon a tanner by the sea side:	10:32
4	men already come unto the **house** where I was,	11:11
4	he came to the **house** of Mary the mother of John,	12:12
3	and to all that were in his **house**.	16:32
3	and assaulted the **house** of Jason,	17:5
4	entered into a certain man's **house**, named Justus,	18:7
2	whose **house** joined hard to the synagogue.	18:7
1	What? have ye not **houses** to eat and to drink in?	1 Co 11:22
4	brethren, ye know the **house** of Stephanas,	16:15
2	earthly **house** of this tabernacle were dissolved,	2 Co 5:1
4	a building of God, an **house** not made with hands,	5:1
1	chiefly they that are of Caesar's **household**.	Phlp 4:22
1	wandering about from **house** to house;	1 Tm 5:13
3	But in a great **house** ... not only vessels of gold	2 Tm 2:20
1	For of this sort are they which creep into **houses**,	3:6
4	not this doctrine, receive him not into your **house**,	2 Jn 1:10

Classical Greek

In classical Greek there is a difference in meaning between *oikia* and *oikos* (3486), "house." *Oikos* is the entire estate, while *oikia* refers just to the house, the building itself. From the time of Herodotus (ca. Fifth Century B.C.) *oikia* assumed the meaning given above. In Koine Greek this distinction disappeared, and this change is reflected in the Septuagint in which both words are used interchangeably (*Liddell-Scott*).

Septuagint Usage

In the Septuagint *oikia* is used about 240 times, almost always to translate the Hebrew term *bayith*, "house, dwelling, home." In the Old

Testament *bayith* is used for a wide variety of meanings. It may refer to a "shelter" or "stall" for animals or even a temporary or nomadic dwelling (i.e., "tent"; cf. Genesis 33:17). The *oikia* could denote many kinds of buildings that are constructed of various kinds of materials (most commonly: stone, lumber, plaster; cf. Leviticus 14:45; 1 Kings 5:8,15-18). However, most frequently *oikia* describes a family dwelling or home (Deuteronomy 6:7). These living quarters were typically two stories and were attached to adjacent homes and/or the city wall (Joshua 2:15-21; cf. Burke, "Home," *International Standard Bible Encyclopedia*, 2:747). Apart from its use as a physical dwelling, *oikia* occasionally refers to the family itself, i.e., the "household" (1 Chronicles 4:21).

New Testament Usage
In the New Testament *oikia* is used in two ways. The first is literal, meaning simply one's house or the place one lives, e.g., Matthew 2:11; 5:15; 7:24-27; 2 Timothy 2:20; 2 John 10. In Mark 12:40 the word is extended to denote property in a more general sense (i.e., estate). Greek, like Hebrew, has no word to explicitly denote the nuclear family. In a distinct parallel to its Hebrew equivalent in the Old Testament (*bayith*), *oikia* can indicate a household, i.e., the family, or the inhabitants of a house, as seen in Matthew 12:25; Mark 6:4; and John 4:53, although when the idea of dynasty or nation is intended, the term used is *oikos* (Matthew 10:6; 15:24; Acts 2:36, etc.). Unlike *oikos*, *oikia* is not used (with or without God's name following) to designate the tabernacle or temple (as *oikos* is, e.g., Matthew 12:4; 21:13, and parallel passages).

The second manner in which the word *oikia* appears in the New Testament is figurative, with one use promising "mansions" (e.g., in "my Father's house," John 14:2) where believers will be accorded places to dwell (*monē* [3301]) when the Lord returns and the kingdom of God is fulfilled. There is some discussion among scholars as to whether this idiom indicates: (1) a heavenly abode for the believer (see Thayer, Vine, Alford and most older scholars); (2) a less localized notion of sanctuary (Goetzmann, "House," *Colin Brown*, 2:250) to be granted the believer; (3) God's family (an expression which may parallel the Pauline concept of adoption in Romans 8:15); (4) or the collective representation of individual believers who would be prepared for the advent of the Spirit (John 14:15-31) by the death, resurrection, and ascension of Jesus.

A second figurative use of *oikia* indicates the believer's present body, contrasted to the body he will have in the resurrection (2 Corinthians 5:1, "If our earthly *house*... were dissolved, we have a building of God, a *house* not made with hands, eternal in the heavens").

STRONG 3614, BAUER 557, MOULTON-MILLIGAN 441, KITTEL 5:131-34, LIDDELL-SCOTT 1203, COLIN BROWN 2:247-50.

3478. οἰκιακός oikiakos noun
Belonging to a household, family member, relative.
CROSS-REFERENCE:
οἰκέω oikeō (3474)

1. **οἰκιακοί** oikiakoi nom pl masc
2. **οἰκιακούς** oikiakous acc pl masc
3. **οἰκειακοί** oikeiakoi nom pl masc
4. **οἰκειακούς** oikeiakous acc pl masc
5. **οἰκιακοῖς** oikiakois dat pl masc

2 much more shall they call them of his **household**?.. Matt 10:25
1 a man's foes shall be they of his own **household**....... 10:36

The word *oikiakos* is related to *oikia* (3477), "house," and in classical Greek literature means "one under control of the master of the house," whether a son or a slave. It is often translated as "members of a household." *Oikiakos* is used only twice in the New Testament. In Matthew 10:36 it refers to relatives who are family members rather than servants ("... a man's foes shall be they of his own household"). Jesus used the example of the lack of trust within human "households" as a contrast with the faithfulness of God's "household" (i.e., Father and Son; cf. Matthew 10:25).

STRONG 3615, BAUER 557, MOULTON-MILLIGAN 441, LIDDELL-SCOTT 1203.

3479. οἰκοδεσποτέω
oikodespoteō verb
To rule, manage a household, keep house.
CROSS-REFERENCES:
δεσπότης despotēs (1197)
οἰκέω oikeō (3474)

1. **οἰκοδεσποτεῖν** oikodespotein inf pres act

1 marry, bear children, **guide the house**,............. 1 Tm 5:14

This late Greek verb is a compound of *oikos* (3477), "house," and *despotēs* (1197), "ruler;"

it denotes the action of ruling over a household, managing its affairs. It also refers to being the head of a family. Its single New Testament use occurs in 1 Timothy 5:14, where younger women are encouraged to marry, bear children, and "guide the house" (NIV: "manage their homes"). Certainly one of the best examples of what Paul meant here is seen in the picture of the woman in Proverbs 31:10-31.

STRONG 3616, BAUER 558, MOULTON-MILLIGAN 441, KITTEL 2:49, LIDDELL-SCOTT 1204, COLIN BROWN 2:508-10.

3480. οἰκοδεσπότης

oikodespotēs noun

Master of a house, head of a household.

CROSS-REFERENCES:
δεσπότης despotēs (1197)
οἰκέω oikeō (3474)

1. **οἰκοδεσπότης** oikodespotēs nom sing masc
2. **οἰκοδεσπότου** oikodespotou gen sing masc
3. **οἰκοδεσπότῃ** oikodespotē dat sing masc
4. **οἰκοδεσπότην** oikodespotēn acc sing masc

```
4  have called the master of the house Beelzebub,..... Matt 10:25
2  So the servants of the householder came and said...... 13:27
3  is like unto a man that is an householder,............ 13:52
3  is like unto a man that is an householder,............ 20:1
2  they murmured against the goodman of the house,..... 20:11
1  There was a certain householder,..................... 21:33
1  that if the goodman of the house had known........... 24:43
3  say ye to the goodman of the house,........... Mark 14:14
1  if the goodman of the house had known what hour Luke 12:39
1  When once the master of the house is risen up,....... 13:25
1  master of the house being angry said to his servant,.... 14:21
3  And ye shall say unto the goodman of the house,...... 22:11
```

Classical Greek

This noun is found only in later Greek (*Bauer*), and like the verb *oikodespoteō*, is a compound of *oikos* (3477), "house," and *despotēs* (1197), "ruler." It denotes one who is empowered to rule over a household. In classical Greek it is often used in connection with a native ruler as opposed to a foreign emperor (*Liddell-Scott*). It also refers to Zodiac symbols. *Oikodespotēs* does not occur in the Septuagint, although the term *despotēs* is found over 60 times.

New Testament Usage

In the New Testament the word occurs 12 times, frequently in the parables of Jesus, and it depicts divine actions as represented by those of "the master of the house." It is rendered "master of the house" in Matthew 10:25; Luke 13:14,25; and 14:21, where context emphasizes the authority of the person spoken of. Elsewhere, it may be rendered (e.g., Matthew 24:43) as "goodman of the house" (an obsolete English term meaning about the same as "master of the house") or as "householder" (e.g., Matthew 13:27,52).

STRONG 3617, BAUER 558, MOULTON-MILLIGAN 441, KITTEL 2:49, LIDDELL-SCOTT 1204, COLIN BROWN 2:508-10.

3481. οἰκοδομέω oikodomeō verb

Build (a home or building), erect, edify, encourage.

COGNATES:
ἀνοικοδομέω anoikodomeō (454)
ἐποικοδομέω epoikodomeō (2010)
οἰκέω oikeō (3474)
οἰκοδομή oikodomē (3482)
οἰκοδόμος oikodomos (3482B)
συνοικοδομέω sunoikodomeō (4776)

SYNONYMS:
ἀνορθόω anorthoō (458)
καταρτίζω katartizō (2645)
κατασκευάζω kataskeuazō (2650)
πήγνυμι pēgnumi (3939)

בָּנָה bānâh (1161), Qal: build (Dt 20:5, 1 Kgs 8:19f., 2 Chr 16:5f.); niphal:be built (1 Kgs 6:7, Neh 7:1, Is 44:26).

בְּנָה bᵉnâh (A1162), Peal: rebuild, build (Ezr 5:3f., 6:7, Dn 4:30 [4:27] —Aramaic); hithpeel: be built, be rebuilt (Ezr 4:16, 21, 5:16—Aramaic).

חָסַם châsam (2733), Stop, muzzle; make a cistern (Sir 48:17).

כּוּן kûn (3679), Hithpolel: be established (Is 54:14).

עָשָׂה ʻāsâh (6449), Make (2 Sm 7:11).

1. **οἰκοδομῶ** oikodomō 1sing indic/subj pres act
2. **οἰκοδομεῖτε** oikodomeite 2pl indic/impr pres act
3. **οἰκοδομεῖ** oikodomei 3sing indic pres act
4. **οἰκοδομοῦντι** oikodomounti
    dat sing masc part pres act
5. **οἰκοδομῶν** oikodomōn
    nom sing masc part pres act
6. **οἰκοδομοῦντες** oikodomountes
    nom pl masc part pres act
7. **οἰκοδομεῖν** oikodomein inf pres act
8. **ᾠκοδόμησεν** ōkodomēsen 3sing indic aor act
9. **οἰκοδομήσαντι** oikodomēsanti
    dat sing masc part aor act
10. **οἰκοδομῆσαι** oikodomēsai inf aor act
11. **οἰκοδομήσω** oikodomēsō 1sing indic fut act
12. **οἰκοδομήσετε** oikodomēsete 2pl indic fut act
13. **ᾠκοδόμουν** ōkodomoun 3pl indic imperf act
14. **οἰκοδομεῖσθε** oikodomeisthe
    2pl indic/impr pres mid
15. **οἰκοδομεῖται** oikodomeitai 3sing indic pres mid
16. **οἰκοδομούμεναι** oikodomoumenai
    nom pl fem part pres mid

οἰκοδομή 3482

17. οἰκοδομούντων oikodomountōn
    gen pl masc/neu part pres mid
18. ᾠκοδομήθη ōkodomēthē 3sing indic aor pass
19. ᾠκοδόμητο ōkodomēto 3sing indic plperf pass
20. οἰκοδομηθήσεται oikodomēthēsetai
    3sing indic fut pass
21. οἰκοδόμησεν oikodomēsen 3sing indic aor act
22. οἰκοδομουμένη oikodomoumenē
    nom sing fem part pres mid
23. οἰκοδομήθη oikodomēthē 3sing indic aor pass
24. οἰκοδομῆσθαι oikodomēsthai inf perf mid

```
8   a wise man, which built his house upon a rock:.... Matt  7:24
8   which built his house upon the sand:..................  7:26
11  and upon this rock I will build my church;..........  16:18
8   and digged a winepress in it, and built a tower,......  21:33
6   The stone which the builders rejected,...............  21:42
2   because ye build the tombs of the prophets,..........  23:29
10  destroy the temple ... and to build it in three days....  26:61
5   destroyest the temple, and buildest it in three days,...  27:40
8   and built a tower, and let it out to husbandmen, Mark  12:1
6   The stone which the builders rejected................  12:10
11  and within three days I will build another...........  14:58
5   destroyest the temple, and buildest it in three days,... 15:29
19  the brow of the hill whereon their city was built,...Luke  4:29
4   He is like a man which built an house,................  6:48
24  because it had been well built. (NASB)...............  6:48
9   is like a man that without a foundation built..........  6:49
8   and he hath built us a synagogue......................  7:5
2   for ye build the sepulchres of the prophets,..........  11:47
2   indeed killed them, and ye build their sepulchres......  11:48
11  I will pull down my barns, and build greater;.........  12:18
10  For which of you, intending to build a tower,........  14:28
7   This man began to build, ... was not able to finish....  14:30
13  they bought, they sold, they planted, they builded;....  17:28
6   The stone which the builders rejected,...............  20:17
18  Forty and six years was this temple in building,.... John  2:20
17  the stone which was set at nought of you builders,..Acts  4:11
8   But Solomon built him an house.......................  7:47
12  what house will ye build me? saith the Lord:..........  7:49
16  were edified; and walking in the fear of the Lord,......  9:31
10  which is able to build you up (NASB)..................  20:32
1   lest I should build upon another man's foundation: Rom  15:20
3   Knowledge puffeth up, but charity edifieth......... 1 Co  8:1
20  which is weak be emboldened to eat those things......  8:10
3   but all things edify not..............................  10:23
3   speaketh in an unknown tongue edifieth himself;.....  14:4
3   but he that prophesieth edifieth the church..........  14:4
15  but the other is not edified..........................  14:17
1   For if I build again the things which I destroyed,....Gal  2:18
2   and edify one another, even as also ye do.......... 1 Th  5:11
14  are built up a spiritual house, an holy priesthood,...1 Pt  2:5
6   the stone which the builders disallowed,...............  2:7
```

Classical Greek and Septuagint Usage
In classical Greek literature the most common meaning of *oikodomeō* is "to build or to erect a structure," such as a house or a temple. This literal use also prevails in the Septuagint where it renders the Hebrew *bānâh*: "So he (Abraham) built an altar there" (Genesis 12:7). In addition, a metaphorical use also appears in the literature contemporary with the New Testament. Philo, for example, used *oikodomeō* to describe the function of the heart upon which the whole body rests and by which it is built up (cf. Michel, "oikodomeō," *Kittel*, 5:138). The metaphorical use also occurs in the Septuagint, particularly in Jeremiah. Here *oikodomeō* is exclusively the work of God in relation to Israel's rebuilding (Jeremiah 31:4 [LXX 38:4]; 33:7 [40:7]).

New Testament Usage
In the New Testament *oikodomeō* occurs with both a literal and a metaphorical sense. The literal use is common in the Gospel narratives, evidenced in such phrases as, "*built* his house upon a rock" (Matthew 7:24); and "I will pull down my barns, and *build* greater" (Luke 12:18). The metaphorical use in the Gospel narratives strikingly emerges in Jesus' promise to "build" His Church (Matthew 16:18).

In the letters of Paul *oikodomeō* takes on an important theological emphasis. Here the metaphorical use predominates as *oikodomeō* denotes the growth and development of the community of believers through the enabling power of the Holy Spirit. Paul envisioned this upbuilding process, on the one hand, as a spiritual activity which was in a special way the particular work of the apostles (2 Corinthians 10:8; 13:10). On the other hand, *oikodomeō* was viewed by Paul as the task of every believer. The people of God are to be built up in and by love (1 Corinthians 8:1; see also, Ephesians 4:16 [*oikodomēn*]) through the encouragement and ministry of fellow-believers who in turn commit themselves to others in the community for their spiritual upbuilding (1 Thessalonians 5:11). Thus *oikodomeō* has more a charismatic and spiritual concern than an ecclesiastical one (see 1 Corinthians 14:12).

In summary, *oikodomeō* describes the activity of spiritual growth within the community of believers. It also denotes the content and purpose of the Church's liturgical life and meetings (Michel, "oikodomeō," *Kittel*, 5:141) as the Church is "being *built* into a spiritual house ... offering spiritual sacrifices acceptable to God through Jesus Christ" (1 Peter 2:5, NIV).

STRONG 3618, BAUER 558, MOULTON-MILLIGAN 441-42, KITTEL 5:136-44, LIDDELL-SCOTT 1204, COLIN BROWN 2:251-53.

3482. οἰκοδομή oikodomē noun
Building, edifice, edification.
CROSS-REFERENCE:
οἰκοδομέω oikodomeō (3481)

בִּירָה bîrāh (1038), Palace (1 Chr 29:1—Codex Alexandrinus only).

בָּנָה bānâh (1161), Build (Ez 17:17).

מִבְנֶה mivneh (4150), Structure (Ez 40:2).

1. **οἰκοδομή** oikodomē nom sing fem
2. **οἰκοδομῆς** oikodomēs gen sing fem
3. **οἰκοδομήν** oikodomēn acc sing fem
4. **οἰκοδομαί** oikodomai nom pl fem
5. **οἰκοδομάς** oikodomas acc pl fem

```
5 to show him the buildings of the temple.......... Matt 24:1
4 see what manner of stones and what buildings..... Mark 13:1
5 Seest thou these great buildings?..................... 13:2
2 and things wherewith one may edify another....... Rom 14:19
3 please his neighbour for his good to edification........ 15:2
1 ye are God's husbandry, ye are God's building...... 1 Co 3:9
3 that prophesieth speaketh unto men to edification,..... 14:3
3 interpret, that the church may receive edifying......... 14:5
3 seek that ye may excel to the edifying................ 14:12
3 Let all things be done unto edifying.................. 14:26
3 we have a building of God,....................... 2 Co 5:1
3 which the Lord hath given us for edification,.......... 10:8
2 we do all things, dearly beloved, for your edifying..... 12:19
3 which the Lord hath given me to edification,.......... 13:10
1 In whom all the building fitly framed together....... Eph 2:21
3 for the edifying of the body of Christ:................. 4:12
3 maketh increase of the body unto the edifying.......... 4:16
3 but that which is good to the use of edifying,........... 4:29
```

Classical Greek
The form *oikodomē* is absent in Attic Greek, although it is found in Aristotle (*Bauer*). Later writers, such as Diodorus Siclus, Plutarch, and Philo also used it (Michel, "oikondomē," *Kittel*, 5:144). A more common term in Koine Greek, its basic meaning is "building" (*Moulton-Milligan*).

Septuagint Usage
Oikodomē occurs 17 times in the Septuagint; however, only 3 of these are canonical. It refers to "siege works" (NIV) built by armies (Ezekiel 17:17) or to regular "buildings" in cities (in a vision, Ezekiel 40:2; cf. Sirach 22:16). Other references include the temple "buildings" (1 Esdras 2:30; 4:51). In Tobit 14:5 some manuscripts employ *oikodomē* to refer to the eternal "house, building" of God (cf. 1 Corinthians 3:9; 2 Corinthians 5:1).

New Testament Usage
The most common New Testament meaning of *oikodomē* is that of a "building," which can be found in the Gospel narratives with literal references primarily to temple buildings. Paul also used the term, but in a figurative sense: "You are God's *building*" (1 Corinthians 3:9) and "we have a *building* from God, an eternal house in heaven, not built by human hands" (2 Corinthians 5:1, NIV). The other occurrences of *oikodomē* in the New Testament denote the act of building up ("edifying") and imply a meaning similar to that of the verb *oikodomeō* (cf. 2 Corinthians 12:19).

Paul declared that the task of every believer is the edification (upbuilding) of the community of believers (Romans 15:2; 1 Corinthians 14:26). Apostolic authority should contribute to this "upbuilding" (2 Corinthians 10:8; 13:10); it is the central criterion for judging the use of charismata in the community of believers (1 Corinthians 14:3,5,12); and leadership given to the Church has *oikodomē* as its goal (Ephesians 4:12). In fact, whatever ministry takes place in the community of believers ought to contribute to this edification (1 Corinthians 14:26; Ephesians 4:29) of the believers in love (Ephesians 4:16).

Oikodomē in the New Testament, then, denotes God's building, the Church, built upon the cornerstone, Jesus Christ (Ephesians 2:20,21). In Paul's epistles it adopts different motifs as the building lives and grows and is "built (*oikodomeō*) up a spiritual house" (1 Peter 2:5).

STRONG 3619, BAUER 558-59, MOULTON-MILLIGAN 442, KITTEL 5:144-47, LIDDELL-SCOTT 1204, COLIN BROWN 2:251-53.

3482B. οἰκοδόμος oikodomos noun
Builder, architect.
CROSS-REFERENCE:
    οἰκοδομέω oikodomeō (3481)

בָּנָה bānâh (1161), Builder (2 Kgs 12:11, 22:6, 2 Chr 34:11).

גָּדַר gādhar (1473), Repairer (Is 58:12).

חָרָשׁ chārāsh (2900), Mason (1 Chr 22:15).

1. **οἰκοδόμων** oikodomōn gen pl masc

```
1 REJECTED BY YOU THE BUILDERS (NASB).... Acts 4:11
```

This noun is a compound of *oikos* (3486), "house," and *demō*, "to build," and can be found in classical Greek from the Fifth Century B.C. denoting the individual who constructs a building. In the Septuagint it generally refers to "builders" (e.g., of the temple, 2 Kings 12:11 [LXX 4 Kings 12:11]), "masons" (1 Chronicles 14:1), or "repairers" (Isaiah 58:12). In the New Testament *oikodomos* occurs only in Acts 4:11 in a quotation of Psalm 118:22. When the same verse is quoted elsewhere in the New Testament, however, the participial form of the verb *oikodomeō* (*hoi oikodomountes*) is used (Matthew 21:42; Mark 12:10; Luke 20:17; 1 Peter 2:7). In each case the reference is to "the builders," namely the Jews who rejected Jesus, "the chief corner stone" (see 1 Peter 2:6).

BAUER 559, MOULTON-MILLIGAN 442, KITTEL 5:136, LIDDELL-SCOTT 1204, COLIN BROWN 2:253-55.

3483. οἰκονομέω oikonomeō verb
To manage a household, be a steward, manage, regulate, administer.
COGNATES:
νόμος nomos (3414)
οἰκέω oikeō (3474)
οἰκονομία oikonomia (3484)
οἰκονόμος oikonomos (3485)

כּוּל kûl (3677), Pilpel: conduct (Ps 112:5 [111:5]).

1. οἰκονομεῖν oikonomein inf pres act
1 for thou mayest be no longer steward............Luke 16:2

This word is best understood by today's term "business manager." Classical usages include citations about the managing of ship cargo, cattle, and other commodities (cf. *Moulton-Milligan*). Found only once in the New Testament, this verb means to perform the function of an *oikonomos*, i.e., to function as a steward, to manage the affairs of a household. It is translated "be no longer steward" in Luke 16:2. See the word study on *oikonomos* at number 3485.

STRONG 3621, BAUER 559, MOULTON-MILLIGAN 442, LIDDELL-SCOTT 1204, COLIN BROWN 2:253-55.

3484. οἰκονομία oikonomia noun
Stewardship, administration, management.
CROSS-REFERENCE:
οἰκονομέω oikonomeō (3483)

מֶמְשָׁלָה memshālāh (4617), Authority (Is 22:21).
מַצָּב matstsāv (4835), Office (Is 22:19).

1. οἰκονομίας oikonomias gen sing fem
2. οἰκονομίαν oikonomian acc sing fem
3. οἰκονομία oikonomia nom sing fem

1 give an account of thy **stewardship**;...............Luke 16:2
2 for my lord taketh away from me the **stewardship**:.....16:3
1 that, when I am put out of the **stewardship**,............16:4
2 a **dispensation** of the gospel is committed unto me...1 Co 9:17
2 That in the **dispensation** of the fulness of times......Eph 1:10
2 If ye have heard of the **dispensation** of the grace........3:2
3 what is the **administration** of the mystery (NASB).......3:9
2 a minister, according to the **dispensation** of God......Col 1:25
2 rather than godly **edifying** which is in faith: so do...1 Tm 1:4

Classical Greek and Septuagint Usage
The word *oikonomia* is derived from the words *oikos* (3486), "house," and *nemō*, "to deal out," or "to administrate." From the time of Xenophon and Plato it represented household administration, the management of a household or of household affairs. Generally it is used for the administration of the state and was eventually used to designate every kind of activity that accrued from the position (Goetzmann, "House," *Colin Brown*, 2:253). It thus takes on the related meanings of "direction, provision," or "administration." The word occurs in the Septuagint only in Isaiah 22:19,21 with its original meaning of "administration, office."

New Testament Usage
In the New Testament *oikonomia* may be extended to include management of the property of others, thus becoming "stewardship" (Luke 16:2-4). In the Pauline epistles it denotes the apostle's attitude toward the duties of his apostolic office. In 1 Corinthians 9:17 Paul used the word to describe the responsibility of preaching the gospel entrusted him by God as a "commission" from which he could not draw back ("A *dispensation* of the gospel is committed unto me"). Paul also used *oikonomia* to designate his responsibility to "fulfil the Word of God" (Colossians 1:25) by which he meant he had been entrusted to impart to the Colossians the unfolding of the plan of God that has been consummated in the Church, the body of Christ. (For a similar passage, cf. Ephesians 3:2.)

In Ephesians 1:10 ("*dispensation* of the fulness of times") and 3:9 ("fellowship of the mystery") *oikonomia* denotes the administration of the plan of God, hidden from eternity in God, by which He, in the fullness of time, will sum up all things in Christ. Finally, in 1 Timothy 1:4 the apostle warned of those who would indulge in speculative knowledge rather than godly "instruction" in faith. With reference to the KJV's translation of *oikonomia* as "dispensation," Vine's comment is appropriate: "A dispensation is not a period or epoch (a common, but erroneous, use of the word), but a mode of dealing, an arrangement or administration of affairs" (*Expository Dictionary*, "Dispensation").

STRONG 3622, BAUER 559-60, MOULTON-MILLIGAN 442, KITTEL 5:151-53, LIDDELL-SCOTT 1204, COLIN BROWN 2:253-56.

3485. οἰκονόμος oikonomos noun
Manager (of a household), steward.
COGNATE:
οἰκονομέω oikonomeō (3483)

SYNONYM:
: ἐπίτροπος epitropos (1996)

פֶּחָה pechāh (6589), Governor (Est 8:9).

1. οἰκονόμος oikonomos nom sing masc
2. οἰκονόμον oikonomon acc sing masc
3. οἰκονόμοι oikonomoi nom pl masc
4. οἰκονόμοις oikonomois dat pl masc
5. οἰκονόμους oikonomous acc pl masc

```
1 Who then is that faithful and wise steward,........ Luke 12:42
2 was a certain rich man, which had a steward;..........  16:1
1 Then the steward said within himself,..................  16:3
2 And the lord commended the unjust steward,..........  16:8
1 Erastus the chamberlain of the city saluteth you,... Rom 16:23
5 and stewards of the mysteries of God................ 1 Co 4:1
4 Moreover it is required in stewards,....................  4:2
5 But is under tutors and governors until the time...... Gal 4:2
2 a bishop must be blameless, as the steward of God;... Tit 1:7
3 as good stewards of the manifold grace of God...... 1 Pt 4:10
```

Classical Greek
In classical Greek *oikonomos* is used like *oikodespotēs* (3480) for a "steward." The word can also mean a "housekeeper" or "housewife." *Oikonomos* can be the one in charge of separate branches of a household such as the inspector of goods, chief cook, porter, accountant, etc. In Philo *oikonomos* is used with *politikos*, "statesman," referring to a statesman and a ruler of the house (cf. *Bauer*). The wise man merits praise because he manages the household well and acts like a statesman outside the house which benefits society (Michel, "oikonomos," *Kittel*, 5:151).

Septuagint Usage
In the Septuagint Eliakim is the most often mentioned of Old Testament stewards. This manager for King Hezekiah is found in 2 Kings (LXX 4 Kings) 18:18,37; 19:2; Isaiah 36:3,22; and 37:2. Other named stewards are: Ahishar (1 Kings 4:6 [LXX 3 Kings 4:6]); Arza, who had his own house (1 Kings 16:9 [LXX 3 Kings 16:9]); and Obadiah, a righteous man who "feared the Lord greatly" and who was steward for Ahab (1 Kings 18:3 [LXX 3 Kings 18:3]).

In 1 Chronicles 29:6 *oikonomos* is used of the various foremen of King David whom he referred to Solomon for building the temple. The word can also mean officials, nobles or governors, etc., which would entail the same basic job description (Esther 1:8; 8:9; 1 Esdras 4:49). Other uses in 1 Esdras include the stewards of Darius in 4:47 and the treasurers of the king in 8:67.

New Testament Usage
Used only 10 times in the New Testament, *oikonomos* signifies the manager of a household or of household affairs (i.e., a steward), a position most often held by a slave, though sometimes by a freedman. He would be one who was entrusted with the management of a house, the control of its cash receipts and expenditures (Luke 16:1-8), and the administration and appropriate care of servants (Luke 12:42). Such managers even assumed responsibility for the children of the household who were not yet come of age (Galatians 4:2). The use of *oikonomos* in Luke 16:1,3,8 seems to designate an employee. But the parallel use of *doulos* (1395) in Matthew 24:45 with *oikonomos* in Luke 12:42 shows that *oikonomos* in Luke 12:42 indicates a slave.

Since an *oikonomos* had a great deal of control over the financial matters of the household, the term took on the connotation of "treasurer." Accordingly, in Romans 16:23, Erastus is called "chamberlain (*oikonomos*) of the city," i.e., the city treasurer of Corinth. In 1 Corinthians 4:1,2 Paul used the term ("stewards," KJV) metaphorically to describe those who have been committed to the preaching of the gospel ("the mysteries of God"), and who, as stewards, are required to be faithful. Likewise, in Titus 1:7 the overseer ("bishop") must be a man of virtue and integrity, of model deportment, for he is one entrusted with the work of God. In 1 Peter 4:10 the apostle used the word to speak of believers generally as those who are responsible to use what they have received in the service of others. Believers are stewards of the gifts of the Spirit and salvation which God has provided for them.

STRONG 3623, BAUER 560, MOULTON-MILLIGAN 442-43, KITTEL 5:149-51, LIDDELL-SCOTT 1204, COLIN BROWN 2:253-55.

3486. οἶκος oikos noun

House, dwelling, home, habitation, household, family.

COGNATES:
: οἰκέω oikeō (3474)
: πάροικος paroikos (3803)

SYNONYM:
: οἰκία oikia (3477)

אֹהֶל 'ōhel (164), Tent (Gn 31:33, Jos 22:6ff., Jb 20:26).

אַרְמוֹן 'armôn (783), Palace (Is 32:14).

אֶרֶץ 'erets (800), Land (Jer 50:16 [27:16]—Codex Alexandrinus only).

οἶκος 3486

בִּירָה bîrāh (1038), Palace (1 Chr 29:19).

בַּיִת bayith (1041), House (Gn 31:14, 2 Sm 7:1f., Jer 7:10f.).

בַּיִת bayith (A1042), House, temple (Ezr 5:16f., 7:19f., Dn 4:4,30 [4:1,27]—Aramaic).

בִּיתָן bîthān (1080), Palace (Est 1:5).

בֵּן bēn (1158), Son, child (1 Chr 2:10, Jer 16:15, Am 3:1).

הֵיכָל hêkhāl (2033), Palace, temple (2 Kgs 20:18, Ezr 3:6, Mi 1:2).

הֵיכָל hêkhāl (A2034), Temple, palace (Ezr 5:14f., Dn 5:2,5—Aramaic).

זְבֻל zᵉvul (2166), Habitation (Is 63:15).

לִשְׁכָּה lishkāh (4099), Chamber (Jer 36:21 [43:21]).

מַחֲנֶה machăneh (4402), Camp (2 Chr 31:2).

מָעוֹן māʽôn (4737), Habitation (Dt 26:15).

מָקוֹם māqôm (4887), House (Jgs 19:29—Codex Alexandrinus only).

מִשְׁכָּן mishkān (5088), Dwelling (Jb 18:21).

נָוָה nāwāh (5297), Habitation (Ps 74:20 [73:20]).

נַחֲלָה nachălāh (5338), Inheritance (Jgs 2:6—Codex Alexandrinus only).

עֶבֶד ʽevedh (5860), Servant (Jer 22:2).

קֹדֶשׁ qōdhesh (7231), Holy place (2 Chr 35:5).

קָהָל qāhāl (7235), Assembly (Dt 23:1—only some Alexandrinus texts).

שָׁכַן shākhan (8331), Dwell (Jb 30:6).

תַּחַת tachath (8809), Place (Ex 16:29).

1. οἶκος oikos nom sing masc
2. οἴκου oikou gen sing masc
3. οἴκῳ oikō dat sing masc
4. οἶκον oikon acc sing masc
5. οἴκων oikōn gen pl masc
6. οἴκοις oikois dat pl masc
7. οἴκους oikous acc pl masc

4 Arise, take up thy bed, and go unto thine **house**.....Matt 9:6
4 And he arose, and departed to his **house**............ 9:7
2 go rather to the lost sheep of the **house** of Israel...... 10:6
6 they that wear soft clothing are in kings' **houses**...... 11:8
4 How he entered into the **house** of God,................ 12:4
4 will return into my **house** from whence I came out;.... 12:44
2 but unto the lost sheep of the **house** of Israel........ 15:24
1 My **house** shall be called the house of prayer;....... 21:13
1 My **house** shall be called the house of prayer;....... 21:13
1 Behold, your **house** is left unto you desolate......... 23:38
4 and it was noised that he was in the **house**......Mark 2:1
4 take up thy bed, and go thy way into thine **house**..... 2:11
4 How he went into the **house** of God,................. 2:26
4 and they went into an **house**......................... 3:19
4 Go **home** to thy friends, and tell them how great..... 5:19
4 cometh to the **house** of the ruler of the synagogue,... 5:38
4 he was entered into the **house** from the people,...... 7:17
4 And when she was come to her **house**,................. 7:30
4 if I send them away fasting to their own **houses**,.... 8:3
4 And he sent him away to his **house**, saying,.......... 8:26
4 And when he was come into the **house**,................ 9:28
1 My **house** shall be called ... the house of prayer?.. 11:17
1 My **house** shall be called ... the house of prayer?.. 11:17

4 he departed to his own **house**...................... Luke 1:23
2 whose name was Joseph, of the **house** of David;....... 1:27
4 he shall reign over the **house** of Jacob for ever;.... 1:33
4 And entered into the **house** of Zacharias,............. 1:40
4 and returned to her own **house**....................... 1:56
3 salvation for us in the **house** of his servant David;... 1:69
2 because he was of the **house** and lineage of David:... 2:4
4 and take up thy couch, and go into thine **house**...... 5:24
4 and departed to his own **house**, glorifying God....... 5:25
4 How he went into the **house** of God,.................. 6:4
4 And they that were sent, returning to the **house**,.... 7:10
4 And He entered the Pharisee's **house**, (NASB)......... 7:36
4 Return to thine own **house**, and show how great....... 8:39
4 besought him that he would come into his **house**:..... 8:41
4 bid them farewell, which are at home at my **house**.... 9:61
3 **house** ye enter, first say, Peace be to this **house**...... 10:5
4 Martha received him into her **house**.................. 10:38
1 and a **house** divided against a house falleth......... 11:17
4 and a **house** divided against a **house** falleth..... 11:17
4 I will return unto my **house** whence I came out....... 11:24
2 which perished between the altar and the **temple**:.... 11:51
4 not have suffered his **house** to be broken through.... 12:39
3 there shall be five in one **house** divided,........... 12:52
1 Behold, your **house** is left unto you desolate........ 13:35
4 went into the **house** of one of the chief Pharisees... 14:1
1 and compel them ... that my **house** may be filled.... 14:23
4 And when he cometh **home**, he calleth together....... 15:6
7 they may receive me into their **houses**.............. 16:4
4 that thou wouldest send him to my father's **house**:... 16:27
4 I tell you, this man went down to his **house**........ 18:14
3 come down; for to day I must abide at thy **house**.... 19:5
3 This day is salvation come to this **house**,.......... 19:9
1 It is written, My **house** is the house of prayer:.... 19:46
1 It is written, My **house** is the **house** of prayer:.... 19:46
4 and brought him into the high priest's **house**....... 22:54
4 not my Father's **house** an house of merchandise..... John 2:16
4 not my Father's house an **house** of merchandise...... 2:16
2 The zeal of thine **house** hath eaten me up........... 2:17
4 And every man went unto his own **house**.............. 7:53
3 but Mary sat still in the **house**.................... 11:20
4 and it filled all the **house** where they were sitting.... Acts 2:2
1 let all the **house** of Israel know assuredly,........ 2:36
4 and breaking bread from **house** to house,............ 2:46
4 And daily in the temple, and in every **house**,....... 5:42
4 made him governor over Egypt and all his **house**,.... 7:10
3 nourished up in his father's **house** three months:... 7:20
1 O ye **house** of Israel,.............................. 7:42
3 for the **house** of Jacob (NASB, margin)............. 7:46
3 But Solomon built him an **house**..................... 7:47
4 what **house** will ye build me? saith the Lord:....... 7:49
7 entering into every **house**, and haling men and...... 8:3
3 and one that feared God with all his **house**,........ 10:2
4 by an holy angel to send for thee into his **house**,... 10:22
3 and at the ninth hour I prayed in my **house**,........ 10:30
4 and we entered into the man's **house**:............... 11:12
3 showed us how he had seen an angel in his **house**,.... 11:13
1 whereby thou and all thy **house** shall be saved...... 11:14
1 And when she was baptized, and her **household**,...... 16:15
4 come into my **house**, and abide there................ 16:15
1 and thou shalt be saved, and thy **house**............. 16:31
4 And when he had brought them into his **house**,....... 16:34
3 Crispus, ... believed on the Lord with all his **house**;... 18:8
2 they fled out of that **house** naked and wounded...... 19:16
7 taught you publicly, and from **house** to house,...... 20:20
4 we entered into the **house** of Philip the evangelist,... 21:8
4 Likewise greet the church that is in their **house**...... Rom 16:5
4 And I baptized also the **household** of Stephanas:.... 1 Co 1:16
3 And if any man hunger, let him eat at **home**;........ 11:34
3 let them ask their husbands at **home**:............... 14:35
4 with the church that is in their **house**,............ 16:19
4 and the church which is in his **house**............... Col 4:15
2 One that ruleth well his own **house**,............... 1 Tm 3:4
2 For if a man know not how to rule his own **house**,.... 3:5
5 ruling their children and their own **houses** well..... 3:12
3 oughtest to behave thyself in the **house** of God,..... 3:15
4 let them learn first to show piety at **home**,......... 5:4
3 Lord give mercy unto the **house** of Onesiphorus;..... 2 Tm 1:16

4	Salute ... the **household** of Onesiphorus.	2 Tm 4:19
7	who subvert whole **houses,**	Tit 1:11
4	beloved Apphia, ... and to the church in thy **house:**	Phlm 1:2
3	as also Moses was faithful in all his **house.**	Heb 3:2
2	inasmuch as he who hath builded the **house**	3:3
1	For every **house** is builded by some man;	3:4
3	And Moses verily was faithful in all his **house,**	3:5
4	But Christ as a son over his own **house;**	3:6
1	whose **house** are we, if we hold fast the confidence	3:6
4	the **house** of Israel and with the house of Judah:	8:8
4	the house of Israel and with the **house** of Judah:	8:8
3	will make with the **house** of Israel after those days,	8:10
4	And having an high priest over the **house** of God;	10:21
2	prepared an ark to the saving of his **house;**	11:7
1	are built up a spiritual **house,** an holy priesthood,	1 Pt 2:5
2	that judgment must begin at the **house** of God:	4:17

Classical Greek

In classical Greek *oikos* appeared very early. It is primarily used for any dwelling place or the building in which one lived. It also includes tents, caves, and cages. Sometimes *oikos* designates a single room or chamber; hence, it is not unusual to find the plural *oikoi* referring to one complete yet single house. *Oikos* can also be used for a temple. The place of worship is identified as the house of the god.

For a while *oikia* (3477), an Ionic form, was used for the dwelling, and *oikos* referred to all property or persons associated with the house (see Goetzmann, "House," *Colin Brown*, 2:247). Although this distinction between *oikia* and *oikos* was maintained in some Attic documents, it was not upheld in all the dialects (cf. *Liddell-Scott*, "oikia"). By the time of the New Testament the two forms were often used interchangeably.

Septuagint Usage

In the Septuagint both *oikos* and *oikia* are used often to translate the Hebrew word *bayith*. Conceptually *bayith* and *oikos* are quite similar in Hebrew and Greek thought; *bayith* can simply refer to a building, or it can refer to other things associated with the domicile such as property or persons. Both Hebrew and Greek use "house" as a word for the family unit (e.g., 2 Samuel 16:5 [LXX 2 Kings 16:5]). The temple or tabernacle of the Lord is called a house even as heathen temples are (e.g., Judges 18:31; 1 Kings 6:1 [LXX 3 Kings 6:1]; 1 Samuel 5:2 [LXX 1 Kings 5:2]). The temple of God is often referred to as "the house" (e.g., 1 Kings 6 [LXX 3 Kings 6]). Furthermore, house can be used to describe an entire nation (e.g., 2 Samuel 6:5 [LXX 2 Samuel 6:5]).

In the Dead Sea Scrolls the Qumran community described itself as the temple of God (1QS 5:6; 8:5,9; 9:6; GD 3:19). (See Gartner, *The Temple and the Community in Qumran and the New Testament.*) This has significant New Testament parallels.

New Testament Usage

In the New Testament *oikos* demonstrates the same meanings found in the Greek and Hebrew literature. Primarily it is used for a building (e.g., Luke 1:40; 4:28) or one's home (1:23). It has a broader application: a large building (Matthew 11:8), the temple (Luke 19:46), a city (Luke 13:35), property (Acts 7:10), and also a family or household (Luke 10:5; Acts 16:31). Like the Old Testament, the New Testament employs "house" to indicate tribes, descendants, or nations. A demon-possessed person can be described as a house of demons (Matthew 12:44; Luke 11:24).

Approaching a more exclusive use of the word, the New Testament describes the Christian community as the "house of God" (1 Timothy 3:15; 1 Peter 4:17). Christians as a whole and not just individually are seen as the temple of the Holy Spirit (Ephesians 2:19-22). Given the Old Testament use of house for temple and the frequent use of compound words from the *oikos* group in the temple context in Ephesians 2, it is obvious that the metaphor the writer has in mind is a building in which God dwells (see Goetzmann, "House," *Colin Brown*, 2:249).

House is used in the epistolary literature to describe a subunit of the church. Groups often met in houses of certain believers, and groups of Christians of a metropolitan church are distinctively identified as associated with a particular household (Acts 12:12; Romans 16:5; 1 Corinthians 1:11; 16:15,19). Finally, Jesus described the Christians' final reward in terms of dwelling places (*oikia* and *monai* [see 3301], John 14:2).

STRONG 3624, BAUER 560-61, MOULTON-MILLIGAN 443, KITTEL 5:119-31, LIDDELL-SCOTT 1204-5, COLIN BROWN 2:247-51.

3487. οἰκουμένη oikoumenē noun

The inhabited earth, the world, the Roman Empire.

COGNATE:
  οἰκέω oikeō (3474)
SYNONYMS:
  αἰών aiōn (163)
  γῆ gē (1087)
  κόσμος kosmos (2862)

1. **οἰκουμένη** oikoumenē nom sing fem
2. **οἰκουμένης** oikoumenēs gen sing fem

3. οἰκουμένῃ oikoumenē dat sing fem
4. οἰκουμένην oikoumenēn acc sing fem

```
3  in all the world for a witness unto all nations;..... Matt 24:14
4  that all the world should be taxed.................... Luke 2:1
2  showed unto him all the kingdoms of the world........ 4:5
3  those things which are coming on the earth:.......... 21:26
4  should be great dearth throughout all the world:.... Acts 11:28
4  These that have turned the world upside down........ 17:6
4  he will judge the world in righteousness.............. 17:31
1  whom all Asia and the world worshippeth............. 19:27
4  sedition among all the Jews throughout the world,..... 24:5
2  and their words unto the ends of the world......... Rom 10:18
4  he bringeth in the firstbegotten into the world,...... Heb 1:6
4  the world to come, whereof we speak................ 2:5
2  temptation, which shall come upon all the world,..... Rev 3:10
4  and Satan, which deceiveth the whole world:.......... 12:9
2  unto the kings of the earth and of the whole world,.... 16:14
```

Classical Greek

Opinions vary as to what *oikoumenē* originally denoted. It could designate the "inhabited earth," as opposed to those areas that were uninhabited. From a technical perspective, *oikoumenē* is the present passive participle from *oikeō* (3474), "to dwell," and designates the portion of the earth that was inhabited (in Greek writings, the world inhabited by Greeks, as distinct from the lands of the barbarian peoples). In those writings that speak of matters touching Roman affairs, *oikoumenē* is used to designate the lands of the Roman Empire. As will be seen later, the connotation of the Greco-Roman pagan world that accompanied this word is never contested in the New Testament. *Oikoumenē* has an extraordinary reference to the whole world including the spirit world. From about the Fourth Century B.C. *oikoumenē* came to indicate the inhabited world in a more general sense. Thus it can be seen that *oikoumenē* could have geographical, cultural, or political nuances in its various usages.

Septuagint Usage

The 41 occurrences of this word in the Septuagint surprisingly reflect only the geographical meaning of the "inhabited world." *Oikoumenē* is found predominantly in the Psalms (17 times) and in Isaiah (13 times). However, the clearest example of the geographic meaning of this word is found in Exodus 16:35. Here Israel ceased from eating manna when they came "to a land inhabited . . . the land of Canaan."

New Testament Usage

Oikoumenē, which occurs 15 times in the New Testament, denotes the "inhabited world" (Luke 4:5; 21:26; Romans 10:18; Hebrews 1:6; Revelation 3:10; 16:14). By extension it came to designate the world's "inhabitants" as in Acts 17:31 and Revelation 12:9, although some of these more universalist references excepted are not free of political connotations in terms of the Roman government. (Cf. Acts 11:28; 17:6; 19:27; 24:5 where *oikoumenō* refers to the Roman Empire or its inhabitants.)

The geographical meaning is well represented. Jesus was shown the kingdoms "of the world" by Satan (Luke 4:5), who also deceives "the whole world" (Revelation 12:9). The gospel is to be preached "in the whole world" (Matthew 24:14). The political meaning (the Roman Empire) is also present. Luke 2:1 says that "all the world" was to be counted in Augustus' census. The apostle Paul was accused of stirring up all the Jews throughout "the world" by his preaching of the gospel (Acts 24:5).

The term is used in Matthew 24:14 to designate the world to which the gospel will have been preached by the time of Christ's return. In Hebrews 2:5 it represents the "world to come" as the *oikoumenē* of the future.

The *oikoumenē* is not to be equated with the Church or with the believing community, but represents the pagan Greco-Roman world under siege by the powers of darkness and thus the field in which the Church is to labor. "The *oikoumenē* is the sphere in which the church lives and which she claims for her Lord, who according to Heb(rew). has been brought into the *oikoumenē* as first-born, and who therefore is its legitimate ruler. An inward-looking ecumenical attitude by the Church is therefore a contradiction in terms" (Flender, "Earth," *Colin Brown*, 1:519).

STRONG 3625, BAUER 561, MOULTON-MILLIGAN 443, KITTEL 5:157-59, LIDDELL-SCOTT 1205, COLIN BROWN 1:517-19.

3487B. οἰκουργός oikourgos adj

Working at home, housekeeping, domestic.

CROSS-REFERENCES:
ἐργάζομαι ergazomai (2021)
οἰκέω oikeō (3474)

1. οἰκουργούς oikourgous acc pl fem

A compound of *oikos* (3486), "house," and *ergon* (2024), "work," *oikourgos* means "working at home." Its only New Testament occurrence is in Titus 2:5. More common is the classical form *oikouros* (3488) (from *oikos* and *ouros* "keeper") which occurs in some New Testament manuscripts at Titus 2:5

meaning "keepers at home," and describes the industriousness by which young women were to demonstrate their Christian walk.

BAUER 561, MOULTON-MILLIGAN 443, LIDDELL-SCOTT 1205.

3488. οἰκουρός oikouros adj

Keeping a home, taking care of household affairs, domestic.

CROSS-REFERENCE:
οἰκέω oikeō (3474)

1. οἰκουρούς oikourous acc pl fem

1 To be discreet, chaste, **keepers at home**, good,........ Tit 2:5

A compound of *oikos* (3486), "house," and *ouros*, "a keeper," *oikouros* indicates one who watches or keeps the house. In classical Greek it can refer to a "watch-dog, rooster," or even a "sacred serpent" that was said to watch over the Acropolis (*Liddell-Scott*). When used of persons it usually refers positively to a female "housekeeper," but can also be found "contemptuously of a man," a "stay at home" during a time of war (ibid.). It does not appear in the Septuagint but does occur once in the New Testament. In Titus 2:5 the KJV renders it "keepers at home" when describing a characteristic of the young women in the church. A few manuscripts here read *oikourgos* (3487B), "working at home" (cf. NIV).

STRONG 3626, BAUER 561, MOULTON-MILLIGAN 443 (see "oikourgos"), LIDDELL-SCOTT 1205.

3489. οἰκτείρω oikteirō verb

To have compassion on someone.

SYNONYMS:
ἐλεέω eleeō (1640)
σπλαγχνίζομαι splanchnizomai (4550)
συμπαθέω sumpatheō (4685)

חָנַן chānan (2706), Be gracious, pity (Pss 37:21 [36:21], 102:14 [101:14], Is 30:18).

יָדַע yādha' (3156), Know; have regard to (Prv 12:10).

נָתַן nāthan (5598), Give (Prv 21:26).

רָחַם rācham (7638), Piel: have compassion (Ex 33:19, Ps 103:13 [102:13], Jer 21:7).

שׁוּב shûv (8178), Return; polel: restore (Ps 60:1 [59:1]).

1. οἰκτείρω oikteirō 1sing subj pres act
2. οἰκτειρήσω oikteirēsō 1sing indic fut act
3. οἰκτίρω oiktirō 1sing subj pres act
4. οἰκτιρήσω oiktirēsō 1sing indic fut act

2 and I will have compassion on whom I will.......... Rom 9:15
1 have compassion on whom I will **have compassion**....... 9:15

Classical Greek and Septuagint Usage

The verb *oikteirō* (also spelled *oiktirō*; cf. *Bauer*) generally means "have pity." Less frequently it is used to describe one way of expressing pity, "bewail, lament" (*Liddell-Scott*). It appears over 30 times in the Septuagint usually translating the Hebrew *chānan*, "have compassion" (e.g., 2 Kings 13:23 [LXX 4 Kings 13:23]), or *rācham*, "show favor" (e.g., Psalm 112:5 [LXX 111:5]). In both classical Greek and the Septuagint *oikteirō* is more than just a feeling or attitude of pity and sympathy, it is the actual expression of such feelings.

New Testament Usage

The single New Testament occurrence, Romans 9:15, continues the classical and Septuagint emphasis on the expression of pity or sympathy. In this instance Paul quoted Exodus 33:19 from the Septuagint: "I will have mercy on whom I will have mercy, and will *have compassion* on whom I will *have compassion*." The purpose in pointing back to the time of Moses was to show that God has always been righteous in His dealings with man. God's "mercy" and "pity" depend on Him alone, without influence by human will or exertion (Romans 9:11). In His sovereignty He chose Israel from among the ancient nations, and by His divine election He presented them with the gospel first; later He presented it to the Gentiles (Romans 9:22-24). Therefore neither Jew nor Gentile has any right to exclude the other from His salvation (Romans 9:30 to 10:1).

STRONG 3627, BAUER 561, KITTEL 5:159-61, LIDDELL-SCOTT 1205, COLIN BROWN 2:598,600.

3490. οἰκτιρμός oiktirmos noun

Pity, mercy, compassion.

COGNATE:
οἰκτίρμων oiktirmōn (3491)

SYNONYM:
ἔλεος eleos (1643)

רַחַם rācham (7641II) Compassion, mercy (Neh 9:27f., Ps 69:16 [68:16], Zec 7:9).

תַּחֲנוּן tachănûn (8800), Supplication (Zec 12:10).

1. οἰκτιρμοί oiktirmoi nom pl masc
2. οἰκτιρμῶν oiktirmōn gen pl masc
3. οἰκτιρμοῦ oiktirmou gen sing masc

2 I beseech you ... brethren, by the **mercies** of God,.. Rom 12:1
2 the Father of **mercies**, and the God of all comfort;.. 2 Co 1:3
1 fellowship of the Spirit, if any bowels and **mercies**,.. Phlp 2:1

2 bowels **of mercies**, kindness, humbleness of mind,.... Col 3:12
2 died without **mercy** under two or three witnesses:...Heb 10:28

Classical Greek
Oiktirmos is a poetic form of *oiktos* that denotes the lamenting that occurred at the death or misfortune of another. It expresses the sympathy and pity one felt towards another that often manifested itself in some form of assistance. Out of this context the word group came to mean "showing pity" or "compassion." It is very similar in meaning to *eleos* (1643).

Septuagint Usage
This noun occurs over 40 times in the Septuagint and is used to translate the Hebrew *chănan*, "to be gracious," and *racham*, "to be compassionate." The *oiktirmos* word group is frequently used with *eleos*. As in the Hebrew, the substantive is plural (e.g., "mercies": Psalm 119:77 [LXX 118:77]; Isaiah 63:15; Daniel 9:9). Note, however, that some English versions of the Bible do not always translate the plural (RSV, for example). The word is often used in the Psalms. As a result, invoking God's mercy became a common element of Jewish prayers (Bultmann, "oiktirō," *Kittel*, 5:160). The meaning of "mercy" and "compassion" is consistent throughout the Old Testament.

New Testament Usage
The word *oiktirmos* occurs five times in the New Testament and retains its Semitic heritage by using the plural form *oiktirmoi*. It expresses the disposition of God towards man, which serves as a model for the believer. God is called the "Father of mercies" (2 Corinthians 1:3), and it is upon the "mercies of God" that Paul based his exhortation in Romans 12:1. The phrase "mercies of God" is said to sum up God's saving acts and plan of salvation; it is the presupposition for the Christian life (Esser, "Mercy," *Colin Brown*, 2:598). As such, Paul expected the Philippian believers to show compassion towards him and one another (Philippians 2:1). He used the word with *splanchna* (see 4551) in Philippians 2:1 which is rendered in the KJV "bowels and mercies." Entrails were seen as the seat of emotions and therefore were associated with mercy, not unlike the English use of the phrase, "have a heart."

With God as the example believers are exhorted to "put on" a heart of compassion (Colossians 3:12). Hebrews 10:28 issues a warning to all who take lightly the things of God. If those who ignored the law of Moses died "without mercy" (*choris oiktirmon*), then what will happen to those who "trample under foot the Son of God" (NASB)?

STRONG 3628, BAUER 561, MOULTON-MILLIGAN 444, KITTEL 5:159-61, LIDDELL-SCOTT 1205, COLIN BROWN 2:593-94,598.

3491. οἰκτίρμων oiktirmōn adj
Compassionate, merciful.
COGNATE:
  οἰκτιρμός oiktirmos (3490)
SYNONYMS:
  ἐλεήμων eleēmōn (1642)
  ἵλεως hileōs (2412)

חַנּוּן channûn (2688), Gracious (Ps 145:8 [144:8]).
חָנַן chānan (2706), Have pity (Ps 109:12 [108:12]).
רַחוּם rachûm (7631), Merciful, compassionate (Dt 4:31, 2 Chr 30:9, Ps 112:4 [111:4]).
רַחֲמָנִי rachămānî (7645), Compassionate (Lam 4:10).

1. οἰκτίρμων oiktirmōn nom sing masc
2. οἰκτίρμονες oiktirmones nom pl masc

2 Be ye therefore **merciful**, as your Father also is..... Luke 6:36
1 Be ye ... **merciful**, as your Father also is **merciful**....... 6:36
1 that the Lord is very pitiful, and of **tender mercy**..... Jas 5:11

Found only three times in the New Testament, this adjective (related to *oikteirō* [3489], "to have compassion on," and to *oiktirmos* [3490], "compassion, pity, mercy") is found twice in Luke 6:36 where Jesus urged His disciples to "be ... *merciful*, as your Father also is *merciful*." Likewise, in James 5:11, the word again refers to God as one who is "*of tender mercy*." This seems to be a variation of the description of God in Psalms 103:8 and 111:4 (Bultmann, "oiktirō," *Kittel*, 5:161).

STRONG 3629, BAUER 561, KITTEL 5:159-61, LIDDELL-SCOTT 1205, COLIN BROWN 2:598.

3492. οἶμαι oimai verb
To suppose, expect.

1. οἶμαι oimai 1sing indic pres mid

1 I **suppose** that even the world itself could not...... John 21:25

This is the contracted form of *oiomai*. See the word study at number 3496.

3493. οἰνοπότης oinopotēs noun
A drinker of wine, drunkard.
CROSS-REFERENCES:
  οἶνος oinos (3494)
  πότος potos (4083)

1. οἰνοπότης oinopotēs nom sing masc

1 Behold a man gluttonous, and **a winebibber**,	Matt 11:19
1 Behold a gluttonous man, and **a winebibber**,	Luke 7:34

Found only twice in the New Testament, this noun, a compound of *oinos*, "wine," and *potēs*, "a drinker," appears in Matthew 11:19 and Luke 7:34. In both cases its companion term "glutton" (*phagos* [5152]) makes it clear that the Pharisees were not merely saying Jesus drank wine in moderation, as was common at meals in those days, but that He was characterized by excessive wine consumption, hence a drunkard (see Brown, "Vine," *Colin Brown*, 3:921). They, of course, were lying, just as they were when they said John the Baptist had a demon (Matthew 11:18; Luke 7:33).

STRONG 3630, BAUER 562, MOULTON-MILLIGAN 444, LIDDELL-SCOTT 1207, COLIN BROWN 3:918,921.

3494. οἶνος oinos noun

Wine, fermented grape juice, fermented juice (of other kinds).

COGNATES:
οἰνοπότης oinopotēs (3493)
οἰνοφλυγία oinophlugia (3495)
πάροινος paroinos (3805)

SYNONYMS:
γλεῦκος gleukos (1092)
ὄξος oxos (3553)

חֲמַר chămar (A2667), Wine (Ezr 6:9, Dn 5:23—Aramaic).
חֶמֶר chemer (2669), Wine (Dt 32:14).
יַיִן yayin (3302), Wine (Gn 19:32ff., 1 Sm 1:14f., Jer 35:5f. [42:5f.]).
יֶקֶב yeqev (3449), Winepress (Dt 15:14).
סֹבֶא sōve' (5618), Drink (Is 1:22).
שֶׁמֶר shemer (8491), Wine (Is 25:6).
תִּירוֹשׁ tîrôsh (8822), New wine (Dt 11:14, 2 Chr 31:5, Hos 7:14).

1. οἶνος oinos nom sing masc
2. οἴνου oinou gen sing masc
3. οἴνῳ oinō dat sing masc
4. οἶνον oinon acc sing masc

4 Neither do men put new **wine** into old bottles:	Matt 9:17
1 else the bottles break, and the **wine** runneth out,	9:17
4 but they put new **wine** into new bottles,	9:17
4 they gave Him **wine** to drink (NASB)	27:34
4 And no man putteth new **wine** into old bottles:	Mark 2:22
1 else the new **wine** doth burst the bottles,	2:22
1 burst the bottles, and the **wine** is spilled,	2:22
4 but new **wine** must be put into new bottles.	2:22
4 they gave him to drink **wine** mingled with myrrh:	15:23
4 and shall drink neither **wine** nor strong drink;	Luke 1:15
4 And no man putteth new **wine** into old bottles:	5:37
1 the new **wine** will burst the bottles, and be spilled,	5:37
4 But new **wine** must be put into new bottles;	5:38
4 came neither eating bread nor drinking **wine**;	7:33
4 and bound up his wounds, pouring in oil and **wine**,	10:34
2 And when they wanted **wine**,	John 2:3
4 They have no **wine**.	2:3
4 tasted the water that was made **wine**,	2:9
4 at the beginning doth set forth good **wine**;	2:10
4 but thou hast kept the good **wine** until now.	2:10
4 Cana of Galilee, where he made the water **wine**.	4:46
4 It is good neither to eat flesh, nor to drink **wine**,	Rom 14:21
3 And be not drunk with **wine**, wherein is excess;	Eph 5:18
3 not given to much **wine**, not greedy of filthy lucre;	1 Tm 3:8
3 but use a little **wine** for thy stomach's sake	5:23
3 not false accusers, not given to much **wine**,	Tit 2:3
4 and see thou hurt not the oil and the **wine**.	Rev 6:6
2 because she made all nations drink of the **wine**	14:8
2 The same shall drink of the **wine** of the wrath	14:10
2 the cup of the **wine** of the fierceness of his wrath.	16:19
2 been made drunk with the **wine** of her fornication.	17:2
2 For all nations have drunk of the **wine** of the wrath	18:3
4 and frankincense, and **wine**, and oil, and fine flour,	18:13
2 treadeth the **winepress** of the fierceness and wrath	19:15

Background and History

Oinos is a common word from antiquity that is found in Homer and other ancient Greek writings, as well as in the Septuagint and papyri. *Oinos* and the Latin word *vinum* may derive from a common Semitic root (*wyn* or *yyn*; cf. Bandstra, "Wine," *International Standard Bible Encyclopedia*, 4:1068). Further Indo-European cognates are the German *Wein*, the French *vin*, the Spanish *vino*, and the English *wine*. As well, Semitic cognates include the Akkadian *inu*, the Arabic *wayn* ("black grapes"), and the Ugaritic *yn* (Harris, "yayin," *Theological Wordbook of the Old Testament*, 1:375f.). Greek *oinos* originally began with a digamma, a consonant obsolete by New Testament times and pronounced like the letter *w*. When it is seen that *oinos* was *woinos*, the etymological connection is clearer.

Various drinks were known and produced in antiquity. The juice of grapes, apples, dates, other fruit, honey, and grains were used for beverages. Modern distilled liquors like whiskey, vodka, and bourbon were unknown in ancient times. Modern distillation did not appear in Europe until the 12th Century A.D.

Beer, made from barley, was common and was the main drink in Mesopotamia until about the time of Nebuchadnezzar (about 600 B.C.) when date wine replaced it in popularity. Due to its high sugar content date wine produced the most highly fermented beverage in antiquity. In Hebrew the term *shēkhār* means "beer" (equivalent to Akkadian *shikāru*). Both *shēkhār* and *shikāru* could also refer to date wine. In the Septuagint *shēkhār* can be translated by *methē* (3149), "wine, alcoholic drink," *methusma* (same as *methē*), *oinos*, and *sikera* (4463), a direct borrowing and transliteration of *shēkhār*. Ancient beer differed from its modern counterpart primarily in the use of hops for flavoring (Limet, "The Cuisine of Ancient Sumer," p.135). Hops were not used until the Middle Ages.

In ancient Palestine wine was a leading product of the land (note the cluster of grapes described by the spies in Numbers 13:23). The Story of Sinuhe also notes the abundance of wine available in Palestine: "It had more wine than water" (see Lichtheim, *Ancient Egyptian Literature*, 1:226). Wine production "was second only to the cultivation of the olive and fig" (Forbes, *Studies in Ancient Technology*, 3:78), and consequently beer was not as popular, although its dangers are noted (Proverbs 20:1, NIV). Beer was the common drink of the Philistines, however.

The process of producing wine required several steps. First, the gathered grapes were pressed, either by a mechanical press or by treading (from which the highest quality wine was produced). Next, the juice was collected and placed in vats to ferment. Naturally occurring molds in the skins caused the sugar in the grapes to change into alcohol. The maximum percentage of alcohol in natural wine is limited by the amount of sugar present (half of the percentage of the sugar) and by the alcohol level itself: if it rises much above 10 or 11 percent the fermenting agents are killed and the process stops (Harris, "yayin," *Theological Wordbook of the Old Testament*; 1:375f.). The fermentation process took only 3 to 4 days, resulting in a beverage with an alcoholic content from 4 to 12 percent (8 to 24 proof). Then the wine was filtered through a linen cloth, stored in jars, and sold. Part of the product was stored in a cool place after being sealed with a stopper and resin or pitch to prevent further fermentation. If the fermentation process were to continue, vinegar, "sour wine," would result. Even so, fermentation could not be completely prevented and consequently 3 years (roughly) was the maximum storage time for wine. Much was boiled down to a syrup in order to preserve it.

Wine was usually diluted with water before consumption; "only 'boozers' drank pure wine" (Forbes, ibid., 3:80; also 3:61-85 for further information). However, Isaiah 1:22 views wine mixed with water as spoiled, reflecting the attitude of the Old Testament period; in New Testament times and after, many did not wish to drink undiluted wine. Rabbi Eliezer in the Talmud (Berakoth 7.5), in fact, forbade the saying of the blessing over wine that was not diluted. Hence Revelation 14:10 says, "The same shall drink of the wine of the wrath of God, which is poured out *without mixture* into the cup of his indignation" (emphasis supplied). For medicinal purposes wine was mixed with vinegar, myrrh (Mark 15:23, offered to the Lord on the cross to deaden the pain or to induce unconsciousness, which He refused), and gall (wormwood, hemlock, also offered to Christ, Matthew 27:34). (Note in Matthew 27:34 the King James Version gives "vinegar" for the word *oinos*, probably out of the opinion that when gall was added the wine became a bitter mixture and that "vinegar" better conveyed this idea.)

Septuagint Usage

In the Septuagint *oinos* appears over 200 times, predominantly translating the Hebrew term *yayin*. While the evils of inebriation are expressed (Proverbs 20:1; 23:29-35), wine is also praised (Psalm 104:15 [LXX 103:15]). Kings are warned to avoid it (Proverbs 31:4,5). An abundance of wine is seen as a sign of affluence (Genesis 49:11,12). It is important to note that the Hebrew word *tîrôsh*, "grape juice, unfermented wine," appearing 38 times in the Old Testament (Harris, "tîrôsh," *Theological Wordbook of the Old Testament*, 2:969), is also almost exclusively translated by *oinos* (36 times). In other words, *oinos* can and does refer to either unfermented or fermented wine in the Septuagint. It is also significant that even grape juice, as a symbol of harmless pleasures, can lead to overindulgence (Hosea 4:11). The Septuagint translates it with *methusma*, not *oinos*.

Nazarites in the Old Testament were forbidden to drink any type of wine whatsoever in order to keep the man of God separate from that which could cloud the mind or spoil his testimony of holiness (Numbers 6:3). Thus John the Baptist was described by the angel as one who would "drink neither wine nor strong drink" (Luke 1:15; see above for a discussion on this verse).

New Testament Usage

In the New Testament *oinos* is used 33 times. Concerning the Parable of the Wineskins, the juice would be acted on by yeast from the old wineskins and would begin to foam. Such gases could split any wineskin, but especially an older one that was already stretched out (Matthew 9:17; Luke 5:37,38). New wine would be grape juice (or a grapeade) made from grape syrup while old wine would be 2 to 3 years old. Old wine was considered better than new wine; hence Jesus' point that those who had drunk the old did not want the new, an obvious allusion to the Pharisees and others who would not accept His new teachings (Luke 5:39).

The Scriptures are abundantly clear in warning firmly against the intoxicating power of alcoholic beverages, even though the world at that time was dealing with drinks of 4 to 12 percent alcoholic content. Modern chemistry commonly produces beverages of 40 to 50 percent alcohol. The fundamentalist, conservative churches in the United States early took a stand for total abstinence, this especially in light of the ruination alcohol brought to certain Indian tribes. However, consumption of alcoholic beverages was common even among evangelical Christians and Puritans until the first half of the 19th Century and the rise of the temperance movement (Tyler, *Freedom's Ferment*, pp.308-12). This stance has been maintained by many groups today in keeping with the teaching of Romans 14:13, "that no man put a stumbling block or an occasion to fall in his brother's way."

First Timothy 5:23 gives Paul's advice to Timothy to no longer drink only water, but to drink "a little wine for thy stomach's sake and thy oft infirmities." Some say this had to do with the effect of the water which grape juice counteracted. Others say this clears the way for Christians to use medicines with alcohol in them for the sake of curing illness. Paul did say "a *little* wine," and the context is clearly one of dealing with a sick person. When Paul warned the Ephesians not to get drunk with wine (5:18), the "wine" refers to all fermented drinks. It does not justify becoming inebriated with beer or distilled liquor.

On the nature of the wine used at the Last Supper it must be kept in mind that ancient man had few beverages to drink, and lack of modern refrigeration prevented them from retaining unfermented fruit and grain beverages. Apart from these juices, only milk and water were available for consumption. Grapes were generally harvested in mid to late summer (Hopkins, "The Subsistence Struggles of Early Israel," p.186) and, to prevent spoilage in the intense heat, had to be processed immediately. Stored wine naturally fermented unless it was boiled down or kept cool, and it is to be expected that by the time of the Last Supper (late March—early April) only fermented juice (or grapeade) was available. Attempts to prevent fermentation by immediately sealing the fresh juice would likely have been considered. However, the discovery of a number of burst vessels shows that such attempts were generally unsuccessful. In spite of sealing, fermentation eventually began and the gases released shattered the vessels (Forbes, *Studies in Ancient Technology*, 3:80). However, today when many satisfying substitutes for alcoholic beverages are available, abstinence is a reasonable alternative to the overwhelming abuse of alcohol.

There have been endless tirades and debates on the nature of the wine made by our Lord at the wedding in Cana (John 2:9,10). Sides are drawn not on the basis of the word *oinos*, but on the view of abstinence held. The issue seems to be whether or not Jesus would create fermented wine and contribute to the further inebriation of the wedding guests. (Had the wine been unfermented, it would not have had time to ferment since it was consumed immediately.) From the Septuagint usage noted above, the *oinos* could be fermented or unfermented. Suffice it to say, the "better" wine of course does not in any way imply or demand a more alcoholic, or even an alcoholic, wine at all (one would presume that any wine that God had made would be better than man-made wine).

Strong 3631, Bauer 562, Moulton-Milligan 444, Kittel 5:162-66, Liddell-Scott 1207, Colin Brown 3:918,922.

3495. οἰνοφλυγία oinophlugia noun
Drunkenness, debauchery.
Cognate:
 οἶνος oinos (3494)
Synonyms:
 κραιπάλη kraipalē (2870)
 μέθη methē (3149)

1. οἰνοφλυγίαις oinophlugiais dat pl fem

1 lusts, excess of wine, revellings, banquetings, ... 1 Pt 4:3

Found only once in the New Testament, this noun, a compound of *oinos* (3494), "wine," and *phluō*, "to bubble up," is found only in 1 Peter 4:3 where it is translated "excess of wine" (KJV;

3496. οἴομαι oiomai verb

To suppose, expect, think.

COGNATE:
πότος potos (4083)

SYNONYMS:
δοκέω dokeō (1374)
ἐνθυμέομαι enthumeomai (1744)
ἡγέομαι hēgeomai (2216)
κρίνω krinō (2892)
λογίζομαι logizomai (3023)
νοέω noeō (3401)
νομίζω nomizō (3406)
ὑπολαμβάνω hupolambanō (5112)
ὑπονοέω huponoeō (5120)
φρονέω phroneō (5262)

הִנֵּה hinnēh (2079), Behold! (Gn 37:7, 40:16, 41:1,17).

1. **οἰέσθω** oiesthō 3sing impr pres mid
2. **οἰόμενοι** oiomenoi nom pl masc part pres mid

2	supposing to add affliction to my bonds:	Phlp 1:16
1	For let not that man think that he shall receive	Jas 1:7

This verb, found quite often in classical Greek from the time of Homer, occurs only three times in the New Testament. In John 21:25 the author of the Gospel supposes that if all the deeds of Jesus were written down the world could not contain the books that would be so generated. In Philippians 1:16 Paul spoke of those who "preach Christ of contention, not sincerely, *supposing*" that jealousy or some other base response would torment Paul in his prison bondage. Finally, in James 1:7 *oiomai* was used by James when he wrote that no one should suppose ("think," KJV) he will receive an answer to his prayer, when he does not ask in faith.

STRONG 3633, BAUER 562, MOULTON-MILLIGAN 444 (see "oimai"), LIDDELL-SCOTT 1208-9.

3497. οἷος hoios rel-pron

Such as, what kind, what sort, what manner of.

1. **οἷον** hoion nom/acc sing masc/neu
2. **οἷος** hoios nom sing masc
3. **οἷοι** hoioi nom pl masc
4. **οἵους** hoious acc pl masc
5. **οἵα** hoia nom sing fem
6. **οἵου** hoiou gen sing neu
7. **οἷα** hoia nom/acc pl neu

5	**such as** was not since the beginning of the world	Matt 24:21
7	as snow; **so as** no fuller on earth can white them	Mark 9:3
5	**such as** was not from the beginning of the creation	13:19
6	Ye know not **what manner** of spirit ye are of	Luke 9:55
1	as **though** the word of God hath taken none effect	Rom 9:6
2	**As** is the earthy, such are they also that are earthy:	1 Co 15:48
2	and **as** is the heavenly, such are they also	15:48
3	Let such an one think this, that, **such as** we are	2 Co 10:11
4	I shall not find you **such as** I would,	12:20
1	and that I shall be found unto you **such as**	12:20
1	Having the same conflict **which** ye saw in me,	Phlp 1:30
3	as ye know **what manner** of men we were among	1 Th 1:5
7	afflictions, **which** came unto me at Antioch,	2 Tm 3:11
4	at Lystra; **what** persecutions I endured:	3:11
2	**such as** was not since men were upon the earth,	Rev 16:18

This word (as well as the forms *hoia* and *hoion*) is a relative pronoun frequently used in comparisons and thus it is difficult to illustrate in English. In Matthew 24:21 and Mark 13:19 the word is used to describe the extent of the "great tribulation" that is to come upon the world in the last days. In Mark 9:3 it is used to indicate the degree to which Jesus' garments shone. According to Thayer, Paul used it with two negative particles to indicate that "the thing (state of the case) is not such as this, that the word of God hath fallen to the ground" (*Greek-English Lexicon*; cf. Romans 9:6). In 1 Corinthians 15:48 it enabled Paul to parallel the "earthy" with "they . . . that are earthy" and the "heavenly" with "they . . . that are heavenly." In 2 Corinthians 10:11 it enabled the apostle to say "such as we are in word by letters . . . such *will we be* also in deed when we are present." In 2 Corinthians 12:20 the word occurs again in a coordinated comparison, allowing the apostle to make the contrast effectively, "*such as* I would . . . *such as* ye would not." In 1 Thessalonians 1:5 KJV translates the word "*what manner*" and in 2 Timothy 3:11 as "what" in the sense of "how great were." In Revelation 16:18 the word is used to describe the extent of an earthquake as "*such as* was not since men were upon the earth."

In Philippians 1:30 it functions as a straightforward relative pronoun, translated "which." The word also occurs in some manuscripts of Luke 9:55 and John 5:5.

STRONG 3634, BAUER 562, MOULTON-MILLIGAN 444, LIDDELL-SCOTT 1209.

3498. ὀκνέω okneō verb

To hesitate, shrink from, delay.

מָנַע mānaʽ (4661), Withhold, keep back; niphal: let hinder (Nm 22:16).

עָצֵל 'ātsēl (6338), Niphal: hesitate (Jgs 18:9).

1. ὀκνῆσαι oknēsai inf aor act
2. ὀκνήσῃς oknēsēs 2sing subj aor act

1 desiring him that he would not delay to come....... Acts 9:38

In nonbiblical contexts this term is used to express the attitude of unwillingness to act, an attitude that halts or holds a person in check (cf. *Liddell-Scott*). *Okneō* is used in the Septuagint in a similar manner. Both Numbers 22:16 and Judges 18:9 are common examples of exhortations to come/go without "hesitation" or "hindrance."

The only New Testament occurrence is in Acts 9:38. The disciples from Lydda, when they heard Peter was near, sent two men to him and urged him: "Please come to us without *delay*" (RSV).

STRONG 3635, BAUER 563, MOULTON-MILLIGAN 444-45, LIDDELL-SCOTT 1212.

3499. ὀκνηρός oknēros adj

Timid, shrinking back from, causing reluctance, troublesome.

SYNONYM:
νωθρός nōthros (3438)

עָצֵל 'ātsēl (6339), Sluggard (Prv 6:6,9, 20:4, 26:13ff.).
עַצְלוּת 'atslûth (6341), Idleness (Prv 31:27 [31:26]).

1. ὀκνηρέ oknēre voc sing masc
2. ὀκνηροί oknēroi nom pl masc
3. ὀκνηρόν oknēron nom/acc sing neu

1 Thou wicked and **slothful** servant,................. Matt 25:26
2 Not **slothful** in business; fervent in spirit;.......... Rom 12:11
3 to me indeed is not **grievous**, but for you it is safe...Phlp 3:1

Classical Greek and Septuagint Usage

Friedrich Hauck defines *oknēros* as "hesitating, anxious, negligent, slothful" (*oknēros*, *Kittel*, 5:166). In the classical era it described one who was slow to act. The Septuagint writers state that the *oknēros* man "lacks the resolve to get to work (Proverbs 6:6,9) . . . lets inconvenience stop him (Proverbs 20:4), or . . . never moves on from the will to the deed (Proverbs 21:25)" (ibid., 5:167).

New Testament Usage

In Matthew 25:26 the servant is called "slothful" ("lazy," NIV) because of his failure to invest that which was committed to him during his master's absence. Verses 24 and 25 indicate that the servant "knew" his master, yet failed to obey and make good use of the opportunity presented to him by his master. The first two servants were called "good and faithful" (verses 21,23) because they made the most of their opportunity for their master's sake, while the "lazy" servant was worried only about his own welfare.

In Romans 12:9ff. Paul urged believers to express their love of God through various activities: "Never *be lacking* in zeal, but keep your spiritual fervor, serving the Lord" (verse 11, NIV).

In Philippians 3:1 Paul told the believers that, "To write the same things to you . . . is not *grievous*." In other words Paul did not hesitate and was not bothered by the idea of reminding them again of things previously said; he knew that such repetition has preventative benefit.

STRONG 3636, BAUER 563, MOULTON-MILLIGAN 445, KITTEL 5:166-67, LIDDELL-SCOTT 1212.

3500. ὀκταήμερος oktaēmeros adj

Eighth day.

1. ὀκταήμερος oktaēmeros nom sing masc

1 Circumcised the **eighth day**, of the stock of Israel,... Phlp 3:5

Two words *oktō* (3501), "eight," and *hēmera* (2232), meaning "day," are combined to mean "eighth day." *Oktaēmeros* is used only once in the New Testament where Paul referred to himself as "circumcised the *eighth day*" (Philippians 3:5), as God had commanded (Genesis 17:12; cf. Joshua 5:2-5).

STRONG 3637, BAUER 563, MOULTON-MILLIGAN 445, LIDDELL-SCOTT 1212.

3501. ὀκτώ oktō num

Eight.

1. ὀκτώ oktō card

1 And when **eight** days were accomplished............Luke 2:21
1 And it came to pass about an **eight** days after these.... 9:28
1 **eighteen**, upon whom the tower in Siloam fell,......... 13:4
1 which had a spirit of infirmity **eighteen** years,.......... 13:11
1 lo, these **eighteen** years, be loosed from this bond..... 13:16
1 who had been thirty-eight years (NASB)............ John 5:5
1 after **eight** days again his disciples were within,........ 20:26
1 AEneas, which had kept his bed **eight** years,........ Acts 9:33
1 not more than **eight** or ten days (NASB).............. 25:6
1 few, that is, **eight** souls were saved by water......... 1 Pt 3:20

Oktō, the common term for the number "eight," is indeclinable. The number "eight" does not seem to have any special significance in the Bible. However there were several significant events that used the number "eight."

In the Old Testament Hebrew male children were circumcised on the "eighth day" after birth (Genesis 17:12; Leviticus 12:3; Luke 1:59; 2:21; Philippians 3:5) and the final gathering for the Feast of Tabernacles was also on the eighth day (Leviticus 23:36). Noah's ark carried eight people (cf. 1 Peter 3:2).

The word is used 10 times in the New Testament: 6 times to express the number "eight" (e.g., Luke 2:21; 9:28; John 20:26; Acts 9:33; 25:6; 1 Peter 3:20); 3 times in conjunction with *deka* (1171), "ten," to express the number 18 (e.g., Luke 13:4,11,16); and once in conjunction with *triakonta* (4984), "thirty," to express the number 38 (e.g., John 5:5).

STRONG 3638, BAUER 563, MOULTON-MILLIGAN 445, KITTEL 2:692, LIDDELL-SCOTT 1213.

3502. ὄλεθρος olethros noun
Destruction, ruin, death.
COGNATE:
    ὀλοθρεύω olothreuō (3508)
SYNONYMS:
    ἀπώλεια apōleia (677)
    καθαίρεσις kathairesis (2478)
    σύντριμμα suntrimma (4790)

אֵיד 'êdh (344), Disaster (Ob 13).

כָּחַד kāchadh (3701), Be hidden, be destroyed; hiphil: destroy (1 Kgs 13:34).

מְשַׁמָּה meshammāh (5103), Desolation (Ez 6:14).

פַּחַד pachadh (6586), Dread (Prv 1:26).

קִמּוֹשׁ qimmôs (7342), Nettles (Hos 9:6).

שֹׁד shōdh (8160), Violence, devastation (Prv 21:7, Jer 48:3 [31:3]).

שָׁדַד shādhadh (8161), Destroyer (Jer 48:8,32 [31:8,32]).

שְׁמָמָה shemāmāh (8463), Desolation (Ez 14:16).

1. ὄλεθρος olethros nom sing masc
2. ὄλεθρον olethron acc sing masc

2 unto Satan for the **destruction** of the flesh,..........1 Co 5:5
1 then sudden **destruction** cometh upon them,..........1 Th 5:3
2 Who shall be punished with everlasting **destruction** .. 2 Th 1:9
2 which drown men in **destruction** and perdition...... 1 Tm 6:9

Classical Greek
The noun *olethros* carries the connotation of sudden destruction, usually involving the loss of life or things. Its cognate forms are similar in meaning: *olothreuō* (3508) means "to destroy"; *exolothreuō* (1826) is an intensive form, meaning "to destroy completely" or "to annihilate"; and *olothreutēs* (3507) is a noun meaning "destroyer." This last form is only found in Christian literature (Hahn, "Destroy," *Colin Brown*, 1:465).

Septuagint Usage
Olethros appears 23 times in the Septuagint and is used to translate eight different Hebrew words. It is often used, especially in the writings of the prophets, to describe the destruction that will result from God's judgment in the last days.

New Testament Usage
This eschatological context is found in two of the four New Testament occurrences of *olethros*. Paul compared the "sudden destruction" that will come with the birth pangs of a woman in labor. Just when men think they are secure, God's judgment will fall, and sinful man will not be able to escape the destruction (1 Thessalonians 5:3). In the second passage, those caught unprepared for Christ's return will suffer "eternal destruction" (*olethron aiōnion*). They shall forever be excluded from the presence of the Lord (2 Thessalonians 1:9).

The most difficult passage containing *olethros* is 1 Corinthians 5:5. Paul delivered a Christian engaged in gross immorality over to Satan "for the destruction of his flesh, that his spirit may be saved in the day of the Lord Jesus" (NASB). Interpretations of this verse have been varied. "In line with ancient ideas of the religio-cultic curse and its effect, Paul obviously believed that the curse will be followed by the (sudden) death of the person thus condemned . . . But the spirit . . . in some unknown way will escape destruction" (Schneider, "olethros," *Kittel* 5:169). Support for this view may be found elsewhere in the New Testament, for example, in Acts 5:1-10 where Ananias and Sapphira fell over dead at the conclusion of Peter's rebuke. Some have taken this passage to refer to a "secret execution" instigated by Paul, while others of a later age used it to justify the torturing and burning of heretics (Hahn, "Destroy," *Colin Brown*, 1:466).

A more moderate view holds that Paul's action was intended to ultimately bring the wayward brother to repentance and restoration to the body of Christ. Although physical death was a possibility (cf. Acts 5), the "destruction" was more in line with the events in the life of Job. First Corinthians 5:11,13 help clarify Paul's intent. The believers were neither to keep company nor to eat with such a person. They were to "put away from among yourselves that wicked man" (verse 13). Dismissed from membership in God's congregation and devoid of the community of faith's redeeming influence, he would be exposed to the full brunt of Satan's attack. Should he continue in the incestuous relationship, sure self-destruction would follow. Those who hold this view speculate that the one restored to fellowship in 2 Corinthians 2:5-10 is the same individual (ibid., 1:466f.).

First Thessalonians 5 contains an apocalyptic section detailing the *destruction* (verse 3), darkness (verse 4), and wrath (verse 9) coming upon those who do not know the salvation that is through the Lord Jesus Christ. Second Thessalonians 1:9 describes the *destruction* that will come to those who neither know God nor the gospel of Jesus (verse 8).

The last reference to *olethros* is found in 1 Timothy 6:9 where those who desire to be rich are caught in temptations and snares that ultimately lead to their ruin and destruction. This fate seems to be realized in this present life, although such individuals are candidates for the "eternal destruction" mentioned earlier.

STRONG 3639, BAUER 563, MOULTON-MILLIGAN 445, KITTEL 5:168-69, LIDDELL-SCOTT 1213-14, COLIN BROWN 1:465-67.

3502B. ὀλιγοπιστία oligopistia noun
Little faith.
CROSS-REFERENCES:
ὀλίγος oligos (3504)
πιστεύω pisteuō (3961)

1. ὀλιγοπιστίαν **oligopistian** acc sing fem

1 you have so little faith. (NIV) .... Matt 17:20

A rare compound of *oligos* (3504), "little," and *pistis* (3963), "faith," *oligopistia* means "little faith." This noun occurs only in Christian writings (*Bauer*) and in the New Testament only in Matthew 17:20. Elsewhere in the Synoptic Gospels the related adjective *oligopistos* (3503) (e.g., Matthew 6:30; 8:26) is used. Byzantine sources tend to substitute *oligopistia* with the more common *apistia* (565), "unbelief." However, Jesus could not have meant the latter in Matthew 17:20. "Little faith" was precisely what Jesus meant, rather than "no faith."

BAUER 563, KITTEL 6:174-228.

3503. ὀλιγόπιστος oligopistos adj
One of little faith, lacking trust.

CROSS-REFERENCES:
ὀλίγος oligos (3504)
πιστεύω pisteuō (3961)

1. ὀλιγόπιστε **oligopiste** voc sing masc
2. ὀλιγόπιστοι **oligopistoi** nom pl masc

2 not much more clothe you, O ye of little faith? ...... Matt 6:30
2 Why are ye fearful, O ye of little faith? 8:26
1 O thou of little faith, wherefore didst thou doubt? 14:31
2 ye of little faith, why reason ye among yourselves, ... 16:8
2 much more will he clothe you, O ye of little faith? Luke 12:28

Oligopistos occurs in the New Testament only in the Synoptic Gospels. It is an adjective composed of two words, *oligos* (3504), "small," and *pistis* (3963), "faith," hence, "little faith." Matthew 6:30 and Luke 12:28 use it to describe the disciples collectively in contexts where they were urged not to be anxious. Matthew related Jesus' use of it in addressing the disciples. When they feared the winds and the sea (8:26); when Peter, fearfully sinking into the sea, cried: "Lord, save me" (14:31); and when the disciples, in confusion and bewilderment over a command of Jesus, were unable to understand (16:8), the Master addressed them as "ye (plural) of little faith."

STRONG 3640, BAUER 563, MOULTON-MILLIGAN 445, KITTEL 6:174-228, LIDDELL-SCOTT 1214.

3504. ὀλίγος oligos adj
Little, small, short, few.
COGNATES:
ὀλιγόπιστος oligopistos (3503)
ὀλιγόψυχος oligopsuchos (3505)
ὀλιγοπιστία oligopistia (3502B)
ὀλίγως oligōs (3506B)
SYNONYM:
μικρός mikros (3262)

אֶחָד 'echādh (259), One; few (Gn 29:20—Sixtine Edition only).

אֶפֶס 'ephes (675), End, only; something left (2 Kgs 14:26—Codex Vaticanus only).

מִזְעָר mizʻār (4347), Few (Is 24:6).

מְעַט meʻaṭ (4746), Small, little (Nm 26:56, Prv 6:10, Hg 1:6).

מִצְעָר mitsʻār (4867), Few (2 Chr 24:24); insignificant (Jb 8:7).

מַת math (5139), A few (Jer 44:28 [51:28]).

1. ὀλίγον **oligon** nom/acc sing masc/neu
2. ὀλίγῳ **oligō** dat sing masc/neu
3. ὀλίγος **oligos** nom sing masc
4. ὀλίγου **oligou** gen sing masc
5. ὀλίγοι **oligoi** nom pl masc
6. ὀλίγων **oligōn** gen pl masc

7. ὀλίγοις **oligois** dat pl masc
8. ὀλίγης **oligēs** gen sing fem
9. ὀλίγην **oligēn** acc sing fem
10. ὀλίγαι **oligai** nom pl fem
11. ὀλίγας **oligas** acc pl fem
12. ὀλίγα **oliga** nom/acc pl neu

5	narrow is the way, ... and **few** there be that find it.	Matt 7:14
5	harvest ... is plenteous, but the labourers are **few**;	9:37
12	And they said, Seven, and **a few** little fishes.	15:34
5	for many be called, but **few** chosen.	20:16
5	For many are called, but **few** are chosen.	22:14
12	thou hast been faithful over **a few things**,	25:21
12	thou hast been faithful over **a few things**,	25:23
1	And when he had gone **a little** farther thence,	Mark 1:19
7	save that he laid his hands upon **a few** sick folk,	6:5
1	apart into a desert place, and rest **a while**:	6:31
12	And they had **a few** small fishes: and he blessed,	8:7
1	that he would thrust out **a little** from the land.	Luke 5:3
1	to whom **little** is forgiven, the same loveth **little**.	7:47
1	to whom **little** is forgiven, the same loveth **little**.	7:47
5	harvest truly is great, but the labourers are **few**:	10:2
11	shall be beaten with **few** stripes.	12:48
5	Lord, are there **few** that be saved?	13:23
3	there was no **small** stir among the soldiers,	Acts 12:18
1	they abode long time with the disciples. (NT)	14:28
8	no **small** dissension and disputation with them,	15:2
10	and of the chief women not **a few**.	17:4
5	women which were Greeks, and of men, not **a few**.	17:12
3	same time there arose no **small** stir about that way.	19:23
9	brought no **small** gain unto the craftsmen;	19:24
2	Almost thou persuadest me to be a Christian.	26:28
2	that whether in **a short** or long time, (NASB)	26:29
4	and no **small** tempest lay on us,	27:20
1	and he that had gathered **little** had no lack.	2 Co 8:15
2	by revelation ... as I wrote afore in **few words**,	Eph 3:3
1	For bodily exercise profiteth **little**:	1 Tm 4:8
2	but use **a little** wine for thy stomach's sake	5:23
11	**a few** days chastened us after their own pleasure;	Heb 12:10
1	Even so the tongue is **a little** member,	Jas 3:5
1	It is even a vapour, that appeareth for **a little** time,	4:14
1	though now **for a season**, if need be,	1 Pt 1:6
10	**few**, that is, eight souls were saved by water.	3:20
1	after that ye have suffered **a while**,	5:10
6	I have written **briefly**, exhorting, and testifying	5:12
12	But I have **a few things** against thee,	Rev 2:14
12	Notwithstanding I have **a few things** against thee,	2:20
12	Thou hast **a few** names even in Sardis	3:4
1	because he knoweth that he hath but **a short** time.	12:12
1	when he cometh, he must continue **a short space**.	17:10

The meaning of this word is consistent throughout classical Greek, Koine, and the New Testament. In the Septuagint it is usually a translation of $m^{e^c}a\underline{t}$. It can refer to size, quantity, degree, or time. Often the use of *oligos* is in a contrast between small and large, little and great, few and many.

In 1 Peter 3:20 "few" refers to eight people. With this word, Jesus stressed that His listeners needed to be careful that they were not among the many in the world who would not enter the kingdom of heaven (Matthew 7:14; 22:14). Believers need to appreciate how much Christ has forgiven them (Luke 7:47) and pray that God will add to the "few" laborers already working in the harvest (Luke 10:2). Thanks be to God who will only let His people suffer from Satan's pressures a "short" while (1 Peter 1:6; 5:10; Revelation 12:12).

STRONG 3641, BAUER 563-64, MOULTON-MILLIGAN 445, KITTEL 5:171-73, LIDDELL-SCOTT 1215, COLIN BROWN 2:427-28.

3505. ὀλιγόψυχος oligopsuchos adj

Discouraged, fainthearted.

CROSS-REFERENCES:
ὀλίγος oligos (3504)
ψυχή psuchē (5425)

מָהַר māhar (4257), Hurry; niphal: be fearful (Is 35:4).

1. ὀλιγοψύχους **oligopsuchous** acc pl masc

1	comfort the **feebleminded**, support the weak,	1 Th 5:14

Oligos (3504), "small," and *psuchē* (5425), signifying "soul" or "life principle," are combined to form an adjective that occurs in the New Testament only in 1 Thessalonians 5:14. There Paul exhorted the brethren not only to show respect to the hard workers among them (verse 12), but to "warn those who are idle, encourage the *timid* ('feebleminded,' KJV; 'fainthearted,' RSV), help the weak, be patient with everyone" (NIV). These general exhortations were given by Paul as instructions for those who would live peaceable, effectual lives while being sanctified "through and through" (verse 23, NIV).

STRONG 3642, BAUER 564, MOULTON-MILLIGAN 445, KITTEL 9:665-66, LIDDELL-SCOTT 1215, COLIN BROWN 3:687.

3506. ὀλιγωρέω oligōreō verb

Think lightly of, to despise, care little for.

מָאַס mā'as (4128), Despise (Prv 3:11).

1. ὀλιγώρει **oligōrei** 2sing impr pres act

1	**despise** not thou the chastening of the Lord,	Heb 12:5

This term is a compound of *oligos* (3504), "little" or "small," and *hōra* (5443), "care" or "concern," hence, "care little for." The single New Testament use of this compound is Hebrews 12:5, a quotation of Proverbs 3:11 where the Hebrew term may be translated "despise." Since the discipline is from the Almighty, a human can hardly reject or refuse it. One might, however, "despise, think lightly of," or "scorn having to accept" the Lord's discipline. Even this is warned against.

STRONG 3643, BAUER 564, MOULTON-MILLIGAN 445-46, LIDDELL-SCOTT 1215, COLIN BROWN 1:462.

3506B. ὀλίγως oligōs adv
Little, scarcely, barely.
CROSS-REFERENCE:
   ὀλίγος oligos (3504)

1. ὀλίγως oligōs
1 those who **barely escape** from the ones (NASB) . . . . . 2 Pt 2:18

This adverb can be found in classical Greek from the Fifth Century B.C. meaning "little, scarcely, barely." It is related to the verb *oligōreō* (3506) and occurs once in some manuscripts at 2 Peter 2:18 (the *Textus Receptus* uses *ontōs* [3552], "really, certainly"). Peter used it to describe new converts who had "barely escaped" the bondage of this world and were still vulnerable to the enticements of false teachers. This verse still offers strong implications for establishing new Christians in orthodox doctrine.

BAUER 564, MOULTON-MILLIGAN 446, LIDDELL-SCOTT 1215.

3507. ὀλοθρευτής olothreutēs noun
Destroyer.
CROSS-REFERENCE:
   ὀλοθρεύω olothreuō (3508)

1. ὀλοθρευτοῦ olothreutou gen sing masc
1 murmured, and were **destroyed of the destroyer** . . . . 1 Co 10:10

This word is used only in Christian writings (*Bauer*) and in the New Testament only at 1 Corinthians 10:10. It is related to the verb *olethreuō* (*olothreuō* [3508] in the New Testament) which means "to destroy, ruin, or slay."

The participle of this verb is used in the Septuagint at Exodus 12:23, and by the New Testament writer of Hebrews 11:28. The Hebrew of Exodus 12:23 is the hiphil participle of *shāchath*, "to ruin, spoil, destroy."

Paul referred to the rebels of Moses' day, such as Korah in Numbers 16, as being killed under God's judgment by a "destroyer" that He sent. In 1 Chronicles 21:12,15 it was a "destroying angel" the Lord sent to punish many Israelites for David's sin. The rabbis believed there was a specific destroying angel which they called *mashchîth* (Schneider, "olethreuō," *Kittel*, 5:168).

STRONG 3644, BAUER 564, MOULTON-MILLIGAN 446, KITTEL 5:169-70, LIDDELL-SCOTT 1217, COLIN BROWN 1:465.

3508. ὀλοθρεύω olothreuō verb
Destroy, spoil.
COGNATES:
   ἐξολοθρεύω exolothreuō (1826)
   ὄλεθρος olethros (3502)
   ὀλοθρευτής olothreutēs (3507)
   ὅλος holos (3513)
SYNONYMS:
   ἀνατρέπω anatrepō (394)
   ἀπόλλυμι apollumi (616)
   ἀφανίζω aphanizō (846)
   διαφθείρω diaphtheirō (1305)
   καθαιρέω kathaireō (2479)
   καταλύω kataluō (2617)
   καταργέω katargeō (2643)
   καταστρέφω katastrephō (2660)
   καταφθείρω kataphtheirō (2673)
   κενόω kenoō (2729)
   λύω luō (3061)
   πορθέω portheō (4058)
   φθείρω phtheirō (5188)

יָרַשׁ yārash (3542), Hiphil: drive out (Jos 3:10).
כָּרַת kārath (3901), Qal: cut down (Jgs 6:25); pual: be cut down (Jgs 6:28); hiphil: be cut off (Nm 4:18).
עָכַר ʿākhar (6138), Bring trouble on (Jos 7:25).
שָׁדַד shādhadh (8161), Destroy (Jer 5:6, 25:36 [32:22]).
שָׁחַת shāchath (8271), Hiphil: destroyer (Jer 22:7).
שָׁמַד shāmadh (8436), Hiphil: destroy (Hg 2:22 [2:23]—Codex Vaticanus only).

1. ὀλοθρεύων olothreuōn nom sing masc part pres act
2. ὀλεθρεύων olethreuōn nom sing masc part pres act
1 he that **destroyed the firstborn** should touch them . . . Heb 11:28

The verb *olathreuō* is related to *apollumi*, which is a strengthened form of *ollumi*, meaning "to destroy utterly." But, where *apollumi* can refer to various kinds of "ruin," *olothreuō* is usually found in references to the destruction of man, especially in the sense of slaying.

The verb *olothreuō* occurs frequently in the Septuagint with regard to "destroying" someone (cf. Exodus 12:23; Joshua 7:25). In the New Testament it appears only as a participle, "the destroyer." The writer to the Hebrews (11:28) recalled the initial Passover when the Lord offered to safeguard Israel from His agent of death, "the destroyer," when he entered all the houses of Egypt "to destroy" their firstborn (cf. Exodus 12:29).

STRONG 3645, BAUER 564, LIDDELL-SCOTT 1217, COLIN BROWN 1:465.

3509. ὁλοκαύτωμα

holokautōma noun

Whole burnt offering.

אִשֶּׁה 'ishsheh (829), Offering by fire (Ex 30:20, Lv 5:12, 23:25).

זֶבַח zevach (2160), Sacrifice (Ex 10:25—Codex Vaticanus only).

כָּלִיל kālîl (3752), A whole burnt offering (Ps 51:19 [50:19]).

מִנְחָה minchāh (4647), Sacrifice (Jos 22:23).

עוֹלָה 'ôlāh (5984), Burnt offering (Lv 9:13f., 2 Chr 7:7, Ez 45:15).

1. ὁλοκαυτωμάτων holokautōmatōn gen pl neu
2. ὁλοκαυτώματα holokautōmata nom/acc pl neu

1 more than all whole **burnt** offerings and sacrifices. Mark 12:33
2 In burnt offerings and sacrifices for sin............ Heb 10:6
2 Sacrifice and offering and **burnt** offerings.............. 10:8

This term is a combination of *holos* (3513), an adjective signifying "whole," and *kautos*, "burnt offering." Mark 12:33 and Hebrews 10:6,8 use it in contexts that point back to the Old Testament sacrificial system (see 1 Samuel 15:22; Hosea 6:6; and Psalm 40:6-8, respectively).

The *holokautōma*, "whole burnt offering," of the old covenant was utterly consumed by fire as an expression of the worshiper's exaltation of God and complete dedication to God (Leviticus 1:3,6,10ff. are illustrative). The burnt offering could follow a sin offering or a guilt (trespass, penalty) offering to indicate reconsecration of the sinner's life to God.

Strong 3646, Bauer 564, Moulton-Milligan 446, Liddell-Scott 1217, Colin Brown 3:417,421,430,434.

3510. ὁλοκληρία holoklēria noun

Soundness, wholeness.

Cross-References:
κληρόω klēroō (2793)
ὅλος holos (3513)

מְתֹם mᵉthōm (5149), Soundness (Is 1:6—Sixtine Edition only).

1. ὁλοκληρίαν holoklērian acc sing fem

1 **perfect soundness** in the presence of you all......... Acts 3:16

A compound of *holos* (3513), "whole, entire," or "complete," and a form of *klēros* (2792), "lot" or that "portion" assigned by lot, *holoklēria* means "soundness or wholeness in all parts." The term occurs only once in the New Testament at Acts 3:16 where one who was lame from birth (3:2) "received strength" (verse 7) so his legs were completely restored and began to function properly. He experienced "perfect soundness" or "complete healing" in his physical person.

Strong 3647, Bauer 564, Moulton-Milligan 446, Kittel 3:767, Liddell-Scott 1217.

3511. ὁλόκληρος holoklēros adj

Complete, sound, perfect, entire.

Cognates:
κληρόω klēroō (2793)
ὅλος holos (3513)

Synonyms:
ἀμφότεροι amphoteroi (295)
ἅπας hapas (532A)
ὅλος holos (3513)
πᾶς pas (3817B)

נָצַב nātsav (5507), Stand; niphal: be healthy (Zec 11:16).

שָׁלֵם shālēm (8400), Whole, uncut (Dt 27:6, Jos 8:31 [9:2]).

תָּמִים tāmîm (8879), Complete, whole (Lv 23:15, Ez 15:5).

1. ὁλόκληροι holoklēroi nom pl masc
2. ὁλόκληρον holoklēron nom/acc sing neu

2 I pray God your **whole** spirit and soul and body..... 1 Th 5:23
1 ye may be perfect and entire, wanting nothing........ Jas 1:4

Classical Greek and Septuagint Usage

A compound of *holos* (3513), "whole, entire, complete," and the noun *klēros* (2792), "lot" or "that which is assigned by lot, portion," *holoklēros* essentially means "complete, entire," or "perfect." In the Septuagint the term describes that which was "whole" (as Deuteronomy 27:6, "unhewn [literally 'whole'] stones"), with no parts missing (cf. Ezekiel 15:5, "whole"; Zechariah 11:16, "healthy"). On occasion with reference to a male (man or animals) the term means "uncastrated" (see *Liddell-Scott*).

New Testament Usage

The term is found twice in the New Testament. Paul used this qualitative adjective in a prayer in 1 Thessalonians 5:23. The Revised Standard Version translates the clause: "May your spirit and soul and body be kept *sound*." In this verse *holoklēros* modifies all three terms "spirit and soul and body."

In James 1:4 our Lord's brother reminded his readers that perseverance makes the individual "mature and *complete*, not lacking anything" (NIV). What constitutes "complete" or how one will be "not lacking anything" is not stated.

However, both words ("mature and complete") must be considered together in light of James' emphasis on "works" as the necessary evidence of real faith (cf. 2:14). James desired that through prayer (1:5) and perseverance (1:4) every believer would mature into someone lacking no Christian virtue.

STRONG 3648, BAUER 564, MOULTON-MILLIGAN 446, KITTEL 3:766-67, LIDDELL-SCOTT 1217.

3512. ὀλολύζω ololuzō verb
Cry out with a loud voice, wail, lament aloud.
CROSS-REFERENCE:
  ὅλος holos (3513)

יָלַל yālal (3321), Hiphil: wail, howl (Is 15:3, Jer 48:20 [31:20], Zec 11:2).

צְוָחָה ts⁽ᵉ⁾wāchāh (6945), Outcry (Is 24:11).

1. ὀλολύζοντες ololuzontes nom pl masc part pres act
1 ye rich men, weep and **howl** for your miseries........Jas 5:1

Classical Greek and Septuagint Usage
In classical Greek *ololuzō* means "cry with a loud voice" (especially in Homeric literature of "women crying aloud to the gods in prayer or thanksgiving," *Liddell-Scott*). *Ololuzō* can be found in the Septuagint exclusively in the prophetic literature where it usually translates the Hebrew term *yālal*, meaning "howl." It is used most frequently in Isaiah where "howling" is an expression of lament: "*Howl* ye, for the day of the LORD is at hand" (Isaiah 13:6; cf. 14:31; 15:2; Amos 8:3).

New Testament Usage
In the New Testament the only occurrence of the onomatopoeic verb *ololuzō* is also in a negative context (James 5:1, NIV), where "to cry with a loud voice" is well expressed as "to wail." Those who become rich at the expense of their hired workers and commit other sins against innocent ones (cf. 5:4-6) face the prospect of weeping and wailing when they endure the misery that is coming upon them as judgment from the Lord (verses 1,4).

STRONG 3649, BAUER 564, MOULTON-MILLIGAN 446, KITTEL 5:173-74, LIDDELL-SCOTT 1217.

3513. ὅλος holos adj
Whole, complete, entire.
COGNATES:
  καθολικός katholikos (2498B)
  καθόλου katholou (2499)
  ὀλοθρεύω olothreuō (3508)
  ὁλοκαύτωμα holokautōma (3509)
  ὁλοκληρία holoklēria (3510)
  ὁλόκληρος holoklēros (3511)
  ὀλολύζω ololuzō (3512)
  ὁλοτελής holotelēs (3514)
  ὅλως holōs (3517)
SYNONYMS:
  ἀμφότεροι amphoteroi (295)
  ἅπας hapas (532A)
  ὁλόκληρος holoklēros (3511)
  πᾶς pas (3817B)

כֹּל kōl (3725), All, whole (Dt 6:5, 1 Kgs 6:10, Ps 56:1f. [55:1f.]).

כָּלִיל kālîl (3752), All, solid (Ex 28:31 [28:27], 39:22 [36:30], Nm 4:6).

תָּמִים tāmîm (8879), Full (Lv 25:30).

1. ὅλον holon nom/acc sing masc/neu
2. ὅλου holou gen sing masc/neu
3. ὅλῳ holō dat sing masc/neu
4. ὅλος holos nom sing masc
5. ὅλους holous acc pl masc
6. ὅλη holē nom sing fem
7. ὅλης holēs gen sing fem
8. ὅλῃ holē dat sing fem
9. ὅλην holēn acc sing fem

1 Now **all** this was done, that it might be fulfilled.....Matt 1:22
9 And Jesus went about **all** Galilee, teaching............ 4:23
9 And his fame went throughout **all** Syria:.............. 4:24
1 not that thy **whole** body should be cast into hell....... 5:29
1 not that thy **whole** body should be cast into hell....... 5:30
1 thy **whole** body shall be full of light................... 6:22
1 thy **whole** body shall be full of darkness............... 6:23
9 And the fame hereof went abroad into **all** that land..... 9:26
8 spread abroad his fame in **all** that country............. 9:31
1 and hid in ... meal, till the **whole** was leavened....... 13:33
9 they sent out into **all** that country round about,...... 14:35
1 if he shall gain the **whole** world,..................... 16:26
9 Why stand ye here **all** the day idle?................... 20:6
1 **All** this was done, that it might be fulfilled........... 21:4
8 love the Lord thy God with **all** thy heart,............. 22:37
8 and with **all** thy soul, and with **all** thy mind........ 22:37
8 and with **all** thy soul, and with **all** thy mind........ 22:37
4 On these two commandments hang **all** the law.......... 22:40
8 in **all** the world for a witness unto all nations;........ 24:14
3 this gospel shall be preached in the **whole** world,...... 26:13
1 **all** this was done, that the scriptures ... fulfilled.... 26:56
1 **all** the council, sought false witness against Jesus,... 26:59
9 and gathered unto him the **whole** band of soldiers...... 27:27
9 throughout **all** the region round about Galilee......Mark 1:28
6 And **all** the city was gathered together at the door..... 1:33
9 And he preached ... throughout **all** Galilee,............ 1:39
9 And ran through that **whole** region round about,........ 6:55
1 shall gain the **whole** world, and lose his own soul?..... 8:36
7 shalt love the Lord thy God with **all** thy heart,....... 12:30
7 with **all** thy soul, and with **all** thy mind,........... 12:30
7 with **all** thy soul, and with **all** thy mind,........... 12:30
7 with **all** thy mind, and with **all** thy strength:....... 12:30
7 And to love him with **all** the heart,.................... 12:33
7 all the heart, and with **all** the understanding,......... 12:33
7 and with **all** the soul, and with **all** the strength,... 12:33
7 and with **all** the soul, and with **all** the strength,... 12:33
1 did cast in all that she had, even **all** her living....... 12:44
1 gospel ... be preached throughout the **whole** world,.... 14:9
1 chief priests and **all** the council sought for witness.... 14:55
1 with the elders and scribes and the **whole** council,..... 15:1
9 and they call together the **whole** band................. 15:16
9 darkness over the **whole** land until the ninth hour...... 15:33

8	abroad throughout **all** the hill country of Judaea	Luke 1:65
7	a fame of him through **all** the region round about	4:14
7	have toiled **all** the night, and have taken nothing:	5:5
8	rumour of him went forth throughout **all** Judaea,	7:17
9	and published throughout the **whole** city	8:39
1	which had spent **all** her living upon physicians,	8:43
1	if he gain the **whole** world, and lose himself,	9:25
7	shalt love the Lord thy God with **all** thy heart,	10:27
7	and with **all** thy soul, and with all thy strength,	10:27
7	and with all thy soul, and with **all** thy strength,	10:27
7	and with all thy strength, and with **all** thy mind;	10:27
1	thy **whole** body also is full of light;	11:34
1	If thy **whole** body therefore be full of light,	11:36
1	the **whole** shall be full of light,	11:36
1	woman took and hid ... till the **whole** was leavened.	13:21
7	teaching throughout **all** Jewry,	23:5
9	a darkness over **all** the earth until the ninth hour	23:44
6	and himself believed, and his **whole** house	John 4:53
1	made a man every whit **whole** on the sabbath day?	7:23
4	Thou wast **altogether** born in sins,	9:34
1	and that the **whole** nation perish not.	11:50
4	but is clean **every whit**: and ye are clean,	13:10
2	without seam, woven from the top **throughout**.	19:23
1	and it filled **all** the house where they were sitting.	Acts 2:2
1	and having favour with **all** the people.	2:47
9	And great fear came upon **all** the church,	5:11
1	made him governor over Egypt and **all** his house.	7:10
9	Now there came a dearth over **all** the land of Egypt	7:11
7	If thou believest with **all** thine heart, thou mayest.	8:37
7	Then had the churches rest throughout **all** Judaea	9:31
7	And it was known throughout **all** Joppa;	9:42
2	of good report among **all** the nation of the Jews,	10:22
7	which was published throughout **all** Judaea,	10:37
1	it came to pass, that a **whole** year they assembled	11:26
9	should be great dearth throughout **all** the world:	11:28
9	through the **whole** island (NASB)	13:6
7	was published throughout **all** the region.	13:49
8	the apostles and elders, with the **whole** church,	15:22
3	Crispus, ... believed on the Lord with **all** his house;	18:8
6	whom **all** Asia and the world worshippeth.	19:27
6	And the **whole** city was filled with confusion:	19:29
6	And **all** the city was moved,	21:30
6	that **all** Jerusalem was in an uproar.	21:31
1	commanded the chief priests and **all** their council	22:30
9	Paul dwelt two **whole** years in his own ... house,	28:30
3	faith is spoken of throughout the **whole** world.	Rom 1:8
9	For thy sake we are killed **all** the day long;	8:36
9	**All** day long I have stretched forth my hands	10:21
7	Gaius mine host, and of the **whole** church,	16:23
1	that a little leaven leaveneth the **whole** lump?	1 Co 5:6
1	**whole** body were an eye, where were the hearing?.	12:17
1	the **whole** were hearing, where were the smelling?.	12:17
6	the **whole** church be come together into one place,	14:23
8	with all the saints which are in **all** Achaia:	2 Co 1:1
1	that he is a debtor to do the **whole** law.	Gal 5:3
1	A little leaven leaveneth the **whole** lump.	5:9
3	my bonds in Christ are manifest in **all** the palace,	Phlp 1:13
8	all the brethren which are in **all** Macedonia:	1 Th 4:10
5	who subvert **whole** houses,	Tit 1:11
3	as also Moses was faithful in **all** his house.	Heb 3:2
3	And Moses verily was faithful in **all** his house,	3:5
1	For whosoever shall keep the **whole** law,	Jas 2:10
1	and able also to bridle the **whole** body.	3:2
1	and we turn about their **whole** body.	3:3
1	the tongue ... that it defileth the **whole** body,	3:6
2	but also for the sins of the **whole** world.	1 Jn 2:2
4	and the **whole** world lieth in wickedness.	5:19
7	temptation, which shall come upon **all** the world,	Rev 3:10
6	the **whole** moon turned blood-red (NIV)	6:12
9	and Satan, which deceiveth the **whole** world:	12:9
6	healed: and **all** the world wondered after the beast.	13:3
7	unto the kings of the earth and of the **whole** world,	16:14

Classical Greek

This term (also spelled *oulos*) is used in classical Greek as an adjective meaning "whole, entire," and as an adverb meaning "wholly, completely." It commonly carries the sense of "complete in all its parts" whether used of people, places, or things (*Liddell-Scott*). Examples of its use are "whole" cities, an "utter" blunder, and a "whole" person, i.e., "safe and sound" (ibid.). Occasionally it can also be found as a substantive (i.e., "the universe"), but according to *Bauer* it is never used this way in the New Testament.

Septuagint Usage

Holos nearly always translates *kōl* in the Septuagint, and it is quite common. The word is used of wholeness in terms of quantity (e.g., Genesis 41:43, the whole land; cf. Exodus 5:12) or of wholeness in terms of length of time (Numbers 11:32; 14:1). Entirety of heart and soul is how God is to be served (Deuteronomy 4:29; 6:5).

New Testament Usage

Holos can refer to a technical completeness including every member or aspect of the subject, such as, being "totally" born in sin (John 9:34), being under obligation to keep the "whole" law (Galatians 5:3), or Jesus dying for the "whole" world (1 John 2:2). In fact, *holos* later interchanges with *pas* (3817B).

On the other hand, it can refer to something "in general, on the whole," or "generally," such as *all* Jerusalem being in an uproar (Acts 21:31), a famine being throughout *all* the world (Acts 11:28), a church's faith being proclaimed throughout the *whole* world (Romans 1:8), or the assembling together of the *whole* church (1 Corinthians 14:23). These need not be taken as absolute statements including every member of the group but as referring to the group as a whole, to the majority or its major members, or as including representatives from every part. Many scholars consider Romans 1:8 an example of hyperbole. One must determine from context what was intended by the word. Rarely will it affect the point being made or have theological significance. According to John 7:23 and 13:10 there is great encouragement in the principle that Jesus cleanses and heals the whole person.

STRONG 3650, BAUER 564-65, MOULTON-MILLIGAN 446-47, KITTEL 5:174-75, LIDDELL-SCOTT 1218.

3514. ὁλοτελής holotelēs adj

Complete to the end, perfect, undamaged, wholly, through and through.

CROSS-REFERENCES:
ὅλος holos (3513)
τελέω teleō (4903)

1. ὁλοτελεῖς holoteleis acc pl masc

1 And the very God of peace sanctify you **wholly**;.....1 Th 5:23

In the only New Testament occurrence of this word Paul prayed that God would sanctify the Thessalonian believers *wholly* (1 Thessalonians 5:23). The adjective is a composite of *holos* (3513), "whole," and *telēs*, "end, purpose." Paul's concern was that the sanctification would be complete. In extra-Biblical literature it occurs in "an inscription recording Nero's announcement of 'complete exemption from taxation' " (Bruce, *Word Biblical Commentary*, 45:129).

STRONG 3651, BAUER 565, MOULTON-MILLIGAN 447, KITTEL 5:175-76, LIDDELL-SCOTT 1219.

3515. Ὀλυμπᾶς Olumpas name
Olympas.

1. Ὀλυμπᾶν Olumpan acc masc

1 **Olympas**, and all the saints which are with them....Rom 16:15

Recipient of a greeting from Paul (Romans 16:15).

3516. ὄλυνθος olunthos noun
Late or summer fig, unripe fig.

פַּג pagh (6532), Unripe fig (S/S 2:13).

1. ὀλύνθους olunthous acc pl masc

1 even as a fig tree casteth her **untimely figs**,..........Rev 6:13

This term, used only once in the New Testament, refers to the late summer figs as opposed to the early figs. "The stars of the heavens fell," John said, "even as a fig tree casteth her *untimely figs*, when she is shaken of a mighty wind" (Revelation 6:13). Though this is the only occurrence of the term in the New Testament, it is also found in secular literature and once in the Septuagint (i.e., Song of Songs 2:13).

STRONG 3653, BAUER 565, KITTEL 7:751-57.

3517. ὅλως holōs adv
Wholly, actually, with a negative: (not) at all.
CROSS-REFERENCE:
ὅλος holos (3513)

1. ὅλως holōs

1 But I say unto you, Swear not **at all**;...............Matt 5:34
1 It is reported **commonly** that there is fornication....1 Co 5:1
1 Now therefore there is **utterly** a fault among you,....... 6:7
1 baptized for the dead, if the dead rise not **at all**?...... 15:29

Holōs is the adverbial form of *holos* (3513), the adjective meaning "whole, entire, complete." This adverb has four basic usages, two of which are seen in the New Testament. The four common usages include the basic sense of the term, which is best translated "wholly" or "altogether." The second sense is best translated "on the whole, speaking generally," or "in short." A third sense may translate "actually" or "really" as in 1 Corinthians 5:1 (NIV); 6:7; and 15:29. Finally, the fourth sense, where the term is used with a negative, may be translated "at all" (i.e., not "at all") as in Matthew 5:34.

STRONG 3654, BAUER 565, MOULTON-MILLIGAN 447, LIDDELL-SCOTT 1218.

3518. ὄμβρος ombros noun
Rainstorm, thunderstorm.

שָׂעִיר sāʿîr (7989), Shower (Dt 32:2).

1. ὄμβρος ombros nom sing masc

1 straightway ye say, There cometh a **shower**;........Luke 12:54

This term, which occurs only once in the New Testament at Luke 12:54, denotes a violent rain, even a thunderstorm. In Greek literature *ombros* can also refer to "water" as an element, an "inundation," and, when used metaphorically, of the "storm" of battle (*Liddell-Scott*). The Septuagint uses *ombros* six times, but only once to translate a Hebrew equivalent. In Deuteronomy 32:2 Moses likened his speech to the Israelites to "showers" (NIV), (Hebrew *sāʿîr*).

Jesus used *ombros* when referring to the common phenomena of nature to teach spiritual truths. Drawing upon the weather patterns of the area, He observed, "When ye see a cloud rise out of the west, straightway ye say, There cometh a *shower*" (Luke 12:54).

STRONG 3655, BAUER 565, MOULTON-MILLIGAN 447, LIDDELL-SCOTT 1221, COLIN BROWN 3:1000,1003.

3518B. ὁμείρομαι homeiromai verb
Yearn for, long for.

חָכָה chākhâh (2542), Piel: long for (Jb 3:21).

1. ὁμειρόμενοι homeiromenoi
nom pl masc part pres mid

ὁμιλέω 3519

1 Having thus a fond **affection** for you, (NASB) .... 1 Th 2:8

Classical Greek and Septuagint Usage
Homeiromai is a rare verb with unknown etymology (cf. *Liddell-Scott*). It means to have a kindly feeling or longing for someone (*Bauer*). The Greek Hesychius equated it with the verb *epithumeō* (1922) (Heidland, "homeiromai," *Kittel*, 5:176). Some suggest that it is a nursery word, derived from the root *smer* meaning "remember." The *ho* at the beginning of the word could come from the interjection *ō* (5434), "Oh!" (*Moulton-Milligan*). It is used in the Septuagint to denote a longing for death (Job 3:21) and a longing for God (Psalm 63:1,2 [LXX 62:1,2]). An inscription on a sepulcher records the parents' sorrow for their deceased son, "We greatly desire him" (ibid.).

New Testament Usage
Homeiromai is found in some New Testament manuscripts at 1 Thessalonians 2:8 as a term of endearment, "Being affectionately desirous of you." The *Textus Receptus* has *himeiromai* (2418) instead of *homeiromai*. Some conjecture that this is merely an alternate spelling and that both words mean the same thing.

BAUER 565, MOULTON-MILLIGAN 447, KITTEL 5:176, LIDDELL-SCOTT 1221.

3519. ὁμιλέω homileō verb
Associate with, talk with, speak, converse, or address.

COGNATES:
ὁμιλία homilia (3520)
ὅμιλος homilos (3521)
συνομιλέω sunomileō (4777)

SYNONYMS:
ἀποκρίνω apokrinō (605B)
διαλέγομαι dialegomai (1250)
ἐρεύγομαι ereugomai (2027)
λαλέω laleō (2953)
λέγω legō (2978)
συμβάλλω sumballō (4671)
φθέγγομαι phthengomai (5187)
φωνέω phōneō (5291)

דָּבַר dāvar (1744), Piel: talk (Dn 1:19).
הָגָה hāghāh (1965), Converse (Sir 11:20).
הָלַךְ hālakh (2050), Go (Prv 15:12).
רָוָה rāwâh (7588), Have enough to drink; piel: satisfy (Prv 5:19).

1. ὁμιλεῖν **homilein** inf pres act
2. ὁμιλήσας **homilēsas** nom sing masc part aor act
3. ὡμίλει **hōmilei** 3sing indic imperf act
4. ὡμίλουν **hōmiloun** 3pl indic imperf act

4 And they **talked** together of all these things .... Luke 24:14
1 while they **communed** together and reasoned, ... 24:15
2 and **talked** a long while, even till break of day, ... Acts 20:11
3 sent for him the oftener, and **communed with** him...... 24:26

Classical Greek and Septuagint Usage
In classical Greek the term *homileō* has a variety of usages. Its basic usage is to portray being in company with someone or something. From this basic sense several nuances in meaning can be seen. It is used in a hostile sense when referring to being in battle with an enemy. It is used of social intercourse, sexual intercourse, as well as business interactions. In a physical sense, it refers to plaster being in contact with something. (For specific examples of the above uses, see *Liddell-Scott*.)

The Septuagint's use of *homileō* is limited to Proverbs where the term denotes "to talk with" or "to converse" (see 15:12; 23:31). In one passage the context suggests the connotation of "to have sexual intercourse" (5:19).

New Testament Usage
In the New Testament the word occurs only four times, exclusively in Luke's writings (Luke 24:14,15; Acts 20:11; 24:26). *Homileō* in these passages expresses the idea of a person dialoguing with another individual or group, for example, the two on the road to Emmaus who "were *talking* with each other" (Luke 24:14,15), and Felix who "talked" with Paul (Acts 24:26). *Homileō* may also describe the actions of a speaker as he addresses a group, as in the case of Paul in Acts 20:11 where he conversed with the believers prior to his departure.

STRONG 3656, BAUER 565, MOULTON-MILLIGAN 447, LIDDELL-SCOTT 1222.

3520. ὁμιλία homilia noun
Companionship, association, intercourse, speech, sermon.

COGNATE:
ὁμιλέω homileō (3519)

SYNONYM:
κοινωνία koinōnia (2815)

לֶקַח leqach (4090), Something persuasive (Prv 7:21).
עֹנָה 'ōnāh (6260), Marital rights (Ex 21:10).

1. ὁμιλίαι **homiliai** nom pl fem

1 evil **communications** corrupt good manners. .... 1 Co 15:33

This substantive, found in Greek literature from Thucydides (Fifth Century B.C.) onward, has two major usages in Greek literature. Its primary use is to denote communion with others. This can refer to a gathering of individuals or of a couple; in this latter sense it can denote sexual intercourse (see Exodus 21:10 in the Septuagint). It is also used to denote instruction or a lecture (cf. the English *homiletics*) or even practice.

Its second major usage is to denote "association" or "company," or in a collective sense, "fellow-sojourners" or "shipmates." This rare term occurs in the New Testament only in 1 Corinthians 15:33 where Paul, quoting from Meander (*Thais* 218; see Orr and Walther, *Anchor Bible*, 32:336), reminded the readers they would be corrupted if they persisted in having evil persons as their *company* (companions).

STRONG 3657, BAUER 565, MOULTON-MILLIGAN 448, LIDDELL-SCOTT 1222.

3521. ὅμιλος homilos noun

Throng, crowd, mass of people.
COGNATE:
ὁμιλέω homileō (3519)
SYNONYMS:
δῆμος dēmos (1211B)
ὄχλος ochlos (3657)
πλῆθος plēthos (3988)

1. ὅμιλος homilos nom sing fem
1 every shipmaster, and all the **company** in ships, ... Rev 18:17

This term, derived from *homos*, "one and the same" or "common," and *ilē*, "band" or "troop" of men, refers to "any assembled crowd" or "throng of people," as opposed to the "chiefs" or "leaders." It can also refer to any assembled group of inanimate objects (cf. *Liddell-Scott*). When referring to warfare it can refer to the "throng" of battle, or less restrictively, to the "battle" itself, or more generally "tumult" or "confusion" (ibid.).

Its only occurrence in the New Testament, Revelation 18:17 (*Textus Receptus*), speaks of "all the *company* in ships" who will lament over the fall of the infamous city Babylon. (Cf. *homilia* [3520].)

STRONG 3658, BAUER 565, MOULTON-MILLIGAN 448, LIDDELL-SCOTT 1222.

3521B. ὁμίχλη homichlē noun

Mist, fog.
חֹשֶׁךְ chōshekh (2932), Darkness (Is 29:18).
כְּפוֹר kᵉphôr (3839), Frost (Ps 147:16 [147:5]).
עֵיפָה ʿêphāh (6107), Darkness (Am 4:13).
עָנָן ʿānān (6281), Mist, cloud mass (Sir 43:22).
עֲרָפֶל ʿărāphel (6441), Thick darkness (Jb 38:9, Jl 2:2, Zep 1:15).

1. ὁμίχλαι homichlai nom pl fem
1 and **mists** driven by a storm, (NASB) .... 2 Pt 2:17

Classical Greek and Septuagint Usage

The noun *homichlē* occurs in Greek literature from the time of Homer (ca. Eighth Century B.C.). It refers to a mist or fog but is not as thick as *nephos*, "cloud," or *nephelē* (3369), "mass of clouds" (*Liddell-Scott*). It may refer to the steam produced in cooking (ibid.). It is commonly used in figurative language as a simile. For example, "The wisdom of God will cover the earth like *mist*" (Sirach 24:3); and "Our lives will be scattered like *mist*" (*Wisdom of Solomon* 2:4). It can also have the sense "darkness" as in Isaiah 29:18 where it translates the Hebrew *hōshek*.

New Testament Usage

Homichlē occurs in some New Testament manuscripts at 2 Peter 2:17, where apostates are likened to mists or clouds that the storm blows along. The point of similarity in the simile suggests a lack of stability. The use of *homichlē* rather than *nephelē* would indicate a very light cloud or mist not able to provide rain, suggesting a lack of spiritual nourishment from their teachings. (The *Textus Receptus* has *nephelē* at 2 Peter 2:17.)

BAUER 565, MOULTON-MILLIGAN 448, LIDDELL-SCOTT 1222, COLIN BROWN 3:1000,1003.

3522. ὄμμα omma noun

Eye.
SYNONYM:
ὀφθαλμός ophthalmos (3652)
עַיִן ʿayin (6084), Eye (Prv 6:4, 7:2, 10:26, 23:5).

1. ὄμματα ommata nom/acc pl neu
2. ὀμμάτων ommatōn gen pl neu
2 compassion, Jesus touched their **eyes;** (NASB) ..... Matt 20:34
1 and when he had spit on his **eyes,** .... Mark 8:23

Classical Greek

This substantive, occurring from Homer onward, has five basic usages in Greek literature (cf. *Liddell-Scott*). First, it refers more commonly to the literal "eye," but it is also used metaphorically in reference to the human soul, "the eye of the soul" (*Bauer*). A second meaning is in reference to the sun, "the eye of heaven." Third, it figuratively refers to light in general, e.g., "that which brings light" or anything that is "dear" or "precious." Fourth, it can refer to a human face, form, or periphrastically, the person himself. And fifth, it denotes the "eyehole" in a helmet (see *Liddell-Scott* for specific examples of the above uses).

Septuagint Usage
In the Septuagint *omma* is used four times to translate the Hebrew term *'ayin*, meaning "eye." All of the occurrences are in Proverbs and use *omma* to refer to "eye" as literally affected by sleep (6:4) and irritated by smoke (10:26). Proverbs also uses "eye" figuratively (cf. 7:2; 23:5).

New Testament Usage
Omma occurs only twice in the New Testament, in Matthew 20:34 and again in Mark 8:23, where Jesus encountered blind men who sought healing. In both instances Jesus placed His hands upon their *eyes*, and they subsequently were able to see. The more common New Testament designation of eyes—*ophthalmos* (3652)—is used in Matthew 20:33 and Mark 8:25. Both writers speak of Jesus' power to give sight to the blind.

STRONG 3659, BAUER 565, MOULTON-MILLIGAN 448, LIDDELL-SCOTT 1222.

3523. ὀμνύω omnuō verb
Swear, make or take an oath, confirm by an oath.

COGNATE:
    συνωμοσία sunōmosia (4797)

אָמַר 'āmar (569), Say (Jgs 15:13—Codex Alexandrinus only).

שָׁבַע shāva' (8123), Niphal: swear (Dt 1:34f., 1 Kgs 1:29f., Jer 12:16); hiphal: make swear, put under oath (1 Sm 20:17, Ezr 10:5).

תָּפַשׂ tāphas (8945), Take hold of; profane (Prv 30:9 [24:32]).

1. ὀμνύει omnuei 3sing indic pres act
2. ὀμνύουσιν omnuousin 3pl indic pres act
3. ὀμνύετε omnuete 2pl impr pres act
4. ὀμνύειν omnuein inf pres act
5. ὤμοσα ōmosa 1sing indic aor act
6. ὤμοσεν ōmosen 3sing indic aor act
7. ὀμόσῃς omosēs 2sing subj aor act
8. ὀμόσῃ omosē 3sing subj aor act
9. ὀμόσας omosas nom sing masc part aor act
10. ὀμόσαι omosai inf aor act
11. ὀμνύναι omnunai inf pres act

10	But I say unto you, Swear not at all;	Matt 5:34
7	Neither **shalt thou swear** by thy head,	5:36
8	Whosoever **shall swear** by the temple, it is nothing;	23:16
8	whosoever **shall swear** by the gold of the temple,	23:16
8	Whosoever **shall swear** by the altar, it is nothing;	23:18
8	but whosoever **sweareth** by the gift that is upon it,	23:18
9	Whoso therefore **shall swear** by the altar,	23:20
1	**sweareth** by it, and by all things thereon.	23:20
9	And whoso **shall swear** by the temple,	23:21
1	**sweareth** by it, and by him that dwelleth therein.	23:21
9	And he that **shall swear** by heaven,	23:22
1	**sweareth** by the throne of God,	23:22
4	Then began he to curse and **to swear**, saying,	26:74
6	sware unto her, Whatsoever thou shalt ask of me,	Mark 6:23
4	But he began to curse and **to swear**, saying,	14:71
6	The oath which he **sware** to our father Abraham,	Luke 1:73
6	knowing that God **had sworn** with an oath to him,	Acts 2:30
6	which God **had sworn** to Abraham,	7:17
5	So I **sware** in my wrath, They shall not enter	Heb 3:11
6	And to whom **sware** he that they should not enter	3:18
5	as he said, As I **have sworn** in my wrath,	4:3
10	because he could **swear** by no greater,	6:13
6	he could swear by no greater, he **sware** by himself,	6:13
2	For men verily **swear** by the greater:	6:16
6	The Lord **sware** and will not repent,	7:21
3	But above all things, my brethren, **swear** not,	Jas 5:12
6	And **sware** by him that liveth for ever and ever,	Rev 10:6

Classical Greek
Omnuō was a common verb in antiquity and is found in Homer's *Iliad* and *Odyssey*, Herodotus, Xenophon, Philo, Josephus, and in many papyri. It is evidently derived from the older form, *omnumi*, of the same meaning. The papyri exhibit the ancient formula of swearing (*omnuō*) by someone, with that name placed in the accusative case. Thus, "I swear by King Ptolemy" (Second Century B.C., Elephantine Egypt papyrus), and "I swear by Nero Claudius Caesar" (First Century A.D., Oxyrhynchus papyrus; cf. *Moulton-Milligan*).

Septuagint Usage
Omnuō is also a common verb in the Septuagint nearly always translating the Hebrew term *shāva'*, "swear." The idea behind this action could be to bind oneself by "seven things" (Genesis 21:28; cf. the related noun *sheva'*, "seven"; Link, "Swear," *Colin Brown*, 3:739). In Genesis 21:24 *omnuō* means "swear" in the sense of "take an oath" (cf. Genesis 21:31; Judges 21:1,18; 2 Samuel 21:2 [LXX 2 Kings 21:2]). In the prophetic literature the phrase "swear by myself" was appropriate only when God promised to make and keep an oath, for only He could fulfill and guarantee such a statement (cf. Jeremiah 22:5; 29:13; Amos 4:2).

New Testament Usage
In the New Testament *omnuō* is used 28 times with the sense of either strongly pledging to

perform a future action or strongly affirming that what is said is indeed the truth (Mark 6:23; Revelation 10:6). It is distinct from *horkizō* (3589), which means to adjure or implore someone divine to accomplish a task (Mark 5:7; Acts 19:13). In Mark 6:23 *omnuō* is used as an oath of future performance, where Herod Antipas *swore* to Salome: "Whatsoever thou shalt ask of me, I will give it to thee, unto the half of my kingdom." Later he felt compelled to give her the head of John the Baptist. (Note that here Herod did not use the formula of swearing in God's name.) In Revelation 10:6 the holy angel swore (*omnuō*) "by him that liveth for ever and ever," namely, God, "that there should be time (delay) no longer" in finishing the judgments of God. Here the angel used the oath as an affirmation of future performance and invoked God the Creator's name as the formula witness.

In the New Testament *omnuō* is used most frequently in the Gospel of Matthew (13 times) and in the Epistle to the Hebrews (7 times). In Matthew 5:34 Jesus exhorted His followers not to swear at all, and in Matthew 23:16-22 He used *omnuō* 10 times in His rebuke of the legalistic oaths of the Pharisees. The word is used three times in Hebrews 6:13,16 where the writer emphasized that God swore His oath to Abraham by Himself because there existed none greater to invoke by which to pledge a truth (cf. Jeremiah 22:5; Amos 4:2).

STRONG 3660, BAUER 565-66, MOULTON-MILLIGAN 448, KITTEL 5:176-185, LIDDELL-SCOTT 1223 (see "omnumi"), COLIN BROWN 3:737-43.

3524. ὁμοθυμαδόν

homothumadon adv
With one accord, together.

יַחַד yachadh (3266), Together (Jb 6:2, 17:6, 34:15).

יַחְדָּו yachdāw (3267), Together, with one accord (Ex 19:8, Jb 2:11, Jer 5:5).

1. ὁμοθυμαδόν homothumadon

1 These all continued **with one accord** in prayer	Acts 1:14
1 they were all **with one accord** in one place.	2:1
1 continuing daily **with one accord** in the temple,	2:46
1 they lifted up their voice to God **with one accord,**	4:24
1 they were all **with one accord** in Solomon's porch.	5:12
1 and ran upon him **with one accord,**	7:57
1 And the people **with one accord** gave heed	8:6
1 but they came **with one accord** to him,	12:20
1 being assembled **with one accord,**	15:25
1 made insurrection **with one accord** against Paul,	18:12
1 they rushed **with one accord** into the theatre.	19:29
1 ye may **with one mind** and one mouth glorify God,	Rom 15:6

Classical Greek and Septuagint Usage

This adverb can be found in classical Greek from the time of Aristotle (ca. Fourth Century B.C.) meaning "with one accord," in the sense of a common agreement of mind or purpose. In the Septuagint *homothumadon* usually translates the Hebrew term *yachadh*, "together, in union." It occurs frequently in the Book of Job regarding Job's "three friends" (2:11), Job's "calamities" (6:2; 16:10; 19:12), and the Lord's reply to Job (40:13). Jeremiah indicted his countrymen who "have known the way of the LORD, and the judgment of their God; but these have *altogether* broken the yoke, and burst the bonds" (Jeremiah 5:5). Therefore the Lord purposed that the walls and ramparts of Zion would languish "together" when they were broken down and the people were carried off into exile (Lamentations 2:8).

New Testament Usage

This adverb is found 10 times in Acts, but only once in the rest of the New Testament (Romans 15:6). In Acts it is always translated "with one accord" in the KJV. Most of the references emphasize the unity experienced by the disciples. They were united in purpose as they awaited the promised empowerment of the Holy Spirit (1:14; 2:1). They were united in their joyous sharing of worship and fellowship afterward (2:46). Led by the Holy Spirit, the apostles and elders of Jerusalem were able to come "with one accord" (15:25) to a unanimous decision in dealing with the difficult question of whether to impose the law of Moses on the new Gentile converts. "With one accord" in these and other instances does not mean that everyone present agreed on everything; rather, they were able to focus on the purposes and motives which united them and which made unified action possible. *Homothumadon* is also used in references to the united hostility of some who opposed the young church and the gospel (7:57; 18:12; 19:29).

In Romans 15:6 Paul used this word when he prayed that the Roman believers would glorify God "with one mind," that is, with a unity of purpose.

STRONG 3661, BAUER 566, MOULTON-MILLIGAN 448, KITTEL 5:185-86, LIDDELL-SCOTT 1224.

3525. ὁμοιάζω homoiazō verb
To be like, to resemble.

ὁμοιοπαθής 3526

CROSS-REFERENCE:
ὅμοιος homoios (3527)

1. ὁμοιάζει homoiazei 3sing indic pres act

1 art a Galilaean, and thy speech **agreeth** thereto.... Mark 14:70

This verb occurs in the New Testament at Mark 14:70 (in *Textus Receptus*) and at Matthew 26:73 in a few manuscripts. In Mark it is translated "agreeth." Bystanders accused Peter of being a follower of Jesus and a Galilean. Despite his denial, they claimed his "speech agreeth" to their charge—that is, his accent was too much like that of the Galileans for him to hide his identity.

STRONG 3662, BAUER 566, LIDDELL-SCOTT 1224.

3526. ὁμοιοπαθής homoiopathēs adj

With the same nature, with like passions or feelings.

CROSS-REFERENCE:
ὅμοιος homoios (3527)

1. ὁμοιοπαθής homoiopathēs nom sing masc
2. ὁμοιοπαθεῖς homoiopatheis nom pl masc

2 We also are men **of like passions** with you,......... Acts 14:15
1 Elias was a man subject to **like passions** as we are,... Jas 5:17

Both occurrences of this adjective in the New Testament are found in statements emphasizing the common humanity of the persons mentioned. In Acts 14:15 Paul and Barnabas stopped the people's attempt to treat them as gods by asserting that they were "men *of like passions* with you," that is, only humans, not gods. James 5:17 encourages believers to pray fervently by pointing out that Elijah, a man who saw extraordinary answers to his prayers, was nevertheless "a man *subject to like passions* as we are." In both cases the term is used to show that those who were thought to be heavenly beings or an especially perfect person were human in every respect. The example of Elijah particularly served to challenge the readers of the epistle to allow the power of God to be released through their prayers, just as it was through the prayer of Elijah.

STRONG 3663, BAUER 566, MOULTON-MILLIGAN 448, KITTEL 5:938-39, LIDDELL-SCOTT 1224.

3527. ὅμοιος homoios adj

Like, similar, resembling.

COGNATES:
ἀφομοιόω aphomoioō (864)
ὁμοιάζω homoiazō (3525)
ὁμοιοπαθής homoiopathēs (3526)
ὁμοιότης homoiotēs (3528)
ὁμοιόω homoioō (3529)
ὁμοίωμα homoiōma (3530)
ὁμοίως homoiōs (3530B)
ὁμοίωσις homoiōsis (3531)
παρομοιάζω paromoiazō (3807)
παρόμοιος paromoios (3808)

SYNONYM:
παρόμοιος paromoios (3808)

דָּמָה dāmâh (1880), Be like (Ez 31:8).
דְּמוּת dᵉmûth (1883), Something like (Is 13:4).
כְּמוֹ kᵉmô (3765), Like (Ex 15:11, 2 Kgs 18:5, Ps 86:8 [85:8]).
כֵּן kēn (3772), Such as (2 Chr 1:12).
מֹשֵׁל mōshel (5093), Equal (Jb 41:33 [41:24]).

1. ὅμοιον homoion nom/acc sing masc/neu
2. ὅμοιος homoios nom sing masc
3. ὅμοιοι homoioi nom pl masc
4. ὁμοία homoia nom sing fem
5. ὅμοιαι homoiai nom pl fem
6. ὁμοίας homoias acc pl fem
7. ὅμοια homoia nom/acc pl neu

4 It is **like** unto children sitting in the markets,...... Matt 11:16
4 The kingdom ... is **like** to a grain of mustard seed,..... 13:31
4 The kingdom of heaven is **like** unto leaven,.......... 13:33
4 the kingdom ... is **like** unto treasure hid in a field;..... 13:44
4 kingdom of heaven is **like** unto a merchant man,..... 13:45
4 the kingdom of heaven is **like** unto a net,............. 13:47
2 is **like** unto a man that is an householder,............. 13:52
4 For the kingdom of heaven is **like** unto a man......... 20:1
4 And the second is **like** unto it,........................ 22:39
4 And the second is **like**, namely this,............ Mark 12:31
2 I will show you to whom he is **like**:................. Luke 6:47
4 He is **like** a man which built an house,............... 6:48
2 is **like** a man that without a foundation built........... 6:49
3 men of this generation? and to what are they **like**?..... 7:31
3 **like** unto children sitting in the marketplace,........... 7:32
3 yourselves like unto men that wait for their lord,...... 12:36
4 Unto what is the kingdom of God **like**?............... 13:18
4 It is **like** a grain of mustard seed,..................... 13:19
4 It is **like** leaven, which a woman took and hid........ 13:21
2 say, I know him not, I shall be a liar **like** unto you: John 8:55
2 others said, He is **like** him: but he said, I am he..... 9:9
1 not to think that the Godhead is **like** unto gold,.... Acts 17:29
7 murders, drunkenness, revellings, and such **like**:...... Gal 5:21
3 we shall be **like** him; for we shall see him as he is... 1 Jn 3:2
1 Sodom ... and the cities about them in **like** manner,.. Jude 7
1 And in the midst ... one **like** unto the Son of man,...Rev 1:13
3 And his feet **like** unto fine brass, as if they burned,... 1:15
3 and his feet are **like** fine brass;....................... 2:18
2 was to look upon **like** a jasper and a sardine stone:... 4:3
2 in sight **like** unto an emerald....................... 4:3
4 there was a sea of glass **like** unto crystal:............. 4:6
1 And the first beast was **like** a lion,................... 4:7
1 and the second beast **like** a calf,..................... 4:7
1 and the fourth beast was **like** a flying eagle.......... 4:7
7 locusts were **like** unto horses prepared unto battle;..... 9:7
3 on their heads were as it were crowns **like** gold,...... 9:7
6 And they had tails **like** unto scorpions,.............. 9:10
5 their tails were **like** unto serpents, and had heads,..... 9:19
2 And there was given me a reed **like** unto a rod:....... 11:1
1 And the beast which I saw was **like** unto a leopard,... 13:2
2 saying, Who is **like** unto the beast?................... 13:4

7 two horns **like** a lamb, and he spake as a dragon....	Rev 13:11
2 upon the cloud one sat **like** unto the Son of man,.....	14:14
7 I saw three unclean spirits **like** frogs come out of......	16:13
4 saying, What city is **like** unto this great city!..........	18:18
2 and her light was **like** unto a stone most precious,.....	21:11
4 and the city was pure gold, **like** unto clear glass........	21:18

Classical Greek
In classical Greek *homoios* means "like" when referring to objects and "of the same status" when referring to individuals. This adjective is also used of possessions shared in common (cf. *Liddell-Scott* for specific references for above examples).

Septuagint Usage
The Septuagint uses *homoios* for the Hebrew word $k^e m\hat{o}$ as in Nehemiah 6:11 where Nehemiah said: "Should such a man *as* I flee?" This adjective is also used for the Hebrew *mîn* translated as "kind" in reference to groups of fowls which are unclean. Included in this list are "every raven after his *kind*; and the owl, and the nighthawk, and the cuckoo, and the hawk after his *kind*" (Leviticus 11:15,16).

New Testament Usage
The prominent use of *homoios* in the New Testament is to introduce parables and to explain imagery in prophetic passages. This adjective is used by the Lord to introduce the parables of the kingdom in Matthew 13. The kingdom of heaven is "*like* to a grain of mustard seed" (verse 31), "*like* unto leaven" (verse 33), "*like* unto treasure" (verse 44), "*like* unto a merchantman" (verse 45), "*like* unto a net" (verse 47), and "*like* unto a man that is a householder" (verse 52).

John used *homoios* 22 times in the Book of Revelation to describe prophetic images. When John saw a vision of Christ, he described Him as "one *like* unto the Son of man" (Revelation 1:13) with "feet *like* unto fine brass, as if they burned in a furnace" (Revelation 1:15). The prophetic hope of believers is that when Christ appears "we shall be *like* him" (1 John 3:2).

STRONG 3664, BAUER 566-67, MOULTON-MILLIGAN 448, KITTEL 5:186-88, LIDDELL-SCOTT 1224-25, COLIN BROWN 2:497,500-503.

3528. ὁμοιότης homoiotēs noun
Resemblance, similarity, likeness, correspondence, in the same way.

COGNATE:
ὅμοιος homoios (3527)

SYNONYMS:
ὁμοίωμα homoiōma (3530)
ὁμοίωσις homoiōsis (3531)

מִין mîn (4464), Kind (Gn 1:12).

1. ὁμοιότητα homoiotēta acc sing fem
1 but was in all points tempted **like** as we are,........	Heb 4:15
1 after the **similitude** of Melchisedec there ariseth.........	7:15

Classical Greek and Septuagint Usage
From classical times the noun *homoiotēs* was used to refer to the similarity or correspondence between persons or between things. This similarity does not mean alike in every detail but alike in some significant respect. The Septuagint uses *homoiotēs* in Genesis 1:11,12 where each plant was created to reproduce its own "kind," meaning that the "offspring" would have a resemblance to the "parent" plant. In the apocryphal 4 Maccabees 15:4 the affections of mother to child are attributed to the "*resemblance* of soul and form" between them.

New Testament Usage
In the New Testament it was said that Christ was tempted "*like as* we are" (Hebrews 4:15). Yet the similarity is not total, since the same verse says that He remained "without sin." In Hebrews 7:15 Christ's coming is said to be "after the *similitude* of Melchizedek," or, more literally translated, "according to the similarity to Melchizedek." The passage goes on to point out significant ways in which Jesus' ministry as our High Priest is similar to the ministry of Melchizedek described in Genesis 14 and Psalm 110.

STRONG 3665, BAUER 567, MOULTON-MILLIGAN 448-49, KITTEL 5:189-90, LIDDELL-SCOTT 1225.

3529. ὁμοιόω homoioō verb
Make alike, be like, compare a person or a thing.

CROSS-REFERENCE:
ὅμοιος homoios (3527)

אוּת 'ûth (224), Niphal: consent (Gn 34:15,22f.).

דָּמָה dāmâh (1880), Qal: be like, do with (S/S 8:14, Ez 31:2, Hos 4:5); niphal: be like (Ps 49:12,20 [48:12,20], Ez 32:2); be wiped out (Zep 1:11); piel: compare, liken (S/S 1:9, Is 46:5, Lam 2:13).

מָשַׁל māshal (5090), Say a proverb; niphal: be like (Pss 28:1 [27:1], 143:7 [142:7]).

עָרַךְ 'ārakh (6424), Set in order, put; compare (Is 40:18).

1. ὁμοιώσωμεν homoiōsōmen 1pl subj aor act
2. ὁμοιώσω homoiōsō 1sing indic fut act

ὁμοίωμα 3530

3. **ὡμοιώθη** hōmoiōthē 3sing indic aor pass
4. **ὡμοιώθημεν** hōmoiōthēmen 1pl indic aor pass
5. **ὁμοιωθῆτε** homoiōthēte 2pl subj aor pass
6. **ὁμοιωθέντες** homoiōthentes
                 nom pl masc part aor pass
7. **ὁμοιωθῆναι** homoiōthēnai inf aor pass
8. **ὁμοιωθήσεται** homoiōthēsetai 3sing indic fut pass
9. **ὁμοιώσομεν** homoiōsomen 1pl indic fut act

5	Be not ye therefore **like** unto them:	Matt 6:8
2	I will **liken** him unto a wise man,	7:24
8	shall be **likened** unto a foolish man,	7:26
2	But whereunto shall I **liken** this generation?	11:16
3	The kingdom of heaven **is likened** unto a man	13:24
3	the kingdom of heaven **likened** unto a certain king,	18:23
3	The kingdom of heaven **is like** unto a certain king,	22:2
8	the kingdom of heaven **be likened** unto ten virgins,	25:1
1	Whereunto **shall we liken** the kingdom of God?	Mark 4:30
2	Whereunto then **shall I liken** the men of this	Luke 7:31
2	the kingdom ... and whereunto shall I **resemble** it?	13:18
2	Whereunto **shall I liken** the kingdom of God?	13:20
6	gods are come down to us **in the likeness** of men	Acts 14:11
4	as Sodoma, and **been made like unto** Gomorrha	Rom 9:29
7	it behoved him **to be made like unto** his brethren,	Heb 2:17

Classical Greek and Septuagint Usage
In classical Greek *homoioō* means "to make alike" or "to be like." The Septuagint uses this verb to translate the Hebrew verb *dāmâh* which also means "to make alike." The translators often used *homoioō* to introduce similies and parables. Isaiah said of God's mercy: "Except the Lord of hosts had left unto us a very small remnant, we should have been as Sodom, and we should have been *like* unto Gomorrah" (Isaiah 1:9; Paul used this same verb when he quoted this verse in Romans 9:29). The maiden in the Song of Solomon described her lover as being "*like* a roe or a young hart" (2:9). Jeremiah introduced a parable when he "*likened* the daughter of Zion to a comely and delicate woman" (Jeremiah 6:2).

New Testament Usage
The New Testament uses the verb *homoioō* to compare persons and things and to introduce parables. The verb introduces the parables of the wheat and the tares (Matthew 13:24), the two debtors (Matthew 18:23), the marriage feast (Matthew 22:2), and the ten virgins (Matthew 25:1). Believers should not pray with vain repetition *like* the heathen (Matthew 6:7,8). After Paul healed the impotent man at Lystra the people said, "The gods are come down to us in the *likeness* of men" (Acts 14:11). The writer to the Hebrews said of Jesus: "Wherefore in all things it behooved him to be *made like* unto his brethren, that he might be a merciful and faithful high priest ... " (Hebrews 2:17).

STRONG 3666, BAUER 567, KITTEL 5:188-89, LIDDELL-SCOTT 1225, COLIN BROWN 2:500-505.

3530. ὁμοίωμα homoiōma noun
Likeness, image, copy, appearance.

COGNATE:
   ὅμοιος homoios (3527)
SYNONYMS:
   εἶδος eidos (1482)
   ὁμοιότης homoiotēs (3528)
   ὁμοίωσις homoiōsis (3531)

דְּמָה dᵉmâh (A1881), Look like (Dn 3:25—Aramaic).

דְּמוּת dᵉmûth (1883), Pattern, likeness (2 Kgs 16:10, Ez 1:22, 10:21).

עַיִן ʿayin (6084), Something like (Ez 1:4—Codex Alexandrinus only).

צֶלֶם tselem (7021), Image (1 Sm 6:5).

תֹּאַר tōʾar (8717), Resemblance (Jgs 8:18).

תַּבְנִית tavnîth (8732), Likeness, image, form (Dt 4:17f., Ps 106:20 [105:20], Ez 8:3).

תְּמוּנָה tᵉmûnāh (8874), Likeness, form (Ex 20:4, Dt 4:12, 5:8).

1. **ὁμοιώματι** homoiōmati dat sing neu
2. **ὁμοιώματα** homoiōmata nom/acc pl neu

1	into an **image made like** to corruptible man,	Rom 1:23
1	after the **similitude** of Adam's transgression,	5:14
1	been planted together in the **likeness** of his death,	6:5
1	sending his own Son in the **likeness** of sinful flesh,	8:3
1	and was made in the **likeness** of men:	Phlp 2:7
2	And the **shapes** of the locusts were **like** unto horses	Rev 9:7

Classical Greek
This noun is rarely found in secular Greek and is usually used to convey the concept of a "copy" rather than an appearance or likeness (*Bauer*). It is also used less frequently to describe something "similar."

Septuagint Usage
The Septuagint uses *homoiōma* to translate the Hebrew *tᵉmûnāh* which is translated "similitude" or "likeness." God commanded Israel not to make "any graven image, or any *likeness* of any thing that is in the heaven above, or that is in the earth beneath, or that is in the water under the earth" (Exodus 20:4). Moses later reminded the new generation of Israel that they were not to make any "graven image, the *similitude* of any figure, the likeness of male or female" (Deuteronomy 4:16). The Septuagint also uses *homoiōma* to translate the Hebrew *dᵉmûth*, as in Isaiah 40:18 where Isaiah asked, "To whom then will ye liken God? or what *likeness* will ye compare unto him?"

New Testament Usage
The New Testament uses *homoiōma* primarily in two ways. The first is the use of the term to indicate something that resembles or is similar, though not necessarily identical, with

something else. John described the locusts of the fifth trumpet judgment as having "*shapes . . . like unto horses prepared unto battle . . .*" (Revelation 9:7). In Romans 1:23 Paul said that mankind had "changed the glory of the uncorruptible God into an image made *like* to corruptible man, and to birds, and four-footed beasts, and creeping things." This act is a direct violation of the command of Exodus 20:4 (see above). Death reigned "even over them that had not sinned after the *similitude* (i.e., in the same way, or having committed the same sins) of Adam's transgression" (Romans 5:14).

The believer has been planted "in the *likeness* of his death" (Romans 6:5). Here *homoiōma* moves beyond similarity to include the sense of sameness or of identical nature. Romans 6:3 presents the beautiful mystery of the believer's spiritual and mystical participation in the death of Christ by submitting himself or herself to the physical waters of baptism. In verse 5 Paul restated the truth of the believer's union with Christ not simply in a death that resembles His but that *is* His. This is the only New Testament use of *homiōma* that bears this degree of exactness.

The use of *homoiōma* in Romans 8:3 and Philippians 2:7 has been the source of great discussion and misunderstanding throughout church history. The phrase "likeness of sinful flesh" appears nowhere else in the New Testament but in Romans 8:3. While the New Testament is replete with statements proclaiming the reality of Jesus' existence in human flesh (John 1:14; Romans 1:3; 1 Timothy 3:16) no other writer, not even Paul, includes the modifier "sinful" in any other passage. It is for this reason that a proper understanding of *homoioma* is imperative in this text.

Here *homoiōma* implies more the idea discussed above, i.e., the concept of similarity. This is not to fall victim to Doscetism which states Jesus' human existence was only an illusion. Rather, as Murray concludes, the word "likeness" by no means suggests any unreality in His human nature; instead, it is necessary because of Paul's use of "sinful" (*New International Commentary on the New Testament, Romans*, p.280). For Paul to have said simply that Jesus came in sinful flesh would have contradicted the clear New Testament teaching of the sinless nature of Jesus (ibid.). By coming in a state of being similar in nature to that which was worldly, historical, and sinful, but that was not by nature sinful, Jesus identified with the misery and pain of human nature without Himself becoming defiled by sin. According to Barth, "In Him the flesh has been deprived of its independence and restored to God who created it . . . God sends His Son in the midst of sin-controlled flesh, in order that there—and if not there, where?—sin and rebellion against God with all its consequences may be struck down" (*Epistle to the Romans*, p.281).

Paul's use of *homoiōma* in Philippians 2:7 is at the heart of the "kenosis" theories. Not only was Jesus in the *morphē theou*, the "form of God" (verse 6), He took on the *morphēn doulou*, the "form of a servant." This phrase "form of a servant" works in parallel with the phrase *en homoiōmati anthrōpōn*, "in the likeness of men." To the same extent that Jesus was divine, He was human. But in His humanity He subjected His desires, drives, emotions, and will to the will of the Father. Thus He showed what it truly means to be human.

S<small>TRONG</small> 3667, B<small>AUER</small> 567, M<small>OULTON</small>-M<small>ILLIGAN</small> 449, K<small>ITTEL</small> 5:191-98, L<small>IDDELL</small>-S<small>COTT</small> 1225, C<small>OLIN</small> B<small>ROWN</small> 2:500-504.

3530B. ὁμοίως homoiōs adv

Likewise, in the same way, similarly, so.

S<small>YNONYMS</small>:
παραπλησίως paraplēsiōs (3759)
ὡσαύτως hōsautōs (5447)

1. ὁμοίως homoiōs

1	Likewise the second also, and the third,	Matt 22:26
1	Likewise also said all the disciples.	26:35
1	Likewise also the chief priests mocking him,	27:41
1	they likewise which are sown on stony ground;	Mark 4:16
1	Likewise also the chief priests mocking	15:31
1	and he that hath meat, let him do likewise.	Luke 3:11
1	so was also James, and John, the sons of Zebedee,	5:10
1	and likewise the disciples of the Pharisees;	5:33
1	should do to you, do ye also to them likewise.	6:31
1	And likewise a Levite, when he was at the place,	10:32
1	said Jesus unto him, Go, and do thou likewise.	10:37
1	you will all likewise perish. (NASB)	13:3
1	but, except ye repent, ye shall all likewise perish.	13:5
1	thy good things, and likewise Lazarus evil things:	16:25
1	Likewise also as it was in the days of Lot;	17:28
1	is in the field, let him likewise not return back.	17:31
1	and likewise his scrip: and he that hath no sword,	22:36
1	these also doeth the Son likewise.	John 5:19
1	and likewise of the fishes as much as they would.	6:11
1	taketh bread, and giveth them, and fish likewise.	21:13
1	And likewise also the men,	Rom 1:27
1	Likewise also the wife unto the husband.	1 Co 7:3
1	and likewise also the husband hath not power	7:4
1	likewise also he that is called, being free,	7:22
1	Moreover he sprinkled with blood	Heb 9:21
1	Likewise also was not Rahab ... justified by works,	Jas 2:25

ὁμοίωσις 3531

1 **Likewise**, ye wives, be in subjection	1 Pt 3:1
1 **Likewise**, ye husbands, dwell with them	3:7
1 **Likewise**, ye younger, submit yourselves	5:5
1 **Likewise** also these filthy dreamers defile the flesh,	Jude 1:8
1 not for a third part of it, and the night **likewise**	Rev 8:12

This adverb is related to the adjective *homoios* (3527), meaning "like" or "resembling." Both adjective and adverb are found frequently in the Septuagint and in the New Testament, with the adverb usually being translated "likewise." Luke 5:10 is an exception, where it is translated "so." Sometimes the word has the grammatical function of a connective (for example see 1 Peter 3:1,7).

STRONG 3668, BAUER 567-68, MOULTON-MILLIGAN 449, LIDDELL-SCOTT 1225 (see "homoios").

3531. ὁμοίωσις homoiōsis noun
Likeness, resemblance, image.

COGNATE:
ὅμοιος homoios (3527)

SYNONYMS:
ὁμοιότης homoiotēs (3528)
ὁμοίωμα homoiōma (3530)

דְּמָה dᵉmâh (A1881), Look like (Dn 7:5—Aramaic).

דְּמוּת dᵉmûth (1883), Likeness (Gn 1:26, Ps 58:4 [57:4], Dn 10:16).

תַּבְנִית tavnîth (8732), Form (Ez 8:10—Codex Alexandrinus only).

תָּכְנִית tokhnîth (8837), Perfection (Ez 28:12).

1. ὁμοίωσιν homoiōsin acc sing fem

1 which are made after the **similitude** of God	Jas 3:9

This word is used eight times in the Septuagint. It is found only once in the New Testament text, at James 3:9 where it expresses a very important Biblical truth: human beings are made in the "likeness" of God. James wrote that men are made "after the *similitude* of God," using the very same wording as Genesis 1:26 in the Septuagint. In both places the words are *kath homoiōsin*, literally "according to the likeness." According to James 3:9, it is contradictory that by the same tongue human beings bless God and curse their *fellowmen* who *are* made in His "likeness."

STRONG 3669, BAUER 568, MOULTON-MILLIGAN 449, KITTEL 5:190-91, LIDDELL-SCOTT 1225.

3532. ὁμοίως homoiōs
See word study at number 3530B.

3533. ὁμολογέω homologeō verb
To agree, confess, profess, admit, acknowledge, promise, praise.

COGNATES:
ἀνοίγω anoigō (453)
ἐξομολογέω exomologeō (1827)
λέγω legō (2978)
ὁμολογία homologia (3534)
ὁμολογουμένως homologoumenōs (3535)
ὀνειδίζω oneidizō (3542)

SYNONYMS:
ἐξομολογέω exomologeō (1827)
ἐπαγγέλλομαι epangellomai (1846)

יָדָה yādhâh (3142), Praise; hiphil: confess (Jb 40:14 [40:9]).

נָדַר nādhar (5265), Vow (Jer 44:25 [51:25]).

שָׁבַע shāvaʿ (8123), Niphal: swear (Ez 16:8—only some Vaticanus texts).

1. **ὁμολογῶ** homologō 1sing indic pres act
2. **ὁμολογεῖ** homologei 3sing indic pres act
3. **ὁμολογοῦσιν** homologousin 3pl indic pres act
4. **ὁμολογῶμεν** homologōmen 1pl subj pres act
5. **ὁμολογοῦντες** homologountes nom pl masc part pres act
6. **ὁμολογούντων** homologountōn gen pl masc part pres act
7. **ὡμολόγησας** hōmologēsas 2sing indic aor act
8. **ὡμολόγησεν** hōmologēsen 3sing indic aor act
9. **ὁμολογήσῃς** homologēsēs 2sing subj aor act
10. **ὁμολογήσῃ** homologēsē 3sing subj aor act
11. **ὁμολογήσαντες** homologēsantes nom pl masc part aor act
12. **ὁμολογήσω** homologēsō 1sing indic fut act
13. **ὁμολογήσει** homologēsei 3sing indic fut act
14. **ὡμολόγουν** hōmologoun 3pl indic imperf act
15. **ὁμολογεῖται** homologeitai 3sing indic pres mid
16. **ὁμολογῶν** homologōn nom sing masc part pres act

12	then **will I profess** unto them, I never knew you:	Matt 7:23
13	Whosoever therefore **shall confess** me before men,	10:32
12	him **will I confess** also before my Father	10:32
8	Whereupon he **promised** with an oath to give her whatsoever	14:7
10	Whosoever **shall confess** me before men,	Luke 12:8
13	him shall the Son of man also **confess**	12:8
8	And he **confessed**, ... I am not the Christ	John 1:20
8	and denied not; he **confessed**, I am not the Christ	1:20
10	that if any man **did confess** that he was Christ,	9:22
14	because of the Pharisees they **did not confess** him,	12:42
8	which God had **assured** to Abraham (NASB)	Acts 7:17
3	no resurrection, ... but the Pharisees **confess** both.	23:8
1	But this I **confess** unto thee,	24:14
9	That if thou **shalt confess** with thy mouth the Lord	Rom 10:9
15	with the mouth **confession** is made unto salvation.	10:10
7	and **hast professed** a good profession before many	1 Tm 6:12
3	They **profess** that they know God;	Tit 1:16
11	**confessed** that they were strangers and pilgrims	Heb 11:13
6	the fruit of our lips **giving thanks** to his name.	13:15
4	If we **confess** our sins, he is faithful and just	1 Jn 1:9
16	the one who **confesses** the Son (NASB)	2:23
2	Every spirit that **confesseth** that Jesus Christ is	4:2
2	**confesseth** not that Jesus Christ is come in the flesh	4:3
10	**shall confess** that Jesus is the Son of God,	4:15

5 confess not that Jesus Christ is come in the flesh... **2 Jn 1:7**
12 but will acknowledge ... before my Father (NIV).... **Rev 3:5**

The meaning of the component parts of *homologeō* is "to say (*legō* [2978]) the same (*homos*) thing." Accordingly, its most basic meaning is to agree with someone or something, or to agree to something. The word has, however, provided a wide range of related meanings (*Liddell-Scott*).

Classical Greek

In classical Greek "the legal connotation is dominant" (Fürst, "Confess," *Colin Brown*, 1:344). The word is regularly found from the Fifth Century B.C. and following to indicate that a person "confessed" or "admitted" to a crime or "openly acknowledged" his guilt. It sometimes means to "agree" with someone else's testimony or to the terms of a contract, even to "consent" to the terms of surrender in a war. In a nonlegal sense, it means to "agree" with someone's statement or proposal, to "consent" to someone's wish or demand, and occasionally, by extension, even to "promise" or "vow." *Homologeō* is also used in the context of war ("to capitulate" to a superior force), in the context of money ("accepting" one's debt), and in the context of Stoic philosophy ("living" according to one's own common sense).

Though "not primarily a religious term" (Michel, "homologeō," *Kittel*, 5:202), both *homologeō* and its noun *homologia* (3534) were commonly used in religious contexts. These same words could indicate not only a worshiper's "confession" of sins to his god but also his "profession" of the god. Followers of a certain deity made confessions to him, or bound themselves with an oath to him in a contractual relationship. Lydian and Phrygian inscriptions indicate that *homologeō* was used for confessing one's sins to a priest (representing the deity) in the hope that the individual would be delivered from sicknesses and disasters (ibid.).

The standard meanings of *homologeō* persist in Hellenistic papyri with heavy emphasis still on legal uses, especially the agreeing to the terms of a contract and the acknowledgment of a debt or receipt of property. Later Jewish writers, including Josephus and Philo, used it in a variety of ways, including the public acknowledgment of something, the praise ("confession") of God, and the confession of sins (*Bauer*).

Septuagint Usage

In the Septuagint there is a preference for the kindred verb *exomologeō* (1827); *homologeō* occurs only three times in the canonical books. In Job 40:14 *homologeō* translates the Hebrew verb *yādhâh*, which usually means "to praise," but here is rendered "to confess" (KJV, NASB), "to acknowledge" (RSV), or "to admit" (NIV). This close link between confession and praise was not strange to ancient Israel. The praise of God was always connected with some past event, be it an act of deliverance or judgment. In the latter case, the one judged was exhorted to praise as a concrete act of acknowledging that God was right (Fürst, "Confess," *Colin Brown*, 1:345).

In a somewhat sarcastic reversal of this, God challenged Job to do a number of things impossible for man. If Job was able to do them, then God would "praise" or "confess" to him that he was right, and could indeed save himself (Job 40:8-14).

In Jeremiah 44:25 (LXX 51:25) *homologeō* translates *nādhar*, "to make a vow." Captive members of the tribe of Judah in Egypt had "vowed" to perform sacrificial rites to the "queen of heaven." Just as they were determined to fulfill their idolatrous vows, so God was determined to fulfill the vow He had sworn by His name: that they would never again invoke His name in the land of Egypt (Jeremiah 44:25,26).

In certain manuscripts this word occurs in Ezekiel 16:8 translating *shāva'*, "to swear." Again the term reflects the concept of making a vow. God tells of how He had "committed" himself to enter into a covenant relationship with destitute Jerusalem, even though she had nothing to offer in return. In light of this truth, her later arrogance and rebellion (Ezekiel 16:15ff.) was all the more reprehensible and worthy of judgment. In the apocryphal books of the Septuagint the word occurs another 11 times, most often meaning to "confess" or "admit," but once meaning to "give thanks."

New Testament Usage

Though the word *homologeō* is generally translated "confess" (18 of 23 times), and only occasionally "profess" (3 times), the dominant meaning in the New Testament actually seems to be the open and public profession of someone or something. Almost half of its uses speak of "confessing" Christ (Matthew 10:32; Luke 12:8; John 12:42; 1 John 2:23) or "confessing" who or what Jesus is ("the Christ" John 9:22; "Lord," Romans 10:9,10; "is come in the flesh,"

1 John 4:2,3; 2 John 7; "the Son of God," 1 John 4:15).

All of these were public professions of what many others were denying. Timothy "professed" (*homologeō*) a good profession (*homologia*) before many witnesses (1 Timothy 6:12). That "profession" is identified in the next verse to be the very same "good confession" (*homologeō* again) that Jesus spoke before Pilate, that is, that He was the King of the Jews, the Christ, the Messiah.

Confessing Christ is an open declaration that one "agrees" with all of Jesus' claims for himself and that he "consents" to Jesus' claims of Lordship over him; in effect, he enters a contractual agreement to accept Jesus as his Saviour and Lord. This profession is necessary for salvation (Romans 10:9,10). Paul demonstrated this by openly declaring before Felix that he followed Christ (Acts 24:14). In John 9:22 the Jews agreed that anyone who confessed Jesus as the Christ would be barred from the synagogue. This threat was enough to cause some who truly believed not to confess (*ouch homologoun*) Him openly (John 12:42). Jesus, likewise, will "confess," or openly acknowledge, before His Father and the angels in heaven those who have confessed Him (Matthew 10:32; Luke 12:8; Revelation 3:5).

John clearly wrote that fellowship with God is based upon the confession of Jesus as the Son of God (1 John 4:15; cf. 2:23). He also warned against deceivers who refuse "to acknowledge" (*hoi me homologountes*) Christ's incarnation (2 John 7), a truth that can be declared only by those who have the Spirit of God (1 John 4:2,3). Indeed, some will maintain they truly know God, but their deeds deny their words. Paul declared such people are "abominable, and disobedient, and unto every good word reprobate" (Titus 1:16). They are liars and the antichrists (1 John 2:22). Thus, the decision to either confess or deny Christ will be evidenced in the life of the individual. This decision is crucial, for Jesus declared each will be treated in accordance with his choice. Those who confess Him now will be acknowledged before the Father, and those who deny Him will be denied before the Father (Matthew 10:32,33). Luke indicated the angels of God will also be present (Luke 12:8). The context of these passages is the final judgment. In Revelation 3:5 the apostle John recorded Jesus' words: "He that overcometh . . . I will confess (*homologēsō*) his name before my Father, and before his angels." Thus, to confess Christ means to have sins forgiven and to enjoy fellowship with God both now and in the world to come.

Homologeō elsewhere suggests public acknowledgments of other sorts. The Pharisees "confessed" their belief in a resurrection and in spirit beings (Acts 23:8). Jesus will "profess" words of condemnation on a religious but disobedient multitude on the Day of Judgment (Matthew 7:23), because they, like those in Titus 1:16, "professed" to know God but had denied Him by their evil deeds. A true confession of Christ involves the heart as well as the lips; a mere proclamation of Christ, even though public, is insufficient without genuine faith and repentance. Conversely, to "believe" on Jesus but not be willing to confess Him is an indication of an inadequate faith, one which loves men's praise more than God's (John 12:42,43).

Several times *homologeō* is used in the sense of "to publicly admit," or "concede" something (John 1:20—twice; Acts 24:14; Hebrews 11:13). First John 1:9 is the only New Testament instance where the word is used for confession of sins, not suggesting a public admission, but an open admission of them to God. Twice the word means "to promise," or "vow" (Matthew 14:7; Acts 7:17). Once it is translated "give thanks" (Hebrews 13:15), reflecting one of the earlier Jewish uses of the term, although the standard meaning "confess" makes good sense here as well.

STRONG 3670, BAUER 568, MOULTON-MILLIGAN 449, KITTEL 5:199-220, LIDDELL-SCOTT 1226, COLIN BROWN 1:344-48.

3534. ὁμολογία homologia noun
Profession, confession, acknowledgment.
CROSS-REFERENCE:
ὁμολογέω homologeō (3533)

נְדָבָה nᵉdhāvāh (5249), Freewill offering (Dt 12:6, Ez 46:12, Am 4:5).

נֶדֶר nedher (5266I), Vow (Lv 22:18).

1. ὁμολογίας homologias gen sing fem
2. ὁμολογίαν homologian acc sing fem

1 they glorify God for your **professed** subjection .... 2 Co 9:13
2 professed a good **profession** before many witnesses. 1 Tm 6:12
2 before Pontius Pilate witnessed a good **confession**; 6:13
1 and High Priest of our **profession**, Christ Jesus; ...... Heb 3:1

1 let us hold fast our **profession**. . . . . Heb 4:14
2 Let us hold fast the **profession** of our faith 10:23

Classical Greek
In classical Greek the compound noun *homologia* primarily means "agreement." This agreement is usually a public rather that a private matter. It can be formalized as a "compact" between parties. For example, in military language it is the "terms of peace, truce, or surrender" (*Liddell-Scott*). The Stoics used *homologia* to mean "conformity with nature" (ibid.). In the papyri *homologia* preserves its classical legal meaning: "contract, agreement" (cf. *Moulton-Milligan*).

Septuagint Usage
In the Septuagint *homologia* translates *nᵉdhāvāh* ("freewill offering," Deuteronomy 12:6,17; Ezekiel 46:12; Amos 4:5). It also translates *nedher*, which means either a "vow" given as a "freewill offering" to the Lord (Leviticus 22:18), or the "(sacrificial) vows" which were made to the "queen of heaven" (Jeremiah 44:25 [LXX 51:25]).

New Testament Usage
Homologia is used six times in the New Testament. It can mean "confession" as an action. Thus, Paul wrote to the Corinthians, "Men will praise God for the obedience that accompanies your confession ('*professed subjection*,' KJV) of the gospel of Christ" (2 Corinthians 9:13, NIV). *Bauer* suggests the translation: "your *confessing* the gospel finds expression in obedient subjection to its requirements."

Homologia, however, is used more often in the passive sense to mean the "confession" or "acknowledgment" that one makes. Thus, not only Timothy "made the good *confession* (of his faith) in the presence of many witnesses," but also Christ Jesus, who "in his testimony before Pontius Pilate made the good *confession*" (1 Timothy 6:12,13, RSV). The writer of the Epistle to the Hebrews used *homologia* three times. Jesus is "the Apostle and High Priest of our profession" (3:1). Therefore, these Hebrew Christians were exhorted to "hold fast (y)our profession" (4:14). This exhortation to endurance is reinforced later in the epistle: "Let us hold fast the profession of our faith without wavering" (10:23). The writer concluded his exhortation with the reminder: "for he is faithful that promised."

Strong 3671, Bauer 568-69, Moulton-Milligan 449, Kittel 5:199-220, Liddell-Scott 1226, Colin Brown 1:344,346-47.

3535. ὁμολογουμένως
homologoumenōs adv
Undeniably, confessedly.
Cross-Reference:
    ὁμολογέω homologeō (3533)

1. ὁμολογουμένως homologoumenōs
1 And **without controversy** great is the mystery . . . . 1 Tm 3:16

This adverb is related to the verb *homologeō* (3533), which has a variety of meanings including "confess, agree," and "assure." The adverb can mean "confessedly, assuredly, admittedly," or "by common consent" (*Liddell-Scott*). In its one New Testament occurrence *homologoumenōs* is translated "without controversy" (1 Timothy 3:16). The "mystery of godliness," the wondrous story of salvation, is acknowledged and affirmed as "great" by all believers.

Strong 3672, Bauer 569, Moulton-Milligan 449-50, Kittel 5:199-220, Liddell-Scott 1226.

3536. ὁμότεχνος **homotechnos** adj
Of the same trade, profession, or craft.

1. ὁμότεχνον homotechnon acc sing masc
1 he was of the **same craft**, he abode with them, ... Acts 18:3

This adjective is a compound of *homou* (3537), "together, along with," and an adjectival form of the word "art" or "skill" (*technē* [4926]). *Homotechnos* could be used to describe any two persons who practice the same profession or skill, whether medical art or manual labor (cf. *Liddell-Scott*). The word is also used substantively to mean "fellow workman" or as a title applied to a good physician (ibid.). Paul was "of the same craft" as Aquila and Priscilla who were tentmakers (Acts 18:3). The use of the term "tentmaker," *skēnopoios* (4490), may actually include a wide variety of leather products, all of which made this craft a very viable one during that period (cf. Gloer, "Tentmaker," *International Standard Bible Encyclopedia*, 4:792). The availability and portability of Paul's craft was an invaluable asset in his practice of supporting his own missionary work (cf. 1 Corinthians 4:12; 1 Thessalonians 2:9). It is more than reasonable to suppose that upon arriving at a new city (Acts 18:2) Paul sought out those who were *homotechnos*, "of the same trade," with whom he could find work.

STRONG 3673, BAUER 569, MOULTON-MILLIGAN 450, LIDDELL-SCOTT 1228.

3537. ὁμοῦ homou adv
Together, along with.

יַחַד yachadh (3266), Both (Jb 34:29).

1. ὁμοῦ homou

| 1 soweth and he that reapeth may rejoice **together**..... John 4:36 |
| 1 So they ran both **together**:........................... 20:4 |
| 1 There were **together** Simon Peter, and Thomas........ 21:2 |
| 1 they were all **together** in one place. (NASB)........ Acts 2:1 |

Homou is an adverb related to the adjective *homos*, "same." *Homou* generally means "together" in the sense of "at the same time" or "at the same place." In John 4:36 and 20:4 the meaning is "together" in the sense of "at the same time." In John 21:2 the meaning is "together" in the sense of "at the same place," although this also includes the sense of "at the same time." Many Greek manuscripts include this word in Acts 2:1, but the *Textus Receptus*, on which the King James Version is based, uses *homothumadon* (3524) instead. The meaning is not substantially changed by the difference in wording.

STRONG 3674, BAUER 569, MOULTON-MILLIGAN 450, LIDDELL-SCOTT 1228.

3538. ὁμόφρων homophrōn adj
Of one mind, united, harmonious.

1. ὁμόφρονες homophrones nom pl masc

| 1 Finally, be ye all **of one mind**,..................... 1 Pt 3:8 |

The only occurrence of this word in the New Testament (in its plural form, *homophrones*) is in 1 Peter 3:8, where it is translated "of one mind." *Homophrōn* was formed by the combination of *homou* (3537), "together," and *phrēn* (5260), "heart, mind understanding" (see *Liddell-Scott*). "Of one mind" in this sense means "united in heart and affections." Peter's exhortation does not mean there will be no differences of opinion. Rather, believers are to focus on the purposes which transcend minor differences of opinion and which thus serve to unite. Precisely because differences of opinion on some things are inevitable, the Bible urges Christians to maintain harmony. Note that the whole verse emphasizes attitudes (compassion, brotherly love) rather than opinions or doctrinal views.

STRONG 3675, BAUER 569, MOULTON-MILLIGAN 450, LIDDELL-SCOTT 1228.

3539. ὅμως homōs adv
Nevertheless, yet, even though.

1. ὅμως homōs

| 1 **Nevertheless** among ... rulers also many believed... John 12:42 |
| 1 And **even** things without life giving sound,......... 1 Co 14:7 |
| 1 **Though** it be but a man's covenant,................. Gal 3:15 |

This adverb has a variety of uses in classical Greek and the Septuagint. Most frequently it means "all the same, nevertheless," but it can also mean "however," and "after all, in spite of all" depending on the sentence construction (*Liddell-Scott*). In the New Testament (John 12:42) it is used in combination with *mentoi* (3175) and is translated "nevertheless."

Two instances of the word in Paul's writings are grammatically difficult. "Nevertheless" would not be a sensible translation in either 1 Corinthians 14:7 (where it is translated "and even") or Galatians 3:15 (where the words "though" and "but" are both required to translate *homōs* [3539]). Some grammarians have suggested treating *homōs* as an adverb in both these verses and translating it as "likewise." This would require only a difference of accent and not of spelling (see *Bauer*). In both these verses, however, the translation "even though" would serve well, and the texts as read in the King James Version are clear enough.

STRONG 3676, BAUER 569, MOULTON-MILLIGAN 450, LIDDELL-SCOTT 1230.

3540. ὄναρ onar noun
Dream.

SYNONYM:
ἐνύπνιον enupnion (1782)

1. ὄναρ onar nom/acc sing neu

| 1 angel of the Lord appeared unto him in **a dream**,... Matt 1:20 |
| 1 And being warned of God in **a dream**................. 2:12 |
| 1 angel of the Lord appeareth to Joseph in **a dream**,... 2:13 |
| 1 angel of the Lord appeareth in **a dream** to Joseph.... 2:19 |
| 1 notwithstanding, being warned of God in **a dream**,... 2:22 |
| 1 I have suffered many things this day in **a dream**.... 27:19 |

Classical Greek

Onar as a noun for "dream" dates back to Homer and is often used in nonbiblical references to dreams believed to be revelatory. In antiquity dreams were much believed in, but still scoffed at because it was debated how to tell genuine direction from false or coincidental dreams (cf. Oepke, "onar," *Kittel* 5:220ff.). Dreams given to righteous people in Bible times were divine messages from God. At times, God gave dreams to unrighteous kings (e.g., Pharaoh and Nebuchadnezzar), but the interpretation came from the righteous. This word is not found in the Septuagint.

New Testament Usage
All six occurrences of this word in the New Testament are in the Gospel of Matthew. In every instance *onar* is found with the preposition *kata* in the phrase *kat' onar*, which is translated "in a dream." Through dreams Joseph received divine guidance and warnings to avoid danger to the child Jesus (Matthew 1:20; 2:13,19,22), and the Wise Men also gave heed to a warning to escape Herod's hand (2:12). "This serves to enforce a basic Matthaean theme that this Jesus is God's chosen and anointed one" (Budd, "Dream," *Colin Brown*, 1:512). A warning which went unheeded was brought to Pilate from his wife, who reported having had a dream about Jesus. Her dream was apparently frightening to her, for she said she had "suffered many things this day in a *dream* because of him" (Matthew 27:19).

STRONG 3677, BAUER 569-70, MOULTON-MILLIGAN 450, KITTEL 5:220-28, LIDDELL-SCOTT 1230, COLIN BROWN 1:511-13.

3541. ὀνάριον onarion noun
Young ass, little donkey.

1. ὀνάριον onarion nom/acc sing neu

1 when he had found a young ass, sat thereon; ...... John 12:14

Classical Greek
In form, *onarion* is a diminutive of *onos* (3551), "ass" or "donkey." If the diminutive form is meant literally *onarion* should mean "little or young donkey." The diminutive force of *onarion*, however, does not always seem to have been intended literally. In some cases, then, *onarion* simply meant "donkey" or "ass" (see *Bauer*). Donkeys were beasts of burden, and their meat was eaten only in an emergency (Michel, "onos," *Kittel*, 5:284). This word is not found in the Septuagint.

New Testament Usage
John is the only New Testament writer to use the word *onarion*. It describes the animal on which Jesus rode into Jerusalem on Palm Sunday (John 12:14). In verse 15 John quoted Zechariah 9:9 which refers to the animal as *pōlos onou*, literally, "colt of an ass" (compare "ass's colt" in the King James Version). Neither way of referring to the animal would necessarily indicate that it was not full grown (and thus capable of bearing the weight of a grown man). On the other hand, both Mark 11:2 and Luke 19:30 refer to the "colt" (*pōlos*) as one on which no one had ever sat. This would indicate that the animal was young even if mature in size and strength.

STRONG 3678, BAUER 570, MOULTON-MILLIGAN 450, KITTEL 5:283-87, LIDDELL-SCOTT 1230, COLIN BROWN 1:117.

3542. ὀνειδίζω oneidizō verb
Scold, reproach, revile.

COGNATES:
ὁμολογέω homologeō (3533)
ὀνειδισμός oneidismos (3543)
ὄνειδος oneidos (3544)

SYNONYMS:
βλασφημέω blasphēmeō (980)
κακολογέω kakologeō (2522)
καταλαλέω katalaleō (2605)
λοιδορέω loidoreō (3032)
ὑβρίζω hubrizō (5036)

גָּדַף gādhaph (1472), Piel: blaspheme (Is 37:6).

חָפַר chāphar (2763), Qal: dig (Ps 35:7 [34:7]); be ashamed (Jer 15:9); hiphil: be ashamed (Is 54:4).

חָרַף chāraph (2884), Qal: reproach (Ps 69:9 [68:9]); piel: defy, reproach (1 Sm 17:10, Ps 55:12 [54:12], Is 37:17).

יָכַח yākhach (3306), Hiphil: rebuke (Is 37:4).

כָּלַם kālam (3757), Be ashamed; hiphil: put to shame (Prv 25:8).

1. ὀνειδίζοντος oneidizontos
    gen sing masc part pres act
2. ὀνειδιζόντων oneidizontōn
    gen pl masc part pres act
3. ὀνειδίζειν oneidizein inf pres act
4. ὠνείδισεν ōneidisen 3sing indic aor act
5. ὀνειδίσωσιν oneidisōsin 3pl subj aor act
6. ὠνείδιζον ōneidizon 3pl indic imperf act
7. ὀνειδιζόμεθα oneidizometha 1pl indic pres mid
8. ὀνειδίζεσθε oneidizesthe 2pl indic pres mid

5 Blessed are ye, when men **shall revile** you, ... Matt 5:11
3 Then began he to **upbraid** the cities wherein 11:20
6 crucified with him also **heaped insults** (NIV) 27:44
6 And they that were crucified with him reviled him. Mark 15:32
4 and **upbraided** them with their unbelief and 16:14
5 **shall reproach** you, and cast out your name as evil, .. Luke 6:22
2 The reproaches of them that **reproached** thee ..... Rom 15:3

ὀνειδισμός 3543

7 For therefore we both labour and **suffer reproach**,...1 Tm 4:10
1 giveth to all men liberally, and **upbraideth** not;.......Jas 1:5
8 If ye **be reproached** for the name of Christ,.........1 Pt 4:14

Classical Greek and Septuagint Usage

The verb *oneidizō* signifies in the active voice "to reproach, to upbraid," or "to revile, to bring reproach against someone, voice a complaint against someone or something." In the passive voice *oneidizō* means "to suffer reproach" or "to be reproached" (cf. *Liddell-Scott*).

In classical Greek the term is sometimes used to denote "reproach" thrown against the gods. It is also used frequently in the Septuagint, especially in the Psalms, in reference to those who "revile" or "scorn" God, the Children of Israel, those who are righteous, etc. (e.g., Psalms 42:10 [LXX 41:10]; 74:10 [73:10]; 89:51 [88:51]).

New Testament Usage

In Matthew 5:11 Jesus indicated to His disciples that they would be "reviled" and persecuted for His sake. In Matthew 11:20 He "reproached" or "scolded" the cities of Galilee when they failed to recognize and respond to the miracles He had performed there. Similarly, Jesus chided his disciples for their unbelief (Mark 16:14). Matthew 27:44 and Mark 15:32 state that the robbers with whom He was crucified "reproached" ("heaped insults upon") Him.

In Romans 15:3 the apostle Paul quoted Psalm 69:9, "The reproaches of them that reproached thee fell on me," illustrating that Christ did not come to please himself but bore on himself the insults and the reproach of men. Likewise, believers should "bear with the failings of the weak" and not live just to please themselves. In the passive voice *oneidizō* means to "suffer reproach, be reproached" (1 Timothy 4:10; 1 Peter 4:14).

STRONG 3679, BAUER 570, MOULTON-MILLIGAN 450, KITTEL 5:239-40, LIDDELL-SCOTT 1230, COLIN BROWN 3:340-41.

3543. ὀνειδισμός oneidismos noun

Reproach, reviling, disgrace, insult.

COGNATE:
  ὀνειδίζω oneidizō (3542)

SYNONYMS:
  ἀτιμία atimia (813)
  ὄνειδος oneidos (3544)
  ὕβρις hubris (5036B)

בִּזָּה bizzāh (996), Plunder (Neh 4:4—only some Sinaiticus texts).

גִּדּוּף giddûph (1450), Reviling (Is 43:28).

חֶרְפָּה cherpāh (2887), Reproach (1 Sm 25:39, Ps 79:12 [78:12], Jer 15:15).

כְּלִמָּה kᵉlimmāh (3759), Scorn, insults (Ez 34:29, 36:6).

תּוֹכֵחָה tôkhēchāh (8762), Rebuke (Is 37:3).

1. ὀνειδισμόν oneidismon acc sing masc
2. ὀνειδισμοί oneidismoi nom pl masc
3. ὀνειδισμοῖς oneidismois dat pl masc

2 The **reproaches** of them that reproached thee......Rom 15:3
1 lest he fall into **reproach** and the snare of the devil. 1 Tm 3:7
3 a gazingstock both by **reproaches** and afflictions;....Heb 10:33
1 Esteeming the **reproach** of Christ greater riches........11:26
1 unto him without the camp, bearing his **reproach**.......13:13

Classical Greek

Oneidismos is essentially indistinguishable in meaning from the word *oneidos* (3544). Both words mean "reproach, disgrace," or "insult," and both are derived from the verb *oneidizō* (3542), which means "to revile" or "to insult." Compared with *oneidos*, however, *oneidismos* occurs quite late in extant Greek literature. The earliest known instances of *oneidismos* are from the Koine period, while *oneidos* is found in the writings of Homer and throughout the classical Greek period.

Septuagint Usage

Both *oneidismos* and *oneidos* are used frequently throughout the Septuagint to translate several different Hebrew words. More often than not, however, the Hebrew term being translated is *cherpāh*, "reproach, blame." This fact bears witness to the interchangeability of these two words in the Koine period. Although found in the writings of Josephus and elsewhere in the Koine period, outside of the Bible the use of *oneidismos* was "comparatively rare" (*Moulton-Milligan*).

Of the many occurrences of *oneidismos* in the Septuagint, especially notable are the several times it is used in Psalm 69 (LXX 68; verses 7,9,10,19,20) and its frequent usage in the Book of Jeremiah. David lamented his unjust treatment from men because of his devotion to God. Because of his zeal for the house of God, the Psalmist said: "The reproaches of them that reproached thee (God) are fallen upon me" (Psalm 69:9 [LXX 68:9]). Likewise, Jeremiah bore the reproach and insults of the people because they regarded the word he brought from God as a reproach (6:10; 20:8). But the reproach and blame which came to those who despised and rejected God's Word was greater and more lasting (23:40; 24:9; 44:12 [LXX 51:12]; 51:51 [28:51]).

New Testament Usage

Oneidismos occurs five times in the New Testament. The first of these is Romans 15:3 where Paul quoted the latter part of Psalm 69:9. (Note that the first part of Psalm 69:9 is applied to Jesus in John 2:17.) Paul said that Christ is the ultimate example of someone bearing the reproach of people because of His devotion to the will of God. The context is an extended exhortation for Christians to accept one another (Romans 14:1 to 15:7). Jesus accepted the reproach of men toward God so believers might be accepted by God. Paul said believers should do the same (15:7). They should not let differences of opinion on insignificant matters break their fellowship with other sincere Christians. If Christ bore the reproach of the believers' sins against God so they might be reconciled to God, they can bear the weaknesses of others and not simply "please" themselves (15:1).

The Book of Hebrews uses *oneidismos* three times, more than all of the rest of the New Testament combined. In each case it signifies the reproach or rejection experienced by those who have identified with Jesus and God's purposes at the expense of being despised by the world. The Christians who first read the words of Hebrews had already experienced "reproaches and afflictions" in being "made a gazing-stock" in the eyes of the unbelieving world (10:33). Moses is cited as an inspiring example of choosing to bear "the reproach of Christ" (i.e., for being identified with God's people) rather than choosing personal comfort and safety (11:26). Psalm 89:50,51, which speaks of bearing the reproach (*oneidismos*) of God's people and God's "anointed" (*christos* [5382] in the Septuagint), was perhaps in mind here (Eichler and Brown, "Possessions," *Colin Brown*, 2:835). Hebrews 13:13 urges believers to join themselves to Christ "without the camp" (i.e., to accept exclusion from the fellowship of those who have rejected Christ). This is what it means to "bear his reproach," to be willing to bear the world's scorn and treatment of Christ in order to be Christ's people.

Some reproaches from the world are inevitable because of the Christian's identification with Christ, but not reproaches for immorality or improper behavior. First Timothy 3:7 states that those considered for leadership positions in the church should "have a good report" even among those outside the church so they do not fall into "*reproach* and the snare of the devil." Here "reproach" is obviously being used in direct contrast to having a "good report."

Oneidismos can also mean a reproach against someone. Jesus reproached or condemned Tyre and Sidon. The same word is also used in the accounts of Jesus being reviled.

STRONG 3680, BAUER 570, MOULTON-MILLIGAN 450, KITTEL 5:241-42, LIDDELL-SCOTT 1230, COLIN BROWN 2:835; 3:340.

3544. ὄνειδος oneidos noun

Reproach, disgrace, censure, rebuke, blame.

COGNATE:
    ὀνειδίζω oneidzō (3542)

SYNONYMS:
    ἀτιμία atimia (813)
    ὀνειδισμός oneidismos (3543)
    ὕβρις hubris (5036B)

חָמָס chāmās (2660), Reproach (Ps 57:3 [56:3]); violence (Prv 3:31, 26:6).

חֶסֶד cheṣedh (2722), Disgrace (Lv 20:17).

חֶרְפָּה cherpāh (2887), Reproach (Gn 30:23, Ps 31:11 [30:11], Is 30:5).

כְּלִמָּה kᵉlimmāh (3759), Shame, humiliation (Prv 18:13, Is 30:3, Mi 2:6).

לַעַג laʿagh (4075), Scorn (Ps 123:4 [122:4]).

1. ὄνειδος oneidos nom/acc sing neu

1 to take away my **reproach** among men.............Luke 1:25

Oneidos is closely related in meaning with *oneidismos* (3543). Both words mean "reproach, disgrace," or "insult," and both are related to the verb *oneidizō* which means "to revile" or "to insult." *Oneidos* appears much earlier in classical Greek literature than *oneidismos* (since Homer, ca. Eighth Century B.C.).

Both *oneidismos* and *oneidos* are used frequently in the Septuagint, often to translate the Hebrew word *cherpah*, "reproach, blame." The only occurrence of *oneidos* in the New Testament is in Luke 1:25. Elizabeth, after becoming pregnant in her old age, felt that her "reproach" had been removed. In that day it was considered something of a public embarrassment not to have had children, and the impending birth of John the Baptist would relieve her of this embarrassment. Compare the similar situation of Rachel in Genesis 30:23, where the Septuagint also uses *oneidos*.

STRONG 3681, BAUER 570, MOULTON-MILLIGAN

450, Kittel 5:238-39, Liddell-Scott 1230, Colin Brown 3:340.

3545. Ὀνήσιμος Onēsimos name
Onesimus.

1. Ὀνησίμου Onēsimou gen masc
2. Ὀνησίμῳ Onēsimō dat masc
3. Ὀνήσιμον Onēsimon acc masc

2 With **Onesimus**, a faithful and beloved brother, ... Col 4:9
3 I beseech thee for my son **Onesimus**, ... Phlm 1:10

Runaway slave converted by Paul in Rome and returned to his master; the letter to Philemon was written by Paul on his behalf (Philemon 10).

3546. Ὀνησίφορος Onēsiphoros name
Onesiphorus.

1. Ὀνησιφόρου Onēsiphorou gen masc
2. Ὀνησιφόρῳ Onēsiphorō dat masc

1 Lord give mercy unto the house of **Onesiphorus**; .... 2 Tm 1:16
1 Salute ... the household of **Onesiphorus**. 4:19

Christian commended for his ministry to Paul, as well as his faithfulness to Paul, when he was in prison (2 Timothy 1:16).

3547. ὀνικός onikos adj
Pertaining to a donkey, large millstone.

1. ὀνικός onikos nom sing masc

1 it were better for him that a **millstone** were hanged Matt 18:6
1 a heavy **millstone** hung around his neck, (NASB) ... Mark 9:42
1 It were better for him that a **millstone** were hanged Luke 17:2

Classical Greek
Onikos is an adjective formed from the noun *onos* (3551), "donkey" or "ass." *Onikos* literally means "of or pertaining to a donkey." In the process of grinding grain in the ancient world the heavy upper millstone was often turned by a donkey. Thus the millstone (*mulos*) came to be called *mulos onikos* because of its relationship to the donkey which moved it. In classical Greek *onikos* can also mean "squared building stones" (*Moulton-Milligan*). This word is not used in the Septuagint.

New Testament Usage
In Matthew 18:6 the two words *mulos onikos* are translated as simply "a millstone," but the sense is "a large millstone," such as could be turned only by a work animal like a donkey. The parallel passage in Luke 17:2 also uses the word *onikos* in the *Textus Receptus* (the basis for the King James Version), but many Greek manuscripts lack *onikos* in this verse. Conversely, the other parallel, Mark 9:42, has the word *onikos* in many manuscripts but not in the *Textus Receptus*. In this verse Jesus said that one would be better off being drowned by having a "millstone" hung around his neck and being thrown into the sea than to offend a little child.

Strong 3684, Bauer 570, Moulton-Milligan 450-51, Liddell-Scott 1231, Colin Brown 3:394.

3548. ὀνίνημι oninēmi verb
Benefit, be useful, help, profit.

1. ὀναίμην onaimēn 1sing opt aor mid

1 Yea, brother, let me **have joy** of thee in the Lord: .. Phlm 1:20

In classical Greek the verb *oninēmi* means "to profit, benefit, help." In the optative mood *oninēmi* principally expresses wishes or protestations. It is not attested in the Septuagint in this mood.

In the New Testament *oninēmi* appears only in Philemon 20. Paul wrote, "Yea, brother, let me *have joy* (benefit) of thee in the Lord." Paul's use of *oninēmi* here may be a deliberate word play on the name Onesimus, which is derived from *onēsis*, "profit" (Philemon 10,11). The church father Ignatius frequently used the optative form *onaimēn* in his epistles (cf. *Bauer*).

Strong 3685, Bauer 570, Moulton-Milligan 451, Liddell-Scott 1231-32.

3549. ὄνομα onoma noun
Name.

Cognates:
 ἐπονομάζω eponomazō (2012)
 ὀνομάζω onomazō (3550)
 ψευδώνυμος pseudōnumos (5416)

זֵכֶר zēkher (2228), Memory (Dt 25:19).

נֶכֶד nekhedh (5408), Posterity (Gn 21:23).

שֵׁם shēm (8428), Name (Gn 38:1-6, 2 Chr 6:7-10, Jer 7:10ff.).

שֻׁם shum (A8430), Name (Ezr 5:1,4,10, Dn 2:20,26—Aramaic).

שֵׁמַע shēma' (8475), News, report (Gn 29:13, Dt 2:25); fame (Is 66:19).

ὄνομα 3549

שֹׁמַע shōmaʿ (8476), Fame, report (Jos 6:27 [6:26], 9:9).

1. ὀνόματα onomata nom/acc pl neu
2. ὄνομα onoma nom/acc sing neu
3. ὀνόματος onomatos gen sing neu
4. ὀνόματι onomati dat sing neu
5. ὀνομάτων onomatōn gen pl neu

2	and thou shalt call his **name** JESUS:	Matt 1:21
2	and they shall call his **name** Emmanuel,	1:23
2	and he called his **name** JESUS.	1:25
2	Hallowed be thy **name**.	6:9
4	have we not prophesied in thy **name**?	7:22
4	and in thy **name** have cast out devils?	7:22
4	and in thy **name** done many wonderful works?	7:22
1	Now the **names** of the twelve apostles are these;	10:2
2	ye shall be hated of all men for my **name's** sake:	10:22
2	receiveth a prophet in the **name** of a prophet	10:41
2	a righteous man in the **name** of a righteous man	10:41
2	a cup of cold water only in the **name** of a disciple,	10:42
4	And in his **name** shall the Gentiles trust.	12:21
4	receive ... little child in my **name** receiveth me.	18:5
2	two or three are gathered together in my **name**,	18:20
3	or wife, or children, or lands, for my **name's** sake,	19:29
4	Blessed is he that cometh in the **name** of the Lord;	21:9
4	Blessed is he that cometh in the **name** of the Lord.	23:39
4	many shall come in my **name**, saying, I am Christ;	24:5
2	ye shall be hated of all nations for my **name's** sake.	24:9
4	they found a man of Cyrene, Simon **by name**:	27:32
2	baptizing them in the **name** of the Father, and	28:19
2	And Simon he **surnamed** Peter;	Mark 3:16
1	**surnamed** them Boanerges, ... The sons of thunder:	3:17
2	And he asked him, What is thy **name**?	5:9
2	saying, My **name** is Legion: for we are many.	5:9
4	one of the rulers of the synagogue, Jairus **by name**;	5:22
2	for his **name** was spread abroad: and he said,	6:14
4	such children in my **name**, receiveth me:	9:37
4	Master, we saw one casting out devils in thy **name**,	9:38
4	man which shall do a miracle in my **name**,	9:39
4	shall give you a cup of water to drink in my **name**,	9:41
4	Blessed is he that cometh in the **name** of the Lord:	11:9
4	kingdom ... that cometh in the **name** of the Lord:	11:10
4	many shall come in my **name**, saying, I am Christ;	13:6
2	ye shall be hated of all men for my **name's** sake:	13:13
2	came to a place which **was named** Gethsemane:	14:32
4	In my **name** shall they cast out devils;	16:17
4	a certain priest **named** Zacharias,	Luke 1:5
3	daughters of Aaron, and her **name** was Elisabeth.	1:5
2	bear thee a son, and thou shalt call his **name** John.	1:13
2	unto a city of Galilee, **named** Nazareth,	1:26
4	virgin espoused to a man whose **name** was Joseph,	1:27
2	and the virgin's **name** was Mary.	1:27
2	bring forth a son, and shalt call his **name** JESUS.	1:31
2	done to me great things; and holy is his **name**.	1:49
4	called him Zacharias, after the **name** of his father.	1:59
2	none of thy kindred that is called by this **name**.	1:61
2	saying, His **name** is John. And they marvelled all.	1:63
2	his **name** was called JESUS,	2:21
2	a man in Jerusalem, whose **name** was Simeon;	2:25
4	he went forth, and saw a publican, **named** Levi,	5:27
2	shall reproach you, and cast out your **name** as evil,	6:22
2	And Jesus asked him, saying, What is thy **name**?	8:30
2	And, behold, there came a man **named** Jairus,	8:41
4	Whosoever shall receive this child in my **name**	9:48
4	Master, we saw one casting out devils in thy **name**;	9:49
4	the devils are subject unto us through thy **name**.	10:17
1	rejoice, because your **names** are written in heaven.	10:20
4	and a certain woman **named** Martha received him	10:38
2	Hallowed be thy **name**. Thy kingdom come.	11:2
4	Blessed is he that cometh in the **name** of the Lord.	13:35
4	And there was a certain beggar **named** Lazarus,	16:20
4	And, behold, there was a man **named** Zacchaeus,	19:2
4	Blessed be the King that cometh in the **name** of	19:38
4	many shall come in my **name**, saying, I am Christ;	21:8
3	before kings and rulers for my **name's** sake.	21:12
2	ye shall be hated of all men for my **name's** sake.	Luke 21:17
4	there was a man **named** Joseph, a counsellor;	23:50
2	went that same day to a village **called** Emmaus,	24:13
2	And the one of them, whose **name** was Cleopas,	24:18
4	remission of sins should be preached in his **name**	24:47
2	was a man sent from God, whose **name** was John.	John 1:6
2	even to them that believe on his **name**:	1:12
2	many believed in his **name**, when they saw	2:23
2	a man of the Pharisees, **named** Nicodemus,	3:1
2	in the **name** of the only begotten Son of God.	3:18
4	I am come in my Father's **name**,	5:43
4	if another shall come in his own **name**,	5:43
2	and he calleth his own sheep by **name**,	10:3
4	the works that I do in my Father's **name**,	10:25
4	King of Israel that cometh in the **name** of the Lord.	12:13
2	Father, glorify thy **name**.	12:28
4	whatsoever ye shall ask in my **name**, that will I do,	14:13
4	If ye shall ask any thing in my **name**, I will do it.	14:14
4	Ghost, whom the Father will send in my **name**,	14:26
4	whatsoever ye shall ask of the Father in my **name**,	15:16
2	things will they do unto you for my **name's** sake,	15:21
4	Whatsoever ye shall ask the Father in my **name**,	16:23
4	Hitherto have ye asked nothing in my **name**:	16:24
4	At that day ye shall ask in my **name**:	16:26
2	I have manifested thy **name** unto the men	17:6
4	Holy Father, keep through thine own **name**	17:11
4	I kept them in thy **name**:	17:12
2	And I have declared unto them thy **name**,	17:26
2	The servant's **name** was Malchus.	18:10
4	that believing ye might have life through his **name**.	20:31
5	the number of **names** ... an hundred and twenty,	Acts 1:15
2	shall call on the **name** of the Lord shall be saved.	2:21
4	be baptized every one of you in the **name** of Jesus	2:38
4	In the **name** of Jesus Christ of Nazareth rise up	3:6
3	And his **name** through faith	3:16
2	faith in his **name** hath made this man strong,	3:16
4	what power, or by what **name**, have ye done this?	4:7
2	that by the **name** of Jesus Christ of Nazareth,	4:10
2	none other **name** under heaven given among men,	4:12
4	that they speak henceforth to no man in this **name**.	4:17
4	not to speak at all nor teach in the **name** of Jesus.	4:18
3	may be done by the **name** of thy holy child Jesus.	4:30
4	But a certain man **named** Ananias,	5:1
4	that ye should not teach in this **name**?	5:28
4	a Pharisee, **named** Gamaliel, a doctor of the law,	5:34
4	that they should not speak in the **name** of Jesus,	5:40
3	were counted worthy to suffer shame for his **name**.	5:41
4	But there was a certain man, **called** Simon,	8:9
3	the kingdom of God, and the **name** of Jesus Christ,	8:12
2	only they were baptized in the **name** of the Lord	8:16
4	a certain disciple at Damascus, **named** Ananias;	9:10
4	inquire in the house of Judas for one **called** Saul,	9:11
4	And hath seen in a vision a man **named** Ananias	9:12
2	to bind all that call on thy **name**.	9:14
2	to bear my **name** before the Gentiles.	9:15
3	great things he must suffer for my **name's** sake.	9:16
2	them which called on this **name** in Jerusalem,	9:21
4	preached boldly at Damascus in the **name** of Jesus.	9:27
4	And he spake boldly in the **name** of the Lord Jesus,	9:29
4	And there he found a certain man **named** AEneas,	9:33
4	was at Joppa a certain disciple **named** Tabitha,	9:36
4	was a certain man in Caesarea **called** Cornelius,	10:1
3	that through his **name** whosoever believeth in him	10:43
4	them to be baptized in the **name** of the Lord.	10:48
4	And there stood up one of them **named** Agabus,	11:28
4	a damsel came to hearken, **named** Rhoda,	12:13
2	a false prophet, a Jew, whose **name** was Barjesus:	13:6
2	for so is his **name** by interpretation	13:8
4	to take out of them a people for his **name**.	15:14
4	all the Gentiles, upon whom my **name** is called,	15:17
3	Men that have hazarded their lives for the **name**	15:26
4	a certain disciple was there, **named** Timotheus,	16:1
4	a certain woman **named** Lydia, a seller of purple,	16:14
4	I command thee in the **name** of Jesus Christ	16:18
4	a woman **named** Damaris, and others with them.	17:34
4	And found a certain Jew **named** Aquila,	18:2
4	entered into a certain man's house, **named** Justus,	18:7

359

ὄνομα 3549

5 But if it be a question of words and **names**,	Acts 18:15
4 a certain Jew **named** Apollos, born at Alexandria,	18:24
2 they were baptized in the **name** of the Lord Jesus.	19:5
2 to call over them which had evil spirits the **name**	19:13
2 and the **name** of the Lord Jesus was magnified.	19:17
4 For a certain man **named** Demetrius, a silversmith,	19:24
4 in a window a certain young man **named** Eutychus,	20:9
4 from Judaea a certain prophet, **named** Agabus.	21:10
3 to die at Jerusalem for the **name** of the Lord Jesus.	21:13
2 away thy sins, calling on the **name** of the Lord.	22:16
2 things contrary to the **name** of Jesus of Nazareth.	26:9
4 they delivered Paul ... unto one **named** Julius,	27:1
4 whose **name** was Publius; who received us,	28:7
3 to the faith among all nations, for his **name**:	Rom 1:5
2 **name** of God is blasphemed among the Gentiles	2:24
2 **name** might be declared throughout all the earth.	9:17
2 call upon the **name** of the Lord shall be saved.	10:13
4 I will confess to thee ... and sing unto thy **name**.	15:9
2 with all that in every place call upon the **name**	1 Co 1:2
3 by the **name** of our Lord Jesus Christ,	1:10
2 or were ye baptized in the **name** of Paul?	1:13
2 should say that I had baptized in mine own **name**.	1:15
4 In the **name** of our Lord Jesus Christ,	5:4
4 but ye are justified in the **name** of the Lord Jesus,	6:11
3 and dominion, and every **name** that is named,	Eph 1:21
4 the Father in the **name** of our Lord Jesus Christ;	5:20
2 and given him a **name** which is above every name:	Phlp 2:9
2 and given him a name which is above every **name**:	2:9
4 That at the **name** of Jesus every knee should bow,	2:10
1 whose **names** are in the book of life.	4:3
4 do all in the **name** of the Lord Jesus,	Col 3:17
2 the **name** of our Lord Jesus Christ may be glorified	2 Th 1:12
2 command ... in the **name** of our Lord Jesus Christ,	3:6
2 that the **name** of God ... be not blasphemed.	1 Tm 6:1
2 Let every one that nameth the **name** of Christ	2 Tm 2:19
2 obtained a more excellent **name** than they.	Heb 1:4
2 I will declare thy **name** unto my brethren,	2:12
2 of love, which ye have showed toward his **name**,	6:10
4 the fruit of our lips giving thanks to his **name**.	13:15
2 Do not they blaspheme that worthy **name**	Jas 2:7
4 who have spoken in the **name** of the Lord,	5:10
4 anointing him with oil in the **name** of the Lord:	5:14
4 If ye be reproached for the **name** of Christ,	1 Pt 4:14
4 but in that **name** let him glorify God. (NASB)	4:16
2 your sins are forgiven you for his **name**'s sake,	1 Jn 2:12
4 should believe on the **name** of his Son Jesus Christ,	3:23
2 you that believe on the **name** of the Son of God;	5:13
2 ye may believe on the **name** of the Son of God.	5:13
3 Because that for his **name**'s sake they went forth,	3 Jn 1:7
2 Our friends salute thee. Greet the friends by **name**.	1:14
2 and for my **name**'s sake hast laboured,	Rev 2:3
2 and thou holdest fast my **name**,	2:13
2 white stone, and in the stone a new **name** written,	2:17
2 thou hast a **name** that thou livest, and art dead.	3:1
1 Thou hast a few **names** even in Sardis	3:4
2 I will not blot out his **name** out of the book of life,	3:5
2 but I will confess his **name** before my Father,	3:5
2 hast kept my word, and hast not denied my **name**.	3:8
2 and I will write upon him the **name** of my God,	3:12
2 and the **name** of the city of my God,	3:12
2 and I will write upon him my new **name**.	3:12
2 and his **name** that sat on him was Death,	6:8
2 And the **name** of the star is called Wormwood:	8:11
2 whose **name** in the Hebrew tongue is Abaddon,	9:11
2 but in the Greek tongue hath his **name** Apollyon.	9:11
1 were slain of men seven thousand: (NT)	11:13
2 and to the saints, and them that fear thy **name**,	11:18
2 and upon his heads the **name** of blasphemy.	13:1
2 to blaspheme his **name**, and his tabernacle,	13:6
1 whose **names** are not written in the book of life	13:8
2 save he ... had the mark, or the **name** of the beast,	13:17
3 the name of the beast, or the number of his **name**.	13:17
2 his Father's **name** written in their foreheads.	14:1
3 and whosoever receiveth the mark of his **name**.	14:11
3 over his mark, and over the number of his **name**,	15:2
2 shall not fear thee, O Lord, and glorify thy **name**?	15:4
2 scorched ... and blasphemed the **name** of God,	16:9
5 scarlet coloured beast, full of **names** of blasphemy,	Rev 17:3
2 And upon her forehead was a **name** written,	17:5
1 whose **names** were not written in the book of life	17:8
2 a **name** written, that no man knew, but he himself.	19:12
2 and his **name** is called The Word of God.	19:13
2 on his vesture and on his thigh a **name** written,	19:16
1 had twelve gates, ... and **names** written thereon,	21:12
1 and in them the **names** of the twelve apostles	21:14
2 and his **name** shall be in their foreheads.	22:4

Classical Greek

The noun *onoma* is derived from the Indo-Germanic word *nomn*, or *enomn* (cf. the Latin *nomen* and the Scandinavian *name*). From the earliest period of the Greek language, *onoma* means *name*, whether of a person or a thing. As with the English word "name," an extended meaning is "fame" or "reputation." To "have a name" means to be notable or, in other contexts, to have *only* a name without the accompanying reality. In business dealings the name represents the person, his property, his interests, or his obligations. In grammar, *onoma* means "noun."

More significant than mere definitions were the various views of the relationship between a name and the thing or person bearing the name. Primitive peoples believed the name provided magical power over the thing, person, god, or demon named. They believed the name itself had an intrinsic and revelatory relationship to its owner. This view persisted in some circles but came to be questioned by the Greek philosophers, beginning in the Sixth and Fifth Centuries B.C. (Bietenhard, "onoma," *Kittel*, 5:246).

Parmenides, the Sophists, and Plato held views somewhat similar to those of modern linguistic science: words (including names) mean what a given language group agree to have them mean. A name may reflect a perception of the thing or person, but a perception may be wrong or partial. Thus *onoma* cannot be simply equated with the nature of what is named (ibid., 5:246f.). In contrast to Plato, Stoic philosophers held that the name represents the very nature of the thing named. Consequently the Stoics believed that etymological analysis of names provides genuine insight into the nature of reality. In a move toward monotheism, the Stoics ascribed all the divine names to one god (Zeus), explaining the various names as descriptions of the multiple aspects of his nature and deeds (ibid., 5:249f.).

Septuagint Usage

Onoma occurs over 1,000 times in the Septuagint, almost always translating the Hebrew *shēm* "name." In a few places it translates other

Hebrew words meaning "report" or "fame" (e.g., Numbers 14:15; Joshua 6:27). The significance attached to names is easily seen in the many etymological explanations of the names of individuals, places, and nations: "Isaac" refers to his parents' laughter (Genesis 17:17; 18:12; 21:6); "Edom" means "red" (Genesis 25:30); "Judah" means "praise" (Genesis 29:35). The basis for the choice of name could have been certain events which took place when the child was born (e.g., Genesis 25:26), or particularities in connection with the complexion of the child (Genesis 25:25). The parents' wishes and expectations for the newborn child could also be expressed by the choice of name; for example, Benjamin; "the son of fortune" (Genesis 35:18) and Solomon; "the peace-loving one" (2 Samuel 12:24).

Giving or changing a name could indicate dominion over that which is named or a change of status: Abram became Abraham, "a father of many nations" (Genesis 17:5); the Jewish exiles received new names from their captor, Nebuchadnezzar (Daniel 1:7), which was a way of giving them Babylonian citizenship so they could help in the government.

Sometimes the name could be personified completely, so that it is mentioned as if it performed the action itself (cf. Psalm 20:1,2 [LXX 19:2]; Malachi 1:11). To disregard the name was to disregard the person (cf. Exodus 20:7; Leviticus 24:16). To pay homage to the name was to show honor to the one who was given that name (Nehemiah 9:5; Psalms 34:3 [LXX 33:3]; 138:2 [137:2]).

God's name is the most important one in the Old Testament. Whether called by His distinctive name "the LORD" (*Yahweh* = *kurios* [2935]) or by the generic term "God" (*Elohim* = *theos* [2292B]), God's identity and nature cannot be known apart from the history of His words and actions in relationship with His people. For this reason God speaks of himself as the God of Abraham, Isaac, and Jacob and as "the LORD thy God, which have brought thee out of the land of Egypt" (Exodus 3:6; 20:2). True knowledge of God's name involves knowledge of this history and participation in this relationship.

In contrast to the beliefs of the primitive pagan world, the Bible makes clear that knowledge and use of God's name does not provide power *over* Him but rather relationship *with* Him and responsibility *to* Him. First of all, His name is known only because He freely chose to reveal it (Genesis 17:1; Exodus 3:14,15). Furthermore, the invoking of His name for magical purposes (or other misuses) is forbidden by the third commandment (Exodus 20:7). Israel was urged "to call on the *name* of the Lord," trusting His faithfulness to the covenant, not because the use of His name could force Him to act. God promised to care for the people and the temple bearing His name, but those privileges and blessings could be forfeited by human unfaithfulness to the relationship (2 Chronicles 7:14-22). Likewise the prophets who spoke "in the name of the LORD" had authority only as faithful proclaimers of what God had spoken to them. Without such a commission, the prophet was false.

In Jewish writings outside of Scripture, Philo reflected the influence of Greek Stoicism when he said God's real name never reaches men. God is being itself, which cannot be named. Thus *kurios*, "Lord" is only the name for God's power to rule and not God's actual name (ibid., 5:264-65).

Josephus is more representative as an example of Jewish reserve in using God's name. In his writings he never used *Yahweh* or *kurios*. Instead of God's name, he used the words *onoma* or *prosēgoria*, "title" (cf. Bietenhard, "Name," *Colin Brown*, 2:653). Likewise the rabbis, in their concern to observe the third commandment, refrained from pronouncing God's name. For *Yahweh*, they often inserted *Adonai*, "Lord."

Family names were not used in Israel, only proper names (the first name). However, by the time of the New Testament there were some attempts to distinguish between persons of the same proper name. For example, the word *bar* ("son") was often placed before the name of the person's father (i.e., Bartholomeus, Bartimeus, Barabbas, Barjesus, etc.). There was also the practice of attaching an indication of one's native land or position to the first name (e.g., Judas Iscariot: "man from Cariot"; Mary Magdlene: "from Magdala"; Simon the tanner, Alexander the coppersmith, etc.). It was not unusual to name a child after the father or another close relative (cf. Luke 1:59f.). The use of Grecian and Latin names was also common, sometimes as an addition (e.g., John Mark, Simon Niger, Joseph Justus).

New Testament Usage

The significance of *onoma* in the New Testament (where it occurs more than 200 times) is similar to its meaning in the Old Testament. An individual's name is occasionally (but not always) noted as being an indication of that person's character or role. The renaming of Simon Peter (Matthew 16:17,18) is an example. Also, as in the Old Testament, *onoma* can mean "fame" or "reputation" (Mark 6:14; Revelation 3:1). To receive someone "in the name" of a prophet, a righteous man, or a disciple meant to recognize and treat someone as being such (Matthew 10:41,42). Usually *onoma* represents the person: that Jesus knew the names of His disciples means that He knew His disciples personally (John 10:3,14); having one's name "written in heaven" means being in a life-giving relationship with God (Luke 10:20). In a few cases, *onoma* simply means "person" (Acts 1:15; Revelation 3:4; 11:13).

Demons have names which reveal their nature (Mark 5:9). The "beast" of Revelation 13 is described as having blasphemous names (13:1), which probably refers to his claims to honors "which belong to God or Christ alone" (Bietenhard, "Name," *Colin Brown*, 2:653). The beast will claim the name of God (cf. 2 Thessalonians 2:4), but "the number of his name" is in reality "the number of a man" (Revelation 13:17,18). To be marked with the beast's name or number will mean identification with the doomed opposition to God (Revelation 14:11). Jesus prophesied many would come falsely "in my name" claiming to be the Christ (Matthew 24:5).

The name of God received important new connotations through the coming of Jesus and the saving events of the gospel. God is now known principally as the One who has acted and revealed himself in the person and work of Jesus, just as in the Old Testament He was known as the One who had spoken and acted in Israel's history.

Jesus came in the name of the Father (i.e., sent by the Father) to accomplish the Father's purposes (John 5:43), but the accomplishment of those purposes brought a revelation of Jesus' own name. Ultimately every knee will bow to Jesus' name, for the name of "Lord" is above every name (Ephesians 1:21; Philippians 2:9-11). "Lord" (*kurios*) is the Septuagint's rendering of *Yahweh*. To call Him "Lord" is to acknowledge that He is God (John 20:28), and to call upon Him as Lord is to find salvation (Romans 10:9,13). To use His name this way, however, does not put His saving power under man's control, since "no man can say that Jesus is the Lord, but by the Holy Ghost" (1 Corinthians 12:3). The saving use of His name is God's gift just as the salvation itself is His gift.

While "Lord" is central to recognizing Jesus' deity and receiving His salvation, other names add perspective concerning His nature and significance for believers. "Jesus" means "Yahweh saves" (see Matthew 1:21). "Christ" has become a name (especially in Paul's writings), although it was originally a title: "Messiah," the "Anointed One." "Son of God," although not a personal name in the ordinary sense, is the "more excellent name" which declares His unique and supreme position (Hebrews 1:4,5). "Immanuel" means "God with us" (Matthew 1:23; cf. Isaiah 7:14). The one who is the "Word of God" (Revelation 19:13) is also truly "God" (John 1:1; 20:28) and can rightfully claim the divine name "I Aᴍ" (John 8:58; Exodus 3:14). Yet He also claims the name of "the Son of man," whose life was devoted to serving and whose death on the cross brought life to all who believe on Him (Matthew 20:28; John 3:14-16).

To believe in Jesus is to believe in (or "on") His name (John 1:12; 1 John 5:13), to accept as true the significance which the New Testament ascribes to His name, His identity, and His saving work. Jesus himself is inseparable from His name. Those who "call on the name" of Jesus are those who believe in Him and pray to Him (Acts 9:14,21; 1 Corinthians 1:2). Because of their identification with Him, their sins are forgiven "for his name's sake" (1 John 2:12), which means because of who Jesus is and what He has done. Also for His name's sake the Church endures the opposition of the world which rejects Christ (Matthew 10:22; 24:9).

The name of Jesus not only identifies who He is, it associates His church with Him. This identification is symbolized by baptism, which can be described as baptism "into Jesus Christ" (Romans 6:3; Galatians 3:27) or "upon (*epi* [1894]) the name of Jesus," that is, upon the authority of Jesus—which refers back to Matthew 28:19 (Acts 2:38; cf. 8:16; 19:5 which replaces *epi* with *eis* [1506B]). To bear His name is to be in relationship with Him, to be devoted to His purposes, to act in the authority of His commission (Luke 24:47), and to share His eternal destiny of bringing glory to the Father. From within such an identification ("abiding" in Jesus), His disciples confidently pray to the Father in Jesus' name (John 14:13,14; 15:7,16; 16:23,24), not for selfish purposes but "according to his will and instruction" (Bietenhard, "Name," *Colin Brown*, 2:654). Requests and thanks to God, prayers for the sick, authoritative words from God, and exorcisms of evil spirits are all spoken in the name of Jesus (Luke 10:17; John 15:16; Acts 3:6; Ephesians 5:20; James 5:14).

Indeed, all believers do should be "in the name of the Lord Jesus" (Colossians 3:17), but only believers can truly act or speak in that Name, since "in His name" implies "in fellowship with Him." Thus, those who truly gather in His name have the assurance of His presence and therefore His power (Matthew 18:20), but the connection between Jesus' name and Jesus' power (Acts 4:7) is not available to those who would use the Name without the relationship (Acts 19:13-16).

Identification with Jesus and His name (through baptism and living as a disciple) means also identification with the triune God (thus the trinitarian wording of the command to baptize disciples "in [into (*eis*)] the name of the Father, and of the Son, and of the Holy Ghost," Matthew 28:19). To respond to Jesus' message and mission is to respond to the Father, in whose name Jesus came (John 5:43). The Father's name is revealed and glorified by Jesus' work on earth and by the believer's submission to the kingdom of God (Matthew 6:9; John 12:28; 17:6,12,26). As the Son glorifies the name of the Father, the Father glorifies the name of the Son through the work of the Spirit, whom the Father sends in the name of the Son (John 14:26; 16:14). Thus, while Jesus has that one "name under heaven given among men, whereby we must be saved" (Acts 4:12), the true significance of Jesus' name involves the name of the Father (whose will Jesus does) and the name of the Spirit (who helps to fulfill in and through the believer, the will of the Father and the Son).

STRONG 3686, BAUER 570-73, MOULTON-MILLIGAN 451-52, KITTEL 5:242-81, LIDDELL-SCOTT 1232, COLIN BROWN 2:648,651-52,654-56.

3550. ὀνομάζω onomazō verb

Name, entitle, call, mention.

COGNATE:
ὄνομα onoma (3549)

SYNONYMS:
ἐπιλέγω epilegō (1935B)
ἐπονομάζω eponomazō (2012)
καλέω kaleō (2535)
λέγω legō (2978)
προσαγορεύω prosagoreuō (4174)
φωνέω phōneō (5291)
χρηματίζω chrēmatizō (5372)

זָכַר zākhar (2226), Qal: remember, mention (Jer 3:16, 20:9, 23:36); hiphil: mention, confess (Jos 23:7, Is 26:13, Am 6:10 [6:11]).

נָקַב nāqav (5529), Qal: blaspheme (Lv 24:16); bestow (Is 62:2); niphal: be designated (1 Chr 12:31, 2 Chr 31:19).

קָרָא qārā' (7410), Call; qal: give (Gn 26:18); niphal: be called (Jer 25:29 [32:15]).

1. ὀνομάζων onomazōn nom sing masc part pres act
2. ὀνομάζειν onomazein inf pres act
3. ὠνόμασεν ōnomasen 3sing indic aor act
4. ὀνομάζεται onomazetai 3sing indic pres mid
5. ὀνομαζέσθω onomazesthō 3sing impr pres mid
6. ὀνομαζόμενος onomazomenos nom sing masc part pres mid
7. ὀνομαζομένου onomazomenou gen sing neu part pres mid
8. ὠνομάσθη ōnomasthē 3sing indic aor pass

```
3  he chose twelve, whom also he named apostles; ..... Luke 6:13
3  Simon, whom he also named Peter, and Andrew ........ 6:14
2  to call over them which had evil spirits the name ... Acts 19:13
8  to preach the gospel, not where Christ was named,  Rom 15:20
4  and such fornication as is not so much as named .... 1 Co 5:1
6  if any man that is called a brother be a fornicator, ...... 5:11
7  and dominion, and every name that is named, ....... Eph 1:21
4  the whole family in heaven and earth is named, ........ 3:15
5  not be once named among you, as becometh saints; ..... 5:3
1  Let every one that nameth the name of Christ ...... 2 Tm 2:19
```

Classical Greek

In classical Greek the verb *onomazō* not only means "to speak of, call" or "address" persons by name, but also "to name" or "specify" things. In the passive voice it can mean "to make famous"; as a passive participle it can mean "persons" or "things" of renown (cf. *Liddell-Scott*). Similarly, in the papyri *onomazō* can be found to mean "to name" (active) and "to be named" (passive). It is also "not uncommon in the sense of 'nominate' to office" (*Moulton-Milligan*).

Septuagint Usage

In the Septuagint *onomazō* translates *zākhar*, which means either "to remember" (Jeremiah 3:16) or "to mention" (Joshua 23:7; Isaiah 19:17; Amos 6:10). It also translates *nāqav*, which means "to specify or designate" (1 Chronicles 12:31; Isaiah 62:2). Furthermore, it may be used negatively to mean "to curse or blaspheme" (Leviticus 24:16). Finally, *onomazō* translates *qārā'*, which means "to call" or "to name" (Genesis 26:18; Deuteronomy 2:20) and as a passive "to be called" (Jeremiah 25:29).

New Testament Usage
In the New Testament *onomazō* retains its classical and Septuagintal meaning: "to give a name, call, name." Thus, Jesus chose the Twelve, "whom also he *named* apostles" (Luke 6:13; cf. Mark 3:14). Included in the Twelve is Simon, "whom he also *named* Peter" (Luke 6:14). Similarly, some in the church at Corinth were "(so) *called*" brothers (1 Corinthians 5:11); and every family on earth "derives its name" from the Father (Ephesians 3:14,15).

The verb *onomazō* is sometimes used with its cognate accusative to mean "to name a name." Thus, the sons of Sceva, a Jewish chief priest, discovered that they had no right "to *call* over them which had evil spirits the name of the Lord Jesus" in an attempted exorcism (Acts 19:13,14). On the other hand, God has exalted Jesus "far above all principality and power . . . and every name that is *named*" (Ephesians 1:21). Moreover, Paul exhorted, "Let every one that nameth the name of Christ depart from iniquity" (2 Timothy 2:19).

Finally, Paul used *onomazō* in the passive voice in the sense "be named" or "be known." His missionary strategy was to preach the gospel "not where Christ *was* (already) *named*," i.e., "known" (Romans 15:20).

STRONG 3687, BAUER 573-74, MOULTON-MILLIGAN 452, KITTEL 5:282, LIDDELL-SCOTT 1232-33, COLIN BROWN 2:648,655.

3551. ὄνος onos noun
Ass, donkey.

אָתוֹן 'āthôn (888), Donkey (Nm 22:22f., 2 Kgs 4:22, 1 Chr 27:30).

חֲמוֹר chămôr (2645), Donkey (Gn 42:26f., Jgs 19:19, Is 1:3).

עַיִר 'ayir (6114I), Donkey (Is 30:6).

פֶּרֶא pere' (6751), Wild donkey (Jb 24:5).

1. ὄνος onos nom sing masc/fem
2. ὄνου onou gen sing masc/fem
3. ὄνον onon acc sing masc/fem

3 and straightway ye shall find **an ass** tied,	Matt 21:2
3 meek, and sitting upon **an ass**,	21:5
3 And brought the **ass**, and the colt,	21:7
3 on the sabbath loose his ox or his **ass** from the stall,	Luke 13:15
1 Which of you shall have **an ass** or an ox	14:5
2 behold, thy King cometh, sitting on **an ass's** colt.	John 12:15

Classical Greek
Onos, the common noun for "donkey" occurs frequently in Greek literature as early as the Eighth Century B.C. It is also used for other animals in classical Greek, such as a "hake" (fish) and a wingless locust (cf. *Liddell-Scott*). Figuratively, it can be found in classical Greek to describe "one who can make nothing of music," "one who gets into a scrape by his own clumsiness," and of "one who gets what he wants" (through stubbornness) (ibid.).

Septuagint Usage
Onos occurs frequently in the Septuagint, usually translating the Hebrew term *chămôr*, "donkey." Frequently it is listed with other animals as part of someone's valued possessions (cf. Genesis 12:16; 24:35; Exodus 13:13; Zechariah 14:15). Donkeys were also used for riding (cf. 2 Samuel [LXX 2 Kings] 17:23; 19:26). In addition to carrying men and women, donkeys were also used as general "beasts of burden" (cf. Genesis 22:3,5; Isaiah 32:20) and might even be used to carry a dead body (1 Kings 13:29 [LXX 4 Kings 13:29]). However, donkeys were not normally used by military personnel (cf. Numbers 22:21; 1 Samuel 25:20 [LXX 1 Kings 25:20]). Thus Jesus' use of the donkey is consistent with His first coming as the "Prince of Peace" (cf. Zechariah 9:9; Matthew 21;1-7; John 12:14).

New Testament Usage
Onos occurs only six times in the Greek New Testament, and four of these cases are in connection with Jesus' triumphal entry into Jerusalem on Palm Sunday (Matthew 21:2,5,7; John 12:15). Both Matthew 21:4,5 and John 12:14,15 record that Jesus' chosen method of entry fulfilled the prophecy of Zechariah 9:9, i.e., that Jerusalem's king would come in a humble manner, riding on a "donkey" (rather than a horse). Matthew specified that two animals were brought to Jesus, an "ass" (*onos*) and a "colt" (*pōlos* [4311]). It is not clear, however, whether Jesus rode on both (alternately?) or whether the older animal was brought along only to calm the younger animal, since it had never been ridden before (see Mark 11:2 and Luke 19:30; see also *onarion* [3541]).

In Luke 13:15 Jesus reminded His critics how they performed necessary work on the Sabbath when they loosed their animals and led them to water. Surely the ox or ass (*onos*) thus cared for was not more valuable than the woman whom Jesus had just healed on the Sabbath! In a similar context, Jesus spoke of setting free "an ass or an ox" which might fall into a pit on the Sabbath (Luke 14:5). Some Greek manuscripts have the word "son" (*huios* [5048]) instead of *onos* in this verse.

STRONG 3688, BAUER 574, MOULTON-MILLIGAN 452, KITTEL 5:283-87, LIDDELL-SCOTT 1233, COLIN BROWN 1:117.

3552. ὄντως ontōs adv
Indeed, certainly, really.

אַךְ 'akh (395), Truly (Jer 10:19).

אָכֵן 'ākhēn (409), Surely (Jer 3:23).

אֻמְנָם 'umnām (562), Really (Nm 22:37).

1. ὄντως ontōs

1 counted John, that he was a prophet **indeed**........	Mark 11:32
1 saying, **Certainly** this was a righteous man.........	Luke 23:47
1 Lord is risen **indeed**, and hath appeared to Simon......	24:34
1 Son ... make you free, ye shall be free **indeed**.......	John 8:36
1 exclaiming, "God is **really** among you!" (NIV).....	1 Co 14:25
1 verily righteousness should have been by the law.....	Gal 3:21
1 Honour widows that are widows **indeed**.............	1 Tm 5:3
1 Now she that is a widow **indeed**, and desolate,..........	5:5
1 that it may relieve them that are widows indeed........	5:16
1 take hold of that which is life **indeed**. (NASB)..........	6:19
1 those that were clean escaped (NT).................	2 Pt 2:18

Ontōs is an adverb whose basic meaning is "really," as in "really existing." In the Septuagint *ontōs* translates three Hebrew terms meaning "able indeed" (really able) (cf. Numbers 22:37) and "truly" (Jeremiah 3:23; 10:19). Often in the New Testament it is translated "indeed" (Mark 11:32; Luke 24:34; John 8:36; 1 Timothy 5:3,5,16), although in 1 Timothy it is used attributively so the translation "real" or "genuine" would also be justified. "Widows indeed" are "real widows." (Some Greek texts use *ontōs*, "real," in this way in 1 Timothy 6:19, where the King James Version has "eternal.")

Ontōs is also translated "certainly" with regard to the centurion's realization of Jesus' identity (Luke 23:47). Paul used *ontōs* in describing the worshipful response of a new convert as a "true" affirmation of the genuineness of the supernatural work in a sinner (1 Corinthians 14:25). Peter also declared that only those who are "clean" ("really true to God") will "escape" the false teachers and prophets (2 Peter 2:18).

STRONG 3689, BAUER 574, MOULTON-MILLIGAN 452, LIDDELL-SCOTT 1234.

3553. ὄξος oxos noun
Vinegar, sour wine.
SYNONYMS:
γλεῦκος gleukos (1092)
οἶνος oinos (3494)

חֹמֶץ chōmets (2663), Vinegar (Nm 6:3, Ps 69:21 [68:21], Prv 25:20).

1. ὄξους oxous gen sing neu
2. ὄξος oxos nom/acc sing neu

2 They gave him **vinegar** to drink mingled with gall:	Matt 27:34
1 took a sponge, and filled it with **vinegar**,..............	27:48
1 And one ran and filled a sponge full **of vinegar**,...	Mark 15:36
2 coming to him, and offering him **vinegar**,..........	Luke 23:36
1 Now there was set a vessel full **of vinegar**:........	John 19:29
1 and they filled a sponge **with vinegar**,.................	19:29
2 When Jesus therefore had received the **vinegar**,.......	19:30

Classical Greek
The noun *oxos* is used in classical Greek to describe "poor wine, ordinary wine" or the "vinegar" made from it (*Liddell-Scott*). *Oxos* is distinguished in the New Testament from *oinos* (3494), "wine," in that the former is cheaper, more tart, and less desirable than the latter. Mixed with water, *oxos* was a favorite drink of the poorer classes and Roman soldiers (*Bauer*). In the kitchen it was used full strength as a table condiment or a cooking seasoning. Physicians attributed medicinal values to it, often prescribing it to reduce fever or to aid digestion (Heidland, "oxos," *Kittel*, 5:288).

Septuagint Usage
Oxos occurs in only four texts in the Septuagint. The Nazarite was to abstain from wine (*oinos*) and *oxos*, "wine vinegar," because of the intoxicating effects of these fermented drinks (Numbers 6:3). In Ruth 2:14 it was used as a condiment to dip bread in. In Psalm 69:21 (LXX 68:21) the Psalmist lamented his enemies' mistreatment of him which included giving him vinegar to drink. The Church saw this text as pointing to Jesus on the cross.

New Testament Usage
All four Gospel writers refer to the use of *oxos* in their accounts of Jesus' crucifixion. The Gospels of Matthew and Mark observe that immediately on arrival at Golgotha, as Jesus was impaled on the cross, He was given *oxos* mingled with "gall" (Matthew 27:34; Mark 15:23). The *oxos* was probably the Roman *posca*, a "mixture of water, egg, and vinegar that was effective in quenching thirst and popular among the soldiers and the poor" (Ladd, "Vinegar," *International Standard Bible Encyclopedia*, 4:987). The "gall" was quite possibly a painkilling drug. Mark assumes

that it was intended to alleviate the agony of crucifixion (Mark 15:36). Matthew agrees with Mark, noting that it was administered after Jesus cried, "*Eli, Eli, lama sabbachthani.*" Some of the bystanders who heard Jesus attempted to restrain the soldier who offered the sour wine, saying, "Let us see whether Elijah will come to save him" (Matthew 27:49).

The Gospel of Luke observes that the soldiers shouted in mockery as they gave Jesus the *oxos*, saying, "If thou be the King of the Jews, save thyself" (Luke 23:37). Possibly they were making sport of the idea of offering such a cheap drink to a "king." John's account emphasizes the aspect of fulfilled prophecy in the act of offering Jesus *oxos* to drink. According to John, Jesus was aware that the Old Testament description of the Suffering Servant was being fulfilled in graphic detail. Doubtless recalling the Psalmist's statement in Psalm 69:21, "In my thirst they gave me *vinegar* to drink," and realizing this had not occurred, Jesus cried, "I thirst" (John 19:28). When He tasted the *oxos* He cried, "It is finished" (i.e., all things are now fulfilled) and died.

Because of the different perspectives of each Evangelist it is impossible to conclusively determine whether the "vinegar" offered to Jesus was done in mockery (by giving Him something undrinkable or by giving Him a drink that might prolong His life and hence His suffering) or to be merciful. However, it is clear that in refusing to drink the "vinegar" Jesus demonstrated His commitment to endure His sufferings alone and without alleviation (cf. Horton, *The Complete Biblical Library, Matthew*, pp.627,635).

STRONG 3690, BAUER 574, MOULTON-MILLIGAN 452-53, KITTEL 5:288-89, LIDDELL-SCOTT 1234, COLIN BROWN 2:28.

3554. ὀξύς oxus adj

Sharp, swift, keen.

SYNONYMS:
ταχινός tachinos (4879)
ταχύς tachus (4884)

חַד chadh (2392), Sharp (Ps 57:4 [56:4], Is 49:2, Ez 5:1).

חָדַד chādhadh (2395), Be swift (Hb 1:8).

חֶרֶשׂ cheres (2895), Potsherd (Jb 41:30 [41:21]).

מָהִיר māhîr (4248), Skilled (Prv 22:29).

קַל qal (7316), Swift (Am 2:15).

שֶׁטֶף shēṭeph (8279II) Flood; something overwhelming (Prv 27:4).

שָׁנַן shānan (8532), Sharp (Is 5:28).

1. ὀξεῖς oxeis nom pl masc
2. ὀξεῖα oxeia nom sing fem
3. ὀξεῖαν oxeian acc sing fem
4. ὀξύ oxu nom/acc sing neu

1 Their feet are **swift** to shed blood:		Rom 3:15
2 out of his mouth went a **sharp** twoedged sword:		Rev 1:16
3 These things saith he which hath the **sharp** sword		2:12
4 a golden crown, and in his hand a **sharp** sickle.		14:14
4 another angel ... he also having a **sharp** sickle.		14:17
4 with a loud cry to him that had the **sharp** sickle,		14:18
4 saying, Thrust in thy **sharp** sickle,		14:18
2 And out of his mouth goeth a **sharp** sword,		19:15

Of the eight times this adjective occurs in the New Testament, seven are in the Book of Revelation. In each instance it means "sharp" or "keen," describing the edge of a sword or sickle (cf. Psalm 57:4 [LXX 56:4]; Isaiah 5:28, "sharp arrows"). This reflects the most common usage of *oxus*. The papyri describe horses used in Egypt rather than donkeys for speedy mail service (*Moulton-Milligan*).

From the basic meaning of "sharp" other meanings developed, such as, "quick, hasty," and "keen" in the sense of "eager." Such is the sense in Romans 3:15, where Paul described sinful mankind as having feet "swift to shed blood," i.e., "eager" or "ready" to do violence to others (cf. Amos 2:15).

STRONG 3691, BAUER 574, MOULTON-MILLIGAN 453, LIDDELL-SCOTT 1236.

3555. ὀπή opē noun

Opening, hole, cavern.

אֲרֻבָּה 'ărubbāh (724), Window (Eccl 12:3).

חָגוּ chāghû (2380), Cleft (Ob 3).

חֹר chōr (2815), Opening (S/S 5:4).

נְקָרָה neqārāh (5549), Cleft (Ex 33:22).

סָעִיף sā'îph (5780), Cleft (Jgs 15:11—Codex Alexandrinus only).

1. ὀπῆς opēs gen sing fem
2. ὀπαῖς opais dat pl fem

2 in mountains, and in dens and caves of the earth.		Heb 11:38
1 at the same **place** sweet water and bitter?		Jas 3:11

Opē is a general word for a hole or opening of any kind, whether in the ground, in a rock, in the roof or wall of a house (i.e., chimneys, doors, windows), or in the human body (i.e., ears, mouth, etc.). In the New Testament it occurs only twice, both times in reference to holes or openings in the ground. In Hebrews 11:38 faithful saints of the past are said to have sought refuge from a hateful world in "caves (*opē*) of the earth," which were really just "holes in the ground." In James 3:11 *opē* refers to a smaller opening or hole ("place" in the King James Version) from which a fountain or spring sends forth water. Unlike the human mouth (3:10), a fountain will not send forth sweet and bitter from the same opening.

STRONG 3692, BAUER 574, LIDDELL-SCOTT 1237.

3556. ὄπισθεν opisthen adv
After, behind, at or on the back.

אַחַר 'achar (313), Following, behind (1 Sm 15:11, 2 Sm 13:34).

1. ὄπισθεν opisthen

1	came **behind** him, and touched the hem of his	Matt 9:20
1	saying, Send her away; for she crieth **after** us.	15:23
1	came in the press **behind**, ... touched his garment.	Mark 5:27
1	Came **behind** him, and touched the border of his	Luke 8:44
1	the cross, that he might bear it **after** Jesus.	23:26
1	were four beasts full of eyes before and **behind**.	Rev 4:6
1	a book written within and **on the backside**,	5:1

Technically this word is an adverb meaning "behind" or "after." As with its English equivalents, however, *opisthen* is sometimes used as a preposition: "behind (something or someone)." Thus in Matthew 9:20 and Luke 8:44, the King James Version adds (in italics) the word "him" after the word "behind," but in the same incident in Mark 5:27, "behind" is left without the addition of "him." The translators were reading *opisthen* as an adverb in Mark but as a preposition in Matthew and Luke. In Matthew 15:23 ("after us") and Luke 23:26 ("after Jesus") *opisthen* is clearly used as a preposition and is translated as "after." Here the Greek text itself supplies the objects of the preposition. The point to be drawn is that following Jesus means full surrender with no going back (Matthew 10:38; Luke 9:62) (Seesemann, "*opisō*," *Kittel*, 5:291).

In Revelation 4:6 and 5:1 *opisthen* is again found as an adverb meaning "behind," although in 5:1 it is translated "back side" in referring to the reverse side of a scroll. In Philippians 3:13 Paul said, "... forgetting those things which are behind ... I press toward the mark." (See also *opisō* [3557].)

STRONG 3693, BAUER 574-75, MOULTON-MILLIGAN 453, KITTEL 5:289-92, LIDDELL-SCOTT 1238, COLIN BROWN 1:492-93.

3557. ὀπίσω opisō adv
After, behind, backwards, afterwards.

אָחוֹר 'āchôr (268), Back (Is 59:14).
אַחַר 'achar (313), After (Gn 41:19, 2 Sm 2:19, Jer 7:6).
אֲחֹרַנִּית 'āchōrannîth (323), Back (1 Kgs 18:37).
אֶל 'el (420), To (1 Kgs 17:10f.).
עִם 'im (6196), With (1 Kgs 1:8).
תַּחַת tachath (8809), In the place of (Dn 8:22).

1. ὀπίσω opisō

1	but he that cometh **after** me is mightier than I,	Matt 3:11
1	And he saith unto them, Follow me, (NT)	4:19
1	he that taketh not his cross, and followeth **after** me,	10:38
1	said unto Peter, Get thee **behind** me, Satan:	16:23
1	any man will come **after** me, let him deny himself,	16:24
1	Neither let him which is in the field return **back**	24:18
1	There cometh one mightier than I **after** me,	Mark 1:7
1	And Jesus said unto them, Come ye **after** me,	1:17
1	left their father Zebedee ... and went **after** him.	1:20
1	rebuked Peter, saying, Get thee **behind** me, Satan:	8:33
1	he said unto them, Whosoever will come **after** me,	8:34
1	And let him that is in the field not turn **back** again	13:16
1	Get thee **behind** me, Satan: for it is written,	Luke 4:8
1	And stood at his feet **behind** him weeping,	7:38
1	If any man will come **after** me, let ... deny himself,	9:23
1	and looking **back**, is fit for the kingdom of God.	9:62
1	doth not bear his cross, and come **after** me,	14:27
1	is in the field, let him likewise not return **back**.	17:31
1	citizens hated him, and sent a message **after** him,	19:14
1	I am Christ; ... go ye not therefore **after** them.	21:8
1	He that cometh **after** me is preferred before me:	John 1:15
1	who coming **after** me is preferred before me,	1:27
1	**After** me cometh a man ... preferred before me;	1:30
1	From that time many of his disciples went **back**;	6:66
1	behold, the world is gone **after** him.	12:19
1	they went **backward**, and fell to the ground.	18:6
1	she turned herself **back**, and saw Jesus standing,	20:14
1	and drew away much people **after** him:	Acts 5:37
1	speaking ... to draw away disciples **after** them.	20:30
1	forgetting those things which are **behind**,	Phlp 3:13
1	For some are already turned aside **after** Satan.	1 Tm 5:15
1	that walk **after** the flesh in the lust of uncleanness,	2 Pt 2:10
1	over to fornication, and going **after** strange flesh,	Jude 1:7
1	heard **behind** me a great voice, as of a trumpet,	Rev 1:10
1	out of his mouth water as a flood **after** the woman,	12:15
1	healed: and all the world wondered **after** the beast.	13:3

Classical Greek
Among classical writers *opisō* (also spelled *opissō*) was an adverb of time ("hereafter, following, after") or of place ("behind, backwards") (*Liddell-Scott*). Bauder notes, however, that it could be used as a noun, adverb, or preposition ("Disciple," *Colin Brown*, 1:492). The use of *opisō* as a preposition is generally regarded as improper, although the phenomenon is common both in the Septuagint and the New Testament (*Bauer*).

Septuagint Usage
Even when used in connection with other Greek words to make particular expressions, *opisō* almost always is associated with the Hebrew word *'achar*, "behind, after" (in a variety of forms). It functions as a temporal adverb: e.g.,

1 Kings 1:6 (LXX 3 Kings 1:6); Ecclesiastes 10:14, and as an adverb of place: e.g., Joel 2:20. But by far its most common use is as an improper preposition (with the genitive case).

In this last use it can depict someone going or pursuing after someone. Thus the pursuit of the Egyptians "after" the Israelites is frequently described by *opisō* (Exodus 14:4,8,9; cf. Joshua 2:5,7). "After" in the sense of "follow after, adhere to" is also common in the Septuagint. This sense holds theological significance in that the phrase "to go *after* other gods" denotes apostasy (Deuteronomy 8:19; 28:14; Judges 2:12,17,19), while "to follow *after* God" is equal to faithfulness (Joshua 14:9). Both of these concepts influenced later Judaism and the New Testament writers (cf. Seeseman, "opizō," *Kittel*, 5:289-292; Bauder, "Disciple," *Colin Brown*, 1:492).

New Testament Usage

In the New Testament *opisō* functions as an adverb or a preposition. Adverbially, in answer to the question "Where?" or "Whither?" it means "behind" or "back." In Luke 7:38 the sinful woman was standing "behind" Jesus at His feet. In Philippians 3:13 *opisō*, with the neuter article, functions as a substantive meaning "those things which are *behind*," as that which a runner leaves in his wake.

As a preposition *opisō* may relate either to time or place. Locally, it means "behind," as in Revelation 1:10, "... and heard *behind* me a great voice"; or Matthew 16:23, "Get thee *behind* me, Satan." As a preposition of time, *opisō* is translated "after" as in Matthew 3:11, "He that cometh after me . . . ."

Like the Septuagint, where the New Testament uses *opisō* as a preposition to express the relation between two persons, a close personal intimacy is usually implied. Jesus' summons, "Follow (*after*) me," demands a severing of ties with one's former life and a rendering of an unconditional commitment to Him (Matthew 4:19; cf. 16:24). The disciple must renounce his own will (Matthew 10:38) and studiously avoid the temptation to return to the things that he renounced to follow Christ (Luke 17:31). False christs will attempt to gain their allegiance; believers must not be misled into following after them (Luke 21:8). Only by this level of self-renunciation and commitment to Christ can one hope to share in His kingdom (Mark 8:34-38). Having understood this aspect of commitment implied in *opisō*, other similar constructions are easily understood, such as Acts 5:37; 20:30; 1 Timothy 5:15.

STRONG 3694, BAUER 575, MOULTON-MILLIGAN 453, KITTEL 5:289-92, LIDDELL-SCOTT 1239, COLIN BROWN 1:492-93.

3558. ὁπλίζω hoplizō verb

To arm, to arm oneself with, equip.

COGNATES:
ὅπλον hoplon (3559)
πανοπλία panoplia (3695)

1. ὁπλίσασθε hoplisasthe 2pl impr aor mid

1 arm yourselves likewise with the same mind: . . . . 1 Pt 4:1

Because this word is most often found in the middle voice, some lexicons spell the term *hoplizomai*, "to arm oneself," or "to equip someone with something." This is its meaning at 1 Peter 4:1, the only New Testament occurrence. *Liddell-Scott* lists other active voice usages in classical Greek. In those places it simply means "to make ready" or "to get ready." It is used of "harnessing horses" as well as equipping and training soldiers for war (ibid.). In 1 Peter 4:1, the text indicates that the believer *should arm himself* (imperative [command] mood) with the same "mind" (*ennoia* [1755], "thought, counsel, resolve") as Jesus had. The idea here is that the believer is to "arm" himself with the expectation that it is not unusual for the disciple of Christ to suffer injustice, persecution, ridicule, or unfair treatment as a result of his profession of faith in Jesus.

STRONG 3695, BAUER 575, MOULTON-MILLIGAN 453 (see "hoplizomai"), KITTEL 5:294-95, LIDDELL-SCOTT 1239, COLIN BROWN 3:959,964.

3559. ὅπλον hoplon noun

Tool, instrument, weapon.

CROSS-REFERENCE:
ὁπλίζω hoplizō (3558)

חֲנִית chănîth (2698), Spear (Ps 46:9 [45:9], Na 3:3).

כְּלִי kᵉlî (3747), Weapon (Jer 21:4, Ez 32:27).

מָגֵן māghēn (4182), Shield (1 Kgs 10:17, Ps 35:2 [34:2], Jer 46:3 [26:3]).

נֶשֶׁק nesheq (5584II) Weapon (2 Kgs 10:2, Ez 39:9f.).

סִרְיוֹן siryōn (5834), Coat of mail (Jer 51:3 [28:3]).

צֵן tsēn (7060), Hook (Am 4:2).

צִנָּה tsinnāh (7065), Shield (1 Sm 17:7, Pss 5:12, 91:4 [90:4]).

שֶׁלַח shelach (8367), Weapon (2 Chr 23:10).
שֶׁלֶט shelet (8377), Shield (2 Chr 23:9).

1. ὅπλα **hopla** nom/acc pl neu
2. ὅπλων **hoplōn** gen pl neu

```
2 cometh ... with lanterns and torches and weapons...John 18:3
1 Neither yield ye your members as instruments.......Rom 6:13
1 and your members as instruments of righteousness......  6:13
1 and let us put on the armour of light..................   13:12
2 by the armour of righteousness on the right hand... 2 Co 6:7
1 For the weapons of our warfare are not carnal,........  10:4
```

Classical Greek and Septuagint Usage

From Homeric times to modern Greek this general word has signified both a tool and a weapon. The related word, *hoplē*, "hoof" (Psalm 69:31 [LXX 68:31]), applies this general meaning even to a horse's weapon or tool, namely, his hoof. In both classical Greek and the Septuagint *hoplon* is often found in the plural *hopla*.

In 1 Samuel 17:7 (LXX 1 Kings 17:7) Goliath's armor-bearer is described in the Septuagint as the carrier of his *hopla*, "arms, weapons." The KJV renders it by the phrase, "one bearing a shield," but the text clearly uses this general word in the plural. In the Tebtunis Papyri (100 B.C.) armed men are referred to as *en hoplois*, "in weapons."

New Testament Usage

The New Testament contains six occurrences of this word. It is used twice in Romans 6:13. Here Paul admonished believers to yield their bodies as *hopla* (plural), "instruments" of righteousness, rather than as *hopla* of unrighteousness. Both the KJV and many of the newer translations prefer "instruments" here, simply because the context does not explicitly denote warfare. In Romans 13:12, however, where again the context is not specifically militaristic, the KJV selects "armor" where "equipment" or even "apparatus" would suffice. Second Corinthians 6:7 could likewise go either way, but later in the same book (10:4) Paul clearly was speaking of the "weapons (*hopla*) of our warfare." Figuratively it points to the spiritual weapons with which God has armed the believer to contend in battle for Him. John 18:3 speaks of the "weapons" the men from the chief priests brought with them, in addition to the tools already mentioned, i.e., lanterns and torches, to arrest Jesus.

In Ephesians 6:11 the Christian soldier is ordered to clothe himself with the "whole armor" of God. Here the word is *panoplia* (3695): a combination of "whole/all" (*pan* [see *pas* (3817B)]) and "weapons/armor" (*hopla*, plural of the word *hoplon*; in English, *panoply*). The completely armed soldier, whether Greek or Roman, was the *hoplitēs*. Paul used this imagery of the *hoplite* (Ephesians 6:13-18) although the word itself is never used in the New Testament. The stress here is not on the ability of the soldier (*hoplite* not being used), but on the quality of all the *hoplon*, warfare equipment.

STRONG 3696, BAUER 575, MOULTON-MILLIGAN 453, KITTEL 5:292-94, LIDDELL-SCOTT 1240.

3560. ὁποῖος **hopoios** intr-pron

Of what sort, manner, or kind.

SYNONYM:
    ποταπός potapos (4076)

1. ὁποῖος **hopoios** nom sing masc
2. ὁποίαν **hopoian** acc sing fem
3. ὁποῖον **hopoion** nom/acc sing neu
4. ὁποῖοι **hopoioi** nom pl masc

```
1 and altogether such as I am, except these bonds.... Acts 26:29
3 fire shall try every man's work of what sort it is..... 1 Co 3:13
4 whatsoever they were, it maketh no matter to me:....Gal 2:6
2 what manner of entering in we had unto you,....... 1 Th 1:9
1 straightway forgetteth what manner of man he was.... Jas 1:24
```

A relative pronoun, *hopoios* expresses quality, manner, or kind. Sometimes it is used as an adverb meaning "as" or "like as" (*Liddell-Scott*). This word is often used in classical Greek but is not found in the Septuagint. The five occurrences of the term in the New Testament are consistent with its primary meaning. Three times it describes persons: e.g., Paul's wish that his accusers could be like him ("such as I am," the same kind of person, Acts 26:29); Paul's indifference to self-declared, pompous, important persons (Galatians 2:6); and James' description of the individual who, after looking in a mirror, immediately forgets what manner of person he was (James 1:24). The term connotes quality of character and of position.

The other occurrences describe the quality of works that endure fiery trials (1 Corinthians 3:13) and the manner of welcome Paul received from the Thessalonian believers (1 Thessalonians 1:9).

STRONG 3697, BAUER 575, MOULTON-MILLIGAN 453, LIDDELL-SCOTT 1241.

3561. ὁπότε **hopote** conj

When, whenever.

1. ὁπότε hopote

1	what David did, **when** himself was an hungered,	Luke 6:3

Hopote is a temporal particle often used as an adverb of time, "when." It is similar to *hote* (3616). It most often refers to events in the past but it also is used to express present and future events. The term sometimes is used in a causal sense and is then translated as "because" or "since" (*Liddell-Scott*). Luke 6:3 is the only place where *hopote* is used in the New Testament. The word is replaced by *hote* in various ancient manuscripts (i.e., *Nestle-Aland 26th*).

STRONG 3698, BAUER 576, MOULTON-MILLIGAN 453, LIDDELL-SCOTT 1241.

3562. ὅπου hopou adv
Where, since, whenever, wherever.

1. ὅπου hopou

1	earth, **where** moth and rust doth corrupt,	Matt 6:19
1	and **where** thieves break through and steal:	6:19
1	**where** neither moth nor rust doth corrupt,	6:20
1	and **where** thieves do not break through nor steal:	6:20
1	For **where** your treasure is, there will your heart	6:21
1	I will follow thee **whithersoever** thou goest.	8:19
1	stony places, **where** they had not much earth:	13:5
1	For **wheresoever** the carcase is,	24:28
1	hard man, reaping **where** thou hast not sown,	25:24
1	thou knewest that I reap **where** I sowed not,	25:26
1	**Wheresoever** this gospel shall be preached	26:13
1	**where** the scribes and the elders were assembled.	26:57
1	Come, see the place **where** the Lord lay.	28:6
1	they uncovered the roof **where** he was:	Mark 2:4
1	pallet **on which** the paralytic was laying (NASB)	2:4
1	fell on stony ground, **where** it had not much earth;	4:5
1	they by the way side, **where** the word is sown;	4:15
1	and entereth in **where** the damsel was lying.	5:40
1	In **what place** soever ye enter into an house,	6:10
1	began to carry about ... **where** they heard he was.	6:55
1	And **whithersoever** he entered, into villages,	6:56
1	And **wheresoever** he taketh him, he teareth him:	9:18
1	**Where** their worm dieth not,	9:44
1	**Where** their worm dieth not,	9:46
1	**Where** their worm dieth not,	9:48
1	see the abomination ... standing **where** it ought not,	13:14
1	**Wheresoever** this gospel shall be preached	14:9
1	And **wheresoever** he shall go in,	14:14
1	**where** I shall eat the passover with my disciples?	14:14
1	is not here: behold the place **where** they laid him.	16:6
1	Lord, I will follow thee **whithersoever** thou goest.	Luke 9:57
1	in the heavens ... **where** no thief approacheth,	12:33
1	**where** your treasure is, there will your heart be	12:34
1	And he said unto them, **Wheresoever** the body is,	17:37
1	**where** I shall eat the passover with my disciples?	22:11
1	beyond Jordan, **where** John was baptizing.	John 1:28
1	The wind bloweth **where** it listeth,	3:8
1	Jerusalem is the place **where** men ... worship.	4:20
1	Cana of Galilee, **where** he made the water wine.	4:46
1	nigh unto the place **where** they did eat bread,	6:23
1	the Son of man ascend up **where** he was before?	6:62
1	and **where** I am, thither ye cannot come.	7:34
1	and **where** I am, thither ye cannot come?	7:36
1	out of the town of Bethlehem, **where** David was?	7:42
1	**whither** I go, ye cannot come.	8:21
1	because he saith, **Whither** I go, ye cannot come.	John 8:22
1	into the place **where** John at first baptized;	10:40
1	but was in that place **where** Martha met him.	11:30
1	Then when Mary was come **where** Jesus was,	11:32
1	**where** Lazarus was which had been dead,	12:1
1	and **where** I am, there shall also my servant be:	12:26
1	**Whither** I go, ye cannot come;	13:33
1	**Whither** I go, thou canst not follow me now;	13:36
1	that **where** I am, there ye may be also.	14:3
1	And **whither** I go ye know, and the way ye know.	14:4
1	whom thou hast given me, be with me **where** I am;	17:24
1	over the brook Cedron, **where** was a garden,	18:1
1	and in the temple, **whither** the Jews always resort;	18:20
1	**Where** they crucified him, and two others	19:18
1	**where** Jesus was crucified was nigh to the city:	19:20
1	place **where** he was crucified there was a garden;	19:41
1	**where** the body of Jesus had lain.	20:12
1	when the doors were shut **where** the disciples were	20:19
1	and walkedst **whither** thou wouldest:	21:18
1	and carry thee **whither** thou wouldest not.	21:18
1	Thessalonica, **where** was a synagogue of the Jews:	Acts 17:1
1	and **there** we stayed seven days (NASB)	20:6
1	to preach the gospel, not **where** Christ was named,	Rom 15:20
1	for **whereas** there is among you envying, and strife,	1 Co 3:3
1	**Where** there is neither Greek nor Jew,	Col 3:11
1	**Whither** the forerunner is for us entered,	Heb 6:20
1	For **where** a testament is, there must also	9:16
1	Now **where** remission of these is,	10:18
1	turned about ... **whithersoever** the governor listeth.	Jas 3:4
1	For **where** envying and strife is,	3:16
1	**Whereas** angels, which are greater in power,	2 Pt 2:11
1	**where** thou dwellest, even **where** Satan's seat is:	Rev 2:13
1	who was slain among you, **where** Satan dwelleth.	2:13
1	**where** also our Lord was crucified.	11:8
1	**where** she hath a place prepared of God,	12:6
1	into her place, **where** she is nourished.	12:14
1	which follow the Lamb **whithersoever** he goeth.	14:4
1	are seven mountains, on **which** the woman sitteth.	17:9
1	**where** the beast and the false prophet are,	20:10

Classical Greek and Septuagint Usage
The word *hopou* is a particle denoting place or circumstance which is translated "where" (*Bauer*). It is a combination of the relative pronoun *ho* (3450) and the indefinite adverb of place *pou* (4085), thus expressing "in which place." It occurs infrequently in the Septuagint and often there is no clear corresponding Hebrew (e.g., Judges 18:10; 20:22; Ruth 3:4).

New Testament Usage
In many of its New Testament uses *hopou* introduces subordinate clauses in the indicative mood. In these cases it describes the location of a noun in the principal clause, as in Matthew 6:19, "treasures upon earth, *where* (*hopou*) moth and rust doth corrupt." When the noun referred to is a person, *hopou* has the force of "in whose house" or "among whom," as in Matthew 26:57, "they ... led him away to Caiaphas, the high priest, *where* (*hopou*) the scribes and the elders were assembled."

Hopou often appears in a figurative sense expressing a logical rather than spacial relationship. In Colossians 3:11 Paul described the domain of the "new man" as "*where* (*hopou*) there is neither Greek nor Jew." In 1 Corinthians

3:3 *hopou* means "since" ("whereas," KJV) and is so translated in NASB: "for *since* (*hopou*) there is jealousy and strife among you...." *Hopou*, followed by the indefinite participle *an* (300) or *ean* (1430) and usually followed by the imperfect tense or subjunctive mode, may mean "whenever" or "wherever" to denote continuity or uncertainty of action or occurrence (Blass and DeBrunner, *Greek Grammar of New Testament*, pp.185f.; cf. *Bauer*).

STRONG 3699, BAUER 576, MOULTON-MILLIGAN 453-54, LIDDELL-SCOTT 1241-42.

3563. ὀπτάνομαι optanomai verb

Be seen, appear.

COGNATES:
αὐτόπτης autoptēs (839)
ἐποπτεύω epopteuō (2013)
ὀπτασία optasia (3564)
ὀπτός optos (3565)

SYNONYMS:
ἀναφαίνω anaphainō (396)
ἐπιφαίνω epiphainō (1998)
ὁράω horaō (3571)
φαίνω phainō (5154)

רָאָה rā'âh (7495), See; niphal: be seen (1 Kgs 8:8).

1. ὀπτανόμενος optanomenos
nom sing masc part pres mid

1 being seen of them forty days,...... Acts 1:3

Optanomai does not appear in classical Greek literature till approximately 164 B.C. (*Moulton-Milligan*). The term is derived from the aorist passive form of *ōphthēn*, "I let myself be seen, I appear" (*Bauer*). In its one use as a passive participle in the New Testament, *optanomai* describes the actual visible appearances, not visions, of Christ during the 40 days following His resurrection. Luke stated that these manifestations served as "infallible proofs" (Acts 1:3).

STRONG 3700, BAUER 576, MOULTON-MILLIGAN 454, KITTEL 5:315-67, LIDDELL-SCOTT 1242, COLIN BROWN 3:516.

3564. ὀπτασία optasia noun

A vision.

COGNATE:
ὀπτάνομαι optanomai (3563)

SYNONYMS:
ὅραμα horama (3568)
ὅρασις horasis (3569)

רָאָה rā'âh (7495), See; niphal: appear (Mal 3:2).

1. ὀπτασίᾳ optasia dat sing fem
2. ὀπτασίαν optasian acc sing fem
3. ὀπτασίας optasias acc pl fem

2 perceived that he had seen a vision in the temple:... Luke 1:22
2 saying, that they had also seen a vision of angels,...... 24:23
1 I was not disobedient unto the heavenly vision:..... Acts 26:19
3 I will come to visions and revelations of the Lord. 2 Co 12:1

Classical Greek and Septuagint Usage
This noun is not a commonly used word in classical Greek and the Septuagint, but it can be found meaning "vision," or simply "appearance" (cf. Sirach 43:2; Malachi 3:2). According to *Bauer*, *optasia* (as "vision") is "that which a Deity permits a human being to see, either of his own Divine Being, or of something else usually hidden from men" (cf. Theodotion's Daniel 9:23; 10:1,7f.). Only by examining the context can it be determined if the "vision" is a supernatural revelation or simply an ordinary sense perception (cf. Aune, "Vision," *International Standard Bible Encyclopedia*, 4:993).

New Testament Usage
Optasia is also used in the New Testament for visions which God causes men to see. The *optasia* consists of images presented visually to the waking mind which give insight into the divine order and reason behind events. The *optasia* ("vision") is a perception of truth revealed by God in contrast to a *phantasma* (5164), "vision," invented by one's own imagination (cf. Mark 6:49). It is difficult to make a clear distinction between dreams and visions in the Bible because visions are called dreams and dreams are called visions (e.g., Acts 2:17; 9:10,12). However, *optasia* is a waking vision while *horama* (3568) is a vision seen in a dream.

Optasia also means intellectual or spiritual perception that comes by means of mystical or religious experience (Luke 1:22; 24:23; Acts 26:19; 2 Corinthians 12:1).

STRONG 3701, BAUER 576, KITTEL 5:372-73, LIDDELL-SCOTT 1242, COLIN BROWN 3:511-12,515,517.

3565. ὀπτός optos adj

Baked, broiled, roasted.

CROSS-REFERENCE:
ὀπτάνομαι optanomai (3563)

צָלִי tsālî (7018), Roasted (Ex 12:8f.).

1. ὀπτοῦ optou gen sing masc

1 And they gave him a piece of a broiled fish,...... Luke 24:42

In the Greek of the pre-Christian era the word *optos* is an adjective that describes anything that is cooked by fire. It was used of bread, fish, or meat—broiled, roasted, or baked; of iron that was forged; of soil that was parched by sun and drought; and of bricks and pottery that were fired (*Liddell-Scott*). The word appears only one time in the New Testament, as a verbal adjective where Luke (24:42,43) tells about the resurrected Jesus eating some "broiled" fish. He did it to prove it was actually He himself who had appeared to the disciples and not a spirit.

STRONG 3702, BAUER 576, MOULTON-MILLIGAN 454, LIDDELL-SCOTT 1242.

3566. ὀπώρα opōra noun
Fruit.
SYNONYM:
καρπός karpos (2561)

קַיִץ qayits (7302), Summer fruit (Jer 40:10,12 [47:10,12], 48:32 [31:32]).

1. ὀπώρα opōra nom sing fem

1 the fruits that thy soul lusted after are departed.... Rev 18:14

Originally *opōra* was the proper name for the fruit-bearing season (late July, August, and early September). By association *opōra* came to mean the "harvest" of the late summer or early autumn, hence the "fruit" itself.

Opōra is related to *opse* (3660) which means "late in the day, finally, or last" and to *opos*, "juice of fruit."

It is found only in the New Testament at Revelation 18:14. There it metaphorically describes the harvest of worldly possessions and pleasures lusted after by Babylon. None of these would be realized. At last—after having waited for them so long as the object of desire—the things lusted for would be taken away forever.

STRONG 3703, BAUER 576, MOULTON-MILLIGAN 454, LIDDELL-SCOTT 1242-43.

3567. ὅπως hopōs conj
How, in what manner, because, that, to, in order that.

1. ὅπως hopōs

1 that they may appear unto men to fast............. Matt 6:16
1 that she may be healed; and she shall live......... Mark 5:23

This is a versatile word used as a conjunction ("that, because"), as a relative adverb ("how, when"), and as a preposition ("to"). *Hopōs* is most often translated "that" and used as a conjunctive to introduce what follows with the meaning "in order that." It is common in classical writings as well as the Septuagint (e.g., Genesis 27:4; Exodus 2:20; Ezekiel 4:17).

Old Testament prophecies fulfilled by episodes in the life of Jesus are introduced by *hopōs*: "*that* it might be fulfilled" (Matthew 2:23; 8:17; 12:17; 13:35).

Hopōs is used as a relative adverb ("how") in Matthew 12:14; 22:15; Mark 3:6; and Luke 24:20. While some translate it as a relative adverb in Acts 3:19, "when (*hopōs*) the times of refreshing shall come," it could be a conjunction, "*that* (*hopōs*) the times of refreshing shall (may) come" (cf. *Bauer*). *Hopōs* is translated as the preposition "to" in Matthew 26:59 ("to put"); Luke 11:37 ("to dine"); Acts 9:24 ("to kill"); Acts 23:23 ("to go").

STRONG 3704, BAUER 576-77, MOULTON-MILLIGAN 454, LIDDELL-SCOTT 1243-44.

3568. ὅραμα horama noun
Vision, spectacle, sight.
COGNATE:
ὁράω horaō (3571)
SYNONYMS:
ὀπτασία optasia (3564)
ὅρασις horasis (3569)

חֵזוּ chēzû (A2468), Night vision, vision (Dn 2:19, 7:7,13,15—Aramaic).
חָזוֹן chāzôn (2469), Vision (Dn 1:17, 8:13,15,17).
חָזוּת chāzûth (2471), Vision (Is 21:2).
חִזָּיוֹן chizzāyôn (2476), Vision (Jb 7:14).
חֲלוֹם chălôm (2573), Dream (Dn 2:1).
חֵלֶם chēlem (A2595), Dream (Dn 2:7,26, 7:1—Aramaic).
מוֹרָא môrā' (4307), Terror (Dt 26:8, Jer 32:21 [39:21]).
מַחֲזֶה machăzeh (4371), Vision (Gn 15:1).
מַרְאָה mar'āh (4919), Vision (Gn 46:2, Nm 12:6).
מַרְאֶה mar'eh (4920), Sight, something seen (Ex 3:3, Eccl 6:9); vision (Dn 8:27, 10:1).
מַשָּׂא mashshā' (5041), Oracle (Is 21:1,11).

1. ὅραμα horama nom/acc sing neu
2. ὁράματος horamatos gen sing neu
3. ὁράματι horamati dat sing neu

1 Jesus ... saying, Tell the vision to no man, ... Matt 17:9
1 When Moses saw it, he wondered at the sight:...... Acts 7:31
3 Ananias; and to him said the Lord in a vision, ... 9:10

3	And hath seen in **a vision** a man named Ananias....	Acts 9:12
3	He saw in **a vision** evidently about the ninth hour.....	10:3
1	what this **vision** which he had seen should mean,......	10:17
2	While Peter thought on the **vision**, the Spirit said......	10:19
1	and in a trance I saw **a vision**,........................	11:5
1	but thought he saw **a vision**............................	12:9
1	And **a vision** appeared to Paul in the night;...........	16:9
1	And after he had seen the **vision**,.....................	16:10
2	spake the Lord to Paul in the night by **a vision**,......	18:9

Classical Greek and Septuagint Usage

Classical writers understood *horama* to mean "that which is seen, visible," "a sight." It did not usually refer to a supernatural vision, although it could. A "dream" could also be called *horama* (*Liddell-Scott*). In the Septuagint the word is used for (1) a "vision" by which God revealed himself to Abraham (Genesis 15:1); (2) a "great sight" of a bush which burned with fire and was not consumed (Exodus 3:3); and (3) "night visions" through which God revealed to Daniel things in the future (Daniel 7:13,15).

New Testament Usage

In the New Testament this Greek noun is used 12 times and is translated "sight" once (Acts 7:31) and "vision" 11 times (e.g., Matthew 17:9). In three of the visions the viewers described in minute detail what they saw.

Matthew's account of Christ's transfiguration describes the appearance of Christ's face and raiment (Matthew 17:2), while Luke's account reveals even the subject of discussion between Christ, Moses, and Elijah, namely Jesus' death on the cross (Luke 9:30,31).

In the account of the conversion of Saul, Luke stated that Saul had seen in a "vision" (*horama*) a man named Ananias coming in and putting his hand on him that he might receive his sight (Acts 9:10,12). In Luke's account of the "door of faith" being opened to the Gentiles, he stated that Cornelius saw in a vision an angel who gave him instructions to send men to a man named Peter, who was in a specific house in a specific city. He would give them specific instructions on what they were to do (Acts 10:3-6). When the three men, sent by Cornelius, arrived at Joppa, God through a vision was showing to Peter how the Gentiles would be included in His plan of salvation for the whole world (Acts 10:9-15). What Peter and Cornelius saw in the visions God gave to them was not some figment of the imagination, but God's glory, power, and plan of salvation for all of mankind through His Son, Jesus Christ.

STRONG 3705, BAUER 577, MOULTON-MILLIGAN 454-55, KITTEL 5:371-72, LIDDELL-SCOTT 1244, COLIN BROWN 3:511-13,515,517.

3569. ὅρασις horasis noun

Sight, appearance, vision.

SYNONYMS:
ὀπτασία optasia (3564)
ὅραμα horama (3568)

זִיו zîw (A2204), Face (Dn 5:6—Aramaic).

חָזָה chāzâh (2463), See (Ez 21:29, Zec 10:2).

חָזוֹן chāzôn (2469), Vision (1 Sm 3:1, Ez 12:22ff., Mi 3:6).

חֲזוֹת chāzôth (A2472), Something visible (Dn 4:11,20 [4:8,17]—Aramaic).

חִזָּיוֹן chizzāyôn (2476), Vision (2 Sm 7:17, Jl 2:28, Zec 13:4).

מַחֲזֶה machāzeh (4371), Vision (Nm 24:4,16, Ez 13:7).

מִצְפָּה mitspāh (4870), Mitzpah (Gn 31:49).

מַרְאָה mar'āh (4919), Vision (1 Sm 3:15, Ez 40:2, Dn 10:7f.).

מַרְאֶה mar'eh (4920), Sight, appearance (Gn 2:9, Na 2:4); vision (Ez 11:24).

מַשָּׂא mashshā' (5041), Oracle (Is 13:1, 19:1).

עַיִן 'ayin (6084), Likeness (Ez 1:22).

רָאָה rā'âh (7495), See (Nm 24:4,16).

רְאִי rᵉ'î (7502), Mirror (Jb 37:18).

רֳאִי rŏ'î (7503), Appearance (1 Sm 16:12).

רֵו rēw (A7585), Appearance (Dn 3:25—Aramaic).

תּוּר tûr (8780), Seek out, reconnoiter; regard (1 Chr 17:17).

1. ὁράσει **horasei** dat sing fem
2. ὁράσεις **horaseis** acc pl fem

2	and your young men shall see **visions**,..............	Acts 2:17
1	was **to look upon** like a jasper and a sardine stone:...	Rev 4:3
1	**in sight** like unto an emerald.........................	4:3
1	And thus I saw the horses in the **vision**,................	9:17

Classical Greek and Septuagint Usage

In classical Greek *horasis* has the primary meaning of "sight," "vision," "the capacity to see," or "the act of seeing" (cf. *Liddell-Scott*). The Septuagint uses the word for (1) God watching over a person's life (Genesis 31:49); (2) a vision by which God revealed to His prophets future events (2 Samuel 7:17 [LXX 2 Kings 7:17]; Isaiah 1:1; Ezekiel 1:1).

New Testament Usage

In the New Testament this Greek noun is used four times and is translated "visions" (Acts 2:17), "appearance" (Revelation 4:3), "sight" (Revelation 4:3), and "vision" (Revelation 9:17). This act or capacity to see is not referring to ordinary physical sight but to a supernatural sight through which God revealed His purpose and plans for His people (cf. 2 Samuel 7:10-

ὁρατός 3570

17), of His glory in the earth (cf. Ezekiel 43:3-5), and of the blessings of the Holy Spirit (cf. Joel 2:28).

STRONG 3706, BAUER 577, MOULTON-MILLIGAN 455, KITTEL 5:370-71, LIDDELL-SCOTT 1244, COLIN BROWN 3:512,515.

3570. ὁρατός horatos adj
Visible, capable of being seen.
CROSS-REFERENCE:
ὁράω horaō (3571)

מַרְאֶה mar'eh (4920), Something impressive (2 Sm 23:21).

רָאָה rā'âh (7495), See (Jb 37:21).

1. ὁρατά horata nom/acc pl neu

1 visible and invisible, whether they be thrones, ... Col 1:16

This word appears only once in the New Testament, in Colossians 1:16. It is the adjectival form of the verb *horaō* (3571), "I see," and signifies that which is visible to human eyesight. The word is commonly used in the writings of Ignatius (ca. A.D. 110) (*Bauer*). He referred to Christ as "the invisible one, the one who is *visible* through us" (ibid.).

Paul used *horatos* in his famous Christological passage of Colossians 1, wherein he proclaimed Christ to be the Lord of creation (verses 15-17) and Lord of the Church (verses 18-20). Here, after pointing out in verse 15 that Christ is the image (*eikōn* [1494]) of the "invisible" (*aoratos* [513], "not-visible") God, Paul proclaimed that this same Christ is also the very Creator of "all things ... visible (*horatos*) and invisible" (verse 16). This is reminiscent of a theme Paul stated earlier in Romans 1:20 that the "invisible" (*aoratos*) things of God are "clearly seen" from His creation.

STRONG 3707, BAUER 577, MOULTON-MILLIGAN 455, KITTEL 5:368-70, LIDDELL-SCOTT 1224.

3571. ὁράω horaō verb
See, look upon or contemplate, perceive, take heed, be visible.
COGNATES:
ἀόρατος aoratos (513)
ἀφοράω aphoraō (865)
καθοράω kathoraō (2501)
ὅραμα horama (3568)
ὁρατός horatos (3570)
προοράω prooraō (4167)
SYNONYMS:
αἰσθάνομαι aisthanomai (143)

ἀναφαίνω anaphainō (396)
ἀτενίζω atenizō (810)
αὐγάζω augazō (820)
ἀφοράω aphoraō (865)
βλέπω blepō (984)
γίνομαι ginomai (1090)
γινώσκω ginōskō (1091)
εἶδον eidon (1481)
ἐμβλέπω emblepō (1676)
ἐμφανίζω emphanizō (1702)
ἐπέρχομαι eperchomai (1889)
ἐπιβλέπω epiblepō (1899)
ἐπιγινώσκω epiginōskō (1906)
ἐπίσταμαι epistamai (1971)
ἐπιφαίνω epiphainō (1998)
ἐπιφαύσκω epiphauskō (2001)
ἐποπτεύω epopteuō (2013)
ἐφίστημι ephistēmi (2168)
θεάομαι theaomai (2277)
θεωρέω theōreō (2311)
ἵστημι histēmi (2449)
καταλαμβάνω katalambanō (2608)
καταμανθάνω katamanthanō (2618)
κατανοέω katanoeō (2627)
νοέω noeō (3401)
οἶδα oida (3471)
ὀπτάνομαι optanomai (3563)
παραγίνομαι paraginomai (3716)
παρακολουθέω parakoloutheō (3738)
προσέχω prosechō (4196)
σκοπέω skopeō (4503)
συνίημι suniēmi (4770)
φαίνω phainō (5154)

אַךְ 'akh (395), Surely (Ex 31:13).

בּוֹא bô' (971), Come (1 Kgs 3:16).

גָּלָה gālâh (1580), Reveal, go away; niphal: be revealed (Is 40:5).

הִנֵּה hinnêh (2079), Behold! (Gn 37:29, Ex 2:13, 14:10).

חָזָה châzâh (2463), See (Ex 24:11, Ez 13:7; seen (2 Sm 24:11).

חֲזָה châzâh (A2464), See (Dn 2:8,41,45, 3:25—Aramaic).

חָלַם châlam (2593), Dream (Gn 41:15, Dn 2:3).

פָּנָה pânâh (6680), Turn (Jb 5:1).

רָאָה rā'âh (7495), Qal: look, see (Lv 13:3, Ps 49:9 [48:9], Jer 1:11); niphal: appear (Ex 4:1, Jgs 13:21, Is 60:2); hiphil: show (Mi 7:15); hithpael: face one another (2 Kgs 14:8, 2 Chr 25:21).

רְאִית re'yyth (7506), Looking (Eccl 5:10).

שׁוּר shûr (8227), See (Jb 34:29).

שָׁכַן shâkhan (8331), Dwell (Ex 25:8 [25:7], Dt 33:16).

1. ὁρᾶτε horate 2pl indic/impr pres act
2. ὁρῶ horō 1sing indic pres act
3. ὁρᾷ hora 3sing indic pres act
4. ὁρῶμεν horōmen 1pl indic pres act
5. ὅρα hora 2sing impr pres act
6. ὁρῶν horōn nom sing masc part pres act
7. ὁρῶντες horōntes nom pl masc part pres act
8. ὁρῶσαι horōsai nom pl fem part pres act

ὁράω 3571

9. ἑώρακα heōraka 1sing indic perf act
10. ἑώρακας heōrakas 2sing indic perf act
11. ἑώρακεν heōraken 3sing indic perf act
12. ἑωράκαμεν heōrakamen 1pl indic perf act
13. ἑωράκατε heōrakate 2pl indic perf act
14. ἑωράκασιν heōrakasin 3pl indic perf act
15. ἑωράκει heōrakei 3sing indic plperf act
16. ἑωρακώς heōrakōs nom sing masc part perf act
17. ἑωρακότες heōrakotes nom pl masc part perf act
18. ἑωρακέναι heōrakenai inf perf act
19. ἑώρων heōrōn 3pl indic imperf act
20. ὤφθην ōphthēn 1sing indic aor pass
21. ὤφθη ōphthē 3sing indic aor pass
22. ὤφθησαν ōphthēsan 3pl indic aor pass
23. ὄψησθε opsēsthe 2pl subj aor mid
24. ὀφθείς ophtheis nom sing masc part aor pass
25. ὀφθέντος ophthentos gen sing masc part aor pass
26. ὀφθέντες ophthentes nom pl masc part aor pass
27. ὀφθήσομαι ophthēsomai 1sing indic fut pass
28. ὄψομαι opsomai 1sing indic fut mid
29. ὄψει opsei 2sing indic fut mid
30. ὀφθήσεται ophthēsetai 3sing indic fut pass
31. ὄψεται opsetai 3sing indic fut mid
32. ὀψόμεθα opsometha 1pl indic fut mid
33. ὄψεσθε opsesthe 2pl indic fut mid
34. ὄψονται opsontai 3pl indic fut mid
35. ἑόρακα heoraka 1sing indic perf act
36. ἑόρακεν heoraken 3sing indic perf act
37. ἑόρακαν heorakan 3pl indic perf act
38. ἑώρακαν heōrakan 3pl indic perf act
39. ὄψῃ opsē 2sing indic fut mid
40. ὄπσονται opsontai 3pl indic fut mid

34	the pure in heart: for they **shall see** God	Matt 5:8
5	**See** thou tell no man; but go thy way,	8:4
1	saying, **See** that no man know it.	9:30
1	Then Jesus said unto them, **Take heed** and beware	16:6
22	there **appeared** unto them Moses and Elias	17:3
1	**Take heed** that ye despise not one of these little	18:10
1	rumours of wars: **see** that ye be not troubled:	24:6
34	and they **shall see** the Son of man coming	24:30
33	unto you, Hereafter **shall** ye **see** the Son of man	26:64
29	And they said, What is that to us? **see** thou to that.	27:4
33	I am innocent of the blood of this ... **see** ye to it.	27:24
33	there **shall** ye **see** him: lo, I have told you.	28:7
34	go into Galilee, and there **shall they see** me.	28:10
5	saith unto him, **See** thou say nothing to any man:	Mark 1:44
1	**Take heed**, beware of the leaven of the Pharisees,	8:15
2	he ... said, I **see** men as trees, walking. (NT)	8:24
21	And there **appeared** unto them Elias with Moses:	9:4
34	And then **shall they see** the Son of man coming	13:26
33	said, I am: and **ye shall see** the Son of man sitting	14:62
33	Galilee: there **shall** ye **see** him, as he said unto you.	16:7
21	And there **appeared** unto him an angel of the Lord	Luke 1:11
11	perceived that he **had seen** a vision in the temple:	1:22
31	And all flesh **shall see** the salvation of God.	3:6
26	Who **appeared** in glory, and spake of his decease	9:31
14	any of those things which they **had seen**.	9:36
1	**Take heed**, and beware of covetousness:	12:15
23	when ye **shall see** Abraham, and Isaac, and Jacob,	13:28
3	**seeth** Abraham afar off, and Lazarus in his bosom.	16:23
33	the days of the Son of man, and ye **shall not see** it.	17:22
34	And then **shall they see** the Son of man coming	21:27
21	there **appeared** an angel unto him from heaven,	22:43
8	stood afar off, **beholding** these things.	Luke 23:49
18	saying, that they **had** also **seen** a vision of angels,	24:23
21	Lord is risen indeed, and hath **appeared** to Simon.	24:34
11	No man **hath seen** God at any time;	John 1:18
9	And I **saw**, and bare record that this is the Son	1:34
33	"Come and **you will see**." (NASB)	1:39
29	thou **shalt see** greater things than these.	1:50
33	Hereafter ye **shall see** heaven open,	1:51
12	and testify that we **have seen**;	3:11
11	what he **hath seen** and heard, that he testifieth;	3:32
31	and he that believeth not the Son **shall not see** life;	3:36
17	**having seen** all the things that he did at Jerusalem	4:45
13	neither heard his voice ... nor **seen** his shape.	5:37
19	followed him, because they **saw** his miracles	6:2
13	That ye also **have seen** me, and believe not.	6:36
11	Not that any man **hath seen** the Father,	6:46
11	save he which is of God, he **hath seen** the Father.	6:46
9	I speak that which I **have seen** with my Father:	8:38
13	and ye do that which ye **have seen** with your father.	8:38
10	art not yet fifty ... and **hast** thou **seen** Abraham?	8:57
10	And Jesus said unto him, Thou **hast** both **seen** him,	9:37
29	thou **shouldest see** the glory of God?	11:40
16	from henceforth ye know him, and **have seen** him.	14:7
16	he that **hath seen** me hath seen the Father;	14:9
11	he that hath seen me **hath seen** the Father;	14:9
14	but now **have** they both **seen** and hated	15:24
33	and again, a little while, and ye **shall see** me,	16:16
33	and again, a little while, and ye **shall see** me:	16:17
33	and again, a little while, and ye **shall see** me?	16:19
28	I **will see** you again, and your heart shall rejoice,	16:22
16	he that saw it bare record, and his record is true:	19:35
34	They **shall look** on him whom they pierced.	19:37
11	told the disciples that she **had seen** the Lord,	20:18
12	We **have seen** the Lord.	20:25
10	because thou **hast seen** me, thou hast believed:	20:29
22	**appeared** unto them cloven tongues like as of fire,	Acts 2:3
34	and your young men **shall see** visions,	2:17
21	God of glory **appeared** unto our father Abraham,	7:2
21	he **showed** himself unto them as they strove,	7:26
21	there **appeared** to him ... an angel of the Lord	7:30
25	the angel which **appeared** to him in the bush.	7:35
15	make it according to the fashion that he **had seen**.	7:44
2	I perceive that thou art in the gall of bitterness,	8:23
24	that **appeared** unto thee in the way as thou camest,	9:17
21	And he **was seen** many days of	13:31
21	And a vision **appeared** to Paul in the night;	16:9
33	**look** ye to it; for I will be no judge of such matters.	18:15
33	**shall see** my face no more.	20:25
10	be his witness unto all men of what thou **hast seen**	22:15
5	saying, **Take heed** what thou doest:	22:26
20	for I **have appeared** unto thee for this purpose,	26:16
27	those things in the which I **will appear** unto thee,	26:16
34	To whom he was not spoken of, they **shall see**:	Rom 15:21
9	have I not **seen** Jesus Christ our Lord?	1 Co 9:1
21	that he **was seen** of Cephas, then of the twelve:	15:5
21	**was seen** of above five hundred brethren at once;	15:6
21	he **was seen** of James; then of all the apostles.	15:7
21	And last of all he **was seen** of me also,	15:8
14	for as many as **have not seen** my face in the flesh;	Col 2:1
11	intruding into those things which he **hath not seen**,	2:18
1	**See** that none render evil for evil unto any man;	1 Th 5:15
21	**seen** of angels, preached unto the Gentiles,	1 Tm 3:16
4	But now we **see** not yet all things put under him.	Heb 2:8
5	for, **See**, saith he, that thou make all things	8:5
30	and unto them that look for him **shall he appear**,	9:28
6	for he endured, as **seeing** him who is invisible.	11:27
31	holiness, without which no man **shall see** the Lord:	12:14
28	with whom, if he come shortly, I **will see** you.	13:23
1	Ye **see** then how that by works a man is justified,	Jas 2:24
7	though now ye **see** him not, yet believing,	1 Pt 1:8
12	which **we have seen** with our eyes,	1 Jn 1:1
12	For the life was manifested, and we **have seen** it,	1:2
12	That which **we have seen** and heard declare we,	1:3
32	we shall be like him; for we **shall see** him as he is.	3:2
11	whosoever sinneth **hath not seen** him,	3:6
11	he that loveth not his brother whom he **hath seen**,	4:20
11	how can he love God whom he **hath not seen**?	4:20

11 but he that doeth evil hath not seen God.	3 Jn 1:11
31 cometh with clouds; and every eye shall see him,	Rev 1:7
21 was seen in his temple the ark of his testament:	11:19
21 And there appeared a great wonder in heaven;	12:1
21 And there appeared another wonder in heaven;	12:3
7 cried when they saw the smoke of her burning,	18:18
5 And he said unto me, See thou do it not:	19:10
34 And they shall see his face;	22:4
5 See thou do it not: for I am thy fellowservant,	22:9

Classical Greek

Various forms of this verb appear in Greek antiquity: *horō*, *horoō*, *orēmi*, and *horeō* (on the formation and forms see *Liddell-Scott*). Its meanings in classical Greek include "see, look" (with the eyes), "look at, view, observe" something. In a metaphorical sense "to see" is "to perceive mentally," "to discern" (ibid.). The idea of "see" is conveyed by multiple Greek terms (e.g., *blepō* [984], *optanomai* [3563], *theōreō* [2311]), and there are many derivatives of *horaō* (e.g., *horama* [3568], *horasis* [3569], *horatos* [3570]).

Since "to see" is to participate in life itself (Michaelis, "horaō," *Kittel*, 5:316), it is easy to imagine the various roles it assumes. It transcends the language barriers of everyday living and enters the vocabulary of philosophy, religion, and science. *Horaō* thus describes ordinary "sight" of physical, tangible objects, but it can also denote spiritual perception, seeing in dreams and visions, and "perceiving" or "understanding" mental complexities. "To see" thus captures the quality of many senses; Michaelis notes that "*horaō* can even be used for *akouō* ('to hear')" (ibid.).

The Greeks viewed "sight" or "seeing" as the main avenue of perception. This is reflected even in their religious systems. The Greeks were a "people of the eye" (ibid., 5:319), in distinction to the Hebrews who were primarily a "people of the ear" (e.g., Deuteronomy 6:4, "Hear . . . O Israel"). Whereas Greeks at times erected visible statues or saw gods in terms of human and animal forms, the Israelites served an unseen God (e.g., Exodus 19:20,21). Later as Greeks like Plato drew distinctions between the "real" and "perceived" world, "sight's" preeminence gave way to the "mind" (*nous* [3426]), which could perceive "true reality." "Nevertheless—and this is worth noting—for the Greeks even supreme and purely intellectual striving is always a seeing" (ibid., 5:321).

Septuagint Usage

Ten Hebrew words are translated by *horaō* (including the form *optesthai*). The majority of times *rā'âh*, "see," is the counterpart. *Horaō* concerns visible seeing, such as the land Abraham saw (Genesis 13:15) or the events witnessed by Joshua (Joshua 8:21). Supernatural visions, sights, and events are also "made to appear," and "sight" or "spiritual perception" plays an important role in the religion of Israel (e.g., Exodus 3:2,3,16; 24:11). God "appears" to individuals (e.g., Exodus 4:5, to Moses; Genesis 12:7; 17:1; 18:1, to Abraham). Prophets "see" the revelation of God and His will for the people, although this may often involve a word from the Lord that needs to be heard (e.g., Ezekiel "sees" visions but speaks a word from the Lord [usually *blepō*]). The spiritual condition of Israel is often depicted as their inability to see and understand (e.g., Isaiah 6:9,10; Ezekiel 12:2).

"Seeing" also involves "mental perception" and "consideration." Thus "appearing" leads to "hearing" (Deuteronomy 31:11) and "to see" means "to discover," "acquire an understanding of" (e.g., 1 Samuel 19:3 [LXX 1 Kings 19:3]). The Septuagint is familiar with all the classical understandings and freely uses *horaō* in both a religious and nonreligious sense (for more on *horaō* in the Old Testament see ibid., and Dahn, "See, Vision, Eye," *Colin Brown*, 3:513f.).

New Testament Usage

As in the Septuagint and classical Greek *horaō* is only one of many terms used to convey the idea of "see, perceive" in the New Testament. The general sense of to "see" with one's eyes is clearly present in the New Testament (e.g., Acts 20:25), although predominantly *horaō* concerns a "seeing" on a supernatural or spiritual plane. Thus visions are "seen" (e.g., Luke 1:22; Acts 2:17; 16:9), and divine revelations or manifestations "appear" (Luke 1:11; 22:43; John 1:51; Acts 2:3; 7:2,30; 9:17; 1 Corinthians 9:1; 1 Timothy 3:16; 1 John 1:1-3). At times the imperative use, *hora* or *horate*, "beware" or "see to, take care of, take care" (cf. *blepete*), occurs. This functions as a warning (Matthew 9:30; Mark 8:15; Luke 12:15; 1 Thessalonians 5:15).

"Sight" during the earthly ministry of Jesus denoted "recognition" that He is indeed who His miracles showed Him to be. Thus in Luke Jesus pronounced His disciples "blessed" because they were seeing the manifestations of the Kingdom that prophets only longed to see (Luke 10:23,24; Greek, *blepō*). In the future mankind "will see" the coming of the Son of

Man (Matthew 24:30; parallel Mark 13:26; Revelation 1:7) and His reigning in glory (Matthew 26:64; parallel Mark 14:62). Future sight is also part of the age to come (Luke 13:28).

John's Gospel makes particular use of the motif of seeing. While God is not seen (John 1:18), He can be known by seeing Jesus: "He that *hath seen* me (Jesus) *hath seen* the Father" (John 14:9). Jesus is seen with the eyes of faith (John 16:16,17,19,22; cf. Hebrews 11:27). Jesus was "seen" by the witnesses who testified of Him (John 19:35; cf. 3:11,32), and the witnesses of the Risen Lord declared they had seen the Lord (John 20:18,25; cf. Acts 22:15; 26:16; 1 Corinthians 15:5-8). Such sight elicits faith, but those who have faith without having seen are blessed (John 20:29; cf. 1 Peter 1:8), and in his first epistle, John wrote that those who insist on sinning have not "seen" Him (1 John 3:2; cf. 3 John 11; cf. Hebrews 12:14).

Thus "seeing" continues to play an important role in the religious language of the New Testament. Sight can even represent "salvation" (cf. Luke 3:6; John 3:36; Hebrews 12:14; 1 John 3:2). "To see" is to grasp by faith that the Son is indeed come and that He offers salvation to all mankind (Romans 15:21).

STRONG 3708, BAUER 577-78, MOULTON-MILLIGAN 455, KITTEL 5:315-67, LIDDELL-SCOTT 1244-45, COLIN BROWN 3:511-13,515-16.

3572. ὀργή orgē noun

Anger, wrath.

COGNATE:
ὀργίζομαι orgizomai (3573)

SYNONYMS:
ἀγανάκτησις aganaktēsis (24)
θυμός thumos (2349)
παροργισμός parorgismos (3812)

אַף 'aph (653), Anger, wrath (Dt 9:19, Ps 110:5 [109:5], Ez 13:13).

זַעַם zaʻam (2279), Wrath, indignation (Ps 102:10 [101:10], Jer 50:25 [27:25], Na 1:6).

זַעַף zaʻaph (2281), Rage (2 Chr 28:9).

חֱמָה chămāh (A2634), Rage (Dn 3:13—Aramaic).

חֵמָה chēmāh (2635), Fury, wrath (Gn 27:44, Ps 6:1, Ez 7:8).

חָרוֹן chārôn (2841), Anger, wrath (Ex 32:12, Ps 88:16 [87:16], Hos 11:9).

חָרָה chārâh (2835), Burn (Nm 12:9).

חֳרִי chŏrî (2853), Fierceness (Is 7:4, Lam 2:3).

כַּעַשׂ kaʻas (3833I), Vexation, anger (Jb 5:2, 10:17).

כַּעַס kaʻas (3833II) Provocation, vexation (Dt 32:19, Prv 12:16, 27:3).

נְאָצָה neʼātsāh (5181), Disgrace (Is 37:3).

סוּפָה sûphāh (5679), Storm (Ps 83:15 [82:15]).

סַעַר saʻar (5787), Tempest (Jer 30:23 [37:23]).

סְעָרָה seʻārāh (5788), Storm (Jer 30:23 [37:23]).

עֶבְרָה ʻevrāh (5887), Wrath (Jb 21:30, Ps 90:9 [89:9], Zep 1:15).

קָצַף qātsaph (7395), Be angry (Nm 16:22).

קֶצֶף qetseph (7397), Wrath, anger (Jos 9:20, 2 Chr 19:2, Is 60:10).

קְצַף qetsaph (A7399), Wrath (Ezr 7:23—Aramaic).

רֹגֶז rōghez (7555), Excitement (Jb 39:24).

1. ὀργή orgē nom sing fem
2. ὀργῆς orgēs gen sing fem
3. ὀργῇ orgē dat sing fem
4. ὀργήν orgēn acc sing fem

2	who ... warned you to flee from the **wrath** to come?	Matt 3:7
2	he had looked round about on them with **anger**,	Mark 3:5
2	warned you to flee from the **wrath** to come?	Luke 3:7
1	distress in the land, and **wrath** upon this people.	21:23
1	but the **wrath** of God abideth on him.	John 3:36
1	For the **wrath** of God is revealed from heaven	Rom 1:18
1	unto thyself **wrath** against the day of **wrath**	2:5
4	unto thyself wrath against the day of **wrath**	2:5
1	but obey unrighteousness, indignation and **wrath**,	2:8
4	Is God unrighteous who taketh **vengeance**?	3:5
4	Because the law worketh **wrath**:	4:15
2	we shall be saved from **wrath** through him.	5:9
4	What if God, willing to show his **wrath**,	9:22
2	the vessels **of wrath** fitted to destruction:	9:22
3	but rather give place unto **wrath**:	12:19
4	a revenger to execute **wrath** upon him that doeth	13:4
4	not only for **wrath**,	13:5
2	and were by nature the children **of wrath**,	Eph 2:3
1	Let all bitterness, and **wrath**, and anger,	4:31
1	because of these things cometh the **wrath** of God	5:6
1	For which things' sake the **wrath** of God cometh	Col 3:6
4	put off all these; anger, **wrath**, malice, blasphemy,	3:8
2	Jesus, which delivered us from the **wrath** to come.	1 Th 1:10
1	for the **wrath** is come upon them to the uttermost.	2:16
4	For God hath not appointed us to **wrath**,	5:9
2	lifting up holy hands, without **wrath** and doubting.	1 Tm 2:8
3	So I sware in my **wrath**, They shall not enter	Heb 3:11
3	as he said, As I have sworn in my **wrath**,	4:3
4	man be swift to hear, slow to speak, slow to **wrath**:	Jas 1:19
1	**wrath** of man worketh not ... righteousness of God.	1:20
2	and from the **wrath** of the Lamb:	Rev 6:16
2	For the great day of his **wrath** is come;	6:17
1	the nations were angry, and thy **wrath** is come,	11:18
2	without mixture into the cup of his **indignation**;	14:10
2	the cup of the wine of the fierceness of his **wrath**.	16:19
2	treadeth the winepress of the fierceness and **wrath**	19:15

Classical Greek

Orgē and its related words (*orgaō*, "wax wanton," and *orgas* [any well-watered, fertile spot of land]) are very common in classical literature. The most basic meaning of *orgē* relates to the inner disposition as evidenced by passion, impulse, and especially outward expressions of displeasure or anger. One might be characterized by an unhappy or "angry" disposition. *Orgē* can express anger against a person or thing, or it may be directed toward no person or thing in particular. The Classical literature has several related words. Among several other meanings, *orgaō* can mean "to be under the influence of passion or anger." An *orgia* is a secret or religious rite, often involving sacrifices, with the worship usually involving sensual and passionate activities. *Orgiazō* refers to the celebration of such a religious *orgia* while the person who participates as a leader or priest is an *orgōn*. A particularly passionate person is a *orgētēs*. (See *Liddell-Scott* for this grouping of words.)

There are several occurrences of *orgē* documented in the papyri literature. *Moulton-Milligan* documents several occurrences when *orgē* is used in the "sense of natural 'anger' or 'passion.'" Also, *orgē* used with the sense of "divine wrath" is documented in the papyri just as it is in the New Testament. The related verb *orgizomai* (3573), "be angry," and the adjective *orgilos* (3574), "quick-tempered," are also found in the papyri.

Septuagint Usage

Orgē is used many times in the Septuagint. In Genesis 27:44 Rebekah spoke to Jacob about Esau's "fury" (*orgē*). In Exodus 4:14 "the anger (*orgē*) of the Lord was kindled against Moses." Again in Deuteronomy 9:19 Moses spoke of the "anger" (*orgē*) of the Lord. Saul's "anger was kindled greatly" (1 Samuel 11:6 [LXX 1 Kings 11:6]). These passages are representative of many other similar occurrences in the Septuagint. It is noteworthy that *orgē* is used often in the Septuagint to refer to God's anger or wrath.

New Testament Usage

Orgē is used frequently in the New Testament. The word most often refers to God's anger or "wrath" (KJV). There are more than 20 occurrences of *orgē* meaning God's wrath, either present or future. With the present tense, *orgē* refers to God's wrath: "He that believeth on the Son hath everlasting life: and he that believeth not the Son shall not see life; but the *wrath* of God abideth on him" (John 3:36). (Also see Romans 1:18 where *orgē* is used with the present tense.)

Orgē refers to God's future judgment on unrighteous people, as in Matthew 3:7 where Jesus referred to the "*wrath* to come." This future judgmental "anger" is mentioned or alluded to as a future happening about 10 times. The final judgmental events are referred to as "the *wrath* of the Lamb" in the Book of Revelation (see Revelation 6:16,17). As is typical of the figurative language of Revelation, 14:10 speaks of "the cup of his *indignation* (*orgē*)" and "the wine of the fierceness of his *wrath*" (16:19). Revelation 19:15 makes a fearful reference to the "*wrath* of Almighty God."

Not only is *orgē* used in reference to God, but also of man and of Jesus. In Mark 3:5 Jesus looked "round about on them with *anger*." *Orgē* is an expression of displeasure and emotion readily evident from His demeanor. Yet *orgē* also refers to human emotional disposition that is not acceptable in the Christian life-style and is spoken of in a negative way (Ephesians 4:31; James 1:19). Paul exhorted the Colossians to "put off all these; *anger* wrath, malice" (Colossians 3:8). *Orgē* refers to God's Old Testament anger toward the Israelite people in a New Testament citation of an Old Testament passage (Hebrews 3:11; 4:3, "have I sworn in my *wrath*"). The New Testament also uses related words like the verb *orgizomai*, "to be angry," and the adjective *orgilos*, "angry."

STRONG 3709, BAUER 578-79, MOULTON-MILLIGAN 455-56, KITTEL 5:382-447, LIDDELL-SCOTT 1246, COLIN BROWN 1:107-8,110-13.

3573. ὀργίζομαι orgizomai verb

To be angry, to be angry at someone.

COGNATES:
 ὀργή orgē (3572)
 ὀργίλος orgilos (3574)
 παροργίζω parorgizō (3811)
 παροργισμός parorgismos (3812)

SYNONYMS:
 θυμόω thumoō (2350)
 παροξύνω paroxunō (3809)
 χολάω cholaō (5356)

אָנֵף 'ānēph (613), Qal: be angry (Pss 2:12, 79:5 [78:5], Is 12:1); hithpael: be angry (1 Kgs 11:9).

אַף 'aph (653), Anger (Dt 11:17—Codex Alexandrinus only).

זָעַם zāʿam (2278), Be enraged (Dn 11:30—Sixtine Edition only).

חָרָה chārâh (2835), Be kindled, burn (Dt 6:15, Jgs 6:39, Ps 124:3 [123:3]).

כָּעַס kāʿaṣ (3832), Be incensed, be vexed (Neh 4:1, Ps 112:10 [111:10]).

מָרַר mārar (5006), Be bitter; hithpalpel: be enraged (Dn 11:11).

עָשֵׁן 'āshen (6478), Smoke (Ps 74:1 [73:1]).

קָצַף qātsaph (7395), Be angry (Gn 40:2, Eccl 5:6 [5:5], Is 57:16).

רָגַז rāghaz (7553), Qal: quarrel, be angry (Gn 45:24, Ps 4:4); hiphil: provoke (Jb 12:6—Codex Alexandrinus only); hithpael: rage (2 Kgs 19:28).

רִיב rîv (7662), Strive (Ps 103:9 [102:9]).

1. ὀργίζεσθε orgizesthe 2pl impr pres mid
2. ὀργιζόμενος orgizomenos nom sing masc part pres mid
3. ὠργίσθη ōrgisthē 3sing indic aor pass
4. ὠργίσθησαν ōrgisthēsan 3pl indic aor pass
5. ὀργισθείς orgistheis nom sing masc part aor pass

2 That whosoever is angry with his brother	Matt 5:22
5 And his lord was wroth,	18:34
3 But when the king heard thereof, he was wroth:	22:7
5 master of the house being angry said to his servant,	Luke 14:21
3 And he was angry, and would not go in:	15:28
1 Be ye angry, and sin not:	Eph 4:26
4 the nations were angry, and thy wrath is come,	Rev 11:18
3 And the dragon was wroth with the woman,	12:17

This word is found eight times in the New Testament and is used in the middle or passive form each time. In classical Greek it is sometimes used in the active form, "to make angry," but not so in either the Septuagint, the New Testament, or papyri (*Bauer*). It represents an inner mental attitude of indignation, wrath, hatred, and fury usually targeted at a specific person, thing, or event (cf. Numbers 22:22; Proverbs 16:30).

New Testament Usage
In the Sermon on the Mount (Matthew 5:22) and in Ephesians 4:31, both Christ and the apostle Paul urged Christians not to "be angry." Christ spoke against "anger" at a brother who is a follower of God, while Paul emphasized that even one with a righteous "anger" must not let it become sin. Revelation 11:18 and 12:17 state that "the nations *were angry*" and "the dragon *was wroth*," as part of the climax of emotions during the Tribulation period.

The remaining four usages are located in parables (Matthew 18:34; 22:7; Luke 14:21; 15:28). In three of the cases the king or lord, representing God, was "angry" at wicked people. In Luke 15:28, however, it is the older brother of the Prodigal Son who "was angry" because of his uncontrolled contempt for his wayward younger brother and because of his discontent with his father for celebrating the brother's return.

STRONG 3710, BAUER 579, MOULTON-MILLIGAN 456, KITTEL 5:382-447, LIDDELL-SCOTT 1246 (see "orgizō"), COLIN BROWN 1:107; 2:419 (see "orgizō").

3574. ὀργίλος orgilos adj
Inclined to anger, quick-tempered, irritable.
CROSS-REFERENCE:
ὀργίζομαι orgizomai (3573)

אַף 'aph (653), Enemy (Ps 18:48 [17:48])

חֵמָה chēmāh (2635), Anger (Prv 22:24, 29:22).

כַּעַס ka'as (3833II) Ill-tempered person (Prv 21:19).

1. ὀργίλον orgilon acc sing masc

1 not selfwilled, not soon angry, not given to wine,	Tit 1:7

Related to the noun *orgē* (3572), "anger, indignation, wrath," the adjective *orgilos*, "quick-tempered, inclined to anger," occurs only once in the New Testament, in Titus 1:7. In this passage Paul used *orgilos* in connection with his instruction concerning the office of a bishop (elder). A person considered for this position must not be "quick-tempered or inclined to anger."

Further study of the concept of *orgē*, "anger," throughout the Old and New Testaments shows the severity with which human anger and its subsequent results are generally viewed. Paul wrote of the putting away of all "anger," listing it among other potential sinful attitudes and practices (Ephesians 4:31; Colossians 3:8; cf. Proverbs 22:24; 29:22). Hence, Paul's instruction concerning the office of a bishop who, in a position of authority and as an example to the body of Christ, should not be *orgilos*, "quick-tempered, inclined to anger."

STRONG 3711, BAUER 579, MOULTON-MILLIGAN 456, KITTEL 4:382-447, LIDDELL-SCOTT 1246, COLIN BROWN 1:107,110.

3575. ὀργυιά orguia noun
Fathom.

1. ὀργυιάς orguias acc pl fem

1 And sounded, and found it twenty fathoms:	Acts 27:28
1 they sounded again, and found it fifteen fathoms.	27:28

The use of *orguia*, "fathom," is rare in the New Testament, occurring twice at its only location, Acts 27:28. The word *orguia* is a technical term used primarily to measure the depth of water. However, there is also some indication that it was a measuring rod for the purpose of measuring land (cf. *Liddell-Scott*).

In early Greek one *orguia* was the distance between the tip of the middle finger of one hand to the tip of the middle finger of the other hand when the arms are outstretched. This distance was approximately equal to 6 feet (1.85 meters).

Paul used *orguia* when he referred to the sailors taking a measure of the sea depth, as "they sounded, and found it twenty *fathoms*; ... they sounded again, and found it fifteen *fathoms*." Fearing they might run aground, the sailors cast out the anchors (Acts 27:29).

STRONG 3712, BAUER 579, MOULTON-MILLIGAN 456, LIDDELL-SCOTT 1246.

3576. ὀρέγομαι oregomai verb

Stretch toward, reach out, yearn for, desire, strive for.

CROSS-REFERENCE:
ὄρεξις orexis (3578)

1. ὀρέγεται oregetai 3sing indic pres mid
2. ὀρέγονται oregontai 3pl indic pres mid
3. ὀρεγόμενοι oregomenoi nom pl masc part pres mid

1 If a man desire the office of a bishop,............. 1 Tm 3:1
3 which while some coveted after,........................ 6:10
2 But now they desire a better country, that is,...... Heb 11:16

Two of its three occurrences in the New Testament are at 1 Timothy 3:1 and 6:10, where each use provides an interesting contrast. In 1 Timothy 3:1 the NASB renders it "aspires to" in reference to a man being an overseer or elder (cf. Acts 20:17,28), in the more common term of our day, pastor. This was not to be an ambitious seeking. The qualifications that follow (1 Timothy 3:2-7) will only fit a person who has a heart with proper motives. A person who has the character and conduct sought by these qualifications is truly "stretching" himself. In contrast, the use of *oregomai* in 1 Timothy 6:10 refers to a person, probably a leader, who "longs for" (NASB; "coveted after," KJV) money. This person believes godliness is a means of financial gain (1 Timothy 6:5) and has a selfish desire for prominence rather than service (cf. Mark 10:42-45). The person who has this kind of "desire" does not have the heart direction that meets the qualifications of 1 Timothy 3:2-7.

The use of *oregomai* in Hebrews 11:16 reflects "desire" in the heroes of faith who did not pursue the material things of this world but sought a "better" city prepared by God.

STRONG 3713, BAUER 579-80, MOULTON-MILLIGAN 456, KITTEL 5:447-48, LIDDELL-SCOTT 1246-47 (see "oregō"), COLIN BROWN 1:460-61.

3577. ὀρεινός oreinos adj

Hilly, mountainous.

1. ὀρεινῇ oreinē dat sing fem
2. ὀρεινήν oreinēn acc sing fem

2 and went into the hill country with haste,............ Luke 1:39
1 abroad throughout all the hill country of Judaea......... 1:65

Classical Greek and Septuagint Usage

Found in the writings of Herodotus, in inscriptions, papyri, the Septuagint, Josephus, and Philo, *oreinos* ("hilly, mountainous") identifies or describes the overall geographical condition of the terrain. It is related to the noun *oros* (3598), "mountain," and is also used more specifically with the sense of a particular geographical location, e.g., "the hill country."

New Testament Usage

In its only two usages in the New Testament, Luke 1:39,65, *oreinos* is found with the definite article (verse 39, *ten oreinen*; verse 65 *te oreine*) to indicate a particular geographical location. Mary went to "the hill country" (verse 39); the news of Zachariah's speaking after a period of dumbness was spread throughout "the hill country" (verse 65).

STRONG 3714, BAUER 580, MOULTON-MILLIGAN 456, LIDDELL-SCOTT 1247, COLIN BROWN 3:1008.

3578. ὄρεξις orexis noun

Strong desire, longing, lust.

COGNATE:
ὀρέγομαι oregomai (3576)

SYNONYMS:
ἐπιθυμία epithumia (1924)
εὐδοκία eudokia (2086)
ὁρμή hormē (3593)

1. ὀρέξει orexei dat sing fem

1 burned in their lust one toward another;............ Rom 1:27

Classical Greek

In its one occurrence in the New Testament (Romans 1:27) *orexis*, "strong desire, longing, lust," is used with an unfavorable connotation. However, in classical use *orexis* is used in a more general sense with reference to one's longings, whether they were good or bad. There may be reference to one's good and natural desires (e.g., sleeping, eating) or to one's evil and corrupt unlawful desires. In the Stoic philosophy the word was used in a neutral sense. In essence it meant to reach or stretch out after something whether it was with one's heart, mind, or body (cf. *Liddell-Scott*).

New Testament Usage
Paul used *orexis* in Romans 1:27 to attack the sexual "desire, lust" of a certain group of people. He did not attack the desires that arise in the course of normal marital sexual relations. Instead, Paul spoke out against the perverted and unnatural sexual *orexei*, "lust," of men towards men, i.e., homosexuality. The context shows that three times Paul asserted, "God gave them up" (verses 24,26,28). Paul interpreted the moral decadence of those who go against the created order of sexual relation between men and women as changing the "truth of God into a lie," and worshiping "the creature more than the Creator" (verse 25). Just as they did not "like to retain God in their knowledge," God then abandoned them (punitively, not merely permissively) to their own "reprobate" minds (verse 28). Paul also noted that these condemnable sins are not simply a thoughtless yielding to temptation, but instead are indulged in deliberately. In fact they are encouraged in others even while "knowing the judgment of God" (verse 32) is inevitable.

STRONG 3715, BAUER 580, MOULTON-MILLIGAN 456, KITTEL 5:447-48, LIDDELL-SCOTT 1247, COLIN BROWN 1:460-61.

3579. ὀρθοποδέω orthopodeō verb
Walk straight or uprightly, act rightly, be straightforward.
CROSS-REFERENCE:
 ὀρθός orthos (3580)

1. ὀρθοποδοῦσιν orthopodousin 3pl indic pres act

1 But when I saw that they **walked not uprightly**....... Gal 2:14

The word *orthopodeō* means "walk straightly" in a literal sense. Figuratively, it is to be "straightforward." Its only occurrence in the New Testament is Galatians 2:14 where Peter (here called Cephas) behaved hypocritically and was confronted by Paul. Peter was not being "*straightforward* about the truth of the gospel" (NASB). Paul cited this experience to the Galatians because it was representative of the problem the Galatians were facing (Galatians 3:1f.). The lack of straightforwardness on the part of Peter and his companions seemed to result, at least partially, from pressure put on the Galatians by the Judaizers who distorted the truth. Straightforwardness about the truth of the gospel is indeed a godly attribute.

STRONG 3716, BAUER 580, MOULTON-MILLIGAN 456, KITTEL 5:451, LIDDELL-SCOTT 1249, COLIN BROWN 3:351-52.

3580. ὀρθός orthos adj
Upright, straight, or a straight way.
COGNATES:
 ἀνορθόω anorthoō (458)
 διόρθωσις diorthōsis (1351)
 ἐπανόρθωσις epanorthōsis (1867)
 ἐπιδιορθόω epidiorthoō (1915)
 κατόρθωμα katorthōma (2705)
 ὀρθοποδέω orthopodeō (3579)
 ὀρθοτομέω orthotomeō (3581)
 ὀρθῶς orthōs (3586)
SYNONYM:
 εὐθύς euthus (2097)

בִּין bîn (1032), Perceive, understand; niphal: have understanding (Prv 15:14).
יָשָׁר yāshār (3596), Upright person, something straight (Prv 12:6, Jer 31:9 [38:9], Ez 1:7).
יֹשֶׁר yōsher (3598), Unrightness (Prv 4:11).
מֵישָׁרִים mêshārîm (4478), What is right (Prv 23:16).
רוֹמָה rômāh (7603), Haughtily (Mi 2:3).

1. ὀρθός orthos nom sing masc
2. ὀρθάς orthas acc pl fem

1 Said with a loud voice, Stand **upright** on thy feet... Acts 14:10
2 And make **straight** paths for your feet,............Heb 12:13

Its two occurrences in the New Testament include a literal sense and a figurative sense. In Acts 14:10 Paul commanded a lame man to stand "upright," whereupon the man was healed. Figuratively, in Hebrews 12:13 the writer exhorted, "... make *straight* paths." The context of verses 12 and 13 is best understood by comparing Isaiah 35:3 (God's promise to heal and save) and Proverbs 4:26 (an exhortation to evaluate whether a person's life goals and directions are based on the Word of God). The description in verse 13 stresses that those who do not advance in their faith may soon become completely disabled and abandon their faith in Christ (cf. verse 15). Those who are not moving towards the Kingdom risk "falling back" from it.

STRONG 3717, BAUER 580, MOULTON-MILLIGAN

456, Kittel 5:449-50, Liddell-Scott 1249, Colin Brown 3:351-52.

3581. ὀρθοτομέω orthotomeō verb
Cut straight; rightly handling, rightly dividing, teach correctly.
CROSS-REFERENCE:
ὀρθός orthos (3580)
יָשַׁר yāshar (3595), Go straight; piel: make straight (Prv 3:6).

1. ὀρθοτομοῦντα orthotomounta
acc sing masc part pres act
1 rightly dividing the word of truth.................2 Tm 2:15

The verb *orthotomeō* is a combination of two smaller words: *orthos* (3580), meaning "straight, on line," or "right," and *tomos*, meaning "a cutting."

Septuagint Usage
It is not found outside of the Bible. In the Septuagint the word is used in Proverbs 3:6 and 11:5 where it is used to translate the intensive form of the verb *yāshar* ("to make straight"). Proverbs 3:5 stresses that the "straight path" comes with trusting God, while 11:5 teaches the "righteousness of the blameless will smooth his way" (NASB). In both, "make or keep straight" is a figurative description of making a straight path through a difficult area directly to the desired destination (cf. *Bauer*).

New Testament Usage
The use of the verb in 2 Timothy 2:15 is part of a metaphor where Timothy is urged to be a "good workman" in his handling of God's Word. The emphasis is on the accurate and competent handling of the task. The RSV's translation, "*rightly handling* the word of truth," places the correct emphasis on accuracy, while the KJV's use of "rightly dividing" gives more of a sense of guiding straight to the goal without distraction or disruption. In both cases the word implies a competent and truthful exposition of Scripture. (See also *Moulton-Milligan* for other metaphoric meanings.)

Strong 3718, Bauer 580, Moulton-Milligan 456-57, Kittel 8:111-12, Liddell-Scott 1249-50, Colin Brown 3:351-52.

3582. ὀρθρίζω orthrizō verb
To rise early in the morning; to be diligent or attentive.

COGNATES:
ὀρθρινός orthrinos (3583)
ὄρθριος orthrios (3584)
ὄρθρος orthros (3585)

שָׁחַר shāchar (8264), Piel: seek, inquire (Jb 7:21, 8:5, Ps 63:1 [62:1]).

שָׁכַם shākham (8326), Hiphil: rise up early (Ex 24:4, 1 Sm 5:3f., Jer 25:3).

1. ὤρθριζεν ōrthrizen 3sing indic imperf act
1 all the people came early in the morning to him.... Luke 21:38

Septuagint Usage
This verb, found only in the Septuagint and the New Testament, means "rise or come early in the morning." It is related to the noun *orthros* (3585), "the time just before daybreak, dawn" (*Liddell-Scott*). The Septuagint mentions that Moses *orthrizō*, "rose early," and then specifically adds the words "in the morning" for clarity (Exodus 24:4). Compare *orthrios* (3584), "pertaining to the morning." The word *orthrizō* is also often used literally in connection with the early morning watch. It frequently carries the connotation of diligence and earnestness in seeking God (Job 8:5; Psalm 78:34 [LXX 77:34]; Isaiah 26:9), in repentance (Hosea 5:15 [LXX 6:1]), and in the fulfilling of one's tasks (Genesis 20:8; Exodus 8:20; etc.), as well as the faithfulness of God (Jeremiah 25:3).

New Testament Usage
This word is used only once in the New Testament, in Luke 21:38. Here it is translated, "And all the people *came early in the morning* to him (Christ) in the temple, for to hear him." In this verse it is probable that the "early in the morning" idea is intended as it is given in contrast with the previous verse which speaks of Christ retiring from the temple and His teaching *for the night*. Then *orthrizō* denotes that the zeal and eagerness of the people to hear the Lord was so great they rose early to be present the next morning.

Strong 3719, Bauer 580, Moulton-Milligan 457, Liddell-Scott 1250.

3583. ὀρθρινός orthrinos adj
In the morning, early, first in the day, pertaining to dawn.
COGNATE:
ὀρθρίζω orthrizō (3582)
SYNONYMS:
ὄρθριος orthrios (3584)
πρωΐα prōia (4263)
πρωϊνός prōinos (4265)

שָׁכַם shākham (8326), Hiphil: morning (Hos 6:4 [6:5], 13:3).

1. ὀρθρινός orthrinos nom sing masc
2. ὀρθριναί orthrinai nom pl fem

1 and the bright and **morning** star.................... Rev 22:16

This adjective is a later form for *orthrios* (3584), "at daybreak, early," and can be found in classical Greek since the Third Century B.C. meaning "morning, pertaining to dawn." It occurs four times in the Septuagint (Hosea 6:4; 13:3; Haggai 2:14; Wisdom of Solomon 11:22) but only in Luke 24:22 and Revelation 22:16 in the New Testament. The earlier form, *orthrios*, is found often in pre-New Testament papyri. In the Luke 24 usage Mary Magdalene and other women came *orthrinos* to the tomb where Jesus had been buried; that is, at the first moments of the sunrise when it would be possible to see their way north of the city to the tomb.

In Revelation 22 Jesus referred to himself as "the bright and *morning* star." As the "morning" star announces the coming of dawn and ushers in a new day, so Jesus proclaimed the coming of God's kingdom that will usher in a "new age."

STRONG 3720, BAUER 580, MOULTON-MILLIGAN 457, LIDDELL-SCOTT 1250.

3584. ὄρθριος orthrios adj

At early morning, at dawn, at the beginning of the morning.

COGNATE:
ὀρθρίζω orthrizō (3582)
SYNONYMS:
ὀρθρινός orthrinos (3583)
πρωΐα prōia (4263)
πρωϊνός prōinos (4265)

1. ὄρθριαι orthriai nom pl fem

1 women ... which were **early** at the sepulchre;....... Luke 24:22

This adjective is the older form of its related term, *orthrinos* (3583). It is found in such literature of antiquity as the hymns of Homer (Seventh—Sixth Centuries B.C.), the Septuagint, Josephus, and in nonliterary papyri. An example of this is found in an Egyptian papyrus of the First Century B.C. which speaks of a man's *orthrios*, i.e., his "first deed" or "morning greeting" (cf. *Moulton-Milligan*).

The New Testament shows only one usage in this form, and that in the *Textus Receptus* of Luke 24:22 (with the older texts giving *orthrinos*). Here the two from Emmaus are telling Jesus, whom they do not recognize, that on the *morning* of the first day of the week "certain women . . . which were *early*" (*orthrios*) discovered the tomb to be empty. This signifies that this occurred at the first dawning.

STRONG 3721, BAUER 580, MOULTON-MILLIGAN 457, LIDDELL-SCOTT 1250.

3585. ὄρθρος orthros noun

Dawn, sun up, early morning; daybreak.

CROSS-REFERENCE:
ὀρθρίζω orthrizō (3582)

אַשְׁמוּרָה 'ashmûrāh (847), Night watch (Ps 63:6 [62:6]).
בֹּקֶר bōqer (1269), Dawn (Jgs 16:2).
שַׁחַר shachar (8266), Daybreak, dawn (Gn 32:26, 1 Sm 9:26, Am 4:13).

1. ὄρθρου orthrou gen sing masc
2. ὄρθρον orthron acc sing masc

1 the first day ... very **early in the morning**,.......... Luke 24:1
1 And **early in the morning** he came again............ John 8:2
2 they entered into the temple **early in the morning**,... Acts 5:21

This noun is found as early as Hesiod (Seventh Century B.C.), as well as in the Septuagint, papyri, and in Josephus. It is found three times in the New Testament; namely, in Luke 24:1, John 8:2, and Acts 5:21. In the Luke passage the women of Galilee are said to have come to the tomb "very *early in the morning*" (*orthros*) on the first day of the week, immediately after the Sabbath Day; they found the tomb empty. In Acts 5:21 the apostles, having been released from prison by the angel of the Lord, are found preaching again at the temple *orthros*, "early in the morning," that is, at dawn or daybreak. John 8:2 (not found in the oldest texts—Augustine said the passage was expurgated out of fear it would teach moral license) shows Jesus arriving at the temple at *daybreak* to teach on that morning in which the scribes and Pharisees brought the accused woman before Him.

STRONG 3722, BAUER 580, MOULTON-MILLIGAN 457, LIDDELL-SCOTT 1250.

3586. ὀρθῶς orthōs adv

Rightly, correctly, properly.

CROSS-REFERENCE:
ὀρθός orthos (3580)

טוֹב ṭôv (3005), Favorable, good (Gn 40:16, Ex 18:17).
יָטַב yāṭav (3296), Hiphil: do well, speak well (Gn 4:7, Dt 18:17); play well (1 Sm 16:17).

כֵּן kēn (3772), Right (Nm 27:7 [27:6]).

1. ὀρθῶς orthōs

1 his tongue was loosed, and he spake **plain**.	Mark 7:35
1 And he said unto him, Thou hast **rightly** judged.	Luke 7:43
1 And he said unto him, Thou hast answered **right**:	10:28
1 we know that thou sayest and teachest **rightly**,	20:21

This word is an adverb related to the adjective *orthos* (3580), "right, straight, correct." *Orthos* was used frequently in classical Greek times and into the Koine period by Josephus and the papyri (cf. *Bauer*). It appears four times in the New Testament. In Mark 7:35 the dumb man healed by Jesus spoke "properly" ("plain," KJV). In all three cases in Luke answers are said to have been given correctly (Luke 7:43; 10:28) or teaching is acknowledged as having been presented correctly (Luke 20:21).

STRONG 3723, BAUER 580, MOULTON-MILLIGAN 457, LIDDELL-SCOTT 1249, COLIN BROWN 3:351.

3587. ὁρίζω horizō verb

To determine, to appoint, to declare, to designate.

COGNATES:
ἀποδιορίζω apodiorizō (587)
ἀφορίζω aphorizō (866)
ἀφρίζω aphrizō (868)
ὅριον horion (3588)
ὁροθεσία horothesia (3597)
προορίζω proorizō (4168)

SYNONYMS:
δείκνυμι deiknumi (1161)
διερμηνεύω diermēneuō (1323)
ἐμφανίζω emphanizō (1702)
ἐξηγέομαι exēgeomai (1817)
ἑρμηνεύω hermēneuō (2043)
καθίστημι kathistēmi (2497)
προχειρίζομαι procheirizomai (4258)
τάσσω tassō (4872)
τίθημι tithēmi (4935)
φράζω phrazō (5255)
χειροτονέω cheirotoneō (5336)

אָסַר ʼāsar (646), Bind (Nm 30:4,8f.,12).

גְּבוּל gᵉvûl (1397), Border (Nm 34:6, Jos 15:12).

גָּבַל gāval (1411), Be a boundary (Jos 18:20).

פָּרַד pāradh (6754), Separate, divide; hiphil: decide (Prv 18:18).

קָרַץ qārats (7460), Wink (Prv 16:30).

רְשַׁם rᵉsham (A7854), Sign (Dn 6:12—Aramaic).

1. ὁρίζει horizei 3sing indic pres act
2. ὥρισεν hōrisen 3sing indic aor act
3. ὥρισαν hōrisan 3pl indic aor act
4. ὁρίσας horisas nom sing masc part aor act
5. ὁρισθέντος horisthentos
gen sing masc part aor pass
6. ὡρισμένος hōrismenos nom sing masc part perf mid
7. ὡρισμένῃ hōrismenē dat sing fem part perf mid
8. ὡρισμένον hōrismenon
nom/acc sing neu part perf mid

8 truly the Son of man goeth, as it **was determined**:	Luke 22:22
7 **determinate** counsel and foreknowledge of God,	Acts 2:23
6 and to testify that it is he which **was ordained**	10:42
3 **determined** to send relief unto the brethren	11:29
4 and **hath determined** the times before appointed,	17:26
2 by that man whom he **hath ordained**;	17:31
5 And **declared** to be the Son of God with power,	Rom 1:4
1 Again, he **limiteth** a certain day, saying in David,	Heb 4:7

Classical Greek

The term *horizō* is a cognate of *horos*, "border," and *horion* (3588), "region." It originally meant "to decide the border," and more generally "to decide, to determine," or "to establish" (cf. *Liddell-Scott*).

Septuagint Usage

In the Septuagint *horizō* is found nearly 20 times. It is often used in the original meaning of "establishing a boundary" (Numbers 34:6; Joshua 13:8,27; 15:12; 18:20; 23:4; Ezekiel 34:6). It appears eight times in Numbers 30, and each time it refers to the voluntary "binding" of oneself with an oath. Proverbs 16:30 speaks of an individual who "brings to pass" (*horizei*) all types of evil with his lips. It can also mean "to decide"; which God is willing to do with all matters brought to Him (Proverbs 18:18).

New Testament Usage

Horizō occurs eight times in the New Testament, and "... with the exception of Ac. 11:29 they are all emphatically theological and christological; they describe the person and work of Jesus Christ" (Schmidt, "horizō," *Kittel*, 5:453). The Scriptures plainly teach that the crucifixion of Christ was neither an accident nor a failure, but was accomplished according to God's "predetermined" plan (Luke 22:22). Peter declared to his fellow Jews on the Day of Pentecost that Jesus was delivered up and crucified by the "*determinate* counsel and foreknowledge of God" (Acts 2:23). But God's plan did not end there, for He also raised Jesus from the dead. In so doing God demonstrated to all that this same Jesus is the One whom He has "appointed" (*horisen*) to judge both the living and the dead (Acts 10:42; 17:31). God is able to appoint such a judge, for He is sovereign over the heavens and the earth. It is He who gives life to all.

In another use of the word *horizō*, it is God who has "determined" the seasons of the earth and established man's dwelling places

(Acts 17:24-26). Also, Christ's resurrection has "declared" (*horisthentos*) Him to be the Son of God with power (Romans 1:4). But before the Day of Judgment, all men have the opportunity to enter into God's "rest" (Hebrews 4:1ff.). This present time of salvation is the day that God has "fixed" (*horizei*) through the accomplishments of His Christ (Hebrews 4:7). The last occurrence of the word is Acts 11:29 where the disciples "determined" for themselves to help the distressed brethren in Judea.

STRONG 3724, BAUER 580-81, MOULTON-MILLIGAN 457, KITTEL 5:452-53, LIDDELL-SCOTT 1250-51, COLIN BROWN 1:472-73.

3588. ὅριον horion noun
Boundary, limit, region, district, zone, border, coast.

COGNATE:
ὁρίζω horizō (3587)

SYNONYM:
μεθόριον methorion (3152)

אֶרֶץ 'erets (800), Land; district (2 Chr 11:23).

בַּת bath (1351), Daughter; town (Jgs 11:26).

גְּבוּל gᵉvûl (1397), Border, boundary (Nm 34:2-11, Jos 18:12ff., Ez 48:1-8).

גְּבוּלָה gᵉvûlāh (1398), Territory, land (Nm 32:33, Jos 19:49); boundary (Is 10:13).

גָּבַל gāval (1411), Be on a border (Zec 9:2).

גּוֹרָל gôrāl (1518), Lot (Jos 16:1, 17:1).

גְּלִילָה gᵉlîlāh (1593), Region (Jos 13:2).

חֹק chōq (2805), Boundaries (Jb 38:10).

יָד yādh (3135), Hand; border (1 Chr 7:29).

מוּל mûl (4272II) Frontier (Jos 22:11—only some Vaticanus texts).

פֵּאָה pe'āh (6523), Side (Ez 47:17—Codex Alexandrinus only).

קֵץ qēts (7377), End (Is 9:7).

שָׂדֶה sādheh (7898), Country (Jgs 20:6).

1. ὁρίων horiōn gen pl neu
2. ὁρίοις horiois dat pl neu
3. ὅρια horia nom/acc pl neu

2	in Bethlehem, and in all the **coasts** thereof,	Matt 2:16
2	in the **borders** of Zabulon and Nephthalim:	4:13
1	that he would depart out of their **coasts**.	8:34
1	a woman of Canaan came out of the same **coasts**,	15:22
3	and came into the **coasts** of Magdala.	15:39
3	and came into the **coasts** of Judaea beyond Jordan;	19:1
1	began to pray him to depart out of their **coasts**.	Mark 5:17
3	and went away to the **region** of Tyre. (NASB)	7:24
1	departing from the **coasts** of Tyre and Sidon,	7:31
1	through the midst of the **coasts** of Decapolis.	7:31
3	and cometh into the **coasts** of Judaea	10:1
1	and expelled them out of their **coasts**.	Acts 13:50

Sophocles and Thucydides (both Fifth Century B.C.), the Septuagint, and papyri all utilize this common word (cf. *Bauer*). A related word is *horizō* (3587), "to determine, set," or "appoint." Thus also *proorizō* (4168), "to foreordain," means to zone or appoint boundaries in advance (Romans 8:30). *Horion* is used in the papyri in astronomical and astrological texts, as well as to denote land "boundaries" (cf. *Moulton-Milligan*). It appears extensively in the Septuagint, generally translating *gᵉvûl*, "border, boundary." *Horion*, always plural in the New Testament, denotes certain geographical limits, some of which are visibly defined by specific geographical features (e.g., "coasts," Matthew 15:39), and others of which are artificially defined by political action or cultural practice (e.g., "borders, regions," Matthew 4:13).

STRONG 3725, BAUER 581, MOULTON-MILLIGAN 457, LIDDELL-SCOTT 1251.

3589. ὁρκίζω horkizō verb
Cause someone to swear, to adjure, to implore.

COGNATES:
ἐνορκίζω enorkizō (1758B)
ἐξορκίζω exorkizō (1828)
ἐξορκιστής exorkistēs (1829)
ἐπιορκέω epiorkeō (1949)
ἐπίορκος epiorkos (1950)
ὅρκος horkos (3590)
ὁρκωμοσία horkōmosia (3591)

SYNONYMS:
διαμαρτύρομαι diamarturomai (1257)
διαστέλλω diastellō (1285)
διατάσσω diatassō (1293)
ἐντέλλομαι entellomai (1765)
ἐξορκίζω exorkizō (1828)
ἐπιτάσσω epitassō (1988)
ἐπιτρέπω epitrepō (1994)
κελεύω keleuō (2724)
λέγω legō (2978)
παραγγέλλω parangellō (3715)
προστάσσω prostassō (4225)
συντάσσω suntassō (4781)
τάσσω tassō (4872)

שָׁבַע shāvaʿ (8123), Swear; hiphil: make one swear, charge (Gn 50:5f., 2 Chr 36:13, S/S 5:9).

1. ὁρκίζω horkizō 1sing indic pres act
2. ὁρκίζομεν horkizomen 1pl indic pres act

1	I **adjure** thee by God, that thou torment me not.	Mark 5:7
2	We **adjure** you by Jesus whom Paul preacheth.	Acts 19:13
1	I **adjure** you by Jesus whom Paul preaches (NASB)	19:13
1	I **charge** you by the Lord that this epistle be read	1 Th 5:27

Classical Greek
This word is found in Xenophon (Fourth Century B.C.), the Septuagint, and in papyri. An example is found in the Hadrumetum tablet,

Third—Second Centuries B.C., saying, "I adjure you, demonic spirit, . . . by the God of Abraan . . . ." (free translation; cf. *Bauer*). It is almost identical to *exorkizō* (1828), "to swear from or out of," also meaning "to adjure" or "to charge with an oath."

Septuagint Usage

Horkizō appears almost 30 times in the Septuagint. Of those occurrences with a Hebrew equivalent, *shāvaʿ* is exclusively translated, and always in the hiphil (causative) stem. Thus the sense is usually "I cause to swear" or "I adjure." The servant of Abraham says, "My master made (caused) me to swear" (Genesis 24:37). This causative aspect is in keeping with the suffix *-izo* in *horkizō* which can denote causation. If an individual himself swears an oath, another expression is used. For instance, when the Lord swears by himself (Genesis 22:16) the Hebrew reads *shāvaʿ* in the niphal (reflexive) aspect. The Septuagint translates this with *omnuō* (3523), "to swear," rather than *horkizō*.

New Testament Usage

The word *horkizō* appears three times in the New Testament (Mark 5:7; Acts 19:13; 1 Thessalonians 5:27 [*Textus Receptus*; other manuscripts use *enorkizō* (1758B), "to adjure in or by"]).

In the Mark 5:7 passage, remarkably, it is the unclean spirit *adjuring* Jesus by God not to torment him; i.e., the unclean spirit did not want Jesus to cast him out nor to put him to the judgment before that appointed day. Acts 19:13 shows certain "vagabond Jews, exorcists," having seen the power of the name *Jesus* as used by the apostle Paul, taking up this name to attempt to cast out demons in Jesus' name. Note that this word is used both to urge someone to swear or to do something in the name of the deity. In the examples cited it is an urging of demons to come out in the name of Jesus. In 1 Thessalonians 5:27 Paul "charged" (literally, "put on oath") the recipients of his letter to be sure it was read to all the believers there.

Strong 3726, Bauer 581, Moulton-Milligan 457, Kittel 5:462-63, Liddell-Scott 1251, Colin Brown 3:737.

3590. ὅρκος horkos noun

Oath.

Cognate:
ὁρκίζω horkizō (3589)

Synonym:
ὁρκωμοσία horkōmosia (3591)

אָלָה ʾālāh (427), Oath (Prv 29:24).

שְׁבוּעָה shᵉvûʿāh (8095), Vow, oath (Nm 30:3, 1 Chr 16:16, Dn 9:11).

שָׁבַע shāvaʿ (8123), Swear; hiphil: make one swear (Ex 13:19).

שִׁבְעָה shivʿāh (8127), Shibah (Gn 26:33).

1. ὅρκος horkos nom sing masc
2. ὅρκου horkou gen sing masc
3. ὅρκῳ horkō dat sing masc
4. ὅρκον horkon acc sing masc
5. ὅρκους horkous acc pl masc

```
5 but shalt perform unto the Lord thine oaths:........ Matt 5:33
2 Whereupon he promised with an oath to give her whatsoever 14:7
5 nevertheless for the oath's sake,...................... 14:9
2 he denied with an oath, I do not know the man........ 26:72
5 yet for his oath's sake, and for their sakes.......... Mark 6:26
4 The oath which he sware to our father Abraham,... Luke 1:73
3 knowing that God had sworn with an oath to him,... Acts 2:30
1 and an oath for confirmation is to them an end...... Heb 6:16
3 confirmed it by an oath:.............................. 6:17
4 neither by any other oath: but let your yea be yea;... Jas 5:12
```

Classical Greek

Horkos can be found in classical Greek as "the object by which one swears, an oath" (*Liddell-Scott*). Oaths in classical Greek generally invoked the names of their gods as witnesses and as a guarantee of the truth of what was said (cf. Schneider, "horkos," *Kittel*, 5:457f.).

Septuagint Usage

In the Septuagint *horkos* translates *ʾālāh* ("to curse") and *shevaʿ* ("to swear"). Since *shivʿāh* means "seven" this may point back to an original practice where a sevenfold blood sacrifice guaranteed the oath (cf. Genesis 21:31). The Old Testament condemns pagan oaths as idolatry (Jeremiah 5:7; 12:16; Amos 8:14; Zephaniah 1:5). Only oaths in the name of Yahweh were acceptable—those who swore falsely by this name profaned the name of God (Leviticus 19:12).

God swears by himself in the Old Testament— only God can verify His own word (Numbers 14:21-23). The oaths of God in the Old Testament deal with His covenant relationship with Israel (Psalm 105:9 [LXX 104:9]). Even God's judgment has the goal of fulfilling this oath (Jeremiah 11:5).

New Testament Usage

By New Testament times the process of swearing oaths had become involved and complex. Jesus prohibited oaths altogether (Matthew 5:33; cf. James 5:12) probably as a reaction to contemporary abuses. Oaths were still not treated lightly: Herod was trapped by his oath when he beheaded John the Baptist (Matthew 14:7-9).

God's oaths in the Old Testament were of great significance to New Testament writers. The promises of the Old Testament oaths are fulfilled in Jesus (Luke 1:73; Acts 2:30; Hebrews 6:16f.). God's word which He swore in the Old Testament is proven true in Jesus Christ.

STRONG 3727, BAUER 581, MOULTON-MILLIGAN 457-58, KITTEL 5:457-62, LIDDELL-SCOTT 1252, COLIN BROWN 3:737-40.

3591. ὁρκωμοσία horkōmosia noun
The act of taking an oath, oath taking, swearing.
COGNATE:
  ὁρκίζω horkizō (3589)
SYNONYM:
  ὅρκος horkos (3590)

אָלָה 'ālāh (427), Oath (Ez 17:18f.).

1. ὁρκωμοσίας horkōmosias gen sing fem

1 as not without an **oath** he was made priest: .... Heb 7:20
1 For those priests were made without an **oath**; 7:21
1 but this with an **oath** by him that said unto him, ... 7:21
1 but the word of the **oath**, which was since the law, ... 7:28

Septuagint Usage
This word is found in the Septuagint in Ezekiel 17:18,19 and refers twice to the oath taking of Zedekiah, King of Judah, and of his breaking this oath taken publicly in the name of Jehovah. The apocryphal book 1 Esdras in 8:90 shows a man crying out to Ezra (Esdras) agreeing that *an oath should be made* to put away unbelieving heathen women from among the faithful. It is related to *horkos* (3590), "an oath," and *horkoō*, "swear, bind by oath."

New Testament Usage
In the New Testament this word appears four times, all in the seventh chapter of Hebrews (7:20,21 [twice],28, KJV). In this passage the writer pointed out that priests under the Old Testament era were consecrated by a ceremony that included no oath from God himself. Yet the Messiah, of whom the quoted Psalm 110:4 speaks, was consecrated as a High Priest forever after the order of Melchizedek and that by an *oath taken* (*horkōmosia*) by God. Since only the Messiah was consecrated as High Priest by God's oath, it followed that His high priesthood was better and more durable than that of any made under the old covenant.

STRONG 3728, BAUER 581, MOULTON-MILLIGAN 458, KITTEL 5:463-64, LIDDELL-SCOTT 1252, COLIN BROWN 3:737,742.

3592. ὁρμάω hormaō verb
Set in motion, rush, set out.
COGNATES:
  ὁρμή hormē (3593)
  ὅρμημα hormēma (3594)

חוּשׁ chûsh (2456), Hiphil: hurry (Jgs 20:37—Codex Alexandrinus only).
פָּנָה pānâh (6680), Turn (Nm 16:42).
פָּשַׁט pāshaṭ (6838), Strip (Na 3:16).
שׁוּב shûv (8178), Return (Jos 4:18).

1. ὥρμησεν hormēsen 3sing indic aor act
2. ὥρμησαν hormēsan 3pl indic aor act

1 the whole herd of swine **ran violently** down .... Matt 8:32
1 and the herd **ran violently** down a steep place ...... Mark 5:13
1 and the herd **ran violently** down a steep place .... Luke 8:33
2 and **ran** upon him with one accord, ... Acts 7:57
2 they **rushed** with one accord into the theatre. 19:29

Classical Greek and Septuagint Usage
This verb can be found in classical Greek meaning "set in motion, urge on," and more frequently "start out, rush headlong" (when used intransitively; cf. *Liddell-Scott*). In the Septuagint *hormaō* translates at least five Hebrew terms, all of which describe the sudden directional movement of someone or something. Frequently this sudden movement was toward someone or something with malcontent (cf. Genesis 31:21; Numbers 16:42; Joshua 4:18; Judges 20:37); it could also mean "flee away" (cf. Nahum 3:16). "In the few passages where it occurs the (word) denotes violent movement uncontrolled by human reason" (Bertram, "hormē," *Kittel*, 5:470). Thus a certain amount of impulsiveness is implicit in its use.

New Testament Usage
In Matthew 8:32 the herd of swine into which the demons went *rushed headlong* (KJV, "ran violently") down the hill and off the cliff. Both Mark and Luke also wrote of the same event (cf. Mark 5:13; Luke 8:33). All three show the wild destructive frenzy that demons impart into flesh when they gain control. In Acts 7:57 it was the fanatic followers of the high priest and others who *rushed* upon Stephen, after hearing his sermon which condemned them, to drag him out of the city and kill him. In Acts 19:29 it was the pagan Gentile followers who, in their zeal for their goddess Diana (Artemis) and hatred for Paul and his companions, *rushed* wildly into

the huge outdoor amphitheater to denounce the Christians.

STRONG 3729, BAUER 581, MOULTON-MILLIGAN 458, KITTEL 5:467-72, LIDDELL-SCOTT 1252-53.

3593. ὁρμή hormē noun
Rush, attack; impulse, desire.
CODGNATE:
ὁρμάω hormaō (3592)
SYNONYMS:
ἐπιθυμία epithumia (1924)
εὐδοκία eudokia (2086)
ὄρεξις orexis (3578)

חֵמָה chēmāh (2635), Heat (Ez 3:14).
מַשָּׂא massā' (5014), Burden (Nm 11:17).
פֶּלֶג pelegh (6631), Channel (Prv 21:1).
קֶצֶף qetseph (7397), Wrath (Zec 7:12—Codex Alexandrinus only).
שׁוֹאָה shô'āh (8177), Ruin (Prv 3:25).
שְׁעָטָה sheʿāṭāh (8543), Galloping (Jer 47:3 [29:3]).

1. ὁρμή hormē nom sing fem

1 there was an **assault** made both of the Gentiles,.... Acts 14:5
1 wherever the **inclination** of the pilot (NASB)........ Jas 3:4

Classical Greek and Septuagint Usage
This word appears in Homeric writings as well as in the Epistle of Aristeas (Second Century B.C.), the Septuagint, Josephus, and Philo of Alexandria. It had a wide range of meanings, usually involving motion, but it could also express such ideas as impulse or eagerness (*Liddell-Scott*). The Leipzig collection of inscriptions read, "He stopped the force of the Barbarian *rush*" (cf. *Moulton-Milligan*). Likewise, the Oxyrhynchus Papyri (Fourth Century A.D.) speak of "two pigs making a *rush* into our piece of land" (ibid.).

New Testament Usage
This noun appears twice in the New Testament, Acts 14:5 and James 3:4. In Acts it provides a vivid description of an *assault* of unbelieving Jews and Gentiles, with the leaders of the city of Iconium, against the synagogue where Paul was preaching. Here the word pictures a violent quick attack and is a reminder of what these first Christian missionary apostles endured to spread the Faith. In James 3:4 the sacred writer pointed out that a large ship is moved by the small wheel and rudder "withersoever the governor listeth" (KJV); literally, "where the *desire* (*hormē*) of the steersman wishes." The lesson here is that the "impulsive" use of a little human tongue can result in great evils.

STRONG 3730, BAUER 581, MOULTON-MILLIGAN 458, KITTEL 5:467-72, LIDDELL-SCOTT 1253.

3594. ὅρμημα hormēma noun
Sudden rush, assault, violent impulse.
CROSS-REFERENCE:
ὁρμάω hormaō (3592)

דָּאָה dā'āh (1723), Swoop (Dt 28:49).
עֶבְרָה 'evrāh (5887), Wrath (Hos 5:10, Am 1:11).
פֶּלֶג pelegh (6631), Stream (Ps 46:4 [45:4]).

1. ὁρμήματι hormēmati dat sing neu

1 Thus **with violence** shall that great city Babylon be.. Rev 18:21

This noun is found only once in the New Testament, in Revelation 18:21, where it is used to convey the rapidity and furiousness with which end-time Babylon will be cast down to destruction. The Septuagint reveals two usages of this word that add understanding to its meaning. In Deuteronomy 28:49 Israel is warned that if it does not serve the Lord, "The LORD shall bring a nation against thee from far, from the end of the earth, as swift as the eagle flieth." Here again dual elements of *hormēna* are seen, i.e., swiftness with fury, anger, indignation. In Hosea 5:10 the Lord cries out in judgment concerning Israel, "I will pour out my wrath upon them like water." Here God's indignation is portrayed as rapidly gushing forth in fierceness and in quantity.

STRONG 3731, BAUER 581, MOULTON-MILLIGAN 458, KITTEL 5:467-72, LIDDELL-SCOTT 1253.

3595. ὄρνεον orneon noun
Bird.
SYNONYM:
πετεινόν peteinon (3932)

עוֹף 'ôph (5991), Bird (Gn 6:20, 40:19, Hos 9:11).
עַיִט 'ayiṭ (6077), Bird of prey (Gn 15:11).
צִפּוֹר tsippôr (7109), Bird (Dt 14:11, Prv 7:23, Ez 39:4).
קָאַת qā'ath (7179I), Owl, pelican, an unclean bird (Is 34:11).

1. ὀρνέου orneou gen sing neu
2. ὄρνεα ornea nom/acc pl neu
3. ὀρνέοις orneois dat pl neu

1 and a cage of every unclean and hateful bird........ Rev 18:2
3 to all the **fowls** that fly in the midst of heaven,........ 19:17
2 and all the **fowls** were filled with their flesh.......... 19:21

The three New Testament appearances of this word are found in Revelation 18:2; 19:17,21.

In 18:2 end-time Babylon is said to have become "a cage of every unclean and hateful *bird*," while in 19:17,21 the *birds* are pictured as coming at God's call to eat the bodies of the soldiers opposing Christ at His return. The KJV translates the word in Revelation 19 as "fowls," perhaps because the related word, *ornis* (3596), is sometimes used of a hen or rooster in classical Greek (see also Matthew 23:37). The use of *orneon* in Deuteronomy 14:11 in the Septuagint ("You shall eat of every clean *bird*") shows that this word does not in itself denote *unclean* birds only.

STRONG 3732, BAUER 581-82, MOULTON-MILLIGAN 458, LIDDELL-SCOTT 1254.

3596. ὄρνις ornis noun
Bird, hen, cock.

1. ὄρνις ornis nom sing fem
2. ὄρνιξ ornix nom sing fem

1 as **a hen** gathereth her chickens under her wings,	Matt 23:37
1 as **a hen** doth gather her brood under her wings,	Luke 13:34

Usage of this term in the Greek world prior to the New Testament shows that the word can denote a cock as well as a hen, the context being the determiner. In addition to domestic fowls, it is also used of birds of prey.

It appears only twice in the New Testament: Luke 13:34 and Matthew 23:37. Both are almost identical passages that utter Christ's lamentation to Jerusalem: "I would have gathered thy children together, even as a *hen* (*ornis*) gathers her young under her wings" (free translation). Here the *bird* is pictured as protectively and lovingly gathering her brood for safety and fellowship. This provides a glimpse of the goodness of God directed toward His people, a reflection of which is seen in nature where God has instilled a maternal instinct even in birds.

STRONG 3733, BAUER 582, MOULTON-MILLIGAN 458-59, LIDDELL-SCOTT 1254.

3597. ὁροθεσία horothesia noun
Fixed boundary, boundary line, border.
CROSS-REFERENCES:
ὁρίζω horizō (3587)
τίθημι tithēmi (4935)

1. ὁροθεσίας horothesias acc pl fem

1 and the **bounds** of their habitation;	Acts 17:26

This word appears in the New Testament only in Acts 17:26, where Paul in his sermon to the Athenians reminded them that God is the ultimate One who determined the "boundaries" wherein the nations and peoples of the earth lived. The word is a combination of *horos*, "boundary, landmark," and a form of *tithēmi* (4935), "I put" or "I place." Thus it conveys the idea of putting up or placing boundaries or landmarks. In order to show the Athenians the sovereignty of the Unknown God, Paul used *horothesia* as a forceful reminder that the Almighty has placed each nation as He willed, and that He should be worshiped for this benign function of His attribute of order, as well as for the other magnanimous expressions of His graciousness.

STRONG 3734, BAUER 582, MOULTON-MILLIGAN 459, LIDDELL-SCOTT 1255.

3598. ὄρος oros noun
Mountain, hill, hill-country.

גִּבְעָה giv'āh (1421), Hill (Ez 34:26).
הָדָר hādhar (1991), Honor; mountain (Is 45:2).
הַר har (2098), Mount, mountain (Ex 34:2ff., 2 Chr 20:10, Ps 104:6,8 [103:6,8]).
הֹר hōr (2099), Hor (Nm 34:7f.).
טוּר ṭûr (A3016), Mountain (Dn 2:35,45—Aramaic).
מָרוֹם mārôm (4953), Height (Jer 31:12 [38:12]).
צוּר tsûr (6962), Rock (Nm 23:9, Jb 29:6).
שְׁפִי sh\ephî (8576), Barren height (Is 41:18).

1. ὄρος oros nom/acc sing neu
2. ὄρους orous gen sing neu
3. ὄρει orei dat sing neu
4. ὄρη orē nom/acc pl neu
5. ὀρέων oreōn gen pl neu
6. ὄρεσιν oresin dat pl neu

1 devil taketh ... into an exceeding high **mountain**,	Matt 4:8
1 seeing the multitudes, he went up into a **mountain**:	5:1
2 A city that is set on **an hill** cannot be hid.	5:14
2 When he was come down from the **mountain**,	8:1
1 he went up into a **mountain** apart to pray:	14:23
1 and went up into a **mountain**, and sat down there.	15:29
1 and bringeth them up into an high **mountain** apart,	17:1
2 And as they came down from the **mountain**,	17:9
3 ye shall say unto this **mountain**,	17:20
4 and goeth into the **mountains**, and seeketh	18:12
1 come to Bethphage, unto the **mount** of Olives,	21:1
3 but also if ye shall say unto this **mountain**,	21:21
2 And as he sat upon the **mount** of Olives,	24:3
4 which be in Judaea flee into the **mountains**:	24:16
1 they went out into the **mount** of Olives.	26:30
1 into a mountain where Jesus had appointed them.	28:16
1 And he goeth up into a **mountain**,	Mark 3:13
6 night and day, he was in the **mountains**,	5:5
4 Now there was there nigh unto the **mountains**	5:11
1 he departed into a **mountain** to pray.	6:46

ὄρος 3598

1	up into an high **mountain** apart by themselves:	Mark 9:2
2	And as they came down from the **mountain**,	9:9
1	Bethphage and Bethany, at the **mount** of Olives,	11:1
3	That whosoever shall say unto this **mountain**,	11:23
1	And as he sat upon the **mount** of Olives	13:3
4	let them that be in Judaea flee to the **mountains**:	13:14
1	they went out into the **mount** of Olives.	14:26
1	and every **mountain** and hill shall be brought low;	Luke 3:5
1	the devil, taking him up into an high **mountain**,	4:5
2	and led him unto the brow of the **hill**	4:29
1	that he went out into a **mountain** to pray,	6:12
3	an herd of many swine feeding on the **mountain**:	8:32
1	and went up into a **mountain** to pray.	9:28
2	when they were come down from the **hill**,	9:37
1	at the **mount** called the mount of Olives,	19:29
2	even now at the descent of the **mount** of Olives,	19:37
4	them which are in Judaea flee to the **mountains**;	21:21
1	in the **mount** that is called the mount of Olives.	21:37
1	and went, as he was wont, to the **mount** of Olives;	22:39
6	Then shall they begin to say to the **mountains**,	23:30
3	Our fathers worshipped in this **mountain**;	John 4:20
3	when ye shall neither in this **mountain**,	4:21
1	And Jesus went up into a **mountain**,	6:3
1	he departed again into a **mountain** himself alone.	6:15
1	Jesus went unto the **mount** of Olives.	8:1
2	unto Jerusalem from the **mount** called Olivet,	Acts 1:12
2	in the wilderness of **mount** Sina an angel	7:30
3	the angel which spake to him in the **mount** Sina,	7:38
4	have all faith, so that I could remove **mountains**,	1 Co 13:2
2	the one from the **mount** Sinai,	Gal 4:24
1	For this Agar is **mount** Sinai in Arabia,	4:25
3	the pattern showed to thee in the **mount**.	Heb 8:5
6	they wandered in deserts, and in **mountains**,	11:38
3	not come unto the **mount** that might be touched,	12:18
2	And if so much as a beast touch the **mountain**,	12:20
3	But ye are come unto **mount** Sion,	12:22
3	when we were with him in the holy **mount**.	2 Pt 1:18
1	and every **mountain** and island were moved	Rev 6:14
5	in the dens and in the rocks of the **mountains**;	6:15
6	And said to the **mountains** and rocks, Fall on us,	6:16
1	and as it were a great **mountain** burning with fire	8:8
1	and, lo, a Lamb stood on the **mount** Sion,	14:1
4	and the **mountains** were not found.	16:20
4	The seven heads are seven **mountains**,	17:9
1	away in the spirit to a great and high **mountain**,	21:10

Classical Greek

This word appears throughout the history of the Greek language, its usage extending from Homer, through the classical era, into Xenophon (Fourth Century B.C.), the Epistle of Aristeas (Second Century B.C.), the Septuagint (Third Century B.C.), Josephus and Philo (First Century A.D.), and down to modern Greek. *Oros*, "mountain," is neuter and should not be confused with the masculine word of the identical spelling meaning the "whey" of milk, nor with *horos*, "boundary, limit, frontier."

In antiquity mountains, perhaps because of their great size, were revered in many cultures. The exterior and peaks could be considered the abode of the gods. For example, in Asia Minor the worship of Cybele, the Great Mother, was usually associated with a mountain (Foerster, "oros," *Kittel*, 5:478). Also, in Ugaritic mythology Mount Zaphon was the abode of Baal (Brown, "Wilderness," *Colin Brown*, 3:1009); and, of course, the famous Mount Olympus was the home of the Greek pantheon. In addition, the Mesopotamian ziggurat was perhaps a representation of a mountain, an attempt to bring the abode of the gods within the reach and sphere of man. The temple of Enlil, the Sumerian wind god, was called "mountain house" (Foerster, "oros," *Kittel*, 5:477). The interior of mountains was also seen as the abode of spirits, and the netherworld could have been pictured as residing under the mountains.

Septuagint Usage

In the Septuagint *oros* translates *har*, "mountain, hill." Mountains were compared with the power of God (Psalm 90:2 [LXX 89:2]) and could be used to give a sense of God's nearness (Exodus 17:9). They were a place of refuge (Judges 6:2) and were used for beacons (Isaiah 13:2). Eschatological expectation is also symbolized by mountains that "drop sweet wine" (Amos 9:13). Very little of the "mountain mythology" found in other cultures appears in the Old Testament. It was not until the pseudepigraphal writings of the Second and First Centuries B.C. that this concept was revived.

That *oros* is found in the papyri, representing "desert, desert burial place," and "desert monastery," can be understood when it is considered that these papyri originated in Egypt. There the desert on either side of the Nile valley is reached by traveling through mountains. Mountains and desert are thus equated (see Wilson, *Intellectual Adventure of Ancient Man, Egypt*, p.38). It is only in Egypt that *oros* refers to the desert as a place of burial (*Liddell-Scott*).

New Testament Usage

Interestingly, the Hebrew word *har* shares with its Grecian counterpart a vagueness foreign to English language precision in dividing between high mountains and low-lying hills. Such detail had to be supplied by adding an additional adjective. For example, Matthew 17:1 describes the scene of the Transfiguration as upon "a *high* mountain," and Matthew 4:8 says that the devil took Jesus "up into an *exceeding high* mountain." Of the 65 New Testament appearances of this word, the King James translators elected to render almost all as "mountain" or "mount," while using the word "hill" on only three occasions (Matthew 5:14, "a city . . . on a *hill*"; Luke 4:29, "led him unto the brow of the *hill*" [Nazareth]; Luke 9:37, "when they were come down from the *hill*" [of transfiguration]). Here the KJV translation refers to the very same elevation called a "hill" in Luke 9:37 as a "mountain" in 9:28, showing that in this case the translators preferred a variety of vocabulary, and were not distinguishing as to the height of the mounds. Modern English usage differentiates clearly between a hill, with a gradual ascent and a lower altitude, and a mountain, which is high, often steep and jagged. But the Biblical reader must avoid reading modern definitions or differences into the sacred accounts which use this general word.

The famed Sermon on the Mount begins in Matthew 5:1 with "he went up into a *mountain*," with Luke 6:17 specifying, "And he came down with them, and stood in the plain." There is no contradiction between Matthew's account and Luke's. Luke portrayed Jesus coming off of the upper height of what was probably an expansive rising ridge and situating himself on (literally) "a place level." The supposition of some that there were two separate sermons, one on "the mount" and another "Sermon on the Plain," is unnecessary and an over-distinction on *oros* which here represents most probably a rolling-hill topography of rises and troughs so characteristic of the Galilean hill country.

Christ spoke figuratively of removing a "mountain," portraying the power of God in response to faith and prayer to do away with great obstacles that human effort alone could not conquer (Matthew 17:20; 21:21; 1 Corinthians 13:2). Likewise, Jesus pictured the testimony of a believer by saying, "A city that is set on a *hill* cannot be hid" (Matthew 5:14).

STRONG 3735, BAUER 582, MOULTON-MILLIGAN 459, KITTEL 5:475-87, LIDDELL-SCOTT 1255, COLIN BROWN 3:1009.

3599. ὀρύσσω orussō verb
Dig, dig a hole or pit.
SYNONYM:
σκάπτω skaptō (4481)

חָתַר gārâh (1667), Piel: stir up (Prv 29:22).
חָפַר châphar (2763), Dig (Gn 26:18, Nm 21:18, Jer 13:7).
חָצַב châtsav (2778), Hew out (Is 5:2, Jer 2:13).
חָתַר châthar (2972), Dig through (Ez 12:7—Codex Alexandrinus only).
כָּרָה kārâh (3868), Qal: dig, cut out (Gn 50:5, 2 Chr 16:14, Ps 57:6 [56:6]); niphal: be dug (Ps 94:13 [93:13]).
נָקַר nāqar (5548), Put out; pual: be hewn (Is 51:1).
פָּתַח pāthach (6858), Open; piel: engrave (Zec 3:9 [3:10]).

1. ὤρυξεν ōruxen 3sing indic aor act

1 and digged a winepress in it, and built a tower,.... Matt 21:33
1 had received one went and digged in the earth,........ 25:18
1 and digged a place for the winefat,................ Mark 12:1

In the New Testament this verb is found only in the Gospels, where it is used three times. In Matthew 25:18 it is used to describe the servant who received one talent, and who promptly "*digged* in the earth, and hid his lord's money." Here the idea conveyed is that of making an effort to hide something of value. Both Matthew 21:33 and Mark 12:1 identically use *orussō* in the Parable of the Wicked Husbandmen (vinekeepers), portraying the owner (God) of the vineyard (Israel) as having "dug" a winepress as part of his complete caretaking activities. Winepresses were usually "dug" below ground level in two compartments—one where the grapes were crushed, and a smaller pitched rectangular recess to receive the juice of the grapes. Here the digging denoted a positive good work; in Matthew 25:18 the digging (to hide the talent) was an evil work.

STRONG 3736, BAUER 582-83, MOULTON-MILLIGAN 459, LIDDELL-SCOTT 1257.

3600. ὀρφανός orphanos adj
Fatherless, orphaned, bereaved, desolate.

יָתוֹם yāthôm (3605), Orphan, fatherless person (Dt 24:17, Ps 94:6 [93:6], Is 1:23).

1. ὀρφανούς orphanous acc pl masc

1 I will not leave you **comfortless**: I will come to you.John 14:18
1 visit the **fatherless** and widows in their affliction,..... Jas 1:27

Classical Greek
In classical Greek the primary meaning of *orphanos* is "fatherless, without parents," or "bereaved." The word is further applied to other situations where one is left "without" someone or something (hence a widow can be called an *orphana*). Classical writers and the papyri also use the phrase "to be left orphan" figuratively in the sense of "abandoned" or "left friendless" (*Bauer*).

ὀρχέομαι 3601

Septuagint Usage

In the Septuagint orphans and widows are the epitome of helplessness. The truly righteous had a duty toward these because they could not demand help. God is the protector of orphans and widows (Psalms 10:14 [LXX 9:35]; 68:5 [67:5]; 82:3 [81:3]). Negatively, the oppression of orphans and widows is one of the sins condemned by the prophets (Isaiah 10:2; Micah 2:2; Zechariah 7:10; Malachi 3:5; and others). In the Old Testament the treatment of the helpless reveals the attitude of the heart. The merciful character of God is revealed best as He cares for those who can give nothing in return. Likewise, the selfishness of man is starkly exposed in their treatment of those with no defense.

New Testament Usage

Orphanos occurs twice in the New Testament: John 14:18 and James 1:27. James continues the Old Testament motif of widows and orphans when he defines the essence of religion in terms of visiting orphans and widows. John 14:18 uses the term figuratively. Jesus promised He would not leave the disciples "orphans" (that is "desolate, alone"). Here the term indicates that the disciples will not be left without guidance, care, or protection.

STRONG 3737, BAUER 583, MOULTON-MILLIGAN 459, KITTEL 5:487-88, LIDDELL-SCOTT 1257-58, COLIN BROWN 2:737-38.

3601. ὀρχέομαι orcheomai verb

Dance.

כָּרַר kārar (3898), Pilpel: dancing (2 Sm 6:16—Codex Alexandrinus only).

פָּזַז pāzaz (6581), Piel: leap (2 Sm 6:16).

רָקַד rāqadh (7833), Qal: dance (Eccl 3:4); piel: dance (1 Chr 15:29, Is 13:21).

שָׂחַק sāchaq (7925), Laugh, play; piel: celebrate (2 Sm 6:21).

1. ὠρχήσατο orchēsato 3sing indic aor mid
2. ὠρχήσασθε orchēsasthe 2pl indic aor mid
3. ὀρχησαμένης orchēsamenēs
        gen sing fem part aor mid

```
2  We have piped unto you, and ye have not danced;  Matt 11:17
1  the daughter of Herodias danced before them,........ 14:6
3  daughter of the said ... came in, and danced,...... Mark 6:22
2  We have piped unto you, and ye have not danced;...Luke 7:32
```

This verb is used four times in the New Testament. In Matthew 11:17 and Luke 7:32 Jesus compared His generation's attitude toward Him and John the Baptist to finicky children who would say, "We have piped unto you, and ye have not *danced*." Even in Jesus' day children may have danced to music. In fact the Old Testament contains many passages describing public dances, usually by groups of women, accompanied by tambourines, and often in a circle (Exodus 15:20; 32:19; Judges 21:19; 2 Samuel 6:14,16; and Psalm 150:4). Dances occurred at both religious occasions and at other times of festivity (2 Samuel 6:14,16; and Matthew 14:6, at a birthday party). An annual dance was given at the Feast of Tabernacles at evening.

In Matthew 14:6 and Mark 6:22 the dancing of Salome at Herod Antipas' birthday party is portrayed by this verb. It delighted Herod so much it generated the rash oath that concluded with John the Baptist being beheaded at the instigation of Herodias, Salome's mother. It is not known whether Salome here danced as a little child or as a sensuous adult. Note also that this word, *orcheomai*, used also in classical Greek, is the root of our present word *orchestra*. (For a splendid brief article on Biblical dancing, see Johnston, "Dance," *International Standard Bible Encyclopedia*, 1:856ff.)

STRONG 3738, BAUER 583, MOULTON-MILLIGAN 459, LIDDELL-SCOTT 1258.

3601B. ὅς hos rel-pron

Who, which, what, that.

1. ὧν hōn gen pl masc/fem/neu
2. οὗ hou gen sing masc/neu
3. ᾧ hō dat sing masc/neu
4. οἷς hois dat pl masc/neu
5. ὅς hos nom sing masc
6. ὅν hon acc sing masc
7. οἵ hoi nom pl masc
8. οὕς hous acc pl masc
9. ἥ hē nom sing fem
10. ἧς hēs gen sing fem
11. ᾗ hē dat sing fem
12. ἥν hēn acc sing fem
13. αἵ hai nom pl fem
14. αἷς hais dat pl fem
15. ἅς has acc pl fem
16. ὅ ho nom/acc sing neu
17. ἅ ha nom/acc pl neu

```
2  agree on ... any thing that they shall ask, (NT)... Matt 18:19
8  and gathered together all they found (NASB) (NT)... 22:10
5  For whosoever shall do the will of God,........... Mark 3:35
5  he be of you that forsaketh not all that he hath,.. Luke 14:33
```

12	might know **wherefore** they cried so against him...	Acts 22:24
10	the world to come, **whereof** we speak..............	Heb 2:5
1	obedience by the **things which** he suffered;..........	5:8

Classical Greek
This term can be found in classical Greek since the Eighth Century B.C. as a demonstrative pronoun ("this, that") and as a relative pronoun ("who, which"). As a demonstrative pronoun *hos* usually appears by the side of *houtos* (3642), *hode* (3455), or the articles *ho* (3450), *hē*, and *to*; however, in post-Homeric Greek literature this usage can only rarely be found (*Liddell-Scott*).

New Testament Usage
In the New Testament *hos* usually occurs as a demonstrative pronoun meaning "those whose" (e.g., Matthew 20:23; Mark 3:13; John 5:21) or "the one whom, this one" (e.g., Mark 15:23; Luke 7:43). It can also have the general meaning of "this, that" (cf. Matthew 13:8; 21:35; 22:5; Luke 23:33; Acts 27:44; Romans 9:21; Jude 22,23).

When used as a relative pronoun it generally agrees in gender and number with the noun or pronoun in the antecedent clause; its case is also determined by the verb, noun, or pronoun that precedes it (*Bauer*). It is generally used to begin a phrase that expressed result or purpose. For example, in Matthew 2 the three Wise Men were detoured from their search for Jesus by Herod, but "when they had heard the king, they departed; and, lo, the star, *which* they saw in the east, went before them" (verse 9). Other examples of its use as a relative pronoun may be found in John 1:47; Acts 13:6; 17:3; and Romans 2:29. In general all of the New Testament occurrences as a relative pronoun correspond to classical usage (Blass and DeBrunner, *Greek Grammar of the New Testament*, pp.153f.).

Hos is also used in a variety of constructions that have their own peculiar meanings. In 2 Corinthians 2:16 it is used with *men* (3173) and *de* (1156) (*hois men ... hois de*) meaning "the (this) one ... and the (this) other." Occasionally *hos* is included in phrases that have more words than necessary (pleonasm) for special emphasis as in Matthew 3:12, "*whose* fan is in *his* hand" (*hou ... autou*) (cf. Luke 3:16; Revelation 3:8; 7:2). When used in the neuter, it often begins explanatory clauses, i.e., "which, this is, which means" (Matthew 27:33; Mark 3:17; Hebrews 7:2; cf. *Bauer*). It has also been used with the particles *an* (300) or *ean* (1430) where it is translated "whosoever, whose, whatever" (ibid.).

STRONG 3739, BAUER 583-85, MOULTON-MILLIGAN 459-60, LIDDELL-SCOTT 1259-60.

3602. ὀσάκις hosakis conj
As often as.

1. ὀσάκις hosakis

1	this do ye, **as oft as** ye drink it,....................	1 Co 11:25
1	For **as often as** ye eat this bread,....................	11:26
1	the earth with all plagues, **as often as** they will......	Rev 11:6

This word appears three times in the New Testament, twice in 1 Corinthians 11:25,26, speaking of the Lord's Table. Christ said, "This do ye, *as oft as* ye drink it, in remembrance of me. For *as often as* ye eat this bread, and drink this cup ...." It assures the believer that each time he partakes in the Lord's Supper, he again and anew "shows" or "declares" (*katangellō* [2576]) his remembrance of the death of the Lord.

In Revelation 11:6 the two end-time witnesses of the Lord (Moses and Elijah or their end-time counterparts; compare Malachi 4:5,6 with Luke 1:17 and Matthew 11:14) can call judgments down upon the wicked *as often as* (*hosakis*) they wish. Here the adverb connects each purposeful desire by the two witnesses with a plague that God will send to substantiate their divinely-given power.

STRONG 3740, BAUER 585, MOULTON-MILLIGAN 460, LIDDELL-SCOTT 1260.

3603. ὅσιος hosios adj
Devout, pious, holy, religiously right, sanctioned.

COGNATES:
  ἀνόσιος anosios (459)
  ὁσιότης hosiotēs (3604)
  ὁσίως hosiōs (3605)

SYNONYMS:
  ἅγιος hagios (39)
  ἱερός hieros (2393)
  σεμνός semnos (4441)

זַךְ zakh (2217), Pure (Prv 20:11).

חֶסֶד cheṣedh (2721), Faithful mercy (Is 55:3).

חָסִיד chāṣîdh (2728), Godly man, saint (Dt 33:8, Pss 30:4 [29:4], 79:2 [78:2]).

יָשָׁר yāshār (3596), Right (Dt 32:4).

מִקְדָּשׁ miqdāsh (4881), Sanctuary (Ps 68:35 [67:35]).

שָׁלוֹם shālôm (8361), Peace (Dt 29:19).

ὅσιος 3603

תָּם tām (8865), Blameless (Prv 29:10).
תֹּם tōm (8866), Upright (Prv 10:29).
תָּמִים tāmîm (8879), Blameless (Prv 2:21).

1. **ὅσιος** hosios nom sing masc
2. **ὅσιον** hosion acc sing masc
3. **ὁσίους** hosious acc pl fem
4. **ὅσια** hosia nom/acc pl neu

```
2  wilt thou suffer thine Holy One to see corruption.... Acts 2:27
4  I will give you the sure mercies of David..............     13:34
2  shalt not suffer thine Holy One to see corruption......     13:35
3  lifting up holy hands, without wrath and doubting... 1 Tm 2:8
2  a lover of good men, sober, just, holy, temperate;....  Tit 1:8
1  For such an high priest became us, who is holy,..... Heb 7:26
1  Lord, and glorify thy name? for thou only art holy:  Rev 15:4
1  O Lord, which art, and wast, and shalt be,............     16:5
```

Classical Greek

In classical Greek the adjective *hosios* is not restricted to a religious connotation but can be used for any moral imperative. It corresponds "to what a man does by disposition in accordance with his inward attitude and the inner acceptance of what is felt to be binding" (Hauck, "hosios," *Kittel*, 5:489). Thus a man would be considered "devout" for following an ancient custom or a natural law (cf. *Liddell-Scott*).

As a substantive the sense that *hosios* takes is often predicated upon its use with two similar terms: *dikaios* (1335B) and *hieros* (2388B). When *hosios* is coupled in antithesis to *dikaios* (a term which denotes that which is customary or allowed by man, often translated "just" or "righteous"), its meaning reflects that which is sanctioned by God. Thus God's decrees (*hosios*) are set over against man's decrees (*dikaios*) (*Bauer*). When *hosios* is coupled in antithesis to *hieros* (a term which denotes that which is hallowed or consecrated to God, often translated "holy"), its meaning refers to that which is permitted and right, but not sanctioned by God. Thus the sacred things (*hieros*) are set over against the permitted (*hosios*).

Septuagint Usage

This term is found over 50 times in the Septuagint, with 26 of these appearing in the Psalms. It is predominately used to translate the Hebrew *chāsîdh*, "one who is faithful, devout," and consistently reflects a religious connotation. God is described as "just and right" (*dikaios kai hosios*) and "holy" (*hosios*) in all His works (Deuteronomy 32:4; Psalm 145:17 [LXX 144:17]). The majority of the references to *hosios* are used substantively to indicate a group of "holy ones" or "saints" (Psalms 79:2 [LXX 78:2]; 149:1ff. [148:1ff.]). Psalm 50:5 (49:5) describes these "saints" (*tous hosious*) as those who are engaged in a covenant relationship, which therefore includes all of Israel. It was not until the time of the Maccabees that a distinct group of people within Judaism became known as the *chāsîdîm* (see 1 Maccabees 7:13 and 2 Maccabees 14:6). These were the spiritual ancestors of the New Testament Pharisees (ibid., 5:491).

New Testament Usage

Although *hosios* developed into a specific title ("pious ones") in the Old Testament, none of the eight New Testament references use it in this sense. The Christians were referred to as the "chosen ones" (*eklektoi* [see 1575]) and the "saints" (*hagioi* [see 39]), but not the "pious ones." This may be due to the perception that the content of *hosios* "is more self-righteous than is in keeping with the New Testament community" (ibid., 5:491). *Hosios* appears three times in the Book of Acts, and each one is an Old Testament quotation applied to Christ. Both Peter (Acts 2:27) and Paul (Acts 13:35) quoted Psalm 16:10 to support Christ's resurrection from the dead. Jesus is the "Holy One" (*ton hosion*) who would not "see corruption," because God raised Him up the third day. Both apostles pointed to David's own death and burial as a sure sign that he wrote concerning someone else (Acts 2:29; 13:36). Paul added that the promises God made to David have been validated for God's children by Christ's resurrection, in fulfillment of Isaiah 55:3 (Acts 13:34). Hebrews 7:26 applies *hosios* to Christ as the believers' High Priest: "Here the word is used absolutely in the way in which elsewhere it can be used only of God. As high priest (*archiereus*), Christ is completely *hosios*, utterly without sin and utterly pure, so that his offering is sufficient once for all" (Seebass, "Holy," *Colin Brown*, 2:238).

In Revelation 15:4 God *alone* is said to be "holy" (*monos hosios*). He is described as "righteous" (*dikaios*) and "the Holy One" (*ho hosios*) in Revelation 16:5, a passage reminiscent of Deuteronomy 32:4.

Two references to *hosios* are found in the Pastoral Epistles and are applied to Christians. Paul desired that men everywhere pray, lifting up "holy" hands (1 Timothy 2:8). These represent freedom from sinful thoughts and deeds and illustrate how a believer is to approach God's throne. Titus 1:8 lists *hosios* as one of the qualifications for the office of overseer, placing it beside *dikaion*, "just."

STRONG 3741, BAUER 585-86, MOULTON-MILLIGAN 460, KITTEL 5:489-92, LIDDELL-SCOTT 1260-61, COLIN BROWN 2:236-38.

3604. ὁσιότης hosiotēs noun

Piety, holiness, devoutness.

COGNATE:
ὅσιος hosios (3603)

SYNONYMS:
ἁγιασμός hagiasmos (38)
ἁγιότης hagiotēs (40)
ἁγιωσύνη hagiōsunē (41)
εὐσέβεια eusebeia (2131)

יֹשֶׁר yōsher (3598), Uprightness (Dt 9:5).
תֹּם tōm (8866), Integrity (1 Kgs 9:4).
תָּמִים tāmîm (8879), Perfect (1 Sm 14:41).

1. ὁσιότητι hosiotēti dat sing fem

1 In holiness and righteousness before him,........... Luke 1:75
1 God is created in righteousness and true holiness..... Eph 4:24

Classical Greek and Septuagint Usage

This noun appears in classical Greek since the Fourth Century B.C. meaning "as many times as, as often as" (cf. *Liddell-Scott*). In the Septuagint *hosiotēs* translates two Hebrew terms, *yōsher* ("straightness, uprightness") and *tōm* ("completeness, integrity"). God told the Israelites that they were not going to possess land because of their "uprightness" but because of the "wickedness" of its inhabitants (Deuteronomy 9:5). God also promised Solomon that He would "establish the throne of thy kingdom upon Israel for ever" (1 Kings 9:5 [LXX 3 Kings 9:5]) if Solomon would live with "integrity of heart, and in *uprightness*" (verse 4).

New Testament Usage

This word is found only two times in the New Testament. In Luke 1:75 Zechariah, the father of John the Baptist, is filled with the Holy Spirit and prophesies (verse 67) that God would allow His people to serve Him "in *holiness* (*hosiotēs*) and righteousness" (verse 75). In this verse "holiness" means belonging to God and "righteousness" means living as one who belongs to God should, instead of serving God in fear (cf. verse 74).

In Ephesians 4:24 Paul urged believers to "put on the new man, which after God is created in righteousness and true *holiness*" (*hosiotēs*). Again "righteousness" is linked with holiness, which in this context (verse 25) speaks of the holy life which is so devoted in piety to God that it refrains from the sinful deeds and habits of the former life.

STRONG 3742, BAUER 585, MOULTON-MILLIGAN 460, KITTEL 5:493, LIDDELL-SCOTT 1261, COLIN BROWN 2:236-37.

3605. ὁσίως hosiōs adv

Holily, devoutly.

CROSS-REFERENCE:
ὅσιος hosios (3603)

1. ὁσίως hosiōs

1 how holily and justly and unblameably............. 1 Th 2:10

This adverb has a single occurrence in the New Testament, in 1 Thessalonians 2:10. Here *hosiōs* is coupled with *dikaiōs* (1339B), "upright, just, righteous," a common practice in classical Greek (*Liddell-Scott*). Bauer renders the word "devoutly, in a manner pleasing to God, in a holy manner." *Hosiōs* has to do with one's actions and attitudes in relation to God.

STRONG 3743, BAUER 585-86, MOULTON-MILLIGAN 460-61, KITTEL 5:489-92, LIDDELL-SCOTT 1260-61.

3606. ὀσμή osmē noun

A smell, odor, scent, fragrance.

CROSS-REFERENCE:
ὄζω ozō (3467)

בְּאֹשׁ be'ōsh (922), Stench (Is 34:3).
בֹּשֶׂם bōsem (1336II) Perfume (Is 3:24).
רֵיחַ rêach (7666), Aroma, scent (Nm 15:13f., S/S 4:11, Ez 20:28).
רֵיחַ rêach (A7667), Smell (Dn 3:27—Aramaic).

1. ὀσμή osmē nom sing fem
2. ὀσμῆς osmēs gen sing fem
3. ὀσμήν osmēn acc sing fem

2 house was filled with the **odour** of the ointment.... John 12:3
3 and maketh manifest the **savour** of his knowledge... 2 Co 2:14
1 To the one we are the **savour** of death unto death;..... 2:16
1 and to the other the **savour** of life unto life............. 2:16
3 and a sacrifice to God for a sweetsmelling **savour**.... Eph 5:2
3 **an odour** of a sweet smell, a sacrifice acceptable,.... Phlp 4:18

Classical Greek and Septuagint Usage

The word comes from the verb *ozō* (3467), meaning "to smell, give off odor," and often refers to an unpleasant odor in Greek literature. *Osmē* can also signify a pleasing odor in the Septuagint, particularly in connection with sacrifices acceptable to God (Genesis 8:21; Leviticus 1:9,13,17; 2:12; Numbers 28:2).

New Testament Usage

In John 12:3 the word *osmē* is used with reference to the "odor" or fragrance of the ointment of spikenard with which Mary anointed the feet of Jesus. He met the criticism of Judas Iscariot by saying she did it in anticipation of His burial. Anointing was a custom commonly observed in connection with preparations for burial.

The word *euōdia* (2156), meaning "good-scentedness, fragrance," is associated with *osmē* in the three other New Testament passages where it occurs. The Greek expression *osmēn euōdias* is rendered "a sweetsmelling *savor*" in Ephesians 5:2 in reference to the effects Godward of the offering and sacrifice of Christ, which no doubt includes both His life and His death on the Cross. In Philippians 4:18 the same expression is translated "an *odor* of a sweet smell," referring to the material assistance sent by the saints at Philippi to the apostle Paul imprisoned in Rome, which he declared to be a sacrifice acceptable and well-pleasing to God.

The knowledge of Christ is said to be a "savor" wherever it penetrates society, to the saved a "*savor* of life unto life," and to those who perish a "*savor* of death unto death" (2 Corinthians 2:14,16). The three times "savor" is used in these two verses it is a translation of *osmē*. The word translated "a sweet savor" in verse 15 is *euōdia*, which gives added force to what Paul was saying. In Paul's reference to always being caused to triumph in Christ, some see a reference to the victorious reception and procession of a Roman general after a significant victory or conquest. On such occasions incense was offered at temple altars. Along with the victors the vanquished were often involved, sometimes suffering death.

STRONG 3744, BAUER 586, MOULTON-MILLIGAN 461, KITTEL 5:493-95, LIDDELL-SCOTT 1261, COLIN BROWN 3:599-601.

3607. ὅσος hosos rel-pron

As great, as far, as long, as much as; how great, how far, how long, how much.

1. ὅσον **hoson** nom/acc sing masc/neu
2. ὅσοι **hosoi** nom pl masc
3. ὅσων **hosōn** gen pl masc
4. ὅσους **hosous** acc pl masc
5. ὅσαι **hosai** nom pl fem
6. ὅσας **hosas** acc pl fem
7. ὅσῳ **hosō** dat sing neu
8. ὅσα **hosa** nom/acc pl neu

8	whatsoever ye would that men should do to you,	Matt 7:12
1	as long as the bridegroom is with them?	9:15
8	for joy thereof goeth and selleth all that he hath,	13:44
8	went and sold all that he had, and bought it.	13:46
2	as many as touched were made perfectly whole.	14:36
8	but have done unto him whatsoever they listed.	17:12
8	Whatsoever ye shall bind on earth	18:18
8	and whatsoever ye shall loose on earth	18:18
8	and his wife, and children, and all that he had,	18:25
8	all things, whatsoever ye shall ask in prayer,	21:22
4	and as many as ye shall find, bid to the marriage.	22:9
4	and gathered together all as many as they found,	22:10
8	All therefore whatsoever they bid you observe,	23:3
1	Inasmuch as ye have done it unto one of the least	25:40
1	Inasmuch as ye did it not to one of the least	25:45
8	observe all ... whatsoever I have commanded you:	28:20
1	as long as they have the bridegroom with them,	Mark 2:19
8	when they had heard what great things he did,	3:8
2	for to touch him, as many as had plagues.	3:10
6	and blasphemies wherewith soever they shall	3:28
8	and tell them how great things the Lord hath done	5:19
8	how great things Jesus had done for him:	5:20
2	whosoever shall not receive you, nor hear you,	6:11
8	and told him all things, both what they had done,	6:30
8	what they had done, and what they had taught.	6:30
2	and as many as touched him were made whole.	6:56
1	but the more he charged them,	7:36
8	they have done unto him whatsoever they listed,	9:13
8	sell whatsoever thou hast, and give to the poor,	10:21
8	What things soever ye desire, when ye pray,	11:24
8	but she of her want did cast in, all that she had,	12:44
8	whatsoever we have heard done in Capernaum,	Luke 4:23
2	all they that had any sick with divers diseases	4:40
8	show how great things God hath done unto thee.	8:39
8	how great things Jesus had done unto him.	8:39
2	And whosoever will not receive you,	9:5
8	told him all that they had done. And he took them,	9:10
3	he will rise and give him as many as he needeth.	11:8
8	Therefore whatsoever ye have spoken in darkness	12:3
8	I fast twice ... I give tithes of all that I possess.	18:12
8	sell all that thou hast, and distribute unto the poor,	18:22
2	But as many as received him,	John 1:12
8	see a man, which told me all things that ever I did:	4:29
8	which testified, He told me all that ever I did.	4:39
8	things that He did in Jerusalem (NASB)	4:45
1	and likewise of the fishes as much as they would.	6:11
2	that ever came before me are thieves and robbers:	10:8
8	all things that John spake of this man were true.	10:41
8	whatsoever thou wilt ask of God, God will give it	11:22
8	Ye are my friends, if ye do whatsoever I command	15:14
8	but whatsoever he shall hear, that shall he speak:	16:13
8	All things that the Father hath are mine:	16:15
8	Whatsoever ye shall ask the Father in my name,	16:23
8	that all things whatsoever thou hast given me	17:7
8	there are also many other things which Jesus did,	21:25
4	even as many as the Lord our God shall call.	Acts 2:39
8	hear in all things whatsoever he shall say unto you.	3:22
2	those that follow after, as many as have spoken,	3:24
2	as many as were of the kindred of the high priest,	4:6
8	and reported all that the chief priests ... had said	4:23
8	For to do whatsoever thy hand and thy counsel	4:28
2	for as many as were possessors of lands or houses	4:34
2	and all, as many as obeyed him, were scattered,	5:36
2	all, even as many as obeyed him, were dispersed.	5:37
8	how much evil he hath done to thy saints	9:13
8	I will show him how great things he must suffer	9:16
8	the coats and garments which Dorcas made,	9:39
2	were astonished, as many as came with Peter,	10:45
2	as many as were ordained to eternal life believed.	13:48
8	they rehearsed all that God had done with them,	14:27
8	declared all things that God had done with them,	15:4
8	declaring what miracles and wonders God had	15:12

2	For **as many as** have sinned without law	Rom 2:12
2	and **as many as** have sinned in the law	2:12
8	we know that **what things soever** the law saith,	3:19
2	Know ye not, that **so many of us as** were baptized	6:3
1	law hath dominion over a man **as long as** he liveth?	7:1
2	For **as many as** are led by the Spirit of God,	8:14
1	**inasmuch** as I am the apostle of the Gentiles,	11:13
8	For **whatsoever** things were written aforetime	15:4
8	**what** God has prepared for those (NIV)	1 Co 2:9
1	is bound by the law **as long as** her husband liveth;	7:39
5	For **all** the promises of God in him are yea,	2 Co 1:20
2	For **as many as** are of the works of the law	Gal 3:10
2	For **as many of you as** have been baptized	3:27
1	Now I say, That the heir, **as long as** he is a child,	4:1
2	**As many as** desire to make a fair show in the flesh,	6:12
2	And **as many as** walk according to this rule,	6:16
2	Let us therefore, **as many as** be perfect,	Phlp 3:15
8	Finally, brethren, **whatsoever** things are true,	4:8
8	**whatsoever** things are honest,	4:8
8	**whatsoever** things are just,	4:8
8	**whatsoever** things are pure,	4:8
8	**whatsoever** things are lovely,	4:8
8	**whatsoever** things are of good report;	4:8
2	for **as many as** have not seen my face in the flesh;	Col 2:1
2	Let **as many** servants **as** are under the yoke	1 Tm 6:1
8	and in **how many things** he ministered unto me	2 Tm 1:18
7	**as** he hath by inheritance obtained	Heb 1:4
2	deliver them **who** ... were ... subject to bondage.	2:15
1	**inasmuch** as he who hath builded the house	3:3
1	And **inasmuch** as not without an oath	7:20
7	**by how much** also he is the mediator	8:6
1	And **as** it is appointed unto men once to die,	9:27
7	**so much the more, as** ye see the day approaching.	10:25
1	yet a little **while**, and he that shall come will come,	10:37
1	yet a little **while**, and he that shall come will come,	10:37
1	I think it meet, **as long as** I am in this tabernacle,	2 Pt 1:13
8	speak evil of those things **which** they know not:	Jude 1:10
8	they know not: but **what** they know naturally,	1:10
8	testimony of Jesus ... and of **all things** that he saw.	Rev 1:2
2	rest in Thyatira, **as many as** have not this doctrine,	2:24
4	**As many as** I love, I rebuke and chasten:	3:19
2	cause that **as many as** would not worship the image	13:15
8	**How much** she hath glorified herself,	18:7
2	sailors, and **as many as** trade by sea, stood afar off,	18:17
1	and the length is as large as the breadth:	21:16

This is a relative and interrogative pronoun. Its wide usage is indicated in ancient inscriptions, the papyri, the Septuagint, classical Greek, and in the writings of Josephus.

Hosos coupled with *an* (300) or *ean* (1430) is translated "whatsoever" (Matthew 7:12, etc.), "as many, much as" (Revelation 3:19, etc.), "wherewith soever" (Mark 3:28), and "whosoever" (Luke 9:5). Without a coupling word it is usually translated by "as many, much as" (Matthew 14:35, etc.). Other renderings are: "all (that)" (Luke 9:10, etc.), "by (or how) many" (Acts 9:13; 2 Timothy 1:18), "so many ... as" (Romans 6:3), "that ever" (John 4:29).

The word is used to denote size or space (Revelation 21:16), time (Romans 7:1), abundance (John 6:11), number (John 1:12; Acts 4:6,34), measure or degree (Mark 7:36; Acts 9:16), and importance (Mark 3:8).

Hosa, the neuter plural of *hosos*, meaning "as much" or "whatsoever things," is sometimes rendered "all that" (Acts 4:23; 14:27).

STRONG 3745, BAUER 586, MOULTON-MILLIGAN 461, LIDDELL-SCOTT 1261-62.

3608. ὅσπερ hosper rel-pron

The very one who.

1. ὅνπερ honper acc sing masc

1 released ... one prisoner, **whomsoever** they desired. Mark 15:6

Hosper is a combination of the relative pronoun *hos* (3601B) and the particle *per*. The addition of the particle *per* intensifies the meaning of the base word to specify the very person or thing. *Hosper* is found in the New Testament as a textual variant in Mark 15:6. It is common in the papyri (*Moulton-Milligan*).

STRONG 3746, BAUER 586, MOULTON-MILLIGAN 461, LIDDELL-SCOTT 1262.

3609. ὀστέον osteon noun

Bone.

גֶּרֶם gerem (1678), Bone (Prv 17:22, 25:15).

גְּרַם gᵉram (A1679), Bone (Dn 6:24—Aramaic).

עֶצֶם ʻetsem (6344), Bone (Ex 13:19, Jb 10:11, Ez 37:1).

עֹצֶם ʻotsem (6346), Frame (Ps 139:15 [138:15]).

1. ὀστοῦν ostoun nom/acc sing neu
2. ὀστέων osteōn gen pl neu
3. ὀστέα ostea nom/acc pl neu

2	but are within full of dead men's **bones**,	Matt 23:27
3	and see; for a spirit hath not flesh and **bones**,	Luke 24:39
1	be fulfilled, A **bone** of him shall not be broken.	John 19:36
2	members of his body, of his flesh, and of his **bones**.	Eph 5:30
2	and gave commandment concerning his **bones**.	Heb 11:22

Of the five occurrences of *osteon* in the New Testament, two refer to Jesus Christ. John (19:36) quoted from Old Testament prophecies regarding the fulfillment of Scripture when the guards at the Crucifixion did not break the legs of Jesus. Luke (24:39) reports a post-Resurrection conversation of Jesus' encounter with His disciples. Bones were regarded as essential for a resurrected body (Marshall, *New International Greek Testament Commentary, Luke*, p.902). *Osteon* is the term used to identify the bone portion of man's anatomy. In the Septuagint it is also used to refer to the dead (Genesis 50:25) or to the totality of human existence—when used with "flesh" (Job 2:5) or even when used alone (Isaiah 66:14). "Flesh" was considered to include the blood in such cases.

ὅστις 3610

Strong 3747, Bauer 586, Moulton-Milligan 461, Liddell-Scott 1263, Colin Brown 1:240-41.

3610. ὅστις hostis rel-pron
Whoever, who, whichever, whatever, anyone who.

1. ὅστις hostis nom sing masc
2. οἵτινες hoitines nom pl masc
3. ἥτις hētis nom sing fem
4. αἵτινες haitines nom pl fem
5. ὅ τι ho ti acc sing neu
6. ἅτινα hatina nom pl neu

1 he said unto them, **Whosoever** will come after me,.. Mark 8:34

Classical Greek
Hostis is an indefinite relative pronoun found in Greek literature from the time of Homer. In the *Iliad* and *Odyssey* Homer used *hostis* both as an indefinite relative pronoun ("anyone," *Odyssey* 1:47; "the man who," *Iliad* 21:347) and in indirect interrogation ("*what man* can he be?" *Iliad* 3:192; *Liddell-Scott*). Herodotus used *hostis* as an indefinite relative pronoun ("who," *Histories* 8:65; *Liddell-Scott*). In classical writings there was a noted distinction between the uses of *hos* (3601B) and *hostis*. The former is translated "who" or "which" while the latter carries a more indefinite translation of "whosoever, whatsoever." This is found to be the case in Homer (*Authenrieth* 213,214; *Liddell-Scott*). Moule points out that there is a difference of opinion as to whether such a distinction still remains in the New Testament (*An Idiom Book of New Testament Greek*, pp.123f.). He cites Moulton and H.J. Cadbury as examples of the two schools of thought (ibid.). *Moulton-Milligan* claims that *hostis* is rare in the papyri.

Septuagint Usage
In the Septuagint *hostis* occurs over 100 times. It can mean "who, whom, which," etc. It is substituted for several Hebrew words or phrases but mainly for '*ăsher* which has the closest meaning to *hostis*. *Hostis* and *hos* are not distinguished in the Septuagint.

New Testament Usage
In the New Testament *hostis* is used in several different ways. In a general or generic sense it means "whoever." For example, in the Sermon on the Mount Jesus gave instruction to His followers, "*Whosoever* shall smite thee on thy right cheek, turn to him the other also" (Matthew 5:39). Secondly, it is used in a qualitative sense to describe someone as belonging to a certain class, i.e., the man "*which* built his house upon a rock" (Matthew 7:24,26). A third use is as a simple relative pronoun, "*which* is called Bethlehem" (Luke 2:4).

Strong 3748, Bauer 586-87, Moulton-Milligan 461-62, Liddell-Scott 1263.

3611. ὀστράκινος ostrakinos adj
Made of earth, of clay.

חָסַף chăsaph (A2739), Clay (Dn 2:34,42—Aramaic).
חֶרֶשׂ cheres (2895), Earthenware vessel, clay pot (Lv 14:5, Nm 5:17, Lam 4:2).

1. ὀστράκινα ostrakina nom/acc pl neu
2. ὀστρακίνοις ostrakinois dat pl neu

2 But we have this treasure in **earthen vessels**,........ 2 Co 4:7
1 **vessels** of gold ... but also of wood and of **earth**;.... 2 Tm 2:20

Classical Greek
This adjective can be traced back to the writings of Hippocrates (Fifth Century B.C.) and is found in the papyri and Septuagint. In these writings various styles of clay vessels are described, for example flat plates, water and wine jugs, pots for boiling meat, and pots used for the preparation of sacrifices. In later writings *ostrakinos* is also used to describe the material from which idols were made (Diognetus 2:7; cf. *Bauer*). Herodotus wrote of a Persian king who melted his gold and silver until they became very fluid, then poured the liquid into *ostrakinos* vessels. When the gold or silver solidified, the vessels were chipped away (Herodotus 3.96; cf. *Liddell-Scott*). Some ancient Egyptians would write the names of their enemies in earthen bowls, then shatter the bowl in an attempt to break the power of this enemy.

Septuagint Usage
In the Septuagint *ostrakinos* is found 15 times and is used to describe the material of which cooking vessels were made. Meat prepared for sacrifices in such vessels is described as "sodden" (KJV) or "boiled" (NASB). Other vessels of this material were used for water (Numbers 5:17), wine (Jeremiah 19:1), and storage (Jeremiah 32:14 [LXX 39:14]; Ezekiel 4:9). In Daniel 2:33,34 the feet of the great image were made of a combination of iron and clay (*ostrakinos*).

New Testament Usage
Ostrakinos is found only twice in the New Testament, in 2 Corinthians 4:7 and 2 Timothy

2:20. Paul used this metaphor to contrast the precious treasure of the gospel (2 Corinthians 4:6) and the human bearers of it (verse 7). This contrast was intended by God so that no one looking at believers would suppose that humans are the source of the power of salvation but that the "excellency of the power may be of God." In 2 Timothy 2:20 Paul used the metaphor of an edifice to describe the Church and the foundation referred to in the previous verse (Guthrie, *Tyndale New Testament Commentaries*, 14:151). Paul was pointing out that there are a variety of people in the Church, some honorable and others less honorable. He explained this to Timothy in order to exhort Timothy to strive for personal sanctification in order to set an example of honor; "in meekness" he was to instruct those who were contrary (cf. verses 21-26).

STRONG 3749, BAUER 587, MOULTON-MILLIGAN 462, LIDDELL-SCOTT 1263, COLIN BROWN 3:913-15.

3612. ὄσφρησις osphrēsis noun
Sense of smell.

1. ὄσφρησις osphrēsis nom sing fem

1 the whole were hearing, where were the **smelling**?..1 Co 12:17

Osphrēsis occurs only once in the New Testament (1 Corinthians 12:17). It is related to the verb *ozō* (3467), "give off an odor," and in its form indicates the action or process of detecting an odor. In 1 Corinthians 12:17 Paul asked the Corinthians, "If the whole body were an eye, where were the hearing? If the whole were hearing, where were the *smelling*?" By asking these rhetorical questions Paul was actually applying his analogy of the parts of the "body." By interchanging sensory organs Paul hoped his readers would see that there is no inferior member but that all the parts of the body must be present and functioning as intended for the sake of the whole body (cf. Fee, *New International Commentary on the New Testament, First Corinthians*, pp.610f.).

STRONG 3750, BAUER 587, MOULTON-MILLIGAN 462, LIDDELL-SCOTT 1264.

3613. ὀσφῦς osphus noun
Waist, loins.

אַלְיָה 'alyāh (454), Fat tail (Lv 3:9, 8:25, 9:19).

חָלָץ chelets (2604), Loins, a person (Gn 35:11, 2 Chr 6:9, Is 11:5).

מָתְנַיִם mothnayim (5158), Loins, belt (Ex 12:11, 2 Kgs 9:1, Is 20:2).

1. ὀσφύος osphuos gen sing fem
2. ὀσφύϊ osphui dat sing fem
3. ὀσφύν osphun acc sing fem
4. ὀσφύες osphues nom pl fem
5. ὀσφύας osphuas acc pl fem

3 and a leathern girdle about his **loins**; .... Matt 3:4
3 and with a girdle of a skin about his **loins**; .... Mark 1:6
4 Let your **loins** be girded about, ... Luke 12:35
1 that of the fruit of his **loins**, according to the flesh,.. Acts 2:30
3 having your **loins** girt about with truth, ... Eph 6:14
1 though they come out of the **loins** of Abraham: ...... Heb 7:5
2 For he was yet in the **loins** of his father, ... 7:10
5 Wherefore gird up the **loins** of your mind, ... 1 Pt 1:13

Classical Greek
In classical Greek *osphus* is generally used literally of the strong trunk of the body that gives stability and power for vigorous action. It is the part of the body where a belt or girdle gives support or binds the clothing out of the way for work, travel, or battle. This concept of physical strength has been variously translated as "loin, waist, hip" or "lumbar region of the lower back."

Septuagint Usage
In the Septuagint *osphus* usually translates the Hebrew term *mothnayim*, "loins," which has a variety of literal and figurative uses. It can simply refer to the place where one would literally wear a belt or girdle (1 Kings 2:5 [LXX 3 Kings 2:5]; Jeremiah 13:1,2,4,11). Note the following figurative use: "And righteousness shall be the girdle of his *loins*" (Isaiah 11:5). The common phrase *gird up the loins* means to prepare for sustained and effective effort, to make ready for action (Exodus 12:11; 1 Kings 18:46 [LXX 3 Kings 18:46]; Job 38:3; 40:7). Physically, the "loins" included the reproductive organs and as such were seen as the source of virility and procreative strength (e.g., Genesis 35:11, "kings shall come out of thy *loins*"). The good wife of Proverbs 31 "girdeth her *loins* with strength, and strengtheneth her arms" (verse 17).

New Testament Usage
In the New Testament *osphus* is used literally only in reference to John the Baptist who wore a "raiment of camel's hair, and a leathern girdle about his *loins*" (Matthew 3:4; cf. Mark 1:6). Other passages use *osphus* figuratively. For example, Jesus told His disciples to make themselves ready for His second coming, "Let

your *loins* be girded about, and your lights burning" (Luke 12:35; cf. the phrase "gird up the loins" in the Old Testament). Both Paul and Peter also exhorted believers to prepare themselves for action, "having your *loins* girt about with truth" (Ephesians 6:14), and "gird up the *loins* of your mind" (1 Peter 1:13). As in the Old Testament, *osphus* is also used to refer to procreative strength and source of successive generations (Hebrews 7:5,10).

The Didache (16:1) exhorts the readers not to let their loins become powerless. *Osphus* had probably by then become established as the sublime metaphor for the inmost source of power—for living, for working, and for passing on a heritage to posterity (*Bauer*). Made in the image of God, man was endowed with an *osphus* that can be spiritually motivated and fulfilled by the power of the indwelling Holy Spirit.

STRONG 3751, BAUER 587, MOULTON-MILLIGAN 462, KITTEL 5:496-97, LIDDELL-SCOTT 1264, COLIN BROWN 1:239.

3614. ὅς hos
See word study at number 3601B.

3615. ὅταν hotan conj
When, whenever.

1. ὅταν hotan

1 Blessed are ye, **when** men shall revile you,	Matt	5:11
1 Therefore **when** thou doest thine alms,		6:2
1 And **when** thou prayest,		6:5
1 **when** thou prayest, enter into thy closet,		6:6
1 Moreover **when** ye fast, be not, as the hypocrites,		6:16
1 **when** the bridegroom shall be taken from them,		9:15
1 But **when** they deliver you up,		10:19
1 But **when** they persecute you in this city,		10:23
1 **When** the unclean spirit is gone out of a man,		12:43
1 is the least of all seeds: but **when** it is grown,		13:32
1 for they wash not their hands **when** they eat bread.		15:2
1 in the regeneration **when** the Son of man shall sit		19:28
1 **When** the lord therefore of the vineyard cometh,		21:40
1 to make one proselyte, and **when** he is made,		23:15
1 **When** ye therefore shall see the abomination		24:15
1 of the fig tree; **When** his branch is yet tender,		24:32
1 So likewise ye, **when** ye shall see all these things,		24:33
1 **When** the Son of man shall come in his glory,		25:31
1 until that day **when** I drink it new with you		26:29
1 **when** the bridegroom shall be taken away	Mark	2:20
1 And unclean spirits, **when** they saw him,		3:11
1 but **when** they have heard, Satan cometh		4:15
1 who, **when** they have heard the word,		4:16
1 But **when** the fruit is brought forth,		4:29
1 which, **when** it is sown in the earth,		4:31
1 But **when** it is sown, it groweth up,		4:32
1 **when** he cometh in the glory of his Father		8:38
1 till the Son of man were risen from the dead.		9:9
1 And **whenever** evening came, (NASB)		11:19
1 And **when** ye stand praying, forgive,	Mark	11:25
1 In the resurrection therefore, **when** they shall rise,		12:23
1 For **when** they shall rise from the dead,		12:25
1 be the sign **when** all these things shall be fulfilled?		13:4
1 **when** ye shall hear of wars and rumours of wars,		13:7
1 But **when** they shall lead you out, and deliver you up,		13:11
1 **when** ye shall see the abomination of desolation,		13:14
1 the fig tree; **When** her branch is yet tender,		13:28
1 **when** ye shall see these things come to pass,		13:29
1 and **whensoever** ye will ye may do them good:		14:7
1 until that day **that** I drink it new in the kingdom		14:25
1 But the days will come, **when** the bridegroom shall	Luke	5:35
1 Blessed are ye, **when** men shall hate you,		6:22
1 **when** they shall separate you from their company,		6:22
1 Woe ... **when** all men shall speak well of you!		6:26
1 which, **when** they hear, receive the word with joy;		8:13
1 **when** he shall come in his own glory,		9:26
1 And he said unto them, **When** ye pray, say,		11:2
1 **When** a strong man armed keepeth his palace,		11:21
1 **When** the unclean spirit is gone out of a man,		11:24
1 therefore **when** thine eye is single,		11:34
1 as **when** the bright shining of a candle doth give		11:36
1 And **when** they bring you unto the synagogues,		12:11
1 **When** ye see a cloud rise out of the west,		12:54
1 And **when** ye see the south wind blow, ye say,		12:55
1 **when** ye shall see Abraham, and Isaac, and Jacob,		13:28
1 **When** thou art bidden of any man to a wedding,		14:8
1 But **when** thou art bidden,		14:10
1 that **when** he that bade thee cometh,		14:10
1 **When** thou makest a dinner or a supper,		14:12
1 But **when** thou makest a feast, call the poor,		14:13
1 that, **when** I am put out of the stewardship,		16:4
1 that, **when** ye fail, they may receive you into		16:9
1 **when** ye shall have done all those things		17:10
1 what sign ... **when** these things shall come to pass?		21:7
1 But **when** ye shall hear of wars and commotions,		21:9
1 And **when** ye shall see Jerusalem compassed		21:20
1 **When** they now shoot forth, ye see and know		21:30
1 likewise ye, **when** ye see these things come to pass,		21:31
1 remember me **when** thou comest into thy kingdom.		23:42
1 and **when** men have well drunk,	John	2:10
1 **when** he is come, he will tell us all things.		4:25
1 **when** the water is troubled, to put me into		5:7
1 but **when** Christ cometh, no man knoweth		7:27
1 **When** Christ cometh, will he do more miracles		7:31
1 **When** ye have lifted up the Son of man,		8:28
1 **When** he speaketh a lie, he speaketh of his own:		8:44
1 As long as I am in the world, I am the light		9:5
1 And **when** he putteth forth his own sheep,		10:4
1 that, **when** it is come to pass, ye may believe		13:19
1 that, **when** it is come to pass, ye might believe.		14:29
1 But **when** the Comforter is come,		15:26
1 that **when** the time shall come,		16:4
1 Howbeit **when** he, the Spirit of truth, is come,		16:13
1 A woman **when** she is in travail hath sorrow,		16:21
1 but as soon as she is delivered of the child,		16:21
1 but **when** thou shalt be old,		21:18
1 **when** thine accusers are also come.	Acts	23:35
1 **When** Lysias the chief captain shall come down,		24:22
1 For **when** the Gentiles, which have not the law,	Rom	2:14
1 **when** I shall take away their sins.		11:27
1 For **while** one saith, I am of Paul;	1 Co	3:4
1 But **when** that which is perfect is come,		13:10
1 How is it then, brethren? **when** ye come together,		14:26
1 **when** he shall have delivered up the kingdom		15:24
1 **when** he shall have put down all rule		15:24
1 But **when** he saith all things are put under him,		15:27
1 And **when** all things shall be subdued unto him,		15:28
1 So **when** this corruptible shall have put on		15:54
1 that there be no gatherings **when** I come.		16:2
1 And **when** I come, whomsoever ye shall approve		16:3
1 **when** I shall pass through Macedonia:		16:5
1 he will come **when** he shall have convenient time.		16:12
1 **when** your obedience is fulfilled.	2 Co	10:6
1 for **when** I am weak, then am I strong.		12:10
1 we are glad, **when** we are weak, and ye are strong:		13:9
1 **When** Christ, who is our life, shall appear,	Col	3:4

1	And **when** this epistle is read among you,	Col 4:16
1	For **when** they shall say, Peace and safety;	1 Th 5:3
1	**When** he shall come to be glorified in his saints,	2 Th 1:10
1	for **when** they have begun to wax wanton	1 Tm 5:11
1	**When** I shall send Artemas unto thee, or Tychicus,	Tit 3:12
1	And again, **when** he bringeth in the firstbegotten	Heb 1:6
1	count it all joy **when** ye fall into divers temptations;	Jas 1:2
1	**when** he shall appear, we may have confidence,	1 Jn 2:28
1	**when** we love God, and keep his commandments.	5:2
1	And **when** those beasts give glory and honour	Rev 4:9
1	And **when** He broke the seventh seal (NASB)	8:1
1	the torment of a scorpion, **when** he striketh a man.	9:5
1	the seventh angel, **when** he shall begin to sound,	10:7
1	And **when** they shall have finished their testimony,	11:7
1	for to devour her child **as soon as** it was born.	12:4
1	**when** he cometh, he must continue a short space.	17:10
1	**when** they shall see the smoke of her burning,	18:9
1	And **when** the thousand years are expired,	20:7

Hotan is a temporal particle used primarily with the subjunctive mood, the mood of contingency meaning "when, whenever." It is a contraction of *hote an* (*hote* [3616] also means "when," and *an* [300] is usually not translatable but generally conveys a sense of vagueness or contingency). *Hotan* is generally used in a temporal clause when there is an element of indefiniteness. One can assume that something will occur, even be repeated, but the exact time of that occurrence cannot be established. As an example, Jesus said to His disciples, "*When* they shall lead you, and deliver you up ..." (Mark 13:11), thus suggesting that there would be frequent arrests. *Hotan* is also used on occasion with the indicative mood (but not in the early Greek literature; cf. *Liddell-Scott*) where it expresses indefinite and repeated actions in past time, "and unclean spirits, *when* they saw him ..." (Mark 3:11); future, "*when* ye shall see Abraham ..." (Luke 13:28); and present, "and *when* ye stand praying ..." (Mark 11:25).
STRONG 3752, BAUER 587-88, MOULTON-MILLIGAN 462-63, LIDDELL-SCOTT 1264-65.

3616. ὅτε hote conj
When, while, since.

1. ὅτε hote

1	**when** Jesus had ended these sayings,	Matt 7:28
1	But **when** the people were put forth, he went in,	9:25
1	**when** Jesus had made an end of commanding	11:1
1	not read what David did, **when** he was an hungred,	12:3
1	But **when** the blade was sprung up,	13:26
1	Which, **when** it was full, they drew to shore,	13:48
1	**when** Jesus had finished these parables,	13:53
1	And **when** he was come into the house,	17:25
1	that **when** Jesus had finished these sayings,	19:1
1	And **when** they drew nigh unto Jerusalem,	21:1
1	And **when** the time of the fruit drew near,	21:34
1	**when** Jesus had finished all these sayings,	26:1
1	And **after** that they had mocked him,	27:31
1	And at even, **when** the sun did set,	Mark 1:32
1	**when** he had need, and was an hungred,	2:25
1	But **when** the sun came up, the plants were (NIV)	4:6
1	And **when** he was alone, ... asked of ... the parable.	Mark 4:10
1	And **when** a convenient day was come,	6:21
1	And **when** he was entered into the house	7:17
1	**When** I brake the five loaves among five thousand,	8:19
1	And **when** the seven among four thousand,	8:20
1	And **when** they came nigh to Jerusalem,	11:1
1	And **when** even was come, he went out of the city.	11:19
1	**when** they killed the passover, his disciples said	14:12
1	And **when** they had mocked him,	15:20
1	Who also, **when** he was in Galilee, followed him,	15:41
1	And **when** eight days were accomplished	Luke 2:21
1	And **when** the days of her purification according to	2:22
1	And **when** he was twelve years old,	2:42
1	**when** the heaven was shut up three years and	4:25
1	what David did, **when** he was hungry, (NASB)	6:3
1	And **when** it was day, he called unto him	6:13
1	until the time come **when** ye shall say,	13:35
1	But **as soon as** this thy son was come,	15:30
1	**when** ye shall desire to see one of the days	17:22
1	And **when** the hour was come, he sat down,	22:14
1	**When** I sent you without purse, and scrip,	22:35
1	And **when** they were come to the place, ... Calvary,	23:33
1	**when** the Jews sent priests ... from Jerusalem	John 1:19
1	**When** therefore he was risen from the dead,	2:22
1	**when** ye shall neither in this mountain,	4:21
1	**when** the true worshippers ... worship ... in spirit	4:23
1	Then **when** he was come into Galilee,	4:45
1	**when** the dead shall hear the voice of the Son	5:25
1	**When** the people ... saw that Jesus was not there,	6:24
1	the night cometh, **when** no man can work.	9:4
1	it was the sabbath day **when** Jesus made the clay,	9:14
1	**when** Jesus was glorified, then remembered they	12:16
1	with him **when** he called Lazarus out of his grave,	12:17
1	These things said Esaias, **when** he saw his glory,	12:41
1	So **after** he had washed their feet,	13:12
1	Therefore, **when** he was gone out, Jesus said,	13:31
1	**when** I shall no more speak unto you in proverbs,	16:25
1	**While** I was with them in the world,	17:12
1	**When** the chief priests ... and officers saw him,	19:6
1	**When** Pilate therefore heard that saying,	19:8
1	Then the soldiers, **when** they had crucified Jesus,	19:23
1	**When** Jesus therefore had received the vinegar,	19:30
1	Thomas, ... was not with them **when** Jesus came.	20:24
1	So **when** they had dined,	21:15
1	**When** thou wast young, thou girdedst thyself,	21:18
1	And **when** they were come in,	Acts 1:13
1	But **when** they believed Philip preaching	8:12
1	And **when** they were come up out of the water,	8:39
1	And **when** Peter was come up to Jerusalem,	11:2
1	And **when** Herod would have brought him forth,	12:6
1	And **when** we had accomplished those days,	21:5
1	And **when** he came upon the stairs, so it was,	21:35
1	**when** the blood of thy martyr Stephen was shed,	22:20
1	And **when** it was day, they knew not the land:	27:39
1	And **when** we came to Rome,	28:16
1	In the day **when** God shall judge the secrets of men	Rom 2:16
1	For **when** ye were the servants of sin,	6:20
1	For **when** we were in the flesh, the motions of sins,	7:5
1	for now is our salvation nearer than **when** we	13:11
1	You know that **when** ye were pagans (NASB)	1 Co 12:2
1	**When** I was a child, I spake as a child,	13:11
1	**when** I became a man, I put away childish things.	13:11
1	But **when** it pleased God,	Gal 1:15
1	But **when** Peter was come to Antioch,	2:11
1	but **when** they were come, he withdrew	2:12
1	But **when** I saw that they walked not uprightly	2:14
1	Even so we, **when** we were children,	4:3
1	But **when** the fulness of the time was come,	4:4
1	**when** I departed from Macedonia,	Phlp 4:15
1	ye also walked some time, **when** ye lived in them.	Col 3:7
1	**when** we were with you, we told you before	1 Th 3:4
1	**when** we were with you, this we commanded you,	2 Th 3:10
1	**when** they will not endure sound doctrine;	2 Tm 4:3
1	But **after** that the kindness and love of God	Tit 3:4
1	loins of his father, **when** Melchisedec met him.	Heb 7:10
1	it is of no strength **at** all while the testator liveth.	9:17
1	**when** once the longsuffering of God waited	1 Pt 3:20

1 Yet Michael ... **when** contending with the devil	Jude 1:9
1 And **when** I saw him, I fell at his feet as dead	Rev 1:17
1 And **when** he had taken the book,	5:8
1 And I saw **when** the Lamb opened one of the seals,	6:1
1 And **when** he had opened the second seal,	6:3
1 And **when** he had opened the third seal,	6:5
1 And **when** he had opened the fourth seal,	6:7
1 And **when** he had opened the fifth seal,	6:9
1 And I beheld **when** he had opened the sixth seal,	6:12
1 And **when** he had opened the seventh seal,	8:1
1 as **when** a lion roareth: and **when** he had cried,	10:3
1 **when** the seven thunders had uttered their voices,	10:4
1 and **as soon as** I had eaten it, my belly was bitter	10:10
1 And **when** the dragon saw that he was cast	12:13
1 **when** I had heard and seen, I fell down to worship	22:8

Hote is a temporal particle used primarily with the indicative mood in the New Testament. *Hote* is generally used as a conjunction in temporal clauses of definiteness, although it may also be used as a substitute for a relative pronoun after a noun denoting time (cf. *Liddell-Scott*). As a conjunction it is used to express (1) an event that has occurred in the past (Matthew 9:25), "*when* the people were put forth" and (Mark 1:32) "*when* the sun did set"; (2) a customary or occasional occurrence in the present (Mark 14:12), "*when* they killed the passover"; and (3) an event which occurred in the past, the result of which continues into the present (1 Corinthians 13:11), "*when* (since) I became a man." *Hote* is frequently used by Matthew as part of a transitional formula, "and it came to pass, *when* ... " (Matthew 7:28).

An example of *hote* used as a substitute for a relative pronoun after a noun denoting time can be seen in Luke 17:22, "The days will come, *when* (*hote*) ye shall desire to see one of the days of the Son of man." Here *hote*, translated "when," serves as a relative pronoun relating back to the noun denoting time, "days." This usage occurs with both the indicative (in future and present tenses) and subjunctive moods. Other examples can be seen at Luke 13:35; John 4:21,23; 5:25; 9:4; 16:25; Romans 2:16; and 2 Timothy 4:3. *Hote* occurs more than 100 times in the New Testament.

STRONG 3753, BAUER 588, MOULTON-MILLIGAN 463, LIDDELL-SCOTT 1265.

3617. ὅτι hoti conj

That, because, since, for.
SYNONYMS:
ἐπεί epei (1878)
ἐπειδή epeidē (1879)

1. ὅτι hoti

1 **Because** it is given unto you to know the mysteries	Matt 13:11
1 **because** they seeing see not;	13:13
1 **because** they counted him as a prophet	Matt 14:5
1 They say unto him, **Because** no man hath hired us	20:7
1 not the devils to speak, **because** they knew him	Mark 1:34
1 saying, My name is Legion: **for** we are many	5:9
1 his brother Philip's wife: **for** he had married her	6:17
1 you say, 'A shower is coming, (NASB) (NT)	Luke 12:54
1 hail; **for** the plague thereof was exceeding great	Rev 16:21

In form, *hoti* is simply the neuter indefinite relative pronoun *ho ti*, meaning "what" or "whatever." The limited demonstrative force of the article *ho* (3450), generalized by the indefinite pronoun *ti* (see 4948), draws specific attention to whatever object or idea is under consideration.

When the pronoun *ho ti* became the conjunction *hoti*, it carried over this demonstrative force and scope into its use as a conjunction. The English word *that* reflects the root idea of *hoti* as it is used in many but not all passages in the New Testament. The uses of *hoti* in classical, Septuagintal, and New Testament texts can be summarized as follows:

(1) *Hoti* frequently introduces an objective or noun clause, calling specific attention to the fact or concept under consideration. This is clear in indirect discourse. *Hoti* also designates what is being quoted or said (Mark 3:28,29). Lexicons list a number of variants. *Hoti* can also introduce what is only perceived, thought, felt, hoped, implied, summarized, or interpreted—whether orally communicated or not. The conjunction calls specific attention to the concept being discussed.

(2) *Hoti* can introduce direct discourse. English would use quotation marks instead of translating the conjunction. But *hoti* still serves the purpose of calling specific attention to the content and form of the quotation as do quotation marks in English.

(3) In many New Testament contexts there is an evident causative force that gives *hoti* the meaning "because, since, for," or even "when." Used in this way it indicates the nature and extent of the influence of the thing said in the subordinate clause on the statement in the main clause. Note, for example, how each subordinate clause in the Beatitudes is introduced with "for" (Matthew 5:3-12), e.g., "*for* theirs is the kingdom of heaven" (verse 3).

STRONG 3754, BAUER 588-89, MOULTON-MILLIGAN 463, LIDDELL-SCOTT 1265.

3618. ὅτου hotou rel-pron

Where, wherever, whereas.

1. ὅτου hotou gen sing neu

This word is the genitive, singular, masculine and neuter form of *hostis*. See the word study at number 3610.

3619. οὗ hou adv

Where, where to.

1. οὗ hou

1 it came and stood over **where** the young child was...	Matt 2:9
1 For **where** two or three are gathered together...	18:20
1 into a mountain **where** Jesus had appointed them...	28:16
1 came to Nazareth, **where** he had been brought up:..	Luke 4:16
1 he found the place **where** it was written,...	4:17
1 city and place, **whither** he himself would come...	10:1
1 and how am I straitened **till** it be accomplished!...	12:50
1 till **thou** hast paid the very last mite...	12:59
1 a sepulchre ... **wherein** never man before was laid...	23:53
1 drew nigh unto the village, **whither** they went:...	24:28
1 the stone from the place **where** the dead was laid..	John 11:41
1 cock shall not crow, **till** thou hast denied me thrice...	13:38
1 **where** abode both Peter, and James, and John,...	Acts 1:13
1 and it filled all the house **where** they were sitting...	2:2
1 in the land of Madian, **where** he begat two sons...	7:29
1 **where** many were gathered together praying...	12:12
1 **where** prayer was wont to be made;...	16:13
1 to Troas in five days; **where** we abode seven days:...	20:6
1 **where** they were gathered together...	20:8
1 at Caesar's ... **where** I ought to be judged:...	25:10
1 **Where** we found brethren,...	28:14
1 for **where** no law is, there is no transgression...	Rom 4:15
1 But **where** sin abounded,...	5:20
1 may bring me on my journey **whithersoever** I go...	1 Co 16:6
1 and **where** the Spirit of the Lord is, there is liberty.	2 Co 3:17
1 **where** Christ sitteth on the right hand of God...	Col 3:1
1 **When** your fathers tempted me, proved me,...	Heb 3:9
1 waters which thou sawest, **where** the whore sitteth,..	Rev 17:15

Hou is an adverb of place derived from the genitive case of the relative pronoun *hos* (3601B), "who, which." The basic meaning is "where," but it may have various nuances in the New Testament.

First, it can refer to a definite geographical place as in Luke 4:16, "And he came to Nazareth, *where* (*hou*) he had been brought up." If it does not follow a noun indicating a place, it would be rendered "the place which" (Matthew 2:9). Second, *hou* can refer to a Biblical reference, as in Luke 4:17, "He found the place *where* (*hou*) it was written." Third, it can refer to an indefinite place "wherever" (Matthew 18:20). An indefinite place is usually indicated by *ean* (1430) or *an* (300) preceding *hou*. Fourth, it may mean "whither" or "where to" when it accompanies a verb of motion: "And they drew nigh unto the village, *whither* (*hou*) they went" (Luke 24:28). Fifth, the word can refer figuratively to a set of circumstances as in Romans 4:15, "Where (*hou*) no law is, there is no transgression."

STRONG 3757, BAUER 589-90, MOULTON-MILLIGAN 464, LIDDELL-SCOTT 1267.

3620. οὐ ou partic

No, not.

1. οὐχ ouch
2. οὐκ ouk
3. οὐ ou

3 let your communication be, Yea, yea; **Nay**, nay:...	Matt 5:37
3 let your communication be, Yea, yea; Nay, **nay**:...	5:37
1 as one having authority, and **not** as the scribes...	7:29
3 But he said, **Nay**; lest while ye gather up the tares,...	13:29
2 he be of you that forsaketh **not** all that he hath,...	Luke 14:33

This objective negative adverb is found in Greek writings from the time of Homer (ca. Eighth Century B.C.). Before consonants the form is *ou*, before unaspirated vowels it is *ouk*, and before aspirated vowels it appears as *ouch*. These differences in spelling are for phonetic reasons only and do not change the meaning of the adverb.

The use of the word is the same throughout Greek literature. It is used as a negative for a statement of fact. As such it is normally used with the indicative mood; however, it is found in the papyri with the participle (*Moulton-Milligan*). In Homer when *ou* is used in a clause the negative is applied to a single word and not the entire clause (Autenrieth, *Homeric Dictionary*, pp.214f.). One method of expressing an affirmative is to negate the opposite of the affirmative. This is known as litotes, and *ou* is the negative frequently found in such constructions (ibid.). Examples are "*not* many days" (John 1:12) and "*not* a few women" (Acts 17:4). The meaning intended is a few days and many women.

In the Septuagint all the commandments of the Decalogue contain *ou* (Exodus 20:13-17; Deuteronomy 5:17-21). This use of *ou*, also found in the New Testament, is referred to as the negative of future prohibition (Matthew 5:21; 19:8; cf. *Bauer*).

When a direct question is asked expecting an affirmative reply, *ou* is used (ibid.). This is true in Homer, the Septuagint, and the New Testament. (When a negative reply is expected, the negative *mē* [3231] is used; cf. ibid.)

In Homer *ou* was sometimes doubled for emphasis (cf. *Liddell-Scott*). In the New Testament *ou* is joined by *mē* for emphasis (ibid.). Jesus is quoted by John (6:37) as saying, "I will in *no* wise cast out." When a verb is preceded by *ou* and therefore made negative, this may be made invalid by the use of *mē* which expects a negative reply. "Have they *not* heard?" (Romans 10:18) means they *have* heard.

STRONG 3756, BAUER 590-91, MOULTON-MILLIGAN 463-64, LIDDELL-SCOTT 1266-67.

3621. οὐά oua intrj

Aha!

1. οὐά oua

1 wagging their heads, and saying, Ah,	Mark 15:29

Oua is an interjection used to express amazement. *Oua* is the adaptation of the Latin *vah!* and was used by later Greeks (ca. Second and Third Century A.D.). In the New Testament *oua* is found only in Mark 15:29 where it is used as an expression of scornful wonder (*Bauer*).

STRONG 3758, BAUER 591, MOULTON-MILLIGAN 464, LIDDELL-SCOTT 1268.

3622. οὐαί ouai intrj

Alas, woe!

1. οὐαί ouai

1 Woe unto thee, Chorazin! ... unto thee, Bethsaida!	Matt 11:21
1 unto thee, Chorazin! woe unto thee, Bethsaida!	11:21
1 Woe unto the world because of offences!	18:7
1 but woe to that man by whom the offence cometh!	18:7
1 But woe unto you, scribes and Pharisees,	23:13
1 Woe unto you, scribes and Pharisees, hypocrites!	23:14
1 Woe unto you, scribes and Pharisees, hypocrites!	23:15
1 Woe unto you, ye blind guides, which say,	23:16
1 Woe unto you, scribes and Pharisees, hypocrites!	23:23
1 Woe unto you, scribes and Pharisees, hypocrites!	23:25
1 Woe unto you, scribes and Pharisees, hypocrites!	23:27
1 Woe unto you, scribes and Pharisees, hypocrites!	23:29
1 And woe unto them that are with child,	24:19
1 but woe unto that man by whom the Son	26:24
1 But woe to them that are with child,	Mark 13:17
1 but woe to that man by whom the Son of man	14:21
1 But woe unto you that are rich!	Luke 6:24
1 Woe unto you that are full! for ye shall hunger.	6:25
1 Woe unto you that laugh now! for ye shall mourn	6:25
1 Woe unto you, when all men shall speak well	6:26
1 Woe unto thee, Chorazin! ... unto thee, Bethsaida!	10:13
1 unto thee, Chorazin! woe unto thee, Bethsaida!	10:13
1 But woe unto you, Pharisees!	11:42
1 Woe unto you, Pharisees!	11:43
1 Woe unto you, scribes and Pharisees, hypocrites!	11:44
1 And he said, Woe unto you also, ye lawyers!	11:46
1 Woe unto you! for ye build the sepulchres	11:47
1 Woe unto you, lawyers!	11:52
1 but woe unto him, through whom they come!	17:1
1 But woe unto them that are with child,	21:23
1 but woe unto that man by whom he is betrayed!	22:22
1 yea, woe is unto me, if I preach not the gospel!	1 Co 9:16
1 Woe unto them! ... have gone in the way of Cain,	Jude 1:11
1 the midst of heaven, saying with a loud voice, Woe,	Rev 8:13
1 saying with a loud voice, Woe, woe, woe,	8:13
1 woe, to the inhabiters of the earth	8:13
1 One woe is past; and, behold, there come two woes	9:12
1 and, behold, there come two woes more hereafter.	9:12
1 The second woe is past; and, behold,	11:14
1 and, behold, the third woe cometh quickly.	11:14
1 Woe to the inhabiters of the earth and of the sea!	12:12
1 afar off for the fear of her torment, saying, Alas,	18:10
1 saying, Alas, alas that great city Babylon,	18:10
1 And saying, Alas, alas, that great city,	18:16
1 And saying, Alas, alas, that great city,	18:16
1 and cried, weeping and wailing, saying, Alas,	18:19
1 and wailing, saying, Alas, alas, that great city,	18:19

Septuagint Usage

The interjection *ouai* is found over 60 times in the Septuagint to express a variety of related emotions. It translates *hôy*, *'ôy*, and occasionally *'î*, *hôwâh*, and *hî*. These all derive from roots meaning "to howl" (Hillyer, "Woe," *Colin Brown*, 3:1051). This term was frequently used by the prophets in oracles of impending judgment (Ezekiel 16:23; Hosea 7:13). The list of woes directed at specific actions in Isaiah 5:8ff. parallels Jesus' denunciation of the Pharisees in Matthew 23:13ff. And yet, coupled with imminent judgment is the sense of warning and sorrow. God did not delight in judging rebellious Israel; He would relent if they would repent (cf. Hosea 11). *Ouai* is used to express the despair of the Philistines (1 Samuel 4:7 [LXX 1 Kings 4:7]), grief over a fallen prophet (1 Kings 13:30 [LXX 3 Kings 13:30]), mourning (Amos 5:16), and lament over realized sin (Lamentations 5:16). It can also express physical pain (Jeremiah 10:19).

New Testament Usage

This term occurs 41 times in the New Testament. The concept of judgment/warning/sorrow found in the Septuagint is carried over into the Synoptic Gospels. The cities of Chorazin and Bethsaida are warned that the miracles they witnessed should have been enough for them to believe, but now a harsh judgment awaits them (Matthew 11:21; Luke 10:13). Judgment dominated Jesus' denunciation of the Pharisee (Matthew 23:13ff.; Luke 11:42ff.), but sorrow was also present as evidenced by His lament over Jerusalem (Matthew 23:37-39). *Ouai* also expresses sorrow for those with children during the siege of Jerusalem (Luke 21:23), sorrow over the fate of Judas (Mark 14:21; Luke 22:22), and the personal grief that would result from failing to preach the gospel (1 Corinthians 9:16). The triple woe announced by an angel in Revelation 8:13 expresses intense sorrow for those who dwell upon the earth during the remaining trumpet judgments. *Ouai* is also used as a noun to represent the tribulations signaled by these trumpet blasts (Revelation 9:12; 11:14; note that similar end-time events, sometimes referred to as "messianic woes," can be found in Jewish apocalyptic literature, e.g., 4 Esdras 4:51 to 5:13; 2 Baruch 24; 1 Enoch 80:2, passim.). The final occurrences of *ouai* express the remorse and sadness felt by the kings, merchants, and sailors who had profited from wicked Babylon as they realize her impending doom (Revelation 18:10,16,19).

STRONG 3759, BAUER 595, MOULTON-MILLIGAN 464, LIDDELL-SCOTT 1268, COLIN BROWN 3:1051-54.

3623. οὐδαμῶς oudamōs adv
By no means, not at all.

1. οὐδαμῶς oudamōs

1 art **not** the least among the princes of Juda: .... Matt 2:6

Oudamōs is an adverb that denotes forceful negation (e.g., "most certainly not, indeed not"). The book of Maccabees in the Septuagint shows several occurrences of this term (e.g., 2 Maccabees 9:7,18; 11:4). However, its only New Testament occurrence is found in Matthew 2:6. Here the seemingly insignificant town of Bethlehem is told that it is by no means inferior in Judah because the Messiah would be born there.

STRONG 3760, BAUER 591, MOULTON-MILLIGAN 464, LIDDELL-SCOTT 1268.

3624. οὐδέ oude conj
And not, nor, neither.

1. οὐδέ oude
2. οὐδ' oud'

1	**Neither** do men light a candle, ... under a bushel, ...	Matt 5:15
1	**neither** will your Father forgive your trespasses.	6:15
1	and where thieves do not break through **nor** steal:	6:20
1	for they sow not, **neither** do they reap, ...	6:26
1	**neither** do they reap, **nor** gather into barns;	6:26
1	they toil not, **neither** do they spin:	6:28
1	That **even** Solomon in all his glory	6:29
1	**neither** can a corrupt tree bring forth good fruit.	7:18
1	not found so great faith, **no, not** in Israel.	8:10
1	**Neither** do men put new wine into old bottles:	9:17
1	**nor** the servant above his lord.	10:24
1	**neither** knoweth any man the Father, save the Son, ...	11:27
1	**neither** for them which were with him, ...	12:4
1	He shall not strive, **nor** cry;	12:19
1	**neither** shall any man hear his voice in the streets.	12:19
1	hearing they hear not, **neither** do they understand.	13:13
1	Do ye not yet understand, **neither** remember	16:9
1	**Neither** the seven loaves of the four thousand, ...	16:10
1	**Neither** tell I you by what authority I do these	21:27
1	did **not** even feel remorse (NASB)	Matt 21:32
1	**neither** durst any man from that day forth ask him	22:46
1	**neither** suffer ye them that are entering to go in.	23:13
2	great tribulation, ... no, **nor** ever shall be.	24:21
1	no, **not** the angels of heaven, but my Father only.	24:36
1	the angels of heaven, **nor** the Son, (NASB)	24:36
1	for ye know neither the day **nor** the hour	25:13
1	not to one of the least of these, ye did it **not** to me. ...	25:45
1	And he answered him to **never** a word;	27:14
1	**neither** was any thing kept secret, but that it	Mark 4:22
1	bind him ... **not** even with a chain (NIV)	5:3
1	and they had **no** leisure so much as to eat.	6:31
1	perceive ye not yet, **neither** understand?	8:17
1	**neither** will your Father which is in heaven forgive	11:26
1	**Neither** do I tell you by what authority I do these	11:33
1	And have ye **not** read this scripture;	12:10
1	**neither** left he any seed: and the third likewise.	12:21
1	no man, no, **not** the angels which are in heaven, ...	13:32
1	no man, ... **neither** the Son, but the Father.	13:32
1	But **neither** so did their witness agree together.	14:59
1	I know not, **neither** understand I what thou sayest.	14:68
1	unto the residue: **neither** believed they them.	16:13
1	Have ye **not** read so much as this, what David did, ..	Luke 6:3
1	**neither** doth a corrupt tree bring forth good fruit.	6:43
1	**nor** of a bramble bush gather they grapes.	6:44
1	**neither** thought I myself worthy to come	7:7
1	I have not found so great faith, **no, not** in Israel.	7:9
1	**neither** any thing hid, that shall not be known	8:17
1	putteth it in a secret place, **neither** under a bushel, ...	11:33
1	Consider the ravens: ... they neither sow **nor** reap;	12:24
1	ravens: ... which neither have storehouse **nor** barn;	12:24
1	If then you **cannot** do (NASB)	12:26
1	the lilies ... they toil not, they spin **not**;	12:27
1	that Solomon in all his glory was **not** arrayed like	12:27
1	no thief approacheth, **neither** moth corrupteth.	12:33
1	and the prophets, **neither** will they be persuaded, ...	16:31
1	**Neither** shall they say, Lo here! or, lo there!	17:21
1	I do not fear God **nor** respect man, (NASB)	18:4
1	would **not** lift up so much as his eyes unto heaven, ...	18:13
1	**Neither** tell I you by what authority I do these	20:8
1	**neither** can they die anymore, (NASB)	20:36
1	adversaries shall not be able to gainsay **nor** resist.	21:15
1	No, **nor** yet Herod: for I sent you to him;	23:15
1	rebuked him, saying, Dost **not** thou fear God, ...	23:40
1	and without him was **not** any thing made	John 1:3
1	not of blood, **nor** of the will of the flesh, ...	1:13
1	**nor** of the will of man, but of God.	1:13
1	if you are not the Christ, **nor** Elijah, (NASB)	1:25
1	Christ, nor Elijah, **nor** the Prophet? (NASB)	1:25
1	For the Father judgeth no man, (NT)	5:22
1	saw that Jesus was not there, **neither** his disciples, ...	6:24
1	For **neither** did his brethren believe in him.	7:5
1	Jesus said unto her, Neither do I condemn thee:	8:11
1	**neither** came I of myself, but he sent me.	8:42
1	**Nor** consider that it is expedient for us, ...	11:50
1	**neither** he that is sent greater than he that sent	13:16
1	because it seeth him not, **neither** knoweth him:	14:17
1	no more can ye, except ye abide in me.	15:4
1	because they have not known the Father, **nor** me.	16:3
1	could **not** contain the books that should be written.	21:25
1	**neither** wilt thou suffer thine Holy One	Acts 2:27
1	**neither** his flesh did see corruption.	2:31
1	for there is no other name (NASB) (NT)	4:12
1	**neither** said **any** of them that ought of the things	4:32
1	**Neither** was there any among them that lacked:	4:34
1	No, **not so much as** to set his foot on:	7:5
1	Thou hast **neither** part **nor** lot in this matter:	8:21
1	and neither did eat **nor** drink.	9:9
1	not lawful for us to receive, **neither** to observe, ...	16:21
1	**Neither** is worshipped with men's hands, ...	17:25
1	We have **not** so much as heard whether there be	19:2
1	**neither** count I my life dear unto myself, ...	20:24
1	**Nor** can they prove to you (NASB)	24:13
1	**neither** with multitude, **nor** with tumult.	24:18
1	**neither** is that circumcision, which is outward	Rom 2:28
1	There is none righteous, no, **not** one:	3:10
1	for where no law is, there is **no** transgression.	4:15

οὐδείς 3625

1	is not subject to the law ... **neither** indeed can be.	Rom 8:7
2	**Neither**, because they are the seed of Abraham,	9:7
1	is not of him that willeth, **nor** of him that runneth,	9:16
1	take heed lest he also spare **not** thee.	11:21
1	**nor** of the princes of this world,	1 Co 2:6
1	Indeed, even now you are **not** yet able, (NASB)	3:2
1	of man's judgment: yea, I judge **not** mine own self.	4:3
1	and such fornication as is **not so much** as named	5:1
1	Is it so, that there is **not** a wise man among you?	6:5
1	Doth **not even** nature itself teach you, that,	11:14
1	have no such custom, **neither** the churches of God.	11:16
2	and **yet** for all that will they not hear me,	14:21
1	if ... be no resurrection ... **then** is Christ not risen:	15:13
1	For if the dead rise not, **then** is not Christ raised:	15:16
1	**neither** doth corruption inherit incorruption.	15:50
1	made glorious had **no** glory in this respect,	2 Co 3:10
1	**nor** for his cause that suffered wrong,	7:12
1	Paul, an apostle, not of men, **neither** by man,	Gal 1:1
1	For I **neither** received it of man,	1:12
1	**Neither** went I up to Jerusalem	1:17
1	**neither** Titus, who was with me, being a Greek,	2:3
1	To whom we gave place by subjection, **no**,	2:5
1	There is neither Jew **nor** Greek,	3:28
1	there is neither bond **nor** free,	3:28
1	ye despised not, **nor** rejected; but received me	4:14
1	For **neither** they themselves who are circumcised	6:13
1	I have not run in vain, **neither** laboured in vain.	Phlp 2:16
1	exhortation was not of deceit, **nor** of uncleanness,	1 Th 2:3
1	**nor** are we trying to trick you. (NIV)	2:3
1	we are not of the night, **nor** of darkness.	5:5
1	**Neither** did we eat any man's bread for nought;	2 Th 3:8
1	to teach, **nor** to usurp authority over the man,	1 Tm 2:12
1	we **cannot** take anything out of it either. (NASB)	6:7
1	whom no man hath seen, **nor** can see:	6:16
2	For if he were on earth, he should **not** be a priest,	Heb 8:4
1	**Neither** by the blood of goats and calves,	9:12
2	Whereupon **neither** the first testament was	9:18
2	**Nor** yet that he should offer himself often,	9:25
1	**neither** hadst pleasure therein;	10:8
2	I will never leave thee, **nor** forsake thee.	13:5
1	**neither** was guile found in his mouth:	1 Pt 2:22
1	that ye shall neither be barren **nor** unfruitful	2 Pt 1:8
1	denieth the Son, the same hath **not** the Father:	1 Jn 2:23
1	sinneth hath not seen him, **neither** known him.	3:6
1	And no man in heaven, **nor** in earth,	Rev 5:3
1	in heaven, nor in earth, **neither** under the earth,	5:3
1	was able to open the book, **neither** to look thereon.	5:3
1	shall hunger no more, **neither** thirst any more;	7:16
1	**neither** shall the sun light on them, nor any heat.	7:16
1	**neither** shall the sun light on them, nor any heat.	7:16
1	the grass of the earth, **neither** any green thing,	9:4
1	**neither** any green thing, **neither** any tree;	9:4
1	did **not** repent of the works (NASB)	9:20
1	there was no longer a place found (NASB) (NT)	12:8
1	had not worshiped the beast **or** his image (NASB)	20:4
1	city had no need of the sun, **neither** of the moon,	21:23

This adverb is a combination of the negative particle *ou* (3620), "not," and the conjunction *de* (1156), "and," thus rendering "and not, nor," or "neither." It is related to the Greek word *mēde* (3234), "and not, but not" (cf. *Liddell-Scott*).

Some New Testament uses are: "nor" (Matthew 6:20,26), "neither" (Matthew 6:15), and "not even" (Matthew 6:29; 1 Corinthians 5:1). *Oude* may also be repeated many times in one sentence to connect negative sentences or clauses of the same kind (*Bauer*).

STRONG 3761, BAUER 591, MOULTON-MILLIGAN 464, LIDDELL-SCOTT 1268.

3625. οὐδείς oudeis num

No, not one, no one, none, nothing, worthless, vain, in no way.

1. οὐδενός **oudenos** card gen masc/neu
2. οὐδείς **oudeis** card nom masc
3. οὐδένα **oudena** card acc masc
4. οὐδεμία **oudemia** card nom fem
5. οὐδεμίαν **oudemian** card acc fem
6. οὐδέν **ouden** card nom/acc neu
7. οὐδενί **oudeni** card dat neu

6	it is thenceforth good for **nothing**,	Matt 5:13
2	**No man** can serve two masters:	6:24
7	**not** found such great faith (NASB)	8:10
2	**No man** putteth a piece of new cloth unto an old	9:16
6	Fear them not ... for there is **nothing** covered,	10:26
2	and **no man** knoweth the Son, but the Father;	11:27
6	did not speak ... without a parable (NASB)	13:34
3	they saw **no man**, save Jesus only.	17:8
6	and **nothing** shall be impossible unto you.	17:20
2	there is **none** good but one, that is, God:	19:17
2	They say unto him, Because **no man** hath hired us.	20:7
6	and found **nothing** thereon, but leaves only,	21:19
1	neither carest thou for **any man**:	22:16
2	And **no man** was able to answer him a word,	22:46
6	Whosoever shall swear by the temple, it is **nothing**;	23:16
6	Whosoever shall swear by the altar, it is **nothing**;	23:18
2	But of that day and hour knoweth **no man**,	24:36
6	and said unto him, Answerest thou **nothing**?	26:62
6	when he was accused ... he answered **nothing**.	27:12
6	When Pilate saw that he could prevail **nothing**,	27:24
2	**No man** also seweth a piece of new cloth on	Mark 2:21
2	And **no man** putteth new wine into old bottles:	2:22
2	**No man** can enter into a strong man's house,	3:27
2	and **no man** could bind him, no, not with chains:	5:3
2	neither could **any man** tame him.	5:4
3	And he suffered **no man** to follow him,	5:37
5	he could there do **no mighty work**,	6:5
6	no more to do **ought** for his father or his mother;	7:12
6	There is **nothing** from without a man,	7:15
3	and would have **no man** know it:	7:24
3	they saw **no man** any more, save Jesus only	9:8
7	This kind can come forth by **nothing**, but by	9:29
2	for there is **no man** which shall do a miracle	9:39
2	there is **none** good but one, that is, God.	10:18
2	There is **no man** that hath left house,	10:29
2	ye shall find a colt tied, whereon **never** man sat;	11:2
6	when he came to it, he found **nothing** but leaves;	11:13
1	we know that thou art true, and carest for **no man**:	12:14
2	And **no man** after that durst ask him any question.	12:34
2	But of that day and that hour knoweth **no man**,	13:32
6	and asked Jesus, saying, Answerest thou **nothing**?	14:60
6	But he held his peace, and answered **nothing**.	14:61
6	asked him again, saying, Answerest thou **nothing**?	15:4
6	Jesus yet answered **nothing**; ... Pilate marvelled.	15:5
7	neither said they any thing **to any man**;	16:8
6	neither said they **any thing** to any man;	16:8
2	**none** of thy kindred that is called by this name.	Luke 1:61
6	And in those days he did eat **nothing**:	4:2
2	**No prophet** is accepted in his own country.	4:24
5	But unto **none** of them was Elias sent,	4:26
2	and **none** of them was cleansed, saving Naaman	4:27
6	have toiled all the night, and have taken **nothing**:	5:5
2	**No man** putteth a piece of a new garment upon	5:36
2	And **no man** putteth new wine into old bottles;	5:37
2	**No man** ... having drunk old wine ... desireth new:	5:39

406

οὐδείς 3625

2	Among those that are born of women there is **not**...Luke	7:28
2	**No man**, when he hath lighted a candle,	8:16
1	had spent all ... neither could be healed of **any**,	8:43
3	he suffered **no man** to go in, save Peter, and	8:51
7	they kept it close, and told **no man** in those days	9:36
6	and told no man in those days **any** of those things	9:36
2	**No man**, having put his hand to the plow,	9:62
6	and **nothing** shall by any means hurt you.	10:19
2	**no man** knoweth who the Son is, but the Father;	10:22
2	**No man**, when he hath lighted a candle,	11:33
6	is **nothing** covered, that shall not be revealed;	12:2
2	**none** of those men which were bidden shall taste	14:24
2	that the swine did eat: and **no man** gave unto him.	15:16
2	**No servant** can serve two masters:	16:13
2	me good? **none** is good, save one, that is, God.	18:19
2	There is **no man** that hath left house, or parents,	18:29
6	And they understood **none** of these things:	18:34
2	on which **no one** yet has ever sat; (NASB)	19:30
6	And after that they durst not ask him **any** question	20:40
1	lacked ye any thing? And they said, **Nothing**.	22:35
6	said Pilate ... I find **no** fault in this man	23:4
6	but he answered him **nothing**.	23:9
6	examined him ... have found **no** fault in this man	23:14
6	and, lo, **nothing** worthy of death is done unto him.	23:15
6	I have found **no** cause of death in him:	23:22
6	but this man hath done **nothing** amiss.	23:41
2	where **no one** had ever lain. (NASB)	23:53
2	**No man** hath seen God at any time;...John	1:18
2	for **no man** can do these miracles that thou doest,	3:2
2	And **no man** hath ascended up to heaven,	3:13
6	A man can receive **nothing**, except it be given him	3:27
2	and **no man** receiveth his testimony.	3:32
2	yet **no man** said, What seekest thou?	4:27
6	The Son can do **nothing** of himself,	5:19
3	For the Father judgeth **no man**,	5:22
6	I can of mine own self do **nothing**:	5:30
2	**No man** can come to me, except	6:44
6	spirit that quickeneth; the flesh profiteth **nothing**:	6:63
2	**no man** can come unto me, except it were given	6:65
2	For there is **no man** that doeth any thing in secret,	7:4
2	**no man** spake openly of him for fear of the Jews.	7:13
2	and yet **none** of you keepeth the law?	7:19
6	he speaketh boldly, and they say **nothing** unto him.	7:26
2	Christ cometh, **no man** knoweth whence he is.	7:27
2	but **no man** laid hands on him,	7:30
2	but **no man** laid hands on him,	7:44
2	hath **no man** condemned thee?	8:10
2	She said, **No man**, Lord.	8:11
3	Ye judge after the flesh; I judge **no man**.	8:15
2	and **no man** laid hands on him;	8:20
6	and that I do **nothing** of myself;	8:28
7	and were never in bondage to **any man**:	8:33
6	If I honour myself, my honour is **nothing**:	8:54
2	the night cometh, when **no man** can work.	9:4
6	If this man were not of God, he could do **nothing**.	9:33
2	**No man** taketh it from me,	10:18
2	and **no man** is able to pluck them out	10:29
6	John did **no** miracle: but all things ... were true.	10:41
6	said unto them, Ye know **nothing** at all,	11:49
6	Perceive ye how ye prevail **nothing**?	12:19
2	Now **no man** at the table knew for what intent	13:28
2	**no man** cometh unto the Father, but by me.	14:6
6	prince of this world ... and hath **nothing** in me.	14:30
6	for without me ye can do **nothing**.	15:5
2	Greater love hath **no man** than this,	15:13
2	the works which **none** other man did,	15:24
2	and **none** of you asketh me, Whither goest thou?	16:5
2	and your joy **no man** taketh from you.	16:22
6	And in that day ye shall ask me **nothing**.	16:23
6	Hitherto have ye asked **nothing** in my name:	16:24
5	now speakest ... plainly, and speakest **no** proverb.	16:29
2	and **none** of them is lost, but the son of perdition;	17:12
3	Of them which thou gavest me have I lost **none**.	18:9
6	and in secret have I said **nothing**.	18:20
3	It is not lawful for us to put **any man** to death:	18:31
5	unto the Jews, ... I find in him **no** fault at all.	18:38
5	that ye may know that I find **no** fault in him.	19:4
5	Thou couldest have **no** power at all against me,....John	19:11
2	in which **no one** had yet been laid. (NASB)	19:41
6	and that night they caught **nothing**.	21:3
2	**none** of the disciples durst ask him, Who art thou?	21:12
7	Neither is there salvation in **any** other:...Acts	4:12
6	they could say **nothing** against it.	4:14
2	And of the rest durst **no man** join himself to them:	5:13
3	when we had opened, we found **no man** within.	5:23
6	and all, ... were scattered, and brought to **nought**.	5:36
7	For as yet he was fallen upon **none** of them:	8:16
3	and when his eyes were opened, he saw **no man**:	9:8
6	And put **no** difference between us and them,	15:9
6	which were there spent their time in **nothing** else,	17:21
2	and **no man** shall set on thee to hurt thee:	18:10
6	And Gallio cared for **none** of those things.	18:17
6	Artemis be regarded as **worthless** (NASB)	19:27
6	I kept back **nothing** that was profitable unto you,	20:20
1	But **none** of these things move me,	20:24
1	I have coveted **no man's** silver, or gold, or apparel.	20:33
2	they were informed concerning thee, are **nothing**;	21:24
6	and strove, saying, We find **no** evil in this man:	23:9
6	to the Jews have I done **no** wrong,	25:10
6	but if there be **none** of these things whereof these	25:11
2	**no man** may deliver me unto them.	25:11
5	**none** accusation of such things as I supposed:	25:18
6	saying **none** other things than those which	26:22
6	that **none** of these things are hidden from him;	26:26
6	This man doeth **nothing** worthy of death	26:31
4	for there shall be **no** loss of any man's life	27:22
1	shall not an hair fall from the head of **any** of you.	27:34
6	shook off the beast into the fire, and felt **no** harm.	28:5
6	I have committed **nothing** against the people,	28:17
6	There is therefore now **no** condemnation...Rom	8:1
2	For **none** of us liveth to himself,	14:7
2	and **no man** dieth to himself.	14:7
6	that there is **nothing** unclean of itself:	14:14
3	I thank God that I baptized **none** of you,...1 Co	1:14
2	Which **none** of the princes of this world knew:	2:8
2	even so the things of God knoweth **no man**,	2:11
1	yet he himself is judged of **no man**.	2:15
2	other foundation can **no man** lay than that is laid,	3:11
6	For I know **nothing** by myself;	4:4
2	there is **nobody** among you wise enough (NASB)	6:5
6	Circumcision is **nothing**,	7:19
6	and uncircumcision is **nothing**,	7:19
6	he knoweth **nothing** yet as he ought to know.	8:2
6	we know that an idol is **nothing** in the world,	8:4
2	and that there is **none** other God but one.	8:4
7	But I have used **none** of these things:	9:15
2	than have **any** man make my boast (NASB)	9:15
2	that **no man** speaking by the Spirit of God	12:3
2	and that **no man** can say that Jesus is the Lord, but	12:3
6	and have not charity, it profiteth me **nothing**.	13:3
2	but unto God: for **no man** understandeth him;	14:2
6	and **none** of them is without signification.	14:10
3	henceforth know we **no man** after the flesh:...2 Co	5:16
3	Receive us; we have wronged **no man**,	7:2
3	wronged no man, we have corrupted **no man**,	7:2
3	corrupted no man, we have defrauded **no man**.	7:2
5	were come into Macedonia, our flesh had **no** rest,	7:5
1	I was chargeable to **no man**:	11:9
6	in **nothing** am I behind the very chiefest apostles,	12:11
6	in nothing am I behind ... though I be **nothing**.	12:11
6	whatsoever they were, it maketh **no** matter to me:....Gal	2:6
6	be somewhat in conference added **nothing** to me:	2:6
2	**no man** is justified by the law in the sight of God,	3:11
2	yet if it be confirmed, **no man** disannulleth,	3:15
6	differeth **nothing** from a servant, though he be lord	4:1
6	for I am as ye are: ye have **not** injured me **at all**.	4:12
6	Christ shall profit you **nothing**.	5:2
6	that ye will be **none** otherwise minded:	5:10
2	For **no man** ever yet hated his own flesh;...Eph	5:29
7	that in **nothing** I shall be ashamed,...Phlp	1:20
3	For I have **no man** likeminded,	2:20
4	**no** church communicated with me ... but ye only.	4:15
6	creature of God is good, and **nothing** to be refused, 1 Tm	4:4
6	For we brought **nothing** into this world,	6:7

407

2	whom **no man** hath seen, nor can see:	1 Tm 6:16
2	**No man** that warreth entangleth himself with	2 Tm 2:4
6	that they strive not about words to **no** profit,	2:14
2	At my first answer **no man** stood with me,	4:16
6	but unto them ... unbelieving is **nothing** pure;	Tit 1:15
6	But without thy mind would I do **nothing**;	Phlm 1:14
6	he left **nothing** that is not put under him.	Heb 2:8
1	because he could swear by **no** greater,	6:13
2	of which **no man** gave attendance at the altar.	7:13
6	tribe Moses spake **nothing** concerning priesthood.	7:14
6	For the law made **nothing** perfect,	7:19
2	holiness, without which **no man** shall see the Lord:	12:14
3	God cannot ... neither tempteth he **any man**:	Jas 1:13
2	the tongue can **no** man tame; it is an unruly evil,	3:8
4	so can **no** fountain both yield salt water and fresh.	3:12
4	that God is light, and in him is **no** darkness at all.	1 Jn 1:5
2	**No man** hath seen God at any time.	4:12
2	which **no man** knoweth saving he that receiveth it.	Rev 2:17
2	he that openeth, and **no man** shutteth;	3:7
2	and shutteth, and **no man** openeth;	3:7
2	before thee an open door, and **no man** can shut it:	3:8
1	increased with goods, and have need of **nothing**;	3:17
2	And **no** man in heaven, nor in earth,	5:3
2	I wept much, because **no man** was found worthy	5:4
2	lo, a great multitude, which **no man** could number,	7:9
2	and **no man** could learn that song but	14:3
2	and **no man** was able to enter into the temple,	15:8
2	for **no man** buyeth their merchandise any more:	18:11
2	a name written, that **no man** knew, but he himself.	19:12

As an adjective *oudeis* means "no" (Luke 4:24; John 16:29). As a substantive it means "no one" or "nobody" (Mark 11:2). In the neuter it (*ouden*) means "nothing" (Matthew 17:20). It is a clear and emphatic negative. It means absolutely nobody or nothing.

Three words were combined into one for strong affirmation. *Ou* (3620) is the negative adverb used primarily with the indicative, the mood of affirmation and reality (as opposed to *mē* [3231] which is used with moods of unreality or contingency). It is an unequivocal negative. This *ou* is combined with the conjunction *de* (1156). The force of this combination in *oude* (3624) is "not even" (Matthew 6:29). The third element, the numeral *heis* (1506A), is the lowest possible number—one. The compound negative affirms: no one, not even to the number of one. The frequent use of *oudeis* reflects a clearly intended emphasis on the exclusive authority of the Law and the Gospel as well as the inescapable consequences of disregarding them.

In addition to the literal use of the neuter *ouden* (as "nothing"), it is used in a general sense as "worthless, meaningless," or "invalid" (*Bauer*; cf. Matthew 23:16,18; John 8:54). *Ouden* is also used in the accusative (of specification) and can be translated "in no respect, in no way," as in Acts 25:10 (where Paul affirmed that he had harmed the Jews in no way). Koine literature of the early Christian times contains parallel examples of these uses of *ouden* (ibid.).

STRONG 3762, BAUER 591-92, MOULTON-MILLIGAN 464-65, LIDDELL-SCOTT 1268-69.

3626. οὐδέποτε oudepote adv
Never.

לֹא (3940), Not; neither (Ex 10:6).

1. οὐδέποτε oudepote

1	I **never** knew you: depart from me,	Matt 7:23
1	saying, It was **never** so seen in Israel.	9:33
1	Jesus saith unto them, Yea; have ye **never** read,	21:16
1	Did ye **never** read in the scriptures,	21:42
1	Peter answered ... yet will I **never** be offended.	26:33
1	saying, We **never** saw it on this fashion.	Mark 2:12
1	Have ye **never** read what David did,	2:25
1	transgressed I **at any time** thy commandment:	Luke 15:29
1	and yet thou **never** gavest me a kid,	15:29
1	officers answered, **Never** man spake like this man.	John 7:46
1	for I have **never** eaten any thing that is common	Acts 10:14
1	unclean hath **at any time** entered into my mouth.	11:8
1	being a cripple ... who **never** had walked:	14:8
1	Charity **never** faileth:	1 Co 13:8
1	can **never** with those sacrifices	Heb 10:1
1	same sacrifices, which can **never** take away sins:	10:11

Oudepote can be found in classical Greek since the Eighth Century B.C. used as both an adverb and conjunction meaning "not ever, not even, never" (*Liddell-Scott*). It appears only a few times in the Septuagint with these same meanings. According to Louw and Nida it is an adverb denoting a negated indefinite point of time (*Greek-English Lexicon*, 1:630) rendering "never, not even," or "at no time."

In the New Testament it is used with the present (Matthew 7:23), past (Mark 2:12), and future tenses (Matthew 26:33), as well as in questions (Matthew 21:16,42). The KJV always translates it "never," with the exception of Luke 15:29 ("neither ... at any time," meaning "not ever").

STRONG 3763, BAUER 592, MOULTON-MILLIGAN 465, LIDDELL-SCOTT 1269.

3627. οὐδέπω oudepō adv
Not yet, never.

טֶרֶם ṭerem (3071), Not yet (Ex 9:30).

1. οὐδέπω oudepō

1	a sepulchre ... wherein **never** man before was laid.	Luke 23:53
1	because that Jesus was **not yet** glorified.	John 7:39
1	a new sepulchre, wherein **never** man yet laid.	19:41
1	For **as yet** they knew not the scripture,	20:9
1	For He had **not yet** fallen upon any (NASB)	Acts 8:16
1	he knoweth nothing yet as he ought to know.	1 Co 8:2

Classical Greek and Septuagint Usage
The adverb and conjunction *oudepō*, literally meaning "not yet," is a compound word made

up of the negative particle *oude* (3624), "and not, nor," and the enclitic particle *pō*, "up to this time, yet." It can be found as early as the Sixth and Fifth Centuries B.C. in the writings of Aeschylus and Plato (cf. *Bauer*). In the Homeric literature *oudepō* is mostly written with a word between *oude* and *pō* (e.g., *oud an pō*, "not yet then") and was always used with the past tense (cf. *Liddell-Scott*). By Plato's time it was being used with the present tense and is also found with the future tense in literature dating from the Fifth Century A.D. (ibid.). In the Septuagint *oudepō* is used only once, at Exodus 9:30 where it translates the Hebrew word *terem* "not yet."

New Testament Usage

In the New Testament *oudepō* occurs only five times: Luke 23:53; John 7:39; 19:41; 20:9; and 1 Corinthians 8:2. All of its uses in the Gospels refer to the true identity of Jesus. John 7:39 explains that Jesus' reference to the coming "rivers of living water" is a description of the Holy Spirit, who "was *not yet* given; because that Jesus was *not yet* glorified" (crucified, resurrected, and ascended). Both Luke and John recorded that when Jesus died He was placed in a tomb "wherein was *never* man *yet* laid" (John 19:41; cf. Luke 23:53). In other words, Jesus' body was not "corrupted" even in death (the Jews considered "used" tombs "unclean"). Even when Jesus died the disciples still did not understand from the Scriptures that He must "rise ... from the dead" (John 20:9).

STRONG 3764, BAUER 592, MOULTON-MILLIGAN 465, LIDDELL-SCOTT 1269.

3628. οὐθέν outhen num

Nothing, no one.

1. οὐθέν outhen card nom/acc neu
2. οὐθενός outhenos card gen masc/neu

2 And they said, "No, nothing." (NASB)		Luke 22:35
1 have found no guilt in this man (NASB)		23:14
1 He made no distinction between us (NASB)		Acts 15:9
1 Artemis will be discredited (NIV) (NT)		19:27
1 none of these things escape his notice (NASB)		26:26
1 and have not charity, I am nothing.		1 Co 13:2

The Greek word *outhen* (meaning "no, no one, nothing, worthless," and "in no way") is a later form of *oudeis* (3625). *Outhen* is never found before the late Fifth or early Fourth Centuries B.C., *oudeis* being the predominant word in use. However, around the late Fifth or early Fourth Centuries B.C., *outhen* became the most frequently used of the two. It was about 130 B.C. that *oudeis* began to reappear on the scene (cf. *Liddell-Scott*). *Oudeis* eventually displaced *outhen* so by the Third Century A.D. *outhen* was no longer found. In *Nestle-Aland 26th*, *outhen* appears 7 times compared to the more than 200 times that *oudeis* is used. The fact that *outhen* still appears in the uncials of the New Testament, being written in a time when *outhen* was no longer in general usage, bears witness to the great care the scribes took in copying the text accurately. For a discussion of how this word was used in the New Testament, see the word study at *oudeis* (3625).

STRONG 3762, BAUER 591-92 (see "oudeis"), MOULTON-MILLIGAN 465, LIDDELL-SCOTT 1269.

3629. οὐκέτι ouketi adv

No longer, no more.

אַיִן 'ayin (375), Not be, be no more (Jb 7:21, Ez 27:36).

אֶפֶס 'ephes (675), No (Am 6:10 [6:11]).

לֹא lō' (3940), No longer, never (Ex 5:7, Jb 7:7, Is 47:1).

1. οὐκέτι ouketi

1 Wherefore they are **no more** twain, but one flesh...		Matt 19:6
1 from that day forth ask him **any more** questions		22:46
1 able to bind him anymore, (NASB) (NT)		Mark 5:3
1 **no more** to do ought for his father or his mother;		7:12
1 they saw no man **any more**, save Jesus only		9:8
1 so then they are **no more** twain, but one flesh.		10:8
1 And no man **after that** durst ask him any question.		12:34
1 I will drink **no more** of the fruit of the vine,		14:25
1 Jesus yet answered nothing; (NT)		15:5
1 And am **no more** worthy to be called thy son:		Luke 15:19
1 and am **no more** worthy to be called thy son.		15:21
1 And **after** that they durst not ask him any question.		20:40
1 For I say unto you, I will not **any more** eat thereof,...		22:16
1 Now we believe, **not** because of thy saying:		John 4:42
1 disciples went back, and walked **no more** with him.		6:66
1 Jesus ... **no longer** continued to walk (NASB)		11:54
1 the world will behold Me **no more**; (NASB)		14:19
1 I will **not** speak much more with you, (NASB)		14:30
1 Henceforth I call you not servants;		15:15
1 and you **no longer** behold Me; (NASB)		16:10
1 and you will **no longer** behold (NASB)		16:16
1 she remembers the anguish **no more**, (NASB)		16:21
1 speak **no more** to you in figurative (NASB)		16:25
1 And I am **no more** in the world, (NASB)		17:11
1 they were **not** able to haul it in (NASB)		21:6
1 away Philip, that the eunuch saw him **no more**:		Acts 8:39
1 shall see my face **no more**.		20:25
1 that they should see his face **no more**.		20:38
1 Christ being raised from the dead dieth **no more**;		Rom 6:9
1 death hath **no more** dominion over him.		6:9
1 Now then it is **no more** I that do it,		7:17
1 **no more** I that do it, but sin that dwelleth in me.		7:20
1 And if by grace, then is it **no more** of works:		11:6
1 otherwise grace is **no more** grace.		11:6
1 But if it be of works, then is it **no more** grace:		11:6
1 otherwise work is **no more** work.		11:6
1 now walkest thou not charitably,		14:15
1 that to spare you I came **not as yet** unto Corinth.		2 Co 1:23
1 yet now henceforth know we him **no more**.		5:16
1 yet not I, but Christ liveth in me:		Gal 2:20

409

οὐκοῦν 3630

1 inheritance be of the law, it is **no more** of promise:	Gal 3:18
1 we are **no longer** under a schoolmaster.	3:25
1 Wherefore thou art **no more** a servant, but a son;	4:7
1 therefore ye are **no more** strangers and foreigners,	Eph 2:19
1 **Not now** as a servant, but above a servant,	Phlm 1:16
1 there is **no more** offering for sin.	Heb 10:18
1 there remaineth **no more** sacrifice for sins,	10:26
1 there shall be delay **no longer** (NASB)	Rev 10:6
1 for no man buyeth their merchandise **any more**:	18:11
1 and thou shalt find them **no more at all**.	18:14

The adverb *ouketi*, meaning "no more, no longer," or "no further," is a combination of the Greek words *ouk* (see 3620), "no, not," and *eti* (2068), "yet, still." Occasionally in extracanonical literature it occurs with a word between (e.g., *ou pampan eti*) or in reverse order (e.g., *etiouk*) (*Liddell-Scott*).

In the New Testament it is used literally when referring to time: "no longer" (Matthew 19:6; Luke 15:19), "never again" (Acts 20:25; Romans 6:9). At times Paul used *ouketi* logically in the "if-then" model of reasoning: "if by grace, then *no longer* by deeds" (Romans 11:6), and "if by the law, then *no longer* by promise" (Galatians 3:18).

STRONG 3765, BAUER 592, MOULTON-MILLIGAN 465, LIDDELL-SCOTT 1269.

3630. οὐκοῦν oukoun conj
So then.

1. οὐκοῦν oukoun

1 Pilate therefore said ... Art thou a king **then**?	John 18:37

The adverb *oukoun* is a compound term stemming from the negative particle *ouk* (see 3620), "no, not," and the conjunction *oun* (3631), "so, therefore." It has two basic usages which prevail from the classical period through the New Testament period. First, it is used in questions which invite assent to an inference, or to an addition to what has already received assent. Two examples of this usage can be seen in the writings of Xenophon (5–4 B.C.), *oukoun dokei soi*, "You think *then*, do you not . . . ?" (cf. *Liddell-Scott*) and in the Gospel of John (18:37), *Oukoun basileus ei su*, "Art thou a king *then*?" (literally, "not therefore a king?"). The anticipated answer to both of these questions is yes. When followed by the negative particle *ou*, a negative answer is expected (ibid.).

Second, *oukoun* is used in affirmative sentences (ibid.). In this sense it might be used in replies or answers that are affirmative. The appropriate translation would be "then, surely then, very well," or "yes." Its only use in the New Testament is in Pilate's question to Jesus (John 18:37) where it serves to introduce a question expecting a positive reply.

STRONG 3766, BAUER 592, MOULTON-MILLIGAN 465, LIDDELL-SCOTT 1270.

3631. οὖν oun partic

Then, now, therefore, so, consequently, in reply, in response, in turn, or the like, to be sure, surely, by all means, indeed, really, above all, certainly, but, however.

1. οὖν oun

1 **Wherefore** if they shall say unto you,	Matt 24:26
1 Watch **therefore**: for ye know not what hour	24:42
1 Watch **therefore**, for ye know neither the day nor	25:13
1 **therefore** to have put my money to the exchangers,	25:27
1 What shall **therefore** the lord of the vineyard do?	Mark 12:9
1 In the resurrection **therefore**, when they shall rise,	12:23
1 Submit yourselves **therefore** to God.	Jas 4:7

Oun is a postpositive conjunction (never occurring first in a sentence). In Homer (early classical Greek) its use was continuative rather than inferential (causative or result) (cf. *Bauer*). There is a strong resurgence of this merely continuative usage in the New Testament narratives, especially in the Gospel of John.

In Homer and many New Testament passages *oun* simply carries along the narrative without reference to cause or result. This reflects the ancient fondness for simple connectives ("such as, and") that seem redundant to the modern reader but that leave room for subtle nuances and insights. J.R. Mantey (Dana and Mantey, *Manual of the Greek New Testament*, p.253) says that *oun* should be translated "then" or "now" in this transitional, continuative, or resumptive sense in about 170 of the 496 times it occurs in the New Testament (Matthew 1:17; Luke 3:18; John 4:27,28).

About 200 times, according to Mantey (ibid.), *oun* should be translated by such inferential words as "therefore, so, consequently, then" (John 4:5,33). Whether *oun* is inferential or not must be determined by the context.

The continuative sense can have the force of a response in some contexts (John 4:7-9). In such cases *oun* could be translated "in reply, in response, in turn, or the like."

Oun is also used for emphasis (John 20:30). Sometimes it is in a group of particles or in a compound word to intensify the emphasis (1 Corinthians 6:7; Philippians 3:8). Possible translations are, "to be sure, surely, by all means, indeed, really, above all, certainly."

Oun can also be used as an adversative ("but" or "however"), (e.g., see Acts 26:21,22; 1 Corinthians 11:20).

STRONG 3767, BAUER 592-93, MOULTON-MILLIGAN 465-66, LIDDELL-SCOTT 1271-72.

3632. οὔπω oupō adv
Not yet.

1. οὔπω oupō

1 Do **not** ye **yet** understand,		Matt 15:17
1 Do ye **not yet** understand, neither remember		16:9
1 things must come to pass, but the end is **not yet**.		24:6
1 perceive ye **not yet**, neither understand?		Mark 8:17
1 "Do you **not yet** understand?" (NASB)		8:21
1 on which no one **yet** has ever sat, (NASB)		11:2
1 such ... needs be; but the end shall **not** be **yet**.		13:7
1 where no one had ever lain. (NASB) (NT)		Luke 23:53
1 mine hour is **not yet** come.		John 2:4
1 For John was **not yet** cast into prison.		3:24
1 and Jesus had **not yet** come to them. (NASB)		6:17
1 My time is **not yet** come:		7:6
1 I go **not** up **yet** unto this feast:		7:8
1 for my time is **not yet** full come.		7:8
1 because his hour was **not yet** come.		7:30
1 for the Holy Ghost was **not yet** given;		7:39
1 for his hour was **not yet** come.		8:20
1 Thou art **not yet** fifty years old,		8:57
1 Now Jesus was **not yet** come into the town,		11:30
1 for I am **not yet** ascended to my Father:		20:17
1 For **as yet** he was fallen upon none of them:		Acts 8:16
1 for **hitherto** ye were not able to bear it,		1 Co 3:2
1 he has **not yet** known as he might (NASB)		8:2
1 I do **not** regard myself as having laid hold (NASB)		Phlp 3:13
1 But now we see **not yet** all things put under him.		Heb 2:8
1 **not yet** resisted unto blood, striving against sin.		12:4
1 and it doth **not yet** appear what we shall be:		1 Jn 3:2
1 and one is, and the other is **not yet** come;		Rev 17:10
1 ten kings, which have received no kingdom as **yet**;		17:12

Oupō is an adverb of time used in negation and in questions. As an adverb of negation it is a strong negative (*Moulton-Milligan*), and in Homeric writings it is used to express the idea of "by no means" (*Homeric Dictionary*). Examples of the negation can be found in Matthew 24:6, "The end is not yet," and John 7:30, "His hour was not yet come." Matthew 15:17 and 16:9 exemplify the use of *oupō* in questions: "Do not ye yet understand?" and in Mark 8:17: "Perceive ye not yet?" *Oupō* occurs 23 times in the New Testament.

STRONG 3768, BAUER 593, MOULTON-MILLIGAN 466, LIDDELL-SCOTT 1272.

3633. οὐρά oura noun
Tail.

זָנָב zānāv (2264), Tail (Dt 28:13, Is 9:14f., 19:15).

1. οὐρά oura nom sing fem
2. οὐραί ourai nom pl fem
3. οὐραῖς ourais dat pl fem
4. οὐράς ouras acc pl fem

4 And they had **tails** like unto scorpions,		Rev 9:10
3 and there were stings in their **tails**:		9:10
3 in their mouth and in their **tails** (NASB)		9:19
2 their **tails** were like unto serpents, and had heads,		9:19
1 his **tail** drew the third part of the stars of heaven,		12:4

This term, which is related to *orros*, "rump," has two primary usages in classical Greek literature. It can refer to either the *tail* of an animal or the rearguard of an army. *Oura* is found in the New Testament only in the Book of Revelation where it occurs five times. It is used to describe the rear appendage of a scorpion, a horse, and a dragon. "Tails like unto scorpions" (Revelation 9:10) contain a venom which is injected into a victim through a sting at the end of the tail. The scorpion is a symbol of wrath. "For their tails were like unto serpents, and had heads" (Revelation 9:19) describes the tails of horses being used for punishment. The statement "and his tail drew the third part of the stars of heaven" (Revelation 12:4) refers to the dragon, the figure of Satan. In all references to a tail in Revelation the idea of punishment and judgment prevails.

STRONG 3769, BAUER 593, MOULTON-MILLIGAN 466, LIDDELL-SCOTT 1272.

3634. οὐράνιος ouranios adj
Heavenly.

COGNATE:
οὐρανός ouranos (3636)
SYNONYM:
ἐπουράνιος epouranios (2016)

שָׁמַיִם shāmayim (8452), Heavens (Dt 28:12—Codex Alexandrinus only).

1. οὐράνιος ouranios nom sing masc
2. οὐρανίου ouraniou gen sing fem
3. οὐρανίῳ ouraniō dat sing fem

1 as your **heavenly** Father is perfect. (NASB)		Matt 5:48
1 your **heavenly** Father will also forgive you:		6:14
1 yet your **heavenly** Father feedeth them.		6:26
1 your **heavenly** Father knoweth that ye have need		6:32
1 which my **heavenly** Father hath not planted,		15:13
1 So shall My **heavenly** Father also do (NASB)		18:35
1 your Father, He who is in **heaven**. (NASB)		23:9
2 a multitude of the **heavenly** host praising God,		Luke 2:13
3 I was not disobedient unto the **heavenly** vision:		Acts 26:19

Ouranios is an adjective used from the time of Homer. In the New Testament it was used by Matthew with the word "father" to designate the dwelling place of God: "our dwelling-in-heaven Father" (Matthew 6:14,26,32). Luke used the word to refer to an army of witnesses that appeared in order to announce the birth of Christ: they are called "a coming-from-heaven host" (Luke 2:13). Paul gave testimony of his Damascus Road experience stating that his commission issued through a vision which came from heaven (Acts 26:19). In all of these instances *ouranios* is aptly translated "heavenly."

STRONG 3770, BAUER 593, MOULTON-MILLIGAN 466, LIDDELL-SCOTT 1272-73, COLIN BROWN 2:188,191-92.

3635. οὐρανόθεν ouranothen adv
From heaven, from the sky.
CROSS-REFERENCE:
οὐρανός ouranos (3636)

1. οὐρανόθεν ouranothen

1 in that he did good, and gave us rain **from heaven**, Acts 14:17
1 I saw in the way a light **from heaven**,............. 26:13

Ouranothen is an adverb of place used in Greek writings since the time of Homer. It occurs twice in the New Testament (Acts 14:17; 26:13). Barnabas and Paul addressed the people of Lystra directing their attention from worshiping the apostles to the worship of God who "gave us rain from heaven" (Acts 14:17). In the third account of Paul's conversion experience Paul told King Agrippa, "At midday, O king, I saw in the way a light from heaven" (Acts 26:13). F.F. Bruce says *ouranothen* is an early poetical form equivalent to *ex ouranou* (Bruce, *Acts of the Apostles*, p.284).

STRONG 3771, BAUER 593, MOULTON-MILLIGAN 466, KITTEL 5:542-43, LIDDELL-SCOTT 1273, COLIN BROWN 2:188,193.

3636. οὐρανός ouranos noun
Heaven.
COGNATES:
ἐπουράνιος epouranios (2016)
μεσουράνημα mesouranēma (3191)
οὐράνιος ouranios (3634)
οὐρανόθεν ouranothen (3635)
SYNONYM:
παράδεισος paradeisos (3719)

אֵל 'ēl (418), God (Is 14:13).
אֱלוֹהַּ 'elôahh (438), God (Jb 22:26).
מָרוֹם mārôm (4953), Window, heavens (Is 24:18,21).
שַׁחַק shachaq (8263), Sky (Ps 89:37 [88:37]).

שָׁמַיִם shāmayim (8452), Heavens, heaven (Gn 1:1, 1 Kgs 8:22f., Ps 57:3 [56:3]).
שְׁמַיִן sh°mayin (A8453), Heaven, sky (Ezr 5:11f., Dn 2:37f., 4:26 [4:23]).

1. οὐρανός ouranos nom sing masc
2. οὐρανοῦ ouranou gen sing masc
3. οὐρανῷ ouranō dat sing masc
4. οὐρανόν ouranon acc sing masc
5. οὐρανέ ourane voc sing masc
6. οὐρανοί ouranoi nom pl masc
7. οὐρανῶν ouranōn gen pl masc
8. οὐρανοῖς ouranois dat pl masc
9. οὐρανούς ouranous acc pl masc

7	Repent ye: for the kingdom of **heaven** is at hand....	Matt 3:2
6	and, lo, the **heavens** were opened unto him,............	3:16
7	And lo a voice from **heaven**, saying,...................	3:17
7	Repent: for the kingdom of **heaven** is at hand..........	4:17
7	for theirs is the kingdom of **heaven**...................	5:3
7	persecuted ... for theirs is the kingdom of **heaven**.....	5:10
8	Rejoice, ... for great is your reward in **heaven**:........	5:12
8	and glorify your Father which is in **heaven**.............	5:16
1	verily I say unto you, Till **heaven** and earth pass,.....	5:18
7	shall be called the least in the kingdom of **heaven**:....	5:19
7	shall be called great in the kingdom of **heaven**.........	5:19
7	in no case enter into the kingdom of **heaven**............	5:20
3	neither by **heaven**; for it is God's throne;.............	5:34
8	be ... children of your Father which is in **heaven**:.....	5:45
8	even as your Father which is in **heaven** is perfect......	5:48
8	no reward of your Father which is in **heaven**............	6:1
8	Our Father which art in **heaven**,.......................	6:9
3	Thy will be done in earth, as it is in **heaven**..........	6:10
3	But lay up for yourselves treasures in **heaven**,.........	6:20
2	Behold the fowls of the **air**: for they sow not,........	6:26
8	your Father which is in **heaven** give good things.......	7:11
7	shall enter into the kingdom of **heaven**;...............	7:21
8	doeth the will of my Father which is in **heaven**........	7:21
7	and Isaac, and Jacob, in the kingdom of **heaven**........	8:11
2	and the birds of the **air** have nests;.................	8:20
7	preach, saying, The kingdom of **heaven** is at hand......	10:7
8	confess also before my Father which is in **heaven**......	10:32
8	also deny before my Father which is in **heaven**.........	10:33
7	least in the kingdom of **heaven** is greater than he.....	11:11
7	the kingdom of **heaven** suffereth violence,.............	11:12
2	Capernaum, which art exalted unto **heaven**,.............	11:23
2	I thank thee, O Father, Lord of **heaven** and earth,.....	11:25
8	shall do the will of my Father which is in **heaven**,....	12:50
7	to know the mysteries of the kingdom **of heaven**,.......	13:11
7	The kingdom of **heaven** is likened unto a man..........	13:24
7	The kingdom of **heaven** is like to a grain.............	13:31
2	birds of the **air** come and lodge in the branches......	13:32
7	The kingdom of **heaven** is like unto leaven,............	13:33
7	the kingdom of **heaven** is like unto treasure hid......	13:44
7	kingdom of **heaven** is like unto a merchant man,.......	13:45
7	the kingdom of **heaven** is like unto a net,............	13:47
7	which is instructed unto the kingdom of **heaven**........	13:52
4	and looking up to **heaven**, he blessed, and brake,......	14:19
2	that he would show them a sign from **heaven**...........	16:1
1	It will be fair weather: for the **sky** is red..........	16:2
1	foul weather ... for the **sky** is red and lowering.....	16:3
2	O ye hypocrites, ye can discern the face of the **sky**;...	16:3
8	but my Father which is in **heaven**......................	16:17
7	give unto thee the keys of the kingdom of **heaven**:.....	16:19
8	thou shalt bind on earth shall be bound in **heaven**.....	16:19
8	thou shalt loose on earth shall be loosed in **heaven**...	16:19
7	Who is the greatest in the kingdom of **heaven**?........	18:1
7	ye shall not enter into the kingdom of **heaven**.........	18:3
7	the same is greatest in the kingdom of **heaven**........	18:4
8	That in **heaven** their angels do always behold.........	18:10
8	the face of my Father which is in **heaven**.............	18:10
8	it is not the will of your Father which is in **heaven**,...	18:14
3	ye shall bind on earth shall be bound in **heaven**:.....	18:18

οὐρανός 3636

3 ye shall loose on earth shall be loosed in **heaven**...	Matt	18:18
8 done for them of my Father which is in **heaven**.......		18:19
7 the kingdom of **heaven** likened unto a certain king,....		18:23
7 eunuchs for the kingdom of **heaven's** sake.............		19:12
7 for of such is the kingdom of **heaven**................		19:14
3 and thou shalt have treasure in **heaven**:.............		19:21
7 hardly enter into the kingdom of **heaven**.............		19:23
7 For the kingdom of **heaven** is like unto a man........		20:1
2 whence was it? from **heaven**, or of men?.............		21:25
2 If we shall say, From **heaven**; he will say unto us,....		21:25
7 The kingdom of **heaven** is like unto a certain king,....		22:2
3 but are as the angels of God in **heaven**...............		22:30
8 for one is your Father, which is in **heaven**............		23:9
7 for ye shut up the kingdom of **heaven** against men:.....		23:13
3 And he that shall swear by **heaven**,..................		23:22
2 and the stars shall fall from **heaven**,................		24:29
7 and the powers of the **heavens** shall be shaken:.......		24:29
3 shall appear the sign of the Son of man in **heaven**:....		24:30
2 see the Son of man coming in the clouds of **heaven**....		24:30
7 his elect ... from one end **of heaven** to the other......		24:31
1 **Heaven** and earth shall pass away,....................		24:35
7 no, not the angels of **heaven**, but my Father only......		24:36
7 the kingdom of **heaven** be likened unto ten virgins,...		25:1
2 of power, and coming in the clouds of **heaven**.........		26:64
2 for the angel of the Lord descended from **heaven**,.....		28:2
3 All power is given unto me in **heaven** and in earth.....		28:18
9 he saw the **heavens** opened, and the Spirit.........	Mark	1:10
7 And there came a voice from **heaven**, saying,............		1:11
2 and the fowls of the **air** came and devoured it up.......		4:4
2 so that the fowls of the **air** may lodge.................		4:32
4 he looked up to **heaven**, and blessed,..................		6:41
4 And looking up to **heaven**, he sighed,.................		7:34
2 seeking of him a sign from **heaven**, tempting him.......		8:11
3 and thou shalt have treasure in **heaven**:...............		10:21
8 your Father also which is in **heaven** may forgive......		11:25
8 neither will your Father which in **heaven** forgive.....		11:26
2 The baptism of John, was it from **heaven**,..............		11:30
2 If we shall say, From **heaven**;......................		11:31
8 but are as the angels which are in **heaven**.............		12:25
2 And the stars of **heaven** shall fall,....................		13:25
8 and the powers that are in **heaven** shall be shaken.....		13:25
2 from ... the earth to the uttermost part **of heaven**.......		13:27
1 **Heaven** and earth shall pass away: but my words......		13:31
3 no man, no, not the angels which are in **heaven**,......		13:32
2 of power, and coming in the clouds of **heaven**.........		14:62
4 he was received up into **heaven**,.......................		16:19
4 the angels were gone away from them into **heaven**,..	Luke	2:15
4 and praying, the **heaven** was opened,...................		3:21
2 and a voice came from **heaven**, which said,............		3:22
1 **heaven** was shut up three years and six months,........		4:25
3 for, behold, your reward is great in **heaven**:............		6:23
2 and the fowls of the **air** devoured it.....................		8:5
4 looking up to **heaven**, he blessed them, and brake.....		9:16
2 that we command fire to come down from **heaven**,.....		9:54
2 Foxes have holes, and birds of the **air** have nests;......		9:58
2 thou, Capernaum, which art exalted to **heaven**,.......		10:15
2 I beheld Satan as lightning fall from **heaven**..........		10:18
8 rejoice, because your names are written in **heaven**....		10:20
2 I thank thee, O Father, Lord of **heaven** and earth,.....		10:21
8 Our Father which art in **heaven**,......................		11:2
3 Thy will be done, as in **heaven**, so in earth............		11:2
2 how much more shall your **heavenly** Father give.......		11:13
2 tempting him, sought of him a sign from **heaven**......		11:16
8 a treasure in the **heavens** that faileth not,............		12:33
2 ye can discern the face of the **sky** and of the earth;....		12:56
2 the fowls of the **air** lodged in the branches of it......		13:19
3 I say unto you, that likewise joy shall be in **heaven**...		15:7
4 I have sinned against **heaven**, and before thee,.........		15:18
4 son said ... Father, I have sinned against **heaven**,......		15:21
4 And it is easier for **heaven** and earth to pass,.........		16:17
4 that lighteneth out of the one part under **heaven**,......		17:24
4 shineth unto the other part under **heaven**;..............		17:24
2 Sodom it rained fire and brimstone from **heaven**,......		17:29
4 would not lift up so much as his eyes unto **heaven**,.....		18:13
3 have treasure in **heaven**: and come, follow me.........		18:22
3 peace in **heaven**, and glory in the highest.............		19:38
2 baptism of John, was it from **heaven**, or of men?......		20:4
2 If we shall say, From **heaven**; he will say,...........	Luke	20:5
2 fearful ... great signs shall there be from **heaven**.......		21:11
7 for the powers **of heaven** shall be shaken.............		21:26
1 **Heaven** and earth shall pass away: but my words.....		21:33
2 there appeared an angel unto him from **heaven**,.......		22:43
4 was parted from them, and carried up into **heaven**.....		24:51
2 I saw the Spirit descending from **heaven**..........	John	1:32
4 Hereafter ye shall see **heaven** open,...................		1:51
4 And no man hath ascended up to **heaven**,.............		3:13
2 but he that came down from **heaven**,.................		3:13
2 even the Son of man which is in **heaven**...............		3:13
2 nothing, except it be given him from **heaven**.........		3:27
2 he that cometh from **heaven** is above all...............		3:31
2 written, He gave them bread from **heaven** to eat.......		6:31
2 Moses gave you not that bread from **heaven**,..........		6:32
2 my Father giveth you the true bread from **heaven**.....		6:32
2 the bread ... he which cometh down from **heaven**,.....		6:33
2 For I came down from **heaven**, not to do mine own.....		6:38
2 I am the bread which came down from **heaven**.........		6:41
2 he saith, I came down from **heaven**?.................		6:42
2 This is the bread which cometh down from **heaven**,....		6:50
2 the living bread which came down from **heaven**:.......		6:51
2 This is that bread which came down from **heaven**;.....		6:58
2 Then came there a voice from **heaven**, saying,.........		12:28
4 and lifted up his eyes to **heaven**, and said,............		17:1
4 And while they looked stedfastly toward **heaven**.....	Acts	1:10
4 why stand ye gazing up into **heaven**?..................		1:11
4 Jesus, which is taken up from you into **heaven**,........		1:11
4 in like manner as ye have seen him go into **heaven**....		1:11
2 And suddenly there came a sound from **heaven**........		2:2
4 devout men, out of every nation under **heaven**.........		2:5
3 And I will show wonders in **heaven** above,............		2:19
9 For David is not ascended into the **heavens**:...........		2:34
4 Whom the **heaven** must receive until the times........		3:21
4 none other name under **heaven** given among men,.....		4:12
4 Lord, thou art God, which hast made **heaven**,.........		4:24
2 and gave them up to worship the host of **heaven**;......		7:42
1 **Heaven** is my throne, and earth is my footstool:.......		7:49
4 looked up stedfastly into **heaven**,......................		7:55
9 And said, Behold, I see the **heavens** opened,...........		7:56
2 there shined round about him a light from **heaven**:.....		9:3
4 And saw **heaven** opened,..............................		10:11
2 and creeping things, and fowls of the **air**.............		10:12
4 and the vessel was received up again into **heaven**.....		10:16
2 let down from **heaven** by four corners;................		11:5
2 and creeping things, and fowls of the **air**..............		11:6
2 But the voice answered me again from **heaven**,........		11:9
2 and all were drawn up again into **heaven**...............		11:10
4 God, which made **heaven**, and earth, and the sea,.....		14:15
2 seeing that he is Lord **of heaven** and earth,............		17:24
2 suddenly there shone from **heaven** a great light........		22:6
2 For the wrath of God is revealed from **heaven**......	Rom	1:18
4 Say not ... Who shall ascend into **heaven**?.............		10:6
3 that are called gods, whether in **heaven** or in earth,..	1 Co	8:5
2 the second man is the Lord from **heaven**..............		15:47
4 have a building of God, ... eternal in the **heavens**....	2 Co	5:1
2 with our house which is from **heaven**:.................		5:2
2 such an one caught up to the third **heaven**............		12:2
2 But though we, or an angel from **heaven**,..........	Gal	1:8
8 both which are in **heaven**, and which are on earth;..	Eph	1:10
8 the whole family in **heaven** and earth is named,.......		3:15
7 same also that ascended up far above all **heavens**,......		4:10
8 knowing that your Master also is in **heaven**;...........		6:9
8 For our conversation is in **heaven**,..................	Phlp	3:20
8 For the hope which is laid up for you in **heaven**,....	Col	1:5
8 that are in **heaven**, and that are in earth,.............		1:16
8 things in earth, or things in **heaven**....................		1:20
4 preached to every creature which is under **heaven**;.....		1:23
8 knowing that ye also have a Master in **heaven**.........		4:1
7 And to wait for his Son from **heaven**,..............	1 Th	1:10
2 Lord ... shall descend from **heaven** with a shout,......		4:16
2 when the Lord Jesus shall be revealed from **heaven**..	2 Th	1:7
6 and the **heavens** are the works of thine hands:......	Heb	1:10
9 high priest, that is passed into the **heavens**,...........		4:14
7 and made higher than the **heavens**;..................		7:26
8 the throne of the Majesty in the **heavens**;.............		8:1
8 that the patterns of things in the **heavens**.............		9:23

413

4 are the figures of the true; but into **heaven** itself, ...	Heb 9:24
8 in **heaven** a better and an enduring substance.	10:34
2 so many as the stars of the **sky** in multitude, ...	11:12
8 of the firstborn, which are written in **heaven**, ...	12:23
7 turn away from him that speaketh from **heaven**:	12:25
4 I shake not the earth only, but also **heaven**, ...	12:26
4 swear not, neither by **heaven**, neither by the earth, . . .	Jas 5:12
1 And he prayed again, and the **heaven** gave rain, ...	5:18
8 that fadeth not away, reserved in **heaven** for you, ...	1 Pt 1:4
2 Ghost sent down from **heaven**;	1:12
4 Who is gone into **heaven**, and is on the right hand	3:22
2 And this voice which came from **heaven** we heard, . . .	2 Pt 1:18
6 that by the word of God the **heavens** were of old, ...	3:5
6 But the **heavens** and the earth, which are now, ...	3:7
6 the **heavens** shall pass away with a great noise, ...	3:10
6 the **heavens** being on fire shall be dissolved, ...	3:12
9 look for new **heavens** and a new earth, ...	3:13
3 For there are three that bear record in **heaven**, ...	1 Jn 5:7
2 which cometh down out of **heaven** from my God:	Rev 3:12
3 and, behold, a door was opened in **heaven**:	4:1
3 and, behold, a throne was set in **heaven**, ...	4:2
3 And no man in **heaven**, nor in earth, ...	5:3
3 And every creature which is in **heaven**, ...	5:13
2 And the stars of **heaven** fell unto the earth, ...	6:13
1 And the **heaven** departed as a scroll	6:14
3 silence in **heaven** about the space of half an hour.	8:1
2 and there fell a great star from **heaven**, ...	8:10
2 and I saw a star fall from **heaven** unto the earth:	9:1
2 another mighty angel come down from **heaven**, ...	10:1
2 and I heard a voice from **heaven** saying unto me, ...	10:4
4 and upon the earth lifted up his hand to **heaven**, ...	10:5
4 that liveth for ever and ever, who created **heaven**, ...	10:6
2 And the voice which I heard from **heaven** spake	10:8
4 These have power to shut **heaven**, ...	11:6
2 heard a great voice from **heaven** saying unto them, . . .	11:12
4 And they ascended up to **heaven** in a cloud;	11:12
2 affrighted, and gave glory to the God of **heaven**.	11:13
3 and there were great voices in **heaven**, saying, ...	11:15
3 And the temple of God was opened in **heaven**, ...	11:19
3 And there appeared a great wonder in **heaven**;	12:1
3 And there appeared another wonder in **heaven**;	12:3
2 his tail drew the third part of the stars of **heaven**, ...	12:4
3 And there was war in **heaven**:	12:7
3 neither was their place found any more in **heaven**.	12:8
3 And I heard a loud voice saying in **heaven**, ...	12:10
6 rejoice, ye **heavens**, and ye that dwell in them.	12:12
3 and his tabernacle, and them that dwell in **heaven**.	13:6
2 so that he maketh fire come down from **heaven**.	13:13
2 a voice from **heaven**, as the voice of many waters, ...	14:2
4 and worship him that made **heaven**, and earth, ...	14:7
2 And I heard a voice from **heaven** saying unto me, ...	14:13
3 angel came out of the temple which is in **heaven**, ...	14:17
3 saw another sign in **heaven**, great and marvellous, ...	15:1
3 tabernacle of the testimony in **heaven** was opened:	15:5
2 And blasphemed the God of **heaven**	16:11
2 came a great voice out of the temple of **heaven**, ...	16:17
2 there fell upon men a great hail out of **heaven**, ...	16:21
2 I saw another angel come down from **heaven**, ...	18:1
2 And I heard another voice from **heaven**, saying, ...	18:4
2 For her sins have reached unto **heaven**, ...	18:5
5 thou **heaven**, and ye holy apostles and prophets;	18:20
3 voice of much people in **heaven**, saying, Alleluia;	19:1
4 I saw **heaven** opened, and behold a white horse;	19:11
3 the armies which were in **heaven** followed him	19:14
2 And I saw an angel come down from **heaven**, ...	20:1
2 and fire came down from God out of **heaven**, ...	20:9
1 whose face the earth and the **heaven** fled away;	20:11
4 And I saw a new **heaven** and a new earth:	21:1
1 first **heaven** and the first earth were passed away;	21:1
2 Jerusalem, coming down from God out of **heaven**, ...	21:2
2 And I heard a great voice out of **heaven** saying, ...	21:3
2 Jerusalem, descending out of **heaven** from God, ...	21:10

This substantive occurs in Greek literature from Homer onward. Its exact etymology is unclear; however, some conjecture that it has an Indo-European root meaning "water" (Bietenhard, *Colin Brown*, 2:188), or that it derives from *horos* meaning "boundary" and *ano* meaning "above," thus "the boundary above" (Aristotle *de Mundo* 400.a7; cf. Traub, "ouranos," *Kittel*, 5:498f.).

Classical Greek

Throughout classical Greek literature the term *ouranos* carries a dual sense. Simply put, it occurs in a literal, cosmological sense to describe what can be seen, the realm visible to mankind. It also occurs in a figurative, mythological sense to describe what cannot be seen, the realm pertaining to the gods. In the former sense *ouranos* may refer to the starry vault of heaven, the outermost regions of the earth, or to the entire order of creation. In the latter sense *ouranos* may occur as an appellation for the pre-Homeric god Uranus, the abode of the gods, or as a mantle for the world. The term never occurs in the plural in classical Greek (cf. *Liddell-Scott*).

Septuagint Usage

In the Septuagint *ouranos*, occurring more than 400 times for the Hebrew *shāmayim*, is used to denote heaven in at least three various senses. First, *ouranos* may refer to the firmament in which are foundations (2 Samuel 22:8 [LXX 2 Kings 22:8]), windows (cf. Genesis 7:11), and pillars (Job 26:11). In this sense it corresponds closely to the classical Greek concept of heaven as a vault stretched out over the earth. Second, it may refer to the area in which the birds fly, the atmosphere between the firmament and the earth (cf. Genesis 1:26,28,30). And third, *ouranos* may refer to a region without boundaries, a region in which God resides and from which God descends, possibly the region beyond the firmament (cf. Genesis 19:24; Exodus 19:18). In the Septuagint the term occurs for the first time in the plural, possibly in order to correspond with its Hebrew counterpart *shāmayim* which is also in the plural, thereby denoting completeness, fullness, or its various aspects.

New Testament Usage

In the New Testament three concepts may be expressed by *ouranos*. The first is the atmosphere that surrounds the earth. It is the place where the birds move (Matthew 6:26) and men observe the weather patterns (Matthew 16:2,3). Secondly, it denotes the cosmos and is mentioned with the earth to express God's creation (Matthew 5:18; Acts 4:24; Revelation 14:7). The third use of *ouranos* expresses the spiritual habitations. It is the place of God's throne (Matthew 5:34) and temple (Revelation 11:19). From heaven God the Father speaks (Matthew 3:17), sends forth good gifts (Luke 11:13), and reveals His wrath against all ungodliness (Romans 1:18).

After His resurrection, Jesus ascended into heaven (Acts 1:11). He sits at the right hand of the Father and appears before Him on our behalf (Hebrews 9:24). A place is being prepared there for His followers (John 14:2,3). All authority in heaven and on earth has been given to Jesus (Matthew 28:18), and He will one day be revealed from heaven (2 Thessalonians 1:7).

The Third Person of the Trinity also has His habitation in heaven. He descended from there upon Jesus as He came up out of the waters of baptism (Matthew 3:16). After His ascension, Jesus poured out the Holy Spirit upon His waiting disciples (Acts 2:4,33). Thus, as the One sent from heaven (1 Peter 1:12), He is called the "heavenly gift" (Hebrews 6:4).

The angels also reside in heaven. Those that appeared to the shepherds in the field are described as a "heavenly host" who returned after making their announcement (Luke 2:13-15). They surround the throne of God singing His praises (Revelation 5:11). Those that rebelled with Satan against God were expelled from heaven (Luke 10:18; Revelation 12:4).

The believer's hope is "laid up ... in heaven" (Colossians 1:5), an imperishable inheritance being reserved (1 Peter 1:4). Even now, the believer is seated in heavenly places in Christ Jesus (Ephesians 2:6)! Treasures and great rewards are laid up in heaven (Matthew 6:20; Luke 6:23) as well as a resurrected body that will one day clothe the believer (2 Corinthians 5:1,2).

The great goal of Biblical prophecy is the establishment of a new heaven and a new earth (Revelation 21:1). This earth, groaning from the corruption of sin (Romans 8:21ff.), will one day be destroyed (2 Peter 3:10; Revelation 20:11). It will be replaced by a new heaven and earth, characterized by righteousness (2 Peter 3:13; Revelation 21:1).

STRONG 3772, BAUER 593-95, MOULTON-MILLIGAN 466, KITTEL 5:497-538, LIDDELL-SCOTT 1273, COLIN BROWN 2:188-96.

3637. Οὐρβανός Ourbanos name
Urbane.

1. Οὐρβανόν Ourbanon acc masc

1 Salute **Urbane**, our helper in Christ, ... Rom 16:9

Recipient of a greeting from Paul; he was Paul's fellow worker (Romans 16:9).

3638. Οὐρίας Ourias name
Uriah.

1. Οὐρίου Ouriou gen masc

1 of her that had been the wife of **Urias**; .... Matt 1:6

The husband of Bathsheba whom King David had killed (Matthew 1:6; cf. 2 Samuel 11:6ff.).

3638B. οὖς ous noun
Ear.

אָזַן 'āzan (237), Listen; piel: ponder (Eccl 12:9).

אֹזֶן 'ōzen (238), Ear, hearing (Ex 11:2, 1 Sm 11:4, Is 42:20).

1. οὖς ous nom/acc sing neu
2. ὦτα ōta nom/acc pl neu
3. ὠσίν ōsin dat pl neu

1	and what ye hear in the **ear**, that preach ye	Matt 10:27
2	He that hath **ears** to hear, let him hear.	11:15
2	Who hath **ears** to hear, let him hear	13:9
3	and their **ears** are dull of hearing,	13:15
3	see with their eyes and hear with their **ears**,	13:15
2	But blessed are ... your **ears**, for they hear.	13:16
2	Who hath **ears** to hear, let him hear.	13:43
2	He that hath **ears** to hear, let him hear.	Mark 4:9
2	If any man have **ears** to hear, let him hear.	4:23
2	If any man have **ears** to hear, let him hear.	7:16
2	and put his fingers into his **ears**,	7:33
2	having **ears**, hear ye not? and do ye not remember?	8:18
2	the voice of thy salutation sounded in mine **ears**,	Luke 1:44
3	This day is this scripture fulfilled in your **ears**.	4:21
2	he cried, He that hath **ears** to hear, let him hear.	8:8
2	Let these sayings sink down into your **ears**:	9:44
1	and that which ye have spoken in the **ear** in closets	12:3
2	He that hath **ears** to hear, let him hear.	14:35
1	smote the servant ... and cut off his right **ear**.	22:50
3	stiffnecked and uncircumcised in heart and **ears**,	Acts 7:51
2	cried out with a loud voice, and stopped their **ears**,	7:57
2	these things came unto the **ears** of the church	11:22
3	and their **ears** are dull of hearing,	28:27
3	see with their eyes, and hear with their **ears**,	28:27
2	and **ears** that they should not hear; unto this day	Rom 11:8
1	as it is written, Eye hath not seen, nor **ear** heard,	1 Co 2:9
1	And if the **ear** shall say, Because I am not the eye,	12:16
2	are entered into the **ears** of the Lord of sabaoth	Jas 5:4
2	and his **ears** are open unto their prayers:	1 Pt 3:12
1	He that hath an **ear**, let him hear	Rev 2:7
1	He that hath an **ear**, let him hear	2:11
1	He that hath an **ear**, let him hear	2:17
1	He that hath an **ear**, let him hear	2:29
1	He that hath an **ear**, let him hear	3:6
1	He that hath an **ear**, let him hear	3:13

1 He that hath **an ear**, let him hear	Rev 3:22
1 If any man have **an ear**, let him hear.	13:9

Classical Greek

Ous is found in Greek writings since the time of Homer. At least three uses of the word can be found in Homer, the following from the *Iliad*: (1) to describe something as unheard or "out of hearing" (*Iliad* 18.272); (2) to describe the "four eared handles" of a drinking cup (*Iliad* 11.633); and (3) to identify the organ of hearing, e.g., " . . . and hit Antiphos by the ear with a sword" (*Iliad* 11.109). Herodotus quoted Xerxes who, in a fit of rage, said, "It is through the ears that you can touch a man to pleasure or to rage" (Histories 7.39). However, the eyes were considered better for belief than were the ears (Histories 1.8). The word *ous* is found to describe the physical organ of animals. For example, the Scythian horses "pricked their ears in consternation" at the braying of the Persian mules and donkeys (Histories, 4.129). In the papyri *ous* is commonly used not only for the human ear but also for a "handle" (Horst, "ous," Kittel, 5:545).

Septuagint Usage

In the Septuagint references are found to the adorning of the ears with earrings (Exodus 35:4). A slave could willingly become the permanent possession of a master by appearing at the city gate with his master and having his ear pierced (Exodus 21:6). In the Old Testament the ear also denotes the sense of hearing and the seat of "insight" (ibid., 5:546). Moses was commanded by God to "rehearse (a memorial) . . . in the ears of Joshua" (Exodus 17:14). This was to be a concentration of instruction, a repetition of the saying. This is a Hebraism that calls the hearer to a greater depth of understanding.

New Testament Usage

In the New Testament there is the literal use of the word *ous*. Mark 7:33 reports that Jesus put His fingers in the ears of a deaf man and gave hearing to him. Luke used *ous* in his record of Malchus losing his right ear to the sword of Peter (Luke 22:50). To say something into one's ear expresses a closeness to that person and denotes a degree of secrecy or confidentiality. This is true not only in the New Testament but is a carryover from classical writings where to speak in the ear of a god was to indicate a personal relationship with that god. However, in Peter this phrase has no indication of an intimate, secret conversation (1 Peter 3:12).

The *ous* is the organ through which the message of Jesus is to be received. The phrase "he who has ears" (or a similar phrase) occurs 15 times in the New Testament accounting for almost 50 percent of the occurrences of the word *ous* in the New Testament. With this phrase hearers are called to a deeper level than mere sense perception, namely, to hear the Word of God which can save them (Marshall, *New International Greek Testament Commentary, Luke*, p.320). One may refuse to hear by stopping his ears (Acts 7:57).

Ous is also used to indicate a mental or spiritual understanding (*Bauer*). The "ears" of the people were "dull of hearing" (Matthew 13:15; Acts 28:27), showing they did not understand or were unable to understand. The "uncircumcised in heart and ears" are those who are dead to or untouched by moral instruction (Acts 7:51).

STRONG 3775, BAUER 595, MOULTON-MILLIGAN 467, KITTEL 5:543-58, LIDDELL-SCOTT 1274.

3639. οὐσία ousia noun

Property, wealth, estate.
COGNATE:
  εἰμί eimi (1498)
SYNONYM:
  ὕπαρξις huparxis (5061)

1. οὐσίας ousias gen sing fem
2. οὐσίαν ousian acc sing fem

1 give me the portion of **goods** that falleth to me	Luke 15:12
2 and there wasted his **substance** with riotous living	15:13

Classical Greek and Septuagint Usage

The word *ousia* can be found in classical Greek of both material items that one owns and immaterial things, i.e., "substance, essence, true nature" (*Liddell-Scott*).

This term is found only twice in the Septuagint and both of these are in the Apocrypha. In Tobit 14:13 a certain man inherited the "estate" of his in-laws whom he had taken exceptional care of in their old age. In the second reference King Ptolemy Philopator issued a letter to his generals and soldiers in Egypt declaring that anyone found aiding a Jew would be severely treated. The offender and his family were to be tortured to death and their "estate" was to be given to the informer (3 Maccabees 3:28). Both of these references seem to indicate that *ousia* was used to represent *all* that an individual owned, the entire estate.

New Testament Usage

This meaning is continued in the only two occurrences of *ousia* in the New Testament. In the Parable of the Prodigal Son, the younger of two sons asked his father to give him his share of the "estate" (*tēs ousias*; Luke 15:12). If the right of the firstborn was followed (see Deuteronomy 21:17), then the younger son received a third of his father's property. The father retained the use and benefits of his property until his death. If the property was sold (which the prodigal apparently did, see verse 13), the new owner could not take possession until the father died (Jeremias, *The Parables of Jesus*, pp.128,129). The father agreed to this highly unusual request, and the boy set off for a distant country. He then proceeded to waste his "wealth" (*tēn ousian*) in wild living (Luke 15:13). This parable could be called "The Parable of the Father's Love." Just as the father in the parable received back his wayward son, so the Heavenly Father lovingly receives back all those who return to Him in repentance.

STRONG 3776, BAUER 596, MOULTON-MILLIGAN 467, LIDDELL-SCOTT 1274-75, COLIN BROWN 2:845-46.

3640. οὖς ous

See word study at number 3638B.

3641. οὔτε oute conj

Neither, and not, neither...nor.

1. οὔτε oute

1	where **neither** moth nor rust doth corrupt,	Matt 6:20
1	where **neither** moth nor rust doth corrupt,	6:20
1	**neither** in this world, **neither** in the world to come.	12:32
1	**neither** in this world, **neither** in the world to come.	12:32
1	For in the resurrection they **neither** marry,	22:30
1	they neither marry, **nor** are given in marriage,	22:30
1	and no man could bind him, **no**, **not** with chains:	Mark 5:3
1	they **neither** marry, **nor** are given in marriage;	12:25
1	they neither marry, **nor** are given in marriage;	12:25
1	I **neither** know **nor** understand what you (NASB)	14:68
1	I neither know **nor** understand what you (NASB)	14:68
1	they **neither** sow nor reap; (NASB)	Luke 12:24
1	they neither sow **nor** reap; (NASB)	12:24
1	If ye then be **not** able to do that ... which is least,	12:26
1	the lilies ... they **neither** toil nor spin (NASB)	12:27
1	the lilies ... they neither toil **nor** spin (NASB)	12:27
1	**neither** fit for the land, nor yet for the dunghill;	14:35
1	neither fit for the land, **nor** yet for the dunghill;	14:35
1	**neither** marry, nor are given in marriage:	20:35
1	neither marry, **nor** are given in marriage:	20:35
1	**Neither** can they die any more:	20:36
1	if thou be not Christ, **nor** Elias,	John 1:25
1	not that Christ, nor Elias, **neither** that prophet?	1:25
1	thou hast **nothing** to draw with,	4:11
1	when ye shall **neither** in this mountain,	4:21
1	nor yet at Jerusalem, worship the Father.	John 4:21
1	Ye have **neither** heard his voice at any time,	5:37
1	neither heard his voice ... **nor** seen his shape.	5:37
1	Ye **neither** know me, nor my Father:	8:19
1	Ye neither know me, **nor** my Father:	8:19
1	**Neither** hath this man sinned, nor his parents:	9:3
1	Neither hath this man sinned, **nor** his parents:	9:3
1	he was **not** abandoned (NIV)	Acts 2:31
1	**nor** did his body undergo decay (NIV)	2:31
1	**none** other name under heaven given among men,	4:12
1	**neither** our fathers nor we were able to bear?	15:10
1	neither our fathers **nor** we were able to bear?	15:10
1	which are **neither** robbers of churches,	19:37
1	**nor** yet blasphemers of your goddess.	19:37
1	**neither** found me in the temple disputing	24:12
1	**neither** in the synagogues, nor in the city:	24:12
1	neither in the synagogues, **nor** in the city:	24:12
1	**Neither** can they prove the things	24:13
1	**Neither** against the law of the Jews,	25:8
1	**neither** against the temple,	25:8
1	**nor** yet against Caesar,	25:8
1	We **neither** received letters out of Judaea	28:21
1	**neither** any of the brethren that came showed	28:21
1	For I am persuaded, that **neither** death, nor life,	Rom 8:38
1	For I am persuaded, that neither death, **nor** life,	8:38
1	**nor** angels, nor principalities, nor powers,	8:38
1	nor angels, **nor** principalities, nor powers,	8:38
1	nor angels, nor principalities, **nor** powers,	8:38
1	**nor** things present, nor things to come,	8:38
1	nor things present, **nor** things to come,	8:38
1	**Nor** height, nor depth, nor any other creature,	8:39
1	Nor height, **nor** depth, nor any other creature,	8:39
1	Nor height, nor depth, **nor** any other creature,	8:39
1	not able to bear it, **neither** yet now are ye able.	1 Co 3:2
1	So then **neither** is he that planteth any thing,	3:7
1	that planteth any thing, **neither** he that watereth;	3:7
1	**neither** fornicators, nor idolaters, nor adulterers,	6:9
1	neither fornicators, **nor** idolaters, nor adulterers,	6:9
1	neither fornicators, nor idolaters, **nor** adulterers,	6:9
1	nor idolaters, nor adulterers, **nor** effeminate,	6:9
1	nor abusers of themselves with mankind,	6:9
1	**Nor** thieves, nor covetous, nor drunkards,	6:10
1	Nor thieves, **nor** covetous, nor drunkards,	6:10
1	Nor thieves, nor covetous, **nor** drunkards,	6:10
1	for **neither**, if we eat, are we the better;	8:8
1	**neither**, if we eat not, are we the worse.	8:8
1	**neither** is the man without the woman,	11:11
1	**neither** the woman without the man, in the Lord.	11:11
1	**neither** received it of man, **neither** was I taught it,	Gal 1:12
1	**neither** circumcision availeth any thing,	5:6
1	neither circumcision ... **nor** uncircumcision;	5:6
1	**neither** circumcision availeth any thing,	6:15
1	**nor** uncircumcision, but a new creature.	6:15
1	was not of deceit, nor of uncleanness, **nor** in guile:	1 Th 2:3
1	For **neither** at any time used we flattering words,	2:5
1	**nor** a cloak of covetousness; God is witness:	2:5
1	**Nor** of men sought we glory, neither of you,	2:6
1	sought we glory, **neither** of you, nor yet of others,	2:6
1	sought we glory, neither of you, **nor** yet of others,	2:6
1	**Neither** can salt water produce fresh. (NASB)	Jas 3:12
1	**neither** doth he himself receive the brethren,	3 Jn 1:10
1	know thy works, that thou art **neither** cold nor hot:	Rev 3:15
1	know thy works, that thou art neither cold **nor** hot:	3:15
1	thou art lukewarm, and **neither** cold nor hot,	3:16
1	thou art lukewarm, and neither cold **nor** hot,	3:16
1	open the book, or to look into it (NASB)	5:3
1	open and to read the book, **neither** to look thereon.	5:4
1	not killed by these plagues yet repented not	9:20
1	idols ... which **neither** can see, nor hear, nor walk:	9:20
1	idols ... which neither can see, **nor** hear, nor walk:	9:20
1	idols ... which neither can see, nor hear, **nor** walk:	9:20
1	**nor** of their sorceries, nor of their fornication,	9:21
1	**nor** of their fornication, nor of their thefts.	9:21
1	nor of their fornication, **nor** of their thefts.	9:21
1	**neither** was their place found any more in heaven.	12:8
1	had not worshipped the beast, **neither** his image,	20:4
1	and there shall be no more death, **neither** sorrow,	21:4

1 shall be no more death, neither sorrow, **nor** crying, Rev 21:4	
1 **neither** shall there be any more pain:	21:4

Oute, when used once in a clause or sentence, is a negative adverb that is translated "neither" or "nothing." The woman at Sychar's well told Jesus, "Thou hast *nothing* (*oute*) to draw with" (John 4:11). When used more than once *oute* is a negative correlative uniting words or clauses and is translated "neither" the first time and "nor" each time after that. In Romans 8:38,39 *oute* appears 10 times, and in 1 Corinthians 6:9,10 it appears 7 times.

STRONG 3777, BAUER 596, MOULTON-MILLIGAN 467, LIDDELL-SCOTT 1275.

3642. οὗτος houtos dem-pron

This, this one, he, (and at) that.

1. τούτου **toutou** gen sing masc/neu
2. τούτων **toutōn** gen pl masc/neu
3. τούτοις **toutois** dat pl masc/neu
4. οὗτος **houtos** nom sing masc
5. τούτῳ **toutō** dat sing masc
6. τοῦτον **touton** acc sing masc
7. οὗτοι **houtoi** nom pl masc
8. τούτους **toutous** acc pl masc
9. αὕτη **hautē** nom sing fem
10. ταύτης **tautēs** gen sing fem
11. ταύτῃ **tautē** dat sing fem
12. ταύτην **tautēn** acc sing fem
13. αὗται **hautai** nom pl fem
14. ταύταις **tautais** dat pl fem
15. ταύτας **tautas** acc pl fem
16. τοῦτ' **tout'** nom/acc sing neu
17. τοῦτο **touto** nom/acc sing neu
18. ταῦτα **tauta** nom/acc pl neu

18 saith unto him, All **these things** will I give thee,	Matt 4:9
8 Therefore whosoever heareth **these** sayings of mine,	7:24
5 and I say **to this man**, Go, and he goeth;	8:9
17 and to my servant, Do **this**, and he doeth it.	8:9
18 While he spake **these things** unto them,	9:18
17 that I may preach ... for **therefore** came I forth.	Mark 1:38

Houtos is the regular demonstrative pronoun used of something or somebody comparatively near at hand or more present to the writer's thought. It means "this" as distinct from "that" (*ekeinos* [1552]), the more remote demonstrative.

Robertson (*Grammar of the Greek New Testament*, p.697) calls *houtos* a doubled demonstrative. Since the Greek article still retains some of its original demonstrative force, the virtual doubling of the article in the stem of *houtos* makes a naturally specific and strong demonstrative pronoun.

Houtos can be used as an adjective ("this") or it can stand by itself as a substantive ("this one," "he").

The substantive can refer to one who is locally near (Matthew 3:17), can express contempt (Matthew 13:55), can refer to what precedes (Matthew 3:15), or can introduce what follows (John 3:19). It can also call attention to a subject more remote in the paragraph but closer to the main concept under discussion (2 John 7). In addition, it may be used in certain idioms as with *men* (3173) and *de* (1156) ("partly . . . partly") in Hebrews 10:33 or *tout' estin* ("that is to say") in Matthew 27:46.

STRONG 3778, BAUER 596, MOULTON-MILLIGAN 467, LIDDELL-SCOTT 1275-76.

3643. οὕτως houtōs adv

In this manner, thus, so, just as, in this way, as follows, without further ado, simply.

אָז 'āz (226), Then (Jb 11:15, Mi 3:4).
זֶה zeh (2172), This (Dt 15:2, Is 63:1).
כֹּה kōh (3662), Thus, this (Nm 8:7, 2 Chr 32:10, Jer 29:4 [36:4]).
כִּי kî (3706), So (2 Sm 16:10).
כֵּן kēn (3772), Just as, as soon as (Gn 41:13, 1 Sm 9:13).

1. οὕτως houtōs
2. οὕτω houtō

1 **Even so** shall it be also unto this wicked generation. Matt 12:45

Houtōs (more rarely *houtō*) is the adverb derived from the demonstrative pronoun *houtos* (3642) by lengthening the final vowel. It describes the manner of the verbal action or state of being. "This" becomes: "thus, so, in this manner." Comparison, summary, or degree of emphasis is often the thrust of the word.

When referring to what has gone before, correlative words may or may not be used as: *kathaper* (2481), *hōsper* (5450), *kath' hoson*, meaning "just as" in Matthew 12:40; Romans 12:4f.; and Hebrews 9:27f. *Houtōs* may be used to point to the moral after figures of speech, parables, and illustrations (Matthew 5:16).

Referring to what follows, *houtōs* may be translated "in this way" or "as follows." Immediately after the adverb, the words to be quoted either follow as direct discourse, or the gist of what was said or done may be given in indirect discourse.

Houtōs may also denote degree or extent in an adjective that it modifies, "so great" (Revelation 16:18), "so frightful" (Hebrews 12:21).

Classical Greek brings out the meaning "without further ado, just, simply." This may be the meaning in John 4:6 when Jesus simply sat on the well while the disciples went to Sychar.

A few times there is an adjective or substantive force: The birth of Jesus was "something like this" (Matthew 1:18); never was seen "anything like this" (Matthew 9:33); "something like this" the Lord has done to me (Luke 1:25).

STRONG 3779, BAUER 597-98, MOULTON-MILLIGAN 467-68, LIDDELL-SCOTT 1276-77.

3644. οὐχί ouchi adv

Not, not so, by no means, no.

1. οὐχί ouchi

1 do **not** even the publicans the same?	Matt 5:46
1 more than others? do **not** even the publicans so?	5:47
1 Is **not** the life more than meat,	6:25
1 Are **not** two sparrows sold for a farthing?	10:29
1 will he **not** lay hold on it, and lift it out?	12:11
1 didst **not** thou sow good seed in thy field?	13:27
1 is **not** his mother called Mary?	13:55
1 And his sisters, are they **not** all with us?	13:56
1 doth he **not** leave the ninety and nine,	18:12
1 didst **not** thou agree with me for a penny?	20:13
1 Not so; but he shall be called John,	Luke 1:60
1 "Is this **not** Joseph's son?" (NASB)	4:22
1 shall they **not** both fall into the ditch?	6:39
1 Are **not** five sparrows sold for two farthings,	12:6
1 I tell you, Nay; but rather division:	12:51
1 I tell you, Nay: but, except ye repent,	13:3
1 I tell you, Nay: but, except ye repent,	13:5
1 sitteth **not** down first, and counteth the cost,	14:28
1 war against another king, sitteth **not** down first,	14:31
1 if she lose one piece, doth **not** light a candle,	15:8
1 And he said, Nay, father Abraham: but if one went	16:30
1 And will **not** rather say unto him,	17:8
1 Jesus answering said, Were there **not** ten cleansed?	17:17
1 who shall **not** receive many times (NASB)	18:30
1 is **not** he that sitteth at meat?	22:27
1 saying, "Are You **not** the Christ? (NASB)	23:39
1 Ought **not** Christ to have suffered these things,	24:26
1 Did **not** our heart burn within us,	24:32
1 Hath **not** the scripture said,	John 7:42
1 saying, "No, but He is like him." (NASB)	9:9
1 Are there **not** twelve hours in the day?	11:9
1 and ye are clean, but **not** all.	13:10
1 therefore said he, Ye are **not** all clean.	13:11
1 manifest thyself unto us, and **not** unto the world?	14:22
1 Whiles it remained, was it **not** thine own?	Acts 5:4
1 Hath **not** my hand made all these things?	7:50
1 shall **not** his uncircumcision be counted for	Rom 2:26
1 By what law? of works? Nay: ... by the law of faith.	3:27
1 is he **not** also of the Gentiles?	3:29
1 shall he **not** with him also freely give us all things?	8:32
1 **not** God made foolish the wisdom of this world?	1 Co 1:20
1 and divisions, are ye **not** carnal, and walk as men?	3:3
1 and another, I am of Apollos; are ye **not** carnal?	3:4
1 ye are puffed up, and have **not** rather mourned,	5:2
1 do **not** ye judge them that are within?	5:12
1 to law before the unjust, and **not** before the saints?	1 Co 6:1
1 Why do ye **not** rather take wrong?	6:7
1 do ye **not** rather suffer yourselves to be defrauded?	6:7
1 shall **not** the conscience of him which is weak	8:10
1 have I **not** seen Jesus Christ our Lord?	9:1
1 or saith **not** the law the same also?	9:8
1 is it **not** the communion of the blood of Christ?	10:16
1 is it **not** the communion of the body of Christ?	10:16
1 are **not** they which eat of the sacrifices partakers	10:18
1 Conscience, I say, **not** thine own, but of the other:	10:29
1 How shall **not** the ministration of the spirit be	2 Co 3:8
1 we will **not** boast of things without our measure,	10:13
1 Are **not** even ye in the presence of our Lord Jesus	1 Th 2:19
1 Are they **not** all ministering spirits,	Heb 1:14
1 was it **not** with them that had sinned,	3:17

Ouchi is a strengthened form of *ou* (3620) found in Greek literature from the time of Homer. Of the 56 occurrences in the New Testament, it is translated 46 times as an interrogative in questions that anticipate an affirmative answer ("do *not* even the publicans the same?" Matthew 5:46). As a simple negative it is a strong "no," usually meaning "not at all" ("Ye are *not* all clean," John 13:11). When *ouchi* is used in answer to a question it is translated "by no means" or "not so" ("*Not* so; ... he shall be called John," Luke 1:60).

STRONG 3780, BAUER 598, MOULTON-MILLIGAN 468, LIDDELL-SCOTT 1266-68 (see "ou").

3645. ὀφειλέτης opheiletēs noun

Debtor, one who is obligated, one who is guilty (or) at fault, transgressor.

COGNATE:
 ὀφείλω opheilō (3648)
SYNONYMS:
 ἁμαρτωλός hamartōlos (266)
 χρεοφειλέτης chreopheiletēs (5367B)

1. ὀφειλέτης opheiletēs nom sing masc
2. ὀφειλέται opheiletai nom pl masc
3. ὀφειλέταις opheiletais dat pl masc

3 forgive us our debts, as we forgive our **debtors**.	Matt 6:12
1 **which owed** him ten thousand talents.	18:24
2 think ye that they were **sinners** above all men	Luke 13:4
1 I am **debtor** both to the Greeks, and ... Barbarians;	Rom 1:14
2 brethren, we are **debtors**, not to the flesh,	8:12
2 pleased them verily; and their **debtors** they are.	15:27
1 that he is a **debtor** to do the whole law.	Gal 5:3

Classical Greek

In classical Greek the word *opheiletēs* denotes a "debtor," someone who owes a debt. It also is used for "one who is under (any kind of) obligation." Included in this is the idea of a moral binding to live in a particular manner.

No instance of the word is found in the Septuagint. One Koine period writing uses *opheiletēs* to refer to a guilty man who must make amends for a great sin committed (1

Enoch 6:3). Rabbinical literature during the New Testament period uses the Hebrew term *chōv* as an equivalent. This denotes not only one legally indebted, but one who is declared guilty and deserving punishment.

New Testament Usage
The New Testament shows three basic usages for this word. One is for an individual who owes another money. This is the literal meaning (see Matthew 18:24). There is the figurative sense of debtor, in which someone is bound or committed to a task, idea, or person (see Romans 1:14; 8:12; Galatians 5:3). A third sense of the word has religious connotations. Jesus taught the disciples to ask God for forgiveness for their debts (wrongdoings or offenses) as they forgave others debts against them (Matthew 6:12). In Luke 13:1-4 Jesus used the words "sinner" and "debtor" as near equivalents in parallel construction, thus conveying the sense of individual sinful fault and failing.

STRONG 3781, BAUER 598, MOULTON-MILLIGAN 468, KITTEL 5:565-66, LIDDELL-SCOTT 1277, COLIN BROWN 2:666-68.

3646. ὀφειλή opheilē noun

Debt, obligation, duty, one's due.
COGNATE:
  ὀφείλω opheilō (3648)
SYNONYM:
  ὀφείλημα opheilēma (3647)

1. ὀφειλήν opheilēn acc sing fem
2. ὀφειλάς opheilas acc pl fem

1 O thou wicked servant, I forgave thee all that debt, Matt 18:32
2 Render therefore to all their dues: .... Rom 13:7
1 Let the husband fulfill his duty to his wife, (NASB) 1 Co 7:3

Classical Greek
Classical Greek gave *opheilē* the literal meaning of "debt" as in a monetary debt. This term was not used by the translators of the Old Testament in the Septuagint though it is thought to correspond to the Rabbinic *hōbah*. Instead, *opheilēma* was used (see 3647 for its meaning and usage).

By the time of the Koine period *opheilē* was found to have kept its literal usage while two other general meanings were added. It retained the idea of a literal sum of money owed in debt. A new connotation of debt grew out of this. It referred to anything one owed another or one's "obligation." Finally, a religious sense of guilt and sin developed from this idea with the Early Church fathers.

New Testament Usage
The New Testament uses *opheilē* in the literal sense to mean "debt," as in a monetary debt (Matthew 18:32). A figurative meaning of "obligation" or "one's due" is also used. For instance, dues are to be paid in respect and honor of others as well as for taxes (Romans 13:7). Another figurative use in the New Testament includes the obligation of sexual relations and other privileges due to married partners (1 Corinthians 7:3). The later Koine religious meaning of "duty" that conveys sin and guilt is not found in the New Testament, but it is found in later Patristic writings.

STRONG 3782, BAUER 598, MOULTON-MILLIGAN 468, KITTEL 5:564, LIDDELL-SCOTT 1277, COLIN BROWN 2:666,668.

3647. ὀφείλημα opheilēma noun

Debt, something owed, one's due, sin.
COGNATE:
  ὀφείλω opheilō (3648)
SYNONYM:
  ὀφειλή opheilē (3646)

מַשָּׁאָה mashshā'āh (5044), Pledge (Dt 24:10).

1. ὀφείλημα opheilēma nom/acc sing neu
2. ὀφειλήματα opheilēmata nom/acc pl neu

2 forgive us our debts, as we forgive our debtors ...... Matt 6:12
1 is the reward not reckoned of grace, but of debt ..... Rom 4:4

Classical Greek
In classical Greek the term *opheilēma* refers to something that is owed or a debt. Literally, it means "a debt of money." It also denotes "something that is legally or justly due to another."

Septuagint Usage
The Septuagint (four texts) keeps this meaning. A debt is seen as a dereliction of one's duty, a falling short of an obligation or owing money (e.g., Deuteronomy 24:10). *Opheilēma* once translates the Hebrew term *nasha'* which means "to lend" or "to borrow" on usury (hence, a "debt"). The apocryphal writings hold to these same definitions (1 Esdras 3:20; 1 Maccabees 15:8).

New Testament Usage
In the New Testament and Koine Greek this term broadens its scope to mean "a failing, fault, or sin." In Matthew 6:12,14 "trespass" is used in parallel construction to draw out the idea of

wrongdoing or an unjust act. Luke's version of this teaching uses the term "sin" in like manner with *opheilēma*, adding to it the unrighteousness and guilt resulting from one's action. Paul used *opheilēma* to illustrate how God "counted" Abraham's faith as "righteous" because of His grace, not Abraham's works. If a man works for an employer, his wage is not dependent on the employer's grace but on his employer's indebtedness to him (Romans 4:4). However, if a person does not work to earn a reward but merely believes in Him who "justifieth the ungodly," then that person's faith is counted as righteousness (verse 5).

STRONG 3783, BAUER 598, MOULTON-MILLIGAN 468, KITTEL 5:565, LIDDELL-SCOTT 1277, COLIN BROWN 2:666-68.

3648. ὀφείλω opheilō verb
Owe, be indebted.

COGNATES:
ὀφειλέτης opheiletēs (3645)
ὀφειλή opheilē (3646)
ὀφείλημα opheilēma (3647)
ὄφελον ophelon (3649)
ὄφελος ophelos (3650)
προσοφείλω prosopheilō (4217)
χρεοφειλέτης chreopheiletēs (5367B)
χρεωφειλέτης chreōpheiletēs (5368)

אֲחַלֵי 'achălê (305I), Would that! Oh that! (2 Kgs 5:3, Ps 119:5 [118:5]).

חוֹב chôv (2420), Pledge (Ez 18:7).

לוּ lû (4001II) Would that! If only! (Nm 14:2 [14:3], Nm 20:3).

נָשָׁא nāsha' (5565), Qal: lender (Is 24:2); borrower (Is 24:2); hiphil: lend (Dt 15:2).

1. ὀφείλετε opheilete 2pl indic/impr pres act
2. ὀφείλεις opheileis 2sing indic pres act
3. ὀφείλει opheilei 3sing indic pres act
4. ὀφείλομεν opheilomen 1pl indic pres act
5. ὀφείλουσιν opheilousin 3pl indic pres act
6. ὀφείλοντι opheilonti dat sing masc part pres act
7. ὀφείλοντες opheilontes nom pl masc part pres act
8. ὤφειλον ōpheilon 1sing indic imperf act
9. ὤφειλεν ōpheilen 3sing indic imperf act
10. ὠφείλομεν ōpheilomen 1pl indic imperf act
11. ὀφειλομένην opheilomenēn acc sing fem part pres mid
12. ὀφειλόμενον opheilomenon nom/acc sing neu part pres mid
13. ὠφείλετε ōpheilete 2pl indic imperf act

9	which **owed** him an hundred pence:	Matt 18:28
2	took him by the throat, ... Pay me that thou **owest**....	18:28
12	cast him into prison, till he should pay the **debt**.	18:30
12	till he should pay all that was **due** unto him.	18:34
3	swear by the gold of the temple, he is a **debtor**!	Matt 23:16
3	sweareth by the gift that is upon it, he is **guilty**.	23:18
9	one **owed** five hundred pence, and the other fifty.	Luke 7:41
6	for we also forgive every one that is **indebted** to us...	11:4
2	How much **owest** thou unto my lord?	16:5
2	And how much **owest** thou? And he said,	16:7
10	we have done that which was our **duty** to do.	17:10
1	ye also **ought** to wash one another's feet.	John 13:14
3	We have a law, and by our law he **ought** to die,	19:7
4	we **ought** not to think that the Godhead is	Acts 17:29
1	**Owe** no man any thing,	Rom 13:8
4	strong **ought** to bear the infirmities of the weak,	15:1
5	**duty** is also to minister unto them in carnal things.	15:27
1	for then **must** ye needs go out of the world.	1 Co 5:10
11	husband render unto the wife **due** benevolence:	7:3
3	pass the flower of her age, and **need** so require,	7:36
3	that he that ploweth **should** plow in hope;	9:10
3	For a man indeed **ought** not to cover his head,	11:7
3	For this cause **ought** the woman to have power	11:10
8	for I **ought** to have been commended of you:	2 Co 12:11
3	the children **ought** not to lay up for the parents,	12:14
5	**ought** men to love their wives as their own bodies.	Eph 5:28
4	We are **bound** to thank God always for you,	2 Th 1:3
4	we are **bound** to give thanks alway to God for you,	2:13
3	If he hath wronged thee, or **oweth** thee ought,	Phlm 18
9	it **behoved** him to be made like unto his brethren,	Heb 2:17
3	And by reason hereof he **ought**, as for the people,	5:3
7	For when for the time ye **ought** to be teachers,	5:12
3	**ought** himself also so to walk, even as he walked.	1 Jn 2:6
4	we **ought** to lay down our lives for the brethren.	3:16
4	we **ought** also to love one another.	4:11
4	We therefore **ought** to receive such,	3 Jn 1:8

Classical Greek

Opheilō, which is used both literally and figuratively, shows very little deviation in meaning from its usage in the classical Greek period down to the New Testament era. In its literal usage Homer employed the verb in a legal or economic sense when he referred to a fine that was "owed" (*Odyssea* 8:332; cf. *Liddell-Scott*). Plato demonstrated its religious or moral sense when he referred to "owing" a sacrifice to a god (*Republic* 331b). In a figurative usage Pindarus employed the term in the sense of "owing" someone a song (*Olympian* 10[11].3; cf. ibid.). Whether it is used literally or figuratively, the underlying sense of the term indicates an obligation that has not been accomplished or fulfilled. From this basic meaning the term came to be used figuratively in expressions of desires or wishes. An example of this usage may be seen in the *Iliad* (10.117): "Now he ought (*ophelen*) to have suffered trial in praying" (ibid.).

Septuagint Usage

In the Septuagint the term occurs both literally and figuratively no less than 22 times, 12 of which occur in the canonical books. Literally, the term occurs in an economic sense in Ezekiel 18:7 where it is used in a participial form: "And hath not oppressed any, *but* hath restored to the debtor (*opheilontos*) his pledge." (Cf. Isaiah 24:2 where it occurs both as a participle and verb in an economic sense.) Figuratively, the term is used in the canonical books mostly to express the speaker's desire for an event that is unattainable; Exodus 16:3 provides a case in point: "Would to God (*ophelon*) we had died by the hand of the Lord in the land of Egypt" (cf. Numbers 14:3; 20:3; 2 Kings 5:3 [LXX 4 Kings 5:3]; Job 14:13; 30:24; and Psalm 119:5 [LXX 118:5]; see *ophelon* [3649]). It is also used figuratively in Proverbs 14:9: "Houses of transgressors will owe (*opheilēsousi*) purification" (cf. Job 6:20). The term occurs in reference to a moral obligation only in the apocryphal books (e.g., 3 Maccabees 7:10; 4 Maccabees 11:3).

New Testament Usage

Opheilō occurs 36 times in the New Testament. Literally it refers to being indebted financially, or figuratively to being indebted morally. It is used in a literal sense mostly in the Gospels. An example may be seen at Matthew 18:28: "But the same servant went out, and found one of his fellow servants, which owed (*opheilen*) him a hundred pence: and he laid hands on him, and took *him* by the throat, saying, Pay me that thou owest (*opheileis*)" (cf. Matthew 18:30,34; 23:16; Luke 7:41; 16:5,7; Philemon 18). The picture of debt is used here in reference to man's guiltiness before God. This debt is too great for any man to pay, either through sacrifices or good works. In a figurative sense the term may express an obligation, something that one can reasonably expect or demand of another. Paul used *opheilō* in this way in Romans 13:8: "*Owe* no man anything, but to love one another" (cf. Luke 17:10; John 19:7, 1 John 3:16; 4:11).

STRONG 3784, BAUER 598-99, MOULTON-MILLIGAN 468-69, KITTEL 5:559-64, LIDDELL-SCOTT 1277, COLIN BROWN 2:662-63,666-69.

3649. ὄφελον *ophelon* partic

Would that, Oh that, if only.

CROSS-REFERENCE:
 ὀφείλω opheilō (3648)

1. ὄφελον *ophelon*

1	and I **would** to God ye did reign,	1 Co 4:8
1	**Would** to God ye could bear with me a little	2 Co 11:1
1	I **would** they were even cut off which trouble you.	Gal 5:12
1	I **would** thou wert cold or hot.	Rev 3:15

In its earlier forms *ophelon* may have been an unaugmented verb used with an infinitive to express a wish. However, many scholars do not think it was an aorist form of *opheilō* without the augment but instead was a participle (cf. *Bauer*). Later the word was used as a particle to introduce wishes that are difficult or seemingly unattainable to fulfill and was usually translated "Oh that" or "would that" (ibid.). It can express such a wish for the past ("I *would* to God ye did reign" [KJV], "I *would* indeed that you had become kings" [NASB], 1 Corinthians 4:8); for the present ("I *would* thou wert cold or hot," Revelation 3:15); or for the future ("I *would* they were even cut off" [KJV], "*Would* that those ... would even mutilate themselves" [NASB], Galatians 5:12). The only other reference is also future. In 2 Corinthians 11:1 Paul asked that the Corinthians would "put up" with him as he presented his argument.

STRONG 3785, BAUER 599, MOULTON-MILLIGAN 469, COLIN BROWN 2:666,668.

3650. ὄφελος *ophelos* noun

Furtherance, advantage, benefit, profit, help.

CROSS-REFERENCE:
 ὀφείλω opheilō (3648)

יָעַל yā'al (3385), Hiphil: be profitable (Jb 15:3).

1. ὄφελος *ophelos* nom/acc sing neu

1	what **advantageth** it me, if the dead rise not?	1 Co 15:32
1	What doth it **profit**, my brethren,	Jas 2:14
1	Depart in peace, ... what doth it **profit**?	2:16

Ophelos is a noun used three times in the New Testament. It is related to the verb *ophellō* meaning "to increase, enlarge, strengthen, make to thrive." In the New Testament it reflects a sense of futility in an action or in the lack of an action. For example, Paul wondered what "advantage" would it be if he were to do battle with wild beasts in Ephesus only to discover that there was no resurrection (1 Corinthians 15:32). James used *ophelos* to describe the futility of a man stating his faith but showing no deed to confirm it. James' illustration was that of a person discovering someone in need of food and clothing and saying, "Have a good day," but giving him nothing. What good or what advantage was that greeting to him? (James 2:14-16).

STRONG 3786, BAUER 599, MOULTON-MILLIGAN 469, LIDDELL-SCOTT 1278.

3651. ὀφθαλμοδουλεία
 ophthalmodouleia noun

Eyeservice.

CROSS-REFERENCES:
δουλόω douloō (1396)
ὀφθαλμός ophthalmos (3652)

1. ὀφθαλμοδουλείαν ophthalmodouleian
   acc sing fem
2. ὀφθαλμοδουλείαις ophthalmodouleiais dat pl fem
3. ὀφθαλμοδουλίᾳ ophthalmodoulia dat sing fem
4. ὀφθαλμοδουλίαν ophthalmodoulian acc sing fem

1	Not with **eyeservice**, as menpleasers;	Eph 6:6
2	obey ... your masters ... not with **eyeservice**,	Col 3:22

The term *ophthalmodouleia* is a combination of two Greek words: *ophthalmos* (3652), "eye," and *douleia* (1391), "service." This word is a Christian coinage used exclusively by the apostle Paul in the New Testament. *Ophthalmodoulos*, the term's root, is found only in post-Christian literature (i.e., *Constitutiones Apostolorum*).

The New Testament uses *ophthalmodouleia* twice, in Ephesians 6:6 and Colossians 3:22, where the apostle Paul was addressing slaves and the work they did. He classified only two types of service: working to please men and working to please the Lord. The first type is an outward show of fidelity and goodwill when the master is watching. When the servant is no longer under surveillance, the hardworking attitude is replaced by a begrudging one. Even if the servant has a genuine desire to please superiors only for the purpose of reaping the rewards they might bestow, this is still considered eyeservice because it is not done to glorify God. Flattery and hypocrisy are all ingredients of this kind of service.

Work, then, is divided along two distinct lines in the New Testament; "eyeservice" (i.e., working for personal, independent gain) and being servants of Christ (i.e., working to please Christ).

STRONG 3787, BAUER 599, KITTEL 2:280, LIDDELL-SCOTT 1278.

3652. ὀφθαλμός ophthalmos noun
Eye.

COGNATES:
μονόφθαλμος monophthalmos (3305)
ὀφθαλμοδουλεία ophthalmodouleia (3651)

SYNONYM:
ὄμμα omma (3522)

מַרְאֶה mar'eh (4920), Appearance (1 Sm 17:42).
עַיִן 'ayin (6084), Eye (Dt 11:7, 2 Chr 7:15, Is 52:8).
עַיִן 'ayin (A6085), Eye (Ezr 5:5, Dn 7:8,20—Aramaic).
עַפְעַפַּיִם 'aph'appayim (6310), Eyelids (Prv 6:25).

פָּנֶה pāneh (6681), Face; before (Ezr 7:28, Jer 38:26 [45:26]).

1. ὀφθαλμός ophthalmos nom sing masc
2. ὀφθαλμοῦ ophthalmou gen sing masc
3. ὀφθαλμῷ ophthalmō dat sing masc
4. ὀφθαλμόν ophthalmon acc sing masc
5. ὀφθαλμοί ophthalmoi nom pl masc
6. ὀφθαλμῶν ophthalmōn gen pl masc
7. ὀφθαλμοῖς ophthalmois dat pl masc
8. ὀφθαλμούς ophthalmous acc pl masc

1	And if thy right **eye** offend thee, pluck it out,	Matt 5:29
4	An **eye** for an **eye**, and a tooth for a tooth:	5:38
2	An **eye** for an **eye**, and a tooth for a tooth:	5:38
1	The light of the body is the **eye**:	6:22
1	if therefore thine **eye** be single,	6:22
1	But if thine **eye** be evil, thy whole body	6:23
3	the mote that is in thy brother's **eye**,	7:3
3	consideredst not the beam that is in thine own **eye**?	7:3
2	Let me pull out the mote out of thine **eye**;	7:4
3	and, behold, a beam is in thine own **eye**?	7:4
2	first cast out the beam out of thine own **eye**,	7:5
2	see ... to cast out the mote out of thy brother's **eye**.	7:5
6	Then touched he their **eyes**, saying,	9:29
5	And their **eyes** were opened;	9:30
8	and their **eyes** they have closed;	13:15
7	lest at any time they should see with their **eyes**	13:15
5	But blessed are your **eyes**, for they see:	13:16
8	And when they had lifted up their **eyes**,	17:8
1	And if thine **eye** offend thee, pluck it out,	18:9
8	than having two **eyes** to be cast into hell fire.	18:9
1	Is thine **eye** evil, because I am good?	20:15
5	Lord, that our **eyes** may be opened.	20:33
6	compassion on them, and touched their **eyes**:	20:34
5	and immediately their **eyes** received sight,	20:34
7	and it is marvellous in our **eyes**?	21:42
5	asleep again: for their **eyes** were heavy.	26:43
1	lasciviousness, an evil **eye**, blasphemy, pride,	Mark 7:22
8	Having **eyes**, see ye not?	8:18
8	After that he put his hands again upon his **eyes**,	8:25
1	And if thine **eye** offend thee, pluck it out:	9:47
8	than having two **eyes** to be cast into hell fire:	9:47
7	the Lord's doing, and it is marvellous in our **eyes**?	12:11
5	asleep again, for their **eyes** were heavy,	14:40
5	For mine **eyes** have seen thy salvation,	Luke 2:30
5	the **eyes** of all them that were in the synagogue	4:20
8	And he lifted up his **eyes** on his disciples,	6:20
3	beholdest ... the mote that is in thy brother's **eye**,	6:41
3	perceivest not the beam that is in thine own **eye**?	6:41
3	let me pull out the mote that is in thine **eye**,	6:42
3	beholdest not the beam that is in thine own **eye**?	6:42
2	cast out first the beam out of thine own **eye**,	6:42
3	to pull out the mote that is in thy brother's **eye**.	6:42
5	Blessed are the **eyes** which see ... things that ye see:	10:23
1	The light of the body is the **eye**:	11:34
1	therefore when thine **eye** is single,	11:34
8	And in hell he lift up his **eyes**, being in torments,	16:23
8	would not lift up so much as his **eyes** unto heaven,	18:13
6	thy peace! but now they are hid from thine **eyes**,	19:42
5	**eyes** were holden that they should not know him.	24:16
5	And their **eyes** were opened, and they knew him;	24:31
8	behold, I say unto you, Lift up your **eyes**,	John 4:35
8	When Jesus then lifted up his **eyes**,	6:5
8	anointed the **eyes** of the blind man with the clay,	9:6
5	How were thine **eyes** opened?	9:10
8	Jesus made clay, and anointed mine **eyes**,	9:11
8	when Jesus made the clay, and opened his **eyes**,	9:14
8	clay upon mine **eyes**, and I washed, and do see.	9:15
8	sayest thou of him, that he hath opened thine **eyes**?	9:17
8	or who hath opened his **eyes**, we know not:	9:21
8	What did he to thee? how opened he thine **eyes**?	9:26
8	and yet he hath opened mine **eyes**.	9:30
8	opened the **eyes** of one that was born blind.	9:32

8	Can a devil open the **eyes** of the blind?	John 10:21
8	this man, which opened the **eyes** of the blind,	11:37
8	And Jesus lifted up his **eyes**, and said, Father,	11:41
8	blinded their **eyes**, and hardened their heart;	12:40
7	that they should not see with their **eyes**,	12:40
8	and lifted up his **eyes** to heaven, and said,	17:1
6	and a cloud received him out of their **sight**.	Acts 1:9
6	and when his **eyes** were opened, he saw no man:	9:8
6	there fell from his **eyes** as it had been scales:	9:18
8	And she opened her **eyes**: and when she saw Peter,	9:40
8	open their **eyes**, and to turn them from darkness	26:18
8	and their **eyes** have they closed;	28:27
7	lest they should see with their **eyes**,	28:27
6	There is no fear of God before their **eyes**.	Rom 3:18
8	**eyes** that they should not see,	11:8
5	Let their **eyes** be darkened that they may not see,	11:10
1	as it is written, **Eye** hath not seen, nor ear heard,	1 Co 2:9
1	Because I am not the **eye**, I am not of the body;	12:16
1	whole body were an **eye**, where were the hearing?	12:17
1	And the **eye** cannot say unto the hand,	12:21
2	In a moment, in the twinkling of an **eye**,	15:52
8	before whose **eyes** Jesus Christ hath been evidently	Gal 3:1
8	ye would have plucked out your own **eyes**,	4:15
8	The **eyes** of your understanding being enlightened;	Eph 1:18
7	but all things are naked and opened unto the **eyes**	Heb 4:13
5	For the **eyes** of the Lord are over the righteous,	1 Pt 3:12
8	Having **eyes** full of adultery,	2 Pt 2:14
7	which we have seen with our **eyes**,	1 Jn 1:1
8	because that darkness hath blinded his **eyes**.	2:11
6	and the lust of the **eyes**, and the pride of life,	2:16
1	cometh with clouds; and every **eye** shall see him,	Rev 1:7
5	and his **eyes** were as a flame of fire;	1:14
8	who hath his **eyes** like unto a flame of fire,	2:18
8	and anoint thine **eyes** with eyesalve,	3:18
6	were four beasts full **of eyes** before and behind.	4:6
6	and they were full **of eyes** within:	4:8
8	a Lamb ... having seven horns and seven **eyes**,	5:6
6	God shall wipe away all tears from their **eyes**.	7:17
5	His **eyes** were as a flame of fire,	19:12
6	And God shall wipe away all tears from their **eyes**;	21:4

Classical Greek

In classical Greek *ophthalmos* means "eye." It is used for the physical eye of the body and is often considered the most important part of the man, linking him to the surrounding world. The eye is the gateway into his innermost being. It is also thought of as man's way of "knowing" and "understanding." A final interpretation is the "dearest" or "best" (i.e., the "apple of the eye"; the "eye of heaven").

Septuagint Usage

The Septuagint most often translates the Hebrew 'ayin which conveys the idea of "seeing, making note of, judging" (Genesis 13:10,14; Isaiah 35:5). Occasionally the eyes of God are referred to (Deuteronomy 11:12). A figurative sense of *ophthalmos* is the ability to "perceive" or "judge." It is often known as the seat of evil impulses (Job 31:1,7; Psalm 17:11 [LXX 16:11]). To keep a matter before one's attention (i.e., "before the eyes") is another application of the term.

New Testament Usage

The New Testament borrows much of the Old Testament use. God's "eyes" are said to be upon His people. The eye is the instrument of moral enlightenment. New Testament uses include the eye as the symbol for judgment, such as in the expressions "an eye for an eye" (Matthew 5:38; cf. Exodus 21:24; Leviticus 24:20; Deuteronomy 19:21) or "having a log (beam) in one's eye" (Matthew 7:3-5). Through the "eye" man is enticed into many sins (Matthew 5:29; 2 Peter 2:14; 1 John 2:16) or directed into moral righteousness (Matthew 6:22).

STRONG 3788, BAUER 599-600, MOULTON-MILLIGAN 469, KITTEL 5:375-78, LIDDELL-SCOTT 1278, COLIN BROWN 3:511-12,516.

3653. ὄφις ophis noun

Snake, serpent.

SYNONYMS:
    δράκων drakōn (1398)
    ἑρπετόν herpeton (2046)

אֶפְעֶה 'eph'eh (679), Viper (Jb 20:16).

נָחָשׁ nāchāsh (5357), Serpent (Gn 3:1f., Nm 21:9, Am 5:19).

שָׂרָף sārāph (8042), Fiery serpent (Nm 21:8).

1. ὄφις ophis nom sing masc
2. ὄφεως opheōs gen sing masc
3. ὄφιν ophin acc sing masc
4. ὄφεις opheis nom/acc pl masc
5. ὄφεων opheōn gen pl masc
6. ὄφεσιν ophesin dat pl masc

3	Or if he ask a fish, will he give him **a serpent**?	Matt 7:10
4	be ye therefore wise as **serpents**,	10:16
4	Ye **serpents**, ye generation of vipers,	23:33
4	They shall take up **serpents**;	Mark 16:18
5	Behold, I give unto you power to tread on **serpents**	Luke 10:19
3	will he for a fish give him **a serpent**?	11:11
3	as Moses lifted up the **serpent** in the wilderness,	John 3:14
5	also tempted, and were destroyed of **serpents**.	1 Co 10:9
1	as the **serpent** beguiled Eve through his subtlety,	2 Co 11:3
6	their tails were like unto **serpents**, and had heads,	Rev 9:19
1	the great dragon was cast out, that old **serpent**,	12:9
2	she is nourished ... from the face of the **serpent**.	12:14
1	the **serpent** cast out of his mouth water as a flood	12:15
3	And he laid hold on the dragon, that old **serpent**,	20:2

Classical Greek

Snakes or serpents were generally feared by Near Eastern peoples for their cunning and deadliness. Evil individuals were often compared to serpents because of their malicious natures (cf. Psalms 58:4; 140:3; Matthew 23:33). Some ancient religions regarded the serpent as a symbol of chaos. They were also described as deities in the underworld—demonic beings—as well as creatures that brought life into existence.

Septuagint Usage

In the Septuagint *ophis* most often transliterates the Hebrew *nāchāsh*, "snake," though it describes no specific species. It also refers to the serpent as an image of the creature which does man the most ultimate evil: Satan. In Genesis 3 Satan used the serpent in tempting Eve to rebel against God which brought about the fall of man. Satan, the archenemy of both God and man, is represented by the serpent or dragon (Isaiah 27:1).

New Testament Usage

New Testament writers maintained this symbolic link between the evil serpent and the devil. The apostle Paul linked the serpent in Eden with the devil who continues to hate mankind and lead him astray (Romans 16:20; 2 Corinthians 11:3). John wrote pictorially of the fifth and sixth plagues describing destructive serpents which God will send to earth (Revelation 9:19). Finally, the serpent or Satan himself will be overcome by God's power (Revelation 20).

STRONG 3789, BAUER 600, MOULTON-MILLIGAN 469, KITTEL 5:566-82, LIDDELL-SCOTT 1279, COLIN BROWN 1:508-9.

3654. ὀφρῦς ophrus noun

Brow (of cliff), eyebrow.

1. ὀφρύος ophruos gen sing fem

1 and led him unto the brow of the hill . . . . Luke 4:29

Ophrus is a noun used in Greek literature from the time of Homer. Its literal meaning is "eyebrow" and is so used by Homer in his *Odyssey* (16.164; cf. *Liddell-Scott*) of an individual who was "nodding with his brows." In the *Iliad ophrus* is used figuratively of a hill (20.151; cf. *Bauer*). The sole use of *ophrus* in the New Testament is found in Luke 4:29. The scene was Nazareth (built on the side of a valley), and Jesus was threatened by a group of people who had disagreed with Him. They took Him to a nearby "cliff" (*ophrus*) to throw Him to His death.

STRONG 3790, BAUER 600, MOULTON-MILLIGAN 469, LIDDELL-SCOTT 1280.

3655. ὀχλέω ochleō verb

Move, disturb, trouble, vex.
CROSS-REFERENCE:
ὄχλος ochlos (3657)

1. ὀχλούμενοι ochloumenoi
nom pl masc part pres mid
2. ὀχλουμένους ochloumenous
acc pl masc part pres mid

1 And they that were vexed with unclean spirits: . . . . . . Luke 6:18
2 and them which were vexed with unclean spirits: . . . . . Acts 5:16

The verb *ochleō* is found in two forms in Greek literature. It appears in Homer's *Iliad* (21.261) to describe pebbles being torn loose from their place by a rush of water (cf. *Liddell-Scott*). The word *ochleō* is related to the noun *ochlos* (3657), "crowd," and also refers to the noise and disturbance made by an unruly mob. *Ochleō* is found twice in the New Testament; it was used only by Luke the physician in a quasi-medical way to describe the condition of persons possessed by unclean spirits (Luke 6:18; Acts 5:16).

STRONG 3791, BAUER 600, MOULTON-MILLIGAN 469-70, LIDDELL-SCOTT 1281.

3656. ὀχλοποιέω ochlopoieō verb

Form a mob, gather a company.
CROSS-REFERENCES:
ὄχλος ochlos (3657)
ποιέω poieō (4020)

1. ὀχλοποιήσαντες ochlopoiēsantes
nom pl masc part aor act

1 gathered a company, and set ... city on an uproar, .. Acts 17:5

This interesting word is a hapax legomenon, a word appearing only once in all of Greek literature. *Ochlopoieō* is translated "gather a company." Its root and context aid in the interpretation of the meaning. In root form it is related to the word *ochlos* (3657) translated "mob, crowd," or "throng," often in the sense of an unruly gathering. Its context describes the type of people making up this gathering: idle men loitering around the agora, ne'er-do-wells, often agitators (see *agoraios* [59]). Luke compounded this word and used it in Acts 17:5, its only appearance in the Bible.

STRONG 3792, BAUER 600, MOULTON-MILLIGAN 470, LIDDELL-SCOTT 1281.

3657. ὄχλος ochlos noun

Crowd, throng, multitude, mob, the common people, populace.
COGNATES:
ἐνοχλέω enochleō (1760)

ὄχλος 3657

ὀχλέω ochleō (3655)
ὀχλοποιέω ochlopoieō (3656)
παρενοχλέω parenochleō (3788)

SYNONYMS:
γλῶσσα glōssa (1094)
δῆμος dēmos (1211B)
ἔθνος ethnos (1477)
λαός laos (2967)
ὅμιλος homilos (3521)
πλῆθος plēthos (3988)
φυλή phulē (5279)

הָמוֹן hāmôn (2066), Multitude (2 Chr 20:15, Dn 11:11).

חַיִל chayil (2524), Army (Is 43:17, Dn 11:25).

חַיִל chayil (A2525), People (Dn 3:4—Aramaic).

טַף ṭaph (3054), Little ones (2 Sm 15:22).

עַם 'am (6194I), Men, people (Nm 20:20, Jer 48:42 [31:42]).

קָהָל qāhāl (7235), Company (Jer 31:8 [38:8], Ez 17:17, 23:46).

רַב rav (7521), Many (Ezr 3:12).

1. ὄχλος ochlos nom sing masc
2. ὄχλου ochlou gen sing masc
3. ὄχλῳ ochlō dat sing masc
4. ὄχλον ochlon acc sing masc
5. ὄχλοι ochloi nom pl masc
6. ὄχλων ochlōn gen pl masc
7. ὄχλοις ochlois dat pl masc
8. ὄχλους ochlous acc pl masc

5	And there followed him great **multitudes** of people	Matt 4:25
8	seeing the **multitudes**, he went up into a mountain:	5:1
5	the **people** were astonished at his doctrine:	7:28
5	great **multitudes** followed him.	8:1
8	Now when Jesus saw great **multitudes** about him,	8:18
5	But when the **multitude** saw it, they marvelled,	9:8
4	saw the minstrels and the **people** making a noise,	9:23
1	But when the **people** were put forth, he went in,	9:25
5	and the **multitudes** marvelled, saying,	9:33
8	But when he saw the **multitudes**,	9:36
7	Jesus began to say unto the **multitudes**	11:7
5	and great **multitudes** followed him,	12:15
5	And all the **people** were amazed, and said,	12:23
7	While he yet talked to the **people**,	12:46
5	great **multitudes** were gathered together unto him,	13:2
1	and the whole **multitude** stood on the shore.	13:2
7	spake Jesus unto the **multitude** in parables;	13:34
8	Then Jesus sent the **multitude** away,	13:36
4	put him to death, he feared the **multitude**,	14:5
5	and when the **people** had heard thereof,	14:13
4	And Jesus went forth, and saw a great **multitude**,	14:14
8	the time is now past; send the **multitude** away,	14:15
8	And he commanded the **multitude** to sit down	14:19
7	and the disciples to the **multitude**.	14:19
8	while he sent the **multitudes** away.	14:22
8	And when he had sent the **multitudes** away,	14:23
4	And he called the **multitude**, and said unto them,	15:10
5	And great **multitudes** came unto him,	15:30
8	Insomuch that the **multitude** wondered,	15:31
4	I have compassion on the **multitude**,	15:32
4	so much bread ... as to fill so great a **multitude**?	15:33
7	And he commanded the **multitude** to sit down	15:35
3	and the disciples to the **multitude**.	15:36
8	And he sent away the **multitude**, and took ship,	15:39
4	And when they were come to the **multitude**,	17:14
5	great **multitudes** followed him; ... he healed them	19:2
1	from Jericho, a great **multitude** followed him.	20:29

1	And the **multitude** rebuked them,	Matt 20:31
1	great **multitude** spread their garments in the way;	21:8
5	**multitudes** that went before, and that followed,	21:9
5	And the **multitude** said, This is Jesus the prophet	21:11
4	But if we shall say, Of men; we fear the **people**;	21:26
8	to lay hands on him, they feared the **multitude**,	21:46
5	And when the **multitude** heard this,	22:33
7	spake Jesus to the **multitude**, and to his disciples,	23:1
1	with him a great **multitude** with swords and staves,	26:47
7	In that same hour said Jesus to the **multitudes**,	26:55
3	was wont to release unto the **people** a prisoner,	27:15
8	chief priests and elders persuaded the **multitude**	27:20
2	and washed his hands before the **multitude**, saying,	27:24
4	they could not come nigh unto him for the **press**,	Mark 2:4
1	and all the **multitude** resorted unto him,	2:13
4	a small ship ... because of the **multitude**,	3:9
1	And the **multitude** cometh together again,	3:20
1	**multitude** sat about him, and they said unto him,	3:32
1	and there was gathered unto him a great **multitude**,	4:1
1	the whole **multitude** was by the sea on the land.	4:1
4	And when they had sent away the **multitude**,	4:36
1	much **people** gathered unto him:	5:21
1	and much **people** followed him, and thronged him.	5:24
3	came in the **press** behind, ... touched his garment.	5:27
3	turned him about in the **press**, and said,	5:30
4	Thou seest the **multitude** thronging thee,	5:31
5	**people** saw them departing, and many knew him,	6:33
4	And Jesus, when he came out, saw much **people**,	6:34
4	while he sent away the **people**.	6:45
4	And when he had called all the **people** unto him,	7:14
2	he was entered into the house from the **people**,	7:17
2	And he took him aside from the **multitude**,	7:33
2	In those days the **multitude** being very great,	8:1
4	I have compassion on the **multitude**,	8:2
3	commanded the **people** to sit down on the ground:	8:6
3	and they did set them before the **people**.	8:6
4	called the **people** unto him with his disciples also,	8:34
4	he saw a great **multitude** about them,	9:14
1	And straightway all the **people**,	9:15
2	And one of the **multitude** answered and said,	9:17
1	Jesus saw that the **people** came running together,	9:25
5	and the **people** resort unto him again;	10:1
2	with his disciples and a great number of **people**,	10:46
1	all the **people** was astonished at his doctrine.	11:18
4	were afraid of the **multitude**, (NASB)	11:32
4	sought to lay hold on him, but feared the **people**:	12:12
1	And the common **people** heard him gladly.	12:37
1	how the **people** cast money into the treasury:	12:41
1	with him a great **multitude** with swords and staves,	14:43
1	**multitude** crying aloud began to desire him to do	15:8
4	But the chief priests moved the **people**,	15:11
3	And so Pilate, willing to content the **people**,	15:15
7	Then said he to the **multitude** that came forth	Luke 3:7
5	**people** asked him, saying, What shall we do then?	3:10
5	and the **people** sought him, and came unto him,	4:42
4	**people** pressed upon him to hear the word of God,	5:1
8	he sat down, and taught the **people** out of the ship.	5:3
5	and great **multitudes** came together to hear,	5:15
4	they might bring him in because of the **multitude**,	5:19
1	and there was a great **company** of publicans	5:29
1	and the **company** of his disciples,	6:17
1	And the whole **multitude** sought to touch him:	6:19
3	and said unto the **people** that followed him,	7:9
1	disciples went with him, and much **people**.	7:11
1	and much **people** of the city was with her.	7:12
8	he began to speak unto the **people** concerning John,	7:24
2	And when much **people** were gathered together,	8:4
4	and could not come at him for the **press**,	8:19
1	the **people** gladly received him:	8:40
5	But as he went the **people** thronged him.	8:42
5	Master, the **multitude** throng thee and press thee,	8:45
5	And the **people**, when they knew it, followed him:	9:11
4	and said unto him, Send the **multitude** away,	9:12
3	gave to the disciples to set before the **multitude**.	9:16
5	he asked them, ... Whom say the **people** that I am?	9:18
1	come down from the hill, much **people** met him.	9:37
2	And, behold, a man of the **company** cried out,	9:38

5	the dumb spake; and the **people** wondered.	Luke 11:14
2	certain woman of the **company** lifted up her voice,	11:27
6	And when the **people** were gathered thick together,	11:29
2	gathered ... an innumerable multitude of **people**,	12:1
2	And one of the **company** said unto him, Master,	12:13
7	And he said also to the **people**,	12:54
3	and said unto the **people**, There are six days in	13:14
1	all the **people** rejoiced for all the glorious things	13:17
5	And there went great **multitudes** with him:	14:25
2	the **multitude** pass by, he asked what it meant.	18:36
2	and could not for the **press**, because he was little of	19:3
2	of the Pharisees from among the **multitude** said	19:39
2	to betray him ... in the absence of the **multitude**.	22:6
1	behold a **multitude**, and he that was called Judas,	22:47
8	said Pilate to the chief priests and to the **people**,	23:4
5	And all the **people** that came together to that sight,	23:48
2	a **multitude** being in that place.	John 5:13
1	And a great **multitude** followed him,	6:2
1	and saw a great **company** come unto him,	6:5
1	when the **people** which stood on the other side	6:22
1	the **people** therefore saw that Jesus was not there,	6:24
7	And there was much murmuring among the **people**	7:12
4	others said, Nay; but he deceiveth the **people**.	7:12
1	The **people** answered and said, Thou hast a devil:	7:20
2	And many of the **people** believed on him, and said,	7:31
2	The Pharisees heard that the **people** murmured	7:32
2	Many of the **people** therefore,	7:40
3	So there was a division among the **people**	7:43
1	this **people** who knoweth not the law are cursed.	7:49
4	but because of the **people** which stand by I said it,	11:42
1	Much **people** of the Jews therefore knew	12:9
1	next day much **people** that were come to the feast,	12:12
1	The **people** therefore that was with him	12:17
1	For this cause the **people** also met him,	12:18
1	**people** therefore, that stood by, and heard it, said	12:29
1	The **people** answered him,	12:34
1	the **number** of names ... an hundred and twenty,	Acts 1:15
1	and a great **company** of the priests were obedient	6:7
5	And the **people** with one accord gave heed	8:6
1	and much **people** was added unto the Lord.	11:24
4	with the church, and taught much **people**.	11:26
8	But when the Jews saw the **multitudes**,	13:45
5	And when the **people** saw what Paul had done,	14:11
7	and would have done sacrifice with the **people**.	14:13
4	and ran in among the **people**, crying out,	14:14
8	these sayings scarce restrained they the **people**,	14:18
8	certain Jews ... who persuaded the **people**,	14:19
1	And the **multitude** rose up together against them:	16:22
4	they troubled the **people** and the rulers of the city,	17:8
8	they came thither also, and stirred up the **people**.	17:13
4	hath persuaded and turned away much **people**,	19:26
2	And they drew Alexander out of the **multitude**,	19:33
4	And when the townclerk had appeased the **people**,	19:35
4	stirred up all the **people**, and laid hands on him,	21:27
3	one thing, some another, among the **multitude**:	21:34
2	borne of the soldiers for the violence of the **people**.	21:35
2	neither raising up the **people**,	24:12
2	neither with **multitude**, nor with tumult.	24:18
1	After this I beheld, and, lo, a great **multitude**,	Rev 7:9
5	**peoples**, and **multitudes**, and nations, and tongues.	17:15
2	voice of much **people** in heaven, saying, Alleluia;	19:1
2	I heard as it were the voice of a great **multitude**,	19:6

Classical Greek

In classical Greek *ochlos* is a crowd or multitude of people viewed collectively rather than as individuals. In many instances the *ochlos* is the mass of the common people in contrast to the nobility or the ruling elite, although it may be a company or troop of men or even an army. On the whole, however, the *ochlos* is characterized by lack of organization and the absence of a leader.

Septuagint Usage

In the Septuagint *ochlos* is used to translate a number of Hebrew terms, including *'am*, "people" (Numbers 20:20), *hāmôn*, "crowd" (2 Chronicles 20:15; Daniel 11:11), and *qāhāl*, "assembly" (Ezekiel 16:40; 17:17). It is the *ochlos* that stones the blasphemer in Leviticus 24:16 (Septuagint), and in Daniel 10:6 the voice of God is like the sound of an *ochlos*.

New Testament Usage

In the New Testament the use of the term is restricted almost entirely to the Gospels and the Book of Acts. The great multitude that followed Jesus for healing and to see miracles and signs was the *ochlos* (see Matthew 4:25; 5:1; Mark 3:32; Luke 4:42). This multitude was very clearly set apart from the ruling elite, the scribes and the Pharisees, who held the *ochlos* in contempt (John 7:31,32,48f.). Yet it was the *ochlos* that was roused against Jesus by those same religious leaders (Matthew 27:20).

Outside the Gospels and Acts, the term occurs only in the Apocalypse. In Revelation 7:9 a great *ochlos* stands before the throne of God and before the Lamb, arrayed in robes of white. In 17:15 the many waters upon which the harlot sits are symbolic of "peoples and *ochloi* and nations," the multitudes caught up in spiritual fornication. In 19:6 John wrote that he heard "as it were the voice of a great multitude (*ochlou*) . . . saying, Alleluia: for the Lord God omnipotent reigneth."

STRONG 3793, BAUER 600-601, MOULTON-MILLIGAN 470, KITTEL 5:582-90, LIDDELL-SCOTT 1281, COLIN BROWN 2:800-801,805.

3658. ὀχύρωμα ochurōma noun

Stronghold, fortress, prison.

בּוֹר bôr (988), Dungeon (Gn 41:14).

בַּיִת bayith (1041), House (Gn 40:14).

בָּצַר bātsar (1245), Piel: fortify (Is 22:10).

בָּצְרָה botsrāh (1249), Bozrah (Jer 49:22 [29:22]).

בִּצָּרוֹן bitstsārôn (1251), Stronghold (Zec 9:12).

הֵיכָל hêkhāl (2033), Palace (Prv 30:28 [24:63]).

מִבְצָר mivtsār (4152), Stronghold, fortification (2 Kgs 8:12, Lam 2:2, Na 3:14).

מַסְגֵּר masgēr (4674), Dungeon (Is 24:22).

מָעוֹז māʿôz (4735), Stronghold (Prv 10:29, Is 23:14).

מַעֲשֶׂה maʿaseh (4801), Works (Jer 48:7 [31:7]).

מְצָד mᵉtsādh (4841), Stronghold (Jer 48:41 [31:41]).

מָצוֹד mātsôdh (4847), Net (Jb 19:6).
מְצוּדָה metsûdhāh (4849), Fortress (2 Sm 22:2).
מָצוֹר mātsôr (4856), Stronghold (Zec 9:3).
עֹז 'ōz (6010), Strength; stronghold (Prv 21:22).
צְרִיחַ tserîach (7161), House (Jgs 9:46—Codex Alexandrinus only).

1. ὀχυρωμάτων ochurōmatōn gen pl neu

1 through God to the pulling down of strong holds;.. 2 Co 10:4

The only occurrence of this word in the New Testament is found in 2 Corinthians 10:4 where Paul stated that the weapons of spiritual warfare are for the "pulling down of strongholds." *Moulton-Milligan* is unable to find a metaphorical meaning of this word in 2 Corinthians 10:4. Thayer believes it to be "arguments and reasonings" one uses against his opponent (*Greek-English Lexicon*). Some scholars believe this verse is an allusion to Proverbs 21:22: "The wise man attacks strong cities and destroys the stronghold in which the ungodly trusted" (cf. Brown, "War," *Colin Brown*, 3:963). Heidland says Paul could have been alluding to the Tower of Babel or the tower at Penuel in his use of this word which corresponds to the usage found in the Septuagint ("ochurōma," *Kittel*, 5:591). Whatever the case, Paul certainly was referring to what is opposed to the knowledge of God (cf. 10:5).

STRONG 3794, BAUER 601, MOULTON-MILLIGAN 470, KITTEL 5:590-91, LIDDELL-SCOTT 1282, COLIN BROWN 3:963.

3659. ὀψάριον opsarion noun

Tiny fish (fishes).
SYNONYM:
ἰχθύς ichthus (2459)

1. ὀψάριον opsarion nom/acc sing neu
2. ὀψαρίων opsariōn gen pl neu
3. ὀψάρια opsaria nom/acc pl neu

3 five barley loaves, and two small fishes:............John 6:9
2 and likewise of the fishes as much as they would........ 6:11
1 they saw a fire of coals there, and fish laid thereon,... 21:9
2 Bring of the fish which ye have now caught........... 21:10
1 taketh bread, and giveth them, and fish likewise....... 21:13

Occurring in John's Gospel (6:9,11; 21:9,10, 13), this word is related to its classical Greek noun *opson*. *Opsarion*, a diminutive form, once indicated a "small, cooked food item eaten with bread" or pickled fish (*Bauer*; cf. *Liddell-Scott*).

Since the Synoptic Gospels say the 5,000 were fed with *duo icthuas*, "two fishes" (compare John 6:9,11 with Matthew 14:17,19; Mark 6:38,41; Luke 9:13,16), it can be reasonably assumed that John's equivalent, *opsarion*, refers to "tiny fishes" which were occasionally cooked on an open fire (John 21:9), eaten at breakfast (John 21:12), or later in the day (Matthew 14:15).

STRONG 3795, BAUER 601, MOULTON-MILLIGAN 470, LIDDELL-SCOTT 1282, COLIN BROWN 1:670-71.

3660. ὀψέ opse adv

Late, late in the day, evening or twilight time, after.

נֶשֶׁף nesheph (5582), Night (Is 5:11).
עֶרֶב 'erev (6394), Evening (Gn 24:11).

1. ὀψέ opse

1 In the end of the sabbath, as it began to dawn..... Matt 28:1
1 since it was already late. (NASB)................Mark 11:11
1 And when even was come, he went out of the city..... 11:19
1 at even, or at midnight, or at the cockcrowing,......... 13:35

Classical Greek
In classical Greek *opse* is primarily an adverb of time meaning "after a long time, at length, late." Examples of its usage can be found in reference to "late in the day, being out late at night, late in life," or even "after" a specific time or event (*Liddell-Scott*). In the Septuagint the term signifies "during the evening hours" or "in the latter part of the day" (Exodus 30:8; Isaiah 5:11).

New Testament Usage
The word has this same meaning in at least one passage in the New Testament also, namely, Mark 13:35. (Note the contrast with *prōi* [4262], "in the morning," in this verse.)

Among the later writers *opse* shows a development toward use as an indeclinable noun (*Bauer*). This use is evidenced in both the Septuagint (Genesis 24:11) and the New Testament. It is so used in Mark 11:19 where the term signifies simply the evening or the latter part of the day.

Another innovation among the late Greek writers was to use *opse* as a preposition with the meaning "after" (ibid.). According to some grammarians it is quite likely this is the intended sense of the word in Matthew 28:1, "*After* the sabbath" rather than "In the end of the sabbath" (Blass and DeBrunner, *Greek Grammar of the New Testament*, p.91).

STRONG 3796, BAUER 601, MOULTON-MILLIGAN 470-71, LIDDELL-SCOTT 1282.

3661. ὄψιμος opsimos adj
Late, later, late or final rain.
CROSS-REFERENCE:
πρόϊμος proimos (4149B)

אָפִיל 'âphîl (663), Something which ripens late (Ex 9:32).

מַלְקוֹשׁ malqôsh (4597), Later rain, spring rain (Dt 11:14, Jer 5:24, Jl 2:23).

1. ὄψιμον opsimon acc sing masc

1 until he receive the early and **latter rain**.............Jas 5:7

Occurring only once in the New Testament (James 5:7), this word is related to the Greek adverb *opse* (3660). In the New Testament *opse* refers to the latter part of the Sabbath Day (Matthew 28:1), or to the Jewish first watch of evening, i.e., until 10 p.m. (Mark 11:19; 13:35).

The "rain" which James described as *opsimos* is the "latter" or "final showers" of the Palestinian farming season. Different from the early ground-softening rains (October—December), these showers prepared the maturing fruits for harvest (February—April). They provided a refreshing moisture which ultimately increased the yield (cf. Exodus 9:32; Deuteronomy 11:14; Hosea 6:3; Joel 2:23,24).

Christ's return, then, was likened by James to the "latter" (later) rains. Just as the farmer patiently waits for his harvest made possible by the early and later rains, so the Christian must wait patiently for the return of Christ and consequently His reward.

STRONG 3797, BAUER 601, MOULTON-MILLIGAN 471, LIDDELL-SCOTT 1282, COLIN BROWN 3:1000,1003.

3662. ὄψιος opsios adj
Late, evening.
SYNONYM:
ἑσπέρα hespera (2055)

1. ὀψία opsia nom sing fem
2. ὀψίας opsias gen sing fem

2 When the **even** was come, they brought unto him....Matt 8:16
2 when it was **evening**, his disciples came to him,........ 14:15
2 when the **evening** was come, he was there alone........ 14:23
2 When it is **evening**, ye say,................................. 16:2
2 when **even** was come, the lord of the vineyard saith.... 20:8
2 Now when the **even** was come,........................... 26:20
2 When the **even** was come, there came a rich man...... 27:57
2 And at **even**, when the sun did set,................ Mark 1:32
2 And the same day, when the **even** was come,.......... 4:35
2 when **even** was come, the ship was in the midst........ 6:47
2 and now the **eventide** was come,....................... 11:11
2 And in the **evening** he cometh with the twelve......... 14:17
2 And now when the **even** was come,..................... 15:42
1 And when **even** was now come,.................... John 6:16
2 Then the same day at **evening**,......................... 20:19

Opsios is related to the adverb *opse* (3660), "late in the day," and among the classical writers it is a temporal adjective meaning "late." The term retains this function in Mark 11:11. The primary use of the word both in the Septuagint and in the New Testament, however, is as a feminine substantive indicating the evening (with the noun *hōra* [5443], "hour," understood).

The term denotes both the time of "lengthening shadows" before sunset (Proverbs 7:9; Jeremiah 6:4) and the time between sunset and total darkness. The New Testament writers also used the term for both periods, with the context often giving some indication of the time intended. Note, for example, Mark 1:32: "And at even, when the sun did set" and John 6:16,17: "When even was now come, his disciples went down unto the sea.... And it was now dark."

STRONG 3798, BAUER 601, MOULTON-MILLIGAN 471, LIDDELL-SCOTT 1282.

3663. ὄψις opsis noun
Outward appearance, face, countenance.
SYNONYMS:
ἰδέα idea (2374)
πρόσωπον prosōpon (4241)

זִיו zîw (A2204), Appearance (Dn 2:31—Aramaic, Codex Alexandrinus only).

מֵצַח mētsach (4860), Forehead (Jer 3:3).

מַרְאָה mar'eh (4920), Appearance, look (Lv 13:20, Ez 23:15); face (S/S 2:14).

עַיִן 'ayin (6084), Eye; surface (Ex 10:5, Nm 22:5); appearance (Ez 1:27).

פֵּאָה pē'āh (6523), Side, edge (Lv 19:27, 21:5).

שְׂאֵת s⁽e⁾ēth (7875), Swelling (Lv 13:43).

תֹּאַר tō'ar (8717), A handsome appearance (1 Kgs 1:6).

1. ὄψις opsis nom sing fem
2. ὄψιν opsin acc sing fem

2 Judge not according to the **appearance**,............. John 7:24
1 and his **face** was bound about with a napkin.......... 11:44
1 **countenance** was as the sun shineth in his strength....Rev 1:16

Classical Greek
Related to the word for "eye," *ophthalmos* (3652), and with the verb "to see," *horaō* (3571), *opsis* has both a subjective and an objective sense in classical Greek. Subjectively—i.e., when the term refers to one who sees something—*opsis* is the power of sight, the act of seeing or, at times, the organs of sight, the eyes. Objectively—i.e., when the term refers to that which is seen—it is the aspect or appearance of

a person or thing, the face or countenance, or even a vision or apparition.

Septuagint Usage
The distinction is carried over into the Septuagint, the objective sense being seen, for example, in the Song of Solomon 2:14 where Solomon told the Shulamite that her *opsis* was lovely. The objective sense is extended even to "the face (surface) of the earth" in Numbers 22:5,11. *Opsis* in its subjective function is found, for example, in the Old Testament apocryphal book Wisdom of Solomon 3:4, "Though they be punished in the *opsis* of men, their hope is full of immortality."

New Testament Usage
John is the only New Testament writer to use the term, and he always used it in its objective sense. John 7:24 records Jesus' admonition to refrain from judging on the basis of outward appearance. In 11:44 John used *opsis* in reference to the face of the resurrected Lazarus, and in Revelation 1:16, to the countenance of Christ as seen in a vision.

STRONG 3799, BAUER 601-2, MOULTON-MILLIGAN 471, LIDDELL-SCOTT 1282-83.

3664. ὀψώνιον opsōnion noun
Wages, pay, compensation, salary.
SYNONYM:
    μισθός misthos (3272)

1. ὀψώνιον opsōnion nom/acc sing neu
2. ὀψώνια opsōnia nom/acc pl neu
3. ὀψωνίοις opsōniois dat pl neu

```
3 and be content with your wages................. Luke 3:14
2 For the wages of sin is death;................... Rom 6:23
3 Who goeth a warfare any time at his own charges?...1 Co 9:7
1 taking wages of them, to do you service........... 2 Co 11:8
```

Classical Greek
Derived from *opsōn*, food prepared over a fire, and a form of *ōneomai* (5441), "to buy," *opsōnion* originally referred to the provisions needed to complete one's meal, and then to the funds needed to purchase such provisions. Thus the money given to a soldier to buy supplies over and above the bread and oil that were provided to him was his *opsōnion*. This usage is quite common in Greek literature. Eventually the term came to denote wages in general, but most often subsistence wages, as opposed to payment commensurate with work completed, for which the Greek used the word *misthos* (3272).

Septuagint Usage
In the Septuagint the term is used, for example, of the wages paid to those who guarded the city of Jerusalem during the rebuilding work (1 Esdras 4:56), and of the payment that Antiochus gave to his military forces (1 Maccabees 3:28). First Maccabees 14:32 states that Simon, son of Mattathias the priest, spent his own money to pay the *opsōnia* of those who defended the land against the enemy.

New Testament Usage
In the New Testament the word occurs but four times, most notably in Romans 6:23. Death is what sin pays out as *opsōnion*; but in striking contrast, God gives freely, as a gift (*charisma* [5321]), eternal life through Christ Jesus. Elsewhere *opsōnion* is, as in classical literature, the soldier's pay (Luke 3:14; 1 Corinthians 9:7) and also the support provided to Paul by some of the churches in which he had ministered (2 Corinthians 11:8).

STRONG 3800, BAUER 602, MOULTON-MILLIGAN 471-72, KITTEL 5:591-92, LIDDELL-SCOTT 1283, COLIN BROWN 3:144-45.

Manuscripts

Egyptian Papyri

Note: (a) designates the section of the New Testament on which the manuscript is based; (b) designates the century in which it is believed the manuscript was written (using the Roman numerals); (c) provides information on the present location of the manuscript.

p1 (a) Gospels; (b) III; (c) Philadelphia, University of Pennsylvania Museum, no. E2746.

p2 (a) Gospels; (b) VI; (c) Florence, Museo Archeologico, Inv. no. 7134.

p3 (a) Gospels; (b) VI, VII; (c) Vienna, Österreichische Nationalbibliothek, Sammlung Papyrus Erzherzog Rainer, no. G2323.

p4 (a) Gospels; (b) III; (c) Paris, Bibliothèque Nationale, no. Gr. 1120, suppl. 2°.

p5 (a) Gospels; (b) III; (c) London, British Museum, P. 782 and P. 2484.

p6 (a) Gospels; (b) IV; (c) Strasbourg, Bibliothèque de la Université, 351^r, 335^v, 379, 381, 383, 384 copt.

p7 (a) Gospels; (b) V; (c) now lost, was in Kiev, library of the Ukrainian Academy of Sciences.

p8 (a) Acts; (b) IV; (c) now lost; was in Berlin, Staatliche Museen, P. 8683.

p9 (a) General Epistles; (b) III; (c) Cambridge, Massachusetts, Harvard University, Semitic Museum, no. 3736.

p10 (a) Paul's Epistles; (b) IV; (c) Cambridge, Massachusetts, Harvard University, Semitic Museum, no. 2218.

p11 (a) Paul's Epistles; (b) VII; (c) Leningrad, State Public Library.

p12 (a) General Epistles; (b) late III; (c) New York, Pierpont Morgan Library, no. G. 3.

p13 (a) General Epistles; (b) III, IV; (c) London, British Museum, P. 1532 (verso), and Florence, Biblioteca Medicea Laurenziana.

p14 (a) Paul's Epistles; (b) V (?); (c) Mount Sinai, St. Catharine's Monastery, no. 14.

p15 (a) Paul's Epistles; (b) III; (c) Cairo, Museum of Antiquities, no. 47423.

p16 (a) Paul's Epistles; (b) III, IV; (c) Cairo, Museum of Antiquities, no. 47424.

p17 (a) General Epistles; (b) IV; (c) Cambridge, England, University Library, gr. theol. f. 13 (P), Add. 5893.

p18 (a) Revelation; (b) III, IV; (c) London, British Museum, P. 2053 (verso).

p19 (a) Gospels; (b) IV, V; (c) Oxford, Bodleian Library, MS. Gr. bibl. d. 6 (P.).

p20 (a) General Epistles; (b) III; (c) Princeton, New Jersey, University Library, Classical Seminary AM 4117 (15).

p21 (a) Gospels; (b) IV, V; (c) Allentown, Pennsylvania, Library of Muhlenberg College, Theol. Pap. 3.

p22 (a) Gospels; (b) III; (c) Glasgow, University Library, MS. 2-x. 1.

p23 (a) General Epistles; (b) early III; (c) Urbana, Illinois, University of Illinois, Classical Archaeological and Art Museum, G. P. 1229.

p24 (a) Revelation; (b) IV; (c) Newton Center, Massachusetts, Library of Andover Newton Theological School.

p25 (a) Gospels; (b) late IV; (c) now lost, was in Berlin, Staatliche Museen, P. 16388.

p26 (a) Paul's Epistles; (b) c. 600; (c) Dallas, Texas, Southern Methodist University, Lane Museum.

p27 (a) Paul's Epistles; (b) III; (c) Cambridge, England, University Library, Add. MS. 7211.

Manuscripts Continued

p28 (a) Gospels; (b) III; (c) Berkeley, California, Library of Pacific School of Religion, Pap. 2.

p29 (a) Acts; (b) III; (c) Oxford, Bodleian Library, MS. Gr. bibl. g. 4 (P.).

p30 (a) Paul's Epistles; (b) III; (c) Ghent, University Library, U. Lib. P. 61.

p31 (a) Paul's Epistles; (b) VII; (c) Manchester, England, John Rylands Library, P. Ryl. 4.

p32 (a) Paul's Epistles; (b) c. 200; (c) Manchester England, John Rylands Library, P. Ryl. 5.

p33 (a) Acts; (b) VI; (c) Vienna, Österreichische Nationalbibliothek, no. 190.

p34 (a) Paul's Epistles; (b) VII; (c) Vienna, Österreichische Nationalbibliothek, no. 191.

p35 (a) Gospels; (b) IV (?); (c) Florence, Biblioteca Medicea Laurenziana.

p36 (a) Gospels; (b) VI; (c) Florence, Biblioteca Medicea Laurenziana.

p37 (a) Gospels; (b) III, IV; (c) Ann Arbor, Michigan, University of Michigan Library, Invent. no. 1570.

p38 (a) Acts; (b) c. 300; (c) Ann Arbor, Michigan, University of Michigan Library, Invent. no. 1571.

p39 (a) Gospels; (b) III; (c) Chester, Pennsylvania, Crozer Theological Seminary Library, no. 8864.

p40 (a) Paul's Epistles; (b) III; (c) Heidelberg, Universitätsbibliothek, Inv. Pap. graec. 45.

p41 (a) Acts; (b) VIII; (c) Vienna, Österreichische Nationalbibliothek, Pap. K.7541-8.

p42 (a) Gospels; (b) VII, VIII; (c) Vienna, Österreichische Nationalbibliothek, KG 8706.

p43 (a) Revelation; (b) VI, VII; (c) London, British Museum, Pap. 2241.

p44 (a) Gospels; (b) VI, VII; (c) New York, Metropolitan Museum of Art, Inv. 14-1-527.

p45 (a) Gospels, Acts; (b) III; (c) Dublin, Chester Beatty Museum; and Vienna, Osterreichische Nationalbibliothek, P. Gr. Vind. 31974.

p46 (a) Paul's Epistles; (b) c. 200; (c) Dublin, Chester Beatty Museum, and Ann Arbor, Michigan, University of Michigan Library, Invent. no. 6238.

p47 (a) Revelation; (b) late III; (c) Dublin, Chester Beatty Museum.

p48 (a) Acts; (b) late III; (c) Florence, Museo Medicea Laurenziana.

p49 (a) Paul's Epistles; (b) late III; (c) New Haven, Connecticut, Yale University Library, P. 415.

p50 (a) Acts; (b) IV, V; (c) New Haven, Connecticut, Yale University Library, P. 1543.

p51 (a) Paul's Epistles; (b) c. 400; (c) London British Museum.

p52 (a) Gospels; (b) early II; (c) Manchester, John Rylands Library, P. Ryl. Gr. 457.

p53 (a) Gospels, Acts; (b) III; (c) Ann Arbor, Michigan, University of Michigan Library, Invent. no. 6652.

p54 (a) General Epistles; (b) V, VI; (c) Princeton, New Jersey, Princeton University Library, Garrett Depos. 7742.

p55 (a) Gospels; (b) VI, VII; (c) Vienna, Österreichische Nationalbibliothek, P. Gr. Vind. 26214.

p56 (a) Acts; (b) V, VI; (c) Vienna, Österreichische Nationalbibliothek, P. Gr. Vind. 19918.

p57 (a) Acts; (b) IV, V; (c) Vienna, Österreichische Nationalbibliothek, P. Gr. Vind. 26020.

p58 (a) Acts; (b) VI; (c) Vienna, Österreichische Nationalbibliothek, P. Gr. Vind. 17973, 36133[54], and 35831.

p59 (a) Gospels; (b) VII; (c) New York, New York University, Washington Square College of Arts and Sciences, Department of Classics, P. Colt. 3.

p60 (a) Gospels; (b) VII; (c) New York, New York University, Washington Square College of Arts and Sciences, Department of Classics, P. Colt. 4.

p61 (a) Paul's Epistles; (b) c. 700; (c) New York, New York University, Washington Square College of Arts and Sciences, Department of Classics, P. Colt. 5.

p62 (a) Gospels; (b) IV; (c) Oslo, University Library.

p63 (a) Gospels; (b) c. 500; (c) Berlin, Staatliche Museen.

p64 (a) Gospels; (b) c. 200; (c) Oxford, Magdalen College Library.

p65 (a) Paul's Epistles; (b) III; (c) Florence, Biblioteca Medicea Laurenziana.

p66 (a) Gospels; (b) c. 200; (c) Cologny/Genève, Bibliothèque Bodmer.

p67 (a) Gospels; (b) c. 200; (c) Barcelona, Fundación San Lucas Evangelista, P. Barc. 1.

p68 (a) Paul's Epistles; (b) VII (?); (c) Leningrad, State Public Library, Gr. 258.

p69 (a) Gospels; (b) III; (c) place (?)

p70 (a) Gospels; (b) III; (c) place (?)

p71 (a) Gospels; (b) IV; (c) place (?)

p72 (a) General Epistles; (b) III, IV; (c) Cologny/Genève, Bibliothèque Bodmer.

p73 (a) Gospels; (b)—; (c) Cologny/Genève, Bibliothèque Bodmer.

p74 (a) Acts, General Epistles; (b) VII; (c) Cologny/Genève, Bibliothèque Bodmer.

p75 (a) Gospels; (b) early III; (c) Cologny/Genève, Bibliothèque Bodmer.

p76 (a) Gospels; (b) VI; (c) Vienna, Österreichische Nationalbibliothek, P. Gr. Vind. 36102.

Major Codices

01, aleph:	Sinaiticus
02, A:	Alexandrinus
03, B:	Vaticanus
04, C:	Ephraemi Rescriptus
05, D:	Bezae Cantabrigiensis
06, E:	Claromontanus

Manuscripts Continued

Majuscules

No.	Contents	Century
01, *aleph*	Total New Testament	4th
02, A	Total New Testament	5th
03, B	New Testament, Revelation	4th
04, C	Total New Testament	5th
05, D	Gospels, Acts	6th
06, D	Paul's Epistles	6th
07, E	Gospels	8th
08, E	Acts	6th
09, F	Gospels	9th
010, F	Paul's Epistles	9th
011, G	Gospels	9th
012, G	Paul's Epistles	9th
013, H	Gospels	9th
015, H	Paul's Epistles	6th
016, I	Paul's Epistles	5th
017, K	Gospels	9th
018, K	Acts, Paul's Epistles	9th
019, L	Gospels	8th
020, L	Acts, Paul's Epistles	9th
021, M	Gospels	9th
022, N	Gospels	6th
023, O	Gospels	6th
024, P	Gospels	6th
025, P	Acts, Paul's Epistles, Revelation	9th
026, Q	Gospels	5th
028, S	Gospels	10th
029, T	Gospels	9th
030, U	Gospels	9th
031, V	Gospels	9th
032, W	Gospels	5th
033, X	Gospels	10th
034, Y	Gospels	9th
036,	Gospels	10th
037,	Gospels	9th
038,	Gospels	9th
039,	Gospels	9th
040,	Gospels	6th-8th
041,	Gospels	9th
042,	Gospels	6th
043,	Gospels	6th
044,	Gospels, Acts, Paul's Epistles	8th-9th

In addition to these manuscripts identified by a letter (letter uncials), there are 200 other numbered majuscule manuscripts. Even though most of these manuscripts are very valuable, there is not enough room to list them all. Our apparatus gives the official numbers, 046, 047 etc.

Minuscules

There are about 2800 of these. A total classification of these is only possible in specialized literature dealing with textual criticism.

Early Versions

Abbrev.	Name	Century
it	Itala, early Latin	II-IV
vul	Vulgate, Latin	IV-V
old syr	Old Syrian	II-III
syr pesh	Peshitta	V
got	Gothic	IV
arm	Armenian	IV-V
geo	Georgian	V
cop	Coptic	VI
nub	Nubian	VI
eth	Ethiopian	VI

Early Church Fathers

Athanasius, deacon of Alexandria; key figure at the Council of Nicea (325) where he attacked Arianism; he defended the Nicean claim that Christ was of the same substance as God; intimate friend of Origen; died 373.

Athenagoras, Christian philosopher of Athens ca. 178; he was one of the most articulate writers of the early Christian apologists.

Augustine, 354–430, convert of Ambrose and bishop of Hippo; his writings have dominated the development of theology in the Western Church since the Middle Ages; wrote *Confessions* and *The City of God*; he advanced the principle "Believe in order to understand."

Basil the Great, 329–379, bishop of Caesarea; one of the Cappadocian fathers and highly influential in the Eastern Church; he was one of the first great defenders of the divinity of the Holy Spirit; his formula "one substance, three persons" is still the accepted expression of the Trinity.

Bede, the Venerable; one of the great church historians of the Middle Ages; wrote *Ecclesiastical History of the English People*; he popularized the calendar which uses the birth of Christ as the baseline.

Chrysostom, 350–407, bishop of Constantinople, known also as "Golden Mouth"; he remains one of the greatest expositors and preachers in the history of the Church.

Clemens Alexandrinus, Clement of Alexandria; one of the founders of Christian literature; he created new terminology in the language of the Greeks to express the ideas of the Faith.

Clemens Romanus, Clement of Rome; traditionally a fellow laborer with Peter and Paul; bishop of Rome in 91; his letter 1 Clement provides insight into the life of the Church shortly after the apostles.

Cyprian, bishop of Carthage in 248, martyred in 258; wrote "The Unity of the Church"; taught the gift of salvation limited to the Roman Catholic Church; he was an outstanding churchman and administrator.

Cyrillus Alexandrinus, Clement of Alexandria, died ca. 444; appointed patriarch of Alexandria in 412; main focus was to oppose Nestorianism; convened the Council of Alexandria, 430, and the Council of Ephesus, 431; his primary contribution was to preserve the unity of Christ, though later he was accused of reviving Apollinarianism.

Cyrillus Hierosolymitanaus, Cyril of Jerusalem, 315–386; bishop of Jerusalem; known widely for his *Catechetical Lectures* which provide detail about the rites and ceremonies of the Church at this time.

Ephraim of Syrus, Ephraim the Syrian, deacon of Edessa; born in early days of Constantine's rule (ca. 306), died 373; known as the "Great Light of the Syrian Church," he was very influential in shaping the ritual of the Syrian church; renowned mystic and teacher, writer of hymns and commentaries.

Eusebius of Caesarea, ca. 260–340; a prolific writer and author of first full scale history of the Church; he was highly instrumental in shaping Byzantium's political ideals.

Gregory Thaumaturgus, disciple of Origen, bishop of Neocaesarea in 240; said to have had the gift to work miracles which he used regularly; wrote *A Declaration of Faith* (on the Trinity), and *Panegyric* which gives insight into the origins of Roman law.

Hippolytus, a bishop and contemporary with Origen; one of the most learned and eminent scholars of the Third Century; he opposed the popes of his day and wrote *Apostolic Tradition* which details the ordaining and ordering of ministers.

Ignatius, bishop of Antioch, martyred ca. 110; a forceful opponent of Docetism; claimed to have the gift of prophesy; he saw the Eucharist as a means of maintaining unity in the Church and stressing the humanity of Jesus.

Irenaeus, 140–202, disciple of Polycarp; bishop of Lyons in 177; countered the Gnostics in his works *Against Heresies* and *Proof of the Apostolic Tradition*; stressed the full humanity and deity of Jesus; he developed idea that the Church preserved the canon of truth for interpreting Scripture.

Early Church Fathers Continued

Jerome, ca. 342–420, also called Hieronymus; one of the most eminent scholars of the Latin fathers; he is the author of the translation of the Scriptures called the Vulgate.

Justin Martyr, martyred 165; Christian philosopher and most noted apologist of the Second Century; he helped to synthesize philosophy and theology; wrote *First Apology* and *Dialogue with Trypho*.

Origen, 185–254; considered by some the greatest scholar and voluminous writer of the Early Church in the East; was responsible for the *Hexapala*; he expressed his faith in the structures of Platonism, and was one of the great champions of allegorical hermeneutics.

Tertullian, died ca. 220; was the first Christian writer to use Latin; rejected any synthesis of theology and philosophy and coined the phrase, "What has Athens to do with Jerusalem"; his writings include *Against Marcion*, defending the use of the Old Testament by Christians, *Against Praxeas*, outlining the doctrine of the Trinity, and *On the Soul*, the first Christian writing on psychology.

Books of the Old and New Testament

Old Testament Books

Genesis
Exodus
Leviticus
Numbers
Deuteronomy
Joshua
Judges
Ruth
1 Samuel
2 Samuel
1 Kings
2 Kings
1 Chronicles
2 Chronicles
Ezra
Nehemiah
Esther
Job
Psalms
Proverbs
Ecclesiastes
Song of Solomon
Isaiah
Jeremiah
Lamentations
Ezekiel
Daniel
Hosea
Joel
Amos
Obadiah
Jonah
Micah
Nahum
Habakkuk
Zephaniah
Haggai
Zechariah
Malachi

New Testament Books

Matthew
Mark
Luke
John
Acts
Romans
1 Corinthians
2 Corinthians
Galatians
Ephesians
Philippians
Colossians
1 Thessalonians
2 Thessalonians
1 Timothy
2 Timothy
Titus
Philemon
Hebrews
James
1 Peter
2 Peter
1 John
2 John
3 John
Jude
Revelation

Books of the Apocrypha and Pseudepigrapha

Old Testament Apocryphal Books

Additions to the Book of Esther
Baruch
Bel and the Dragon
Ecclesiasticus (Sirach)
1 Esdras
2 Esdras
Judith
Letter of Jeremiah
1 Maccabees
2 Maccabees
Prayer of Azariah
Prayer of Manasseh
Song of the Three Young Men
Susanna
Tobit
Wisdom of Solomon

New Testament Apocryphal Books

Gospels
Arabic Gospel of the Infancy
Armenian Gospel of the Infancy
Assumption of the Virgin
Book of the Resurrection of Christ by Bartholomew the Apostle
Gospel According to the Egyptians
Gospel According to the Hebrews
Gospel of Bartholomew
Gospel of Basilides
Gospel of the Birth of Mary
Gospel of the Ebionites
Gospel of Marcion
Gospel of Matthias
Gospel of the Nazarenes
Gospel of Peter
Gospel of Philip
Gospel of Pseudo-Matthew
Gospel of Thomas
History of Joseph the Carpenter
Protevangelium of James

Acts
Acts of Andrew
Acts of Andrew
Acts of Andrew and Matthias
Acts of Andrew and Paul
Acts of Barnabas
Acts of James the Great
Acts of John
Acts of John by Prochorus
Acts of Paul
Acts of Peter
Acts of Peter and Andrew
Acts of Peter and Paul
Acts of Philip
Acts of Pilate
Acts of Thaddaeus
Acts of Thomas
Apostolic History of Abdias
Ascents of James
Fragmentary Story of Andrew
Martyrdom of Matthew
Passion of Paul
Passion of Peter
Passion of Peter and Paul
Preaching of Peter
Slavonic Acts of Peter

Epistles
Apocryphal Epistle of Titus
Epistle of the Apostles
Epistle to the Laodiceans
Epistle of Lentalus
Epsitles of Christ and Abgarus
Epistles of Paul and Seneca
Third Epistle to the Corinthians

Apocalypses
Apocalypse of James
Apocalypse of Paul
Apocalypse of Peter
Revelation of Stephen
Apocalypse of Thomas
Apocalypse of the Virgin

Books of the Pseudepigrapha

Apocalypse of Baruch
Apocryphon of Genesis
Aristeas
Assumption of Moses
3 Baruch
Book of Mysteries
Damascus Document
Description of the New Jerusalem
Enoch
2 Enoch
Hodayoth
Jubilees
Life of Adam and Eve
Liturgy of Three Tongues of Fire
Lives of the Prophets
3 Maccabees
4 Maccabees
Martyrdom of Isaiah
Paralipomena of Jeremiah
Psalms of Joshua
Psalms of Solomon
Pseudo-Jeremianic work
Sibylline Oracles
Testament of Job
Testament of Levi
Testaments of the Twelve Patriarchs
War Scroll

Orders and Tractates of the Mishnah and the Talmud

Division 1: Zeraim *Seeds*
Berakoth *Blessings*
Peah *Gleanings*
Demai *Produce not Certainly Tithed*
Kilaim *Two Kinds*
Shebiith *The Seventh Year*
Terumoth *Heave Offerings*
Maaseroth *Tithes*
Maaser Sheni *Second Tithe*
Hallah *Dough Offering*
Orlah *The Fruit of Young Trees*
Bikkurim *First Fruits*

Division 2: Moed *Feast*
Shabbath *Sabbath*
Erubin *Mixtures*
Pesahim *Passover*
Shekalim *The Shekel Dues*
Yoma *The Day of Atonement*
Sukkah *The Feast of Tabernacles*
Yom Tob *Festival Days*
Rosh ha-Shanah *New Year*
Taanith *The Days of Fasting*
Megillah *Scroll of Esther*
Moed Katan *Minor Feast*
Hagigah *The Festival Offering*

Division 3: Nashim *Women*
Yebamoth *Sisters-in-law*
Ketuboth *Marriage Deeds*
Nedarim *Vows*
Nazir *Nazirite Vow*
Sotah *The Suspected Adulteress*
Gittin *Bills of Divorce*
Kiddushin *Betrothals*

Division 4: Nezekin *Damages*
Baba Kamma *First Gate*
Baba Metzia *Middle Gate*
Baba Bathra *Last Gate*
Sanhedrin *The Sanhedrin*
Makkoth *Stripes*
Shebuoth *Oaths*
Eduyoth *Testimonies*
Abodah Zarah *Unlawful Worship*
Aboth *Fathers*
Horayoth *Instructions*

Division 5: Kodashim *Sacred Things*
Zebahim *Animal Offerings*
Menahoth *Meal Offerings*
Hullin *Slaughtering of Animals*
Bekhoroth *Firstlings*
Arakhin *Valuations*
Temurah *Substituted Offering*
Kerithoth *Excisions*
Meilah *Trespass*
Tamid *The Daily Whole Offering*
Middoth *Measurements*
Kinnim *Nests*

Division 6: Tohoroth *Cleannesses*
Kelim *Vessels*
Oholoth *Tents*
Negaim *Plagues*
Parah *The Red Heifer*
Tohoroth *Cleannesses*
Mikwaoth *Pools of Water*
Niddah *The Menstruant*
Makshirin *Predisposers*
Zabim *Persons that Suffer a Flux*
Tebul Yom *One Immersed on the Day*
Yadaim *Hands*
Uktzin *Stalks*

Bibliography

Resource Tools

BAUER (BAGD)
Bauer, Walter, William F. Arndt, and F. Wilbur Gingrich. *A Greek-English Lexicon of the New Testament and other Early Christian Literature.* Rev. ed. by F. Wilbur Gingrich and Frederick W. Danker. Chicago: The University of Chicago Press. 1979.

COLIN BROWN (NIDNTT)
Brown, Colin, ed. *The New International Dictionary of New Testament Theology.* 4 vols. Grand Rapids: Zondervan Publishing House. 1975.

KITTEL (TDNT)
Kittel, G., and G. Friedrich. *Theological Dictionary of the New Testament.* Trans. by G. W. Bromiley. 10 vols. Grand Rapids: William B. Eerdmans Publishing Co. 1972.

LIDDELL–SCOTT (LSJ)
Liddell, H. G., and R. Scott. *A Greek-English Lexicon.* 9th. ed. Ed. by H. Stuart Jones and R. McKenzie. Oxford: Clarendon. 1940.

MOULTON–MILLIGAN (M-M)
Moulton, J.H., and G. Milligan. *The Vocabulary of the Greek Testament Illustrated from the Papyri and Other Non-Literary Sources.* London: Hodder and Stoughton. 1914–1930. Reprint. Grand Rapids: Wm. B. Eerdmans Publishing Company. 1985.

STRONG
Strong, James. *The Exhaustive Concordance of the Bible.* 1890. Reprint. Nashville: Abingdon Press. 1977.

(Parenthetical abbreviations found in Study Bible.)

Modern Greek Texts

Aland, K. et al. in cooperation with the Institute for New Testament Textual Research. *The Greek New Testament.* 2nd ed. London: United Bible Societies. 1968. (Also known as UBS.)

Aland, K. et al. in cooperation with the Institute for New Testament Textual Research. *The Greek New Testament.* 3rd ed. New York: United Bible Societies. 1975. (Also known as UBS.)

Nestle, E., and K. Aland. *Novum Testamentum Graece.* 25th ed. Stuttgart: Wurtembergische Bibelanstalt. 1963. (Also known as Nestle-Aland or NA 25.)

Nestle, E., and K. Aland. et al. *Novum Testamentum Graece.* 26th ed. Stuttgart: Deutsche Bibelstiftung. 1979. (Also known as Nestle-Aland or NA 26.)

General Bibliography

Abbott, T. K. *Ephesians and Colossians*. The International Critical Commentary. Ed. by S. R. Driver, A. Plummer, and C. A. Briggs. Edinburgh: T. and T. Clark. 1968.

Abbott-Smith, G. *A Manual Greek Lexicon of the New Testament*. New York: Charles Scribner's Sons. 1937.

Achtemeier, Paul J. *Harper's Bible Dictionary*. New York: Harper and Row. 1985.

Albright, W. F., and C. S. Mann. *Matthew*. Vol. 26 of *The Anchor Bible*. Ed. by William Foxwell Albright and David Noel Freedman. Garden City, NY: Doubleday and Company, Inc. 1971.

Alford, Henry. *Alford's Greek Testament*. 3 vols. Grand Rapids: Baker Book House. 1980.

Allen, W. C. *A Critical and Exegetical Commentary on the Gospel According to St. Matthew*. The International Critical Commentary. Ed. by S. R. Driver, A. Plummer, and C. A. Briggs. Edinburgh: T. and T. Clark. 1912.

Archer, Gleason L. *Encyclopedia of Bible Difficulties*. Grand Rapids: Zondervan Publishing House. 1982.

Bauckham, Richard J. *Jude, 2 Peter*. Vol. 50 of *Word Biblical Commentary*. Ed. by David A. Hubbard, et al. Waco, TX: Word Books. 1983.

Barclay, William. *The Gospel of John*. The Daily Study Bible. Rev. ed. Philadelphia: The Westminster Press. 1975.

Barclay, William. *The Gospel of Mark*. The Daily Study Bible. Rev. ed. Philadelphia: The Westminster Press. 1975.

Barclay, William. *New Testament Words*. Philadelphia: The Westminster Press. 1974.

Barrett, C. K. *A Commentary on the Epistle to the Romans*. Harper's New Testament Commentaries. Ed. by Henry Chadwick. New York: Harper and Row. 1957.

Barrett, C. K. *A Commentary on the First Epistle to the Corinthians*. Harper's New Testament Commentaries. Ed. by Henry Chadwick. New York: Harper and Row. 1968.

Barrett, C. K. *The New Testament Background: Selected Documents*. New York: Harper and Row. 1961.

Barth, Karl. *The Epistle to the Romans*. Trans. by Edwyn C. Hoskyns. London: Oxford University Press. 1933.

Barth, Karl. *The Word of God and the Word of Man*. Trans. by Douglas Horton. New York: Harper and Brothers, Publishers. 1957.

Bauer, Walter. *Griechisch-deutsches Worterbuch zu den Schriften des Neuen Testaments und der fruhchristlichen Literatur*. Ed. by Kurt and Barbara Aland. New York: Walter de Gruyter. 1988.

Bauer, Walter, William F. Arndt, and F. Wilbur Gingrich. *A Greek-English Lexicon of the New Testament and other Early Christian Literature*. Rev. ed. by F. Wilbur Gingrich and Frederick W. Danker. Chicago: The University of Chicago Press. 1979.

Baylis, Charles P. "The Woman Caught in Adultery: A Test of Jesus as the Greater Prophet." *Biblio Theca Sacra* 146 (April–June 1989): 171-184.

Beasley-Murray, G. R. *Baptism in the New Testament*. Grand Rapids: William B. Eerdmans Publishing Co. 1973.

Bickerman, E. J. "The Name of Christians." *Harvard Theological Review* 42, no. 1 (January 1949): 109-124.

Bibliography Continued

Bigg, Charles. *A Critical and Exegetical Commentary on the Epistles of St. Peter and St. Jude.* The International Critical Commentary. Ed. by S. R. Driver, A. Plummer, and C. A. Briggs. Edinburgh: T. and T. Clark. 1978.

Black, David Alan. "Ephesian Address." *Grace Theological Journal* 2 (1981): 59-73.

Blass, F. *Philology of the Gospels.* Amsterdam: B. R. Gruner. 1969.

Blass, F., and A. DeBrunner. *A Greek Grammar of the New Testament and Other Early Christian Literature.* Trans. by Robert W. Funk. Chicago: The University of Chicago Press. 1974.

Blum, Edwin A. *2 Peter.* In *Hebrews—Revelation.* Vol. 12 of *The Expositor's Bible Commentary.* Ed. by Frank E. Gaebelein. Grand Rapids: Zondervan Publishing House. 1981.

Bornkamm, Gunther. *Jesus of Nazareth.* Trans. by Irene and Fraser McLuskey. New York: Harper. 1960.

Botterweck, G. Johannes, and Helmer Ringgren, eds. *Theological Dictionary of the Old Testament.* 5 vols. Trans. by Geoffrey Bromiley, et al. Grand Rapids: William B. Eerdmans Publishing Co. 1974.

Brown, Colin, ed. *The New International Dictionary of New Testament Theology.* 4 vols. Grand Rapids: Zondervan Publishing House. 1975.

Brown, Raymond E. *The Gospel According to St. John.* Vols. 29 and 29a of *The Anchor Bible.* Ed. by William Foxwell Albright and David Noel Freedman. Garden City, NY: Doubleday and Company, Inc. 1978.

Brown, Francis, Samuel Driver, and Charles A. Briggs. *The New Brown-Driver-Briggs-Gesenius Hebrew and English Lexicon of the Old Testament.* Peabody, MA: Hendrickson Publishers. 1979.

Bruce, A. B. *The Synoptic Gospels.* In *The Synoptic Gospels and John.* Vol. 1 of *The Expositor's Greek Testament.* Ed. by W. Robertson Nicoll. Grand Rapids: William B. Eerdmans Publishing Co. 1951.

Bruce, F. F. *The Acts of the Apostles.* Vol. 5 of *Tyndale New Testament Commentaries.* Ed. by R. V. G. Tasker. Grand Rapids: William B. Eerdmans Publishing Co. 1952.

Bruce, F. F. *The Acts of the Apostles: The Greek Text.* London: The Tyndale Press. 1956.

Bruce, F. F. *The Book of Acts.* The New International Commentary on the New Testament. Ed. by F. F. Bruce. Grand Rapids: William B. Eerdmans Publishing Co. 1979.

Bruce, F. F. *The Epistle of Paul to the Romans.* Vol. 6 of *Tyndale New Testament Commentaries.* Ed. by R. V. G. Tasker. Grand Rapids: William B. Eerdmans Publishing Co. 1963.

Bruce, F. F. *The Epistle to the Hebrews.* The New International Commentary on the New Testament. Ed. by F. F. Bruce. Grand Rapids: William B. Eerdmans Publishing Co. 1964.

Bruce, F. F. *The Epistles to the Colossians, to Philemon, and to the Ephesians.* The New International Commentary on the New Testament. Ed. by F. F. Bruce. Grand Rapids: William B. Eerdmans Publishing Co. 1984.

Bruce, F. F. *1 and 2 Thessalonians.* Word Biblical Commentary. Ed. by David A. Hubbard, et al. Waco, TX: Word Books. 1982.

Bruce, F. F. *Galatians.* New International Greek Testament Commentary. Ed. by I. Howard Marshall and W. Ward Gasque. Grand Rapids: William B. Eerdmans Publishing Co. 1982.

Bruce, F. F. *The Gospel of John: Introduction, Exposition, and Notes.* Grand Rapids: William B. Eerdmans Publishing Co. 1983.

Bruce, F. F. *The Hard Sayings of Jesus.* The Jesus Library. Ed. by Michael Green. Downers Grove, IL: InterVarsity Press. 1983.

Bruce, F. F. *New Testament Development of Old Testament Themes*. Grand Rapids: William B. Eerdmans Publishing Co. 1969.

Bruce, F. F. *Paul, Apostle of the Heart Set Free*. Grand Rapids: William B. Eerdmans Publishing Co. 1977.

Bruce, F. F., and E. K. Simpson. *Ephesians and Colossians*. The New International Commentary on the New Testament. Ed. by F. F. Bruce. Grand Rapids: William B. Eerdmans Publishing Co. 1975.

Bultmann, Rudolf. *The Gospel of John*. Trans. by G. R. Beasley-Murray. Philadelphia: The Westminster Press. 1975.

Bultmann, Rudolf. *Primitive Christianity in its Contemporary Setting*. Trans. by R. H. Fuller. New York: The World Publishing Company. 1972.

Burdick, Donald W. *Oida and Ginōskō in the Pauline Epistles*. In *New Dimensions in New Testament Study*. Ed. by Richard N. Longenecker and Merrill C. Tenney. Grand Rapids: Zondervan Publishing House. 1974.

Burrows, Millar. *The Dead Sea Scrolls*. New York: Viking Press. 1955.

Carson, D. A. *Matthew*. In *Matthew, Mark, and Luke*. Vol. 8 of *The Expositor's Bible Commentary*. Ed. by Frank E. Gaebelein. Grand Rapids: Zondervan Publishing House. 1984.

Casson, Lionel. *Ships and Seamanship in the Ancient World*. Princeton: Princeton University Press. 1971.

Chamberlain, William D. *An Exegetical Grammar of the Greek New Testament*. New York: The Macmillan Company. 1952.

Charles, R. H. *The Revelation of St. John*. 2 vols. The International Critical Commentary. Ed. by S. R. Driver, A. Plummer, and C. A. Briggs. Edinburgh: T. and T. Clark. 1971.

Clark, Stephen B. *Man and Woman in Christ: An Examination of the Roles of Men and Women in the Light of Scripture and the Social Sciences*. Ann Arbor, MI: Servant Books. 1980.

Conzelmann, Hans. *1 Corinthians*. Ed. by George W. McRae, and trans. by James W. Leitch. *Hermeneia*. Ed. by Helmut Koester, et al. Philadelphia: Fortress Press. 1975.

Cook, Barbara. *Ordinary Women, Extraordinary Strength*. Lynnwood: Aglow Publications. 1988.

Craigie, Peter C. *Deuteronomy*. The New International Commentary on the Old Testament. Ed. by R. K. Harrison. Grand Rapids: William B. Eerdmans Publishing Co. 1976.

Cranfield, C. E. B. *The Epistle to the Romans*. 2 vols. The International Critical Commentary. Rev. ed. Ed. by J. A. Emerton and C. E. B. Cranfield. Edinburgh: T. and T. Clark. 1979.

Cross, F. L. *The Oxford Dictionary of the Christian Church*. Oxford: Oxford University Press. 1974.

Dana, H. E., and Julius R. Mantey. *A Manual of the Greek New Testament*. New York: The Macmillan Co. 1955.

Daube, David. "Jesus and the Samaritan Woman: The Meaning of *Sugchraomai*." *Journal of Biblical Literature* 69 (1950): 137-147.

Davids, Peter H. *The Epistle of James: A Commentary on the Greek Text*. New International Greek Testament Commentary. Ed. by I. Howard Marshall and W. Ward Gasque. Grand Rapids: William B. Eerdmans Publishing Co. 1982.

Deissmann, G. Adolf. *Bible Studies*. Winona Lake, IN: Alpha Publications. 1979.

Dibelius, Martin. *James*. Trans. by Michael A. Williams. *Hermeneia*. Ed. by Helmut Koester, et al. Philadelphia: Fortress Press. 1976.

Dodd, C. H. *The Apostolic Preaching of the Cross*. Grand Rapids: Baker Book House. 1980.

Dodd, C. H. *The Interpretation of the Fourth Gospel*. Cambridge: Cambridge University Press. 1972.

Bibliography Continued

Doerksen, Vernon. *James*. Chicago: Moody Press. 1983.

Dods, Marcus. *The Epistle to the Hebrews*. In *Thessalonians–James*. Vol. 4 of *The Expositor's Greek Testament*. Ed. by W. Robertson Nicoll. Grand Rapids: William B. Eerdmans Publishing Co. 1974.

Douglas, J. D., ed. *The Illustrated Bible Dictionary*. 3 vols. Wheaton: Tyndale House Publishers. 1980.

Douglas, J. D. *New Bible Dictionary*. 2d ed. Wheaton: Tyndale House Publishers. 1982.

Dunn, James D. G. *Jesus and the Spirit*. Philadelphia: The Westminster Press. 1975.

Dunn, James D. G. *Romans 9–16*. Vol. 38b of *Word Biblical Commentary*. Ed. by David A. Hubbard, et al. Waco, TX: Word Books. 1988.

Eadie, John. *Ephesians*. Vol. 2 of *The John Eadie Greek Text Commentaries*. Grand Rapids: Baker Book House. 1979.

Earle, Ralph. *Word Meanings in the New Testament*. 6 vols. Grand Rapids: Baker Book House. 1984.

Edersheim, Alfred. *The Life and Times of Jesus the Messiah*. 2 vols. Grand Rapids: William B. Eerdmans Publishing Co. 1972.

Eichrodt, Walter. *Theology of the Old Testament*. 2 vols. Trans. by J. A. Baker. Philadelphia: The Westminster Press. 1967.

Ellis, E. Earle. *Paul's Use of the Old Testament*. Grand Rapids: William B. Eerdmans Publishing Co. 1957.

Ellis, E. Earle. *Prophecy and Hermeneutic in Early Christianity*. Grand Rapids: William B. Eerdmans Publishing Co. 1978.

English, E. Schugler. *Rethinking the Rapture*. Traveller's Rest, SC: Southern Bible Book House. 1954.

Fee, Gordon D. *1 and 2 Timothy, Titus. A Good News Commentary*. Ed. by W. Ward Gasque. San Francisco: Harper and Row. 1984.

Fee, Gordon D. *The First Epistle to the Corinthians. The New International Commentary on the New Testament*. Ed. by F. F. Bruce. Grand Rapids: William B. Eerdmans Publishing Co. 1987.

Fitzmyer, Joseph A. *The Gospel According to Luke*. Vol. 28 of *The Anchor Bible*. Ed. by William Foxwell Albright and David Noel Freedman. Garden City, NY: Doubleday and Company, Inc. 1982.

Forbes, R. J., ed. *Studies in Ancient Technology*. 9 vols. Leiden: E. J. Brill. 1965.

Ford, J. Massyngberde. *Revelation*. Vol. 38 of *The Anchor Bible*. Ed. by William Foxwell Albright and David Noel Freedman. Garden City, NY: Doubleday and Company, Inc. 1975.

Foulkes, Francis. *The Epistle of Paul to the Ephesians*. Vol. 10 of *Tyndale New Testament Commentaries*. Ed. by R. V. G. Tasker. Grand Rapids: William B. Eerdmans Publishing Co. 1983.

Furnish, Victor Paul. *2 Corinthians*. Vol. 32a of *The Anchor Bible*. Ed. by William Foxwell Albright and David Noel Freedman. Garden City, NY: Doubleday and Company, Inc. 1984.

Gartner, Betril Edgar. *The Temple and the Community in Qumran and the New Testament*. Cambridge: Cambridge University Press. 1965.

Gehman, Henry Snyder, ed. *The New Westminster Dictionary of the Bible*. Philadelphia: The Westminster Press. 1970.

Gemsler, B. *The Rîv or Controversy Pattern in Hebrew Mentality*. In *Wisdom in Israel and in the Ancient Near East*. Ed. by M. Noth and D. W. Thomas. *Supplements to Vetus Testamentum*, vol. 3. Leiden: E. J. Brill. 1969.

Gesenius, Wilhelm. *Gesenius' Hebrew Grammar.* 2d English ed., ed. and rev. by E. Kautzsch and A. E. Cowley. Oxford: Clarendon Press. 1910.

Glover, T. R. *The Conflict of Religions in the Early Roman Empire.* Washington: Canon Press. 1974.

Grant, Robert McQueen. *Gnosticism and Early Christianity.* 2d ed. New York: Columbia University Press. 1966.

Green, Michael. *The Second Epistle of Peter and the Epistle of Jude.* Vol. 18 of *Tyndale New Testament Commentaries.* Ed. by R. V. G. Tasker. Grand Rapids: William B. Eerdmans Publishing Co. 1975.

Green, Samuel G. *Handbook to the Grammar of the Greek Testament.* London: The Religious Tract Society. N.d.

Greenlee, J. Harold. *A Concise Exegetical Grammar of New Testament Greek.* Grand Rapids: William B. Eerdmans Publishing Co. 1963.

Greenlee, J. Harold. *A New Testament Greek Morpheme Lexicon.* Grand Rapids: Zondervan Publishing House. 1983.

Grimm, C. L. Wilibald. *A Greek-English Lexicon of the New Testament.* 4th ed., trans. and rev. by Joseph Henry Thayer. Edinburgh: T. and T. Clark. 1956.

Gundry, Robert. *Matthew: A Commentary on His Literary and Theological Art.* Grand Rapids: William B. Eerdmans Publishing Co. 1982.

Guthrie, Donald. *The Letter to the Hebrews.* Vol. 20 of *Tyndale New Testament Commentaries.* Ed. by R. V. G. Tasker. Grand Rapids: William B. Eerdmans Publishing Co. 1983.

Guthrie, Donald. *The Pastoral Epistles.* Vol. 14 of *Tyndale New Testament Commentaries.* Ed. by R. V. G. Tasker. Grand Rapids: William B. Eerdmans Publishing Co. 1957.

Guthrie, Donald, and J. A. Motyer. *The New Bible Commentary: Revised.* Grand Rapids: William B. Eerdmans Publishing Co. 1981.

Guthrie, W. K. C. *The Greeks and Their Gods.* Boston: Beacon Press. 1949.

Hagner, Donald A. *Hebrews. A Good News Commentary.* Ed. by W. Ward Gasque. San Francisco: Harper and Row. 1983.

Harner, Philip B. *The "I Am" of the Fourth Gospel.* Facet Books: Biblical Series, no. 26. Philadelphia: Fortress Press. 1970.

Hastings, James, et al., eds. *Dictionary of the Bible.* New York: Charles Scribner's Sons. 1951.

Hatch, Edwin, and Henry A. Redpath, eds. *A Concordance to the Septuagint.* 2 vols. Reprint. Grand Rapids: Baker Book House. 1983.

Hawthorne, Gerald F. *Philippians.* Vol. 43 of *Word Biblical Commentary.* Ed. by David A. Hubbard, et al. Waco, TX: Word Books. 1983.

Hemer, Colin J. *The Letters to the Seven Churches of Asia in Their Local Setting.* Journal for the Study of the New Testament Supplement Series, vol. 11. Ed. by David Hill. Sheffield, England: JSOT Press. 1986.

Hendriksen, William. *Exposition of the Pastoral Epistles. New Testament Commentary.* Grand Rapids: Baker Book House. 1957.

Hengel, Martin. *Judaism and Hellenism.* Trans. by John Bowden. Philadelphia: Fortress Press. 1981.

Hiebert, D. Edmond. *1 Timothy.* Chicago: Moody Press. 1957.

Hiebert, D. Edmond. *The Thessalonian Epistles.* Chicago: Moody Press. 1971.

Bibliography Continued

Hiebert, D. Edmond. *Titus*. In *Ephesians–Philemon*. Vol. 11 of *The Expositor's Bible Commentary*. Ed. by Frank E. Gaebelein. Grand Rapids: Zondervan Publishing House. 1978.

Hobart, William Kirk. *The Medical Language of St. Luke*. Dublin: Hodges, Figgis, and Co. 1882.

Hodge, Charles. *A Commentary on 1 and 2 Corinthians*. Edinburgh: The Banner of Truth Trust. 1974.

Hopkins, David C. "Life on the Land: The Subsistence Struggles of Early Israel." *Biblical Archeologist* 50 (September 1987): 179-190.

Hort, Fenton John Anthony. *Judaistic Christianity*. Ed. by J. O. F. Murray. Grand Rapids: Baker Book House. 1980.

Horton, Stanley M. *What the Bible Says about the Holy Spirit*. Springfield, MO: Gospel Publishing House. 1976.

Howard, J. Keir. "Neither Male nor Female: An Examination of the Status of Women in the New Testament." *Evangelical Quarterly* 55, no. 1 (1983): 31-42.

Hughes, Philip E. *The Second Epistle to the Corinthians*. *The New International Commentary on the New Testament*. Ed. by F. F. Bruce. Grand Rapids: William B. Eerdmans Publishing Co. 1962.

Jackson, F. J. Foakes, and Kirsopp Lake. *The Beginnings of Christianity*. 5 vols. London: Macmillan and Company, Limited. 1920.

Jagersma, Henk. *A History of Israel from Alexander the Great to Bar Kochba*. Trans. by John Bowden. Philadelphia: Fortress Press. 1986.

Jart, Una. "The Precious Stones in the Revelation of St. John 21:18-21." *Studia Theologica* 24 (1970): 150-181.

Jeremias, Joachim. *The Eucharistic Words of Jesus*. London: SCM Press. 1966.

Jeremias, Joachim. *Jerusalem in the Time of Jesus*. Philadelphia: Fortress Press. 1987.

Jeremias, Joachim. *The Parables of Jesus*. New York: Charles Scribner's Sons. 1963.

Kaseman, Ernst. *Perspectives on Paul*. Trans. by Margaret Kohl. Philadelphia: Fortress Press. 1974.

Kee, H. C. *The Linguistic Background of Shame in the New Testament*. In *On Language, Culture, and Religion: In Honor of Eugene A. Nida*. Ed. by Matthew Black and William A. Smalley. The Hague: Mouton. 1974.

Kelly, J. N. D. *A Commentary on the Epistles of Peter and Jude*. Thornapple Commentaries. Reprint. Grand Rapids: Baker Book House. 1981.

Kent, Homer. *The Pastoral Epistles*. Chicago: Moody Press. 1958.

Kittel, G., and G. Friedrich. *Theological Dictionary of the New Testament*. Trans. by G. W. Bromiley. 10 vols. Grand Rapids: William B. Eerdmans Publishing Co. 1972.

Kitto, H. D. F. *The Greeks*. Middlesex: Penguin Books. 1951.

Klein, Ralph W. *1 Samuel*. Vol. 10 of *Word Biblical Commentary*. Ed. by John D. Watts, et al. Waco, TX: Word Books. 1983.

Knight, George W. "*Authenteō* in Reference to Women in 1 Timothy 2:12." *New Testament Studies* 30 (1984): 143-157.

Knowling, R. J. *The Acts of the Apostles*. In *Acts–1 Corinthians*. Vol. 2 of *The Expositor's Greek Testament*. Ed. by W. Robertson Nicoll. Grand Rapids: William B. Eerdmans Publishing Co. 1974.

Koester, Helmut. *History, Culture and Religion of the Hellenistic Age*. Philadelphia: Fortress Press. 1982.

Kroeger, Catarine C. "Ancient Heresies and a Strange Greek Verb." *The Reformed Journal* 29, no. 3 (1979): 12-15.

Kummel, Werner Georg. *Introduction to the New Testament*. Rev. ed. Ed. by Howard Clark Kee. Nashville: Abingdon Press. 1975.

Ladd, George Eldon. *The Presence of the Future*. Grand Rapids: William B. Eerdmans Publishing Co. 1974.

Lane, William L. *The Gospel of Mark*. *The New International Commentary on the New Testament*. Ed. by F. F. Bruce. Grand Rapids: William B. Eerdmans Publishing Co. 1978.

Lenski, R. C. H. *The Interpretation of the Acts of the Apostles*. Minneapolis: Augsburg Publishing House. 1964. Lenski, R. C. H. *The Interpretation of the Epistles of St. Peter, St. John, and St. Jude*. Minneapolis: Augsburg Publishing House. 1966.

Lenski, R. C. H. *The Interpretation of the Epistles to the Hebrews and James*. Minneapolis: Augsburg Publishing House. 1966.

Lenski, R. C. H. *The Interpretation of St. Paul's Epistles to the Colossians, to the Thessalonians, to Timothy, to Titus, and to Philemon*. Minneapolis: Augsburg Publishing House. 1966.

Lenski, R. C. H. *The Interpretation of St. Paul's First and Second Epistles to the Corinthians*. Minneapolis: Augsburg Publishing House. 1964.

Lichtheim, Miriam. *The Old and Middle Kingdoms*. Vol. 1 of *Ancient Egyptian Literature*. Los Angeles: University of California Press. 1975.

Liddell, H. G., and R. Scott. *A Greek-English Lexicon*. 9th ed., ed. by H. Stuart Jones and R. McKenzie. Oxford: Clarendon Press. 1940.

Liefeld, Walter L. *Luke*. In *Matthew, Mark, and Luke*. Vol. 8 of *The Expositor's Bible Commentary*. Ed. by Frank E. Gaebelein. Grand Rapids: Zondervan Publishing House. 1984.

Lightfoot, J. B. *The Epistle of St. Paul to the Galatians*. Grand Rapids: Zondervan Publishing House. 1974.

Lightfoot, J. B. *Matthew–Mark*. Vol. 2 of *A Commentary on the New Testament from the Talmud and Hebraica*. Grand Rapids: Baker Book House. 1979.

Lightfoot, J. B. *Saint Paul's Epistle to the Philippians*. Grand Rapids: Zondervan Publishing House. 1953.

Lightfoot, J. B. *Saint Paul's Epistles to the Colossians and to Philemon*. New York: The Macmillan Company. 1897.

Lightfoot, R. H. *St. John's Gospel: A Commentary*. Ed. by C. F. Evans. Oxford: Oxford University Press. 1956.

Limet, Henri. "The Cuisine of Ancient Sumer." *Biblical Archeologist* 50 (September 1987): 132-147.

Lockyer, Hebert, ed. *Nelson's Illustrated Bible Dictionary*. Nashville: Thomas Nelson. 1986.

Lohse, Eduard. *Colossians and Philemon*. Ed. by Helmut Koester, and trans. by William R. Poehlmann and Robert J. Karris. *Hermeneia*. Ed. by Helmut Koester, et al. Philadelphia: Fortress Press. 1982.

Bibliography Continued

Longenecker, Richard N. *The Acts of the Apostles.* In *John–Acts.* Vol. 9 of *The Expositor's Bible Commentary.* Ed. by Frank E. Gaebelein. Grand Rapids: Zondervan Publishing House. 1981.

Louw, Johannes P. and Eugene A. Nida, eds. *Greek-English Lexicon of the New Testament Based on Semantic Domains.* 2 vols. New York: United Bible Societies. 1988.

Machen, J. Gresham. *New Testament Greek for Beginners.* New York: The Macmillan Company. 1957.

Mackie, George M. *Bible Manners and Customs.* New York: Flemming H. Revell Co. N.d.

Marshall, I. Howard. *The Acts of the Apostles.* Vol. 5 of *Tyndale New Testament Commentaries.* Ed. by R. V. G. Tasker. Grand Rapids: William B. Eerdmans Publishing Co. 1980.

Marshall, I. Howard. *The Gospel of Luke. New International Greek Testament Commentary.* Ed. by I. Howard Marshall and W. Ward Gasque. Grand Rapids: William B. Eerdmans Publishing Co. 1978.

Marshall, I. Howard. *The Meaning of Reconciliation.* In *Unity and Diversity in New Testament Theology: Essays in Honor of George E. Ladd.* Ed. by Robert A. Guelich. Grand Rapids: William B. Eerdmans Publishing Co. 1978.

Mayor, Joseph B. *The Epistle of St. James.* Minneapolis: Klock and Klock Christian Publishers. 1977.

McDonald, H. Dermot. *Commentary on Colossians and Philemon.* Waco, TX: Word Books. 1982.

Metzger, Bruce M. *Lexical Aids for Students of New Testament Greek.* Princeton: Bruce M. Metzger. 1978.

Metzger, Bruce M. *A Textual Commentary on the Greek New Testament.* London: United Bible Societies. 1971.

Miranda, Jose. *Christianity is Communism.* In *Third World Liberation Theologies.* Ed. by Deane William Ferm. Maryknoll, NY: Orbis Books. 1986.

Moffatt, James. *The Revelation of St. John the Divine.* In *1 Peter–Revelation.* Vol. 5 of *The Expositor's Greek Testament.* Ed. by W. Robertson Nicoll. Grand Rapids: William B. Eerdmans Publishing Co. 1951.

Moo, Douglas J. "1 Timothy 2:11-15: Meaning and Significance." *Trinity Journal* 1, no. 1 (1980): 62-83.

Morris, Leon. *The First and Second Epistles to the Thessalonians. The New International Commentary on the New Testament.* Ed. by F. F. Bruce. Grand Rapids: William B. Eerdmans Publishing Co. 1959.

Morris, Leon. *The Gospel According to John. The New International Commentary on the New Testament.* Ed. by F. F. Bruce. Grand Rapids: William B. Eerdmans Publishing Co. 1973.

Morris, Leon. *Hebrews.* In *Hebrews–Revelation.* Vol. 12 of *The Expositor's Bible Commentary.* Ed. by Frank E. Gaebelein. Grand Rapids: Zondervan Publishing House. 1981.

Morris, Leon. *The Revelation of St. John.* Vol. 20 of *Tyndale New Testament Commentaries.* Ed. by R. V. G. Tasker. Grand Rapids: William B. Eerdmans Publishing Co. 1969.

Morrish, George. *A Concordance of the Septuagint.* Grand Rapids: Zondervan Publishing House. 1976.

Moule, C. F. D. *An Idiom Book of New Testament Greek.* Cambridge: Cambridge University Press. 1986.

Moulton, J. H., and W. F. Howard. *Accidence and Word Formation.* Vol. 2 of *Grammar of New Testament Greek.* Edinburgh: T. and T. Clark. 1979.

Moulton, J. H., and G. Milligan. *The Vocabulary of the Greek Testament Illustrated from the Papyri and Other Non-Literary Sources.* London: Hodder and Stoughton. 1914-1930. Reprint. Grand Rapids: William B. Eerdmans Publishing Co. 1985.

Moulton, W. F., et al. *A Concordance to the Greek New Testament.* Edinburgh: T. and T. Clark. 1897.

Mounce, Robert H. *Revelation. The New International Commentary on the New Testament.* Ed. by F. F. Bruce. Grand Rapids: William B. Eerdmans Publishing Co. 1977.

Muhly, James D. *The Bronze Age Setting.* In *The Coming of the Age of Iron.* Ed. by Theodore A. Wertime and James D. Muhly. New Haven: Yale University Press. 1980.

Muller, J. J. *The Epistles of Paul to the Philippians and to Philemon. The New International Commentary on the New Testament.* Ed. by F. F. Bruce. Grand Rapids: William B. Eerdmans Publishing Co. 1955.

Murphy-O'Connor, Jerome. "1 Corinthians 11:2-16 Once Again." *Catholic Biblical Quarterly* 50, no. 2 (April 1988): 265-274.

Murray, John. *The Epistle to the Romans. The New International Commentary on the New Testament.* Ed. by F. F. Bruce. Grand Rapids: William B. Eerdmans Publishing Co. 1965.

Negev, Abraham. "Understanding the Nabateans." *Biblical Archeology Review* 14 (November–December 1988): 26-45.

Orr, William F., and James Arthur Walther. *1 Corinthians.* Vol. 26 of *The Anchor Bible.* Ed. by William Foxwell Albright and David Noel Freedman. Garden City, NY: Doubleday and Company, Inc. 1976.

O'Brien, Peter T. *Colossians and Philemon.* Vol. 44 of *Word Biblical Commentary.* Ed. by David A. Hubbard, et al. Waco, TX: Word Books. 1982.

Osiek, Carolyn. *Galatians.* Vol. 22 of *New Testament Message: A Biblical Theological Commentary.* Wilmington: Michael Glazier, Inc. 1980.

Pfeifer, Charles F., and Howard F. Vos. *The Wycliffe Historical Geography of Bible Lands.* Chicago: Moody Press. 1967.

Plummer, Alfred. *A Critical and Exegetical Commentary on the Gospel According to St. Luke. The International Critical Commentary.* Ed. by S. R. Driver, A. Plummer, and C. A. Briggs. Edinburgh: T. and T. Clark. 1969.

Radford, Lewis B. *The Epistle to Colossians and the Epistle to Philemon. Westminster Commentaries.* Ed. by Walter Lock and D. C. Simpson. London: Melhuen and Co. Ltd. 1931.

Rapinsky, Michael. "The Camel in Ancient Arabia." *Antiquity* 49 (1979): 295-298.

Reicke, Bo Ivar. *The New Testament Era: The World of the Bible from 500 B.C. to A.D. 100.* Philadelphia: Fortress Press. 1968.

Reiling, J., and J. L. Swellengvebel. *A Translator's Handbook on the Gospel of Luke.* London: United Bible Society. 1971.

Ridderbos, Herman J. *Paul: An Outline of His Theology.* Trans. by Rohn Richard deWitt. Grand Rapids: William B. Eerdmans Publishing Co. 1975.

Ridderbos, Herman J. *Studies in Scripture and its Authority.* Grand Rapids: William B. Eerdmans Publishing Co. 1978.

Rienecker, Fritz. *Linguistic Key to the Greek New Testament.* 2 vols. Grand Rapids: Zondervan Publishing House. 1980.

Robertson, Archibald Thomas. *A Grammar of the Greek New Testament in the Light of Historical Research.* Nashville: Broadman Press. 1934.

Robertson, Archibald Thomas. *Word Pictures in the New Testament.* 6 vols. Nashville: Broadman Press. 1931.

Bibliography Continued

Robinson, J. Armitage. *Commentary on Ephesians.* Grand Rapids: Kregel Publications. 1979.

Rose, H. J. *A Handbook of Greek Mythology.* New York: E. P. Dutton and Co., Inc. 1959.

Russell, David S. *The Method and Message of Jewish Apocalyptic.* Philadelphia: The Westminster Press. 1964.

Sanday, William, and Arthur Headlam. *A Critical and Exegetical Commentary on the Epistle to the Romans. The International Critical Commentary.* Ed. by S. R. Driver, A. Plummer, and C. A. Briggs. Edinburgh: T. and T. Clark. 1897.

Scarborough, John. *Facets of Hellenic Life.* Boston: Houghton Mifflin Company. 1976.

Schmithals, Walter. *Paul and the Gnostics.* Trans. by John E. Steely. Nashville: Abingdon Press. 1972.

Selwyn, Edward Gordon. *The First Epistle of St. Peter.* Grand Rapids: Baker Book House. 1981.

Sevier, Paul. *Images of the Church in the New Testament.* Philadelphia: The Westminster Press. 1960.

Sherwin-White, Adrian Nicholas. *Roman Society and Roman Law in the New Testament.* Grand Rapids: Baker Book House. 1978.

Sidebottom, E. M. *James, Jude, 2 Peter. The New Century Bible Commentary.* Grand Rapids: William B. Eerdmans Publishing Co. 1982.

Smalley, Stephen. *1, 2, 3 John.* Vol. 51 of *Word Biblical Commentary.* Ed. by David A. Hubbard, et al. Waco, TX: Word Books. 1984.

Smith, J. B. *Greek-English Concordance to the New Testament.* Scottsdale, PA: Herald Press. 1974.

Smyth, Herbert Weir. *Greek Grammar.* Cambridge: Harvard University Press. 1984.

Snodgrass, Anthony M. *Iron and Early Metallurgy in the Mediterranean.* In *The Coming of the Age of Iron.* Ed. by Theodore A. Wertime and James D. Muhly. New Haven: Yale University Press. 1980.

Spence, H. D. M., and J. Marshall Lang. *St. Luke.* In *Mark and Luke.* Vol. 16 of *The Pulpit Commentary.* Grand Rapids: William B. Eerdmans Publishing Co. 1950.

Stagg, Frank. *New Testament Theology.* Nashville: Broadman Press. 1962.

Stagg, Frank. *Polarities of Man's Existence in Biblical Perspective.* Philadelphia: The Westminster Press. 1973.

Stein, Robert H. *The Method and Message of Jesus' Teachings.* Philadelphia: The Westminster Press. 1978.

Summers, Ray. *Worthy is the Lamb.* Nashville: Broadman Press. 1951.

Temkin, Owsei. *The Falling Sickness.* 2d ed. Baltimore: The Johns Hopkins Press. 1971.

Tenney, Merrill C. *The Zondervan Pictorial Encyclopedia of the Bible.* 5 vols. Grand Rapids: Zondervan Publishing House. 1975.

Thayer, Joseph Henry. *Thayer's Greek-English Lexicon of the New Testament.* Grand Rapids: Associated Publishers Authors, Inc. N.d.

Theissen, Henry C. *Introduction to the New Testament.* Grand Rapids: William B. Eerdmans Publishing Co. 1950.

Thrall, Margaret E. *Greek Participles in the New Testament*. Grand Rapids: William B. Eerdmans Publishing Co. 1962.

Tigoy, Jeffrey H. "On the Term Phylacteries." *Harvard Theological Review* 72 (January–April 1979): 45-54.

Trench, Richard C. *Synonyms of the New Testament*. 8th ed. Greenwood: The Attic Press, Inc. 1961.

Turner, Nigel. *Christian Words*. Nashville: Thomas Nelson Publishers. 1982.

Turner, Nigel. *Grammatical Insights into the New Testament*. Edinburgh: T. and T. Clark. 1965.

Turner, Nigel. *Style*. Vol. 4 of *A Grammar of New Testament Greek*. Edinburgh: T. and T. Clark. 1976.

Turner, Nigel. *Syntax*. Vol. 3 of *A Grammar of New Testament Greek*. Edinburgh: T. and T. Clark. 1980.

Tyler, Alice F. *Freedom's Ferment*. New York: Harper and Row. 1962.

Vaughan, Curtis. *Colossians*. In *Ephesians–Philemon*. Vol. 11 of *The Expositor's Bible Commentary*. Ed. by Frank E. Gaebelein. Grand Rapids: Zondervan Publishing House. 1978.

Vaughan, Curtis, and Virtus E. Gideon. *A Greek Grammar of the New Testament*. Nashville: Broadman Press. 1979.

Vincent, Marvin R. *The Epistles to the Philippians and to Philemon*. The International Critical Commentary. Ed. by S. R. Driver, A. Plummer, and C. A. Briggs. Edinburgh: T. and T. Clark. 1972.

Vincent, Marvin R. *Word Studies in the New Testament*. 4 vols. Grand Rapids: William B. Eerdmans Publishing Co. 1946.

Vine, W. E. *An Expository Dictionary of New Testament Words*. Nashville: Royal Publishers, Inc. 1952.

Walbank, F. W. *A Historical Commentary on Polybius*. 3 vols. Oxford: Clarendon Press. 1967.

Waldbaum, Jane C. *The First Archaeological Appearance of Iron and the Transition to the Iron Age*. In *The Coming of the Iron Age*. Ed. by Theodore A. Wertime and James D. Muhly. New Haven: Yale University Press. 1980.

Walters, Peter. *The Text of the Septuagint*. Ed. by D. W. Gooding. Cambridge: Cambridge University Press. 1973.

Walvoord, John F. *The Revelation of Jesus Christ*. Chicago: Moody Press. 1966.

Ward, Ronald A. *Commentary on 1 and 2 Timothy and Titus*. Waco, TX: Word Books. 1980.

Wescott, B. F. *The Epistle to the Hebrews*. Grand Rapids: William B. Eerdmans Publishing Co. 1955.

Wessel, Walter W. *Mark*. In *Matthew, Mark and Luke*. Vol. 8 of *The Expositor's Bible Commentary*. Ed. by Frank E. Gaebelein. Grand Rapids: Zondervan Publishing House. 1984.

Wight, Fred H. *Manners and Customs of Bible Lands*. Chicago: Moody Press. 1953.

Wigram, George W. *The Englishman's Greek Concordance*. Grand Rapids: Baker Book House. 1979.

Wilkinson, John. *Jerusalem as Jesus Knew It: Archaelogy as Evidence*. London: Thames and Hudson. 1978.

Wilson, John A. *The Intellectual Adventure of Ancient Man*. Ed. by H. and H. A. Frankfort. Chicago: The University of Chicago Press. 1946.

Wolff, Hans Walter. *Hosea*. Ed. by Paul D. Hanson, and trans. by Gary Stansell. *Hermeneia*. Ed. by Frank M. Cross, et al. Philadelphia: Fortress Press. 1974.

Bibliography Continued

Wood, A. Skevington. *Ephesians.* In *Ephesians–Philemon.* Vol. 11 of *The Expositor's Bible Commentary.* Ed. by Frank E. Gaebelein. Grand Rapids: Zondervan Publishing House. 1978.

Wurthwein, Ernst. *The Text of the Old Testament.* Trans. by Erroll F. Rhodes. Grand Rapids: William B. Eerdmans Publishing Co. 1979.

Yeager, Randolph O. *The Renaissance New Testament.* 8 vols. Gretna, LA: Pelican Publishing Company. 1980.

Young, Edward J. *The Book of Isaiah.* 3 vols. *The New International Commentary on the Old Testament.* Grand Rapids: William B. Eerdmans Publishing Co. 1972.

Zarins, Zuris. "The Camel in Ancient Arabia: A Further Note." *Antiquity* 52 (1978): 44-46.

Zockler, Otto. *The Proverbs of Solomon.* Ed. and trans. by Charles A. Aiken. In *Proverbs, Ecclesiastes, and the Song of Solomon.* Vol. 10 of *Commentary on the Holy Scriptures by John Lange.* Ed. and trans. by Philip Schaff. Grand Rapids: Zondervan Publishing House. 1969.

General Reference Sources by Title

This list is provided to make it easier for the reader to find the source material in those instances where only the title of the general reference is cited in text without the editor(s) or compiler(s).

The Analytical Greek Lexicon Revised. Harold K. Moulton. Grand Rapids: Zondervan Publishing House. 1977.

The Assyrian Dictionary. Ed. by A. Leo Oppenheim. 21 vols. Chicago: The Oriental Institute of the University of Chicago. 1968.

Biblico-Theological Lexicon of New Testament Greek. August Hermann Cremer. 4th ed. Edinburgh: T. and T. Clark. 1962.

A Concise Hebrew and Aramaic Lexicon of the Old Testament. William L. Holladay. Grand Rapids: William B. Eerdmans Publishing Co. 1980.

A Critical Lexicon and Concordance to the English and Greek New Testament. Ethelbert W. Bullinger. 8th ed. London: The Lamp Press, Ltd. 1957.

A Dictionary of Life in Bible Times. Willy Corswant. Trans. by Arthur Heathcote. London: Hodder and Stoughton. 1960.

Expository Dictionary of Bible Words. Lawrence O. Richards. Grand Rapids: Zondervan Publishing House. 1985.

An Expository Dictionary of New Testament Words. W. E. Vine. Nashville: Royal Publishers, Inc. 1952.

A Greek-English Lexicon of the New Testament and Other Early Christian Literature. W. A. Bauer, William F. Arndt, and F. Wilbur Gingrich. 2nd ed. Revised and augmented by F. Wilbur Gingrich and Frederick W. Danker. Chicago: The University of Chicago Press. 1979.

A Greek-English Lexicon. H. G. Liddell and R. Scott. 9th ed. Ed. by H. Stuart Jones and R. McKenzie. Oxford: Oxford University Press. 1940.

Greek-English Lexicon of the New Testament. Joseph Henry Thayer. 4th ed. Grand Rapids: Baker Book House. 1979.

Greek-English Lexicon of the New Testament Based on Semantic Domains. Ed. by Johannes P. Louw and Eugene A. Nida. 2 vols. New York: United Bible Societies. 1988.

A Homeric Dictionary. Georg Autenreith. Trans. by Robert P. Keep. Norman, OK: University of Oklahoma Press. 1972. *The International Standard Bible Encyclopedia.* Ed. by Geoffrey W. Bromiley. 4 vols. Grand Rapids: William B. Eerdmans Publishing Co. 1979.

The Interpreter's Dictionary of the Bible. Ed. by George Arthur Buttrick. 5 vols. Nashville: Abingdon Press. 1962.

The New Bible Dictionary. Ed. by J. D. Douglas. 2d ed. Wheaton: Tyndale House Publishers. 1982.

The New International Dictionary of New Testament Theology. Ed. by Colin Brown. 4 vols. Grand Rapids: Zondervan Publishing House. 1975.

Bibliography Continued

The New Standard Jewish Encyclopedia. Ed. by Cecil Roth and Geoffrey Wigoder. 5th ed. Garden City, NY: Doubleday and Company, Inc. 1977.

The New Westminster Dictionary of the Bible. Ed. by Henry Snyder Gehman. Philadelphia: The Westminster Press. 1970.

A Patristic Greek Lexicon. G. W. H. Lampe. Oxford: The Clarendon Press. 1961.

A Reader's Greek-English Lexicon of the New Testament. Sakae Kubo. Berrien Springs: Andrews University Press. 1975.

Theological Dictionary of the New Testament. Ed. by G. Kittel and G. Friedrich. 10 vols. Trans. by G. W. Bromiley. Grand Rapids: William B. Eerdmans Publishing Co. 1964-1977.

Theological Wordbook of the Old Testament. Ed. by R. Laird Harris, Gleason J. Archer, Jr., and Bruce K. Waltke. 2 vols. Chicago: Moody Press. 1980.

The Vocabulary of the Greek Testament Illustrated from the Papyri and Other Non-Literary Sources. J. H. Moulton and G. Milligan. London: Hodder and Stoughton. 1914-1930. Reprint. Grand Rapids: William B. Eerdmans Publishing Co. 1985.

The Zondervan Pictorial Bible Dictionary. Ed. by Merrill C. Tenney. Grand Rapids: Zondervan Publishing House. 1972.

Literature of Antiquity

The "Literature of Antiquity" (8th century B.C. to 16th century A.D.) refers to the noncanonical quotations and references found in one or all of the volumes of the *Greek-English Dictionary*. Also included are the sources where these materials may be found in print, many of which contain English translations.

Aeschylus.*
 Agamemnon.
 Prometheus Bound.

Anaxandrides.

The Apostolic Fathers.*
 1 Clement.
 The Didache.
 The Epistle of Barnabas.
 The Epistle to Diognetus.
 The Epistle to the Philippians of St. Polycarp.
 The Epistles of St. Ignatius.
 The Martyrdom of Polycarp.
 The Shepherd of Hermas.

Aristophanes.*
 Thesmophriazusae.

Aristotle.*
 Analytica Priora (Prior Analytics).
 The Athenian Constitution.
 De Caelo (On the Heavens).
 Ethica Nicomachea (Nichomachean Ethics).
 Historia Animalium (The History of Animals).
 De Longitudine et Brevitate Vitae (On Length and Shortness of Life).
 Meteorologica.
 Mirabilia (*De Mirabilibus Auscultationibus*, On Marvelous Things Heard).
 Politics.
 Problemata (Problems).
 Rhetorica (Rhetoric).

The Babylonian Talmud. Ed. by I. Epstein. London: The Soncino Press. 1948.

Cicero.*
 In Verrem.
 Letters to Atticus.

Demosthenes.*
 De Corona and De Falsa Legatione.
 Orations.

Diodorus Siculus.*
 Library of History.

Bibliography Continued

Diogenes Laertius.*
Lives of Eminent Philosophers.

Dionysius of Halicarnassus.*
Roman Antiquities.

Epictetus.*
Discourses.

Epicurus. *To Menoeceus.* In *Letters, Principal Doctrines and Vatican Sayings.* Trans. by Russel M. Geer. Indianapolis: The Bobbs-Merrill Company, Inc. 1964.

Euripides.*
Supplices.

Flavius Josephus. *The Complete Works of Flavius Josephus.* Trans. by William Whiston. Grand Rapids: Kregel Publications. 1960.
Against Apion.
Antiquities of the Jews.
Wars of the Jews.

Herodotus.*

Hesiod.*
Fragmenta.
Theogony.
Works and Days.

Hippocrates.*
De Fracturis (On Fractures).
Prognostikon (The Book of Prognostics).

Homer.*
Iliad.
Odyssey.

Justin. *Apology.* In *St. Justin Martyr.* Vol. 6, *The Fathers of the Church.* Washington, D.C.: The Catholic University of America Press. 1977.

Lucian.*
Tyrannicida (The Tyrannicide).
Philopseudes (The Lover of Lies).

Lycurgus. In *Minor Attic Orators.**

Marcus Aurelius. *Lucretius, Epictetus, Marcus Aurelius.* Trans. by George Long. *Great Books of the Western World.* Chicago: William Benton, Publisher. 1971.

Methodius. *The Symposium: A Treatise on Chastity.* Trans. by Herbert Musurillo. Vol. 27 of *Ancient Christian Writers.* New York: Newman Press. 1958.

The Mishna: Translated from the Hebrew with Introduction and Brief Explanatory Notes. Trans. by Herbert Danby. Oxford: Oxford University Press. 1933.

Mishnayoth. 7 vols. Ed. by Philip Blackman. New York: Judaica Press, Inc. 1964.

The Old Testament Pseudepigrapha. 2 vols. Ed. by James H. Charlesworth. Garden City, NY: Doubleday and Company, Inc. 1983.

Pausanias.*
  Description of Greece.

Philo.*
  De Mutatione Nominum (On the Change of Names).
  De Opificio Mundi (On the Creation).
  Quid Rerum Divinarum Heres (Who Is the Heir of Divine Things?).
  De Specialibus Legibus (On the Special Books).
  De Somniis (On Dreams).
  De Vita Mosis (The Life of Moses).

Philostratus.*
  Vitae Sophistarum (The Lives of the Sophists).

Pindar.*
  The Odes of Pindar.

Plato.*
  Euthyphro, Apology, Crito, Phaedo, Phaedrus.
  Legum Allegoriae.
  Lysis, Symposium, Gorgias.
  Philebus.
  Republic.
  Timaeus, Critias, Clitophon, Menexenus, Epistulae.

Pliny.*
  Natural History.

Plotinus.*

Plutarch.*
  Demetrius.
  Moralia.

Polybius.*
  The Histories.

Propertius.*

Seneca.*
  Moral Essays.

The Talmud of the Land of Israel. Ed. by Jacob Neusner, et al. Chicago: University of Chicago Press. 1988.

Bibliography Continued

Tertullian. *Against Marcion.* In *Latin Christianity: Its Founder Tertullian.* Vol. 3 of *The Ante-Nicene Fathers.* Ed. by Alexander Roberts and James Donaldson. Edinburgh. 1867. Reprint. Grand Rapids: William B. Eerdmans Publishing Co. 1973.

Theophrastus.*
  Characteres.

Thucydides.*

Vettius Valens. *Astrologus.* In *The Greek Anthology and other Ancient Greek Epigrams.* Ed. and trans. by Peter Jay. New York: Oxford University Press. 1973.

Xenophon.*
  Anabasis.
  Constitution of the Lacedaimonians. In *Scripta Minora.*
  Cyropaedia (Institutio Cyri.).
  Memorabilia.

**The Loeb Classical Library.* Cambridge: Harvard University Press.